Baker's Greek New Testament Library

Timothy Friberg and Barbara Friberg, Editors

1. *Analytical Greek New Testament*
2. *Analytical Concordance of the Greek New Testament,*
   vol. 1: *Lexical Focus*
3. *Analytical Concordance of the Greek New Testament,*
   vol. 2: *Grammatical Focus*
4. *Analytical Lexicon of the Greek New Testament*

Timothy Friberg and **Barbara Friberg** are field linguists and teachers of graduate linguistics working in Southeast Asia. Timothy holds a Ph.D. from the University of Minnesota. Barbara earned an M.A. in linguistics at the University of Saigon and an M.S. in computer science at the University of Minnesota.

Neva F. Miller was a research consultant for the Summer Institute of Linguistics in Dallas, Texas. She taught Greek, Bible, and Christian education for thirty years at Vennard College in University Park, Iowa.

An
of the Greek

Analytical Lexicon
of the
Greek New Testament

Timothy Friberg
Barbara Friberg
Neva F. Miller

 Baker Books

A Division of Baker Book House Co
Grand Rapids, Michigan 49516

©2000 by Timothy Friberg and Barbara Friberg

Published by Baker Books
a division of Baker Book House Company
P.O. Box 6287, Grand Rapids MI 49516-6287

Printed in the United States of America

Library of Congress Cataloging-in-Publication Data

Friberg, Timothy.
    Analytical lexicon of the Greek New Testament / Timothy Friberg, Barbara Friberg, Neva F. Miller.
       p.   cm. — (Baker's Greek New Testament library)
    Includes bibliographical references (p.   ).
    ISBN 0-8010-2135-9
    1. Greek language, Biblical—Glossaries, vocabularies, etc. 2. Bible. N.T.—Language, style—Dictionaries. I. Friberg, Barbara. II. Miller, Neva F. III. Title. IV. Series.

PA881.F75 2000
487'.4—dc21
                                        00-024983

For information about academic books, resources for Christian leaders, and all new releases available from Baker Book House, visit our web site:
http://www.bakerbooks.com

Contents

Introduction

The *Analytical Lexicon of the Greek New Testament* (*ANLEX*) is an entirely new work, though very much resting on the work of past and present scholars. It is contemporary, representing for the user the best scholarship available at the present time in the areas of New Testament Greek, translation theory, linguistics, and lexicography.

The Development of *ANLEX*

The *Analytical Greek New Testament* (*AGNT*) appeared in 1981 after more than five years of development. From the beginning, both a companion concordance and a lexicon were envisaged. The concordance was published in 1991 as the *Analytical Concordance of the Greek New Testament* in two volumes, one with a lexical focus and the other with a grammatical focus. The lexicon itself was worked on from 1980. From the beginning, the lemma entries were developed afresh and have gone through several stages of refining.

The analytical part of the lexicon, on the other hand, sprang nearly fully formed as an offspring of *AGNT*. To the basic vocabulary of *AGNT*, itself using the text of the third edition of the United Bible Societies' *Greek New Testament*, we have aimed to include in *ANLEX* every reflex found in the following versions of the Greek New Testament:

The Greek New Testament
   1st edition. Edited by Kurt Aland, Matthew Black, Bruce M. Metzger, and Allen Wikgren. United Bible Societies, 1966.
   2d edition. Edited by Kurt Aland, Matthew Black, Carlo M. Martini, Bruce M. Metzger, and Allen Wikgren. United Bible Societies, 1968.
   3d edition. Edited by Kurt Aland, Matthew Black, Carlo M. Martini, Bruce M. Metzger, and Allen Wikgren. United Bible Societies, 1975 (corrected printing 1983).

4th edition. Edited by Barbara Aland, Kurt Aland, Johannes Karavidopoulos, Carlo M. Martini, and Bruce M. Metzger. United Bible Societies, 1993 (corrected printing 1994).

Novum Testamentum Graece
25th edition. Edited by Erwin Nestle and Kurt Aland. Stuttgart: Württembergische Bibelanstalt, 1963.
26th edition. Edited by Kurt Aland, Matthew Black, Carlo M. Martini, Bruce M. Metzger, and Allen Wikgren. Stuttgart: Deutsche Bibelstiftung, 1979.
27th edition. Edited by Barbara Aland, Kurt Aland, Johannes Karavidopoulos, Carlo M. Martini, and Bruce M. Metzger. Stuttgart: Deutsche Bibelgesellschaft, 1993.

The Englishman's Greek New Testament. Reprinted Grand Rapids: Zondervan, 1974 (= Stephanus's 1550 text).

The Greek New Testament according to the Majority Text
1st edition. Edited by Zane C. Hodges and Arthur L. Farstad. Nashville: Nelson, 1982.
2d edition. Edited by Zane C. Hodges and Arthur L. Farstad. Nashville: Nelson, 1985.

The New Testament in the Original Greek according to the Byzantine/Majority Textform. Edited by Maurice A. Robinson and William G. Pierpont. Atlanta: Original Word, 1991.

Additionally, we have aimed to include all reflexes found in the critical apparatuses and comments of these editions of the Greek New Testament. We are convinced that this represents the overwhelmingly vast majority of readings of all extant manuscripts, but we are open to corrections and additions from users of *ANLEX*.

After going through numerous printings, *AGNT* was ripe for revision. This was appropriate for both of *AGNT*'s lines. The first line, containing the Greek text, has been upgraded to be equivalent to the fourth edition of the United Bible Societies' *Greek New Testament*. The second line, *AGNT*'s morphological-grammatical analysis, was revised in several ways: correction, simplification (especially of complex tags), and enhancement. This revision of *AGNT* is fully reflected in the present lexicon. The print revision of *AGNT* (scheduled for publication by Baker Book House in 2001) will also include two additional lines: the third line contains the lemma form, and the fourth line contains an English reference gloss of the lemma.

The Analytical Lexicon as Lexicon

This work is first and foremost a lexicon. More than fifteen years in preparation, it has been developed as the original work of the last-named editor, both out of her decades-long experience in teaching and researching New Testament Greek and out of her interaction with the very best scholarship available, through both personal discussions and extensive consulting of the published literature.[1]

The lexicon is aimed at users who want at their fingertips a complete lexicon with meanings and definitions, yet who do not require the more technical discussions found, for example, in Bauer, Arndt, Gingrich, and Danker's *Greek-English Lexicon of the New Testament*. Furthermore, *ANLEX* is provided for users who want an analysis of the reflex forms of Greek words found in the text.

Several features of the lexicon make it particularly attractive. First, each lexical entry consists of a keyword or lemma (dictionary or citation form) by which the form is uniquely identified. The first part of the lemma (up to the first comma or to the end of the boldface type, whichever comes first) is the minimal identifying form. This form is reproduced as the homebase form in the right column of the reflex entries of *ANLEX* (to be explained below). It is also the form given interlinearly in the revised *AGNT*.

The larger lemma gives more than this minimal identification. For nouns we give the nominative article (indicating gender) and, if declinable, the genitive ending. For adjectives we give the two or three nominative-case terminations. In the case of nouns and adjectives, these added endings are frequently longer than those found in some scholarly works. This is usually for the express purpose of showing the shift of an accent caused by a long (genitive-case) ending vowel, but has been generalized. Thus for κρίμα, for which the genitive form is κρίματος, we give the genitive ending as ατος, whereas some scholarly works give merely τος. For verbs the lemma is almost invariably given in the first-person singular form of the present tense.

For several reasons, we frequently give two or more forms of verbs in the lemma entry. First, sometimes verbs borrow from several forms for their full expression, for example, forming their present system from one verb form and their aorist system from another (not unlike English *go* and *went*). Second, two verbs may have developed variation (not to exclude dialect variation), and thus all relevant information has been given in the lemma form.

Notwithstanding our innovation in other areas of the lexicon, in matters of lemma presentation there is a certain convention that is so widespread that not to have followed it would have confused readers of all textual-type persuasions. In particular we refer to the choice of certain spellings or words for purposes of lexical or lemma presentation. The following guidelines explain our choices for lexical presentation, especially with regard to the use of *and*, *or*, and *also*—with or without parentheses

---

1. See the bibliography for a list of scholarly literature this volume is most indebted to.

(examples from the lexicon are given following each guideline). In these guidelines, the following distinction should be noted: "alternate" refers to word-form and spelling variation within conventional New Testament Greek lexicography, which of course necessarily reflects the dominant text form presented in multiple editions of the Greek New Testament over the last one hundred or more years; "variant" refers to word-form and spelling variation outside of that conventional lexicography, forms that the dominant text tradition would consider merely variant readings.

1. All variant forms that accompany a lemma are enclosed within parentheses, whether they are verbs, nouns, adjectives, etc. In distinction, alternate forms appear without parentheses:

   βλαστάνω (and βλαστάω)
   καθίστημι and καθιστάνω

2. For verbs, if present-system forms from both lemmas occur, the lemmas are joined by *and*:

   αὐξάνω and αὔξω
   ἐπισκοπέω (and ἐπισκοπεύω)

3. For verbs, if present-system forms occur from only one lemma and forms in other tenses occur from the other lemma, the lemmas are joined by *and*:

   ῥίπτω and ῥιπτέω

4. For verbs, if variant spelling occurs only in principal parts and present-system forms are all derived from one lemma, variant principal parts are joined by *and*:

   λαμβάνω   fut. mid. λήμψομαι (and λήψομαι)

5. For verbs, if no present-system forms from both lemmas occur and if forms in other tenses may be derived from either of the alternate forms equally well, alternate lemmas are joined by *or*:

   ἀπονίζω or ἀπονίπτω

6. For verbs, if no present-system forms from both lemmas occur and if forms in other tenses may not be derived from either of the lemma forms equally well, variant principal parts or reflexes are joined by *or* to correlate with *or* between the lemma forms:

ἐγκαινίζω (or ἐνκαινίζω)   1aor. ἐνεκαίνισα; pf. pass. ἐγκεκαίνισμαι (or ἐνκεκαίνισμαι)

7. For nonverbs, alternate lemmas are joined by *and*:

   Βαριωνᾶ and Βαριωνᾶς

8. For nonverbs, variant lemmas are joined by *also*:

   Ἀχάζ, ὁ (also Ἄχαζ, Ἄχας)

9. For nonverbs, forms with variant case endings are joined by *or*:

   γένος, ους (or ως), το, dative γένει

When a lemma has no status within conventional lexicography, we present it as its own lemma, write-up and all. In such a case it has no parenthesis set, unless of course it has its own variant forms:

   ἐπιπνίγω
   Δονεῖ, ὁ (also Δονεί)

The meaning given for any entry generally consists of a definition and a gloss. The definition, printed in roman type, is a clarifying description of the entry. It supports and is subordinate to the gloss. The gloss, printed in italic type, is a set of one or more English words that are thought best to represent the sense of the Greek word. We have tried to avoid achieving a "thesaurus" effect, the mere listing of as many synonyms as possible.

Our choice of terminology favors contemporary expression over against archaisms and otherwise outdated forms. Because the lexicon is not a revision of any existing work, all English vocabulary was weighed for its appropriateness to the Greek expression. Both scholarly vocabulary and theological terminology have been avoided. We also have exercised care that specific theological frameworks are not promoted and others demoted. Our aim has been openness, so that doctrine can be developed more directly and intuitively from the source text.

An entry may begin with *strictly*, denoting the basic sense of the item. This designation may then be followed by *hence*, giving derived or contextually developed senses of the form.

A frequently encountered device is the division between *literal* and *figurative*. Thus for ἁμαρτάνω the literal meaning is "miss the mark, be in error," while the figurative application of the term with respect to God and fellow man is "sin, do wrong, transgress." In fact, only the figurative usage of ἁμαρτάνω (which may also be its most frequent usage) means "sin." Figurative usage usually comprises "dead metaphors," that is, expressions of language that, once created fresh for an occasion, became fixed and regular. *Metaphorical*, on the other hand, is used in the lexicon to explain "live metaphors," either the special creation of the author thus cited or thought to be sufficiently new as to involve special reader/listener attention.

Other presentational divisions include the distinction between *active* and *passive*, between *transitive* and *intransitive*, etc. The active/passive distinction is used not only for appropriate Greek verbal forms but also for nouns and adjectives that may have active and passive senses. For example, the adjective θεοστυγής is noted as originally having a passive sense ("hated by God"), which in New Testament usage has become active ("hateful toward God"). Such words are not infrequently abstract nouns that have been built on underlying verbal ideas.

Scripture references are frequently given to illustrate the form in question. References in parentheses may represent others not cited; references not given in parentheses are unique to the discussion at hand. (See the discussion of variant readings for apparent "phantom" references.)

Greek technical terms from business, law, religion, etc. are frequently indicated by *technical term*.

The infinitive form is used in discussing a verb unless it is particularized to a reflex in some actual context. Within each lemma, keywords are abbreviated by the initial letter (β., λ., μ.) when the form is identical to that of the lemma form, but accents on final syllables are ignored.[2] Vowel-initial forms are abbreviated as either the initial vowel (ἁ.) or diphthong (αὐ.), depending on which is necessary to show the breathing mark. Forms not identical with the lemma (except, as noted above, for final-syllable accents) are written out in full.

Our division of meanings by numbers and letters is meant as an aid to the user. We do not divide beyond normal "semicolon" divisions, except when there is subordination that might tend toward confusion. Thus, a division between only literal and figurative will not normally be accompanied by numbers. But if there is subordinate division under the same literal discussion, numbering is employed.

The principal parts of verbs included immediately after the lemma represent those parts underlying the reflexes found in the lexicon. All verb forms are built on one of the six basic principal parts (the numbered items in the list below). Additionally, it is sometimes useful to add other forms, even though built on these basic six, for the convenience of the reader. The following chart shows all forms (according to the traditional order) potentially found in the principal parts listing:

---

2. This exception allows for final-syllable interplay of grave and acute accents and for "second" accents imposed by a following clitic.

1. present active
     present middle/passive
     imperfect active
     imperfect middle/passive
2. future active
     future middle
3. aorist active
     aorist middle
4. perfect active
     pluperfect active
5. perfect middle/passive
     pluperfect middle/passive
6. aorist passive
     future passive

Principal parts are always separated by semicolons, as are any tenses within a given principal part. When the lemma form is nonactive (= deponent), designations for middle and passive are not generally given. An exception to this occurs when not indicating middle and passive would result in two identical tense designations, as, for example, with the aorist. Passive is also given with the tense designation of a principal part (aorist, etc.) when the form represents one or more instances of a true passive of an otherwise deponent verb. Additionally, active is indicated to designate active principal parts of an otherwise deponent lemma. And finally, voice indications are also indicated when not to have them might confuse the reader as to the order of principal parts.

Whereas it is the user's responsibility and privilege to determine which meaning or submeaning is appropriate for a given Greek reflex in context, sometimes our discussion of a word weighs the choices involved. Three terms are frequently used in evaluating those choices, listed here in order of increasing validity:

perhaps	A meaning is not strongly supported grammatically and/or exegetically, but it is proposed by some interpreters and should **perhaps** be considered.
possibly	Because the grammatical and exegetical factors impacting the term allow ambiguity, two or more equally valid alternatives are **possible**.
probably	Grammatical and exegetical factors, perhaps also reinforced by consensus, make one alternative more **probable**.

In a given entry, then, the reader might find *possibly* under the discussion of one facet of the meaning and *probably* under another. This means that the editors, weighing the term in context and consulting commentaries, consider that the meaning with *probably* more likely reflects the author's intent than does the meaning labeled *possibly*.

Variant Readings

A dictionary or lexicon is an alphabetic listing of the word forms of a language together with, among other things, definitions of those forms. Such a work may be monolingual (as, e.g., a dictionary of and in the English language) or bilingual, defining words of one language in those of another (as in the present lexicon). Dictionaries or lexicons are statements of language. By definition, language is a social convention whereby individuals communicate verbally among themselves (indeed language has neither definition nor existence apart from social interaction). Since no one individual controls the entire language in question, a dictionary is not a description of a single individual's speech but an expression of the language as spoken by more than one person.

With regard to New Testament Greek lexicons, much insight has been gained from studying the usages of words in extra–New Testament contexts, both Christian and non-Christian. New Testament Greek is not the special language it was once thought to be; rather, it was the language of everyday communication (along with local languages like Aramaic, Lycaonian, etc.) in the world of the New Testament. In a New Testament lexicon, it is impossible to fully separate out the meaning of words in specific contexts from the wider usage those same words had in countless conversations. In fact, although in some contexts we may identify a specialized or restricted meaning of a word, the terms *specialized* and *restricted* are only meaningful as limitations on the wider context of a word's full meaning.

Lexicons of New Testament Greek traditionally call some forms variant readings, usually abbreviated *v.l.* (= *varia lectio*). Readings so identified vary from those found in the text serving as the basis of the lexicon. Variant readings are evidence of manuscript variation.

It would be an easy thing if there were only two manuscripts of the Greek New Testament. Then every time there was variance between the two, each could be represented in the scholarly reference work by its own unique code, say, A and B. When neither code was indicated, the user would understand the texts of these manuscripts to be in agreement. This ideal situation would assure that the reference work was manuscript neutral, not choosing one over the other, but rather only identifying and defining variation. Further to our illustration, the work would not change in time with respect to the statement of manuscript evidence, assuming that only those two manuscripts continued extant and were not supplemented by later discoveries.

There are, however, thousands of extant New Testament manuscripts, some few covering the entire New Testament, many others only some portion of it. Furthermore, scholarly reference works are not based on a given New Testament manuscript, but rather on some critical edition of the assembled manuscript evidence. Some editions of the Greek New Testament follow more closely a small set of manuscripts, while others follow sets of larger membership. The point is that there is no equivalence between a given edition and a specific manuscript. Furthermore, editions are regularly updated, revised, and changed.

We have chosen in this analytical lexicon not to indicate that any readings are variant. Our preference is to be neutral with respect to any scholarly position on the identity of the New Testament text. This means that we do not pick between various editions of the Greek New Testament for purposes of stating the language defined in the lexicon. Just as we stated above that a lexicon is validly an expression of the language as spoken by more than one person, so by loose analogy we have chosen to record all so-called variants as valid and full-fledged entries in our lexicon (with exceptions as stated below). Whereas this is not a lexicon of first-century Greek in all its local expressions and registers, we present this as a lexicon of New Testament Greek in its various manuscript variations. The editors of the lexicon are not neutral with respect to the important question of the identity of the New Testament text, but we choose that our lexicon will be.

What then are the practical implications of such a choice? In fact, there are very few observed differences between the lexicon as presented and as we might have formulated it had we adopted a particular text-type as the base. The major difference is that the user of any edition of the Greek New Testament will find the item being searched for as a full-fledged member of the lexicon, not as having some questioned status as a variant. We assume that most users will approach our lexicon because they have a specific word in a particular context that they are looking for information about—either its grammatical parsing or definition. Every individual form that we have been able to identify as occurring in any Greek New Testament manuscript has been included with grammatical/morphological parsing. Each item is followed by a pointer to the home-base/lemma form, where general information, a supporting definition, and a gloss are given. Among the subparts of the definition, scriptural references illustrative to each are usually given. It has been our practice, as much as possible, to illustrate the subparts of a definition with forms common to all manuscript families. Of course, this is not always possible. In such cases, references are given that are variant to some edition.

We anticipate that only one kind of user will become aware of unmarked variant readings. It is that user who, instead of looking up specific forms, wants to study an entire lemma or a particular reference. He may encounter, as he works his way through the definition, certain references to the keyword that occur not in the text proper of his edition of the Greek New Testament but in the critical apparatus, assuming it is complete with respect to that reference. We give below a short lemma write-up that includes a reference (AC 16.39; indeed another instance of this verb is found at AC 28.19) that is variant to one or more editions of the Greek New Testament:

ἐπικράζω   *shout threats against* someone (AC 16.39)

As is obvious, this write-up is identical in form to that of a "normal" lemma. And the only difference between this write-up and that found in other lexicons is the absence of *v.l.* following the reference notation (see BAGD, p. 295; Mounce, *Analytical Lexicon to the Greek New Testament*, p. 206; Perschbacher's *New Analytical Greek Lexicon* does not list this word).

There were in Koine Greek certain vowels that, as the language changed, increasingly came to be pronounced alike. These vowels were often interchanged in spelling. This is one kind of variant that we do not give independent status to. Our practice is to refer the user to the standard form by use of *see X* in the right column of reflex lines.[3] Other (mis)spelling differences are also handled in the same way, sometimes including those of proper nouns.[4] Both spelling and name variants are illustrated below:

ἰδώς	VPRANM-S	see εἰδώς
Ἀπολλωνίδα	N-AF-S	see Ἀπολλωνίαν

The Analytical Lexicon as Analytical

Although *ANLEX* and *AGNT* are unique and separate works, each able by itself to serve the user independently of the other, they are together a unified work. The unifying factor is the system of grammatical tags (coded morphological analyses). Indeed the use of grammatical tags makes the lexicon efficient to use, both because the statement of each form's parsing is perfectly regular, taken from the table of abbreviations, and because the placement of the prepared tag allows the reader's eyes always to find the tag at the same place on the page everywhere throughout the work. The

---

3. "Standard" in this case is determined by criteria other than manuscript membership. We are not saying that any one form or reading is more basic and thus correct, but rather we are going with the conventional wisdom that some forms are nonstandard spellings, even if they occurred in the autographs.

4. On the other hand, we indicate some forms by putting them in parentheses immediately following the lemma entry: (*also X*).

Abbreviations and Symbols

N noun / P pronoun

P pronoun	N nominative	M masculine	1 1st person	S singular
–	G genitive	F feminine	2 2d person	P plural
	D dative	N neuter	3 3d person	
	A accusative	–	–	
	V vocative			

V verb

I indicative	P present	A active	N nominative	M masculine	1 1st person	S singular
M imperative	I imperfect	M middle	G genitive	F feminine	2 2d person	P plural
N infinitive	F future	P passive	D dative	N neuter	3 3d person	–
O optative	A aorist	E either middle or passive	A accusative	–	–	
P participle	R perfect	D middle deponent	V vocative			
R participle (imperative sense)	L pluperfect	O passive deponent	–			
S subjunctive		N middle or passive deponent				

A adjective

B adverb	C cardinal	N nominative	M masculine	1 1st person	S singular
P pronominal	D demonstrative	G genitive	F feminine	2 2d person	P plural
–	I indefinite	D dative	N neuter	–	–
	M comparative	A accusative	–		
	O ordinal	V vocative			
	R relative	–			
	S superlative				
	T interrogative				
	–				

D determiner (definite article)

N nominative	M masculine	S singular
G genitive	F feminine	P plural
D dative	N neuter	
A accusative		
V vocative		

P preposition

G genitive
D dative
A accusative

C conjunction

C coordinating
H superordinating (hyperordinating)
S subordinating

Q particle

N negative
S sentence
T interrogative
V verbal

Complex Tags

+	intertag connector
–	antecedentless relative
/	"or"
!	"or" (order is significant)
<	function, "used as"
&	"and," crasis

tagging system of abbreviations and symbols is explained on the accompanying chart and is fully described in the appendix to *AGNT*.

The chart of abbreviations and symbols used in *AGNT* has been simplified somewhat for purposes of *ANLEX*. The reason for this is straightforward: the analysis in *AGNT* is based on context; in the lexicon, on the other hand, there is no context. Here we give the reflex alone, pulled out of its New Testament context. A given reflex in the lexicon may represent the single occurrence of a word in the whole New Testament or it may represent thousands, as in the case of καί.

The differences between the chart of abbreviations and symbols as used in *AGNT* and their use in *ANLEX* may be summarized as follows.

1. The two intertag "or" connectors (/ and !) find no use here. What are alternate analysis choices in *AGNT* are given on separate lines of *ANLEX*.
2. Analysis tags in *AGNT* frequently have a functional description of the basic morphological form. Most of these, being contextual, are not found in the pages of *ANLEX*. Some have been retained, however, if they are relevant apart from context, for example:

ἀγαπήσεις	VIFA--2S	ἀγαπάω
	VIFA--2S^VMPA--2S	"

   In addition to the simple analysis tag of the form ἀγαπήσεις, VIFA--2S, which incidentally does not occur separately in the Greek New Testament, we give VIFA--2S^VMPA--2S, a complex analysis tag showing that the future indicative form is used imperatively, a distinct Hebraistic influence.[5] That is not the case with other forms.
3. The minus sign (–) preceding a relative pronoun that in context is without antecedent is absent in *ANLEX*, again due to lack of a context.[6]
4. The plus sign (+) indicates in *AGNT* that there is a relationship between the form under analysis and something in its context. Since there is no context indicated for the reflexes in *ANLEX*, the plus sign is in general absent. We have retained it, however, following articles that function demonstratively. Thus for ὁ, both DNMS and DNMS+ will be found in the lexicon, indicating that the reflex in question has both articular and demonstrative functions in the New Testament. The use of the plus sign typically represents articles that do not have an overt head noun.[7]

---

5. Other futures, for example ἐρεῖς, appear sometimes as simple futures, sometimes as functional imperatives.

6. This is an innovation in revised *AGNT* not present in the first edition.

7. A specialized demonstrative function of ὁ (i.e., that with following μέν or δέ) is represented by a complex tag: DNMS^APDNM-S. For details, consult the appendix in revised *AGNT*.

5. The symbol R (= participle [imperative sense]) as second place in a verbal tag does not appear in *ANLEX*, again for the reason that participles used imperatively are contextually determined, something beyond the scope of our treatment of reflexes in isolation.

6. The fourth column of verbal tags allows for E (= either middle or passive) and N (= middle or passive deponent). These two forms are not found in *ANLEX*, for they are conflating devices that may confuse the reader. Rather we have doubled the representation in the lexicon of each reflex that has the tag E or N in *AGNT*. For verbal reflexes analyzed as E in *AGNT*, we give M (= middle) on one line and P (= passive) on the following line; for those analyzed as N in *AGNT*, we give D (= middle deponent) on one line and O (= passive deponent) on the following line. The reader is reminded here of the convention followed in *AGNT* with respect to these symbols: E represents contextual ambiguity, whereas N represents ambiguity of form apart from context. Thus in the lexicon, Greek verbs with D and O in tenses other than future and aorist do not represent distinct reflexes.[8]

ANLEX is designed to be used without *AGNT*—whether revised or unrevised. But if it is used with unrevised *AGNT*, a few differences should be noted.

1. *AGNT* used X, Y, Z to represent first-, second-, and third-person; in revised *AGNT* and *ANLEX* person is represented as 1, 2, 3.

2. Οὐ (also οὐκ and οὐχ) and μή are called negative particles by some Greek grammarians and adverbs by others. *AGNT* considered them adverbs and accordingly gave them the analysis tag AB. In revised *AGNT* we thought it appropriate to distinguish them from adverbs in general and so have given them the tag QN (which did not previously exist), that is, negative particles.

3. The symbol @ used in *AGNT* is changed to ^ in *ANLEX* and revised *AGNT*.

Though the appendix of *AGNT* contains a full discussion of the choices underlying the grammatical analysis of New Testament Greek in the volumes of this series, it is appropriate here to summarize for the reader several major points.

---

8. A search of the literature may expose an apparent discrepancy in this regard. For example, BAGD labels περιεργάζομαι a middle deponent; but in *ANLEX* we analyze the present-tense περιεργαζομένους on successive lines as VPPDAM-P (middle) and VPPOAM-P (passive). This word occurs in the New Testament only at 2TH 3.11 and is for us ambiguously either middle or passive in form. To the editors of BAGD, it is apparently (for reasons that are not stated, though we may guess at them) a middle deponent. See the discussion of deponency in the appendix (§5.3) to *AGNT* and in appendix 2 in *ANLEX*.

Generally speaking, nouns are nouns, pronouns pronouns, and adjectives adjectives. In our analytical system, we give a major category to nouns (N) and one to adjectives (A), but where do pronouns fit?

Pronouns that are noun substitutes and never function adjectivally are given the initial tag NP, meaning that they are of the noun class, specifically the pronoun subclass. Among these are the expected ἐγώ, σύ, αὐτός, and many more.

But many other pronouns sometimes function as adjectives modifying some overt noun and at other times stand alone for an unexpressed noun. These we have seen as basically adjectives in that they modify or otherwise limit a noun form. In this function we give them the adjective designation A-. But in other functions they are pronouns, standing for a noun and not merely modifying it. In this latter function we give them the analogical designation AP, meaning a pronominal subclass of the adjective class. In fact, the AP function of these words may outnumber the modifying (A-) function, especially among the distinct sets: demonstratives (D), interrogatives (T), indefinites (I), and relatives (R). These, among others, may be either A- (modifying) or AP (pronominal).

A few Greek pronoun forms may be variously analyzed as AP/A- or NP. Αὐτός, for example, really comprises two functions: NP ("he, she, it") and AP/A- ("same").

But there is one more important extension of this principle, and that is to regular adjectives. An adjective can modify a noun, as with ὁ ἄνθρωπος ὁ καλός ("the good man"), or it may stand alone in reference to a noun, as with ὁ καλός ("the good [one])." Surely all Greek lexicons identify καλός as an adjective, thus, καλός, ή, όν.

There are other adjectives, however, that have almost "crossed over" and become nouns, at least in some particular function. Thus ἱερόν ("temple") seems to have a life of its own, even though it is demonstrably from the adjective ἱερός, ά, όν. Many lexicons would identify two lemmas here: a noun meaning "temple" and an adjective meaning "sacred, holy, pertaining to a temple." If we had done this, ἱερόν ("temple") would have been tagged beginning with N- and ἱερόν ("sacred") beginning with A-.

Rather than multiply lemmas, we have chosen to keep such as adjectives, so long as there was first-century usage of the term as an adjective.[9] Thus for many "nouns" in *ANLEX* and in *AGNT*, we use AP rather than N- to tell the reader that this form is a substantival use of an adjective. Indeed, under the adjective lemma entry, a subentry comments on the substantival usage of the adjective. AP, then, strictly means adjective class, pronominal subclass, but in fact there is congruity in tagging the substantival

9. As explained in the appendix to *AGNT*, this was our criterion for determining not only adjective lemma status, but also for determining whether verbs have lemma representation as active voice or nonactive (deponent).

usage of an adjective as AP. If pronouns (AP or NP) are forms that stand *for a noun*, then substantival usages of adjectives marked as AP may be understood as standing *as* or *for a noun*.[10]

Every reflex that may be potentially identified stands in *ANLEX* in the left column, usually on a line of its own, with the grammatical analysis in the center column and the homebase or lemma form in the right column. A reflex may also occur as the lemma entry itself. That is, it is given a line of its own when there is information to be added about it (i.e., the grammatical analysis or its homebase form). When it has no grammatical analysis (only in the case of indeclinables in the lexicon, though such reflexes receive analysis in *AGNT*) and when it is identical with the lemma form, a reflex will not be given its own independent line. This is especially the case with Aramaic forms and many indeclinable names. For example, Μόλοχ appears only as a lemma entry and not on its own reflex line. An alternate spelling, Μολόχ, appears on its own line, with the only information provided being a pointer in the right column to the lemma form.

The form of the reflex is exactly that of the form in the Greek text, with several conventional differences. If the ultimate (final) syllable on a form in the text bears a grave accent, it will appear in the left column of the reflex line with an acute accent. For example, καλὸς in context (*AGNT*) appears as καλός in isolation (*ANLEX*). Further, enclitics that lose their accents and/or put them on the previous word, are here given with their accents. For example, γέ for γε in context.[11]

Reflexes are alphabetized according to the Greek alphabet. Reflexes spelled identically but having different accentuation, breathing, and diacritical markings are treated as distinct entries. Our conventions for alphabetizing otherwise identically spelled forms are the following:

> capital letter (A) before lowercase letter (α)
> smooth breathing (ἀ) before rough breathing (ἁ)
> no dieresis (αι) before dieresis (αϊ)
> no iota subscript (α) before iota subscript (ᾳ)
> earlier accented syllable (άα) before later accented syllable (αά)
> acute (ά) before circumflex (ᾶ)
> lemma entry before reflex entry

10. The above discussion notwithstanding, we note that because *ANLEX* is a context-less expression of given reflexes, we use the AP tag for forms that have somehow "crossed over" and may be recognized as nouns/substantives apart from context. On the other hand, substantival forms that are contextually determined (and marked AP in *AGNT*) are here in *ANLEX* marked A-. See appendix 1 for a list of adjectives-become-substantives and the criteria we used in identifying them.

11. The accent sometimes given to the preceding word in context is deleted in *ANLEX*.

Movable *nu* (ν) and movable *sigma* (ς) are added where appropriate. The alphabetic ordering of such forms is undertaken without regard to the parentheses marks (i.e., such words are alphabetized according to their full spellings).

In some Greek texts, Aramaic forms are given without accentuation. Furthermore, some apparatuses do not accent Greek forms. These two kinds of accentless forms are accented in the left column of the lexicon. In a rare case the reader may have to decide which of two accented reflexes represents the unaccented form.

The center column represents the coded grammatical analysis. If two or more analyses are possible for a given reflex, they appear in alphabetic order in the center column, each on its own line. Lack of a grammatical tag means that the form is generally a non-Hellenized foreign loanword, the form of which does not indicate its analysis in Greek.

The right column points the reader to the homebase form. If the homebase form is identical to the one immediately above it, the reader will be referred upward by ditto marks (") in the right column.

In the rare case when two lemmas (in basic reduced form) are identical, they are distinguished by I and II. For example, the adjective δοῦλος, η, ον and the noun δοῦλος, ου, ὁ are identical in form prior to the first comma and so are distinguished by roman numerals.

Sometimes instead of a homebase form in the right column, the reader will find *see X* pointing the reader to another reflex. In addition to spelling variations (see p. 16), this convention is used when the original reflex is unusual in some sense, defying correct or easy analysis. The kinds of reflexes most frequently bearing a *see X* identification will be those missing an augment or having one vowel when another is expected (e.g., ο for ω, ει for η, etc.). Such deviations from standard form reflect variations from an accepted spelling or grammatical norm and in no way automatically consign the reflex to "variant" status. If a form (especially nonverbs) is given in the lemma entry as part of the parenthetical *also X* designation, its reflex line will not receive the *see X* notation. The homebase form thus given is in fact the minimal form of the lemma employed and will direct the reader to the main entry with its listing of alternative forms.

Ancillary Materials

Appendix 1 is a list of "crossed-over" adjectives, that is, forms showing regular substantival use (AP) that may well be analyzed as nouns (regardless of whether an adjectival use remains).[12]

---

12. See above for a fuller description of crossed-over adjectives.

In the lexicon we use the notational system for deponency developed in *AGNT* and explained there. There is, however, another way to look at deponency. In order for the reader to be adequately informed of this other "semantic" view, we include as appendix 2 a short essay by Neva F. Miller.

Appendix 3 is a glossary of terms used in the lexicon and in the field of linguistics and translation. Committed to helping those in early stages of using the Greek New Testament at very least, we are attempting to translate expressions into the best English equivalents. The terms in the glossary express some of the dynamics of that process.

Acknowledgments

A work of this sort is not done in isolation. In addition to the works cited in the bibliography, we have been helped immeasurably by colleagues and friends.

Of course this work, in part coming out of *AGNT*, owes a debt of gratitude to those who helped so selflessly there. Beyond that there are many who helped specifically on this volume. Two men have served as contributing editors in the many details that make this volume so valuable. Hilary Evans, M.D., went through the critical apparatuses of the third edition of the United Bible Societies' *Greek New Testament* and the twenty-sixth edition of Nestle-Aland's *Novum Testamentum Graece*, carefully recording every variant encountered. The resultant list appears as an important appendix to the *Analytical Concordance of the Greek New Testament*. Unfortunately, due to oversight, Dr. Evans was not there acknowledged. All forms that he culled from these apparatuses also appear in this volume. Robert E. Smith has further provided variant readings from Stephanus's Textus Receptus, from Henry Alford's *Greek New Testament*, and from the Majority Text. Bob was crucially involved in the revision of *AGNT*, making corrections and offering suggestions that strengthen the contribution of that volume. Those changes are reflected in the present volume. He was contributing editor for more than a decade of *ANLEX*'s development.

Additionally, competent Greek scholars helped check our work for completeness, consistency, comprehension, and correctness. Robert L. Merz, a retired teacher, was heavily involved in checking the concordance volumes and continued this tedious work for *ANLEX*, always in a cheerful and supportive manner. Robert L. Morris, a teacher and church administrator on a denominational level, spent much time checking the exegetical accuracy of the meaning entries. His expertise in New Testament studies and his profound respect for Greek as the language of the New Testament made this for him a genuine labor of love.

The last-named editor wishes to acknowledge with heartfelt gratitude her sister, Mrs. Harmon T. Jacobs. Glada, I couldn't have done it without you.

Thanks are also due Baker Book House for its long and faithful support to this entire series of Greek references. In particular we wish to thank David Aiken, who has represented the publisher on this lexical undertaking, for his cheerful spirit, high standards, and incredible patience.

We dedicate *ANLEX* to all those who are content not merely to know the truth of God's Word in their own language but who spend their lives translating that Word into other languages for other peoples.

We value your insight and are open to receiving correspondence about general assumptions or specific choices made in the development of *ANLEX*. Direct correspondence to:

Analytical Greek New Testament Project
Baker Book House
P.O. Box 6287
Grand Rapids MI 49516-6287
U.S.A.

For more information about *ANLEX* in electronic form, please contact Silver Mountain Software at info@silvermnt.com.

Bibliography

Alford, Henry. *The Greek New Testament*. 4 vols. Fifth (vols. 3–4) and seventh (vols. 1–2) editions. London: Rivingtons/Cambridge: Deighton, Bell, 1871–77. Reprinted Grand Rapids: Guardian, 1976.

Bartholomew, Doris A., and Louise C. Schoenals. *Bilingual Dictionaries for Indigenous Languages*. Mexico City: Summer Institute of Linguistics, 1983.

Bauer, Walter, William F. Arndt, F. Wilbur Gingrich, and Frederick W. Danker. *A Greek-English Lexicon of the New Testament and Other Early Christian Literature*. Second edition. Chicago: University of Chicago Press, 1979.

Blass, Friedrich W., Albert Debrunner, and Robert W. Funk. *Greek Grammar of the New Testament*. Chicago: University of Chicago Press, 1961.

Clapp, Philip S., Barbara Friberg, and Timothy Friberg. *Analytical Concordance to the Greek New Testament*. 2 vols. Grand Rapids: Baker, 1991.

Friberg, Barbara, and Timothy Friberg. *Analytical Greek New Testament*. Grand Rapids: Baker, 1981.

Goodwin, W. W. *Syntax of the Moods and Tenses of the Greek Verb*. Second edition. Boston: Ginn, 1890. (See also *Greek Grammar* by W. W. Goodwin and C. B. Gulick [Boston: Ginn, 1930].)

Liddell, Henry G., Robert Scott, and Henry S. Jones. *A Greek-English Lexicon*. Ninth edition. New York: Oxford University Press, 1940.

Louw, Johannes P., and Eugene A. Nida. *Greek-English Lexicon of the New Testament Based on Semantic Domains*. 2 vols. New York: United Bible Societies, 1988.

Miller, Neva F. *The Epistle to the Hebrews: An Analytical and Exegetical Handbook*. Dallas: Summer Institute of Linguistics, 1988.

Moulton, James H., and George Milligan. *The Vocabulary of the Greek New Testament Illustrated from the Papyri*. Reprinted Grand Rapids: Eerdmans, 1952.

Moulton, William F., Alfred S. Geden, and Harold K. Moulton. *A Concordance to the Greek Testament*. Fifth edition. Edinburgh: Clark, 1978.

Mounce, William D. *The Analytical Lexicon to the Greek New Testament*. Grand Rapids: Zondervan, 1993.

————. *The Morphology of Biblical Greek*. Grand Rapids: Zondervan, 1994.

Newman, Barclay M., Jr. *A Concise Greek-English Dictionary of the New Testament*. London: United Bible Societies, 1971.

Perschbacher, Wesley J. *The New Analytical Greek Lexicon*. Peabody, Mass.: Hendrickson, 1990.

Robertson, Archibald T. *A Grammar of the Greek New Testament*. Second edition. Nashville: Broadman, 1934.

Wigram, George V. *The Analytical Greek Lexicon*. Reprinted Grand Rapids: Zondervan, 1967 (originally London: Bagster, 1852).

Abbreviations

New Testament Books

MT	Matthew
MK	Mark
LU	Luke
JN	John
AC	Acts
RO	Romans
1C	1 Corinthians
2C	2 Corinthians
GA	Galatians
EP	Ephesians
PH	Philippians
CO	Colossians
1TH	1 Thessalonians
2TH	2 Thessalonians
1T	1 Timothy
2T	2 Timothy
TI	Titus
PM	Philemon
HE	Hebrews
JA	James
1P	1 Peter
2P	2 Peter
1J	1 John
2J	2 John
3J	3 John
JU	Jude
RV	Revelation

General

act.	active
AGNT	*Analytical Greek New Testament*
ANLEX	*Analytical Lexicon of the Greek New Testament*
1aor.	first aorist
2aor.	second aorist
fut.	future
1fut.	first future
2fut.	second future
gen.	genitive
impf.	imperfect
inf.	infinitive
mid.	middle
NT	New Testament
pass.	passive
pf.	perfect
ptc.	participle

A, α indeclinable; first letter of the Greek alphabet; (1) α' (or A') as a cardinal number *one*; as an ordinal number *first*, used in the title of several NT letters; (2) A (or ἄλφα [q.v.]) as a symbolic letter in combination with Ω (q.v.), the last letter of the Greek alphabet ΑΩ *beginning and end, first and last* (RV 1.11)

ἄ	APRAN-P	ὅς
	APRNN-P	"

Ἀαρών, ὁ indeclinable; *Aaron*, masculine proper noun

Ἀβαδδών, ὁ (also **Ἀβαδών, Ἀββααδδών, Ἀββαδών, Βαττών**) indeclinable; transliterated from *Abaddon*, the Hebrew name for the ruling angel of the underworld (abyss); translated into Greek as Ἀπολλύων (*Destroyer*) (RV 9.11)

Ἀβαδών		Ἀβαδδών
ἀβαρῆ	A--AM-S	ἀβαρής

ἀβαρής, ές, gen. οὖς literally *light in weight*; figuratively in the NT *not financially burdensome, not a bother* or *expense* to anyone (2C 11.9)

ἀββά, ὁ (also **ἀββᾶ**) indeclinable; transliterated from the Aramaic *Abba* (*father*); translated into Greek as ὁ πατήρ (*father*); used as a vocative (MK 14.36)

ἀββᾶ		ἀββά
Ἀββααδδών		Ἀβαδδών
Ἀββαδών		"
Ἀβειληνῆς	N-GF-S	Ἀβιληνή
Ἄβελ		Ἄβελ
Ἀβέλ		"

Ἄβελ, ὁ (also **Ἄβελ, Ἀβέλ**) indeclinable; *Abel*, masculine proper noun

Ἀβιά, ὁ indeclinable; *Abijah*, masculine proper noun

Ἀβιάθαρ		Ἀβιαθάρ

Ἀβιαθάρ, ὁ (also **Ἀβιάθαρ**) indeclinable; *Abiathar*, masculine proper noun (MK 2.26)

Ἀβιληνή, ῆς, ἡ (also **Ἀβειληνή, Ἀβιλλιανή**) *Abilene*, a district of the Syrian Decapolis northwest of Damascus

Ἀβιληνῆς	N-GF-S	Ἀβιληνή
Ἀβιλλιανῆς	N-GF-S	"

Ἀβιούδ, ὁ indeclinable; *Abiud*, masculine proper noun

Ἀβραάμ, ὁ indeclinable; *Abraham*, masculine proper noun

ἄβυσσον	N-AF-S	ἄβυσσος

ἄβυσσος, ου, ἡ literally *bottomless pit*, transliterated into English as *abyss*; (1) as the place where dead people go *depths, underworld* (RO 10.7); (2) as a place for shutting away the devil and evil spirits *abyss, bottomless pit, very deep and large hole* (LU 8.31; RV 20.3)

ἀβύσσου	N-GF-S	ἄβυσσος
Ἄγαβος	N-NM-S	Ἄγαβος

Ἄγαβος, ου, ὁ (also **Ἄγαβος**) *Agabus*, masculine proper noun

Ἄγαβος	N-NM-S	Ἄγαβος

ἄγαγε	VMAA--2S	ἄγω
ἀγαγεῖν	VNAA	"
ἀγάγετε	VMAA--2P	"
ἀγάγη	VSAA--3S	"
ἀγαγόντα	VPAAAM-S	"
ἀγαγόντες	VPAANM-P	"
ἀγαγών	VPAANM-S	"
ἀγάγωσι(ν)	VSAP--3P	"
ἀγαθά	A--AN-P	ἀγαθός
	A--NN-P	"
ἀγαθάς	A--AF-P	"
ἀγαθέ	A--VM-S	"
ἀγαθή	A--NF-S	"
ἀγαθῇ	A--DF-S	"
ἀγαθήν	A--AF-S	"
ἀγαθῆς	A--GF-S	"
ἀγαθοεργεῖν	VNPA	ἀγαθοεργέω

ἀγαθοεργέω contracted form ἀγαθουργέω; *do good, provide benefits, show kindness* (1T 6.18)

ἀγαθοεργός, όν *doing good, acting kindly*; substantivally ὁ ἀ. *well-doer* (RO 13.3)

ἀγαθοεργῷ	AP-DM-S	ἀγαθοεργός
ἀγαθοῖς	A--DM-P	ἀγαθός
	A--DN-P	"
ἀγαθόν	AB	"
	A--AM-S	"
	A--AN-S	"
	A--NN-S	"
ἀγαθοποιεῖτε	VMPA--2P	ἀγαθοποιέω

ἀγαθοποιέω 1aor. inf. ἀγαθοποιῆσαι; *do good*; (1) as showing goodwill toward someone *do good to, benefit* (LU 6.9), opposite κακοποιέω (*do wrong to*); (2) of actions that fulfill moral law *do what is right* (3J 11), opposite ἁμαρτάνω (*sin, do wrong*); (3) of citizenship worthy of imitation *behave well, live in the right way* (1P 2.15)

ἀγαθοποιῆσαι	VNAA	ἀγαθοποιέω
ἀγαθοποιῆτε	VSPA--2P	"

ἀγαθοποιΐα, ας, ἡ (1) as morally good action *doing what is right, living in the right way* (probably 1P 4.19); (2) as helpful action *doing good, well-doing* (possibly 1P 4.19)

ἀγαθοποιΐα	N-DF-S	ἀγαθοποιΐα
ἀγαθοποιΐαις	N-DF-P	"

ἀγαθοποιός, όν of one who behaves in a way that is good *upright, doing good*; substantivally ὁ ἀ. *well-doer, one who does right* (1P 2.14), opposite κακοποιός (*evildoer, criminal*)

ἀγαθοποιοῦντας	VPPAAM-P	ἀγαθοποιέω
ἀγαθοποιοῦντες	VPPANM-P	"
ἀγαθοποιοῦσαι	VPPANF-P	"
ἀγαθοποιῶν	AP-GM-P	ἀγαθοποιός
	VPPANM-S	ἀγαθοποιέω

ἀγαθός, ή, όν *good*, opposite κακός (*bad*); (1) of the moral character of persons *good, upright, worthy* (JN 7.12); (2) of outward performance *capable, excellent, good* (LU 19.17); (3) of the quality of things *good, beneficial*; of soil *fertile*; of gifts *beneficial*; of words *useful*; of deeds *good*; (4) substantivally τὸ ἀγαθόν as what is morally good *the good, what is good, right*; τὰ ἀγαθά as what is for one's well-being *good things, fine things* (LU 16.25); of materially valuable things *goods, possessions, treasures* (LU 12.18); ὁ ἀ. *the Good One* (i.e. God) (MT 19.17); *the good person* (RO 5.7); (5) neuter as an adverb *in a good way, helpfully* (2C 5.10)

ἀγαθός	A--NM-S	ἀγαθός
ἀγαθοῦ	A--GM-S	"
	A--GN-S	"
ἀγαθουργέω		see ἀγαθοεργέω
ἀγαθουργῶν	VPPANM-S	ἀγαθοεργέω
ἀγαθούς	A--AM-P	ἀγαθός
ἀγαθῷ	A--DM-S	"
	A--DN-S	"
ἀγαθῶν	A--GM-P	"
	A--GN-P	"

ἀγαθωσύνη, ης, ἡ (1) as a quality of moral excellence *being good, goodness, uprightness* (RO 15.14); (2) as a quality of relationship with others *willingness to give* or *share, generosity, goodness* (GA 5.22)

ἀγαθωσύνη	N-NF-S	ἀγαθωσύνη
ἀγαθωσύνη	N-DF-S	"
ἀγαθωσύνης	N-GF-S	"
ἀγαλλιαθῆναι	VNAP	ἀγαλλιάω
ἀγαλλιάσαντες	VPAANM-P	"
ἀγαλλιάσει	N-DF-S	ἀγαλλίασις
ἀγαλλιάσεως	N-GF-S	"
ἀγαλλιᾶσθε	VIPM--2P	ἀγαλλιάω
	VMPM--2P	"
ἀγαλλιασθῆναι	VNAP	"

ἀγαλλίασις, εως, ἡ *gladness, (extreme) joy, feeling of great happiness*, often implied by words and body movements, such as jumping, smiling, etc.

ἀγαλλίασις	N-NF-S	ἀγαλλίασις
ἀγαλλιᾶτε	VIPA--2P	ἀγαλλιάω

ἀγαλλιάω usually mid. ἀγαλλιάομαι; 1aor. ἠγαλλίασα, mid. ἠγαλλιασάμην; 1aor. pass. ἠγαλλιάθην; as feeling and expressing supreme joy *be glad, rejoice exceedingly, be very happy*

ἀγαλλιώμεθα	VSPM--1P	ἀγαλλιάω
ἀγαλλιῶμεν	VSPA--1P	"
ἀγαλλιώμενοι	VPPMNM-P	"
ἀγάμοις	N-DM-P	ἄγαμος

ἄγαμος, ου, ὁ and **ἡ** *unmarried person*, either man or woman, *single person* (1C 7.8); a woman separated or divorced from her husband (1C 7.11)

ἄγαμος	N-NF-S	ἄγαμος
	N-NM-S	"
ἀγανακτεῖν	VNPA	ἀγανακτέω

ἀγανακτέω 1aor. ἠγανάκτησα; *be indignant, be angry, be displeased* (MT 21.15); *express displeasure* or *vexation* (MT 20.24)

ἀγανάκτησιν	N-AF-S	ἀγανάκτησις

ἀγανάκτησις, εως, ἡ as a feeling or expression of strong opposition and displeasure *indignation, anger*, aroused by something thought to be wrong (2C 7.11)

ἀγανακτοῦντες	VPPANM-P	ἀγανακτέω
ἀγανακτῶν	VPPANM-S	"
ἀγαπᾷ	VIPA--3S	ἀγαπάω
	VSPA--3S	"
ἀγάπαις	N-DF-P	ἀγάπη
ἀγαπᾶμε	VIPP--1S	see ἀγαπῶμαι
ἀγαπᾶν	VNPA	ἀγαπάω
ἀγαπᾷς	VIPA--2S	"
ἀγαπᾶτε	VIPA--2P	"
	VMPA--2P	"
	VSPA--2P	"
ἀγαπάτω	VMPA--3S	"

ἀγαπάω mid./pass. ἀγαπῶμαι; fut. ἀγαπήσω; 1aor. ἠγάπησα; pf. ἠγάπηκα, ptc. ἠγαπηκώς; pf. pass. ptc. ἠγαπημένος; 1fut. pass. ἀγαπηθήσομαι; *love*, especially of love as based on evaluation and choice, a matter of will and action; (1) toward persons *love, be loyal to, regard highly* (EP 5.25); (2) toward God (MT 22.37); (3) from God (JN 3.16); (4) toward things *value, delight in, strive for* (LU 11.43); *long for* (2T 4.8); (5) ἀγάπην ἀγαπᾶν *show love* (JN 17.26)

ἀγάπη, ης, ἡ *love*; (1) especially as an attitude of appreciation resulting from a conscious evaluation and choice; used of divine and human love *love, devotion*; (2) plural αἱ ἀγάπαι *love feasts, fellowship meals*, meals in which members of a Christian community eat together in fellowship (JU 12)

ἀγάπη	N-NF-S	ἀγάπη
ἀγάπη	N-DF-S	"
ἀγαπηθήσεται	VIFP--3S	ἀγαπάω
ἀγάπην	N-AF-S	ἀγάπη
ἀγάπης	N-GF-S	"
ἀγαπήσαντα	VPAAAM-S	ἀγαπάω
ἀγαπήσαντι	VPAADM-S	"
ἀγαπήσαντος	VPAAGM-S	"
ἀγαπήσας	VPAANM-S	"
ἀγαπήσατε	VMAA--2P	"
ἀγαπήσει	VIFA--3S	"
ἀγαπήσεις	VIFA--2S	"
	VIFA--2S^VMPA--2S	"
ἀγαπήσητε	VSAA--2P	"
ἀγαπήσω	VIFA--1S	"
ἀγαπητά	A--AN-P	ἀγαπητός
	A--NN-P	"
ἀγαπητέ	A--VM-S	"
ἀγαπητῇ	A--DF-S	"
ἀγαπητήν	A--AF-S	"
ἀγαπητοί	A--NM-P	"
	A--VM-P	"
ἀγαπητοῖς	A--DM-P	"
ἀγαπητόν	A--AM-S	"
	A--NN-S	"

ἀγαπητός, ή, όν (1) *beloved, dear, very much loved* (AC 15.25; possibly 1T 6.2); (2) of one not only greatly loved but also unique, the only one of a class *only beloved, one dear* (MT 3.17); (3) *worthy of love* (probably 1T 6.2)

ἀγαπητός	A--NM-S	ἀγαπητός
ἀγαπητοῦ	A--GM-S	"

ἀγαπητῷ	A--DM-S	"
	A--DN-S	"
ἀγάπομεν	VIPA--1P	see ἀγαπῶμεν
ἀγαπῶ	VIPA--1S	ἀγαπάω
ἀγαπῶμαι	VIPP--1S	"
ἀγαπῶμεν	VIPA--1P	"
	VSPA--1P	"
ἀγαπῶν	VPPANM-S	"
ἀγαπῶντας	VPPAAM-P	"
ἀγαπῶντι	VPPADM-S	"
ἀγαπώντων	VPPAGM-P	"
ἀγαπῶσι(ν)	VIPA--3P	"
	VPPADM-P	"
Ἄγαρ		Ἁγάρ
Ἄγαρ		"

Ἁγάρ, ἡ (also Ἄγαρ, Ἅγαρ) indeclinable; *Hagar*, feminine proper noun

ἀγγαρεύουσι(ν)	VIPA--3P	ἀγγαρεύω
ἀγγαρεύσει	VIFA--3S	"

ἀγγαρεύω (or ἐγγαρεύω) fut. ἀγγαρεύσω; 1aor. ἠγγάρευσα; from ἄγγαρος (a Persian *messenger* or *courier* with authority to compel others to assist him); *press into service, compel, require* another *to carry a burden*

ἀγγεῖα	N-AN-P	ἀγγεῖον
ἀγγείοις	N-DN-P	"

ἀγγεῖον, ου, τό *utensil, bottle, container* for liquids (MT 25.4)

ἀγγεῖον	N-AN-S	ἀγγεῖον

ἀγγελία, ας, ἡ *message*; (1) as the content of what is announced *message* (1J 1.5); (2) as an announced requirement *directive, command* (1J 3.11)

ἀγγελία	N-NF-S	ἀγγελία
ἀγγέλλουσα	VPPANF-S	ἀγγέλλω

ἀγγέλλω 1aor. ἤγγειλα; *announce, tell* something to someone (JN 20.18)

ἄγγελοι	N-NM-P	ἄγγελος
ἀγγέλοις	N-DM-P	"
ἄγγελον	N-AM-S	"

ἄγγελος, ου, ὁ as one sent to tell or bring a message *messenger*; (1) of persons *messenger, envoy, one sent* (MK 1.2); (2) of divine messengers and agents of God *angel* (LU 1.26); (3) of demonic powers as Satan's messengers *(evil) angel* (MT 25.41); (4) specifically in RV 1.20; 2.1, 8, 12, 18; 3.1, 7, 14 probably *minister*, one overseeing a group of believers under Jesus' supervision, *messenger*

ἄγγελος	N-NM-S	ἄγγελος
ἀγγέλου	N-GM-S	"
ἀγγέλους	N-AM-P	"
ἀγγέλῳ	N-DM-S	"
ἀγγέλων	N-GM-P	"
ἄγγη	N-AN-P	ἄγγος

ἄγγος, ους, τό *utensil, container*; for holding wet objects, such as fish *(woven) basket* (MT 13.48)

ἄγε	VMPA--2S	ἄγω
	VMPA--2S^QS	"
ἄγει	VIPA--3S	"
ἄγειν	VNPA	"

ἀγέλη, ης, ἡ a group of animals kept by people for domestic use *herd* (of pigs), *drove, flock*

ἀγέλη	N-NF-S	ἀγέλη

ἀγέλην	N-AF-S	"

ἀγενεαλόγητος, ον literally *without genealogy* or *ancestral record*; in the NT of holding an office independently of natural descent *without (relying on) ancestral line, without (record of) descent* (HE 7.3)

ἀγενεαλόγητος	A--NM-S	ἀγενεαλόγητος
ἀγενῆ	AP-AN-P	ἀγενής

ἀγενής, ές, gen. οὖς strictly *not born into a noble family*; hence *insignificant, inferior, lowborn*; substantivally τὰ ἀγενῆ *common people, unimportant people* (1C 1.28)

ἄγεσθαι	VNPP	ἄγω
ἄγεσθε	VIPP--2P	"
ἄγετε	VMPA--2P	"
	VMPA--2P^QS	"
ἅγια	AP-AN-P	ἅγιος
	AP-NN-P	"
	A--NN-P	"
ἁγία	A--NF-S	"
ἁγίᾳ	A--DF-S	"
ἁγιάζει	VIPA--3S	ἁγιάζω
ἁγιάζεται	VIPP--3S	"
ἁγιαζόμενοι	VPPPNM-P	"
ἁγιαζομένους	VPPPAM-P	"
ἁγιάζον	VPPANN-S	"

ἁγιάζω 1aor. ἡγίασα; pf. pass. ἡγίασμαι, ptc. ἡγιασμένος; 1aor. pass. ἡγιάσθην; 1fut. pass. ἁγιασθήσομαι; *make holy, consecrate, sanctify*; (1) of things set apart for sacred purposes *consecrate, dedicate* (MT 23.19); (2) of God's name *treat as holy, revere* (MT 6.9); (3) of persons; (a) objectively, of Christ and his church acknowledged as being God's own possession *set apart for a holy purpose, dedicate, consecrate* (1C 6.11); (b) subjectively, of spiritual and moral preparation *sanctify, make holy, purify* (1TH 5.23); (4) specifically in 1C 7.14 of an unbelieving partner in a Christian home set aside for God's purpose *sanctified, consecrated, accepted* or *acknowledged* by God

ἁγιάζω	VIPA--1S	ἁγιάζω
ἁγιάζων	VPPANM-S	"
ἅγιαι	A--NF-P	ἅγιος
ἁγίαις	A--DF-P	"
ἁγίαν	A--AF-S	"
ἁγίας	A--AF-S	"
	A--GF-S	"
ἁγιάσαι	VOAA--3S	ἁγιάζω
ἁγιάσας	VPAANM-S	"
ἁγιάσατε	VMAA--2P	"
ἁγιάσῃ	VSAA--3S	"
ἁγιασθήτω	VMAP--3S	"
ἁγιασμόν	N-AM-S	ἁγιασμός

ἁγιασμός, οῦ, ὁ (1) as the process of making holy *dedicating, sanctifying*; (a) as the operation of the Spirit making holy, causing to belong completely to God, *sanctifying work* (1P 1.2); (b) as the careful moral behavior that expresses one's dedication to God *pure way of life, upright behavior, holy living* (1TH 4.3, 4, 7), opposite ἀκαθαρσία (*uncleanness, impurity*); (2) as the moral goal of the purifying process *holiness, right behavior* (RO 6.22)

ἁγιασμός	N-NM-S	ἁγιασμός
ἁγιασμῷ	N-DM-S	"

ἁγίασον   VMAA--2S   ἁγιάζω
ἅγιε   A--VM-S   ἅγιος
ἅγιοι   AP-NM-P   "
    AP-VM-P   "
    A--NM-P   "
    A--VM-P   "
ἁγίοις   AP-DM-P   "
    A--DM-P   "
ἅγιον   AP-AN-S   "
    A--AM-S   "
    A--AN-S   "
    A--NN-S   "

ἅγιος, ία, ον as the quality of persons or things that can be brought near or into God's presence *holy*; (1) of things set apart for God's purpose *dedicated, sacred, holy* (MT 4.5), opposite κοινός (*not consecrated, common*); (2) of persons *holy, pure, consecrated to God* (LU 1.70); (3) of supernatural beings, as God (JN 17.11), Christ (LU 1.35), the Spirit of God (MK 12.36), angels (MK 8.38) *holy*; (4) superlative ἁγιώτατος, τάτη, ον *most holy, very pure* or *sincere* (JU 20); (5) as a substantive; (a) ὁ ἅ. *the Holy One*, as a designation for God (1J 2.20) and Christ (MK 1.24); plural οἱ ἅγιοι *the holy ones*, as a designation for angels (1TH 3.13); as human beings belonging to God *saints, God's people, believers* (AC 9.13); (b) neuter τὸ ἅγιον *what is holy, what is dedicated to God* (MT 7.6); as a place dedicated to God *sanctuary, holy place* (HE 9.1); plural ἅγια *holy place, (outer) sanctuary* (HE 9.2); ἅγια ἁγίων *most sacred place, inner sanctuary, very holy place* (HE 9.3)

ἅγιος   A--NM-S   ἅγιος
    A--VM-S   "

ἁγιότης, ητος, ἡ as a state *holiness, sanctity*; as a quality of God's character to be shared by the Christian in his own character *holiness* (HE 12.10); *moral purity* (2C 1.12)

ἁγιότητι   N-DF-S   ἁγιότης
ἁγιότητος   N-GF-S   "
ἁγίου   A--GM-S   ἅγιος
    A--GN-S   "
ἁγίους   AP-AM-P   "
    A--AM-P   "
ἁγίῳ   A--DM-S   "
    A--DN-S   "
ἁγίων   AP-GM-P   "
    AP-GN-P   "
    A--GM-P   "

ἁγιωσύνη, ης, ἡ *holiness, dedication*, as a quality of life expressed in careful obedience to God (RO 1.4)

ἁγιωσύνη   N-DF-S   ἁγιωσύνη
ἁγιωσύνην   N-AF-S   "
ἁγιωσύνης   N-GF-S   "
ἁγιωτάτῃ   A-SDF-S   ἅγιος
ἀγκάλας   N-AF-P   ἀγκάλη

ἀγκάλη, ης, ἡ of the body *arm*, especially as bent to hold something (LU 2.28)

ἄγκιστρον, ου, τό *fishhook, hook* on the end of a line (MT 17.27)

ἄγκιστρον   N-AN-S   ἄγκιστρον

ἄγκυρα, ας, ἡ literally *anchor* for a boat or ship, a heavy weight, usually of stone or metal, attached to a rope

or chain and dropped overboard to keep a ship or boat from moving; metaphorically, of what provides security or support (HE 6.19)

ἄγκυραν   N-AF-S   ἄγκυρα
ἀγκύρας   N-AF-P   "
ἁγνά   A--NN-P   ἁγνός
ἁγνάς   A--AF-P   "

ἄγναφος, ον of cloth *unbleached, unshrunken, new*

ἀγνάφου   A--GN-S   ἄγναφος

ἁγνεία, ας, ἡ (also **ἁγνία**) (1) as a moral quality *purity, virginity* (1T 4.12); (2) as conformity to acceptable standards of sexual behavior *propriety, purity* (1T 5.2)

ἁγνείᾳ   N-NF-S   ἁγνεία
ἁγνείᾳ   N-DF-S   "
ἁγνευομένους   VPPPAM-P   ἁγνεύω

ἁγνεύω *be (morally) clean, keep oneself pure* (JU 24)

ἁγνή   A--NF-S   ἁγνός
ἁγνήν   A--AF-S   "
ἁγνία   N-NF-S   ἁγνεία
ἁγνίζει   VIPA--3S   ἁγνίζω

ἁγνίζω 1aor. ἥγνισα; pf. ἥγνικα; pf. pass. ἥγνισμαι; 1aor. pass. ἡγνίσθην; *purify*; (1) literally, of ceremonial washings and purifications *purify, cleanse* from ritual defilement (JN 11.55); middle (with the aorist passive) *purify oneself, dedicate oneself, become (ritually) acceptable*; of fulfilling requirements under a vow *be purified, be (ceremonially) cleansed* (AC 21.26); (2) figuratively, of moral cleansing *purify* (1P 1.22)

ἁγνίσατε   VMAA--2P   ἁγνίζω
ἁγνισθείς   VPAPNM-S   "
ἁγνίσθητι   VMAP--2S   "

ἁγνισμός, οῦ, ὁ as the process of ceremonial cleansing *purification* (AC 21.26)

ἁγνισμοῦ   N-GM-S   ἁγνισμός
ἁγνίσωσι(ν)   VSAA--3P   ἁγνίζω
ἀγνοεῖ   VIPA--3S   ἀγνοέω
ἀγνοεῖν   VNPA   "
ἀγνοεῖται   VIPP--3S   "
ἀγνοεῖτε   VIPA--2P   "
ἀγνοείτω   VMPA--3S   "

ἀγνοέω impf. ἠγνόουν; 1aor. ἠγνόησα; (1) as lacking information *be ignorant, not know*, often with ὅτι following (RO 1.13); (2) as lacking ability to understand *be mistaken, be in error, not understand* (HE 5.2); (3) as due to inexcusable moral ignorance *disregard, fail to understand* (RO 10.3); (4) as refusal to pay attention *ignore* (1C 14.38)

ἀγνόημα, ατος, τό as what is done wrong without deliberate intent *sin committed in ignorance, (unconscious) error, oversight* (HE 9.7)

ἀγνοημάτων   N-GN-P   ἀγνόημα
ἀγνοήσαντες   VPAANM-P   ἀγνοέω

ἄγνοια, ας, ἡ *ignorance, lack of knowing better* (EP 4.18)

ἀγνοίᾳ   N-DF-S   ἄγνοια
ἀγνοίαις   N-DF-P   "
ἄγνοιαν   N-AF-S   "
ἀγνοίας   N-GF-S   "
ἁγνόν   A--AM-S   ἁγνός
ἀγνοοῦμεν   VIPA--1P   ἀγνοέω
ἀγνοούμενοι   VPPPNM-P   "
ἀγνοούμενος   VPPPNM-S   "

ἀγνοοῦντες   VPPANM-P   "
ἀγνοοῦσι(ν)   VIPA--3P   "
     VPPADM-P   "

ἀγνός, ή, όν (1) of persons, as characterized by moral purity *pure, free from sin* (1T 5.22); as being without intent to do wrong in a matter *innocent, blameless* (2C 7.11); (2) of things without moral defect *harmless, acceptable, pure* (PH 4.8)

ἀγνός   A--NM-S   ἀγνός

ἀγνότης, ητος, ἡ as a quality of behavior that is morally clean *purity, sincerity, blamelessness* (2C 6.6)

ἀγνότητι   N-DF-S   ἀγνότης
ἀγνότητος   N-GF-S   "
ἀγνούς   A--AM-P   ἀγνός
ἀγνοῶν   VPPANM-S   ἀγνοέω

ἀγνῶς adverb; of actions characterized by right motives *purely, sincerely* (PH 1.17)

ἀγνῶς   AB   ἀγνῶς

ἀγνωσία, ας, ἡ *ignorance*, especially denoting a lack of knowledge of God and of spiritual discernment, *failure to understand* (1P 2.15)

ἀγνωσίαν   N-AF-S   ἀγνωσία

ἄγνωστος, ον *unknown, not recognized* (AC 17.23)

ἀγνώστῳ   A--DM-S   ἄγνωστος
ἀγόμενα   VPPPAN-P   ἄγω
ἀγομένοις   VPPPDN-P   "
ἀγομένους   VPPPAM-P   "
ἀγομένων   VPPPGN-P   "
ἄγονται   VIPP--3P   "
ἄγοντες   VPPANM-P   "

ἀγορά, ᾶς, ἡ *marketplace*; a place for trading and business, especially as the center of public life *forum, public square*

ἀγορᾷ   N-DF-S   ἀγορά
ἀγοράζει   VIPA--3S   ἀγοράζω
ἀγοράζοντας   VPPAAM-P   "
ἀγοράζοντες   VPPANM-P   "

ἀγοράζω impf. ἠγόραζον; 1aor. ἠγόρασα; 1aor. pass. ἠγοράσθην; literally *buy, purchase, do business in the marketplace* (MT 13.44); figuratively, as being no longer controlled by sin *set free*; from the analogy of buying a slave's freedom for a price paid by a benefactor *redeem* (1C 6.20)

ἀγόραιοι   AP-NF-P   ἀγοραῖος
ἀγοραῖοι   AP-NF-P   "

ἀγοραῖος, ον (also **ἀγόραιος**) *belonging to the marketplace, frequenting the marketplace*; substantivally οἱ ἀγοραῖοι *market people, loafers, idle people in the marketplace* (AC 17.5); substantivally αἱ ἀγοραῖοι (ἡμέραι) the days when courts of justice are in session *court days, sessions* (AC 19.38)

ἀγοραῖς   N-DF-P   ἀγορά
ἀγοραίων   AP-GM-P   ἀγοραῖος
ἀγοράν   N-AF-S   ἀγορά
ἀγορᾶς   N-GF-S   "
ἀγοράσαι   VNAA   ἀγοράζω
ἀγοράσαντα   VPAAAM-S   "
ἀγοράσαντος   VPAAGM-S   "
ἀγοράσας   VPAANM-S   "
ἀγοράσατε   VMAA--2P   "
ἀγορασάτω   VMAA--3S   "

ἀγοράσομεν   VIFA--1P   "
ἀγόρασον   VMAA--2S   "
ἀγοράσωμεν   VSAA--1P   "
ἀγοράσωσι(ν)   VSAA--3P   "
ἄγουσι(ν)   VIPA--3P   ἄγω

ἄγρα, ας, ἡ as an action *catching, hunting*; εἰς ἄγραν *to catch, for a catch* (LU 5.4); passive, of what is taken *catch*; of the amount of fish taken by one drawing-in of the net *draft, catch* (LU 5.9)

ἄγρᾳ   N-DF-S   ἄγρα
ἀγράμματοι   A--NM-P   ἀγράμματος

ἀγράμματος, ον strictly *unable to write*; hence *unable to read or write, illiterate; uneducated, unlearned* (AC 4.13)

ἄγραν   N-AF-S   ἄγρα

ἀγραυλέω *live outdoors, stay in the open air*; of shepherds *stay in the fields* (LU 2.8)

ἀγραυλοῦντες   VPPANM-P   ἀγραυλέω
ἀγρεύσωσι(ν)   VSAA--3P   ἀγρεύω

ἀγρεύω 1aor. ἤγρευσα; of hunting or fishing *take, catch*; figuratively in the NT, of taking advantage of someone in an unguarded moment *catch in a mistake, try to get someone to make a wrong statement* (MK 12.13)

ἄγρια   A--NN-P   ἄγριος

ἀγριέλαιος, ου, ἡ *wild olive tree* (RO 11.24), opposite καλλιέλαιος (*cultivated olive tree*); *sprout* or *shoot from an uncultivated olive tree* (RO 11.17)

ἀγριέλαιος   N-NF-S   ἀγριέλαιος
ἀγριελαίου   N-GF-S   "
ἄγριον   A--AN-S   ἄγριος
     A--NN-S   "

ἄγριος, ία, ον literally, of plants and animals *found in the open field* or *forest, wild* (MT 3.4); figuratively, of strong natural occurrences *stormy, fierce*; of sea waves *raging, violent* (JU 13)

Ἀγρίππα   N-GM-S   Ἀγρίππας
     N-VM-S   "

Ἀγρίππας, α, ὁ *Agrippa*, masculine proper noun

Ἀγρίππας   N-NM-S   Ἀγρίππας
ἀγρόν   N-AM-S   ἀγρός

ἀγρός, οῦ, ὁ (1) *field*, especially as cultivated for agriculture (MT 13.24); (2) *country, rural area*, as opposed to a city or village (MK 16.12); (3) plural *lands, farms*, (small, unwalled) *villages* or *hamlets* (LU 9.12)

ἀγρός   N-NM-S   ἀγρός
ἀγροῦ   N-GM-S   "
ἀγρούς   N-AM-P   "
ἀγρυπνεῖτε   VMPA--2P   ἀγρυπνέω

ἀγρυπνέω literally *be awake, watch, stay alert*; figuratively *be on the lookout for, be watchful* (MK 13.33); of diligent concern for others *keep watch over, care for* (HE 13.17)

ἀγρυπνία, ας, ἡ *lack of sleep, wakefulness*; plural *sleepless nights*

ἀγρυπνίαις   N-DF-P   ἀγρυπνία
ἀγρυπνοῦντες   VPPANM-P   ἀγρυπνέω
ἀγρυπνοῦσι(ν)   VIPA--3P   "
ἀγρῷ   N-DM-S   ἀγρός
ἀγρῶν   N-GM-P   "

ἄγω fut. ἄξω; 2aor. ἤγαγον; 1aor. pass. ἤχθην; 1fut. pass. ἀχθήσομαι; *lead, bring*; (1) as conducting or accompanying someone or something *bring* or *take along* (1TH

4.14); figuratively, of the influence of God's Spirit *lead, guide* (RO 8.14); (2) as a legal technical term implying use of force *lead away, arrest, take into custody* (MK 13.11); (3) of time *spend, celebrate, observe* certain days (AC 19.38); τρίτην ταύτην ἡμέραν ἄγει probably *this third day he spends*; perhaps impersonally *this is now the third day* (LU 24.21); (4) intransitively, as moving away from a point of reference *go, depart*; ἄγωμεν *let us go* (MT 26.46); (5) present imperative as an interjection intended to call attention to the following statement ἄγε νῦν *come now! look here! now listen!* (JA 4.13)

ἄγω	VIPA--1S	ἄγω

ἀγωγή, ῆς, ἡ *manner* or *way of life, conduct, behavior* (2T 3.10)

ἀγωγῇ	N-DF-S	ἀγωγή
ἄγωμεν	VSPA--1P	ἄγω

ἀγών, ἀγῶνος, ὁ (1) literally *(athletic) contest*; metaphorically *race* (i.e. *course*) *of life* (HE 12.1); (2) of exertion and self-denial in the face of opposition *conflict, struggle, fight*; figuratively, of intense nonphysical *struggle, conflict* (1TH 2.2)

ἀγῶνα	N-AM-S	ἀγών
ἀγῶνι	N-DM-S	"

ἀγωνία, ας, ἡ as great inner tension or conflict *agony, anguish, anxiety* (LU 22.44)

ἀγωνία	N-DF-S	ἀγωνία
ἀγωνίζεσθε	VMPD--2P	ἀγωνίζομαι
	VMPO--2P	"

ἀγωνίζομαι pf. ἠγώνισμαι; (1) literally, of public games *engage in a contest, contend for a prize* (1C 9.25); figuratively, of any heroic effort *strive earnestly, make every effort, try very hard* (CO 1.29); (2) of fighting with weapons, literally *fight, struggle* (JN 18.36); figuratively, of great nonphysical effort and struggle *strive earnestly, do one's very best* (CO 4.12)

ἀγωνιζόμεθα	VIPD--1P	ἀγωνίζομαι
	VIPO--1P	"
ἀγωνιζόμενοι	VPPDNM-P	"
	VPPONM-P	"
ἀγωνιζόμενος	VPPDNM-S	"
	VPPONM-S	"
ἀγωνίζου	VMPD--2S	"
	VMPO--2S	"
ἄγωσι(ν)	VSPA--3P	ἄγω

Ἀδάμ, ὁ indeclinable; *Adam*, masculine proper noun

ἀδάπανον	A--AN-S	ἀδάπανος

ἀδάπανος, ον *free of charge, without expense* (1C 9.18)

Ἀδδί		Ἀδδί

Ἀδδί, ὁ (also **Ἀδδεί**) indeclinable; *Addi*, masculine proper noun (LU 3.28)

ἀδελφαί	N-NF-P	ἀδελφή
ἀδελφάς	N-AF-P	"
ἀδελφέ	N-VM-S	ἀδελφός

ἀδελφή, ῆς, ἡ *sister*; literally, female sibling with at least one parent in common (AC 23.16); figuratively, female member of the Christian community (RO 16.1)

ἀδελφή	N-NF-S	ἀδελφή
ἀδελφῇ	N-DF-S	"
ἀδελφήν	N-AF-S	"
ἀδελφῆς	N-GF-S	"
ἀδελφοί	N-NM-P	ἀδελφός
	N-VM-P	"

ἀδελφοῖς	N-DM-P	"
ἀδελφόν	N-AM-S	"

ἀδελφός, οῦ, ὁ *brother*; (1) literally, male sibling with at least one parent in common (JN 1.41); figuratively, members of the Christian community, and of associates in religious work *(spiritual) brother, fellow Christian, fellow believer* (RO 8.29); (2) in Jewish usage *fellow countryman* (AC 3.22); (3) of one of equal rank and dignity (MT 23.8); (4) of a neighbor or member of one's in-group *brother, friend* (MT 5.22)

ἀδελφός	N-NM-S	ἀδελφός

ἀδελφότης, ητος, ἡ literally, as a group of people united for a common purpose *brotherhood*; figuratively, as a group of fellow believers *brotherhood, community of believers* (1P 2.17)

ἀδελφότητα	N-AF-S	ἀδελφότης
ἀδελφότητι	N-DF-S	"
ἀδελφοῦ	N-GM-S	ἀδελφός
ἀδελφούς	N-AM-P	"
ἀδελφῷ	N-DM-S	"
ἀδελφῶν	N-GM-P	"
ᾅδῃ	N-VM-S	ᾅδης
ᾅδῃ	N-DM-S	"
ἄδηλα	A--NN-P	ἄδηλος
ἄδηλον	A--AF-S	"

ἄδηλος, ον (1) *not clear, unseen, unmarked* (LU 11.44); (2) *not clear, vague, indistinct* (1C 14.8)

ἀδηλότης, ητος, ἡ *uncertainty*; of riches that are soon gone *insecurity* (1T 6.17)

ἀδηλότητι	N-DF-S	ἀδηλότης

ἀδήλως adverb; *uncertainly, indistinctly*; of running a race without a fixed goal *aimlessly* (1C 9.26)

ἀδήλως	AB	ἀδήλως
ἀδημονεῖν	VNPA	ἀδημονέω

ἀδημονέω (and **ἀκηδεμονέω**) *be upset, be distressed, be (deeply) troubled* (MK 14.33)

ἀδημονῶν	VPPANM-S	ἀδημονέω
ᾅδην	N-AM-S	ᾅδης

ᾅδης, ου, ὁ *Hades* (literally *unseen place*); (1) the place of the dead *underworld* (AC 2.27); (2) usually in the NT as the temporary underworld prison where the souls of the ungodly await the judgment (LU 16.23); (3) personified as following along after Death (RV 6.8)

ᾅδης	N-NM-S	ᾅδης

ἀδιάκριτος, ον with active sense; (1) as being without uncertainty *unwavering, unshakable* (possibly JA 3.17); (2) without making distinctions *impartial, free from prejudice* (probably JA 3.17)

ἀδιάκριτος	A--NF-S	ἀδιάκριτος
ἀδιάλειπτον	A--AF-S	ἀδιάλειπτος

ἀδιάλειπτος, ον *unceasing, unfailing, without stopping*

ἀδιάλειπτος	A--NF-S	ἀδιάλειπτος

ἀδιαλείπτως adverb; *unceasingly, continuously*

ἀδιαλείπτως	AB	ἀδιαλείπτως

ἀδιαφθορία, ας, ἡ of freedom from corruption *sincerity, honesty, integrity* (TI 2.7)

ἀδιαφθορίαν	N-AF-S	ἀδιαφθορία
ἀδικεῖσθε	VIPP--2P	ἀδικέω
ἀδικεῖτε	VIPA--2P	"

ἀδικέω fut. ἀδικήσω; 1aor. ἠδίκησα; pf. ἠδίκηκα; 1aor. pass. ἠδικήθην; (1) intransitively, of acting unjustly *be* *in the wrong* (RV 22.11); as violating law *do wrong* (CO 3.25); (2) transitively, with the accusative of a person *do wrong to, act unjustly toward, injure* (AC 7.26); passive *suffer wrong* or *injustice* (1C 6.7); with the accusative of the thing *harm, damage, hurt* (RV 7.2); passive *be harmed by, suffer damage* (2P 2.13)

ἀδικηθέντος	VPAPGM-S	ἀδικέω
ἀδικηθῇ	VSAP--3S	"

ἀδίκημα, ατος, τό as a completed act of deliberate wrong-doing *wrong, crime, (act of) injustice* (AC 24.20)

ἀδίκημα	N-AN-S	ἀδίκημα
	N-NN-S	"
ἀδικήματα	N-AN-P	"
ἀδικῆσαι	VNAA	ἀδικέω
ἀδικήσαντος	VPAAGM-S	"
ἀδικησάτω	VMAA--3S	"
ἀδικήσει	VIFA--3S	"
ἀδικήσῃ	VSAA--3S	"
ἀδικήσῃς	VSAA--2S	"
ἀδικήσητε	VSAA--2P	"
ἀδικήσουσι(ν)	VIFA--3P	"
ἀδικήσωσι(ν)	VSAA--3P	"

ἀδικία, ας, ἡ generally *disregard for what is right*; (1) as disregard for divine law *unrighteousness, wrongdoing* (HE 8.12), correlated with ἀνομία (*lawlessness, wickedness*) and opposite δικαιοσύνη (*righteousness, uprightness*); (2) as disregard for human rights *injustice, unrighteousness, violation of justice* (RO 1.18); (3) as disregard for the respect and obedience due to God *wickedness, unrighteousness, wrongdoing* (1J 1.9), correlated with ἁμαρτία (*sin*); (4) as disregard for truth *wrong, evil* (1C 13.6), opposite ἀλήθεια (*truth*)

ἀδικία	N-NF-S	ἀδικία
ἀδικίᾳ	N-DF-S	"
ἀδικίαις	N-DF-P	"
ἀδικίαν	N-AF-S	"
ἀδικίας	N-GF-S	"
ἄδικοι	AP-NM-P	ἄδικος
	A--NM-P	"
ἀδικοκριτάς	N-AM-P	ἀδικοκριτής

ἀδικοκριτής, ου, ὁ *unjust judge*, a judge who does not correctly follow the law in his legal decisions (TI 1.9)

ἄδικος, ον generally *characterized by violation of divine law*; (1) as doing contrary to what is right, *unrighteous, wrong* (MT 5.45), opposite δίκαιος (*righteous, just*); (2) as characterized by disregard for God *ungodly, unjust* (2P 2.9), opposite εὐσεβής (*devout, godly*); (3) as characterized by lack of integrity *dishonest, untrustworthy* (LU 16.10), opposite πιστός (*trustworthy, faithful*); (4) of things obtained by wrong means *unjust, dishonest* (LU 16.11); (5) substantivally, of a person not a member of a Christian community *unbeliever* (1C 6.1)

ἄδικος	AP-NM-S	ἄδικος
	A--NM-S	"
ἀδίκου	A--GM-S	"
ἀδικούμενοι	VPPMNM-P	ἀδικέω
	VPPPNM-P	"
ἀδικούμενον	VPPPAM-S	"
ἀδικοῦντας	VPPAAM-P	"
ἀδίκους	AP-AM-P	ἄδικος
ἀδικοῦσι(ν)	VIPA--3P	ἀδικέω

ἀδικῶ	VIPA--1S	"
ἀδίκῳ	A--DM-S	ἄδικος
ἀδίκων	AP-GM-P	"
ἀδικῶν	VPPANM-S	ἀδικέω

ἀδίκως adverb; characterized by wrongdoing *unjustly*; passive, of suffering injustice *undeservedly, without good reason* (1P 2.19)

ἀδίκως	AB	ἀδίκως
Ἀδμείν		Ἀδμίν
Ἀδμί		"

Ἀδμίν, ὁ (also **Ἀδμείν, Ἀδμί, Ἀρμίν**) indeclinable; *Admin*, masculine proper noun (LU 3.33)

ἀδόκιμοι	A--NM-P	ἀδόκιμος
ἀδόκιμον	A--AM-S	"

ἀδόκιμος, ον strictly *failing to meet the test*; hence *worthless, unqualified*; (1) of athletic endeavor *disqualified* (1C 9.27); (2) of false profession of faith *rejected, proven false* (2T 3.8); (3) of proven inability to do good *unfit, untrustworthy, worthless* (TI 1.16)

ἀδόκιμος	A--NF-S	ἀδόκιμος
	A--NM-S	"
ἄδολον	A--AN-S	ἄδολος

ἄδολος, ον *without deceit, honest*; passive *pure, unadulterated*, of milk (1P 2.2)

ᾄδοντας	VPPAAM-P	ᾄδω
ᾄδοντες	VPPANM-P	"
ᾅδου	N-GM-S	ᾅδης
ᾄδουσι(ν)	VIPA--3P	ᾄδω
Ἀδραμυντηνῷ	A--DN-S	Ἀδραμυντηνός
Ἀδραμυντηνῷ	A--DN-S	"

Ἀδραμυντηνός, ή, όν (also **Ἀδραμυντηνός, Ἀδραμυντηνός**) *from Adramyttium*, an Aegean seaport in Mysia in northwestern Asia Minor (AC 27.2)

Ἀδραμυττηνῷ	A--DN-S	Ἀδραμυντηνός
Ἀδρίᾳ	N-DM-S	Ἀδρίας
Ἀδρίᾳ	N-DM-S	"

Ἀδρίας, ου, ὁ (also **Ἀδρίας**) *Adriatic Sea*, between Crete and Sicily in the Mediterranean, and north between Italy and Greece (AC 27.27)

ἁδρότης, ητος, ἡ *abundance*; characterized by *fullness* or *ripeness*; of a money collection *great liberality, generous gift* (2C 8.20)

ἁδρότητι	N-DF-S	ἁδρότης
ἀδύνατα	AP-NN-P	ἀδύνατος

ἀδυνατέω fut. ἀδυνατήσω; *be powerless, be unable*; only impersonally in the NT ἀδυνατεῖ *be impossible*

ἀδυνατήσει	VIFA--3S	ἀδυνατέω
ἀδύνατον	AP-AN-S	ἀδύνατος
	A--NN-S	"

ἀδύνατος, ον (1) active, of one with no ability *powerless, incapable* (AC 14.8); figuratively and substantivally οἱ ἀδύνατοι *those who do not strongly believe* (RO 15.1); (2) passive *impossible*; impersonally *(it is) impossible* (MT 19.26); substantivally τὸ ἀδύνατον *what is impossible* (RO 8.3)

ἀδύνατος	A--NM-S	ἀδύνατος
ἀδυνάτων	A--GM-P	"
ἀδυσβάστακτα	A--AN-P	see δυσβάστακτα

ᾄδω *sing, produce musical sounds* or *notes with the voice*

ἀεί adverb; (1) *always, forever* (1P 3.15); (2) referring to the past *always, from the beginning* (2P 1.12); (3) of a frequently recurring action *continually, constantly* (2C 4.11)

ἀεί	AB	ἀεί
ἀέρα	N-AM-S	ἀήρ
ἀέρος	N-GM-S	"
ἀετοί	N-NM-P	ἀετός

ἀετός, οῦ, ὁ (1) as a large bird with great strength and speed *eagle* (RV 12.14); (2) as an eater of decaying flesh *vulture* (LU 17.37)

ἀετοῦ	N-GM-S	ἀετός
ἀετῷ	N-DM-S	"
ἄζυμα	AP-NN-P	ἄζυμος
ἄζυμοι	A--NM-P	"
ἀζύμοις	AP-DN-P	"

ἄζυμος, ον (1) *without fermentation*; of bread *unleavened, made without yeast*; substantivally τὰ ἄζυμα *unleavened bread* made into flat cakes (Hebrew *matzoth*) eaten by Jews at Passover season; metaphorically in 1C 5.7, 8 of a life free from sinful corruption; (2) by metonymy for the Passover *festival of unleavened bread* (MT 26.17)

ἀζύμων	AP-GN-P	ἄζυμος

Ἀζώρ, ὁ indeclinable; *Azor*, masculine proper noun

Ἄζωτον	N-AF-S	Ἄζωτος

Ἄζωτος, ου, ἡ *Azotus*, NT name for the Philistine city of Ashdod along the Mediterranean coast (AC 8.40)

ἀηδία, ας, ἡ strictly *unpleasantness, what excites hatred*; hence *dislike, enmity* (LU 23.12)

ἀηδία	N-DF-S	ἀηδία
ἀηλί		ἠλί

ἀήρ, έρος, ὁ (1) as the space immediately above the earth *air, atmosphere* (1C 14.9); (2) as a substance *air*; equivalent to *nothing* in 1C 9.26; (3) as the space between heaven and earth inhabited by spirit-beings *sky, air* (EP 2.2)

ἀήρ	N-NM-S	ἀήρ
ἀθά		see μαράνα θά
ἀθᾶ		see μαράνα θά

ἀθανασία, ας, ἡ *immortality, endless existence*, opposite τὸ θνητόν (*what is subject to death*)

ἀθανασίαν	N-AF-S	ἀθανασία

ἀθάνατος, ον having a quality of endless existence *deathless, immortal* (1T 1.17), opposite θνητός (*mortal, subject to death*); substantivally ὁ ἀ. *the immortal one* (RV 6.8)

ἀθάνατος	A--NM-S	ἀθάνατος
ἀθανάτῳ	A--DM-S	"
ἀθεμίτοις	A--DF-P	ἀθέμιτος
ἀθέμιτον	A--NN-S	"

ἀθέμιτος, ον of what is contrary to (higher) law *unlawful, illegal*; (1) of pagan idolatry *forbidden, disgusting* (1P 4.3); (2) impersonally ἀθέμιτόν ἐστιν with an infinitive following *it is unlawful, not right, not allowed* (AC 10.28)

ἄθεοι	A--NM-P	ἄθεος

ἄθεος, ον strictly *atheistic*; as estrangement from God *godless, without God* (EP 2.12)

ἄθεσμος, ον *lawless, unprincipled*, opposite δίκαιος (*righteous, just*); substantivally ὁ ἀ. of a person who breaks through the restraint of law to satisfy selfish desire *the lawless one, the licentious person* (2P 2.7)

ἀθέσμων	A--GM-P	ἄθεσμος

ἀθετεῖ	VIPA--3S	ἀθετέω
ἀθετεῖτε	VIPA--2P	"

ἀθετέω fut. ἀθετήσω; 1aor. ἠθέτησα; strictly *regard as nothing, set aside*; (1) of a legal enactment *annul, declare invalid* (GA 3.15); (2) of God's setting aside human intelligence as a means of knowing God *frustrate, thwart* (1C 1.19); (3) as directed toward people and events *reject, turn one's back on, refuse* (JN 12.48)

ἀθετῆσαι	VNAA	ἀθετέω
ἀθετήσας	VPAANM-S	"
ἀθέτησιν	N-AF-S	ἀθέτησις

ἀθέτησις, εως, ἡ (1) as a legal technical term *annulment, setting aside* as being no longer in force (HE 7.18); (2) of Christ's dealing with sin *removal, putting away, doing away with* (HE 9.26)

ἀθέτησις	N-NF-S	ἀθέτησις
ἀθετήσω	VIFA--1S	ἀθετέω
ἀθετοῦσι(ν)	VIPA--3P	"
ἀθετῶ	VIPA--1S	"
ἀθετῶν	VPPANM-S	"

Ἀθῆναι, Ἀθηνῶν, αἱ *Athens*, capital city of Attica in Greece

Ἀθηναῖοι	AP-NM-P	Ἀθηναῖος
	A--VM-P	"

Ἀθηναῖος, αία, ον *Athenian, inhabiting Athens*; substantivally *citizen of Athens, Athenian*

Ἀθήναις	N-DF-P	Ἀθῆναι
Ἀθηνῶν	N-GF-P	"

ἀθλέω *strive, compete*; in the athletic arena *take part in a contest*

ἀθλῇ	VSPA--3S	ἀθλέω
ἀθλήσῃ	VSAA--3S	"
ἄθλησιν	N-AF-S	ἄθλησις

ἄθλησις, εως, ἡ literally *contest, challenge*; figuratively *combat, struggle, conflict* (HE 10.32)

ἀθροίζω pf. pass. ptc. ἠθροισμένος; only passive in the NT *gather together, assemble in a group* (LU 24.33)

ἀθυμέω *be discouraged, feel like giving up, lack motivation* (CO 3.21)

ἀθυμῶσι(ν)	VSPA--3P	ἀθυμέω
ἄθῳον	A--AN-S	ἄθῳος
ἄθῳος	A--NM-S	"

ἄθῳος, ον (also ἀθῷος) *innocent, guiltless* (MT 27.24)

ἀθῷος	A--NM-S	ἄθῳος
αἱ	DNFP	ὁ
	DNFP+	"
	DNFP^APDNF-P	"
	DVFP	"
αἵ	APRNF-P	ὅς
αἰγείοις	A--DN-P	αἴγειος

αἴγειος, εία, ον (also αἴγιος) *of a goat*; of clothing ἐν αἰγείοις δέρμασιν *in goatskins* (HE 11.37)

αἰγιαλόν	N-AM-S	αἰγιαλός

αἰγιαλός, οῦ, ὁ *seashore, beach*

αἰγιαλῷ	N-DM-S	αἰγιαλός
αἰγίοις	A--DN-P	αἴγειος
Αἰγύπτιοι	AP-NM-P	Αἰγύπτιος
Αἰγύπτιον	AP-AM-S	"

Αἰγύπτιος, ία, ον *Egyptian*; substantivally, as a national name *Egyptian* (AC 7.24)

Αἰγύπτιος	AP-NM-S	Αἰγύπτιος

Αἰγυπτίων   AP-GM-P   "

Αἴγυπτον   N-AF-S   Αἴγυπτος

Αἴγυπτος, ου, ἡ (also Ἔγυπτος) *Egypt*, a country of northern Africa

Αἴγυπτος   N-NF-S   Αἴγυπτος

Αἰγύπτου   N-GF-S   "

Αἰγύπτῳ   N-DF-S   "

αἰγῶν   N-GM-P   αἴξ

ἀϊδίοις   A--DM-P   ἀΐδιος

           A--DN-P   "

ἀΐδιος, ον *everlasting, eternal, always existing*

ἀΐδιος   A--NF-S   ἀΐδιος

αἰδοῦς   N-GF-S   αἰδώς

αἰδώς, οῦς, ἡ *reverence, respect*; of women *modesty* (1T 2.9)

Αἰθιόπων   N-GM-P   Αἰθίοψ

Αἰθίοψ, οπος, ὁ *Ethiopian, inhabitant of Ethiopia*, a country in Africa south of Egypt

Αἰθίοψ   N-NM-S   Αἰθίοψ

αἷμα, ατος, τό *blood*; (1) human *blood* (JN 19.34); by metonymy *human nature, physical descent* (HE 2.14); (2) of sacrificial animals *blood* (HE 9.7); (3) idiomatically αἱ. ἐκχεῖν literally *pour out blood*, i.e. *kill* (RV 16.6); ῥύσις αἵματος *menstrual flow, hemorrhage* (MK 5.25); πηγὴ αἵματος literally *fountain of blood*, i.e. *bleeding* (MK 5.29); (4) by metonymy, of another's murder (MT 23.30); of Christ's atoning sacrifice *death*, the blood of Christ (RO 3.25); (5) in apocalyptic language, the red color of blood as symbolizing disaster (AC 2.19)

αἷμα   N-AN-S   αἷμα

      N-NN-S   "

αἵματα   N-AN-P   "

      N-NN-P   "

αἱματεκχυσία, ας, ἡ from αἷμα (*blood*) and ἐκχέω (*pour out*); *shedding* or *pouring out of blood*, especially referring to the killing and offering sacrifices (HE 9.22)

αἱματεκχυσίας   N-GF-S   αἱματεκχυσία

αἵματι   N-DN-S   αἷμα

αἵματος   N-GN-S   "

αἱμάτων   N-GN-P   "

αἱμορροέω from αἷμα (*blood*) and ῥέω (*flow*); *suffer with a hemorrhage, bleed, lose blood* (MT 9.20)

αἱμορροοῦσα   VPPANF-S   αἱμορροέω

Αἰνέα   N-VM-S   Αἰνέας

Αἰνέαν   N-AM-S   "

Αἰνέας, ου, ὁ *Aeneas*, masculine proper noun

αἰνεῖν   VNPA   αἰνέω

αἰνεῖτε   VMPA--2P   "

αἰνέσεως   N-GF-S   αἴνεσις

αἴνεσις, εως, ἡ as an action *praise*, a speaking of how excellent a person, thing, or event is (HE 13.15)

αἰνέω *praise, speak in praise of*; in the NT used only of praise for God

αἴνιγμα, ατος, τό (1) as a saying difficult to understand *riddle, enigma*; (2) as revelation obscurely expressed ἐν αἰνίγματι *dimly, indistinctly* (1C 13.12)

αἰνίγματι   N-DN-S   αἴνιγμα

αἶνον   N-AM-S   αἶνος

αἶνος, ου, ὁ *praise*, what is spoken to extol or honor someone

αἰνοῦντα   VPPAAM-S   αἰνέω

αἰνοῦντες   VPPANM-P   "

αἰνούντων   VPPAGM-P   "

Αἰνών, ἡ indeclinable; *Aenon*, a place where springs are found along the Jordan River valley (JN 3.23)

αἰνῶν   VPPANM-S   αἰνέω

αἴξ, αἰγός, ὁ and ἡ *goat*, either male or female (LU 15.29)

αἶρε   VMPA--2S   αἴρω

αἴρει   VIPA--3S   "

αἴρεις   VIPA--2S   "

αἱρέομαι   VIPM--1S   αἱρέω

αἱρέσεις   N-AF-P   αἵρεσις

      N-NF-P   "

αἱρέσεως   N-GF-S   "

αἵρεσιν   N-AF-S   "

αἵρεσις, έσεως, ἡ strictly *choice* or *option*; (1) of a separatist group characterized by loyalty to a certain school of thought and practice *sect, party, school* (AC 5.17); (2) of such separatist groups claiming status within the Christian community *heretical sect, party, division* (1C 11.19); (3) in a religious sense, of belief contrary to established doctrine *heresy, false teaching* (2P 2.1)

αἵρεσις   N-NF-S   αἵρεσις

αἵρεται   VIPP--3S   αἴρω

αἵρετε   VMPA--2P   "

αἱρετίζω 1aor. ἡρέτισα; *choose*; in a strengthened sense *choose with delight*, perhaps in the sense of *adopt* (MT 12.18)

αἱρετικόν   A--AM-S   αἱρετικός

αἱρετικός, ή, όν denoting loyalty to a separatist group *heretical, factious, causing divisions* (TI 3.10)

αἱρέω fut. mid. αἱρήσομαι; 2aor. mid. εἱλόμην and εἱλάμην; (1) active *take, grasp*; (2) middle in the NT, of taking for oneself *choose, select* (2TH 2.13); as choosing between alternatives *prefer* (PH 1.22)

αἱρήσομαι   VIFM--1S   αἱρέω

αἱρήσωμαι   VSAM--1S   "

αἱρόμενον   VPPPAM-S   αἴρω

αἴροντος   VPPAGM-S   "

αἴρω fut. ἀρῶ; 1aor. ἦρα; pf. ἦρκα; pf. pass. ἦρμαι; 1aor. pass. ἤρθην; fut. pass. ἀρθήσομαι; (1) literally, as lifting up something *take up, pick, raise* (MT 17.27; RV 10.5); absolutely, of a ship *weigh anchor, depart* (AC 27.13); hyperbolically, of a mountain *arise* (MT 21.21); idiomatically αἴρειν τοὺς ὀφθαλμοὺς ἄνω literally *raise one's eyes*, i.e. *look up* (JN 11.41); αἴρειν τὸν σταυρόν literally *take up the cross*, i.e. *be prepared to suffer to the point of death* (MT 16.24); αἴρειν τὴν ψυχήν τινος literally *lift up someone's soul*, i.e. *keep someone in suspense* without being able to come to a conclusion (JN 10.24); (2) as lifting up and carrying something away *remove, carry off, take away* (JN 11.39); idiomatically αἴρειν ἀπό literally *take from*, i.e. *cause to no longer experience* (MT 21.43); (3) of removing by force; (a) *do away with, kill, execute* (JN 19.15); (b) *sweep away* as with a flood (MT 24.39); (c) *destroy, do away with* (JN 11.48); (d) as a religious technical term, of the effect of Christ's paying the complete penalty for sin *remove, take away* (JN 1.29)

αἴρω   VIPA--1S   αἴρω

αἴρων   VPPANM-S   "

ἄρωσι(ν)   VSPA--3P   "

αἷς   APRDF-P   ὅς

αἰσθάνομαι   2aor. ἠσθόμην; as indicating an inner thought process; intellectually *perceive, understand*; spiritually *discern, perceive* (LU 9.45)

αἰσθήσει   N-DF-S   αἴσθησις

αἴσθησις, εως, ἡ   as a moral action of recognizing distinctions and making a decision about behavior *perception, insight, capacity for understanding* (PH 1.9)

αἰσθητήρια   N-AN-P   αἰσθητήριον

αἰσθητήριον, ου, τό   as the ability to make moral decisions *sense, ability to understand, power to discriminate* (HE 5.14)

αἴσθωνται   VSAD--3P   αἰσθάνομαι
αἰσχροκερδεῖς   A--AM-P   αἰσχροκερδής
αἰσχροκερδῆ   A--AM-S   "

αἰσχροκερδής, ές   *covetous of, eager for dishonest gain, greedy in a shameful way* (1T 3.8)

αἰσχροκερδῶς   adverb; *covetously, greedily, with eagerness for dishonest gain* (1P 5.2)

αἰσχροκερδῶς   AB   αἰσχροκερδῶς

αἰσχρολογία, ας, ἡ   *dirty talk, filthy* or *obscene language* or *speech* (CO 3.8)

αἰσχρολογίαν   N-AF-S   αἰσχρολογία
αἰσχρόν   A--NN-S   αἰσχρός

αἰσχρός, ά, όν   literally *ugly, deformed*, opposite καλός (*good, beautiful*); figuratively in the NT, of what is *disgraceful, shameful* (1C 11.6); of effort for gain *dishonest* (TI 1.11)

αἰσχρότης, ητος, ἡ   literally *ugliness*; figuratively *indecency*; in a concrete sense, equivalent to αἰσχρολογία (EP 5.4)

αἰσχρότης   N-NF-S   αἰσχρότης
αἰσχροῦ   A--GN-S   αἰσχρός
αἰσχύνας   N-AF-P   αἰσχύνη
αἰσχυνέσθω   VMPM--3S   αἰσχύνω

αἰσχύνη, ης, ἡ   (1) as a feeling *shame, embarrassment, humiliation* (LU 14.9); (2) as an experience that comes to one, either deservedly (JU 13) or undeservedly (HE 12.2) *shame, disgrace*; (3) of conduct that causes shame *shameful ways, dishonorable deeds* (2C 4.2)

αἰσχύνη   N-NF-S   αἰσχύνη
αἰσχύνῃ   N-DF-S   "
αἰσχύνης   N-GF-S   "
αἰσχυνθήσομαι   VIFP--1S   αἰσχύνω
αἰσχυνθῶμεν   VSAP--1P   "
αἰσχυνθῶσι(ν)   VSAP--3P   "
αἰσχύνομαι   VIPM--1S   "

αἰσχύνω   1aor. pass. ᾐσχύνθην; fut. pass. αἰσχυνθήσομαι; only middle/passive in the NT; middle *be ashamed, feel ashamed* or *embarrassed* (LU 16.3); passive, in the sense of being disappointed or disillusioned *be put to shame, admit defeat, be disgraced* (PH 1.20)

αἰτεῖ   VIPA--3S   αἰτέω
αἰτεῖν   VNPA   "
αἰτεῖς   VIPA--2S   "
αἰτεῖσθαι   VNPM   "
αἰτεῖσθε   VIPM--2P   "
αἰτεῖτε   VIPA--2P   "
               VMPA--2P   "
αἰτείτω   VMPA--3S   "

αἰτέω   mid. αἰτέομαι; fut. αἰτήσω, mid. αἰτήσομαι; 1aor. ᾔτησα, mid. ᾐτησάμην; pf. ᾔτηκα; active/middle *ask (for), request* (MT 7.10); *ask for, demand* (LU 23.23); as making a request in prayer *ask for* (MT 21.22)

αἴτημα, ατος, τό   as what has been requested or demanded *request, petition, demand*; as distinct from δέησις (*plea, entreaty*), αἴ. is the content of the request or petition

αἴτημα   N-AN-S   αἴτημα
αἰτήματα   N-AN-P   "
               N-NN-P
αἰτῆσαι   VNAA   αἰτέω
αἰτήσας   VPAANM-S   "
αἰτήσασθε   VMAM--2P   "
αἰτήσει   VIFA--3S   "
               VIFA--3S^VMAA--3S
αἰτήσεις   VIFA--2S   "
αἰτήσεσθαι   VNFM   "
αἰτήσεσθε   VIFM--2P   "
αἰτήσῃ   VSAA--3S   "
               VSAM--2S
αἰτήσῃς   VSAA--2S   "
αἰτήσηται   VSAM--3S   "
αἰτήσητε   VSAA--2P   "
αἰτήσομαι   VIFM--1S   "
αἴτησον   VMAA--2S   "
αἰτήσουσι(ν)   VIFA--3P   "
αἰτήσωμαι   VSAM--1S   "
αἰτήσωμεν   VSAA--1P   "
αἰτήσωνται   VSAM--3P   "
αἰτῆτε   VSPA--2P   "

αἰτία, ας, ἡ   (1) *cause, reason, grounds* (MT 19.3); as the grounds in a particular situation *case* (MT 19.10); (2) as a legal technical term *(formal) charge, ground for accusation* (AC 23.28); αἰτίαν φέρειν *bring accusation* (AC 25.18)

αἰτία   N-NF-S   αἰτία
αἰτιάματα   N-AN-P   αἰτίωμα
αἰτίαν   N-AF-S   αἰτία

αἰτιάομαι   1aor. ᾐτιασάμην; *accuse, charge with something* (RO 3.9)

αἰτίας   N-AF-P   αἰτία
               N-GF-S   "
αἵτινες   APRNF-P   ὅστις
αἴτιοι   AP-NM-P   αἴτιος
αἴτιον   AP-AN-S   "

αἴτιος, ία, ον   of being the cause of something *responsible, guilty*; substantivally in the NT; (1) in a good sense ὁ αἴ. *the cause, source* (HE 5.9); (2) in a bad sense τὸ αἴτιον equivalent to αἰτία *(basis of) guilt, crime* (LU 23.4); αἴτιον θανάτου *reason for capital punishment, grounds for the death penalty* (LU 23.22)

αἴτιος   AP-NM-S   αἴτιος
αἰτίου   AP-GN-S   "

αἰτίωμα, ατος, τό (also **αἰτίαμα**)   as a legal technical term *charge, complaint, accusation* (AC 25.7)

αἰτιώματα   N-AN-P   αἰτίωμα
αἰτοῦμαι   VIPM--1S   αἰτέω
αἰτούμεθα   VIPM--1P   "
αἰτούμενοι   VPPMNM-P   "
αἰτοῦντι   VPPADM-S   "
αἰτοῦσα   VPPANF-S   "

αἰτοῦσι(ν)   VIPA--3P   "
   VPPADM-P   "
αἰτώμεθα   VSPM--1P   "
αἰτῶμεν   VSPA--1P   "
αἰτῶν   VPPANM-S   "

αἰφνίδιος, ον (also **ἐφνίδιος**)   *sudden, unforeseen, unexpected*

αἰφνίδιος   A--NF-S   αἰφνίδιος
   A--NM-S   "

αἰχμαλωσία, ας, ἡ   *captivity, state of captivity* as a result of war (RV 13.10); in a concrete sense *group of captives, prisoners of war, captive multitude* (EP 4.8)

αἰχμαλωσίαν   N-AF-S   αἰχμαλωσία
αἰχμαλωσίας   N-GF-S   "
αἰχμαλωτεύοντες   VPPANM-P   αἰχμαλωτεύω

αἰχμαλωτεύω   1aor. ἠχμαλώτευσα; as a military technical term *take captive, lead captive*; figuratively in the NT, of Christ's activity at his ascension (EP 4.8)

αἰχμαλωτίζει   VIPA--3S   αἰχμαλωτίζω
αἰχμαλωτίζοντα   VPPAAM-S   "
αἰχμαλωτίζοντες   VPPANM-P   "

αἰχμαλωτίζω   1aor. pass. ἠχμαλωτίσθην; 1fut. pass. αἰχμαλωτισθήσομαι; (1) literally, as a military technical term *take prisoner, lead captive*; passive *be carried off as prisoner* (LU 21.24); (2) figuratively; (a) in a bad sense of the inner religious and moral struggle resulting in subjection to sin *take captive, make prisoner* (RO 7.23); as leading someone astray *carry away, gain control over* (2T 3.6); (b) in a good sense, as subjecting one's thoughts to Christ *take captive, take control of* (2C 10.5)

αἰχμαλωτισθήσεται   VIFP--3S   αἰχμαλωτίζω
αἰχμαλωτισθήσονται   VIFP--3P   "
αἰχμαλώτοις   N-DM-P   αἰχμάλωτος

αἰχμάλωτος, ώτου, ὁ   literally *captive*; figuratively, of someone in moral or spiritual bondage (LU 4.18)

αἰών, ῶνος, ὁ   *era, time, age*; (1) as a segment of contemporary time *lifetime, era, present age* (LU 16.8); (2) of time gone by *past, earliest times* (LU 1.70); (3) of prolonged and unlimited time *eternity* (1T 1.17); (4) of time to come *eternity, age to come* (LU 20.35); idiomatically εἰς τὸν αἰῶνα literally *into the age*, i.e. *forever, eternally* (JN 6.51); εἰς τοὺς αἰῶνας τῶν αἰώνων literally *into the ages of the ages*, i.e. *forever and ever, forevermore* (HE 1.8); (5) plural, as a spatial concept, of the creation as having a beginning and moving forward through long but limited time *universe, world* (HE 1.2; 9.26; 11.3)

αἰών   N-NM-S   αἰών
αἰῶνα   N-AM-S   "
αἰῶνας   N-AM-P   "
αἰῶνι   N-DM-S   "
αἰώνια   A--NN-P   αἰώνιος
αἰωνίαν   A--AF-S   "
αἰωνίοις   A--DM-P   "
αἰώνιον   AB   "
   A--AF-S   "
   A--AM-S   "
   A--AN-S   "
   A--NN-S   "

αἰώνιος, ον (sometimes **ος, ία, ον**)   *eternal, everlasting*, opposite πρόσκαιρος (*temporary, transitory*); (1) of God

without beginning or end, eternal (RO 16.26); (2) *without beginning* (RO 16.25); (3) *without end, everlasting* (2C 5.1); (4) neuter singular αἰώνιον as an adverb *for all time, forever* (PM 15)

αἰώνιος   A--NF-S   αἰώνιος
αἰωνίου   A--GF-S   "
   A--GM-S   "
   A--GN-S   "
αἰωνίους   A--AF-P   "
αἰωνίων   A--GM-P   "
αἰῶνος   N-GM-S   αἰών
αἰώνων   N-GM-P   "
αἰῶσι(ν)   N-DM-P   "

ἀκαθαρσία, ας, ἡ   literally *worthless material, waste*; of graves *decayed flesh*, causing ceremonial *uncleanness, defilement* (MT 23.27); figuratively, moral *uncleanness, impurity* (1TH 2.3), opposite ἁγιασμός (*holy living*); of sexual vice *immorality, indecency, sexual impurity* (RO 1.24)

ἀκαθαρσία   N-NF-S   ἀκαθαρσία
ἀκαθαρσίᾳ   N-DF-S   "
ἀκαθαρσίαν   N-AF-S   "
ἀκαθαρσίας   N-GF-S   "
ἀκάθαρτα   A--AN-P   ἀκάθαρτος
   A--NN-P   "

ἀκαθάρτης, ητος, ἡ   *uncleanness* (RV 17.4)

ἀκαθάρτητος   N-GF-S   ἀκαθάρτης
ἀκαθάρτοις   A--DN-P   ἀκάθαρτος
ἀκάθαρτον   A--AM-S   "
   A--AN-S   "
   A--NN-S   "
   A--VN-S   "

ἀκάθαρτος, ον   *unclean*; (1) in religious observance, of what is ritually not acceptable *defiled, unclean* (AC 10.14); especially used of everything related to idolatry (2C 6.17); (2) morally, of vices *indecent, filthy*; (3) of demons πνεῦμα ἀκάθαρτον *evil spirit, spirit that causes one to be unclean* (MT 10.1); substantivally *what is unclean* translated according to the context (RV 17.4)

ἀκάθαρτος   A--NM-S   ἀκάθαρτος
ἀκαθάρτου   A--GN-S   "
ἀκαθάρτῳ   A--DN-S   "
ἀκαθάρτων   A--GN-P   "

ἀκαιρέομαι   impf. ἠκαιρούμην; *have no opportunity, lack occasion* or *(suitable) time* (PH 4.10)

ἀκαίρως   of an inopportune time *inconveniently, at an unfavorable time* (2T 4.2)

ἀκαίρως   AB   ἀκαίρως

ἄκακος, ον   (1) active, of one who does no evil *upright, without fault, harmless* (HE 7.26); (2) passive, of one not expecting to be involved in evil *innocent, naïve, unsuspecting*; substantivally ὁ ἄ. *unsuspecting person* (RO 16.18)

ἄκακος   A--NM-S   ἄκακος
ἀκάκων   A--GM-P   "

ἄκανθα, ης, ἡ   *thorn*; by synecdoche, of prickly plants in neglected fields *thornbush, prickly weed, thistle*

ἄκανθαι   N-NF-P   ἄκανθα
ἀκάνθας   N-AF-P   "
ἀκάνθινον   A--AM-S   ἀκάνθινος

ἀκάνθινος, η, ον   *thorny, made from thorny branches*

ἀκανθῶν	N-GF-P	ἄκανθα
ἄκαρπα	A--NN-P	ἄκαρπος
ἄκαρποι	A--NM-P	"
ἀκάρποις	A--DN-P	"

ἄκαρπος, ον literally *unfruitful, without fruit, barren*; figuratively, of moral, mental, or spiritual barrenness *useless, unproductive* (1C 14.14; EP 5.11)

ἄκαρπος	A--NM-S	ἄκαρπος
ἀκάρπους	A--AM-P	"
ἀκατάγνωστον	A--AM-S	ἀκατάγνωστος

ἀκατάγνωστος, ον *blameless, above criticism, beyond reproach* (TI 2.8)

ἀκατακάλυπτον	A--AF-S	ἀκατακάλυπτος

ἀκατακάλυπτος, ον *uncovered, without (head) covering, unveiled*

ἀκατακαλύπτῳ	A--DF-S	ἀκατακάλυπτος
ἀκατάκριτον	A--AM-S	ἀκατάκριτος

ἀκατάκριτος, ον as a legal technical term *uncondemned, without proper trial*

ἀκατακρίτους	A--AM-P	ἀκατάκριτος

ἀκατάλυτος, ον strictly, of what cannot be brought to an end *indestructible*; hence *endless, everlasting* (HE 7.16)

ἀκαταλύτου	A--GF-S	ἀκατάλυτος
ἀκαταπάστους	A--AM-P	ἀκατάπαυστος

ἀκατάπαυστος, ον (also **ἀκατάπαστος**) *unceasing, restless*; as characterized by strong sensual desire *never satisfied* (2P 2.14)

ἀκαταπαύστου	A--GF-S	ἀκατάπαυστος
ἀκαταπαύστους	A--AM-P	"

ἀκαταστασία, ας, ἡ *instability, unrest*; (1) of political unrest *turmoil, revolution, insurrection* (LU 21.9); (2) of social unrest *rioting, tumult, disturbance* due to mob action (2C 6.5); (3) of community disruption *confusion, disorder, unruliness* (JA 3.16)

ἀκαταστασία	N-NF-S	ἀκαταστασία
ἀκαταστασίαι	N-NF-P	"
ἀκαταστασίαις	N-DF-P	"
ἀκαταστασίας	N-AF-P	"
	N-GF-S	"
ἀκατάστατον	A--NN-S	ἀκατάστατος

ἀκατάστατος, ον (1) of a person often changing his mind about something *unstable, restless, unsteady, fickle* (JA 1.8); (2) of the tongue *not subject to control, unruly* (JA 3.8)

ἀκατάστατος	A--NM-S	ἀκατάστατος
ἀκατάσχετον	A--NN-S	ἀκατάσχετος

ἀκατάσχετος, ον *uncontrollable* (JA 3.8)

Ἀκελδαμάχ		Ἀκελδαμάχ
Ἀκέλδαμα		"
Ἀκελδαμά		"
Ἀκελδαμάκ		"
Ἀκελδαμάχ		"

Ἀκελδαμάχ, τό (also **Ἀκελδαιμάχ, Ἀκέλδαμα, Ἀκελδαμά, Ἀκελδαμάκ, Ἀκελδαμάχ, Ἀχελδαμάχ**) indeclinable; *Akeldama*, transliterated from the Aramaic phrase meaning *Field of Blood*; formerly the potter's field, traditionally located near Jerusalem on the southern side of the Valley of Hinnom (AC 1.19)

ἀκέραιοι	A--NM-P	ἀκέραιος

ἀκέραιος, ον literally *pure, unmixed*, as wine; figuratively in the NT, of a character marked by integrity and innocence of evil *pure, sincere, harmless* (PH 2.15)

ἀκεραίους	A--AM-P	ἀκέραιος
ἀκηδεμονεῖν	VNPA	ἀδημονέω
ἀκήκοα	VIRA--1S	ἀκούω
ἀκηκόαμεν	VIRA--1P	"
ἀκηκόασι(ν)	VIRA--3P	"
ἀκηκόατε	VIRA--2P	"
ἀκηκοότας	VPRAAM-P	"
ἀκλινῆ	A--AF-S	ἀκλινής

ἀκλινής, ές strictly *bending to neither side*; hence *steady, unwavering* (HE 10.23)

ἀκμάζω 1aor. ἤκμασα; literally *be at the prime, be fully ripe*; used figuratively in RV 14.18 of conditions on earth fully ready for judgment

ἀκμήν adverbial accusative from ἀκμή (*point of time*); as an adverb of time extended longer than expected or necessary *still, even yet* (MT 15.16)

ἀκμήν	AB	ἀκμήν
ἀκοαί	N-NF-P	ἀκοή
ἀκοαῖς	N-DF-P	"
ἀκοάς	N-AF-P	"

ἀκοή, ῆς, ἡ *ability to hear, hearing*; (1) as the sense organ for hearing *ear*; idiomatically ἠνοίγησαν αὐτοῦ αἱ ἀκοαί literally *his ears were opened*, i.e. *he could hear* (MK 7.35); εἰσφέρειν εἰς τὰς ἀκοάς literally *bring into the ears*, i.e. *speak about* (AC 17.20); (2) as the act of hearing *listening*; idiomatically ἀκοῇ ἀκούειν literally *hear with hearing*, i.e. *listen carefully, again and again* (AC 28.26); (3) passive; (a) as what is heard *rumor, report, news* (MT 4.24); (b) *message*; ὁ λόγος τῆς ἀκοῆς *the message heard* (HE 4.2)

ἀκοή	N-NF-S	ἀκοή
ἀκοῇ	N-DF-S	"
ἀκοήν	N-AF-S	"
ἀκοῆς	N-GF-S	"
ἀκολοθοῦντες	VPPANM-P	ἀκολουθέω
ἀκολούθει	VMPA--2S	"
ἀκολουθεῖ	VIPA--3S	"
ἀκολουθεῖν	VNPA	"
ἀκολουθείτω	VMPA--3S	"

ἀκολουθέω (and **ἀκολοθέω, ἀκωλυθέω**) impf. ἠκολούθουν; fut. ἀκολουθήσω; 1aor. ἠκολούθησα; pf. ἠκολούθηκα; (1) literally *follow, go along behind, come after* (MK 10.52); of a crowd *go along with, accompany* (MT 21.9); figuratively, of discipleship and self-commitment *follow, go after, obey* (MT 9.9); (2) generally, of observance of laws and customs *obey, follow*

ἀκολουθῇ	VIPA--3S	see ἀκολουθεῖ
ἀκολουθῆσαι	VNAA	ἀκολουθέω
ἀκολουθήσαντες	VPAANM-P	"
ἀκολουθησάντων	VPAAGM-P	"
ἀκολουθήσατε	VMAA--2P	"
ἀκολουθήσει	VIFA--3S	"
ἀκολουθήσεις	VIFA--2S	"
ἀκολουθήσουσι(ν)	VIFA--3P	"
ἀκολουθήσω	VIFA--1S	"
ἀκολουθήσωσι(ν)	VSAA--3P	"
ἀκολουθοῦντα	VPPAAM-S	"
ἀκολουθοῦντας	VPPAAM-P	"

ἀκολουθοῦντες	VPPANM-P	"
ἀκολουθοῦντι	VPPADM-S	"
ἀκολουθούσης	VPPAGF-S	"
ἀκολουθοῦσι(ν)	VIPA--3P	"
	VPPADM-P	"
ἀκολουθῶν	VPPANM-S	"
ἄκουε	VMPA--2S	ἀκούω
ἀκούει	VIPA--3S	"
ἀκούειν	VNPA	"
ἀκούεις	VIPA--2S	"
ἀκούεται	VIPP--3S	"
ἀκούετε	VIPA--2P	"
	VMPA--2P	"
ἀκουέτω	VMPA--3S	"
ἀκούητε	VSPA--2P	"
ἀκούομεν	VIPA--1P	"
ἀκούοντα	VPPAAM-S	"
	VPPANN-P	"
ἀκούοντας	VPPAAM-P	"
ἀκούοντες	VPPANM-P	"
ἀκούοντι	VPPADM-S	"
ἀκούοντος	VPPAGM-S	"
ἀκουόντων	VPPAGM-P	"
ἀκούουσι(ν)	VIPA--3P	"
	VPPADM-P	"
ἀκοῦσαι	VNAA	"
ἀκούσαντες	VPAANM-P	"
ἀκουσάντων	VPAAGM-P	"
ἀκούσας	VPAANM-S	"
ἀκούσασα	VPAANF-S	"
ἀκούσασαι	VPAANF-P	"
ἀκούσασι(ν)	VPAADM-P	"
ἀκούσατε	VMAA--2P	"
ἀκουσάτω	VMAA--3S	"
ἀκουσάτωσαν	VMAA--3P	"
ἀκούσει	VIFA--3S	"
ἀκούσεσθε	VIFM--2P	"
	VIFM--2P^VMAM--2P	"
ἀκούσετε	VIFA--2P	"
ἀκούση	VIFM--2S	"
	VSAA--3S	"
ἀκούσητε	VSAA--2P	"
ἀκουσθεῖσι(ν)	VPAPDN-P	"
ἀκουσθῆ	VSAP--3S	"
ἀκουσθήσεται	VIFP--3S	"

ἄκουσμα, ατος, τό *thing heard, rumor, report* (HE 4.2)

ἀκούσμασι(ν)	N-DN-P	ἄκουσμα
ἀκούσομαι	VIFM--1S	ἀκούω
ἀκουσόμεθα	VIFM--1P	"
ἀκούσονται	VIFM--3P	"
ἀκούσοντες	VPFANM-P	"
ἀκούσουσι(ν)	VIFA--3P	"
	VPPADM-P	"
ἀκουστόν	A--NN-S	ἀκουστός

ἀκουστός, ή, όν *audible, able to be heard*; idiomatically ἀκουστὸν ἐγένετο τοῖς ἀποστόλοις literally *it became audible to the apostles*, i.e. *the apostles heard the report* (AC 11.1)

ἀκούσω	VSAA--1S	ἀκούω
ἀκούσων	VPFANM-S	"
ἀκούσωσι(ν)	VSAA--3P	"

ἀκούω fut. ἀκούσω and ἀκούσομαι; 1aor. ἤκουσα; pf. ἀκήκοα; 1aor. pass. ἠκούσθην; *hear, listen to*; (1) followed by the genitive to indicate sense perception *hear* (AC 9.7); (2) followed by the accusative to indicate understanding of what was said *hear* (AC 9.4); (3) as a legal technical term *give a hearing, grant a court trial* (JN 7.51); (4) of being informed about something *learn* or *hear (of)* (MT 14.13); (5) impersonally ἀκούεται *it is reported* (1C 5.1); (6) of discipleship *listen to, pay attention to, obey* (LU 9.35); (7) of inner comprehension *understand, be aware of, listen to* (GA 4.21)

ἀκούω	VIPA--1S	ἀκούω
	VSPA--1S	"
ἀκούων	VPPANM-S	"
ἀκούωσι(ν)	VSPA--3P	"

ἀκρασία, ας, ἡ *lack of self-control, self-indulgence*

ἀκρασίαν	N-AF-S	ἀκρασία
ἀκρασίας	N-GF-S	"
ἀκρατεῖς	A--NM-P	ἀκρατής

ἀκρατής, ές *without self-control, lacking in moral restraint, intemperate* (2T 3.3)

ἄκρατος, ον literally *unmixed, pure, undiluted*, as wine; figuratively, of God's anger *at full strength, very strong* (RV 14.10)

ἀκράτου	A--GM-S	ἄκρατος

ἀκρίβεια, ας, ἡ *exactness, strict conformity, accuracy*; κατὰ ἀ. *strictly, very carefully, thoroughly* (AC 22.3)

ἀκρίβειαν	N-AF-S	ἀκρίβεια
ἀκριβεστάτην	A-SAF-S	ἀκριβής
ἀκριβέστερον	ABM	"
	A-MAN-S	"

ἀκριβής, ές *exact, strict, accurate*; comparative neuter as an adverb ἀκριβέστερον *more exactly* or *accurately* (AC 18.26); substantivally τι ἀκριβέστερον *something more accurate* (AC 23.20); superlative ἀκριβέστατος, τάτη, ον *strictest* (AC 26.5)

ἀκριβόω 1aor. ἠκρίβωσα; *find out exactly, inquire accurately*

ἀκριβῶς adverb; characterized by exactness and thoroughness; (1) in information *accurately* (1TH 5.2); (2) in effort *thoroughly, diligently* (MT 2.8); (3) in ethical behavior *carefully* (EP 5.15)

ἀκριβῶς	AB	ἀκριβῶς
ἀκρίδας	N-AF-P	ἀκρίς
ἀκρίδες	N-NF-P	"
ἀκρίδων	N-GF-P	"

ἀκρίς, ίδος, ἡ *locust*, an insect similar to a grasshopper, often consumed as food

ἀκροαταί	N-NM-P	ἀκροατής

ἀκροατήριον, ου, τό as a place for a hearing *audience room, auditorium, hall*; as a place for a judicial hearing *courtroom* (AC 25.23)

ἀκροατήριον	N-AN-S	ἀκροατήριον

ἀκροατής, οῦ, ὁ *hearer (only)*, as contrasted with one who acts on what he hears

ἀκροατής	N-NM-S	ἀκροατής

ἀκροβυστία, ας, ἡ (1) as a state, of the male sexual organ with *the foreskin not cut off* (AC 11.3); (2) by metonymy, of the state of an uncircumcised man *uncircumcision* (GA 5.6), opposite περιτομή (*circumcision*); (3) with the abstract for concrete *Gentiles, non-Jewish people, pa-*

gans (RO 3.30); (4) figuratively, in a negative sense of lack of relationship with God and righteousness *uncircumcision* (CO 2.13)

ἀκροβυστία	N-NF-S	ἀκροβυστία
ἀκροβυστίᾳ	N-DF-S	"
ἀκροβυστίαν	N-AF-S	"
ἀκροβυστίας	N-GF-S	"
ἀκρογωνιαῖον	A--AM-S	ἀκρογωνιαῖος

ἀκρογωνιαῖος, α, ον literally *lying at the extreme angle*; ἀ. (λίθος) *cornerstone; capstone*, the final stone placed at the top of a building structure to integrate it; figuratively, of the place of Christ in the believing community (EP 2.20)

ἀκρογωνιαίου	A--GM-S	ἀκρογωνιαῖος

ἀκροθίνιον, ου, τό (1) often plural, as the best of produce, at the top of the pile *firstfruits*; (2) as the best part of goods captured in battle *most valuable plunder, booty, spoils* (HE 7.4)

ἀκροθινίων	N-GN-P	ἀκροθίνιον

ἄκρον, ου, τό *high point, extremity*; of a mountain *top*; of a staff *top, tip, end* (HE 11.21); of a finger *tip* (LU 16.24); of the sky or heavens *farthest boundary, end* (MT 24.31)

ἄκρον	N-AN-S	ἄκρον
ἄκρου	N-GN-S	"
ἄκρων	N-GN-P	"
Ἀκύλα	N-GM-S	Ἀκύλας
Ἀκύλαν	N-AM-S	"

Ἀκύλας, α, ὁ, accusative **αν** *Aquila*, masculine proper noun

Ἀκύλας	N-NM-S	Ἀκύλας
ἀκυροῖ	VIPA--3S	ἀκυρόω
ἀκυροῦντες	VPPANM-P	"

ἀκυρόω 1aor. ἠκύρωσα; (1) as a legal technical term *make invalid* or *void, annul* (GA 3.17); (2) of depriving divine law of authority by placing priority on human traditions *make of no effect, disregard* (MK 7.13)

ἀκωλουθεῖ	VIPA--3S	ἀκολουθέω

ἀκωλύτως adverb; *without hindrance, freely* (AC 28.31)

ἀκωλύτως	AB	ἀκωλύτως

ἄκων, ἄκουσα, ἄκον *unwilling*; as an adverb *unwillingly* (1C 9.17)

ἄκων	A--NM-S	ἄκων
ἄλα	N-AN-S	ἄλας
	N-NN-S	"
ἀλάβαστρον	N-AF-S	ἀλάβαστρος
	N-AM-S	"
	N-AN-S	"

ἀλάβαστρος, ου, ὁ and ἡ and ἀλάβαστρον, ου, τό *alabaster*; by metonymy, a container for perfumed ointment *alabaster jar, flask, (small) bottle*

ἀλαζόνας	N-AM-P	ἀλαζών

ἀλαζονεία, ας, ἡ (also **ἀλαζονία**) characterized by presumption in word or action *arrogance, pretension* (JA 4.16); in regard to one's possessions *false pride, conceit, boasting* (1J 2.16)

ἀλαζονεία	N-NF-S	ἀλαζονεία
ἀλαζονείαις	N-DF-P	"
ἀλαζόνες	N-NM-P	ἀλαζών
ἀλαζονία	N-NF-S	ἀλαζονεία

ἀλαζών, όνος, ὁ of one who arrogantly presumes too much about himself *boaster, braggart, show-off*

ἀλαλάζον	VPPANN-S	ἀλαλάζω
ἀλαλάζοντας	VPPAAM-P	"
ἀλαλαζόντων	VPPAGM-P	"

ἀλαλάζω strictly *raise the war cry* (ἀλαλά); (1) of a death wail *cry out, wail loudly* (MK 5.38); (2) of the loud sound of a cymbal *clash, clang* (1C 13.1)

ἀλαλήτοις	A--DM-P	ἀλάλητος

ἀλάλητος, ον of something that arouses such strong emotions one cannot find words to speak of it *inexpressible, unutterable* (RO 8.26)

ἄλαλον	A--AN-S	ἄλαλος
	A--VN-S	"

ἄλαλος, ον *unable to speak, mute*; substantivally *mute person* (MK 7.37)

ἀλάλους	A--AM-P	ἄλαλος

ἅλας and ἅλα, ατος, τό (also ἅλς, ἁλός, ὁ) literally *salt* (MK 9.50a, b); figuratively, as having a quality of effectiveness (CO 4.6)

ἅλας	N-NN-S	ἅλας
Ἄλασσα	N-NF-S	Λασαία
ἅλατι	N-DN-S	ἅλας
ἀλεεύς	N-NM-S	ἁλιεύς

ἀλείφω impf. ἤλειφον; 1aor. ἤλειψα, mid. ἠλειψάμην; *anoint*, of external physical application of oil or perfumed ointment (MK 6.13); middle *anoint oneself* or part of one's body (MT 6.17)

ἀλείψαι	VMAM--2S	ἀλείφω
ἀλείψαντες	VPAANM-P	"
ἀλείψασα	VPAANF-S	"
ἀλείψωσι(ν)	VSAA--3P	"
ἀλέκτορα	N-AM-S	ἀλέκτωρ

ἀλεκτοροφωνία, ας, ἡ *crowing of a cock* or *rooster*; generally of time, the third watch of the night (from midnight to 3:00 A.M.) *cockcrow, before dawn* (MK 13.35)

ἀλεκτοροφωνίας	N-GF-S	ἀλεκτοροφωνία

ἀλέκτωρ, ορος, ὁ *cock, rooster, male chicken*

ἀλέκτωρ	N-NM-S	ἀλέκτωρ

Ἀλεξανδρεύς, έως, ὁ *Alexandrian, native of Alexandria*, a city in Egypt

Ἀλεξανδρεύς	N-NM-S	Ἀλεξανδρεύς
Ἀλεξανδρέων	N-GM-P	
Ἀλεξανδρῖνον	A--AN-S	Ἀλεξανδρῖνος

Ἀλεξανδρῖνος, η, ον *Alexandrian, of Alexandria*, a city in Egypt

Ἀλεξανδρίνῳ	A--DN-S	Ἀλεξανδρῖνος
Ἀλέξανδρον	N-AM-S	Ἀλέξανδρος

Ἀλέξανδρος, ου, ὁ *Alexander*, masculine proper noun

Ἀλέξανδρος	N-NM-S	Ἀλέξανδρος
Ἀλεξάνδρου	N-GM-S	"

ἄλευρον, ου, τό *wheat flour, meal, ground wheat*

ἀλεύρου	N-GN-S	ἄλευρον

ἀλήθεια, ας, ἡ (1) of what has certainty and validity *truth* (EP 4.21), opposite πλάνη (*going astray, wandering*); (2) of the real state of affairs, especially as divinely disclosed *truth* (RO 1.18), opposite μῦθος (*fiction, myth*); (3) of the concept of the gospel message as being absolute *truth* (2TH 2.12); (4) of true-to-fact statements *truth, fact* (LU 4.25), opposite ψεῦδος (*lie, falsehood*); (5) of what is characterized by love of truth *truthfulness, uprightness, fidelity* (1C 5.8; 13.6), opposite ἀδικία (*wrong, evil*); (6) of reality as opposed to pretense or mere appearance *truth, sincerity* (PH 1.18), opposite πρόφασις (*pretext, excuse*); idiomatically ἐν ἀληθείᾳ literally *in truth*, i.e. *really, truly, indeed* (MT 22.16); κατὰ ἀλήθειαν literally *according to truth*, i.e. *rightly* (RO 2.2); ἐπ᾽ ἀληθείας literally *on truth*, i.e. *really, actually* (AC 4.27)

ἀλήθεια	N-NF-S	ἀλήθεια
ἀληθείᾳ	N-DF-S	"
ἀλήθειαν	N-AF-S	"
ἀληθείας	N-GF-S	"
ἀληθεῖς	A--NM-P	ἀληθής
ἀληθές	A--AN-S	"
	A--NN-S	"
ἀληθεύοντες	VPPANM-P	ἀληθεύω

ἀληθεύω *tell the truth, be truthful* (GA 4.16); of upholding the gospel *speak what is true* (about God); *be faithful to the truth* (EP 4.15)

ἀληθεύων	VPPANM-S	ἀληθεύω
ἀληθῆ	A--AF-S	ἀληθής
	A--AN-P	"
	A--NN-P	"

ἀληθής, ές *true*; (1) of statements that agree with facts *true* (TI 1.13); (2) of things characterized by reality *genuine, true, real* (JN 6.55); substantivally *true thing, fact* (JN 19.35); (3) of persons characterized by integrity *trustworthy, truthful, honest* (RO 3.4), opposite ψευδής (*lying, false*)

ἀληθής	A--NF-S	ἀληθής
	A--NM-S	"
ἀληθιναί	A--NF-P	ἀληθινός
ἀληθινή	A--NF-S	"
ἀληθινῆς	A--GF-S	"
ἀληθινοί	A--NM-P	"
ἀληθινόν	A--AM-S	"
	A--AN-S	"
	A--NN-S	"

ἀληθινός, ή, όν (1) of words that conform to facts *true, correct, dependable* (JN 19.35); (2) of what conforms to reality *genuine, real, true* (1J 2.8); substantivally *true thing, reality* (HE 9.24); (3) of persons characterized by integrity and trustworthiness *true, dependable*; substantivally, as a person who is what he claims to be *(the) true one* (RV 3.7)

ἀληθινός	A--NM-S	ἀληθινός
	A--VM-S	"
ἀληθινῷ	A--DM-S	"
ἀληθινῶν	A--GN-P	"
ἀληθοῦς	A--GF-S	ἀληθής
ἀληθοῦσαι	VPPANF-P	ἀλήθω

ἀλήθω of processing grain into meal or flour *grind*

ἀληθῶς adverb; (1) as qualifying a verb of telling *truly, in truth* (LU 9.27); (2) as attributing genuine existence to a thing, state, or quality as opposed to what is imagined *really, truly, actually* (JN 1.47)

ἀληθῶς	AB	ἀληθῶς
ἁλί	N-DM-S	ἅλας
ἁλιεῖς	N-AM-P	ἁλιεύς
	N-NM-P	"
ἁλιεύειν	VNPA	ἁλιεύω

ἁλιεύς, έως, ὁ (also ἁλεεύς) literally in the NT *one who earns his living by catching fish, fisher(man)* (MT 4.18);

metaphorically, of one who evangelizes or wins disciples to Christ (MT 4.19)

ἁλιεύω *fish, catch fish* (JN 21.3)

ἁλίζω 1aor. pass. ἡλίσθην; 1fut. pass. ἁλισθήσομαι; literally *salt, season with salt, preserve by salting* (MT 5.13); figuratively in MK 9.49 probably of God's judgment (fire), applied to test believers and punish unbelievers

ἁλισγέω fut. pass. ἁλισγηθήσομαι; *pollute, make ceremonially impure* (MK 9.49)

ἁλισγηθήσεται	VIFP--3S	ἁλισγέω

ἁλίσγημα, ατος, τό of the effect of contact with idols *(ceremonial) pollution, ritual defilement* (AC 15.20)

ἁλισγημάτων	N-GN-P	ἁλίσγημα
ἁλισθήσεται	VIFP--3S	ἁλίζω
ἀλλ᾽	A--AN-P	ἄλλος
	A--NN-P	"
	CC	ἀλλά
	CH	"
	CS	"
ἄλλα	A--AN-P	ἄλλος
	A--NN-P	"

ἀλλά an adversative conjunction indicating contrast, difference, or limitation *but, however, yet, nevertheless, at least*; (1) after a negative; (a) to introduce a contrast *but, however, yet, nevertheless* (MT 7.21); (b) to provide ascensive force to a statement οὐ μόνον . . . ἀ. καί *not only . . . but also* (AC 26.29); with οὐ μόνον implied *even more than that* (2C 7.11); (c) to introduce a main point after questions with an implied negative answer *rather, instead* (LU 13.5); (d) to negate an incorrect declaration *rather, instead* (LU 1.60); (e) to introduce an exception *except, however* (2C 1.13); (2) to provide transition between independent clauses, with limiting or differing force *but, yet, however* (MK 14.36); (3) to strengthen a command *now, then, so* (MK 16.7; AC 10.20); (4) in the consequence clause of conditional sentences to change thought direction *yet, certainly, at least* (MK 14.29)

ἀλλά	CC	ἀλλά
	CH	"
	CS	"
ἀλλαγησόμεθα	VIFP--1P	ἀλλάσσω
ἀλλαγήσονται	VIFP--3P	"
ἄλλαι	A--NF-P	ἄλλος
ἀλλάξαι	VNAA	ἀλλάσσω
ἀλλάξει	VIFA--3S	"
ἀλλάξεις	VIFA--2S	"
ἄλλας	A--AF-P	ἄλλος

ἀλλάσσω (and ἀλλάττω) fut. ἀλλάξω; 1aor. ἤλλαξα; 2fut. pass. ἀλλαγήσομαι; literally *make otherwise*; (1) *change, alter, transform* (1C 15.51); (2) *exchange, give in exchange* (RO 1.23)

ἀλλάττω	VIPA--1S	ἀλλάσσω

ἀλλαχόθεν adverb of place *from another place, by some other way* (JN 10.1)

ἀλλαχόθεν	AB	ἀλλαχόθεν

ἀλλαχοῦ adverb of place *elsewhere, somewhere else, in another direction* (MK 1.38)

ἀλλαχοῦ	AB	ἀλλαχοῦ
ἄλλη	A--NF-S	ἄλλος
ἄλλη	A--DF-S	"

ἀλληγορέω   as aiming to convey other than the literal meaning *allegorize, speak* or *explain allegorically, talk figuratively, illustrate with an (implied) comparison* (GA 4.24)

ἀλληγορούμενα	VPPPNN-P	ἀλληγορέω
ἀλλήλοις	NPDM1P	ἀλλήλων
	NPDM2P	"
	NPDM3P	"
	NPDN3P	"
ἀλληλουϊά	QS	ἀλληλουϊά

ἀλληλουϊά (also ἀλληλουϊά)   transliterated from the Hebrew; literally *praise Yahweh (Jehovah)*; transliterated into English as *hallelujah, alleluia,* used as a worship formula

ἀλληλουϊά	QS	ἀλληλουϊά
ἀλλήλους	NPAM1P	ἀλλήλων
	NPAM2P	"
	NPAM3P	"

ἀλλήλων   genitive of the reciprocal pronoun; dative ἀλλήλοις, accusative ἀλλήλους; *one another, each other, mutually,* applicable to first-, second-, or third-person referents

ἀλλήλων	NPGM1P	ἀλλήλων
	NPGM2P	"
	NPGM3P	"
ἄλλην	A--AF-S	ἄλλος
ἄλλης	A--GF-S	"
ἄλλο	A--AN-S	"
	A--NN-S	"

ἀλλογενής, ές   *foreign, alien, of another race, kinship group,* or *nation*; substantively *foreigner* (LU 17.18)

ἀλλογενής	AP-NM-S	ἀλλογενής
ἄλλοι	A--NM-P	ἄλλος

ἀλλοιόω   1aor. pass. ἠλλοιώθην; *change*; passive *be changed, become different* (LU 9.29)

ἄλλοις	A--DM-P	ἄλλος
	A--DN-P	"

ἅλλομαι   1aor. ἡλάμην; of quick movement; (1) of animate beings *leap, spring up* (AC 3.8); (2) of inanimate things, as water *well up, bubble up* with a continuous flow (JN 4.14)

ἁλλόμενος	VPPDNM-S	ἅλλομαι
	VPPONM-S	"
ἁλλομένου	VPPDGN-S	"
	VPPOGN-S	"
ἄλλον	A--AM-S	ἄλλος

ἄλλος, η, ο   *other, another*; (1) generally *another* person or thing of the same kind (AC 4.12), as contrasted with ἕτερος (*another* of a different kind or form) (GA 1.6–7); (2) used correlatively, in contrast (οἱ μὲν) ἄλλοι . . . (οἱ δὲ) ἄλλοι *some . . . others* (MK 6.15); (3) with cardinal numbers *more* (MT 25.16); (4) with the article ἡ ἄλλη *the other* (of two) (MT 12.13); οἱ ἄλλοι *the others, the rest* (1C 14.29); (τὰ) ἄλλα *other things* (MK 7.4)

ἄλλος	A--NM-S	ἄλλος
ἀλλοτρία	A--DF-S	ἀλλότριος
ἀλλοτρίαις	A--DF-P	"
ἀλλοτρίαν	A--AF-S	"

ἀλλοτριεπίσκοπος, ου, ὁ (also ἀλλοτριοεπίσκοπος)   strictly, one who interferes in the affairs of others, *meddler, busybody*; found only in 1P 4.15, variously suggested to mean; (1) one who has his eye on someone else's possessions, as a thief; (2) one who dishonestly takes for himself what is entrusted to him; (3) one who meddles in things that do not concern him; (4) *informer, spy*; the third alternative is generally preferred

ἀλλοτριεπίσκοπος	N-NM-S	ἀλλοτριεπίσκοπος
ἀλλοτριοεπίσκοπος	N-NM-S	"
ἀλλοτρίοις	AP-DM-P	ἀλλότριος
	A--DM-P	"
	A--DN-P	"
ἀλλότριον	A--AM-S	"

ἀλλότριος, ία, ον   (1) *belonging to another, not one's own* (LU 16.12), opposite τὸ ὑμέτερον (*your own property, what is yours*); (2) of lands *strange, foreign* (AC 7.6); (3) as a substantive; (a) *stranger, foreigner, alien* (JN 10.5); (b) *enemy, hostile alien* (HE 11.34)

ἀλλότριος	A--NM-S	ἀλλότριος
ἀλλοτρίῳ	AP-DM-S	"
	A--DM-S	"
	A--DN-S	"
ἀλλοτρίων	AP-GM-P	"
ἄλλου	A--GM-S	ἄλλος
ἄλλους	A--AM-P	"

ἀλλόφυλος, ον   *of alien descent, foreign*; from a Jewish viewpoint *Gentile, heathen, non-Jewish*; substantively *Gentile, non-Jew* (AC 10.28)

ἀλλοφύλους	AP-AM-P	ἀλλόφυλος
ἀλλοφύλῳ	AP-DM-S	"
ἀλλοφύλων	AP-GM-P	"
ἄλλῳ	A--DM-S	ἄλλος
ἄλλων	A--GM-P	"

ἄλλως   adverb *otherwise, in another way* (1T 5.25)

ἄλλως	AB	ἄλλως

Ἁλμεί, ὁ   indeclinable; *Almi*, masculine proper noun (LU 3.33)

ἀλοάω   as processing grain *thresh*; as done with oxen *tread, thresh out* the chaff from the grain

ἄλογα	A--NN-P	ἄλογος
ἄλογον	A--NN-S	"

ἄλογος, ον   (1) of animals *unable to reason* (2P 2.12; JU 10); (2) of faulty human reasoning *without basis, contrary to reason, absurd* (AC 25.27)

ἀλόη, ης, ἡ   *aloes*, aromatic dried sap of the aloe plant, used for embalming the dead (JN 19.39)

ἀλόης	N-GF-S	ἀλόη
ἀλοῶν	VPPANM-S	ἀλοάω
ἀλοῶντα	VPPAAM-S	"
ἁλυκόν	A--NN-S	ἁλυκός

ἁλυκός, ή, όν   *salty*; substantively *salt spring* (JA 3.12)

ἄλυπος, ον   *free from grief* or *sorrow, relieved of anxiety*; comparative ἀλυπότερος, τέρα, ον *less anxious, free from all anxiety* (PH 2.28)

ἀλυπότερος	A-MNM-S	ἄλυπος
ἀλύσει	N-DF-S	ἅλυσις
ἁλύσεις	N-AF-P	
	N-NF-P	"
ἁλύσεσι(ν)	N-DF-P	"
ἅλυσιν	N-AF-S	"

ἅλυσις, εως, ἡ   (1) *chain* (LU 8.29); in distinction from πέδη (*fetter, shackle*) for the feet, *handcuff* (MK 5.4); (2) by metonymy *imprisonment* (EP 6.20)

ἀλυσιτελές   A--NN-S   ἀλυσιτελής

ἀλυσιτελής, ές   *unprofitable, of no advantage, detrimental* (HE 13.17)

ἀλύτοις   A--DM-P   ἄλυτος

ἄλυτος, ον   of chains *not to be loosed, unbreakable* (JU 6)

ἄλφα, τό   indeclinable; literally *alpha*, the name of the first letter of the Greek alphabet α, A; figuratively, as a title for Christ *the Beginning* (RV 1.8)

Ἀλφαῖος, ου, ὁ (also **Ἀλφαῖος**)   *Alphaeus*, masculine proper noun

Ἀλφαίου   N-GM-S   Ἀλφαῖος
Ἀλφαίου   N-GM-S   "

ἅλων, ωνος, ἡ   *threshing floor*; by metonymy *threshed grain* lying on the threshing floor waiting to be winnowed; metaphorically in MT 3.12 and LU 3.17 of Christ's work of saving and judging

ἅλωνα   N-AF-S   ἅλων
ἀλώπεκες   N-NF-P   ἀλώπηξ
ἀλώπεκι   N-DF-S   "

ἀλώπηξ, εκος, ἡ   literally *fox* (MT 8.20); figuratively *crafty, sly person* (LU 13.32)

ἅλωσιν   N-AF-S   ἅλωσις

ἅλωσις, εως, ἡ   as the catching of animals for food *taking, capture*; εἰς ἅ. *to be caught* or *taken* (2P 2.12)

ἅμα   expressing coincidence of action; (1) as an adverb of time *at the same time* (AC 27.40); (2) as an improper preposition with the dative to denote what belongs together in time and place *in association with, together with* (MT 13.29)

ἅμα   AB   ἅμα
    PD   "
ἀμαθεῖς   A--NM-P   ἀμαθής

ἀμαθής, ές   *unlearned, ignorant, uneducated*; substantivally *untaught people* (2P 3.16)

ἀμαράντινον   A--AM-S   ἀμαράντινος

ἀμαράντινος, η, ον   literally *unfading*, as flowers; figuratively *enduring, lasting* (1P 5.4)

ἀμάραντον   A--AF-S   ἀμάραντος

ἀμάραντος, ον   literally, of a flower in bloom *unfading*; figuratively *enduring, eternally fresh, everlasting* (1P 1.4)

ἁμάρτανε   VMPA--2S   ἁμαρτάνω
ἁμαρτάνει   VIPA--3S   "
ἁμαρτάνειν   VNPA   "
ἁμαρτάνετε   VIPA--2P   "
    VMPA--2P   "
ἁμαρτάνητε   VSPA--2P   "
ἁμαρτάνοντα   VPPAAM-S   "
ἁμαρτάνοντας   VPPAAM-P   "
ἁμαρτάνοντες   VPPANM-P   "
ἁμαρτάνοντι   VPPADM-P   "
ἁμαρτανόντων   VPPAGM-P   "
ἁμαρτάνουσι(ν)   VPPADM-P   "

ἁμαρτάνω   fut. ἁμαρτήσω; 1aor. ἡμάρτησα; 2aor. ἥμαρτον; pf. ἡμάρτηκα; literally *miss the mark, be in error*; figuratively, of offending against God, man, religious or moral law *sin, do wrong, transgress*, opposite ἀγαθοποιέω (*do what is right*)

ἁμαρτάνων   VPPANM-S   ἁμαρτάνω
ἁμάρτῃ   VSAA--3S   "

ἁμάρτημα, ατος, τό   as a result of ἁμαρτάνω (*sin, do wrong*); strictly *error, fault*; as an offense against law, incurring guilt because of its wrong intent *sin, sinful act, wrongdoing*

ἁμάρτημα   N-NN-S   ἁμάρτημα
ἁμαρτήματα   N-NN-P   "
ἁμαρτήματος   N-GN-S   "
ἁμαρτημάτων   N-GN-P   "
ἁμαρτήσαντας   VPAAAM-P   ἁμαρτάνω
ἁμαρτήσαντος   VPAAGM-S   "
ἁμαρτησάντων   VPAAGM-P   "
ἁμαρτήσασι(ν)   VPAADM-P   "
ἁμαρτήσει   VIFA--3S   "
ἁμαρτήσῃ   VSAA--3S   "
ἁμαρτήσομεν   VIFA--1P   "
ἁμαρτήσωμεν   VSAA--1P   "
ἁμαρτήσωσι(ν)   VSAA--3P   "
ἁμάρτητε   VSAA--2P   "

ἁμαρτία, ας, ἡ   *sin*; (1) of an act, a departure from doing what is right, equivalent to ἁμάρτημα *sin, wrongdoing* (1J 5.17); (2) as the moral consequence of having done something wrong *sin, guilt* (AC 3.19; 1J 1.7); (3) as the nature of wrongdoing viewed as the rejection of God by self-assertive human beings *sin, evil* (RO 5.12, 13; cf. 1.21); (4) especially in Johannine usage as a moral condition of human beings in revolt against God *sin, being evil, sinfulness* (JN 9.34; 15.24); (5) especially in Pauline usage as an abstract moral principle or force personified as evil in character *sin, evil* (RO 6.12); (6) especially in Hebrews as a deceiving power personified as leading human beings to guilt and destruction (HE 3.13; 12.1)

ἁμαρτία   N-NF-S   ἁμαρτία
ἁμαρτίᾳ   N-DF-S   "
ἁμαρτίαι   N-NF-P   "
ἁμαρτίαις   N-DF-P   "
ἁμαρτίαν   N-AF-S   "
ἁμαρτίας   N-AF-P   "
    N-GF-S   "
ἁμαρτιῶν   N-GF-P   "
ἁμάρτυρον   A--AM-S   ἁμάρτυρος

ἁμάρτυρος, ον   *without witness* or *evidence* (AC 14.17)

ἁμαρτωλοί   AP-NM-P   ἁμαρτωλός
    AP-VM-P   "
    A--NM-P   "
ἁμαρτωλοῖς   AP-DM-P   "
ἁμαρτωλόν   AP-AM-S   "

ἁμαρτωλός, όν   (1) *sinful, guilty, shown to be wrong* (RO 7.13); (2) substantivally, as one who lives in opposition to the divine will *sinner* (JA 4.8); (3) in the Pharisaic view, a Jew who is not religious or does not observe Jewish traditional rules *sinner, outcast* (MK 2.16); (4) in the Jewish view *Gentile, non-Jew* (GA 2.15)

ἁμαρτωλός   AP-NM-S   ἁμαρτωλός
    A--NF-S   "
    A--NM-S   "
ἁμαρτωλούς   AP-AM-P   "
ἁμαρτωλῷ   AP-DM-S   "
    A--DF-S   "
    A--DM-S   "
ἁμαρτωλῶν   AP-GM-P   "
    A--GM-P   "
Ἀμασίαν   N-AM-S   Ἀμασίας

Ἀμασίας, ου, ὁ   *Amaziah*, masculine proper noun (MT 1.8)

| Ἀμασίας | N-NM-S | Ἀμασίας |
| ἄμαχον | A--AM-S | ἄμαχος |

ἄμαχος, ον   *not disposed to fight* or *quarrel, peaceable*

| ἀμάχους | A--AM-P | ἄμαχος |

ἀμάω   1aor. ἤμησα; of cutting grass or standing grain in a field *mow, cut down* (JA 5.4)

| ἀμέθυσος | N-NF-S | ἀμέθυστος |

ἀμεθύστινος, η, ον   *made of amethyst* (RV 21.20)

| ἀμεθύστινος | A--NM-S | ἀμεθύστινος |

ἀμέθυστος, ου, ἡ (also ἀμέθυσος)   *amethyst*, a gem of deep purple or violet, so-called from its supposed power to ward off drunkenness (μέθυσις) (RV 21.20)

ἀμέθυστος	N-NF-S	ἀμέθυστος
Ἀμειναδάβ		Ἀμιναδάβ
ἀμέλει	VMPA--2S	ἀμελέω

ἀμελέω   1aor. ἠμέλησα; *neglect, be unconcerned about, care nothing for* someone or something (HE 2.3); absolutely *pay no attention* (MT 22.5)

ἀμελήσαντες	VPAANM-P	ἀμελέω
ἀμελήσω	VIFA--1S	"
ἄμεμπτοι	A--NM-P	ἄμεμπτος

ἄμεμπτος, ον   (1) of persons *blameless, faultless, without guilt* (LU 1.6); (2) of things *faultless, without defect* (HE 8.7)

ἄμεμπτος	A--NF-S	ἄμεμπτος
	A--NM-S	"
ἀμέμπτους	A--AF-P	"

ἀμέμπτως   adverb; *blamelessly, free from all fault*

| ἀμέμπτως | AB | ἀμέμπτως |

ἀμέριμνος, ον   *free from care* or *anxiety, not worried*

| ἀμερίμνους | A--AM-P | ἀμέριμνος |
| ἀμετάθετον | A--AN-S | ἀμετάθετος |

ἀμετάθετος, ον   *never changing, unalterable* (HE 6.18); neuter as a substantive *unchangeableness, immutability* (HE 6.17)

| ἀμεταθέτων | A--GN-P | ἀμετάθετος |
| ἀμετακίνητοι | A--NM-P | ἀμετακίνητος |

ἀμετακίνητος, ον   *immovable, firm* (1C 15.58)

| ἀμεταμέλητα | A--NN-P | ἀμεταμέλητος |
| ἀμεταμέλητον | A--AF-S | " |

ἀμεταμέλητος, ον   (1) of God's gifts and calling *incapable of being changed, not to be taken back, inflexible* (RO 11.29); (2) of the beneficial results of repentance *with nothing to feel sorry about, leaving no feeling of regret* (2C 7.10)

| ἀμετανόητον | A--AF-S | ἀμετανόητος |

ἀμετανόητος, ον   *not feeling sorry, unrepentant, hardened in heart* (RO 2.5)

| ἄμετρα | A--AN-P | ἄμετρος |

ἄμετρος, ον   of what cannot be measured *immeasurable*; idiomatically εἰς τὰ ἄμετρα literally *into what is not measured*, i.e. *beyond limits, extravagantly, excessively* (2C 10.13, 15)

ἀμήν   transliterated from the Hebrew *amen*; usually translated into Greek by γένοιτο (*let it be so, truly*); (1) liturgically, used as a particle of strong affirmation and assent at the end of a doxology *this is indeed true* (RO 11.36) or a prayer of thanksgiving *that is the way it should be* (1C 14.16); (2) used with λέγω to emphasize

that what is being said is a solemn declaration of what is true (JN 1.51); (3) figuratively and substantivally ὁ Ἀ. *the Amen*, used by Christ of himself as the one speaking what is true (RV 3.14)

| ἀμήν | QS | ἀμήν |
| ἀμησάντων | VPAAGM-P | ἀμάω |

ἀμήτωρ, gen. ορος   strictly *without mother*; in the NT, as denoting one who holds an office independently of maternal descent *without record of a mother* (HE 7.3)

| ἀμήτωρ | A--NM-S | ἀμήτωρ |
| ἀμίαντον | A--AF-S | ἀμίαντος |

ἀμίαντος, ον   (1) literally *undefiled, unsoiled*; (2) figuratively, in a religious and moral sense *pure*; (a) of persons *pure, spotless* (HE 7.26); (b) of things *unspoiled, undefiled, pure* (JA 1.27); of an eternal inheritance *beyond the reach of decay or change* (1P 1.4); of marriage *intact, pure* (HE 13.4)

| ἀμίαντος | A--NF-S | ἀμίαντος |
| | A--NM-S | " |

Ἀμιναδάβ, ὁ (also Ἀμειναδάβ, Ἀμιναδάμ)   indeclinable; *Aminadab*, masculine proper noun

Ἀμιναδάμ		Ἀμιναδάβ
ἄμμον	N-AF-S	ἄμμος
	N-NN-S	"

ἄμμος, ου, ἡ (also ἄμμον, ου, τό)   (1) *sand* (RO 9.27); (2) by metonymy *sandy shore, beach* (RV 12.18)

ἄμμος	N-NF-S	ἄμμος
ἄμμῳ	N-DF-S	"
Ἀμμών		Ἀμών
Ἀμμών		"

ἀμνός, οῦ, ὁ   literally *lamb*, an offspring of a sheep; metaphorically, of Christ as one suffering innocently and representatively as the all-sufficient sacrifice to provide atonement (JN 1.29)

ἀμνός	N-NM-S	ἀμνός
ἀμνοῦ	N-GM-S	"
ἀμοιβάς	N-AF-P	ἀμοιβή

ἀμοιβή, ῆς, ἡ   *recompense, repayment, return* for benefits received (1T 5.4)

| ἄμορφα | A--AN-P | ἄμορφος |

ἄμορφος, ον   *shapeless, ugly, deformed* (1C 12.2)

| ἄμπελον | N-AF-S | ἄμπελος |

ἄμπελος, ου, ἡ   literally *grapevine* (MT 26.29); metaphorically, of Christ as sustaining and spiritually nurturing his disciples (JN 15.1); by metonymy, to indicate the produce that a plant produces (RV 14.19)

ἄμπελος	N-NF-S	ἄμπελος
ἀμπέλου	N-GF-S	"
ἀμπελουργόν	N-AM-S	ἀμπελουργός

ἀμπελουργός, οῦ, ὁ   as one who takes care of a vineyard *vinedresser, gardener* (LU 13.7)

| ἀμπέλῳ | N-DF-S | ἄμπελος |

ἀμπελών, ῶνος, ὁ   *vineyard*, a piece of land where grapevines are cultivated

ἀμπελῶνα	N-AM-S	ἀμπελών
ἀμπελῶνι	N-DM-S	"
ἀμπελῶνος	N-GM-S	"
Ἀμπλίαν	N-AM-S	Ἀμπλιᾶτος
Ἀμπλιάν	N-AM-S	"
Ἀμπλιᾶν	N-AM-S	"
Ἀμπλίατον	N-AM-S	"

Ἀμπλιᾶτον   N-AM-S   "

Ἀμπλιᾶτος, ου, ὁ (also Ἀμπλίας, Ἀμπλιάς, Ἀμπλιᾶς, Ἀμπλίατος) *Ampliatus*, masculine proper noun (RO 16.8)

ἀμύνομαι   1aor. ἠμυνάμην; only middle in the NT; (1) negatively *ward off from oneself, repel*; (2) positively in AC 7.24 of assuming the role of a protector *defend, rescue, help out*

ἀμφιάζει   VIPA--3S   ἀμφιέζω
ἀμφιβάλλοντας   VPPAAM-P   ἀμφιβάλλω

ἀμφιβάλλω   strictly *throw around*; hence, as a fishing technical term for throwing out a circular fishing net *cast (a net)* (MK 1.16)

ἀμφίβληστρον, ου, τό   strictly *what is thrown*; hence, as a fishing technical term *casting net* (MT 4.18)

ἀμφίβληστρον   N-AN-S   ἀμφίβληστρον
ἀμφιέζει   VIPA--3S   ἀμφιέζω

ἀμφιέζω and ἀμφιάζω   literally *clothe, dress, put garments on* someone; figuratively, of the beauty and form God has given to even common field flowers *adorn, cover* (LU 12.28)

ἀμφιέννυμι   pf. pass. ἠμφίεσμαι; literally *clothe, dress* (MT 11.8); figuratively, of the beauty and form God has given to even common field flowers *adorn, cover* (MT 6.30)

ἀμφιέννυσι(ν)   VIPA--3S   ἀμφιέννυμι
Ἀμφίπολιν   N-AF-S   Ἀμφίπολις

Ἀμφίπολις, εως, ἡ   *Amphipolis*, capital city of southeastern Macedonia, a military post on the highway from Rome to Asia (AC 17.1)

ἄμφοδον, ου, τό   *road leading around (part of a) city, thoroughfare, (open) street* (MK 11.4)

ἄμφοδον   N-AN-S   ἄμφοδον
ἀμφόδου   N-GN-S   "
ἀμφότερα   A--AN-P   ἀμφότεροι

ἀμφότεροι, αι, α   usually substantivally in the NT; (1) *both* (MT 9.17); (2) when involving more than two *all* (AC 19.16)

ἀμφότεροι   A--NM-P   ἀμφότεροι
ἀμφοτέροις   A--DM-P   "
ἀμφοτέρους   A--AM-P   "
ἀμφοτέρων   A--GM-P   "
ἄμω   A--NM-P   see ἄμωμοι
ἄμωμα   A--NN-P   ἄμωμος
ἀμώμητα   A--NN-P   ἀμώμητος
ἀμώμητοι   A--NM-P   "

ἀμώμητος, ον   *(morally) blameless, without reproach* (2P 3.14)

ἄμωμοι   A--NM-P   ἄμωμος

ἄμωμον, ου, τό   *amomum*, a spice plant native to India, used in precious ointment (RV 18.13)

ἄμωμον   A--AM-S   ἄμωμος
    N-AN-S   ἄμωμον

ἄμωμος, ον   (1) literally, of the absence of defects in sacrificial animals *unblemished*; used metaphorically of Christ as God's sacrificial lamb (HE 9.14); (2) in a religious and moral sense *blameless, without fault* (EP 1.4)

ἄμωμος   A--NF-S   ἄμωμος
ἀμώμου   A--GM-S   "
ἀμώμους   A--AM-P   "

Ἀμών, ὁ (also Ἀμμών, Ἀμμῶν, Ἀμώς) indeclinable; *Amon*, masculine proper noun (MT 1.10), son of Manasseh, father of Josiah

Ἀμώς, ὁ   indeclinable; *Amos*, masculine proper noun (LU 3.25); see also Ἀμών

ἄν   a particle untranslated by a single English word but adding possibility or uncertainty of time to the action of a verb or making a relative or conjunction indefinite; (1) denoting possibility (often ἐάν) *if (ever)*, e.g. εἰ ἐμὲ ᾔδειτε, καὶ τὸν πατέρα μου ἂν ᾔδειτε *if you had known me, you would have known my Father also* (JN 8.19); (2) denoting uncertainty as in rhetorical (AC 8.31; 17.18) or indirect (LU 1.62; AC 5.24) questions; (3) denoting indefinite future time (*-ever*); (a) with a relative pronoun ὃς ἄν *whoever*, ὅσοι ἄν *as many as, whoever*; (b) with a conjunction ὅταν *whenever*, ἕως ἄν *until*, ὡς ἄν *as soon as*, ὅπου ἄν *wherever*, ἡνίκα ἐάν or ἄν *whenever*

ἄν   QV   ἄν

ἀνά   (1) used as a preposition with the accusative ἀ. μέσον *in the midst, among* (MT 13.25); *in the middle, between* (1C 6.5); (2) used as an adverb distributively with numbers *each, apiece* (JN 2.6); ἀ. δύο *by twos, two by two* (LU 10.1); ἀ. μέρος *one after another, in turn* (1C 14.27); (3) as a prefix to verbs ἀνα- *up, back, again*

ἀνά   AB   ἀνά
    PA   "
ἀνάβα   VMAA--2S   ἀναβαίνω

ἀναβαθμός, οῦ, ὁ   (1) as the act of ascending *step (up)*; (2) as the means of ascending *step*; plural *(flight of) stairs, steps* (AC 21.35)

ἀναβαθμούς   N-AM-P   ἀναβαθμός
ἀναβαθμῶν   N-GM-P   "
ἀναβαίνει   VIPA--3S   ἀναβαίνω
ἀναβαίνειν   VNPA   "
ἀναβαίνομεν   VIPA--1P   "
ἀναβαῖνον   VPPAAN-S   "
    VPPANN-S   "
ἀναβαίνοντα   VPPAAM-S   "
    VPPANN-P   "
ἀναβαίνοντας   VPPAAM-P   "
ἀναβαίνοντες   VPPANM-P   "
ἀναβαινόντων   VPPAGM-P   "
ἀναβαίνουσι(ν)   VIPA--3P   "

ἀναβαίνω   fut. mid. ἀναβήσομαι; 2aor. ἀνέβην; pf. ἀναβέβηκα; (1) literally, of upward movement *go* or *come up, ascend*, especially of the road to Jerusalem, located on mountainous terrain (MT 20.17); with the translation suited to the context: of a ship *embark, climb aboard* (MT 14.32); of plants *grow, spring up* (MT 13.7); of a mountain *climb, ascend* (MT 5.1); of smoke *rise, mount upward* (RV 8.4); (2) figuratively, of thoughts *arise, enter the mind* (LU 24.38); of information *reach, come to* (AC 21.31); idiomatically ἀναβαίνειν ἐπὶ καρδίαν literally *arise in the heart*, i.e. *begin to think* (1C 2.9)

ἀναβαίνω   VIPA--1S   ἀναβαίνω
ἀναβαίνων   VPPANM-S   "

ἀναβάλλω   2aor. mid. ἀνεβαλόμην; active/middle *postpone, defer*; legally, of a trial *adjourn* (AC 24.22)

ἀναβάντα   VPAAAM-S   ἀναβαίνω

ἀναβάντες	VPAANM-P	"
ἀναβάντων	VPAAGM-P	"
ἀναβάς	VPAANM-S	"
ἀνάβατε	VMAA--2P	"
ἀναβέβηκα	VIRA--1S	"
ἀναβέβηκε(ν)	VIRA--3S	"
ἀνάβηθι	VMAA--2S	"
ἀναβῆναι	VNAA	"
ἀναβήσεται	VIFD--3S	"
ἀνάβητε	VMAA--2P	"

ἀναβιβάζω 1aor. ἀνεβίβασα; causal of ἀναβαίνω (*come or go up, ascend*); *cause to come up* or *go up* or *ascend*; of a net be brought to shore *draw, pull up* (MT 13.48)

ἀναβιβάσαντες	VPAANM-P	ἀναβιβάζω
ἀναβλέπουσι(ν)	VIPA--3P	ἀναβλέπω

ἀναβλέπω 1aor. ἀνέβλεψα; (1) strictly *look up* (MT 14.19); (2) of recovery from blindness *see again, regain sight* (MT 11.5); (3) of one born blind *gain sight, become able to see, receive sight* (JN 9.11)

ἀναβλέψαι	VNAA	ἀναβλέπω
ἀναβλέψαντος	VPAAGM-S	"
ἀναβλέψας	VPAANM-S	"
ἀναβλέψασαι	VPAANF-P	"
ἀναβλέψατε	VMAA--2P	"
ἀναβλέψῃ	VSAA--3S	"
ἀναβλέψῃς	VSAA--2S	"
ἀνάβλεψιν	N-AF-S	ἀνάβλεψις

ἀνάβλεψις, εως, ἡ *recovery of sight, ability to see again* (LU 4.18)

ἀνάβλεψον	VMAA--2S	ἀναβλέπω
ἀναβλέψω	VSAA--1S	"

ἀναβοάω 1aor. ἀνεβόησα; *cry out, cry aloud, shout* (MT 27.46)

ἀναβοήσας	VPAANM-S	ἀναβοάω

ἀναβολή, ῆς, ἡ *delay*; as a legal technical term *postponement* of a court case (AC 25.17)

ἀναβολήν	N-AF-S	ἀναβολή
ἀναγαγεῖν	VNAA	ἀνάγω
ἀναγαγών	VPAANM-S	"

ἀνάγαιον, ου, τό (also **ἀνώγαιον, ἀνώγεον**) *upper room* of a house, *room upstairs*

ἀνάγαιον	N-AN-S	ἀνάγαιον
ἀναγγεῖλαι	VNAA	ἀναγγέλλω
ἀνάγγειλον	VMAA--2S	"
ἀναγγελεῖ	VIFA--3S	"
ἀναγγέλλειν	VNPA	"
ἀναγγέλλομεν	VIPA--1P	"
ἀναγγέλλοντες	VPPANM-P	"
ἀναγγέλλουσα	VPPANF-S	"

ἀναγγέλλω fut. ἀναγγελῶ; 1aor. ἀνήγγειλα; 2aor. pass. ἀνηγγέλην; (1) as carrying back news of happenings *report, inform* (AC 14.27); (2) generally *announce, proclaim, openly declare* (AC 19.18); in religious usage *preach, teach, declare* (AC 20.20)

ἀναγγέλλων	VPPANM-S	ἀναγγέλλω
ἀναγγελῶ	VIFA--1S	"
ἀναγεγεννημένοι	VPRPNM-P	ἀναγεννάω
ἀνάγει	VIPA--3S	ἀνάγω

ἀναγεννάω 1aor. ἀνεγέννησα; pf. pass. ἀναγεγέννημαι; literally *regenerate, father anew, bring to birth again*; figuratively, of God's act in bringing about a spiritual rebirth causing a definite change for the better; active *cause to be born again, regenerate* (1P 1.3); passive *be born again* (1P 1.23)

ἀναγεννήσας	VPAANM-S	ἀναγεννάω
ἀνάγεον	N-AN-S	see ἀνάγαιον
ἀνάγεσθαι	VNPP	ἀνάγω
ἀναγινώσκει	VIPA--3S	ἀναγινώσκω
ἀναγινώσκεις	VIPA--2S	"
ἀναγινώσκεται	VIPP--3S	"
ἀναγινώσκετε	VIPA--2P	"
ἀναγινώσκηται	VSPP--3S	"
ἀναγινωσκομένας	VPPPAF-P	"
ἀναγινωσκομένη	VPPPNF-S	"
ἀναγινωσκόμενος	VPPPNM-S	"
ἀναγινώσκοντες	VPPANM-P	"
ἀναγινώσκοντος	VPPAGM-S	"

ἀναγινώσκω impf. ἀνεγίνωσκον; 2aor. ἀνέγνων; 1aor. pass. ἀνεγνώσθην; (1) *read* (MT 12.3); (2) used mainly of public reading *read aloud* (LU 4.16)

ἀναγινώσκων	VPPANM-S	ἀναγινώσκω
ἀναγκάζεις	VIPA--2S	ἀναγκάζω
ἀναγκάζουσι(ν)	VIPA--3P	"

ἀναγκάζω impf. ἠνάγκαζον; 1aor. ἠνάγκασα; 1aor. pass. ἠναγκάσθην; (1) of compulsion outwardly *compel, force* (AC 26.11); of friendly pressure *(strongly) urge, constrain* (MT 14.22); (2) passive, of compulsion inwardly *feel obliged to, feel compelled* (AC 28.19)

ἀναγκαῖα	A--NN-P	ἀναγκαῖος
ἀναγκαίας	A--AF-P	"
ἀναγκαῖον	A--NN-S	"

ἀναγκαῖος, αία, ον (1) of what compels or makes needful *necessary, indispensable, pressing* (TI 3.14); (2) neuter in an impersonal construction ἀναγκαῖόν (ἐστιν) *it is necessary* (HE 8.3); comparative ἀναγκαιότερόν (ἐστιν) *it is more necessary, needful* (PH 1.24); (3) of persons connected by natural ties τοὺς ἀναγκαίους φίλους *close* or *intimate friends* (AC 10.24)

ἀναγκαιότερον	A-MNN-S	ἀναγκαῖος
ἀναγκαίους	A--AM-P	"
ἀνάγκαις	N-DF-P	ἀνάγκη
ἀνάγκασον	VMAA--2S	ἀναγκάζω
ἀναγκαστικῶς	AB	ἀναγκαστῶς

ἀναγκαστῶς (also **ἀναγκαστικῶς**) adverb; *in a forced manner, unwillingly, out of obligation* (1P 5.2), opposite ἑκουσίως (*willingly, voluntarily*)

ἀναγκαστῶς	AB	ἀναγκαστῶς

ἀνάγκη, ης, ἡ (1) *necessity, compulsion, force*; (a) from a feeling of inward necessity *constraint, compelling obligation* (1C 9.16); (b) as brought about by circumstances *what is inevitable* (MT 18.7); (c) as arising from the divine order of things *necessity* (RO 13.5); (2) as difficult circumstances that come on one with compelling force *distress, trouble, tribulation* (LU 21.23); (3) impersonally ἀ. (ἐστίν) *it is necessary* (HE 9.16)

ἀνάγκη	N-NF-S	ἀνάγκη
ἀνάγκῃ	N-DF-S	"
ἀνάγκην	N-AF-S	"
ἀνάγκης	N-GF-S	"
ἀναγνόντες	VPAANM-P	ἀναγινώσκω
ἀναγνούς	VPAANM-S	"
ἀναγνῶναι	VNAA	"

ἀναγνωρίζω   1aor. pass. ἀνεγνωρίσθην; with middle sense *make oneself known again, cause to be recognized* (AC 7.13)

ἀναγνώσει	N-DF-S	ἀνάγνωσις
ἀναγνωσθῇ	VSAP--3S	ἀναγινώσκω
ἀναγνωσθῆναι	VNAP	"
ἀνάγνωσιν	N-AF-S	ἀνάγνωσις

ἀνάγνωσις, εως, ἡ   *reading, public reading*

ἀναγνῶτε	VSAA--2P	ἀναγινώσκω
ἀναγομένοις	VPPPDM-P	ἀνάγω

ἀνάγω   2aor. ἀνήγαγον; 1aor. pass. ἀνήχθην; (1) literally, of movement from a lower to a higher point *lead, bring up, conduct* (LU 4.5); figuratively, of sacrifice *offer up, bring* (AC 7.41); (2) middle or passive, as a nautical technical term *put (out) to sea, set sail* (AC 28.11)

ἀναδείκνυμι   1aor. ἀνέδειξα; strictly *lift up and show, show forth*; (1) as setting apart by some outward expression *appoint, commission, give a task to* (LU 10.1); (2) as making public what is hidden *disclose, reveal, show clearly* (AC 1.24)

ἀναδείκνυναι	VNPA	ἀναδείκνυμι
ἀναδείξεως	N-GF-S	ἀνάδειξις

ἀνάδειξις, εως, ἡ   strictly *showing forth, making known publicly*; hence, of John the Baptist on publicly beginning his work as forerunner to which he had already been consecrated *manifestation, public appearance* (LU 1.80)

ἀνάδειξον	VMAA--2S	ἀναδείκνυμι
ἀναδεξάμενος	VPADNM-S	ἀναδέχομαι

ἀναδέχομαι   1aor. ἀνεδεξάμην; *accept, receive*; (1) of guests *welcome, receive* (AC 28.7); (2) of a promise *receive, accept, take up* (HE 11.17)

ἀναδίδωμι   2aor. ἀνέδων; *hand over, deliver, present* (AC 23.33)

ἀναδόντες	VPAANM-P	ἀναδίδωμι

ἀναζάω   1aor. ἀνέζησα; literally, of the dead *become alive again, rise again, return to life*; metaphorically, of sin personified *revive, become (suddenly) active, spring into life* (RO 7.9); figuratively, of one morally and spiritually dead *become alive again, live in a new and different way* (LU 15.24)

ἀναζητέω   impf. ἀνεζήτουν; 1aor. ἀνεζήτησα; *search out, look for, discover*

ἀναζητῆσαι	VNAA	ἀναζητέω
ἀναζητοῦντες	VPPANM-P	"
ἀναζητῶν	VPPANM-S	"

ἀναζώννυμι   1aor. mid. ἀνεζωσάμην; only middle in the NT; literally, of long Eastern robes *gird up, bind up*; idiomatically, of preparing the mind for action ἀναζώννυναι τὰς ὀσφύας τῆς διανοίας literally *tie up at the waist the clothes of the mind*, i.e. *get mentally ready, get set to learn* (1P 1.13)

ἀναζωπυρεῖν	VNPA	ἀναζωπυρέω

ἀναζωπυρέω   literally, of fire *rekindle, revive, fan into flame*; figuratively, of spiritual gifts *stir up* (into new life), *reactivate, excite into fresh activity* (2T 1.6)

ἀναζωσάμενοι	VPAMNM-P	ἀναζώννυμι

ἀναθάλλω   2aor. ἀνέθαλον; literally, of plants *shoot up, become green* or *flourish again*; figuratively *become active again, revive* (one's care for someone), *renew* (concern) (PH 4.10)

ἀνάθεμα, ατος, τό   strictly *what is placed* or *set up*; (1) as what has been dedicated to a divinity *votive offering, consecrated gift* (LU 21.5); (2) in a negative sense, as someone delivered over to divine wrath *curse, one accursed* (GA 1.8); (3) as a binding oath with dreadful consequences expected if not carried out *curse* (AC 23.14)

ἀνάθεμα	N-NN-S	ἀνάθεμα
ἀναθέμασι(ν)	N-DN-P	"
ἀναθέματι	N-DN-S	"
ἀναθεματίζειν	VNPA	ἀναθεματίζω

ἀναθεματίζω   1aor. ἀνεθεμάτισα, ptc. ἀναθεματίσας (AC 23.12); as calling on God to punish if what is solemnly spoken is not true or carried out; (1) transitively *bind (with an oath), bring (under a curse)* (AC 23.14); (2) intransitively *curse, utter curses* (MK 14.71)

ἀναθεωρέω   *look at again and again, examine attentively, observe carefully* (AC 17.23); of mental attention *consider, reflect on* (HE 13.7)

ἀναθεωροῦντες	VPPANM-P	ἀναθεωρέω
ἀναθεωρῶν	VPPANM-S	"

ἀνάθημα, ατος, τό   *votive offering*, often set up in a temple, *gift consecrated to God* (LU 21.5)

ἀναθήμασι(ν)	N-DN-P	ἀνάθημα

ἀναίδεια, ας, ἡ (also ἀναιδία)   (1) in a negative sense, as insensitivity to what is proper *shamelessness, boldness, insolence* (possibly LU 11.8); (2) in a positive sense *persistence, tenacious insistence* without regard to time, place, or person (possibly LU 11.8)

ἀναίδειαν	N-AF-S	ἀναίδεια
ἀναιδίαν	N-AF-S	"
ἀναιρεθῆναι	VNAP	ἀναιρέω
ἀναιρεῖ	VIPA--3S	"
ἀναιρεῖν	VNPA	"
ἀναιρεῖσθαι	VNPP	"
ἀναιρέσει	N-DF-S	ἀναίρεσις
ἀναίρεσιν	N-AF-S	"

ἀναίρεσις, εως, ἡ   strictly *taking up* or *away*; hence, as an action *murder, killing* (AC 8.1)

ἀναιρέω   fut. ἀναιρήσω and ἀνελῶ; 2aor. ἀνεῖλον and ἀνεῖλα, mid. ἀνειλόμην and ἀνειλάμην; 1aor. pass. ἀνηρέθην; (1) active *take away, do away with, destroy*; (a) of persons *kill, murder*, usually in a violent way (MT 2.16); (b) of things *do away with, abolish* (HE 10.9); (2) middle *take up (for oneself)*; of exposed infants *take up* (to rear), *adopt* (AC 7.21)

ἀναιρουμένων	VPPPGM-P	ἀναιρέω
ἀναιρούντων	VPPAGM-P	"
ἀναίτιοι	A--NM-P	ἀναίτιος

ἀναίτιος, ον   *innocent, without guilt, not having done anything wrong*; substantively οἱ ἀναίτιοι *innocent people* (MT 12.7)

ἀναιτίους	A--AM-P	ἀναίτιος

ἀνακαθίζω   1aor. ἀνεκάθισα; *sit up(right)* from a reclining position

ἀνακαινίζειν	VNPA	ἀνακαινίζω

ἀνακαινίζω   figuratively in the NT *renew, restore* to a more desirable state (HE 6.6)

ἀνακαινούμενον	VPPPAM-S	ἀνακαινόω
ἀνακαινοῦται	VIPP--3S	"

ἀνακαινόω   as causing something to be new and better *renew, restore*; figuratively and passive in the NT, of spiritual rebirth or renewal *be renewed*

ἀνακαινώσει	N-DF-S	ἀνακαίνωσις
ἀνακαινώσεως	N-GF-S	"

ἀνακαίνωσις, εως, ἡ   figuratively in the NT, as the action by which a person becomes spiritually new and different *renewing, renewal* (TI 3.5)

ἀνακαλυπτόμενον	VPPPNN-S	ἀνακαλύπτω

ἀνακαλύπτω   pf. pass. ἀνακεκάλυμμαι; *uncover, unveil*; passive, of the face *be unveiled, be uncovered, be without a veil*

ἀνακαλύψατε	VMAA--2P	ἀνακαλύπτω

ἀνακάμπτω   fut. ἀνακάμψω; 1aor. ἀνέκαμψα; strictly *bend back* to a previous position; (1) literally *return, go back* (MT 2.12); (2) figuratively; (a) of a religious greeting that does not benefit a home unworthy of it *return, come back* (LU 10.6); (b) of changing to a former belief *turn back* (2P 2.21)

ἀνακάμψαι	VNAA	ἀνακάμπτω
ἀνακάμψει	VIFA--3S	"
ἀνακάμψω	VIFA--1S	"

ἀνάκειμαι   impf. ἀνεκείμην; (1) generally *lie, recline* (MK 5.40); (2) predominately in the NT of being at a table, where in the Roman style reclining couches were used *recline at table, sit to eat, be at table* (MT 9.10)

ἀνακειμένοις	VPPDDM-P	ἀνάκειμαι
	VPPODM-P	"
ἀνακείμενον	VPPDAN-S	"
	VPPOAN-S	"
ἀνακείμενος	VPPDNM-S	"
	VPPONM-S	"
ἀνακειμένου	VPPDGM-S	"
	VPPOGM-S	"
ἀνακειμένους	VPPDAM-P	"
	VPPOAM-P	"
ἀνακειμένων	VPPDGM-P	"
	VPPOGM-P	"
ἀνάκειται	VIPD--3S	"
	VIPO--3S	"
ἀνακεκαλυμμένῳ	VPRPDN-S	ἀνακαλύπτω
ἀνακεκύλισται	VIRP--3S	ἀνακυλίω
ἀνακεφαλαιοῦται	VIPP--3S	ἀνακεφαλαιόω

ἀνακεφαλαιόω   1aor. mid. ἀνεκεφαλαιωσάμην; (1) *sum up, include* under one principle (RO 13.9); (2) of bringing everything together under the control of one person *gather* (everything) *together, unify, make into one* (EP 1.10)

ἀνακεφαλαιώσασθαι	VNAD	ἀνακεφαλαιόω
ἀνακλιθῆναι	VNAP	ἀνακλίνω
ἀνακλιθήσονται	VIFP--3P	"
ἀνακλῖναι	VNAA	"
ἀνακλινεῖ	VIFA--3S	"
ἀνακλίνεσθε	VIPM--2P	"

ἀνακλίνω   fut. ἀνακλινῶ; 1aor. ἀνέκλινα; 1aor. pass. ἀνεκλίθην; 1fut. pass. ἀνακλιθήσομαι; (1) active *lay* (someone) *down*; of a child *put to bed* (LU 2.7); *cause to lie or sit down, make to recline* (at table) (LU 12.37); (2) passive *lie down, recline* or *sit down at a meal* (MT 14.19); figuratively, of participation in Christ's kingdom (MT 8.11; LU 13.29)

ἀνακράζω   1aor. ἀνέκραξα; 2aor. ἀνέκραγον; *cry out*; (1) of the loud cry of demonized or frightened people *cry aloud, scream, shout* (MK 1.23); (2) of an aroused multitude *shout out, howl, yell* (LU 23.18)

ἀνακράζων	VPPANM-S	ἀνακράζω
ἀνακράξας	VPAANM-S	"

ἀνακραυγάζω   1aor. ἀνεκραύγασα; *cry out* (LU 4.35)

ἀνακραύγασαν	VPAANN-S	ἀνακραυγάζω
ἀνακριθῶ	VSAP--1S	ἀνακρίνω
ἀνακρίναντα	VPAAAM-S	"
ἀνακρίναντες	VPAANM-P	"
ἀνακρίνας	VPAANM-S	"
ἀνακρίνει	VIPA--3S	"
ἀνακρίνεται	VIPP--3S	"
ἀνακρινόμεθα	VIPP--1P	"
ἀνακρίνοντες	VPPANM-P	"
ἀνακρίνουσι(ν)	VPPADM-P	"

ἀνακρίνω   1aor. ἀνέκρινα; 1aor. pass. ἀνεκρίθην; (1) generally, of the process of evaluation *examine, question, study carefully* (AC 17.11); (2) as sifting evidence in judicial hearings *hold a preliminary hearing, cross-examine, investigate, interrogate* (AC 28.18); (3) as passing judgment on personal behavior *call to account, criticize, judge* (1C 14.24)

ἀνακρίνω	VIPA--1S	ἀνακρίνω
ἀνακρίνων	VPPANM-S	"
ἀνακρίσεως	N-GF-S	ἀνάκρισις

ἀνάκρισις, εως, ἡ   as an evaluative action *investigation*; as a legal technical term *preliminary hearing, judicial examination* (AC 25.26)

ἀνακυλίω   pf. pass. ἀνακεκύλισμαι; of a circular gravestone *roll away, roll back* (MK 16.4)

ἀνακύπτω   1aor. ἀνέκυψα; *stand erect, lift up the head, raise oneself up*; literally, of a body bent by disease *straighten up* (LU 13.11); figuratively, of taking courage *stand up, be strong* (LU 21.28)

ἀνακύψαι	VNAA	ἀνακύπτω
ἀνακύψας	VPAANM-S	"
ἀνακύψατε	VMAA--2P	"
ἀναλάβετε	VMAA--2P	ἀναλαμβάνω
ἀναλαβόντες	VPAANM-P	"
ἀναλαβών	VPAANM-S	"
ἀναλαμβάνειν	VNPA	"

ἀναλαμβάνω   2aor. ἀνέλαβον; 1aor. pass. ἀνελήμφθην (and ἀνελήφθην); (1) as causing to go up *lift up, take up*; passive *be taken up* (AC 1.11); (2) of persons or things *pick up, lift up and carry (away)* (EP 6.16); *carry along* (EP 6.13); (3) of a travel companion *bring* or *take along* (AC 23.31); *get, pick up* (2T 4.11); (4) *bring* or *take on board* (AC 20.13)

ἀναλημφθείς	VPAPNM-S	ἀναλαμβάνω
ἀναλήμψεως	N-GF-S	ἀνάλημψις

ἀνάλημψις, εως, ἡ (also ἀνάληψις)   as an action *taking* or *receiving up*; specifically in LU 9.51 of Jesus' approaching death, resurrection, and ascension into heaven (cf. ἔξοδος [*departure, death*] in LU 9.31)

ἀναληφθείς	VPAPNM-S	ἀναλαμβάνω
ἀναλήψεως	N-GF-S	ἀνάλημψις

ἀναλίσκω and ἀναλόω   fut. ἀναλώσω; 1aor. ἀνήλωσα; 1aor. pass. ἀνηλώθην; (1) literally *use up*; of fire *consume, burn up* (LU 9.54); (2) figuratively; (a) active, of annihilation of enemies *destroy* (2TH 2.8); (b) passive, of the effects of strife within a group *be ruined, be destroyed* (GA 5.15)

ἀνάλλομαι   1aor. ἀνήλατο; *jump up, leap up* (AC 14.10)

ἀναλογία, ας, ἡ   as showing the correspondence between two things *right relationship, comparison, proportion*; κατὰ τὴν ἀναλογίαν *in agreement with, in proportion to* (RO 12.6)

ἀναλογίαν	N-AF-S	ἀναλογία

ἀναλογίζομαι   1aor. ἀνελογισάμην; *consider (attentively), think about carefully* (HE 12.3)

ἀναλογίσασθε	VMAD--2P	ἀναλογίζομαι
ἀναλοῖ	VIPA-3S	ἀναλίσκω
ἄναλον	A--NN-S	ἄναλος

ἄναλος, ον   *deprived of saltiness, saltless, insipid* (MK 9.50)

ἀναλῦσαι	VNAA	ἀναλύω
ἀναλύσεως	N-GF-S	ἀνάλυσις
ἀναλύσῃ	VSAA--3S	ἀναλύω

ἀνάλυσις, εως, ἡ   as an action *breaking up, dissolution*; euphemistically, of departure from life *death* (2T 4.6)

ἀναλύω   1aor. ἀνέλυσα; 1aor. pass. ἀνελύθην; (1) transitively *loose, untie* (AC 16.26); (2) intransitively *depart, return* (LU 12.36); euphemistically *die, depart from life* (PH 1.23)

ἀναλωθήσεται	VIFP--3S	ἀναλίσκω
ἀναλωθῆτε	VSAP--2P	"
ἀναλῶσαι	VNAA	"
ἀναλώσει	VIFA--3S	ἀναλίσκω

ἀναμάρτητος, ον   *having not sinned, without sin, guiltless*; substantivally ὁ ἀ. *the one who has done nothing wrong* (JN 8.7)

ἀναμάρτητος	A--NM-S	ἀναμάρτητος
ἀναμένειν	VNPA	ἀναμένω

ἀναμένω   *wait for, await, expect* (1TH 1.10)

ἀναμέσον	PA&A--AN-S	see ἀνά and μέσον
ἀναμιμνῄσκεσθε	VMPP--2P	ἀναμιμνῄσκω
ἀναμιμνῃσκομένου	VPPPGM-S	"

ἀναμιμνῄσκω   fut. ἀναμνήσω; 1aor. pass. ἀνεμνήσθην; *remind, cause to remember, make mention of* (1C 4.17); passive *be reminded, recall, remember* (MK 14.72)

ἀναμιμνῄσκω	VIPA--1S	ἀναμιμνῄσκω
ἀναμνήσει	VIFA--3S	"
ἀναμνησθείς	VPAPNM-S	"
ἀναμνησθέντες	VPAPNM-P	"
ἀνάμνησιν	N-AF-S	ἀνάμνησις

ἀνάμνησις, εως, ἡ   *means of remembering, remembrance, reminder* (HE 10.3); εἰς τὴν ἐμὴν ἀνάμνησιν *as my memorial, in remembrance* or *memory of me* (1C 11.24)

ἀνάμνησις	N-NF-S	ἀνάμνησις
ἀνανεοῦσθαι	VNPP	ἀνανεόω
ἀνανεοῦσθε	VMPP--2P	"

ἀνανεόω   *renew*; passive *be renewed, be revived, be made new* or *different* (EP 4.23)

ἀνανήφω   1aor. ἀνένηψα; strictly *become sober again*; hence *come to one's senses, no longer think wrong thoughts*; figuratively, of spiritual recovery (2T 2.26)

ἀνανήψωσι(ν)	VSAA--3P	ἀνανήφω
Ἀνανία	N-VM-S	Ἀνανίας
Ἀνανία	N-VM-S	"
Ἀνανίαν	N-AM-S	"

Ἀνανίαν	N-AM-S	"
Ἀνανίας	N-NM-S	"

Ἀνανίας, ου, ὁ (also Ἀνανίας)   *Ananias, masculine proper noun*

Ἀνανίας	N-NM-S	Ἀνανίας
ἀναντιρήτως	AB	ἀναντιρρήτως

ἀναντίρρητος, ον   *not to be contradicted, indisputable, undeniable* (AC 19.36)

ἀναντιρρήτων	A--GN-P	ἀναντίρρητος

ἀναντιρρήτως (also ἀναντιρήτως)   adverb; *without raising any question, without objection, without hesitation* (AC 10.29)

ἀναντιρρήτως	AB	ἀναντιρρήτως
ἀνάξιοι	A--NM-P	ἀνάξιος

ἀνάξιος, ον   *unworthy, not competent, inadequate* (1C 6.2)

ἀναξίως   adverb; *unworthily, in an improper* or *careless manner* (1C 11.27)

ἀναξίως	AB	ἀναξίως
ἀναπαήσονται	VIFP--3P	ἀναπαύω
ἀναπαύεσθε	VIPM--2P	"
	VMPM--2P	"
ἀναπαύεται	VIPM--3S	"
ἀναπαυόμενον	VPPMAM-S	"
ἀναπαύου	VMPM--2S	"
ἀναπαύσασθε	VMAM--2P	"
ἀναπαῦσθαι	VNPM	"
ἀνάπαυσιν	N-AF-S	ἀνάπαυσις

ἀνάπαυσις, εως, ἡ   (1) as a ceasing from activity *stopping, interruption* (RV 4.8); (2) as a resting from labor or carrying burdens *rest, repose*; figuratively, of spiritual rest (MT 11.29); (3) by metonymy *resting place, settled habitation* (MT 12.43)

ἀναπαύσομαι	VIFM--1S	ἀναπαύω
ἀνάπαυσον	VMAA--2S	"
ἀναπαύσονται	VIFM--3P	"
ἀναπαύσω	VIFA--1S	"
ἀναπαύσωνται	VSAM--3P	"

ἀναπαύω   fut. ἀναπαύσω, mid. ἀναπαύσομαι; 1aor. ἀνέπαυσα; pf. pass. ἀναπέπαυμαι; 1aor. pass. ἀνεπαύθην; 2fut. pass. ἀναπαήσομαι; (1) transitively *cause to rest, refresh*; figuratively, of giving spiritual rest (MT 11.28); passive, of receiving encouragement *be refreshed*; (2) middle, of taking bodily rest, as in sleep *rest* (MT 26.45); of taking one's ease *rest* (LU 12.19); of remaining quiet or restful *rest, be still* (RV 6.11); (3) figuratively, with ἐπί of the Spirit's resting place *remain on, continue to be with* (1P 4.14)

ἀναπείθει	VIPA--3S	ἀναπείθω

ἀναπείθω   *persuade*; in a bad sense *induce, incite, persuade* to a different opinion (AC 18.13)

ἀνάπειρος, ον (also ἀνάπηρος)   *crippled, maimed, mutilated*; substantivally (LU 14.13)

ἀναπείρους	A--AM-P	ἀνάπειρος
ἀναπέμπεται	VIPP--3S	ἀναπέμπω

ἀναπέμπω   fut. ἀναπέμψω; 1aor. ἀνέπεμψα; literally *send up* or *back*; figuratively, as a legal technical term *send (up)* to a higher or proper tribunal or official (LU 23.7); *send (back)* to the previous tribunal or official (LU 23.11)

ἀναπέμψαι	VNAA	ἀναπέμπω

ἀναπέμψω VSAA--1S "

ἀναπέπαυται VIRP--3S ἀναπαύω

ἀνάπεσαι VMAM--2S ἀναπίπτω

ἀνάπεσε VMAA--2S "

ἀναπεσεῖν VNAA "

ἀναπεσῇς VSAA--2S "

ἀνάπεσον VMAA--2S "

ἀναπεσών VPAANM-S "

ἀναπηδάω 1aor. ἀνεπήδησα; *jump up, leap up* (MK 10.50)

ἀναπηδήσας VPAANM-S ἀναπηδάω

ἀναπήρους A--AM-P ἀνάπειρος

ἀναπίπτω 2aor. ἀνέπεσον; (1) *lie down, recline*, especially at a meal; *take one's place at table, sit down* (MT 15.35); (2) *lean close to, lean back on* (JN 13.25)

ἀναπίρους A--AM-P see ἀναπείρους

ἀναπληροῦται VIPP--3S ἀναπληρόω

ἀναπληρόω fut. ἀναπληρώσω; 1aor. ἀνεπλήρωσα; (1) literally *fill up, make complete*; figuratively, of filling up the measure of sins *sin to the limit* (1TH 2.16); (2) of prophecy *fulfill, confirm, cause to happen*; passive *be fulfilled, happen* (MT 13.14); (3) of filling or taking someone's place *replace, make up for* someone's absence (1C 16.17); *fill a position* (1C 14.16); (4) of making good a lack *supply* (PH 2.30); (5) of observing the law *fulfill, obey* (GA 6.2)

ἀναπληρῶν VPPANM-S ἀναπληρόω

ἀναπληρῶσαι VNAA "

ἀναπληρώσατε VMAA--2P "

ἀναπληρώσετε VIFA--2P "

ἀναπληρώσῃ VSAA--3S "

ἀναπολόγητος, ον *without excuse, indefensible, inexcusable*

ἀναπολόγητος A--NM-S ἀναπολόγητος

ἀναπολογήτους A--AM-P "

ἀναπράσσω (or **ἀναπράττω**) 1aor. ἀνέπραξα; *demand, exact payment* (LU 19.23)

ἀνάπτει VIPA--3S ἀνάπτω

ἀναπτύξας VPAANM-S ἀναπτύσσω

ἀναπτύσσω 1aor. ἀνέπτυξα; of a book rolled up in the form of a scroll *unroll, open* (LU 4.17)

ἀνάπτω 1aor. pass. ἀνήφθην; as causing burning to begin *kindle, set on fire, light*; passive *be kindled, be burning*

ἀναρίθμητος, ον *unable to be numbered, countless, innumerable* (HE 11.12)

ἀναρίθμητος A--NF-S ἀναρίθμητος

ἀνασείει VIPA--3S ἀνασείω

ἀνασείω 1aor. ἀνέσεισα; literally *shake up, swing up and down*; figuratively *stir up, incite*, often of moving a crowd to mob action

ἀνασκάπτω pf. pass. ptc. ἀνεσκαμμένος; *dig up* (AC 15.16)

ἀνασκευάζοντες VPPANM-P ἀνασκευάζω

ἀνασκευάζω strictly *pack up* baggage (τὰ σκευή); hence *tear down, upset, unsettle*; figuratively, of unsettling someone's mind *upset, trouble the mind* (AC 15.24)

ἀνασπάσει VIFA--3S ἀνασπάω

ἀνασπάω fut. ἀνασπάσω; 1aor. pass. ἀνεσπάσθην; *pull or draw out* (LU 14.5); *pull or draw up* (AC 11.10)

ἀνάστα VMAA--2S ἀνίστημι

ἀναστάν VPAANN-S "

ἀναστάντες VPAANM-P "

ἀναστάς VPAANM-S "

ἀναστᾶσα VPAANF-S "

ἀναστᾶσαν VPAAAF-S "

ἀναστάσει N-DF-S ἀνάστασις

ἀναστάσεως N-GF-S "

ἀνάστασιν N-AF-S "

ἀνάστασις, εως, ἡ (1) intransitively, of coming back to life after having died *arising, resurrection* (MT 22.23); (2) by metonymy, of Jesus as the author of resurrection (JN 11.25); (3) figuratively, as advancing to a higher status *rising* (LU 2.34)

ἀνάστασις N-NF-S ἀνάστασις

ἀναστατοῦντες VPPANM-P ἀναστατόω

ἀναστατόω 1aor. ἀνεστάτωσα; (1) as creating a public disturbance *trouble, disturb, upset* (AC 17.6); (2) as agitating for a political uprising against established authority *start a revolt, stir up a rebellion* (AC 21.38)

ἀναστατώσαντες VPAANM-P ἀναστατόω

ἀναστατώσας VPAANM-S "

ἀνασταυροῦντας VPPANM-P ἀνασταυρόω

ἀνασταυρόω literally, of a Roman form of cruel execution by affixing the body to a raised pole and crosspiece *crucify*; figuratively in HE 6.6 of rejection of Christ by apostates, probably *crucify, hang up*; possibly *crucify anew* or *again*

ἀναστενάζω 1aor. ἀνεστέναξα; *sigh deeply, groan inwardly* (MK 8.12)

ἀναστενάξας VPAANM-S ἀναστενάζω

ἀναστῇ VSAA--3S ἀνίστημι

ἀνάστηθι VMAA--2S "

ἀναστῆναι VNAA "

ἀναστῆσαι VNAA "

ἀναστήσας VPAANM-S "

ἀναστήσει VIFA--3S "

 VIFA--3S^VMAA--3S "

ἀναστήσειν VNFA "

ἀναστήσεται VIFM--3S "

ἀναστησόμεθα VIFM--1P "

ἀναστήσονται VIFM--3P "

ἀναστήσω VIFA--1S "

 VSAA--1S "

ἀναστράφητε VMAP--2P ἀναστρέφω

ἀναστρέφεσθαι VNPP "

ἀναστρεφομένους VPPPAM-P "

ἀναστρεφομένων VPPPGM-P "

ἀναστρέφω fut. ἀναστρέψω; 1aor. ἀνέστρεψα; 2aor. pass. ἀνεστράφην; (1) transitively *overturn, upset* (JN 2.15); (2) passive, with a reflexive sense of turning back and forth in a place *live, stay* (MT 17.22); figuratively, of moral conduct *act, behave, live* (1T 3.15); passive, as living with suffering as a part of Christian experience *be treated, go through* (HE 10.33); (3) intransitively *return* to a place (AC 5.22)

ἀναστρέψαντες VPAANM-P ἀναστρέφω

ἀναστρέψω VIFA--1S "

ἀναστροφαῖς N-DF-P ἀναστροφή

ἀναστροφή, ῆς, ἡ strictly *turning about in a place*; hence, of a way of life *conduct, behavior*

ἀναστροφῇ N-DF-S ἀναστροφή

ἀναστροφήν N-AF-S "

ἀναστροφῆς N-GF-S "

ἀναστῶσι(ν) VSAA--3P ἀνίστημι

ἀνασῳζομένους   VPPPAM-P   ἀνασῴζω

ἀνασῴζω figuratively in the NT *save, deliver* or *rescue* (from sin) (HE 10.14)

ἀνατάξασθαι   VNAD   ἀνατάσσομαι

ἀνατάσσομαι 1aor. ἀνεταξάμην; literally *arrange in proper order*; figuratively, of writing in an organized way *compose, compile, draw up* (LU 1.1)

ἀνατεθραμμένος   VPRPNM-S   ἀνατρέφω
ἀνατείλαντος   VPAAGM-S   ἀνατέλλω
ἀνατείλη   VSAA--3S   "
ἀνατέλλει   VIPA--3S   "
ἀνατέλλοντος   VPPAGM-S   "
ἀνατέλλουσαν   VPPAAF-S   "

ἀνατέλλω 1aor. ἀνέτειλα; pf. ἀνατέταλκα; with an indication of upward movement; (1) transitively *cause to spring up* or *rise* (MT 5.45); (2) intransitively; (a) literally, of the sun *rise, come up* (MK 4.6); of a cloud *appear* (LU 12.54); (b) figuratively, of one's family origin *be descended, arise from* (HE 7.14); (c) metaphorically, of increased understanding of spiritual things made possible through Christ's return, likened to the appearance of the morning star *rise, shine forth* (2P 1.19)

ἀνατέταλκε(ν)   VIRA--3S   ἀνατέλλω

ἀνατίθημι 2aor. mid. ἀνεθέμην; only middle in the NT; (1) as setting forth one's cause *declare, refer to* (for counsel) (AC 25.14); (2) as giving additional information with a request for consideration *explain, communicate, put before* (GA 2.2)

ἀνατολή, ῆς, ἡ with an indication of an upward movement; (1) of a star *rising* (MT 2.2, 9); (2) of the direction of the sun's rising, especially in the plural *east, eastern lands* (MT 8.11); (3) metaphorically, of the coming of Christ *sunrise, rising sun, light of dawn* (LU 1.78)

ἀνατολή   N-NF-S   ἀνατολή
ἀνατολῆ   N-DF-S   "
ἀνατολῆς   N-GF-S   "
ἀνατολικά   A--AN-P   ἀνατολικός

ἀνατολικός, ή, όν *eastern* (AC 19.1)

ἀνατολῶν   N-GF-P   ἀνατολή
ἀνατρέπουσι(ν)   VIPA--3P   ἀνατρέπω

ἀνατρέπω 1aor. ἀνέτρεψα; literally *overturn, upset, overthrow* (JN 2.15); figuratively *upset, ruin*, especially as the effect of false teaching (2T 2.18; TI 1.11)

ἀνατρέφω 1aor. mid. ἀνεθρεψάμην; pf. pass. ἀνατέθραμμαι; 2aor. pass. ἀνετράφην; in relation to child rearing; (1) as physical nurturing *bring up, nourish, care for* (AC 7.20); (2) as mental and spiritual nurturing *rear, train, educate* (AC 7.21)

ἀναφαίνεσθαι   VNPP   ἀναφαίνω

ἀναφαίνω 1aor. ἀνέφανα; (1) *bring to light, cause to appear*; passive *appear* (LU 19.11); (2) active, as a nautical technical term *come in sight of, sight (land)* (AC 21.3)

ἀναφάναντες   VPAANM-P   ἀναφαίνω
ἀναφανέντες   VPAPNM-P   "
ἀναφέρει   VIPA--3S   ἀναφέρω
ἀναφέρειν   VNPA   "

ἀναφέρω 2aor. ἀνήνεγκα and ἀνήνεγκον; literally *bring* or *take up, lead up* (MT 17.1); as a religious technical term for offering sacrifices *offer up, bring* (to an altar) (HE 7.27); figuratively, of Christ's taking sins on himself in order to atone for them *bear, take away* (HE 9.28)

ἀναφέρωμεν   VSPA--1P   ἀναφέρω

ἀναφωνέω 1aor. ἀνεφώνησα; *cry out loudly, exclaim* (LU 1.42)

ἀναχθέντες   VPAPNM-P   ἀνάγω
ἀναχθῆναι   VNAP   "
ἀνάχυσιν   N-AF-S   ἀνάχυσις

ἀνάχυσις, εως, ἡ *pouring out, flooding* as in a wide stream; figuratively and in a negative sense, of moral dissipation and reckless living *excess, extreme degree* (1P 4.4)

ἀναχωρεῖτε   VMPA--2P   ἀναχωρέω

ἀναχωρέω 1aor. ἀνεχώρησα; (1) *depart, go away* (MT 2.14); (2) as departing to go to one's own country *return* (MT 2.12); (3) as retreating to a secluded place *withdraw, retire* (MT 12.15)

ἀναχωρήσαντες   VPAANM-P   ἀναχωρέω
ἀναχωρησάντων   VPAAGM-P   "
ἀναχωρήσας   VPAANM-S   "
ἀνάψαντες   VPAANM-P   ἀνάπτω
ἀναψύξεως   N-GF-S   ἀνάψυξις

ἀνάψυξις, εως, ἡ strictly *recovery of breath*; literally, as a relief from heat *coolness, refreshing, relaxation*; figuratively, of the messianic age as relief from distressing circumstances *rest, refreshing* (AC 3.20)

ἀναψύξω   VSAA--1S   ἀναψύχω

ἀναψύχω 1aor. ἀνέψυξα; (1) transitively, strictly *give someone a breathing space*; hence *refresh, cheer up, encourage* (2T 1.16); (2) intransitively *be refreshed, be cheered up* (in someone's company) (RO 15.32)

ἀναψύχω   VIPA--1S   ἀναψύχω
ἄνδρα   N-AM-S   ἀνήρ
ἀνδραποδισταῖς   N-DM-P   ἀνδραποδιστής

ἀνδραποδιστής, οῦ, ὁ *kidnapper, slave trader* (1T 1.10)

ἄνδρας   N-AM-P   ἀνήρ
ἀνδράσι(ν)   N-DM-P   "
Ἀνδρέα   N-DM-S   Ἀνδρέας
Ἀνδρέαν   N-AM-S   "

Ἀνδρέας, ου, ὁ *Andrew*, masculine proper noun

Ἀνδρέας   N-NM-S   Ἀνδρέας
Ἀνδρέου   N-GM-S   "
ἄνδρες   N-NM-P   ἀνήρ
    N-VM-P   "
ἀνδρί   N-DM-S   "
ἀνδρίζεσθε   VMPD--2P   ἀνδρίζομαι
    VMPO--2P   "

ἀνδρίζομαι *behave like a man, be brave* (1C 16.13)

Ἀνδρόνικον   N-AM-S   Ἀνδρόνικος

Ἀνδρόνικος, ου, ὁ *Andronicus*, masculine proper noun (RO 16.7)

ἀνδρός   N-GM-S   ἀνήρ
ἀνδροφόνοις   N-DM-P   ἀνδροφόνος

ἀνδροφόνος, ου, ὁ *murderer* (1T 1.9)

ἀνδρῶν   N-GM-P   ἀνήρ
ἀναβαίνομεν   VIIA--1P   ἀναβαίνω
ἀνέβαινον   VIIA--3P   "
ἀνεβάλετο   VIAM--3S   ἀναβάλλω
ἀνέβη   VIAA--3S   ἀναβαίνω
ἀνέβημεν   VIAA--1P   "
ἀνέβην   VIAA--1S   "
ἀνέβησαν   VIAA--3P   "
ἀνεβίβασαν   VIAA--3P   ἀναβιβάζω

ἀνέβλεψα	VIAA--1S	ἀναβλέπω
ἀνέβλεψαν	VIAA--3P	"
ἀνέβλεψε(ν)	VIAA--3S	"
ἀνεβόησε(ν)	VIAA--3S	ἀναβοάω
ἀνεγίνωσκε(ν)	VIIA--3S	ἀναγινώσκω

ἀνεγκλησία, ας, ἡ strictly, of one who has not been called up before a judge for any reason; hence *blamelessness, innocence* (PH 3.14)

ἀνεγκλησίας	N-GF-S	ἀνεγκλησία
ἀνέγκλητοι	A--NM-P	ἀνέγκλητος
ἀνέγκλητον	A--AM-S	"

ἀνέγκλητος, ον strictly *not having been called up* or *arraigned* before a judge; hence *free from reproach, blameless, not accused of having done anything wrong* (1T 3.10)

ἀνέγκλητος	A--NM-S	ἀνέγκλητος
ἀνεγκλήτους	A--AM-P	"
ἀνεγνωρίσθη	VIAP--3S	ἀναγνωρίζω
ἀνέγνωσαν	VIAA--3P	ἀναγινώσκω
ἀνέγνωτε	VIAA--2P	"
ἀνέδειξε(ν)	VIAA--3S	ἀναδείκνυμι
ἀνέζησαν	VIAA--3S	ἀναζάω
ἀνέζησε(ν)	VIAA--3S	"
ἀνεζήτουν	VIIA--3P	ἀναζητέω
ἀνεθάλετε	VIAA--2P	ἀναθάλλω
ἀνεθεματίσαμεν	VIAA--1P	ἀναθεματίζω
ἀνεθεμάτισαν	VIAA--3P	"
ἀνεθέμην	VIAM--1S	ἀνατίθημι
ἀνέθετο	VIAM--3S	"
ἀνέθη	VIAP--3S	ἀνίημι
ἀνεθρέψατο	VIAM--3S	ἀνατρέφω
ἀνεῖλαν	VIAA--3P	ἀναιρέω
ἀνείλατε	VIAA--2P	"
ἀνείλατο	VIAM--3S	"
ἀνεῖλε(ν)	VIAA--3S	"
ἀνεῖλες	VIAA--2S	"
ἀνείλετε	VIAA--2P	"
ἀνείλετο	VIAM--3S	"
ἀνεῖλον	VIAA--3S	"
ἀνείχεσθε	VIIM--2P	ἀνέχω
ἀνεκάθισε(ν)	VIAA--3S	ἀνακαθίζω

ἀνεκδιήγητος, ον of what cannot be told because it is too wonderful for words *indescribable, inexpressible* (2C 9.15)

ἀνεκδιηγήτῳ	A--DF-S	ἀνεκδιήγητος
ἀνέκειτο	VIID--3S	ἀνάκειμαι
	VIIO--3S	"

ἀνεκλάλητος, ον of what cannot be spoken *unspeakable, inexpressible* (1P 1.8)

ἀνεκλαλήτῳ	A--DF-S	ἀνεκλάλητος
ἀνέκλειπτον	A--AM-S	ἀνέκλειπτος

ἀνέκλειπτος, ον of what can never decrease or cease to exist *inexhaustible, unfailing*; figuratively, of the reward for good works (LU 12.33)

ἀνεκλίθη	VIAP--3S	ἀνακλίνω
ἀνέκλιναν	VIAA--3S	"
	VIIA--3S	"
ἀνέκλινε(ν)	VIAA--3S	"
	VIIA--3S	"
ἀνέκοψε(ν)	VIAA--3S	ἐγκόπτω
ἀνέκραγε(ν)	VIAA--3S	ἀνακράζω

ἀνέκραγον	VIAA--3P	"
ἀνέκραξαν	VIAA--3P	"
ἀνέκραξε(ν)	VIAA--3S	"

ἀνεκτός, όν *bearable, endurable*; comparative ἀνεκτότερος, τέρα, ον *more tolerable* or *able to be endured*

ἀνεκτότερον	A-MNN-S	ἀνεκτός
ἀνέκυψε(ν)	VIAA--3S	ἀνακύπτω
ἀνελάβετε	VIAA--2P	ἀναλαμβάνω
ἀνελεήμονας	A--AM-P	ἀνελεήμων

ἀνελεήμων, ον *unmerciful, without compassion, pitiless* (RO 1.31)

ἀνελεῖ	VIFA--3S	ἀναιρέω
ἀνελεῖν	VNAA	"

ἀνέλεος, ον (also ἀνίλεως) *merciless, pitiless, without compassion* (JA 2.13)

ἀνέλεος	A--NF-S	ἀνέλεος
ἀνέλεως	A--NF-S	see ἀνέλεος
ἀνελήμφθη	VIAP--3S	ἀναλαμβάνω
ἀνελήφθη	VIAP--3S	"
ἀνελθών	VPAANM-S	ἀνέρχομαι
ἀνελοῖ	VOAA--3S	ἀναιρέω
ἀνελύθη	VIAP--3S	ἀναλύω
ἀνέλωσι(ν)	VSAA--3P	ἀναιρέω
ἀνεμιζομένῳ	VPPPDM-S	ἀνεμίζω

ἀνεμίζω only passive in the NT *be moved by the wind*; of sea waves *be tossed* or *driven* by the wind (JA 1.6)

ἀνεμνήσθη	VIAP--3S	ἀναμιμνήσκω
ἄνεμοι	N-NM-P	ἄνεμος
ἀνέμοις	N-DM-P	"
ἄνεμον	N-AM-S	"

ἄνεμος, ου, ὁ as rapidly moving air *wind*; οἱ τέσσαρες ἄνεμοι *the four directions, all directions* (MT 24.31); figuratively *rapid shift* or *change* in doctrine (EP 4.14)

ἄνεμος	N-NM-S	ἄνεμος
ἀνέμου	N-GM-S	"
ἀνέμους	N-AM-P	"
ἀνέμῳ	N-DM-S	"
ἀνέμων	N-GM-P	"
ἀνένδεκτον	A--NN-S	ἀνένδεκτος

ἀνένδεκτος, ον *impossible*; *unavoidable, inevitable*; used impersonally in LU 17.1

ἀνενέγκαι	VNAA	ἀναφέρω
ἀνενέγκας	VPAANM-S	"
ἀνενεγκεῖν	VNAA	"
ἀνενεχθείς	VPAPNM-S	"
ἀνέντες	VPAANM-P	ἀνίημι
ἀνεξεραύνητα	A--NN-P	ἀνεξεραύνητος

ἀνεξεραύνητος, ον (also ἀνεξερεύνητος) *impossible to search out* or *fully understand, unsearchable, unfathomable* (RO 11.33)

ἀνεξερεύνητα	A--NN-P	ἀνεξεραύνητος
ἀνεξίκακον	A--AM-S	ἀνεξίκακος

ἀνεξίκακος, ον of bearing difficulties without resentment *patient, forbearing, tolerant* (2T 2.24)

ἀνεξιχνίαστοι	A--NF-P	ἀνεξιχνίαστος
ἀνεξιχνίαστον	A--AN-S	"

ἀνεξιχνίαστος, ον strictly *not to be tracked out* or *detected*; *unsearchable*; hence, of God's ways *impossible to understand, inscrutable* (RO 11.33); of spiritual blessing given through Christ *too much to be measured, infinite, beyond one's ability to imagine* (EP 3.8)

ἀνέξομαι VIFM--1S ἀνέχω
ἀνέξονται VIFM--3P "
ἀνεπαίσχυντον A--AM-S ἀνεπαίσχυντος
ἀνεπαίσχυντος, ον *having no cause* or *need to be ashamed* (2T 2.15)
ἀνέπαυσαν VIAA--3P ἀναπαύω
ἀνέπεισαν VIAA--3P ἀναπείθω
ἀνέπεμψα VIAA--1S ἀναπέμπω
ἀνέπεμψαν VIAA--3P "
ἀνέπεμψε(ν) VIAA--3S "
ἀνέπεσαν VIAA--3P ἀναπίπτω
ἀνέπεσε(ν) VIAA--3S "
ἀνέπεσον VIAA--3P "
ἀνεπίλημπτοι A--NM-P ἀνεπίλημπτος
ἀνεπίλημπτον A--AF-S "
A--AM-S "
ἀνεπίλημπτος, ον (also **ἀνεπίληπτος**) strictly *not to be laid hold of*; hence, of moral conduct *blameless, above criticism, without fault* (1T 5.7)
ἀνεπίληπτοι A--NM-P ἀνεπίλημπτος
ἀνεπίληπτον A--AF-S "
A--AM-S "
ἀνεπλήρωσαν VIAA--3P ἀναπληρόω
ἀνέπραξα VIAA--1S ἀναπράσσω
ἄνερ N-VM-S ἀνήρ
ἀνέρχομαι 2aor. act. ἀνῆλθον; of movement from a lower to a higher place *go* or *come up, ascend*
ἀνέσεισαν VIAA--3P ἀνασείω
ἄνεσιν N-AF-S ἄνεσις
ἄνεσις, εως, ἡ *relaxing*; (1) literally, of confinement, relaxation of custody *mitigation, measure of freedom* (AC 24.23); (2) figuratively; (a) *refreshment, rest, relief* from tension (2C 7.5); (b) as release from burdensome expense *relief* (2C 8.13)
ἄνεσις N-NF-S ἄνεσις
ἀνεσκαμμένα VPRPAN-P ἀνασκάπτω
ἀνεσπάσθη VIAP--3S ἀνασπάω
ἀνεστέναξε(ν) VIAA--3S ἀναστενάζω
ἀνέστη VIAA--3S ἀνίστημι
ἀνέστησαν VIAA--3P "
ἀνέστησε(ν) VIAA--3S "
ἀνεστράφημεν VIAP--1P ἀναστρέφω
ἀνέστρεψε(ν) VIAA--3S "
ἀνεσχόμην VIAM--1S ἀνέχω
ἀνετάζειν VNPA ἀνετάζω
ἀνετάζεσθαι VNPP "
ἀνετάζω as a legal technical term *examine thoroughly, question, interrogate*, often with lashing or some form of torture
ἀνέτειλε(ν) VIAA--3S ἀνατέλλω
ἀνετράφη VIAP--3S ἀνατρέφω
ἀνέτρεψε(ν) VIAA--3S ἀνατρέπω
ἄνευ preposition with the genitive *without*; (1) with a person *without* another's *knowledge* or *consent, independent of* (MT 10.29); (2) with a thing *without, apart from* (1P 3.1)
ἄνευ PG ἄνευ
ἀνεύθετος, ον *unfavorably situated, in a poor location*; of a harbor *inconvenient, unsuitable* (AC 27.12)
ἀνευθέτου A--GM-S ἀνεύθετος
ἀνεῦραν VIAA--3P ἀνευρίσκω

ἀνευρίσκω 2aor. ἀνεῦρα and ἀνεῦρον; *find, discover* by diligent search
ἀνεῦρον VIAA--3P ἀνευρίσκω
ἀνευρόντες VPAANM-P "
ἀνεφέρετο VIIP--3S ἀναφέρω
ἀνεφώνησε(ν) VIAA--3S ἀναφωνέω
ἀνέχεσθαι VNPM ἀνέχω
ἀνέχεσθε VIPM--2P "
VMPM--2P "
ἀνεχόμεθα VIPM--1P "
ἀνεχόμενοι VPPMNM-P "
ἀνέχω impf. mid. ἀνειχόμην; fut. mid. ἀνέξομαι; 2aor. mid. ἀνεσχόμην; only middle in the NT; (1) as exercising self-restraint and tolerance *endure (patiently), put up with, bear with* (EP 4.2); (2) *accept* as valid, *listen to* (2T 4.3; HE 13.22)
ἀνεχώρησαν VIAA--3P ἀναχωρέω
ἀνεχώρησε(ν) VIAA--3S "
ἀνεψιός, οῦ, ὁ *a child of one's uncle or aunt (first) cousin* (CO 4.10)
ἀνεψιός N-NM-S ἀνεψιός
ἀνέψυξε(ν) VIAA--3S ἀναψύχω
ἀνέῳγε(ν) VIRA--3S ἀνοίγω
ἀνεῳγμένας VPRPAF-P "
ἀνεῳγμένη VPRPNF-S "
ἀνεῳγμένην VPRPAF-S "
ἀνεῳγμένης VPRPGF-S "
ἀνεῳγμένον VPRPAM-S "
ἀνεῳγμένος VPRPNM-S "
ἀνεῳγμένους VPRPAM-P "
ἀνεῳγμένων VPRPGM-P "
ἀνεῳγότα VPRAAM-S "
ἀνέῳξε(ν) VIAA--3S "
ἀνεῴχθη VIAP--3S "
ἀνεῳχθῆναι VNAP "
ἀνεῴχθησαν VIAP--3P "
ἀνήγαγον VIAA--3P ἀνάγω
ἀνήγγειλαν VIAA--3P ἀναγγέλλω
ἀνήγγειλε(ν) VIAA--3S "
ἀνηγγέλη VIAP--3S "
ἀνήγγελλον VIIA--3P "
ἀνήγεσθε VIIP--2P ἀνάγω
ἄνηθον, ου, τό as an aromatic plant used for seasoning *dill* (MT 23.23)
ἄνηθον N-AN-S ἄνηθον
ἀνῆκε(ν) VIIA--3S ἀνήκω
ἀνῆκον VPPAAN-S "
ἀνήκοντα VPPANN-P "
ἀνήκω of what pertains to a person or thing *relate to, belong to*; used impersonally in the NT ἀνήκει *it is fitting* or *right*; τὸ ἀνῆκον *what is proper, one's duty* (PM 8); with the imperfect to denote an imperatival sense, what should or should not take place ἃ οὐκ ἀνῆκεν *what is not* or *should not be fitting* (EP 5.4)
ἀνήλατο VIAD--3S ἀνάλλομαι
ἀνῆλθε(ν) VIAA--3S ἀνέρχομαι
ἀνῆλθον VIAA--1S "
ἀνήμεροι A--NM-P ἀνήμερος
ἀνήμερος, ον literally *untamed, not gentle*; figuratively, of persons *brutal, savage, fierce* (2T 3.3)
ἀνήνεγκε(ν) VIAA--3S ἀναφέρω

ἀνήρ, ἀνδρός, ὁ   *man*; (1) in contrast to a woman *man, male* (MK 6.44); (2) as distinct from a boy *(adult) man* (1C 13.11); (3) in a marital context, whenever γυνή *(woman, wife)* is present or implied in the passage *husband* (1C 7.3); (4) in a general sense, as equivalent to τὶς *someone, a person* (JN 1.30); calling attention to an individual ἀ. τις *a certain man* (LU 8.27)

ἀνήρ	N-NM-S	ἀνήρ
ἀνῃρέθη	VIAP--3S	ἀναιρέω
ἀνήφθη	VIAP--3S	ἀνάπτω
ἀνήχθη	VIAP--3S	ἀνάγω
ἀνήχθημεν	VIAP--1P	"
ἀνήχθησαν	VIAP--3P	"
ἀνθ᾿	PG	ἀντί
ἀνθεματίσαντες	VPAANM-P	ἀναθεματίζω
ἀνθέξεται	VIFM--3S	ἀντέχω
ἀνθέστηκε(ν)	VIRA--3S	ἀνθίστημι
ἀνθεστηκότες	VPRANM-P	"
ἀνθίστανται	VIPM--3P	"
ἀνθίστατο	VIIM--3S	"

ἀνθίστημι   2aor. ἀνέστην; pf. ἀνθέστηκα; *set against*; in the NT all forms have a middle sense; (1) *set oneself against, oppose, resist, refuse to yield* (GA 2.11); (2) with an impersonal sense *oppose, resist* something (RO 9.19); (3) absolutely, as taking a firm stand *stand firm, stand one's ground* (EP 6.13)

ἀνθομολογέομαι   impf. ἀνθωμολογούμην; as openly or publicly confessing what is due someone *acknowledge*; hence, of what is due God *praise, thank* (LU 2.38)

ἄνθος, ους, τό   *blossom, flower*; in the NT *wild* or *field flower*

ἄνθος	N-NN-S	ἄνθος
ἄνθρακας	N-AM-P	ἄνθραξ

ἀνθρακιά, ᾶς, ἡ   *charcoal fire; heap of live coals*

ἀνθρακιάν	N-AF-S	ἀνθρακιά

ἄνθραξ, ακος, ὁ   *coal, charcoal, burning ember* or *coal*; idiomatically σωρεύειν ἄνθρακας πυρὸς ἐπὶ τὴν κεφαλήν literally *heap coals of fire on the head*, used proverbially in RO 12.20 in the sense of causing someone more quickly to feel ashamed and change his ways (cf. Proverbs 25.21–22)

ἀνθρωπάρεσκοι	A--NM-P	ἀνθρωπάρεσκος

ἀνθρωπάρεσκος, ον   *desiring to please people*; substantivally, one who sacrifices principle to please someone of superior authority *people-pleaser* (EP 6.6)

ἄνθρωπε	N-VM-S	ἄνθρωπος
ἀνθρωπίνη	A--DF-S	ἀνθρώπινος
ἀνθρωπίνης	A--GF-S	"
ἀνθρώπινον	AB	"

ἀνθρώπινος, η, ον   (1) as distinct from animal nature *human* (JA 3.7); (2) as distinct from divine nature *human, common to man* (1C 2.13); neuter as an adverb *humanly, in human terms* (RO 6.19)

ἀνθρώπινος	A--NM-S	ἀνθρώπινος
ἀνθρωπίνων	A--GF-P	"
ἄνθρωποι	N-NM-P	ἄνθρωπος
ἀνθρώποις	N-DM-P	"

ἀνθρωποκτόνος, ου, ὁ   *murderer*

ἀνθρωποκτόνος	N-NM-S	ἀνθρωποκτόνος
ἄνθρωπον	N-AM-S	ἄνθρωπος

ἄνθρωπος, ου, ὁ   (1) as a generic term *human being, person* (AC 10.26); plural *people, mankind, one's fellow men* (MT 23.5); (2) as a form of address: in friendly relation *friend* (LU 5.20); as a reproach *man, my good fellow* (LU 12.14); in rhetorical speaking ὦ ἄνθρωπε κενέ *you foolish man! you fool!* (JA 2.20); (3) with the translation according to the context *man, adult male* (LU 7.25), *husband* (MT 19.10), *son* (MT 10.35); (4) idiomatically in Pauline usage as distinguishing between various aspects of a person; (a) between two sides of human nature ὁ ἔξω (ἀ.) *the outer person, physical body* in contrast to ὁ ἔσω (ἀ.) *the inner being* (intellectual, emotional, spiritual aspects) (2C 4.16); (b) between a former and a new and different way of living παλαιὸς ἀ. *former person* or *self, old pattern of behavior* in contrast to καινὸς ἀ. *new person* or *self, new pattern of behavior* (EP 4.22, 24); (c) between a person not indwelt by God's Spirit ψυχικὸς ἀ. *natural (unredeemed) person* in contrast to a person who has God's Spirit πνευματικὸς (ἀ.) *spiritual (redeemed) person* (1C 2.14)

ἄνθρωπος	N-NM-S	ἄνθρωπος
ἀνθρώπου	N-GM-S	"
ἀνθρώπους	N-AM-P	"
ἀνθρώπῳ	N-DM-S	"
ἀνθρώπων	N-GM-P	"
ἀνθυπατεύοντος	VPPAGM-S	ἀνθυπατεύω

ἀνθυπατεύω   *be proconsul* (AC 18.12)

ἀνθύπατοι	N-NM-P	ἀνθύπατος
ἀνθύπατον	N-AM-S	

ἀνθύπατος, ου, ὁ   as a head of government in a Roman senatorial province *proconsul, governor of a province*

ἀνθύπατος	N-NM-S	ἀνθύπατος
ἀνθυπάτου	N-GM-S	
ἀνθυπάτῳ	N-DM-S	
ἀνθωμολογεῖτο	VIID--3S	ἀνθομολογέομαι
	VIIO--3S	
ἀνιέντες	VPPANM-P	ἀνίημι

ἀνίημι   2aor. ἀνῆν, subjunctive ἀνῶ, ptc. ἀνείς; 1aor. pass. ἀνέθην; basically, of relaxation of tension; (1) of chains *loose, unfasten* (AC 16.26); (2) with a person as object *abandon, desert* (HE 13.5); (3) with an activity as object *give up, cease from* (EP 6.9)

ἀνίλεως	A--NF-S	ἀνέλεος
ἀνίπτοις	A--DF-P	ἄνιπτος

ἄνιπτος, ον   *unwashed*; used of disregarding of Jewish rules for washing hands before a meal (MT 15.20)

ἀνιστάμενος	VPPMNM-S	ἀνίστημι
ἀνίστασθαι	VNPM	"
ἀνίσταται	VIPM--3S	"

ἀνίστημι   fut. ἀναστήσω, mid. ἀναστήσομαι; 1aor. ἀνέστησα, ptc. ἀναστήσας; 2aor. ἀνέστην, imperative ἀνάστα and ἀνάστηθι; (1) transitively (future and first aorist active); (a) of persons *cause to stand up* or *rise, raise up* (AC 9.41); (b) of bringing a dead person to life *raise up* (AC 2.24); (c) in a statement not understood by Jesus' opponents as a metaphor, of the body as a temple *erect, put up* (MK 14.58); (d) of causing someone to appear *raise up, send* (AC 3.22); (2) intransitively (second aorist active and future middle); (a) *rise (up), stand up, arise* (MK 14.57); (b) as appearing in history *come into existence, arise, appear* (AC 7.18); (c) in Hebrew idiom marking the beginning of an action *rise, get up, get ready* (MT 9.9); (d) of a building *rise, be put up* (MK 13.2)

Ἀνμεί, ὁ indeclinable; *Anmi*, masculine proper noun (LU 3.33)

Ἄννα	N-GM-S	Ἄννας
	N-NF-S	Ἄννα

Ἄννα, ας, ἡ (also Ἅννα) *Anna*, feminine proper noun (LU 2.36)

Ἄννα	N-GM-S	Ἄννας
	N-NF-S	Ἄννα
Ἄνναν	N-AM-S	Ἄννας
Ἄνναν	N-AM-S	"
Ἄννας	N-NM-S	

Ἄννας, α, ὁ (also Ἅννας) *Annas*, masculine proper noun

Ἄννας	N-NM-S	Ἄννας
ἀνόητοι	A--NM-P	ἀνόητος
	A--VM-P	"
ἀνοήτοις	A--DM-P	"

ἀνόητος, ον (1) of persons *without understanding, foolish* (GA 3.3), opposite σοφός (*wise, skillful*); substantivally (LU 24.25); (2) of things *foolish, senseless, not to be thought on* (1T 6.9)

ἀνοήτους	A--AF-P	ἀνόητος

ἄνοια, ας, ἡ (1) as a lack of understanding *folly, foolishness* (2T 3.9); (2) as irrational anger *fury, extreme rage* (LU 6.11)

ἄνοια	N-NF-S	ἄνοια
ἀνοίας	N-GF-S	"
ἀνοίγει	VIPA--3S	ἀνοίγω
ἀνοίγειν	VNPA	"
ἀνοίγεται	VIPP--3S	"
ἀνοίγῃ	VSPA--3S	"
ἀνοιγήσεται	VIFP--3S	"

ἀνοίγω fut. ἀνοίξω; 1aor. ἀνέῳξα, ἤνοιξα, and ἠνέῳξα; second perfect ἠνέῳγα; pf. pass. ἀνέῳγμαι and ἠνέῳγμαι; 1aor. pass. ἀνεῴχθην, ἠνοίχθην, and ἠνεῴχθην; 2aor. pass. ἠνοίγην; 1fut. pass. ἀνοιχθήσομαι; 2fut. pass. ἀνοιγήσομαι; (1) transitively *open* (AC 12.14); *give entrance* or *access to* (MT 25.11); idiomatically ἀνοίγειν τοὺς ὀφθαλμούς literally *open the eyes*, i.e. *cause to see* (MT 9.30); with a figurative sense, literally *open the eyes of the mind*, i.e. *cause to understand* (AC 26.18); ἀνοίγειν τὸ στόμα literally *open the mouth*, i.e. *begin to speak* (MT 5.2); ἀνοίγειν θύραν literally *open a door*, i.e. *make possible* (CO 4.3); αἱ ἀκοαὶ ἀνοίγουσιν literally *the ears open*, i.e. *become able to hear* (MK 7.35); (2) intransitively (second perfect) idiomatically τὸ στόμα ἀνοίγειν πρὸς literally *open the mouth toward*, i.e. *speak the whole truth* (2C 6.11)

ἀνοίγων	VPPANM-S	ἀνοίγω
ἀνοιγῶσι(ν)	VSAP--3P	"
ἀνοικοδομεῖσθε	VMPM--2P	ἀνοικοδομέω

ἀνοικοδομέω fut. ἀνοικοδομήσω; literally *build up again, rebuild*; figuratively, of restoring the Davidic dynasty through Christ *establish again* (AC 15.16)

ἀνοικοδομήσω	VIFA--1S	ἀνοικοδομέω
ἀνοῖξαι	VNAA	ἀνοίγω
ἀνοίξαντες	VPAANM-P	"
ἀνοίξας	VPAANM-S	"
ἀνοίξει	N-DF-S	ἄνοιξις
ἀνοίξῃ	VSAA--3S	ἀνοίγω

ἄνοιξις, εως, ἡ as an action *opening*; idiomatically, of speaking a message ἐν ἀνοίξει τοῦ στόματός μου literally *in the opening of my mouth*, i.e. *when I begin to speak* (EP 6.19)

ἄνοιξον	VMAA--2S	ἀνοίγω
ἀνοίξω	VIFA--1S	"
ἀνοίξωσι(ν)	VSAA--3P	"
ἀνοιχθήσεται	VIFP--3S	"
ἀνοιχθῶσι(ν)	VSAP--3P	"

ἀνομία, ας, ἡ as what is contrary to law; (1) as a general state of wrong *lawlessness, wickedness, iniquity* (1J 3.4); (2) as an individual violation of law *sin, wrong(doing), (practice of) lawlessness* (MT 7.23)

ἀνομία	N-NF-S	ἀνομία
ἀνομίᾳ	N-DF-S	"
ἀνομίαι	N-NF-P	"
ἀνομίαν	N-AF-S	"
ἀνομίας	N-GF-S	"
ἀνομιῶν	N-GF-P	"
ἀνόμοις	AP-DM-P	ἄνομος
	A--DN-P	"

ἄνομος, ον *lawless*; (1) as having no law, not subject to law (1C 9.21c); substantivally, of Gentiles not under the Mosaic law *pagan, non-Jew* (1C 9.21a, b, d); (2) as not obeying the moral or civil law *wicked, godless* (2P 2.8); substantivally, of the Antichrist *the lawless one* (2TH 2.8)

ἄνομος	AP-NM-S	ἄνομος
	A--NM-S	"
ἀνόμους	AP-AM-P	"
ἀνόμων	AP-GM-P	"

ἀνόμως adverb; as being without the Mosaic law *without (the) law, apart from (the) law, in ignorance of (the) law*

ἀνόμως	AB	ἀνόμως

ἀνόνητος, ον *useless, unprofitable* (1T 6.9)

ἀνονήτους	A--AF-P	ἀνόνητος

ἀνορθόω fut. ἀνορθώσω; 1aor. pass. ἀνορθώθην; (1) as rebuilding a fallen structure *rebuild, restore*; figuratively, of restoring the Davidic dynasty through Christ (AC 15.16); (2) passive, of the healing of a person crippled into a bent position *straighten up, become erect again* (LU 13.13); (3) of strengthening bodily limbs *straighten*; used metaphorically in HE 12.12 of encouraging believers to steadfast faith *brace up*, i.e. *cause to be strong again*

ἀνορθώθη	VIAP--3S	see ἀνωρθώθη
ἀνορθώσατε	VMAA--2P	ἀνορθόω
ἀνορθώσω	VIFA--1S	"
ἀνόσιοι	A--NM-P	ἀνόσιος
ἀνοσίοις	A--DM-P	"

ἀνόσιος, ον of those who reject religious obligations *unholy, ungodly, impious* (2T 3.2); substantivally (1T 1.9)

ἀνοχή, ῆς, ἡ as self-restraint *forbearance, toleration, patience*

ἀνοχῇ	N-DF-S	ἀνοχή
ἀνοχῆς	N-GF-S	"

ἀνταγωνίζομαι literally *carry on a contest* or *struggle against, contend*; figuratively, of struggling against evil *do everything possible against, fight against* (HE 12.4)

ἀνταγωνιζόμενοι VPPDNM-P ἀνταγωνίζομαι
    VPPONM-P "

ἀντάλλαγμα, ατος, τό *what is given in exchange, purchase price*; in an abstract sense *equivalent, substitute* (MT 16.26)

ἀντάλλαγμα N-AN-S ἀντάλλαγμα

ἀνταναπληρόω as mutually and representatively making up a lack within a community *fill up, make up, complete* (CO 1.24)

ἀνταναπληρῶ VIPA--1S ἀντανaπληρόω

ἀνταποδίδωμι fut. ἀνταποδώσω; 2aor. inf. ἀνταποδοῦναι; 1fut. pass. ἀνταποδοθήσομαι; *give back, repay*; (1) in a positive sense, of incurred obligation *return, give in return, repay* (LU 14.14); (2) in a negative sense, of deserved punishment or revenge *pay back, requite* (RO 12.19)

ἀνταποδοθήσεται VIFP--3S ἀνταποδίδωμι

ἀνταπόδομα, ατος, τό *paying back* for something; (1) positively, as a reward *recompense, repayment* (LU 14.12); (2) negatively, as a punishment *retribution, recompense* (RO 11.9)

ἀνταπόδομα N-AN-S ἀνταπόδομα
    N-NN-S "
ἀνταποδόσεως N-GF-S ἀνταπόδοσις
ἀνταπόδοσιν N-AF-S "

ἀνταπόδοσις, εως, ἡ as an action *repaying*; (1) in a positive sense *reward* (CO 3.24); (2) in a negative sense *retribution, paying back* (RO 2.5)

ἀνταποδοῦναι VNAA ἀνταποδίδωμι
ἀνταποδώσω VIFA--1S "
ἀνταποκριθῆναι VNAO ἀνταποκρίνομαι

ἀνταποκρίνομαι 1aor. ἀνταπεκρίθην; (1) *answer back, reply against* (LU 14.6); (2) *contradict, dispute* (RO 9.20)

ἀνταποκρινόμενος VPPDNM-S ἀνταποκρίνομαι
    VPPONM-S "
Ἀντείπας N-NM-S Ἀντιπᾶς
ἀντειπεῖν VNAA ἀντεῖπον

ἀντεῖπον second aorist used in place of the missing aorist of ἀντιλέγω; *speak against, contradict, reply* (LU 21.15; AC 4.14)

ἀντελάβετο VIAM--3S ἀντιλαμβάνω
ἀντέλεγον VIIA--3P ἀντιλέγω
ἀντελοιδόρει VIIA--3S ἀντιλοιδορέω
ἀντέστη VIAA--3S ἀνθίστημι
ἀντέστην VIAA--1S "
ἀντέστησαν VIAA--3P "
ἀντέτυπτε VIAA--3S ἀντιτύπτω
ἀντέχεσθε VMPM--2P ἀντέχω
ἀντεχόμενον VPPMAM-S "

ἀντέχω fut. mid. ἀνθέξομαι; only middle in the NT; (1) of holding closely to someone or something *cling to, hold firmly to, be devoted to* (MT 6.24); of sound doctrine *adhere to, hold fast* (TI 1.9); (2) as feeling helpful concern for others *help, support* (1TH 5.14)

ἀντί preposition with the genitive, originally with a local sense *over against, opposite*; used figuratively in the NT (1) to indicate a replacement *instead of, in place of* (LU 11.11; MT 20.28 and MK 10.45 also belong here; JN 1.16 indicates a successive replacement); (2) to indicate one thing as equivalent to another *for, as, in place of* (1C 11.15); (3) in the sense of ὑπέρ *on behalf of,*

for, for the sake of (MT 17.27); (4) to indicate a cause: ἀ. τούτου *for this reason, that is why* (EP 5.31); ἀνθ᾽ ὧν *because, in return for which* (LU 1.20); (5) to indicate a result ἀνθ᾽ ὧν, implying one thing for another *so then, therefore* (LU 12.3)

ἀντί PG ἀντί
ἀντιβάλλετε VIPA--2P ἀντιβάλλω

ἀντιβάλλω literally *put* or *place against, toss back and forth*; figuratively, of words or ideas *argue about, discuss together* (LU 24.17)

ἀντιγράφοις N-DN-P ἀντίγραφον

ἀντίγραφον, ου, τό of a book *copy*; *book* that has been copied (MK 16 shorter ending)

ἀντιγράφων N-GN-P ἀντίγραφον
ἀντιδιαθεμένους VPAMAM-P ἀντιδιατίθημι
ἀντιδιατιθεμένους VPPMAM-P "

ἀντιδιατίθημι only middle in the NT; strictly *set oneself against*; hence *oppose, express an opposite opinion* (2T 2.25)

ἀντίδικος, ου, ὁ *adversary, enemy*; in a lawsuit *opponent, accuser* (MT 5.25); as one who is constantly hostile toward another *adversary* (1P 5.8)

ἀντίδικος N-NM-S ἀντίδικος
ἀντιδίκου N-GM-S "
ἀντιδίκῳ N-DM-S "
ἀντιθέσεις N-AF-P ἀντίθεσις

ἀντίθεσις, εως, ἡ as an action *(illogical) objection, contradiction, argument* (1T 6.20)

ἀντικαθίστημι 2aor. ἀντικατέστην; (1) transitively *place against*; (2) intransitively (second aorist) *withstand, resist* (HE 12.4)

ἀντικαλέσωσι(ν) VSAA--3P ἀντικαλέω

ἀντικαλέω 1aor. ἀντεκάλεσα; as giving a return invitation *invite back* or *in return* (LU 14.12)

ἀντικατέστητε VIAA--2P ἀντικαθίστημι

ἀντίκειμαι *be opposed, be hostile to, be in opposition to* (GA 5.17); participle as a substantive ὁ ἀντικείμενος *the enemy, opponent* (LU 13.17); of the Antichrist *the adversary* (2TH 2.4)

ἀντικείμενοι VPPDNM-P ἀντίκειμαι
    VPPONM-P "
ἀντικείμενος VPPDNM-S "
    VPPONM-S "
ἀντικειμένῳ VPPDDM-S "
    VPPODM-S "
ἀντικειμένων VPPDGM-P "
    VPPOGM-P "
ἀντίκειται VIPD--3S "
    VIPO--3S "
ἀντικρύ PG ἀντικρυς

ἄντικρυς (also **ἀντικρύ**) adverb; *opposite*; used as an improper preposition with the genitive *opposite, against* to indicate an offshore location near to a coastal city (AC 20.15)

ἄντικρυς PG ἄντικρυς
ἀντιλαμβάνεσθαι VNPM ἀντιλαμβάνω
ἀντιλαμβανόμενοι VPPMNM-P "
ἀντιλαμβάνοντες VPPANM-P "

ἀντιλαμβάνω 2aor. mid. ἀντελαβόμην; (1) active *receive back* or *in return* (RO 1.27); (2) predominately middle in the NT; (a) *help, take the part of, come to the aid of*

(AC 20.35); (b) *benefit from, receive benefit from* something (probably 1T 6.2); (c) *devote oneself to* something (perhaps 1T 6.2)

ἀντιλέγει   VIPA--3S   ἀντιλέγω
ἀντιλέγειν   VNPA   "
ἀντιλέγεται   VIPP--3S   "
ἀντιλεγόμενον   VPPPAN-S   "
ἀντιλέγοντα   VPPAAM-S   "
ἀντιλέγοντας   VPPAAM-P   "
ἀντιλέγοντες   VPPANM-P   "
ἀντιλεγόντων   VPPAGM-P   "

ἀντιλέγω ἀντεῖπον (q.v.) is used as the second aorist; (1) *contradict, speak against, refute* (AC 13.45); (2) followed by μή with an infinitive *deny* (LU 20.27); (3) as contradicting an authority *be obstinate* or *stubborn* (RO 10.21); (4) as rejecting evidence *speak against, reject* (LU 2.34)

ἀντιλήμψεις   N-AF-P   ἀντίλημψις
ἀντίλημψις, εως, ἡ (also ἀντίληψις) as an action; strictly *laying hold of*; hence *help, assistance*; plural *helpful deeds*; by metonymy *those who help* (1C 12.28)

ἀντιλήψεις   N-AF-P   ἀντίλημψις
ἀντιλογία, ας, ἡ as a statement of (1) opposite opinion *contradiction, dispute* (HE 6.16); (2) contrary evidence *doubt, denial, controversy* (HE 7.7); (3) defiance against authority *rebellion, hostility* (JU 11)

ἀντιλογία   N-DF-S   ἀντιλογία
ἀντιλογίαν   N-AF-S   "
ἀντιλογίας   N-GF-S   "

ἀντιλοιδορέω as returning an insult *revile in return, retaliate, answer back* (1P 2.23)

ἀντίλυτρον, ου, τό literally, as a price paid or means used to set someone free from captivity or bondage *ransom*; figuratively, of Christ's atonement for sin *price of redemption, means of deliverance* (1T 2.6)

ἀντίλυτρον   N-AN-S   ἀντίλυτρον
ἀντιμετρέω 1fut. pass. ἀντιμετρηθήσομαι; *measure in (re)turn, give back a (corresponding) measure, repay* (LU 6.38)

ἀντιμετρηθήσεται   VIFP--3S   ἀντιμετρέω
ἀντιμισθία, ας, ἡ with an emphasis on receiving what is due in exchange; (1) in a positive sense *reward, recompense, fair exchange* (2C 6.13); (2) in a negative sense *requital, retribution, due penalty* (RO 1.27)

ἀντιμισθίαν   N-AF-S   ἀντιμισθία
Ἀντιοχέα   N-AM-S   Ἀντιοχεύς
Ἀντιόχεια, ας, ἡ *Antioch*; (1) a large city in Syria (AC 11.19); (2) a city in Pisidia in southern Galatia (AC 13.14)

Ἀντιόχεια   N-DF-S   Ἀντιόχεια
Ἀντιόχειαν   N-AF-S   "
Ἀντιοχείας   N-GF-S   "
Ἀντιοχεύς, έως, ὁ *man from Antioch* (AC 6.5)

ἀντιπαρέρχομαι 2aor. ἀντιπαρῆλθον; in relation to a point of reference *pass by on the opposite* or *other side* (LU 10.31)

ἀντιπαρῆλθε(ν)   VIAA--3S   ἀντιπαρέρχομαι
Ἀντίπας   N-NM-S   Ἀντιπᾶς
Ἀντιπᾶς, ᾶ, ὁ (also Ἀντείπας, Ἀντίπας) *Antipas*, masculine proper noun (RV 2.13)

Ἀντιπᾶς   N-NM-S   Ἀντιπᾶς

Ἀντιπατρίδα   N-AF-S   Ἀντιπατρίς
Ἀντιπατρίς, ίδος, ἡ *Antipatris*, a city in Judea on the road from Jerusalem to Caesarea (AC 23.31)

ἀντιπέρα   PG   ἀντιπέρα
ἀντιπέρα (also ἀντίπερα, ἀντιπέραν) adverb; in relation to one position as opposed to another position with something between *opposite, on the other side*; used in the NT as an improper preposition with the genitive *opposite, across* (the sea) *from* (i.e. the eastern shore of the sea) (LU 8.26)

ἀντιπέρα   PG   ἀντιπέρα
ἀντιπέραν   PG   "
ἀντιπίπτετε   VIPA--2P   ἀντιπίπτω
ἀντιπίπτω strictly *fall against, rush against*; hence *strive against, resist, oppose* (AC 7.51)

ἀντιστῆναι   VNAA   ἀνθίστημι
ἀντίστητε   VMAA--2P   "
ἀντιστρατευόμενον   VPPMAM-S   ἀντιστρατεύω
ἀντιστρατεύω only middle in the NT; strictly *take the field against, wage war against*; figuratively, of sin personified as a ruling, hostile force *oppose* (RO 7.23)

ἀντιτάσσεται   VIPM--3S   ἀντιτάσσω
ἀντιτασσόμενος   VPPMNM-S   "
ἀντιτασσομένων   VPPMGM-P   "
ἀντιτάσσω only middle in the NT; strictly *set in array against*; as setting oneself against *oppose, resist, be hostile toward* (AC 18.6)

ἀντίτυπα   A--AN-P   ἀντίτυπος
ἀντίτυπον   AB   "
    A--NN-S   "
ἀντίτυπος, ον strictly *struck back, echoed*; hence *answering to, corresponding to*; neuter as an adverb; of baptism fulfilling a type presented in Noah's flood *in a way corresponding to* (1P 3.21); substantivally τὸ ἀ. *copy, exact representation, antitype* (HE 9.24)

ἀντιτύπτω impf. ἀντέτυπτον; *beat in turn, give back blow for blow* (1P 2.23)

ἀντίχριστοι   N-NM-P   ἀντίχριστος
ἀντίχριστος, ου, ὁ as an opponent of Christ *antichrist* (1J 2.18b); as a proper noun for Christ's adversary in the end-times *Antichrist* (1J 2.18a)

ἀντίχριστος   N-NM-S   ἀντίχριστος
ἀντιχρίστου   N-GM-S   "
ἀντλεῖν   VNPA   ἀντλέω
ἀντλέω 1aor. ἤντλησα; pf. ptc. ἠντληκώς; generally, remove a liquid, such as water, from a well or storage jar *draw, dip out*

ἄντλημα, ατος, τό *container for drawing water, bucket, pail* (JN 4.11)

ἄντλημα   N-AN-S   ἄντλημα
ἀντλῆσαι   VNAA   ἀντλέω
ἀντλήσατε   VMAA--2P   "
ἀντοφθαλμεῖν   VNPA   ἀντοφθαλμέω
ἀντοφθαλμέω strictly *look in the face*; hence, of a ship against the wind *bear up against, face into* (AC 27.15)

ἄνυδροι   A--NF-P   ἄνυδρος
ἄνυδρος, ον *without water*; ἄ. τόπος *dry place, desert* (MT 12.43); metaphorically, of a person who teaches and behaves in a way without value to others: a spring *without water* (2P 2.17), a cloud *without rain* (JU 12)

ἀνύδρων   A--GM-P   ἄνυδρος

ἀνυπόκριτον	A--AF-S	ἀνυπόκριτος

ἀνυπόκριτος, ον literally *without hypocrisy*; hence *genuine, sincere*

ἀνυπόκριτος	A--NF-S	ἀνυπόκριτος
ἀνυποκρίτου	A--GF-S	"
ἀνυποκρίτῳ	A--DF-S	"
ἀνυπότακτα	A--AN-P	ἀνυπότακτος
ἀνυπότακτοι	A--NM-P	"
ἀνυποτάκτοις	A--DM-P	"
ἀνυπότακτον	A--AN-S	"

ἀνυπότακτος, ον strictly *not under orders*; hence (1) *independent, not subject* (HE 2.8); (2) in a negative sense *insubordinate, rebellious* (TI 1.10); substantivally *rebellious person* (1T 1.9); of children *disobedient, undisciplined, spoiled* (TI 1.6)

ἄνω adverb of place; (1) *above* (GA 4.26), opposite κάτω (*below*); substantivally τὰ ἄ. *what is above, the world above, heaven* (JN 8.23); (2) as a direction *up, upward* (JN 11.41); ἕως ἄ. *to the top* or *brim* (JN 2.7)

ἄνω	AB	ἄνω
ἀνῶ	VSAA--1S	ἀνίημι
ἀνώγαιον	N-AN-S	ἀνάγαιον
ἀνώγεον	N-AN-S	"

ἄνωθεν adverb; (1) of place *from above* (JN 3.31; perhaps 3.3, 7); ἄ. ἕως κάτω *from top to bottom* (MT 27.51); (2) of past time *from an earlier period, from the beginning, from the first* (AC 26.5); (3) of future time, indicating repetition *anew, again* (GA 4.9; probably JN 3.3, 7)

ἄνωθεν	AB	ἄνωθεν
ἀνωρθώθη	VIAP--3S	ἀνορθόω
ἀνωτερικά	A--AN-P	ἀνωτερικός

ἀνωτερικός, ή, όν *upper, higher*; of the inland regions of a mountainous country *interior* (AC 19.1)

ἀνώτερον	ABM	ἀνώτερος

ἀνώτερος, τέρα, ον proper comparative of ἄνω (*above*); only neuter as a comparative adverb in the NT; (1) of a more honorable place at table *superior, better, higher* (LU 14.10); (2) as referring to a previous statement *above, preceding* (HE 10.8)

ἀνωφελεῖς	A--NF-P	ἀνωφελής
ἀνωφελές	A--AN-S	"

ἀνωφελής, ές *useless, unprofitable*; substantivally τὸ ἀνωφελές *uselessness* (HE 7.18); of controversies *harmful, futile* (TI 3.9)

ἄξει	VIFA--3S	ἄγω
ἄξια	A--AN-P	ἄξιος
	A--NN-P	"
ἀξία	A--NF-S	"

ἀξίνη, ης, ἡ as a tool for cutting (down) trees or wood *ax*

ἀξίνη	N-NF-S	ἀξίνη
ἀξίνην	N-AF-S	"
ἄξιοι	A--NM-P	ἄξιος
ἄξιον	A--AM-S	"
	A--AN-S	"
	A--NN-S	"

ἄξιος, ία, ον strictly *bringing up the other beam of the scales, equivalent*; (1) of things in relation to other things *corresponding, comparable, worthy* (AC 26.20); of price *of equal value* (RO 8.18); impersonally ἄξιόν ἐστιν *it is proper, fitting, worthwhile* (2TH 1.3); (2) of persons,

followed by the genitive, in a good sense *worthy of, entitled to* (LU 15.19); in a bad sense *deserving of, worthy of* (LU 12.48)

ἄξιος	A--NM-S	ἄξιος
ἀξιοῦμεν	VIPA--1P	ἀξιόω
ἀξιοῦντες	VPPANM-P	"
ἀξίους	A--AM-P	ἄξιος
ἀξιούσθωσαν	VMPP--3P	ἀξιόω

ἀξιόω impf. ἠξίουν; 1aor. ἠξίωσα; pf. pass. ἠξίωμαι; 1aor. pass. ἠξιώθην; 1fut. pass. ἀξιωθήσομαι; (1) *make worthy* (2TH 1.11); (2) *think of as worthy, consider worthy* or *deserving* (1T 5.17); (3) *think fitting* to do something, *prefer, regard as right* to do (AC 15.38); (4) *want, request, desire* (AC 13.42; 28.22)

ἀξιωθήσεται	VIFP--3S	ἀξιόω

ἀξίως adverb; *worthily, suitably, in a manner proper to*

ἀξίως	AB	ἀξίως
ἀξιώσῃ	VSAA--3S	ἀξιόω
ἄξων	VPFANM-S	ἄγω
ἀόρατα	A--NN-P	ἀόρατος
ἀόρατον	A--AM-S	"

ἀόρατος, ον *unable to be seen*; of God *invisible* (CO 1.15); substantivally τὰ ἀόρατα *the invisible world* (CO 1.16); *the invisible attributes* of God (RO 1.20)

ἀοράτου	A--GM-S	ἀόρατος
ἀοράτῳ	A--DM-S	"
Ἀουλίαν	N-AF-S	Ἰουλία
ἀπ᾽	PG	ἀπό
ἀπάγαγε	VMAA--2S	ἀπάγω
ἀπαγάγετε	VMAA--2P	"
ἀπαγαγών	VPAANM-S	"
ἀπαγγεῖλαι	VNAA	ἀπαγγέλλω
ἀπαγγείλατε	VMAA--2P	"
ἀπάγγειλον	VMAA--2S	"
ἀπαγγελεῖ	VIFA--3S	"
ἀπαγγέλλει	VIPA--3S	"
ἀπαγγέλλομεν	VIPA--1P	"
ἀπαγγέλλοντας	VPPAAM-P	"
ἀπαγγέλλοντες	VPPANM-P	"
ἀπαγγέλλουσα	VPPANF-S	"
ἀπαγγέλλουσι(ν)	VIPA--3P	"

ἀπαγγέλλω impf. ἀπήγγελλον; fut. ἀπαγγελῶ; 1aor. ἀπήγγειλα; 2aor. pass. ἀπηγγέλην; (1) as carrying back word from a happening *report (back), inform, tell* (MT 2.8); (2) as announcing something *proclaim, declare* (MT 12.18); (3) as acknowledging something publicly *confess* (LU 8.47); as announcing what must be done *order, command* (AC 17.30)

ἀπαγγέλλω	VIPA--1S	ἀπαγγέλλω
ἀπαγγέλλων	VPPANM-S	"
ἀπαγγελοῦντας	VPFAAM-P	"
ἀπαγγελῶ	VIFA--1S	"
ἄπαγε	VMPA--2S	ἀπάγω
ἀπάγει	VIPA--3S	"
ἀπάγειν	VNPA	"
ἀπάγετε	VMPA--2P	"
ἀπαγόμενοι	VPPPNM-P	"
ἀπαγομένους	VPPPAM-P	"
ἀπάγουσα	VPPANF-S	"
ἀπάγουσι(ν)	VIPA--3P	"

ἀπάγχω 1aor. mid. ἀπηγξάμην; only middle in the NT; (1) active *strangle*; (2) middle *choke* or *strangle oneself, hang oneself* (MT 27.5)

ἀπάγω 2aor. ἀπήγαγον; 1aor. pass. ἀπήχθην; (1) *lead away, conduct*, as an animal to water (LU 13.15); figuratively and passive, of persons *be deceived, be influenced* (1C 12.2); (2) as a legal technical term *bring before* (MT 26.57); (3) of a prisoner or condemned person *lead away* (MK 14.44); (4) intransitively, of a road *lead (away) to, extend to* (figuratively in MT 7.14)

| ἀπάγων | VPPANM-S | ἀπάγω |

ἀπαίδευτος, ον *uneducated, uninstructed*; of speculations *stupid, foolish* (2T 2.23)

| ἀπαιδεύτους | A--AF-P | ἀπαίδευτος |

ἀπαίρω 1aor. pass. ἀπήρθην; *take away*; passive *be taken away* or *withdrawn* (MT 9.15)

| ἀπαίτει | VMPA--2S | ἀπαιτέω |

ἀπαιτέω (1) generally *demand, desire* (1P 3.15); (2) of property that has been requisitioned or stolen *ask for, demand back* (LU 6.30); figuratively, of the concept of life as a loan from God *demand, ask for in return* (LU 12.20)

ἀπαιτήσουσι(ν)	VIFA--3P	ἀπαιτέω
ἀπαιτοῦντι	VPPADM-S	"
ἀπαιτοῦσι(ν)	VIPA--3P	"

ἀπαλγέω pf. ἀπήλγηκα; strictly *become without pain or feeling*; hence *become callous, lose sensitivity, feel no shame* (EP 4.19)

ἀπαλλαγῆναι	VNAP	ἀπαλλάσσω
ἀπαλλάξῃ	VSAA--3S	"
ἀπαλλάξωσι(ν)	VSAA--3P	"
ἀπαλλάσσεσθαι	VNPP	"

ἀπαλλάσσω 1aor. ἀπήλλαξα; pf. pass. ἀπήλλαγμαι; 2aor. pass. ἀπηλλάγην; (1) *set free, liberate, release* (HE 2.15); (2) passive, of a judicial settlement *get oneself delivered from, come to a settlement with, be rid of* (LU 12.58); (3) intransitively and passive, of an end or change of state *stop, leave*; of disease *go away*, i.e. *be healed of* (AC 19.12)

ἀπαλλοτρίόω pf. pass. ἀπηλλοτρίωμαι; *alienate, estrange*; only passive in the NT *be a stranger to, be separated from* (EP 4.18)

ἀπαλός, ή, όν strictly *easily yielding to pressure*; hence, of sprouting branches *soft, tender* (MT 24.32)

ἀπαλός	A--NM-S	ἀπαλός
ἄπαν	A--NN-S	ἅπας
ἄπαντα	AP-AN-P	"
	AP-NN-P	"
	A--AM-S	"
	A--AN-P	"
ἄπαντας	AP-AM-P	"

ἀπαντάω fut. ἀπαντήσω; 1aor. ἀπήντησα; *meet someone* (MK 14.13); *come forward, come out (to meet)* (LU 17.12)

ἄπαντες	AP-NM-P	ἅπας
	A--NM-P	"
ἀπαντῆσαι	VNAA	ἀπαντάω
ἀπαντήσει	VIFA--3S	"
ἀπάντησιν	N-AF-S	ἀπάντησις

ἀπάντησις, εως, ἡ as an action *meeting, encountering*; εἰς ἀπάντησιν *to meet* (MT 25.6)

| ἀπάντων | A--GN-P | ἅπας |

ἅπαξ adverb; *once*; (1) as a strictly numerical concept in the sense of one time *once* (2C 11.25); *once a year* (HE 9.7); (2) of something done uniquely *only once, once for all* (HE 9.28); (3) idiomatically ἅ. καὶ δίς literally *once and twice*, i.e. *more than once, several times* (PH 4.16)

| ἅπαξ | AB | ἅπαξ |
| ἀπαράβατον | A--AF-S | ἀπαράβατος |

ἀπαράβατος, ον strictly *not transient*; hence, of what is fixed and not subject to change *permanent, never changing* (HE 7.24)

ἀπαρασκεύαστος, ον *unprepared, not ready* (2C 9.4)

| ἀπαρασκευάστους | A--AM-P | ἀπαρασκεύαστος |
| ἀπαρθῇ | VSAP--3S | ἀπαίρω |

ἀπαρνέομαι fut. ἀπαρνήσομαι; 1aor. ἀπηρνησάμην; 1fut. pass. ἀπαρνηθήσομαι; *deny*; (1) in the NT mainly of denying relationship to a person *reject, disown* (MT 26.34); (2) as choosing to live in a selfless way *deny* or *disregard oneself* (MT 16.24)

ἀπαρνηθήσεται	VIFP--3S	ἀπαρνέομαι
ἀπαρνησάσθω	VMAD--3S	"
ἀπαρνήσει	VIFD--2S	see ἀπαρνήσῃ
ἀπαρνήσῃ	VIFD--2S	ἀπαρνέομαι
	VSAD--2S	"
ἀπαρνήσομαι	VIFD--1S	"
ἀπαρνήσωμαι	VSAD--1S	"

ἀπάρτι adverb of time *from now on* (JN 13.19)

| ἀπάρτι | AB | ἀπάρτι |
| ἀπαρτισμόν | N-AM-S | ἀπαρτισμός |

ἀπαρτισμός, οῦ, ὁ of bringing something to a successful conclusion *completion* (LU 14.28)

ἀπαρχή, ῆς, ἡ (1) in Mosaic ceremonial law, a technical term for the first portion of grain and fruit harvests and flocks offered to God *firstfruits, first offering* (RO 11.16); (2) figuratively, of persons as the first of a set or category *first*: as the first converts in an area (RO 16.5), as the first to be resurrected (1C 15.20), as the first of their category to be dedicated to God (RV 14.4); (3) of the Holy Spirit, given to believers as the first portion and pledge of all that God will give to redeemed people *foretaste* (RO 8.23)

| ἀπαρχή | N-NF-S | ἀπαρχή |
| ἀπαρχήν | N-AF-S | " |

ἅπας, ασα, αν as expressing the totality of any object; (1) substantivally, without a noun, masculine *all, everybody* (MT 24.39); neuter *all, everything* (MK 8.25); (2) with a noun and the article, of persons *the whole* (people), *all the* (people) (LU 3.21); of things *all, the whole* (LU 4.6)

ἅπας	A--NM-S	ἅπας
ἅπασα	A--NF-S	"
ἅπασαν	A--AF-S	"
ἅπασι(ν)	A--DM-P	"

ἀπασπάζομαι 1aor. ἀπησπασάμην; *take one's leave of, say good-bye to* (AC 21.6)

ἀπάται	N-NF-P	ἀπάτη
ἀπάταις	N-DF-P	"
ἀπατάτω	VMPA--3S	ἀπατάω

ἀπατάω 1aor. pass. ἠπατήθην; *deceive, mislead* (EP 5.6); passive *be led astray, be deceived* (1T 2.14)

ἀπάτη, ης, ἡ   (1) *trickery, deceitfulness, deception* (CO 2.8); of the appeal of riches *temptation, seduction, delusion* (MT 13.22); of the attractiveness of sin *deceit, deception* (HE 3.13); (2) of pleasure that involves one in sin *deceitful pleasure, evil fun, dissipation* (2P 2.13)

ἀπάτη	N-NF-S	ἀπάτη
ἀπάτῃ	N-DF-S	"
ἀπατηθεῖσα	VPAPNF-S	ἀπατάω
ἀπάτης	N-GF-S	ἀπάτη
ἀπατῶν	VPPANM-S	ἀπατάω

ἀπάτωρ, gen. ορος   strictly *without father, fatherless*; in the NT, as denoting one who holds an office independently of ancestral line or paternal descent *without record of a father* (HE 7.3)

ἀπάτωρ	A--NM-S	ἀπάτωρ

ἀπαύγασμα, ατος, τό   active *radiance, outshining, effulgence* (probably HE 1.3); passive *reflection* (possibly HE 1.3)

ἀπαύγασμα	N-NN-S	ἀπαύγασμα
ἀπαφρίζοντα	VPPANN-P	ἀπαφρίζω

ἀπαφρίζω   *cause to splash up like foam, cast off like foam* (JU 13)

ἀπαχθῆναι	VNAP	ἀπάγω
ἀπέβησαν	VIAA--3P	ἀποβαίνω
ἀπέβλεπε(ν)	VIIA--3S	ἀποβλέπω
ἀπέδειξε(ν)	VIAA--3S	ἀποδείκνυμι
ἀπεδέξαντο	VIAD--3P	ἀποδέχομαι
ἀπεδέξατο	VIAD--3S	"
ἀπέδετο	VIAM--3S	ἀποδίδωμι
ἀπεδέχετο	VIID--3S	ἀποδέχομαι
	VIIO--3S	"
ἀπεδέχθησαν	VIAP--3P	"
ἀπεδήμησε(ν)	VIAA--3S	ἀποδημέω
ἀπεδίδουν	VIIA--3P	ἀποδίδωμι
ἀπεδοκίμασαν	VIAA--3P	ἀποδοκιμάζω
ἀπεδοκιμάσθη	VIAP--3S	"
ἀπέδοντο	VIAM--3P	ἀποδίδωμι
ἀπέδοσθε	VIAM--2P	"
ἀπέδοτο	VIAM--3S	"
ἀπέδωκε(ν)	VIAA--3S	"
ἀπέθανε(ν)	VIAA--3S	ἀποθνήσκω
ἀπεθάνετε	VIAA--2P	"
ἀπεθάνομεν	VIAA--1P	"
ἀπέθανον	VIAA--1S	"
	VIAA--3P	"
ἀπέθεντο	VIAM--3P	ἀποτίθημι
ἀπέθετο	VIAM--3S	"
ἀπέθνησκε(ν)	VIIA--3S	ἀποθνήσκω
ἀπέθνησκε(ν)	VIIA--3S	"
ἀπεῖδον	VSAA--1S	see ἀπίδω

ἀπείθεια, ας, ἡ   in the NT in relation to God *disobedience*; often shown as the result of ἀπιστία (*unbelief*)

ἀπειθείᾳ	N-DF-S	ἀπείθεια
ἀπείθειαν	N-AF-S	"
ἀπειθείας	N-GF-S	"
ἀπειθεῖς	A--AM-P	ἀπειθής
	A--NM-P	"

ἀπειθέω   1aor. ἠπείθησα; (1) in relation to God *disobey, be disobedient* (RO 11.30); (2) of the most severe form of disobedience, in relation to the gospel message *disbelieve, refuse to believe, be an unbeliever* (AC 14.2)

ἀπειθής, ές   of one who will not be persuaded to obey some authority *disobedient*; substantivally *disobedient person* (LU 1.17)

ἀπειθής	A--NM-S	ἀπειθής
ἀπειθήσαντες	VPAANM-P	ἀπειθέω
ἀπειθήσασι(ν)	VPAADM-P	"
ἀπειθοῦντα	VPPAAM-S	"
ἀπειθοῦντες	VPPANM-P	"
ἀπειθοῦντι	VPPADM-S	"
ἀπειθούντων	VPPAGM-P	"
ἀπειθοῦσι(ν)	VIPA--3P	"
	VPPADM-P	"
ἀπειθῶν	VPPANM-S	"
ἀπειλάς	N-AF-P	ἀπειλή

ἀπειλέω   impf. ἠπείλουν; 1aor. mid. ἠπειλησάμην; as expressing intention to harm if a condition is not met *threaten, warn* (AC 4.17); absolutely, of Christ's refusal to retaliate *threaten to get even* (1P 2.23)

ἀπειλή, ῆς, ἡ   *threat, threatening*

ἀπειλῇ	N-DF-S	ἀπειλή
ἀπειλήν	N-AF-S	"
ἀπειλῆς	N-GF-S	"
ἀπειλησώμεθα	VSAM--1P	ἀπειλέω

ἄπειμι (I)   ptc. ἀπών; from ἀπό (*away from*) and εἰμί (*be*); *be absent* or *away* (2C 13.10), opposite πάρειμι (*be present, be here*)

ἄπειμι (II)   impf. ἀπῄειν; from ἀπό (*away from*) and εἶμι (*go*); *go away, depart*; simply *go, come* (AC 17.10)

ἄπειμι	VIPA--1S	ἄπειμι (I)
ἀπειπάμεθα	VIAM--1P	ἀπεῖπον

ἀπεῖπον   used as the second aorist of an obsolete verb ἀπολέγω; 2aor. mid. ἀπειπάμην; with a middle sense *renounce, disown* (2C 4.2)

ἀπείραστος, ον   *without temptation*; in the active sense, of one who does not tempt; in the passive sense, of one who cannot be tempted *incapable of being tempted* (JA 1.13)

ἀπείραστος	A--NM-S	ἀπείραστος

ἄπειρος, ον   denoting lack of knowledge or inability to do something *inexperienced in, unskilled in, unacquainted with* (HE 5.13)

ἄπειρος	A--NM-S	ἄπειρος
ἀπεῖχε(ν)	VIIA--3S	ἀπέχω
ἀπεκαλύφθη	VIAP--3S	ἀποκαλύπτω
ἀπεκάλυψας	VIAA--2S	"
ἀπεκάλυψε(ν)	VIAA--3S	"
ἀπεκατεστάθη	VIAP--3S	ἀποκαθιστάνω
ἀπεκατέστη	VIAA--3S	"
ἀπεκατήλλαξε(ν)	VIAA--3S	ἀποκαταλλάσσω
ἀπεκδέχεται	VIPD--3S	ἀπεκδέχομαι
	VIPO--3S	"

ἀπεκδέχομαι   impf. ἀπεξεδεχόμην; *expect, (eagerly) await, look for* (RO 8.23); absolutely *wait patiently* (RO 8.25)

ἀπεκδεχόμεθα	VIPD--1P	ἀπεκδέχομαι
	VIPO--1P	"
ἀπεκδεχόμενοι	VPPDNM-P	"
	VPPONM-P	"
ἀπεκδεχομένοις	VPPDDM-P	"
	VPPODM-P	"
ἀπεκδεχομένους	VPPDAM-P	"
	VPPOAM-P	"

ἀπεκδύομαι 1aor. ἀπεξεδυσάμην; (1) literally, of clothes *undress, take off, strip off*; (2) figuratively; (a) as firmly renouncing a former sinful life *change one's character, no longer behave as before* (CO 3.9); (b) as rendering an enemy helpless *disarm, take away the power of* (CO 2.15)

ἀπεκδυσάμενοι	VPADNM-P	ἀπεκδύομαι
ἀπεκδυσάμενος	VPADNM-S	"
ἀπεκδύσει	N-DF-S	ἀπέκδυσις

ἀπέκδυσις, εως, ἡ as an action, of clothes *stripping off, undressing*; figuratively, of believers *being set free* from their sinful nature through union with Christ *putting off, removal* (CO 2.11)

ἀπεκεφάλισα	VIAA--1S	ἀποκεφαλίζω
ἀπεκεφάλισε(ν)	VIAA--3S	"
ἀπέκοψαν	VIAA--3P	ἀποκόπτω
ἀπέκοψε(ν)	VIAA--3S	"
ἀπεκριθείς	VPAONM-S	see ἀποκριθείς
ἀπεκρίθη	VIAO--3S	ἀποκρίνομαι
ἀπεκρίθην	VIAO--1S	"
ἀπεκρίθης	VIAO--2S	"
ἀπεκρίθησαν	VIAO--3P	"
ἀπεκρίνατο	VIAD--3S	"
ἀπεκρίνεται	VIPD--3S	"
	VIPO--3S	"
ἀπέκρυψας	VIAA--2S	ἀποκρύπτω
ἀπέκρυψε(ν)	VIAA--3S	"
ἀπεκτάνθη	VIAP--3S	ἀποκτείνω
ἀπεκτάνθησαν	VIAP--3P	"
ἀπέκτειναν	VIAA--3P	"
ἀπεκτείνατε	VIAA--2P	"
ἀπέκτεινε(ν)	VIAA--3S	"
ἀπεκύησε(ν)	VIAA--3S	ἀποκυέω
ἀπεκύλισε(ν)	VIAA--3S	ἀποκυλίω
ἀπέλαβε(ν)	VIAA--3S	ἀπολαμβάνω
ἀπέλαβες	VIAA--2S	"
ἀπελάλει	VIIA--3S	ἀπολαλέω

ἀπελαύνω 1aor. ἀπήλασα; as causing to move away from a point of reference by threat or force *drive off* or *away, send away, expel* (AC 18.16)

ἀπελεγμόν	N-AM-S	ἀπελεγμός

ἀπελεγμός, οῦ, ὁ strictly *refutation, proving to be wrong*; hence *disrepute, bad name, discredit* (AC 19.27)

ἀπέλειπον	VIIA--3P	ἀπολείπω
ἀπέλειχον	VIIA--3P	ἀπολείχω

ἀπελεύθερος, ου, ὁ literally, of a person who has been freed from slavery *emancipated slave, freedman*; figuratively, of Christians, set free from sin by Christ *free person* (1C 7.22)

ἀπελεύθερος	N-NM-S	ἀπελεύθερος
ἀπελεύσομαι	VIFD--1S	ἀπέρχομαι
ἀπελευσόμεθα	VIFD--1P	"
ἀπελεύσονται	VIFD--3P	"
ἀπεληλύθεισαν	VILA--3P	"
ἀπελήλυθε(ν)	VIRA--3S	"
ἀπελθεῖν	VNAA	"
ἀπέλθη	VSAA--3S	"
ἀπέλθητε	VSAA--2P	"
ἀπελθόντα	VPAAAM-S	"
ἀπελθόντες	VPAANM-P	"
ἀπελθόντι	VPAADM-S	"
ἀπελθόντων	VPAAGM-P	"
ἀπελθοῦσα	VPAANF-S	"
ἀπελθοῦσαι	VPAANF-P	"
ἀπέλθω	VSAA--1S	"
ἀπελθών	VPAANM-S	"
ἀπέλθωσι(ν)	VSAA--3P	"
ἀπέλιπον	VIAA--1S	ἀπολείπω
Ἀπελλῆν	N-AM-S	Ἀπελλῆς

Ἀπελλῆς, οῦ, ὁ *Apelles*, masculine proper noun

Ἀπελλῆς	N-NM-S	Ἀπελλῆς
ἀπελογεῖτο	VIID--3S	ἀπολογέομαι
	VIIO--3S	"
ἀπελογοῦντο	VIID--3P	"
	VIIO--3P	"
ἀπελούσασθε	VIAM--2P	ἀπολούω
ἀπελπίζοντες	VPPANM-P	ἀπελπίζω

ἀπελπίζω pf. ἀπήλπικα; (1) *despair, be without hope* (EP 4.19); (2) *expect nothing in return* (LU 6.35)

ἀπέλυε(ν)	VIIA--3S	ἀπολύω
ἀπελύθησαν	VIAP--3P	"
ἀπελύοντο	VIIM--3P	"
ἀπέλυσαν	VIAA--3P	"
ἀπέλυσε(ν)	VIAA--3S	"
ἀπέμεινε(ν)	VIAA--3S	ἀπομένω

ἀπέναντι improper preposition with the genitive; (1) literally, of place *opposite, in front of, before* (MT 27.61); figuratively, of something happening before the eyes of onlookers *in the presence of, before* (someone's eyes) (MT 27.24; AC 3.16); (2) denoting defiant action *against, contrary to* (AC 17.7)

ἀπέναντι	PG	ἀπέναντι
ἀπενέγκατε	VMAA--2P	ἀποφέρω
ἀπενεγκεῖν	VNAA	"
ἀπενεχθῆναι	VNAP	"
ἀπενίψατο	VIAM--3S	ἀπονίζω
ἀπεξεδέχετο	VIID--3S	ἀπεκδέχομαι
	VIIO--3S	"
ἀπέπεμψας	VIAA--2S	ἀποπέμπω
ἀπέπεσαν	VIAA--3P	ἀποπίπτω
ἀπέπεσον	VIAA--3P	"
ἀπεπλανήθησαν	VIAP--3P	ἀποπλανάω
ἀπέπλευσαν	VIAA--3P	ἀποπλέω
ἀπέπλυναν	VIAA--3P	ἀποπλύνω
ἀπεπνίγη	VIAP--3S	ἀποπνίγω
ἀπέπνιξαν	VIAA--3P	"
ἀπεράντοις	A--DF-P	ἀπέραντος

ἀπέραντος, ον of a series that has no end *endless, interminable* (1T 1.4)

ἀπερίσπαστος, ον *not distracted, with undisturbed mind* (1C 7.35)

ἀπερισπάστους	A--AM-P	ἀπερίσπαστος

ἀπερισπάστως adverb; *without distraction, in an undisturbed way* (1C 7.35)

ἀπερισπάστως	AB	ἀπερισπάστως
ἀπερίτμητοι	A--VM-P	ἀπερίτμητος

ἀπερίτμητος, ον literally *uncircumcised*; substantivally, figuratively, and idiomatically ἀπερίτμητοι καρδίαις καὶ τοῖς ὠσίν literally *people uncircumcised in hearts and ears*, i.e. *stubborn, obstinate people* (AC 7.51)

ἀπερριμμένων	VPRPGM-P	ἀπορίπτω

ἀπέρχεσθαι	VNPD	ἀπέρχομαι
	VNPO	"
ἀπέρχῃ	VSPD--2S	"
	VSPO--2S	"

ἀπέρχομαι fut. ἀπελεύσομαι; 2aor. act. ἀπῆλθον; pf. act. ἀπελήλυθα; pluperfect act. ἀπεληλύθειν; (1) *go away, depart* (JA 1.24); figuratively, of disease *leave* (MK 1.42); (2) with εἰς and indication of place *go (away)* (to) (MK 1.35); (3) of discipleship *go after, follow, go with* (MK 1.20); idiomatically, of following wrong sexual practices ἀπέρχεσθαι ὀπίσω σαρκὸς ἑτέρας literally *go after strange flesh*, i.e. *take part in unnatural sexual intercourse, practice homosexuality* (JU 7); (4) of a report spread, *go out* (MT 4.24)

ἀπερχομένων	VPPDGF-P	ἀπέρχομαι
	VPPOGF-P	"
ἀπέσπασε(ν)	VIAA--3S	ἀποσπάω
ἀπεσπάσθη	VIAP--3S	"
ἀπεστάθη	VIAP--3S	ἀφίστημι
ἀπεστάλη	VIAP--3S	ἀποστέλλω
ἀπεστάλην	VIAP--1S	"
ἀπέσταλκα	VIRA--1S	"
ἀπεστάλκαμεν	VIRA--1P	"
ἀπεστάλκαν	VIRA--3P	"
ἀπεστάλκασι(ν)	VIRA--3P	"
ἀπεστάλκατε	VIRA--2P	"
ἀπέσταλκε(ν)	VIRA--3S	"
ἀπέσταλμαι	VIRP--1S	"
ἀπεσταλμένα	VPRPNN-P	"
ἀπεσταλμένοι	VPRPNM-P	"
ἀπεσταλμένος	VPRPNM-S	"
ἀπεσταλμένους	VPRPAM-P	"
ἀπεστέγασαν	VIAA--3P	ἀποστεγάζω
ἀπέστειλα	VIAA--1S	ἀποστέλλω
ἀπεστείλαμεν	VIAA--1P	"
ἀπέστειλαν	VIAA--3P	"
ἀπέστειλας	VIAA--2S	"
ἀπέστειλε(ν)	VIAA--3S	"
ἀπεστερημένος	VPRPNM-S	ἀποστερέω
ἀπεστερημένων	VPRPGM-P	"
ἀπεστέρησθαι	VNRP	"
ἀπέστη	VIAA--3S	ἀφίστημι
ἀπέστησαν	VIAA--3P	"
ἀπέστησε(ν)	VIAA--3S	"
ἀπεστραμμένων	VPRPGM-P	ἀποστρέφω
ἀπεστράφησαν	VIAP--3P	"
ἀπέστρεψε(ν)	VIAA--3S	"
ἀπετάξατο	VIAM--3S	ἀποτάσσω
ἀπεφθέγξατο	VIAD--3S	ἀποφθέγγομαι
ἀπέχει	VIPA--3S	ἀπέχω
ἀπέχεσθαι	VNPM	"
ἀπέχεσθε	VMPM--2P	"
ἀπέχετε	VIPA--2P	"
ἀπέχῃς	VSAA--2S	"
ἀπέχον	VPPANN-S	"
ἀπέχοντα	VPPAAM-S	"
ἀπέχοντος	VPPAGM-S	"
ἀπέχουσαι	VPPANF-P	"
ἀπέχουσαν	VPPAAF-S	"
ἀπέχουσι(ν)	VIPA--3P	"

ἀπέχω impf. ἀπεῖχον; 2aor. mid. ἀπεσχόμην; (1) transitively; (a) of commercial receipts *receive* in *full (payment)* (PH 4.18); (b) of persons *receive back, have back* (PM 15); (2) intransitively; (a) of a measurement of distance *be distant, be a given distance away* (MT 14.24); (b) figuratively, of separation or distance from a person *be far from* (MT 15.8); (3) impersonally, in MK 14.41 ἀπέχει *it in is enough* is possibly Jesus' assertion that his atoning work is at the point of completion *the account is closed* (cf. JN 19.30); or it may be a rebuke to his disciples *that is enough*, i.e. *stop sleeping*; (4) middle *keep away, abstain from* something (AC 15.29); *keep hands off* someone (AC 5.39)

ἀπέχω	VIPA--1S	ἀπέχω
ἀπεχωρίσθη	VIAP--3S	ἀποχωρίζω
ἀπήγαγε(ν)	VIAA--3S	ἀπάγω
ἀπήγαγον	VIAA--3P	"
ἀπήγγειλαν	VIAA--3P	ἀπαγγέλλω
ἀπήγγειλε(ν)	VIAA--3S	"
ἀπηγγέλη	VIAP--3S	"
ἀπηγγέλλη	VIAP--3S	see ἀπηγγέλη
ἀπήγγελλον	VIIA--1S	ἀπαγγέλλω
ἀπήγξατο	VIAM--3S	ἀπάγχω
ἀπῆγον	VIIA--3P	ἀπάγω
ἀπῆεσαν	VIIA--3P	ἄπειμι (II)
ἀπήλασε(ν)	VIAA--3S	ἀπελαύνω
ἀπηλγηκότες	VPRANM-P	ἀπαλγέω
ἀπῆλθα	VIAA--1S	ἀπέρχομαι
ἀπῆλθαν	VIAA--3P	"
ἀπῆλθε(ν)	VIAA--3S	"
ἀπῆλθον	VIAA--1S	"
	VIAA--3P	"
ἀπήλλαξε(ν)	VIAA--3S	ἀπαλλάσσω
ἀπηλλάσσοντο	VIIP--3P	"
ἀπηλλάχθαι	VNRP	"
ἀπηλλοτριωμένοι	VPRPNM-P	ἀπαλλοτριόω
ἀπηλλοτριωμένους	VPRPAM-P	"
ἀπηλπικότες	VPRANM-P	ἀπελπίζω
ἀπήνεγκαν	VIAA--3P	ἀποφέρω
ἀπήνεγκε(ν)	VIAA--3S	"
ἀπήντησαν	VIAA--3P	ἀπαντάω
ἀπήντησε(ν)	VIAA--3S	"
ἀπήρθη	VIAP--3S	ἀπαίρω
ἀπησπασάμεθα	VIAD--1P	ἀπασπάζομαι
ἀπήχθη	VIAP--3S	ἀπάγω
ἀπίδω	VSAA--1S	ἀφοράω
ἄπιστε	A--VF-S	ἄπιστος

ἀπιστέω impf. ἠπίστουν; 1aor. ἠπίστησα; (1) *not believe, refuse to believe, be distrustful* (LU 24.11); (2) as acting disloyally *be unfaithful, prove false* (RO 3.3; 2T 2.13)

ἀπιστήσας	VPAANM-S	ἀπιστέω
ἀπιστήσασι(ν)	VPAADM-P	"

ἀπιστία, ας, ἡ (1) as failure to trust *unbelief, lack of trust, lack of faith* (MK 6.6); (2) as failure to be trustworthy *unfaithfulness* (RO 3.3)

ἀπιστία	N-NF-S	ἀπιστία
ἀπιστίᾳ	N-DF-S	"
ἀπιστίαν	N-AF-S	"
ἀπιστίας	N-GF-S	"
ἄπιστοι	AP-NM-P	ἄπιστος

ἄπίστοις   AP-DM-P   "
    A--DM-P   "

ἄπιστον   A--AF-S   "
    A--AM-S   "
    A--NN-S   "

ἄπιστος, ον (1) *not believable, incredible, impossible to be true* (AC 26.8); (2) *lacking in faith, unbelieving, not trusting* (JN 20.27); substantivally, as one who does not believe God's message about Christ *unbeliever, pagan* (1T 5.8); plural *nonbelievers, non-Christians, pagans* (1C 6.6); (3) as a quality of behavior *lacking in faithfulness, unfaithful, untrustworthy*; substantivally *unreliable person* (RV 21.8)

ἄπιστος   AP-NM-S   ἄπιστος
    A--NF-S   "
    A--NM-S   "
    A--VF-S   "

ἀπίστου   AP-GM-S   "
    A--GF-S   "

ἀπιστοῦμεν   VIPA--1P   ἀπιστέω
ἀπιστοῦντες   VPPANM-P   "
ἀπιστούντων   VPPAGM-P   "
ἀπιστοῦσι(ν)   VPPADM-P   "
ἀπίστων   AP-GM-P   ἄπιστος
ἀπιστῶν   VPPANM-S   ἀπιστέω

ἀπλότης, ητος, ἡ (1) *simplicity*; as a moral trait *purity of motive, sincerity, integrity* (EP 6.5); (2) as an openness and sincerity in sharing with others *generosity, liberality* (RO 12.8)

ἀπλότητα   N-AF-S   ἀπλότης
ἀπλότητι   N-DF-S   "
ἀπλότητος   N-GF-S

ἀπλοῦς, ῆ, οῦν strictly *single, without folds*; hence *simple, sincere, innocent*; of the eye *healthy, clear* (MT 6.22); superlative ἀπλούστατος, τάτη, ον *quite innocent, without any guile* (MT 10.16)

ἀπλοῦς   A--NM-S   ἀπλοῦς
ἀπλούστατοι   A-SNM-P   "

ἀπλῶς adverb; *in simplicity, openly*; of giving *wholeheartedly, generously, without reserve* (JA 1.5)

ἀπλῶς   AB   ἀπλῶς

ἀπό preposition with the genitive, with the basic meanings *separation off, motion away from*; (1) to denote separation from a person or place *from, away from* (LU 16.18); (2) to denote a point from which something begins *from, out from* (LU 24.47); (3) to indicate distance from a point *away from, from, far from* (2TH 1.9); ἀ. μακρόθεν *from afar* (MT 26.58); with detailed measurement ὡς ἀ. *about* (JN 11.18); (4) to indicate source or origin *from, out of* (JN 1.44); (5) to indicate cause or reason *because of, on account of, as a result of, for* (HE 5.7); (6) to indicate means *with, with the help of, by* (RV 18.15; LU 15.16); (7) to show the originator of the action in a verb *from, by* (1J 1.5); (8) in adverbial expressions: ἀ. μέρους *in part, partly* (RO 11.25); ἀ. μιᾶς *alike, unanimously, as one* (LU 14.18); ἀ. τῆς καρδίας *from the heart, sincerely* (MT 18.35)

ἀπό   PG   ἀπό

ἀποβαίνω fut. mid. ἀποβήσομαι; 2aor. ἀπέβην; literally *go away from*; from a ship or boat *step off, get out of, disembark (from)* (LU 5.2); idiomatically, of a resultant state ἀποβαίνειν εἰς literally *go away into*, i.e. *turn out, end up in, lead to* (LU 21.13)

ἀποβάλητε   VSAA--2P   ἀποβάλλω
ἀποβάλλειν   VNPA   "

ἀποβάλλω 2aor. ἀπέβαλον; literally, of a garment *throw off, take off* (MK 10.50); figuratively, of losing or rejecting a quality or state *throw away, cause to cease, do away with* (HE 10.35)

ἀποβαλώμεθα   VSAM--1P   ἀποβάλλω
ἀποβαλών   VPAANM-S   "
ἀποβάντες   VPAANM-P   ἀποβαίνω
ἀποβήσεται   VIFD--3S   "

ἀποβλέπω impf. ἀπέβλεπον; strictly *look away from all else* to one single object; hence *carefully think about, concentrate on, pay attention to* (HE 11.26)

ἀπόβλητον   A--NN-S   ἀπόβλητος

ἀπόβλητος, ον a verbal adjective from ἀποβάλλω (*throw off, take off*); *rejected, thrown away as worthless* (1T 4.4)

ἀποβολή, ῆς, ἡ strictly *being cast off*; (1) from God's favor *rejection* (RO 11.15); (2) from life itself *loss, destruction* (AC 27.22)

ἀποβολή   N-NF-S   ἀποβολή
ἀπογεγραμμένων   VPRPGM-P   ἀπογράφω
ἀπογενόμενοι   VPADNM-P   ἀπογίνομαι

ἀπογίνομαι 2aor. ἀπεγενόμην; literally *die*; figuratively in the NT, in relation to doing wrong *cease from, have nothing to do with, be finished with* (1P 2.24)

ἀπογράφεσθαι   VNPM   ἀπογράφω
    VNPP   "

ἀπογραφή, ῆς, ἡ as an inventory of citizens in a country *census, registration, listing* (LU 2.2)

ἀπογραφή   N-NF-S   ἀπογραφή
ἀπογραφῆς   N-GF-S   "

ἀπογράφω 1aor. mid. ἀπεγραψάμην; pf. pass. ἀπογέγραμμαι; (1) literally, of an official listing of citizens *enroll, register*; middle *enroll* or *register oneself* (LU 2.3); passive *be registered* or *enrolled* (LU 2.1); (2) figuratively, of records kept in heaven *be enrolled* or *written, be listed* (HE 12.23)

ἀπογράψασθαι   VNAM   ἀπογράφω
ἀποδεδειγμένον   VPRPAM-S   ἀποδείκνυμι
ἀποδεδοκιμασμένον   VPRPAM-S   ἀποδοκιμάζω

ἀποδείκνυμι (and ἀποδεικνύω) 1aor. ἀπέδειξα; pf. pass. ἀποδέδειγμαι; strictly *point out from* something; (1) as demonstrating approval *show clearly to be genuine, endorse* (AC 2.22); (2) as demonstrating by argument *prove, show to be true* (AC 25.7); (3) as making a demonstration publicly *exhibit, put on display* (1C 4.9); as putting oneself on display *proclaim* oneself, *claim to be* (2TH 2.4)

ἀποδεικνύντα   VPPAAM-S   ἀποδείκνυμι
ἀποδεικνύοντα   VPPAAM-S   "
ἀποδεῖξαι   VNAA   "
ἀποδείξει   N-DF-S   ἀπόδειξις

ἀπόδειξις, εως, ἡ strictly *showing forth*; hence *demonstration, proof, evidence* (1C 2.4)

ἀποδεκατεύω *tithe, give one part out of ten* (LU 18.12)

ἀποδεκατεύω   VIPA--1S   ἀποδεκατεύω
ἀποδεκατοῦν   VNPA   ἀποδεκατόω
ἀποδεκατοῦτε   VIPA--2P   "

ἀποδεκατόω inf. ἀποδεκατοῦν; (1) *pay tithes, give one-tenth* or *one part out of every ten of* something (MT 23.23); (2) *collect a tithe from* someone (HE 7.5)

ἀποδεκατῶ	VIPA--1S	ἀποδεκατόω
ἀπόδεκτον	A--NN-S	ἀπόδεκτος

ἀπόδεκτος, ον a verbal adjective from ἀποδέχομαι (*welcome, receive*); of what can be accepted *acceptable, pleasing*

ἀποδεξάμενοι	VPADNM-P	ἀποδέχομαι
ἀποδεξάμενος	VPADNM-S	"
ἀποδέξασθαι	VNAD	"
ἀποδέξωνται	VSAD--3P	"

ἀποδέχομαι impf. ἀπεδεχόμην; 1aor. ἀπεδεξάμην; (1) as giving a friendly reception to someone *welcome, receive favorably* (LU 8.40); (2) as understanding and receiving a message favorably *receive, accept* (AC 2.41); (3) as being content with what someone has done *recognize, acknowledge, praise for* (AC 24.3)

ἀποδεχόμεθα	VIPD--1P	ἀποδέχομαι
	VIPO--1P	"

ἀποδημέω 1aor. ἀπεδήμησα; (1) as going away from one's home or country *go (away) on a journey, leave home* (LU 15.13); (2) metaphorically *be away from, be absent from* (the Lord), i.e. *be still alive* (2C 5.6)

ἀπόδημος, ον of absence in a foreign land *away on a journey, away from home* (MK 13.34)

ἀπόδημος	A--NM-S	ἀπόδημος
ἀποδημοῦμεν	VIPA--1P	ἀποδημέω
ἀποδημῶν	VPPANM-S	"
ἀποδιγνύοντα	VPPAAM-S	see ἀποδεικνύοντα
ἀποδιδόναι	VNPA	ἀποδίδωμι
ἀποδιδόντες	VPPANM-P	"
ἀποδιδότω	VMPA--3S	"
ἀποδιδοῦν	VPPANN-S	"
ἀποδιδούς	VPPANM-S	"

ἀποδίδωμι impf. ἀπεδίδουν; fut. ἀποδώσω; 1aor. ἀπέδωκα; 2aor. subjunctive second-person singular ἀποδῷς, third-person singular ἀποδῷ, imperative ἀπόδος and ἀπόδοτε, mid. ἀπεδόμην, third-person singular ἀπέδετο; 1aor. pass. ἀπεδόθην; (1) as fulfilling an obligation or expectation *give, give back*, with what is given derived from the context; *pay* taxes or wages (MT 20.8); *award* a crown (2T 4.8); *yield* fruit (RV 22.2); *give* a witness (AC 4.33); (2) of divine or human retribution or reward *repay, recompense* (MT 6.4); (3) as returning something *give back, hand back, pay back* (LU 19.8); (4) middle, as giving up something one possesses for sale *sell* (AC 5.8)

ἀποδίδωμι	VIPA--1S	ἀποδίδωμι
ἀποδίδωσι(ν)	VIPA--3S	"
ἀποδιορίζοντες	VPPANM-P	ἀποδιορίζω

ἀποδιορίζω strictly *separate off by placing boundaries*; hence *set up distinctions, separate, cause divisions* (JU 19)

ἀποδοθῆναι	VNAP	ἀποδίδωμι

ἀποδοκιμάζω 1aor. ἀπεδοκίμασα; pf. pass. ἀποδεδοκίμασμαι; 1aor. pass. ἀπεδοκιμάσθην; strictly *throw out as the result of a test*; hence (1) of things *reject, declare useless* (MT 21.42); (2) of persons *reject, think of as unworthy* (HE 12.17)

ἀποδοκιμασθῆναι	VNAP	ἀποδοκιμάζω

ἀπόδος	VMAA--2S	ἀποδίδωμι
ἀπόδοτε	VMAA--2P	"
ἀποδοῦναι	VNAA	"
ἀποδούς	VPAANM-S	"

ἀποδοχή, ῆς, ἡ as a favorable reception *acceptance, approval*

ἀποδοχῆς	N-GF-S	ἀποδοχή
ἀποδῶ	VSAA--3S	ἀποδίδωμι
ἀποδώῃ	VOAA--3S	"
ἀποδῷς	VSAA--2S	"
ἀποδώσει	VIFA--3S	"
ἀποδώσεις	VIFA--2S	"
	VIFA--2S^VMAA--2S	"
ἀποδώσονται	VIFM--3P	"
ἀποδώσοντες	VPFANM-P	"
ἀποδώσουσι(ν)	VIFA--3P	"
ἀποδώσω	VIFA--1S	"
ἀποθανεῖν	VNAA	ἀποθνήσκω
ἀποθανεῖσθε	VIFD--2P	"
ἀποθανεῖται	VIFD--3S	"
ἀποθάνῃ	VSAA--3S	"
ἀποθανόντα	VPAANN-P	"
ἀποθανόντες	VPAANM-P	"
ἀποθανόντι	VPAADM-S	"
ἀποθανόντος	VPAAGM-S	"
ἀποθανοῦνται	VIFM--3P	"
ἀποθάνωμεν	VSAA--1P	"
ἀποθανών	VPAANM-S	"
ἀποθέμενοι	VPAMNM-P	ἀποτίθημι
ἀποθέσθαι	VNAM	"
ἀπόθεσθε	VMAM--2P	"

ἀπόθεσις, εως, ἡ (1) as an action *putting off* or *away, removal* (1P 3.21); (2) idiomatically and euphemistically ἀ. τοῦ σκηνώματος literally *taking down of the tent dwelling*, i.e. *death* (2P 1.14)

ἀπόθεσις	N-NF-S	ἀπόθεσις
ἀποθήκας	N-AF-P	ἀποθήκη

ἀποθήκη, ης, ἡ of any place where natural produce is laid up or stored *barn, storehouse, granary*

ἀποθήκη	N-NF-S	ἀποθήκη
ἀποθήκην	N-AF-S	"
ἀποθησαυρίζοντας	VPPAAM-P	ἀποθησαυρίζω

ἀποθησαυρίζω strictly *store up, lay up in store*; hence, of good works that will provide rewarding benefits in the future life *treasure up, lay up* (1T 6.19)

ἀποθλίβουσι(ν)	VIPA--3P	ἀποθλίβω

ἀποθλίβω of crowds pushing inward *press against, crowd in on* (LU 8.45)

ἀποθνήσκει	VIPA--3S	ἀποθνήσκω
ἀποθνήσκει	VIPA--3S	"
ἀποθνήσκειν	VNPA	"
ἀποθνήσκειν	VNPA	"
ἀποθνήσκεις	VIPA--2S	"
ἀποθνήσκῃ	VSPA--3S	"
ἀποθνήσκομεν	VIPA--1P	"
ἀποθνήσκομεν	VIPA--1P	"
ἀποθνήσκοντες	VPPANM-P	"
ἀποθνήσκοντες	VPPANM-P	"
ἀποθνήσκουσα	VPPANF-S	"
ἀποθνήσκουσι(ν)	VIPA--3P	"
ἀποθνήσκουσι(ν)	VIPA--3P	"

ἀποθνήσκω   VIPA--1S   "

ἀποθνήσκω (and **ἀποθνῄσκω**) impf. ἀπέθνησκον; fut. mid. ἀποθανοῦμαι; 2aor. ἀπέθανον; (1) literally, of natural death *die, suffer death* (MT 22.24), opposite ζάω (*live, be alive*) and μένω (*remain, abide*); of plants and animals *decay, die* (JN 12.24); (2) figuratively; (a) of not responding to something due to separation from it *have no part in, become dead to* (RO 6.2); (b) of spiritual dying as the separation of the soul from God *lose (eternal) life, die* (JN 6.50); (3) of being subject to death as a human being *be mortal* (HE 7.8); *face death* (1C 15.31)

ἀποθνήσκω   VIPA--1S   ἀποθνήσκω
ἀποθνήσκωμεν   VSPA--1P   "
ἀποθνήσκωμεν   VSPA--1P   "
ἀποθνήσκων   VPPANM-S   "
ἀποθνήσκων   VPPANM-S   "
ἀποθώμεθα   VSAM--1P   ἀποτίθημι
ἀποίσῃ   VIFA--3S   ἀποφέρω
ἀποίσουσι(ν)   VIFA--3P   "
ἀποκαθιστᾷ   VIPA--3S   ἀποκαθιστάνω
ἀποκαθιστάνει   VIPA--3S   "
ἀποκαθιστάνεις   VIPA--2S   "

ἀποκαθιστάνω (and **ἀποκατιστάνω**) and **ἀποκαθ- ίστημι** fut. ἀποκαταστήσω; 2aor. ἀπεκατέστην; 1aor. pass. ἀπεκατεστάθην; strictly *restore to an earlier condition*; hence (1) *restore, establish again* (AC 1.6); (2) as a medical technical term *cure, restore* (to health) (MK 3.5); (3) passive, of persons being reunited *be sent back, be brought together again* (HE 13.19)

ἀποκαλύπτεσθαι   VNPP   ἀποκαλύπτω
ἀποκαλύπτεται   VIPP--3S   "

ἀποκαλύπτω fut. ἀποκαλύψω; 1aor. ἀπεκάλυψα; 1aor. pass. ἀπεκαλύφθην; with a basic meaning *uncover, reveal*; figuratively in the NT; (1) generally *disclose, make known, reveal* (MT 10.26); (2) of divine revelation; (a) active *reveal, make known* (MT 11.25); (b) passive *be revealed, be shown* (RO 1.17, 18); (3) passive, of persons *appear, be revealed, be made (fully) known* (LU 17.30)

ἀποκαλυφθῇ   VSAP--3S   ἀποκαλύπτω
ἀποκαλυφθῆναι   VNAP   "
ἀποκαλυφθήσεται   VIFP--3S   "
ἀποκαλυφθῶσι(ν)   VSAP--3P   "
ἀποκαλύψαι   VNAA   "
ἀποκαλύψει   N-DF-S   ἀποκάλυψις
   VIFA--3S   ἀποκαλύπτω
ἀποκαλύψεις   N-AF-P   ἀποκάλυψις
ἀποκαλύψεων   N-GF-P   "
ἀποκαλύψεως   N-GF-S   "
ἀποκάλυψιν   N-AF-S   "

ἀποκάλυψις, εως, ἡ literally, as an action *uncovering, disclosing, revealing*; figuratively in the NT; (1) generally, of what God discloses or makes known *revelation, disclosure*, e.g. his plan of redemption (EP 3.3); (2) as an end-time event *revelation, appearing* (RO 2.5; 1P 1.7); (3) of particular forms of disclosure, as through vision (RV 1.1) and personal guidance (GA 2.2)

ἀποκάλυψις   N-NF-S   ἀποκάλυψις
ἀποκάλυψον   VMAA--2S   ἀποκαλύπτω

ἀποκαραδοκία, ας, ἡ strictly *watching* with the head stretched forward alertly; hence *eager expectation, earnest waiting* (RO 8.19)

ἀποκαραδοκία   N-NF-S   ἀποκαραδοκία
ἀποκαραδοκίαν   N-AF-S   "
ἀποκαταλλαγέντες   VPAPNM-P   ἀποκαταλλάσσω
ἀποκαταλλάγητε   VSAP--2P   "
ἀποκαταλλάξαι   VNAA   "
ἀποκαταλλάξῃ   VSAA--3S   "

ἀποκαταλλάσσω 1aor. ἀποκατήλλαξα; pf. pass. ἀποκατήλ- λαγμαι; 2aor. pass. ἀποκατηλλάγην; strictly *transfer from one state to another quite different state*; hence, of broken interpersonal relations *reconcile, restore* (from enmity to favor) (EP 2.16)

ἀποκατασταθῶ   VSAP--1S   ἀποκαθιστάνω
ἀποκαταστάνει   VIPA--3S   "
ἀποκαταστάσεως   N-GF-S   ἀποκατάστασις

ἀποκατάστασις, εως, ἡ as an action *restoring, restoration* of a thing to its former good state (AC 3.21)

ἀποκαταστῆσαι   VNAA   ἀποκαθιστάνω
ἀποκαταστήσει   VIFA--3S   "
ἀποκατεστάθη   VIAP--3S   "
ἀποκατέστη   VIAA--3S   "
ἀποκατηλλάγητε   VIAP--2P   ἀποκαταλλάσσω
ἀποκατήλλακται   VIRP--3S   "
ἀποκατήλλαξε(ν)   VIAA--3S   "

ἀπόκειμαι literally *be put away, stored up, reserved* (LU 19.20); figuratively, of the certainties of man's future as established by God *be awaiting, be appointed, exist* (CO 1.5)

ἀποκειμένην   VPPDAF-S   ἀπόκειμαι
   VPPOAF-S   "
ἀπόκειται   VIPD--3S   "
   VIPO--3S   "
ἀποκεκρυμμένην   VPRPAF-S   ἀποκρύπτω
ἀποκεκρυμμένον   VPRPAN-S   "
ἀποκεκρυμμένου   VPRPGN-S   "
ἀποκεκυλισμένον   VPRPAM-S   ἀποκυλίω
ἀποκεκύλισται   VIRP--3S   "

ἀποκεφαλίζω 1aor. ἀπεκεφάλισα; as a form of execution *behead, cut off the head*

ἀποκλείσῃ   VSAA--3S   ἀποκλείω

ἀποκλείω 1aor. ἀπέκλεισα; strictly *close off from an area, exclude*; hence, of a door *close, shut* (LU 13.25)

ἀποκόπτω fut. ἀποκόψω; 1aor. ἀπέκοψα; (1) of bodily limbs or parts *cut off* (MK 9.43); of ropes (AC 27.32); (2) of removing male testicles *castrate, emasculate, make a eunuch of*; middle *emasculate oneself*; used sarcastically in GA 5.12 of carrying an error in doctrine to its logical extreme

ἀπόκοψον   VMAA--2S   ἀποκόπτω
ἀποκόψονται   VIFM--3P   "
ἀποκόψωνται   VSAM--3P   "
ἀποκριθείς   VPAONM-S   ἀποκρίνομαι
ἀποκριθεῖσα   VPAONF-S   "
ἀποκριθέν   VPAONN-S   "
ἀποκριθέντες   VPAONM-P   "
ἀποκριθῇ   VIAO--3S   "
ἀποκριθῆναι   VNAO   "
ἀποκριθήσεται   VIFO--3S   "
ἀποκριθήσονται   VIFO--3P   "
ἀποκρίθητε   VMAO--2P   "
ἀποκριθῆτε   VSAO--2P   "
ἀποκριθῶσι(ν)   VSAO--3P   "

ἀπόκριμα, ατος, τό   literally, as a legal technical term *official decision, sentence*; figuratively in 2C 1.9 of a feeling that death is sure to take place

ἀπόκριμα	N-AN-S	ἀπόκριμα
ἀποκρίνεσθαι	VNPD	ἀποκρίνομαι
	VNPO	"
ἀποκρίνεται	VIPD--3S	"
	VIPO--3S	"
ἀποκρίνῃ	VIPD--2S	"
	VIPO--2S	"

ἀποκρίνομαι   1aor. mid. ἀπεκρινάμην; 1aor. pass. ἀπεκρίθην; 1fut. ἀποκριθήσομαι; (1) *answer, reply*, as a somewhat formal response or reaction to a speech, exhortation, question, or request, generally followed by a direct quoted answer (JN 1.21); (2) Hebraistically, as a formula to control the flow of discourse; (a) *continue* (MT 11.25); (b) *begin, speak up* (MT 14.28); (c) *answer* or often left untranslated or translated as a single verb when combined with a form of speech verb, such as εἶπεν (LU 1.19), λέγει (LU 11.45), ἔφη (LU 23.3), λέγοντες (MT 25.37)

ἀποκρίσει	N-DF-S	ἀπόκρισις
ἀποκρίσεσι(ν)	N-DF-P	"
ἀπόκρισιν	N-AF-S	"

ἀπόκρισις, εως, ἡ   as a response *an answer, a reply*

ἀποκρύπτω   1aor. ἀπέκρυψα; pf. pass. ptc. ἀποκεκρυμμένος; literally *hide away, conceal* (MT 25.18); figuratively, of knowledge that cannot be known except through divine revelation *keep secret* or *hidden* (LU 10.21)

ἀπόκρυφοι	A--NM-P	ἀπόκρυφος
ἀπόκρυφον	A--NN-S	"

ἀπόκρυφος, ον   literally *kept secret, hidden (away)* (MK 4.22); figuratively, of unrevealed knowledge *concealed, secret* (CO 2.3); possibly substantivally ἀπόκρυφον *hidden thing, secret* (LU 8.17)

ἀποκταίνει	VIPA--3S	ἀποκτείνω
ἀποκταινεῖ	VIFA--3S	"
ἀποκτανθείς	VPAPNM-S	"
ἀποκτανθῆναι	VNAP	"
ἀποκτανθῶσι(ν)	VSAP--3P	"
ἀποκτεῖναι	VNAA	"
ἀποκτεινάντων	VPAAGM-P	"
ἀποκτείνας	VPAANM-S	"
ἀποκτείνει	VIPA--3S	"
ἀποκτείνεσθαι	VNPP	"
ἀποκτείνοντες	VPPANM-P	"
ἀποκτεινόντων	VPPAGM-P	"
ἀποκτείνουσα	VPPAVF-S	"

ἀποκτείνω (and ἀποκταίνω, ἀποκτέμνω, ἀποκτέννω, ἀποκτένω)   fut. ἀποκτενῶ; 1aor. ἀπέκτεινα; 1aor. pass. ἀπεκτάνθην; (1) as depriving a person of physical life *kill, slay, put to death* (MT 14.5); (2) of anything personified, as depriving a person of spiritual life, i.e. causing separation from God, such as sin (RO 7.11) or law (2C 3.6); (3) figuratively, of forcefully causing a condition or state of affairs to cease *do away with, eliminate* (EP 2.16)

ἀποκτείνωμεν	VSAA--1P	ἀποκτείνω
ἀποκτείνωσι(ν)	VSAA--3P	"
ἀποκτέμνει	VIPA--3S	"

ἀποκτένει	VIPA--3S	"
ἀποκτενεῖ	VIFA--3S	"
ἀποκτενεῖν	VNFA	"
ἀποκτενεῖτε	VIFA--2P	"
ἀποκτέννει	VIPA--3S	"
ἀποκτέννεσθαι	VNPP	"
ἀποκτέννοντες	VPPANM-P	"
ἀποκτεννόντων	VPPAGM-P	"
ἀποκτέννουσα	VPPAVF-S	"
ἀποκτενόντων	VPPAGM-P	"
ἀποκτένουσα	VPPAVF-S	"
ἀποκτενοῦσι(ν)	VIFA--3P	"
ἀποκτενῶ	VIFA--1S	"
ἀποκύει	VIPA--3S	ἀποκυέω
ἀποκυεῖ	VIPA--3S	"

ἀποκυέω   1aor. ἀπεκύησα; literally, of motherhood *give birth to, bear*; figuratively in the NT; (1) of sin personified *produce, cause to bring forth* (JA 1.15); (2) of God's spiritual fathering *bring into being (spiritually), bring forth into new life* (JA 1.18)

ἀποκυλίσαι	VNAA	ἀποκυλίω
ἀποκυλίσει	VIFA--3S	"

ἀποκυλίω   fut. ἀποκυλίσω; 1aor. ἀπεκύλισα; pf. pass. ἀποκεκύλισμαι; of a stone at the entrance of a tomb *roll away, roll back* (MT 28.2)

ἀπολαβεῖν	VNAA	ἀπολαμβάνω
ἀπολάβετε	VMAA--2P	"
ἀπολάβῃ	VSAA--3S	"
ἀπολάβητε	VSAA--2P	"
ἀπολάβομεν	VSAA--1P	see ἀπολάβωμεν
ἀπολαβόμενοι	VPAMNM-P	ἀπολαμβάνω
ἀπολαβόμενος	VPAMNM-S	"
ἀπολάβωμεν	VSAA--1P	"
ἀπολάβωσι(ν)	VSAA--3P	"

ἀπολαλέω   impf. ἀπελάλουν; *speak out freely* (AC 18.25)

ἀπολαμβάνειν	VNPA	ἀπολαμβάνω
ἀπολαμβάνομεν	VIPA--1P	"
ἀπολαμβάνοντες	VPPANM-P	"

ἀπολαμβάνω   fut. mid. ἀπολήμψομαι; 2aor. ἀπέλαβον, mid. ptc. ἀπολαβόμενος; of what is due, sought, or needed; (1) *receive, obtain, gain* (LU 16.25); (2) *recover, receive in return, get back* (LU 6.34); (3) middle, of persons *take aside, lead away* (MK 7.33); (4) *welcome* (3J 8); (5) *welcome back, receive back* (LU 15.27)

ἀπόλαυσιν	N-AF-S	ἀπόλαυσις

ἀπόλαυσις, εως, ἡ   *enjoyment, pleasure*

ἀπολείπεται	VIPP--3S	ἀπολείπω

ἀπολείπω (and ἀπολιμπάνω)   impf. ἀπέλειπον; 2aor. ἀπέλιπον; (1) *leave behind* (2T 4.13); *leave as an example* (1P 2.21); (2) in a bad sense *desert, abandon* (JU 6); (3) passive, of what is allowed to remain in order to be available *be reserved, continue to exist* (HE 4.9; 10.26)

ἀπολεῖσθε	VIFM--2P	ἀπόλλυμι
ἀπολεῖται	VIFM--3S	"

ἀπολείχω   impf. ἀπέλειχον; of an animal, such as a dog, that passes its tongue over a surface *lick, lick off* (LU 16.21)

ἀπολελυμένην	VPRPAF-S	ἀπολύω
ἀπολελυμένον	VPRPAM-S	"
ἀπολέλυσαι	VIRP--2S	"
ἀπολελύσθαι	VNRP	"

ἀπολέσαι	VNAA	ἀπόλλυμι
ἀπολέσας	VPAANM-S	"
ἀπολέσασα	VPAANF-S	"
ἀπολέσει	VIFA--3S	"
ἀπολέσῃ	VSAA--3S	"
ἀπολέσηται	VSAA--2P	"
ἀπολέσητε	VSAA--2P	"
ἀπολέσθαι	VNAM	"
ἀπολέσομεν	VSAA--1P	"
ἀπολέσουσι(ν)	VIFA--3P	"
ἀπολέσω	VIFA--1S	"
	VSAA--1S	"
ἀπολέσωμεν	VSAA--1P	"
ἀπολέσωσι(ν)	VSAA--3P	"
ἀπολήθειτε	VOAP--2P	"
ἀπολήμψεσθε	VIFD--2P	ἀπολαμβάνω
ἀπόλησθε	VSAM--2P	ἀπόλλυμι
ἀπόληται	VSAM--3S	"
ἀπόλητε	VSAA--2P	"
ἀπολήψεσθε	VIFD--2P	ἀπολαμβάνω
ἀπολιμπάνων	VPPANM-S	ἀπολείπω
ἀπολιπόντας	VPAAAM-P	"
ἀπόλυε	VMPA--2S	ἀπόλλυμι
ἀπολλύει	VIPA--3S	"
ἀπόλλυμαι	VIPM--1S	"
ἀπολλύμεθα	VIPM--1P	"
ἀπολλυμένην	VPPMAF-S	"
ἀπολλύμενοι	VPPMNM-P	"
	VPPPNM-P	"
ἀπολλυμένοις	VPPMDM-P	"
	VPPPDM-P	"
ἀπολλυμένου	VPPMGN-S	"

ἀπόλλυμι fut. ἀπολέσω and ἀπολῶ, mid. ἀπολοῦμαι; 1aor. ἀπώλεσα; 2aor. mid. ἀπωλόμην; second perfect ἀπόλωλα; (1) active *ruin, destroy*; (a) of persons *destroy, kill, bring to ruin* (MT 2.13); (b) with an impersonal object *destroy, bring to nothing* (1C 1.19); (c) of a reward *lose, be deprived of* (MT 10.42), opposite τηρέω (*maintain, keep*); (2) middle *be ruined, be destroyed* (second perfect active as middle); (a) of persons *die, perish, lose one's life* (MT 8.25); (b) of things *be lost, be ruined* (MT 9.17); (c) of transitory things *pass away, cease to exist, perish* (1P 1.7)

ἀπόλλυνται	VIPM--3P	ἀπόλλυμι
ἀπόλλυται	VIPM--3S	"
	VIPP--3S	"

Ἀπολλύων, ονος, ὁ as the evil angel who rules over the demons *Apollyon, Destroyer*, Greek translation of the Hebrew *Abaddon* (transliterated into Greek as Ἀβαδδών) (RV 9.11)

Ἀπολλύων	N-NM-S	Ἀπολλύων
Ἀπολλώ	N-AM-S	Ἀπολλῶς
	N-GM-S	"
Ἀπολλῶ	N-AM-S	"
	N-GM-S	"
Ἀπολλών	N-AM-S	"
Ἀπολλών	N-AM-S	"

Ἀπολλωνία, ας, ἡ *Apollonia*, a city in Macedonia (AC 17.1)

Ἀπολλωνίαν	N-AF-S	Ἀπολλωνία
Ἀπολλωνίδα	N-AF-S	see Ἀπολλωνίαν

Ἀπολλώνιος, ου, ὁ		*Apollonius*, masculine proper noun (AC 18.24)
Ἀπολλώνιος	N-NM-S	Ἀπολλώνιος
Ἀπολλώς	N-NM-S	Ἀπολλῶς

Ἀπολλῶς, ῶ, ὁ (also Ἀπολλώς) *Apollos*, masculine proper noun

Ἀπολλῶς	N-NM-S	Ἀπολλῶς
ἀπολογεῖσθαι	VNPD	ἀπολογέομαι
	VNPO	"

ἀπολογέομαι impf. ἀπελογούμην; 1aor. mid. ἀπελογησάμην; 1aor. pass. ἀπολογήθην; *speak in one's own defense, defend oneself* (LU 12.11)

ἀπολογηθῆναι	VNAO	ἀπολογέομαι
ἀπολογήσησθε	VSAD--2P	"

ἀπολογία, ας, ἡ *defense*; as a legal technical term, a speech in defense of oneself *reply, verbal defense* (2T 4.16); as a religious technical term *defense* of the gospel message from false teaching (PH 1.7)

ἀπολογία	N-NF-S	ἀπολογία
ἀπολογία	N-DF-S	"
ἀπολογίαν	N-AF-S	"
ἀπολογίας	N-GF-S	"
ἀπολογοῦμαι	VIPD--1S	ἀπολογέομαι
	VIPO--1S	"
ἀπολογούμεθα	VIPD--1P	"
	VIPO--1P	"
ἀπολογουμένου	VPPDGM-S	"
	VPPOGM-S	"
ἀπολογουμένων	VPPDGM-P	"
	VPPOGM-P	"
ἀπολομένου	VPAMGM-S	ἀπόλλυμι
ἀπόλονται	VIPP--3P	"
ἀπολοῦνται	VIFM--3P	"
ἀπόλουσαι	VMAM--2S	ἀπολούω

ἀπολούω 1aor. mid. ἀπελουσάμην; *wash*; middle *wash oneself*; figuratively and middle in the NT, of the relation of baptism to pardon for sins, as a break from the sinful past *wash away* one's sins (AC 22.16); *become pure* (1C 6.11)

ἀπολύει	VIPA--3S	ἀπολύω
ἀπολύειν	VNPA	"
ἀπολύεις	VIPA--2S	"
ἀπολύετε	VMPA--2P	"
ἀπολυθέντες	VPAPNM-P	"
ἀπολυθήσεσθε	VIFP--2P	"
ἀπολυθῆτε	VSAP--2P	"
ἀπόλυνται	VIPP--3P	ἀπόλλυμι
ἀπολῦσαι	VNAA	ἀπολύω
ἀπολύσας	VPAANM-S	"
ἀπολύσασα	VPAANF-S	"
ἀπολύσει	VIFA--3S	"
ἀπολύσετε	VIFA--2P	"
ἀπολύσῃ	VSAA--3S	"
ἀπολύσῃς	VSAA--2S	"
ἀπολύσητε	VSAA--2P	"
ἀπόλυσον	VMAA--2S	"
ἀπολύσω	VIFA--1S	"
	VSAA--1S	"
ἀπολυτρώσεως	N-GF-S	ἀπολύτρωσις
ἀπολύτρωσιν	N-AF-S	"

ἀπολύτρωσις, εως, ἡ   (1) literally, as an action a buying back of a slave or captive through payment of a ransom; hence *setting free, release* (HE 11.35); (2) figuratively; (a) of rescue from sin *redemption, deliverance* (RO 3.24); (b) of the release of the body from earthly limitations and mortality *liberation, deliverance* (RO 8.23); (c) of Christ as the one who sets free from sin *redeemer, deliverer* (1C 1.30)

ἀπολύτρωσις   N-NF-S   ἀπολύτρωσις

ἀπολύω   impf. ἀπέλυον; fut. ἀπολύσω; 1aor. ἀπέλυσα; pf. pass. ἀπολέλυμαι; 1aor. pass. ἀπελύθην; fut. pass. ἀπολυθήσομαι; (1) of a prisoner or debtor *set free, release, pardon* (MT 27.15); (2) of divorce *send away, dismiss, let go* (MT 1.19; 19.3); (3) of a crowd or assembly *dismiss, send away* (MT 14.15); (4) middle *go away, depart* (AC 28.25); (5) euphemistically, for death *let die, let depart* (LU 2.29)

ἀπολύων   VPPANM-S   ἀπολύω
ἀπολῶ   VIFA--1S   ἀπόλλυμι
ἀπολωλός   VPRAAN-S   "
ἀπολωλότα   VPRAAN-P   "
ἀπολωλώς   VPRANM-S   "
ἀπόλωνται   VSAM--3P   "
ἀπομασσόμεθα   VIPM--1P   ἀπομάσσω

ἀπομάσσω   mid. ἀπομάσσομαι; *wipe off, wipe clean*; only middle in the NT *wipe oneself off, wipe (dust) off of one's feet* (LU 10.11)

ἀπομένω   1aor. ἀπέμεινα; *remain or stay behind* (LU 2.43)

ἀπονέμοντες   VPPANM-P   ἀπονέμω

ἀπονέμω   literally *assign, apportion off, distribute*; idiomatically ἀπονέμειν τιμήν literally *assign honor to*, i.e. *show respect to* (1P 3.7)

ἀπονίζω or ἀπονίπτω   1aor. mid. ἀπενιψάμην; *wash off*; middle *wash (oneself) off*; used symbolically to assert innocence *wash* (one's hands) (MT 27.24)

ἀπόντες   VPPANM-P   ἄπειμι (I)

ἀποπέμπω   1aor. ἀπέπεμψα; (1) *send off or away, dismiss*; (2) *send* on a mission, equivalent to ἀποστέλλω (JN 17.3)

ἀποπίπτω   1aor. ἀπέπεσα; *fall off or from* (AC 9.18)

ἀποπλανᾶν   VNPA   ἀποπλανάω

ἀποπλανάω   1aor. pass. ἀπεπλανήθην; (1) active *lead astray, mislead*; figuratively, of false teachers *deceive, cause to believe what is not true* (MK 13.22); (2) passive *wander away*; figuratively and idiomatically ἀποπλανᾶσθαι ἀπὸ τῆς πίστεως literally *go astray from the faith*, i.e. *no longer believe God's message about Christ* (1T 6.10)

ἀποπλεῖν   VNPA   ἀποπλέω
ἀποπλεύσαντες   VPAANM-P   "

ἀποπλέω   1aor. ἀπέπλευσα; as a nautical technical term, of ships *sail away*; with εἰς *sail from* one point *to* another (AC 13.4)

ἀποπληρόω   fut. ἀποπληρώσω; strictly *fill quite full, satisfy*; hence, of a claim or duty *carry out, submit to fulfill* (GA 6.2)

ἀποπληρώσετε   VIFA--2P   ἀποπληρόω

ἀποπλύνω   fut. ἀποπλυνῶ; *wash, rinse* (LU 5.2)

ἀποπνίγω   1aor. ἀπέπνιξα; 2aor. pass. ἀπεπνίγην; transitively *choke (out)* (MT 13.7); passive *be choked*; by falling into the sea *drown* (LU 8.33)

ἀπορεῖσθαι   VNPM   ἀπορέω

ἀπορέω   impf. ἠπόρουν; active/middle (1) *be at a loss, be perplexed, be uncertain* (AC 25.20); (2) *be inwardly disturbed* (MK 6.20)

ἀπορία, ας, ἡ   *perplexity, anxiety, dismay* (LU 21.25)

ἀπορίᾳ   N-DF-S   ἀπορία

ἀπορίπτω (or ἀπορρίπτω)   1aor. ἀπέριψα; pf. pass. ἀπέριμμαι (or ἀπέρριμμαι); (1) transitively *throw down or away*; (2) intransitively *throw oneself down*; from a ship *cast oneself overboard, jump overboard* (AC 27.43)

ἀπορίψαντας   VPAAAM-P   ἀπορίπτω
ἀπορίψαντες   VPAANM-P   "
ἀπορούμαι   VIPM--1S   ἀπορέω
ἀπορούμενοι   VPPMNM-P   "
ἀπορούμενος   VPPMNM-S   "
ἀπορρίψαντας   VPAAAM-P   ἀπορίπτω

ἀπορφανίζω   1aor. pass. ptc. ἀπορφανισθείς; literally *make an orphan of*; figuratively and passive, of an unwanted separation *be torn away from, be deprived of, be (unwillingly) separated from* (1TH 2.17)

ἀπορφανισθέντες   VPAPNM-P   ἀπορφανίζω

ἀποσκευάζω   1aor. mid. ἀπεσκευασάμην; probably *pack up and leave* (AC 21.15)

ἀποσκευασάμενοι   VPAMNM-P   ἀποσκευάζω

ἀποσκίασμα, ατος, τό   literally *shadow* as caused by an object that blocks rays of light; τροπῆς ἀ. *shifting shadow* caused by the changing position of light-giving bodies, such as the sun or moon; figuratively *changeableness, variation* (JA 1.17)

ἀποσκίασμα   N-NN-S   ἀποσκίασμα
ἀποσκιάσματος   N-GN-S   "
ἀποσπᾶν   VNPA   ἀποσπάω
ἀποσπᾶν   VNPA   "
ἀποσπασθέντας   VPAPAM-P   "
ἀποσπασθέντων   VPAPGM-P   "

ἀποσπάω   1aor. ἀπέσπασα; 1aor. pass. ἀπεσπάσθην; literally *draw away, pull or drag away*; of a sword *draw out* (MT 26.51); figuratively, of alienating persons from someone *tear away, lure away, draw away* (AC 20.30); passive *withdraw, be separated from* (LU 22.41)

ἀποσταλέντι   VPAPDN-S   ἀποστέλλω
ἀποσταλῶσι(ν)   VSAP--3P   "
ἀποστάντα   VPAAAM-S   ἀφίστημι
ἀποστάς   VPAANM-S   "

ἀποστασία, ας, ἡ   as a condition resulting from changing loyalties *revolt, desertion*; as a religious technical term; (1) *apostasy, rebellion* (2TH 2.3); (2) *defection, abandonment* (AC 21.21)

ἀποστασία   N-NF-S   ἀποστασία
ἀποστασίαν   N-AF-S   "

ἀποστάσιον, ου, τό   as a legal technical term, the act of putting away a wife *divorce* (MT 19.7); by metonymy *certificate of divorce* (MT 5.31)

ἀποστάσιον   N-AN-S   ἀποστάσιον
ἀποστασίου   N-GN-S   "

ἀπόστασις, εως, ἡ   strictly, as an action *standing away from*; hence (1) *rebellion, defection*; (2) *departure from, removal from*; (3) *distance, interval* (HE 11.1)

ἀπόστασις   N-NF-S   ἀπόστασις

ἀποστάτης, ου, ὁ   *deserter, rebel, apostate* (JA 2.11)

ἀποστάτης   N-NM-S   ἀποστάτης

ἀποστεγάζω   1aor. ἀπεστέγασα; *unroof, remove* or *break through a roof* (MK 2.4)

ἀποστεγάσαντες	VPAANM-P	ἀποστεγάζω
ἀποστεῖλαι	VNAA	ἀποστέλλω
ἀποστείλαντα	VPAAAM-S	"
ἀποστείλαντας	VPAAAM-P	"
ἀποστείλαντες	VPAANM-P	"
ἀποστείλαντος	VPAAGM-S	"
ἀποστείλας	VPAANM-S	"
ἀποστείλῃ	VSAA--3S	"
ἀπόστειλον	VMAA--2S	"
ἀποστείλω	VSAA--1S	"
ἀποστελεῖ	VIFA--3S	"
ἀποστέλλει	VIPA--3S	"
ἀποστέλλειν	VNPA	"
ἀποστέλλῃ	VSPA--3S	"
ἀποστελλόμενα	VPPPNN-P	"
ἀποστέλλουσι(ν)	VIPA--3P	"

ἀποστέλλω   fut. ἀποστελῶ; 1aor. ἀπέστειλα; pf. ἀπέσταλκα; pf. pass. ἀπέσταλμαι; 1aor. pass. ἀπεστάλην; (1) *send forth, send out* (MK 11.1); in relation to a sender *send with a commission, send with authority, send for a purpose* (MT 11.10); (2) when used with other verbs that indicate the action in the situation was performed by someone else, *have* something done (e.g. MT 2.16 ἀποστείλας ἀνεῖλεν *he had (them) killed*); (3) idiomatically ἀποστέλλειν τὸ δρέπανον literally *send the sickle*, i.e. *begin to harvest* (MK 4.29)

ἀποστέλλω	VIPA--1S	ἀποστέλλω
ἀποστελῶ	VIFA--1S	"
ἀποστερεῖσθε	VIPP--2P	ἀποστερέω
ἀποστερεῖτε	VIPA--2P	"
	VMPA--2P	"

ἀποστερέω   1aor. ἀπεστέρησα; pf. pass. ptc. ἀπεστερημένος; (1) active, as obtaining something by deceiving another *deprive, defraud, steal* (1C 6.8); figuratively, of marital rights *withhold, deprive* (1C 7.5); (2) passive *permit oneself to be defrauded; let oneself be robbed* (1C 6.7)

ἀποστερήσῃς	VSAA--2S	ἀποστερέω
ἀποστῇ	VSAA--3S	ἀφίστημι
ἀποστῆναι	VNAA	"
ἀποστήσονται	VIFM--3P	"
ἀπόστητε	VMAA--2P	"
ἀποστήτω	VMAA--3S	"

ἀποστολή, ῆς, ἡ   strictly *a sending off, mission*; hence, a position as a special messenger *apostleship, office of an apostle* (AC 1.25)

ἀποστολήν	N-AF-S	ἀποστολή
ἀποστολῆς	N-GF-S	"
ἀπόστολοι	N-NM-P	ἀπόστολος
	N-VM-P	"
ἀποστόλοις	N-DM-P	"
ἀπόστολον	N-AM-S	"

ἀπόστολος, ου, ὁ   (1) as one who is sent on a mission with full authority *apostle, messenger, envoy* (JN 13.16); (2) as a commissioned representative of a congregation *delegate, missionary, representative* (2C 8.23); (3) in the NT used especially of a messenger for God; (a) generally (LU 11.49); (b) more specifically as a person who tells the gospel message *apostle* (RO 16.7); often of a person who has the special task of founding and establishing churches *apostle, messenger* (of God) (EP 2.20); (c) especially of the Twelve chosen by Jesus *apostle* (LU 6.13)

ἀπόστολος	N-NM-S	ἀπόστολος
ἀποστόλου	N-GM-S	"
ἀποστόλους	N-AM-P	"
ἀποστόλων	N-GM-P	"
ἀποστοματίζειν	VNPA	ἀποστοματίζω

ἀποστοματίζω   strictly *require* or *provoke* someone *to speak without thinking*; hence *question closely, ask hostile questions, try to catch in an unguarded moment* (LU 11.53)

ἀποστραφῇς	VSAP--2S	ἀποστρέφω
ἀποστρέφειν	VNPA	"
ἀποστρεφόμενοι	VPPPNM-P	"
ἀποστρεφομένων	VPPPGM-P	"
ἀποστρέφοντα	VPPAAM-S	"

ἀποστρέφω   fut. ἀποστρέψω; 1aor. ἀπέστρεψα, mid. ἀποστρέφομαι; 2aor. pass. ἀπεστράφην; (1) transitively; (a) as turning someone away from correct behavior or belief *mislead, cause to go astray* (LU 23.14); with one's attention as the object τὴν ἀκοὴν ἀποστρέφειν literally *turn away the ear*, i.e. *stop listening* (2T 4.4); (b) as causing someone to change from incorrect to correct behavior *cause to turn away from, stop* (RO 11.26; possibly AC 3.26); (c) *put back, return* something (MT 26.52; 27.3); (2) intransitively *turn away from, stop* (possibly AC 3.26); (3) middle and second aorist passive *turn away from, refuse help, reject* (2T 1.15; AC 7.39)

ἀποστρέψει	VIFA--3S	ἀποστρέφω
ἀπόστρεψον	VMAA--2S	"
ἀποστρέψουσι(ν)	VIFA--3P	"

ἀποστυγέω   *hate, abhor*; of evil *hate utterly, shrink away from* (RO 12.9)

ἀποστυγοῦντες	VPPANM-P	ἀποστυγέω
ἀποσυνάγωγοι	A--NM-P	ἀποσυνάγωγος

ἀποσυνάγωγος, ον   as a religious technical term relating to Jewish disciplinary measures in varying degrees of severity *expelled from the synagogue; (completely) excommunicated; cut off from the rights and privileges of a Jew; put under the ban* or *curse* (JN 9.22)

ἀποσυνάγωγος	A--NM-S	ἀποσυνάγωγος
ἀποσυναγώγους	A--AM-P	"
ἀπόσχεσθε	VMAM--2P	ἀπέχω
ἀποταξάμενοι	VPAMNM-P	ἀποτάσσω
ἀποταξάμενος	VPAMNM-S	"
ἀποτάξασθαι	VNAM	"
ἀποτάσσεται	VIPM--3S	"

ἀποτάσσω   1aor. mid. ἀπεταξάμην; only middle in the NT *part from, take leave of, say good-bye to* (MK 6.46); figuratively, of possessions *renounce, give up* (LU 14.33)

ἀποτελεσθεῖσα	VPAPNF-S	ἀποτελέω

ἀποτελέω   1aor. pass. ἀπετελέσθην; literally *complete, finish*; of cures *perform* (LU 13.32); figuratively and passive, of something that has completed its action *run its course, reach a final stage* (JA 1.15)

ἀποτελοῦμαι	VIPM--1S	ἀποτελέω
ἀποτελῶ	VIPA--1S	"

ἀποτίθημι   2aor. mid. ἀπεθέμην; 1aor. pass. ἀπετέθην; only middle/passive in the NT; (1) literally *put off*; of clothes *take off and lay down* (AC 7.58); figuratively *get rid of, cease from, give up* (RO 13.12); (2) *put away* (MT 14.3)

ἀποτιναξάμενος	VPAMNM-S	ἀποτινάσσω
ἀποτινάξας	VPAANM-S	"
ἀποτινάξατε	VMAA--2P	"
ἀποτινάσσετε	VMPA--2P	"

ἀποτινάσσω 1aor. ἀπετίναξα; *shake off* something in order to get rid of it; of a snake from the hand (AC 28.5); of dust from the feet (LU 9.5)

ἀποτίνω fut. ἀποτίσω; as a legal technical term, of damages to be paid off *repay, make good, compensate* (PM 19)

ἀποτίσω	VIFA--1S	ἀποτίνω
ἀποτολμᾷ	VIPA--3S	ἀποτολμάω

ἀποτολμάω *be bold, speak out fearlessly* (RO 10.20)

ἀποτομία, ας, ἡ strictly *abruptness, steepness* in the terrain; hence *severity, sternness* (RO 11.22), opposite χρηστότης (*goodness, kindness*)

ἀποτομία	N-NF-S	ἀποτομία
ἀποτομίαν	N-AF-S	"

ἀποτόμως adverb; *severely, sharply, harshly*

ἀποτόμως	AB	ἀποτόμως
ἀποτρέπου	VMPM--2S	ἀποτρέπω

ἀποτρέπω *turn* someone *away from* something; only middle in the NT *turn oneself away from, avoid, shun* (2T 3.5)

ἀπουσία, ας, ἡ *absence, being away* (PH 2.12), opposite παρουσία (*being present, presence*)

ἀπουσία	N-DF-S	ἀπουσία
ἀποφέρεσθαι	VNPP	ἀποφέρω

ἀποφέρω fut. ἀποίσω, third-person singular ἀποίσῃ (JN 21.18); 2aor. ἀπήνεγκα; 1aor. pass. ἀπηνέχθην; (1) of persons *carry off, take away, transport* (LU 16.22); of a prisoner *lead away* (by force) (MK 15.1; JN 21.18); (2) of things *take, bring* from one place to another (AC 19.12)

ἀποφεύγοντας	VPPAAM-P	ἀποφεύγω

ἀποφεύγω 2aor. ἀπέφυγον; literally *escape, flee from*; figuratively *be free from, be rid of, escape* (2P 1.4)

ἀποφθέγγεσθαι	VNPD	ἀποφθέγγομαι
	VNPO	"

ἀποφθέγγομαι 1aor. ἀπεφθεγξάμην; *speak out (loudly and clearly), declare (emphatically)*

ἀποφθέγγομαι	VIPD--1S	ἀποφθέγγομαι
	VIPO--1S	"

ἀποφορτίζομαι of the cargo of a ship *unload* (AC 21.3)

ἀποφορτιζόμενον	VPPDNN-S	ἀποφορτίζομαι
	VPPONN-S	"
ἀποφυγόντας	VPAAAM-P	ἀποφεύγω
ἀποφυγόντες	VPAANM-P	"
ἀπόχρησει	N-DF-S	ἀπόχρησις

ἀπόχρησις, εως, ἡ as an action *consuming* (by use), *using up* (CO 2.22)

ἀποχωρεῖ	VIPA--3S	ἀποχωρέω
ἀποχωρεῖτε	VMPA--2P	"

ἀποχωρέω 1aor. ἀπεχώρησα; *go away from* someone, *depart* (MT 7.23); in a stronger sense *desert, abandon* (AC 13.13); of unclean spirits *withdraw, leave* (LU 9.39)

ἀποχωρήσαντες	VPAANM-P	ἀποχωρέω
ἀποχωρήσας	VPAANM-S	"

ἀποχωρίζω 1aor. pass. ἀπεχωρίσθην; (1) of persons *cause to leave, separate*; (2) passive *be separated from* someone, *part company, go on one's own way* (AC 15.39); of things *be swept aside, be split off, disappear* (RV 6.14)

ἀποχωρισθῆναι	VNAP	ἀποχωρίζω
ἀποψυχόντων	VPPAGM-P	ἀποψύχω

ἀποψύχω physically *faint dead away, lose consciousness*; in an extreme sense *stop breathing, die* (perhaps LU 21.26); of an effect of fear *feel fainthearted, be dismayed* (probably LU 21.26)

Ἀππίου	N-GM-S	Ἀππίου Φόρον

Ἀππίου Φόρον, τό *Appii Forum, Forum* or *Marketplace of Appius*, a market town on the Appian Way, 43 Roman miles south of Rome (AC 28.15)

ἀπρόσιτον	A--AN-S	ἀπρόσιτος

ἀπρόσιτος, ον *unapproachable, not to be approached, inaccessible* (1T 6.16)

ἀπρόσκοποι	A--NM-P	ἀπρόσκοπος
ἀπρόσκοπον	A--AF-S	"

ἀπρόσκοπος, ον strictly *not stumbling* or *jarring against* anything; hence *blameless, void of offense* (PH 1.10); of the conscience *clear* (AC 24.16); in relation to others *giving no offense, causing no trouble* (1C 10.32)

ἀπροσωπολήμπτως (also **ἀπροσωπολήπτως**) adverb; *impartially, without respect of persons* (1P 1.17)

ἀπροσωπολήμπτως	AB	ἀπροσωπολήμπτως
ἀπροσωπολήπτως	AB	"

ἄπταιστος, ον strictly *not stumbling*; hence, in a moral sense *free from offense, without fault* (JU 24)

ἀπταίστους	A--AM-P	ἄπταιστος
ἅπτει	VIPA--3S	ἅπτω
ἅπτεσθαι	VNPM	"
ἅπτεσθε	VMPM--2P	"
ἅπτεται	VIPM--3S	"
ἅπτηται	VSPM--3S	"
ἅπτου	VMPM--2S	"
ἀπτύξας	VPAANM-S	see ἀναπτύξας

ἅπτω 1aor. ἦψα, mid. ἡψάμην; (1) active, of a fire *light, kindle* (AC 28.2; LU 22.55); (2) middle; (a) literally *touch, take hold of, hold* (JN 20.17); of food *touch, eat* (CO 2.21); (b) figuratively and euphemistically ἅπτεσθαι γυναικός literally *touch a woman*, i.e. *have sexual intercourse with a woman* (1C 7.1); with the implication of conveying divine blessing or power through physical contact *touch* (MK 10.13; LU 8.46); in a negative sense *harm* (1J 5.18)

Ἀπφία, ας, ἡ *Apphia*, feminine proper noun (PM 2)

Ἀπφίᾳ	N-DF-S	Ἀπφία
ἀπωθεῖσθε	VIPM--2P	ἀπωθέω

ἀπωθέω 1aor. mid. ἀπωσάμην; literally *push aside, thrust off from oneself, drive away* (AC 7.27); figuratively *reject, repudiate, refuse to listen to* (RO 11.1)

ἀπώλεια, ας, ἡ *destruction, ruin*; (1) transitively, as the result of disregard for the value of something *waste* (MK 14.4); (2) intransitively, of the destruction that one experiences *(utter) ruin, (complete) loss* (1T 6.9); as the eternal punishment of the wicked *destruction* (2P 3.7)

ἀπώλεια	N-NF-S	ἀπώλεια
ἀπωλείαις	N-DF-P	"
ἀπώλειαν	N-AF-S	"
ἀπωλείας	N-GF-S	"

ἀπώλεσα	VIAA--1S	ἀπόλλυμι
ἀπώλεσε(ν)	VIAA--3S	"
ἀπώλετο	VIAM--3S	"
ἀπώλλυντο	VIIP--3P	"
ἀπώλοντο	VIAM--3P	"
ἀπών	VPPANM-S	ἄπειμι (1)
ἀπωσάμενοι	VPAMNM-P	ἀπωθέω
ἀπώσαντο	VIAM--3P	"
ἀπώσατο	VIAM--3S	"
Ἀρ		see Ἁρμαγεδών

ἄρα   inferential particle; (1) denoting transition in natural sequence to show correspondence *accordingly, then* (MT 12.28; LU 11.48); (2) denoting logical inference *therefore, consequently, so; you may be sure, then* (RO 7.25); (3) in questions, drawing an inference from what precedes, referring to (a) possibility *then* (MT 19.25) or (b) uncertainty *perhaps* (AC 12.18); (4) emphasizing the result in the consequence clause of conditional sentences *in that case, then, as a result* (1C 15.14)

ἄρα	CH	ἄρα
	QT	"

ἄρα   an interrogative inferential particle indicating anxiety or impatience, used only in direct questions *then, indeed, ever* (GA 2.17); often left untranslated (LU 18.8)

ἄρα	CH	ἄρα
	QT	"

ἀρά, ᾶς, ἡ   originally *wish, prayer*; more commonly a prayer for evil to come on someone *curse* (RO 3.14)

Ἄραβες	N-NM-P	Ἄραψ

Ἀραβία, ας, ἡ   *Arabia*; (1) a country east and south of Damascus (GA 1.17); (2) a name for the Sinai Peninsula as inhabited by Arabs (GA 4.25)

Ἀραβίᾳ	N-DF-S	Ἀραβία
Ἀραβίαν	N-AF-S	"

Ἄραβοι, ων, οἱ   from Ἄραψ (*Arab, Arabian*); perhaps incorrectly from the genitive plural Ἀράβων *Arabs* (AC 2.11)

Ἄραβοι	N-NM-P	Ἄραβοι
ἄραγε	CH	see ἄρα and γέ
ἀράγε	QT	see ἄρα and γέ
ἄραι	VNAA	αἴρω

Ἀράμ, ὁ   indeclinable; *Aram*, masculine proper noun

ἄραντες	VPAANM-P	αἴρω
ἄρας	VPAANM-S	"
ἀρᾶς	N-GF-S	ἀρά
ἄρατε	VMAA--2P	αἴρω
ἀράτω	VMAA--3S	"

ἄραφος, ον (also ἄρραφος)   of a robe *not sewn, seamless* (JN 19.23)

ἄραφος	A--NM-S	ἄραφος

Ἄραψ, βος, ὁ   *Arab, Arabian* (AC 2.11)

ἀργά	A--NN-P	ἀργός
ἀργαί	A--NF-P	"
ἀργεῖ	VIPA--3S	ἀργέω

ἀργέω   *be idle, do nothing*; literally, of a field *be left unplowed and unseeded*; figuratively οὐκ ἀργεῖ of God's judgment that is already prepared for the wicked literally *not be idle*, i.e. *be in force, not be delayed* (2P 2.3)

ἀργή	A--NF-S	ἀργός
ἀργοί	A--NM-P	"
ἀργόν	A--AN-S	"

ἀργός, ή, όν   from ἀ (*not*) and ἔργον (*work*); *inactive, not working*; (1) of persons with nothing to do *idle, unemployed* (MT 20.3); (2) of persons wanting nothing to do *lazy, idle, neglectful* (1T 5.13); (3) of things *useless, unprofitable, worthless* (JA 2.20; possibly MT 12.36); (4) of what is said *without careful thought, careless* (possibly MT 12.36)

ἀργούς	A--AM-P	ἀργός
ἀργυρᾶ	A--AN-P	ἀργυροῦς
	A--NN-P	"
ἀργύρια	N-AN-P	ἀργύριον

ἀργύριον, ου, τό   (1) as a metal *silver* (1C 3.12); (2) by metonymy *money* (AC 8.20); as a specific silver coin *piece of silver*, (Attic) *drachma* (AC 19.19); (Hebrew) *silver shekel* (MT 26.15)

ἀργύριον	N-AN-S	ἀργύριον
	N-NN-S	"
ἀργυρίου	N-GN-S	"
ἀργυρίῳ	N-DN-S	"

ἀργυροκόπος, ου, ὁ   *silversmith, worker in silver* (AC 19.24)

ἀργυροκόπος	N-NM-S	ἀργυροκόπος
ἄργυρον	N-AM-S	ἄργυρος

ἄργυρος, ου, ὁ   as a metal *silver* (AC 17.29); by metonymy *money* (MT 10.9)

ἄργυρος	N-NM-S	ἄργυρος
ἀργύρου	N-GM-S	"
ἀργυροῦν	A--AM-S	ἀργυροῦς

ἀργυροῦς, ᾶ, οῦν   *(made of) silver* (AC 19.24)

ἀργυροῦς	A--AM-P	ἀργυροῦς
ἀργύρῳ	N-DM-S	ἄργυρος
ἀρεῖ	VIFA--3S	αἴρω
Ἄρειον	A--AM-S	Ἄρειος Πάγος
Ἀρειοπαγίτης	N-NM-S	see Ἀρεοπαγίτης

Ἄρειος Πάγος, ὁ (also Ἄριος Πάγος)   transliterated into English as *Areopagus*, meaning *Hill of Ares* (the Greek god of war); (1) a hill northwest of the Acropolis in Athens and overlooking the marketplace (AC 17.19); (2) by metonymy, an advisory council meeting there *council of Areopagus* (AC 17.22)

Ἀρείου	A--GM-S	Ἄρειος Πάγος
Ἀρεμαθείας	N-GM-S	Ἀριμαθαία
ἄρενα	N-AM-S	ἄρσην
Ἀρεοπαγείτης	N-NM-S	see Ἀρεοπαγίτης

Ἀρεοπαγίτης, ου, ὁ   *Areopagite*, a member of the court or council that met on the Areopagus, a hill in Athens (AC 17.34)

Ἀρεοπαγίτης	N-NM-S	Ἀρεοπαγίτης
ἀρέσαι	VNAA	ἀρέσκω
ἀρεσάσης	VPAAGF-S	"
ἀρέσει	VIFA--3S	"
ἀρέσῃ	VSAA--3S	"

ἀρεσκεία, ας, ἡ   subjectively *desire* or *willingness to please*, in either a good or bad sense; objectively *pleasing, what pleases* (CO 1.10)

ἀρεσκείαν	N-AF-S	ἀρεσκεία
ἀρέσκειν	VNPA	ἀρέσκω
ἀρεσκέτω	VMPA--3S	"
ἀρέσκοντες	VPPANM-P	"
ἀρεσκόντων	VPPAGM-P	"

ἀρέσκω   impf. ἤρεσκον; 1aor. ἤρεσα; (1) of having favor *please, be pleasing to, be acceptable to* someone (MT

14.6); (2) of seeking favor *(strive to) please, accommodate, win over* (GA 1.10)

ἀρέσκω	VIPA--1S	ἀρέσκω
ἀρεστά	A--AN-P	ἀρεστός
ἀρεστόν	A--NN-S	"

ἀρεστός, ή, όν *pleasing, acceptable*; neuter plural τὰ ἀρεστά as a substantive *pleasing things* (JN 8.29); impersonally οὐκ ἀρεστόν ἐστιν *it is not desirable, right, proper* (AC 6.2)

Ἀρέτα	N-GM-S	Ἀρέτας

Ἀρέτας, α, ὁ *Aretas*, masculine proper noun (2C 11.32)

ἀρετάς	N-AF-P	ἀρετή

ἀρετή, ῆς, ἡ (1) generally, of a good quality of any kind *excellence, goodness, valor*; (2) as ascribed to God *excellence, praise*; concretely *wonderful deed* (1P 2.9); (3) as a manifestation of God's grace *goodness, power* (2P 1.3); (4) as a moral characteristic *virtue, uprightness, goodness* (2P 1.5), opposite κακία (*depravity, vice*)

ἀρετή	N-NF-S	ἀρετή
ἀρετῇ	N-DF-S	"
ἀρετήν	N-AF-S	"
ἀρετῆς	N-GF-S	"
ἄρη	VSAA--3S	αἴρω
Ἀρηί		Ἀρνί

ἀρήν, ἀρνός, ὁ as young offspring of sheep *lamb* (LU 10.3)

ἄρης	VSAA--2S	αἴρω
ἀρθῇ	VSAP--3S	"
ἀρθήσεται	VIFP--3S	"
ἄρθητι	VMAP--2S	"
ἀρθήτω	VMAP--3S	"
ἀρθῶσι(ν)	VSAP--3P	"

ἀριθμέω 1aor. ἠρίθμησα; pf. pass. ἠρίθμημαι; as determining quantity *count, number, reckon*

ἀριθμῆσαι	VNAA	ἀριθμέω
ἀριθμόν	N-AM-S	ἀριθμός

ἀριθμός, οῦ, ὁ (1) as an identification of quantity *number* (LU 22.3); (2) *total, sum, number* (AC 6.7)

ἀριθμός	N-NM-S	ἀριθμός
ἀριθμοῦ	N-GM-S	"
ἀριθμῷ	N-DM-S	"

Ἀριμαθαία, ας, ἡ (also **Ἀρεμαθεία, Ἀριμαθαία, Ἀριμαθία**) *Arimathea*, a city in Judea

Ἀριμαθαίας	N-GF-S	Ἀριμαθαία
Ἀριμαθαίας	N-GF-S	"
Ἀριμαθείας	N-GF-S	see Ἀριμαθαίας
Ἀριμαθίας	N-GF-S	Ἀριμαθαία
Ἄριον	A--AM-S	Ἄρειος Πάγος
Ἀρίου	A--GM-S	"
Ἀρίσταρχον	N-AM-S	Ἀρίσταρχος

Ἀρίσταρχος, ου, ὁ *Aristarchus*, masculine proper noun

Ἀρίσταρχος	N-NM-S	Ἀρίσταρχος
Ἀριστάρχου	N-GM-S	"

ἀριστάω 1aor. ἠρίστησα; (1) *take the first meal* of the day, *eat breakfast* (JN 21.12); (2) of any meal *eat, dine* (LU 11.37)

ἀριστερά	AP-NF-S	ἀριστερός

ἀριστερός, ά, όν *left*, opposite δεξιός (*right*); plural, of weapons used with the left hand *for defense* (2C 6.7); substantivally ἡ ἀριστερά *the left hand* (MT 6.3); the *left side, on the left*, i.e. *less important position* (MK 10.37; LU 23.33)

ἀριστερῶν	A--GN-P	ἀριστερός
ἀριστήσατε	VMAA--2P	ἀριστάω
ἀριστήσῃ	VSAA--3S	"
ἀριστήσω	VSAA--1S	"

Ἀριστόβουλος, ου, ὁ *Aristobulus*, masculine proper noun (RO 16.10)

Ἀριστοβούλου	N-GM-S	Ἀριστόβουλος

ἄριστον, ου, τό (1) strictly, the early meal of the day *breakfast, lunch* (LU 14.12); (2) later extended in meaning, the more important meal *noon meal, dinner* (MT 22.4); (3) generally *meal* (LU 11.38)

ἄριστον	N-AN-S	ἄριστον
ἀρίστου	N-GN-S	"
ἀρκεῖ	VIPA--3S	ἀρκέω
ἀρκεῖσθε	VMPP--2P	"
ἀρκέσῃ	VSAA--3S	"
ἀρκεσθησόμεθα	VIFP--1P	"
ἀρκετόν	A--NN-S	ἀρκετός

ἀρκετός, ή, όν *sufficient, enough, adequate*

ἀρκετός	A--NM-S	ἀρκετός

ἀρκέω 1aor. ἤρκεσα; 1fut. pass. ἀρκεσθήσομαι; (1) active *be enough, be sufficient, be adequate* (2C 12.9); (2) passive *be satisfied, be contented with* something (LU 3.14)

ἄρκος, ου, ὁ and ἡ (also **ἄρκτος**) *bear* (RV 13.2)

ἄρκου	N-GF-S	ἄρκος
	N-GM-S	"
ἀρκούμενοι	VPPPNM-P	ἀρκέω
ἀρκούμενος	VPPPNM-S	"
ἀρκοῦσι(ν)	VIPA--3P	"
ἄρκτου	N-GF-S	ἄρκος
	N-GM-S	"

ἅρμα, ατος, τό (1) as a travel vehicle *chariot, carriage* (AC 8.28); (2) as used in war *war chariot* (RV 9.9)

ἅρμα	N-AN-S	ἅρμα
Ἀρμαγεδδών		Ἀρμαγεδών

Ἀρμαγεδών, τό (also **Ἀρμαγεδδών, Ἀρ Μαγεδών**) indeclinable; *Armageddon*, a Hebrew place-name meaning *Mount* or *Hill of Megiddo* and generally identified as the fortress overlooking a pass through the Carmel Range into Galilee (RV 16.16)

ἅρματι	N-DN-S	ἅρμα
ἅρματος	N-GN-S	"
ἁρμάτων	N-GN-P	"
Ἀρμίν		Ἀδμίν

ἁρμόζω 1aor. mid. ἡρμοσάμην; transitively *fit together, join*; active/middle *promise to, give in marriage, be engaged to*; figuratively, of union with Christ (2C 11.2)

ἁρμός, οῦ, ὁ of the parts where bones come together *joint* (HE 4.12)

ἁρμῶν	N-GM-P	ἁρμός
ἄρνας	N-AM-P	ἀρήν
Ἀρνεί		Ἀρνί
ἀρνεῖσθαι	VNPD	ἀρνέομαι
	VNPO	"

ἀρνέομαι impf. ἠρνούμην; fut. ἀρνήσομαι; 1aor. ἠρνησάμην; pf. ἤρνημαι; (1) in relation to a question or demand *deny* (LU 8.45), opposite ὁμολογέω (*admit, confess*); (2) in relation to a claim *refuse, disown, not* consent to (HE 11.24); (3) in relation to God or a person *deny, disown, renounce* (1J 2.23); (4) in relation to the Christian faith, usually in the sense of apostasy *deny, repudiate* (1T 5.8); (5) as saying no to oneself in order to live wholly for Christ *disregard, pay no attention to one's own desires* (LU 9.23); as turning from ungodly conduct *renounce, deny* (TI 2.12); (6) as acting contrary to one's true character *be untrue, be false to oneself* (2T 2.13)

ἀρνησάμενοι	VPADNM-P	ἀρνέομαι
ἀρνησάμενος	VPADNM-P	"
ἀρνήσασθαι	VNAD	"
ἀρνησάσθω	VMAD--3S	"
ἀρνήσεται	VIFD--3S	"
ἀρνήση	VIFD--2S	"
ἀρνήσηται	VSAD--3S	"
ἀρνήσομαι	VIFD--1S	"
ἀρνησόμεθα	VIFD--1P	"

Ἀρνί, ὁ (also Ἀρηί, Ἀρνεί, Ἀρνίν) indeclinable; *Arni*, masculine proper noun (LU 3.33)

ἀρνία	N-AN-P	ἀρνίον
Ἀρνίν		Ἀρνί

ἀρνίον, ου, τό originally a diminutive of ἀρήν; *sheep, lamb* (RV 13.11); metaphorically in Revelation (except 13.11) as a designation of Christ, the atoning sacrifice *lamb*; plural as a designation of Christ's followers, needing help and care *lambs* (JN 21.15)

ἀρνίον	N-NN-S	ἀρνίον
ἀρνίου	N-GN-S	"
ἀρνίῳ	N-DN-S	
ἀρνός	N-GM-S	ἀρήν
ἀρνούμεθα	VIPD--1P	ἀρνέομαι
	VIPO--1P	"
ἀρνούμενοι	VPPDNM-P	"
	VPPONM-P	"
ἀρνούμενος	VPPDNM-S	"
	VPPONM-S	"
ἀρνουμένων	VPPDGM-P	"
	VPPOGM-P	"
ἀρνοῦνται	VIPD--3P	"
	VIPO--3P	"
ἀρξάμενοι	VPAMNM-P	ἄρχω
ἀρξάμενον	VPAMAN-S	"
ἀρξάμενος	VPAMNM-S	"
ἀρξαμένου	VPAMGM-S	"
ἀρξαμένων	VPAMGM-P	"
ἄρξασθαι	VNAM	"
ἄρξεσθε	VIFM--2P	"
ἄρξη	VIFM--2S	"
ἄρξησθε	VIFM--2P	see ἄρξεσθε
	VSAM--2P	ἄρχω
ἄρξηται	VSAM--3S	"
ἄρξονται	VIFM--3P	"
ἄρξωνται	VSAM--3P	"
ἄρον	VMAA--2S	αἴρω
ἀροτριᾶν	VNPA	ἀροτριάω

ἀροτριάω as preparing soil for planting *plow* (LU 17.7)

ἀροτριῶν	VPPANM-S	ἀροτριάω
ἀροτριῶντα	VPPAAM-S	"

ἄροτρον, ου, τό as an instrument for cultivating soil for planting *plow* (LU 9.62)

ἄροτρον	N-AN-S	ἄροτρον
ἀροῦσι(ν)	VIFA--3P	αἴρω
ἅρπαγας	AP-AM-P	ἅρπαξ
ἁρπαγέντα	VPAPAM-S	ἁρπάζω
ἅρπαγες	AP-NM-P	ἅρπαξ
	A--NM-P	"

ἁρπαγή, ῆς, ἡ (1) as an action of carrying off someone's belongings by force *robbery, plundering* (HE 10.34); (2) concretely *what has been seized, plunder, booty* (probably MT 23.25); (3) as an attitude *greediness, covetousness* (LU 11.39; perhaps MT 23.25)

ἁρπαγήν	N-AF-S	ἁρπαγή
ἁρπαγῆς	N-GF-S	"
ἁρπαγησόμεθα	VIFP--1P	ἁρπάζω
ἁρπαγμόν	N-AM-S	ἁρπαγμός

ἁρπαγμός, οῦ, ὁ (1) literally *something seized and held, plunder*; (2) figuratively in PH 2.6 of Jesus' equality with God οὐχ ἁρπαγμόν; (a) possibly, as not forcefully grasping something one does not have *something not to be seized, not a prize to be seized*; (b) probably, as not forcefully retaining something for one's own advantage *something not to be held onto, not a piece of good fortune*

ἁρπάζει	VIPA--3S	ἁρπάζω
ἁρπάζειν	VNPA	"
ἁρπάζετε	VMPA--2P	"
ἁρπάζοντες	VPPANM-P	"
ἁρπάζουσι(ν)	VIPA--3P	"

ἁρπάζω fut. ἁρπάσω; 1aor. ἥρπασα; 1aor. pass. ἡρπάσθην; 2aor. pass. ἡρπάγην; (1) as forcibly taking someone or something *snatch, seize, take away* (JN 6.15); (2) as the action of thieves and wild beasts *steal, carry off, drag away* (JN 10.12); (3) of seed already sown *carry off, snatch away* (MT 13.19); (4) of an ecstatic vision or experience *catch up* or *away* (2C 12.2); (5) ἁ. in MT 11.12 has two possible meanings: (a) *seize on eagerly, appropriate* (the kingdom); (b) *attack and seize* (the kingdom) as a violent or forcible person would do; since ἁ. is used with βιάζεται (*suffer violently, be treated violently*) and βιασταί (*violent people*), the second is preferable

ἅρπαξ, gen. αγος (1) *vicious, ravenous, destructive*, like a wild animal (MT 7.15); (2) *violently greedy* (LU 18.11); substantivally *robber, swindler* (1C 6.10)

ἅρπαξ	A--NM-S	ἅρπαξ
ἅρπαξι(ν)	AP-DM-P	"
ἁρπάσαι	VNAA	ἁρπάζω
ἁρπάσαντες	VPAANM-P	"
ἁρπάσατε	VIAA--2P	"
ἁρπάσει	VIFA--3S	"
ἁρπάση	VSAA--3S	"

ἀρραβών, ῶνος, ὁ transliterated from the Hebrew; literally, as a legal and commercial technical term, an advance transaction that guarantees the validity of a contract or a full purchase price *down payment, first installment, pledge*; figuratively in the NT, of the gift of the Holy Spirit to believers (2C 1.22)

ἀρραβών	N-NM-S	ἀρραβών
ἀρραβῶνα	N-AM-S	"
ἄρραφος	A--NM-S	ἄραφος

ἄρρενα	AP-AN-P	ἄρσην
	A--AM-S	"
ἄρρενες	AP-NM-P	"
ἄρρεσι(ν)	AP-DM-P	"
ἄρρητα	A--AN-P	ἄρρητος

ἄρρητος, ον (1) of what cannot be expressed in words *inexpressible, unspeakable*; (2) of what should not or must not be expressed *too sacred* (2C 12.4)

ἀρρωστέω *be sick* or *ill* (MT 14.14)

ἄρρωστοι	A--NM-P	ἄρρωστος
ἀρρώστοις	A--DM-P	"

ἄρρωστος, ον strictly *without strength*; hence *sickly, infirm, disabled*; substantivally *sick person* (MK 6.5)

ἀρρωστοῦντας	VPPAAM-P	ἀρρωστέω
ἀρρώστους	A--AM-P	ἄρρωστος
ἄρσεν	AP-AN-S	ἄρσην
	AP-NN-S	"
ἄρσενα	AP-AM-S	"
	A--AM-S	"
ἄρσενες	AP-NM-P	"
ἀρσενοκοῖται	N-NM-P	ἀρσενοκοίτης
ἀρσενοκοίταις	N-DM-P	"

ἀρσενοκοίτης, ου, ὁ an adult male who practices sexual intercourse with another adult male or a boy *homosexual, sodomite, pederast*

ἄρσεσι(ν)	AP-DM-P	ἄρσην

ἄρσην, εν, gen. ενος (also **ἄρρην**) *male, of the male sex*, opposite θῆλυς (*female*); substantivally τὸ ἄρσεν *(the) male sex* (MT 19.4), *male child* (RV 12.5); ὁ ἄ. *(the) male, (the) man* (RO 1.27)

Ἀρτεμᾶν	N-AM-S	Ἀρτεμᾶς

Ἀρτεμᾶς, ᾶ, ὁ *Artemas*, masculine proper noun (TI 3.12)

Ἀρτέμιδος	N-GF-S	Ἄρτεμις

Ἄρτεμις, ιδος, ἡ *Artemis*, name of a Greek goddess (Roman Diana)

Ἄρτεμις	N-NF-S	Ἄρτεμις
ἀρτέμονα	N-AM-S	see ἀρτέμωνα

ἀρτέμων, ωνος, ὁ a cloth hoisted on a ship to catch the wind *sail*; probably *foresail*, a small sail hoisted in wind too strong for larger sails (AC 27.40)

ἀρτέμωνα	N-AM-S	ἀρτέμων

ἄρτι adverb of time; (1) *now, at the present moment* (JN 9.19); (2) of the immediate present *presently, right now, at once* (MT 26.53); idiomatically ἡ ἄ. ὥρα literally *the present hour*, i.e. *this very moment* (1C 4.11); (3) of the immediate past *just now, recently* (MT 9.18); (4) in prepositional phrases: ἕως ἄ. *until now, up to now, hitherto* (MT 11.12); ἀπ' ἄ. *from this time, henceforth, from now on* (JN 13.19)

ἄρτι	AB	ἄρτι
ἀρτιγέννητα	A--NN-P	ἀρτιγέννητος

ἀρτιγέννητος, ον *newly* or *recently born* (1P 2.2)

ἄρτιος, ία, ον of one able to meet all demands *qualified, fully ready, perfectly fit* (2T 3.17)

ἄρτιος	A--NM-S	ἄρτιος
ἄρτοι	N-NM-P	ἄρτος
ἄρτοις	N-DM-P	"
ἄρτον	N-AM-S	"

ἄρτος, ου, ὁ (1) *bread, loaf of bread* (MT 4.3); (2) by metonymy *food, nourishment* (LU 15.17)

ἄρτος	N-NM-S	ἄρτος

ἄρτου	N-GM-S	"
ἄρτους	N-AM-P	"
ἀρτυθήσεται	VIFP--3S	ἀρτύω
ἀρτύσεται	VIFM--3S	"
ἀρτύσετε	VIFA--2P	"

ἀρτύω fut. ἀρτύσω; pf. pass. ἤρτυμαι; 1fut. pass. ἀρτυθήσομαι; literally *prepare, make ready*; of food, *season, make tasty* (LU 14.34); idiomatically, of profitable or beneficial speech ἅλατι ἠρτυμένος literally *seasoned with salt*, i.e. *wisely spoken* (CO 4.6)

ἄρτῳ	N-DM-S	ἄρτος
ἄρτων	N-GM-P	"

Ἀρφαξάδ, ὁ indeclinable; *Arphaxad*, masculine proper noun (LU 3.36)

ἀρχάγγελος, ου, ὁ *archangel, chief angel, very important leader among the angels*

ἀρχάγγελος	N-NM-S	ἀρχάγγελος
ἀρχαγγέλου	N-GM-S	"
ἀρχαί	N-NF-P	ἀρχή
ἀρχαῖα	A--NN-P	ἀρχαῖος
ἀρχαίοις	A--DM-P	"
ἀρχαῖον	A--AM-S	"

ἀρχαῖος, αία, ον (1) of what was first or early in time *ancient, old* (RV 12.9); (2) of a disciple of long standing *veteran, early* (disciple) (AC 21.16); (3) of what existed in former times *ancient, old* (2P 2.5); (4) substantivally οἱ ἀρχαῖοι *people who lived long ago* (MT 5.21); τὰ ἀρχαῖα *what is old, what existed before* (2C 5.17)

ἀρχαῖος	A--NM-S	ἀρχαῖος
ἀρχαίου	A--GM-S	"
ἀρχαῖς	N-DF-P	ἀρχή
ἀρχαίῳ	A--DM-S	ἀρχαῖος
ἀρχαίων	A--GF-P	"
	A--GM-P	"
ἀρχάς	N-AF-P	ἀρχή
ἄρχειν	VNPA	ἄρχω

Ἀρχέλαος, ου, ὁ *Archelaus*, masculine proper noun (MT 2.22)

Ἀρχέλαος	N-NM-S	Ἀρχέλαος
ἀρχεύς	N-NM-S	see ἀρχιερεύς

ἀρχή, ῆς, ἡ strictly *primacy*; (1) in relation to place *corner* of a cloth (AC 10.11); (2) in relation to time *beginning* of anything (MT 24.8), *(the) first* (JN 2.11), opposite τέλος (*end, cessation*); of first teaching *elementary* (HE 6.1); ἀπ' ἀρχῆς, ἐξ ἀρχῆς *from the first, originally* (JN 6.64; 15.27); ἐν ἀρχῇ, κατ' ἀρχάς *in the beginning, at the first* (JN 1.1; HE 1.10); τὴν ἀρχήν in JN 8.25 is probably adverbial *at all*, possibly *to begin with*; (3) in relation to rank *(position of) power, rule, domain* (EP 1.21); as a person with authority or a supernatural being *ruler, authority* (RO 8.38)

ἀρχή	N-NF-S	ἀρχή
ἀρχῇ	N-DF-S	"
ἀρχηγόν	N-AM-S	ἀρχηγός

ἀρχηγός, οῦ, ὁ (1) strictly *one who goes first on the path*; hence *leader, prince, pioneer* (HE 2.10); (2) as one who causes something to begin *originator, founder, initiator* (HE 12.2)

ἀρχήν	N-AF-S	ἀρχή
ἀρχῆς	N-GF-S	"

ἀρχιδεσμοφύλαξ, ακος, ὁ   as the chief officer in charge of a place where prisoners are bound and kept *chief jailer* (AC 16.36; cf. Genesis 39.21–23 Septuagint)

ἀρχιδεσμοφύλαξ	N-NM-S	ἀρχιδεσμοφύλαξ

ἀρχιερατικός, όν *high priestly, belonging to the chief priest* (AC 4.6)

ἀρχιερατικοῦ	A--GN-S	ἀρχιερατικός
ἀρχιερέα	N-AM-S	ἀρχιερεύς
ἀρχιερεῖ	N-DM-S	"
ἀρχιερεῖς	N-AM-P	"
	N-NM-P	"

ἀρχιερεύς, έως, ὁ *high priest, chief priest*; plural *principal priests, most important priests* (MT 2.4)

ἀρχιερεύς	N-NM-S	ἀρχιερεύς
ἀρχιερεῦσι(ν)	N-DM-P	"
ἀρχιερέων	N-GM-P	"
ἀρχιερέως	N-GM-S	"

ἀρχιλῃστής, οῦ, ὁ *robber chieftain, chief of a robber band* (JN 18.40)

ἀρχιλῃστής	N-NM-S	ἀρχιλῃστής
ἀρχιποίμενος	N-GM-S	ἀρχιποίμην

ἀρχιποίμην, ενος, ὁ literally, as one who directs other shepherds *chief shepherd*; metaphorically, of Christ as in charge of leaders of Christian communities (1P 5.4)

Ἄρχιππος, ου, ὁ *Archippus*, masculine proper noun

Ἀρχίππῳ	N-DM-S	Ἄρχιππος
ἀρχισυνάγωγοι	N-NM-P	ἀρχισυνάγωγος
ἀρχισυνάγωγον	N-AM-S	"

ἀρχισυνάγωγος, ου, ὁ *president, chief officer, leader of a (Jewish) synagogue*

ἀρχισυνάγωγος	N-NM-S	ἀρχισυνάγωγος
ἀρχισυναγώγου	N-GM-S	"
ἀρχισυναγώγῳ	N-DM-S	"
ἀρχισυναγώγων	N-GM-P	"

ἀρχιτέκτων, ονος, ὁ *architect, head* or *master builder* (1C 3.10)

ἀρχιτέκτων	N-NM-S	ἀρχιτέκτων

ἀρχιτελώνης, ου, ὁ *chief tax collector, tax commissioner* (LU 19.2)

ἀρχιτελώνης	N-NM-S	ἀρχιτελώνης

ἀρχιτρίκλινος, ου, ὁ as the slave or steward responsible for managing a feast or important meal *head waiter, butler, master of the feast* (JN 2.8)

ἀρχιτρίκλινος	N-NM-S	ἀρχιτρίκλινος
ἀρχιτρικλίνῳ	N-DM-S	"
ἀρχόμεθα	VIPM--1P	ἄρχω
ἀρχόμενος	VPPMNM-S	"
ἀρχομένων	VPPMGN-P	"
ἄρχοντα	N-AM-S	ἄρχων
ἄρχοντας	N-AM-P	"
ἄρχοντες	N-NM-P	"
	N-VM-P	"
ἄρχοντι	N-DM-S	"
ἄρχοντος	N-GM-S	"
ἀρχόντων	N-GM-P	"

ἀρχοστάσια, ων, τά equivalent to ἡ ἀρχαιρεσία *tendency to choose and follow one leader above others* (1C 3.3)

ἀρχοστάσια	N-NN-P	ἀρχοστάσια
ἄρχουσι(ν)	N-DM-P	ἄρχων

ἄρχω fut. mid. ἄρξομαι; 1aor. mid. ἠρξάμην; literally *be first*; (1) active *rule over, be leader of* (MK 10.42); (2) middle *begin, start* (MT 20.8); predominately as an auxiliary verb with a present infinitive used to draw attention to some element in the story *begin (to)* (MT 26.37)

ἄρχων, οντος, ὁ strictly, the present participle of ἄρχω (*be first*); used as a substantive; (1) as a high official; (a) one exercising authority *official, (respected) leader* (MT 9.18); (b) one invested with power and dignity *ruler, lord, prince* (RO 13.3); (2) of the devil as the leader of the evil spirits in the supernatural world *prince, ruler* (MT 9.34)

ἄρχων	N-NM-S	ἄρχων
ἀρῶ	VIFA--1S	αἴρω

ἄρωμα, ατος, τό usually plural *spices, aromatic oils, perfumed salves*, especially for embalming the dead

ἀρώματα	N-AN-P	ἄρωμα
ἀρωμάτων	N-GN-P	"
ἀρῶσι	VIFA--3P	αἴρω
ἅς	APRAF-P	ὅς
Ἀσά		Ἀσάφ
ἀσαίνεσθαι	VNPP	see σαίνεσθαι
ἀσάλευτον	A--AF-S	ἀσάλευτος

ἀσάλευτος, ον literally *immovable, fixed* (AC 27.41); figuratively *firm, unchangeable, enduring* (HE 12.28)

ἀσάλευτος	A--NF-S	ἀσάλευτος

Ἀσάφ, ὁ (also Ἀσά, Ἀσσά) indeclinable; *Asaph* or *Asa*, masculine proper noun

ἄσβεστον	A--AN-S	ἄσβεστος

ἄσβεστος, ον of fire that cannot be put out *inextinguishable, unquenchable*

ἀσβέστου	A--GN-S	ἄσβεστος
ἀσβέστῳ	A--DN-S	"
ἀσεβεῖ	A--DM-S	ἀσεβής

ἀσέβεια, ας, ἡ as disregard for religious belief or practice *irreverence, godlessness, impiety*

ἀσεβείᾳ	N-DF-S	ἀσέβεια
ἀσέβειαν	N-AF-S	"
ἀσεβείας	N-AF-P	"
	N-GF-S	"
ἀσεβεῖν	VNPA	ἀσεβέω
ἀσεβεῖς	A--AM-P	ἀσεβής
	A--NM-P	"
ἀσεβειῶν	N-GF-P	ἀσέβεια
ἀσεβέσι(ν)	A--DM-P	ἀσεβής

ἀσεβέω 1aor. ἠσέβησα; as living without regard for religion either in belief or in practice *be ungodly, live wickedly, act profanely* (2P 2.6)

ἀσεβῆ	A--AM-S	ἀσεβής
ἀσεβήν	A--AM-S	see ἀσεβῆ

ἀσεβής, ές *ungodly, irreverent, godless* (2P 3.7); usually as a substantive ὁ ἀ. *ungodly* or *wicked person* (JU 15)

ἀσεβής	A--NM-S	ἀσεβής
ἀσεβί	A--DM-S	see ἀσεβεῖ
ἀσεβῶν	A--GM-P	ἀσεβής

ἀσέλγεια, ας, ἡ as living without any moral restraint *licentiousness, sensuality, lustful indulgence* (2C 12.21); especially as indecent and outrageous sexual behavior *debauchery, indecency, flagrant immorality* (RO 13.13)

ἀσέλγεια	N-NF-S	ἀσέλγεια
ἀσελγείᾳ	N-DF-S	"
ἀσελγείαις	N-DF-P	"

ἀσέλγειαν   N-AF-S   "

ἀσελγείας   N-GF-S   "

ἄσημος, ον strictly *not marked*; hence *obscure, insignificant*; of a city *unimportant, inferior* (AC 21.39)

ἀσήμου   A--GF-S   ἄσημος

Ἀσήρ, ὁ indeclinable; *Asher*, masculine proper noun; name of a tribe of Israel

ἀσθενεῖ   VIPA--3S   ἀσθενέω

ἀσθένεια, ας, ἡ as a state of incapacity *weakness, impotence*; literally, as bodily ailment *sickness, disease, infirmity* (LU 5.15); as physical inability *weakness* (HE 11.34), opposite δύναμις (*might, strength*); figuratively, as a quality of character *weakness, lack of insight* (RO 6.19); *timidity, feeling of inadequacy* (1C 2.3)

ἀσθένεια   N-NF-S   ἀσθένεια

ἀσθενείᾳ   N-DF-S   "

ἀσθενείαις   N-DF-P   "

ἀσθένειαν   N-AF-S   "

ἀσθενείας   N-AF-P   "

    N-GF-S   "

ἀσθενεῖς   A--AM-P   ἀσθενής

    A--NM-P   "

ἀσθενειῶν   N-GF-P   ἀσθένεια

ἀσθενές   A--AN-S   ἀσθενής

    A--NN-S   "

ἀσθενέσι(ν)   A--DM-P   "

ἀσθενέστερα   A-MNN-P   "

ἀσθενεστέρῳ   A-MDN-S   "

ἀσθενέω 1aor. ἠσθένησα; *be weak, be powerless*; (1) literally, of bodily ailment *be sick, be ill, be diseased* (LU 4.40); figuratively, of incapability of any kind *be weak, be incapable* (2C 12.10); of religious or moral weakness *be weak* (in faith) (RO 4.19); (2) economically *be in need, be poor* (AC 20.35)

ἀσθενῆ   A--AM-S   ἀσθενής

    A--AN-P   "

ἀσθένημα, ατος, τό *weakness, incapability*; figuratively τὰ ἀσθενήματα as the result of a conscience being bound to legalistic requirements *scruples, weaknesses, qualms, misgivings* (RO 15.1)

ἀσθενήματα   N-AN-P   ἀσθένημα

ἀσθενής, ές *weak, powerless*; (1) literally, of bodily ailment *weak, ill, sick* (AC 4.9), opposite ἰσχυρός (*strong, robust*); substantivally ὁ ἀ. *(the) sick person* (LU 10.9); of physical or intellectual inability *weak, inadequate* (MT 26.41); (2) figuratively, of what is less effective *weak, feeble, not strong* (1C 4.10); substantivally τὸ ἀσθενές *weak thing* (1C 1.27), opposite τὸ ἰσχυρόν (*strong thing*); of what is in a hopeless condition morally *weak, helpless* (RO 5.6); (3) comparative ἀσθενέστερος, τέρα, ον *weaker* (1P 3.7)

ἀσθενής   A--AM-S   ἀσθενής

    A--NF-S   "

    A--NM-S   "

ἀσθενήσας   VPAANM-S   ἀσθενέω

ἀσθενήσασαν   VPAAAF-S   "

ἀσθενοῦμεν   VIPA--1P   "

ἀσθενοῦντα   VPPAAM-S   "

ἀσθενοῦντας   VPPAAM-P   "

ἀσθενούντων   VPPAGM-P   "

ἀσθενοῦς   A--GM-S   ἀσθενής

ἀσθενοῦσα   VPPANF-S   ἀσθενέω

ἀσθενοῦσαν   VPPAAF-S   "

ἀσθενοῦσι(ν)   VPPADM-P   "

ἀσθενῶ   VIPA--1S   "

    VSPA--1S   "

ἀσθενῶμεν   VSPA--1P   "

ἀσθενῶν   A--GM-P   ἀσθενής

    A--GN-P   "

    VPPANM-S   ἀσθενέω

Ἀσία, ας, ἡ *Asia*, Roman province in western Asia Minor (AC 2.9)

Ἀσία   N-NF-S   Ἀσία

Ἀσίᾳ   N-DF-S   "

Ἀσίαν   N-AF-S   "

Ἀσιανοί   N-NM-P   Ἀσιανός

Ἀσιανός, οῦ, ὁ *native of Asia, Asian*, a person belonging to the Roman province of Asia in western Asia Minor (AC 20.4)

Ἀσιάρχης, ου, ὁ *Asiarch*, an officer or deputy in the province of Asia, a member of the assembly that met in Ephesus (AC 19.31)

Ἀσιαρχῶν   N-GM-P   Ἀσιάρχης

Ἀσίας   N-GF-S   Ἀσία

ἀσιτία, ας, ἡ as going without food *fasting, abstinence, being without appetite for food* (AC 27.21)

ἀσιτίας   N-GF-S   ἀσιτία

ἄσιτοι   A--NM-P   ἄσιτος

ἄσιτος, ον *fasting, without appetite for food* (AC 27.33)

ἀσκέω strictly *work* in various materials to fashion something; hence *engage in, practice*; absolutely, with an infinitive following *do one's best to, strive to, exert oneself to* (AC 24.16)

ἀσκοί   N-NM-P   ἀσκός

ἀσκός, οῦ, ὁ *leather bag*; especially *bottle made of skin, wineskin* (MT 9.17)

ἀσκούς   N-AM-P   ἀσκός

ἀσκῶ   VIPA--1S   ἀσκέω

ἀσμένως adverb; *gladly, joyfully* (AC 21.17)

ἀσμένως   AB   ἀσμένως

ἄσοφοι   A--NM-P   ἄσοφος

ἄσοφος, ον *without wisdom, foolish, unwise* (EP 5.15)

ἀσπάζεσθαι   VNPD   ἀσπάζομαι

    VNPO   "

ἀσπάζεται   VIPD--3S   "

    VIPO--3S   "

ἀσπάζομαι 1aor. ἠσπασάμην; strictly *embrace*; hence *greet, salute, express good wishes*; literally, of those entering a house *greet, salute* (LU 1.40); of meeting someone along the road *greet* (LU 10.4); of departing *take leave of, say good-bye to* (AC 20.1); in letters (often imperatively) *greet* someone, *remember* (the writer) *to* someone (RO 16.3); of short official visits *pay one's respects to* (AC 25.13); figuratively, of treating someone affectionately *be fond of, be friendly to* (MT 5.47); of things *be happy about, welcome, anticipate* (HE 11.13)

ἀσπάζομαι   VIPD--1S   ἀσπάζομαι

    VIPO--1S   "

ἀσπαζομένους   VPPDAM-P   "

    VPPOAM-P   "

ἀσπαζομένων   VPPDGM-P   "

    VPPOGM-P   "

ἀσπάζονται VIPD--3P "
    VIPO--3P "
ἀσπάζου VMPD--2S "
    VMPO--2S "
ἀσπασαι VMAD--2S "
ἀσπασάμενοι VPADNM-P "
ἀσπασάμενος VPADNM-S "
ἀσπάσασθε VMAD--2P "
ἀσπάσησθε VSAD--2P "
ἀσπασμόν N-AM-S ἀσπασμός
ἀσπασμός, οῦ, ὁ   as the use of set words or phrases to express a welcome or farewell *greeting, salutation*; (1) as a formal spoken greeting (MT 23.7); (2) as a written greeting at the close of a letter (1C 16.21)
ἀσπασμός N-NM-S ἀσπασμός
ἀσπασμοῦ N-GM-S "
ἀσπασμούς N-AM-P "
ἀσπασόμενοι VPADNM-P see ἀσπασάμενοι
ἀσπίδων N-GF-P ἀσπίς
ἄσπιλοι A--NM-P ἄσπιλος
ἄσπιλον A--AF-S "
    A--AM-S "
ἄσπιλος, ον   literally *spotless, without defect* (1P 1.19); figuratively, in a moral sense *pure, clean, uncorrupted* (JA 1.27)
ἀσπίλου A--GM-S ἄσπιλος
ἀσπίλους A--AM-P "
ἀσπίς, ίδος, ἡ   generally a snake with deadly venom *asp, viper* (RO 3.13)
ἄσπονδοι A--NM-P ἄσπονδος
ἄσπονδος, ον   strictly *unwilling to make a treaty*; hence *irreconcilable, unforgiving* (2T 3.3)
ἀσπόνδους A--AM-P ἄσπονδος
Ἀσσά Ἀσάφ
ἀσσάριον, ου, τό   diminutive of the Roman copper coin *as*; *assarion, penny*, worth about one-sixteenth of a denarius; the smallest coin, like a cent or halfpenny
ἀσσαρίου N-GN-S ἀσσάριον
ἀσσαρίων N-GN-P "
Ἀσσάρωνα N-AM-S Σαρών
*Ασσον N-AF-S *Ασσος
ἇσσον   comparative of ἄγχι (*near*); adverbially *nearer; very close, very near* (AC 27.13)
ἇσσον ABM ἇσσον
*Ασσος, ου, ἡ   *Assos*, a coastal city in Mysia in the Roman province of Asia in western Asia Minor
ἀστατέω   as being without a permanent home *be homeless* or *unsettled, wander from place to place* (1C 4.11)
ἀστατοῦμεν VIPA--1P ἀστατέω
ἀστεῖον A--AN-S ἀστεῖος
ἀστεῖος, εία, ον   strictly *belonging to a city*; hence *well-bred, acceptable, well-pleasing* (possibly AC 7.20); of bodily appearance *well-formed, beautiful, noble* (HE 11.23; possibly AC 7.20)
ἀστεῖος A--NM-S ἀστεῖος
ἀστέρα N-AM-S ἀστήρ
ἀστέρας N-AM-P "
ἀστέρες N-NM-P "
ἀστέρος N-GM-S "
ἀστέρων N-GM-P "

ἀστήρ, έρος, ὁ   literally *(single) star, luminous (heavenly) body like a star* (MT 2.2); metaphorically, of spiritual leaders, of Christ (RV 22.16), of those in charge of churches as Christ's messengers (RV 1.20), and of false teachers (JU 13)
ἀστήρ N-NM-S ἀστήρ
ἀστήρικτοι A--NM-P ἀστήρικτος
ἀστήρικτος, ον   having a tendency to change one's views and attitudes *unstable, unsteady, not settled* (2P 2.14); substantivally, of someone not settled in his thinking *unstable person* (2P 3.16)
ἀστηρίκτους A--AF-P ἀστήρικτος
ἄστοργοι A--NM-P ἄστοργος
ἄστοργος, ον   *devoid of natural affection, unloving, heartless*
ἀστόργους A--AM-P ἄστοργος
ἀστοχέω   1aor. ἠστόχησα; strictly *miss the mark*; hence *depart from, deviate from, go astray*, especially as failing to follow Christian teachings and principles (2T 2.18)
ἀστοχήσαντες VPAANM-P ἀστοχέω
ἄστρα N-NN-S ἄστρον
ἀστραπαί N-NF-P ἀστραπή
ἀστραπή, ῆς, ἡ   as a natural phenomenon *lightning* (MT 24.27); as light radiating from a lamp *bright beam, ray* (LU 11.36)
ἀστραπή N-NF-S ἀστραπή
ἀστραπῇ N-DF-S "
ἀστραπήν N-AF-S "
ἀστράπτει VIPA--3S ἀστράπτω
ἀστράπτουσα VPPANF-S "
ἀστραπτούσαις VPPADF-P "
ἀστραπτούσῃ VPPADF-S "
ἀστράπτω   as giving off a very bright light *flash, gleam*; of lightning *flash* (LU 17.24); of clothing *be dazzling, gleam, shine brilliantly* (LU 24.4)
ἄστροις N-DN-P ἄστρον
ἄστρον, ου, τό   *star, constellation of stars* (LU 21.25)
ἄστρον N-AN-S ἄστρον
ἄστρων N-GN-P "
Ἀσύγκριτον N-AM-S Ἀσύγκριτος
Ἀσύγκριτος, ου, ὁ (also Ἀσύνκριτος)   *Asyncritus*, masculine proper noun (RO 16.14)
ἀσύμφωνοι A--NM-P ἀσύμφωνος
ἀσύμφωνος, ον   literally *not harmonious*; figuratively, of persons *unable to come to an agreement, disagreeing, discordant* (AC 28.25)
ἀσύνετοι A--NM-P ἀσύνετος
ἀσύνετος, ον   *without understanding, unintelligent* (MT 15.16); in a moral sense *foolish, senseless* (RO 1.31)
ἀσύνετος A--NF-S ἀσύνετος
ἀσυνέτους A--AM-P "
ἀσυνέτῳ A--DN-S "
ἀσύνθετος, ον   strictly *covenant-breaking*; hence *not keeping a promise, untrustworthy, treacherous* (RO 1.31)
ἀσυνθέτους A--AM-P ἀσύνθετος
Ἀσύνκριτον N-AM-S Ἀσύγκριτος
ἀσφάλεια, ας, ἡ   literally, a state of being secured from falling *firmness, safety, security* (1TH 5.3); as a legal technical term for keeping a prisoner securely guarded *security* (AC 5.23); figuratively, of what qualified instruction affords *certainty, truth, reliability* (LU 1.4)

ἀσφάλεια	N-NF-S	ἀσφάλεια
ἀσφαλείᾳ	N-DF-S	"
ἀσφάλειαν	N-AF-S	"
ἀσφαλές	A--AN-S	ἀσφαλής
	A--NN-S	"
ἀσφαλῆ	A--AF-S	"
ἀσφαλῆν	A--AF-S	see ἀσφαλῆ

ἀσφαλής, ές (1) literally *firm, secure* (HE 6.19); figuratively, of a state of knowledge *certain, reliable, sure*; substantivally τὸ ἀσφαλές as what is certain or definite *the truth, the facts* (AC 21.34); (2) of a course of action *safe, free from danger* (PH 3.1)

ἀσφαλίζω 1aor. mid. ἠσφαλισάμην; 1aor. pass. ἠσφαλίσθην; middle for active in the NT; (1) of a prisoner *tie up, fasten* (AC 16.24); (2) of a tomb *make secure, guard* (MT 27.64)

ἀσφαλισάμενος	VPAMNM-S	ἀσφαλίζω
ἀσφαλίσασθαι	VNAM	"
ἀσφαλίσασθε	VMAM--2P	"
ἀσφαλισθῆναι	VNAP	"

ἀσφαλῶς adverb; literally, of guarding a prisoner *securely, safely* (AC 16.23); *under guard* (MK 14.44); figuratively, of knowing something *beyond doubt, for sure, certainly* (AC 2.36)

ἀσφαλῶς	AB	ἀσφαλῶς
ἀσχήμονα	AP-NN-P	ἀσχήμων
ἀσχημονεῖ	VIPA--3S	ἀσχημονέω
ἀσχημονεῖν	VNPA	"

ἀσχημονέω (and αὐσχημονέω) (1) as defying moral standards *act disgracefully, behave improperly* (1C 7.36); (2) as defying social standards *be ill-mannered* or *rude* (1C 13.5)

ἀσχημοσύνη, ης, ἡ strictly *shamelessness*; (1) as a concrete term *shameless deed, indecent behavior* (RO 1.27); (2) as being without proper clothing to cover private body parts *nakedness, shame*; metaphorically in RV 16.15 for spiritual unpreparedness *shameful condition*

ἀσχημοσύνη	N-NF-S	ἀσχημοσύνη
ἀσχημοσύνην	N-AF-S	"

ἀσχήμων, ον *unattractive, indecent, unpresentable*, of the parts of the body that should be kept private and covered; substantivally τὰ ἀσχήμονα *the unpresentable parts* (1C 12.23)

ἀσωτία, ας, ἡ strictly, the disposition of an ἄσωτος (*having no hope of safety*); the act of one who has abandoned himself to reckless immoral behavior *debauchery, dissipation, incorrigibility*

ἀσωτία	N-NF-S	ἀσωτία
ἀσωτίας	N-GF-S	"

ἀσώτως adverb; of living in a wild, abandoned manner *recklessly, riotously, loosely* (LU 15.13)

ἀσώτως	AB	ἀσώτως

ἀτακτέω 1aor. ἠτάκτησα; strictly *set oneself outside the order*; hence *be idle* or *lazy, evade one's responsibilities* (2TH 3.7)

ἄτακτος, ον (1) strictly, of soldiers who will not obey orders *disorderly*; hence *unruly, undisciplined*; (2) of persons who evade responsibilities *idle, lazy*; substantivally *lazy person* (1TH 5.14)

ἀτάκτους	A--AM-P	ἄτακτος

ἀτάκτως adverb; *in a disorderly manner*; figuratively, of persons who live irresponsibly *idly, lazily*

ἀτάκτως	AB	ἀτάκτως
ἄταφα	A--NN-P	ἄταφος

ἄταφος, ον strictly *without a grave*; hence *unburied* (RV 11.8)

ἄτεκνος, ον *childless, without children*

ἄτεκνος	A--NM-S	ἄτεκνος
ἀτενίζετε	VIPA--2P	ἀτενίζω
ἀτενίζοντες	VPPANM-P	"

ἀτενίζω 1aor. ἠτένισα; *look* or *stare intently at, fix one's eyes on*

ἀτενίσαι	VNAA	ἀτενίζω
ἀτενίσαντες	VPAANM-P	"
ἀτενίσας	VPAANM-S	"
ἀτενίσασα	VPAANF-S	"
ἀτένισον	VMAA--2S	"

ἄτερ preposition with the genitive *without, apart from* (LU 22.6)

ἄτερ	PG	ἄτερ
ἀτιμάζεις	VIPA--2S	ἀτιμάζω
ἀτιμάζεσθαι	VNPM	"
	VNPP	"
ἀτιμάζετε	VIPA--2P	"

ἀτιμάζω 1aor. ἠτίμασα; 1aor. pass. ἠτιμάσθην; (1) of persons *treat with disrespect, dishonor, treat shamefully* (MK 12.4); (2) of the body when used for immoral purposes *degrade, abuse* (RO 1.24)

ἀτιμάσαντες	VPAANM-P	ἀτιμάζω
ἀτιμασθῆναι	VNAP	"

ἀτιμάω 1aor. ἠτίμησα; *treat with disrespect, dishonor, treat shamefully* (MK 12.4)

ἀτιμία, ας, ἡ *dishonor, disgrace, shame* (1C 11.14); of a container εἰς ἀτιμίαν *for common* or *ordinary use* (RO 9.21); of a manner of speaking κατὰ ἀτιμίαν *slightingly, in a foolish* or *disparaging way* (2C 11.21)

ἀτιμία	N-NF-S	ἀτιμία
ἀτιμίᾳ	N-DF-S	"
ἀτιμίαν	N-AF-S	"
ἀτιμίας	N-GF-S	"
ἄτιμοι	A--NM-P	ἄτιμος

ἄτιμος, ον *without honor, despised, dishonored* (MT 13.57); comparative ἀτιμώτερος, τέρα, ον *less respectable, more insignificant* (1C 12.23)

ἄτιμος	A--NM-S	ἄτιμος
ἀτιμότερα	A-MAN-P	"

ἀτιμόω pf. pass. ptc. ἠτιμωμένος; *treat with disrespect, dishonor, treat shamefully* (MK 12.4)

ἄτινα	APRNN-P	ὅστις
ἀτμίδα	N-AF-S	ἀτμίς

ἀτμίς, ίδος, ἡ (1) literally *steam, mist, vapor*; figuratively in JA 4.14 for the transient nature of earthly life; (2) ἀ. καπνοῦ *rising cloud of smoke* (AC 2.19)

ἀτμίς	N-NF-S	ἀτμίς

ἄτομος, ον strictly, of something too small to be cut *indivisible*; hence, of the smallest measure of time; substantivally ἐν ἀτόμῳ *in a moment* or *instant* (1C 15.52)

ἀτόμῳ	AP-DN-S	ἄτομος
ἄτοπον	AP-AN-S	ἄτοπος
	AP-NN-S	"
	A--AN-S	"

ἄτοπος, ον   strictly *out of place*; hence *unusual, unexpected, surprising* (AC 28.6); in a moral sense *improper, wrong, evil*; neuter as a substantive ἄτοπον *what is bad, crime* (LU 23.41)

ἀτόπων   A--GM-P   ἄτοπος

Ἀττάλεια, ας, ἡ (also Ἀτταλία) *Attalia*, a seaport along the Mediterranean Sea in Pamphylia in Asia Minor (AC 14.25)

Ἀττάλειαν   N-AF-S   Ἀττάλεια
Ἀτταλίαν   N-AF-S   "

αὐγάζω 1aor. inf. αὐγάσαι; (1) transitively *see distinctly, discern*; figuratively, of understanding the gospel message (probably 2C 4.4); (2) intransitively *be clearly evident* (possibly 2C 4.4)

αὐγάσαι   VNAA   αὐγάζω
αὐγή, ῆς, ἡ as the point of time when daylight appears *dawn, daybreak, sunrise* (AC 20.11)

αὐγῆς   N-GF-S   αὐγή
Αὐγοῦστος, ου, ὁ (also Αὔγυστος) *Augustus*, a Latin title (with its Greek equivalent Σεβαστός given to Roman emperors) (LU 2.1); the adjective αὐ. means *worthy of reverence, revered*

Αὐγούστου   N-GM-S   Αὐγοῦστος
αὐθάδεις   A--NM-P   αὐθάδης
αὐθάδη   A--AM-S   "
αὐθάδης, ες strictly, of one who pleases himself; hence *self-willed, stubborn, arrogant* (TI 1.7)

αὐθαίρετοι   A--NM-P   αὐθαίρετος
αὐθαίρετος, ον strictly, of one who chooses his own course of action; hence *of one's own free will, acting spontaneously* or *voluntarily* (2C 8.3)

αὐθαίρετος   A--NM-S   αὐθαίρετος
αὐθεντεῖν   VNPA   αὐθεντέω
αὐθεντέω strictly, of one who acts on his own authority; hence *have control over, domineer, lord it over* (1T 2.12)

αὐλέω 1aor. ηὔλησα; *play the flute* or *pipe* (αὐλός), *pipe* (a tune) (MT 11.17)

αὐλή, ῆς, ἡ strictly *unroofed enclosure* surrounded by walls or rooms; (1) *courtyard, (sheep)fold* (JN 10.1); (2) *(royal) court, palace* (MT 26.3); (3) *(outer) court* of the temple (RV 11.2); (4) *dwelling, house*, from the layout of a Middle Eastern house around a central court (LU 11.21)

αὐλῇ   N-DF-S   αὐλή
αὐλήν   N-AF-S   "
αὐλῆς   N-GF-S   "
αὐλητάς   N-AM-P   αὐλητής
αὐλητής, οῦ, ὁ *flute player, one who plays on a pipe*, hired for occasions of festivity (RV 18.22) or mourning (MT 9.23)

αὐλητῶν   N-GM-P   αὐλητής
αὐλίζομαι impf. ηὐλιζόμην; 1aor. ηὐλίσθην; *spend the night, find lodging* (MT 21.17)

αὐλός, οῦ, ὁ a musical wind instrument shaped like a tube *flute, pipe* (1C 14.7)

αὐλός   N-NM-S   αὐλός
αὐλούμενον   VPPPNN-S   αὐλέω
αὐξάνει   VIPA--3S   αὐξάνω
αὐξάνειν   VNPA   "
αὔξανε(ν)   VIIA--3S   "

αὐξάνεσθε   VMPP--2P   "
αὐξάνετε   VMPA--2P   "
αὐξάνητε   VSPA--2P   "
αὐξανόμενα   VPPPNN-P   "
αὐξανομένης   VPPPGF-S   "
αὐξανόμενοι   VPPPNM-P   "
αὐξανόμενον   VPPPAN-S   "
    VPPPNN-S   "
αὐξάνοντα   VPPANN-P   "
αὐξάνουσι(ν)   VIPA--3P   "

αὐξάνω and αὔξω impf. ηὔξανον; fut. αὐξήσω; 1aor. ηὔξησα; 1aor. pass. ηὐξήθην; (1) transitively *cause to grow* or *increase*, as plants; figuratively, of the effect of giving out the gospel message (1C 3.6); (2) passive, with an intransitive sense *grow, increase* (MT 13.32); figuratively, of growth in relation to spiritual things (CO 1.6); (3) intransitively *grow*; literally, of plants (MT 6.28) and children (LU 1.80); of a people *increase, become more in number* (AC 7.17); figuratively *increase* of a state in relation to spiritual things (AC 6.7); of an increase in status *become more important* (JN 3.30)

αὐξάνων   VPPANM-S   αὐξάνω
αὔξει   VIPA--3S   "
αὐξηθῇ   VSAP--3S   "
αὐξηθῆτε   VSAP--2P   "
αὐξῆσαι   VNAA   "
αὐξήσει   VIFA--3S   "
αὐξήσῃ   VSAA--3S   "
αὔξησιν   N-AF-S   αὔξησις
αὔξησις, εως, ἡ as an action *growth, increase*; used figuratively in the NT of the church as Christ's body, whether increasing in numbers or spiritual maturity

αὐξήσωμεν   VSAA--1P   αὐξάνω
αὔριον adverb; *tomorrow*; (1) literally *next day* (AC 23.20); (2) with an indeterminate time *soon, in a short time* (MT 6.30)

αὔριον   AB   αὔριον
αὐστηρός, ά, όν as a personal quality *severe, exacting, stern*

αὐστηρός   A--NM-S   αὐστηρός
αὐσχημονεῖ   VIPA--3S   εὐσχημονέω
αὐτά   AP-AN-P   αὐτός
    NPAN3P   "
    NPNN3P   "
αὗται   APDNF-P   οὗτος
    A-DNF-P   "
αὐταῖς   A--DF-P   αὐτός
    NPDF3P   "
αὐτάρκεια, ας, ἡ (1) as ability to supply the necessities of life without help from others *self-sufficiency, adequacy*; αὐ. ἔχειν *have enough to live on* (2C 9.8); (2) as a state of mind satisfied with its lot *contentment, satisfaction* (1T 6.6)

αὐτάρκειαν   N-AF-S   αὐτάρκεια
αὐταρκείας   N-GF-S   "
αὐτάρκης, ες of a happy state of mind *content, satisfied* (PH 4.11)

αὐτάρκης   A--NM-S   αὐτάρκης
αὐτάς   A--AF-P   αὐτός
    NPAF3P   "

αὐτή	A--NF-S	"
	NPNF3S	"
αὐτῇ	A--DF-S	αὐτός
	NPDF3S	"
αὕτη	APDNF-S	οὗτος
	A-DNF-S	"
αὐτήν	A--AF-S	αὐτός
	NPAF2S	"
	NPAF3S	"
αὐτῆς	A--GF-S	"
	NPGF2S	"
	NPGF3S	"
αὐτῆς	NPGF3S	ἑαυτοῦ
αὐτό	AP-AN-S	αὐτός
	AP-NN-S	"
	A--AN-S	"
	A--NN-S	"
	NPAN3S	"
	NPNN3S	"
αὐτοί	NPNM1P	"
	NPNM2P	"
	NPNM3P	"
αὐτοῖς	A--DN-P	"
	NPDM2P	"
	NPDM3P	"
	NPDN3P	"
αὐτοῖς	NPDM3P	ἑαυτοῦ

αὐτοκατάκριτος, ον of a person who shows by his own actions that he is wrong or guilty *self-condemned* (TI 3.11)

αὐτοκατάκριτος	A--NM-S	αὐτοκατάκριτος
αὐτομάτη	A--NF-S	αὐτόματος

αὐτόματος, η, ον of something that happens without visible cause *of its own self, spontaneously*

αὐτόν	A--AM-S	αὐτός
	NPAM3S	"
αὐτόπται	N-NM-P	αὐτόπτης

αὐτόπτης, ου, ὁ of one who sees an event for himself *eyewitness* (LU 1.2)

αὐτός, ή, ὁ (1) as an intensive pronoun to emphasize identity, setting the individual person or thing apart from others, used of all persons, genders, and numbers; (a) in the nominative case to intensify the subject *-self, -selves* e.g. αὐ. ἐγώ *I myself* (2C 10.1); αὐτοὶ ὑμεῖς *you yourselves* (JN 3.28); αὐ. σώσει *he himself will save* (MT 1.21); (b) in an oblique case to add emphasis or contrast to any lexical unit *-self, -selves* e.g. σοῦ αὐτῆς *of you yourself* (LU 2.35); (2) as equivalent to a demonstrative pronoun to direct attention exclusively to a person or thing, placed in the predicate position *even, very, just* (JN 5.36b); (3) as a third-person pronoun in oblique cases to refer to an expressed or implied antecedent *him, her, it* (MT 2.2); (4) as an adjective preceded by the article in the attributive position, with or without a noun *the same* (MT 5.46; 26.44)

αὐτός	AP-NM-S	αὐτός
	A--NM-S	"
	NPNM1S	"
	NPNM2S	"
	NPNM3S	"

αὐτοῦ adverb of place; strictly *in the very place*; hence *here, in this place* (MT 26.36); *there, in that place* (AC 18.19)

αὐτοῦ	AB	αὐτοῦ
	A--GN-S	αὐτός
	NPGM1S	"
	NPGM3S	"
	NPGN3S	"
αὐτοῦ	NPGM3S	ἑαυτοῦ
αὐτούς	NPAM1P	αὐτός
	NPAM3P	"

αὐτόφωρος, ον referring to one who is unexpectedly found doing something; substantivally ἐπ᾽ αὐτοφώρῳ *(caught) in the (very) act* (JN 8.4)

αὐτοφώρῳ	A--DN-S	αὐτόφωρος

αὐτόχειρ, ρος of using one's hands to do something; substantivally *with one's own hand, by hand* (AC 27.19)

αὐτόχειρες	A--NM-P	αὐτόχειρ
αὐτῷ	AP-DN-S	αὐτός
	A--DM-S	"
	A--DN-S	"
	NPDM3S	"
	NPDN3S	"
αὐτῷ	NPDM3S	ἑαυτοῦ
αὐτῶν	AP-GN-P	αὐτός
	A--GN-P	"
	NPGF3P	"
	NPGM2P	"
	NPGM3P	"
	NPGN3P	"
αὐτῶν	NPGM1P	ἑαυτοῦ
αὐχεῖ	VIPA--3S	αὐχέω

αὐχέω as talking with much confidence about something *boast, pride oneself, declare boastfully*

αὐχμηρός, ά, όν of a place *filthy, dark, dismal* (2P 1.19)

αὐχμηρῷ	A--DM-S	αὐχμηρός
ἀφ᾽	PG	ἀπό
ἀφαίοντα	VIPP--3P	see ἀφαίονται
ἀφαίονται	VIPP--3P	ἀφίημι
ἀφαιρεθήσεται	VIFP--3S	ἀφαιρέω
ἀφαίρει	VIPA--3S	"
ἀφαιρεῖν	VNPA	"
ἀφαιρεῖται	VIPM--3S	"

ἀφαιρέω (and **ἀφερέω**) 2fut. ἀφελῶ; 2aor. ἀφεῖλον; 1fut. pass. ἀφαιρεθήσομαι; (1) active/middle *take away, remove* (LU 1.25); *take off, cut off* (MT 26.51); (2) passive *be taken away from, be deprived of* (LU 10.42)

ἀφαιρῇ	VSPA--3S	ἀφαιρέω
ἀφαιρήσει	VIFA--3S	"

ἀφανής, ές *out of sight, hidden, unable to be known about*

ἀφανής	A--NF-S	ἀφανής
ἀφανίζει	VIPA--3S	ἀφανίζω
ἀφανιζομένη	VPPPNF-S	"
ἀφανίζουσι(ν)	VIPA--3P	"

ἀφανίζω 1aor. pass. ἠφανίσθην; (1) active *cause to disappear, make invisible* or *unrecognizable*; of one's face *disfigure, neglect (appearance), make ugly* (MT 6.16); of treasures *ruin, destroy* (MT 6.19); (2) passive *perish, disappear* (AC 13.41)

ἀφανισθήσονται	VIFP--3P	ἀφανίζω
ἀφανίσθητε	VMAP--2P	

ἀφανισμός, οῦ, ὁ   *vanishing away, disappearance, doing away with* (HE 8.13)

| ἀφανισμοῦ | N-GM-S | ἀφανισμός |

ἄφαντος, ον   *invisible, out of sight*; ἄ. γενέσθαι *disappear or vanish* (LU 24.31)

| ἄφαντος | A--NM-S | ἄφαντος |

ἀφεδρών, ῶνος, ὁ   *toilet, latrine, sewer*

ἀφεδρῶνα	N-AM-S	ἀφεδρών
ἀφεθῇ	VSAP--3S	ἀφίημι
ἀφέθησαν	VIAP--3P	"
ἀφεθήσεται	VIFP--3S	"
ἀφεθήσομαι	VIFP--1S	"
ἀφεθήσονται	VIFP--3P	"

ἀφειδία, ας, ἡ   as *not sparing one's body severe self-control, nonindulgence, asceticism* (CO 2.23)

ἀφειδία	N-DF-S	ἀφειδία
ἀφείλατο	VIAM--3S	ἀφαιρέω
ἀφεῖλε(ν)	VIAA--3S	"
ἀφείλετο	VIAM--3S	"
ἀφεῖναι	VNAA	ἀφίημι
ἀφείονται	VIPP--3P	"
ἀφείς	VPAANM-S	"
ἀφεῖς	VIPA--2S	"
ἀφελεῖ	VIFA--3S	ἀφαιρέω
ἀφελεῖν	VNAA	"
ἀφέλῃ	VSAA--3S	"

ἀφελότης, ητος, ἡ   strictly *smoothness, evenness*; hence *sincerity, simplicity* of heart, *humbleness* (AC 2.46)

ἀφελότητι	N-DF-S	ἀφελότης
ἀφελπίζοντες	VPPANM-P	see ἀπελπίζοντες
ἀφέλωμαι	VSAM--1S	ἀφαιρέω
ἀφέντες	VPAANM-P	ἀφίημι
ἀφέονται	VIPP--3P	"
ἀφέοντε	VIPP--3P	"
αφερεῖ	VIPA--3S	ἀφαιρέω
ἄφες	VMAA--2S	ἀφίημι
ἀφέσει	N-DF-S	ἄφεσις
ἄφεσιν	N-AF-S	"

ἄφεσις, εως, ἡ   (1) of captivity *release, liberation, deliverance* (LU 4.18); (2) of an obligation or debt *cancellation, pardon*; (3) predominately in relation to sins *forgiveness, cancellation of guilt* (MT 26.28); in the new covenant, ἄ. involves not a passing over of sins as in the old covenant (cf. πάρεσις [*passing over, overlooking*] in RO 3.25), but their *removal* from the mind of God, *taking away* (HE 10.18; cf. 10.3)

ἄφεσις	N-NF-S	ἄφεσις
ἄφετε	VMAA--2P	ἀφίημι
ἀφέωνται	VIRP--3P	"
ἀφῇ	VSAA--3S	"

ἀφή, ῆς, ἡ   strictly *fastening, connection*; as a medical technical term for what binds the parts of the body together *ligament, sinew* (EP 4.16)

ἀφῆκα	VIAA--1S	ἀφίημι
ἀφήκαμεν	VIAA--1P	"
ἀφῆκαν	VIAA--3P	"
ἀφῆκας	VIAA--2S	"
ἀφήκατε	VIAA--2P	"
ἀφῆκε(ν)	VIAA--3S	"
ἀφῆκες	VIAA--2S	"
ἀφῆς	N-GF-S	ἀφή

ἀφήσει	VIFA--3S	ἀφίημι
ἀφήσεις	VIFA--2S	"
	VIFA--2S^VMAA--2S	"
ἀφήσουσι(ν)	VIFA--3P	"
ἀφήσω	VIFA--1S	"
ἀφῆτε	VSAA--2P	"

ἀφθαρσία, ας, ἡ   a state of *not being subject to decay or death immortality, incorruptibility* (RO 2.7); ἐν ἀφθαρσίᾳ (EP 6.24) has three possible alternatives: (1) as qualifying love *unceasing, undying*; (2) as qualifying grace *with incorruptibility, eternally*; (3) as qualifying Christ and Christians *in immortal life*

ἀφθαρσία	N-DF-S	ἀφθαρσία
ἀφθαρσίαν	N-AF-S	"
ἄφθαρτοι	A--NM-P	ἄφθαρτος
ἄφθαρτον	A--AF-S	"
	A--AM-S	"
	A--AN-S	"

ἄφθαρτος, ον   *not subject to decay or death immortal, incorruptible, imperishable*; substantivally *immortal character* (1P 3.4)

ἀφθάρτου	A--GF-S	ἄφθαρτος
	A--GM-S	"
ἀφθάρτῳ	A--DM-S	"

ἀφθονία, ας, ἡ   strictly *freedom from envy*; hence *willingness, readiness* (TI 2.7)

| ἀφθονίαν | N-AF-S | ἀφθονία |

ἀφθορία, ας, ἡ   strictly *not subject to corruption*; hence, in relation to teaching that is free from error *soundness, purity, integrity* (TI 2.7)

ἀφθορίαν	N-AF-S	ἀφθορία
ἀφίδω	VSAA--1S	ἀφοράω
ἀφίεμεν	VIPA--1P	see ἀφίομεν
ἀφιέναι	VNPA	ἀφίημι
ἀφίενται	VIPP--3P	"
ἀφίεται	VIPP--3S	"
ἀφίετε	VIPA--2P	"
	VMPA--2P	"
ἀφιέτω	VMPA--3S	"

ἀφίημι   impf. ἤφιον; fut. ἀφήσω; 1aor. ἀφῆκα; 2aor. imperative ἄφες and ἄφετε, inf. ἀφεῖναι; (1) *send off* or *away, let go* (MT 27.50); (2) as a legal technical term *divorce* (1C 7.11); (3) *abandon, leave behind* (MT 26.56); (4) of duty and obligation *reject, set aside, neglect* (MK 7.8); (5) of toleration *let go, leave in peace, allow* (MK 11.6); (6) of sins or debts *forgive, pardon, cancel* (LU 7.47); (7) *give* or *utter* a loud cry (MK 15.37)

ἀφίημι	VIPA--1S	ἀφίημι
ἀφίησι(ν)	VIPA--3S	"
ἀφίκετο	VIAD--3S	ἀφικνέομαι

ἀφικνέομαι   2aor. ἀφικόμην; *arrive at, come to, reach*; of a report *reach, become known* (RO 16.19)

| ἀφιλάγαθοι | A--NM-P | ἀφιλάγαθος |

ἀφιλάγαθος, ον   *not loving what is good, hating good* (*things* or *people*) (2T 3.3)

| ἀφιλάργυρον | A--AM-S | ἀφιλάργυρος |

ἀφιλάργυρος, ον   *not loving money, not greedy*; *liberal, generous*

ἀφιλάργυρος	A--NM-S	ἀφιλάργυρος
ἀφίλετο	VIAM--3S	ἀφαιρέω
ἄφιξιν	N-AF-S	ἄφιξις

ἄφιξις, εως, ἡ   as motion away from a point of reference *departure* (AC 20.29)

ἀφίομεν	VIPA--1P	ἀφίημι
ἀφίονται	VIPP--3P	see ἀφίενται
ἀφίουσι(ν)	VIPA--3P	ἀφίημι
ἀφίστανται	VIPM--3P	ἀφίστημι
ἀφίστασο	VMPM--2S	"
ἀφίστατο	VIIM--3S	"

ἀφίστημι   mid. ἀφίσταμαι; fut. mid. ἀποστήσομαι; 1aor. ἀπέστησα; 2aor. ἀπέστην; (1) transitively *cause to revolt, mislead, alienate* (AC 5.37); (2) intransitively (second aorist active, present middle, future middle); (a) *go away, withdraw* (LU 2.37); (b) *desert* (with the object with an ἀπό phrase) (AC 15.38); in a religious sense *fall away, become apostate* (LU 8.13); (c) *keep away* (with an ἀπό phrase); figuratively, of moral behavior *keep away, abstain* (2T 2.19)

ἀφίωνται	VIRP--3P	ἀφίημι

ἄφνω   adverb; *suddenly, unexpectedly, unawares*

ἄφνω	AB	ἄφνω

ἀφόβως   adverb; (1) *fearlessly, boldly* (PH 1.14); (2) *securely, peacefully* (LU 1.74); (3) in a bad sense *impudently, shamelessly* (possibly JU 12); *without regard for God, irreverently* (possibly JU 12)

ἀφόβως	AB	ἀφόβως

ἀφομοιόω   pf. pass. ptc. ἀφωμοιωμένος; *make like, liken*; passive *be like, resemble, portray* (HE 7.3)

ἀφοράω   2aor. ἀπεῖδον, subjunctive ἀφίδω; (1) strictly *look away* or *from*; hence, as giving attention to one thing to the exclusion of all else *look with undivided attention, fix one's eyes* (with an εἰς phrase) (HE 12.2); (2) *learn, find out, ascertain* (PH 2.23)

ἀφοριεῖ	VIFA--3S	ἀφορίζω
ἀφορίζει	VIPA--3S	"

ἀφορίζω   impf. ἀφώριζον; fut. ἀφοριῶ and ἀφορίσω; 1aor. ἀφώρισα; pf. pass. ptc. ἀφωρισμένος; 1aor. pass. ἀφωρίσθην; strictly *mark off by boundaries*; hence (1) *separate, sever, take away* (MT 13.49); (2) as excluding from a society *cut off, excommunicate, drive out* (LU 6.22); (3) of separation for a special purpose *set apart, appoint* (RO 1.1)

ἀφοριοῦσι(ν)	VIFA--3P	ἀφορίζω
ἀφορίσας	VPAANM-S	"
ἀφορίσατε	VMAA--2P	"
ἀφορίσει	VIFA--3S	"
ἀφορίσθητε	VMAP--2P	"
ἀφορίσωσι(ν)	VSAA--3P	"

ἀφορμή, ῆς, ἡ   strictly *starting point* or *base of operations* for an expedition; hence (1) *occasion, opportunity, favorable circumstance* (RO 7.8; GA 5.13); (2) *pretext, excuse* (2C 11.12)

ἀφορμήν	N-AF-S	ἀφορμή
ἀφορῶντες	VPPANM-P	ἀφοράω
ἀφρίζει	VIPA--3S	ἀφρίζω

ἀφρίζω   of a person stricken with a frenzy or seizure *foam* or *froth at the mouth*

ἀφρίζων	VPPANM-S	ἀφρίζω
ἄφρον	A--VM-S	ἄφρων
ἄφρονα	A--AM-S	"
ἄφρονες	A--NM-P	
	A--VM-P	

ἀφρόνων	A--GM-P	"

ἀφρός, οῦ, ὁ   as a medical technical term *foam* or *froth* appearing at the mouth during a seizure (LU 9.39)

ἀφροσύνη, ης, ἡ   morally or intellectually, not using one's ability to understand *foolishness, lack of sense, (boastful) folly* (2C 11.1)

ἀφροσύνη	N-NF-S	ἀφροσύνη
ἀφροσύνη	N-DF-S	
ἀφροσύνης	N-GF-S	
ἀφροῦ	N-GM-S	ἀφρός

ἄφρων, ον, gen. ονος   as not using common sense *foolish, senseless, silly* (RO 2.20), opposite φρόνιμος (*wise, sensible*); substantively *foolish person, fool* (LU 11.40)

ἄφρων	A--NM-S	ἄφρων
	A--VM-S	"

ἀφυπνόω   1aor. ἀφύπνωσα; *fall asleep, begin to sleep* (LU 8.23)

ἀφύπνωσε(ν)	VIAA--3S	ἀφυπνόω

ἀφυστερέω   pf. pass. ptc. ἀφυστερημένος; of wages owed *withhold, keep back* (JA 5.4)

ἀφυστερημένος	VPRPNM-S	ἀφυστερέω
ἀφῶμεν	VSAA--1P	ἀφίημι
ἀφωμοιωμένος	VPRPNM-S	ἀφομοιόω
ἀφῶν	N-GF-S	ἀφή
ἄφωνα	A--AN-P	ἄφωνος
ἄφωνον	A--NN-S	"

ἄφωνος, ον   (1) as being unable to speak *mute, silent, voiceless*; of idols (1C 12.2); of a lamb being sheared, *mute, silent* (AC 8.32); (2) *incapable of speech* (2P 2.16); (3) of sounds incapable of conveying meaning *inarticulate, without meaning* (1C 14.10)

ἄφωνος	A--NM-S	ἄφωνος
ἀφώριζε(ν)	VIIA--3S	ἀφορίζω
ἀφώρισε(ν)	VIAA--3S	"
ἀφωρισμένος	VPRPNM-S	"
Ἄχαζ		Ἀχάζ

Ἀχάζ, ὁ (also Ἄχαζ, Ἄχας)   indeclinable; *Ahaz*, masculine proper noun

Ἀχαΐα	N-NF-S	Ἀχαΐα
Ἀχαΐᾳ	N-DF-S	"

Ἀχαΐα, ας, ἡ (also Ἀχαία)   *Achaia*, in NT times a Roman province including Greece to the south of Thessaly

Ἀχαΐα	N-NF-S	Ἀχαΐα
Ἀχαΐᾳ	N-DF-S	"
Ἀχαΐαν	N-AF-S	"
Ἀχαΐαν	N-AF-S	"
Ἀχαΐας	N-GF-S	"
Ἀχαΐας	N-GF-S	"

Ἀχαϊκός, οῦ, ὁ   *Achaicus*, masculine proper noun (1C 16.17)

Ἀχαϊκοῦ	N-GM-S	Ἀχαϊκός
ἀχάριστοι	A--NM-P	ἀχάριστος

ἀχάριστος, ον   *ungrateful, not thankful*; substantivally *ungrateful person* (LU 6.35)

ἀχαρίστους	A--AM-P	ἀχάριστος
Ἄχας		Ἀχάζ
Ἀχείμ		Ἀχίμ
ἀχειροποίητον	A--AF-S	ἀχειροποίητος
	A--AM-S	"

ἀχειροποίητος, ον   *not made by (human) hands, not hand-crafted* (MK 14.58); of spiritual circumcision *not done by human hands* (CO 2.11)

ἀχειροποιήτῳ	A--DF-S	ἀχειροποίητος
Ἀχελδαμάχ		Ἀκελδαμάχ
ἀχθῆναι	VNAP	ἄγω
ἀχθήσεσθε	VIFP--2P	"

Ἀχίμ, ὁ (also Ἀχείμ)   indeclinable; *Achim*, masculine proper noun

ἀχλύς, ύος, ἡ   *mist, mistiness, gloom*; as a medical technical term for sight impairment *failure of sight, dimness* (AC 13.11)

ἀχλύς	N-NF-S	ἀχλύς
ἀχρεῖοι	A--NM-P	ἀχρεῖος
ἀχρεῖον	A--AM-S	"

ἀχρεῖος, ον   strictly *of no use*; hence, of persons *unprofitable, unworthy, not deserving praise*

ἀχρειόω   1aor. pass. ἠχρεώθην; literally *make useless*; figuratively *do what is totally wrong*; only passive in the NT *become depraved, become (morally) worthless, become corrupt* (RO 3.12)

ἀχρηστοι	A--NM-P	ἄχρηστος
ἄχρηστον	A--AM-S	"

ἄχρηστος, ον   of a person *useless, unprofitable* (PM 11)

ἄχρι(ς)   (1) as a conjunction expressing time up to a point *until* (RV 7.3); (2) as an improper preposition with the genitive; (a) of time *within, during* (AC 20.6); (b) of place *as far as, to* (AC 28.15); (c) figuratively, of manner expressing extent *to (the point of)* (AC 22.4); (3) as an improper preposition with a relative pronoun in the genitive, used as a conjunction to express extent of time; ἄ. ἧς ἡμέρας *up to the day in which, until the time when* (MT 24.38); ἄ. οὗ *until the time when* (AC 7.18); ἄ. οὗ *while, as long as* (HE 3.13)

ἄχρι(ς)	CS	ἄχρι(ς)
	PG	"

ἄχυρον, ου, τό   *chaff, husks, straw broken up* by treading out grain

ἄχυρον	N-AN-S	ἄχυρον
ἄψαι	VMAM--2S	ἅπτω
ἁψάμενος	VPAMNM-S	"
ἅψαντες	VPAANM-P	"
ἁψάντων	VPAAGM-P	"
ἅψας	VPAANM-S	"
ἅψασθαι	VNAM	"
ἅψεσθαι	VNFM	"

ἀψευδής, ές   *incapable of lying* or *deceit, .truthful, trustworthy*, used only of God in the NT (TI 1.2)

ἀψευδής	A--NM-S	ἀψευδής
ἅψῃ	VSAM--2S	ἅπτω
ἅψηται	VSAM--3S	"
Ἀψίνθιον	N-NM-S	Ἄψινθος
ἀψίνθιον	N-AN-S	ἄψινθος
ἄψινθον	N-AF-S	"

Ἄψινθος, ου, ὁ (also Ἀψίνθιον, ου, τό)   *Absinthos*, masculine (also neuter) proper noun of a star meaning *Bitterness, Wormwood*, used symbolically in RV 8.11

Ἄψινθος	N-NM-S	Ἄψινθος

ἄψινθος, ου, ἡ (also ἀψίνθιον, ου, τό)   *wormwood, absinthe*, a bitter, dark green oil made from certain strong-smelling plants with white or yellow flowers, alcoholic in effect; called *wormwood* from its use as a medicine to kill intestinal worms (RV 8.11)

ἄψυχα	A--NN-P	ἄψυχος

ἄψυχος, ον   *lifeless, inanimate*; substantivally τὰ ἄψυχα *the things without life* (1C 14.7)

ἄψωμαι	VSAM--1S	ἅπτω
ἄψωνται	VSAM--3P	"

β B

β′ indeclinable; *beta*, second letter of the Greek alphabet; as a cardinal number *two*; as an ordinal number *second*, in the title of several NT letters

Βάαλ, ὁ indeclinable; *Baal*, masculine proper noun of Semitic male deity (RO 11.4)

Βαβυλών, ῶνος, ἡ *Babylon*; (1) as the country *Babylonia* (MT 1.11); (2) as the capital of the country *Babylon*; (3) symbolically in Revelation of a world power hostile to God *Babylon* (RV 14.8)

Βαβυλών	N-NF-S	Βαβυλών
	N-VF-S	"
Βαβυλῶνι	N-DF-S	"
Βαβυλῶνος	N-GF-S	"
βάδους	N-AM-P	βάτος (II)
βαθέα	AP-AN-P	βαθύς
βαθεῖ	A--DM-S	"
βαθέος	A--GM-S	"
βαθέως	A--GM-S	"
βάθη	N-AN-P	βάθος
βαθμόν	N-AM-S	βαθμός

βαθμός, οῦ, ὁ *step, stair*; figuratively, of dignity of office or social status *standing, rank, degree (of respect)* (1T 3.13)

βαθμούς	N-AM-P	βαθμός

βάθος, ους, τό literally, as indicating distance below a surface *depth, deep place*; of earth (MT 13.5); of sea (LU 5.4); in contrast to height (RO 8.39); figuratively, of a great or extreme degree of anything; as a quality in relation to God *depths, inexhaustibility* (RO 11.33); in relation to man *depths, extremity* (2C 8.2); τὰ βάθη as knowledge difficult to understand *deep secrets, deep-laid plans* (1C 2.10)

βάθος	N-AN-S	βάθος
	N-NN-S	"
βάθους	N-GN-S	"
βαθύ	A--NN-S	βαθύς

βαθύνω 1aor. ἐβάθυνα; (1) transitively *deepen, hollow out, excavate*; (2) intransitively *go down deep, dig deep* (probably LU 6.48, but either transitive or intransitive is possible)

βαθύς, εῖα, ύ literally, of extent below a surface *deep* (JN 4.11); figuratively, of the morning *early, at earliest dawn* (LU 24.1); of an extreme degree of anything: of sleep *deep, profound* (AC 20.9); substantivally, plural τὰ βαθέα of satanic influence *depths, deep secrets* (RV 2.24)

βαία	N-AN-P	βάιον

βάιον, ου, τό *palm branch* (JN 12.13)

Βαλαάκ		Βαλάκ

Βαλαάμ, ὁ indeclinable; *Balaam*, masculine proper noun

Βαλάκ, ὁ (also **Βαλαάκ**) indeclinable; *Balak*, masculine proper noun (RV 2.14)

βαλάντια	N-AN-P	βαλλάντιον
βαλάντιον	N-AN-S	"
βαλαντίου	N-GN-S	"
βάλε	VMAA--2S	βάλλω
βαλεῖ	VIFA--3S	"
βαλεῖν	VNAA	"
βάλετε	VMAA--2P	"
βαλέτω	VMAA--3S	"
βάλη	VSAA--3S	"
βάλητε	VSAA--2P	"
βαλλάντια	N-AN-P	βαλλάντιον

βαλλάντιον, ου, τό (also **βαλάντιον**) *moneybag, purse, pouch*

βαλλάντιον	N-AN-S	βαλλάντιον
βαλλαντίου	N-GN-S	"
βάλλει	VIPA--3S	βάλλω
βάλλειν	VNPA	"
βάλλεται	VIPP--3S	"
βάλλη	VSPA--3S	"
βάλληται	VSPP--3S	"
βάλλομεν	VIPA--1P	"
βαλλόμενα	VPPPAN-P	"
βαλλόμενον	VPPPAM-S	"
βάλλοντας	VPPAAM-P	"
βάλλοντες	VPPANM-P	"
βαλλόντων	VPPAGM-P	"
βάλλουσα	VPPANF-S	"
βάλλουσαν	VPPAAF-S	"
βάλλουσι(ν)	VIPA--3P	"
Βάλλς		Βόες

βάλλω fut. βαλῶ; 2aor. ἔβαλον; pf. βέβληκα; pf. pass. βέβλημαι; pluperfect pass. ἐβεβλήμην; 1aor. pass. ἐβλήθην; 1fut. pass. βληθήσομαι; (1) transitively, as a powerful movement of throwing or propelling *throw, cast*, with the context determining in what sense: *scatter* (seed), *cast* (lots), *pour* (liquid), *throw* (stones), *throw* (into hell), *let* (fruit) *fall*, etc.; (2) transitively, of putting or placing someone or something somewhere: *put* (money into a treasury box), *put* (a sword into its scabbard), *place* (someone into a pool), *put* (a burden on someone), *lay down* (crowns before a throne), etc.; (3) intransitively, as a sudden and fast downward movement; of a storm *beat down, rush down* (AC 27.14)

βάλλω	VIPA--1S	βάλλω
βαλόντες	VPAANM-P	"
βαλόντων	VPAAGM-P	"
βαλοῦμεν	VIFA--1P	"
βαλοῦσα	VPAANF-S	"
βαλοῦσι(ν)	VIFA--3P	"
βάλω	VSAA--1S	"
βαλῶ	VIFA--1S	"
βάλωσι(ν)	VSAA--3P	"
βαπτίζει	VIPA--3S	βαπτίζω

βαπτίζειν	VNPA	"
βαπτίζεις	VIPA--2S	"
βαπτίζομαι	VIPP--1S	"
βαπτιζόμενοι	VPPPNM-P	"
βαπτίζονται	VIPP--3P	"
βαπτίζοντες	VPPANM-P	"
βαπτίζοντος	VPPAGM-S	"

βαπτίζω fut. βαπτίσω; 1aor. ἐβάπτισα, mid. ἐβαπτισάμην; pf. pass. ptc. βεβαπτισμένος; 1aor. pass. ἐβαπτίσθην; 1fut. pass. βαπτισθήσομαι; strictly *dip, immerse* in water; middle *dip oneself, wash*; in the NT predominately of the use of water in a religious and symbolic sense; (1) of Jewish ritual washings *wash, cleanse, purify by washing* (MK 7.4); (2) as a symbolic rite indicating an aspect of relation to Christ; (a) of John the Baptist's preparatory baptizing with water *baptize* (MT 3.6); (b) of Jesus' transitional baptizing with water (JN 3.22); (c) of Christian baptism with water, identifying a believer with the death of Christ (AC 2.41; RO 6.3); (3) figuratively, in reference to ideas associated with baptism, as an act of commitment and identification; with Moses (1C 10.2); of receiving the Holy Spirit (MT 3.11b); of trial and martyrdom (LU 12.50)

βαπτίζω	VIPA--1S	βαπτίζω
βαπτίζων	VPPANM-S	"
βαπτίζωνται	VSPP--3P	"
βάπτισαι	VMAM--2S	"
βαπτίσαντες	VPAANM-P	"
βαπτίσει	VIFA--3S	"
βαπτισθείς	VPAPNM-S	"
βαπτισθέντες	VPAPNM-P	"
βαπτισθέντος	VPAPGM-S	"
βαπτισθῆναι	VNAP	"
βαπτισθήσεσθε	VIFP--2P	"
βαπτισθήτω	VMAP--3S	"

βάπτισμα, ατος, τό literally, as the result of baptizing with water *baptism, ordinance of baptism*, used specifically of John's baptism (MT 3.7) and Christian baptism (RO 6.4); figuratively, of martyrdom or a trial by suffering (LU 12.50)

βάπτισμα	N-AN-S	βάπτισμα
	N-NN-S	"
βαπτίσματι	N-DN-S	"
βαπτίσματος	N-GN-S	"
βαπτισμοῖς	N-DM-P	βαπτισμός

βαπτισμός, οῦ, ὁ as a religious technical term related to ceremonial rites of purification by the use of water *act of dipping, immersion*; (1) of an inanimate object *washing* (MK 7.4; possibly HE 6.2); (2) of a person *baptism* (possibly HE 6.2)

βαπτισμούς	N-AM-P	βαπτισμός
βαπτισμῷ	N-DM-S	"
βαπτισμῶν	N-GM-P	"
βαπτίσονται	VIFP--3P	βαπτίζω
βαπτιστήν	N-AM-S	βαπτιστής

βαπτιστής, οῦ, ὁ *one who baptizes, baptist, baptizer*; used in the NT as a surname for John as the forerunner of Jesus *the Baptist*

βαπτιστής	N-NM-S	βαπτιστής
βαπτιστοῦ	N-GM-S	"
βαπτίσωνται	VSAM--3P	βαπτίζω

βάπτω fut. βάψω; 1aor. ἔβαψα; pf. pass. ptc. βεβαμμένος; (1) *dip in* or *under, immerse* in a liquid (LU 16.24); (2) as coloring cloth *dip into dye, dye* (RV 19.13)

βάρ, ὁ indeclinable; transliterated from the Aramaic for *son*; used in the NT as the prefix for a family name or a surname, e.g. B. Ἰωνᾶ *son of Jonah* (MT 16.17)

Βαραββᾶν	N-AM-S	Βαραββᾶς

Βαραββᾶς, ᾶ, ὁ *Barabbas*, masculine proper noun

Βαραββᾶς	N-NM-S	Βαραββᾶς

Βαράκ, ὁ indeclinable; *Barak*, masculine proper noun (HE 11.32)

Βαραχίας, ου, ὁ *Barachiah, Berekiah*, masculine proper noun (MT 23.35)

Βαραχίου	N-GM-S	Βαραχίας
βάρβαροι	AP-NM-P	βάρβαρος
βαρβάροις	AP-DM-P	"

βάρβαρος, ον strictly *stammering, stuttering, uttering unintelligible sounds*; hence, of strange speech or foreign language (i.e. non-Greek in language and culture in the NT) *barbarian, foreign, strange*; as a substantive *non-Greek, uncivilized person, barbarian* (RO 1.14), opposite Ἕλλην (*Greek*)

βάρβαρος	AP-NM-S	βάρβαρος
βαρέα	A--AN-P	βαρύς
βάρει	N-DN-S	βάρος
βαρεῖαι	A--NF-P	βαρύς
βαρεῖς	A--NM-P	"
βαρείσθω	VMPP--3S	βαρέω

βαρέω pf. pass. ptc. βεβαρημένος; 1aor. pass. ἐβαρήθην; *weigh down, burden* only passive in the NT; (1) of oppressive financial obligation *burden* (1T 5.16); of difficult obligations and troubles *burden, trouble* (2C 1.8); (2) of becoming insensitive through indulgent behavior *become dull, be preoccupied* with something (LU 21.34); figuratively and idiomatically ἦσαν βεβαρημένοι ὕπνῳ literally *they were burdened by sleep*, i.e. *they were sound asleep* (LU 9.32); ἦσαν αὐτῶν οἱ ὀφθαλμοὶ βεβαρημένοι literally *their eyes were weighed down*, i.e. *they were very sleepy* (MT 26.43)

βαρέως adverb; *heavily*; figuratively, of mental comprehension *with difficulty, dully, stupidly* (MT 13.15)

βαρέως	AB	βαρέως
βάρη	N-AN-P	βάρος
βαρηθῶσι(ν)	VSAP--3P	βαρέω
Βαρθολομαῖον	N-AM-S	Βαρθολομαῖος

Βαρθολομαῖος, ου, ὁ *Bartholomew*, masculine proper noun

Βαρθολομαῖος	N-NM-S	Βαρθολομαῖος
Βαριησοῦ	N-GM-S	Βαριησοῦς
Βαριήσουαν	N-AM-S	"
Βαριησοῦμ		"
Βαριησοῦν	N-AM-S	"
Βαριϊσοῦν	N-AM-S	"

Βαριησοῦς, οῦ, ὁ (also **Βαριησοῦμ** [indeclinable], **Βαριϊσοῦς, Βαρσοῦμα** [indeclinable]) *Bar-Jesus*, masculine proper noun meaning *son of Jesus* or *Joshua* (AC 13.6)

Βαριησοῦς	N-NM-S	Βαριησοῦς
Βαριησοῦς	N-NM-S	"
Βαριτιμίας	N-NM-S	Βαρτιμαῖος

Βαριωνᾶ and **Βαριωνᾶς, ᾶ, ὁ** *Bar-Jonah*, surname of the apostle Simon Peter, meaning *son of Jonah* (MT 16.17)

Βαριωνᾶ	N-VM-S	Βαριωνᾶ
Βαρνάβα	N-GM-S	Βαρναβᾶς
Βαρναβᾶ	N-GM-S	"
Βαρνάβᾳ	N-DM-S	"
Βαρναβᾷ	N-DM-S	"
Βαρνάβαν	N-AM-S	"
Βαρναβᾶν	N-AM-S	"
Βαρνάβας	N-NM-S	"

Βαρναβᾶς, ᾶ, ὁ (also **Βαρνάβας**) *Barnabas*, masculine proper noun; translated *son of encouragement* in AC 4.36

Βαρναβᾶς	N-NM-S	Βαρναβᾶς

βάρος, ους, τό literally *burden, weight*; figuratively in the NT; (1) *burden, hardship* with the meaning suiting the context; *(daily) toil* (MT 20.12); *oppressive suffering* (GA 6.2); *difficult duty* (RV 2.24); (2) as a large amount, *weight, great extent* (2C 4.17); ἐν βάρει εἶναι literally *be in weight* may mean either *insist on one's importance, claim high status* or *make demands* (1TH 2.7)

βάρος	N-AN-S	βάρος
βαρούμενοι	VPPPNM-P	βαρέω
Βαρσαβᾶν	N-AM-S	Βαρσαββᾶς
Βαρσαββᾶν	N-AM-S	"

Βαρσαββᾶς, ᾶ, ὁ (also **Βαρσαβᾶς**) *Barsabbas*, masculine proper noun

Βαρσαββᾶς	N-NM-S	Βαρσαββᾶς
Βαρσοῦμα		Βαριησοῦς
Βαρτίμαιος	N-NM-S	Βαρτιμαῖος

Βαρτιμαῖος, ου, ὁ (also **Βαριτιμίας, Βαρτίμαιος**) *Bartimaeus*, masculine proper noun; translated as *son of Timaeus* in MK 10.46

Βαρτιμαῖος	N-NM-S	Βαρτιμαῖος
βαρυνθῶσι(ν)	VSAP--3P	βαρύνω
βαρυνόμενοι	VPPPNM-P	"

βαρύνω 1aor. ἐβάρυνα; 1aor. pass. ἐβαρύνθην; *weigh down, burden* (AC 3.14)

βαρύς, εῖα, ύ *heavy*; figuratively in the NT; (1) of rules and regulations *difficult to obey, burdensome, oppressive* (2C 10.10); (2) of important matters *very significant, serious, momentous*; comparative βαρύτερος, τέρα, ον *more important*; substantively τὰ βαρύτερα of laws *the more important matters* (MT 23.23); (3) as a characteristic of a person *fierce, cruel, vicious* (AC 20.29)

βαρύτερα	A-MAN-P	βαρύς

βαρύτιμος, ον *very expensive, of great price, very valuable* (MT 26.7)

βαρυτίμου	A--GN-S	βαρύτιμος
βασανιζομένη	VPPPNF-S	βασανίζω
βασανιζόμενον	VPPPNN-S	"
βασανιζόμενος	VPPPNM-S	"
βασανιζομένους	VPPPAM-P	"

βασανίζω impf. ἐβασάνιζον; 1aor. ἐβασάνισα; 1aor. pass. ἐβασανίσθην; 1fut. pass. βασανισθήσομαι; strictly *rub on the touchstone* (βάσανος), a Lydian stone used to test the genuineness of metals; hence *test* or *make proof of* anything; (1) of bodily disease *torment, cause great pain*; passive *be in great pain* (MT 8.6); (2) passive, of birth pangs *suffer pain, be in anguish* (RV 12.2); (3) figuratively, of any severe distress *afflict, torment, harass* (MT 8.29); (4) passive, of a boat in a storm *be tossed* or *buffeted about* (MT 14.24)

βασανίσαι	VNAA	βασανίζω
βασανίσῃς	VSAA--2S	"
βασανισθήσεται	VIFP--3S	"
βασανισθήσονται	VIFP--3P	"
βασανισθῶσι(ν)	VSAP--3P	"
βασανισμόν	N-AM-S	βασανισμός

βασανισμός, οῦ, ὁ strictly *testing by torture*; hence, of extreme distress *torture, tormenting* (RV 9.5b); passive, as the condition of those tortured *torment* (RV 9.5a; 14.11)

βασανισμός	N-NM-S	βασανισμός
βασανισμοῦ	N-GM-S	"
βασανισταῖς	N-DM-P	βασανιστής

βασανιστής, οῦ, ὁ as a legal technical term, one who examines by using torture *judicial examiner, tormentor*; in the NT *jailer, torturer, prison guard* (MT 18.34)

βασάνοις	N-DF-P	βάσανος

βάσανος, ου, ἡ strictly *touchstone* for testing the genuineness of metals by rubbing against it; hence *torture, torment*; (1) as severe bodily affliction *tormenting pain, painful affliction* (MT 4.24); (2) as the suffering of the unrighteous dead *torment* (LU 16.23)

βασάνου	N-GF-S	βάσανος
βάσεις	N-NF-P	βάσις
βασιλέα	N-AM-S	βασιλεύς
βασιλεῖ	N-DM-S	"

βασιλεία, ας, ἡ (1) abstractly, the power exercised by a king *kingship, royal rule, reign* (AC 1.6); (2) concretely, the territory ruled by a king *kingdom, realm* (MT 4.8); (3) predominately in the NT of the rule of God as promised, prophesied, and fulfilled through the spiritual rule of God in the hearts of people now (RO 14.17) and ultimately to be fulfilled in the messianic reign of Christ on earth *reign, kingdom* (LU 1.33)

βασιλεία	N-NF-S	βασιλεία
βασιλείᾳ	N-DF-S	"
βασιλεῖαι	N-NF-P	"
βασιλείαν	N-AF-S	"
βασιλείας	N-AF-P	"
	N-GF-S	"
βασιλείοις	AP-DN-P	βασίλειος
βασίλειον	AP-AN-S	"
	A--NN-S	"

βασίλειος, ον *royal, kingly, belonging to* or *fit for a king*; neuter as a substantive τὸ βασίλειον *ruler's home, palace*

βασιλεῖς	N-AM-P	βασιλεύς
	N-NM-P	"
βασιλειῶν	N-GF-P	βασιλεία
βασιλεῦ	N-VM-S	βασιλεύς
βασιλεύει	VIPA--3S	βασιλεύω
βασιλεύειν	VNPA	"
βασιλευέτω	VMPA--3S	"
βασιλευόντων	VPPAGM-P	"
βασιλεύουσι(ν)	VIPA--3S	"

βασιλεύς, έως, ὁ (1) generally one possessing royal authority *king, monarch* (MT 1.6); (2) of God as possessing supreme power to rule (MT 5.35); (3) of Christ as appointed by God to rule over all (RV 19.16)

βασιλεύς	N-NM-S	βασιλεύς
	N-VM-S	"
βασιλεῦσαι	VNAA	βασιλεύω

βασιλεύσει	VIFA--3S	"
βασιλεύσῃ	VSAA--3S	"
βασιλεῦσι(ν)	N-DM-P	βασιλεύς
βασιλεύσομεν	VIFA--1P	βασιλεύω
βασιλεύσουσι(ν)	VIFA--3P	"

βασιλεύω fut. βασιλεύσω; 1aor. ἐβασίλευσα; (1) *be king, reign, rule* (MT 2.22); (2) aorist *become king, be made king, obtain royal power* (RV 19.6); (3) of the rule of God and Christ and those called to rule with Christ *reign* (RV 20.4); (4) figuratively, of the dominating quality of something as sin (RO 5.21a), death (RO 5.14), grace (RO 5.21b) *reign, rule over, control completely*

βασιλέων	N-GM-P	βασιλεύς
βασιλέως	N-GM-S	"
βασιλικήν	A--AF-S	βασιλικός
βασιλικῆς	A--GF-S	"
βασιλικόν	A--AM-S	"

βασιλικός, ή, όν *royal*; of law as given from God as king (JA 2.8); substantively ὁ β. *royal officer, palace official* (JN 4.46)

βασιλικός	AP-NM-S	βασιλικός

βασιλίσκος, ου, ὁ diminutive of βασιλεύς; *petty king, minor king* (JN 4.46)

βασιλίσκος	N-NM-S	βασιλίσκος

βασίλισσα, ης, ἡ *queen*, in the NT a female ruler with complete authority over her domain

βασίλισσα	N-NF-S	βασίλισσα
βασιλίσσης	N-GF-S	"

βάσις, εως, ἡ strictly *step, stepping*; by metonymy *(human) foot* (AC 3.7)

βασκαίνω 1aor. ἐβάσκανα; originally *cause harm with unfavorable words*; in the NT *bewitch, cast the evil eye on, put a spell on* someone (probably used ironically in GA 3.1); figuratively *cunningly deceive* (possibly GA 3.1)

βαστάζει	VIPA--3S	βαστάζω
βαστάζειν	VNPA	"
βαστάζεις	VIPA--2S	"
βαστάζεσθαι	VNPP	"
βαστάζετε	VMPA--2P	"
βαστάζοντες	VPPANM-P	"
βαστάζοντος	VPPAGN-S	"

βαστάζω fut. βαστάσω; 1aor. ἐβάστασα; (1) *take up, lift up, pick up* (JN 10.31); (2) *carry, bear* (MK 14.13); figuratively, of anything burdensome or difficult *bear, endure, put up with* (MT 20.12); (3) *bear away, remove* (JN 20.15); figuratively, of healing disease (MT 8.17); (4) *steal, pilfer, carry off* (JN 12.6); (5) figuratively, of serving as a source of supply *support, provide for* (RO 11.18)

βαστάζω	VIPA--1S	βαστάζω
βαστάζων	VPPANM-S	"
βαστάξαι	VNAA	see βαστάσαι
βαστάσαι	VNAA	βαστάζω
βαστάσασα	VPAANF-S	"
βαστάσασι	VPAADM-P	"
βαστάσει	VIFA--3S	"

βάτος, ου, ἡ and ὁ (I) *thornbush, bramble, prickly bush*
βάτος, ου, ὁ (II) (also **βάδος**) *bath*, a Hebrew liquid measure estimated as containing 21.5 liters, between 5 and 6 gallons (LU 16.6)

βάτου	N-GF-S	βάτος (I)
	N-GM-S	"
βάτους	N-AM-P	βάτος (II)
βάτραχοι	N-NM-P	βάτραχος

βάτραχος, ου, ὁ *frog* (RV 16.13)

βατράχους	N-AM-P	βάτραχος
βατταλογεῖτε	VIPA--2P	βατταλογέω

βατταλογέω 1aor. ἐβατταλόγησα; *use many (meaningless) words, babble, use vain repetitions* (MT 6.7)

βατταλογήσητε	VSAA--2P	βατταλογέω
Βαττών		Ἀβαδδών
βάτῳ	N-DF-S	βάτος (I)
βάψας	VPAANM-S	βάπτω
βάψῃ	VSAA--3S	"
βάψω	VIFA--1S	"

βδέλυγμα, ατος, τό (1) generally, as what is extremely hated or abhorred *abomination, detestable thing* (LU 16.15); (2) as anything connected with idolatry *abomination* (RV 17.4); (3) as what is connected with the worship of the Antichrist τὸ β. τῆς ἐρημώσεως *the abomination of desolation, the detestable thing that causes desecration* of God's sanctuary (MT 24.15)

βδέλυγμα	N-AN-S	βδέλυγμα
	N-NN-S	"
βδελυγμάτων	N-GN-P	"
βδελυκτοί	A--NM-P	βδελυκτός

βδελυκτός, ή, όν of someone considered extremely bad *abominable, abhorrent, detestable* (TI 1.16)

βδελύσσομαι pf. ptc. ἐβδελυγμένος; *abhor, detest, loathe* something (RO 2.22); passive *be abominable, be detestable* (RV 21.8)

βδελυσσόμενος	VPPDVM-S	βδελύσσομαι
	VPPOVM-S	"
βεβαία	A--NF-S	βέβαιος
βεβαίαν	A--AF-S	"

βέβαιος, αία, ον (also **βλίβαιος**) *steadfast, firm, sure*; (1) literally, of an anchor *secure, firm* (HE 6.19); figuratively, of what can be depended on *reliable, certain, trustworthy* (RO 4.16); (2) as a legal technical term; (a) of law *legally enforced, valid* (HE 2.2); (b) of a contracted agreement or testament *valid, in force* (HE 9.17); (3) comparative βεβαιότερος, τέρα, ον *more sure, altogether reliable* (2P 1.19)

βέβαιος	A--NM-S	βέβαιος
βεβαιότερον	A-MAM-S	"
βεβαιούμενοι	VPPPNM-P	βεβαιόω
βεβαιοῦντος	VPPAGM-S	"
βεβαιοῦσθαι	VNPP	"

βεβαιόω fut. βεβαιώσω; 1aor. ἐβεβαίωσα; 1aor. pass. ἐβεβαιώθην; *confirm, establish, make sure*; (1) in relation to things *prove valid, confirm, verify* (RO 15.8); (2) in relation to persons *strengthen inwardly, make unwavering, establish* (2C 1.21); passive *increase in inward strength* (CO 2.7)

βεβαιῶν	VPPANM-S	βεβαιόω

βεβαίως adverb; *certainly, firmly, steadfastly* (HE 3.6)

βεβαίως	AB	βεβαίως
βεβαιῶσαι	VNAA	"
βεβαιώσει	N-DF-S	βεβαίωσις
	VIFA--3S	βεβαιόω
βεβαίωσιν	N-AF-S	βεβαίωσις

βεβαίωσις, εως, ἡ   strictly, a legal technical term for furnishing a guarantee *legally valid confirmation*; hence, as an action *confirmation, verification, making sure* (HE 6.16)

βεβαμμένον	VPRPAN-S	βάπτω
βεβάπτικα	VIRA--1S	βαπτίζω
βεβαπτισμένοι	VPRPNM-P	"
βεβαρημένοι	VPRPNM-P	βαρέω
βεβήλοις	A--DM-P	βέβηλος

βέβηλος, ον   strictly *open and accessible to all*, opposite ἱερός (*sacred*); (1) of things *profane, godless, worldly* (1T 6.20); (2) substantivally οἱ βέβηλοι of persons *ungodly, irreligious, profane people* (HE 12.16)

βέβηλος	A--NM-S	βέβηλος
βεβήλους	A--AF-P	"
	A--AM-P	"
βεβηλοῦσι(ν)	VIPA--3P	βεβηλόω

βεβηλόω   1aor. ἐβεβήλωσα; as disregarding what is to be kept sacred or holy *desecrate, violate, ritually defile* (MT 12.5)

βεβηλῶσαι	VNAA	βεβηλόω
βέβληκε(ν)	VIRA--3S	βάλλω
βεβληκότος	VPRAGM-S	"
βεβλημένην	VPRPAF-S	"
βεβλημένον	VPRPAM-S	"
	VPRPAN-S	"
βεβλημένος	VPRPNM-S	"
βέβληται	VIRP--3S	"
βεβρωκόσι(ν)	VPRADM-P	βιβρώσκω
Βεεζεβούλ		Βεελζεβούλ
Βεελζεβούβ		"

Βεελζεβούλ, ὁ (also Βεεζεβούλ, Βεελζεβούβ) indeclinable; *Beelzebul*, masculine proper noun for a Philistine deity meaning *lord of flies*; in the NT a name for the devil as ruler over the demons (MT 12.24)

Βελζεθά		Βηθζαθά
βέλη	N-AN-P	βέλος
Βελιάβ		Βελιάρ
Βελίαλ		"
Βελιάλ		"
Βελιάν		"

Βελιάρ, ὁ (also Βελιάβ, Βελίαλ, Βελιάλ, Βελιάν) indeclinable; *Belial*, masculine proper noun meaning *worthlessness*, a designation for the devil (2C 6.15)

βελόνη, ης, ἡ   *pointed instrument* for sewing, *needle* (LU 18.25)

βελόνης	N-GF-S	βελόνη

βέλος, ους, τό   as something thrown *pointed weapon, arrow, dart*; metaphorically, of Satan's temptations as weapons of attack (EP 6.16)

βέλτιον	ABM	βελτίων

βελτίων, ον   comparative of ἀγαθός (*good*); *better*; neuter βέλτιον as an adverb; *very well* (2T 1.18)

Βενιαμείν		Βενιαμίν

Βενιαμίν, ὁ (also Βενιαμείν) indeclinable; *Benjamin*, masculine proper noun

Βερενίκη	N-NF-S	Βερνίκη
Βερηνίκη	N-NF-S	"

Βερνίκη, ης, ἡ (also Βερενίκη, Βερηνίκη) *Bernice*, feminine proper noun

Βερνίκη	N-NF-S	Βερνίκη
Βερνίκης	N-GF-S	"

Βέροια, ας, ἡ   *Beroea* or *Berea*, city in Macedonia

Βεροίᾳ	N-DF-S	Βέροια

Βεροιαῖος, αία, ον (also Βερροιαῖος)   *belonging to Beroea* or *Berea*; as a substantive *Beroean* or *Berean, person from Beroea* or *Berea* (AC 20.4)

Βεροιαῖος	AP-NM-S	Βεροιαῖος
Βέροιαν	N-AF-S	Βέροια
Βέροιας	N-GF-S	"
Βεροῖος	AP-NM-S	see Βεροιαῖος
Βέρου	N-GF-S	see Βέροιας
Βερροιαῖος	AP-NM-S	Βεροιαῖος
Βεωορσόρ		Βοσόρ
Βεώρ		
Βηδσαϊδά		Βηθσαϊδά
Βηδσαϊδάν		
Βηζαθά		Βηθζαθά

Βηθαβαρά, ᾶς, ἡ (also Βηθαραβά, Βιθαρά) *Bethabara*, possibly the name for a site east of the Jordan River where John baptized (JN 1.28)

Βηθαβαρᾷ	N-DF-S	Βηθαβαρά

Βηθανία, ας, ἡ   *Bethany*; (1) a village on the Mount of Olives near Jerusalem (MT 21.17); (2) possible name for a site east of the Jordan River where John baptized (JN 1.28)

Βηθανία	N-AF-S	see Βηθανίαν
	N-NF-S	Βηθανία
Βηθανίᾳ	N-DF-S	"
Βηθανίαν	N-AF-S	"
Βηθανίας	N-GF-S	"
Βηθαραβᾷ	N-DF-S	Βηθαβαρά
Βηθεσδά		Βηθζαθά

Βηθζαθά, ἡ (also Βελζεθά, Βηζαθά, Βηθεσδά) indeclinable; (1) *Bethzatha*, name of the northeastern section of ancient Jerusalem; possibly the name of the pool located there (JN 5.2); (2) *Bethesda*, possibly the name of the pool in northeastern Jerusalem

Βηθλέεμ, ἡ (also Βηθλεέμ) indeclinable; *Bethlehem*, a town in Judea 7 kilometers or about 4.5 miles south of Jerusalem

Βηθλεέμ		Βηθλέεμ

Βηθσαϊδά, ἡ (also Βηδσαϊδά, Βηδσαϊδάν, Βηθσαϊδάν, Βησσαϊδά) indeclinable; *Bethsaida*; (1) a town in Galilee north of the Sea of Galilee near the inlet of the Jordan River; (2) possible name for a pool in Jerusalem (JN 5.2); see Βηθζαθά

Βηθσαϊδάν		Βηθσαϊδά

Βηθφαγή, ἡ   indeclinable; *Bethphage*, a village on the Mount of Olives east of Jerusalem

βῆμα, ατος, τό   (1) as a distance measured by one stride, approximately 2.5 feet, less than 1 meter *step, stride* (AC 7.5); (2) as an elevated platform ascended by steps; (a) *judicial bench, tribunal, judge's seat* (MT 27.19); (b) as a seat for a king or high official *rostrum, throne* (AC 12.21)

βῆμα	N-AN-S	βῆμα
βήματι	N-DN-S	"
βήματος	N-GN-S	"
Βηρέα	N-AM-S	Νηρεύς

βήρυλλος, ου, ὁ   *beryl*, a valuable stone or gem of sea-green color (RV 21.20)

βήρυλλος N-NM-S βήρυλλος
Βησσαϊδά Βηθσαϊδά
βία, ας, ἡ (1) of persons *bodily strength, force, violence* (AC 21.35); (2) of the forces of nature *violence*; of the force of waves against a ship *pounding* (AC 27.41)
βία N-DF-S βία
βιάζεται VIPM--3S βιάζω
    VIPP--3S "
βιάζω always with a component of force; (1) intransitively *use force, violence*; in a good sense *press (in), try hard to (enter), enter forcibly* (into) (LU 16.16; cf. 13.24); (2) transitively and passive *suffer violently, be treated violently*; MT 11.12's kingdom of heaven may fit here with two possible meanings: in a bad sense *suffer violently* at the hands of opponents (cf. βιασταὶ ἁρπάζουσιν [*violent people are seizing (it)*] in the next clause and MT 23.13); in a good sense (forceful people) *lay hold of* (it)
βιαίας A--GF-S βίαιος
βίαιος, αία, ον *violent, forcible, vehement* (AC 2.2)
βίαν N-AF-S βία
βίας N-GF-S "
βιασταί N-NM-P βιαστής
βιαστής, οῦ, ὁ *violent person, violator, one who uses force,* usually in a bad sense (MT 11.12)
βιβλαρίδιον, ου, τό (also βιβλιδάριον) diminutive of βίβλος; *little book, small scroll*
βιβλαρίδιον N-AN-S βιβλαρίδιον
βιβλάριον, ου, τό diminutive of βίβλος; *little book, small scroll* (RV 10.2)
βιβλάριον N-AN-S βιβλάριον
βιβλία N-AN-P βιβλίον
    N-NN-P
βιβλιδάριον N-AN-S βιβλαρίδιον
βιβλίδιον, ου, τό diminutive of βιβλίον; *small book* or *scroll, document* (RV 10.10)
βιβλίδιον N-AN-S βιβλίδιον
βιβλίοις N-DN-P βιβλίον
βιβλίον, ου, τό (1) *book, scroll, roll of a book, writing* (JN 20.30); (2) legally *document*; of divorce *certificate* (MT 19.7); (3) *written record* (RV 17.8)
βιβλίον N-AN-S βιβλίον
    N-NN-S "
βιβλίου N-GN-S "
βιβλίῳ N-DN-S "
βιβλίοις N-DF-P βίβλος
βίβλος, ου, ἡ strictly *inner bark of papyrus reed* used for paper; (1) as an object, a written document in the form of a *scroll* or *book* (AC 19.19); (2) by metonymy, of the content *book* (LU 20.42); *written record* (MT 1.1)
βίβλος N-NF-S βίβλος
βίβλου N-GF-S "
βίβλους N-AF-P "
βίβλῳ N-DF-S "
βιβρώσκω pf. βέβρωκα; *eat, consume* (JN 6.13)
Βιθαρᾶ N-DF-S Βηθαβαρά
Βιθυνία, ας, ἡ *Bithynia,* a province in the northern part of Asia Minor
Βιθυνίαν N-AF-S Βιθυνία
Βιθυνίας N-GF-S "
βίον N-AM-S βίος

βίος, ου, ὁ *life*; (1) of earthly life in its daily functions, such as preoccupation with food, clothing, and shelter (2T 2.4); (2) of the means of subsistence *property, goods, one's living* (1J 3.17)
βίου N-GM-S βίος
βιόω 1aor. ἐβίωσα; of life on earth *live, spend one's (earthly) life* (1P 4.2)
βιῶσαι VNAA βιόω
βίωσιν N-AF-S βίωσις
βίωσις, εως, ἡ as how one spends his earthly life *kind* or *manner of life, way of living* (AC 26.4)
βιωτικά A--AN-P βιωτικός
βιωτικαῖς A--DF-P "
βιωτικός, ή, όν *pertaining to (daily) life, of daily matters,* having to do with this life (LU 21.34); substantivally βιωτικά *matters of this life, ordinary matters* (1C 6.3)
βλαβεράς A--AF-P βλαβερός
βλαβερός, ή, όν *harmful, injurious, hurtful* (1T 6.9)
βλάβητε VSAA--2P βλάπτω
βλάπτω 1aor. ἔβλαψα; *harm, injure, hurt*
βλαστᾷ VSPA--3S βλαστάνω
βλαστάνη VSPA--3S "
βλαστάνω (and βλαστάω) 1aor. ἐβλάστησα; (1) transitively, of the earth or soil *produce, yield* (JA 5.18); (2) intransitively, of the beginning growth of plants and trees *sprout, bud, put forth leaves* (MT 13.26)
βλαστήσασα VPAANF-S βλαστάνω
Βλάστον N-AM-S Βλάστος
Βλάστος, ου, ὁ *Blastus,* masculine proper noun (AC 12.20)
βλάσφημα A--AN-P βλάσφημος
βλασφημεῖ VIPA--3S βλασφημέω
βλασφημεῖν VNPA "
βλασφημεῖς VIPA--2S "
βλασφημείσθω VMPP--3S "
βλασφημεῖται VIPP--3S "
βλασφημέω impf. ἐβλασφήμουν; 1aor. ἐβλασφήμησα; 1fut. pass. βλασφημηθήσομαι; *speak injuriously*; (1) in relation to people *slander, revile, defame* someone's reputation (TI 3.2); (2) in relation to God *blaspheme, insult* (MT 26.65); (3) in relation to the things of God, such as the gospel message (TI 2.5), one's way of life (RO 14.16) *speak evil about, revile*; (4) in relation to supernatural beings, as angels and heavenly dignitaries *speak evil about, insult* (JU 8); (5) in relation to idols regarded as divinities *blaspheme, insult* (AC 19.37)
βλασφημηθήσεται VIFP--3S βλασφημέω
βλασφημῆσαι VNAA "
βλασφημήσαντι VPAADM-S "
βλασφημήση VSAA--3S "
βλασφημήσωσι(ν) VSAA--3P "
βλασφημῆται VSPP--3S "
βλασφημία, ας, ἡ (1) generally *harmful, abusive speech* against someone's reputation; *slander, reviling, evil speaking* (CO 3.8); (2) predominantly of speech that is against the nature and power of God *blasphemy, insult, outrage* (MT 26.65)
βλασφημία N-NF-S βλασφημία
βλασφημίαι N-NF-P "
βλασφημίαν N-AF-S "
βλασφημίας N-AF-P "
    N-GF-S "

βλάσφημοι   A--NM-P   βλάσφημος
βλάσφημον   AP-AM-S   "
     A--AF-S   "

βλάσφημος, ον   of abusive, reproachful speech *blasphemous, slanderous, insulting* (AC 6.11); substantivally *blasphemer* (1T 1.13); τὰ βλάσφεμα *blasphemous speech* (RV 13.5)

βλασφημοῦμαι   VIPP--1S   βλασφημέω
βλασφημούμεθα   VIPP--1P   "
βλασφημούμενοι   VPPPNM-P   "
βλασφημοῦντας   VPPAAM-P   "
βλασφημοῦντες   VPPANM-P   "
βλασφημούντων   VPPAGM-P   "
βλασφημοῦσι(ν)   VIPA--3P   "
βλάψαν   VPAANN-S   βλάπτω
βλάψει   VIFA--3S   "
βλάψῃ   VSAA--3S   "

βλέμμα, ατος, τό   as the result of an act of seeing *look, glance; what one sees, sight* (2P 2.8)

βλέμματι   N-DN-S   βλέμμα
βλέπε   VMPA--2S   βλέπω
βλέπει   VIPA--3S   "
βλέπειν   VNPA   "
βλέπεις   VIPA--2S   "
βλέπετε   VIPA--2P   "
     VMPA--2P   "
βλεπέτω   VMPA--3S   "
βλέπῃ   VSPA--3S   "
βλέπῃς   VSPA--2S   "
βλέπομεν   VIPA--1P   "
βλεπόμενα   VPPPAN-P   "
     VPPPNN-P   "
βλεπομένη   VPPPNF-S   "
βλεπόμενον   VPPPAN-S   "
βλεπομένων   VPPPGN-P   "
βλέποντα   VPPAAM-S   "
βλέποντας   VPPAAM-P   "
βλέποντες   VPPANM-P   "
βλεπόντων   VPPAGM-P   "
βλέπουσι(ν)   VIPA--3P   "

βλέπω   fut. βλέψω; 1aor. ἔβλεψα; *see, look at*; (1) of sense perception *see* (MT 7.3); (2) in contrast to being blind *be able to see* (LU 7.21); figuratively, of spiritual perception *see, understand, be aware of* (JN 9.39; RO 11.8); (3) of careful observing *look at, regard* (MT 5.28; JN 13.22); (4) of mental functions; (a) as directing one's attention *take notice of, regard, consider* (1C 1.26); (b) as taking warning *watch, beware, take heed* (MK 13.9); (c) as mentally perceiving *discover, find, become aware of* (RO 7.23)

βλέπω   VIPA--1S   βλέπω
βλέπωμεν   VSPA--1S   "
βλέπων   VPPANM-S   "
βλέπωσι(ν)   VSPA--3P   "
βλέψετε   VIFA--2P   "
βλέψον   VMAA--2S   "
βληθείς   VPAPNM-S   βάλλω
βληθείσῃ   VPAPDF-S   "
βληθέν   VPAPNN-S   "
βληθῇ   VSAP--3S   "
βληθῆναι   VNAP   "

βληθήσεται   VIFP--3S   "
βληθήσῃ   VIFP--2S   "
βληθήσονται   VIFP--3P   "
βλήθητι   VMAP--2S   "
βλητέον   A--NN-S   βλητέος

βλητέος, α, ον   a verbal adjective from βάλλω (*throw, cast*); *requiring to be cast* or *put*; of wine in wineskins *must be stored* (LU 5.38)

βλιβαία   A--NF-S   βέβαιος
Βόαζ   Βόες
βοαί   N-NF-P   βοή

Βοανηργές, ὁ   indeclinable; *Boanerges*, masculine plural Aramaic nickname given by Jesus to James and John, the sons of Zebedee; translated *sons of thunder* (MK 3.17)

βόας   N-AM-P   βοῦς

βοάω   1aor. ἐβόησα; *cry out, shout, call loudly*; (1) absolutely *exult, shout for joy* (GA 4.27); (2) as solemnly proclaiming *cry, call out, shout* (JN 1.23); (3) as a crowd raising an outcry *cry, shout* (AC 17.6); (4) as crying for help *call to, call out* (LU 9.38); (5) as crying out in anguish *shout, cry* (MK 15.34; MT 27.46)

Βόες, ὁ (also Βόλλς, Βόαζ, Βοές, Βόοζ, Βοόζ, Βόος, Βοός)   indeclinable; *Boaz*, masculine proper noun

Βοές   Βόες

βοή, ῆς, ἡ   *cry, shout*; of workers seeking fair compensation *outcry* (JA 5.4)

βοήθει   VMPA--2S   βοηθέω

βοήθεια, ας, ἡ   (1) *help, aid* (HE 4.16); (2) plural, a nautical technical term for safety devices for a ship *supports*, such as ropes (AC 27.17)

βοηθείαις   N-DF-P   βοήθεια
βοήθειαν   N-AF-S   "
βοηθείας   N-AF-P   "
βοηθεῖν   VNPA   βοηθέω
βοηθεῖτε   VMPA--2P   "

βοηθέω   1aor. ἐβοήθησα; strictly *run to the aid of one who cries for help*; hence *help, come to the aid of, rescue* (MT 15.25)

βοηθῆσαι   VNAA   βοηθέω
βοήθησον   VMAA--2S   "

βοηθός, όν   *helpful*; substantivally *helper* (HE 13.6)

βοηθός   AP-NM-S   βοηθός
βόησον   VMAA--2S   βοάω
βόθρον   N-AM-S   βόθρος

βόθρος, ου, ὁ   *pit, cistern* (MT 15.14)

βόθυνον   N-AM-S   βόθυνος

βόθυνος, ου, ὁ   a hole of some kind dug into the ground *pit, well, cistern* (MT 12.11)

βολή, ῆς, ἡ   *a throw* or *a cast*; the distance an object can be thrown; ὡσεὶ λίθου βολήν *about a stone's throw away* (LU 22.41)

βολήν   N-AF-S   βολή
βολίδι   N-DF-S   βολίς

βολίζω   1aor. ἐβόλισα; strictly, as a nautical technical term *heave the lead* (βολίς); hence *take soundings, drop a weighted line* (AC 27.28)

βολίς, ίδος, ἡ   *anything thrown*; (1) *missile*, such as *arrow* (HE 12.20) or *javelin*; (2) as a nautical technical term *sounding lead*, a weight attached to a line used to measure the depth of a body of water

βολίσαντες VPAANM-P βολίζω

Βόοζ Βόες

Βοόζ "

Βόος "

Βοός "

βόρβορος, ου, ὁ *slime, mud, mire* (2P 2.22)

βορβόρου N-GM-S βόρβορος

βορρᾶ N-GM-S βορρᾶς

βορρᾶς, ᾶ, ὁ as one of the four directions *north*

βόσκε VMPA--2S βόσκω

βόσκειν VNPA "

βοσκομένη VPPPNF-S "

βοσκομένων VPPPGM-P "

βόσκοντες VPPANM-P "

βόσκω (1) active, of herdsmen tending flocks or herds *feed, pasture, tend while grazing* (MT 8.33); (2) passive, of grazing animals *feed, be feeding* (MT 8.30)

Βοσόρ, ὁ (also **Βεωορσόρ, Βεώρ, Βοσύρ**) indeclinable; *Bosor*, masculine proper noun (2P 2.15)

Βοσύρ Βοσόρ

βοτάνη, ης, ἡ generally, any of the smaller green plants *grass, herb(s), fodder* (HE 6.7)

βοτάνην N-AF-S βοτάνη

βότρυας N-AM-P βότρυς

βότρυς, υος, ὁ as the fruit from grapevines *cluster* or *bunch of grapes* (RV 14.18)

βουλάς N-AF-P βουλή

βούλει VIPD--2S βούλομαι

VIPO--2S "

βούλεσθε VIPD--2P "

VIPO--2P "

βούλεται VIPD--3S "

VIPO--3S "

βουλεύεται VIPM--3S βουλεύω

βουλεύομαι VIPM--1S "

βουλευόμενος VPPMNM-S "

βουλεύσεται VIFM--3S "

βουλευτής, οῦ, ὁ a member of a legislative or advisory body *councilor, council member*; in the NT a member of the Sanhedrin, the Jewish Supreme Court (MK 15.43)

βουλευτής N-NM-S βουλευτής

βουλεύω impf. mid. ἐβουλευόμην; fut. mid. βουλεύσομαι; 1aor. mid. ἐβουλευσάμην; only middle in the NT; (1) *deliberate, consider, think about carefully* (LU 14.31); (2) *decide, purpose* (JN 11.53)

βουλή, ῆς, ἡ (1) as an inward thought process leading toward a decision *deliberation, motive* (1C 4.5); (2) as the result of inner deliberation *resolve, decision, purpose, plan* (AC 5.38); (3) as the result of community deliberation *counsel* (AC 27.12); as the divine will *counsel, purpose* (AC 2.23)

βουλή N-NF-S βουλή

βουλῇ N-DF-S "

βουληθείς VPAONM-S βούλομαι

βουληθῇ VSAO--3S "

βούλημα, ατος, τό as the result of deciding *intention, purpose, will* (RO 9.19)

βούλημα N-AN-S βούλημα

βουλήματι N-DN-S "

βουλήματος N-GN-S "

βουλήν N-AF-S βουλή

βουλῆς N-GF-S "

βούληται VSPD--3S βούλομαι

VSPO--3S "

βούλοιτο VOPD--3S "

VOPO--3S "

βούλομαι second-person singular βούλει (LU 22.42); impf. ἐβουλόμην; 1aor. ἐβουλήθην and ἠβουλήθην; (1) of a person desiring something *wish, want, desire* (AC 25.22); (2) of a person deliberating and deciding something *will, determine, intend* (2C 1.15); (3) of God *wish, want* (2P 3.9); *decide, will* (JA 1.18)

βούλομαι VIPD--1S βούλομαι

VIPO--1S "

βουλόμεθα VIPD--1P "

VIPO--1P "

βουλόμενοι VPPDNM-P "

VPPONM-P "

βουλόμενος VPPDNM-S "

VPPONM-S "

βουλομένου VPPDGM-S "

VPPOGM-S "

βουλομένους VPPDAM-P "

VPPOAM-P "

βοῦν N-AM-S βοῦς

βουνοῖς N-DM-P βουνός

βουνός, οῦ, ὁ *hill, rising ground, mound*

βουνός N-NM-S βουνός

βοῦς, βοός, ὁ and **ἡ** *bull, cow*; plural *cattle*

βοῦς N-NM-S βοῦς

βοῶν N-GM-P "

βοῶντα VPPAAN-P βοάω

βοῶντες VPPANM-P "

βοῶντος VPPAGM-S "

βοώντων VPPAGM-P "

βραβεῖον, ου, τό literally *prize; award* for victory in games (1C 9.24); figuratively, as a spiritual benefit *reward, prize* (PH 3.14)

βραβεῖον N-AN-S βραβεῖον

βραβευέτω VMPA--3S βραβεύω

βραβεύω strictly *be judge* or *umpire in public games*; hence *preside, direct, control* (CO 3.15)

βραδεῖς A--VM-P βραδύς

βραδύνει VIPA--3S βραδύνω

βραδυνεῖ VIFA--3S "

βραδύνω fut. βραδυνῶ; intransitively *delay, be slow about something*

βραδύνω VSPA--1S βραδύνω

βραδυπλοέω *sail slowly* (AC 27.7)

βραδυπλοοῦντες VPPANM-P βραδυπλοέω

βραδύς, εῖα, ύ literally *slow*, opposite ταχύς (*quick, prompt*); figuratively, of mental and spiritual slowness *slow, dull, stupid* (JA 1.19); substantivally οἱ βραδεῖς *slow learners, stupid people* (LU 24.25)

βραδύς A--NM-S βραδύς

βραδύτης, ητος, ἡ *slowness, delay, tardiness* (2P 3.9)

βραδύτητα N-AF-S βραδύτης

βραχεῖς A--AM-P βραχύς

βραχέων A--GM-P "

A--GN-P "

βραχίονι N-DM-S βραχίων

βραχίονος N-GM-S "

βραχίων, ονος, ὁ   *arm*; in the NT used to express God's powerful activity in analogy to human activity (LU 1.51)

βραχίων	N-NM-S	βραχίων
βραχύ	AB	βραχύς
	A--AN-S	"

βραχύς, εῖα, ύ   *short, little*; (1) of time *brief, short* (LU 22.58); neuter singular βραχύ as an adverb *for a short time, briefly* (AC 5.34; possibly HE 2.7); (2) of space *little*, neuter singular as an adverb *short distance* (AC 27.28); (3) of degree or quantity *little, few*; substantivally *small amount* (JN 6.7); neuter singular as an adverb *by little (degree), in a small amount* (probably HE 2.7 as Psalm 8.5 Septuagint)

βρέξαι	VNAA	βρέχω
βρέξῃ	VSAA--3S	"
βρέφη	N-AN-P	βρέφος
	N-NN-P	"

βρέφος, ους, τό   (1) *unborn child, babe* (LU 1.41); (2) *newborn child, infant, baby* (LU 2.12); (3) *childhood* (2T 3.15); (4) metaphorically, of a new or immature Christian (1P 2.2)

βρέφος	N-AN-S	βρέφος
	N-NN-S	"
βρέφους	N-GN-S	"
βρέχει	VIPA--3S	βρέχω
βρέχειν	VNPA	"
βρέχῃ	VSPA--3S	"

βρέχω   1aor. ἔβρεξα; (1) *make wet, moisten*, as with tears (LU 7.38); (2) *send rain, cause to rain* (MT 5.45); (3) impersonally βρέχει *it rains* (JA 5.17); (4) intransitively, of rain *fall* (RV 11.6)

βριμάομαι   1aor. ἐβριμησάμην; *be indignant* (JN 11.33)

βρονταί	N-NF-P	βροντή

βροντή, ῆς, ἡ   as the loud, rolling sound that follows a flash of lightning *thunder*

βροντήν	N-AF-S	βροντή
βροντῆς	N-GF-S	"
βροντῶν	N-GF-P	"

βροχή, ῆς, ἡ   *rain*

βροχή	N-NF-S	βροχή
βρόχον	N-AM-S	βρόχος

βρόχος, ου, ὁ   *noose* or *slip cord*, used in hunting for catching or in captivity for restraining; figuratively *restraint, restriction* (1C 7.35)

βρυγμός, οῦ, ὁ   as the sound made by striking the teeth together *gnashing, grinding, grating* (MT 8.12)

βρυγμός	N-NM-S	βρυγμός
βρύει	VIPA--3S	βρύω

βρύχω   impf. ἔβρυχον; as making sounds by striking the teeth together *gnash, grate, grind*; idiomatically βράχειν τοὺς ὀδόντας literally *grind the teeth*, i.e. *be furious* (AC 7.54)

βρύω   strictly *be full to bursting*; hence *send forth, cause to pour* or *gush out* (JA 3.11)

βρωθῇ	VSAP--3S	βιβρώσκω

βρῶμα, ατος, τό   (1) generally *food, something to eat* (RO 14.15); (2) specifically *solid food, meat*, in contrast to γάλα (*milk*); figuratively *mature doctrine* (1C 3.2); (3) figuratively, of Jesus' being spiritually sustained by doing God's will *source of strength* (JN 4.34)

βρῶμα	N-AN-S	βρῶμα
	N-NN-S	"
βρώμασι(ν)	N-DN-P	"
βρώματα	N-AN-P	"
	N-NN-P	"
βρώματι	N-DN-S	"
βρώματος	N-GN-S	"
βρωμάτων	N-GN-P	"
βρώσει	N-DF-S	βρῶσις
βρώσεως	N-GF-S	"
βρώσιμον	A--AN-S	βρώσιμος

βρώσιμος, ον   *eatable, edible, useful for food*; substantivally τι βρώσιμον *something to eat* (LU 24.41)

βρῶσιν	N-AF-S	βρῶσις

βρῶσις, εως, ἡ   (1) as an action *eating* (1C 8.4); often with πόσις (*drinking*) (RO 14.17); (2) as a corrosive action on metals *rust, corrosion, eating into* (usually taken to be the meaning in MT 6.19, 20, though possibly a burrowing insect like *woodworm* is intended); as what is eaten *meal* (HE 12.16)

βρῶσις	N-NF-S	βρῶσις
βυθίζεσθαι	VNPP	βυθίζω
βυθίζουσι(ν)	VIPA--3P	"

βυθίζω   (1) literally and passive, of a ship *sink* (LU 5.7); (2) figuratively and active, of causing serious consequences *plunge* (into ruin), *thrust down* (1T 6.9)

βυθός, οῦ, ὁ   *depth*; of the open sea *deep*; ἐν τῷ βυθῷ *adrift at sea* (2C 11.25)

βυθῷ	N-DM-S	βυθός
βυρσεῖ	N-DM-S	βυρσεύς

βυρσεύς, έως, ὁ   a person who prepares animal skins for use *tanner, leather dresser*

βυρσέως	N-GM-S	βυρσεύς
βύσσινον	AP-AN-S	βύσσινος
	AP-NN-S	"

βύσσινος, η, ον   *made of fine linen*; neuter as a substantive τὸ βύσσινον *fine linen goods, linen garment* (RV 18.12)

βυσσίνου	AP-GN-S	βύσσινος
βυσσίνων	AP-GN-P	"
βύσσον	N-AF-S	βύσσος

βύσσος, ου, ἡ   a shiny white cloth made from bleached flax *fine linen* (LU 16.19)

βύσσου	N-GF-S	βύσσος
βωμόν	N-AM-S	βωμός

βωμός, οῦ, ὁ   strictly *elevated spot*, as a pedestal; hence *altar* (AC 17.23)

γ indeclinable; third letter of the Greek alphabet; as a cardinal number *three*; as an ordinal number *third* (AC 2.15); used in the superscription of 3 John

Γαββαθά, τό (also **Γαββαθᾶ**) indeclinable; *Gabbatha*, an Aramaic place-name in Jerusalem called in Greek λιθόστρωτον (*Stone Pavement*) (JN 19.13)

Γαββαθᾶ		Γαββαθά

Γαβριήλ, ὁ indeclinable; *Gabriel*, masculine proper noun; name of an angel (LU 1.19)

γάγγραινα, ης, ἡ a medical technical term for spreading ulcers *gangrene, cancer* (2T 2.17)

γάγγραινα	N-NF-S	γάγγραινα

Γάδ, ὁ indeclinable; *Gad*, masculine proper noun; one of the tribes of Israel (RV 7.5)

Γαδαρηνός, ή, όν (also **Γαζαρηνός**) *from Gadara*, a city in Perea, a region east of the Jordan River; substantivally *Gadarene* (MT 8.28)

Γαδαρηνῶν	AP-GM-P	Γαδαρηνός

Γάζα, ης, ἡ *Gaza*, a chief Philistine city in southwestern Palestine, along the seacoast route to Egypt (AC 8.26)

γάζα, ης, ἡ from the Persian word for treasure; *treasury* (AC 8.27)

Γάζαν	N-AF-S	Γάζα
Γαζαρηνῶν	AP-GM-P	Γαδαρηνός
γάζης	N-GF-S	γάζα

γαζοφυλάκιον, ου, τό literally *treasury, treasure room* (JN 8.20); by metonymy *collection box, chest for offerings* or *contributions* (MK 12.41)

γαζοφυλάκιον	N-AN-S	γαζοφυλάκιον
γαζοφυλακίου	N-GN-S	"
γαζοφυλακίῳ	N-DN-S	"
Γάϊον	N-AM-S	Γάϊος
Γάϊον	N-AM-S	"
Γάϊος	N-NM-S	"

Γάϊος, ου, ὁ (also **Γαῖος**) *Gaius*, masculine proper noun

Γάϊος	N-NM-S	Γάϊος
Γαΐῳ	N-DM-S	"
Γαΐῳ	N-DM-S	"

γάλα, γάλακτος, τό *milk*, in contrast to βρῶμα (*food*) and στερεός (*solid food*); literally, as food (1C 9.7); metaphorically, of spiritual nourishment through elementary doctrinal instruction (1C 3.2)

γάλα	N-AN-S	γάλα
γάλακτος	N-GN-S	"
Γαλάται	N-VM-P	Γαλάτης

Γαλάτης, ου, ὁ *Galatian, inhabitant of Galatia* (GA 3.1)

Γαλατία, ας, ἡ (also **Γαλλία**) *Galatia*, the name of (a) a large interior, mountainous region in Asia Minor and (b) a Roman province in the southern part of the region

Γαλατίαν	N-AF-S	Γαλατία
Γαλατίας	N-GF-S	"
Γαλατικήν	A--AF-S	Γαλατικός

Γαλατικός, ή, όν *Galatian*; with χώρα *Galatian region* or *country* (AC 16.6; 18.23)

γαλήνη, ης, ἡ *calm, tranquillity, stillness* on the surface of a body of water

γαλήνη	N-NF-S	γαλήνη

Γαλιλαία, ας, ἡ *Galilee*, a district of Palestine north of Samaria (MT 2.22)

Γαλιλαία	N-NF-S	Γαλιλαία
	N-VF-S	"
Γαλιλαίᾳ	N-DF-S	"
Γαλιλαίαν	N-AF-S	"
Γαλιλαίας	N-GF-S	"
Γαλιλαῖοι	AP-NM-P	Γαλιλαῖος
	A--NM-P	"
	A--VM-P	"

Γαλιλαῖος, αία, ον *Galilean*; substantivally *inhabitant of Galilee, Galilean*

Γαλιλαῖος	A--NM-S	Γαλιλαῖος
Γαλιλαίου	A--GM-S	"
Γαλιλαίους	AP-AM-P	"
Γαλιλαίων	AP-GM-P	"
Γαλλίαν	N-AF-S	Γαλατία

Γαλλίων, ωνος, ὁ *Gallio*, masculine proper noun

Γαλλίων	N-NM-S	Γαλλίων
Γαλλίωνι	N-DM-S	"
Γαλλίωνος	N-GM-S	"

Γαμαλιήλ, ὁ indeclinable; *Gamaliel*, masculine proper noun

γαμεῖν	VNPA	γαμέω
γαμείτω	VMPA--3S	"
γαμείτωσαν	VMPA--3P	"

γαμέω impf. ἐγάμουν; 1aor. ἔγημα and ἐγάμησα; 1aor. pass. ἐγαμήθην; *marry* (MT 5.32); (1) absolutely *enter into marriage, marry* (MT 19.10); (2) of both sexes *marry* (1T 4.3); (3) of a woman *marry* (MK 10.12); (4) passive *get married, be married* (MK 10.12; 1C 7.39)

γαμηθῇ	VSAP--3S	γαμέω
γαμηθῆναι	VNAP	"
γαμῆσαι	VNAA	"
γαμήσας	VPAANM-S	"
γαμήσασα	VPAANF-S	"
γαμησάτωσαν	VMAA--3P	"
γαμήσῃ	VSAA--3S	"
γαμήσῃς	VSAA--2S	"
γαμίζονται	VIPP--3P	γαμίζω
γαμίζοντες	VPPANM-P	"

γαμίζω and **γαμίσκω** impf. pass. ἐγαμιζόμην; (1) active *give* (a woman) *in marriage* (MT 24.38; probably 1C 7.38); as equivalent to γαμέω (perhaps 1C 7.38); (2) passive, of women *be given in marriage, be married* (MT 22.30; LU 20.34, 35)

γαμίζων	VPPANM-S	γαμίζω

γαμίσκονται	VIPP--3P	"
γαμίσκοντες	VPPANM-P	"
γάμον	N-AM-S	γάμος

γάμος, ου, ὁ (1) *wedding, wedding feast* (JN 2.1); generally plural *wedding festivities, wedding celebration* (MT 22.2); (2) by metonymy, as the place where the wedding takes place *wedding hall* (MT 22.10); (3) as the married state *marriage* (HE 13.4); (4) *wedding ceremony*; figuratively, as the inauguration of the messianic kingdom by celebrating the union of Christ and the church (RV 19.7)

γάμος	N-NM-S	γάμος
γάμου	N-GM-S	"
γαμοῦντες	VPPANM-P	γαμέω
γάμους	N-AM-P	γάμος
γαμοῦσι(ν)	VIPA--3P	γαμέω
γάμῳ	N-DM-S	γάμος
γάμων	N-GM-P	"
γαμῶν	VPPANM-S	γαμέω

γάρ a conjunction basically introducing an explanation; (1) expressing cause or reason *for, because* (JN 2.25); (2) giving grounds for a conclusion, exhortation, or warning *for* (HE 2.2); (3) giving an explanation *for, you see* (MK 5.42); (4) expressing continuation like δέ (*but, and*) *indeed, certainly, to be sure* (RO 2.25); (5) as an inferential particle qualifying a whole sentence, usually in direct speech responses; (a) as an exclamation to point to a self-evident conclusion; (i) to make a strong denial *of course not, no indeed, by no means* (AC 8.31; 16.37; JA 1.7); (ii) to make a strong affirmation *yes indeed* (AC 19.35); τί γ. *why not? so what?* (PH 1.18); (b) to express skepticism about someone else's conclusion *Why should you say that? Come now, you know better than that!* (MT 27.23)

γάρ	CS	γάρ
	QS	"
γαστέρες	N-NF-P	γαστήρ

γαστήρ, τρός, ἡ (1) as the inward parts of the body *belly, stomach*; figuratively, of one who lives only to satisfy his appetite for food *glutton* (TI 1.12); (2) of a woman *womb* (LU 1.31); idiomatically ἐν γαστρὶ ἔχειν literally *have in the womb*, i.e. *be pregnant* (MT 1.18)

γαστρί	N-DF-S	γαστήρ
Γαύδην		Καῦδα

γέ an enclitic particle intensifying a word, always adding emphasis but not always translated; (1) as limiting *at least* (LU 11.8); (2) as intensifying *indeed, even* (RO 8.32); (3) often combined with other particles: εἰ δὲ μή γε *otherwise* (MT 6.1); καί γε as limiting *at least* (LU 19.42); as intensifying *even* (AC 2.18); *though* (AC 17.27); καίτοιγε *and yet, of course, although* (JN 4.2); μήτιγε *not to mention, let alone* (1C 6.3)

γέ	QS	γέ
γεγαμηκόσι(ν)	VPRADM-P	γαμέω
γεγενήμεθα	VIRP--1P	γίνομαι
γεγενημένα	VPRPNN-P	"
γεγενημένον	VPRPAN-S	"
γεγενημένους	VPRPAM-P	"
γεγενημένῳ	VPRPDM-S	"
γεγενῆσθαι	VNRP	"
γεγένησθε ·	VIRP--2P	"
γεγέννηκα	VIRA--1S	γεννάω

γεγέννημαι	VIRP--1S	"
γεγεννήμεθα	VIRP--1P	"
γεγεννημένα	VPRPNN-P	"
γεγεννημένον	VPRPAM-S	"
	VPRPNN-S	"
γεγεννημένος	VPRPNM-S	"
γεγεννημένου	VPRPGM-S	"
γεγέννηται	VIRP--3S	"
γέγονα	VIRA--1S	γίνομαι
γεγόναμεν	VIRA--1P	"
γέγοναν	VIRA--3P	"
γέγονας	VIRA--2S	"
γεγόνασι(ν)	VIRA--3P	"
γεγόνατε	VIRA--2P	"
γεγόνει	VILA--3S	"
γέγονε(ν)	VIRA--3S	"
γεγονέναι	VNRA	"
γεγονός	VPRAAN-S	"
	VPRANN-S	"
γεγονότα	VPRAAM-S	"
γεγονότας	VPRAAM-P	"
γεγονότες	VPRANM-P	"
γεγονότι	VPRADN-S	"
γεγονυῖα	VPRANF-S	"
γεγονώς	VPRANM-S	"
γεγραμμένα	VPRPAN-P	γράφω
	VPRPNN-P	"
γεγραμμένας	VPRPAF-P	"
γεγραμμένη	VPRPNF-S	"
γεγραμμένην	VPRPAF-S	"
γεγραμμένοι	VPRPNM-P	"
γεγραμμένοις	VPRPDN-P	"
γεγραμμένον	VPRPAN-S	"
	VPRPNN-S	"
γεγραμμένος	VPRPNM-S	"
γεγραμμένων	VPRPGM-P	"
	VPRPGN-P	"
γέγραπται	VIRP--3S	"
γέγραφα	VIRA--1S	"
γεγυμνασμένα	VPRPAN-P	γυμνάζω
γεγυμνασμένην	VPRPAF-S	"
γεγυμνασμένοις	VPRPDM-P	"

Γεδεών, ὁ indeclinable; *Gideon*, masculine proper noun (HE 11.32)

Γέεννα		γέεννα

γέεννα, ης, ἡ (also Γέεννα) *Gehenna*; literally *valley of Hinnom*, a ravine south of Jerusalem where fires were kept burning to consume the dead bodies of animals, criminals, and refuse; figuratively in the Gospels and James for *hell*, a fiery place of eternal punishment for the ungodly dead (MT 5.22)

γέενναν	N-AF-S	γέεννα
γεέννῃ	N-DF-S	"
γεέννης	N-GF-S	"
Γεθσημανεί		Γεθσημανί
Γεθσημανεῖ		"
Γεθσημανῆ		"

Γεθσημανί, τό (also Γεθσημανεί, Γεθσημανεῖ, Γεθσημανῆ) indeclinable; *Gethsemane*; strictly *oil press*; name of an olive orchard on the Mount of Olives overlooking Jerusalem from the east

γείτονας	N-AF-P	γείτων
	N-AM-P	"
γείτονες	N-NM-P	"

γείτων, ονος, ὁ and ἡ *neighbor*, one living nearby and sharing ethnic and cultural similarities

γελάσετε	VIFA--2P	γελάω
γελάσουσι(ν)	VIFA--3P	"

γελάω fut. γελάσω; *laugh, be merry*, in both good and bad senses

γελῶντες	VPPAVM-P	γελάω

γέλως, ωτος, ὁ *laughter*; by metonymy *merrymaking, rejoicing* (JA 4.9)

γέλως	N-NM-S	γέλως
γέμει	VIPA--3S	γέμω
γεμίζεσθαι	VNPP	γεμίζω

γεμίζω 1aor. ἐγέμισα; 1aor. pass. ἐγεμίσθην; *fill an object with something* (JN 2.7); passive *be filled, become full* (MK 4.37)

γεμίσαι	VNAA	γεμίζω
γεμίσας	VPAANM-S	"
γεμίσατε	VMAA--2P	"
γεμισθῇ	VSAP--3S	"
γέμον	VPPAAN-S	γέμω
γέμοντα	VPPAAN-P	"
	VPPANN-P	"
γεμόντων	VPPAGN-P	"
γεμούσας	VPPAAF-P	"
γέμουσι(ν)	VIPA--3P	"

γέμω *be full of* something, *contain*

γέμων	VPPANM-S	γέμω
γεναμένης	VPADGF-S	γίνομαι
γεναμένου	VPADGN-S	"
γεναμένων	VPADGN-P	"

γενεά, ᾶς, ἡ strictly *birth*, the circumstances relating to one's *origin*; (1) literally, those descended from a common ancestor *race, clan, descendants* (perhaps AC 8.33); as an ethnic group *kind* (LU 16.8); (2) generally, all those living at the same time *generation, contemporaries* (MT 12.41); (3) the time span of one generation *age, generation, period* (MT 1.17); (4) specifically in AC 8.33's quotation from Isaiah 53.8 Septuagint, possibly *origin*; more probably *posterity, descendants*

γενεά	N-NF-S	γενεά
	N-VF-S	"
γενεᾷ	N-DF-S	"
γενεαί	N-NF-P	"
γενεαῖς	N-DF-P	"

γενεαλογέω *trace* or *give account of descent*; only passive in the NT *have descent traced, be descended from* (HE 7.6)

γενεαλογία, ας, ἡ *genealogy, record of ancestry, family tree*

γενεαλογίαις	N-DF-P	γενεαλογία
γενεαλογίας	N-AF-P	"
γενεαλογούμενος	VPPPNM-S	γενεαλογέω
γενεάν	N-AF-S	γενεά
γενεάς	N-AF-P	"
γενεᾶς	N-GF-S	"
γενεθλίοις	A--DN-P	γενέθλιος

γενέθλιος, ον *having to do with birth*; γ. ἡμέρα *birthday* (MK 6.21)

γένει	N-DN-S	γένος

γενέσει	N-DF-S	γένεσις
γενέσεως	N-GF-S	"
γενέσθαι	VNAD	γίνομαι
γενέσθε	VMAD--2P	"
γενέσθω	VMAD--3S	"

γενέσια, ίων, τό originally a day observed on the birthday of a deceased person; in the NT *birthday feast* or *celebration* (MT 14.6)

γενεσίοις	N-DN-P	γενέσια

γένεσις, εως, ἡ (1) *birth* (LU 1.14); (2) as a historical record of a family line *origin, genealogy, lineage* (MT 1.1); (3) *existence, life*; πρόσωπον τῆς γενέσεως αὐτοῦ *face he was born with, his natural face* (JA 1.23); ὁ τροχὸς τῆς γενέσεως *the course of life, the (whole) round of existence* (JA 3.6)

γένεσις	N-NF-S	γένεσις
γενεσίων	N-GN-P	γενέσια

γενετή, ῆς, ἡ *birth* (JN 9.1)

γενετῆς	N-GF-S	γενετή
γενεχλίοις	A--DN-P	see γενεθλίοις
γενεῶν	N-GF-P	γενεά
γένη	N-AN-P	γένος
	N-NN-P	"
γενηθέντας	VPAOAM-P	γίνομαι
γενηθέντες	VPAONM-P	"
γενηθέντων	VPAOGN-P	"
γενηθῇ	VSAO--3S	"
γενηθῆναι	VNAO	"
γενηθῆτε	VMAO--2P	"
γενηθήτω	VMAO--3S	"
γενηθῶμεν	VSAO--1P	"

γένημα, ατος, τό literally, as increase of harvest *product, fruit, yield* (LU 22.18); figuratively, as the result of giving generously *benefit, outcome* (2C 9.10)

γενήματα	N-AN-P	γένημα
γενήματος	N-GN-S	"
Γεννησαρέθ		Γεννησαρέτ
Γενησαρέτ		"
γενήσεσθε	VIFD--2P	γίνομαι
γενήσεται	VIFD--3S	"
γένησθε	VSAD--2P	"
γενησόμενον	VPFDAN-S	"
γενήσονται	VIFD--3P	"
γένηται	VSAD--3S	"
γεννᾶται	VIPP--3S	γεννάω

γεννάω fut. γεννήσω; 1aor. ἐγέννησα; pf. γεγέννηκα; pf. pass. γεγέννημαι; 1aor. pass. ἐγεννήθην; (1) literally; (a) of men *father, become the father of* (MT 1.2); (b) of women *bear, give birth to* (LU 1.13); (c) passive, of both men and women *be born (of)* (GA 4.23); (2) figuratively; (a) of God's part in Jesus' resurrection (AC 13.33) and his messianic exaltation to the position of highest honor (HE 1.5) *(officially) become father of, publicly acknowledge*; (b) passive, of the spiritual new birth *be born, be regenerated* (JN 3.3); (c) of the influence of a leader on his disciples *become a father of* (1C 4.15); (d) as producing a result *give rise to, cause* (2T 2.23)

γεννηθείς	VPAPNM-S	γεννάω
γεννηθέν	VPAPNN-S	"
γεννηθέντος	VPAPGM-S	"
γεννηθέντων	VPAPGM-P	"

γεννηθῇ	VSAP--3S	"
γεννηθῆναι	VNAP	"

γέννημα, ατος, τό what is produced or born; of man *offspring, child*; plural, of vipers *brood*; used metaphorically of a kind or class of person, ungodly and rebellious toward God (MT 12.34)

γεννήματα	N-VN-P	γέννημα
γεννήματος	N-GN-S	"
γεννήσαντα	VPAAAM-S	γεννάω
Γεννησάρ		Γεννησαρέτ
Γεννησαράτ		"
Γεννησαρέθ		

Γεννησαρέτ, ἡ (also **Γενησαρέθ, Γενησαρέτ, Γεννησάρ, Γεννησαράτ, Γεννησαρέθ**) indeclinable; *Gennesaret*, another name for the Sea of Galilee (LU 5.1); also a small fertile plain bordering the lake on the northwest (MT 14.34)

γεννήσει	N-DF-S	γέννησις
	VIFA--3S	γεννάω
γεννήσεται	VIFM--3S	"
γεννήσῃ	VSAA--3S	"

γέννησις, εως, ἡ *birth* (MT 1.18)

γέννησις	N-NF-S	γέννησις
γεννησόμενον	VPFMAN-S	γεννάω
γεννητοῖς	AP-DM-P	γεννητός

γεννητός, ή, όν of human beings as distinct from God or angels *born*; substantivally *one born, human being, person* (MT 11.11)

γεννόμενον	VPPPNN-S	see γεννώμενον
γεννώμενον	VPPPNN-S	γεννάω
γεννωμένου	VPPPGN-S	"
γεννῶνται	VIPP--3P	"
γεννῶσα	VPPANF-S	"
γεννῶσι(ν)	VIPA--3P	"
γένοισθε	VOAD--2P	γίνομαι
γένοιτο	VOAD--3S	"
γενόμενα	VPADAN-P	"
γενόμεναι	VPADNF-P	"
γενομένην	VPADAF-S	"
γενομένης	VPADGF-S	"
γενόμενοι	VPADNM-P	"
γενομένοις	VPADDM-P	"
	VPADDN-P	"
γενόμενον	VPADAM-S	"
	VPADAN-S	"
γενόμενος	VPADNM-S	"
γενομένου	VPADGM-S	"
	VPADGN-S	"
γενομένους	VPADAM-P	"
γενομένων	VPADGF-P	"
	VPADGM-P	"
	VPADGN-P	"

γένος, ους (or **ως**), **τό**, dative **γένει** (1) of common ancestry *posterity, descendant, family* (RV 22.16); (2) of common identity as an ethnic group *race, people, nation* (AC 7.19); of common identity of believers *nation, people* (1P 2.9); (3) of members of a family circle *kindred, relatives, (extended) family* (AC 7.13); (4) of a distinctive species of something *kind, class* (1C 12.10)

γένος	N-AN-S	γένος
	N-NN-S	"

γένους	N-GN-S	"
γένωμαι	VSAD--1S	γίνομαι
γενώμεθα	VSAD--1P	"
γένωνται	VSAD--3P	"

Γερασηνός, ή, όν (also **Γεργεσηνός, Γεργεσινός, Γεργυστηνός, Γερσινός**) *from Gerasa*, a city in Perea, east of the Jordan River; substantivally *Gerasene, native of Gerasa*

Γερασηνῶν	AP-GM-P	Γερασηνός
Γερασηνῶν	AP-GM-P	see Γερασηνῶν
Γεργαρσηνῶν	AP-GM-P	see Γερασηνῶν
Γεργεσηνῶν	AP-GM-P	Γερασηνός
Γεργεσινῶν	AP-GM-P	"
Γεργυστηνῶν	AP-GM-P	"

γερουσία, ας, ἡ *council of elders, senate*; especially of the Sanhedrin, the Jewish supreme court in Jerusalem (AC 5.21)

γερουσίαν	N-AF-S	γερουσία
Γερσινῶν	AP-GM-P	Γερασηνός

γέρων, οντος, ὁ *old man* (JN 3.4)

γέρων	N-NM-S	γέρων

γεύομαι fut. γεύσομαι; 1aor. ἐγευσάμην; (1) literally, as testing a liquid by sipping *taste* (MT 27.34); as partaking of food *eat, partake of, enjoy* (AC 10.10); (2) figuratively *come to know, experience, partake of* (HE 2.9)

γευσάμενος	VPADNM-S	γεύομαι
γευσαμένους	VPADAM-P	"
γεύσασθαι	VNAD	"
γεύσεται	VIFD--3S	"
γεύσῃ	VSAD--2S	"
γεύσηται	VSAD--3S	"
γεύσονται	VIFD--3P	"
γεύσωνται	VSAD--3P	"
γεωργεῖται	VIPP--3S	γεωργέω

γεωργέω *prepare ground for planting, cultivate, till*; passive *be cultivated* (HE 6.7)

γεώργιον, ου, τό *field, cultivated land, farm*; metaphorically, for a community of believers (1C 3.9)

γεώργιον	N-NN-S	γεώργιον
γεωργοί	N-NM-P	γεωργός
γεωργοῖς	N-DM-P	"
γεωργόν	N-AM-S	"

γεωργός, οῦ, ὁ *one who tills the soil, farmer* (2T 2.6); *vineyard keeper, vinedresser, gardener* (MK 12.1)

γεωργός	N-NM-S	γεωργός
γεωργούς	N-AM-P	"
γεωργῶν	N-GM-P	"

γῆ, γῆς, ἡ *earth*; (1) as receiving seed or rain *soil, ground, earth* (MT 13.5); (2) as a place to lay a foundation *ground* (LU 6.49); (3) *land* (MK 4.1), in contrast to θάλασσα (*sea*); (4) *earth* (MT 5.18), in contrast to οὐρανός (*heaven*); (5) as a specific territory *land, region, country* (MT 2.20); (6) as the whole inhabited *earth* (LU 21.35); by metonymy *mankind, world* (MT 5.13); ἐπὶ τῆς γῆς *among people* (LU 18.8)

γῆ	N-NF-S	γῆ
	N-VF-S	"
γῇ	N-DF-S	"
γήμας	VPAANM-S	γαμέω
γήμῃ	VSAA--3S	"
γήμῃς	VSAA--2S	"
γῆν	N-AF-S	γῆ
γήρᾳ	N-DN-S	γῆρας

γῆρας, ους, τό   *old age* (LU 1.36)

γηράσῃς	VSAA--2S	γηράσκω
γηράσκον	VPPANN-S	"

γηράσκω   1aor. ἐγήρασα; *grow old, become old* (JN 21.18); figuratively, of the old covenant *become obsolete* (HE 8.13)

γήρει	N-DN-S	γῆρας
γῆς	N-GF-S	γῆ
γίνεσθαι	VNPD	γίνομαι
	VNPO	"
γίνεσθε	VMPD--2P	"
	VMPO--2P	"
γινέσθω	VMPD--3S	"
	VMPO--3S	"
γίνεται	VIPD--3S	"
	VIPO--3S	"

γίνομαι   impf. ἐγινόμην; fut. γενήσομαι; 2aor. ἐγενόμην; pf. act. γέγονα; pf. mid./pass. γεγένημαι; 1aor. pass. ἐγενήθην; (1) as what comes into existence *become, come to be, originate,* with the distinctive sense arising from the context; (a) of persons *be born, appear* (RO 1.3); (b) of fruits *be produced* (MT 21.19); (c) of events *arise, come about, happen, take place* (MK 4.37); (d) of divisions of the day *come, arrive* (LU 4.42); (2) of what is created; (a) *be made, be done, be brought into existence* (JN 1.3); (b) of miracles *take place, be performed* (AC 4.22); (c) of commands *be fulfilled, be performed, be carried out* (MT 6.10); (d) of institutions *be established* (MK 2.27); (3) to indicate the progress of a narrative καὶ ἐγένετο *and it came to pass, it happened* (MK 1.9); the phrase may be left untranslated; (4) of persons or things that enter into a new condition *become* something (MT 5.45); (5) to denote change of location *come, go, arrive at, be at* (AC 20.16b); (6) to express a characteristic of someone or something *be, become* (MT 10.16; HE 11.6); (7) with the genitive of possessor *belong to* (LU 20.14); (8) with the dative of person *belong to* (RO 7.3); (9) in a strong negative formula μὴ γένοιτο *let it not be, God forbid, don't even think about it, how ridiculous* (RO 6.2; GA 3.21)

γινόμενα	VPPDAN-P	γίνομαι
	VPPOAN-P	"
γινόμεναι	VPPDNF-P	"
	VPPONF-P	"
γινομένας	VPPDAF-P	"
	VPPOAF-P	"
γινομένη	VPPDNF-S	"
	VPPONF-S	"
γινομένῃ	VPPDDF-S	"
	VPPODF-S	"
γινομένης	VPPDGF-S	"
	VPPOGF-S	"
γινόμενοι	VPPDNM-P	"
	VPPONM-P	"
γινομένοις	VPPDDN-P	"
	VPPODN-P	"
γινόμενον	VPPDAM-S	"
	VPPDAN-S	"
	VPPDNN-S	"
	VPPOAM-S	"
	VPPOAN-S	"
	VPPONN-S	"
γινομένου	VPPDGN-S	"
	VPPOGN-S	"
γινομένων	VPPDGN-P	"
	VPPOGN-P	"
γίνονται	VIPD--3P	"
	VIPO--3P	"
γίνου	VMPD--2S	"
	VMPO--2S	"
γινώμεθα	VSPD--1P	"
	VSPO--1P	"
γίνωνται	VSPD--3P	"
	VSPO--3P	"
γίνωσκε	VMPA--2S	γινώσκω
γινώσκει	VIPA--3S	"
γινώσκειν	VNPA	"
γινώσκεις	VIPA--2S	"
γινώσκεται	VIPP--3S	"
γινώσκετε	VIPA--2P	"
	VMPA--2P	"
γινωσκέτω	VMPA--3S	"
γινώσκῃ	VSPA--3S	"
γινώσκητε	VSPA--2P	"
γινώσκομαι	VIPP--1S	"
γινώσκομεν	VIPA--1P	"
γινωσκομένη	VPPPNF-S	"
γινώσκοντες	VPPANM-P	"
γινώσκουσι(ν)	VIPA--3P	"
	VPPADM-P	"

γινώσκω   impf. ἐγίνωσκον; fut. mid. γνώσομαι; 2aor. ἔγνων; pf. ἔγνωκα; pf. pass. ἔγνωσμαι; 1aor. pass. ἐγνώσθην; 1fut. pass. γνωσθήσομαι; (1) of intelligent comprehension *know, come to understand, ascertain* (LU 8.10); (2) with a person as the object *know, be acquainted with* (2C 5.16); (3) as learning something through sense perception *learn of, become aware of, find out, perceive* (MK 5.29); (4) euphemistically *have sexual intercourse* (MT 1.25); (5) of recognition of a claim *acknowledge, recognize* (MT 7.23); (6) of certainty gained through experience *know, come to know, be sure of*; (a) of a thing (JN 8.32); (b) of a person (JN 2.24; 1J 2.3)

γινώσκω	VIPA--1S	γινώσκω
γινώσκωμεν	VSPA--1P	"
γινώσκων	VPPANM-S	"
γινώσκωσι(ν)	VSPA--3P	"

γλεῦκος, ους, τό   strictly *unfermented juice of grapes;* hence *sweet new wine* (AC 2.13)

γλεύκους	N-GN-S	γλεῦκος
γλυκύ	A--AN-S	γλυκύς
	A--NN-S	"

γλυκύς, εῖα, ύ   literally *sweet,* opposite πικρός (*bitter*); substantivally τὸ γλυκύ *sweet, fresh water* (JA 3.11); figuratively, of a book delightful to read *pleasant* (RV 10.9)

γλῶσσα, ης, ἡ   *tongue;* (1) literally, the organ of speech and taste *tongue* (MK 7.33); figuratively, as a means of verbal communication *tongue, language* (AC 2.11); (2) by metonymy *tribe, people,* or *nation* that speaks a common language (RV 5.9); (3) as a religious technical term for glossalalia *tongues(-speaking),* understood variously to be unintelligible ecstatic utterance (1C 14.2), heavenly language (1C 13.1), or foreign languages not learned through natural means by the speaker (AC 2.4); (4) as the shape of fire *forked flames* (AC 2.3)

γλῶσσα	N-NF-S	γλῶσσα
γλῶσσαι	N-NF-P	"
γλώσσαις	N-DF-P	"
γλῶσσαν	N-AF-S	"
γλώσσας	N-AF-P	"
γλώσσῃ	N-DF-S	"
γλώσσης	N-GF-S	"

γλωσσόκομον, ου, τό originally *box* or *case for the mouthpiece* or *reed of musical instruments*; generally, any *case* or *container*; in the NT *purse, moneybag* (JN 12.6)

γλωσσόκομον	N-AN-S	γλωσσόκομον
γλωσσῶν	N-GF-P	γλῶσσα

γναφεύς, έως, ὁ from γνάφος (*teasel* or *thistle used to raise the nap of cloth*); one who prepares a material, such as wool, for cloth by cleaning, shrinking, and thickening it *bleacher, whitener, fuller* (MK 9.3)

γναφεύς	N-NM-S	γναφεύς
γνήσιε	A--VM-S	γνήσιος
γνήσιον	A--AN-S	"

γνήσιος, ία, ον (1) literally, of children *legitimate, lawful, born in wedlock*; figuratively, of spiritual relationship *true, genuine* (1T 1.2); (2) as a commendable quality of integrity *genuine, sincere*; substantivally *genuineness, sincerity* (2C 8.8)

γνησίῳ	A--DN-S	γνήσιος

γνησίως adverb; *sincerely, genuinely* (PH 2.20)

γνησίως	AB	γνησίως
γνοῖ	VSAA--3S	γινώσκω
γνόντα	VPAAAM-S	"
γνόντες	VPAANM-P	"
γνούς	VPAANM-S	"

γνόφος, ου, ὁ *darkness (that conceals), thick darkness* (HE 12.18)

γνόφῳ	N-DM-S	γνόφος
γνῶ	VSAA--1S	γινώσκω
γνῷ	VSAA--3S	"
γνῶθι	VMAA--2S	"

γνώμη, ης, ἡ basically, the *mind* as the instrument of knowing; (1) as the direction of one's thinking *intention, disposition, will* (1C 1.10); (2) as the result of one's consideration *resolve, decision, purpose* (AC 20.3); (3) as advice, distinct from command *counsel, opinion, judgment* (1C 7.25); (4) as the result of sharing another's consideration *consent, previous knowledge, agreement* (PM 14)

γνώμη	N-NF-S	γνώμη
γνώμῃ	N-DF-S	"
γνώμην	N-AF-S	"
γνώμης	N-GF-S	"
γνῶναι	VNAA	γινώσκω
γνωριζέσθω	VMPP--3S	γνωρίζω
γνωρίζομεν	VIPA--1P	"

γνωρίζω fut. γνωρίσω; 1aor. ἐγνώρισα; 1aor. pass. ἐγνωρίσθην; (1) as a causative *make known, reveal, declare* (LU 2.15); (2) as the result of consideration *know* (PH 1.22)

γνωρίζω	VIPA--1S	γνωρίζω
γνωρίουσι(ν)	VIFA--3P	"
	VIFA--3P^VMAA--3P	"

γνωρίσαι	VNAA	"
γνωρίσας	VPAANM-S	"
γνωρίσει	VIFA--3S	"
γνωρίσῃ	VSAA--3S	"
γνωρισθέντος	VPAPGN-S	"
γνωρισθῇ	VSAP--3S	"
γνωρίσουσι(ν)	VIFA--3P	"
γνωρίσω	VIFA--1S	"
γνῷς	VSAA--2S	γινώσκω
γνώσει	N-DF-S	γνῶσις
γνώσεις	N-NF-P	"
γνώσεσθε	VIFD--2P	γινώσκω
γνώσεται	VIFD--3S	"
γνώσεως	N-GF-S	γνῶσις
γνώσῃ	VIFD--2S	γινώσκω
γνωσθέντες	VPAPNM-P	"
γνωσθῇ	VSAP--3S	"
γνωσθήσεται	VIFP--3S	"
γνωσθήτω	VMAP--3S	"
γνῶσι(ν)	VSAA--3P	"
γνῶσιν	N-AF-S	γνῶσις

γνῶσις, εως, ἡ basically, as the possession of information *what is known, knowledge*; (1) as a characteristic of God and man *knowledge* (RO 11.33; 1C 8.1); (2) as the result of divine enlightenment *knowledge, understanding, insight* (LU 1.77); (3) of heretical claims to higher forms of knowledge available only to a select few *gnosis, (esoteric) knowledge* (1T 6.20)

γνῶσις	N-NF-S	γνῶσις
γνώσομαι	VIFD--1S	γινώσκω
γνωσόμεθα	VIFD--1P	"
γνώσονται	VIFD--3P	"
γνωστά	A--AN-P	γνωστός
γνώστην	N-AM-S	γνώστης

γνώστης, ου, ὁ one thoroughly acquainted with or practiced in something *expert, one skilled in* or *familiar with* (AC 26.3)

γνωστοί	AP-NM-P	γνωστός
γνωστοῖς	AP-DM-P	"
γνωστόν	A--NN-S	"

γνωστός, ή, όν (1) of something clearly recognizable *known, made known, remarkable* (AC 4.16); (2) *well-known*; substantivally, of persons *acquaintance, friend* (LU 2.44); (3) of what can be known *intelligible, knowable* (RO 1.19)

γνωστός	A--NM-S	γνωστός
γνώσωσι(ν)	VSAA--3P	see γνῶσι(ν)
γνῶτε	VMAA--2P	γινώσκω
	VSAA--2P	"
γνώτω	VMAA--3S	"
γογγύζετε	VMPA--2P	γογγύζω
γογγύζοντος	VPPAGM-S	"
γογγύζουσι(ν)	VIPA--3P	"

γογγύζω impf. ἐγόγγυζον; 1aor. ἐγόγγυσα; from the sound that suggests the sense; (1) as expressing dissatisfaction *grumble, complain, murmur* (MT 20.11); (2) as expressing skepticism or speculation about someone *mutter, complain secretly, speak in a low voice* (JN 7.32)

γογγύζωμεν	VSPA--1P	γογγύζω

γογγυσμός, οῦ, ὁ (1) as an expression of dissatisfaction *grumbling, complaining* (AC 6.1); (2) as an expression of speculation and skepticism about someone *murmuring, whispering, secret talk* (JN 7.12)

γογγυσμός	N-NM-S	γογγυσμός
γογγυσμοῦ	N-GM-S	"
γογγυσμῶν	N-GM-P	"
γογγυσταί	N-NM-P	γογγυστής

γογγυστής, οῦ, ὁ as a person dissatisfied with his circumstances or place in life *murmurer, grumbler, complainer* (JU 16)

γόης, ητος, ὁ originally one who tried to control the wind by wailing and howling; then a *magician* who deceives with chants; hence *impostor, deceiver* (2T 3.13)

γόητες	N-NM-P	γόης
Γολγόθ		Γολγοθᾶ
Γολγοθά	N-AF-S	"
	N-NF-S	"

Γολγοθᾶ, ἡ (also **Γολγόθ** [indeclinable], **Γολγοθά**), accusative **Γολγοθᾶ, Γολγοθᾶν** (also **Γολγοθά, Γολγοθάν**) transliterated from the Aramaic *Golgotha*; translated into Greek as κρανίου τόπος (*place of a skull*), a place near Jerusalem (MT 27.33)

Γολγοθᾶ	N-AF-S	Γολγοθᾶ
	N-NF-S	"
Γολγοθάν	N-AF-S	"
Γολγοθᾶν	N-AF-S	"
γόμον	N-AM-S	γόμος

Γόμορρα, ων, τά and **ας, ἡ** *Gomorrah*, name of a ruined city probably located in the depression of land now covered by the Dead Sea

Γόμορρα	N-NF-S	Γόμορρα
	N-NN-P	"
Γομόρρας	N-GF-S	"
Γομόρροις	N-DN-P	"
Γομόρρων	N-GN-P	"

γόμος, ου, ὁ *load, freight*; of a ship *cargo*

γόνασι(ν)	N-DN-P	γόνυ
γόνατα	N-AN-P	"
γονεῖς	N-AM-P	γονεύς
	N-NM-P	"

γονεύς, έως, ὁ *parent*; only plural in the NT οἱ γονεῖς, έων *parents* (LU 2.43)

γονεῦσι(ν)	N-DM-P	γονεύς
γονέων	N-GM-P	"

γόνυ, ατος, τό *knee*; by synecdoche, *person* (PH 2.10)

γόνυ	N-AN-S	γόνυ
	N-NN-S	"

γονυπετέω 1aor. ἐγονυπέτησα; from γόνυ (*knee*) and πίπτω (*fall*); *fall on one's knees, kneel down* before someone

γονυπετήσαντες	VPAANM-P	γονυπετέω
γονυπετήσας	VPAANM-S	"
γονυπετῶν	VPPANM-S	"

γράμμα, ατος, τό (1) literally *what is written*; (2) of the alphabet *letter* (GA 6.11); by extension plural γράμματα, of education *letters, learning* (JN 7.15); (3) as a piece of writing *letter, document, book* (AC 28.21); (4) as a promissory note *record of debts, contract, account* (LU 16.6)

γράμμα	N-NN-S	γράμμα
γράμμασι(ν)	N-DN-P	"
γράμματα	N-AN-P	"
	N-NN-P	"

γραμματεῖς	N-AM-P	γραμματεύς
	N-NM-P	"
	N-VM-P	"

γραμματεύς, έως, ὁ (1) one skilled in Jewish law and theology *scribe, expert, scholar* (MT 2.4); (2) as a town official *secretary, town clerk* (AC 19.35)

γραμματεύς	N-NM-S	γραμματεύς
γραμματεῦσι(ν)	N-DM-P	"
γραμματέων	N-GM-P	"
γράμματι	N-DN-S	γράμμα
γράμματος	N-GN-S	"
γραπτόν	A--AN-S	γραπτός

γραπτός, ή, όν *written* (RO 2.15)

γραφαί	N-NF-P	γραφή
γραφαῖς	N-DF-P	"
γραφάς	N-AF-P	"
γράφε	VMPA--2S	γράφω
γράφει	VIPA--3S	"
γράφειν	VNPA	"
γράφεις	VIPA--2S	"
γράφεσθαι	VNPP	"

γραφή, ῆς, ἡ (1) *writing*; (2) in the NT only of sacred writing *scripture*; used to designate the Scripture(s) as a whole or any particular part or single passage

γραφή	N-NF-S	γραφή
γραφῇ	N-DF-S	"
γράφην	VNPA	see γράφειν
γραφήν	N-AF-S	γραφή
γραφῆς	N-GF-S	"
γράφηται	VSPP--3S	γράφω
γράφομεν	VIPA--1P	"
γραφόμενα	VPPPAN-P	"

γράφω impf. ἔγραφον; 1aor. ἔγραψα; pf. γέγραφα; pf. pass. γέγραμμαι; 2aor. pass. ἐγράφην; (1) of the activity of writing *write* (GA 6.11); (2) as covering something with writing or drawing *write, engrave* (RV 5.1); (3) as making a record *write down, record* (RV 1.19); (4) as making a literary composition *compose, write* (AC 23.25); (5) as drawing up a legal composition *set down, draw up* (MK 10.4); γέγραπται *it is written*, used for legal attestation of the law and Old Testament witnesses (MT 4.4)

γράφω	VIPA--1S	γράφω
γράφων	VPPANM-S	"
γραφῶν	N-GF-P	γραφή
γράψαι	VNAA	γράφω
γράψαντες	VPAANM-P	"
γράψας	VPAANM-S	"
γράψῃς	VSAA--2S	"
γράψον	VMAA--2S	"
γράψω	VIFA--1S	"
	VSAA--1S	"
γραώδεις	A--AM-P	γραώδης

γραώδης, ες *characteristic of old women, old-womanish*; by implication *silly, absurd* (1T 4.7)

γρηγορεῖτε	VMPA--2P	γρηγορέω

γρηγορέω 1aor. ἐγρηγόρησα; (1) literally *watch, be* or *keep awake* (MK 13.34); figuratively *be watchful, vigilant, alert* (MT 24.42); (2) as an antonym for the metaphor of sleep as death *be awake, be alive* (1TH 5.10)

γρηγορῇ	VSPA--3S	γρηγορέω
γρηγορῆσαι	VNAA	"
γρηγορήσατε	VMAA--2P	"
γρηγορήσῃς	VSAA--2S	"
γρηγοροῦντας	VPPAAM-P	"
γρηγοροῦντες	VPPANM-P	"
γρηγορῶμεν	VSPA--1P	"
γρηγορῶν	VPPANM-S	"
Γύλλιον	N-AN-S	Τρωγύλλιον
γυμνά	A--NN-P	γυμνός
γύμναζε	VMPA--2S	γυμνάζω

γυμνάζω pf. pass. ptc. γεγυμνασμένος; literally *exercise naked, train* in gymnastic discipline; figuratively in the NT, of mental and spiritual training and discipline *control oneself, exercise self-control* (1T 4.7)

γυμνασία, ας, ἡ *physical exercise, bodily training* (1T 4.8)

γυμνασία	N-NF-S	γυμνασία
γυμνήν	A--AF-S	γυμνός
γυμνητεύομεν	VIPA--1P	γυμνιτεύω
γυμνιτεύομεν	VIPA--1P	"

γυμνιτεύω (and **γυμνητεύω**) *be poorly clothed, wear ragged clothing* (1C 4.11)

γυμνοί	A--NM-P	γυμνός
γυμνόν	A--AM-S	"

γυμνός, ή, όν (1) literally; (a) *naked, unclothed, bare*; substantively *naked person* (MK 14.52); (b) *poorly dressed, (partially) naked* (JA 2.15); (c) *without an outer garment*, thus unpresentable for public appearance (JN 21.7); (2) figuratively; (a) *without bodily form, without body* (2C 5.3); (b) of things disclosed *easy to be known, exposed, not hidden* (HE 4.13); (c) substantively *person spiritually unprepared* (RV 3.17)

γυμνός	A--NM-S	γυμνός

γυμνότης, ητος, ἡ (1) *nakedness*; figuratively, of spiritual unpreparedness (RV 3.18); (2) *lack of sufficient clothing, destitution* (RO 8.35)

γυμνότης	N-NF-S	γυμνότης

γυμνότητι	N-DF-S	"
γυμνότητος	N-GF-S	"
γυμνοῦ	A--GN-S	γυμνός
γυμνούς	A--AM-P	"
γύναι	N-VF-S	γυνή
γυναῖκα	N-AF-S	"
γυναικάρια	N-AN-P	γυναικάριον

γυναικάριον, ου, τό diminutive of γυνή; literally *little woman*; used with a derogatory sense *idle, frivolous, silly woman* (2T 3.6)

γυναῖκας	N-AF-P	γυνή

γυναικεῖος, εία, ον *of* or *belonging to woman, female, feminine*; euphemistically σκεῦος γυναικεῖον literally *feminine partner*, i.e. *woman, wife* (1P 3.7)

γυναικείῳ	A--DN-S	γυναικεῖος
γυναῖκες	N-NF-P	γυνή
	N-VF-P	"
γυναικί	N-DF-S	"
γυναικός	N-GF-S	"
γυναικῶν	N-GF-P	"
γυναιξί(ν)	N-DF-P	"

γυνή, αικός, ἡ *woman*; (1) as distinct from a male *female, woman* (AC 5.14); (2) as a married woman *wife* (LU 1.5); γ. χήρα *widow* (LU 4.26); a bride or fiancée legally considered as *wife* (MT 1.20)

γυνή	N-NF-S	γυνή

Γώγ, ὁ indeclinable; *Gog*, name of an enemy nation hostile to Messiah's reign; perhaps symbolic (RV 20.8)

γωνία, ας, ἡ *corner*; literally, street *corner* (MT 6.5); of a building *cornerstone, keystone, capstone* (MT 21.42); figuratively, of the four directional extremities of the earth *corner* (RV 7.1); of something done obscurely ἐν γωνίᾳ *in a corner* (AC 26.26)

γωνίᾳ	N-DF-S	γωνία
γωνίαις	N-DF-P	"
γωνίας	N-AF-P	"
	N-GF-S	"

δ'	CC	δέ
	CH	"
	CS	"
Δαβίδ		Δαυίδ
Δαδδαῖον	N-AM-S	Θαδδαῖος
δαίμονες	N-NM-P	δαίμων
δαιμόνια	N-AN-P	δαιμόνιον
	N-NN-P	"
δαιμονίζεται	VIPD--3S	δαιμονίζομαι
	VIPO--3S	"

δαιμονίζομαι 1aor. ptc. δαιμονισθείς; of demon possession or oppression *be possessed by, be tormented* or *vexed by, be demonized* (MT 4.24)

δαιμονιζόμενοι	VPPDNM-P	δαιμονίζομαι
	VPPONM-P	"
δαιμονιζόμενον	VPPDAM-S	"
	VPPOAM-S	"
δαιμονιζόμενος	VPPDNM-S	"
	VPPONM-S	"
δαιμονιζομένου	VPPDGM-S	"
	VPPOGM-S	"
δαιμονιζομένους	VPPDAM-P	"
	VPPOAM-P	"
δαιμονιζομένῳ	VPPDDM-S	"
	VPPODM-S	"
δαιμονιζομένων	VPPDGM-P	"
	VPPOGM-P	"
δαιμονίοις	N-DN-P	δαιμόνιον

δαιμόνιον, ου, τό (1) *heathen god, minor divinity* (AC 17.18); (2) predominately *demon, evil spirit*, regarded as a supernatural and independent being neither human nor divine (MT 7.22)

δαιμόνιον	N-AN-S	δαιμόνιον
	N-NN-S	"
δαιμονίου	N-GN-S	"
δαιμονισθείς	VPAONM-S	δαιμονίζομαι
δαιμονίῳ	N-DN-S	δαιμόνιον

δαιμονιώδης, ες pertaining to or proceeding from demons *demonic, devilish* (JA 3.15)

δαιμονιώδης	A--NF-S	δαιμονιώδης
δαιμονίων	N-GN-P	δαιμόνιον
δαίμονος	N-GM-S	δαίμων
δαιμόνων	N-GM-P	"

δαίμων, ονος, ὁ *demon, evil spirit* (MT 8.31)

| δάκνετε | VIPA--2P | δάκνω |

δάκνω *bite*; literally, of animals and reptiles; figuratively, as acting spitefully or injuriously toward others *cause harm to* (GA 5.15)

δάκρυον, ου, τό of crying *tear* (RV 7.17); plural *tears, weeping* (MK 9.24)

| δάκρυον | N-AN-S | δάκρυον |
| δάκρυσι(ν) | N-DN-P | " |

δακρύω	1aor. ἐδάκρυσα; *weep, shed tears, cry* (JN 11.35)
δακρύων	N-GN-P	δάκρυον
δακτύλιον	N-AM-S	δακτύλιος

δακτύλιος, ου, ὁ *ring* to be worn on a finger, often displaying the seal of the owner (LU 15.22)

| δάκτυλον | N-AM-S | δάκτυλος |

δάκτυλος, ου, ὁ literally *finger* (MK 7.33); figuratively, as an expression of someone's activity *power, authority* (MT 23.4); used to express God's direct and concrete intervention in likeness of human activity (LU 11.20)

δακτύλου	N-GM-S	δάκτυλος
δακτύλους	N-AM-P	"
δακτύλῳ	N-DM-S	"
δακτύλων	N-GM-P	"

Δαλμανουθά, ἡ (also **Δαλμανοῦναι, Δαλμανουνθά, Δαλμοῦναι**) indeclinable; *Dalmanutha*, a district along the western shore of the Sea of Galilee (MK 8.10)

| Δαλμανοῦναι | | Δαλμανουθά |
| Δαλμανουνθά | | " |

Δαλματία, ας, ἡ *Dalmatia*, a region of southern Illyricum across the Adriatic Sea from southern Italy (2T 4.10)

Δαλματίαν	N-AF-S	Δαλματία
Δαλμοῦναι		Δαλμανουθά
δαμάζεται	VIPP--3S	δαμάζω

δαμάζω 1aor. ἐδάμασα; pf. pass. δεδάμασμαι; literally *subdue, tame* (JA 3.7); figuratively, of the tongue *bring under control, restrain* (JA 3.8)

| δαμάλεως | N-GF-S | δάμαλις |

δάμαλις, εως, ἡ *heifer, young cow* that has not yet had its first calf (HE 9.13)

Δάμαρις, ιδος, ἡ *Damaris*, feminine proper noun (AC 17.34)

| Δάμαρις | N-NF-S | Δάμαρις |
| δαμάσαι | VNAA | δαμάζω |

Δαμασκηνός, ή, όν *from Damascus*; substantively *Damascene, native of Damascus* (2C 11.32)

| Δαμασκηνῶν | AP-GM-P | Δαμασκηνός |
| Δαμασκόν | N-AF-S | Δαμασκός |

Δαμασκός, οῦ, ἡ *Damascus*, capital city of Syria

| Δαμασκῷ | N-DF-S | Δαμασκός |

Δάν, ὁ indeclinable; *Dan*, masculine proper noun; name of one of the tribes of Israel

δανείζετε	VIPA--2P	δανίζω
	VMPA--2P	"
δανείζητε	VSPA--2P	"
δανείζουσι(ν)	VIPA--3P	"

δάνειον, ου, τό *loan, debt* (MT 18.27)

δάνειον	N-AN-S	δάνειον
δανείσασθαι	VNAM	δανίζω
δανείσητε	VSAA--2P	"
δανειστῇ	N-DM-S	δανιστής
δανίζετε	VMPA--2P	δανίζω

δανίζουσι(ν) VIPA--3P "

δανίζω (and **δανείζω**) 1aor. ἐδάνισα, mid. ἐδανισάμην; (1) active *lend* (money) (LU 6.34); (2) middle *borrow* (money) (MT 5.42)

Δανιήλ, ὁ indeclinable; *Daniel*, masculine proper noun (MT 24.15)

δάνιον	N-AN-S	δάνειον
δανίσασθαι	VNAM	δανίζω
δανίσητε	VSAA--2P	"
δανιστῇ	N-DM-S	δανιστής

δανιστής, οῦ, ὁ (also **δανειστής**) *money lender, creditor* (LU 7.41)

δαπανάω fut. δαπανήσω; 1aor. ἐδαπάνησα; *spend (freely)*; (1) of one's property *spend, waste, use up* (LU 15.14); (2) as spending on someone *pay expenses* (AC 21.24; possibly 2C 12.15); (3) figuratively *exert great effort, wear oneself out* (possibly 2C 12.15)

δαπάνη, ης, ἡ *expense, cost* (LU 14.28)

δαπάνην	N-AF-S	δαπάνη
δαπανήσαντος	VPAAGM-S	δαπανάω
δαπανήσασα	VPAANF-S	"
δαπανήσητε	VSAA--2P	"
δαπάνησον	VMAA--2S	"
δαπανήσω	VIFA--1S	"
δαρήσεσθε	VIFP--2P	δέρω
δαρήσεται	VIFP--3S	"
Δαυείδ		Δαυίδ

Δαυίδ, ὁ (also **Δαβίδ, Δαυείδ**) indeclinable; *David*, masculine proper noun

δέ conjunctive particle; (1) most commonly to denote continuation and further thought development, taking its specific sense from the context *and*; contrast *but*; transition *then, now* (with no temporal sense); (2) to emphasize contrast; as a correlative with μέν *(on the one hand) . . . but (on the other hand)* (MT 3.11); after a negative *but rather, instead* (HE 4.13); (3) to introduce background material into a narrative *now* (with no temporal sense) or left untranslated (JN 11.18; this use is especially characteristic of John's Gospel); (4) to resume an interrupted discourse *and, then*, or left untranslated (LU 4.1); (5) used with other particles: δὲ καὶ *but also, but even* (MT 10.30); καὶ . . . δέ *and indeed, and also, but also* (1J 1.3)

δέ	CC	δέ
	CH	"
	CS	"
δεδάμασται	VIRP--3S	δαμάζω
δεδεκάτωκε(ν)	VIRA--3S	δεκατόω
δεδεκάτωται	VIRP--3S	"
δέδεκται	VIRD--3S	δέχομαι
	VIRO--3S	"
δεδεκώς	VPRANM-S	δέω
δέδεμαι	VIRP--1S	"
δεδεμένα	VPRPNN-P	"
δεδεμένην	VPRPAF-S	"
δεδεμένον	VPRPAM-S	"
	VPRPNN-S	"
δεδεμένος	VPRPNM-S	"
δεδεμένους	VPRPAM-P	"
δέδεσαι	VIRP--2S	"
δεδέσθαι	VNRP	"

δέδεται	VIRP--3S	"
δεδικαίομαι	VIRP--1S	see δεδικαίωμαι
δεδικαίωμαι	VIRP--1S	δικαιόω
δεδικαιωμένοις	VPRPDM-P	"
δεδικαιωμένος	VPRPNM-S	"
δεδικαίωται	VIRP--3S	"
δεδιωγμένοι	VPRPNM-P	διώκω
δεδοκιμάσμεθα	VIRP--1P	δοκιμάζω
δεδοκιμασμένον	VPRPAM-S	"
δεδομένην	VPRPAF-S	δίδωμι
δεδομένον	VPRPNN-S	"
δεδόξασμαι	VIRP--1S	δοξάζω
δεδοξασμένη	VPRPDF-S	"
δεδοξασμένον	VPRPNN-S	"
δεδόξασται	VIRP--3S	"
δέδοται	VIRP--3S	δίδωμι
δεδουλεύκαμεν	VIRA--1P	δουλεύω
δεδουλωμένας	VPRPAF-P	δουλόω
δεδουλωμένοι	VPRPNM-P	"
δεδούλωται	VIRP--3S	"
δέδωκα	VIRA--1S	δίδωμι
δέδωκας	VIRA--2S	"
δεδώκει	VILA--3S	"
δεδώκεισαν	VILA--3P	"
δέδωκε(ν)	VIRA--3S	"
δεδωκότι	VPRADM-S	"
δεδωκώς	VPRANM-S	"
δεδωρημένης	VPRDGF-S	δωρέομαι
	VPROGF-S	"
δεδώρηται	VIRD--3S	"
	VIRO--3S	"
δέη	VSPA--3S	δεῖ
δεηθέντων	VPAOGM-P	δέομαι
δεήθητε	VMAO--2P	"
δεήθητι	VMAO--2S	"
δεήσει	N-DF-S	δέησις
δεήσεις	N-AF-P	"
δεήσεσι(ν)	N-DF-P	"
δεήσεως	N-GF-S	"
δέησιν	N-AF-S	"

δέησις, εως, ἡ *plea, entreaty*; as addressed to God *prayer, request, petition*

δέησις	N-NF-S	δέησις
δεθῆναι	VNAP	δέω

δεῖ present subjunctive δέῃ; impf. ἔδει; an impersonal verb from δέω (*bind*); (1) as expressing compulsion, necessity, or inevitability in an event *it is necessary, one must, one has to* (MT 17.10); (2) as expressing the will of God or law *it is necessary* or *binding* (LU 13.14); (3) of the compulsion of duty *one ought, one should, one has to, one must* (AC 5.29); (4) of the compulsion of valid expectation or what is fitting *it is proper, it must be, it is right* (2T 2.6); (5) imperfect ἔδει, of something needful that was left undone *should have, ought to have* (MT 18.33)

δεῖ	VIPA--3S	δεῖ

δεῖγμα, ατος, τό strictly *what is shown*; hence *proof, example* (JU 7)

δεῖγμα	N-AN-S	δεῖγμα

δειγματίζω 1aor. ἐδειγμάτισα; *expose, make an example of*; as a warning *make a (public) example* of someone, *publicly disgrace* (MT 1.19)

δειγματίσαι	VNAA	δειγματίζω
δεικνύειν	VNPA	δείκνυμι
δεικνύεις	VIPA--2S	"

δείκνυμι and **δεικνύω** fut. δείξω; 1aor. ἔδειξα; pf. δέδειχα; 1aor. pass. ἐδείχθην; (1) as drawing attention to something *point out, show, cause to see* (AC 7.3); (2) as exhibiting something *show, cause to be seen* (JN 2.18); (3) as indicating something verbally *teach, explain, demonstrate* (AC 10.28)

δείκνυμι	VIPA--1S	δείκνυμι
δεικνύοντος	VPPAGM-S	"
δείκνυσι(ν)	VIPA--3S	"

δειλία, ας, ἡ as a shameful state of fear from lack of courage *cowardice, timidity* (2T 1.7)

δειλίας	N-GF-S	δειλία
δειλιάτω	VMPA--3S	δειλιάω

δειλιάω *be timid, be afraid, be cowardly* (JN 14.27)

δειλινόν	A--AN-S	δειλινός

δειλινός, ή, όν *in the afternoon*; τὸ δειλινόν as an adverb *toward evening* (AC 3.1)

δειλοί	A--NM-P	δειλός
δειλοῖς	A--DM-P	"

δειλός, ή, όν *timid, fearful, cowardly* (MT 8.26); substantivally, of persons showing fear in a shameful way *coward* (RV 21.8)

δεῖν	VNPA	δεῖ

δεῖνα, ὁ, ἡ, and **τό** in the NT used of a person one cannot or will not name *so-and-so, a certain person, such a one* (MT 26.18)

δεῖνα	N-AM-S	δεῖνα
δεινά	A--NN-P	δεινός

δεινός, ή, όν of punishment *terrible, severe*; of events that display great power or force *dreadful*; substantivally ἄλλα δεινά *other severe afflictions* (MK 16.14)

δεινῶς adverb; characterized by an extreme degree; (1) of suffering *terribly, fearfully* (MT 8.6); (2) of opposition *fiercely, exceedingly*

δεινῶς	AB	δεινῶς
δεῖξαι	VNAA	δείκνυμι
δείξατε	VMAA--2P	"
δειξάτω	VMAA--3S	"
δείξει	VIFA--3S	"
δεῖξον	VMAA--2S	"
δείξω	VIFA--1S	"
	VSAA--1S	"

δειπνέω fut. δειπνήσω; 1aor. ἐδείπνησα; *eat, dine, take the main meal*

δειπνῆσαι	VNAA	δειπνέω
δειπνήσω	VIFA--1S	"
	VSAA--1S	"
δείπνοις	N-DN-P	δεῖπνον

δειπνοκλήτωρ, ορος, ὁ one who invites people to a feast or dinner *host* (MT 20.28; cf. LU 14.8–10)

δειπνοκλήτωρ	N-NM-S	δειπνοκλήτωρ

δεῖπνον, ου, τό (1) *(principal) meal* (JN 12.2); (2) a main evening meal *dinner, supper* (LU 14.12); (3) a formal meal *dinner, banquet* (MT 23.6); (4) figuratively, as a sacred meal with symbolic meaning attached κυριακὸν δ. *Lord's Supper* (1C 11.20); as a future feast celebrating the union of Christ and his followers *supper* (RV 19.9)

δεῖπνον	N-AN-S	δεῖπνον
δείπνου	N-GN-S	"
δείπνῳ	N-DN-S	"
δείραντες	VPAANM-P	δέρω
δεισιδαιμονεστέρους	A-MAM-P	δεισιδαίμων

δεισιδαιμονία, ας, ἡ from δείδω (*fear*) and δαίμων (*divinity*); (1) in a good sense *reverence toward the gods, pious attitude toward divinities*; (2) in a bad sense *superstition*; (3) in a neutral sense, a system of beliefs *religion* (AC 25.19)

δεισιδαιμονίας	N-GF-S	δεισιδαιμονία

δεισιδαίμων, ον, gen. **ονος** from δείδω (*fear*) and δαίμων (*divinity*); (1) in a bad sense *superstitious*; (2) in a neutral sense in the NT, of carefulness and precision in religion *religious*; comparative δεισιδαιμονέστερος, τέρα, ον *very religious* (AC 17.22)

δειχθέντα	VPAPAM-S	δείκνυμι

δέκα indeclinable; as a cardinal number *ten* (MT 25.1); as a relatively short period of time ἡμερῶν δ. *ten days, few days, short time* (RV 2.10)

δεκαδύο indeclinable; as a cardinal number *twelve* (RV 21.16)

δεκαοκτώ indeclinable; as a cardinal number *eighteen* (LU 13.4)

δεκαπέντε indeclinable; as a cardinal number *fifteen*; ἡμέρας δ. *two weeks* (GA 1.18)

Δεκαπόλει	N-DF-S	Δεκάπολις
Δεκαπόλεως	N-GF-S	"

Δεκάπολις, εως, ἡ *Decapolis*, a district lying mainly east of the Jordan River just south of the Sea of Galilee; originally a league of ten cities (αἱ δέκα πόλεις)

δεκάτας	APOAF-P	δέκατος

δεκατέσσαρες, gen. **σάρων** as a cardinal number *fourteen*

δεκατέσσαρες	A-CNF-P	δεκατέσσαρες
δεκατεσσάρων	A-CGN-P	"
δεκάτη	APONF-S	δέκατος
δεκάτην	APOAF-S	"
δεκάτης	APOGF-S	"
δέκατον	A-ONN-S	"

δέκατος, η, ον (1) as an ordinal number *tenth* (JN 1.39); (2) substantivally ἡ δεκάτη *the tenth (part)* of anything given for a purpose (HE 7.2, 4); as the proportionate sacred gift prescribed by Mosaic law *tithe, tenth* (HE 7.8, 9); τὸ δέκατον *the tenth (part)* of an object, series, or amount (RV 11.13)

δέκατος	A-ONM-S	δέκατος

δεκατόω pf. δεδεκάτωκα; pf. pass. δεδεκάτωμαι; (1) active *collect, receive tithes* from someone (HE 7.6); (2) passive *pay tithes, be tithed* (HE 7.9)

δεκτήν	A--AF-S	δεκτός
δεκτόν	A--AM-S	"

δεκτός, ή, όν a verbal adjective from δέχομαι (*receive, accept*); *acceptable, welcome, pleasing* (LU 4.24); of time *favorable, appropriate, acceptable* (LU 4.19)

δεκτός	A--NM-S	δεκτός
δεκτῷ	A--DM-S	"
δελεαζόμενος	VPPPNM-S	δελεάζω
δελεάζοντες	VPPANM-P	"

δελεάζουσι(ν)   VIPA--3P   "

δελεάζω   related to δέλεαρ (*bait*); literally *lure, entrap*; figuratively *lead astray, entice* or *allure into wrongdoing* (2P 2.14)

δένδρα   N-AN-P   δένδρον
    N-NN-P   "

δένδρον, ου, τό   *tree, large bush*

δένδρον   N-AN-S   δένδρον
    N-NN-S   "

δένδρου   N-GN-S   "

δένδρων   N-GN-P   "

δέξαι   VMAD--2S   δέχομαι

δεξαμένη   VPADNF-S   "

δεξάμενοι   VPADNM-P   "

δεξάμενος   VPADNM-S   "

δέξασθαι   VNAD   "

δέξασθε   VMAD--2P   "

δέξηται   VSAD--3S   "

δεξιά   AP-NF-S   δεξιός
    A--AN-P   "
    A--NF-S   "

δεξιᾷ   AP-DF-S   "
    A--DF-S   "

δεξιάν   AP-AF-S   "
    A--AF-S   "

δεξιάς   AP-AF-P   "

δεξιᾶς   AP-GF-S   "
    A--GF-S   "

δεξιοβόλος, ου, ὁ   a military technical term (found only in AC 23.23); as an armed bodyguard, perhaps *spearman* or *bowman*; see δεξιολάβος

δεξιοβόλους   N-AM-P   δεξιοβόλος

δεξιοῖς   AP-DN-P   δεξιός

δεξιολάβος, ου, ὁ   a military technical term for a light-armed foot soldier *spearman, guard, infantryman* (AC 23.23)

δεξιολάβους   N-AM-P   δεξιολάβος

δεξιόν   A--AM-S   δεξιός
    A--AN-S   "

δεξιός, ά, όν   *right*, opposite ἀριστερός (*left*); (1) used with a noun ἡ δεξιὰ χείρ *the right hand* (LU 6.6), ὁ δ. ὀφθαλμός *the right eye* (MT 5.29), etc.; ὅπλα δεξιά *weapons for the right side, offensive weapons*, such as a sword; (used metaphorically in 2C 6.7); τὰ δεξιὰ μέρη *the parts toward the right side, the right side* (JN 21.6); (2) used absolutely and substantivally; (a) ἡ δεξιά and τὰ δεξιά *the right hand* (MT 25.33; AC 2.33); (b) idiomatically ἐκ δεξιῶν καθίζειν literally *sit on the right side of*, i.e. *be in a high position, be greatly honored* (MT 20.21); καθίζειν ἐν δεξιᾷ literally *cause to sit at the right hand*, i.e. *give special honor to, place in high position* (EP 1.20); δεξιὰς διδόναι literally *give right hands*, i.e. *make an agreement* (GA 2.9)

δεξιός   A--NM-S   δεξιός

δεξιῶν   AP-GN-P   "
    A--GN-P   "

δέξωνται   VSAD--3P   δέχομαι

δέομαι   1aor. ἐδεήθην; *ask*; (1) used predominately as an orienter for direct or indirect discourse *ask urgently, seek, beg* someone in relation to something (LU 8.28); δ. σου followed with direct discourse *tell me, please*

(AC 8.34); (2) as an orienter for prayer *make petition, plead, ask in prayer* (LU 10.2)

δέομαι   VIPD--1S   δέομαι
    VIPO--1S   "

δεόμεθα   VIPD--1P   "
    VIPO--1P   "

δεόμενοι   VPPDNM-P   "
    VPPONM-P   "

δεόμενος   VPPDNM-S   "
    VPPONM-S   "

δέον   VPPANN-S   δεῖ

δέοντα   VPPAAN-P   "

δέος, ους, τό   *fear, awe, reverence* (HE 12.28)

δέους   N-GN-S   δέος

Δερβαῖος, αία, ον   (also **Δουβέριος, Δούβριος**)   *from Derbe*; substantivally *Derbean* (AC 20.4)

Δερβαῖος   AP-NM-S   Δερβαῖος

Δέρβη, ης, ἡ   *Derbe*, a city in Lycaonia, in the Roman province of Galatia

Δέρβην   N-AF-S   Δέρβη

δέρει   VIPA--3S   δέρω

δέρεις   VIPA--2S   "

δέρμα, ατος, τό   *(animal) skin, hide* (HE 11.37)

δέρμασι(ν)   N-DN-P   δέρμα

δερματίνην   A--AF-S   δερμάτινος

δερμάτινος, η, ον   *made of leather* or *skin, leather* (MK 1.6)

δέροντες   VPPANM-P   δέρω

δέρριν   N-AF-S   δέρρις

δέρρις, εως, ἡ   *covering made of skin*; *leather clothing* (MK 1.6)

δέρω   1aor. ἔδειρα; 2aor. pass. ἐδάρην; 2fut. pass. δαρήσομαι; literally *remove the skin, flay*; figuratively in the NT *beat, strike repeatedly, whip* (MT 21.35)

δέρων   VPPANM-S   δέρω

δεσμά   N-AN-P   δεσμός
    N-NN-P   "

δέσμας   N-AF-P   δέσμη

δεσμείοις   N-DM-P   see δεσμίοις

δεσμεύουσι(ν)   VIPA--3P   δεσμεύω

δεσμεύω (and **δεσμέω**)   impf. pass. ἐδεσμευόμην; (1) *bind, confine* with chains (LU 8.29); (2) *bind up, tie up* in a bundle as a load, *bind together*; figuratively *contrive and impose many restrictions* (MT 23.4)

δεσμεύων   VPPANM-S   δεσμεύω

δέσμη, ῆς, ἡ   as grain or weeds tied together *bundle* (MT 13.30)

δέσμιοι   N-NM-P   δέσμιος

δεσμίοις   N-DM-P   "

δέσμιον   N-AM-S   "

δέσμιος, ου, ὁ   *prisoner*

δέσμιος   N-NM-S   δέσμιος

δεσμίους   N-AM-P   "

δεσμίων   N-GM-P   "

δεσμοῖς   N-DM-P   δεσμός
    N-DN-P   "

δεσμός, οῦ, ὁ   literally *bond, fetter*; plural οἱ δεσμοί and τὰ δεσμά *bonds, fetters* (AC 16.26); by metonymy *imprisonment, prison* (PH 1.7); figuratively, as an impediment or binding condition causing physical disability tongue-tied condition (MK 7.35); crippled condition (LU 13.16)

δεσμός	N-NM-S	δεσμός
δεσμοῦ	N-GM-S	"
δεσμούς	N-AM-P	"
δεσμοφύλακι	N-DM-S	δεσμοφύλαξ

δεσμοφύλαξ, ακος, ὁ prison guard, jailer

δεσμοφύλαξ	N-NM-S	δεσμοφύλαξ
δεσμῶν	N-GM-P	δεσμός
	N-GN-P	"
δεσμώτας	N-AM-P	δεσμώτης

δεσμωτήριον, ου, τό prison, jail

δεσμωτήριον	N-AN-S	δεσμωτήριον
δεσμωτηρίου	N-GN-S	"
δεσμωτηρίῳ	N-DN-S	"

δεσμώτης, ου, ὁ prisoner, person tied up in jail

δέσποτα	N-VM-S	δεσπότης
δεσπόταις	N-DM-P	"
δεσπότας	N-AM-P	"
δεσπότῃ	N-DM-S	"
δεσπότην	N-AM-S	"

δεσπότης, ου, ὁ (1) master, owner, lord, especially as the ruler over a household (TI 2.9); (2) as a title for God as the one who has supreme power Master, Sovereign, Lord (LU 2.29); as a title for Christ Lord, Master (2P 2.1)

δεσπότης	N-NM-S	δεσπότης
	N-VM-S	"

δεῦρο adverb; here; (1) of place, used as an imperative come, come here (AC 7.3); followed by an imperative come (and) (MT 19.21); (2) of time ἄχρι τοῦ δ. until now (RO 1.13)

δεῦρο	AB	δεῦρο
	AB^VMAA--2S	"

δεῦτε serving as the plural of δεῦρο (here); adverb; (1) with an imperative following come! come on! come now! (MT 21.38); (2) absolutely come (MT 22.4); with ὀπίσω come after, follow (MT 4.19)

δεῦτε	AB	δεῦτε
	AB^VMAA--2P	"
δευτέρα	A-ONF-S	δεύτερος
δευτέρα	A-ODF-S	"
δευτεραῖοι	A--NM-P	δευτεραῖος

δευτεραῖος, αία, ον on the second day (AC 28.13)

δευτέραν	A-OAF-S	δεύτερος
δευτέρας	A-OGF-S	"
δεύτερον	ABO	"
	A-OAN-S	"
	A-ONN-S	"

δευτερόπρωτος, ον a word of uncertain meaning; used only to qualify Sabbath in LU 6.1; literally second-first Sabbath; several attempts at explaining the now-lost cultural understanding include (1) the first Sabbath after the second day of unleavened bread in the Passover season; (2) the first Sabbath of the second year in a sabbatical cycle of seven years; (3) first but one, i.e. the next Sabbath after that

δευτεροπρώτῳ	A--DN-S	δευτερόπρωτος

δεύτερος, τέρα, ον (1) as an ordinal number second (RV 2.11); (2) of what follows in a series; in time (MT 26.42); in place (AC 12.10); in a succession of persons (MT 22.26); in a succession of events afterward, later (JU 5); (3) neuter as an adverb (τὸ) δεύτερον of enumerations second (1C 12.28); for the second time, again (JN 3.4; 2C 13.2); ἐκ δευτέρου second time (MT 26.42); (4) substantivally ὁ δ. the second one (MT 22.26)

δεύτερος	A-ONM-S	δεύτερος
δευτέρου	A-OGM-S	"
	A-OGN-S	"
δευτέρῳ	A-ODM-S	"
	A-ODN-S	"
δέχεται	VIPD--3S	δέχομαι
	VIPO--3S	"
δέχηται	VSPD--3S	"
	VSPO--3S	"

δέχομαι 1aor. mid. ἐδεξάμην; pf. δέδεγμαι; 1aor. pass. ἐδέχθην; (1) receive, accept (AC 3.21); as showing hospitality welcome, entertain (LU 16.4); (2) as assenting to God's message receive, accept, believe (MT 11.14); (3) as taking something into one's hand, take, grasp (EP 6.17); (4) as taking a favorable attitude toward something take well to, approve, accept (MT 11.14; 1C 2.14)

δεχόμενος	VPPDNM-S	δέχομαι
	VPPONM-S	"
δέχονται	VIPD--3P	"
	VIPO--3P	"
δέχωνται	VSPD--3P	"
	VSPO--3P	"

δέω 1aor. ἔδησα; pf. δέδεκα; pf. pass. δέδεμαι; 1aor. pass. ἐδέθην; (1) bind (together), tie (up) (MT 13.30), opposite λύω (loose, untie); (2) of burial procedures wrap up (JN 19.40); (3) of arrest and imprisonment bind, tie up (MK 6.17); (4) figuratively, of mutual commitment to the marriage vow be restricted (RO 7.2); (5) of physical incapacity cause to be ill (LU 13.16); (6) the binding and loosing (λύω) in MT 16.19 and 18.18 may be interpreted (a) according to Jewish rabbinic custom: to declare what is forbidden and permitted or (b) according to the understanding of early church fathers: to impose or remove the ban of excommunication; cf. JN 20.23

δή intensive particle; (1) denoting that a statement is definitely true surely, indeed (MT 13.23); (2) adding a note of urgency to commands and exhortations now, then, therefore (LU 2.15)

δή	QS	δή
δηλαυγῶς	AB	τηλαυγῶς
δηλοῖ	VIPA--3S	δηλόω
δῆλον	A--AM-S	δῆλος
	A--NN-S	"

δῆλος, η, ον strictly clearly visible; hence clear, plain, evident (MT 26.73); impersonally, with ὅτι following δῆλόν (ἐστιν) it is clear that (GA 3.11)

δηλοῦντος	VPPAGN-S	δηλόω

δηλόω fut. δηλώσω; 1aor. ἐδήλωσα; 1aor. pass. ἐδηλώθην; (1) show clearly, make clear or plain (1C 3.13); (2) indicate, signify (HE 9.8); (3) declare, impart information (1C 1.11); (4) of something divinely communicated reveal, make known (2P 1.14)

δηλῶ	VIPA--1S	δηλόω
δηλώσας	VPAANM-S	"
δηλώσει	VIFA--3S	"

Δημᾶς, ᾶ, ὁ   *Demas*, masculine proper noun
Δημᾶς   N-NM-S   Δημᾶς
δημηγορέω   impf. ἐδημηγόρουν; *address public assembly,*
give a speech (AC 12.21)
Δημήτριος, ου, ὁ   *Demetrius*, masculine proper noun
Δημήτριος   N-NM-S   Δημήτριος
Δημητρίῳ   N-DM-S   "
δημιουργός, οῦ, ὁ   literally *one who works for the people in*
public affairs, builder, architect, artisan; figuratively, of
the divine activity *maker, builder* (HE 11.10)
δημιουργός   N-NM-S   δημιουργός
δῆμον   N-AM-S   δῆμος
δῆμος, ου, ὁ   (1) as the population of a city *people, popu-*
lace; (2) as the populace gathered for any purpose *mob,*
crowd (AC 17.5); (3) as the citizens gathered to trans-
act business *(popular) assembly* (AC 19.30)
δῆμος   N-NM-S   δῆμος
δημοσίᾳ   AB   δημόσιος
                          A--DF-S
δημόσιος, ία, ον   *belonging to the people, public*; (1) of a
building for public use τήρησις δημοσίᾳ *prison, jail* (AC
5.18); (2) substantivally δημοσίᾳ *in the open* used as
an adverb *publicly, openly before the people* (AC 16.37)
δήμῳ   N-DM-S   δῆμος
δηνάρια   N-AN-P   δηνάριον
δηνάριον, ου, τό   *denarius*, a Roman silver coin equivalent
to a laborer's average daily wage
δηνάριον   N-AN-S   δηνάριον
δηναρίου   N-GN-S   "
δηναρίων   N-GN-P   "
δήποτ'   AB   δήποτε
δήποτε   adverb; *at any time*; with a relative *whatever time*
(JN 5.4)
δήποτε   AB   δήποτε
δήπου   adverb of affirmation *of course, surely* (HE 2.16)
δήπου   QS   δήπου
δήραντες   VPAANM-P   see δείραντες
δῆσαι   VNAA   δέω
δήσαντες   VPAANM-P   "
δήσας   VPAANM-S   "
δήσατε   VMAA--2P   "
δήσῃ   VSAA--3S   "
δήσῃς   VSAA--2S   "
δήσητε   VSAA--2P   "
δήσουσι(ν)   VIFA--3P   "
δι'   PA   διά
                          PG   "
Δία   N-AM-S   Ζεύς
διά   preposition; **I.** with the genitive; (1) spatial *through,*
by way of (JN 10.1); (2) temporal; (a) of a whole duration of time *through, throughout* (LU 5.5); (b) of time
within which something takes place *during, within* (MT
26.61); (c) of an interval of time *after* (AC 24.17); (3)
modal; (a) denoting manner *through, in, with* (LU 8.4);
(b) of accompanying circumstance *with, among, in*
spite of (AC 14.22); (4) causal; (a) of the efficient cause
in consequence of, by, on the basis of, on account of
(RO 12.1); (b) of the intermediate agent of an action *by,*
through, by agency of (GA 1.1; 1C 1.9); **II.** with the accusative; (1) spatial *through* (LU 17.11); (2) causal, to
indicate a reason *on account of, because of, for the sake*

of (MT 13.21); (3) in direct questions δ. τί *why?* (MT
9.11); (4) in answers giving reason and inferences δ.
τοῦτο *therefore, for this reason* (MK 11.24)
διά   PA   διά
                          PG   "
διαβαίνω   2aor. διέβην; *pass through, cross over* (LU 16.26);
of a sea *cross* from one side to the other (AC 16.9); of
the miraculous crossing of the Red Sea *go through* (HE
11.29)
διαβάλλω   1aor. pass. διεβλήθην; *bring charges, bring com-*
plaint against, accuse (LU 16.1)
διαβάς   VPAANM-S   διαβαίνω
διαβεβαιόομαι   *strongly maintain, confidently assert, insist*
(TI 3.8)
διαβεβαιοῦνται   VIPD--3P   διαβεβαιόομαι
                          VIPO--3P   "
διαβεβαιοῦσθαι   VNPD   "
                          VNPO   "
διάβημα, ατος, τό   *step*; plural and figuratively, of the
course of a person's life *steps* (JA 4.12)
διαβήματα   N-NN-P   διάβημα
διαβῆναι   VNAA   διαβαίνω
διαβλέπω   fut. διαβλέψω; 1aor. διέβλεψα; (1) *look intently*
or *steadily* (MK 8.25); (2) with an infinitive following *see*
clearly or *distinctly* (LU 6.42)
διαβλέψεις   VIFA--2S   διαβλέπω
διάβολε   AP-VM-S   διάβολος
διάβολοι   A--NM-P   "
διάβολον   AP-AM-S   "
διάβολος, ον   *slanderous* (2T 3.3); substantivally ὁ δ. *the*
slanderer; predominately, as a specific name for Satan
as the accuser *the devil* (MT 4.1)
διάβολος   AP-NM-S   διάβολος
διαβόλου   AP-GM-S   "
διαβόλους   A--AF-P   "
διαβόλῳ   AP-DM-S   "
διάγγειλον   VMAA--2S   διαγγέλλω
διαγγελῇ   VSAP--3S   "
διάγγελλε   VMPA--2S   "
διαγγέλλω   2aor. διήγγειλα; 2aor. pass. διηγγέλην; (1) *pro-*
claim far and wide, preach, make known (LU 9.60); (2)
of a public notification *announce, certify, give notice*
of (AC 21.26)
διαγγέλλων   VPPANM-S   διαγγέλλω
διαγενομένου   VPADGM-S   διαγίνομαι
                          VPADGN-S   "
διαγενομένων   VPADGF-P   "
διαγίνομαι   2aor. διεγενόμην; of time *pass, elapse, be over*
(MK 16.1)
διαγινώσκειν   VNPA   διαγινώσκω
διαγινώσκω   fut. mid. διαγνώσομαι; as a legal technical
term; (1) *decide, determine* (AC 24.22); (2) as judicial
inquiry *(thoroughly) examine, inquire into, investigate*
(AC 23.15)
διαγνωρίζω   1aor. διεγνώρισα; *give an exact report, tell ac-*
curately (LU 2.17)
διάγνωσιν   N-AF-S   διάγνωσις
διάγνωσις, εως, ἡ   strictly *act of discernment, determina-*
tion; as a legal technical term *judicial hearing, deci-*
sion, judgment (AC 25.21)
διαγνώσομαι   VIFD--1S   διαγινώσκω

διαγογγύζω impf. διεγόγγυζον; as expressing dissatis-faction *complain, grumble (aloud), mutter* (LU 19.7)

διάγοντες   VPPANM-P   διάγω

διαγρηγορέω 1aor. διεγρηγόρησα; *keep awake;* aorist *be-come fully awake* (LU 9.32)

διαγρηγορήσαντες   VPAANM-P   διαγρηγορέω

διάγω of time *spend, pass* (TI 3.3); often with βίον *spend one's life, live (daily)* (1T 2.2)

διάγωμεν   VSPA--1P   διάγω
διαδεξάμενοι   VPADNM-P   διαδέχομαι

διαδέχομαι 1aor. διεδεξάμην; *receive (in turn), succeed to;* of an object or possession *have handed down* (AC 7.45)

διάδημα, ατος, τό *band* or *fillet* worn around the head as a sign of royalty *diadem, crown, tiara* (RV 12.3)

διαδήματα   N-AN-P   διάδημα
                     N-NN-P
διαδιδόναι   VNPA   διαδίδωμι

διαδίδωμι impf. pass. third-person singular διεδίδετο; 1aor. διέδωκα; 2aor. imperative διάδος; *distribute, give out, assign* (LU 18.22); of spoils *divide up, share, dis-tribute* (LU 11.22)

διαδίδωσι(ν)   VIPA--3S   διαδίδωμι
διαδιδώσουσι(ν)   VIFA--3P   "
διάδος   VMAA--2S   "
διαδοῦναι   VNAA   "
διάδοχον   N-AM-S   διάδοχος

διάδοχος, ου, ὁ *successor,* one who takes over the position or responsibility of another (AC 24.27)

διαζώννυμι 1aor. διέζωσα, mid. διεζωσάμην; pf. pass. ptc. διεζωσμένος; (1) active *tie around one's waist* (JN 13.4); (2) middle *gird* or *tie around oneself;* of an outer garment *put on* (JN 21.7)

διαθέμενος   VPAMNM-S   διατίθημι
διαθεμένου   VPAMGM-S   "
διαθῆκαι   N-NF-P   διαθήκη

διαθήκη, ης, ἡ basically *settlement;* (1) as a legal techni-cal term in settling an inheritance, as common in the Greek and Roman world *last will and testament* (prob-ably HE 9.16, 17); (2) between two or more persons, a binding *contract, agreement, treaty* (GA 3.15); (3) pre-dominately in the NT, as in the Old Testament and Sep-tuagint, a declaration of the will of God concerning his self-commitment, promises, and conditions by which he entered into relationship with man *covenant, agreement* (LU 1.72; MK 14.24; possibly HE 9.16, 17)

διαθήκη   N-NF-S   διαθήκη
διαθήκη   N-DF-S   "
διαθήκην   N-AF-S   "
διαθήκης   N-GF-S   "
διαθηκῶν   N-GF-P   "
διαθήσομαι   VIFM--1S   διατίθημι
διαιρέσεις   N-NF-P   διαίρεσις

διαίρεσις, εως, ἡ (1) what is apportioned out *division, allotment, distribution* (possibly 1C 12.4–6); (2) as a state of difference in the nature of things *variety, di-versity, distinction* (probably 1C 12.4–6)

διαιρέω 2aor. διεῖλον; *distribute, apportion, divide (out)*
διαιροῦν   VPPANN-S   διαιρέω

διακαθαίρω 1aor. inf. διακαθᾶραι; as thoroughly sepa-rating chaff from grain on a threshing floor *clean thor-oughly;* used metaphorically in LU 3.17

διακαθᾶραι   VNAA   διακαθαίρω
διακαθαριεῖ   VIFA--3S   διακαθαρίζω

διακαθαρίζω fut. διακαθαριῶ; as thoroughly separating chaff from grain on a threshing floor *cause to be thor-oughly cleaned;* used metaphorically in MT 3.12

διακατελέγχομαι impf. διακατηλεγχόμην; as maintaining a discussion strenuously and thoroughly *vigorously* or *powerfully refute, confound completely* (AC 18.28)

διακατηλέγχετο   VIID--3S   διακατελέγχομαι
                     VIIO--3S   "
διακελεύει   VIPA--3S   διακελεύω

διακελεύω *order, command* (JN 8.5)

διακόνει   VMPA--2S   διακονέω
διακονεῖ   VIPA--3S   "
διακονεῖν   VNPA   "
διακονείτωσαν   VMPA--3P   "

διακονέω impf. διηκόνουν; fut. διακονήσω; 1aor. διηκόνησα; 1aor. pass. διηκονήθην; (1) generally, of services of any kind *serve* (MT 4.11); (2) of supplying with life's necessities *support, take care of, minister to* (MT 25.44); (3) of table service *wait on, serve* (LU 12.37); (4) of religious service relating the physical needs of believers *serve as deacon, perform duties of deacon* (1T 3.10)

διακονῇ   VSPA--3S   διακονέω
διακονηθεῖσα   VPAPNF-S   "
διακονηθῆναι   VNAP   "
διακονῆσαι   VNAA   "
διακονήσαντες   VPAANM-P   "
διακονήσει   VIFA--3S   "
διακονήσων   VPFANM-S   "

διακονία, ας, ἡ (1) generally *service* (HE 1.14); (2) as charitable giving *aid, support, arrangement for provi-sion* (AC 6.1); (3) as preparing meals *serving, prepara-tion* (LU 10.40); (4) as the role or position of one serv-ing God in a special way *task, office, ministry* (RO 12.7; 1T 1.12)

διακονία   N-NF-S   διακονία
διακονίᾳ   N-DF-S   "
διακονίαν   N-AF-S   "
διακονίας   N-GF-S   "
διακονιῶν   N-GF-P   "
διάκονοι   N-NM-P   διάκονος
διακόνοις   N-DM-P   "
διάκονον   N-AF-S   "
                     N-AM-S   "

διάκονος, ου, ὁ and ἡ (1) generally of a person who ren-ders helpful service *servant, helper* (MT 20.26; possi-bly RO 16.1); (2) as an official in the church; *deacon,* both masculine (1T 3.8) and feminine (probably RO 16.1); (3) as a government official *minister, agent* (RO 13.4); (4) as one who serves a high official *attendant, servant* (MT 22.13)

διάκονος   N-NM-S   διάκονος
διακονουμένη   VPPPDF-S   διακονέω
διακονοῦντες   VPPANM-P   "
διακονούντων   VPPAGM-P   "
διακόνους   N-AM-P   διάκονος

διακονοῦσαι	VPPANF-P	διακονέω
διακονῶν	VPPANM-S	"
διακόσιαι	A-CNF-P	διακόσιοι
διακοσίας	A-CAF-P	

διακόσιοι, αι, α as a cardinal number *two hundred*

διακοσίους	A-CAM-P	διακόσιοι
διακοσίων	A-CGM-P	"
	A-CGN-P	"
διακούσομαι	VIFD--1S	διακούω

διακούω fut. mid. διακούσομαι; as a legal technical term *give a hearing, hear a case through* (AC 23.35)

διακριθῇ	VSAP--3S	διακρίνω
διακριθῆτε	VSAP--2P	"
διακρῖναι	VNAA	"
διακρίναντα	VPAAAM-S	"
διακρίνει	VIPA--3S	"
διακρίνειν	VNPA	"
διακρινέτωσαν	VMPA--3P	"
διακρινόμενοι	VPPMNM-P	"
διακρινόμενον	VPPMAM-S	"
διακρινόμενος	VPPMNM-S	"
διακρινομένους	VPPMAM-P	"
διακρινομένῳ	VPPMDM-S	"
διακρίνοντα	VPPAAM-S	"

διακρίνω impf. mid. διεκρινόμην; 1aor. pass. διεκρίθην; (1) as evaluating the difference between things *discern, distinguish, differentiate* (MT 16.3); (2) as making a distinction between persons by evaluation *make a difference, decide between, pass judgment on* (AC 15.9); (3) as a legal technical term for arbitration *judge a dispute, settle a difference* (1C 6.5); (4) in the aorist tense, the middle sense is conveyed with the passive form; (a) as debating an issue *dispute, contend, argue* (AC 11.2); (b) as being undecided within oneself *doubt, hesitate, waver* (JA 1.6)

διακρίνων	VPPANM-S	διακρίνω
διακρίσεις	N-AF-P	διάκρισις
	N-NF-P	"
διάκρισιν	N-AF-S	"

διάκρισις, εως, ἡ (1) as the ability to evaluate and decide *discernment, differentiation* (1C 12.10); (2) of divergent opinions *disputing, judgment, argument* (RO 14.1)

διάκρισις	N-NF-S	διάκρισις

διακωλύω impf. διεκώλυον; *prevent, restrain, dissuade* (MT 3.14)

διαλαλέω impf. διελάλουν; *discuss thoroughly, deliberate, talk over in detail* (LU 6.11); passive, of a report *be talked about, be told everywhere* (LU 1.65)

διαλέγεται	VIPD--3S	διαλέγομαι
	VIPO--3S	"

διαλέγομαι impf. διελεγόμην; 1aor. mid. διελεξάμην; 1aor. pass. διελέχθην; (1) of a reasoned discussion *discuss, discourse with, conduct a discussion* (AC 18.4); (2) of disputations *contend, argue, dispute* (MK 9.34); (3) of speaking to someone in order to convince *address, speak, reason with* (HE 12.5)

διαλεγόμενον	VPPDAM-S	διαλέγομαι
	VPPOAM-S	"
διαλεγόμενος	VPPDNM-S	"
	VPPONM-S	"

διαλεγομένου	VPPDGM-S	"
	VPPOGM-S	"
διαλεγομένων	VPPDGM-P	"
	VPPOGM-P	"

διαλείπω 2aor. διέλιπον; *stop, cease, leave off* doing something (LU 7.45)

διάλεκτον	N-AF-S	διάλεκτος

διάλεκτος, ου, ἡ of the form of speech characteristic of a nation or region *dialect, language, way of speaking*

διαλέκτῳ	N-DF-S	διάλεκτος

διαλιμπάνω impf. διελίμπανον; *cease, stop, leave off* doing something (AC 8.24)

διαλλάγηθι	VMAP--2S	διαλλάσσω

διαλλάσσω 2aor. pass. διηλλάγην; as dealing with mutual hostility *change from enmity to friendship, reconcile*; only passive in the NT *become reconciled, make peace with* someone (MT 5.24)

διαλογίζεσθαι	VNPD	διαλογίζομαι
	VNPO	
διαλογίζεσθε	VIPD--2P	"
	VIPO--2P	"

διαλογίζομαι impf. διελογιζόμην; (1) as reasoning inwardly *think about thoroughly, consider carefully, reason out* (LU 1.29); (2) as reasoning with others *discuss, argue, debate* (MK 9.33)

διαλογιζόμενοι	VPPDNM-P	διαλογίζομαι
	VPPONM-P	
διαλογιζομένων	VPPDGM-P	"
	VPPOGM-P	
διαλογίζονται	VIPD--3P	"
	VIPO--3P	
διαλογισμοί	N-NM-P	διαλογισμός
διαλογισμοῖς	N-DM-P	"
διαλογισμόν	N-AM-S	"

διαλογισμός, ου, ὁ (1) in a positive sense *thought (process), reasoning, design* (LU 2.35); (2) in a negative sense *doubt, dispute, argument* (LU 24.38); κριταὶ διαλογισμῶν πονηρῶν *judges with evil motives* (JA 2.4)

διαλογισμός	N-NM-S	διαλογισμός
διαλογισμοῦ	N-GM-S	"
διαλογισμούς	N-AM-P	"
διαλογισμῶν	N-GM-P	"

διαλύω impf. pass. διελυόμην; 1aor. pass. διελύθην; *dissolve, break up*; literally and passive, of a ship's stern *be broken up* (AC 27.41); figuratively, of a crowd *disperse, scatter* (AC 5.36)

διαμαρτυράμενοι	VPADNM-P	διαμαρτύρομαι
διαμαρτύρασθαι	VNAD	"
διαμαρτύρεται	VIPD--3S	"
	VIPO--3S	"
διαμαρτύρηται	VSPD--3S	"
	VSPO--3S	"

διαμαρτύρομαι 1aor. διεμαρτυράμην; (1) *solemnly witness, bear witness (to), testify (about)* (AC 20.24); (2) as giving a solemn warning *admonish, earnestly ask, strongly tell* (1T 5.21); (3) *strongly urge, insist* (AC 2.40)

διαμαρτύρομαι	VIPD--1S	διαμαρτύρομαι
	VIPO--1S	"
διαμαρτυρόμενος	VPPDNM-S	"
	VPPONM-S	"

διαμάχομαι impf. διεμαχόμην; *protest strongly, argue vehemently* (AC 23.9)

διαμεῖναι	VNAA	διαμένω
διαμείνη	VSAA--3S	"
διαμεμενηκότες	VPRANM-P	"
διαμεμερισμένοι	VPRPNM-P	διαμερίζω
διαμένει	VIPA--3S	διαμένω
διαμένεις	VIPA--2S	"
διαμένη	VSPA--3S	"

διαμένω impf. διέμενον; 1aor. διέμεινα; pf. διαμεμένηκα; (1) of things *remain (unchanged), continue to exist* (GA 2.5); (2) of persons *remain constant, stand by* (LU 22.28); (3) of circumstances *continue unchanged, be permanent* (2P 3.4)

διαμεριζόμεναι	VPPMNF-P	διαμερίζω
	VPPPNF-P	"
διαμεριζόμενοι	VPPMNM-P	"
διαμερίζονται	VIPM--3P	"

διαμερίζω impf. διεμέριζον; 1aor. διεμέρισα, mid. διεμερισάμην; pf. pass. ptc. διαμεμερισμένος; 1aor. pass. διεμερίσθην; (1) *divide, separate*; passive *be separated off, be dispersed* (AC 2.3); (2) *distribute, divide up, share* (LU 22.17); middle *divide up among* (MT 27.35); (3) figuratively and passive *be divided against, be opposed to* (LU 11.17)

διαμερίσατε	VMAA--2P	διαμερίζω
διαμερισθεῖσα	VPAPNF-S	"
διαμερισθήσεται	VIFP--3S	"
διαμερισθήσονται	VIFP--3P	"
διαμερισμόν	N-AM-S	διαμερισμός

διαμερισμός, οῦ, ὁ *division, opposition, dissension* (LU 12.51), in contrast to εἰρήνη (*peace*)

Δίαν	N-AM-S	Ζεύς
διανεμηθῇ	VSAP--3S	διανέμω

διανέμω 1aor. pass. διενεμήθην; *distribute*; passive, of a report *be spread (abroad), be circulated, be told everywhere* (AC 4.17)

διανεύω *signify by a nod of the head, beckon, make signs by gesturing* with some part of the body (LU 1.22)

διανεύων	VPPANM-S	διανεύω

διανοέομαι impf. διενοούμην; *consider, think over, intend* (1P 1.12)

διανόημα, ατος, τό as the result of considering something *thought, idea* (LU 11.17)

διανοήματα	N-AN-P	διανόημα

διάνοια, ας, ἡ (1) as the seat of perception and thinking *mind, understanding, intellect* (MK 12.30); (2) as an inner disposition of mind and heart *attitude, thought, way of thinking* (LU 1.51); (3) as a function of the intellect resulting in insight *comprehension, understanding, idea* (1J 5.20)

διάνοια	N-NF-S	διάνοια
διανοίᾳ	N-DF-S	"
διάνοιαν	N-AF-S	"
διανοίας	N-GF-S	"
διανοῖγον	VPPANN-S	διανοίγω

διανοίγω 1aor. διήνοιξα; 1aor. pass. διηνοίχθην; (1) *open*; idiomatically ἄρσην διανοίων μήτραν literally *male that opens the womb*, i.e. *firstborn son* (LU 2.23); (2) figuratively, of the eyes, ears, heart, or mind in enabling someone to perceive or understand *open* (LU 24.45);

(3) of what has been hidden or obscure *explain, interpret, open up* (LU 24.32)

διανοίγων	VPPANM-S	διανοίγω
διανοίχθητι	VMAP--2S	"
διανοιῶν	N-GF-P	διάνοια

διανυκτερεύω *spend the whole night, pass the night* (LU 6.12)

διανυκτερεύων	VPPANM-S	διανυκτερεύω
διανύσαντες	VPAANM-P	διανύω

διανύω 1aor. διήνυσα; *complete, finish* something (AC 21.7); *continue* (the voyage) is also possible here, as in classical writers

διαπαντός *continually* (AC 10.2)

διαπαντός	AB	διαπαντός
διαπαρατριβαί	N-NF-P	διαπαρατριβή

διαπαρατριβή, ῆς, ἡ strictly *rubbing against*; hence *mutual irritation, constant friction, continual arguing*

διαπεράσαι	VNAA	διαπεράω
διαπεράσαντες	VPAANM-P	"
διαπεράσαντος	VPAAGM-S	"

διαπεράω 1aor. διεπέρασα; *cross from one point to another pass over, go across, cross (over)*

διαπερῶν	VPPAAN-S	διαπεράω
διαπερῶσι(ν)	VSPA--3P	"
διαπλεύσαντες	VPAANM-P	διαπλέω

διαπλέω 1aor. διέπλευσα; as crossing a sea *sail through* or *over* (AC 27.5)

διαπονέομαι impf. διεπονούμην; 1aor. διεπονήθην; *be greatly annoyed, be much disturbed, be upset* (AC 4.2)

διαπονηθείς	VPAONM-S	διαπονέομαι
διαπονούμενοι	VPPDNM-P	"
	VPPONM-P	"
διαπορεῖν	VNPA	διαπορέω
διαπορεῖσθαι	VNPM	"
διαπορεύεσθαι	VNPD	διαπορεύομαι
	VNPO	"

διαπορεύομαι impf. διεπορευόμην; *travel throughout* an area (AC 16.4); *pass through* (LU 6.1); of a crowd *go by* (LU 18.36)

διαπορευόμενος	VPPDNM-S	διαπορεύομαι
	VPPONM-S	"
διαπορευομένου	VPPDGM-S	"
	VPPOGM-S	"

διαπορέω impf. διηπόρουν; of mental perplexity *be utterly at a loss, be thoroughly perplexed, be bewildered* (AC 2.12)

διαπραγματεύομαι 1aor. διεπραγματευσάμην; *gain by trading, earn*

διαπρίω impf. pass. διεπριόμην; strictly *divide with a saw*; hence *cut to the quick, infuriate*; only passive in the NT *be infuriated, be enraged*

διαρήσσονται	VIFM--3P	διαρρήγνυμι
διαρήσσων	VPPANM-S	"

διαρθρόω *render capable of articulate speech* (LU 1.64)

διαρθρώθη	VIAP--3S	διαρθρόω

διαρπάζω fut. διαρπάσω; 1aor. διήρπασα; *plunder thoroughly, despoil, carry off as plunder*

διαρπάσαι	VNAA	διαρπάζω
διαρπάσει	VIFA--3S	"
διαρπάση	VSAA--3S	"
διαρπάστω	VMAA--3S	"

διαρρήγνυμι (and **διαρήγνυμι**) and **διαρρήσσω** (and **δια-ρήσσω**) impf. pass. διερρησόμην; 1aor. διέρρηξα; (1) of a garment *tear, rip in two* (MT 26.65); (2) of chains and fetters *break* (LU 8.29); (3) of nets *tear, break* (LU 5.6)

διαρρήξαντες	VPAANM-P	διαρρήγνυμι
διαρρήξας	VPAANM-S	"
διαρρήσσων	VPPANM-S	"

διασαφέω 1aor. διεσάφησα; strictly *make thoroughly clear*; hence *explain* (MT 13.36); as telling in detail *report, tell all about* (MT 18.31)

διασάφησον	VMAA--2S	διασαφέω
διασείσητε	VSAA--2P	διασείω

διασείω 1aor. διέσεισα; strictly *shake violently* or *thoroughly*; hence *extort money from* someone, *harass, intimidate* (LU 3.14)

διασκορπίζω 1aor. διεσκόρπισα; 1aor. pass. διεσκορπίσθην; 1fut. pass. διασκορπισθήσομαι; *scatter, disperse* (MT 26.31); of property *waste, squander* (LU 15.13)

διασκορπίζων	VPPANM-S	διασκορπίζω
διασκορπισθήσεται	VIFP--3S	"
διασκορπισθήσονται	VIFP--3P	"
διασκορπίσω	VIFA--1S	"
διασπαρέντες	VPAPNM-P	διασπείρω
διασπασθῇ	VSAP--3S	διασπάω

διασπάω pf. pass. inf. διεσπάσθαι; 1aor. pass. διεσπάσθην; *tear apart, tear to pieces, pull apart*

διασπείρω 2aor. pass. διεσπάρην; *scatter abroad, disperse*

διασπορά, ᾶς, ἡ strictly *scattering*, as of seed, *sowing*; hence (1) of persons *dispersion*; in the NT the portion of the Jews living outside Palestine *Dispersion* (JN 7.35); (2) of place, *regions where scattered people are living*; transliterated into English as *Diaspora* (JA 1.1)

διασπορᾷ	N-DF-S	διασπορά
διασποράν	N-AF-S	διασπορά
διασπορᾶς	N-GF-S	"
διαστάσης	VPAAGF-S	διΐστημι
διαστελλόμενον	VPPPAN-S	διαστέλλω

διαστέλλω impf. mid. διεστελλόμην; 1aor. mid. διεστειλάμην; only middle in the NT; (1) *order, give (strict) orders, command* (HE 12.20); (2) when followed by a negative *prohibit, forbid* (MT 16.20)

διάστημα, ατος, τό as a period of time between two events *interval* (AC 5.7)

διάστημα	N-NN-S	διάστημα
διαστήσαντες	VPAANM-P	διΐστημι

διαστολή, ῆς, ἡ *distinction, difference*

διαστολή	N-NF-S	διαστολή
διαστολήν	N-AF-S	"
διαστρέφοντα	VPPAAM-S	διαστρέφω

διαστρέφω 1aor. διέστρεψα; pf. pass. ptc. διεστραμμένος; (1) literally, of an object on the potter's wheel *become misshapen*; figuratively *pervert, corrupt, distort* (AC 13.10); passive, of the truth *be perverted, be distorted* (AC 20.30); in a moral sense *be depraved* (LU 9.41); (2) as causing someone to err *mislead* (AC 13.8)

διαστρέφων	VPPANM-S	διαστρέφω
διαστρέψαι	VNAA	"

διασῴζω 1aor. διέσωσα; 1aor. pass. διεσώθην; (1) *bring safely through, save, rescue* (AC 27.43); (2) passive, of sickness *be completely healed, be restored to health* (MT 14.36); of imminent death *escape, be rescued from* (AC 28.4)

διασωθέντα	VPAPAM-S	διασῴζω
διασωθέντες	VPAPNM-P	"
διασωθῆναι	VNAP	"
διασῶσαι	VNAA	"
διασώσῃ	VSAA--3S	"
διασώσωσι(ν)	VSAA--3P	"
διαταγάς	N-AF-P	διαταγή
διαταγείς	VPAPNM-S	διατάσσω

διαταγή, ῆς, ἡ as how a matter has been arranged *ordinance, direction, disposition* (AC 7.53)

διαταγῇ	N-DF-S	διαταγή

διάταγμα, ατος, τό as what has been imposed by decree *command, edict* (HE 11.23)

διάταγμα	N-AN-S	διάταγμα
διαταξάμενος	VPAMNM-S	διατάσσω
διατάξομαι	VIFM--1S	"
διατάξωμαι	VSAM--1S	"

διαταράσσω 1aor. pass. διεταράχθην; *greatly disturb, perplex, throw into great confusion*; only passive in the NT *be greatly perplexed* or *troubled* (LU 1.29)

διατάσσομαι	VIPM--1S	διατάσσω

διατάσσω fut. mid. διατάξομαι; 1aor. διέταξα, mid. διεταξάμην; pf. διατέταχα; 1aor. pass. διετάχθην; 2aor. pass. ptc. διαταγείς; strictly *arrange carefully, make precise arrangement*; hence *order, direct, command* (MT 11.1); middle with the same sense (AC 24.23); passive *be ordered* or *ordained* (GA 3.19)

διατάσσων	VPPANM-S	διατάσσω
διαταχθέντα	VPAPAN-P	"
διατελεῖτε	VIPA--2P	διατελέω

διατελέω intransitively, persevere in a certain course of action *continue, remain*, followed by a participle or adjective to denote what one is persevering in (AC 27.33)

διατεταγμένον	VPRPAN-S	διατάσσω
διατεταγμένος	VPRMNM-S	"
διατεταχέναι	VNRA	"

διατηρέω impf. διετήρουν; of words to be carefully remembered *keep, treasure up* (LU 2.51); of moral abstinence, with ἑαυτόν *keep oneself free from, wholly abstain from, avoid* something (AC 15.29)

διατηροῦντες	VPPANM-P	διατηρέω

διατί *for what? for what reason* or *purpose?*

διατί	QT	διατί
διατίθεμαι	VIPM--1S	διατίθημι

διατίθημι fut. mid. διαθήσομαι; 2aor. mid. διεθέμην; middle in the NT; (1) as related to a covenant *make a covenant, ordain, arrange* (AC 3.25); (2) in relation to disposing of property *make a will* (HE 9.16); (3) as assigning a kingdom or domain *appoint*; idiomatically διατιθέναι βασιλείαν literally *designate ruling*, i.e. *give authority to rule* (LU 22.29)

διατρίβοντες	VPPANM-P	διατρίβω
διατριβόντων	VPPAGM-P	"

διατρίβω impf. διέτριβον; 1aor. διέτριψα; strictly *rub through, wear away*; hence, of spending or passing time in a place *remain, stay, tarry* (JN 3.22)

διατρίψαντες	VPAANM-P	διατρίβω
διατρίψας	VPAANM-S	"
διατροφάς	N-AF-P	διατροφή

διατροφή, ῆς, ἡ   *sustenance, food, means of subsistence* (1T 6.8)

διατροφήν	N-AF-S	διατροφή

διαυγάζω   1aor. διηύγασα; *shine through*; of the day *dawn, break*; used metaphorically in 2P 1.19, possibly to refer to Christ's return

διαυγάσαι	VNAA	διαυγάζω
διαυγάση	VSAA--3S	"

διαυγής, ές   of an object through which light can shine *transparent, translucent, radiant* (RV 21.21)

διαυγής	A--NM-S	διαυγής

διαφανής, ές   *transparent* (RV 21.21)

διαφανής	A--NM-S	διαφανής
διαφέρει	VIPA--3S	διαφέρω
διαφέρετε	VIPA--2P	"
διαφερομένων	VPPPGM-P	"
διαφέροντα	VPPAAN-P	"

διαφέρω   impf. mid./pass. διεφερόμην; 1aor. διήνεγκα; (1) transitively, as transporting something through an area *carry through* (MK 11.16); as telling a message throughout an area *spread, tell everywhere* (AC 13.49); passive, of a ship in shifting winds *be driven about, drift about* (AC 27.27); (2) intransitively *differ, be different* (GA 4.1); as differing advantageously *be superior to, be worth more than* (MT 6.26); (3) absolutely τὰ διαφέροντα *the essential things, the things that matter* or *are of greater value* (RO 2.18); (4) impersonally διαφέρει *it matters, it makes a difference* (GA 2.6)

διαφεύγω   2aor. διέφυγον; *escape, get away* (AC 27.42)

διαφημίζειν	VNPA	διαφημίζω

διαφημίζω   1aor. διεφήμισα; 1aor. pass. διεφημίσθην; of news or a report *spread abroad, tell everywhere, proclaim widely*

διαφθεῖραι	VNAA	διαφθείρω
διαφθείραντας	VPAAAM-P	"
διαφθείρει	VIPA--3S	"
διαφθείρεται	VIPP--3S	"
διαφθείροντας	VPPAAM-P	"

διαφθείρω   1aor. διέφθειρα; pf. pass. ptc. διεφθαρμένος; 2aor. pass. διεφθάρην; (1) *spoil, ruin, destroy utterly* (RV 8.9); of a moth in clothes *eat, consume* (LU 12.33); passive, of persons *waste away, become weak* (2C 4.16); (2) morally *corrupt, lead astray, ruin*; passive *be depraved* (1T 6.5)

διαφθορά, ᾶς, ἡ   *corruption, destruction, ruin*; of the body *decay, dissolution* (AC 2.27)

διαφθοράν	N-AF-S	διαφθορά
διάφορα	A--AN-P	διάφορος
διαφόροις	A--DM-P	"

διάφορος, ον   (1) *different, diverse, of varying kinds* (RO 12.6); (2) comparative διαφορώτερος, τέρα, ον *superior, more valuable* or *important* (HE 1.4)

διαφορωτέρας	A-MGF-S	διάφορος
διαφορώτερον	A-MAN-S	"
διαφύγη	VSAA--3S	διαφεύγω
διαφύγοι	VOAA--3S	"
διαφυλάξαι	VNAA	διαφυλάσσω

διαφυλάσσω   1aor. διεφύλαξα; *carefully guard* or *keep, protect* (LU 4.10)

διαχειρίζω   1aor. mid. διεχειρισάμην; only middle in the NT *lay hands on violently, seize and kill, murder*

διαχειρίσασθαι	VNAM	διαχειρίζω
διαχλευάζοντες	VPPANM-P	διαχλευάζω

διαχλευάζω   *jeer outright at, make fun of, ridicule* (AC 2.13)

διαχωρίζεσθαι	VNPP	διαχωρίζω

διαχωρίζω   *separate*; only passive in the NT *be separated* from someone, *go away, depart* (LU 9.33)

διγαμία, ας, ἡ   *second marriage* (TI 1.9)

διγαμίας	N-GF-S	διγαμία

δίγαμος, ον   *married for the second time*; substantivally δίγαμοι *twice-married persons* (TI 1.9)

διγάμους	A--AM-P	δίγαμος
διδακτικόν	A--AM-S	διδακτικός

διδακτικός, ή, όν   *skillful in teaching, able to teach* (1T 3.2)

διδακτοί	A--NM-P	διδακτός
διδακτοῖς	A--DM-P	"

διδακτός, ή, όν   *taught*; (1) of persons *instructed, taught* (JN 6.45); (2) of words *imparted, learned, taught* (1C 2.13a); substantivally (1C 2.13b)

διδάξαι	VNAA	διδάσκω
διδάξει	VIFA--3S	"
διδάξη	VSAA--3S	"
δίδαξον	VMAA--2S	"
διδάξωσι(ν)	VSAA--3P	"
διδάσκαλε	N-VM-S	διδάσκαλος

διδασκαλία, ας, ἡ   (1) active *instruction, act of teaching* (RO 12.7); (2) passive *what is taught, teaching, doctrine* (EP 4.14)

διδασκαλία	N-NF-S	διδασκαλία
διδασκαλίᾳ	N-DF-S	"
διδασκαλίαις	N-DF-P	"
διδασκαλίαν	N-AF-S	"
διδασκαλίας	N-AF-P	"
	N-GF-S	"
διδάσκαλοι	N-NM-P	διδάσκαλος
διδάσκαλον	N-AM-S	"

διδάσκαλος, ου, ὁ   *teacher*; as a title of dignity and respect *master, teacher* (MT 10.24); in the NT equivalent to ῥαββί, a designation for teacher meaning *my great one* (JN 1.38)

διδάσκαλος	N-NM-S	διδάσκαλος
διδασκάλους	N-AM-P	"
διδασκάλων	N-GM-P	"
δίδασκε	VMPA--2S	διδάσκω
διδάσκει	VIPA--3S	"
διδάσκειν	VNPA	"
διδάσκεις	VIPA--2S	"
διδάσκεσθαι	VNPP	"
διδάσκη	VSPA--3S	"
διδάσκοντες	VPPANM-P	"
διδάσκοντι	VPPADM-S	"
διδάσκοντος	VPPAGM-S	"
διδασκόντων	VPPAGM-P	"

διδάσκω   impf. ἐδίδασκον; fut. διδάξω; 1aor. ἐδίδαξα; 1aor. pass. ἐδιδάχθην; *teach, instruct* (MT 4.23); passive *be taught, learn* (GA 1.12)

διδάσκω	VIPA--1S	διδάσκω
διδάσκων	VPPANM-S	"
	VPPAVM-S	"
διδαχαῖς	N-DF-P	διδαχή

113

διδαχή, ῆς, ἡ (1) active, as an activity *teaching, instruction* (1C 14.6); (2) passive *what is taught, teaching, doctrine* (JN 7.16)

διδαχή	N-NF-S	διδαχή
διδαχῇ	N-DF-S	"
διδαχήν	N-AF-S	"
διδαχῆς	N-GF-S	"
διδόασι(ν)	VIPA--3P	δίδωμι
διδόμενον	VPPPNN-S	"
διδόναι	VNPA	"
διδόντα	VPPAAM-S	"
	VPPAAN-P	"
διδόντες	VPPANM-P	"
διδόντι	VPPADM-S	"
διδόντος	VPPAGM-S	"
δίδοται	VIPP--3S	"
δίδοτε	VMPA--2P	"
δίδου	VMPA--2S	"
διδούς	VPPANM-S	"
δίδραχμα	N-AN-P	δίδραχμον

δίδραχμον, ου, τό *double drachma, two-drachma piece,* a silver coin worth two Attic drachmas, two Roman denarii, or a Jewish half-shekel, a tax for the temple, expected of all Jewish males each year

Δίδυμον	N-AM-S	Δίδυμος

Δίδυμος, ου, ὁ *Didymus,* masculine proper noun meaning *twin,* Greek for *Thomas* (JN 11.16)

Δίδυμος	N-NM-S	Δίδυμος
διδῶ	VSPA--1S	δίδωμι

δίδωμι by-form διδῶ (RV 3.9); impf. ἐδίδουν; fut. δώσω; 1aor. ἔδωκα, subjunctive δώσῃ (JN 17.2); 2aor. ἔδων; pf. δέδωκα; pluperfect ἐδεδώκειν; pf. pass. δέδομαι; 1aor. pass. ἐδόθην; 1fut. pass. δοθήσομαι; with a basic meaning *give,* the translation varying widely to suit the context; (1) of persons; (a) of what is given by a person in superior position to one in subordinate position; as a task, equivalent to τίθημι, *appoint, assign* (AC 13.20); as authority to carry out a task *entrust, grant, put* (MT 9.8; JN 3.35); as a favor or privilege *give, bestow* (MT 4.9); (b) of what is given by a person in inferior position to one in superior position; as an acknowledgment *devote, offer, bring* (LU 2.24); as a service gift *surrender, give up* (MT 20.28); (2) of things; (a) as implying a transfer of place or possession *give, present* (MK 2.26); *put, place* (LU 15.22; figuratively and metaphorically in 2C 6.3); *give out, hand over* (MT 5.31); (b) as giving something valuable in return *yield, give back, pay* (MT 13.8; MK 14.11); (c) as giving something valuable to gain a return *invest, put* (LU 19.23); (3) of events; (a) as giving opportunity *permit, allow* (LU 1.73); *leave place for, let experience* (RO 12.19); (b) as causing to happen *produce, make* (AC 2.19); (4) idiomatically διδόναι δεξιάς literally *give right hands,* i.e. *make an agreement* (GA 2.9); διδόναι στόμα literally *give mouth,* i.e. *help to say* (LU 21.15); διδόναι ἐργασίαν literally *give effort,* i.e. *do one's best, strive, try hard* (LU 12.58); διδόναι δόξαν τῷ θεῷ literally *give glory to God,* i.e. *swear before God to tell the truth* (JN 9.24)

δίδωμι	VIPA--1S	δίδωμι
δίδωσι(ν)	VIPA--3S	"
διέβησαν	VIAA--3P	διαβαίνω

διέβλεψε(ν)	VIAA--3P	διαβλέπω
διεβλήθη	VIAP--3S	διαβάλλω
διεγείραντες	VPAANM-P	διεγείρω
διεγείρειν	VNPA	"
διεγείρετο	VIIP--3S	"
διεγείρουσι(ν)	VIPA--3P	"

διεγείρω impf. pass. διεγειρόμην; 1aor. διήγειρα; 1aor. pass. διηγέρθην; (1) active *cause to wake up, awaken* (LU 8.24); figuratively, of mental activity *rouse up, stir up* (2P 1.13); (2) passive *become awake, wake up* (MK 4.39); metaphorically, of a calm sea *become stormy* or *turbulent* (JN 6.18)

διεγείρω	VIPA--1S	διεγείρω
διεγερθείς	VPAPNM-S	"
διεγνώρισαν	VIAA--3P	διαγνωρίζω
διεγόγγυζον	VIIA--3P	διαγογγύζω
διεδίδετο	VIIP--3S	διαδίδωμι
διεδίδοτο	VIAA--3S	"
διέδωκε(ν)	VIAA--3S	"
διεζώσατο	VIAM--3S	διαζώννυμι
διέζωσε(ν)	VIAA--3S	"
διεζωσμένος	VPRMNM-S	"
διέθετο	VIAM--3S	διατίθημι
διεῖλε(ν)	VIAA--3S	διαιρέω
διεκρίθη	VIAP--3S	διακρίνω
διεκρίθητε	VIAP--2P	"
διεκρίναμεν	VIAA--1P	"
διέκρινε(ν)	VIAA--3S	"
διεκρίνομεν	VIIA--1P	"
διεκρίνοντο	VIIM--3P	"
διεκώλυε(ν)	VIIA--3S	διακωλύω
διελαλεῖτο	VIIP--3S	διαλαλέω
διελάλουν	VIIA--3P	"
διελέγετο	VIID--3S	διαλέγομαι
	VIIO--3S	"
διέλειπε(ν)	VIIA--3S	διαλείπω
διελέξατο	VIAD--3S	διαλέγομαι
διελεύσεται	VIFD--3S	διέρχομαι
διελέχθη	VIAO--3S	διαλέγομαι
διελέχθησαν	VIAO--3P	"
διεληλυθότα	VPRAAM-S	διέρχομαι
διελθεῖν	VNAA	"
διελθόντα	VPAAAM-S	"
διελθόντες	VPAANM-P	"
διέλθω	VSAA--1S	"
διέλθωμεν	VSAA--1P	"
διελθών	VPAANM-S	"
διελίμπανε(ν)	VIAA--3S	διαλιμπάνω
διελίμπανον	VIAA--3S	"
διέλιπε(ν)	VIAA--3S	διαλείπω
διελογίζεσθε	VIID--2P	διαλογίζομαι
	VIIO--2P	"
διελογίζετο	VIID--3S	"
	VIIO--3S	"
διελογίζοντο	VIID--3P	"
	VIIO--3P	"
διελογίσαντο	VIAD--3P	"
διελύετο	VIIP--3S	διαλύω
διελύθη	VIAP--3S	"
διελύθησαν	VIAP--3P	"
διεμαρτυράμεθα	VIAD--1P	διαμαρτύρομαι

διεμαρτύρατο	VIAD--3S	"
διεμαρτύρετο	VIID--3S	"
	VIIO--3S	"
διεμαρτύρω	VIAD--2S	"
διεμάχοντο	VIID--3P	διαμάχομαι
	VIIO--3P	"
διέμενε(ν)	VIIA--3S	διαμένω
διεμέριζον	VIIA--3P	διαμερίζω
διεμερίζοντο	VIIM--3P	"
διεμέρισαν	VIAA--3P	"
διεμερίσαντο	VIAM--3P	"
διεμερίσθη	VIAP--3S	"
διενέγκη	VSAA--3S	διαφέρω

διενθυμέομαι of the significance of something *ponder on, consider carefully, think about seriously* (AC 10.19)

διενθυμουμένου	VPPDGM-S	διενθυμέομαι
	VPPOGM-S	"
διενοοῦντο	VIID--3P	διανοέομαι
διεξελθοῦσα	VPAANF-S	διεξέρχομαι

διεξέρχομαι 2aor. act. διεξῆλθον; *come out* (AC 28.3)

διέξοδος, ου, ἡ strictly *passage through*; hence, either *street crossing* or more probably *outlet* where a main street cuts through the city boundary and out into the country; αἱ διέξοδοι τῶν ὁδῶν *thoroughfares* (MT 22.9)

διεξόδους	N-AF-P	διέξοδος
διεπέρασε(ν)	VIAA--3S	διαπεράω
διεπονοῦντο	VIID--3P	διαπονέομαι
διεπορεύετο	VIID--3S	διαπορεύομαι
	VIIO--3S	"
διεπορεύοντο	VIID--3P	"
	VIIO--3P	"
διεπραγματεύσαντο	VIAD--3P	διαπραγματεύομαι
διεπραγματεύσατο	VIAD--3S	"
διεπρίοντο	VIIP--3P	διαπρίω
διερήγνυτο	VIIP--3S	διαρρήγνυμι
διερήσσετο	VIIP--3S	"

διερμηνεία, ας, ἡ *explanation, translation, interpretation* (1C 12.10)

διερμηνεία	N-NF-S	διερμηνεία
διερμήνευε(ν)	VIIA--3S	διερμηνεύω
διερμηνεύει	VIPA--3S	"
διερμηνευέτω	VMPA--3S	"
διερμηνεύῃ	VSPA--3S	"
διερμηνευομένη	VPPPNF-S	"
διερμηνευομένων	VPPPGF-P	"
διερμηνεύουσι(ν)	VIPA--3P	"
διερμήνευσε(ν)	VIAA--3S	"

διερμηνευτής, οῦ, ὁ *interpreter, translator* (1C 14.28)

διερμηνευτής	N-NM-S	διερμηνευτής

διερμηνεύω 1aor. διερμήνευσα; *translate* (AC 9.36); *interpret, explain* (LU 24.27; 1C 12.30)

διερμηνεύων	VPPANM-S	διερμηνεύω
διέρρηξε(ν)	VIAA--3S	διαρρήγνυμι
διερρήγνυτο	VIIP--3S	"
διέρρησσε(ν)	VIIA--3S	"
διερρήσσετο	VIIP--3S	"
διέρρητο	VIIP--3S	see διερρήσσετο
διέρχεσθαι	VNPD	διέρχομαι
	VNPO	"
διέρχεται	VIPD--3S	"
	VIPO--3S	"

διέρχομαι impf. διηρχόμην; fut. διελεύσομαι; 2aor. act. διῆλθον; pf. act. διελήλυθα; (1) *go through, pass through* a place (AC 13.6); of a sword *pierce, penetrate* (figuratively in LU 2.35); (2) of travel from place to place *go about, travel throughout* (LU 9.6); (3) of death *extend to, come to* (RO 5.12); (4) figuratively, of a report *spread, be told everywhere* (LU 5.15)

διέρχομαι	VIPD--1S	διέρχομαι
	VIPO--1S	"
διερχόμενοι	VPPDNM-P	"
	VPPONM-P	"
διερχόμενον	VPPDAM-S	"
	VPPOAM-S	"
διερχόμενος	VPPDNM-S	"
	VPPONM-S	"
διέρχωμαι	VSPD--1S	"
	VSPO--1S	"

διερωτάω 1aor. διηρώτησα; *ascertain by inquiry, find out by inquiring* (AC 10.17)

διερωτήσαντες	VPAANM-P	διερωτάω
διεσάφησαν	VIAA--3P	διασαφέω
διεσάφησε(ν)	VIAA--3S	"
διεσκόρπισα	VIAA--1S	διασκορπίζω
διεσκόρπισας	VIAA--2S	"
διεσκόρπισε(ν)	VIAA--3S	"
διεσκορπίσθησαν	VIAP--3P	"
διεσκορπισμένα	VPRPAN-P	"
διεσπακέναι	VNRA	διασπάω
διεσπάρησαν	VIAP--3P	διασπείρω
διεσπαρμένα	VPRPAN-P	"
διεσπάσθαι	VNRP	διασπάω
διεστειλάμεθα	VIAM--1P	διαστέλλω
διεστείλατο	VIAM--3S	"
διεστέλλετο	VIIM--3S	"
διέστη	VIAA--3S	διΐστημι
διεστραμμένα	VPRPAN-P	διαστρέφω
διεστραμμένη	VPRPVF-S	"
διεστραμμένης	VPRPGF-S	"
διεσώθησαν	VIAP--3P	διασώζω
διέταξα	VIAA--1S	διατάσσω
διεταξάμην	VIAM--1S	"
διετάξατο	VIAM--3S	"
διέταξε(ν)	VIAA--3S	"
διεταράχθη	VIAP--3S	διαταράσσω
διετήρει	VIIA--3S	διατηρέω

διετής, ές of a child's age *two years old*; substantivally *two-year old child* (MT 2.16)

διετία, ας, ἡ *period of two years*

διετίαν	N-AF-S	διετία
διετίας	N-GF-S	"
διετοῦς	A--GM-S	διετής
διέτριβε(ν)	VIIA--3S	διατρίβω
διέτριβον	VIIA--3P	"
διετρίψαμεν	VIAA--1P	"
διέτριψαν	VIAA--3P	"
διεφέρετο	VIIP--3S	διαφέρω
διεφήμισαν	VIAA--3P	διαφημίζω
διεφημίσθη	VIAP--3S	"
διεφθάρη	VIAP--3S	διαφθείρω
διεφθάρησαν	VIAP--3P	"
διεφθαρμένων	VPRPGM-P	"

διέφθειρε(ν)	VIIA--3S	"
διεχειρίσασθε	VIAM--2P	διαχειρίζω
διήγειραν	VIAA--3P	διεγείρω
διηγείρετο	VIIP--3S	"
διηγεῖτο	VIID--3S	διηγέομαι
	VIIO--3S	"

διηγέομαι fut. διηγήσομαι; 1aor. διηγησάμην; set out something in detail *tell, relate, describe fully* (LU 8.39)

διηγήσαντο	VIAD--3P	διηγέομαι
διηγήσατο	VIAD--3S	"
διηγήσεται	VIFD--3S	"
διήγησιν	N-AF-S	διήγησις

διήγησις, εως, ἡ *narrative, account, story*, giving details in orderly sequence (LU 1.1)

διηγήσωνται	VSAD--3P	διηγέομαι
διηγοῦ	VMPD--2S	"
	VMPO--2S	"
διηγούμενον	VPPDAM-S	"
	VPPOAM-S	"
διηκόνει	VIIA--3S	διακονέω
διηκονήσαμεν	VIAA--1P	"
διηκόνησε(ν)	VIAA--3S	"
διηκόνουν	VIIA--3P	"
διῆλθε(ν)	VIAA--3S	διέρχομαι
διῆλθον	VIAA--1S	"
	VIAA--3P	"
διηνεκές	A--AN-S	διηνεκής

διηνεκής, ές strictly *stretched the whole length*; hence *continuous, uninterrupted*; idiomatically, of time εἰς τὸ διηνεκές literally *to the whole length*, i.e. *continually* (HE 10.1); *eternally, always, forever* (HE 7.3)

διήνοιγε(ν)	VIIA--3S	διανοίγω
διηνοίγησαν	VIAP--3P	"
διηνοιγμένους	VPRPAM-P	"
διήνοιξε(ν)	VIAA--3S	"
διηνοίχθησαν	VIAP--3P	"
διηπόρει	VIIA--3S	διαπορέω
διηπόρουν	VIIA--3P	"
διηπορούντο	VIIM--3P	"
διηρμήνευε(ν)	VIIA--3S	διερμηνεύω
διηρμήνευσε(ν)	VIAA--3S	"
διήρχετο	VIID--3S	διέρχομαι
	VIIO--3S	"
διήρχοντο	VIID--3P	"
	VIIO--3P	"
διθάλασσον	A--AM-S	διθάλασσος

διθάλασσος, ον *washed on both sides by the sea*; τόπος δ. *reef, shoal, sandbank* formed where two opposing currents flow together (AC 27.41)

διϊκνέομαι intransitively, as moving into and through something producing a marked effect *go through, thoroughly penetrate* (HE 4.12)

διϊκνούμενος	VPPDNM-S	διϊκνέομαι
	VPPONM-S	"

διΐστημι 1aor. διέστησα; 2aor. διέστην; (1) transitively (first aorist), strictly *set at an interval* from a former position; idiomatically βραχύ διαστῆσαι (τὴν ναῦν) literally *set (the ship) at an interval*, i.e. *sail a little farther* (AC 27.28); (2) intransitively (second aorist) *go away, depart* from someone (LU 24.51); of a time interval *pass* (LU 22.59)

διϊστορέω *examine carefully* (AC 17.23)

διϊστορῶν	VPPANM-S	διϊστορέω
διϊσχυρίζετο	VIID--3S	διϊσχυρίζομαι
	VIIO--3S	"

διϊσχυρίζομαι impf. διϊσχυριζόμην; *insist, assert, firmly maintain*

διϊσχυριζόμενος	VPPDNM-S	διϊσχυρίζομαι
	VPPONM-S	"
δικάζετε	VMPA--2P	δικάζω

δικάζω 1aor. pass. ἐδικάσθην; *judge, condemn* (LU 6.37)

δίκαια	A--NN-P	δίκαιος
δικαία	A--NF-S	"
δίκαιαι	A--NF-P	"
δικαίαν	A--AF-S	"
δικαίας	A--GF-S	"
δίκαιε	A--VM-S	"
δίκαιοι	A--NM-P	"
δικαιοῖ	VIPA--3S	δικαιόω
δικαίοις	A--DM-P	δίκαιος

δικαιοκρισία, ας, ἡ as a quality of a righteous judge *righteous judgment, fair* or *just verdict* (RO 2.5)

δικαιοκρισίας	N-GF-S	δικαιοκρισία
δίκαιον	A--AM-S	δίκαιος
	A--AN-S	"
	A--NN-S	"

δίκαιος, αία, ον (1) morally and ethically, of persons *righteous, upright, just* (MT 5.45), opposite ἄδικος (*unrighteous*); from a legal viewpoint *law-abiding, honest, good* (in behavior) (1T 1.9), opposite ἄθεσμος (*lawless*); from a religious viewpoint, as rightly related to God *righteous, just* (LU 1.6); *put right* (RO 2.13); substantivally οἱ δίκαιοι *the righteous, people rightly related to God* (MT 13.43; singular in RO 1.17); (2) of God *just, righteous, fair* (2T 4.8); (3) of Christ *just, innocent* (LU 23.47); (4) of things *righteous, innocent* (MT 23.35); (5) neuter δίκαιον used impersonally *it is right, proper* (EP 6.1); *what is right* (LU 12.57)

δίκαιος	A--NM-S	δίκαιος

δικαιοσύνη, ης, ἡ (1) *righteousness, uprightness*, generally denoting the characteristics of δίκαιος (*righteous, just*) (MT 5.6); (2) legally *justice, uprightness, righteousness* (PH 3.6); (3) as an attribute of God *righteousness, integrity* (RO 3.5); (4) of the right behavior that God requires of persons *righteousness, good behavior, uprightness* (MT 5.20), opposite ἀδικία (*unrighteousness, wrongdoing*); (5) in Pauline thought of the divine action by which God puts a person right with himself and which then becomes a dynamic power in the believer's life *making right(eous); state of having been made righteous* (RO 1.17)

δικαιοσύνη	N-NF-S	δικαιοσύνη
δικαιοσύνη	N-DF-S	"
δικαιοσύνην	N-AF-S	"
δικαιοσύνης	N-GF-S	"
δικαίου	A--GM-S	δίκαιος
	A--GN-S	"
δικαιούμενοι	VPPPNM-P	δικαιόω
δικαιοῦν	VNPA	"
δικαιοῦντα	VPPAAM-S	"
δικαιοῦντες	VPPANM-P	"
δικαίους	A--AM-P	δίκαιος

δικαιοῦσθαι	VNPP	δικαιόω
δικαιοῦσθε	VIPP--2P	"
δικαιοῦται	VIPP--3S	"

δικαιόω fut. δικαιώσω; 1aor. ἐδικαίωσα; pf. pass. δεδικαίωμαι; 1aor. pass. ἐδικαιώθην; 1fut. pass. δικαιωθήσομαι; (1) generally *make right* or *just*; (2) as behaving in a way expected of the one δίκαιος (*righteous, just*) *obey God's requirements, live right, do right* (RV 22.11); (3) as demonstrating that someone is δίκαιος *vindicate, show to be right* (LU 10.29); (4) as acknowledging that someone is just *justify, vindicate* (LU 7.29); (5) as a religious technical term; (a) of imputed righteousness, as God's judging and saving activity in relation to persons *justify, declare righteous, put right with* (himself) (RO 3.24); (b) experientially, of imparted righteousness as freedom from sin's power *make free, release, set free*; passive *be set free* (RO 6.7)

δικαιῶ	A--DM-S	δίκαιος
δικαιωθέντες	VPAPNM-P	δικαιόω
δικαιωθῆναι	VNAP	"
δικαιωθῇς	VSAP--2S	"
δικαιωθήσεται	VIFP--3S	"
δικαιωθήσῃ	VIFP--2S	"
δικαιωθήσονται	VIFP--3P	"
δικαιωθήτω	VMAP--3S	"
δικαιωθῶμεν	VSAP--1P	"

δικαίωμα, ατος, τό (1) of God's requirements *ordinance, regulation, commandment* (LU 1.6); (2) of fulfillment of a legal requirement *righteous deed, act of justice*, by Christ (RO 5.18), by God (RV 15.4), by saints (RV 19.8); (3) as an act of justification equivalent to δικαίωσις *removal of guilt, acquittal* (RO 5.16)

δικαίωμα	N-AN-S	δικαίωμα
	N-NN-S	"
δικαιώμασι(ν)	N-DN-P	"
δικαιώματα	N-AN-P	"
	N-NN-P	"
δικαιώματος	N-GN-S	"
δικαίων	A--GM-P	δίκαιος
δικαιῶν	VPPANM-S	δικαιόω

δικαίως adverb; (1) legally *justly, with strict justice* (1P 2.23); (2) ethically *in a right way, honestly, with integrity* (TI 2.12); (3) deservedly, *fairly* (LU 23.41)

δικαίως	AB	δικαίως
δικαιῶσαι	VNAA	δικαιόω
δικαιώσει	VIFA--3S	"
δικαίωσιν	N-AF-S	δικαίωσις

δικαίωσις, εως, ἡ strictly, an act of *making right* or *just*; hence *justification, acquittal, vindication* (RO 4.25); εἰς δικαίωσιν ζωῆς *righteous act that sets free and gives life* (RO 5.18)

δικασθῆτε	VSAP--2P	δικάζω
δικαστήν	N-AM-S	δικαστής

δικαστής, οῦ, ὁ *judge*, one who pronounces the verdict in a court case

δίκη, ης, ἡ as penal justice *penalty, punishment* (2TH 1.9); in popular pagan belief, *Dike*, the goddess of justice (AC 28.4)

δίκη	N-NF-S	δίκη
δίκην	N-AF-S	"

δίκτυα	N-AN-P	δίκτυον
	N-NN-P	"

δίκτυον, ου, τό *net, fishing net*

δίκτυον	N-AN-S	δίκτυον
	N-NN-S	"

δίλογος, ον strictly *saying the same thing twice*; hence, of speaking one thing and meaning another *hypocritical, insincere, deceitful* (1T 3.8)

διλόγους	A--AM-P	δίλογος

διό inferential conjunction; *for this reason, therefore, for this purpose* (MT 27.8); δ. καί of a self-evident inference *and so, so also, so therefore* (LU 1.35)

διό	CH	διό
διοδεύσαντες	VPAANM-P	διοδεύω

διοδεύω impf. διώδευον; 1aor. διώδευσα; (1) transitively *go through, travel through* a place (AC 17.1); (2) intransitively *go about* from one place to another (LU 8.1)

Διονύσιος, ου, ὁ *Dionysius*, masculine proper noun

Διονύσιος	N-NM-S	Διονύσιος

διόπερ inferential conjunction; a strengthened form of διό; *therefore, for this very reason, on this very account* (1C 8.13)

διόπερ	CH	διόπερ

διοπετής, ές (also **Διοπετής, διοσπετής**) strictly *fallen from Zeus*; neuter as a substantive τὸ διοπετές as the goddess image at Ephesus, reputed to be a *stone fallen from heaven* (AC 19.35)

Διοπετοῦς	AP-GN-S	διοπετής
διοπετοῦς	AP-GN-S	"

διόρθωμα, ατος, τό what has been set straight, especially internal improvements in administration *reform* (AC 24.2)

διορθωμάτων	N-GN-P	διόρθωμα
διορθώσεως	N-GF-S	διόρθωσις

διόρθωσις, εως, ἡ (1) as a process of setting things straight *reformation* (probably HE 9.10); (2) as the result of setting things right *new order* (possibly HE 9.10)

διορυγῆναι	VNAA	διορύσσω
διορύσσουσι(ν)	VIPA--3P	"

διορύσσω 1aor. pass. διωρύχθην; of a thief who gains entrance into a house by digging through a wall *break in* or *through, dig through*

διορυχθῆναι	VNAP	διορύσσω
Διός	N-GM-S	Ζεύς
Διοσκόροις	N-DM-P	Διόσκουροι

Διόσκουροι, ων, οἱ (also **Διόσκοροι**) *Dioscuri*, meaning *heavenly twins*, name of Greek gods Castor and Pollux, twin sons of Zeus and Leda, regarded as patrons of sailors (AC 28.11)

Διοσκύροις	N-DM-P	Διόσκουροι
διοσπετῆς	AP-GN-S	διοπετής

διότι a conjunction from διά (*because of*) and ὅτι (*that*); (1) in causal clauses *because* (1C 15.9; possibly RO 8.21); (2) to introduce an inferential clause *therefore* (AC 13.35); (3) as equivalent to the causal conjunction ὅτι *because, for that, inasmuch as* (LU 1.13); (4) as equivalent to the declarative ὅτι *that* (possibly RO 8.21)

διότι	CH	διότι
	CS	"

Διοτρέφης, ους, ὁ (also **Διοτρεφής**) *Diotrephes*, masculine proper noun (3J 9)

Διοτρέφης	N-NM-S	Διοτρέφης
Διοτρεφής	N-NM-S	"
διπλᾶ	A--AN-P	διπλοῦς
διπλῆς	A--GF-S	"
διπλότερον	A-MAM-S	"
διπλοῦν	A--AN-S	"

διπλοῦς, ῆ, οῦν *double, twofold* (1T 5.17); comparative **διπλότερος, τέρα, ον** *twofold more, twice as much* (MT 23.15); substantivally, neuter διπλοῦν and τὰ διπλᾶ *double* (RV 18.6)

διπλόω 1aor. ἐδίπλωσα; *double*; διπλώσατε τὰ διπλᾶ *pay back double* or *twice as much* (RV 18.6)

διπλώσατε	VMAA--2P	διπλόω

δίς adverb; *twice* (MK 14.30); idiomatically ἅπαξ καὶ δ. literally *once and again*, i.e. *several times* (PH 4.16); δ. ἀποθάνων *being completely dead* (JU 12)

δίς	AB	δίς
δισμυριάδες	N-NF-P	δισμυριάς

δισμυριάς, άδος, ἡ *double myriad*, i.e. 20,000; idiomatically δισμυριάδες μυριάδων literally *20,000 x 10,000*, i.e. *countless, great number of*, used to emphasize an extremely large number (RV 9.16)

διστάζω 1aor. ἐδίστασα; *doubt, waver, be of two minds* about something

δίστομον	A--AF-S	δίστομος

δίστομος, ον strictly *having two mouths*; hence, of a sword *double-edged, two-edged*

δίστομος	A--NF-S	δίστομος

δισχίλιοι, αι, α as a cardinal number *two thousand*; substantivally *two thousand* (MK 5.13)

δισχίλιοι	APCNM-P	δισχίλιοι
διϋλίζοντες	VPPAVM-P	διϋλίζω

διϋλίζω *strain* or *filter thoroughly, filter* or *strain out*, as insects from wine (MT 23.24)

διχάζω 1aor. ἐδίχασα; strictly *divide in two, separate*; hence *disunite, cause to rebel, turn* someone *against* another (MT 10.35)

διχάσαι	VNAA	διχάζω

διχοστασία, ας, ἡ strictly *standing apart*; hence *disunity, dissension, division* within a community

διχοστασία	N-NF-S	διχοστασία
διχοστασίαι	N-NF-P	"
διχοστασίας	N-AF-P	"

διχοτομέω fut. διχοτομήσω; of an ancient form of severe punishment *cut in two, cut in pieces*; figuratively *punish with greatest severity*

διχοτομήσει	VIFA--3S	διχοτομέω
διψᾷ	VSPA--3S	διψάω

διψάω fut. διψήσω; 1aor. ἐδίψησα; literally *thirst, be thirsty, suffer from thirst* (MT 25.35); figuratively *long earnestly for, have strong desire for* (MT 5.6)

δίψει	N-DN-S	δίψος
διψήσει	VIFA--3S	διψάω
διψήση	VSAA--3S	"
διψήσουσι(ν)	VIFA--3P	"

δίψος, ους, τό *thirst* (2C 11.27)

δίψυχοι	AP-VM-P	δίψυχος

δίψυχος, ον strictly *having two minds*; hence *doubting, hesitating, double-minded*; substantivally *fickle person* (JA 4.8)

δίψυχος	A--NM-S	δίψυχος
διψῶ	VIPA--1S	διψάω
	VSPA--1S	"
διψῶμεν	VIPA--1P	"
διψῶν	VPPANM-S	"
διψῶντα	VPPAAM-S	"
διψῶντες	VPPANM-P	"
διψῶντι	VPPADM-S	"
διωγμοῖς	N-DM-P	διωγμός
διωγμόν	N-AM-S	"

διωγμός, οῦ, ὁ literally *pursuit, chase*; figuratively *persecution* (MT 13.21)

διωγμός	N-NM-S	διωγμός
διωγμοῦ	N-GM-S	"
διωγμούς	N-AM-P	"
διωγμῶν	N-GM-P	"
διώδευε(ν)	VIIA--3S	διοδεύω
δίωκε	VMPA--2S	διώκω
διώκεις	VIPA--2S	"
διώκετε	VMPA--2P	"
διώκομαι	VIPP--1S	"
διώκομεν	VIPA--1P	"
διωκόμενοι	VPPPNM-P	"
διώκοντα	VPPANN-P	"
διώκονται	VIPP--3P	"
διώκοντας	VPPAAM-P	"
διώκοντες	VPPANM-P	"
διωκόντων	VPPAGM-P	"
διώκουσι(ν)	VIPA--3P	"
διώκτην	N-AM-S	διώκτης

διώκτης, ου, ὁ *persecutor*, one who is preoccupied with causing others to suffer (1T 1.13)

διώκω impf. ἐδίωκον; fut. διώξω; 1aor. ἐδίωξα; pf. pass. ptc. δεδιωγμένος; 1aor. pass. ἐδιώχθην; (1) as making haste *press forward, hasten, run* (figuratively in PH 3.12); (2) of hostile pursuit *persecute* (JN 5.16); *drive out, expel* (MT 23.34); (3) figuratively, as being zealous; for a person *run after, pursue* (LU 17.23); as an earnest striving after something *pursue, follow after, seek after* (1T 6.11)

διώκω	VIPA--1S	διώκω
διώκωμεν	VSPA--1P	"
διώκων	VPPANM-S	"
διώκωνται	VSPP--3P	"
διώκωσι(ν)	VSPA--3P	"
διωξάτω	VMAA--3S	"
διώξετε	VIFA--2P	"
διώξητε	VSAA--2P	"
διώξουσι(ν)	VIFA--3P	"
διώξωσι(ν)	VSAA--3P	"
διωχθήσονται	VIFP--3P	"

δόγμα, ατος, τό (1) as a fixed and authoritative decision or requirement *decree, command* (LU 2.1; AC 17.7); (2) as a fixed rule or set of rules *law, ordinance* (AC 16.4)

δόγμα	N-NN-S	δόγμα
δόγμασι(ν)	N-DN-P	"
δόγματα	N-AN-P	"
δογματίζεσθε	VIPP--2P	δογματίζω

δογματίζω active *decree, ordain*; only passive in the NT *submit to rules, obey regulations* decreed by others (CO 2.20)

δογμάτων	N-GN-P	δόγμα
δοθεῖσα	VPAPNF-S	δίδωμι
δοθεῖσαν	VPAPAF-S	"
δοθείσῃ	VPAPDF-S	"
δοθείσης	VPAPGF-S	"
δοθέντος	VPAPGN-S	"
δοθῇ	VSAP--3S	"
δοθῆναι	VNAP	"
δοθήσεται	VIFP--3S	"
δοῖ	VSAA--3S	"
δοκεῖ	VIPA--3S	δοκέω
δοκεῖν	VNPA	"
δοκεῖς	VIPA--2S	"
δοκεῖτε	VIPA--2P	"
	VMPA--2P	"

δοκέω impf. ἐδόκουν; fut. δόξω; 1aor. ἔδοξα; (1) transitively, of subjective opinion *think, presume, suppose* (MT 6.7); often followed by an infinitive translated as a finite verb (1C 3.18); *choose, be disposed to* (1C 11.16); (2) intransitively *seem, have the appearance, appear* (AC 17.18); of having a reputation for something *be recognized as, count for, be regarded as* (GA 2.6); (3) impersonally δοκεῖ μοι *it seems to me, I think*; used with the dative of person and an infinitive to express one's will or pleasure *it seems best* or *good, decide* (LU 1.3)

δοκῇ	VSPA--3S	δοκέω
δοκιμάζει	VIPA--3S	δοκιμάζω
δοκιμάζειν	VNPA	"
δοκιμάζεις	VIPA--2S	"
δοκιμαζέσθωσαν	VMPP--3P	"
δοκιμάζεται	VIPP--3S	"
δοκιμάζετε	VIPA--2P	"
	VMPA--2P	"
δοκιμαζέτω	VMPA--3S	"
δοκιμαζομένου	VPPPGN-S	"
δοκιμάζοντες	VPPANM-P	"
δοκιμάζοντι	VPPADM-S	"

δοκιμάζω fut. δοκιμάσω; 1aor. ἐδοκίμασα; pf. pass. δεδοκίμασμαι; (1) as making an examination *put to the test, examine, prove (by testing)* (LU 14.19); as testing or proving the will of God *prove* (RO 12.2); as testing oneself by self-examination *test, examine* (2C 13.5); as being aware of the progress of history *test* (the times) (LU 12.56); (2) as accepting the result of an examination of a person *regard as approved, consider qualified, approve* (1C 16.3); as accepting the result of examination of a thing *think of as valuable* or *worthwhile* (RO 1.28)

δοκιμάζω	VIPA--1S	δοκιμάζω
δοκιμάζων	VPPANM-S	"
δοκιμάσαι	VNAA	"
δοκιμάσει	VIFA--3S	"
δοκιμάσητε	VSAA--2P	"
δοκιμασθήσεται	VIFP--3S	"

δοκιμασία, ας, ἡ as seeking proof of genuineness by testing or trial *testing, examination*; πειράζειν ἐν δοκιμασίᾳ *put to the test* (HE 3.9)

δοκιμασία	N-DF-S	δοκιμασία

δοκιμή, ῆς, ἡ (1) as having the quality of having stood the test *mature* or *approved character* (RO 5.4); (2) as the experience of testing *ordeal* (2C 8.2); (3) as the proof of genuineness *evidence* (2C 13.3)

δοκιμή	N-NF-S	δοκιμή
δοκιμῇ	N-DF-S	"
δοκιμήν	N-AF-S	"
δοκιμῆς	N-GF-S	"

δοκίμιον, ου, τό (1) *means of testing, criterion, test*; (2) as the act of testing *trial, proving* (JA 1.3); (3) as the result of testing *proof, genuineness* (1P 1.7)

δοκίμιον	N-NN-S	δοκίμιον
δόκιμοι	A--NM-P	δόκιμος
δοκίμοις	A--DM-P	"
δόκιμον	A--AM-S	"

δόκιμος, ον (1) as a qualification that results from trial and examination *approved, reliable*; substantivally οἱ δόκιμοι *the tried and true people* (1C 11.19); (2) of a characteristic of a person who has stood the test *trustworthy, respected, esteemed* (RO 14.18); (3) of something that has stood the test *genuine* (RO 16.10)

δόκιμος	A--NM-S	δόκιμος
δοκόν	N-AF-S	δοκός

δοκός, οῦ, ἡ *beam of wood, shaft of timber*

δοκός	N-NF-S	δοκός
δοκοῦμεν	VIPA--1P	δοκέω
δοκοῦν	VPPAAN-S	"
δοκοῦντα	VPPANN-P	"
δοκοῦντες	VPPANM-P	"
δοκούντων	VPPAGM-P	"
δοκοῦσα	VPPANF-S	"
δοκοῦσι(ν)	VIPA--3P	"
	VPPADM-P	"
δοκῶ	VIPA--1S	"
δοκῶν	VPPANM-S	"
δόλιοι	A--NM-P	δόλιος

δόλιος, ία, ον *deceitful, treacherous, dishonest* (2C 11.13)

δολιόω impf. third-person plural ἐδολιοῦσαν; *deceive, deal treacherously, use fraud* (RO 3.13)

δολοῖ	VIPA--3S	δολόω
δόλον	N-AM-S	δόλος

δόλος, ου, ὁ strictly *bait for fish*; hence *deceit, treachery, fraud*

δόλος	N-NM-S	δόλος
δόλου	N-GM-S	"
δολοῦντες	VPPANM-P	δολόω

δολόω as changing something to cause it to be false *distort, falsify, adulterate* (2C 4.2)

δόλῳ	N-DM-S	δόλος

δόμα, ατος, τό what has been given *gift, present*

δόμα	N-AN-S	δόμα
δόματα	N-AN-P	"
Δονεί		Δονεί

Δονεῖ, ὁ (also **Δονεί**) indeclinable; *Doni*, masculine proper noun

δόντα	VPAAAM-S	δίδωμι
δόντι	VPAADM-S	"
δόντος	VPAAGM-S	"

δόξα, ης, ἡ (1) as a manifestation of light *radiance, brightness, splendor* (AC 22.11); (2) as a manifestation of God's excellent power *glory, majesty* (RO 9.23); (3) as an excellent reputation *honor, glory, praise* (JN 5.44); (4) as a state characterized by honor, power, and remarkable appearance *glory, splendor* (LU 24.26); (5) of a person created in the image of God *reflection, glory* (1C 11.7); (6) δόξαι as angelic powers around God *angelic beings, majesties, dignities* (JU 8)

δόξα	N-NF-S	δόξα
δοξάζειν	VNPA	δοξάζω
δοξάζεται	VIPP--3S	"
δοξαζέτω	VMPA--3S	"
δοξάζηται	VSPP--3S	"
δοξάζητε	VSPA--2P	"
δοξαζόμενος	VPPPNM-S	"
δοξάζοντες	VPPANM-P	"

δοξάζω impf. ἐδόξαζον; fut. δοξάσω and δοξήσω; 1aor. ἐδόξασα; pf. pass. δεδόξασμαι; 1aor. pass. ἐδοξάσθην; (1) as giving or sharing a high status *glorify, make great* (RO 8.30); (2) as enhancing the reputation of God or man *praise, honor, magnify* (MK 2.12); (3) as putting into a position of power and great honor, especially in the future life *glorify* (JN 7.39); (4) passive; (a) of things greatly valued and excellent *be wonderful, be glorious* (1P 1.8); (b) of persons receiving great honor *be glorified, be praised* (LU 4.15)

δοξάζω	VIPA--1S	δοξάζω
δοξάζων	VPPANM-S	"
δόξαν	N-AF-S	δόξα
δόξαντες	VPAANM-P	δοκέω
δόξας	N-AF-P	δόξα
δοξάσαι	VNAA	δοξάζω
δοξάσατε	VMAA--2P	"
δοξάσει	VIFA--3S	"
δοξάσῃ	VSAA--3S	"
δοξασθῇ	VSAP--3S	"
δοξασθῶσι(ν)	VSAP--3P	"
δόξασον	VMAA--2S	"
δοξάσω	VIFA--1S	"
	VSAA--1S	"
δοξάσωσι(ν)	VSAA--3P	"
δόξῃ	N-DF-S	δόξα
	VSAA--3S	δοκέω
δόξης	N-GF-S	δόξα
δοξήσει	VIFA--3S	δοξάζω
δόξητε	VSAA--2P	δοκέω
δόξω	VSAA--1S	"

Δορκάς, άδος, ἡ *Dorcas*, feminine proper noun

Δορκάς	N-NF-S	Δορκάς
δός	VMAA--2S	δίδωμι
δόσει	N-DF-S	δόσις
δόσεως	N-GF-S	"
δόσιν	N-AF-S	"

δόσις, εως, ἡ (1) as an action *giving* (PH 4.15); (2) as what is given *gift* (JA 1.17)

δόσις	N-NF-S	δόσις
δότε	VMAA--2P	δίδωμι
δότην	N-AM-S	δότης

δότης, ου, ὁ *one who gives, giver* (2C 9.7)

δότω	VMAA--3S	δίδωμι
Δουβέριος	AP-NM-S	Δερβαῖος
Δούβριος	AP-NM-S	"
δοῦλα	A--AN-P	δοῦλος (I)

δουλαγωγέω literally *lead into slavery, cause to live the life of a slave*; figuratively, of disciplining one's physical body *bring under control, subdue, make ready to serve* (1C 9.27)

δουλαγωγῶ	VIPA--1S	δουλαγωγέω
δούλας	N-AF-P	δούλη
δοῦλε	N-VM-S	δοῦλος (II)

δουλεία, ας, ἡ literally, as a condition *slavery, bondage*, opposite ἐλευθερία (*freedom, liberty*); figuratively, of an enslaved moral or spiritual condition characterized by fear of breaking rules *bondage, lack of freedom* (GA 4.24)

δουλείαν	N-AF-S	δουλεία
δουλείας	N-GF-S	"
δουλεύει	VIPA--3S	δουλεύω
δουλεύειν	VNPA	"
δουλεύετε	VIPA--2P	"
	VMPA--2P	"
δουλευέτωσαν	VMPA--3P	"
δουλεύοντες	VPPANM-P	"
δουλεύουσι(ν)	VIPA--3P	"
δουλεῦσαι	VNAA	"
δουλεύσει	VIFA--3S	"
δουλεύσουσι(ν)	VIFA--3P	"
δουλεύσωσι(ν)	VSAA--3P	"

δουλεύω fut. δουλεύσω; 1aor. ἐδούλευσα; pf. δεδούλευκα; (1) of relationship *be a slave, be subjected* (JN 8.33); (2) of action or behavior *perform the duties of a slave, serve, obey* (MT 6.24); (3) figuratively, of spiritual service to God *serve, obey* (AC 20.19); of spiritual or moral enslavement to sin, appetites, etc. *be a slave to, be controlled by* (RO 6.6)

δουλεύω	VIPA--1S	δουλεύω
δουλεύων	VPPANM-S	"

δούλη, ης, ἡ literally *female slave, maidservant, slave woman*; figuratively, of a woman's relationship to God or Christ *servant, handmaiden* (LU 1.38)

δούλη	N-NF-S	δούλη
δούλης	N-GF-S	"
δουλίαν	N-AF-S	see δουλείαν
δουλίας	N-GF-S	see δουλείας
δοῦλοι	N-NM-P	δοῦλος (II)
	N-VM-P	"
δούλοις	N-DM-P	"
δοῦλον	N-AM-S	"

δοῦλος, η, ον (I) of being in a servile condition *enslaved, performing the service of a slave*; figuratively, of unquestioning obedience, in either a good or bad sense *subservient, enslaved, subject* (RO 6.19)

δοῦλος, ου, ὁ (II) (1) generally, as one who serves in obedience to another's will *slave, servant* (JN 15.15); (2) literally, in contrast to (a) a master *slave* (MT 8.9); (b) a freeman *bondman, slave* (CO 3.11), opposite ἐλεύθερος (*freeman*) and πολίτης (*citizen*); (c) a son *(house) servant, family servant* (GA 4.7); (d) a believer regarded as a brother *slave* (PM 16); (3) figuratively; (a) of relationship to God, Christ, one's fellow man *servant* (GA 1.10); (b) of being controlled by sin *slave* (JN 8.34)

δοῦλος	N-NM-S	δοῦλος (II)
δούλου	N-GM-S	"

δούλους N-AM-P "

δουλόω fut. δουλώσω; 1aor. ἐδούλωσα; pf. pass. δεδούλωμαι; 1aor. pass. δεδουλώθην; literally, as requiring absolute obedience *enslave, make* someone *a slave* (AC 7.6); figuratively *gain control over* someone; with ἑαυτόν as the object of one who gives up personal rights for the sake of others *make oneself a slave, submit oneself to* (1C 9.19); passive *be enslaved, be subject to* (GA 4.3); *be under obligation, be bound to* (1C 7.15)

δούλῳ N-DM-S δοῦλος (II)
δουλωθέντες VPAPNM-P δουλόω
δούλων N-GM-P δοῦλος (II)
δουλώσουσι(ν) VIFA--3P δουλόω
δοῦναι VNAA δίδωμι
δούς VPAANM-S "

δοχή, ῆς, ἡ a substantive from δέχομαι (*receive, accept*); strictly *reception of guests*; hence *meal for guests, banquet, feast* (LU 5.29)

δοχήν N-AF-S δοχή
δράκοντα N-AM-S δράκων
δράκοντι N-DM-S "
δράκοντος N-GM-S "

δράκων, οντος, ὁ literally, as a monstrous reptile *serpent, dragon*; metaphorically in Revelation as a designation for the devil (RV 12.9)

δράκων N-NM-S δράκων
δραμόντες VPAANM-P τρέχω
δραμών VPAANM-S "

δράσσομαι strictly *catch with the hand*; hence *catch, seize, lay hold of* (1C 3.19)

δρασσόμενος VPPDNM-S δράσσομαι
  VPPONM-S "
δραχμάς N-AF-P δραχμή

δραχμή, ῆς, ἡ *drachma*, Attic silver coin approximately equal to the Roman denarius, with significant purchasing power

δραχμήν N-AF-S δραχμή

δρέπανον, ου, τό *sickle*, a knifelike instrument with a curved blade used for reaping grain by hand

δρέπανον N-AN-S δρέπανον
δρόμον N-AM-S δρόμος

δρόμος, ου, ὁ from ἔδραμον, aorist of τρέχω (*run*); (1) *racecourse, course, place for running*; (2) as the circuit followed by the sun, moon, and stars *course*; (3) figuratively, of one's purpose in life and obligations in relation to it *task, mission* (AC 13.25)

Δρούσιλλα, ης, ἡ *Drusilla*, feminine proper noun (AC 24.24)

Δρούσιλλαν N-AF-S Δρούσιλλα
Δρουσίλλῃ N-DF-S "
δυναίμην VOPD--1S δύναμαι
  VOPO--1S "
δύναιντο VOPD--3P "
  VOPO--3P "

δύναμαι impf. ἠδυνάμην and ἐδυνάμην; fut. δυνήσομαι; 1aor. ἠδυνήθην and ἠδυνάσθην; of capacity or ability *be able, be capable of, can, have power to*; with an infinitive supplied or implied of what one is able to do (MT 3.9; 16.3)

δύναμαι VIPD--1S δύναμαι
  VIPO--1S "

δυνάμεθα VIPD--1P "
  VIPO--1P "
δυνάμει N-DF-S δύναμις
δυνάμεις N-AF-P "
  N-NF-P "
δυνάμενα VPPDAN-P δύναμαι
  VPPOAN-P "
δυνάμεναι VPPDNF-P "
  VPPONF-P "
δυναμένη VPPDNF-S "
  VPPONF-S "
δυνάμενοι VPPDNM-P "
  VPPONM-P "
δυνάμενον VPPDAM-S "
  VPPOAM-S "
δυνάμενος VPPDNM-S "
  VPPONM-S "
δυναμένου VPPDGM-S "
  VPPDGN-S "
  VPPOGM-S "
  VPPOGN-S "
δυναμένους VPPDAM-P "
  VPPOAM-P "
δυναμένῳ VPPDDM-S "
  VPPODM-S "
δυναμένων VPPDGM-P "
  VPPOGM-P "
δυνάμεσι(ν) N-DF-P δύναμις
δυνάμεων N-GF-P "
δυνάμεως N-GF-S "
δύναμιν N-AF-S "

δύναμις, εως, ἡ (1) as able to produce a strong effect *power, might, strength* (AC 1.8), opposite ἀσθένεια (*weakness*); plural, as universal or supernatural rulers *powers* (MT 24.29); (2) as capacity for something *ability, capability* (2C 8.3); (3) as ability to communicate through language *meaning, force* (1C 14.11); (4) as supernatural manifestations of power *miracle, wonder, powerful deed* (HE 2.4); (5) as the value and usefulness of money *wealth, resources, riches* (RV 18.3)

δύναμις N-NF-S δύναμις
δυναμούμενοι VPPPNM-P δυναμόω
δυναμοῦσθε VMPP--2P "

δυναμόω 1aor. pass. ἐδυναμώθην; as causing someone to be able *strengthen, empower, make strong*

δύνανται VIPD--3P δύναμαι
  VIPO--3P "
δύναντος VPAAGM-S δύνω
δύνασαι VIPD--2S δύναμαι
  VIPO--2S "
δύνασε VIPD--2S see δύνασαι
  VIPO--2S see δύνασαι
δύνασθαι VNPD δύναμαι
  VNPO "
δύνασθε VIPD--2P "
  VIPO--2P "
δυνάστας N-AM-P δυνάστης

δυνάστης, ου, ὁ as one who is in a position to command others *ruler, sovereign, potentate* (1T 6.15); *court official, high official* (AC 8.27)

δυνάστης N-NM-S δυνάστης

δυνατά	A--NN-P	δυνατός
δύναται	VIPD--3S	δύναμαι
	VIPO--3S	"
δυνατεῖ	VIPA--3S	δυνατέω

δυνατέω (1) absolutely *be strong* or *powerful* (2C 13.3); (2) followed by a complementary infinitive *be able to, be powerful enough to, can* (RO 14.4)

δυνατοί	AP-NM-P	δυνατός
	A--NM-P	"
δυνατόν	A--AN-S	"
	A--NN-S	"

δυνατός, ή, όν (1) of one who possesses power *powerful, mighty, strong*; (a) substantivally τὸ δυνατόν as an attribute of God, equivalent to δύναμις (RO 9.22); (b) substantivally, as a designation for God ὁ δ. *the Mighty One* (LU 1.49); (c) as an attribute of persons *able, strong* (2C 12.10); (d) of persons, as being in a position to do something *be able, be capable* (LU 14.31); substantivally οἱ δυνατοί *important, influential people* (AC 25.5); (2) neuter, of what is possible δυνατόν (ἐστιν) *it is possible, it can be* (MT 26.39)

δυνατός	AP-NM-S	δυνατός
	A--NM-S	"
δύνῃ	VIPD--2S	δύναμαι
	VIPO--2S	"
δυνηθῆτε	VSAO--2P	"
δυνήσεσθε	VIFD--2P	"
δυνήσεται	VIFD--3S	"
δυνήσῃ	VIFD--2S	"
δυνησόμεθα	VIFD--1P	"
δυνήσονται	VIFD--3P	"
δύνηται	VSPD--3S	"
	VSPO--3S	"
δύνοντος	VPPAGM-S	δύνω

δύνω 1aor. ἔδυσα; 2aor. ἔδυν; *sink, go down*; of the sun *set*

δύνωνται	VSPD--3P	δύναμαι
	VSPO--3P	"

δύο, gen. and accusative δύο, dative δυσί often substantivally; (1) as a cardinal number *two* (MT 4.18); (2) to indicate a comparatively small number δ. ἢ τρεῖς *two or three* (MT 18.20); οἱ δ. *both* (JN 20.4); δ. δ. *two by two* (MK 6.7); (3) with prepositions: κατὰ δ. *two at a time* (1C 14.27); ἀνὰ δ. *two apiece, two each* (LU 9.3); εἰς δ. *in two, into two parts* (MK 15.38)

δύο	APCAM-P	δύο
	APCAN-P	"
	APCGM-P	"
	APCGN-P	"
	APCNF-P	"
	APCNM-P	"
	A-CAF-P	"
	A-CAM-P	"
	A-CAN-P	"
	A-CGM-P	"
	A-CGN-P	"
	A-CNF-P	"
	A-CNM-P	"
	A-CNN-P	"
δύσαντος	VPAAGM-S	δύνω
δυσβάστακτα	A--AN-P	δυσβάστακτος

δυσβάστακτος, ον of burdens *hard to bear, difficult* (LU 11.46)

δυσεντερία	N-DF-S	δυσεντέριον

δυσεντέριον, ου, τό (also **δυσεντερία, ας, ἡ**) as an infectious intestinal disease *dysentery* (AC 28.8)

δυσεντερίῳ	N-DN-S	δυσεντέριον

δυσερμήνευτος, ον *hard to explain, not easy to make clear* (HE 5.11)

δυσερμήνευτος	A--NM-S	δυσερμήνευτος
δύσεως	N-GF-S	δύσις
δυσί(ν)	APCDM-P	δύο
	A-CDF-P	"
	A-CDM-P	"

δύσις, εως, ἡ of the sun *setting*; as the direction in which the sun sets *west*

δύσκολον	A--NN-S	δύσκολος

δύσκολος, ον followed by an infinitive *hard, difficult* to do something (MK 10.24)

δυσκόλως adverb; *with difficulty, hardly*

δυσκόλως	AB	δυσκόλως

δυσμή, ῆς, ἡ of the sun *going down, setting*; as the direction in which the sun sets *west*, usually plural

δυσμῶν	N-GF-P	δυσμή
δυσνόητα	A--NN-P	δυσνόητος

δυσνόητος, ον *hard to understand*; substantivally δυσνόητα *things difficult to understand* (2P 3.16)

δυσφημέω as speaking against someone's reputation *slander, revile, defame* (1C 4.13)

δυσφημία, ας, ἡ strictly *evil language*; hence *slander, reproach, evil report* (2C 6.8)

δυσφημίας	N-GF-S	δυσφημία
δυσφημούμενοι	VPPPNM-P	δυσφημέω
δῶ	VSAA--3S	δίδωμι

δώδεκα indeclinable; (1) as a cardinal number *twelve* (MT 14.20); (2) οἱ δ. the apostles appointed by Jesus *the Twelve* (MK 3.14; 4.10)

δωδέκατος, η, ον as an ordinal number *twelfth*; substantivally ὁ δ. *the twelfth one* (RV 21.20)

δωδέκατος	A-ONM-S	δωδέκατος

δωδεκάφυλον, ου, τό as the major division of Israel *the twelve tribes* (AC 26.7)

δωδεκάφυλον	N-NN-S	δωδεκάφυλον
δώῃ	VOAA--3S	δίδωμι
δώῃ	VSAA--3S	"

δῶμα, ατος, τό as the area on top of a house with a flat roof *roof, housetop*

δῶμα	N-AN-S	δῶμα
δώματος	N-GN-S	"
δωμάτων	N-GN-P	"
δῶμεν	VSAA--1P	δίδωμι
δῶρα	N-AN-P	δῶρον
	N-NN-P	"

δωρεά, ᾶς, ἡ *gift, free gift, benefit*; in the NT used only of spiritual and supernatural gifts that are freely given by God to believers, including eternal life (JN 4.10), the Holy Spirit (AC 2.38), righteousness, i.e. state of being put right with God (RO 5.17), enabling grace for appointed ministry (EP 3.7)

δωρεά	N-NF-S	δωρεά
δωρεᾷ	N-DF-S	"

δωρεάν   accusative of δωρεά (*gift*) used as an adverb; (1) of a gift bestowed without payment *freely, gratis, as a gift* (MT 10.8); (2) of something endured without cause *undeservedly, without reason* (JN 15.25); (3) of something done without due result *in vain, to no purpose* (GA 2.21)

δωρεάν	AB	δωρεάν
	N-AF-S	δωρεά
δωρεᾶς	N-GF-S	"

δωρέομαι   1aor. ἐδωρησάμην; pf. δεδώρημαι; as God's giving to man *give, grant, bestow* (2P 1.3); as a person responding favorably to a request *grant, give* (MK 15.45)

δώρημα, ατος, τό   what has been given *gift, free gift, present*; used in the NT of what God has given to man (JA 1.17)

δώρημα	N-NN-S	δώρημα
δώροις	N-DN-P	δῶρον

δῶρον, ου, τό   *gift, present, offering*; (1) as a gift to show honor and respect (MT 2.11); (2) as a support gift to maintain divine service (LU 21.1); by metonymy, a receptacle for gifts *offering box* (LU 21.4); (3) as a gift offered to God (MT 8.4); (4) as God's gift of salvation (EP 2.8)

δῶρον	N-AN-S	δῶρον
	N-NN-S	"

δωροφορία, ας, ἡ   *bringing of a gift, gift-bearing* (RO 15.31)

δωροφορία	N-NF-S	δωροφορία
δώρῳ	N-DN-S	δῶρον
δῷς	VSAA--2S	δίδωμι
δώσει	VIFA--3S	"
δώσεις	VIFA--2S	"
δώσῃ	VSAA--3S	"
δῶσι(ν)	VSAA--3P	"
δώσομεν	VIFA--1P	"
δώσουσι(ν)	VIFA--3P	"
δώσω	VIFA--1S	"
δώσωμεν	VSAA--1P	"
δώσωσι(ν)	VSAA--3P	"
δῶτε	VSAA--2P	"

ε E

ε´ indeclinable; fifth letter of the Greek alphabet; used as a cardinal number *five*; as an ordinal number *fifth* (AC 19.9)

ἔα particle; perhaps related to the imperative of ἐάω (*let alone!*); used as an exclamation of surprise or displeasure *ah! ha!* (LU 4.34)

ἔα		QS		ἔα

ἐάν conjunction; *if, if at any time, whenever*; a combination of the conditional εἰ and the particle ἄν to denote uncertainty or indefiniteness; (1) with the subjunctive; (a) to introduce a hypothetical condition *if (ever)* (MK 3.24); (b) to indicate a realizable future contingency *if, whenever* (JN 3.12); (c) to show time uncertainty *whenever, when* (JN 14.3); (2) with the indicative to express possibility as with the subjunctive *if, when* (1TH 3.8); (3) with other particles: ἐ. μή *if not, unless, except* (MT 5.20); ἐ. τε . . . ἐ. τε *whether . . . or whether* (RO 14.8); (4) after a relative, to express a condition ὃς ἐ. *whoever* (MT 5.19); ὃ ἐ. *whatever* (MT 16.19); ὅστις ἐ. *who(so)ever* (GA 5.10); ὅπου ἐ. *wherever* (MT 8.19)

ἐάν		CS		ἐάν
		QV		"

ἐάνπερ conjunction; a reinforced form of ἐάν (*if*), *if indeed, if only, on condition that* (HE 3.14)

ἐάνπερ		CS		ἐάνπερ
ἐᾷς		VIPA--2S		ἐάω
ἐάσαντες		VPAANM-P		"
ἐάσατε		VMAA--2P		"
ἐάσει		VIFA--3S		"
ἐᾶτε		VMPA--2P		"
ἑαυτά		NPAN2P		ἑαυτοῦ
ἑαυταῖς		NPDF2P		"
ἑαυτάς		NPAF2P		"
		NPAF3P		"
ἑαυτῇ		NPDF3S		"
ἑαυτήν		NPAF3S		"
ἑαυτῆς		NPGF3S		"
ἑαυτό		NPAN3S		"
ἑαυτοῖς		NPDM1P		"
		NPDM2P		"
		NPDM3P		"
ἑαυτόν		NPAM3S		"

ἑαυτοῦ, ῆς, οῦ (also αὑτοῦ) a reflexive pronoun referring action in a verb back to its own subject; plural ἑαυτῶν; (1) with the third-person *himself, herself, itself* (MT 18.4); (2) used also for the first-person and second-person plural *ourselves* (RO 8.23), *yourselves* (MT 23.31); (3) as equivalent to the reciprocal pronoun ἀλλήλων (MT 21.38); (4) used in place of the possessive pronoun *his, her, their* (MT 8.22); (5) used with prepositions: (a) ἀφ᾽ ἑ. *of one's own accord, voluntarily, spon-*

taneously (JN 5.19); (b) δι᾽ ἑ. *by itself, in its own nature* (RO 14.14); (c) ἐν ἑαυτῷ *to* or *within oneself*, used of not speaking audibly (LU 7.39; MK 2.8) or of being aware of something inwardly (AC 12.11); (d) εἰς ἑαυτὸν ἔρχεσθαι *come to oneself, come to one's senses* (LU 15.17); (e) ἐξ ἑαυτῶν *of* (our) *own strength* (2C 3.5); (f) καθ᾽ ἑαυτόν expressing manner *by oneself* (AC 28.16); *against itself* (MT 12.25)

ἑαυτοῦ		NPGM3S		ἑαυτοῦ
		NPGN3S		"
ἑαυτούς		NPAM1P		"
		NPAM2P		"
		NPAM3P		"
ἑαυτῷ		NPDM3S		"
ἑαυτῶν		NPGF3P		"
		NPGM1P		"
		NPGM2P		"
		NPGM3P		"
		NPGN3P		"

ἐάω impf. εἴων; fut. ἐάσω; 1aor. εἴασα, imperative ἔασον (AC 5.38); (1) as allowing something to be done *let, permit, suffer* (MT 24.43); (2) as leaving someone or something alone *let go* (AC 5.38); idiomatically ἐᾶτε ἕως τούτου literally *leave off until this*, i.e. *stop this, that's enough* (LU 22.51); (3) as allowing something to remain somewhere *leave* (AC 27.40)

ἐβάθυνε(ν)		VIAA--3S		βαθύνω
ἔβαλαν		VIAA--3P		βάλλω
ἔβαλε(ν)		VIAA--3S		"
ἔβαλλον		VIIA--3P		"
ἔβαλον		VIAA--3P		"
ἐβάπτιζε(ν)		VIIA--3S		βαπτίζω
ἐβαπτίζοντο		VIIP--3P		"
ἐβάπτισα		VIAA--1S		"
ἐβαπτίσαντο		VIAM--3P		"
ἐβάπτισας		VIAA--2S		"
ἐβαπτίσατο		VIAM--3S		"
ἐβάπτισε(ν)		VIAA--3S		"
ἐβαπτίσθη		VIAP--3S		"
ἐβαπτίσθημεν		VIAP--1P		"
ἐβαπτίσθησαν		VIAP--3P		"
ἐβαπτίσθητε		VIAP--2P		"
ἐβαρήθημεν		VIAP--1P		βαρέω
ἐβάρησα		VIAA--1S		"
ἐβαρύνατε		VIAA--2P		βαρύνω
ἐβαρύνθη		VIAP--3S		"
ἐβασάνιζε(ν)		VIIA--3S		βασανίζω
ἐβασάνισαν		VIAA--3P		"
ἐβασίλευσαν		VIAA--3P		βασιλεύω
ἐβασίλευσας		VIAA--2S		"
ἐβασιλεύσατε		VIAA--2P		"
ἐβασίλευσε(ν)		VIAA--3S		"

124

ἐβάσκανε(ν)	VIAA--3S	βασκαίνω
ἐβάσταζε(ν)	VIIA--3S	βαστάζω
ἐβαστάζετο	VIIP--3S	"
ἐβάστασαν	VIAA--3P	"
ἐβάστασας	VIAA--2S	"
ἐβάστασε(ν)	VIAA--3S	"
ἐβδελυγμένοις	VPRDDM-P	βδελύσσομαι
	VPRODM-P	"
ἐβδόμη	A-ODF-S	ἕβδομος

ἐβδομήκοντα indeclinable; as a cardinal number *seventy* (AC 23.23)

ἐβδομηκονταέξ indeclinable; as a cardinal number *seventy-six* (AC 27.37)

ἐβδομηκοντάκις adverb; *seventy times*; ἑ. ἑπτά in MT 18.22 may be *seventy times seven* (490), but more probably *seventy-seven times* (77), as in Genesis 4.24

ἐβδομηκοντάκις	AB	ἐβδομηκοντάκις
ἐβδόμην	A-OAF-S	ἕβδομος
ἐβδόμης	A-OGF-S	"

ἕβδομος, η, ον as an ordinal number *seventh*; substantivally ἡ ἐβδόμη *the seventh day* (HE 4.4)

ἕβδομος	A-ONM-S	ἕβδομος
ἐβδόμου	A-OGM-S	"
ἐβεβαιώθη	VIAP--3S	βεβαιόω
ἐβέβλητο	VILP--3S	βάλλω

Ἕβερ, ὁ (also **Ἐβέρ**) indeclinable; *Eber*, masculine proper noun (LU 3.35)

Ἐβέρ		Ἕβερ
Ἕβερ		see Ἕβερ
ἐβλάστησε(ν)	VIAA--3S	βλαστάνω
ἐβλασφήμει	VIIA--3S	βλασφημέω
ἐβλασφήμησαν	VIAA--3P	"
ἐβλασφήμησε(ν)	VIAA--3S	"
ἐβλασφήμουν	VIIA--3P	"
ἔβλεπε(ν)	VIIA--3S	βλέπω
ἔβλεπον	VIIA--3P	"
ἔβλεψα	VIAA--1S	"
ἐβλήθη	VIAP--3S	βάλλω
ἐβλήθησαν	VIAP--3P	"
ἐβοήθησα	VIAA--1S	βοηθέω
ἐβοήθησε(ν)	VIAA--3S	"
ἐβόησε(ν)	VIAA--3S	βοάω
ἐβούλετο	VIID--3S	βούλομαι
	VIIO--3S	"
ἐβουλεύοντο	VIIM--3P	βουλεύω
ἐβουλεύσαντο	VIAM--3P	"
ἐβουλεύσατο	VIAM--3S	"
ἐβουλήθη	VIAO--3S	βούλομαι
ἐβουλήθημεν	VIAO--1P	"
ἐβουλήθην	VIAO--1S	"
ἐβουλόμην	VIID--1S	"
	VIIO--1S	"
ἐβούλοντο	VIID--3P	"
	VIIO--3P	"
ἐβόων	VIIA--3P	βοάω
Ἑβραηκοῖς	A--DN-P	see Ἑβραϊκοῖς
Ἑβραΐδι	A--DF-S	Ἑβραΐς
Ἑβραΐδι	A--DF-S	"
Ἑβραϊκοῖς	A--DN-P	Ἑβραϊκός

Ἑβραϊκός, ή, όν a language *Hebrew* (LU 23.38); possibly *Aramaic*

Ἑβραῖοι	N-NM-P	Ἑβραῖος
Ἑβραῖοι	N-NM-P	"
Ἑβραῖος	N-NM-S	"

Ἑβραῖος, ου, ὁ (also **Ἐβραῖος**) *Hebrew*; (1) racially, one descended from Abraham (PH 3.5); (2) nationally, a Jew in contrast to a Gentile (2C 11.22); (3) linguistically, a native Palestinian Jew who spoke Hebrew (possibly Aramaic) as a mother tongue in contrast to a Greek-speaking Jew who was probably an immigrant to Palestine (AC 6.1)

Ἑβραῖος	N-NM-S	Ἑβραῖος
Ἑβραίους	N-AM-P	"
Ἑβραίους	N-AM-P	"

Ἑβραΐς, ΐδος, ἡ (also **Ἐβραΐς**) as a language *Hebrew*; τῇ Ἑβραΐδι διαλέκτῳ *the Hebrew dialect*, referring to the particular form of Hebrew (possibly Aramaic) spoken in Palestine (AC 21.40; 22.2)

Ἑβραϊστί (also **Ἐβραϊστί**) adverb; *in the Hebrew language* (JN 5.2), in contrast to Ἑλληνικός (*Greek language*); possibly *in the Aramaic language*

Ἑβραϊστί	AB	Ἑβραϊστί
Ἑβραίων	N-GM-P	Ἑβραῖος
Ἑβραίων	N-GM-P	"
ἐβρειμήσατο	VIAD--3S	βριμάομαι
ἔβρεξε(ν)	VIAA--3S	βρέχω
ἐβριμήσατο	VIAD--3S	βριμάομαι
ἔβρυχον	VIIA--3P	βρύχω
ἐγάμησε(ν)	VIAA--3S	γαμέω
ἐγαμίζοντο	VIIP--3P	γαμίζω
ἐγάμουν	VIIA--3P	γαμέω
ἐγγαμίζοντες	VPPANM-P	ἐκγαμίζω
ἐγγαρεύσῃ	VSAA--3S	ἀγγαρεύω
ἐγγεγραμμένη	VPRPNF-S	ἐγγράφω
ἐγγέγραπται	VIRP--3S	"
ἐγγιεῖ	VIFA--3S	ἐγγίζω
ἐγγίζει	VIPA--3S	"
ἐγγίζειν	VNPA	"
ἐγγίζομεν	VIPA--1P	"
ἐγγίζοντες	VPPANM-P	"
ἐγγίζοντι	VPPADM-S	"
ἐγγίζοντος	VPPAGM-S	"
ἐγγιζόντων	VPPAGM-P	"
ἐγγίζουσαν	VPPAAF-S	"
ἐγγίζουσι(ν)	VIPA--3P	"

ἐγγίζω fut. ἐγγίσω (Attic fut. ἐγγιῶ); 1aor. ἤγγισα; pf. ἤγγικα; intransitively in the NT *approach, draw near, be near*; (1) with the dative of person or place *draw near to, approach* (AC 9.3); (2) with εἰς *draw near, approach* a place (MK 11.1); (3) absolutely, of approaching in space *be near* (MT 26.46); of approaching in time *draw near, be at hand* (LU 22.1); perfect *have come* (RO 13.12)

ἐγγίζωμεν	VSPA--1P	ἐγγίζω
ἐγγίσαι	VNAA	"
ἐγγίσαντος	VPAAGM-S	"
ἐγγίσας	VPAANM-S	"
ἐγγίσατε	VMAA--2P	"
ἐγγίσει	VIFA--3S	"
ἔγγιστα	ABS	ἐγγύς

ἐγγράφω (or **ἐνγράφω**) pf. pass. ἐγγέγραμμαι; literally *enroll, enter into a register, record* (LU 10.20); figuratively, of a spiritual impression made on the heart *write in, inscribe on* (2C 3.2)

ἔγγυος, ον literally *under good security*; substantivally ὁ ἔ. *pledge, down payment*; metaphorically, of Christ as guaranteeing fulfillment of the new covenant *guarantor, surety* (HE 7.22)

ἔγγυος	AP-NM-S	ἔγγυος

ἐγγύς adverb; (1) of space *near, close to* (JN 3.23); absolutely *close by, near at hand, neighboring* (JN 19.42); (2) of time *near, imminent, close* (MT 26.18); (3) figuratively, of close or intimate relationship *near, close to* (EP 2.17); (4) comparative ἐγγύτερον *nearer* (RO 13.11); superlative ἔγγιστα *nearest, closest*

ἐγγύς	AB	ἐγγύς
	PD	"
	PG	"
ἐγγύτερον	ABM	"
	PG	"
ἐγεγόνει	VILA--3S	γίνομαι
ἐγέγραπτο	VILP--3S	ἐγγράφω
ἔγειραι	VMPA--2S	see ἔγειρε
ἐγεῖραι	VNAA	ἐγείρω
ἐγείραντα	VPAAAM-S	"
ἐγείραντες	VPAANM-P	"
ἐγείραντι	VPAADM-S	"
ἐγείραντος	VPAAGM-S	"
ἐγείρας	VPAANM-S	"
ἔγειρε	VMPA--2S	"
ἐγείρει	VIPA--3S	"
ἐγείρειν	VNPA	"
ἐγείρεσθε	VMPP--2P	"
ἐγείρεται	VIPP--3S	"
ἐγείρετε	VMPA--2P	"
ἐγείρηται	VSPP--3S	"
ἐγείρομαι	VIPP--1S	"
ἐγείρονται	VIPP--3P	"
ἐγείροντι	VPPADM-S	"
ἐγείρου	VMPM--2S	"
ἐγείρουσι(ν)	VIPA--3P	"

ἐγείρω fut. ἐγερῶ; 1aor. ἤγειρα; pf. pass. ἐγήγερμαι; 1aor. pass. ἠγέρθην; 1fut. pass. ἐγερθήσομαι; (1) transitively and literally, of a sleeping person; (a) active *wake, rouse* (MT 8.25); (b) passive with an intransitive meaning *wake up, awaken* (MT 1.24); figuratively, of a state of watchfulness or readiness *become aware, think carefully, pay attention* (EP 5.14); (2) transitively and literally, of persons sitting or lying down; (a) active *raise up, help to rise, lift up* (AC 3.7); (b) passive with an intransitive meaning *rise, get up* (MT 9.19); (c) as an imperatival formula *get up! stand up!* (MK 2.9); (d) figuratively, as healing the sick *raise up, restore to health* (JA 5.15); (e) figuratively, as bringing back from death *raise, cause to rise* (MT 10.8); of the resurrection of Jesus (AC 5.30); (3) transitively; (a) active, as causing a person to appear in history *raise up, bring into being* (MT 3.9); (b) passive with an intransitive meaning *appear, rise* (MT 11.11); (4) transitively, passive with an intransitive meaning, of nations fighting each other ἐγείρεσθαι ἐπί *rise up against* (MT 24.7); (5) transitively, of buildings *erect, restore* (JN 2.20); metaphorically, of

the body as a dwelling place belonging to God *make alive again, resurrect* (JN 2.19)

ἐγέμισαν	VIAA--3P	γεμίζω
ἐγέμισε(ν)	VIAA--3S	"
ἐγεμίσθη	VIAP--3S	"
ἐγένεσθε	VIAD--2P	γίνομαι
ἐγένετο	VIAD--3S	"
ἐγενήθη	VIAO--3S	"
ἐγενήθημεν	VIAO--1P	"
ἐγενήθην	VIAO--1S	"
ἐγενήθησαν	VIAO--3P	"
ἐγενήθητε	VIAO--2P	"
ἐγεννήθη	VIAP--3S	γεννάω
ἐγεννήθημεν	VIAP--1P	"
ἐγεννήθης	VIAP--2S	"
ἐγεννήθησαν	VIAP--3P	"
ἐγέννησα	VIAA--1S	"
ἐγέννησαν	VIAA--3P	"
ἐγέννησε(ν)	VIAA--3S	"
ἐγενόμεθα	VIAD--1P	γίνομαι
ἐγενόμην	VIAD--1S	"
ἐγένοντο	VIAD--3P	"
ἐγένου	VIAD--2S	"
ἐγερεῖ	VIFA--3S	ἐγείρω
ἐγερεῖς	VIFA--2S	"
ἐγερθείς	VPAPNM-S	"
ἐγερθέντες	VPAPNM-P	"
ἐγερθέντι	VPAPDM-S	"
ἐγερθῇ	VSAP--3S	"
ἐγερθῆναι	VNAP	"
ἐγερθήσεται	VIFP--3S	"
ἐγερθήσονται	VIFP--3P	"
ἐγέρθητε	VMAP--2P	"
ἐγέρθητι	VMAP--2S	"
ἔγερσιν	N-AF-S	ἔγερσις

ἔγερσις, εως, ἡ strictly, as an action *waking, rousing*; hence, of a person *coming back to life* after having been dead *resurrection* (MT 27.53)

ἐγερῶ	VIFA--1S	ἐγείρω
ἐγεύσασθε	VIAD--2P	γεύομαι
ἐγεύσατο	VIAD--3S	"
ἐγηγερμένον	VPRPAM-S	ἐγείρω
ἐγήγερται	VIRP--3S	"
ἔγημα	VIAA--1S	γαμέω
ἐγίνετο	VIID--3S	γίνομαι
	VIIO--3S	"
ἐγίνοντο	VIID--3P	
	VIIO--3P	
ἐγίνωσκε(ν)	VIIA--3S	γινώσκω
ἐγινώσκετε	VIIA--2P	"
ἐγίνωσκον	VIIA--3P	"

ἐγκάθετος, ον (also ἐνκάθετος) *hired to lie in wait, bribed*; substantivally *spy* (LU 20.20)

ἐγκαθέτους	AP-AM-P	ἐγκάθετος

ἐγκαίνια, ίων, τά (also ἐνκαίνια) *feast of renovation or dedication*; among the Jews *Feast of Rededication, Hannukah*, or *Feast of Lights*, an annual festival commemorating the purification and rededication of the temple by Judas Maccabeus in 165 B.C. (JN 10.22)

ἐγκαίνια	N-NN-P	ἐγκαίνια

ἐγκαινίζω (or ἐνκαινίζω)   1aor. ἐνεκαίνισα; pf. pass. ἐγκεκαίνισμαι (or ἐνκεκαίνισμαι); (1) *make new, renew*; as opening a way not there before *open, dedicate* (HE 10.20); (2) as solemnly bringing a covenant into effect *put into effect, inaugurate, establish* (HE 9.18)

ἐγκακεῖν	VNPA	ἐγκακέω
ἐγκακεῖτε	VMPA--2P	"

ἐγκακέω (and ἐκκακέω, ἐνκακέω)   1aor. ἐνεκάκησα; (1) strictly *act badly* in some circumstance; with a participle following *become weary* or *tired* of doing something (2TH 3.13); (2) as failing to hold out successfully *give up, become discouraged, lose heart* (2C 4.1)

ἐγκακήσητε	VSAA--2P	ἐγκακέω
ἐγκακήσωμεν	VSAA--1P	"
ἐγκακοῦμεν	VIPA--1P	"
ἐγκακῶμεν	VSPA--1P	"
ἐγκαλεῖσθαι	VNPP	ἐγκαλέω
ἐγκαλείτωσαν	VMPA--3P	"
ἐγκαλέσει	VIFA--3S	"

ἐγκαλέω   impf. ἐνεκάλουν; fut. ἐγκαλέσω; *call in, summon*; as a legal technical term *accuse, bring charges against, institute proceedings against* someone (AC 23.28)

ἐγκαλοῦμαι	VIPP--1S	ἐγκαλέω
ἐγκαλούμενον	VPPPAM-S	"
ἐγκαταλειπόμενοι	VPPPNM-P	ἐγκαταλείπω
ἐγκαταλείποντες	VPPANM-P	"

ἐγκαταλείπω (and ἐνκαταλείπω)   impf. ἐγκατέλειπον; fut. ἐγκαταλείψω; 2aor. ἐγκατέλιπον; 1aor. pass. ἐγκατελείφθην; (1) of a posterity *leave behind* (RO 9.29); (2) *forsake, abandon, desert* (MT 27.46); (3) as allowing to remain *leave* (AC 2.27); (4) of ceasing from an activity *leave off, stop* (HE 10.25)

ἐγκαταλείπω	VIPA--1S	ἐγκαταλείπω
ἐγκαταλείψεις	VIFA--2S	"
ἐγκαταλίπω	VSAA--1S	"
ἐγκατέλειπας	VIIA--2S	see ἐγκατέλειπες
ἐγκατέλειπε(ν)	VIIA--3S	ἐγκαταλείπω
ἐγκατέλειπες	VIIA--2S	"
ἐγκατέλειπον	VIIA--3P	"
ἐγκατελείφθη	VIAP--3S	"
ἐγκατέλιπας	VIAA--2S	see ἐγκατέλιπες
ἐγκατέλιπε(ν)	VIAA--3S	ἐγκαταλείπω
ἐγκατέλιπες	VIAA--2S	"
ἐγκατέλιπον	VIAA--3P	"

ἐγκατοικέω (and ἐνκατοικέω)   *live* or *dwell among* (2P 2.8)

ἐγκατοικῶν	VPPANM-S	ἐγκατοικέω

ἐγκαυχάομαι (and ἐνκαυχάομαι)   *boast about* someone or something; *take pride in* (2TH 1.4)

ἐγκαυχᾶσθαι	VNPD	ἐγκαυχάομαι
	VNPO	"
ἐγκεκαίνισται	VIRP--3S	ἐγκαινίζω

ἐγκεντρίζω (and ἐνκεντρίζω)   1aor. ἐνεκέντρισα; 1aor. pass. ἐνεκεντρίσθην; 1fut. pass. ἐγκεντρισθήσομαι; literally, as cutting into one plant to insert another plant so the two grow as one plant *graft in*; figuratively, of Gentiles partaking of salvation provided through the Messiah to the Jews (RO 11.17–24)

ἐγκεντρίσαι	VNAA	ἐγκεντρίζω
ἐγκεντρισθήσονται	VIFP--3P	"
ἐγκεντρισθῶ	VSAP--1S	"

ἔγκλημα, ατος, τό   (1) as a legal technical term *charge, accusation* (AC 25.16); (2) generally *reproach, blame* (AC 23.29)

ἔγκλημα	N-AN-S	ἔγκλημα
ἐγκλήματος	N-GN-S	"
ἔγκλησιν	N-AF-S	ἔγκλησις

ἔγκλησις, εως, ἡ   an action *accusing, accusation, reproach, blame* (AC 23.25)

ἐγκομβόομαι   1aor. ἐνεκομβωσάμην; strictly *clothe oneself with a garment* by tying it on with a κόμβος (*string, band*); figuratively, of taking on an essential characteristic τὴν ταπεινοφροσύνην ἐγκομβοῦσθαι *be humble, act humbly* (1P 5.5)

ἐγκομβώσασθε	VMAD--2P	ἐγκομβόομαι

ἐγκοπή, ῆς, ἡ (also ἐκκοπή, ἐνκοπή)   from the military practice of making a trench or ditch to slow down a pursuing enemy *impediment, blockage*; figuratively *hindrance, obstacle* (1C 9.12)

ἐγκοπήν	N-AF-S	ἐγκοπή
ἐγκόπτεσθαι	VNPP	ἐγκόπτω

ἐγκόπτω (and ἀνακόπτω, ἐνκόπτω)   impf. pass. ἐνεκοπτόμην; 1aor. ἐνέκοψα; strictly *knock* or *cut into*; hence *hinder, impede, thwart* (GA 5.7); *delay, detain* (AC 24.4)

ἐγκόπτω	VSPA--1S	ἐγκόπτω

ἐγκράτεια, είας, ἡ   *self-control*, especially in matters related to sex

ἐγκράτεια	N-NF-S	ἐγκράτεια
ἐγκρατείᾳ	N-DF-S	"
ἐγκράτειαν	N-AF-S	"
ἐγκρατείας	N-GF-S	"
ἐγκρατεύεται	VIPD--3S	ἐγκρατεύομαι
	VIPO--3S	"

ἐγκρατεύομαι   *exercise self-control, control* oneself, *abstain from* something (1C 7.9)

ἐγκρατεύονται	VIPD--3P	ἐγκρατεύομαι
	VIPO--3P	"
ἐγκρατῆ	A--AM-S	ἐγκρατής

ἐγκρατής, ές   as having a firm hold over one's desires *self-controlled, disciplined* (TI 1.8)

ἐγκρῖναι	VNAA	ἐγκρίνω

ἐγκρίνω (or ἐνκρίνω)   1aor. ἐνέκρινα; *reckon* or *count in* or *among, classify with, consider as belonging to* (2C 10.12)

ἐγκρύπτω   1aor. ἐνέκρυψα; *hide* or *conceal in*; of yeast in dough *put in, mix in*

ἔγκυος, ον (also ἔνκυος)   *pregnant, with child* (LU 2.5)

ἐγκύῳ	A--DF-S	ἔγκυος
ἔγνω	VIAA--3S	γινώσκω
ἔγνωκα	VIRA--1S	"
ἐγνώκαμεν	VIRA--1P	"
ἔγνωκαν	VIRA--3P	"
ἔγνωκας	VIRA--2S	"
ἐγνώκατε	VIRA--2P	"
ἐγνώκειτε	VILA--2P	"
ἔγνωκε(ν)	VIRA--3S	"
ἐγνωκέναι	VNRA	"
ἐγνώκετε	VIRA--2P	"
ἐγνωκότες	VPRANM-P	"
ἔγνων	VIAA--1S	"
ἐγνώρισα	VIAA--1S	γνωρίζω
ἐγνωρίσαμεν	VIAA--1P	"

ἐγνώρισαν	VIAA--3P	"
ἐγνώρισας	VIAA--2S	"
ἐγνώρισε(ν)	VIAA--3S	"
ἐγνωρίσθη	VIAP--3S	"
ἔγνως	VIAA--2S	γινώσκω
ἔγνωσαν	VIAA--3P	"
ἐγνώσθη	VIAP--3S	"
ἔγνωσται	VIRP--3S	"
ἐγόγγυζον	VIIA--3P	γογγύζω
ἐγόγγυσαν	VIAA--3P	"
ἔγραφε(ν)	VIIA--3S	γράφω
ἐγράφη	VIAP--3S	"
ἔγραψα	VIAA--1S	"
ἔγραψαν	VIAA--3P	"
ἔγραψας	VIAA--2S	"
ἐγράψατε	VIAA--2P	"
ἔγραψε(ν)	VIAA--3S	"
ἐγρηγόρησε(ν)	VIAA--3S	γρηγορέω
Ἔγυπτον	N-AF-S	Αἴγυπτος
ἐγχρῖσαι	VNAA	ἐγχρίω
ἐγχρίσῃ	VSAA--3S	
ἔγχρισον	VMAA--2S	"

ἐγχρίω 1aor. ἐνέχρισα; *rub on, anoint*; of eyesalve *put on, anoint, smear on* (RV 3.18)

ἐγώ first-person personal pronoun ἐμοῦ (μου), ἐμοί (μοι), ἐμέ (με); plural ἡμεῖς, ἡμῶν, ἡμῖν, ἡμᾶς; with reference to the speaker *I, me, we, us*; when used with a verb ἐ. and ἡμεῖς intensify and emphasize the subject of that verb or show contrast to a previous referent

ἐγώ	NPN-1S	ἐγώ
ἐδάκρυσε(ν)	VIAA--3S	δακρύω

ἐδαφίζω Attic fut. ἐδαφιῶ; *dash to the ground, overthrow*; of a city *level to the ground, raze*; of persons *kill* (both meanings are present in LU 19.44)

ἐδαφιοῦσι(ν)	VIFA--3P	ἐδαφίζω

ἔδαφος, ους, τό strictly *bottom* of anything; hence *ground* (AC 22.7)

ἔδαφος	N-AN-S	ἔδαφος
ἐδεεῖτο	VIID--3S	see ἐδεῖτο
	VIIO--3S	see ἐδεῖτο
ἐδέετο	VIID--3S	δέομαι
	VIIO--3S	"
ἐδεήθη	VIAO--3S	δέομαι
ἐδεήθην	VIAO--1S	"
ἔδει	VIIA--3S	δεῖ
ἐδειγμάτισε(ν)	VIAA--3S	δειγματίζω
ἔδειξα	VIAA--1S	δείκνυμι
ἔδειξαν	VIAA--3P	"
ἔδειξε(ν)	VIAA--3S	"
ἔδειραν	VIAA--3P	δέρω
ἐδεῖτο	VIID--3S	δέομαι
	VIIO--3S	"
ἐδεξάμεθα	VIAD--1P	δέχομαι
ἐδέξαντο	VIAD--3P	"
ἐδέξασθε	VIAD--2P	"
ἐδέξατο	VIAD--3S	"
ἐδεσμεῖτο	VIIP--3S	δεσμεύω
ἐδεσμεύετο	VIIP--3S	"
ἔδετο	VIID--3S	see ἐδεῖτο
	VIIO--3S	see ἐδεῖτο

ἐδέχετο	VIID--3S	δέχομαι
	VIIO--3S	"
ἐδήλου	VIIA--3S	δηλόω
ἐδηλοῦτο	VIIP--3S	"
ἐδηλώθη	VIAP--3S	"
ἐδήλωσε(ν)	VIAA--3S	"
ἐδημηγόρει	VIIA--3S	δημηγορέω
ἔδησαν	VIAA--3P	δέω
ἔδησε(ν)	VIAA--3S	"
ἐδίδαξα	VIAA--1S	διδάσκω
ἐδίδαξαν	VIAA--3P	"
ἐδίδαξας	VIAA--2S	"
ἐδίδαξε(ν)	VIAA--3S	"
ἐδίδασκε(ν)	VIIA--3S	"
ἐδίδασκον	VIIA--3P	"
ἐδιδάχθην	VIAP--1S	"
ἐδιδάχθησαν	VIAP--3P	"
ἐδιδάχθητε	VIAP--2P	"
ἐδίδοσαν	VIIA--3P	δίδωμι
ἐδίδου	VIIA--3S	"
ἐδίδουν	VIIA--3P	"
ἐδικαιώθη	VIAP--3S	δικαιόω
ἐδικαιώθητε	VIAP--2P	"
ἐδικαίωσαν	VIAA--3P	"
ἐδικαίωσε(ν)	VIAA--3S	"
ἐδίστασαν	VIAA--3P	διστάζω
ἐδίστασας	VIAA--2S	"
ἐδίψησα	VIAA--1S	διψάω
ἐδίωκε(ν)	VIIA--3S	διώκω
ἐδίωκον	VIIA--1S	"
	VIIA--3P	"
ἐδίωξα	VIAA--1S	"
ἐδίωξαν	VIAA--3P	"
ἐδίωξε(ν)	VIAA--3S	"
ἐδόθη	VIAP--3S	δίδωμι
ἐδόθησαν	VIAP--3P	"
ἐδόκει	VIIA--3S	δοκέω
ἐδοκιμάσαμεν	VIAA--1P	δοκιμάζω
ἐδοκίμασαν	VIAA--3P	"
ἐδόκουν	VIIA--3P	δοκέω
ἐδολιοῦσαν	VIIA--3P	δολιόω
ἔδοξα	VIAA--1S	δοκέω
ἐδόξαζε(ν)	VIIA--3S	δοξάζω
ἐδόξαζον	VIIA--3P	"
ἔδοξαν	VIAA--3P	δοκέω
ἐδόξασα	VIAA--1S	δοξάζω
ἐδόξασαν	VIAA--3P	"
ἐδόξασας	VIAA--2S	"
ἐδόξασε(ν)	VIAA--3S	"
ἐδοξάσθη	VIAP--3S	"
ἔδοξε(ν)	VIAA--3S	δοκέω
ἐδουλεύσατε	VIAA--2P	δουλεύω
ἐδούλευσε(ν)	VIAA--3S	"
ἐδουλώθητε	VIAP--2P	δουλόω
ἐδούλωσα	VIAA--1S	"
ἑδραῖοι	A--NM-P	ἑδραῖος

ἑδραῖος, αία, ον strictly *sedentary, seated*; hence *steadfast, firm, settled* in one's thinking or belief

ἑδραῖος	A--NM-S	ἑδραῖος

ἑδραίωμα, ατος, τό *foundation, mainstay, support* (1T 3.15)

ἑδραίωμα	N-NN-S	ἑδραίωμα
ἔδραμε(ν)	VIAA--3S	τρέχω
ἔδραμον	VIAA--1S	"
	VIAA--3P	"
ἔδυ	VIAA--3S	δύνω
ἐδυναμώθησαν	VIAP--3P	δυναμόω
ἐδύναντο	VIID--3P	δύναμαι
	VIIO--3P	"
ἐδύνασθε	VIID--2P	"
	VIIO--2P	"
ἐδύνατο	VIID--3S	"
	VIIO--3S	"
ἔδυσε(ν)	VIAA--3S	δύνω
ἔδωκα	VIAA--1S	δίδωμι
ἐδώκαμεν	VIAA--1P	"
ἔδωκαν	VIAA--3P	"
ἔδωκας	VIAA--2S	"
ἐδώκατε	VIAA--2P	"
ἔδωκε(ν)	VIAA--3S	"
ἐδωρήσατο	VIAD--3S	δωρέομαι
Ἑζεκίαν	N-AM-S	Ἑζεκίας
Ἑζεκίαν	N-AM-S	"
Ἑζεκίας	N-NM-S	"

Ἑζεκίας, ου, ὁ (also **Ἐζεκίας**) *Hezekiah*, masculine proper noun

Ἑζεκίας	N-NM-S	Ἑζεκίας
ἐζημιώθην	VIAP--1S	ζημιόω
ἔζησα	VIAA--1S	ζάω
ἔζησαν	VIAA--3P	"
ἔζησε(ν)	VIAA--3S	"
ἐζῆτε	VIIA--2P	"
ἐζήτει	VIIA--3S	ζητέω
ἐζητεῖτε	VIIA--2P	"
ἐζητεῖτο	VIIP--3S	"
ἐζητήσαμεν	VIAA--1P	"
ἐζήτησαν	VIAA--3P	"
ἐζήτησε(ν)	VIAA--3S	"
ἐζητοῦμεν	VIIA--1P	"
ἐζήτουν	VIIA--3P	"
ἐζυμώθη	VIAP--3S	ζυμόω
ἐζωγρημένοι	VPRPNM-P	ζωγρέω
ἔζων	VIIA--1S	ζάω
ἐζώννυες	VIIA--2S	ζωννύω
ἐθαμβήθησαν	VIAP--3P	θαμβέω
ἐθαμβοῦντο	VIIP--3P	"
ἐθανατώθητε	VIAP--2P	θανατόω
ἐθαύμαζε(ν)	VIIA--3S	θαυμάζω
ἐθαύμαζον	VIIA--3P	"
ἐθαύμασα	VIAA--1S	"
ἐθαύμασαν	VIAA--3P	"
ἐθαύμασας	VIAA--2S	"
ἐθαύμασε(ν)	VIAA--3S	"
ἐθαυμάσθη	VIAP--3S	"
ἔθαψαν	VIAA--3P	θάπτω
ἐθεάθη	VIAP--3S	θεάομαι
ἐθεασάμεθα	VIAD--1P	"
ἐθεάσαντο	VIAD--3P	"
ἐθεάσασθε	VIAD--2P	"
ἐθεάσατο	VIAD--3S	"
ἐθεᾶτο	VIID--3S	"
ἔθει	N-DN-S	ἔθος

ἐθελοθρησκεία	N-DF-S	ἐθελοθρησκία

ἐθελοθρησκία, ας, ἡ (also **ἐθελοθρησκεία**) *self-made religion, self-imposed worship, self-willed observance* (CO 2.23)

ἐθελοθρησκία	N-DF-S	ἐθελοθρησκία
ἐθεμελίωσας	VIAA--2S	θεμελιόω
ἔθεντο	VIAM--3P	τίθημι
ἐθεράπευε(ν)	VIIA--3S	θεραπεύω
ἐθεραπεύθη	VIAP--3S	"
ἐθεραπεύθησαν	VIAP--3P	"
ἐθεράπευον	VIIA--3P	"
ἐθεραπεύοντο	VIIP--3P	"
ἐθεράπευσε(ν)	VIAA--3S	"
ἐθερίσθη	VIAP--3S	θερίζω
ἐθερμαίνοντο	VIIM--3P	θερμαίνω
ἔθεσθε	VIAM--2P	τίθημι
ἔθεσι(ν)	N-DN-P	ἔθος
ἔθετο	VIAM--3S	τίθημι
ἐθεώρει	VIIA--3S	θεωρέω
ἐθεώρησαν	VIAA--3P	"
ἐθεώρουν	VIIA--1S	"
	VIIA--3P	"
ἐθεωροῦντες	VPPANM-P	see θεωροῦντες
ἔθη	N-AN-P	ἔθος
ἔθηκα	VIAA--1S	τίθημι
ἔθηκαν	VIAA--3P	"
ἔθηκας	VIAA--2S	"
ἔθηκε(ν)	VIAA--3S	"
ἐθήλασαν	VIAA--3P	θηλάζω
ἐθήλασας	VIAA--2S	"
ἐθηριομάχησα	VIAA--1S	θηριομαχέω
ἐθησαυρίσατε	VIAA--2P	θησαυρίζω

ἐθίζω pf. pass. ptc. εἰθισμένος; from ἔθος (*custom, usage*); *carry out a custom*; κατὰ τὸ εἰθισμένον *in the customary way, according to the custom* (LU 2.27)

ἐθνάρχης, ου, ὁ as a title for the leading official of a tribe, people, or nation *ethnarch, governor, chief* (2C 11.32)

ἐθνάρχης	N-NM-S	ἐθνάρχης
ἔθνει	N-DN-S	ἔθνος
ἔθνεσι(ν)	N-DN-P	"
ἔθνη	N-AN-P	"
	N-NN-P	"
	N-VN-P	"
ἐθνικοί	AP-NM-P	ἐθνικός

ἐθνικός, ή, όν *national*; substantivally in the NT, having to do with non-Jewish peoples *foreign, Gentile* (3J 7); in a negative sense *heathen, pagan*, in contrast to adherents to Judaism (MT 18.17)

ἐθνικός	AP-NM-S	ἐθνικός
ἐθνικῶν	AP-GM-P	"

ἐθνικῶς adverb; denoting a way of life in contrast to the Jewish *like the heathen, after the manner of the Gentiles* (GA 2.14)

ἐθνικῶς	AB	ἐθνικῶς

ἔθνος, ους, τό (1) generally *nation, people* (LU 7.5); (2) plural τὰ ἔθνη used to designate non-Jews *Gentiles, nations, foreigners* (RO 15.10, 11), opposite λαός (*people*); in a negative sense *pagans, heathen* (MT 6.32)

ἔθνος	N-AN-S	ἔθνος
	N-NN-S	"
ἔθνους	N-GN-S	"

129

ἐθνῶν	N-GN-P	"
ἐθορύβουν	VIIA--3P	θορυβέω

ἔθος, ους, τό (1) *habit, custom, usage* (LU 22.39); (2) as fixed or traditional law and order *custom, law* (AC 6.14)

ἔθος	N-AN-S	ἔθος
	N-NN-S	"
ἔθου	VIAM--2S	τίθημι
ἐθρέψαμεν	VIAA--1P	τρέφω
ἔθρεψαν	VIAA--3P	"
ἐθρέψατε	VIAA--2P	"
ἐθρηνήσαμεν	VIAA--1P	θρηνέω
ἐθρήνουν	VIIA--3P	"
ἐθύθη	VIAP--3S	θύω
ἐθυμώθη	VIAP--3S	θυμόω
ἔθυον	VIIA--3P	θύω
ἔθυσας	VIAA--2S	"
ἔθυσε(ν)	VIAA--3S	"
ἐθῶν	N-GN-P	ἔθος

εἰ conditional particle *if, since*; (1) with the indicative to express a condition of fact regarded as true or settled *since, because* (RO 2.17); (2) in conditional sentence with the imperfect, aorist, or pluperfect indicative in the conditional clause and usually ἄν in the consequence clause to express a contrary-to-fact (unreal) condition *if* (JN 11.21); (3) with the optative to express a general or remote possibility *if* (1P 3.14); (4) εἰ καί with the indicative to express concession to something that is true *even if, although, even though* (CO 2.5); (5) with the indicative or subjunctive in indirect questions to imply a likelihood or improbability *whether, if perhaps* (MT 27.49; PH 3.12); (6) as an interrogative particle to introduce direct questions, left untranslated (LU 13.23); (7) after verbs of emotion *that* (MK 15.44); (8) Hebraistically, in oath formulas to express a strong negative *surely not, certainly not* (HE 4.3); (9) in combination with other particles following: εἰ δὲ μή *if not, otherwise* (JN 14.2); εἰ μὲν οὖν *if then, if therefore* (HE 7.11); εἰ μέντοι *if however* (JA 2.8); εἰ μή *except, unless, if not* (MT 12.4); εἰ πως *if somehow, if perhaps* (AC 27.12); εἴτε . . . εἴτε *if . . . if, whether . . . or* (1C 12.26; see εἴτε); εἰ μήν, used as an oath formula *surely, certainly* (HE 6.14); (10) in combination with the indefinite pronoun: εἴ τις *whoever, everyone who* (MT 16.24); εἴ τι *whatever, everything that* (MT 18.28)

εἰ	ABR	εἰ
	CC	"
	CS	"
	QT	"
εἶ	VIPA--2S	εἰμί
εἴα	VIIA--3S	ἐάω
εἴασαν	VIAA--3P	"
εἴασε(ν)	VIAA--3S	"
εἴδαμεν	VIAA--1P	εἶδον
εἴδαν	VIAA--3P	"
εἴδε	QS	ἴδε

εἰδέα, ας, ἡ (also **ἰδέα**) as what someone or something looks like *appearance, (outward) form* (MT 28.3)

εἰδέα	N-NF-S	εἰδέα
εἴδει	N-DN-S	εἶδος
εἴδε(ν)	VIAA--3S	εἶδον

εἰδέναι	VNRA	οἶδα
εἶδες	VIAA--2S	εἶδον
εἴδετε	VIAA--2P	"
εἰδῇ	VSRA--3S	οἶδα
εἰδῇς	VSRA--2S	"
εἰδήσουσι(ν)	VIFA--3P	"
εἰδῆτε	VSRA--2P	"
εἴδομεν	VIAA--1P	εἶδον

εἶδον used as the second aorist of ὁράω (*see*); see also ἴδε and οἶδα; (1) literally, as perception by sight *see, perceive, look at* (MT 2.2); (2) as sense perception of any kind *become aware of, feel* (MT 27.54); (3) as taking note by observation *consider, pay attention to, look at* (RO 11.22); (4) as experientially coming to know or realize something *know, see, experience* (LU 2.26); (5) in the sense of making a friendly call *visit (with), see* (LU 8.20); (6) in the sense of coming to know someone personally *know, learn to know, get acquainted with* (LU 9.9)

εἶδον	VIAA--1S	εἶδον
	VIAA--3P	"

εἶδος, ους, τό (1) with a passive sense, as what is visible to the eye *form, (external) appearance* (LU 3.22); (2) with an active sense *sight, what one sees* (2C 5.7); (3) *(particular) kind, sort* (1TH 5.22)

εἶδος	N-AN-S	εἶδος
	N-NN-S	"
εἴδοσαν	VIAA--3P	οἶδα
εἰδόσι(ν)	VPRADM-P	"
εἰδότα	VPRANN-P	"
εἰδότας	VPRAAM-P	"
εἰδότες	VPRANM-P	"
εἰδότι	VPRADM-S	"
εἴδους	N-GN-S	εἶδος
εἰδυῖα	VPRANF-S	οἶδα
εἰδῶ	VSRA--1S	"
εἴδωλα	N-AN-P	εἴδωλον

εἰδωλεῖον, ου, τό *idol temple, heathen temple* (1C 8.10)

εἰδωλείῳ	N-DN-S	εἰδωλεῖον
εἰδωλόθυτα	AP-AN-P	εἰδωλόθυτος
εἰδωλόθυτον	AP-AN-S	"
	AP-NN-S	"

εἰδωλόθυτος, ον *sacrificed to an idol*; neuter singular and plural as substantives, as remains of victims sacrificed to an idol and reserved for eating *meat offered to an idol, idol food* (AC 21.25; 1C 8.10)

εἰδωλοθύτων	AP-GN-P	εἰδωλόθυτος
εἰδωλολάτραι	N-NM-P	εἰδωλολάτρης
εἰδωλολάτραις	N-DM-P	"
εἰδωλολατρεία	N-NF-S	εἰδωλολατρία
εἰδωλολατρείαις	N-DF-P	"
εἰδωλολατρείας	N-GF-S	"

εἰδωλολάτρης, ου, ὁ *idolater, one who worships idols* (1C 5.11), opposite *one who is God-fearing* or *devout* (θεοσεβής)

εἰδωλολάτρης	N-NM-S	εἰδωλολάτρης

εἰδωλολατρία, ας, ἡ (also **εἰδωλολατρεία**) *idolatry, worship of idols*

εἰδωλολατρία	N-NF-S	εἰδωλολατρία
εἰδωλολατρίαις	N-DF-P	"
εἰδωλολατρίας	N-GF-S	"

εἴδωλον, ου, τό strictly *form, copy, figure*; hence (1) an object resembling a person or animal and worshiped as a god *idol, image* (RV 9.20); (2) *idol, false god*, with reference to demonic power involved in idol worship (1C 10.19)

εἴδωλον	N-NN-S	εἴδωλον
εἰδώλου	N-GN-S	"
εἰδώλῳ	N-DN-S	"
εἰδώλων	N-GN-P	"
εἰδῶμεν	VSRA--1P	οἶδα
εἰδώς	VPRANM-S	"
εἴη	VOPA--3S	εἰμί
εἴης	VOPA--2S	"
εἰθισμένον	VPRPAN-S	ἐθίζω

εἰκῇ adverb; strictly *at random, without plan* or *system*; hence (1) *thoughtlessly, rashly* (possibly 1C 15.2); (2) *without cause* (CO 2.18); (3) *without result, in vain, for nothing* (GA 3.4); (4) *without purpose, for no purpose* (RO 13.4; possibly 1C 15.2)

εἰκῇ	AB	εἰκῇ
εἰκόνα	N-AF-S	εἰκών
εἰκόνι	N-DF-S	"
εἰκόνος	N-GF-S	"

εἴκοσι(ν) indeclinable; as a cardinal number *twenty*

εἰκοσιπέντε indeclinable; as a cardinal number *twenty-five* (JN 6.19)

εἰκοσιτέσσαρες, gen. **άρων** as a cardinal number *twenty-four* (RV 5.8)

εἰκοσιτέσσαρες	A-CNM-P	εἰκοσιτέσσαρες

εἰκοσιτρεῖς, τρία as a cardinal number *twenty-three* (1C 10.8)

εἰκοσιτρεῖς	A-CNF-P	εἰκοσιτρεῖς

εἴκω 1aor. εἶξα; *yield, give place, submit* (GA 2.5)

εἰκών, όνος, ἡ (1) as an artistic representation, such as on a coin or statue *image, likeness* (MT 22.20); (2) as an embodiment or living manifestation of God *form, appearance* (CO 1.15); (3) as a visible manifestation of an invisible and heavenly reality *form, substance* (HE 10.1)

εἰκών	N-NF-S	εἰκών
εἵλατο	VIAM--3S	αἱρέω
εἵλετο	VIAM--3S	"
εἰλευθέρωσε(ν)	VIAA--3S	see ἠλευθέρωσε(ν)
εἰλημμένην	VPPPAF-S	λαμβάνω
εἴληπται	VIRP--3S	"
εἴληφα	VIRA--1S	"
εἴληφας	VIRA--2S	"
εἴληφε(ν)	VIRA--3S	"
εἰληφώς	VPRANM-S	"

εἰλικρίνεια, ας, ἡ strictly *judged by the light of the sun*; hence *clearness, purity*; morally *purity of motive, integrity* (2C 2.17)

εἰλικρινεία	N-DF-S	εἰλικρίνεια
εἰλικρινείας	N-GF-S	"
εἰλικρινεῖς	A--NM-P	εἰλικρινής
εἰλικρινῆ	A--AF-S	"

εἰλικρινής, ές, gen. **οῦς** strictly *tested by sunlight*; hence *sincere* (2P 3.1); morally *spotless, pure* (PH 1.10)

εἰλισσόμενον	VPPPNN-S	ἑλίσσω
εἷλκον	VIIA--3P	ἕλκω
εἵλκυσαν	VIAA--3P	"
εἵλκυσε(ν)	VIAA--3S	"
εἱλκωμένος	VPRPNM-S	ἑλκόω

εἶμι *go*; Attic present used as the future of ἔρχομαι; possibly for εἰμί in JN 7.34, 36; 12.26; 14.3; 17.24

εἶμι	VIPA--1S	εἶμι

εἰμί inf. εἶναι; impf. mid. ἤμην; fut. mid. ἔσομαι; **I.** as a predicate *be*, relating to what exists; (1) to denote God's existence (HE 11.6); ὁ ὤν *the one who is, exists* (RV 1.4); (2) to denote Christ's self-designation of himself ἐγώ εἰ. *I am* (JN 8.58); (3) to denote temporal existence *live* (MT 23.30); (4) to denote a sojourn in a place *stay, reside* (MT 2.13); (5) to denote what happens, such as phenomena and events *be, take place, occur, happen* (ἦν JN 9.16); (6) with indications of time (JN 4.6b); (7) of what is on the scene (MK 8.1) or available (AC 7.12); (8) impersonally ἔστιν followed by an infinitive *it is possible* (HE 9.5); **II.** as a copulative verb; (1) linking subject to predicate (MK 3.11); (2) introducing an explanation or equivalence in another language τοῦτ᾽ ἔστιν and ὅ ἐστιν *that is, which means* (MT 27.46; MK 3.17); (3) constructed with a variety of adverbs, prepositions, nouns, etc., translated according to the context

εἰμί	VIPA--1S	εἰμί
εἶναι	VNPA	"
εἵνεκεν	PG	ἕνεκα
εἵνεκν	PG	see εἵνεκεν
εἴξαμεν	VIAA--1P	εἴκω
εἶπα	VIAA--1S	εἶπον
εἶπαν	VIAA--3P	"
εἴπας	VPAANM-S	"
εἶπας	VIAA--2S	"
εἴπατε	VIAA--2P	"
	VMAA--2P	"
εἰπάτω	VMAA--3S	"
εἰπάτωσαν	VMAA--3P	"
εἰπέ	VMAA--2S	"
εἰπεῖν	VNAA	"
εἶπε(ν)	VIAA--3S	"

εἴπερ conditional particle; a strengthened form of εἰ (*if, since*): *if indeed, if after all, since* (RO 3.30)

εἴπερ	CS	εἴπερ
εἶπες	VIAA--2S	εἶπον
εἴπῃ	VSAA--3S	"
εἴπῃς	VSAA--2S	"
εἴπητε	VSAA--2P	"

εἶπον used as the second aorist of λέγω (*say, speak, tell*); also used with the first aorist endings (e.g. εἶπα); the future (ἐρῶ), perfect (εἴρηκα), pluperfect (εἰρήκειν), perfect passive (εἴρημαι), and first aorist passive (ἐρρέθην) are supplied from an obsolete verb εἴρω (*say*); (1) with the accusative *say, tell* something (MT 26.44); (2) absolutely *speak, say* (MT 2.8); (a) with a qualifying adverb, e.g. ὁμοίως εἰπεῖν *speak in the same way* (MT 26.35); (b) with a qualifying adverbial phrase, e.g. εἰπεῖν ἐν παραβολαῖς *talk parabolically, speak in parables* (MT 22.1); εἰπεῖν ἐν ἑαυτῷ *say inwardly, think* (LU 7.39); (c) to introduce direct discourse *say* (MT 2.8); (d) to introduce indirect discourse with ὅτι following *say*; (3) with the context determining various modifications of meaning *command, tell* (MK 5.43); *foretell, say before-*

hand (MT 28.6); *call, designate* with the double accusative (JN 15.15); (4) idiomatically ὡς ἔπος εἰπεῖν literally *as to speak a word*, i.e. *one might say, that is* (HE 7.9)

εἶπον	VIAA--1S	εἶπον
	VIAA--3P	"
εἰπόν	VMAA--2S	"
εἰπόντα	VPAAAM-S	"
εἰπόντες	VPAANM-P	"
εἰπόντι	VPAADM-S	"
εἰπόντος	VPAAGM-S	"
εἰπόντων	VPAAGM-P	"
εἰποῦσα	VPAANF-S	"
εἴπω	VSAA--1S	"
εἴπωμεν	VSAA--1P	"
εἰπών	VPAANM-S	"

εἴπως conditional particle and indefinite adverb; *if somehow, if perhaps*

εἴπως	CC&ABI	εἴπως
εἴπωσι(ν)	VSAA--3P	εἶπον
εἰργάζετο	VIID--1S	ἐργάζομαι
	VIIO--1S	"
εἰργάζοντο	VIID--3P	"
	VIIO--3P	"
εἰργασάμεθα	VIAD--1P	"
εἰργάσαντο	VIAD--3P	"
εἰργάσασθε	VIAD--2P	"
εἰργάσατο	VIAD--3S	"
εἴργασθε	VIAD--2P	see εἰργάσασθε
εἰργασμένα	VPRPNN-P	ἐργάζομαι
εἰργασόμεθα	VIAD--1P	"
εἴρηκα	VIRA--1S	εἶπον
εἴρηκαν	VIRA--3P	"
εἴρηκας	VIRA--2S	"
εἰρήκασι(ν)	VIRA--3P	"
εἰρήκατε	VIRA--2P	"
εἰρήκει	VILA--3S	"
εἴρηκε(ν)	VIRA--3S	"
εἰρηκέναι	VNRA	"
εἰρηκότος	VPRAGM-S	"
εἰρημένα	VPRPAN-P	"
εἰρημένοις	VPRPDN-P	"
εἰρημένον	VPRPAN-S	"
	VPRPNN-S	"
εἰρηνεύετε	VMPA--2P	εἰρηνεύω
εἰρηνεύοντες	VPPANM-P	"

εἰρηνεύω fut. εἰρηνεύσω; intransitively *keep peace, live at peace* with someone (RO 12.18)

εἰρήνη, ης, ἡ *peace*; (1) literally, as a state of *peace* (LU 14.32), opposite πόλεμος (*armed conflict, war*); figuratively, as an agreement between persons (JA 3.18), in contrast to διαμερισμός (*division, dissension*); (2) as a greeting or farewell corresponding to the Hebrew word *shalom: health, welfare, peace* (to you) (1T 1.2); (3) as a religious disposition characterized by inner rest and harmony *peace, freedom from anxiety* (RO 15.13); (4) as a state of reconciliation with God (GA 5.22); (5) of an end-time condition, as the salvation of mankind brought about through Christ's reign (LU 2.14; AC 10.36)

εἰρήνη	N-NF-S	εἰρήνη

εἰρήνη	N-DF-S	"
εἰρήνην	N-AF-S	"
εἰρήνης	N-GF-S	"
εἰρηνική	A--NF-S	εἰρηνικός
εἰρηνικόν	A--AM-S	"

εἰρηνικός, ή, όν *peaceful, peaceable, free from worry*

εἰρηνοποιέω 1aor. εἰρηνοποίησα; *make peace* (CO 1.20)

εἰρηνοποιήσας	VPAANM-S	εἰρηνοποιέω
εἰρηνοποιοί	AP-NM-P	εἰρηνοποιός

εἰρηνοποιός, όν of establishing a friendly relationship between persons *peace-making*; substantivally *peacemaker* (MT 5.9)

εἴρηται	VIRP--3S	εἶπον

εἰς preposition with the accusative *into, in*; (1) spatially, denoting motion toward a place, after verbs of going, sending, moving *to, toward, into* (MT 9.7); (2) denoting direction of address after verbs of speaking, telling, teaching, preaching *to* (MK 13.10); (3) temporally, with an indication of the time up to which something continues *until, to* (MT 10.22); (4) modally, to indicate degree or intensity εἰς τέλος *to the end, to the utmost, completely* (1TH 2.16); (5) logically, (a) to indicate purpose *in order to, with a view to, for the purpose of* (MT 26.28); (b) to indicate reason *for, because of, in view of* (MT 12.41); εἰς τοῦτο *for this reason, therefore* (MK 1.38); (c) to denote the purpose of a divine appointment (HE 1.14) or a human appointment in the Lord's will (AC 13.2); (d) to denote a specific goal, the direction of an action to an intended end *to, unto, for, with a view to* (MT 3.11); (6) denoting relationship; (a) in a neutral sense *with reference to, regarding* (EP 5.32); (b) in a hostile sense *against* (RO 8.7); (c) in a friendly sense *toward, for, in* (RO 15.26); (7) in uncommon usage; (a) of presence in a place, where ἐν (*in*) might be expected *in* (AC 19.22b); (b) in Semitic fashion to replace a predicate nominative or a predicate accusative after verbs such as γίνομαι (*become, come to be*) (MT 21.42), εἰμί (*be*) (MT 19.5), λογίζομαι (*think*) (RO 4.3), ἔχω (*have*) (MT 21.46): *as, for*

εἰς	PA	εἰς

εἷς, μία, ἕν, gen. **ἑνός, μιᾶς, ἑνός** often substantivally; (1) as a cardinal number *one* (MT 5.29); (2) emphatically, in contrast to more than one *only one, single* (MK 12.6); *one and the same* (LU 12.52); *alone* (LU 18.19); (3) as equivalent to τὶς *someone, certain one, anyone* (MT 19.16); (4) in special combinations: (a) εἷς ἕκαστος *each one, every one, every single one* (EP 4.16); (b) εἷς τὸν ἕνα *one another, one and the other* (1TH 5.11); (c) εἷς . . . καὶ εἷς *the one . . . and the other* (MT 20.21); (d) καθ᾽ ἕνα, καθ᾽ ἕν *one by one, one after the other* (1C 14.31); (e) ἀπὸ μιᾶς *one by one, one after the other* (LU 14.18); (5) from the Hebrew, as an ordinal number *first*, in time notations (MT 28.1)

εἷς	APCNM-S	εἷς
	A-CNM-S	"
εἰσάγαγε	VMAA--2S	εἰσάγω
εἰσαγαγεῖν	VNAA	"
εἰσαγάγη	VSAA--3S	"
εἰσαγαγών	VPAANM-S	"
εἰσάγειν	VNPA	"
εἰσάγεσθαι	VNPP	"

εἰσάγω   2aor. εἰσήγαγον; (1) *bring* or *lead* someone into something *conduct* (JN 18.16); *bring in* someone, *introduce* someone (HE 1.6); (2) *bring* or *carry* something *in* (AC 7.45)

εἰσακουσθείς	VPAPNM-S	εἰσακούω
εἰσακουσθήσονται	VIFP--3P	"
εἰσακούσονται	VIFD--3P	"

εἰσακούω   fut. mid. εἰσακούσομαι; 1aor. pass. εἰσηκούσθην; 1fut. pass. εἰσακουσθήσομαι; (1) active *hear, listen to attentively*; passive *be heard* (MT 6.7); (2) middle *listen to, pay attention to, obey* (1C 14.21); (3) passive, with reference to prayer *be heard, be answered* (AC 10.31)

εἰσδέξομαι	VIFD--1S	εἰσδέχομαι

εἰσδέχομαι   fut. εἰσδέξομαι; *receive, welcome, accept* (2C 6.17)

εἰσδραμοῦσα	VPAANF-S	εἰστρέχω

εἴσειμι   inf. εἰσιέναι; impf. εἰσήειν; from εἰς (*into*) and εἰμι (*go*); *go into, enter* (AC 3.3)

εἰσελεύσεσθαι	VNFD	εἰσέρχομαι
εἰσελεύσεται	VIFD--3S	"
εἰσελεύσομαι	VIFD--1S	"
εἰσελευσόμεθα	VIFD--1P	"
εἰσελεύσονται	VIFD--3P	"
εἰσελήλυθαν	VIRA--3P	"
εἰσεληλύθασι(ν)	VIRA--3P	"
εἰσεληλύθατε	VIRA--2P	"
εἰσέλθατε	VMAA--2P	"
εἰσελθάτω	VMAA--3S	"
εἴσελθε	VMAA--2S	"
εἰσελθεῖν	VNAA	"
εἰσέλθετε	VMAA--2P	"
εἰσελθέτω	VMAA--3S	"
εἰσέλθῃ	VSAA--3S	"
εἰσέλθῃς	VSAA--2S	"
εἰσέλθητε	VSAA--2P	"
εἰσελθόντα	VPAAAM-S	"
	VPAANN-P	"
εἰσελθόντες	VPAANM-P	"
εἰσελθόντι	VPAADM-S	"
εἰσελθόντος	VPAAGM-S	"
εἰσελθόντων	VPAAGM-P	"
εἰσελθοῦσα	VPAANF-S	"
εἰσελθοῦσαι	VPAANF-P	"
εἰσελθούσης	VPAAGF-S	"
εἰσέλθωμεν	VSAA--1P	"
εἰσελθών	VPAANM-S	"
εἰσέλθωσι(ν)	VSAA--3P	"
εἰσενεγκεῖν	VNAA	εἰσφέρω
εἰσενέγκῃς	VSAA--2S	"
εἰσενέγκωσι(ν)	VSAA--3P	"
εἰσενεχθῆναι	VNAP	"
εἰσεπήδησαν	VIAA--3P	εἰσπηδάω
εἰσεπήδησε(ν)	VIAA--3S	"
εἰσεπορεύετο	VIID--3S	εἰσπορεύομαι
	VIIO--3S	"
εἰσέρχεσθε	VIPD--2P	εἰσέρχομαι
	VIPO--2P	"
εἰσερχέσθωσαν	VMPD--3P	"
	VMPO--3P	"

εἰσέρχεται	VIPD--3S	"
	VIPO--3S	"
εἰσέρχησθε	VSPD--2P	"
	VSPO--2P	"

εἰσέρχομαι   fut. εἰσελεύσομαι; 2aor. act. εἰσῆλθον; pf. act. εἰσελήλυθα; (1) literally, in a local sense *go* or *come into, enter* (MT 2.21); (2) figuratively; (a) of the birth of Jesus *come into* (the world) (HE 10.5); (b) of demons *enter in, take possession of* (MK 9.25); (c) of persons; (i) in a good sense *come into, enter into, begin to enjoy* (MT 5.20); (ii) in a bad sense *begin to experience, meet, encounter* (MT 26.41); (d) as the first stage of an activity *begin, come up* (LU 9.46)

εἰσερχόμεθα	VIPD--1P	εἰσέρχομαι
	VIPO--1P	"
εἰσερχομένην	VPPDAF-S	"
	VPPOAF-S	"
εἰσερχόμενοι	VPPDNM-P	"
	VPPONM-P	"
εἰσερχόμενον	VPPDNN-S	"
	VPPONN-S	"
εἰσερχόμενος	VPPDNM-S	"
	VPPONM-S	"
εἰσερχομένου	VPPDGM-S	"
	VPPOGM-S	"
εἰσερχομένους	VPPDAM-P	"
	VPPOAM-P	"
εἰσέρχονται	VIPD--3P	"
	VIPO--3P	"
εἰσερχώμεθα	VSPD--1P	"
	VSPO--1P	"
εἰσήγαγε(ν)	VIAA--3S	εἰσάγω
εἰσήγαγον	VIAA--3P	"
εἰσήει	VIIA--3S	εἴσειμι
εἰσηκούσθη	VIAP--3S	εἰσακούω
εἰσήλθαμεν	VIAA--1P	εἰσέρχομαι
εἰσῆλθαν	VIAA--3P	"
εἰσήλθατε	VIAA--2P	"
εἰσῆλθε(ν)	VIAA--3S	"
εἰσῆλθες	VIAA--2S	"
εἰσήλθετε	VIAA--2P	"
εἰσήλθητε	VSAA--2P	see εἰσέλθητε
εἰσήλθομεν	VIAA--1P	εἰσέρχομαι
εἰσῆλθον	VIAA--1S	"
	VIAA--3P	"
εἰσηνέγκαμεν	VIAA--1P	εἰσφέρω
εἰσήνεγκε(ν)	VIAA--3S	"
εἰσίασι(ν)	VIPA--3P	εἴσειμι
εἰσιέναι	VNPA	"
εἰσί(ν)	VIPA--3P	εἰμί

εἰσκαλέομαι   1aor. εἰσεκαλεσάμην; *invite in, call in* (AC 10.23)

εἰσκαλεσάμενος	VPADNM-S	εἰσκαλέομαι
εἴσοδον	N-AF-S	εἴσοδος

εἴσοδος, ου, ἡ   (1) as an action *coming in, access, entrance* (HE 10.19); (2) as the reception given *acceptance, welcome* (1TH 1.9)

εἴσοδος	N-NF-S	εἴσοδος
εἰσόδου	N-GF-S	"

εἰσπηδάω   1aor. εἰσεπήδησα; *leap* or *spring in, rush in* (AC 16.29)

εἰσπορεύεται   VIPD--3S   εἰσπορεύομαι
                VIPO--3S   "

εἰσπορεύομαι   impf. εἰσεπορευόμην; (1) literally *go or come in, enter* (MK 1.21); (2) figuratively; (a) of things; (i) of food entering the mouth (MK 7.15, 18); (ii) of desire entering the heart (MK 4.19); (b) of persons entering into God's kingdom (LU 18.24)

εἰσπορευόμεναι   VPPDNF-P   εἰσπορεύομαι
                 VPPONF-P   "

εἰσπορευόμενοι   VPPDNM-P   "
                 VPPONM-P   "

εἰσπορευόμενον   VPPDNN-S   "
                 VPPONN-S   "

εἰσπορευόμενος   VPPDNM-S   "
                 VPPONM-S   "

εἰσπορευομένους   VPPDAM-P   "
                 VPPOAM-P   "

εἰσπορευομένων   VPPDGM-P   "
                 VPPOGM-P   "

εἰσπορεύονται   VIPD--3P   "
                 VIPO--3P   "

εἰστήκει   VILA--3S   ἵστημι
εἰστήκεισαν   VILA--3P   "

εἰστρέχω   2aor. εἰσέδραμον; *run in(to)* (AC 12.14)

εἰσφέρει   VIPA--3S   εἰσφέρω
εἰσφέρεις   VIPA--2S   "
εἰσφέρεται   VIPP--3S   "

εἰσφέρω   1aor. εἰσήνεγκα; 2aor. εἰσήνεγκον; literally *bring* or *carry in* (LU 5.18, 19); of forcefully bringing someone into court or before rulers *drag in* (LU 12.11); idiomatically, of conveying a message εἰσφέρειν εἰς τὰς ἀκοάς literally *bring into the ears*, i.e. *announce, tell* (AC 17.20); figuratively, of temptation *lead into, bring into* (MT 6.13)

εἰσφέρωσι(ν)   VSPA--3P   εἰσφέρω

εἶτα (also **εἶτεν**)   adverb; (1) temporally *then, afterward, next* (MK 4.17); (2) in enumerations *then, next* (1T 2.13); to make a transition to a new point in an argument *furthermore, then, besides* (HE 12.9)

εἶτα   AB   εἶτα

εἶτε   see also εἰ; a conditional disjunctive conjunction bringing together two objects in one's thoughts while keeping them distinct from each other *if, whether* (1C 12.26); εἴτε . . . εἴτε *if . . . if* (RO 12.6–8); *whether . . . or* (1C 3.22)

εἶτε   CC   εἶτε
       CS+   "
εἶτεν   AB   εἶτα
εἶχαν   VIIA--3P   ἔχω
εἶχε(ν)   VIIA--3S   "
εἶχες   VIIA--2S   "
εἴχετε   VIIA--2P   "
εἴχομεν   VIIA--1P   "
εἶχον   VIIA--1S   "
       VIIA--3P   "
εἴχοσαν   VIIA--3P   "

εἴωθα   second perfect of obsolete present ἔθω; pluperfect εἰώθειν; with the present meaning *be accustomed, be in the habit of* (LU 4.16); pluperfect with the past meaning *was accustomed* (MT 27.15)

εἰώθει   VILA--3S   εἴωθα

εἰωθός   VPRAAN-S
εἴων   VIIA--3P   ἐάω

ἐκ   before a vowel ἐξ; preposition with the genitive; (1) spatially, denoting motion away from a place, after verbs of going, sending, escaping, moving *from, out of, away from* (MK 7.31); (2) denoting direction from which something comes *from, out of* (LU 5.3); (3) denoting origin as to family, race, city *from, out of* (LU 2.36); (4) denoting source, cause, motive, reason *from, of, by* (MT 5.37; JN 1.13); (5) denoting the distinguishing mark of a class, group, party *from, of* (AC 11.2); (6) used in periphrasis; (a) for the partitive genitive, after words denoting number *of* (JN 1.35; 6.60); (b) after an interrogative or indefinite pronoun *of* (LU 11.5; JN 6.64); (c) used with εἶναι *belong to, be one of* (MT 26.73); (d) after verbs of filling *with* (JN 12.3); (e) denoting price or value *for (the amount of)* (MT 20.2); (7) temporally; (a) denoting time from when *from, since, for* (JN 9.32); (b) showing sequence of time ἡμέραν ἐξ ἡμέρας *day after day* (2P 2.8); ἐκ δευτέρου *for the second time, again* (MT 26.42); ἐκ τρίτου *for the third time* (MT 26.44); (8) adverb; (a) ἐκ μέτρου *by measure, sparingly* (JN 3.34); (b) ἐκ μέρους *individually, in particular* (1C 12.27); (c) ἐκ λύπης *reluctantly, grudgingly* (2C 9.7); ἐκ συμφώνου *mutually, by common consent* (1C 7.5)

ἐκ   PG   ἐκ
ἐκαθάρισε(ν)   VIAA--3S   καθαρίζω
ἐκαθαρίσθη   VIAP--3S   "
ἐκαθαρίσθησαν   VIAP--3P   "
ἐκαθέζετο   VIID--3S   καθέζομαι
       VIIO--3S   "
ἐκαθεζόμην   VIID--1S   "
       VIIO--1S   "
ἐκαθέρισε(ν)   VIAA--3S   see ἐκαθάρισε(ν)
ἐκάθευδε(ν)   VIIA--3S   καθεύδω
ἐκάθευδον   VIIA--3P   "
ἐκάθισαν   VIAA--3P   see ἐκάθισαν
ἐκάθητο   VIID--3S   κάθημαι
       VIIO--3S   "
ἐκάθισα   VIAA--1S   καθίζω
ἐκάθισαν   VIAA--3P   "
ἐκάθισε(ν)   VIAA--3S   "
ἐκάκωσαν   VIAA--3P   κακόω
ἐκάκωσε(ν)   VIAA--3S   "
ἐκάλεσα   VIAA--1S   καλέω
ἐκάλεσαν   VIAA--1P   "
ἐκάλεσε(ν)   VIAA--3S   "
ἐκάλουν   VIIA--3P   "
ἐκάμμυσαν   VIAA--3P   καμμύω
ἐκαμψαν   VIAA--3P   κάμπτω
ἐκανόνισε(ν)   VIAA--3S   κανονίζω
ἐκαρτέρησε(ν)   VIAA--3S   καρτερέω
ἐκάστη   AP-NF-S   ἕκαστος
ἐκάστην   A--AF-S   "
ἕκαστοι   AP-NM-S   "
ἑκάστοις   AP-DM-P   "
ἕκαστον   AP-AM-S   "
       AP-AN-S   "
       A--AM-S   "
       A--AN-S   "
       A--NN-S   "

ἕκαστος, η, ον (1) adjectivally *each, every* (LU 6.44); (2) substantivally *each one, every one* (MT 16.27); strengthened form εἷς ἕ. *every single one* (MT 26.22); ἀνὰ εἷς ἕ. *every single one* (RV 21.21); καθ᾽ ἓν ἕκαστον *one after the other, in detail* (AC 21.19)

ἕκαστος	AP-NM-S	ἕκαστος
	A--NM-S	"

ἑκάστοτε adverb of time *at any time, always* (2P 1.15)

ἑκάστοτε	AB	ἑκάστοτε
ἑκάστου	AP-GM-S	ἕκαστος
	A--GM-S	"
	A--GN-S	"
ἑκάστῳ	AP-DM-S	"
	A--DM-S	"
ἐκατέστησας	VIAA--2S	καθίστημι

ἑκατόν indeclinable; as a cardinal number *one hundred*
ἑκατονταετής, ές *hundred years old* (RO 4.19)

ἑκατονταετής	A--NM-S	ἑκατονταετής
ἑκατονταπλασίονα	AB	ἑκατονταπλασίων
	A--AM-S	"
	A--AN-P	"

ἑκατονταπλασίων, ον of quantity *hundredfold* (LU 8.8); substantivally, neuter plural as an adverb *hundred times as much* (MT 19.29)

ἑκατοντάρχας	N-AM-P	ἑκατοντάρχης
ἑκατοντάρχῃ	N-DM-S	"

ἑκατοντάρχης, ου, ὁ (also ἑκατόνταρχος) strictly, as a Roman officer, *commander of a hundred soldiers*; hence *centurion, captain, commander*

ἑκατοντάρχης	N-NM-S	ἑκατοντάρχης
ἑκατόνταρχον	N-AM-S	"
ἑκατόνταρχος	N-NM-S	"
ἑκατοντάρχου	N-GM-S	"
ἑκατοντάρχους	N-AM-P	"
ἑκατοντάρχων	N-GM-P	"
ἑκατονταρχῶν	N-GM-P	"
ἐκαυματίσθη	VIAP--3S	καυματίζω
ἐκαυματίσθησαν	VIAP--3P	"
ἐκαυματώθη	VIAP--3S	καυματόω

ἐκβαίνω 2aor. ἐξέβην; with ἀπό *go* or *come out from* (HE 11.15)

ἔκβαλε	VMAA--2S	ἐκβάλλω
ἐκβαλεῖν	VNAA	"
ἐκβάλετε	VMAA--2P	"
ἐκβάλῃ	VSAA--3S	"
ἐκβάλλει	VIPA--3S	"
ἐκβάλλειν	VNPA	"
ἐκβάλλεις	VIPA--2S	"
ἐκβάλλεται	VIPP--3S	"
ἐκβάλλετε	VMPA--2P	"
ἐκβάλλῃ	VSPA--3S	"
ἐκβαλλόμενοι	VPPMNM-P	"
ἐκβαλλομένους	VPPPAM-P	"
ἐκβάλλοντα	VPPAAM-S	"
ἐκβάλλουσι(ν)	VIPA--3P	"

ἐκβάλλω fut. ἐκβαλῶ; 2aor. ἐξέβαλον; pluperfect ἐκβεβλήκειν; 1aor. pass. ἐξεβλήθην; 1fut. pass. ἐκβληθήσομαι; (1) as ejection by force *throw out, expel, drive out* (MT 8.16); (2) as expelling or excluding without force *repudiate, send away, let go* (JN 6.37); (3) as taking out or removing from something *bring out, bring forth* (MT 12.35); *take out* (LU 10.35); *pull out, tear out and throw away* (MK 9.47); *leave out* (of consideration), *omit* (RV 11.2)

ἐκβάλλω	VIPA--1S	ἐκβάλλω
ἐκβάλλων	VPPANM-S	"
ἐκβάλλωσι(ν)	VSPA--3P	"
ἐκβαλόντες	VPAANM-P	"
ἐκβαλόντος	VPAAGM-S	"
ἐκβαλοῦσα	VPAANF-S	"
ἐκβαλοῦσι(ν)	VIFA--3P	"
ἐκβάλω	VSAA--1S	"
ἐκβαλών	VPAANM-S	"
ἐκβάλωσι(ν)	VSAA--3P	"
ἔκβασιν	N-AF-S	ἔκβασις

ἔκβασις, εως, ἡ *way out, way of escape* (1C 10.13); *outcome, result, end* (of a way of life) (HE 13.7)

ἐκβεβλήκει	VILA--3S	ἐκβάλλω

ἐκβλαστάνω 1aor. ἐξεβλάστησα; of plants *sprout up* (MK 4.5)

ἐκβληθέντος	VPAPGN-S	ἐκβάλλω
ἐκβληθήσεται	VIFP--3S	"
ἐκβληθήσονται	VIFP--3P	"

ἐκβολή, ῆς, ἡ as a nautical technical term *throwing overboard* of a ship's cargo because of a stormy sea, *jettisoning* (AC 27.18)

ἐκβολήν	N-AF-S	ἐκβολή
ἐκγαμίζονται	VIPP--3P	ἐκγαμίζω
ἐκγαμίζοντες	VPPANM-P	"

ἐκγαμίζω (and ἐγγαμίζω, ἐκγαμίσκω) (1) active *give* (a woman) *in marriage* (MT 24.38; probably 1C 7.38); *marry* (perhaps 1C 7.38); (2) passive, of women *be given in marriage* (MT 22.30)

ἐκγαμίζων	VPPANM-S	ἐκγαμίζω
ἐκγαμίσκονται	VIPP--3P	"
ἐκγαμίσκοντες	VPPANM-P	"
ἔκγονα	AP-AN-P	ἔκγονος

ἔκγονος, ον *born of, descended from*; substantivally τό ἔκγονον *descendant*; more specifically *grandchild* (1T 5.4)

ἐκδαπανάω 1fut. pass. ἐκδαπανηθήσομαι; *spend completely, exhaust*; figuratively and passive, of sacrificing one's life to help others *be spent, give oneself completely* (2C 12.15)

ἐκδαπανηθήσομαι	VIFP--1S	ἐκδαπανάω
ἐκδεδεμένον	VPRPAN-S	ἐκδέω
ἐκδέχεσθε	VMPD--2P	ἐκδέχομαι
	VMPO--2P	"
ἐκδέχεται	VIPD--3S	"
	VIPO--3S	"

ἐκδέχομαι impf. ἐξεδεχόμην; (1) of things *expect, await, look for* (HE 11.10); (2) of persons *wait for, expect* (AC 17.16); (3) of future events *wait for, expect to happen* (JN 5.3); followed by ἕως *wait until* (HE 10.13)

ἐκδέχομαι	VIPD--1S	ἐκδέχομαι
	VIPO--1S	"
ἐκδεχόμενος	VPPDNM-S	"
	VPPONM-S	"
ἐκδεχομένου	VPPDGM-S	"
	VPPOGM-S	"
ἐκδεχομένων	VPPDGM-P	"
	VPPOGM-P	"

ἐκδέω pf. pass. ἐκδέδεμαι; *bind on* or *to*; passive *be tied* or *fastened together* (AC 10.11)

ἔκδηλος, ον of what is clearly manifest *quite evident, very plain, easy to know about* (2T 3.9)

ἔκδηλος	A--NF-S	ἔκδηλος

ἐκδημέω 1aor. inf. ἐκδημῆσαι; (1) literally *leave one's country, be away from* where one normally belongs; (2) figuratively; (a) as dying *be away from, be absent from* (the body) (2C 5.8, 9); (b) as staying alive physically *be away from* (heaven) (2C 5.6)

ἐκδημῆσαι	VNAA	ἐκδημέω
ἐκδημοῦμεν	VIPA--1P	"
ἐκδημοῦντες	VPPANM-P	"

ἐκδίδωμι fut. mid. ἐκδώσομαι; 2aor. mid. ἐξεδόμην; only middle in the NT *lease, let out for hire, rent out* (MT 21.33)

ἐκδιηγέομαι *tell (in detail), narrate fully, recount in full*

ἐκδιηγῆται	VSPD--3S	ἐκδιηγέομαι
	VSPO--3S	"
ἐκδιηγούμενοι	VPPDNM-P	"
	VPPONM-P	"
ἐκδικεῖς	VIPA--2S	ἐκδικέω

ἐκδικέω fut. ἐκδικήσω; 1aor. ἐξεδίκησα; (1) as helping someone secure justice *avenge, get justice for* (LU 18.3); (2) as bringing someone to judgment for something *punish* (2C 10.6) *take revenge* (RV 6.10)

ἐκδικῆσαι	VNAA	ἐκδικέω
ἐκδικήσεως	N-GF-S	ἐκδίκησις
ἐκδίκησιν	N-AF-S	"

ἐκδίκησις, εως, ἡ (1) as an act of retributive justice *vengeance, punishment, revenge* (LU 21.22); (2) ἐκδίκησιν ποιεῖν *give justice, see to it that justice is done* (LU 18.7)

ἐκδίκησις	N-NF-S	ἐκδίκησις
ἐκδίκησον	VMAA--2S	ἐκδικέω
ἐκδικήσω	VIFA--1S	"

ἔκδικος, ον of deciding by legal process *avenging, maintaining* or *defending the right*; substantivally, one who carries out a judicial sentence *avenger, punisher* (RO 13.4)

ἔκδικος	AP-NM-S	ἔκδικος
ἐκδικοῦντες	VPPANM-P	ἐκδικέω

ἐκδιώκω fut. ἐκδιώξω; 1aor. ἐξεδίωξα; strictly *chase away, drive away, banish*; hence *persecute severely, harass* (1TH 2.15)

ἐκδιῶξαι	VNAA	ἐκδιώκω
ἐκδιωξάντων	VPAAGM-P	"
ἐκδιώξουσι(ν)	VIFA--3P	"
ἐκδόσεται	VIFM--3S	"
ἔκδοτον	A--AM-S	ἔκδοτος

ἔκδοτος, ον *delivered* or *given up, handed over* (AC 2.23)

ἐκδοχή, ῆς, ἡ of future events *looking for, expectation* (HE 10.27)

ἐκδοχή	N-NF-S	ἐκδοχή
ἐκδυσάμενοι	VPAMNM-P	ἐκδύω
ἐκδύσαντες	VPAANM-P	"
ἐκδύσασθαι	VNAM	"

ἐκδύω 1aor. ἐξέδυσα, mid. ἐξεδυσάμην; (1) active and literally, of garments *strip, take off* (MT 27.28); (2) middle *strip off, undress (oneself)*; figuratively, of death, with a metaphor of the body as a garment *be unclothed, be without body, die* (2C 5.4)

ἐκδώσεται	VIFM--3S	ἐκδίδωμι

ἐκεῖ adverb of place; (1) *there, in that place* (MT 2.15); (2) *there, to that place* (MT 2.22)

ἐκεῖ	AB	ἐκεῖ

ἐκεῖθεν adverb of place *from there, from that point*

ἐκεῖθεν	AB	ἐκεῖθεν
ἐκεῖνα	A-DAN-P	ἐκεῖνος
ἐκεῖναι	APDNF-P	"
	A-DNF-P	"
ἐκείναις	A-DDF-P	"
ἐκείνας	A-DAF-P	"
ἐκείνη	APDNF-S	"
	A-DNF-S	"
ἐκείνη	A-DDF-S	"
ἐκείνην	A-DAF-S	"
ἐκείνης	APDGF-S	"
	A-DGF-S	"
ἐκεῖνο	APDAN-S	"
	APDNN-S	"
	A-DAN-S	"
	A-DNN-S	"
ἐκεῖνοι	APDNM-P	"
	A-DNM-P	"
ἐκείνοις	APDDM-P	"
	A-DDM-P	"
ἐκεῖνον	APDAM-S	"
	A-DAM-S	"

ἐκεῖνος, η, ο a demonstrative adjective referring to an entity relatively absent from the discourse setting; often substantivally, as a pronoun *that (person), that (thing)*; plural *those*; (1) absolutely, as a far demonstrative in contrast to a near demonstrative (οὗτος *this, these*) *that, those* (MK 4.11); (2) resumptively, in referring back to a previously mentioned person or thing *that one*, often weakened to *he, she, it* (JN 5.37); (3) as a more remote antecedent in referring to the first of two persons or things previously mentioned *the former* (LU 18.14); (4) to relate to a well-known or notorious personality *that one, that man* (JN 7.11); (5) with a noun referring to time, to relate to the past (MT 3.1) or the future (MT 24.19); (6) ἐκείνης genitive of place, with τῆς ὁδοῦ to be understood (LU 19.4)

ἐκεῖνος	APDNM-S	ἐκεῖνος
	A-DNM-S	"
ἐκείνου	APDGM-S	"
	A-DGM-S	"
	A-DGN-S	"
ἐκείνους	APDAM-P	"
	A-DAM-P	"
ἐκείνῳ	APDDM-S	"
	A-DDM-S	"
ἐκείνων	APDGM-P	"
	A-DGF-P	"
	A-DGM-P	"
	A-DGN-P	"

ἐκεῖσε adverb of place; (1) *there, to that place*; (2) as equivalent to ἐκεῖ *there, in that place* (AC 21.3)

ἐκεῖσε	AB	ἐκεῖσε

ἔκειτο	VIID--3S	κεῖμαι
	VIIO--3S	"
ἐκέκραξα	VIAA--1S	κράζω
ἐκέλευον	VIIA--3P	κελεύω
ἐκέλευσα	VIAA--1S	"
ἐκέλευσε(ν)	VIAA--3S	"
ἐκένωσε(ν)	VIAA--3S	κενόω
ἐκέρασε(ν)	VIAA--3S	κεράννυμι
ἐκέρδησα	VIAA--1S	κερδαίνω
ἐκέρδησας	VIAA--2S	"
ἐκέρδησε(ν)	VIAA--3S	"
ἐκεφαλαίωσαν	VIAA--3P	κεφαλιόω
ἐκεφαλίωσαν	VIAA--3P	"

ἐκζητέω 1aor. ἐξεζήτησα; 1aor. pass. ἐξεζητήθην; 1fut. pass. ἐκζητηθήσομαι; (1) of diligent investigation *scrutinize, search out* (1P 1.10); (2) of careful search for someone or something *seek out, search for* (HE 11.6); (3) from the Hebrew, of a thorough demand for justice *bring charges against, require of* (LU 11.50, 51)

ἐκζητηθῇ	VSAP--3S	ἐκζητέω
ἐκζητηθήσεται	VIFP--3S	"
ἐκζητήσας	VPAANM-S	"
ἐκζητήσεις	N-AF-P	ἐκζήτησις

ἐκζήτησις, εως, ἡ as an action *aimless arguing, speculation, controversy* (1T 1.4)

ἐκζητήσωσι(ν)	VSAA--3P	ἐκζητέω
ἐκζητοῦσι(ν)	VPPADM-P	"
ἐκζητῶν	VPPANM-S	"
ἐκηρύξαμεν	VIAA--1P	κηρύσσω
ἐκήρυξαν	VIAA--3P	"
ἐκήρυξε(ν)	VIAA--3S	"
ἐκήρυσσε(ν)	VIIA--3S	"
ἐκήρυσσον	VIIA--3P	"
ἐκηρύχθη	VIAP--3S	"
ἐκθαμβεῖσθαι	VNPP	ἐκθαμβέω
ἐκθαμβεῖσθε	VMPP--2P	"

ἐκθαμβέω 1aor. pass. ἐξεθαμβήθην; only passive in the NT; (1) *be (utterly) amazed, be astonished* (MK 9.15); (2) *be alarmed, be greatly disturbed* (MK 14.33); (3) *be frightened* (MK 16.5, 6)

ἔκθαμβοι	A--NM-P	ἔκθαμβος

ἔκθαμβος, ον *utterly astonished, amazed, awestruck* (AC 3.11)

ἐκθαυμάζω impf. ἐξεθαύμαζον; *wonder greatly, be baffled* (MK 12.17)

ἔκθετα	A--AN-P	ἔκθετος

ἔκθετος, ον strictly *placed outside*; hence, of newborn babies put out to die or be picked up by others *exposed, abandoned* (AC 7.19)

ἐκινδύνευε(ν)	VIIA--3S	κινδυνεύω
ἐκινδύνευον	VIIA--3P	"
ἐκινήθη	VIAP--3S	κινέω
ἐκινήθησαν	VIAP--3P	"

ἐκκαθαίρω 1aor. ἐξεκάθαρα; *clean out, cleanse thoroughly, purge out*; figuratively, of removing wrongdoing (1C 5.7; 2T 2.21)

ἐκκαθάρατε	VMAA--2P	ἐκκαθαίρω
ἐκκαθάρῃ	VSAA--3S	"

ἐκκαίω 1aor. pass. ἐξεκαύθην; of a fire *set aflame, kindle*; in the NT passive and idiomatically ἐκκαίεσθαι ἐν τῇ

ὀρέξει literally *burn with longing*, i.e. *have strong desire* (RO 1.27)

ἐκκακεῖν	VNPA	ἐγκακέω
ἐκκακήσητε	VSAA--2P	"
ἐκκακοῦμεν	VIPA--1P	"
ἐκκακῶμεν	VSPA--1P	"

ἐκκεντέω 1aor. ἐξεκέντησα; *pierce* or *stab (deeply)* with a lance or sword; thus, *kill*

ἐκκεχυμένον	VPRPNN-S	ἐκχέω
ἐκκέχυται	VIRP--3S	"

ἐκκλάω 1aor. pass. ἐξεκλάσθην; of branches *break off*

ἐκκλεῖσαι	VNAA	ἐκκλείω

ἐκκλείω 1aor. ἐξέκλεισα; 1aor. pass. ἐξεκλείσθην; literally, as a withdrawal of fellowship or association *shut out, exclude* (GA 4.17); figuratively, as making something impossible *exclude, eliminate, leave no place for* (RO 3.27)

ἐκκλησία, ας, ἡ (1) in a general sense, as a gathering of citizens *assembly, meeting* (AC 19.32); (2) as the assembled people of Israel *congregation* (HE 2.12); (3) as the assembled Christian community *church, congregation, meeting* (RO 16.5); (4) as the totality of Christians living in one place *church* (AC 8.1); (5) as the universal body of believers *church* (EP 1.22)

ἐκκλησία	N-NF-S	ἐκκλησία
ἐκκλησία	N-DF-S	"
ἐκκλησίαι	N-NF-P	"
ἐκκλησίαις	N-DF-P	"
ἐκκλησίαν	N-AF-S	"
ἐκκλησίας	N-AF-P	"
	N-GF-S	"
ἐκκλησιαστικάς	A--AF-P	ἐκκλησιαστικός

ἐκκλησιαστικός, ή, όν of what has to do with the church, especially in its organized form *ecclesiastical, church-related* (2P 2.10)

ἐκκλησιῶν	N-GF-P	ἐκκλησία
ἐκκλίνατε	VMAA--2P	ἐκκλίνω
ἐκκλινάτω	VMAA--3S	"
ἐκκλίνετε	VMPA--2P	"

ἐκκλίνω 1aor. ἐξέκλινα; (1) as morally deviating from a right path *turn aside, turn away* (RO 3.12); (2) as declining to follow false teachers *turn away (from), avoid, shun* (RO 16.17); (3) as turning from doing what is bad *avoid, turn away (from), stop* (1P 3.11)

ἐκκολυμβάω 1aor. ἐξεκολύμβησα; *swim away, swim off to land* (AC 27.42)

ἐκκολυμβήσας	VPAANM-S	ἐκκολυμβάω

ἐκκομίζω impf. pass. ἐξεκομιζόμην; of a body being taken to a burial place *carry out* (LU 7.12)

ἐκκοπήν	N-AF-S	ἐγκοπή
ἐκκοπήσῃ	VIFP--2S	ἐκκόπτω
ἐκκόπτεσθαι	VNPP	"
ἐκκόπτεται	VIPP--3S	"

ἐκκόπτω fut. ἐκκόψω; 1aor. ἐξέκοψα; 2aor. pass. ἐξεκόπην; 2fut. pass. ἐκκοπήσομαι; literally, of a tree *cut down* (MT 3.10); of a branch *cut off*; used metaphorically in RO 11.22, 24; of a hand *cut off* (MT 5.30); figuratively, of removing the opportunity for something *eliminate, do away with, remove* (2C 11.12)

ἐκκόψεις	VIFA--2S	ἐκκόπτω
	VIFA--2S^VMAA--2S	"

ἔκκοψον VMAA--2S "
ἐκκόψω VSAA--1S "

ἐκκρεμάννυμι impf. mid. ἐξεκρεμάμην; *let hang from*; only middle in the NT, as listening earnestly to a speaker *hang on* someone's words, *listen attentively to* (LU 19.48)

ἔκλαιε(ν) VIIA--3S κλαίω
ἔκλαιον VIIA--1S "
 VIIA--3P "

ἐκλαλέω 1aor. ἐξελάλησα; *speak out, tell* (someone), *inform* (AC 23.22)

ἐκλαλῆσαι VNAA ἐκλαλέω

ἐκλάμπω fut. ἐκλάμψω; of the sun *shine out* or *forth, be radiant* or *resplendent*; figuratively, of the lives of the righteous (MT 13.43)

ἐκλάμψουσι(ν) VIFA--3P ἐκλάμπω

ἐκλανθάνομαι pf. ἐκλέλησμαι; *completely forget* (HE 12.5)

ἔκλασα VIAA--1S κλάω
ἔκλασε(ν) VIAA--3S "
ἐκλάσθησαν VIAP--3P "
ἔκλαυσαν VIAA--3P κλαίω
ἐκλαύσατε VIAA--2P "
ἔκλαυσε(ν) VIAA--3S "
ἐκλέγονται VIPM--3P ἐκλέγω

ἐκλέγω impf. mid. ἐξελεγόμην; 1aor. mid. ἐξελεξάμην; pf. pass. ἐκλέλεγμαι; only middle/passive in the NT; (1) middle *choose out, select* (for oneself) (MK 13.20); (2) *choose from among* (a number) (AC 1.24); (3) *choose for* (some purpose) (EP 1.4), opposite μισέω (*reject, not choose*); (4) absolutely ἐκλελεγμένος *chosen* (LU 9.35)

ἔκλειπε(ν) VIIA--3S ἐκλείπω
ἐκλείπῃ VSPA--3S "
ἐκλείπητε VSPA--2P "
ἐκλείποντος VPPAGM-S "
ἐκλειπόντος VPPAGM-S "

ἐκλείπω fut. ἐκλείψω; 2aor. ἐξέλιπον; intransitively in the NT; (1) generally *leave off, cease*; of faith *fail* (LU 22.32); of money *be used up* (LU 16.9); of years *come to an end* (HE 1.12); of the sun *cease to give light, be shut out, be eclipsed* (LU 23.45); (2) *leave, depart* (AC 18.19)

ἔκλεισε(ν) VIAA--3S κλείω
ἐκλείσθη VIAP--3S "
ἐκλείσθησαν VIAP--3P "
ἐκλείψουσι(ν) VIFA--3P ἐκλείπω
ἐκλεκτῇ A--DF-S ἐκλεκτός
ἐκλεκτῆς A--GF-S "
ἐκλεκτοί AP-NM-P "
 A--NM-P "
ἐκλεκτοῖς AP-DM-P "
 A--DM-P "
ἐκλεκτόν A--AM-S "
 A--NN-S "

ἐκλεκτός, ή, όν (1) generally, of a quality of persons or things *choice, select, excellent* (1P 2.4, 6); (2) in the Gospels of those who respond positively to the privileges of God's grace (MT 22.14) and place trust in him (substantivally in LU 18.7); (3) of the basis of salvation in God's calling people to belong to himself *elect, chosen* (CO 3.12); substantivally, of the community of believers *elect* (MT 24.24); (4) substantivally, of the Messiah *the Chosen One* (LU 23.35)

ἐκλεκτός A--NM-S ἐκλεκτός
ἐκλεκτούς AP-AM-P "
ἐκλεκτῶν AP-GM-P "
 A--GM-P "
ἐκλελεγμένος VPRPNM-S ἐκλέγω
ἐκλέλησθε VIRD--2P ἐκλανθάνομαι
 VIRO--2P "
ἐκλελυμένοι VPRPNM-P ἐκλύω
ἐκλεξαμένοις VPAMDM-P ἐκλέγω
ἐκλεξάμενος VPAMNM-S "
ἐκλεξαμένους VPAMAM-P "
ἔκλεψαν VIAA--3P κλέπτω
ἐκλήθη VIAP--3S καλέω
ἐκλήθημεν VIAP--1P "
ἐκλήθης VIAP--2S "
ἐκλήθητε VIAP--2P "
ἐκληρώθημεν VIAP--1P κληρόω
ἔκλιναν VIAA--3P κλίνω
ἐκλίπῃ VSAA--3S ἐκλείπω
ἐκλίπητε VSAA--2P "
ἐκλιπόντος VPAAGM-S "

ἐκλογή, ῆς, ἡ (1) as an action *choosing out, selection, election* (2P 1.10); (2) passive, of the divine selection for a purpose or task *what is chosen* or *selected, choice* (AC 9.15); (3) ἡ ἐ. *elect, chosen ones*, as the community of believers, equivalent to ἐκλεκτοί (RO 11.7); (4) of God's *choice* of Israel, as the community of people selected to carry out God's plan of redemption for mankind (RO 11.28)

ἐκλογή N-NF-S ἐκλογή
ἐκλογήν N-AF-S "
ἐκλογῆς N-GF-S "
ἐκλυθήσονται VIFP--3P ἐκλύω
ἐκλυθῶσι(ν) VSAP--3P "
ἐκλυόμενοι VPPPNM-P "
ἐκλύου VMPP--2S "
ἐκλυσάμενοι VPAMNM-P "
ἐκλύσω VIFA--1S "

ἐκλύω 1aor. pass. ἐξελύθην; 1fut. pass. ἐκλυθήσομαι; only passive in the NT; (1) physically *become weary* or *exhausted, give out* (MT 15.32); (2) psychologically *lose heart, faint, get discouraged* (GA 6.9)

ἐκμάξασα VPAANF-S ἐκμάσσω
ἐκμάσσειν VNPA "

ἐκμάσσω impf. ἐξέμασσον; 1aor. ἐξέμαξα; *wipe (off), (wipe) dry*

ἐκμυκτηρίζω impf. ἐξεμυκτήριζον; strictly *turn one's nose up at* someone; hence *ridicule, sneer at, scoff at*

ἐκνεύω 1aor. ἐξένευσα; *withdraw*; of getting away unnoticed from a place *disappear, slip away* (JN 5.13)

ἐκνήφω 1aor. ἐξένηψα; literally *become sober* after being drunk; figuratively, of regaining proper control of one's thinking *come to one's senses, stop thinking foolish thoughts* (1C 15.34)

ἐκνήψατε VMAA--2P ἐκνήφω
ἐκοιμήθη VIAO--3S κοιμάομαι
ἐκοιμήθησαν VIAO--3P "
ἐκοινώνησαν VIAA--3P κοινωνέω
ἐκοινώνησε(ν) VIAA--3S "
ἐκολάφισαν VIAA--3P κολαφίζω
ἐκολλήθη VIAP--3S κολλάω

ἐκολλήθησαν	VIAP--3P	"
ἐκολοβώθησαν	VIAP--3P	κολοβόω
ἐκολόβωσε(ν)	VIAA--3S	"
ἐκομισάμην	VIAM--1S	κομίζω
ἐκομίσαντο	VIAM--3P	"
ἐκομίσατο	VIAM--3S	"
ἐκόπασε(ν)	VIAA--3S	κοπάζω
ἐκοπίασα	VIAA--1S	κοπιάω
ἐκοπιάσαμεν	VIAA--1P ·	
ἐκοπίασας	VIAA--2S	"
ἐκοπίασε(ν)	VIAA--3S	"
ἔκοπτον	VIIA--3P	κόπτω
ἐκόπτοντο	VIIM--3P	"
ἐκόσμησαν	VIAA--3P	κοσμέω
ἐκόσμουν	VIIA--3P	"
ἐκοῦσα	A--NF-S	ἑκών
ἐκούσιον	A--AN-S	ἑκούσιος

ἑκούσιος, ία, ον of what is done without compulsion *voluntary, spontaneous*; substantivally κατὰ ἑκούσιον *of one's own free will*, i.e. *willingly, freely* (PM 14)

ἑκουσίως adverb; (1) *willingly, voluntarily, spontaneously* (1P 5.2), opposite ἀναγκαστῶς (*unwillingly*); (2) *deliberately, intentionally* (HE 10.26)

ἑκουσίως	AB	ἑκουσίως
ἐκούφιζον	VIIA--3P	κουφίζω
ἐκόψασθε	VIAM--2P	κόπτω

ἔκπαλαι adverb of time; *for a long time* (2P 2.3); *long ago, long since, of old* (2P 3.5)

ἔκπαλαι	AB	ἔκπαλαι
ἐκπειράζοντες	VPPANM-P	ἐκπειράζω

ἐκπειράζω fut. ἐκπειράσω; 1aor. ἐξεπείρασα; (1) *put to the test, try out, tempt* (MT 4.7); (2) *try to trap* or *catch in a mistake* (LU 10.25)

ἐκπειράζωμεν	VSPA--1P	ἐκπειράζω
ἐκπειράζων	VPPANM-S	"
ἐκπειράσεις	VIFA--2S	"
	VIFA--2S^VMAA--2S	"

ἐκπέμπω 1aor. ἐξέπεμψα; 1aor. pass. ἐξεπέμφθην; *send off* or *away* (AC 17.10); passive *be sent out* (AC 13.4)

ἐκπεμφθέντες	VPAPNM-P	ἐκπέμπω
ἐκπεπλήρωκε(ν)	VIRA--3S	ἐκπληρόω
ἐκπέπτωκας	VIRA--2S	ἐκπίπτω
ἐκπέπτωκε(ν)	VIRA--3S	"
ἐκπερισσοῦ	AB	ἐκπερισσῶς

ἐκπερισσῶς (also **ἐκπερισσοῦ**) adverb; *excessively*; as a manner of speaking *vehemently, emphatically, insistently* (MK 14.31)

ἐκπερισσῶς	AB	ἐκπερισσῶς
ἐκπεσεῖν	VNAA	ἐκπίπτω
ἐκπέσητε	VSAA--2P	ἐκπίπτω
ἐκπέσωμεν	VSAA--1P	"
ἐκπέσωσι(ν)	VSAA--3P	"

ἐκπετάννυμι 1aor. ἐξεπέτασα; *spread out, stretch out*; as holding out the hands in an imploring gesture *stretch out, extend*

ἐκπεφευγέναι	VNRA	ἐκφεύγω

ἐκπηδάω 1aor. ἐξεπήδησα; strictly *leap forth*; hence *rush out* (AC 14.14)

ἐκπηδήσας	VPAANM-S	ἐκπηδάω
ἐκπίπτει	VIPA--3S	ἐκπίπτω
ἐκπίπτοντες	VPPANM-P	"

ἐκπίπτω 1aor. ἐξέπεσα; 2aor. ἐξέπεσον; pf. ἐκπέπτωκα; basically *fall out of* or *down from*; (1) literally; (a) of withered blossoms *fall off* (JA 1.11); (b) of fetters *fall off* (AC 12.7); (c) as a nautical technical term, of ships *drift off course, be driven onto rocks, run aground* (AC 27.17); (2) figuratively; (a) of the loss of favor or grace *lose, no longer experience* (GA 5.4); (b) of the nonfulfillment of a divine promise *fail, lose effect* (RO 9.6)

ἐκπλεῦσαι	VNAA	ἐκπλέω

ἐκπλέω impf. ἐξέπλουν; 1aor. ἐξέπλευσα; (1) with εἰς *sail away to* a place; (2) with ἀπό *sail away from* a place

ἐκπληρόω pf. ἐκπεπλήρωκα; *fill up*; figuratively, of promises *fulfill (exactly), perform, accomplish* (AC 13.33)

ἐκπλήρωσιν	N-AF-S	ἐκπλήρωσις

ἐκπλήρωσις, εως, ἡ literally *filling up, completion*; of a designated span of days *completion, fulfilling* (AC 21.26)

ἐκπλήσσεσθαι	VNPP	ἐκπλήσσω
ἐκπλησσόμενος	VPPPNM-S	

ἐκπλήσσω (and **ἐκπλήττω**) impf. pass. ἐξεπλησσόμην; 2aor. pass. ἐξεπλάγην; only passive in the NT; (1) *be amazed* or *astounded, be struck with astonishment* (MT 7.28); (2) *be overwhelmed, be bewildered* (MT 19.25)

ἐκπλήττεσθαι	VNPP	ἐκπλήσσω
ἐκπληττόμενος	VPPPNM-S	"
ἐκπλοκῆς	N-GF-S	ἐμπλοκή

ἐκπνέω 1aor. ἐξέπνευσα; literally *breathe out*; euphemistically *expire, die* (MK 15.37)

ἐκπορεύεσθαι	VNPD	ἐκπορεύομαι
	VNPO	
ἐκπορεύεσθω	VMPD--3S	"
	VMPO--3S	"
ἐκπορεύεται	VIPD--3S	"
	VIPO--3S	"

ἐκπορεύομαι impf. ἐξεπορευόμην; fut. ἐκπορεύσομαι; (1) literally; (a) absolutely *go from* or *out of* a place, *depart from* (MK 6.11); *go out* (AC 9.28); (b) of the dead coming out of tombs *emerge, come forth* (JN 5.29); (c) of demons *come out* (MT 17.21); (d) of a journey *set out* (MK 10.17); (2) figuratively; (a) of words or thoughts *proceed from, go* or *come out of* the mouth, i.e. *be spoken* (MT 15.11); (b) of a report *spread abroad, tell everywhere* (LU 4.37); (c) of the Spirit *proceed from* (JN 15.26); (d) of water *flow out, stream forth* (RV 22.1)

ἐκπορευόμενα	VPPDNN-P	ἐκπορεύομαι
	VPPONN-P	"
ἐκπορευομένη	VPPDNF-S	"
	VPPONF-S	"
ἐκπορευόμενοι	VPPDNM-P	"
	VPPONM-P	"
ἐκπορευομένοις	VPPDDM-P	"
	VPPODM-P	"
ἐκπορευόμενον	VPPDAM-S	"
	VPPDNN-S	"
	VPPOAM-S	"
	VPPONN-S	"
ἐκπορευόμενος	VPPDNM-S	"
	VPPONM-S	"
ἐκπορευομένου	VPPDGM-S	"
	VPPDGN-S	"
	VPPOGM-S	"
	VPPOGN-S	"

ἐκπορευομένῳ	VPPDDN-S	"
	VPPODN-S	"
ἐκπορευομένων	VPPDGM-P	"
	VPPOGM-P	"
ἐκπορεύονται	VIPD--3P	"
	VIPO--3P	"
ἐκπορεύσονται	VIFD--3P	"
ἐκπορνεύσασαι	VPAANF-P	ἐκπορνεύω

ἐκπορνεύω 1aor. ἐξεπόρνευσα; *indulge in flagrant immorality, be given to fornication, misbehave sexually* (JU 7)

ἐκπτύω 1aor. ἐξέπτυσα; literally *spit out*, used anciently as a gesture to ward off illness or demonic threat, probably the symbolic sense of GA 4.14 *reject, disdain*

ἐκπυρόω 1fut. pass. ἐκπυρωθήσομαι; of the end of the world *set on fire, destroy by fire* (2P 3.10)

ἐκπυρωθήσεται	VIFP--3S	ἐκπυρόω
ἔκραζε(ν)	VIIA--3S	κράζω
ἔκραζον	VIIA--3P	"
ἔκραξα	VIAA--1S	"
ἔκραξαν	VIAA--3P	"
ἔκραξε(ν)	VIAA--3S	"
ἐκραταιοῦτο	VIIP--3S	κραταιόω
ἐκρατεῖτε	VIIA--2P	κρατέω
ἐκρατήσαμεν	VIAA--1P	"
ἐκράτησαν	VIAA--3P	"
ἐκρατήσατε	VIAA--2P	"
ἐκράτησε(ν)	VIAA--3S	"
ἐκρατοῦντο	VIIP--3P	"
ἐκραύγαζον	VIIA--3P	κραυγάζω
ἐκραύγασαν	VIAA--3P	"
ἐκραύγασε(ν)	VIAA--3S	"

ἐκριζόω 1aor. ἐξερίζωσα; 1aor. pass. ἐξεριζώθην; 1fut. pass. ἐκριζωθήσομαι; literally *uproot, pull out by the roots* (LU 17.6; used metaphorically in JU 12)

ἐκριζωθέντα	VPAPNN-P	ἐκριζόω
ἐκριζωθήσεται	VIFP--3S	"
ἐκριζώθητι	VMAP--2S	"
ἐκριζώσητε	VSAA--2P	"
ἐκρίθη	VIAP--3S	κρίνω
ἐκρίθησαν	VIAP--3P	"
ἔκρινα	VIAA--1S	"
ἔκρινας	VIAA--2S	"
ἔκρινε(ν)	VIAA--3S	"
ἐκρινόμεθα	VIIP--1P	"
ἐκρύβη	VIAP--3S	κρύπτω
ἔκρυψα	VIAA--1S	"
ἔκρυψαν	VIAA--3P	"
ἔκρυψας	VIAA--2S	"
ἐκρύψατε	VIAA--2P	"
ἔκρυψε(ν)	VIAA--3S	"
ἐκστάσει	N-DF-S	ἔκστασις
ἐκστάσεως	N-GF-S	"

ἔκστασις, εως, ἡ strictly *being put out of place*; hence (1) as an abnormal state of mind *distraction, terror, amazement* (MK 5.42); (2) as a partially suspended consciousness *ecstasy, trance* (AC 10.10)

ἔκστασις	N-NF-S	ἔκστασις

ἐκστρέφω pf. pass. ἐξέστραμμαι; *pervert, turn aside* from correct behavior; only passive in the NT *be perverted* or *corrupt* (TI 3.11)

ἐκσῴζω 1aor. ἐξέσωσα; *bring out safely* (AC 27.39)

ἐκσῶσαι	VNAA	ἐκσῴζω
ἐκταράσσουσι(ν)	VIPA--3P	ἐκταράσσω

ἐκταράσσω *agitate, disturb*; of the population of a city *throw into confusion, cause to be disturbed, stir up* (AC 16.20)

ἐκτεθέντα	VPAPAM-S	ἐκτίθημι
ἐκτεθέντος	VPAPGM-S	"
ἐκτείνας	VPAANM-S	ἐκτείνω
ἐκτείνειν	VNPA	"
ἔκτεινον	VMAA--2S	"

ἐκτείνω fut. ἐκτενῶ; 1aor. ἐξέτεινα; *stretch out*; literally, as a graphic gesture of the hand *stretch out* or *forth, hold out* (MT 8.3); with hostile intent *lay hands on, arrest* (LU 22.53); euphemistically, of crucifixion *stretch out* (the hands) (JN 21.18)

ἐκτελέσαι	VNAA	ἐκτελέω

ἐκτελέω 1aor. ἐξετέλεσα; *completely finish, bring to completion* (LU 14.29, 30)

ἐκτένεια, ας, ἡ *perseverance, earnestness, zeal*; ἐν ἐκτενείᾳ *earnestly, persistently* (AC 26.7)

ἐκτενείᾳ	N-DF-S	ἐκτένεια
ἐκτενεῖς	VIFA--2S	ἐκτείνω
ἐκτενέστερον	ABM	ἐκτενής
ἐκτενῆ	A--AF-S	"

ἐκτενής, ές strictly *extended*; hence *earnest, eager*; of love *intense, fervent* (1P 4.8); comparative ἐκτενέστερος, τέρα, ον; neuter as an adverb *very fervently, (even) more earnestly* (LU 22.44)

ἐκτενής	A--NF-S	ἐκτενής

ἐκτενῶς adverb; strictly *in an extended way*; hence *eagerly, fervently, earnestly*

ἐκτενῶς	AB	ἐκτενῶς
ἕκτη	A-ONF-S	ἕκτος
ἕκτην	A-OAF-S	"
ἕκτης	A-OGF-S	"
ἐκτησάμην	VIAD--1S	κτάομαι
ἐκτήσατο	VIAD--3S	"

ἐκτίθημι impf. mid. ἐξετιθέμην; 2aor. mid. ἐξεθέμην; 1aor. pass. ἐξετέθην; only middle and passive in the NT; literally *place outside*; passive, of newborn babies left out to die *expose, abandon* (AC 7.21); figuratively and middle *explain* something, *set forth* (AC 11.4)

ἐκτιναξάμενοι	VPAMNM-P	ἐκτινάσσω
ἐκτιναξάμενος	VPAMNM-S	"
ἐκτινάξατε	VMAA--2P	"

ἐκτινάσσω 1aor. ἐξετίναξα, mid. ἐξετιναξάμην; (1) of dust clinging to the feet *shake off*, as a symbolic act denoting disassociation (MT 10.14); (2) of clothes *shake out*, as a symbolic act of protesting innocence (AC 18.6)

ἔκτισας	VIAA--2S	κτίζω
ἔκτισε(ν)	VIAA--3S	"
ἐκτίσθη	VIAP--3S	"
ἐκτίσθησαν	VIAP--3P	"
ἔκτισται	VIRP--3S	"

ἐκτός adverb; (1) *outside, without*; τὸ ἐ. *the outside* (part) (MT 23.26); ἐ. εἰ μή *unless, except* (1C 14.5); (2) as an improper preposition with the genitive *outside of, apart from* (2C 12.2); *except, besides* (1C 15.27); *independent of* (1C 6.18)

ἐκτός AB ἐκτός
  PG "

ἕκτος, η, ον as an ordinal number *sixth* (LU 1.36); substantivally ὁ ἕ. *the sixth one* (RV 21.20)

ἕκτος A-ONM-S ἕκτος
ἐκτραπῇ VSAP--3S ἐκτρέπω
ἐκτραπήσονται VIFP--3P "
ἐκτρεπόμενος VPPMNM-S "

ἐκτρέπω 2aor. pass. ἐξετράπην; 2fut. pass. ἐκτραπήσομαι; only passive with the middle sense in the NT; (1) *swerve, turn aside* or *away* (probably the sense in the Pastoral Epistles and HE 12.13); (2) as a medical technical term, of a limb *be dislocated* or *put out of joint* (perhaps HE 12.13)

ἐκτρέφει VIPA--3S ἐκτρέφω
ἐκτρέφετε VMPA--2P "

ἐκτρέφω (1) of the body *nourish, feed* (figuratively in EP 5.29); (2) of children *rear, bring up, educate* (EP 6.4)

ἔκτρομος A--NM-S ἔντρομος

ἔκτρωμα, ατος, τό as a birth that takes place contrary to the normal course of nature *untimely* or *abnormal birth, miscarriage* (1C 15.8)

ἐκτρώματι N-DN-S ἔκτρωμα
ἕκτῳ A-ODM-S ἕκτος
ἐκύκλευσαν VIAA--3P κυκλεύω
ἐκύκλωσαν VIAA--3P κυκλόω
ἐκυλίετο VIIM--3S κυλίω
  VIIP--3S "
ἐκύλισον VIAA--3P "
ἐκφέρειν VNPA ἐκφέρω
ἐκφέρουσα VPPANF-S "

ἐκφέρω fut. ἐξοίσω; 1aor. ἐξήνεγκα; (1) *bring* or *carry out* (AC 5.15); (2) of a blind person *lead out* (MK 8.23); (3) of growth through natural processes *produce, yield* (HE 6.8)

ἐκφεύγω fut. mid. ἐκφεύξομαι; 2aor. ἐξέφυγον; second perfect ἐκπέφευγα; (1) intransitively *flee out, (make an) escape, run away* (AC 19.16); (2) transitively and figuratively, of severe trials or judgment *escape, avoid* (LU 21.36)

ἐκφεύξῃ VIFD--2S ἐκφεύγω
ἐκφευξόμεθα VIFD--1P "
ἐκφεύξονται VIFD--3P "
ἐκφευξώμεθα VIFD--1P see ἐκφευξόμεθα
ἐκφοβεῖν VNPA ἐκφοβέω

ἐκφοβέω *terrify, frighten* (2C 10.9)

ἔκφοβοι A--NM-P ἔκφοβος

ἔκφοβος, ον *terrified, frightened, extremely afraid*

ἔκφοβος A--NM-S ἔκφοβος
ἐκφυγεῖν VNAA ἐκφεύγω
ἐκφύγωσι(ν) VSAA--3P "
ἐκφύῃ VSPA--3S ἐκφύω

ἐκφύω literally *cause to grow, generate*; of tree branches *put forth* (leaves), *sprout*

ἐκφωνέω *cry out* (LU 16.24)

ἐκφωνήσας VPAANM-S ἐκφωνέω
ἐκχέαι VNAA ἐκχέω
ἐκχέατε VMAA--2P "
ἐκχέετε VMPA--2P "
ἐκχεῖται VIPP--3S "

ἐκχέω and **ἐκχύννω** (and **ἐκχύνω**) impf. pass. ἐξεχυννόμην; fut. ἐκχεῶ; 1aor. ἐξέχεα; pf. pass. ἐκκέχυμαι; 1aor. pass. ἐξεχύθην; 1fut. pass. ἐκχυθήσομαι; *pour out*; (1) literally; (a) of fluids *pour out* (RV 16.1); *spill* (MT 9.17); of blood *shed*; idiomatically αἷμα ἐκκύννειν/ἐκχεῖν literally *pour out blood*, i.e. *murder* (MT 23.35; RO 3.15); (b) of solids *scatter* (JN 2.15); (2) figuratively; (a) of spiritual gifts and benefits *give in abundance, cause to fully experience, generously provide* (AC 2.33); (b) passive, of rushing headlong into some type of behavior *give oneself over to, plunge into, devote oneself to* (JU 11)

ἐκχεῶ VIFA--1S ἐκχέω
ἐκχυθήσεται VIFP--3S "
ἐκχυννόμενον VPPPNN-S "
ἐκχυνόμενον VPPPNN-S "
ἐκχωρείτωσαν VMPA--3P ἐκχωρέω

ἐκχωρέω *go out, depart, get out of* someplace (LU 21.21)

ἐκψύχω 1aor. ἐξέψυξα; *breathe one's last, expire, die* (AC 5.5)

ἐκωλύθη VIAP--3S κωλύω
ἐκωλύθην VIAP--1S "
ἐκωλύομεν VIIA--1P "
ἐκώλυον VIIA--3P "
ἐκωλύσαμεν VIAA--1P "
ἐκωλύσατε VIAA--2P "
ἐκώλυσε(ν) VIAA--3S "

ἑκών, οῦσα, όν *willing, voluntary, of one's own free will* (RO 8.20)

ἑκών A--NM-S ἑκών
ἔλαβε(ν) VIAA--3S λαμβάνω
ἔλαβες VIAA--2S "
ἐλάβετε VIAA--2P "
ἐλάβομεν VIAA--1P "
ἔλαβον VIAA--1S "
  VIAA--3S "
ἐλάβοσαν VIAA--3P see ἔλαβον
ἔλαθε(ν) VIAA--3S λανθάνω
ἔλαθον VIAA--3P "

ἐλαία, ας, ἡ (1) *olive tree* (RO 11.17); τὸ ὄρος τῶν ἐλαιῶν *the Mount of Olives*, the mountain looking down on Jerusalem from the east (MT 21.1); (2) as the fruit of the olive tree *olive* (JA 3.12)

ἐλαία N-DF-S ἐλαία
ἐλαῖαι N-NF-P "
ἐλαίας N-AF-P "
  N-GF-S "

ἔλαιον, ου, τό (1) *olive oil* (MT 25.3); (2) as used for anointing *oil* (LU 7.46); figuratively, as a symbol of a festive occasion (HE 1.9); (3) by metonymy *olive orchard* (RV 6.6)

ἔλαιον N-AN-S ἔλαιον
ἐλαίου N-GN-S "
ἐλαίῳ N-DN-S "

ἐλαιών, ῶνος, ὁ *olive grove* or *orchard*; in the NT the name of the mountain looking down on Jerusalem from the east *Mount of Olives, Olivet* (AC 1.12)

ἐλαιῶν N-GF-P ἐλαία
ἐλαιῶνος N-GM-S ἐλαιών
ἐλάκησε(ν) VIAA--3S λακάω
ἐλάλει VIIA--3S λαλέω

ἐλάλη	VIIA--3S	see ἐλάλει
ἐλαλήθη	VIAP--3S	λαλέω
ἐλάλησα	VIAA--1S	"
ἐλαλήσαμεν	VIAA--1P	"
ἐλάλησαν	VIAA--3P	"
ἐλαλήσατε	VIAA--2P	"
ἐλάλησε(ν)	VIAA--3S	"
ἐλαλοῦμεν	VIIA--1P	"
ἐλάλουν	VIIA--1S	"
	VIIA--3P	"
ἐλάμβανον	VIIA--3P	λαμβάνω
Ἐλαμεῖται	N-NM-P	Ἐλαμίτης
Ἐλαμῖται	N-NM-P	"

Ἐλαμίτης, ου, ὁ (also **Ἐλαμείτης**) *Elamite, inhabitant of Elam*, a district north of the Persian Gulf (AC 2.9)

ἐλαμψε(ν)	VIAA--3S	λάμπω
ἐλάσατε	VMAA--2P	ἐλεάω
ἐλάσσονι	A-MDM-S	ἐλάσσων
ἐλάσσω	A-MAM-S	"

ἐλάσσων, ἔλασσον and **ἐλάττων, ἔλαττον** comparative of an ancient word ἐλαχύς (*short, small, little*) used as the comparative of μικρός (*small*); *smaller*; of age *younger*; substantivally *younger person* (RO 9.12); of quality *inferior* (JN 2.10); of number *less, fewer*; substantivally, neuter as an adverb *less* (1T 5.9); of position *inferior, subordinate* (HE 7.7)

ἐλατόμησε(ν)	VIAA--3S	λατομέω
ἐλάτρευσαν	VIAA--3P	λατρεύω
ἔλαττον	ABM	ἐλάσσων
	A-MNN-S	"

ἐλαττονέω 1aor. ἠλαττόνησα; *have less* or *too little*

ἐλαττοῦσθαι	VNPM	ἐλαττόω
	VNPP	"

ἐλαττόω 1aor. ἠλάττωσα; pf. pass. ἠλάττωμαι; 1aor. pass. ἠλαττώθην (and ἐλαττώθην); (1) in a comparative way *make less, lower, inferior in position* (HE 2.7); (2) passive *be worse off* or *inferior* (2C 12.13); (3) intransitively *diminish in status, become less important* (JN 3.30)

ἐλαττώθητε	VIAP--2P	ἐλαττόω
ἐλαύνειν	VNPA	ἐλαύνω
ἐλαυνόμενα	VPPPNN-P	"
ἐλαυνόμεναι	VPPPNF-P	"
ἐλαυνομένη	VPPPNF-S	"
ἐλαύνοντας	VPPAAM-P	"

ἐλαύνω impf. pass. ἠλαυνόμην; pf. ἐλήλακα; (1) of an impelling force *drive, urge forward* (LU 8.29); (2) absolutely, of impelling a boat forward by oars *row* (MK 6.48)

ἐλαφρία, ας, ἡ strictly *lightness* in weight; hence, of lack of stability in behavior *vacillation, fickleness, levity* (2C 1.17)

ἐλαφρία	N-DF-S	ἐλαφρία
ἐλαφρόν	A--NN-S	ἐλαφρός

ἐλαφρός, ά, όν literally, of weight *light*; figuratively, of a burden or trial *easy to bear, insignificant* (MT 11.30); *limited* in extent, *light* (2C 4.17)

ἔλαχε(ν)	VIAA--3S	λαγχάνω
ἐλαχίστη	A-SNF-S	ἐλάχιστος
ἐλάχιστον	A-SAN-S	"

ἐλάχιστος, ίστη, ον superlative of the ancient word ἐλαχύς (*short, small, little*) used as the superlative of μικρός

(*small*); (1) *smallest, least* (MT 5.19); substantivally *least important one* (1C 15.9); (2) as an elative *very small, quite unimportant, insignificant* (JA 3.4); substantivally *a very little thing* (LU 12.26); (3) a colloquial comparative formed from the superlative ἐλαχιστότερος, τέρα, ον *the very least* (EP 3.8)

ἐλάχιστος	A-SNM-S	ἐλάχιστος
ἐλαχιστοτέρῳ	A-MDM-S	"
ἐλαχίστου	A-SGN-S	"
ἐλαχίστῳ	A-SDN-S	"
ἐλαχίστων	A-SGF-P	"
	A-SGM-P	"
	A-SGN-P	"
ἐλεᾷ	VIPA--3S	ἐλεάω

Ἐλεάζαρ, ὁ indeclinable; *Eleazar*, masculine proper noun

ἐλεᾶτε	VMPA--2P	ἐλεάω

ἐλεάω with same meaning as ἐλεέω, serving as the present-tense by-form; *show mercy to, pity* (JU 22, 23); absolutely *be merciful, feel pity* (RO 9.16)

ἔλεγε(ν)	VIIA--3S	λέγω
ἐλέγετε	VIIA--2P	"
ἐλέγετο	VIIP--3S	"
ἐλεγμόν	N-AM-S	ἐλεγμός

ἐλεγμός, οῦ, ὁ as a process *rebuking, reproof, convicting* (2T 3.16)

ἐλέγξαι	VNAA	ἐλέγχω
ἐλέγξει	VIFA--3S	"
ἔλεγξιν	N-AF-S	ἔλεγξις

ἔλεγξις, εως, ἡ as an action *rebuking, rebuke, reproof* (2P 2.16)

ἔλεγξον	VMAA--2S	ἐλέγχω
ἔλεγον	VIIA--1S	λέγω
	VIIA--3P	"
ἐλέγοσαν	VIIA--3P	see ἔλεγον
ἔλεγχε	VMPA--2S	ἐλέγχω
ἐλέγχει	VIPA--3S	"
ἐλέγχειν	VNPA	"
ἐλέγχεσθαι	VNPP	"
ἐλέγχεται	VIPP--3S	"
ἐλέγχετε	VMPA--2P	"
ἐλεγχθῇ	VSAP--3S	"
ἐλεγχόμενα	VPPPNN-P	"
ἐλεγχόμενοι	VPPPNM-P	"
ἐλεγχόμενος	VPPPNM-S	"
ἔλεγχον	N-AM-S	ἔλεγχος

ἔλεγχος, ου, ὁ strictly *trying* or *testing* for the purpose of proving; (1) objectively *proof, means of proof, evidence* (possibly HE 11.1); in a negative sense *reproof, correction* (2T 3.16); (2) subjectively *inner conviction, confident assurance* (possibly HE 11.1)

ἔλεγχος	N-NM-S	ἔλεγχος

ἐλέγχω fut. ἐλέγξω; 1aor. ἤλεγξα; 1aor. pass. ἠλέγχθην; (1) in the NT, generally as showing someone that he has done something wrong and summoning him to repent *bring to light, expose* (JN 3.20); *convince, convict* (JA 2.9); (2) in the sense of setting right *reprove, correct* (1T 5.20); in an intensified sense *rebuke, discipline, punish* (HE 12.5)

ἐλέγχω	VIPA--1S	ἐλέγχω
ἐλέει	N-DN-S	ἔλεος
ἐλεεῖ	VIPA--3S	ἐλεέω

ἐλεεινός, ή, όν *miserable, pitiful, wretched*; substantivally ὁ ἐ. *the miserable person* (RV 3.17); comparative ἐλεεινότερος, τέρα, ον *more miserable*; comparative as superlative *most miserable* (1C 15.19)

ἐλεεινός	A--NM-S	ἐλεεινός
ἐλεεινότεροι	A-MNM-P	"
ἐλεεῖτε	VMPA--2P	ἐλεέω

ἐλεέω fut. ἐλεήσω; 1aor. ἠλέησα; pf. pass. ἠλέημαι; 1aor. pass. ἠλεήθην; 1fut. pass. ἐλεηθήσομαι; active, of helping someone because of pity *take pity, be merciful, show mercy* (MT 9.27); passive *find mercy, be shown mercy* (MT 5.7)

ἐλεηθέντες	VPAPNM-P	ἐλεέω
ἐλεηθήσονται	VIFP--3P	"
ἐλεηθῶσι(ν)	VSAP--3P	"
ἐλεήμονες	A--NM-P	ἐλεήμων
ἐλεημοσύναι	N-NF-P	ἐλεημοσύνη
ἐλεημοσύνας	N-AF-P	"

ἐλεημοσύνη, ης, ἡ *sympathy, charitableness, compassion*; concretely in the NT, as benevolent activity toward the poor *donation, almsgiving, charitable giving* (MT 6.2)

ἐλεημοσύνη	N-NF-S	ἐλεημοσύνη
ἐλεημοσύνην	N-AF-S	"
ἐλεημοσυνῶν	N-GF-P	"

ἐλεήμων, ον, gen. ονος *merciful, compassionate, sympathetic* (HE 2.17); substantivally, of a person who shows pity to others *merciful person* (MT 5.7)

ἐλεήμων	A--NM-S	ἐλεήμων
ἐλεῆσαι	VNAA	ἐλεέω
ἐλεήσῃ	VSAA--3S	"
ἐλέησον	VMAA--2S	"
ἐλεήσω	VIFA--1S	"
ἐλεινός	A--NM-S	ἐλεεινός
Ἐλεισάβετ		Ἐλισάβετ
ἔλειχον	VIIA--3P	λείχω
ἔλεον	N-AM-S	ἔλεος

ἔλεος, ους, τό (also **ἔλεος, ου, ὁ**) *mercy, compassion*, used of attitudes of both God and man; (1) as an attitude and emotion roused by the affliction of another *pity, compassion, sympathy* (LU 1.78); (2) especially of gracious action demonstrating God's compassion *mercy, lovingkindness, faithfulness* (RO 11.31)

ἔλεος	N-AN-S	ἔλεος
	N-NN-S	"
ἐλέους	N-GN-S	"
ἐλεοῦτος	VPPAGM-S	ἐλεέω
ἐλεδόρησαν	VIAA--3P	see ἐλοιδόρησαν
ἐλευθέρα	A--NF-S	ἐλεύθερος
ἐλευθέρας	AP-GF-S	"

ἐλευθερία, ας, ἡ as a state of being free *freedom, liberty*, opposite δουλεία (*slavery, bondage*); (1) of a life rescued from spiritual and moral wrongdoing *freedom* (2C 3.17); (2) of a conscience no longer dominated by binding scruples *freedom, liberty* (1C 10.29); (3) of a way of life no longer dominated by legal constraint *liberty* (GA 2.4); (4) as the liberation of nature from decay and corruption *freedom* (RO 8.21)

ἐλευθερία	N-NF-S	ἐλευθερία
ἐλευθερίᾳ	N-DF-S	"
ἐλευθερίαν	N-AF-S	"
ἐλευθερίας	N-GF-S	"

ἐλεύθεροι	AP-NM-P	ἐλεύθερος
	A--NM-P	"

ἐλεύθερος, έρα, ον *free*; (1) of political and social freedom allowing for self-determination *free, independent, not bound* (JN 8.33); substantivally ὁ ἐ. *the freeman* (1C 7.22), opposite δοῦλος (*slave, servant*); (2) of freedom from taxation *exempt* (MT 17.26); (3) spiritually, of freedom from sin and death *free* (JN 8.36); (4) morally, of freedom from self-seeking through self-control *free* (1P 2.16)

ἐλεύθερος	AP-NM-S	ἐλεύθερος
	A--NM-S	"
ἐλευθέρους	AP-AM-P	"
ἐλευθεροῦται	VIPP--3S	ἐλευθερόω

ἐλευθερόω fut. ἐλευθερώσω; 1aor. ἠλευθέρωσα; 1aor. pass. ἠλευθερώθην; 1fut. pass. ἐλευθερωθήσομαι; (1) of spiritual and moral freedom *set free, make free* (JN 8.32); (2) of freedom from binding legalism *make free* (GA 5.1); (3) of nature's deliverance from decay and corruption *free, deliver, liberate* (RO 8.21)

ἐλευθερωθέντες	VPAPNM-P	ἐλευθερόω
ἐλευθερωθῆναι	VNAP	"
ἐλευθερωθήσεται	VIFP--3S	"
ἐλευθέρων	AP-GM-P	ἐλεύθερος
ἐλευθερώσει	VIFA--3S	ἐλευθερόω
ἐλευθέρωσε(ν)	VIAA--3S	"
ἐλευθερώσῃ	VSAA--3S	"
ἐλεύκαναν	VIAA--3P	λευκαίνω
ἐλεύσεται	VIFD--3S	ἔρχομαι
ἐλεύσεως	N-GF-S	ἔλευσις

ἔλευσις, εως, ἡ abstract form of ἐλεύσομαι, the future of ἔρχομαι (*come, go*); *coming, advent, appearing* (AC 7.52)

ἐλεύσομαι	VIFD--1S	ἔρχομαι
ἐλευσόμεθα	VIFD--1P	"
ἐλεύσονται	VIFD--3P	"
ἐλεφάντινον	A--AN-S	ἐλεφάντινος

ἐλεφάντινος, η, ον *ivory, made of ivory* (RV 18.12)

ἐλεῶ	VSPA--1S	ἐλεέω
ἐλεῶν	VPPANM-S	"
ἐλεῶντος	VPPAGM-S	ἐλεάω
ἐληλακότες	VPRANM-P	ἐλαύνω
ἐλήλυθα	VIRA--1S	ἔρχομαι
ἐλήλυθαν	VIRA--3P	"
ἐλήλυθας	VIRA--2S	"
ἐληλύθει	VILA--3S	"
ἐληλύθεισαν	VILA--3P	"
ἐλήλυθε(ν)	VIRA--3S	"
ἐληλυθέναι	VNRA	"
ἐληλυθότα	VPRAAM-S	"
ἐληλυθότες	VPRANM-P	"
ἐληλυθότων	VPRAGM-P	"
ἐληλυθυῖαν	VPRAAF-S	"
ἐλθάτω	VMAA--3S	"
ἐλθέ	VMAA--2S	"
ἐλθεῖν	VNAA	"
ἐλθέτω	VMAA--3S	"
ἔλθῃ	VSAA--3S	"
ἔλθῃς	VSAA--2S	"
ἔλθητε	VSAA--2P	"
ἐλθόν	VPAANN-S	"

143

ἐλθόντα	VPAAAM-S	"
	VPAANN-P	"
ἐλθόντας	VPAAAM-P	"
ἐλθόντες	VPAANM-P	"
ἐλθόντι	VPAADM-S	"
ἐλθόντος	VPAAGM-S	"
ἐλθόντων	VPAAGM-P	"
	VPAAGN-P	"
ἐλθοῦσα	VPAANF-S	"
ἐλθοῦσαι	VPAANF-P	"
ἐλθούσης	VPAAGF-S	"
ἔλθω	VSAA--1S	"
ἐλθών	VPAANM-S	"
ἔλθωσι(ν)	VSAA--3P	"
Ἐλιακείμ		Ἐλιακίμ

Ἐλιακίμ, ὁ (also **Ἐλιακείμ**) indeclinable; *Eliakim*, masculine proper noun

ἔλιγμα, ατος, τό what has been rolled or is in the shape of a roll *roll, package* (JN 19.39)

ἔλιγμα	N-AN-S	ἔλιγμα

Ἐλιέζερ, ὁ indeclinable; *Eliezer*, masculine proper noun (LU 3.29)

ἐλιθάσθην	VIAP--1S	λιθάζω
ἐλιθάσθησαν	VIAP--3P	"
ἐλιθοβόλησαν	VIAA--3P	λιθοβολέω
ἐλιθοβόλουν	VIIA--3P	"
ἑλίξεις	VIFA--2S	ἑλίσσω

Ἐλιούδ, ὁ indeclinable; *Eliud*, masculine proper noun

Ἐλισάβετ, ἡ (also **Ἐλεισάβετ**) indeclinable; *Elizabeth*, feminine proper noun

Ἐλισαῖος, ου, ὁ (also **Ἐλισαῖος, Ἐλισσαῖος**) *Elisha*, masculine proper noun (LU 4.27)

Ἐλισαίου	N-GM-S	Ἐλισαῖος
Ἐλισαίου	N-GM-S	"
Ἐλισσαίου	N-GM-S	"
ἑλισσόμενον	VPPPNN-S	ἑλίσσω
ἑλισσόμενος	VPPPNM-S	"

ἑλίσσω (and **εἱλίσσω**) fut. ἑλίξω; *roll up* something, as a scroll

ἕλκη	N-AN-P	ἕλκος

ἕλκος, ους, τό strictly *wound*; by metonymy *ulcer, ulcerated sore, abscess*

ἕλκος	N-NN-S	ἕλκος
ἕλκουσι(ν)	VIPA--3P	ἕλκω

ἑλκόω pf. pass. εἵλκωμαι; strictly *wound sorely*; by metonymy *cause sores, ulcerate*; only passive in the NT *be covered with sores* or *ulcers* (LU 16.20)

ἑλκύσαι	VNAA	ἕλκω
ἑλκύσῃ	VSAA--3S	"
ἑλκύσω	VIFA--1S	"

ἕλκω impf. εἷλκον; the future (ἑλκύσω) and first aorist (εἵλκυσα) are formed as if from ἑλκύω; *tug, draw, drag*; literally; (1) of a sword *draw, unsheath* (JN 18.10); (2) of a person, forcibly led *drag* (AC 21.30); (3) of a net *haul, drag* (JN 21.6); (4) as a legal technical term *lead by force, drag into court* (JA 2.6); figuratively, of a strong pull in the mental or moral life *draw, attract* (JN 6.44)

ἑλκῶν	N-GN-P	ἕλκος
Ἑλλάδα	N-AF-S	Ἑλλάς

Ἑλλάς, άδος, ἡ *Greece, Hellas*; in the NT limited to the southern portion of modern Greece, the Roman province of Achaia (AC 20.2)

Ἕλλην, ηνος, ὁ *Greek, Hellene*; (1) culturally, a person of Greek language and civilization, *Greek* (RO 1.14), opposite βάρβαρος (*foreigner*); (2) in a religious sense *Gentile, non-Jew, pagan* (JN 7.35), opposite Ἰουδαῖος (*Jew*)

Ἕλλην	N-NM-S	Ἕλλην
Ἕλληνας	N-AM-P	"
Ἕλληνες	N-NM-P	"
Ἕλληνι	N-DM-S	"
Ἑλληνίδων	N-GF-P	Ἑλληνίς
Ἑλληνικῇ	AP-DF-S	Ἑλληνικός
Ἑλληνικοῖς	A--DN-P	"

Ἑλληνικός, ή, όν *Greek*; usually substantivally ἡ Ἑλληνική, of the *Greek language* (RV 9.11), in contrast to Ἑβραϊστί (*Hebrew language*)

Ἑλληνίς, ίδος, ἡ (1) *Gentile* or *non-Jewish woman* (MK 7.26); (2) as an adjective *Gentile, Greek*, with γυνή (AC 17.12)

Ἑλληνίς	N-NF-S	Ἑλληνίς
Ἑλληνιστάς	N-AM-P	Ἑλληνιστής

Ἑλληνιστής, οῦ, ὁ *Hellenist*, a Greek-speaking Jew in contrast to one speaking a Semitic language

Ἑλληνιστί adverb; *in the Greek language*

Ἑλληνιστί	AB	Ἑλληνιστί
Ἑλληνιστῶν	N-GM-P	Ἑλληνιστής
Ἕλληνος	N-GM-S	Ἕλλην
Ἑλλήνων	N-GM-P	"
Ἕλλησι(ν)	N-DM-P	"
Ἑλλινηκοῖς	A--DN-P	see Ἑλληνικοῖς
ἐλλόγα	VMPA--2S	ἐλλογέω
ἐλλογᾶται	VIPP--3S	"
ἐλλόγατο	VIIP--3S	"
ἐλλόγει	VMPA--2S	"
ἐλλογεῖται	VIPP--3S	"

ἐλλογέω (and **ἐλλογάω**) inf. ἐλλογεῖν, imperative ἐλλόγα; (1) as a commercial technical term *reckon in, charge to* someone's account (PM 18); (2) figuratively, of God's dealing with sins *keep record, take into account* (RO 5.13)

Ἑλμαδάμ, ὁ (also **Ἑλμασάμ, Ἑλμωδάμ**) indeclinable; *Elmadam*, masculine proper noun (LU 3.28)

Ἑλμασάμ		Ἑλμαδάμ
Ἑλμωδάμ		"
ἐλογιζόμην	VIID--1S	λογίζομαι
	VIIO--1S	"
ἐλογίζοντο	VIID--3P	"
	VIIO--3P	"
ἐλογίσθη	VIAP--3S	"
ἐλογίσθημεν	VIAP--1P	"
ἐλοιδόρησαν	VIAA--3P	λοιδορέω
ἐλόμενος	VPAMNM-S	αἱρέω
ἐλούετο	VIIM--3S	λούω
ἔλουσε(ν)	VIAA--3S	"
ἐλπίδα	N-AF-S	ἐλπίς
ἐλπίδι	N-DF-S	"
ἐλπίδι	N-DF-S	see ἐλπίδι
ἐλπίδος	N-GF-S	ἐλπίς
ἐλπίζει	VIPA--3S	ἐλπίζω

ἐλπίζετε	VIPA--2P	"
ἐλπίζομεν	VIPA--1P	"
ἐλπιζομένων	VPPPGN-P	"
ἐλπίζουσαι	VPPANF-P	"

ἐλπίζω fut. ἐλπιῶ; 1aor. ἤλπισα; pf. ἤλπικα; *hope, hope for*; (1) in the sense of counting on something *expect, await, hope for* (LU 6.34); (2) as relying on a basis of confidence *hope in, trust in, confide in* (1C 15.19)

ἐλπίζω	VIPA--1S	ἐλπίζω
ἐλπίζων	VPPANM-S	"
ἐλπιοῦσι(ν)	VIFA--3P	"

ἐλπίς, ίδος, ἡ *hope*; (1) as an expected and awaited good *hope, expectation, prospect* (AC 27.20); (2) as hopeful *confidence* in a trustworthy person *hope* (1TH 2.19); (3) as expectation of a divinely provided future *(the) hope* (CO 1.27); (4) as a Christian attitude of patient waiting, along with πίστις and ἀγάπη *hope* (1C 13.13); (5) in combination with prepositions: ἐπ' ἐλπίδι *in (the) expectation of* something (RO 5.2); παρ' ἐλπίδα *contrary to (all) expectation* (RO 4.18)

ἐλπίς	N-NF-S	ἐλπίς
ἐλπίσατε	VMAA--2P	ἐλπίζω
ἔλυε(ν)	VIIA--3S	λύω
ἐλύετο	VIIP--3S	"
ἐλύθη	VIAP--3S	"
ἐλύθησαν	VIAP--3P	"
ἐλυμαίνετο	VIIM--3S	λυμαίνω

Ἐλύμας, α, ὁ *Elymas*, masculine proper noun (AC 13.8)

Ἐλύμας	N-NM-S	Ἐλύμας
ἐλυπήθη	VIAP--3S	λυπέω
ἐλυπήθησαν	VIAP--3P	"
ἐλυπήθητε	VIAP--2P	"
ἐλύπησα	VIAA--1S	"
ἐλύπησε(ν)	VIAA--3S	"
ἔλυσε(ν)	VIAA--3S	λύω
ἐλυτρώθητε	VIAP--2P	λυτρόω
ἐλωεί		ἐλωΐ
ἐλωΐ		"

ἐλωΐ (also ἐλωεί, ἐλωΐ, ἐλωΐ) transliterated from the Aramaic word meaning *my God*; see also ἠλί

ἐλωΐ		ἐλωΐ
ἐμά	A--AN1P	ἐμός
	A--NN1P	"
ἔμαθε(ν)	VIAA--3S	μανθάνω
ἔμαθες	VIAA--2S	"
ἐμάθετε	VIAA--2P	"
ἐμαθητεύθη	VIAP--3S	μαθητεύω
ἐμαθήτευσε(ν)	VIAA--3S	"
ἔμαθον	VIAA--1S	μανθάνω
ἐμαρτύρει	VIIA--3S	μαρτυρέω
ἐμαρτυρεῖτο	VIIP--3S	"
ἐμαρτυρήθη	VIAP--3S	"
ἐμαρτυρήθησαν	VIAP--3P	"
ἐμαρτυρήσαμεν	VIAA--1P	"
ἐμαρτύρησαν	VIAA--3P	"
ἐμαρτύρησε(ν)	VIAA--3S	"
ἐμαρτύρουν	VIIA--3P	"
ἐμάς	A--AF1P	ἐμός
ἐμαστίγωσε(ν)	VIAA--3S	μαστιγόω
ἐμασῶντο	VIID--3P	μασάομαι
	VIIO--3P	"

ἐματαιώθησαν	VIAP--3P	ματαιόω
ἐμαυτόν	NPAM1S	ἐμαυτοῦ

ἐμαυτοῦ, ῆς reflexive pronoun of the first-person *myself*; (1) as a possessive genitive with a noun *my own* (1C 10.33); (2) with a verb *myself* (JN 14.21); (3) with prepositions: (a) ἀπ' ἐ. *on my own (authority), of my own accord* (JN 7.17); *of my own free will* (JN 10.18); (b) ὑπ' ἐμαυτόν *under my authority* (LU 7.8); (c) περὶ ἐ. *about or concerning myself* (JN 8.14); (d) πρὸς ἐμαυτόν *to myself* (JN 12.32); (e) ὑπὲρ ἐ. *on my own behalf, for myself* (2C 12.5)

ἐμαυτοῦ	NPGM1S	ἐμαυτοῦ
ἐμαυτῷ	NPDM1S	"
ἐμάχοντο	VIID--3P	μάχομαι
	VIIO--3P	"
ἐμβαίνοντος	VPPAGM-S	ἐμβαίνω

ἐμβαίνω 2aor. ἐνέβην, ptc. ἐμβάς; *step in(to), go in(to)* (JN 5.4); of a ship *get into, embark* (MT 8.23)

ἐμβαλεῖν	VNAA	ἐμβάλλω

ἐμβάλλω 2aor. ἐνέβαλον, inf. ἐμβαλεῖν; *throw* or *cast into, put into* (LU 12.5)

ἐμβάντα	VPAAAM-S	ἐμβαίνω
ἐμβάντες	VPAANM-P	"
ἐμβάντι	VPAADM-S	"
ἐμβάντος	VPAAGM-S	"
ἐμβάντων	VPAAGM-P	"
ἐμβαπτάμενος	VPPMNM-S	ἐμβάπτω

ἐμβαπτίζω *dip (in, into)*; middle *dip for oneself* (MK 14.20)

ἐμβαπτόμενος	VPPMNM-S	ἐμβάπτω

ἐμβάπτω (or ἐνβάπτω) 1aor. ἐνέβαψα; (1) active *dip (one's hand) in* something (MT 26.23); (2) middle *dip (for food) in* a dish (MK 14.20)

ἐμβάς	VPAANM-S	ἐμβαίνω

ἐμβατεύω strictly *step in* or *on, stand on*; figuratively in the NT, only in CO 2.18, in a warning against dependence on ecstatic, nonrational visions; perhaps *examine in detail, investigate* (what one has seen or claims to have seen in ecstasy); or more probably *take one's stand on, base one's authority on* (what one has seen or claims to have seen in ecstasy); a second-century inscription leads some to see it as a religious technical term for the second step of an initiate into a mystery religion as he entered an inner sanctuary *enter into mysteries*

ἐμβατεύων	VPPANM-S	ἐμβατεύω
ἐμβάψας	VPAANM-S	ἐμβάπτω
ἐμβῆναι	VNAA	ἐμβαίνω

ἐμβιβάζω 1aor. ἐνεβίβασα; *cause to step in* or *on*; of a ship *put on board, make to embark* (AC 27.6)

ἐμβλέποντες	VPPANM-P	ἐμβλέπω

ἐμβλέπω impf. ἐνέβλεπον; 1aor. ἐνέβλεψα; literally, as an attentive looking on someone or something *fix one's gaze (earnestly) on, look at attentively* (LU 22.61); absolutely *see clearly* (MK 8.25); *be able to see* (AC 22.11); figuratively, as giving careful attention *consider, think about* (MT 6.26)

ἐμβλέψας	VPAANM-S	ἐμβλέπω
ἐμβλέψασα	VPAANF-S	"
ἐμβλέψατε	VMAA--2P	"

ἐμβριμάομαι (and ἐμβριμόομαι) present act. ptc. ἐμβριμῶν (JN 11.38); 1aor. mid. ἐνεβριμησάμην; 1aor. pass. ἐνεβριμήθην; (1) as emphasizing what is forbidden to do *sternly warn, admonish strictly* (MT 9.30); (2) as expressing intense agitation *be deeply moved, groan* (JN 11.33); (3) as expressing anger or displeasure *scold, reproach, grumble at* (MK 14.5)

ἐμβριμησάμενος	VPADNM-S	ἐμβριμάομαι
ἐμβριμούμενος	VPPDNM-S	"
	VPPONM-S	
ἐμβριμώμενος	VPPDNM-S	
	VPPONM-S	
ἐμβριμῶν	VPPANM-S	"
ἐμέ	NPA-1S	ἐγώ
ἐμεγάλυνε(ν)	VIAA--3S	μεγαλύνω
	VIIA--3S	"
ἐμεγαλύνετο	VIIP--3S	"
ἐμεθύσθησαν	VIAP--3P	μεθύσκω
ἐμείναμεν	VIAA--1P	μένω
ἔμειναν	VIAA--3P	"
ἔμεινε(ν)	VIAA--3S	"
ἔμελε(ν)	VIIA--3S	μέλει
ἐμελέτησαν	VIAA--3P	μελετάω
ἔμελλε(ν)	VIIA--3S	μέλλω
ἔμελλον	VIIA--3P	
ἐμέμψαντο	VIAD-3P	μέμφομαι
ἔμενε(ν)	VIIA--3S	μένω
ἔμενον	VIIA--3P	"
ἐμέρισε(ν)	VIAA--3S	μερίζω
ἐμερίσθη	VIAP-3S	"
ἐμέσαι	VNAA	ἐμέω
ἐμεσίτευσε(ν)	VIAA--3S	μεσιτεύω
ἐμέτρησαν	VIAA--3P	μετρέω
ἐμέτρησε(ν)	VIAA--3S	"

ἐμέω 1aor. ἤμεσα; *spit out, vomit* (RV 3.16)

ἐμή	A--NF1S	ἐμός
ἐμῇ	A--DF1S	"
ἐμήν	A--AF1S	"
ἐμήνυσε(ν)	VIAA--3S	μηνύω
ἐμῆς	A--GF1S	ἐμός
ἔμιξε(ν)	VIAA--3S	μίγνυμι
ἐμίσει	VIIA--3S	μισέω
ἐμίσησα	VIAA--1S	"
ἐμίσησαν	VIAA--3P	"
ἐμίσησας	VIAA--2S	"
ἐμίσησε	VIAA--3S	"
ἐμισθώσατο	VIAM--3S	μισθόω
ἐμίσουν	VIIA--3P	μισέω

ἐμμαίνομαι *be (furiously) enraged against, be (insanely) angry against* someone (AC 26.11)

ἐμμαινόμενος	VPPDNM-S	ἐμμαίνομαι
	VPPONM-S	"

Ἐμμανουήλ, ὁ indeclinable; *Emmanuel*, masculine proper noun applied to Jesus, interpreted as *God (is) with us* (MT 1.23)

Ἐμμαοῦς, ἡ (also Οὐλαμμαούς) indeclinable; *Emmaus*, a village in Judea near Jerusalem (LU 24.13)

ἐμμένει	VIPA--3S	ἐμμένω
ἐμμένειν	VNPA	"

ἐμμένω 1aor. ἐνέμεινα; literally, of a place *remain* or *stay in* (AC 28.30); figuratively, of keeping oneself to something *persevere in, persist in, continue firm in* (AC 14.22); of the terms of a covenant *abide by, carefully obey* (GA 3.10)

Ἐμμόρ	Ἐμμώρ
Ἐμμώρ	"

Ἐμμώρ, ὁ (also Ἐμμόρ, Ἑμμώρ, Ἐμόρ) indeclinable; *Hamor*, masculine proper noun (AC 7.16)

ἐμνημόνευον	VIIA--3P	μνημονεύω
ἐμνημόνευσαν	VIIA--3P	"
ἐμνημόνευσε(ν)	VIAA--3S	"
ἐμνήσθη	VIAP--3S	μιμνήσκω
ἐμνήσθημεν	VIAP--1P	"
ἐμνήσθην	VIAP--1S	"
ἐμνήσθησαν	VIAP--3P	"
ἐμνηστευμένη	VPRPDF-S	μνηστεύω
ἐμνηστευμένην	VPRPAF-S	"
ἐμοί	A--NM1P	ἐμός
	NPD-1S	ἐγώ
ἐμοῖς	A--DN1P	ἐμός
ἐμοίχευσε(ν)	VIAA--3S	μοιχεύω
ἐμόλυναν	VIAA--3P	μολύνω
ἐμολύνθησαν	VIAP--3P	"
ἐμόν	A--AM1S	ἐμός
	A--AN1S	"
	A--NN1S	"
Ἐμόρ	Ἐμμώρ

ἐμός, ή, όν (1) first-person possessive adjective *my* (MT 18.20); as adding emphasis *my own* (1C 16.21); (2) substantivally τὸ ἐμόν *my property, my money, what is mine* (MT 25.27)

ἐμός	A--NM1S	ἐμός
ἐμοσχοποίησαν	VIAA--3P	μοσχοποιέω
ἐμοῦ	A--GN1S	ἐμός
	NPG-1S	ἐγώ
ἐμούς	A--AM1P	ἐμός

ἐμπαιγμονή, ῆς, ἡ *mocking, ridicule, derision* (2P 3.3)

ἐμπαιγμονῇ	N-DF-S	ἐμπαιγμονή
ἐμπαιγμονῆς	N-GF-S	"

ἐμπαιγμός, οῦ, ὁ *mocking, scorn, derision* (HE 11.36)

ἐμπαιγμῶν	N-GM-P	ἐμπαιγμός
ἐμπαίζειν	VNPA	ἐμπαίζω
ἐμπαίζοντες	VPPANM-P	

ἐμπαίζω fut. ἐμπαίξω; 1aor. ἐνέπαιξα; 1aor. pass. ἐνεπαίχθην; 1fut. pass. ἐμπαιχθήσομαι; (1) as expressing verbal mockery and derision *ridicule, make fun of, mock someone* (MT 27.29); absolutely (MT 20.19); (2) as outwitting someone *make a fool of, trick, deceive* (MT 2.16)

ἐμπαῖκται	N-NM-P	ἐμπαίκτης

ἐμπαίκτης, ου, ὁ one who makes fun of another *mocker, scoffer, scorner*

ἐμπαῖξαι	VNAA	ἐμπαίζω
ἐμπαίξας	VPAANM-S	"
ἐμπαίξουσι(ν)	VIFA--3P	"
ἐμπαιχθήσεται	VIFP--3S	"

ἐμπέμπω 1aor. ἐνέπεμψα; *send* (LU 19.14)

ἐμπεπλησμένοι	VPRPVM-P	ἐμπίπλημι

ἐμπεριπατέω (and ἐνπεριπατέω) fut. ἐμπεριπατήσω; literally *walk about* in a place, *move among* the people in a place; figuratively, of God's presence among his people *live among, live with* (2C 6.16)

ἐμπεριπατήσω	VIFA--1S	ἐμπεριπατέω
ἐμπεσεῖν	VNAA	ἐμπίπτω
ἐμπεσεῖται	VIFD--3S	"
ἐμπέσῃ	VSAA--3S	

ἐμπεσόντος   VPAAGM-S   "

ἐμπεσοῦνται   VIFD--3P   "

ἐμπίπλημι (or **ἐμπίμπλημι**) or **ἐμπιπλάω**   1aor. ἐνέπλησα; pf. pass. ἐμπέπλησμαι; 1aor. pass. ἐνεπλήσθην; (1) active *satisfy, fill with* something (LU 1.53); (2) passive *be satisfied, have enough of* something (JN 6.12); figuratively *enjoy* something, *have one's fill of* (RO 15.24)

ἐμπιπλῶν   VPPANM-S   ἐμπίπλημι

ἐμπίπρασθαι   VNPP   ἐμπίπρημι

ἐμπίπρημι or **ἐμπίμπρημι**   1aor. ἐνέπρησα; (1) *burn, set on fire* (MT 22.7); as a sickness *burn with fever* (probably AC 28.6); (2) *become distended, swell up* (possibly AC 28.6)

ἐμπίπτουσι(ν)   VIPA--3P   ἐμπίπτω

ἐμπίπτω   fut. mid. ἐμπεσοῦμαι; 2aor. ἐνέπεσον; literally *fall into* something, e.g. as into a fire or a pit (MT 12.11); figuratively *experience suddenly, be beset by, encounter* as robbers (LU 10.36)

ἐμπλακέντες   VPAPNM-P   ἐμπλέκω

ἐμπλέκεται   VIPM--3S   "

    VIPP--3S   "

ἐμπλέκω   2aor. pass. ἐνεπλάκην; *entangle*; figuratively and passive in the NT *be involved in* (2T 2.4)

ἐμπλησθῶ   VSAP--1S   ἐμπίπλημι

ἐμπλοκή, ῆς, ἡ (also **ἐκπλοκή**)   *plaiting* or *interweaving*; of the hair *braiding*, using costly and extravagant ways of dressing the hair, probably including interwoven ornaments (1P 3.3)

ἐμπλοκῆς   N-GF-S   ἐμπλοκή

ἐμπνέω (and **ἐνπνέω**)   *breathe (on)*; figuratively and idiomatically ἐμπνεῖν ἀπειλῆς literally *breathe out threat*, i.e. *strongly threaten* (AC 9.1)

ἐμπνέων   VPPANM-S   ἐμπνέω

ἐμπορεύομαι   fut. ἐμπορεύσομαι; literally *travel for business, carry on business, trade* (JA 4.13); figuratively, of deceiving another for one's own advantage *exploit, cheat* (2P 2.3)

ἐμπορευσόμεθα   VIFD--1P   ἐμπορεύομαι

ἐμπορεύσονται   VIFD--3P   "

ἐμπορευσώμεθα   VSPD--1P   "

ἐμπορία, ας, ἡ   *business, trade* (MT 22.5)

ἐμπορίαν   N-AF-S   ἐμπορία

ἐμπόριον, ου, τό   a place set aside for trade and business *market, emporium*; with οἶκος *house of trade, marketplace* (JN 2.16)

ἐμπορίου   N-GN-S   ἐμπόριον

ἔμποροι   N-NM-P   ἔμπορος

ἔμπορος, ου, ὁ   strictly *passenger by sea, traveler*; hence *one who travels about for trading, merchant, wholesale dealer* in contrast to a retailer (MT 13.45)

ἐμπόρῳ   N-DM-S   ἔμπορος

ἔμπροσθεν   (1) adverb of place *in front, ahead* (LU 19.4), opposite ὄπισθεν (*behind, on the back*); of position *on the front* (surface) (RV 4.6); figuratively *what lies ahead* (PH 3.13); (2) improper preposition with the genitive; (a) of place *in front of, before* (MT 5.24); (b) of being face to face with someone *in the presence of, before* (MT 27.29); (c) as a legal technical term, of appearing before a judge or high official *before* (MT 27.11); (d) with a verb expressing or implying forward motion *ahead of, before* (MT 6.2; 11.10); (e) expressing supe-

rior rank or position *higher than, before* (JN 1.15); (f) expressing a relevant viewpoint *in the sight of, in the opinion of* (MT 11.26)

ἔμπροσθεν   AB   ἔμπροσθεν

    PG   "

ἐμπτύειν   VNPA   ἐμπτύω

ἐμπτύσαντες   VPAANM-P   "

ἐμπτυσθήσεται   VIFP--3S   "

ἐμπτύσουσι(ν)   VIFA--3P   "

ἐμπτύω   fut. ἐμπτύσω; 1aor. ἐνέπτυσα; 1fut. pass. ἐμπτυσθήσομαι; *spit on* or *at* (MT 26.67); passive *be spit on* (LU 18.32), to be understood as a gesture of extreme contempt

ἐμφανῆ   A--AM-S   ἐμφανής

ἐμφανής, ές   *visible, manifest* (AC 10.40); figuratively, of God's self-revelation inwardly communicated *clearly evident, well-known* (RO 10.20)

ἐμφανής   A--NM-S   ἐμφανής

ἐμφανίζειν   VNPA   ἐμφανίζω

ἐμφανίζουσι(ν)   VIPA--3P   "

ἐμφανίζω   fut. ἐμφανίσω; 1aor. ἐνεφάνισα; 1aor. pass. ἐνεφανίσθην; (1) literally *make visible, show, manifest* (JN 14.22); passive *become visible, appear* (MT 27.53); figuratively, of Jesus' self-revelation inwardly communicated *manifest, make known, reveal* (JN 14.21); (2) of a semiofficial report *inform, report, make known* (AC 23.22); (3) as a legal technical term *bring charges, formally accuse* (AC 24.1)

ἐμφανίσατε   VMAA--2P   ἐμφανίζω

ἐμφανισθῆναι   VNAP   "

ἐμφανίσω   VIFA--1S   "

ἔμφοβοι   A--NM-P   ἔμφοβος

ἔμφοβος, ον   *terrified, startled, afraid*

ἔμφοβος   A--NM-S   ἔμφοβος

ἐμφόβων   A--GF-P   "

ἐμφυσάω   1aor. ἐνεφύσησα; *breathe into* or *on* someone, as a symbolic and spiritually creative act conveying God's power or blessing (JN 20.22; cf. Genesis 2.7)

ἔμφυτον   A--AM-S   ἔμφυτος

ἔμφυτος, ον   *implanted, engrafted*; metaphorically, of the Word of God *place in, put within* (JA 1.21)

ἐμφωνέω   *call, express* (in certain terms) (LU 16.24)

ἐμῷ   A--DM1S   ἐμός

    A--DN1S   "

ἐμῶν   A--GN1P   "

ἐμώρανε(ν)   VIAA--3S   μωραίνω

ἐμωράνθησαν   VIAP--3P   "

ἐν   preposition with the dative; the primary idea is *within, in, withinness*, denoting static position or time, but the many and varied uses can be determined only by the context; the chief categories of usage are as follows: (1) of place; (a) denoting a position within boundaries *in, within* (JN 8.20); (b) denoting a specific location *on* (2C 3.3); (c) denoting nearness *at, near* (HE 1.3); (d) with a plural noun, denoting close relationship *among, within* (GA 1.16b); (e) with a name identifying where a quoted passage is found *in* (MK 1.2); (f) psychologically, describing processes, qualities, possessions within God or man *in* (MT 5.28); (g) denoting a single identity selected as a specimen or illustration *in the case of* (1C 4.2); (h) expressing an occasion or sphere of activity *at, in, on the grounds of* (AC 7.29a; RO 1.9b); (i) designating close personal relationship, especially with God, Christ, or the Spirit (GA 2.20a); (2) of time; (a) denoting a point of time for an event *in, on, at* (JN 6.44); (b) denoting a boundary of time *within, during* (MT 27.40); (c) denoting an activity that serves to time an event *in, while, during, when* (MK 15.7); (3) of cause; (a) denoting means or instrument *by, with* (HE 9.22); (b) denoting personal agency *by, with the help of, through* (MT 9.34); (c) denoting cause or reason *because of, on account of, by (reason of)* (JN 16.30); (d) denoting manner, especially in adverbial phrases: ἐν χαρᾷ *with joy, joyfully* (RO 15.32), ἐν σπουδῇ *zealously, eagerly* (RO 12.8), ἐν χάριτι *graciously* (GA 1.6), etc.

ἐν	PD	ἐν
ἕν	APCAN-S	εἰς
	APCNN-S	"
	A-CAN-S	"
	A-CNN-S	"
ἕνα	APCAM-S	"
	A-CAM-S	"
ἐνάγει	VIPA--3S	ἐνάγω

ἐναγκαλίζομαι 1aor. ἐνηγκαλισάμην; *take into one's arms, embrace*

ἐναγκαλισάμενος	VPADNM-S	ἐναγκαλίζομαι

ἐνάγω *lead into, lead onto, urge, persuade* (RO 2.4)

ἐνάλιος, ον *marine, living in* or *belonging to the sea;* neuter as a substantive τὸ ἐνάλιον *sea animal, creature of the sea* (JA 3.7)

ἐναλίων	AP-GN-P	ἐνάλιος

ἐνάλλομαι *leap on* (AC 19.16)

ἐναλλόμενος	VPPDNM-S	ἐνάλλομαι

ἐνανθρωπέω 1aor. ptc. ἐνανθρωπήσας; *take on human form* (1J 4.17)

ἐνανθρωπήσαντα	VPAAAM-S	ἐνανθρωπέω

ἔναντι an adverb used as an improper preposition with the genitive; literally, of place *in the presence of, over against, opposite* (LU 1.8); figuratively, of a relevant viewpoint *in the eyes of, in the sight of* (AC 7.10)

ἔναντι	PG	ἔναντι
ἐναντία	A--AN-P	ἐναντίος
ἐναντίας	A--GF-S	"

ἐναντίον neuter of ἐναντίος (*opposite*); (1) used as an improper preposition with the genitive; literally *before, in the presence of* (AC 8.32); figuratively, of a relevant viewpoint *in the eyes of, in the judgment of* (LU 1.6); (2) used as an adverb with the article τοὐναντίον *on the other hand, on the contrary, instead* (2C 2.7)

ἐναντίον	A--AN-S	ἐναντίος
	PG	ἐναντίον

ἐναντιόομαι *set oneself against, be hostile toward, oppose* (AC 13.45)

ἐναντίος, α, ον literally, of direction *opposite;* substantivally ἐξ ἐναντίας *opposite, over against* someone (MK 15.39); of the wind *contrary, blowing against* (MT 14.24); figuratively, of attitudes *hostile, contrary, opposed to* (1TH 2.15)

ἐναντίος	A--NM-S	ἐναντίος
ἐναντιούμενοι	VPPDNM-P	ἐναντιόομαι
ἐναντίους	A--AM-P	ἐναντίος
ἐναντίων	A--GM-P	"

ἐναργής, ές *clear, evident* (HE 4.12)

ἐναργής	A--NM-S	ἐναργής
ἐναρξάμενοι	VPADNM-P	ἐνάρχομαι
ἐναρξάμενος	VPADNM-S	"

ἐνάρχομαι 1aor. ἐνηρξάμην; *begin, commence, make a beginning*

ἐνάτη	A-ODF-S	ἔνατος
ἐνάτην	A-OAF-S	"
ἐνάτης	A-OGF-S	"

ἔνατος, η, ον (also **ἔννατος**) as an ordinal number *ninth* (MK 15.34); substantivally ἡ ἐνάτη *the ninth hour* (AC 10.30); ὁ ἔ. *the ninth one* (RV 21.20)

ἔνατος	A-ONM-S	ἔνατος
ἐναυάγησα	VIAA--1S	ναυαγέω
ἐναυάγησαν	VIAA--3P	"
ἐναφίετε	VIPA--2P	ἐναφίημι

ἐναφίημι *allow, permit* (MK 7.12)

ἐνβαπτάμενος	VPPMNM-S	ἐμβάπτω
ἐνβαπτιζόμενος	VPPMNM-S	ἐμβαπτίζω
ἐνβάψας	VPAANM-S	ἐμβάπτω
ἐνγεγραμμένη	VPRPNF-S	ἐγγράφω
ἐνγέγραπται	VIRP--3S	"
ἐνδεδυμένοι	VPRMNM-P	ἐνδύω
ἐνδεδυμένοις	VPRMDM-P	"
ἐνδεδυμένον	VPRMAM-S	"
ἐνδεδυμένος	VPRMNM-S	"
ἐνδεδύσθαι	VNRM	"

ἐνδεής, ές as lacking basic needs *poor, needy, impoverished;* substantivally *poverty-stricken person* (AC 4.34)

ἐνδεής	A--NM-S	ἐνδεής

ἔνδειγμα, ατος, τό *evidence, plain indication, proof* (2TH 1.5)

ἔνδειγμα	N-NN-S	ἔνδειγμα
ἐνδεικνύμενοι	VPPMNM-P	ἐνδείκνυμι
ἐνδεικνυμένους	VPPMAM-P	"

ἐνδείκνυμι 1aor. mid. ἐνεδειξάμην; only middle in the NT; (1) as giving outward proof *show, demonstrate* (HE 6.10); (2) as perpetrating something openly against someone *do to* (2T 4.14)

ἐνδείκνυνται	VIPM--3P	ἐνδείκνυμι
ἐνδείκνυσθαι	VNPM	"
ἐνδείξασθαι	VNAM	"
ἐνδείξασθε	VMAM--2P	"
ἐνδείξηται	VSAM--3S	"
ἔνδειξιν	N-AF-S	ἔνδειξις

ἔνδειξις, εως, ἡ (1) strictly *pointing out;* hence *sign, indication, proof* (PH 1.28); (2) as public information *demonstration, proof, showing forth* (RO 3.25)

ἔνδειξις	N-NF-S	ἔνδειξις
ἐνδείξωμαι	VSAM--1S	ἐνδείκνυμι

ἔνδεκα indeclinable; as a cardinal number *eleven*

ἐνδεκάτην	A-OAF-S	ἐνδέκατος

ἐνδέκατος, η, ον as an ordinal number *eleventh;* substantivally ἡ ἐνδεκάτη *the eleventh hour* (MT 20.6)

ἐνδέκατος	A-ONM-S	ἐνδέκατος
ἐνδέχεται	VIPD--3S	ἐνδέχομαι
	VIPO--3S	"

ἐνδέχομαι only impersonally in the NT ἐνδέχεται *it is possible;* impersonally with a negative οὐκ ἐνδέχεται *it is unthinkable, it cannot be* (LU 13.33) ἐνδημέω   1aor. ἐνεδήμησα; literally *stay at home, be in one's own land*; idiomatically ἐνδημεῖν ἐν τῷ σώματι literally *be at home in the body*, i.e. *be (physically) alive (on earth)* (2C 5.6); ἐνδημεῖν πρὸς τὸν κύριον literally *be at home in the presence of the Lord*, i.e. *be in heaven* (2C 5.8)

ἐνδημῆσαι	VNAA	ἐνδημέω
ἐνδημοῦντες	VPPANM-P	"
ἐνδιδύσκουσι(ν)	VIPA--3P	ἐνδιδύσκω

ἐνδιδύσκω   impf. mid. ἐνεδιδυσκόμην; *clothe, dress, put clothing on* someone (MK 15.17); middle *clothe oneself in, dress (oneself) in* (LU 16.19)

ἔνδικον	A--AF-S	ἔνδικος
	A--NN-S	

ἔνδικος, ον   strictly *based on what is right*; hence *fair, just, deserved*

ἐνδόμησις	N-NF-S	ἐνδώμησις

ἐνδοξάζομαι   1aor. ἐνεδοξάσθην; as being the object of honor and praise, *be shown as wonderful, be honored*

ἐνδοξασθῇ	VSAO--3S	ἐνδοξάζομαι
ἐνδοξασθῆναι	VNAO	"
ἔνδοξοι	A--NM-P	ἔνδοξος
ἐνδόξοις	A--DN-P	"
ἔνδοξον	A--AF-S	"

ἔνδοξος, ον   (1) of human distinction *honored, esteemed* (1C 4.10); comparative ἐνδοξότερος, τέρα, ον *more honorable*; substantivally *more honorable person* (MT 20.28); (2) of clothing *splendid, fine* (LU 7.25); (3) of spiritual excellence *glorious, splendid, wonderful* (EP 5.27); substantivally ἔνδοξα *wonderful things, splendid deeds* (LU 13.17)

ἐνδοξότερος	A-MNM-S	ἔνδοξος
ἐνδόξῳ	A--DM-S	"

ἔνδυμα, ατος, τό   literally *clothing, garment*, especially *outer garment, cloak* (MT 3.4); as a wedding garment *robe* (MT 22.11); idiomatically ἔρχεσθαι ἐν ἐνδύμασιν προβάτων literally *wear sheep's clothing*, i.e. *only pretend to be harmless*, of the ways of a false teacher, disguising destructive intentions (MT 7.15)

ἔνδυμα	N-AN-S	ἔνδυμα
	N-NN-S	"
ἐνδύμασι(ν)	N-DN-P	"
ἐνδύματος	N-GN-S	"
ἐνδυναμοῦ	VMPP--2S	ἐνδυναμόω
ἐνδυναμοῦντι	VPPADM-S	"
ἐνδυναμοῦσθε	VMPP--2P	"

ἐνδυναμόω   1aor. ἐνεδυνάμωσα; 1aor. pass. ἐνεδυναμώθην; (1) of spiritual and moral strengthening *enable, empower, make strong* (1T 1.12); (2) passive *become strong, become able* (AC 9.22); usually of religious and moral strength *grow strong* (RO 4.20)

ἐνδυναμώσαντι	VPAADM-S	ἐνδυναμόω
ἐνδυνόντες	VPPANM-S	ἐνδύνω

ἐνδύνω   *slip in, enter secretly, worm one's way in* (2T 3.6)

ἐνδύουσι(ν)	VIPA--3P	ἐνδύω
ἐνδυσάμενοι	VPAMNM-P	"
ἐνδυσάμενος	VPAMNM-S	"
ἐνδύσαντες	VPAANM-P	"
ἐνδύσασθαι	VNAM	"
ἐνδύσασθε	VMAM--2P	"
ἐνδύσατε	VMAA--2P	"

ἐνδύσεσθαι	VNFM	"
ἐνδύσεως	N-GF-S	ἔνδυσις
ἐνδύσησθε	VSAM--2P	ἐνδύω
ἐνδύσηται	VSAM--3S	"

ἔνδυσις, εως, ἡ   as an action *dressing up, putting on* or *wearing* clothes (1P 3.3)

ἐνδυσώμεθα	VSAM--1P	ἐνδύω

ἐνδύω   fut. ἐνδύσω; 1aor. ἐνέδυσα, mid. ἐνεδυσάμην; pf. pass. ἐνδέδυμαι; (1) literally; (a) active *dress, clothe* someone (LU 15.22); (b) middle *clothe oneself with, draw on, put on* something (LU 8.27); (2) figuratively, of taking on or being invested with spiritual gifts or qualities *receive* (LU 24.49)

ἐνδώμησις, εως, ἡ   (also ἐνδόμησις)   strictly *thing built in, interior structure*; the meaning in RV 21.18 is uncertain, perhaps *what is added on*, i.e. the coping or top layer of a structured wall; other suggestions include *building material* or *foundation*

ἐνδώμησις	N-NF-S	ἐνδώμησις
ἐνέβη	VIAA--3S	ἐμβαίνω
ἐνέβημεν	VIAA--1P	"
ἐνέβησαν	VIAA--3P	"
ἐνεβίβασε(ν)	VIAA--3S	ἐμβιβάζω
ἐνέβλεπε(ν)	VIIA--3S	ἐμβλέπω
ἐνέβλεπον	VIIA--1S	"
ἐνέβλεψα	VIAA--1S	"
ἐνέβλεψε(ν)	VIAA--3S	"
ἐνεβριμήθη	VIAO--3S	ἐμβριμάομαι
ἐνεβριμήσατο	VIAD--3S	"
ἐνεβριμοῦντο	VIID--3P	"
	VIIO--3P	"
ἐνεβριμῶντο	VIID--3P	"
	VIIO--3P	"
ἐνέγκαι	VNAA	φέρω
ἐνέγκαντες	VPAANM-P	"
ἐνέγκας	VPAANM-S	"
ἐνέγκατε	VMAA--2P	"
ἔνεγκε	VMAA--2S	"
ἐνεγκεῖ	VNAA	see ἐνεγκεῖν
ἐνεγκεῖν	VNAA	φέρω
ἐνεδείξασθε	VIAM--2P	ἐνδείκνυμι
ἐνεδείξατο	VIAM--3S	"
ἐνεδιδύσκετο	VIIM--3S	ἐνδιδύσκω

ἐνέδρα, ας, ἡ   (also ἔνεδρον, ου, τό)   strictly *sitting in* or *on a spot*; hence *plot, ambush, lying in wait*

ἐνέδραν	N-AF-S	ἐνέδρα
ἐνεδρεύοντες	VPPANM-P	ἐνεδρεύω
ἐνεδρεύουσι(ν)	VIPA--3P	"

ἐνεδρεύω   literally *lie in wait* or *in ambush for* (AC 23.21); figuratively *make plans against, plot against* (LU 11.54)

ἔνεδρον	N-AN-S	ἐνέδρα
ἐνεδυναμοῦτο	VIIP--3S	ἐνδυναμόω
ἐνεδυναμώθη	VIAP--3S	"
ἐνεδυναμώθησαν	VIAP--3P	"
ἐνεδυνάμωσε(ν)	VIAA--3S	"
ἐνέδυσαν	VIAA--3P	ἐνδύω
ἐνεδύσασθε	VIAM--2P	"
ἐνεδύσατο	VIAM--3S	"

ἐνειλέω   1aor. ἐνείλησα; *wrap up* or *confine in* something; of a shroud for burial *wrap in* (MK 15.46)

ἐνείλησε(ν)	VIAA--3S	ἐνειλέω

ἔνειμι   ptc. ἐνών; *be in* or *within*; τὰ ἐνόντα *the things on the inside*; *what is within* (LU 11.41)

ἐνεῖχε(ν)	VIIA--3S	ἐνέχω

ἕνεκα, ἕνεκεν, and εἵνεκεν   improper preposition with the genitive, expressing reason or purpose *on account of, for the sake of, because of, by reason of*

ἕνεκα	PG	ἕνεκα
ἐνεκαίνισε(ν)	VIAA--3S	ἐγκαινίζω
ἐνεκάλουν	VIIA--3P	ἐγκαλέω
ἕνεκεν	PG	ἕνεκα
ἐνεκεντρίσθης	VIAP--2S	ἐγκεντρίζω
ἐνεκοπτόμην	VIIP--1S	ἐγκόπτω
ἐνέκοψε(ν)	VIAA--3S	"
ἐνέκρυψε(ν)	VIAA--3S	ἐγκρύπτω
ἐνελογεῖται	VIPP--3S	ἐλλογέω
ἐνελογεῖτο	VIIP--3S	"
ἐνέμειναν	VIAA--3P	ἐμμένω
ἐνέμεινε(ν)	VIAA--3S	"
ἐνένευον	VIIA--3P	ἐννεύω

ἐνενήκοντα   indeclinable; as a cardinal number *ninety* (LU 15.7)

ἐνεοί	A--NM-P	ἐνεός

ἐνεός, ά, όν (also ἐννεός)   of a result of being frightened or amazed *speechless, astounded, unable to say anything* (AC 9.7)

ἐνέπαιζον	VIIA--3P	ἐμπαίζω
ἐνέπαιξαν	VIAA--3P	"
ἐνεπαίχθη	VIAP--3S	"
ἐνέπεμψα	VIAA--1S	ἐμπέμπω
ἐνέπεμψαν	VIAA--3P	"
ἐνέπλησε(ν)	VIAA--3S	ἐμπίπλημι
ἐνεπλήσθησαν	VIAP--3P	"
ἐνέπρησε(ν)	VIAA--3S	ἐμπίπρημι
ἐνέπτυον	VIIA--3P	ἐμπτύω
ἐνέπτυσαν	VIAA--3P	"
ἐνεργεῖ	VIPA--3S	ἐνεργέω

ἐνέργεια, ας, ἡ   *function, activity*; in the NT used of supernatural activity *energy, operation, working*

ἐνέργεια	N-NF-S	ἐνέργεια
ἐνέργειαν	N-AF-S	"
ἐνεργείας	N-GF-S	"
ἐνεργεῖν	VNPA	ἐνεργέω
ἐνεργεῖται	VIPM--3S	"

ἐνεργέω   1aor. ἐνήργησα; pf. ἐνήργηκα; (1) intransitively; (a) active *be at work, be active, work* (EP 2.2); (b) middle, with an impersonal subject *be at work in, be active in* (2C 4.12); (2) transitively *produce, effect, (set at) work* (GA 3.5)

ἐνέργημα, ατος, τό   *what has been done*; in the NT, what has been effected by divine energy *work, operation, activity* (1C 12.6); ἐνεργήματα δυνάμεων *power for working miracles* (1C 12.10)

ἐνεργήματα	N-NN-P	ἐνέργημα
ἐνεργημάτων	N-GN-P	"

ἐνεργής, ές   *effective, able to cause* something *to happen, powerful*

ἐνεργής	A--NF-S	ἐνεργής
	A--NM-S	"
ἐνεργήσας	VPAANM-S	ἐνεργέω
ἐνεργουμένη	VPPMNF-S	"
ἐνεργουμένην	VPPMAF-S	"

ἐνεργουμένης	VPPMGF-S	"
ἐνεργοῦντος	VPPAGM-S	"
	VPPAGN-S	"
ἐνεργοῦσι(ν)	VIPA--3P	"
ἐνεργῶν	VPPANM-S	"
ἐνέστηκε(ν)	VIRA--3S	ἐνίστημι
ἐνεστηκότα	VPRAAM-S	"
ἐνεστῶσαν	VPRAAF-S	"
ἐνεστῶτα	VPRANN-P	"
ἐνεστῶτος	VPRAGM-S	"
ἐνετειλάμην	VIAD--1S	ἐντέλλομαι
ἐνετείλατο	VIAD--3S	"
ἐνετρεπόμεθα	VIIP--1P	ἐντρέπω
ἐνετύλιξε(ν)	VIAA--3S	ἐντυλίσσω
ἐνέτυχε(ν)	VIAA--3S	ἐντυγχάνω
ἐνέτυχον	VIAA--3P	"

ἐνευλογέω   1fut. pass. ἐνευλογηθήσομαι; as a benefiting that includes all races and peoples *act kindly toward, bless by means of* or *through* someone; used of Abraham in quotation from Genesis 22.18 (AC 3.25)

ἐνευλογηθήσονται	VIFP--3P	ἐνευλογέω
ἔνευσε(ν)	VIAA--3S	νεύω
ἐνεφάνισαν	VIAA--3P	ἐμφανίζω
ἐνεφάνισας	VIAA--2S	"
ἐνεφανίσθησαν	VIAP--3P	"
ἐνεφύσησε(ν)	VIAA--3S	ἐμφυσάω
ἐνέχειν	VNPA	ἐνέχω
ἐνέχεσθε	VMPP--2P	"
ἐνεχθεῖσαν	VPAPAF-S	φέρω
ἐνεχθείσης	VPAPGF-S	"
ἐνεχθῆναι	VNAP	"

ἐνέχω   impf. ἐνεῖχον; strictly *hold fast to, hold within*; (1) active, of having hostile feelings *hold a grudge against, feel resentful toward*, colloquially *have it in for* (MK 6.19); absolutely δεινῶς ἐνέχειν *be very hostile to, harass violently, press on fiercely* (LU 11.53); (2) passive with the dative *let oneself be entangled in, be subject to, be under the control of* (GA 5.1)

ἐνηργεῖτο	VIIM--3S	ἐνεργέω
ἐνήργηκε(ν)	VIRA--3S	"
ἐνήργησε(ν)	VIAA--3S	"
ἐνήρξασθε	VIAD--2P	ἐνάρχομαι
ἐνήρξατο	VIAD--3S	"

ἐνθάδε   adverb of place; (1) *here, to this place* (JN 4.15); (2) *here, in this place* (LU 24.41)

ἐνθάδε	AB	ἐνθάδε

ἔνθεν   adverb of place *from here, from this place*

ἔνθεν	AB	ἔνθεν
ἐνθυμεῖσθε	VIPD--2P	ἐνθυμέομαι
	VIPO--2P	"

ἐνθυμέομαι   1aor. ἐνεθυμήθην; of inner reflection *consider, ponder on, think about*

ἐνθυμηθέντος	VPAOGM-S	ἐνθυμέομαι
ἐνθυμήσεις	N-AF-P	ἐνθύμησις
ἐνθυμήσεων	N-GF-P	"
ἐνθυμήσεως	N-GF-S	"

ἐνθύμησις, εως, ἡ   what one is thinking about or pondering on *reflection, consideration, thought*

ἐνθυμουμένου	VPPPGM-S	ἐνθυμέομαι

ἔνι   for ἔνεστι(ν); *there exists*; only impersonally and negatively in the NT οὐκ ἔ. *there is not* or *no*

ἔνι VIPA--3S ἔνι
ἑνί APCDM-S εἷς
 APCDN-S "
 A-CDM-S "
 A-CDN-S "
ἑνιαυτόν N-AM-S ἑνιαυτός
ἐνιαυτός, οῦ, ὁ (1) *year* (JN 11.49); κατ᾽ ἐνιαυτόν *every year, annually* (HE 9.25); (2) a cycle of seasons or years, perhaps sabbatical years (GA 4.10); (3) as an extended period *time, age, era* (LU 4.19)
ἑνιαυτοῦ N-GM-S ἑνιαυτός
ἑνιαυτούς N-AM-P "
ἑνίκησα VIAA--1S νικάω
ἑνίκησαν VIAA--3P "
ἑνίκησε(ν) VIAA--3S "
ἑνίοτε adverb; *sometimes* (MT 17.15)
ἑνίοτε AB ἑνίοτε
ἑνίστημι fut. mid. ἐνστήσομαι; 2aor. ἐνέστην; pf. ἐνέστηκα, ptc. ἐνεστηκώς and ἐνεστώς; intransitively and in a temporal sense in the NT; (1) in past tenses *have come, be present, be here* (2TH 2.2); perfect participle as an adjective *present* (GA 1.4); (2) with a connotation of warning or threat *be imminent, impend, be at hand* (1C 7.26)
ἑνισχύθη VIAP--3S ἐνισχύω
ἐνίσχυσε(ν) VIAA--3S "
ἐνισχύω 1aor. ἐνίσχυσα; 1aor. pass. ἐνισχύθην; (1) transitively *strengthen, impart strength* (LU 22.43); (2) intransitively *grow strong, regain strength* (AC 9.19)
ἐνισχύων VPPANM-S ἐνισχύω
ἔνιψα VIAA--1S νίπτω
ἐνιψάμην VIAM--1S "
ἐνίψατο VIAM--3S "
ἔνιψε(ν) VIAA--3S "
ἐγκαθέτους AP-AM-P ἐγκάθετος
ἐγκαίνια N-NN-P ἐγκαίνια
ἐγκακεῖν VNPA ἐγκακέω
ἐγκακήσητε VSAA--2P "
ἐγκακήσωμεν VSAA--1P "
ἐγκακοῦμεν VIPA--1P "
ἐγκακῶμεν VSPA--1P "
ἐγκαταλείψεις VIFA--2S ἐγκαταλείπω
ἐγκατελείφθη VIAP--3S "
ἐγκατέλιπε(ν) VIAA--3S "
ἐγκατοικῶν VPPANM-S ἐγκατοικέω
ἐγκαυχᾶσθαι VNPD ἐγκαυχάομαι
 VNPO "
ἐγκεκαίνισται VIRP--3S ἐγκαινίζω
ἐγκεντρίσαι VNAA ἐγκεντρίζω
ἐγκεντρισθήσονται VIFP--3P "
ἐγκεντρισθῶ VSAP--1S "
ἐγκοπήν N-AF-S ἐγκοπή
ἐγκόπτεσθαι VNPP ἐγκόπτω
ἐγκόπτω VSPA--1S "
ἐγκρῖναι VNAA ἐγκρίνω
ἐγκύφ A--DF-S ἔγκυος
ἐννάτῃ A-ODF-S ἔνατος
ἐννάτην A-OAF-S "
ἐννάτης A-OGF-S "
ἔννατος A-ONM-S "
ἐννέα indeclinable; as a cardinal number *nine*

ἐννενηκονταεννέα indeclinable; as a cardinal number *ninety-nine* (MT 18.12)
ἐννεοί A--NM-P ἐνεός
ἐννεύω impf. ἐνένευον; *nod at, make signs* by a nod of the head; by a hand gesture *motion to* someone, *beckon* (LU 1.62)
ἔννοια, ας, ἡ the mental conception that follows consideration or deliberation *way of thinking, insight, idea* (1P 4.1); in relation to behavior *intent, resolution* (HE 4.12)
ἔννοιαν N-AF-S ἔννοια
ἐννοιῶν N-GF-P "
ἔννομος, ον strictly *within law*; hence *lawful, legal, according to law* (AC 19.39); as a personal characteristic *committed to law, obedient to law* (1C 9.21)
ἔννομος A--NM-S ἔννομος
ἐννόμῳ A--DF-S "
ἐννόμως adverb; in relation to obligation to obey a system of law *while subject to law, when controlled by law* (RO 2.12)
ἐννόμως AB ἐννόμως
ἔννυχα AB ἔννυχος
ἔννυχον AB "
ἔννυχος, ον *at night*; accusative neuter plural as an adverb *by night, in the night*; πρωΐ ἔννυχα λίαν *early in the morning while it was still quite dark* (MK 1.35)
ἐνοήσαμεν VIAA--1P νοέω
ἐνόησαν VIAA--3P "
ἐνοικείτω VMPA--3S ἐνοικέω
ἐνοικέω fut. ἐνοικήσω; 1aor. ἐνῴκησα; *dwell in, live in*; in the NT used of spiritual indwelling *indwell, live in* (RO 8.11); *dwell among* (2C 6.16); personification of sin *live in* (RO 7.17)
ἐνοικήσω VIFA--1S ἐνοικέω
ἐνοικοδομεῖσθε VIPP--2P ἐνοικοδομέω
ἐνοικοδομέω *build in*; *build together* (1P 2.5)
ἐνοικοῦν VPPAAN-S ἐνοικέω
ἐνοικοῦντας VPPAAM-P "
ἐνοικοῦντος VPPAGN-S "
ἐνοικοῦσα VPPANF-S "
ἐνοικοῦσαν VPPAAF-S "
ἐνομίζαμεν VIIA--1P see ἐνομίζομεν
ἐνόμιζε(ν) VIIA--3S νομίζω
ἐνομίζετο VIIP--3S "
ἐνομίζομεν VIIA--1P "
ἐνόμιζον VIIA--3P "
ἐνομίζοντο VIIP--3P "
ἐνομίσαμεν VIAA--1P "
ἐνόμισαν VIAA--3P "
ἐνόμισας VIAA--2S "
ἐνόντα VPPAAN-P ἔνειμι
ἐνορκίζω (1) of an oath *cause to swear, put under oath*; (2) *appeal to earnestly, adjure* (1TH 5.27)
ἐνορκίζω VIPA--1S ἐνορκίζω
ἑνός APCGM-S εἷς
 APCGN-S "
 A-CGM-S "
 A-CGN-S "
ἐνοσφίσατο VIAM--3S νοσφίζω
ἑνότης, ητος, ἡ as a state *oneness, unity, unison*
ἑνότητα N-AF-S ἑνότης

151

ἑνότητος   N-GF-S   "

ἐνοχλέω   (1) *trouble, annoy*; (2) absolutely *cause trouble* (HE 12.15); passive *be afflicted, suffer* (LU 6.18)

ἐνοχλῇ   VSPA--3S   ἐνοχλέω

ἐνοχλούμενοι   VPPPNM-P   "

ἔνοχοι   A--NM-P   ἔνοχος

ἔνοχον   A--AM-S   "

ἔνοχος, ον   literally *held fast in, caught in*; (1) of spiritual bondage *subject to, held in, under the control of* (HE 2.15); (2) as a legal technical term, with the genitive denoting the guilt or punishment *guilty of* (MK 3.29); *liable to, answerable to* (MT 5.22a, b); *deserving of* (MT 5.22c; 26.66); (3) with the genitive denoting what one has transgressed against *guilty of doing wrong against* (1C 11.27); of law *guilty of violating* or *disobeying* (JA 2.10)

ἔνοχος   A--NM-S   ἔνοχος

ἐνπεριπατήσω   VIFA--1S   ἐμπεριπατέω

ἐνπνέων   VPPANM-S   ἐμπνέω

ἐνστήσονται   VIFM--3P   ἐνίστημι

ἔνταλμα, ατος, τό   what has been ordered *commandment, precept, ordinance*

ἐντάλμασι(ν)   N-DN-P   ἔνταλμα

ἐντάλματα   N-AN-P   "

ἐνταφιάζειν   VNPA   ἐνταφιάζω

ἐνταφιάζω   1aor. ἐνεταφίασα; *prepare for burial, bury*

ἐνταφιάσαι   VNAA   ἐνταφιάζω

ἐνταφιασμόν   N-AM-S   ἐνταφιασμός

ἐνταφιασμός, οῦ, ὁ   *preparation for burial, burial, entombment* (MK 14.8)

ἐνταφιασμοῦ   N-GM-S   ἐνταφιασμός

ἐντειλάμενος   VPADNM-S   ἐντέλλομαι

ἐντελεῖται   VIFD--3S   "

ἐντέλλεται   VIPD--3S   "

     VIPO--3S   "

ἐντέλλομαι   1aor. ἐνετειλάμην; pf. act. ἐντέταλκα (AC 13.47); pf. pass. ἐντέταλμαι; (1) *give orders to, command, enjoin* (MT 17.9); (2) *commission, direct* (MK 13.34); (3) of a covenant *ordain, make* (HE 9.20)

ἐντέλλομαι   VIPD--1S   ἐντέλλομαι

     VIPO--1S   "

ἐντέταλκε(ν)   VIRA--3S   "

ἐντέταλται   VIRD--3S   "

     VIRO--3S   "

ἐντετυλιγμένον   VPRPAN-S   ἐντυλίσσω

ἐντετυπωμένη   VPRPNF-S   ἐντυπόω

ἐντεῦθεν   adverb; (1) of place *from here, from this place* (JN 7.3); ἐ. καὶ ἐ. strictly *from here and from there*; hence *(one) on each side* (JN 19.18); (2) of source or reason *from this (cause)* (JA 4.1)

ἐντεῦθεν   AB   ἐντεῦθεν

ἐντεύξεις   N-AF-P   ἔντευξις

ἐντεύξεως   N-GF-S   "

ἔντευξις, εως, ἡ   from ἐντυγχάνω (*meet, encounter*); strictly *meeting with*; hence *conversation*; as a form of prayer *intercession* (1T 2.1); *prayer of thanksgiving* (1T 4.5)

ἐντιθείς   VPPANM-S   ἐντίθημι

ἐντίθημι   ptc. ἐντιθείς; *put in, implant*; figuratively *instill, let know about, impart* (AC 18.4)

ἔντιμον   A--AM-S   ἔντιμος

ἔντιμος, ον   (1) *honored, respected, esteemed* (PH 2.29); (2) of rank *distinguished*; comparative ἐντιμότερος, τέρα, ον *more distinguished, surpassing in honor*; substantively *more honorable person* (LU 14.8); (3) as a measure of value *highly prized, valuable* (LU 7.2)

ἔντιμος   A--NM-S   ἔντιμος

ἐντιμότερος   A-MNM-S   "

ἐντίμους   A--AM-P   "

ἐντολαί   N-NF-P   ἐντολή

ἐντολαῖς   N-DF-P   "

ἐντολάς   N-AF-P   "

ἐντολή, ῆς, ἡ   (1) of the Old Testament law *commandment, precept, ordinance* (LU 23.56); (2) of official commands *edict, decree, order* (JN 11.57); (3) of authoritative but not official directions *order, command* (LU 15.29)

ἐντολή   N-NF-S   ἐντολή

ἐντολήν   N-AF-S   "

ἐντολῆς   N-GF-S   "

ἐντολῶν   N-GF-P   "

ἐντόπιοι   AP-NM-P   ἐντόπιος

ἐντόπιος, ία, ον   strictly *in* or *of a place*; hence *local*; substantively οἱ ἐντόπιοι *local residents, people living in a place* (AC 21.12)

ἐντός   adverb of place *within, inside*; in the NT only as an improper preposition with the genitive *inside, within* (MT 23.26; probably LU 17.21); *among (you), in (your) midst* (perhaps LU 17.21)

ἐντός   AB   ἐντός

     PG   "

ἐντραπῇ   VSAP--3S   ἐντρέπω

ἐντραπήσονται   VIFP--3P   "

ἐντρέπομαι   VIPP--1S   "

ἐντρεπόμενος   VPPPNM-S   "

ἐντρέπω   2aor. pass. ἐνετράπην; 2fut. pass. ἐντραπήσομαι; strictly *turn back* or *about*; (1) active *put to shame, make ashamed, reprove* (1C 4.14); (2) passive *be put to shame, be ashamed* (TI 2.8); (3) passive with the middle sense; strictly *turn oneself toward* someone; hence *respect, reverence, have regard for* (MT 21.37)

ἐντρέπων   VPPANM-S   ἐντρέπω

ἐντρεφόμενος   VPPPNM-S   ἐντρέφω

ἐντρέφω   as the process of educating and training from childhood *bring up, rear, nourish* (1T 4.6)

ἔντρομος, ον   (also ἔκτρομος)   as caused by extreme fear *trembling* (HE 12.21)

ἔντρομος   A--NF-S   ἔντρομος

     A--NM-S   "

ἐντροπή, ῆς, ἡ   as caused by a sense of failure *shame, humiliation, reproach*

ἐντροπήν   N-AF-S   ἐντροπή

ἐντρυφάω   as wrongfully enjoying something, as a sport *revel in, carouse in, openly indulge in* (2P 2.13)

ἐντρυφῶντες   VPPANM-P   ἐντρυφάω

ἐντυγχάνει   VIPA--3S   ἐντυγχάνω

ἐντυγχάνειν   VNPA   "

ἐντυγχάνω   2aor. ἐνέτυχον; (1) *meet up with, encounter*; (2) of approaching someone with a petition *turn to, appeal to*; in a negative sense *complain to, make a complaint against* (AC 25.24); (3) with ὑπέρ as directing a petition toward God for someone *intercede for, pray for*

(RO 8.27); with κατά as a petition made against someone *intercede against* (RO 11.2)

ἐντυλίσσω 1aor. ἐνετύλιξα; pf. pass. ἐντετύλιγμαι; (1) of burial preparation *wrap (up)* (MT 27.59); (2) of a cloth *roll* or *fold up* (JN 20.7)

ἐντυπόω pf. pass. ptc. ἐντετυπωμένος; *engrave, carve, impress (on)* (2C 3.7)

ἐνυβρίζω 1aor. ἐνύβρισα; *insult, outrage, treat despitefully* (HE 10.29)

ἐνυβρίσας	VPAANM-S	ἐνυβρίζω
ἔνυξε(ν)	VIAA--3S	νύσσω
ἐνύπνια	N-AN-P	ἐνύπνιον

ἐνυπνιάζομαι fut. ἐνυπνιασθήσομαι; (1) of receiving an impression of seeing something during sleep *dream, envisage during sleep*; as seeing through supernatural impression (AC 2.17); (2) as promoting deluding teachings through false dreams *fantasize, dream (up)* (JU 8)

ἐνυπνιαζόμενοι	VPPDNM-P	ἐνυπνιάζομαι
	VPPONM-P	"
ἐνυπνιασθήσονται	VIFO--3P	"
ἐνυπνίοις	N-DN-P	ἐνύπνιον

ἐνύπνιον, ου, τό what is communicated during sleep *dream, vision, dream revelation* (AC 2.17)

ἐνύσταξαν	VIAA--3P	νυστάζω
ἐνφωνήσας	VPAANM-S	ἐμφωνέω
ἐνῴκησε(ν)	VIAA--3S	ἐνοικέω

ἐνώπιον neuter of ἐνώπιος (*in sight* or *in front*); used as an improper preposition with the genitive; (1) of place *before, in front of* (RV 4.10); (2) of doing something in someone's presence *in the presence of, in the sight of, before* (JN 20.30); (3) metaphorically *in the sight of, in the eyes of* (GA 1.20); (4) as acknowledging the opinion or judgment of another *in the opinion of, in the eyes of* (AC 4.19); (5) special uses; (a) with ἁμαρτάνω *sin* or *do wrong against* (LU 15.18); (b) *by the authority of, on behalf of* (RV 13.12, 14; 19.20)

ἐνώπιον	PG	ἐνώπιον

Ἐνώς, ὁ indeclinable; *Enos*, masculine proper noun (LU 3.38)

ἐνωτίζομαι 1aor. ἐνωτισάμην; from ἐν (*in*) and ὠτίον (*ear*); *listen carefully to, pay attention to* (AC 2.14)

ἐνωτίζω 1aor. ἐνώτισα; from ἐν (*in*) and ὠτίον (*ear*); *cause (another) to hear, make (someone) pay attention* (AC 2.14)

ἐνωτίσασθε	VMAD--2P	ἐνωτίζομαι
ἐνωτίσατε	VMAA--2P	ἐνωτίζω
Ἐνώχ		Ἐνώχ

Ἐνώχ, ὁ (also Ἑνώχ) indeclinable; *Enoch*, masculine proper noun

ἐξ	PG	ἐκ

ἕξ indeclinable; as a cardinal number *six*

ἐξαγαγεῖν	VNAA	ἐξάγω
ἐξαγαγέτωσαν	VMAA--3P	"
ἐξαγαγόντες	VPAANM-P	"
ἐξαγαγών	VPAANM-S	"
ἐξαγγείλητε	VSAA--2P	ἐξαγγέλλω

ἐξαγγέλλω 1aor. ἐξήγγειλα; *report widely, proclaim throughout, tell everywhere*

ἐξάγει	VIPA--3S	ἐξάγω
ἐξαγοραζόμενοι	VPPMNM-P	ἐξαγοράζω

ἐξαγοράζω 1aor. ἐξηγόρασα; (1) active *buy back, buy up*; figuratively, of Jesus' liberating atonement *deliver, redeem* (GA 3.13); (2) middle, of making the most of an opportunity *make the best use of, take advantage of* (EP 5.16)

ἐξαγοράσῃ	VSAA--3S	ἐξαγοράζω
ἐξάγουσι(ν)	VIPA--3P	ἐξάγω

ἐξάγω 2aor. ἐξήγαγον; *lead out, bring out* from a place

ἐξαίρετε	VMPA--2P	ἐξαίρω

ἐξαιρέω 2aor. ἐξεῖλον, mid. ἐξειλάμην; (1) active *take out, tear out, remove* (MT 5.29); (2) middle *deliver, rescue, set free* (AC 12.11; probably 26.17); *choose out* (perhaps AC 26.17)

ἐξαιρούμενος	VPPMNM-S	ἐξαιρέω

ἐξαίρω 1aor. ἐξῆρα; *exclude, expel, drive out* (1C 5.13)

ἐξαιτέω 1aor. mid. ἐξῃτησάμην; only middle in the NT *ask for, demand*; in LU 22.31 the aorist tense allows one to infer that the request has been granted

ἐξαίφνης adverb; *suddenly, unexpectedly*

ἐξαίφνης	AB	ἐξαίφνης

ἐξακολουθέω fut. ἐξακολουθήσω; 1aor. ἐξηκολούθησα; *follow*; figuratively in the NT; (1) of a kind of teaching *obey, follow* (2P 1.16); (2) of a way of life *closely imitate, follow after, comply with* (2P 2.2)

ἐξακολουθήσαντες	VPAANM-P	ἐξακολουθέω
ἐξακολουθήσουσι(ν)	VIFA--3P	"
ἐξακόσια	APCNN-P	ἐξακόσιοι
ἐξακόσιαι	APCNF-P	"

ἐξακόσιοι, αι, α as a cardinal number *six hundred*; substantivally (RV 13.18)

ἐξακόσιοι	APCNM-P	ἐξακόσιοι
ἐξακοσίων	A-CGM-P	"
ἐξαλειφθῆναι	VNAP	ἐξαλείφω

ἐξαλείφω fut. ἐξαλείψω; 1aor. ἐξήλειψα; 1aor. pass. ἐξηλείφθην; (1) of tears *wipe away* (RV 7.17); (2) of a written record *do away with, erase* (RV 3.5); of a record of misdeeds *remove, eliminate* (AC 3.19)

ἐξαλείψας	VPAANM-S	ἐξαλείφω
ἐξαλείψει	VIFA--3S	"
ἐξαλείψω	VIFA--1S	"

ἐξάλλομαι *leap* or *jump up, spring up* (AC 3.8)

ἐξαλλόμενος	VPPDNM-S	ἐξάλλομαι
	VPPONM-S	"
ἐξανάστασιν	N-AF-S	ἐξανάστασις

ἐξανάστασις, εως, ἡ strictly *arising up*; hence *resurrection from* the dead, *becoming alive again* (PH 3.11)

ἐξαναστατώσας	VPAANM-S	ἐξανίστημι
ἐξαναστήσῃ	VSAA--3S	"

ἐξανατέλλω 1aor. ἐξανέτειλα; intransitively, of a fast-growing plant *spring up, sprout up*

ἐξανέστησαν	VIAA--3P	ἐξανίστημι
ἐξανέτειλε(ν)	VIAA--3S	ἐξανατέλλω

ἐξανίστημι 1aor. ἐξανέστησα; 2aor. ἐξανέστην; (1) transitively, as a Hebraism for fathering offspring *become the father* (MK 12.19); (2) intransitively *rise up, stand forth* (AC 15.5)

ἐξανοίγω 1aor. ptc. ἐξανοίξαντες; *to open (fully)* (AC 12.16)

ἐξανοίξαντες	VPAANM-P	ἐξανοίγω
ἐξαπατάτω	VMPA--3S	ἐξαπατάω

ἐξαπατάω   1aor. ἐξηπάτησα; 1aor. pass. ἐξηπατήθην; *deceive completely, entice, delude*

ἐξαπατηθεῖσα	VPAPNF-S	ἐξαπατάω
ἐξαπατήσῃ	VSAA--3S	"
ἐξαπατῶσι(ν)	VIPA--3P	"
ἐξαπεστάλη	VIAP--3S	ἐξαποστέλλω
ἐξαπέστειλαν	VIAA--3P	"
ἐξαπέστειλε(ν)	VIAA--3S	"

ἐξάπινα   adverb; *suddenly, immediately* (MK 9.8)

ἐξάπινα	AB	ἐξάπινα

ἐξαπορέομαι   1aor. ἐξηπορήθην; *be greatly perplexed, be in utmost despair*

ἐξαπορηθῆναι	VNAO	ἐξαπορέομαι
ἐξαπορούμενοι	VPPDNM-P	"
	VPPONM-P	"

ἐξαποστέλλω   fut. ἐξαποστελῶ; 1aor. ἐξαπέστειλα; 2aor. pass. ἐξαπεστάλην; (1) as on a mission *send, send out, dispatch* (AC 22.21); (2) as removing someone from a place *send away, dismiss* (AC 17.14); (3) with a double accusative ἐξαποστέλλειν τινὰ κενόν *send away empty-handed* (LU 1.53)

ἐξαποστέλλω	VIPA--1S	ἐξαποστέλλω
ἐξαποστελῶ	VIFA--1S	"
ἐξάρατε	VMAA--2P	ἐξαίρω
ἐξαρεῖτε	VIFA--2P	"
ἐξαρθῇ	VSAP--3S	"

ἐξαρπάζω   1aor. ἐξήρπασα; *snatch away* (AC 23.25)

ἐξαρπάσαντες	VPAANM-P	ἐξαρπάζω

ἐξαρτίζω   1aor. ἐξήρτισα; pf. pass. ἐξήρτισμαι; literally *finish, complete*; figuratively in the NT; (1) of thorough spiritual and moral preparedness *equip completely, make adequate* (2T 3.17); (2) as ending a prescribed time *be up, be over* (AC 21.5)

ἐξαρτίσαι	VNAA	ἐξαρτίζω

ἐξαστράπτω   *flash forth* or *gleam like lightning*; of a garment *glisten* (LU 9.29)

ἐξαστράπτων	VPPANM-S	ἐξαστράπτω

ἐξαυτῆς   adverb; strictly *at the very time*; hence *immediately, instantly, at once*

ἐξαυτῆς	AB	ἐξαυτῆς
ἐξέβαλε(ν)	VIAA--3S	ἐκβάλλω
ἐξέβαλλον	VIIA--3P	"
ἐξεβάλομεν	VIAA--1P	"
ἐξέβαλον	VIAA--3P	"
ἐξέβησαν	VIAA--3P	ἐκβαίνω
ἐξεβλάστησε(ν)	VIAA--3S	ἐκβλαστάνω
ἐξεβλήθη	VIAP--3S	ἐκβάλλω
ἐξεγαμίζοντο	VIIP--3P	ἐκγαμίζω
ἐξεγείρει	VIPA--3S	ἐξεγείρω

ἐξεγείρω   fut. ἐξεγερῶ; 1aor. ἐξήγειρα; (1) *cause to appear in history, call into being, raise up* (RO 9.17); (2) of the dead *cause to live again, raise up* (1C 6.14)

ἐξεγερεῖ	VIFA--3S	ἐξεγείρω
ἐξεδέξαντο	VIAD--3P	ἐκδέχομαι
ἐξέδετο	VIAM--3S	ἐκδίδωμι
ἐξεδέχετο	VIID--3S	ἐκδέχομαι
	VIIO--3S	"
ἐξεδίκησε(ν)	VIAA--3S	ἐκδικέω
ἐξεδίωξε(ν)	VIAA--3S	ἐκδιώκω
ἐξέδοτο	VIAM--3S	ἐκδίδωμι
ἐξέδυσαν	VIAA--3P	ἐκδύω

ἐξεζήτησαν	VIAA--3P	ἐκζητέω
ἐξεθαμβήθη	VIAP--3S	ἐκθαμβέω
ἐξεθαμβήθησαν	VIAP--3P	"
ἐξεθαύμαζον	VIIA--3P	ἐκθαυμάζω
ἐξέθεντο	VIAM--3P	ἐκτίθημι
ἐξέθετο	VIAM--3S	"
ἐξέθρεψαν	VIAA--3P	ἐκτρέφω
ἕξει	VIFA--3S	ἔχω
ἐξειλάμην	VIAM--1S	ἐξαιρέω
ἐξείλατο	VIAM--3S	"
ἐξείλετο	VIAM--3S	"
ἐξειλόμην	VIAM--1S	"

ἔξειμι   inf. ἐξιέναι, ptc. ἐξιών; impf. ἐξῄειν; from ἐκ (*out*) and εἶμι (*go*); (1) *go out, go away, depart* (AC 17.15); (2) *go on a journey* (AC 20.7); (3) ἐξιέναι ἐπὶ τὴν γῆν *get to land* (AC 27.43)

ἕξεις	VIFA--2S	ἔχω
ἐξεκαύθησαν	VIAP--3P	ἐκκαίω
ἐξεκέντησαν	VIAA--3P	ἐκκεντέω
ἐξεκλάσθησαν	VIAP--3P	ἐκκλάω
ἐξεκλείσθη	VIAP--3S	ἐκκλείω
ἐξέκλιναν	VIAA--3P	ἐκκλίνω
ἐξεκομίζετο	VIIP--3S	ἐκκομίζω
ἐξεκόπης	VIAP--2S	ἐκκόπτω
ἐξεκρέματο	VIAM--3S	ἐκκρεμάννυμι
ἐξεκρέμετο	VIAM--3S	"
ἔξελε	VMAA--2S	ἐξαιρέω
ἐξελέγξαι	VNAA	ἐξελέγχω
ἐξελέγοντο	VIIM--3P	ἐκλέγω

ἐξελέγχω   *search thoroughly, test, convict, condemn* (JU 15)

ἐξελεξαμένους	VPAMAM-P	ἐκλέγω
ἐξελεξάμην	VIAM--1S	"
ἐξελέξαντο	VIAM--3P	"
ἐξελέξασθε	VIAM--2P	"
ἐξελέξατο	VIAM--3S	"
ἐξελέξω	VIAM--2S	"
ἐξελέσθαι	VNAM	ἐξαιρέω
ἐξελεύσεται	VIFD--3S	ἐξέρχομαι
ἐξελεύσονται	VIFD--3P	"
ἐξελήλυθα	VIRA--1S	"
ἐξελήλυθασι(ν)	VIRA--3P	"
ἐξεληλύθατε	VIRA--2P	"
ἐξεληλύθει	VILA--3S	"
ἐξελήλυθε(ν)	VIRA--3S	"
ἐξεληλυθός	VPRAAN-S	"
ἐξεληλυθότας	VPRAAM-P	"
ἐξεληλυθυῖαν	VPRAAF-S	"
ἐξέληται	VSAM--3S	ἐξαιρέω
ἐξέλθατε	VMAA--2P	ἐξέρχομαι
ἔξελθε	VMAA--2S	"
ἐξελθεῖν	VNAA	"
ἐξέλθῃ	VSAA--3S	"
ἐξέλθῃς	VSAA--2S	"
ἐξέλθητε	VSAA--2P	"
ἐξελθόντα	VPAAAM-S	"
	VPAANN-P	"
ἐξελθόντες	VPAANM-P	"
ἐξελθόντι	VPAADM-S	"
ἐξελθόντος	VPAAGM-S	"
	VPAAGN-S	"
ἐξελθόντων	VPAAGM-P	"

ἐξελθοῦσα	VPAANF-S	"
ἐξελθοῦσαι	VPAANF-P	"
ἐξελθοῦσαν	VPAAAF-S	"
ἐξελθούσῃ	VPAADF-S	"
ἐξελθών	VPAANM-S	"
ἐξελκόμενος	VPPPNM-S	ἐξέλκω

ἐξέλκω *pull out, drag away*; figuratively and passive, of the pull of strong desires *be allured, be drawn away* (JA 1.14)

ἐξέμαξε(ν)	VIAA--3S	ἐκμάσσω
ἐξέμασσε(ν)	VIIA--3S	"
ἐξεμυκτήριζον	VIIA--3P	ἐκμυκτηρίζω
ἐξενέγκαντες	VPAANM-P	ἐκφέρω
ἐξενέγκατε	VMAA--2P	"
ἐξενεγκεῖν	VNAA	"
ἐξένευσε(ν)	VIAA--3S	ἐκνεύω
ἐξένισε(ν)	VIAA--3S	ξενίζω
ἐξενοδόχησε(ν)	VIAA--3S	ξενοδοχέω
ἐξεπείρασαν	VIAA--3P	ἐκπειράζω
ἐξέπεμψαν	VIAA--3P	ἐκπέμπω
ἐξέπεσαν	VIAA--3P	ἐκπίπτω
ἐξεπέσατε	VIAA--2P	"
ἐξέπεσε(ν)	VIAA--3S	"
ἐξέπεσον	VIAA--3P	"
ἐξεπέτασα	VIAA--1S	ἐκπετάννυμι
ἐξεπήδησαν	VIAA--3P	ἐκπηδάω
ἐξεπλάγησαν	VIAP--3P	ἐκπλήσσω
ἐξέπλει	VIIA--3S	ἐκπλέω
ἐξεπλεύσαμεν	VIAA--1P	"
ἐξέπλευσε(ν)	VIAA--3S	"
ἐξεπλήσσετο	VIIP--3S	ἐκπλήσσω
ἐξεπλήσσοντο	VIIP--3P	"
ἐξέπνευσε(ν)	VIAA--3S	ἐκπνέω
ἐξεπορεύετο	VIID--3S	ἐκπορεύομαι
	VIIO--3S	"
ἐξεπορεύοντο	VIID--3P	"
	VIIO--3P	"
ἐξεπτύσατε	VIAA--2P	ἐκπτύω

ἐξέραμα, ατος, τό *what is vomited out, vomit*

ἐξέραμα	N-AN-S	ἐξέραμα

ἐξεραυνάω 1aor. ἐξηραύνησα; as making a thorough investigation *search out diligently, inquire carefully, seek intently*

ἐξέρχεσθαι	VNPD	ἐξέρχομαι
	VNPO	"
ἐξέρχεσθε	VMPD--2P	"
	VMPO--2P	"
ἐξέρχεται	VIPD--3S	"
	VIPO--3S	"

ἐξέρχομαι fut. ἐξελεύσομαι; 2aor. act. ἐξῆλθον and ἐξῆλθα; pf. act. ἐξελήλυθα; (1) literally *go* or *come out of* (JN 4.30); *go forth* or *away, depart* (MK 1.35), opposite μένω (*remain*); from a ship *disembark* (MK 6.54); of liquids *flow out* (JN 19.34); with an infinitive of purpose *go forth* or *out* to do something (MT 11.7); (2) figuratively, of thoughts and words *proceed, go forth, come out* (JA 3.10); (3) of evil spirits that leave a person *come* or *go out* (MK 1.25); (4) euphemistically *leave* the world, *die* (1C 5.10); (5) in John's Gospel of Jesus' birth *come forth* from God (JN 8.42); (6) figuratively *be gone, disappear* (AC 16.19)

ἐξερχόμενοι	VPPDNM-P	ἐξέρχομαι
	VPPONM-P	"
ἐξερχόμενος	VPPDNM-S	"
	VPPONM-S	"
ἐξερχομένων	VPPDGM-P	"
	VPPOGM-P	"
ἐξέρχονται	VIPD--3P	"
	VIPO--3P	"
ἐξερχώμεθα	VSPD--1P	"
	VSPO--1P	"
ἐξεστακέναι	VNRA	ἐξίστημι
ἐξέστανε	VIIA--3S	"
ἐξέστη	VIAA--3S	"
ἐξέστημεν	VIAA--1P	"
ἐξέστησαν	VIAA--3P	"

ἔξεστι(ν) ptc. ἐξόν; impersonal verb; (1) as denoting that there are no hindrances to an action or that the opportunity for it occurs *it is possible*, followed by an infinitive (AC 2.29); (2) predominately as denoting that an action is not prevented by a higher court or by law *it is permitted, it is lawful, it may be done* (MK 10.2)

ἔξεστι(ν)	VIPA--3S	ἔξεστι(ν)
ἐξέστραπται	VIRP--3S	ἐκστρέφω

ἐξετάζω 1aor. ἐξήτασα; (1) as making a careful effort to get information *search out, inquire diligently* (MT 2.8); (2) as interrogating someone *question, examine* (JN 21.12)

ἐξετάραξαν	VIAA--3P	ἐκταράσσω
ἐξετάσαι	VNAA	ἐξετάζω
ἐξετάσατε	VMAA--2P	"
ἔξετε	VIFA--2P	ἔχω
ἐξετείνατε	VIAA--2P	ἐκτείνω
ἐξέτεινε(ν)	VIAA--3S	"
ἐξετίθετο	VIIM--3S	ἐκτίθημι
ἐξετράπησαν	VIAP--3P	ἐκτρέπω
ἐξέφυγον	VIAA--1S	ἐκφεύγω
	VIAA--3P	"
ἐξέχεαν	VIAA--3P	ἐκχέω
ἐξέχεε(ν)	VIAA--3S	"
ἐξεχεῖτο	VIIP--3S	"
ἐξέχοντας	VPPAAM-P	ἐξέχω
ἐξεχύθη	VIAP--3S	ἐκχέω
ἐξεχύθησαν	VIAP--3P	"
ἐξεχύνετο	VIIP--3S	"
ἐξεχύννετο	VIIP--3S	"

ἐξέχω *stand out, be prominent* (MT 20.28)

ἐξέψυξε(ν)	VIAA--3S	ἐκψύχω
ἐξεῶσαι	VNAA	see ἐξῶσαι
ἐξέωσε(ν)	VIAA--3S	see ἐξῶσε(ν)
ἐξήγαγε(ν)	VIAA--3S	ἐξάγω
ἐξήγαγον	VIAA--1S	"
ἐξήγγειλαν	VIAA--3P	ἐξαγγέλλω
ἐξήγειρα	VIAA--1S	ἐξεγείρω
ἐξήγειρε(ν)	VIAA--3S	"
ἐξηγεῖτο	VIID--3S	ἐξηγέομαι
	VIIO--3S	"

ἐξηγέομαι 1aor. ἐξηγησάμην; (1) as giving a description or detailed report *explain, report, describe* (AC 10.8); (2) of God's self-revelation through Christ *reveal, make fully known* (JN 1.18)

ἐξηγησάμενος	VPADNM-S	ἐξηγέομαι

155

ἐξηγήσατο	VIAD--3S	"
ἐξηγόρασε(ν)	VIAA--3S	ἐξαγοράζω
ἐξηγουμένων	VPPDGM-P	ἐξηγέομαι
	VPPOGM-P	"
ἐξηγοῦντο	VIID--3P	"
	VIIO--3P	"
ἐξήεσαν	VIIA--3P	ἔξειμι

ἐξήκοντα indeclinable; as a cardinal number *sixty*

ἐξῆλθαν	VIAA--3P	ἐξέρχομαι
ἐξήλθατε	VIAA--2P	"
ἐξῆλθε(ν)	VIAA--3S	"
ἐξῆλθες	VIAA--2S	"
ἐξήλθετε	VIAA--2P	"
ἐξήλθομεν	VIAA--1P	"
ἐξῆλθον	VIAA--1S	"
	VIAA--3P	"
ἐξήλλατο	VIID--3S	ἐξάλλομαι
ἐξήνεγκαν	VIAA--3P	ἐκφέρω
ἐξήνεγκε(ν)	VIAA--3S	"
ἐξηπάτησε(ν)	VIAA--3S	ἐξαπατάω
ἐξηραμμένην	VPRPAF-S	ξηραίνω
ἐξήρανε(ν)	VIAA--3S	"
ἐξηράνθη	VIAP--3S	"
ἐξηράνθησαν	VIAP--3P	"
ἐξήρανται	VIRP--3S	"
ἐξηραύνησαν	VIAA--3P	ἐξερευνάω
ἐξηρτισμένος	VPRPNM-S	ἐξαρτίζω
ἐξήρχετο	VIID--3S	ἐξέρχομαι
	VIIO--3S	"
ἐξήρχοντο	VIID--3P	"
	VIIO--3P	"

ἑξῆς adverb; *next in order*; in the NT always of time and with the article τῇ ἑ. (ἡμέρᾳ) *on the next day* (LU 9.37)

ἑξῆς	AB	ἑξῆς
ἕξητε	VIFA--2P	see ἕξετε
ἐξητήσατο	VIAM--3S	ἐξαιτέω

ἐξηχέω pf. pass. ἐξήχημαι; transitively *cause to sound forth* or *be heard*; only passive in the NT *sound forth, ring out*; metaphorically, of a message *be heard everywhere* (1TH 1.8)

ἐξήχηται	VIRP--3S	ἐξηχέω
ἐξιέναι	VNPA	ἔξειμι
ἕξιν	N-AF-S	ἕξις
ἐξιόντες	VPPANM-P	ἔξειμι
ἐξιόντων	VPPAGM-P	"

ἕξις, εως, ἡ literally, as a condition of body or mind acquired through practice *skill*; in the NT *practice, exercise, doing again and again* (HE 5.14)

ἐξίσταντο	VIIM--3P	ἐξίστημι
ἐξιστάνων	VPPANM-S	"
ἐξίστασθαι	VNPM	"
ἐξίστατο	VIIM--3S	"

ἐξίστημι and **ἐξιστάνω** mid. ἐξίσταμαι; impf. ἐξέστανον, mid. ἐξιστάμην; 1aor. ἐξέστησα; 2aor. ἐξέστην; pf. ἐξέστηκα; (1) transitively and literally *remove* something from a place, *alter, change*; figuratively in the NT, as causing someone to be amazed beyond comprehension *confuse, astound, amaze* (AC 8.9); (2) intransitively (all middle forms, second aorist active, and perfect active) and figuratively; (a) *lose one's mind, be insane, be out of one's senses* (2C 5.13); (b) of a min-

gling of awe and fear *be astonished, be astounded* (MK 5.42)

ἐξιστῶν	VPPANM-S	ἐξίστημι
ἐξισχύσητε	VSAA--2P	ἐξισχύω

ἐξισχύω 1aor. ἐξίσχυσα; *be fully able, be strong enough* (EP 3.18)

ἔξοδον	N-AF-S	ἔξοδος

ἔξοδος, ου, ἡ (1) literally *going out, exodus, departure*; historically, of the exodus of Israel from Egypt (HE 11.22); (2) euphemistically, of the end of earthly life *departure, death* (LU 9.31)

ἐξόδου	N-GF-S	ἔξοδος
ἐξοίσουσι(ν)	VIFA--3P	ἐκφέρω
ἐξολεθρευθήσεται	VIFP--3S	ἐξολεθρεύω
	VIFP--3S^VMAP--3S	"
ἐξολεθρεῦσαι	VNAA	"

ἐξολεθρεύω 1fut. pass. ἐξολεθρευθήσομαι; *utterly destroy, root out, completely cut off* (AC 3.23)

ἐξομολογεῖσθε	VMPM--2P	ἐξομολογέω

ἐξομολογέω fut. mid. ἐξομολογήσομαι; 1aor. ἐξωμολόγησα; (1) active *agree, promise, fully consent* (LU 22.6); (2) middle; (a) of sins openly *confess, acknowledge, admit* (MT 3.6); (b) of grateful acknowledgment to God *extol, praise, thank* (MT 11.25); (3) of open expression of allegiance to someone *confess, acknowledge* (PH 2.11)

ἐξομολογήσεται	VIFM--3S	ἐξομολογέω
ἐξομολογήσηται	VSAM--3S	"
ἐξομολογήσομαι	VIFM--1S	"
ἐξομολογοῦμαι	VIPM--1S	"
ἐξομολογούμενοι	VPPMNM-P	"
ἐξόν	VPPANN-S	ἔξεστι(ν)
ἐξορκίζειν	VNPA	ἐξορκίζω
ἐξορκίζομεν	VIPA--1S	"

ἐξορκίζω *cause to swear, adjure, put under oath*

ἐξορκίζω	VIPA--1S	ἐξορκίζω

ἐξορκιστής, οῦ, ὁ strictly *one who administers an oath*; in the NT one who drives out demons by magical formulas *exorcist* (AC 19.13)

ἐξορκιστῶν	N-GM-P	ἐξορκιστής
ἐξορύξαντες	VPAANM-P	ἐξορύσσω

ἐξορύσσω 1aor. ἐξώρυξα; (1) of a roof *dig through, open up* (MK 2.4); (2) of eyes *tear out, gouge out* (GA 4.15)

ἐξουδενέω (or **ἐξουδενόω**) 1aor. pass. ἐξουδενήθην (or ἐξουδενώθην); *treat with contempt, reject* (MK 9.12)

ἐξουδενηθῇ	VSAP--3S	ἐξουδενέω
ἐξουδενημένος	VPRPNM-S	"
ἐξουδενωθῇ	VSAP--3S	"
ἐξουθενεῖς	VIPA--2S	ἐξουθενέω
ἐξουθενεῖτε	VMPA--2P	"
ἐξουθενείτω	VMPA--3S	"

ἐξουθενέω (or **ἐξουθενόω**) 1aor. ἐξουθένησα; pf. pass. ἐξουθένημαι; 1aor. pass. ἐξουθενήθη (or ἐξουθενώθη); (1) as treating someone or something as of no account *despise, disdain, make light of* (RO 14.3); (2) as making something or someone as of no account *disregard, reject, despise* (1TH 5.20)

ἐξουθενηθείς	VPAPNM-S	ἐξουθενέω
ἐξουθενηθῇ	VSAP--3S	"
ἐξουθενημένα	VPRPAN-P	"
ἐξουθενημένος	VPRPNM-S	"

ἐξουθενημένους	VPRPAM-P	"
ἐξουθενήσας	VPAANM-S	"
ἐξουθενήσατε	VIAA--2P	"
ἐξουθενήσῃ	VSAA--3S	"
ἐξουθενοῦντας	VPPAAM-P	"
ἐξουθενοῦντες	VPPANM-P	"
ἐξουθενωθῇ	VSAP--3S	"

ἐξουσία, ας, ἡ *authority, right, power*; (1) as denoting the power of decision making, especially as the unlimited possibility of action proper to God *authority, power* (AC 1.7); (2) as denoting God's power displayed through the sphere of nature *power, authority* (RV 9.10, 19); (3) as denoting limited authority to act, given to Satan in his sphere of dominion *power, sphere of power, dominion* (AC 26.18); (4) as Jesus' divinely given and unrestricted exercise of freedom to act *power, authority* (JN 10.18); (5) as authority imparted to a community to act in ordering relationships within it *right, control, authority* (2C 13.10); (6) as those in whom authority for ruling rests, both supernatural and human, especially in the plural *officials, authorities, dignitaries, (the) government* (CO 1.16); (7) 1C 11.10 variously interpreted, including (a) a woman ought to have *authority* over her own head (to unveil) and (b) a woman ought to have *(a sign* or *symbol of) authority* on her head (a head-covering, pointing to the authority of her husband)

ἐξουσία	N-NF-S	ἐξουσία
ἐξουσίᾳ	N-DF-S	"
ἐξουσιάζει	VIPA--3S	ἐξουσιάζω
ἐξουσιάζοντες	VPPANM-P	"

ἐξουσιάζω 1fut. pass. ἐξουσιασθήσομαι; as having and exercising ἐξουσία (*authority, power*) in its various senses; (1) *have the right* or *freedom to exercise authority over, have (independent) control of* (1C 7.4); (2) *have the power* or *mastery over* something; passive *be mastered* or *controlled by* (1C 6.12)

ἐξουσίαι	N-NF-P	ἐξουσία
ἐξουσίαις	N-DF-P	"
ἐξουσίαν	N-AF-S	"
ἐξουσίας	N-AF-P	"
	N-GF-S	"
ἐξουσιασθήσομαι	VIFP-1S	ἐξουσιάζω
ἐξουσιαστική	A--NF-S	ἐξουσιαστικός

ἐξουσιαστικός, ή, όν *having the characteristics of authority, authoritative* (MK 1.27)

ἐξουσι(ν)	VIFA--3P	ἔχω
ἐξουσιῶν	N-GF-P	ἐξουσία

ἐξοχή, ῆς, ἡ literally *standing out, prominence*; figuratively, of persons in high position *distinction, prominence*; οἱ κατ᾽ ἐξοχήν *the prominent* or *chief ones* (AC 25.23)

ἐξοχήν	N-AF-S	ἐξοχή

ἐξυπνίζω 1aor. ἐξύπνισα; of sleeping persons *cause to wake up, rouse*; figuratively, of dead persons *awaken, cause to become alive again* (JN 11.11)

ἐξυπνίσω	VSAA--1S	ἐξυπνίζω
ἔξυπνος, ον	*awakened, aroused from sleep* (AC 16.27)	
ἔξυπνος	A--NM-S	ἔξυπνος
ἐξυρημένη	VPRPDF-S	ξυράω

ἔξω adverb of place; (1) *outside, without, out of doors* (MK 11.4); (2) as an adjective οἱ ἔ. of those who are not a part of the believing community *those outside* (1C 5.12, 13); idiomatically ὁ ἔ. ἄνθρωπος literally *the outer, exterior person*, i.e. *the body, the physical part of a person* (2C 4.16); (3) as an improper preposition with the genitive *outside (of), out of* (LU 13.33)

ἔξω	AB	ἔξω
	PG	"

ἔξωθεν adverb of place; opposite ἔσωθεν (*from the inside, within*); (1) *from the outside, outwardly, externally* (MK 7.18); (2) as a substantive, with the article οἱ ἔ. *those on the outside, nonbelievers* (1T 3.7); τὸ ἔ. *the outside of* something (MT 23.25); (3) as an adjective *external, outer* (1P 3.3); (4) as an improper preposition with the genitive *from outside* (MK 7.15); *outside* (RV 11.2a)

ἔξωθεν	AB	ἔξωθεν
	PG	"

ἐξωθέω 1aor. ἐξῶσα; (1) *expel, drive out, push out* (AC 7.45); (2) as a nautical technical term, of a ship *run aground, beach* (AC 27.39)

ἐξωμολόγησε(ν)	VIAA--3S	ἐξομολογέω
ἐξῶσαι	VNAA	ἐξωθέω
ἔξωσε(ν)	VIAA--3S	"
ἐξῶσε(ν)	VIAA--3S	"
ἐξώτερον	A-MAN-S	ἐξώτερος

ἐξώτερος, τέρα, ον an adjectival comparative of ἔξω (*outside*); in Hellenistic Greek (including the NT period) the comparative has largely replaced the superlative, often retaining the superlative meaning *farthest out, extreme* (MT 8.12)

ἔοικα the perfect of an obsolete verb εἴκω (*appear, resemble*); *be like, resemble*

ἔοικε(ν)	VIRA--3S	ἔοικα
ἑόρακα	VIRA--1S	ὁράω
ἑόρακαν	VIRA--3P	"
ἑόρακε(ν)	VIRA--3S	"

ἑορτάζω *celebrate a festival, take part in a feast*; metaphorically, of the Christian life likened to a Passover feast kept with unleavened bread (1C 5.8)

ἑορτάζωμεν	VSPA--1P	ἑορτάζω

ἑορτή, ῆς, ἡ *celebration, festival, feast* (CO 2.16); predominately of a specific Jewish festival ἡ ἑ. *Passover (feast)* (JN 2.23); of other Jewish festivals, such as Tabernacles or Booths (JN 7.2)

ἑορτή	N-NF-S	ἑορτή
ἑορτῇ	N-DF-S	"
ἑορτήν	N-AF-S	"
ἑορτῆς	N-GF-S	"
ἐπ᾽	PA	ἐπί
	PD	"
	PG	"
ἐπαγαγεῖν	VNAA	ἐπάγω
ἐπαγγειλάμενον	VPADAM-S	ἐπαγγέλλομαι
ἐπαγγειλάμενος	VPADNM-S	"

ἐπαγγελία, ας, ἡ (1) originally *announcement, declaration*; in later Greek *agreement, promise, assurance* (AC 23.21); (2) predominately of God's pronouncements that provide assurance of what he intends to do *promise*

(EP 6.2); by metonymy *thing promised, what was promised* (AC 1.4)

ἐπαγγελία	N-NF-S	ἐπαγγελία
ἐπαγγελία	N-DF-S	"
ἐπαγγελίαι	N-NF-P	"
ἐπαγγελίαις	N-DF-P	"
ἐπαγγελίαν	N-AF-S	"
ἐπαγγελίας	N-AF-P	"
	N-GF-S	"
ἐπαγγελιῶν	N-GF-P	"

ἐπαγγέλλομαι 1aor. pass. ἐπηγγειλάμην; pf. ἐπήγγελμαι; (1) as a divine or human declaration, offering to do something *(make a) promise, offer* (JA 1.12); (2) as what one is asserting about himself *profess, lay claim to* (1T 2.10)

ἐπαγγελλομέναις	VPPDDF-P	ἐπαγγέλλομαι
	VPPODF-P	"
ἐπαγγελλόμενοι	VPPDNM-P	"
	VPPONM-P	"

ἐπάγγελμα, ατος, τό (1) as a declaration of intentions *promise, announcement* (2P 3.13); (2) as the content of a promise *thing promised* (2P 1.4)

ἐπάγγελμα	N-AN-S	ἐπάγγελμα
ἐπαγγέλματα	N-AN-P	"
ἐπάγοντες	VPPANM-P	ἐπάγω

ἐπάγω 1aor. ptc. ἐπάξας; 2aor. ἐπήγαγον; *bring on*; figuratively and in a bad sense *bring on, cause to happen* (2P 2.1)

ἐπαγωνίζεσθαι	VNPD	ἐπαγωνίζομαι
	VNPO	"

ἐπαγωνίζομαι *make a strenuous effort on behalf of, struggle for* (JU 3)

ἔπαθε(ν)	VIAA--3S	πάσχω
ἐπάθετε	VIAA--2P	"
ἔπαθον	VIAA--1S	"
ἐπαθροιζομένων	VPPPGM-P	ἐπαθροίζω

ἐπαθροίζω *collect more, assemble besides*; middle, of a crowd *gather (thick) together, crowd around* (LU 11.29)

ἐπαιδεύθη	VIAP-3S	παιδεύω
ἐπαίδευον	VIIA--3P	"
ἐπαινέσατε	VMAA--2P	ἐπαινέω
ἐπαινεσάτωσαν	VMAA--3P	"
ἐπαινέσω	VSAA--1S	"
Ἐπαίνετον	N-AM-S	Ἐπαίνετος
Ἐπαινετόν	N-AM-S	"

Ἐπαίνετος, ου, ὁ (also Ἐπαινετός) *Epenetus*, masculine proper noun (RO 16.5)

ἐπαινέω fut. ἐπαινέσω; 1aor. ἐπήνεσα; as expressing a high evaluation of someone's actions *praise, commend, approve of* (1C 11.2)

ἔπαινον	N-AM-S	ἔπαινος

ἔπαινος, ου, ὁ (1) as an expression of high evaluation; (a) from people *praise, approval, commendation* (RO 2.29); (b) from God *commendation, praise* (1C 4.5); (c) to God *praise* (PH 1.11); (2) by metonymy, of an object of praise *something praiseworthy, what deserves to be praised* (PH 4.8)

ἔπαινος	N-NM-S	ἔπαινος
ἐπαινῶ	VIPA--1S	ἐπαινέω
ἐπαινῶν	VPPANM-S	"
ἐπαίρεται	VIPM--3S	ἐπαίρω

ἐπαιρόμενον	VPPMAN-S	"
ἐπαίροντας	VPPAAM-P	"

ἐπαίρω 1aor. ἐπῆρα; pf. ἐπήρκα; 1aor. pass. ἐπήρθην; (1) active; (a) literally *lift up, raise, elevate* (1T 2.8); of a sail *hoist* (AC 27.40); (b) idiomatically ἐπαίρειν φωνήν literally *raise the voice*, i.e. *speak loudly, cry out* (LU 11.27); ἐπαίρειν τὴν κεφαλήν literally *lift up the head*, i.e. *have courage, take courage* (LU 21.28); ἐπαίρειν τὴν πτέραν literally *lift up one's heel against*, i.e. *turn against, oppose someone* (JN 13.18); ἐπαίρειν τοὺς ὀφθαλμούς literally *lift up the eyes*, i.e. *look closely, notice* (MT 17.8); (2) passive; (a) *be taken up, ascend* (AC 1.9); (b) figuratively, of exalting oneself; in self-assertion *boast, be arrogant* (2C 11.20); in opposition to someone *oppose, rise up against* (2C 10.5)

ἔπαισε(ν)	VIAA--3S	παίω
ἐπαισχύνεσθε	VIPD--2P	ἐπαισχύνομαι
	VIPO--2P	"
ἐπαισχύνεται	VIPD--3S	"
	VIPO--3S	"
ἐπαισχύνθη	VIAO--3S	"
ἐπαισχυνθῇ	VSAO--3S	"
ἐπαισχυνθῇς	VSAO--2S	"
ἐπαισχυνθήσεται	VIFO--3S	"

ἐπαισχύνομαι 1aor. ἐπαισχύνθην; 1fut. ἐπαισχυνθήσομαι; (1) as denoting a sense of guilt and remorse *be ashamed* (RO 6.21); (2) as denoting fear of embarrassment that one's expectations may prove false *be ashamed, be embarrassed (to), hesitate (to)* (RO 1.16); (3) as denoting reluctance through fear of humiliation *be ashamed, be afraid (to), lack courage to stand up for* (MK 8.38)

ἐπαισχύνομαι	VIPD--1S	ἐπαισχύνομαι
	VIPO--1S	"
ἐπαιτεῖν	VNPA	ἐπαιτέω

ἐπαιτέω strictly *ask for more*; hence *beg*

ἐπαιτῶν	VPPANM-S	ἐπαιτέω

ἐπακολουθέω 1aor. ἐπηκολούθησα; *follow, come after, accompany*; (1) literally, as going along in someone's footsteps *follow along behind*; figuratively, as following in someone's course of life *imitate, live in the same way* (1P 2.21); (2) as pursuing a matter or devoting oneself to it *dedicate oneself to, give attention to* (1T 5.10); (3) of time *appear as a sequel, accompany, follow on* (MK 16.20)

ἐπακολουθήσητε	VSAA--2P	ἐπακολουθέω
ἐπακολουθοῦντα	VPPAAM-S	"
ἐπακολουθούντων	VPPAGN-P	"
ἐπακολουθοῦσι(ν)	VIPA--3P	"

ἐπακούω 1aor. ἐπήκουσα; (1) *hear, listen favorably to, attend to* (2C 6.2); (2) *obey*

ἐπακροάομαι impf. ἐπηκροώμην; *listen to someone, hear*

ἐπάν temporal conjunction; *when(ever), as soon as*

ἐπάν	CS	ἐπάν
ἐπανάγαγε	VMAA--2S	ἐπανάγω
ἐπαναγαγεῖν	VNAA	"
ἐπαναγαγών	VPAANM-S	"

ἐπάναγκες adverb; *necessarily, of necessity*; substantivally τὰ ἐ. *the necessary things, essentials, essential requirements* (AC 15.28)

ἐπάναγκες	AB	ἐπάναγκες

ἐπανάγω   2aor. ἐπανήγαγον; (1) *bring back, bring up*; (2) intransitively in the NT; (a) as a nautical technical term *put out* (to sea), *push off* (from shore) (LU 5.3); (b) *return* (MT 21.18)

ἐπανάγων	VPPANM-S	ἐπανάγω

ἐπαναμιμνήσκω   *remind, cause to think again about, mention again* (RO 15.15)

ἐπαναμιμνήσκων	VPPANM-S	ἐπαναμιμνήσκω
ἐπαναπαήσεται	VIFO--3S	ἐπαναπαύομαι
ἐπαναπαύεται	VIPD--3S	"
	VIPO--3S	"
ἐπαναπαύῃ	VIPD--2S	"
	VIPO--2S	"

ἐπαναπαύομαι   fut. ἐπαναπαύσομαι; pf. ἐπαναπέπαυμαι; 2fut. ἐπαναπαήσομαι; with a basic meaning *rest on*; (1) *continue, remain with* (LU 10.6); (2) as finding comfort through confident dependence on something *rely on, trust in* (RO 2.17)

ἐπαναπαύσεται	VIFD--3S	ἐπαναπαύομαι
ἐπαναπέπαυται	VIRD--3S	"
	VIRO--3S	"
ἐπαναστήσεται	VIFM--3P	ἐπανίστημι
ἐπαναστήσονται	VIFM--3P	"
ἐπανελθεῖν	VNAA	ἐπανέρχομαι
ἐπανελθών	VPAANM-S	"
ἐπανέρχεσθαι	VNPD	"
	VNPO	"

ἐπανέρχομαι   2aor. act. ἐπανῆλθον; *return, come* or *go back*

ἐπανῆλθε(ν)	VIAA--3S	ἐπανέρχομαι

ἐπανίστημι   fut. mid. ἐπαναστήσομαι; only middle in the NT, of hostile action *rise up against, rebel against*

ἐπανόρθωσιν	N-AF-S	ἐπανόρθωσις

ἐπανόρθωσις, εως, ἡ   as an action related to faults *correcting, amendment, making upright again* (2T 3.16)

ἐπάνω   adverb; (1) of place *above, over* (LU 11.44); (2) with numbers *more than* (1C 15.6); (3) as an improper preposition with the genitive *over, above, on* (MT 5.14); (4) figuratively, of the exercise of authority *over* (LU 19.17); of a superior status *above* (JN 3.31)

ἐπάνω	AB	ἐπάνω
	PG	"
ἐπάξας	VPAANM-S	ἐπάγω
ἐπᾶραι	VNAA	ἐπαίρω
ἐπάραντες	VPAANM-P	"
ἐπάρας	VPAANM-S	"
ἐπάρασα	VPAANF-S	"
ἐπάρατε	VMAA--2P	"
ἐπάρατοι	A--NM-P	ἐπάρατος

ἐπάρατος, ον   *accursed, cursed, under curse* (JN 7.49)

ἐπαρκείσθω	VMPP--3S	ἐπαρκέω
ἐπαρκείτω	VMPA--3S	"
ἐπαρκέσῃ	VSAA--3S	"

ἐπαρκέω   1aor. ἐπήρκεσα; strictly *ward off* something from someone; hence *help, aid, relieve*

ἐπαρρησιάζετο	VIID--3S	παρρησιάζομαι
	VIIO--3S	"
ἐπαρρησιασάμεθα	VIAD--1P	"
ἐπαρρησιάσατο	VIAD--3S	"

ἐπαρχεία, ας, ἡ   (also ἐπαρχία)   as denoting an area ruled over by a governor or prefect *province, prefecture*

ἐπαρχεία	N-DF-S	ἐπαρχεία
ἐπαρχείας	N-GF-S	"

ἐπάρχειος, ον   *belonging to a governor* or *prefect* of a province; substantivally *province*; ἐπιβὰς τῇ ἐπαρχείᾳ *after he had arrived in the province* (AC 25.1)

ἐπαρχείῳ	AP-DF-S	ἐπάρχειος
ἐπαρχία	N-DF-S	ἐπαρχεία
ἐπαρχίας	N-GF-S	"
ἐπαρχίῳ	AP-DF-S	see ἐπαρχείῳ
ἐπάταξε(ν)	VIAA--3S	πατάσσω
ἐπατήθη	VIAP--3S	πατέω

ἔπαυλις, εως, ἡ   strictly *place to spend the night, lodging*; in the NT *dwelling place, residence, homestead* (AC 1.20)

ἔπαυλις	N-NF-S	ἔπαυλις
ἐπαύοντο	VIIM--3P	παύω

ἐπαύριον   adverb of time *tomorrow*; τῇ ἐ. *on the next* or *following day*

ἐπαύριον	AB	ἐπαύριον
ἐπαυσάμην	VIAM--1S	παύω
ἐπαύσαντο	VIAM--3P	παύω
ἐπαύσατο	VIAM--3S	"

ἐπαυτοφώρῳ   *in the very act* (JN 8.4)

ἐπαυτοφώρῳ	AB	ἐπαυτοφώρῳ
Ἐπαφρᾶ	N-GM-S	Ἐπαφρᾶς

Ἐπαφρᾶς, ᾶ, ὁ   *Epaphras*, masculine proper noun; probably a shortened form of Ἐπαφρόδιτος

Ἐπαφρᾶς	N-NM-S	Ἐπαφρᾶς
ἐπαφρίζοντα	VPPANN-P	ἐπαφρίζω

ἐπαφρίζω   intransitively *foam up*; transitively *cause to splash up like foam*; *cast up to the surface*; metaphorically in JU 13 of living shamefully in an abandoned way

Ἐπαφρόδιτον	N-AM-S	Ἐπαφρόδιτος

Ἐπαφρόδιτος, ου, ὁ   *Epaphroditus*, masculine proper noun

Ἐπαφροδίτου	N-GM-S	Ἐπαφρόδιτος
ἐπαχύνθη	VIAP--3S	παχύνω
ἐπέβαλαν	VIAA--3P	ἐπιβάλλω
ἐπέβαλε(ν)	VIAA--3S	"
ἐπέβαλλε(ν)	VIIA--3S	"
ἐπέβαλον	VIAA--3P	"
ἐπέβημεν	VIAA--1P	ἐπιβαίνω
ἐπέβην	VIAA--1S	"
ἐπεβίβασαν	VIAA--3P	ἐπιβιβάζω
ἐπέβλεψε(ν)	VIAA--3S	ἐπιβλέπω
ἐπεγέγραπτο	VILP--3S	ἐπιγράφω

ἐπεγείρω   1aor. ἐπήγειρα; *rouse up, awaken*; figuratively in the NT *incite, stir up, instigate*

ἐπεγένετο	VIAD--3S	ἐπιγίνομαι
ἐπεγίνωσκε(ν)	VIIA--3S	ἐπιγινώσκω
ἐπεγίνωσκον	VIIA--3P	"
ἐπεγνωκέναι	VNRA	"
ἐπεγνωκόσι(ν)	VPRADM-P	"
ἐπέγνωμεν	VIAA--1P	"
ἐπέγνωσαν	VIAA--3P	"
ἐπεγνώσθην	VIAP--1S	"
ἐπέγνωτε	VIAA--2P	"
ἐπέδειξε(ν)	VIAA--3S	ἐπιδείκνυμι
ἐπεδημοῦμεν	VIIA--1P	ἐπιδημέω
ἐπεδίδου	VIIA--3S	ἐπιδίδωμι
ἐπεδόθη	VIAP--3S	"
ἐπέδωκαν	VIAA--3P	"

ἐπεζήτει	VIIA--3S	ἐπιζητέω
ἐπεζήτησε(ν)	VIAA--3S	"
ἐπεζήτουν	VIIA--3P	"
ἐπέθανε(ν)	VIAA--3S	see ἀπέθανε(ν)
ἐπέθεντο	VIAM--3P	ἐπιτίθημι
ἐπέθηκαν	VIAA--3P	"
ἐπέθηκε(ν)	VIAA--3S	"
ἐπεθύμει	VIIA--3S	ἐπιθυμέω
ἐπεθύμησα	VIAA--1S	"
ἐπεθύμησαν	VIAA--3P	"

ἐπεί conjunction; (1) with a causal sense *since, because* (MT 18.32); (2) inferentially *else, otherwise, in that case* (HE 9.26); (3) with a temporal sense *when, after* (LU 7.1)

ἐπεί	CS	ἐπεί
ἐπεῖδε(ν)	VIAA--3S	ἐπεῖδον

ἐπειδή conjunction; (1) with a causal sense *since, because* (1C 1.21); (2) with a temporal sense *when, after* (LU 7.1)

ἐπειδή	CS	ἐπειδή

ἐπειδήπερ a causal conjunction with reference to a well-known fact *since indeed, inasmuch as, considering that* (LU 1.1)

ἐπειδήπερ	CS	ἐπειδήπερ

ἐπεῖδον the second aorist of ἐφοράω (*gaze on*); strictly *fix one's gaze on, look at*; hence *regard, concern oneself with* (AC 4.29)

ἔπειθε(ν)	VIIA--3S	πείθω
ἐπείθετο	VIIP--3S	"
ἔπειθον	VIIA--3P	"
ἐπείθοντο	VIIP--3P	"

ἔπειμι ptc. ἐπιών, οὖσα, όν; from ἐπί (*on*) and εἶμι (*go*); in the NT predominately of time immediately succeeding *come on, succeed*; τῇ ἐπιούσῃ *on the next* (day) (AC 7.26); *on the next* (night) (AC 23.11)

ἐπείνασα	VIAA--1S	πεινάω
ἐπείνασαν	VIAA--3P	"
ἐπείνασε(ν)	VIAA--3S	"

ἐπείπερ causal conjunction; *since indeed* (RO 3.30)

ἐπείπερ	CS	ἐπείπερ
ἐπείραζε(ν)	VIIA--3S	πειράζω
ἐπείραζον	VIIA--3P	"
ἐπείρασαν	VIAA--3P	"
ἐπείρασας	VIAA--2S	"
ἐπείρασε(ν)	VIAA--3S	"
ἐπειράσθησαν	VIAP--3S	"
ἐπειράσω	VIAM--2S	πειράομαι
ἐπειρᾶτο	VIID--3S	"
	VIIO--3S	"
ἐπειρῶντο	VIID--3P	"
	VIIO--3P	"

ἐπεισαγωγή, ῆς, ἡ strictly *bringing in besides*; hence *(further) introduction*, either as an addition or replacement (HE 7.19)

ἐπεισαγωγή	N-NF-S	ἐπεισαγωγή
ἔπεισαν	VIAA--3P	πείθω
ἐπεισελεύσεται	VIFD--3S	ἐπεισέρχομαι

ἐπεισέρχομαι fut. ἐπεισελεύσομαι; as happening suddenly and forcibly *come in on, take by surprise* (LU 21.35)

ἐπείσθησαν	VIAP--3P	πείθω

ἔπειτα an adverb marking the sequence of one thing after another; (1) temporally *later, next, after that* (GA 1.18, 21; 2.1); (2) in enumeration *then, next, in the next place* (HE 7.27)

ἔπειτα	AB	ἔπειτα
ἐπεῖχε(ν)	VIIA--3S	ἐπέχω
ἐπεκάθισαν	VIAA--3P	ἐπικαθίζω
ἐπεκάθισε(ν)	VIAA--3S	"
ἐπεκάλεσαν	VIAA--3P	ἐπικαλέω
ἐπεκαλέσαντο	VIAM--3P	"
ἐπεκαλύφθησαν	VIAP--3P	ἐπικαλύπτω
ἐπέκειλαν	VIAA--3P	ἐπικέλλω

ἐπέκεινα adverb of place *farther on, on yonder side*; improper preposition with the genitive *beyond* (AC 7.43)

ἐπέκεινα	PG	ἐπέκεινα
ἐπέκειντο	VIID--3P	ἐπίκειμαι
	VIIO--3P	"
ἐπέκειτο	VIID--3S	"
	VIIO--3S	"
ἐπεκέκλητο	VILM--3S	ἐπικαλέω
ἐπεκέρδησα	VIAA--1S	ἐπικερδαίνω
ἐπεκλήθη	VIAP--3S	ἐπικαλέω
ἐπέκρινε(ν)	VIAA--3S	ἐπικρίνω

ἐπεκτείνομαι literally *reach out toward, strain forward to*; figuratively *try hard for* (PH 3.13)

ἐπεκτεινόμενος	VPPDNM-S	ἐπεκτείνομαι
	VPPONM-S	"
ἐπελάβετο	VIAD--3S	ἐπιλαμβάνομαι
ἐπελάθετο	VIAD--3S	ἐπιλανθάνομαι
ἐπελάθοντο	VIAD--3P	"
ἐπέλαμψε(ν)	VIAA--3S	ἐπιλάμπω
ἐπέλειχον	VIIA--3P	ἐπιλείχω
ἐπελεύσεται	VIFD--3S	ἐπέρχομαι
ἐπέλθη	VSAA--3S	"
ἐπελθοί	VOAA--3S	"
ἐπελθόντος	VPAAGN-S	"
ἐπελθόντων	VPAAGN-P	"
ἐπελθών	VPAANM-S	"
ἐπέλθωσι(ν)	VSAA--3P	"
ἐπέλυε(ν)	VIIA--3S	ἐπιλύω
ἐπέμεινα	VIAA--1S	ἐπιμένω
ἐπεμείναμεν	VIAA--1P	"
ἐπεμελήθη	VIAO--3S	ἐπιμελέομαι
ἐπέμενε(ν)	VIIA--3S	ἐπιμένω
ἐπέμενον	VIIA--3P	"
ἐπέμφθη	VIAP--3S	πέμπω
ἐπέμφθησαν	VIAP--3P	"
ἔπεμψα	VIAA--1S	"
ἐπέμψαμεν	VIAA--1P	"
ἐπέμψατε	VIAA--2P	"
ἔπεμψε(ν)	VIAA--3S	"
ἐπενδύσασθαι	VNAM	ἐπενδύω
ἐπενδύτην	N-AM-S	ἐπενδύτης

ἐπενδύτης, ου, ὁ an outer garment that is taken off for working *coat, outer garment, outer robe* (JN 21.7)

ἐπενδύω 1aor. mid. ἐπενεδυσάμην; only middle in the NT *be (further) clothed with, put on (in addition)*; metaphorically, of the resurrection body (2C 5.2, 4)

ἐπενεγκεῖν	VNAA	ἐπιφέρω
ἐπένευσε(ν)	VIAA--3S	ἐπινεύω
ἐπενθήσατε	VIAA--2P	πενθέω

ἐπέπεσαν	VIAA--3P	ἐπιπίπτω
ἐπέπεσε(ν)	VIAA--3S	"
ἐπέπεσον	VIAA--3P	"
ἐπέπληξε(ν)	VIAA--3S	ἐπιπλήσσω
ἐπέπνιξαν	VIAA--3P	ἐπιπνίγω
ἐπεποίθει	VILA--3S	πείθω
ἐπερίσσευον	VIIA--3P	περισσεύω
ἐπερίσσευσαν	VIAA--3P	"
ἐπερίσσευσε(ν)	VIAA--3S	"
ἐπέρριψαν	VIAA--3P	ἐπιρίπτω

ἐπέρχομαι fut. ἐπελεύσομαι; 2aor. act. ἐπῆλθον; (1) *come along, appear* (MT 20.28); *come from* (AC 14.19); (2) of time *come (on), approach* (EP 2.7); of events in an unexpected time *come on, overtake* (AC 13.40); (3) as coming against, i.e. with a hostile intent *attack, come on* (LU 11.22); (4) of what comes from heaven *come (down) on* (AC 1.8)

ἐπερχομέναις	VPPDDF-P	ἐπέρχομαι
	VPPODF-P	"
ἐπερχομένοις	VPPDDM-P	"
	VPPODM-P	"
ἐπερχομένων	VPPDGN-P	"
	VPPOGN-P	"
ἐπερωτᾶν	VNPA	ἐπερωτάω
ἐπερωτᾷς	VIPA--2S	"
ἐπερωτάτωσαν	VMPA--3P	"

ἐπερωτάω impf. ἐπηρώτων; fut. ἐπερωτήσω; 1aor. ἐπηρώτησα; 1aor. pass. ἐπηρωτήθην; (1) of inquiry in general *ask, put a question, inquire* (MK 9.32, 33); (2) as a legal technical term *interrogate, examine, question* (AC 5.27); (3) as seeking to know God *ask after, desire to know* (RO 10.20); (4) as making a request for something *ask for, demand* (MT 16.1)

ἐπερωτηθείς	VPAPNM-S	ἐπερωτάω

ἐπερώτημα, ατος, τό as what is asked; (1) *question*; (2) *appeal, request* (1P 3.21)

ἐπερώτημα	N-NN-S	ἐπερώτημα
ἐπερωτῆσαι	VNAA	ἐπερωτάω
ἐπερωτήσας	VPAANM-S	"
ἐπερωτήσατε	VMAA--2P	"
ἐπερώτησον	VMAA--2S	"
ἐπερωτήσω	VIFA--1S	"
ἐπερωτήσωσι(ν)	VSAA--3P	"
ἐπερωτῶ	VIPA--1S	"
ἐπερωτῶντα	VPPAAM-S	"
ἐπερωτῶσι(ν)	VIPA--3P	"
	VPPADM-P	"
ἔπεσα	VIAA--1S	πίπτω
ἔπεσαν	VIAA--3P	"
ἔπεσε(ν)	VIAA--3S	"
ἐπεσκέψασθε	VIAD--2P	ἐπισκέπτομαι
ἐπεσκέψατο	VIAD--3S	"
ἐπεσκίαζε(ν)	VIIA--3S	ἐπισκιάζω
ἐπεσκίασε(ν)	VIAA--3S	"
ἔπεσον	VIAA--1S	πίπτω
ἐπέσπαρκε(ν)	VIRA--3S	ἐπισπείρω
ἐπέσπειρε(ν)	VIAA--3S	"
ἐπέστειλα	VIAA--1S	ἐπιστέλλω
ἐπεστείλαμεν	VIAA--1P	"
ἐπέστη	VIAA--3S	ἐφίστημι
ἐπεστήριξαν	VIAA--3P	ἐπιστηρίζω

ἐπέστησαν	VIAA--3P	ἐφίστημι
ἐπεστράφητε	VIAP--2P	ἐπιστρέφω
ἐπέστρεψα	VIAA--1S	"
ἐπέστρεψαν	VIAA--3P	"
ἐπεστρέψατε	VIAA--2P	"
ἐπέστρεψε(ν)	VIAA--3S	"
ἐπέσχε(ν)	VIAA--3S	ἐπέχω
ἐπέταξας	VIAA--2S	ἐπιτάσσω
ἐπέταξε(ν)	VIAA--3S	"
ἐπετίθεσαν	VIIA--3P	ἐπιτίθημι
ἐπετίθουν	VIIA--3P	"
ἐπετίμα	VIIA--3S	ἐπιτιμάω
ἐπετίμησαν	VIAA--3P	"
ἐπετίμησε(ν)	VIAA--3S	"
ἐπετίμων	VIIA--3P	"
ἐπετράπη	VIAP--3S	ἐπιτρέπω
ἐπέτρεψε(ν)	VIAA--3S	"
ἐπέτυχε(ν)	VIAA--3S	ἐπιτυγχάνω
ἐπέτυχον	VIAA--3P	"

ἐπευλογέω 1fut. pass. ἐπευλογηθήσομαι; *bless, act kindly toward* (AC 3.25)

ἐπευλογηθήσονται	VIFP--3P	ἐπευλογέω
ἐπεφάνη	VIAP--3S	ἐπιφαίνω
ἐπέφερον	VIIA--3P	ἐπιφέρω
ἐπεφώνει	VIIA--3S	ἐπιφωνέω
ἐπεφώνουν	VIIA--3P	"
ἐπέφωσκε(ν)	VIIA--3S	ἐπιφώσκω
ἔπεχε	VMPA--2S	ἐπέχω
ἐπέχειν	VNPA	"
ἐπεχείρησαν	VIAA--3P	ἐπιχειρέω
ἐπεχείρουν	VIIA--3P	"
ἐπέχοντες	VPPANM-P	ἐπέχω
ἐπέχουσαι	VPPANF-P	"
ἐπέχρισε(ν)	VIAA--3S	ἐπιχρίω

ἐπέχω impf. ἐπεῖχον; 2aor. ἐπέσχον; (1) transitively *hold fast, hold on to* (PH 2.16); (2) intransitively; (a) of mental processes *fix attention on, observe, take note of* (LU 14.7); (b) of a constant state of readiness *be alert for, watch out for* (1T 4.16); (c) of additional time spent in a place *delay, stay on* (AC 19.22)

ἐπέχων	VPPANM-S	ἐπέχω
ἐπήγαγον	VIAA--3P	ἐπάγω
ἐπηγγείλαντο	VIAD--3P	ἐπαγγέλλομαι
ἐπηγγείλατο	VIAD--3S	"
ἐπήγγελται	VIRD--3S	"
	VIRO--3S	"
	VIRP--3S	"
ἐπήγειραν	VIAA--3P	ἐπεγείρω
ἐπηκολούθησε(ν)	VIAA--3S	ἐπακολουθέω
ἐπήκουσα	VIAA--1S	ἐπακούω
ἐπηκροῶντο	VIID--3P	ἐπακροάομαι
	VIIO--3P	"
ἐπῆλθαν	VIAA--3P	ἐπέρχομαι
ἐπῆλθον	VIAA--3P	"
ἐπήνεσε(ν)	VIAA--3S	ἐπαινέω
ἔπηξε(ν)	VIAA--3S	πήγνυμι
ἐπῆραν	VIAA--3P	ἐπαίρω
ἐπηρεάζοντες	VPPANM-P	ἐπηρεάζω
ἐπηρεαζόντων	VPPAGM-P	"
ἐπηρεάζουσι(ν)	VIPA--3P	"

ἐπηρεάζω (1) of ill treatment *mistreat, insult, abuse* (LU 6.28); (2) of false accusation *revile, slander* (1P 3.16)

ἐπῆρε(ν)	VIAA--3S	ἐπαίρω
ἐπήρθη	VIAP--3S	"
ἐπῆρκε(ν)	VIRA--3S	"
ἐπήρκεσε(ν)	VIAA--3S	ἐπαρκέω
ἐπήρωσε(ν)	VIAA--3S	πηρόω
ἐπηρώτα	VIIA--3S	ἐπερωτάω
ἐπηρώτησαν	VIAA--3P	"
ἐπηρώτησε(ν)	VIAA--3S	"
ἐπηρώτων	VIIA--3P	"

ἐπί preposition with a basic meaning *on*, but with a wide range of meanings according to the context; **I.** with the genitive emphasizing contact; (1) in answer to "where?" *on* (LU 2.14); (2) with verbs of motion answering "to what place? where?" *on, in* (HE 6.7); (3) expressing immediate proximity *at, by, near* (JN 21.1); (4) in legal procedures *in the presence of, before* an official court (AC 25.10); (5) figuratively, related to rule and authority *over* (RO 9.5); (6) figuratively; (a) as giving a basis *on the basis* or *evidence of* (1T 5.19); (b) *based on, in view of* (LU 4.25); (7) as relating in historical timing *in the time of, under (the rule of)* (MK 2.26); **II.** with the dative emphasizing position; (1) of place *on, in* (MK 6.39); of proximity *at, near, by* (MT 24.33); (2) of hostility *against* (LU 12.52); (3) of time *at, in, in the time of, during* (HE 9.26); (4) of cause or occasion *because, on account of, on the basis of, from (the fact that)* (RO 5.12); (5) figuratively, of aim or purpose *for (the purpose of)* (EP 2.10); (6) figuratively, of power, authority, control *over* (LU 12.44); **III.** with the accusative emphasizing motion or direction; (1) of place *on* (MT 14.29); *across, over* (MT 27.45); *as far as, to, up to* (MK 16.2); (2) of hostile intent *against* (MT 26.55); (3) figuratively, of goal or purpose *for* (MT 3.7); (4) figuratively, of making addition to something already present *on, on top of* (PH 2.27); (5) figuratively, in relation to feelings that are directed toward a person or thing: (believe) *on* (AC 9.42), (hope) *for* (1P 1.13), (have compassion) *on, toward* (MT 15.32), etc.; (6) of extension of time, answering "when?" or "for how long?" *for, over a period of* (LU 4.25); (7) to indicate number, in answering "how many times?" with ἐ. untranslated (AC 10.16); (8) to indicate degree or measure, in answering "how much?" ἐφ᾽ ὅσον *to the degree that, insofar as* (MT 25.40); ἐ. τὸ χεῖρον *to the worse, from bad to worse* (2T 3.13)

ἐπί	PA	ἐπί
	PD	"
	PG	"
ἐπίασαν	VIAA--3P	πιάζω
ἐπιάσατε	VIAA--2P	"
ἐπίασε(ν)	VIAA--3S	"
ἐπιάσθη	VIAP--3S	"
ἐπιβαίνειν	VNPA	ἐπιβαίνω

ἐπιβαίνω 2aor. ἐπέβην; pf. ἐπιβέβηκα; strictly *step on*; (1) of an animal *mount, get on*; perfect participle ἐπιβεβηκώς *having mounted*, i.e. *riding on* (MT 21.5); of a ship *go on board, embark* (AC 27.2); (2) as entering a country or region *set foot in, enter, come to* (AC 20.18)

ἐπιβαλεῖν	VNAA	ἐπιβάλλω
ἐπιβάλλει	VIPA--3S	"
ἐπιβάλλον	VPPAAN-S	"

ἐπιβάλλουσι(ν)	VIPA--3P	"

ἐπιβάλλω 2aor. ἐπέβαλον; strictly *cast over, throw on*; (1) transitively; (a) of a violent movement *throw* something *over* someone (RV 18.19); metaphorically in 1C 7.35 *put a noose on*, i.e. *put a restriction on*; (b) *lay* (hands) *on, seize* (MK 14.46); (c) *put* (a patch) *on, sew on* (MT 9.16); (d) *put* (a hand) *to, start* (LU 9.62); (2) intransitively; (a) of waves *splash into, break over, dash against* (MK 4.37); (b) of legal inheritance *fall to, belong to* (LU 15.12); (3) in MK 14.72 καὶ ἐπιβαλὼν ἔκλαιεν has two possible meanings: (a) *put one's mind on, think seriously about*; thus *and when he thought seriously about the matter, he wept*; (b) *set oneself to, begin to*; thus *and he began to weep*

ἐπιβάλλων	VPPANM-S	ἐπιβάλλω
ἐπιβαλόντες	VPAANM-P	"
ἐπιβαλοῦσι(ν)	VIFA--3P	"
ἐπιβάλω	VSAA--1S	"
ἐπιβαλών	VPAANM-S	"
ἐπιβάντες	VPAANM-P	ἐπιβαίνω

ἐπιβαρέω 1aor. ἐπεβάρησα; (1) as expecting too much financial support *weigh down, (put a) burden (on), be burdensome to* (1TH 2.9); (2) *press too heavily on, be too severe with* (2C 2.5)

ἐπιβαρῆσαι	VNAA	ἐπιβαρέω
ἐπιβαρῶ	VSPA--1S	"
ἐπιβάς	VPAANM-S	ἐπιβαίνω
ἐπιβεβηκώς	VPRANM-S	"

ἐπιβιβάζω 1aor. ἐπεβίβασα; as putting someone on an animal to ride *set on, mount on*

ἐπιβιβάσαντες	VPAANM-P	ἐπιβιβάζω
ἐπιβιβάσας	VPAANM-S	"

ἐπιβλέπω 1aor. ἐπέβλεψα; (1) in a positive sense *look or gaze on*, in the sense of *have regard for, consider, help* (LU 9.38); (2) in a negative sense *care too much about, be partial toward, notice* (JA 2.3)

ἐπιβλέψαι	VNAA	ἐπιβλέπω
ἐπιβλέψητε	VSAA--2P	"
ἐπίβλεψον	VMAA--2S	"

ἐπίβλημα, ατος, τό strictly *what has been put over or on*; hence *patch*

ἐπίβλημα	N-AN-S	ἐπίβλημα
	N-NN-S	"

ἐπιβοάω *cry out loudly* (AC 25.24)

ἐπιβουλαῖς	N-DF-P	ἐπιβουλή

ἐπιβουλή, ῆς, ἡ a purpose or design against someone *plot, conspiracy*

ἐπιβουλή	N-NF-S	ἐπιβουλή
ἐπιβουλῆς	N-GF-S	"
ἐπιβοῶντες	VPPANM-P	ἐπιβοάω
ἐπιγαμβρεύσει	VIFA--3S	ἐπιγαμβρεύω
	VIFA--3S^VMAA--3S	"

ἐπιγαμβρεύω fut. ἐπιγαμβρεύσω; of a levirate marriage (see Deuteronomy 25.5–6), in which a man marries his brother's childless widow *marry afterward, marry as next of kin* (MT 22.24)

ἐπιγεγραμμένα	VPRPAN-P	ἐπιγράφω
ἐπιγεγραμμένη	VPRPNF-S	"
ἐπίγεια	A--AN-P	ἐπίγειος
	A--NN-P	"

ἐπίγειος, ον (1) strictly *existing on earth, belonging to earth*; hence *earthly, terrestrial* (1C 15.40), opposite ἐπουράνιος (*heavenly*); (2) substantivally τὰ ἐπίγεια *earthly things, what happens on earth* (JN 3.12); (3) belonging to human existence *of people, human* (JA 3.15), opposite θεῖος (*divine*)

ἐπίγειος	A--NF-S	ἐπίγειος
ἐπιγείων	A--GM-P	"
	A--GN-P	"
ἐπιγενομένου	VPADGM-S	ἐπιγίνομαι

ἐπιγίνομαι 2aor. ἐπεγενόμην; *happen, occur*; of wind *come up, spring up* (AC 28.13)

ἐπιγινώσκει	VIPA--3S	ἐπιγινώσκω
ἐπιγινώσκεις	VIPA--2S	"
ἐπιγινώσκετε	VIPA--2P	"
	VMPA--2P	"
ἐπιγινωσκέτω	VMPA--3S	"
ἐπιγινωσκόμενοι	VPPPNM-P	"
ἐπιγινώσκοντες	VPPANM-P	"

ἐπιγινώσκω fut. mid. ἐπιγνώσομαι; 2aor. ἐπέγνων; pf. ἐπέγνωκα; 1aor. pass. ἐπεγνώσθην; (1) with no emphasis on the ἐπι- prefix; (a) *recognize, know* (MT 11.27; cf. LU 10.22); (b) *perceive, notice, become aware of* (MK 5.30; cf. LU 8.46); (c) *learn of, find out* (LU 7.37); (d) *acknowledge, understand* (2C 1.13); (2) with the preposition intensifying the meaning; (a) *know exactly, fully, completely* (LU 1.4); (b) especially in relation to higher and spiritual knowledge received through revelation *fully know, perfectly know* (CO 1.6)

ἐπιγνόντες	VPAANM-P	ἐπιγινώσκω
ἐπιγνόντως	VPAAGM-P	"
ἐπιγνούς	VPAANM-S	"
ἐπιγνοῦσα	VPAANF-S	"
ἐπιγνοῦσι(ν)	VPAADM-P	"
ἐπιγνῶ	VSAA--3S	"
ἐπιγνῶναι	VNAA	"
ἐπιγνῷς	VSAA--2S	"
ἐπιγνώσει	N-DF-S	ἐπίγνωσις
ἐπιγνώσεσθε	VIFD--2P	ἐπιγινώσκω
ἐπιγνώσεως	N-GF-S	ἐπίγνωσις
ἐπιγνωσθῇ	VSAP--3S	ἐπιγινώσκω
ἐπίγνωσιν	N-AF-S	ἐπίγνωσις

ἐπίγνωσις, εως, ἡ *knowledge, true knowledge*; in the NT of content, used especially of intensive religious and moral knowledge, what one comes to know and appropriate through faith in Christ *(full) knowledge, acknowledgment, recognition* (CO 1.10; 2T 2.25)

ἐπίγνωσις	N-NF-S	ἐπίγνωσις
ἐπιγνώσομαι	VIFD--1S	ἐπιγινώσκω

ἐπιγραφή, ῆς, ἡ as writing put on an object for identification *inscription* (MK 15.26); as what is written on a coin *legend, inscription* (MT 22.20)

ἐπιγραφή	N-NF-S	ἐπιγραφή
ἐπιγραφήν	N-AF-S	"

ἐπιγράφω fut. ἐπιγράψω; pf. pass. ἐπιγέγραμμαι; pluperfect pass. ἐπεγεγράμμην; 2aor. pass. ἐπεγράφην; literally *write in* or *on, engrave, inscribe* (MK 15.26); figuratively, as making a deep impression on the heart or the mind *write on* (HE 8.10)

ἐπιγράψω	VIFA--1S	ἐπιγράφω
ἔπιδε	VMAA--2S	ἐπεῖδον

ἐπιδεικνύμεναι	VPPMNF-P	ἐπιδείκνυμι

ἐπιδείκνυμι 1aor. ἐπέδειξα; literally, as causing to be seen *show, exhibit, demonstrate* (MT 16.1); figuratively, as proving to be true *show beyond doubt, prove, demonstrate convincingly* (AC 18.28)

ἐπιδεικνύς	VPPANM-S	ἐπιδείκνυμι
ἐπιδεῖξαι	VNAA	"
ἐπιδείξασθαι	VNAM	"
ἐπιδείξατε	VMAA--2P	"
ἐπιδεξάμενος	VPADNM-S	ἐπιδέχομαι
ἐπιδέχεται	VIPD--3S	"
	VIPO--3S	"

ἐπιδέχομαι 1aor. ἐπεδεξάμην; (1) as showing hospitality *receive (kindly), welcome, entertain* (3J 10); (2) as welcoming someone as a companion *accept, take along* (AC 15.40); (3) as acknowledging someone's authority *accept, admit* (3J 9)

ἐπιδεχομένους	VPPDAM-P	ἐπιδέχομαι
	VPPOAM-P	"

ἐπιδημέω as living away from one's home *dwell among another people, temporarily *reside among, stay in* a place as a visitor

ἐπιδημήσας	VPAANM-S	ἐπιδημέω
ἐπιδημοῦντες	VPPANM-P	"
ἐπιδιατάσσεται	VIPD--3S	ἐπιδιατάσσομαι
	VIPO--3S	"

ἐπιδιατάσσομαι *introduce in addition*; as a legal technical term involving a last will or testament *add a codicil, add to* (GA 3.15)

ἐπιδιδούς	VPPANM-S	ἐπιδίδωμι

ἐπιδίδωμι impf. third-person singular ἐπεδίδου; fut. ἐπιδώσω; 1aor. ἐπέδωκα; 1aor. pass. ἐπεδόθην; (1) *give* or *hand over, deliver* something *to* someone (LU 4.17); (2) as yielding to a superior force *give oneself up* or *over to, surrender* (AC 27.15)

ἐπιδίδωσι(ν)	VIPA--3S	ἐπιδίδωμι

ἐπιδιορθόω 1aor. ἐπεδιόρθωσα, mid. ἐπεδιορθωσάμην; *(further) set in order, correct, straighten out* (TI 1.5)

ἐπιδιορθώσῃ	VSAM--2S	ἐπιδιορθόω
ἐπιδιορθώσῃς	VSAA--2S	"
ἐπιδόντες	VPAANM-P	ἐπιδίδωμι
ἐπιδυέτω	VMPA--3S	ἐπιδύω

ἐπιδύω of the sun *go down on, set on* or *during* an event (EP 4.26)

ἐπιδῷ	VSAA--3S	ἐπιδίδωμι
ἐπιδώσει	VIFA--3S	"
ἐπιδώσω	VIFA--1S	"

ἐπιείκεια, ας, ἡ *gentleness, graciousness* (2C 10.1); as a commendable attribute for a ruler *forbearance, clemency* (AC 24.4)

ἐπιεικείᾳ	N-DF-S	ἐπιείκεια
ἐπιεικείας	N-GF-S	"
ἐπιεικεῖς	A--AM-P	ἐπιεικής
ἐπιεικές	A--NN-S	"
ἐπιεικέσι(ν)	A--DM-P	"
ἐπιεικῆ	A--AM-S	"

ἐπιεικής, ές *gentle, kind, forbearing* (1T 3.3); substantivally τὸ ἐπιεικές equivalent to ἡ ἐπιείκεια *gentleness, forbearance* (PH 4.5)

ἐπιεικής	A--NF-S	ἐπιεικής
ἔπιε(ν)	VIAA--3S	πίνω

ἐπιζητεῖ	VIPA--3S	ἐπιζητέω
ἐπιζητεῖτε	VIPA--2P	"

ἐπιζητέω impf. ἐπεζήτουν; 1aor. ἐπεζήτησα; (1) with regard to persons *search for, look for, seek out* (LU 4.42); (2) of intellectual inquiry *inquire about, want to know* (AC 19.39); (3) of yearning of the heart *desire, seek after, wish for* (MT 6.32); (4) as making an effort to get what one wants *demand, strive for, require* (MT 12.39)

ἐπιζητήσας	VPAANM-S	ἐπιζητέω
ἐπιζητοῦμεν	VIPA--1P	"
ἐπιζητοῦσι(ν)	VIPA--3P	"
ἐπιζητῶ	VIPA--1S	"

ἐπιθανάτιος, ον *condemned to death, sentenced to die* (1C 4.9)

ἐπιθανατίους	A--AM-P	ἐπιθανάτιος
ἐπιθεῖναι	VNAA	ἐπιτίθημι
ἐπιθείς	VPAANM-S	"
ἐπιθέντα	VPAAAM-S	"
ἐπιθέντες	VPAANM-P	"
ἐπιθέντος	VPAAGM-S	"
ἐπίθες	VMAA--2S	"
ἐπιθέσεως	N-GF-S	ἐπίθεσις

ἐπίθεσις, εως, ἡ as a symbolic action conveying power or blessing or transferring authority *laying* or *placing on* (of hands)

ἐπιθῇ	VSAA--3S	ἐπιτίθημι
ἐπιθῇς	VSAA--2S	"
ἐπιθήσει	VIFA--3S	"
ἐπιθήσεται	VIFM--3S	"
ἐπιθήσουσι(ν)	VIFA--3P	"
ἐπιθύειν	VNPA	ἐπιθύω
ἐπιθυμεῖ	VIPA--3S	ἐπιθυμέω
ἐπιθυμεῖτε	VIPA--2P	"

ἐπιθυμέω impf. ἐπεθύμουν; 1aor. ἐπεθύμησα; (1) generally, of a strong impulse toward something *desire, long for* (LU 16.21); (2) in a good sense of natural or commendable desire *long for, earnestly desire* (LU 22.15); (3) in a bad sense of unrestricted desire for a forbidden person or thing *lust for* or *after, crave, covet* (MT 5.28; AC 20.33)

ἐπιθυμῆσαι	VNAA	ἐπιθυμέω
ἐπιθυμήσεις	VIFA--2S	"
	VIFA--2S^VMAA--2S	"
ἐπιθυμήσετε	VIFA--2P	"
ἐπιθυμήσῃς	VSAA--2S	"
ἐπιθυμήσουσι(ν)	VIFA--3P	"
ἐπιθυμητάς	N-AM-P	ἐπιθυμητής

ἐπιθυμητής, οῦ, ὁ *one who ardently desires*; in the NT *one who craves for* or *greatly desires forbidden things* (1C 10.6)

ἐπιθυμία, ας, ἡ (1) in a neutral sense *strong impulse* or *desire* (MK 4.19); (2) in a good sense of natural and legitimate desire *(eager) longing, (earnest) desire* (1TH 2.17); (3) in a bad sense of unrestrained desire for something forbidden *lust, craving, evil desire* (1T 6.9)

ἐπιθυμία	N-NF-S	ἐπιθυμία
ἐπιθυμίᾳ	N-DF-S	"
ἐπιθυμίαι	N-NF-P	"
ἐπιθυμίαις	N-DF-P	"
ἐπιθυμίαν	N-AF-S	"
ἐπιθυμίας	N-AF-P	"
	N-GF-S	"

ἐπιθυμιῶν	N-GF-P	"
ἐπιθυμοῦμεν	VIPA--1P	ἐπιθυμέω
ἐπιθυμοῦσι(ν)	VIPA--3P	"
ἐπιθυμῶν	VPPANM-S	"

ἐπιθύω *offer sacrifice* (AC 14.13)

ἐπιθῶ	VSAA--1S	ἐπιτίθημι

ἐπικαθίζω 1aor. ἐπεκάθισα; intransitively *sit (down) on* (MT 21.7)

ἐπικαλεῖσθαι	VNPP	ἐπικαλέω
ἐπικαλεῖσθε	VIPM--2P	"
ἐπικαλεῖται	VIPP--3S	"
ἐπικαλεσάμενος	VPAMNM-S	"
ἐπικαλεσαμένου	VPAMGM-S	"
ἐπικαλέσασθαι	VNAM	"
ἐπικαλέσηται	VSAM--3S	"
ἐπικαλέσονται	VIFM--3P	"
ἐπικαλέσωνται	VSAM--3P	"

ἐπικαλέω fut. mid. ἐπικαλέσομαι; 1aor. ἐπεκάλεσα, mid. ἐπεκαλεσάμην; pf. pass. ἐπικέκλημαι; pluperfect mid. ἐπεκεκλήμην; 1aor. pass. ἐπεκλήθην; (1) active, in speaking of a person *call, name, give a surname* (MT 10.25); passive *be called, be named* (AC 1.23); (2) passive with ὄνομα (*name*), idiomatically, denoting that one person belongs to another whose name is attached to him ἐπικαλεῖσθαι τὸ ὄνομά τινος ἐπί τινα literally *have someone's name called on someone*, i.e. *belong to, be the person of* (AC 15.17); (3) middle, as a legal technical term for appealing to a higher court *appeal, call* or *summon as witness* (2C 1.23); (4) middle, as invoking God's name in prayer *call on* (AC 2.21)

ἐπικαλοῦμαι	VIPM--1S	ἐπικαλέω
ἐπικαλουμένοις	VPPMDM-P	"
ἐπικαλούμενον	VPPMAM-S	"
	VPPPAM-S	"
ἐπικαλούμενος	VPPPNM-S	"
ἐπικαλουμένου	VPPPGM-S	"
ἐπικαλουμένους	VPPMAM-P	"
ἐπικαλουμένων	VPPMGM-P	"

ἐπικάλυμμα, ατος, τό literally *covering*; figuratively, of a *cover-up* for evil, *pretext, excuse* (1P 2.16)

ἐπικάλυμμα	N-AN-S	ἐπικάλυμμα

ἐπικαλύπτω 1aor. pass. ἐπεκαλύφθην; literally *cover (over), hide*; figuratively, of God's dealing with sin *forgive* (RO 4.7)

ἐπικατάρατοι	A--NM-P	ἐπικατάρατος

ἐπικατάρατος, ον *cursed, (even more) accursed, being under (severe) curse*, i.e. *condemned by God*

ἐπικατάρατος	A--NM-S	ἐπικατάρατος

ἐπίκειμαι impf. ἐπεκείμην; literally *be placed on, lie on* (JN 11.38); figuratively *be (laid) on*; of a storm *beat on, rage around* (AC 27.20); of a crowd *press against, throng* (LU 5.1); of legal ordinances *be imposed, be in control over* (HE 9.10); of persistent demands *continue insisting* (LU 23.23)

ἐπικείμενα	VPPDNN-P	ἐπίκειμαι
	VPPONN-P	"
ἐπικείμενον	VPPDAN-S	"
	VPPOAN-S	"
ἐπικειμένου	VPPDGM-S	"
	VPPOGM-S	"

ἐπικεῖσθαι VNPD "
           VNPO "
ἐπίκειται VIPD--3S "
           VIPO--3S "
ἐπικέκλησαι VIRM--2S ἐπικαλέω
ἐπικέκληται VIRP--3S "
ἐπικέκλητο VILM--3S see ἐπεκέκλητο
ἐπικέλλω 1aor. ἐπέκειλα; as a nautical technical term *bring* (a ship) *to shore; run aground* (AC 27.41)
ἐπικερδαίνω 1aor. ἐπεκέρδησα; *gain besides* or *in addition* (MT 25.20)
ἐπικεφάλαιον, ου, τό *poll tax, head tax, tax on individuals* (MK 12.14)

ἐπικεφάλαιον N-AN-S ἐπικεφάλαιον
ἐπικέψεται VIFD--3S see ἐπισκέψεται
ἐπικληθείς VPAPNM-S ἐπικαλέω
ἐπικληθέν VPAPAN-S "
ἐπικληθέντα VPAPAM-S "
Ἐπικούρειος, ου, ὁ (also Ἐπικούριος) *Epicurean*, a follower of the pleasure-seeking philosophy of Epicurus (AC 17.18)

Ἐπικουρείων N-GM-P Ἐπικούρειος
ἐπικουρία, ας, ἡ *help, assistance* (AC 26.22)
ἐπικουρίας N-GF-S ἐπικουρία
Ἐπικουρίων N-GM-P Ἐπικούρειος
ἐπικράζοντες VPPANM-P ἐπικράζω
ἐπικραζόντων VPPAGM-P "
ἐπικράζω *shout threats against* someone (AC 16.39)
ἐπικράνθη VIAP--3S πικραίνω
ἐπικράνθησαν VIAP--3P "
ἐπικρίνω 1aor. ἐπέκρινα; *decide*; of an official decision *determine, pronounce sentence, adjudge* (LU 23.24)
ἐπιλαβέσθαι VNAD ἐπιλαμβάνομαι
ἐπιλαβόμενοι VPADNM-P "
ἐπιλαβόμενος VPADNM-S "
ἐπιλαβομένου VPADGM-S "
ἐπιλαβοῦ VMAD--2S "
ἐπιλαβών VPAANM-S "
ἐπιλάβωνται VSAD--3P "
ἐπιλαθέσθαι VNAD ἐπιλανθάνομαι
ἐπιλαμβάνεται VIPD--3S ἐπιλαμβάνομαι
           VIPO--3S "
ἐπιλαμβάνομαι 2aor. act. ptc. ἐπιλαβών (MK 14.72); 2aor. mid. ἐπελαβόμην; (1) literally, as taking a firm hold, often with the hand *grasp, take hold of, seize* (LU 23.26); (2) figuratively; (a) as listening to someone's words with a hostile intent *catch, fasten on, take hold of* (LU 20.20); (b) as drawing someone to oneself in order to help *take hold of, be concerned with, help* (HE 2.16); (c) as seeking to experience something *take hold of, have* (1T 6.12)
ἐπιλάμπω 1aor. ἐπέλαμψα; of a light *shine out, shine all around* (AC 12.7)
ἐπιλανθάνεσθε VMPD--2P ἐπιλανθάνομαι
           VMPO--2P "
ἐπιλανθάνομαι pf. pass. ἐπιλέλησμαι; 2aor. ἐπελαθόμην; (1) literally *forget* (MK 8.14); (2) figuratively; (a) *neglect, disregard, care nothing for* (HE 13.2); (b) *escape notice, be overlooked* or *forgotten* (LU 12.6)
ἐπιλανθανόμενος VPPDNM-S ἐπιλανθάνομαι
           VPPONM-S "

ἐπιλεγομένη VPPPNF-S ἐπιλέγω
ἐπιλέγω 1aor. mid. ἐπελεξάμην; (1) active *call* or *name*; passive *be called* or *named* (JN 5.2); (2) middle *choose, select for oneself* (AC 15.40)
ἐπιλείπω fut. ἐπιλείψω; strictly *leave behind*; hence, of time *run out of, be short of, fail* (HE 11.32)
ἐπιλείχω impf. ἐπέλειχον; as moving the tongue over an object *lick* (LU 16.21)
ἐπιλείψει VIFA--3S ἐπιλείπω
ἐπιλελησμένον VPRPNN-S ἐπιλανθάνομαι
ἐπιλεξάμενος VPAMNM-S ἐπιλέγω
ἐπιλησμονή, ῆς, ἡ *forgetfulness*; ἀκροατὴ ἐ. *forgetful hearer* (JA 1.25)
ἐπιλησμονῆς N-GF-S ἐπιλησμονή
ἐπίλοιπα A--AN-P ἐπίλοιπος
ἐπίλοιπον A--AM-S "
ἐπίλοιπος, ον of a part from a whole that remains or continues *rest, still left*; substantivally τὰ ἐπίλοιπα *the remaining portion, what is left over* (LU 24.43); of time *remaining, future* (1P 4.2)
ἐπιλυθήσεται VIFP--3S ἐπιλύω
ἐπιλύσεως N-GF-S ἐπίλυσις
ἐπίλυσις, εως, ἡ literally *loosing, liberation*; figuratively, as explaining what is obscure *explanation, exposition, interpretation* (2P 1.20)
ἐπιλύω impf. ἐπέλυον; 1fut. pass. ἐπιλυθήσομαι; literally *release, set free*; figuratively, as clarifying parables *explain, interpret* (MK 4.34); as putting an end to a dispute *resolve, decide, settle* (AC 19.39)
ἐπιμαρτυρέω *bear witness, attest* (a preceding assertion), *affirm* (1P 5.12)
ἐπιμαρτυρῶν VPPANM-S ἐπιμαρτυρέω
ἐπιμεῖναι VNAA ἐπιμένω
ἐπιμείναντες VPAANM-P "
ἐπιμείνῃς VSAA--2S "
ἐπιμείνωσι(ν) VSAA--3P "
ἐπιμέλεια, ας, ἡ *care, attention*; ἐπιμελείας τυχεῖν *be cared for, get needed care* (AC 27.3)
ἐπιμελείας N-GF-S ἐπιμέλεια
ἐπιμελεῖσθε VIPO--2P ἐπιμελέομαι
ἐπιμελέομαι 1aor. ἐπεμελήθην; fut. ἐπιμελήσομαι; only passive in the NT; (1) *care for, take care of* (LU 10.34); (2) *look after, have charge of* (1T 3.5)
ἐπιμελήθητι VMAO--2S ἐπιμελέομαι
ἐπιμελήσεται VIFO--3S "
ἐπιμελῶς adverb; *carefully, diligently* (LU 15.8)
ἐπιμελῶς AB ἐπιμελῶς
ἐπίμενε VMPA--2S ἐπιμένω
ἐπιμένειν VNPA "
ἐπιμένετε VIPA--2P "
ἐπιμένῃς VSPA--2S "
ἐπιμένομεν VIPA--1P "
ἐπιμενόντων VPPAGM-P "
ἐπιμενοῦμεν VIFA--1P "
ἐπιμένω impf. ἐπέμενον; fut. ἐπιμενῶ; 1aor. ἐπέμεινα; *stay, remain*; (1) literally, as prolonging one's time in a place *remain on, stay on* (AC 10.48); (2) figuratively *continue, persevere, persist (in)* (RO 6.1)
ἐπιμενῶ VIFA--1S ἐπιμένω
ἐπιμένωμεν VSPA--1P "
ἐπιμένωσι(ν) VSPA--3P "

ἐπινεύω 1aor. ἐπένευσα; strictly *nod to*; hence *give consent, assent to, agree to* (AC 18.20)

ἐπίνοια, ας, ἡ *thought, purpose, intention* (AC 8.22)

ἐπίνοια	N-NF-S	ἐπίνοια
ἔπινον	VIIA--3P	πίνω
ἐπίομεν	VIAA--1P	"
ἔπιον	VIAA--3P	"
ἐπίοντι	VPPADN-S	ἔπειμι

ἐπιορκέω fut. ἐπιορκήσω; (1) *swear falsely, commit perjury*; (2) *break one's oath* or *vow*; either meaning is possible in MT 5.33

ἐπιορκήσεις	VIFA--2S	ἐπιορκέω
	VIFA--2S^VMPA--2S	"
ἐπιόρκοις	AP-DM-P	ἐπίορκος

ἐπίορκος, ον of one who violates his oath *perjured, swearing falsely*; substantively *perjurer* (1T 1.10)

ἐπιούσῃ	VPPADF-S	ἔπειμι
ἐπιούσιον	A--AM-S	ἐπιούσιος

ἐπιούσιος, ον of a daily and needed portion of food *daily, sufficient for the day* (MT 6.11); compare the provision of manna in the Old Testament

ἐπιπεπτωκός	VPRANN-S	ἐπιπίπτω
ἐπιπεσόντες	VPAANM-P	"
ἐπιπεσών	VPAANM-S	"
ἐπιπίπτειν	VNPA	"

ἐπιπίπτω 2aor. ἐπέπεσον; pf. ἐπιπέπτωκα; (1) literally *fall on* someone, *throw oneself on* (AC 20.10); idiomatically ἐπιπίπτειν ἐπὶ τὸν τράχηλον literally *fall on the neck*, i.e. *embrace, hug affectionately* (LU 15.20; AC 20.37); (2) *press* or *push against* (MK 3.10); (3) figuratively, of unexpected events, misfortunes, apprehensions *come on, seize, happen suddenly to* (AC 19.17); of the Holy Spirit in relation to a person *come down on, fall on* (AC 10.44)

ἐπιπλήξῃς	VSAA--2S	ἐπιπλήσσω
ἐπιπλήσσοντι	VPPADM-S	"

ἐπιπλήσσω 1aor. ἐπέπληξα; strictly *inflict with blows*; hence *reprove, rebuke (sharply)* (1T 5.1)

ἐπιπνίγω 1aor. ἐπέπνιξα; *suffocate*; figuratively, of plants overcrowded by other plants *choke (out)* (LU 8.7)

ἐπιποθεῖ	VIPA--3S	ἐπιποθέω

ἐπιποθέω 1aor. ἐπεπόθησα; *long for, have great affection for, yearn for* someone (PH 1.8); πρὸς φθόνον ἐπιποθεῖ τὸ πνεῦμα ὃ κατῴκισεν ἐν ἡμῖν (JA 4.5) is difficult: possibly *(God) zealously yearns over the spirit that he has caused to dwell in us* or *the Spirit he has caused to dwell in us is deeply jealous*

ἐπιποθήσατε	VMAA--2P	ἐπιποθέω
ἐπιπόθησιν	N-AF-S	ἐπιπόθησις

ἐπιπόθησις, εως, ἡ *great longing, earnest desire*

ἐπιπόθητοι	A--VM-P	ἐπιπόθητος

ἐπιπόθητος, ον *longed for, very dear, yearned over* (PH 4.1)

ἐπιποθία, ας, ἡ *great longing, yearning, earnest desire* (RO 15.23)

ἐπιποθίαν	N-AF-S	ἐπιποθία
ἐπιποθοῦντες	VPPANM-P	ἐπιποθέω
ἐπιποθούντων	VPPAGM-P	"
ἐπιποθῶ	VIPA--1S	"
ἐπιποθῶν	VPPANM-S	"

ἐπιπορεύομαι *go* or *journey to, come to, arrive* (LU 8.4)

ἐπιπορευομένων	VPPDGM-P	ἐπιπορεύομαι
	VPPOGM-P	"

ἐπίπρασκον	VIIA--3P	πιπράσκω
ἔπιπτε(ν)	VIIA--3S	πίπτω
ἐπιράπτει	VIPA--3S	ἐπιράπτω

ἐπιράπτω (and ἐπιρράπτω) of attaching a piece of cloth *sew* or *stitch on* (MK 2.21)

ἐπιράσθησαν	VIAP--3S	see ἐπειράσθησαν

ἐπιρίπτω (or ἐπιρρίπτω) 1aor. ἐπέριψα (or ἐπέρριψα); *throw on*; literally, as putting clothes on a riding animal as a kind of saddle cloth *throw on* (LU 19.35); idiomatically τὴν μέριμναν ἐπιρίπτειν ἐπί literally *cast cares on*, i.e. *stop worrying and trust completely* (1P 5.7)

ἐπιρίψαντες	VPAANM-P	ἐπιρίπτω
ἐπιρίψατε	VIAA--2S	"
ἐπιρράπτει	VIPA--3S	ἐπιράπτω
ἐπιρρίψαντες	VPAANM-P	ἐπιρίπτω
ἐπισείσαντες	VPAANM-P	ἐπισείω

ἐπισείω 1aor. ἐπέσεισα; (1) as a threatening gesture *shake* (one's hand or weapon) *at* someone; (2) as stirring a crowd to action *wave* or *beckon on, urge on, incite* (AC 14.19)

ἐπίσημοι	A--NM-P	ἐπίσημος
ἐπίσημον	A--AM-S	"

ἐπίσημος, ον (1) in a positive sense *outstanding, well-known* (RO 16.7); (2) in a negative sense *notorious, infamous, having a bad reputation* (MT 27.16)

ἐπισιτισμόν	N-AM-S	ἐπισιτισμός

ἐπισιτισμός, οῦ, ὁ *provisions, (supply of) food, something to eat*

ἐπισκέπτεσθαι	VNPD	ἐπισκέπτομαι
	VNPO	"
ἐπισκέπτεσθε	VIPD--2P	"
	VIPO--2P	"
ἐπισκέπτη	VIPD--2S	"
	VIPO--2S	"

ἐπισκέπτομαι 1aor. ἐπεσκεψάμην; (1) as looking after the sick *visit, go to help, look after* (MT 25.36); (2) as responsible ministry to someone *seek out, visit* (AC 15.36); (3) as finding a suitable person for an official position *choose, select, look for* (AC 6.3); (4) of God's gracious oversight of his people *visit, come to help* (LU 1.68); *be concerned about, show care for* (AC 15.14)

ἐπισκευάζομαι 1aor. ἐπεσκευασάμην; *make preparations, prepare*; of a journey *prepare, get ready for* (AC 21.15)

ἐπισκευασάμενοι	VPADNM-P	ἐπισκευάζομαι
ἐπισκέψασθαι	VNAD	ἐπισκέπτομαι
ἐπισκέψασθε	VMAD--2P	"
ἐπισκέψεται	VIFD--3S	"
ἐπισκεψώμεθα	VSAD--1P	"

ἐπισκηνόω 1aor. ἐπεσκήνωσα; literally *reside in a tent, take up residence* in a place; figuratively, of God's power sent to live in a person *rest on, indwell* (2C 12.9)

ἐπισκηνώσῃ	VSAA--3S	ἐπισκηνόω
ἐπισκιάζουσα	VPPANF-S	ἐπισκιάζω

ἐπισκιάζω 1aor. ἐπεσκίασα; literally, as darkening by partially blocking out a source of light *overshadow, cast a shadow on* (AC 5.15); of a cloud *cover* (MT 17.5); figuratively, of the effectual presence of God *overshadow, rest on, come to* (LU 1.35)

ἐπισκιάσει	VIFA--3S	ἐπισκιάζω
ἐπισκιάσῃ	VSAA--3S	"
ἐπισκοπεύοντες	VPPANM-P	ἐπισκοπέω

ἐπισκοπέω (and ἐπισκοπεύω)   (1) as denoting the responsibilities of elders and church officials (ἐπίσκοποι) *care for, watch out for* (1P 5.2); (2) of community responsibility for its members *see to, look after* (HE 12.15)

ἐπισκοπή, ῆς, ἡ   (1) as the presence of divine power to benefit or save *coming visitation* (LU 19.44; probably 1P 2.12); (2) as a demonstration of the divine power to punish *visitation, reckoning* (perhaps 1P 2.12); (3) as the position of an overseer *office, responsibility* (AC 1.20)

ἐπισκοπήν	N-AF-S	ἐπισκοπή
ἐπισκοπῆς	N-GF-S	"
ἐπισκόποις	N-DM-P	ἐπίσκοπος
ἐπίσκοπον	N-AM-S	"

ἐπίσκοπος, ου, ὁ   *overseer, one who watches over* the welfare of others; (1) of Christ *guardian, keeper* (1P 2.25); (2) of church leaders *bishop, overseer, pastor* (1T 3.2)

ἐπίσκοπος	N-NM-S	ἐπίσκοπος
ἐπισκοποῦντες	VPPANM-P	ἐπισκοπέω
ἐπισκόπους	N-AM-P	ἐπίσκοπος

ἐπισπάομαι   as a medical technical term *pull over the foreskin* to conceal former circumcision, *become uncircumcised, conceal circumcision* (1C 7.18)

ἐπισπάσθω	VMPD--3S	ἐπισπάομαι
	VMPO--3S	"

ἐπισπείρω   1aor. ἐπέσπειρα; *sow afterward; sow in* or *among* a previous sowing (MT 13.25)

ἐπίσταμαι   (1) of intellectual apprehension *understand, comprehend* (MK 14.68); (2) of recognition or acquaintance with something *know (about)* (AC 26.26); (3) of recognition of persons *be acquainted with, know (about)* (AC 19.15)

ἐπίσταμαι	VIPD--1S	ἐπίσταμαι
	VIPO--1S	"
ἐπιστάμεθα	VIPD--1P	"
	VIPO--1P	"
ἐπιστάμενος	VPPDNM-S	"
	VPPONM-S	"
ἐπίστανται	VIPD--3P	"
	VIPO--3P	"
ἐπιστάντες	VPAANM-P	ἐφίστημι
ἐπιστάς	VPAANM-S	"
ἐπιστᾶσα	VPAANF-S	"
ἐπίστασθαι	VNPD	ἐπίσταμαι
	VNPO	"
ἐπίστασθε	VIPD--2P	"
	VIPO--2P	"
ἐπίστασιν	N-AF-S	ἐπίστασις

ἐπίστασις, εως, ἡ   strictly *stopping, checking, halt in a march*; hence, as what creates hindrance to normal activity; (1) of people roused up against someone *attack, disturbance, rioting* (AC 24.12); (2) of the onset of multitudinous duties *burden, pressure, heavy responsibility* (2C 11.28)

ἐπίστασις	N-NF-S	ἐπίστασις
ἐπιστάτα	N-VM-S	ἐπιστάτης
ἐπίσταται	VIPD--3S	ἐπίσταμαι
	VIPO--3S	"

ἐπιστάτης, ου, ὁ   as a person of high status *master, lord*, used as a title by which to address Jesus (LU 5.5)

ἐπιστεῖλαι	VNAA	ἐπιστέλλω

ἐπιστέλλω   1aor. ἐπέστειλα; as transmitting a message or direction by letter or messenger *send word to, write to, instruct by letter*

ἐπίστευε(ν)	VIIA--3S	πιστεύω
ἐπιστεύετε	VIIA--2P	"
ἐπιστεύθη	VIAP--3S	"
ἐπιστεύθην	VIAP--1S	"
ἐπιστεύθησαν	VIAP--3P	"
ἐπίστευον	VIIA--3P	"
ἐπίστευσα	VIAA--1S	"
ἐπιστεύσαμεν	VIAA--1P	"
ἐπίστευσαν	VIAA--3P	"
ἐπίστευσας	VIAA--2S	"
ἐπιστεύσατε	VIAA--2P	"
ἐπίστευσε(ν)	VIAA--3S	"
ἐπιστῆ	VSAA--3S	ἐφίστημι
ἐπίστηθι	VMAA--2S	"

ἐπιστήμη, ης, ἡ   *knowledge, understanding, experience* (PH 4.8)

ἐπιστήμης	N-GF-S	ἐπιστήμη

ἐπιστήμων, ον, gen. ονος   *understanding, knowledgeable, well-instructed, skilled* (JA 3.13)

ἐπιστήμων	A--NM-S	ἐπιστήμων
ἐπιστηρίζοντες	VPPANM-P	ἐπιστηρίζω

ἐπιστηρίζω   1aor. ἐπεστήριξα; of attitude or belief *strengthen, establish, cause to be firm*

ἐπιστηρίζων	VPPANM-S	ἐπιστηρίζω
ἐπιστολαί	N-NF-P	ἐπιστολή
ἐπιστολαῖς	N-DF-P	"
ἐπιστολάς	N-AF-P	"

ἐπιστολή, ῆς, ἡ   a transmitted message *letter, epistle* (AC 9.2); metaphorically, of the church as a message produced by Christ, especially as a commendation of the success of the founding apostle (2C 3.2, 3)

ἐπιστολή	N-NF-S	ἐπιστολή
ἐπιστολῇ	N-DF-S	"
ἐπιστολήν	N-AF-S	"
ἐπιστολῆς	N-GF-S	"
ἐπιστολῶν	N-GF-P	"
ἐπιστομίζειν	VNPA	ἐπιστομίζω
ἐπιστόμιζε(ν)	VIPA--3S	"

ἐπιστομίζω   strictly *apply a muzzle* or *bridle*; hence, of false teachers *silence, prevent from teaching, stop the mouth* (TI 1.11)

ἐπιστραφείς	VPAPNM-S	ἐπιστρέφω
ἐπιστραφήτω	VMAP--3S	"
ἐπιστραφῶσι(ν)	VSAP--3P	"
ἐπιστρέφειν	VNPA	"
ἐπιστρέφετε	VIPA--2P	"
ἐπιστρέφητε	VSPA--2P	"
ἐπιστρέφουσι(ν)	VPPADM-P	"

ἐπιστρέφω   fut. ἐπιστρέψω; 1aor. ἐπέστρεψα; 2aor. pass. ἐπεστράφην; (1) intransitively, active and middle with aorist passive; (a) literally, of physical movement *turn around, turn (about)* (JN 21.20); *return, turn back* (AC 15.36); (b) figuratively, of religious or moral change *change one's ways, repent* (MK 4.12); of a change of mind or course of action *come to believe again in, turn back to, return to* (LU 17.4; GA 4.9); (2) transitively, of religious or moral change *turn, bring back, cause to change* (JA 5.19, 20)

ἐπιστρέψαι	VNAA	ἐπιστρέφω
ἐπιστρέψαντες	VPAANM-P	"
ἐπιστρέψας	VPAANM-S	"
ἐπιστρέψατε	VMAA--2P	"
ἐπιστρεψάτω	VMAA--3S	"
ἐπιστρέψει	VIFA--3S	"
ἐπιστρέψῃ	VSAA--3S	"
ἐπιστρέψητε	VSAA--2P	"
ἐπίστρεψον	VMAA--2S	"
ἐπιστρέψουσι(ν)	VPPADM-P	"
ἐπιστρέψω	VIFA--1S	"
ἐπιστρέψωσι(ν)	VSAA--3P	"

ἐπιστροφή, ῆς, ἡ literally *turning toward, turning about*; figuratively in the NT *change of one's beliefs* (possibly AC 15.3); *change in one's way of life* (possibly AC 15.3)

ἐπιστροφήν	N-AF-S	ἐπιστροφή
ἐπιστώθη	VIAP--3S	πιστόω
ἐπιστώθης	VIAP--2S	"
ἐπισυναγαγεῖν	VNAA	ἐπισυνάγω
ἐπισυνάγει	VIPA--3S	"

ἐπισυνάγω fut. ἐπισυνάξω; 1aor. inf. ἐπισυνάξαι (LU 13.34); 2aor. inf. ἐπισυναγαγεῖν (MT 23.37); pf. pass. ἐπισύνηγμαι; 1aor. pass. ἐπισυνήχθην; 1fut. pass. ἐπισυναχθήσομαι; *gather (together) people to a place, assemble, convene* (MK 13.27); passive *come together* (MK 1.33); of fowls or birds of prey *cause to come to the same place, gather* (MT 23.37); passive *be gathered* (LU 17.37)

ἐπισυναγωγή, ῆς, ἡ strictly, in a passive sense; an action *being gathered together*; of a community of believers *meeting together* (HE 10.25); as an end-time event at Christ's return *assembling, gathering together* (2TH 2.1)

ἐπισυναγωγήν	N-AF-S	ἐπισυναγωγή
ἐπισυναγωγῆς	N-GF-S	"
ἐπισυνάξαι	VNAA	ἐπισυνάγω
ἐπισυνάξει	VIFA--3S	"
ἐπισυνάξουσι(ν)	VIFA--3P	"
ἐπισυναχθεισῶν	VPAPGF-P	"
ἐπισυναχθήσονται	VIFP--3P	"
ἐπισυνηγμένη	VPRPNF-S	"
ἐπισυντρέχει	VIPA--3S	ἐπισυντρέχω

ἐπισυντρέχω of crowds *run together* to a place (MK 9.25)

ἐπισύστασιν	N-AF-S	ἐπισύστασις

ἐπισύστασις, εως, ἡ (1) *being gathered together against, riotous meeting, disturbance* (AC 24.12); (2) as the pressure of daily responsibilities *burden* (2C 11.28)

ἐπισύστασις	N-NF-S	ἐπισύστασις

ἐπισφαλής, ές *insecure, unsafe*; of a voyage in stormy seas *hazardous, dangerous* (AC 27.9)

ἐπισφαλοῦς	A--GM-S	ἐπισφαλής
ἐπίσχυον	VIIA--3P	ἐπισχύω

ἐπισχύω impf. ἐπίσχυον; intransitively *add strength, grow strong*; figuratively, of pressing a point *insist on, persist in, be emphatic about* (LU 23.5)

ἐπισωρεύσουσι(ν)	VIFA--3P	ἐπισωρεύω

ἐπισωρεύω fut. ἐπισωρεύσω; *heap together, pile up*; metaphorically, as increasing the amount of something *surround oneself with, accumulate (largely), gather around oneself* (2T 4.3)

ἐπιταγή, ῆς, ἡ (1) *command, order* (1C 7.25); κατ' ἐπιταγήν *by command* (2C 8.8); (2) as the exercise of official leadership *authority* (TI 2.15)

ἐπιταγήν	N-AF-S	ἐπιταγή
ἐπιταγῆς	N-GF-S	"
ἐπιτάξῃ	VSAA--3S	ἐπιτάσσω
ἐπιτάσσει	VIPA--3S	"
ἐπιτάσσειν	VNPA	"

ἐπιτάσσω 1aor. ἐπέταξα; as exercising authority to give specific instructions *order, command, instruct* (LU 4.36)

ἐπιτάσσω	VIPA--1S	ἐπιτάσσω
ἐπιτεθῇ	VSAP--3S	ἐπιτίθημι
ἐπιτελεῖν	VNPA	ἐπιτελέω
ἐπιτελεῖσθαι	VNPP	"
ἐπιτελεῖσθε	VIPM--2P	"
	VIPP--2P	"
ἐπιτελεῖται	VIPP--3S	"
ἐπιτελέσαι	VNAA	"
ἐπιτελέσας	VPAANM-S	"
ἐπιτελέσατε	VMAA--2P	"
ἐπιτελέσει	VIFA--3S	"
ἐπιτελέσῃ	VSAA--3S	"

ἐπιτελέω fut. ἐπιτελέσω; 1aor. ἐπετέλεσα; (1) in a temporal sense *finish, end, successfully complete* what has been begun (GA 3.3); (2) as bringing something about *accomplish, complete, perfect* (2C 7.1); of ritual duties *perform* (HE 9.6); as setting up a tent *erect* (HE 8.5); (3) passive, as experiencing purposeful trials *undergo, endure, go through* (1P 5.9)

ἐπιτελοῦντες	VPPANM-P	ἐπιτελέω
ἐπιτελῶ	VIPA--1S	"
ἐπιτέτραπται	VIRA--3S	ἐπιτρέπω
ἐπιτήδεια	A--AN-P	ἐπιτήδειος

ἐπιτήδειος, εία, ον *necessary*; substantivally τὰ ἐπιτήδεια τοῦ σώματος *what is necessary for the body, physical needs* (JA 2.16)

ἐπιτηδείῳ	A--DM-S	ἐπιτήδειος
ἐπιτιθέασι(ν)	VIPA--3P	ἐπιτίθημι
ἐπιτίθει	VMPA--2S	"
ἐπιτιθείς	VPPANM-S	"
ἐπιτίθεσθαι	VNPP	"
ἐπιτιθῇ	VSPA--3S	"

ἐπιτίθημι impf. third-person plural ἐπετίθεσαν; fut. ἐπιθήσω, mid. ἐπιθήσομαι; 1aor. ἐπέθηκα; 2aor. ἐπέθην, mid. ἐπεθέμην; (1) active; (a) literally *lay on, put* or *place on* (MT 27.29); ritually *lay hands on* (MK 5.23); (b) figuratively, of blows *inflict* (LU 10.30); as increasing an existing quantity *add on* or *to* (RV 22.18); as giving an additional name *nickname* or *surname* (MK 3.16, 17); (c) idiomatically ἐπιτιθέναι ζυγὸν ἐπὶ τὸν τράχηλον literally *put a yoke on the neck*, i.e. *impose many requirements* (AC 15.10); (2) middle, as giving to someone what he needs *furnish, provide* (AC 28.10); of hostile intent *set on, attack* (AC 18.10)

ἐπιτίθησι(ν)	VIPA--3S	ἐπιτίθημι
ἐπιτιμᾶν	VNPA	ἐπιτιμάω

ἐπιτιμάω impf. ἐπετίμων; 1aor. ἐπετίμησα; strictly *appraise someone, assess* a penalty, *charge someone as being blamable*; hence *rebuke, reprove* (JU 9); *warn, strongly admonish, threaten* (MK 3.12; 8.30)

ἐπιτιμῆσαι	VOAA--3S	ἐπιτιμάω

ἐπιτιμήσας VPAANM-S "
ἐπιτίμησον VMAA--2S "
ἐπιτιμία, ας, ἡ as a religious technical term for group discipline assessed and carried out with proper authority *punishment* (2C 2.6)
ἐπιτιμία N-NF-S ἐπιτιμία
ἐπιτιμῶν VPPANM-S ἐπιτιμάω
ἐπιτρέπεται VIPP--3S ἐπιτρέπω
ἐπιτρέπῃ VSPA--3S "
ἐπιτρέπω 1aor. ἐπέτρεψα; pf. pass. ἐπιτέτραμμαι; 2aor. pass. ἐπετράπην; *allow, permit, let* someone do something (MT 8.21)
ἐπιτρέπω VIPA--1S ἐπιτρέπω
ἐπιτρέψαι VNAA "
ἐπιτρέψαντος VPAAGM-S "
ἐπιτρέψῃ VSAA--3S "
ἐπίτρεψον VMAA--2S "
ἐπιτροπεύοντος VPPAGM-S ἐπιτροπεύω
ἐπιτροπεύω *hold the office of governor* (ἐπίτροπος), *be in charge, be procurator* (LU 3.1)
ἐπιτροπή, ῆς, ἡ *full authority* to carry out an assignment, *commission, trust* (AC 26.12)
ἐπιτροπῆς N-GF-S ἐπιτροπή
ἐπίτροπος, ου, ὁ *one put in charge* or *control*; (1) over things *steward, manager, foreman* (LU 8.3); (2) over persons *governor*; over children *guardian* (GA 4.2)
ἐπιτρόπου N-GM-S ἐπίτροπος
ἐπιτρόπους N-AM-P "
ἐπιτρόπῳ N-DM-S "
ἐπιτυγχάνω 2aor. ἐπέτυχον; strictly *light on, meet up with, find*; hence *obtain, get, attain*, with the genitive of the thing obtained (HE 6.15; probably RO 11.7); as equivalent to τυγχάνω *experience* (possibly RO 11.7)
ἐπιτυχεῖν VNAA ἐπιτυγχάνω
ἐπιτύχοντες VPAANM-S "
ἐπιφαινόντων VPPAGN-P ἐπιφαίνω
ἐπιφαίνω 1aor. ἐπέφανα; 2aor. pass. ἐπεφάνην; intransitively in the NT; (1) *show oneself, appear* (AC 27.20); metaphorically, of God's intervention *give light, shine on* (LU 1.79); (2) passive *become known, be manifested, appear* (TI 2.11)
ἐπιφᾶναι VNAA ἐπιφαίνω
ἐπιφάνεια, ας, ἡ as a visible manifestation of a divine being *appearance*; in the NT only of Christ; (1) in his first coming to earth (2T 1.10); (2) in his future coming (1T 6.14)
ἐπιφανεία N-DF-S ἐπιφάνεια
ἐπιφάνειαν N-AF-S "
ἐπιφανείας N-GF-S "
ἐπιφανῆ A-AF-S ἐπιφανής
ἐπιφανής, ές strictly *in full and clear view*; hence *splendid, glorious, wonderful* (AC 2.20)
ἐπιφαύσει VIFA--3S ἐπιφαύσκω
ἐπιφαύσκω fut. ἐπιφαύσω; *shine on, give light to*, figuratively, of spiritual enlightenment *cause to understand* (EP 5.14)
ἐπιφέρειν VNPA ἐπιφέρω
ἐπιφέρεσθαι VNPP "
ἐπιφέρω 2aor. ἐπήνεγκον; basically *cause to experience, impose on*; (1) of punishment *bring on, inflict* (RO 3.5); (2) of an accusation *bring (against), pronounce* (JU 9)

ἐπιφέρων VPPANM-S ἐπιφέρω
ἐπιφωνέω impf. ἐπεφώνουν; *cry out (loudly) against* someone, *shout (at)*
ἐπιφωσκούσῃ VPPADF-S ἐπιφώσκω
ἐπιφώσκω impf. ἐπέφωσκον; of the beginning of day *dawn, become light*
ἐπιχειρέω impf. ἐπεχείρουν; 1aor. ἐπεχείρησα; as setting one's hand to do something *undertake, try, attempt*
ἐπιχείρησις, εως, ἡ as an action *attempt* or *attack* on someone (AC 12.3)
ἐπιχείρησις N-NF-S ἐπιχείρησις
ἐπιχέω of liquids *pour on, pour over* (LU 10.34)
ἐπιχέων VPPANM-S ἐπιχέω
ἐπιχορηγέω 1aor. ἐπεχορήγησα; 1fut. pass. ἐπιχορηγηθήσομαι; (1) literally, of one who provides out of his own expense *furnish, supply* (2C 9.10); figuratively *provide in addition, add* (2P 1.5); (2) of the supply of spiritual benefits *give, grant, bestow* (2P 1.11); (3) passive, of vigor supplied to the body *be supported* (CO 2.19)
ἐπιχορηγηθήσεται VIFP--3S ἐπιχορηγέω
ἐπιχορηγήσατε VMAA--2P "
ἐπιχορηγία, ας, ἡ literally *supply, support, provision* (metaphorically in EP 4.16); figuratively, of the supply of spiritual benefits (PH 1.19)
ἐπιχορηγίας N-GF-S ἐπιχορηγία
ἐπιχορηγούμενον VPPPNN-S ἐπιχορηγέω
ἐπιχορηγῶν VPPANM-S "
ἐπιχρίω 1aor. ἐπέχρισα; *smear on, anoint, rub on*
ἐπιψαύσεις VIFA--2S ἐπιψαύω
ἐπιψαύω fut. ἐπιψαύσω; *touch*; figuratively, of persons *be in contact with* (EP 5.14)
ἐπλανήθησαν VIAP--3P πλανάω
ἐπλάνησε(ν) VIAA--3S "
ἔπλασας VIAA--2S πλάσσω
ἐπλάσθη VIAP--3S "
ἐπλάτυναν VIAA--3P πλατύνω
ἐπλέομεν VIIA--1P πλέω
ἐπλεόνασε(ν) VIAA--3S πλεονάζω
ἐπλεονέκτησα VIAA--1S πλεονεκτέω
ἐπλεονεκτήσαμεν VIAA--1P "
ἐπλεονέκτησε(ν) VIAA--3S "
ἔπλευσε(ν) VIAA--3S πλέω
ἐπλήγη VIAP--3S πλήσσω
ἐπληθύνετο VIIP--3S πληθύνω
ἐπληθύνθη VIAP--3S "
ἐπληθύνοντο VIIP--3P "
ἐπλήρου VIIA--3S πληρόω
ἐπληροῦντο VIIP--3P "
ἐπληροῦτο VIIP--3S "
ἐπληρώθη VIAP--3S "
ἐπληρώθημεν VIAP--1P "
ἐπληρώθησαν VIAP--3P "
ἐπλήρωσαν VIAA--3P "
ἐπληρώσατε VIAA--2P "
ἐπλήρωσε(ν) VIAA--3S "
ἔπλησαν VIAA--3P πίμπλημι
ἐπλήσθη VIAP--3S "
ἐπλήσθησαν VIAP--3P "
ἐπλήσσοντι VPPADM-S πλήσσω
ἐπλούτησαν VIAA--3P πλουτέω
ἐπλουτήσατε VIAA--2P "

ἐπλουτίσθητε	VIAP--2P	πλουτίζω
ἔπλυναν	VIAA--3P	πλύνω
ἔπλυνον	VIIA--3P	"
ἔπνευσαν	VIAA--3P	πνέω
ἔπνιγε(ν)	VIIA--3S	πνίγω
ἐπνίγοντο	VIIP--3P	"
ἔπνιξαν	VIAA--3P	"
ἐποίει	VIIA--3S	ποιέω
ἐποιεῖτε	VIIA--2P	"
ἐποίησα	VIAA--1S	"
ἐποιήσαμεν	VIAA--1P	"
ἐποιησάμην	VIAM--1S	"
ἐποίησαν	VIAA--3P	"
ἐποιήσαντο	VIAM--3P	"
ἐποίησας	VIAA--2S	"
ἐποιήσατε	VIAA--2P	"
ἐποίησε(ν)	VIAA--3S	"
ἐποικοδομεῖ	VIPA--3S	ἐποικοδομέω
ἐποικοδομεῖσθε	VIPP--2P	"
	VMPP--2P	"

ἐποικοδομέω 1aor. ἐποικοδόμησα; 1aor. pass. ἐποικοδομήθην; literally, as adding to the foundation of a building *build on*, *build further* (metaphorically in 1C 3.10); figuratively, as adding to a spiritual foundation *build up*, *make more able*, *cause to be strong* (CO 2.7)

ἐποικοδομηθέντες	VPAPNM-P	ἐποικοδομέω
ἐποικοδομῆσαι	VNAA	"
ἐποικοδόμησε(ν)	VIAA--3S	"
ἐποικοδομούμενοι	VPPPNM-P	"
ἐποικοδομοῦντες	VPPANM-P	"
ἐποίουν	VIIA--3P	ποιέω
ἐποιοῦντο	VIIM--3P	"

ἐποκέλλω 1aor. ἐπώκειλα; of a ship *run aground*, *run ashore* (AC 27.41)

ἐπολέμει	VIIA--3S	πολεμέω
ἐπολέμησαν	VIAA--3P	"
ἐπολέμησε(ν)	VIAA--3S	"
ἐπολέμουν	VIIA--3S	"
ἐπονομάζῃ	VIPM--2S	ἐπονομάζω

ἐπονομάζω strictly *name after*, *give an additional name*; hence *classify by name*, *call*; only middle in the NT *call oneself* (RO 2.17)

ἐπόπται	N-NM-P	ἐπόπτης
ἐποπτεύοντες	VPPANM-P	ἐποπτεύω
ἐποπτεύσαντες	VPAANM-P	"

ἐποπτεύω 1aor. ἐπώπτευσα; *look on*, *observe*, *watch*

ἐπόπτης, ου, ὁ as an attentive onlooker *eyewitness*, *observer* (2P 1.16)

ἐπορεύετο	VIID--3S	πορεύομαι
	VIIO--3S	"
ἐπορεύθη	VIAO--3S	"
ἐπορεύθησαν	VIAO--3P	"
ἐπορευόμεθα	VIID--1P	"
	VIIO--1P	"
ἐπορευόμην	VIID--1S	"
	VIIO--1S	"
ἐπορεύοντο	VIID--3P	"
	VIIO--3P	"
ἐπόρθει	VIIA--3S	πορθέω
ἐπόρθουν	VIIA--1S	"

ἐπόρνευσαν	VIAA--3P	πορνεύω

ἔπος, ους, τό *word*; idiomatically, to introduce another way of saying something ὡς ἔ. εἰπεῖν literally *as to speak a word*, i.e. *so to speak*, *if one may say so*, *one might say* (HE 7.9)

ἔπος	N-AN-S	ἔπος
ἐπότιζε(ν)	VIIA--3S	ποτίζω
ἐπότιζον	VIIA--3P	"
ἐπότισα	VIAA--1S	"
ἐποτίσαμεν	VIAA--1P	"
ἐποτίσατε	VIAA--2P	"
ἐπότισε(ν)	VIAA--3S	"
ἐποτίσθημεν	VIAP--1P	"
ἐπουράνια	A--AN-P	ἐπουράνιος
	A--NN-P	"
ἐπουράνιοι	A--NM-P	"
ἐπουρανίοις	A--DN-P	"
ἐπουράνιον	A--AF-S	"

ἐπουράνιος, ον (1) as an adjective, with reference to heaven as the dwelling of God and what belongs there *heavenly* (HE 12.22), opposite ἐπίγειος (*earthly*); (2) substantivally; (a) οἱ ἐπουράνιοι *dwellers in heaven*, *heavenly beings* (PH 2.10); (b) τὰ ἐπουράνια what is derived from God *heavenly things*, *divine* or *spiritual things* (JN 3.12); (c) τὰ ἐπουράνια as the dwelling place of God *heaven*, *the heavenly world*, *the heavenly places* (EP 3.10); (3) as an adjective, with reference to the sky as the realm of the sun, moon, and stars *in the sky*, *celestial* (1C 15.40)

ἐπουράνιος	A--NM-S	ἐπουράνιος
ἐπουρανίου	A--GF-S	"
	A--GM-S	"
ἐπουρανίῳ	A--DF-S	"
ἐπουρανίων	A--GM-P	"
	A--GN-P	"
ἐπράθη	VIAP--3S	πιπράσκω
ἔπραξα	VIAA--1S	πράσσω
ἐπράξαμεν	VIAA--1P	"
ἔπραξαν	VIAA--3P	"
ἐπράξατε	VIAA--2P	"
ἔπραξε(ν)	VIAA--3S	"
ἔπρεπε(ν)	VIIA--3S	πρέπω
ἐπρήσθησαν	VIAP--3P	πίμπρημι
ἐπρίσθησαν	VIAP--3P	πρίζω
ἐπροφήτευον	VIIA--3P	προφητεύω
ἐπροφητεύσαμεν	VIAA-1P	"
ἐπροφήτευσαν	VIAA--3P	"
ἐπροφήτευσε(ν)	VIAA--3S	"

ἑπτά indeclinable; as a cardinal number *seven* (MT 15.34); in Jewish usage often designating a round or complete number (MT 12.45)

ἔπταισαν	VIAA--3P	πταίω

ἑπτάκις adverb; *seven times*, possibly indicating a relatively larger number than one would expect

ἑπτάκις	AB	ἑπτάκις

ἑπτακισχίλιοι, αι, α as a cardinal number *seven thousand* (RO 11.4)

ἑπτακισχιλίους	A-CAM-P	ἑπτακισχίλιοι
ἑπταπλασίονα	A--AN-P	ἑπταπλασίων

ἑπταπλασίων, ον, gen. **ονος**   *sevenfold, seven times more,* i.e. much more than one would expect; substantively ἑπταπλασίονα *seven times as much* (LU 18.30)

ἔπτυσε(ν)	VIAA--3S	πτύω
ἐπτώχευσε(ν)	VIAA--3S	πτωχεύω
ἐπύθετο	VIAD--3S	πυνθάνομαι
ἐπύθοντο	VIAD--3P	"
ἐπυνθάνετο	VIID--3S	"
	VIIO--3S	"
ἐπυνθάνοντο	VIID--3P	"
	VIIO--3P	"
ἐπώκειλαν	VIAA--3P	ἐποκέλλω
ἐπῳκοδόμησε(ν)	VIAA--3S	ἐποικοδομέω
ἐπώλησε(ν)	VIAA--3S	πωλέω
ἐπώλουν	VIIA--3P	"
ἐπωνόμασε(ν)	VIAA--3S	ἐπονομάζω
ἐπωρώθη	VIAP--3S	πωρόω
ἐπωρώθησαν	VIAP--3P	"
ἐπώρωσε(ν)	VIAA--3S	"
ἐραβδίσθην	VIAP--1S	ῥαβδίζω
ἐράντισε(ν)	VIAA--3S	ῥαντίζω
ἐράπισαν	VIAA--3P	ῥαπίζω
Ἔραστον	N-AM-S	Ἔραστος

Ἔραστος, ου, ὁ   *Erastus,* masculine proper noun

Ἔραστος	N-NM-S	Ἔραστος
ἐραυνᾷ	VIPA--3S	ἐραυνάω
ἐραυνᾶτε	VIPA--2P	"
	VMPA--2P	"

ἐραυνάω (and **ἐρευνάω**)   1aor. ἠραύνησα and ἐρεύνησα; (1) as making a thorough investigation *try to find out, search, examine* (JN 5.39); (2) of the Spirit's investigation *search (deeply), fathom* (1C 2.10)

ἐραύνησον	VMAA--2S	ἐραυνάω
ἐραυνῶν	VPPANM-S	"
ἐραυνῶντες	VPPANM-P	"
ἔργα	N-AN-P	ἔργον
	N-NN-P	"
ἐργάζεσθαι	VNPD	ἐργάζομαι
	VNPO	"
ἐργάζεσθε	VIPD--2P	"
	VIPO--2P	"
	VMPD--2P	"
	VMPO--2P	"
ἐργάζεται	VIPD--3S	"
	VIPO--3S	"
ἐργάζῃ	VIPD--2S	"
	VIPO--2S	"

ἐργάζομαι   1aor. ἠργασάμην and εἰργασάμην; (1) intransitively; (a) *work, be active* (1C 4.12); (b) of business practice *trade* (MT 25.16); (2) transitively; (a) *do, accomplish, perform, carry out* something (JN 6.28); (b) of duties and rites *practice, perform, minister* (1C 9.13); (c) as making one's living *earn by working;* ἐργάζεσθαι θάλασσαν *make one's living on the sea, trade by sea* (RV 18.17); (d) of effectiveness in anything, either negative (MT 7.23) or positive (JA 1.20) *accomplish, bring about*

ἐργάζομαι	VIPD--1S	ἐργάζομαι
	VIPO--1S	"
ἐργαζόμεθα	VIPD--1P	"
	VIPO--1P	"

ἐργαζόμενοι	VPPDNM-P	"
	VPPDVM-P	"
	VPPONM-P	"
	VPPOVM-P	"
ἐργαζόμενον	VPPDAM-S	"
	VPPOAM-S	"
ἐργαζόμενος	VPPDNM-S	"
	VPPONM-S	"
ἐργαζομένους	VPPDAM-P	"
	VPPOAM-P	"
ἐργαζομένῳ	VPPDDM-S	"
	VPPODM-S	"
ἐργάζονται	VIPD--3P	"
	VIPO--3P	"
ἐργάζου	VMPD--2S	"
	VMPO--2S	"
ἐργαζώμεθα	VSPD--1P	"
	VSPO--1P	"
ἐργάσῃ	VSAD--2S	"

ἐργασία, ας, ἡ   (1) *work, labor, practice* or *pursuit* of something (EP 4.19); (2) a work carried on as a business *trade, craft* (AC 19.25); as the product of such business *gain, profit* (AC 16.16); (3) idiomatically διδόναι ἐργασίαν literally *give effort,* i.e. *do one's best, strive, try hard* (LU 12.58)

ἐργασίαν	N-AF-S	ἐργασία
ἐργασίας	N-GF-S	"
ἐργασώμεθα	VSAD--1P	ἐργάζομαι
ἐργάται	N-NM-P	ἐργάτης
	N-VM-P	"
ἐργάτας	N-AM-P	"
ἐργάτην	N-AM-S	"

ἐργάτης, ου, ὁ   literally *worker, laborer* (MT 10.10); metaphorically, of one who engages in spiritual activity *doer, laborer,* used in good and bad senses (LU 10.2; 2C 11.13)

ἐργάτης	N-NM-S	ἐργάτης
ἐργατῶν	N-GM-P	"
ἔργοις	N-DN-P	ἔργον

ἔργον, ου, τό   (1) generally *work;* (a) active, anything done or to be done *deed, work, action* (JN 3.21); (b) passive, anything achieved or made as the product of an action or process *workmanship, deed, accomplishment* (1C 3.13); (2) in contrast to rest *work, activity* (HE 4.3, 4); *deed* (1J 3.18) in contrast to word (λόγος); as a corollary or complement to faith, as a practical demonstration or proof of it *work(s), deed(s)* (JA 2.18); (3) as God's activity in the world *work(s), deed(s), act(s)* (JN 5.20); (4) as human duties and occupations *work, task* (AC 14.26); (5) in a weakened sense *matter, thing, undertaking* (AC 5.38)

ἔργον	N-AN-S	ἔργον
	N-NN-S	"
ἔργου	N-GN-S	"
ἔργῳ	N-DN-S	"
ἔργων	N-GN-P	"
ἐρεθίζετε	VMPA--2P	ἐρεθίζω

ἐρεθίζω   1aor. ἠρέθισα; *arouse, excite, kindle;* in a bad sense *make resentful, irritate, rouse to anger* (CO 3.21); in a good sense *incite, stimulate* (2C 9.2)

ἐρεῖ	VIFA--3S	εἶπον

ἐρείδω   1aor. ἤρεισα; as becoming immovable *become fixed, stay on* something; of a ship's bow run aground *jam* or *stick fast* (AC 27.41)

ἔρεις	N-AF-P	ἔρις
ἐρεῖς	VIFA--2S	εἶπον
	VIFA--2S^VMAA--2S	"
ἐρείσασα	VPAANF-S	ἐρείδω
ἐρεῖτε	VIFA--2P	εἶπον
	VIFA--2P^VMAA--2P	"

ἐρεύγομαι   fut. ἐρεύξομαι; literally *spit* or *spew out, disgorge*; figuratively, of sudden and emphatic speech *utter, speak out, announce* (MT 13.35)

ἐρευνᾷ	VIPA--3S	ἐραυνάω
ἐρευνᾶτε	VIPA--2P	"
	VMPA--2P	"
ἐρεύνησον	VMAA--2S	"
ἐρευνῶν	VPPANM-S	"
ἐρευνῶτες	VPPANM-P	"
ἐρεύξομαι	VIFD--1S	ἐρεύγομαι

ἐρημία, ας, ἡ   *uninhabited region, desolate place, desert*

ἐρημίᾳ	N-DF-S	ἐρημία
ἐρημίαις	N-DF-P	"
ἐρημίας	N-GF-S	"
ἐρήμοις	AP-DF-P	ἔρημος
	A--DM-P	"
ἔρημον	AP-AF-S	"
	A--AM-S	"

ἔρημος, ον   (1) of an empty or uninhabited place *abandoned, lonely, desolate* (LU 4.42); (2) of persons *abandoned, forsaken, desolate* (GA 4.27); (3) substantivally ἡ ἔ. an uncultivated or uninhabited place *desert, wilderness* (LU 15.4)

ἔρημος	A--NF-S	ἔρημος
	A--NM-S	"
ἐρήμου	AP-GF-S	"
ἐρήμους	AP-AF-P	"
ἐρημοῦται	VIPP--3S	ἐρημόω

ἐρημόω   pf. pass. ptc. ἠρημωμένος; 1aor. pass. ἠρημώθην; only passive in the NT; (1) of a kingdom *be brought to ruin, become desolate, be devastated* (MT 12.25); (2) of a prosperous city *be depopulated, be destroyed, be ruined* (RV 18.17)

ἐρήμῳ	AP-DF-S	ἔρημος
	A--DM-S	"
ἐρημώσεως	N-GF-S	ἐρήμωσις

ἐρήμωσις, εως, ἡ   as an action *desolation, devastation, destruction* (LU 21.20); τὸ βδέλυγμα τῆς ἐρημώσεως, a Hebraism meaning *the detestable thing that causes desolation* or *abandonment* (MT 24.15)

ἐρήμωσις	N-NF-S	ἐρήμωσις
ἔριδες	N-NF-P	ἔρις
ἔριδι	N-DF-S	"
ἔριδος	N-GF-S	"

ἐρίζω   fut. ἐρίσω; *quarrel, angrily dispute, strive* with harsh words (MT 12.19)

ἐριθεία, ας, ἡ   from ἐριθεύω (*serve for hire*), which is from ἔριθος (*day-laborer*); as denoting an attitude of self-seeking *selfish ambition, self-interest, rivalry* (PH 2.3)

ἐριθεία	N-NF-S	ἐριθεία
ἐριθείαι	N-NF-P	"
ἐριθείαν	N-AF-S	"

ἐριθείας	N-GF-S	"
ἐριμμένοι	VPRPNM-P	ῥίπτω
ἔριν	N-AF-S	ἔρις

ἔριον, ου, τό   *wool*; as the curly hair of sheep *fleece, wool* (RV 1.14); as the processed hair *wool* (HE 9.19)

ἔριον	N-NN-S	ἔριον
ἐρίου	N-GN-S	"

ἔρις, ιδος, ἡ   *strife, debate, discord* (RO 1.29); plural *quarrels, rivalries* (1C 1.11)

ἔρις	N-NF-S	ἔρις
ἐρίσει	VIFA--3S	ἐρίζω
ἔρισι	N-DF-P	ἔρις
ἐρίφια	N-AN-P	ἐρίφιον

ἐρίφιον, ου, τό   diminutive of ἔριφος; *kid* (LU 15.29), *goat* (MT 25.33)

ἐρίφιον	N-AN-S	ἐρίφιον
ἔριφον	N-AM-S	ἔριφος

ἔριφος, ου, ὁ   *he-goat, kid, young goat*; plural *goats*, including male and female

ἐρίφων	N-GM-P	ἔριφος
ἔριψαν	VIAA--3P	see ἔρριψαν
Ἑρμᾶν	N-AM-S	Ἑρμᾶς

Ἑρμᾶς, ᾶ, ὁ   *Hermas*, masculine proper noun (RO 16.14)

Ἑρμῆν	N-AM-S	Ἑρμῆς

ἑρμηνεία, ας, ἡ   *interpretation, explanation, translation*; as an endowment of the Spirit, the ability to make words intelligible that would otherwise not be understood (1C 12.10)

ἑρμηνεία	N-NF-S	ἑρμηνεία
ἑρμηνείαν	N-AF-S	"
ἑρμηνεύειν	VNPA	ἑρμηνεύω
ἑρμηνεύεται	VIPP--3S	"
ἑρμηνευόμενον	VPPPNN-S	"
ἑρμηνευόμενος	VPPPNM-S	"

ἑρμηνευτής, οῦ, ὁ   *interpreter, translator* (1C 14.28)

ἑρμηνευτής	N-NM-S	ἑρμηνευτής

ἑρμηνεύω   (1) as transferring from a foreign to a familiar language *translate, interpret* (JN 1.42); (2) as making clear what is difficult to understand *expound, explain* (LU 24.27)

Ἑρμῆς, οῦ, ὁ   *Hermes*; (1) masculine proper noun (RO 16.14); (2) name of a Greek god (AC 14.12)

Ἑρμογένης, ους, ὁ   *Hermogenes*, masculine proper noun (2T 1.15)

Ἑρμογένης	N-NM-S	Ἑρμογένης
ἐροῦμεν	VIFA--1P	εἶπον
ἐροῦσι(ν)	VIFA--3P	"
ἑρπετά	N-AN-P	ἑρπετόν
	N-NN-P	"

ἑρπετόν, οῦ, τό   *reptile, creeping animal* (AC 10.12)

ἑρπετῶν	N-GN-P	ἑρπετόν
ἐρραβδίσθην	VIAP--1S	ῥαβδίζω
ἐρραμμένον	VPRPAN-S	ῥαίνω
ἐρράντισε(ν)	VIAA--3S	ῥαντίζω
ἐρραντισμένοι	VPRPNM-P	"
ἐρραντισμένον	VPRPAN-S	"
ἐρράπισαν	VIAA--3P	ῥαπίζω
ἐρρέθη	VIAP--3S	εἶπον
ἐρρέθησαν	VIAP--3P	"
ἐρρήθη	VIAP--3S	"
ἔρρηξε(ν)	VIAA--3S	ῥήγνυμι

ἐρριζωμένοι	VPRPNM-P	ῥιζόω
ἐρριμμένοι	VPRPNM-P	ῥίπτω
ἔρριπται	VIRP--3S	"
ἐρρίψαμεν	VIAA--1P	"
ἔρριψαν	VIAA--3P	"
ἐρρύσατο	VIAD--3S	ῥύομαι
ἐρρύσθην	VIAP--1S	"
ἔρρωσ᾽	VMRP--2P	see ἔρρωσθε
	VMRP--2P^QS	see ἔρρωσθε
	VMRP--2S	see ἔρρωσο
	VMRP--2S^QS	see ἔρρωσο
ἔρρωσθε	VMRP--2P	ῥώννυμι
	VMRP--2P^QS	"
ἔρρωσο	VMRP--2S	"
	VMRP--2S^QS	"
ἐρυθρᾷ	A--DF-S	ἐρυθρός
ἐρυθράν	A--AF-S	"
ἐρυθρός, ά, όν	as a color *red*	
ἐρυσάμην	VIAD--1S	ῥύομαι
ἐρύσατο	VIAD--3S	"
ἐρύσθην	VIAP--1S	"
ἔρχεσθαι	VNPD	ἔρχομαι
	VNPO	"
ἔρχεσθε	VMPD--2P	"
	VMPO--2P	"
ἐρχέσθω	VMPD--3S	"
	VMPO--3S	"
ἔρχεται	VIPD--3S	"
	VIPO--3S	"
ἔρχῃ	VIPD--2S	"
	VIPO--2S	"
ἔρχηται	VSPD--3S	"
	VSPO--3S	"

ἔρχομαι impf. ἠρχόμην; fut. ἐλεύσομαι; 2aor. act. ἦλθον and ἦλθα; pf. act. ἐλήλυθα; with a basic meaning *come, go*, used of persons and things, events and situations; used both literally and figuratively, with the meaning varying according to the context and the accompanying preposition; (1) of persons; (a) as coming forward publicly *come, appear, show up* (MT 11.14); (b) as the future coming of the Messiah *going to come, will come* (JN 4.25); (c) figuratively, as the spiritual coming of God (JN 14.23); of Christ (JN 14.18), of the Spirit (JN 15.26); (d) as the coming of persons to God (JN 14.6); (2) of events *happen to* someone or something (PH 1.12); (3) of time in a future sense of time *coming, will come* (JN 16.4)

ἔρχομαι	VIPD--1S	ἔρχομαι
	VIPO--1S	"
ἐρχόμεθα	VIPD--1P	"
	VIPO--1P	"
ἐρχόμενα	VPPDAN-P	"
	VPPOAN-P	"
ἐρχομένη	VPPDNF-S	"
	VPPONF-S	"
ἐρχομένην	VPPDAF-S	"
	VPPOAF-S	"
ἐρχομένης	VPPDGF-S	"
	VPPOGF-S	"
ἐρχόμενοι	VPPDNM-P	"
	VPPONM-P	"

ἐρχόμενον	VPPDAM-S	"
	VPPDAN-S	"
	VPPDNN-S	"
	VPPOAM-S	"
	VPPOAN-S	"
	VPPONN-S	"
ἐρχόμενος	VPPDNM-S	"
	VPPONM-S	"
ἐρχομένου	VPPDGM-S	"
	VPPOGM-S	"
ἐρχομένους	VPPDAM-P	"
	VPPOAM-P	"
ἐρχομένῳ	VPPDDM-S	"
	VPPDDN-S	"
	VPPODM-S	"
	VPPODN-S	"
ἐρχομένων	VPPDGM-P	"
	VPPOGM-P	"
ἔρχονται	VIPD--3P	"
	VIPO--3P	"
ἔρχου	VMPD--2S	"
	VMPO--2S	"
ἔρχωμαι	VSPD--1S	"
	VSPO--1S	"
ἐρῶ	VIFA--1S	εἶπον
ἐρώτα	VIPA--3S	see ἐρωτᾷ
ἐρωτᾷ	VIPA--3S	ἐρωτάω
	VSPA--3S	"
ἐρωτᾶν	VNPA	"
ἐρωτᾷς	VIPA--2S	"
ἐρωτᾶτε	VIPA--2P	"

ἐρωτάω fut. ἐρωτήσω; 1aor. ἠρώτησα; (1) as seeking information *ask, inquire, question* (MT 19.17); (2) as making a request *ask, demand, beg* someone to do something (JN 4.40); as making a request to God *ask, pray* (JN 16.26)

ἐρωτῆσαι	VNAA	ἐρωτάω
ἐρωτήσατε	VMAA--2P	"
ἐρωτήσετε	VIFA--2P	"
ἐρωτήσῃ	VSAA--3S	"
ἐρώτησον	VMAA--2S	"
ἐρωτήσουσι(ν)	VIFA--3P	"
ἐρωτήσω	VIFA--1S	"
	VSAA--1S	"
ἐρωτήσωμεν	VSAA--1P	"
ἐρωτήσωσι(ν)	VSAA--3P	"
ἐρωτῶ	VIPA--1S	"
ἐρωτῶμεν	VIPA--1P	"
ἐρωτῶν	VPPANM-S	"
ἐρωτῶντες	VPPANM-P	"
ἐρωτώντων	VPPAGM-P	"
ἐσαλεύθη	VIAP--3S	σαλεύω
ἐσάλευσε(ν)	VIAA--3S	"
ἐσάλπισε(ν)	VIAA--3S	σαλπίζω
ἔσβεσαν	VIAA--3P	σβέννυμι
ἐσεβάσθησαν	VIAO--3P	σεβάζομαι
ἐσείσθη	VIAP--3S	σείω
ἐσείσθησαν	VIAP--3P	"
ἔσεσθαι	VNFD	εἰμί
ἔσεσθε	VIFD--2P	"
	VIFD--2P^VMPA--2P	"

173

ἔση	VIFD--2S	"
ἐσήμαινε(ν)	VIIA--3S	σημαίνω
ἐσήμανε(ν)	VIAA--3S	"
ἐσθής, ῆτος, ἡ	*clothing, robe, garment*	
ἐσθήσεσι(ν)	N-DF-P	ἐσθής
ἐσθῆτα	N-AF-S	"
ἔσθητε	VSPA--2P	ἐσθίω
ἐσθῆτι	N-DF-S	ἐσθής
ἐσθίει	VIPA--3S	ἐσθίω
ἐσθίειν	VNPA	"
ἐσθίετε	VIPA--2P	"
	VMPA--2P	"
ἐσθιέτω	VMPA--3S	"
ἐσθίη	VSPA--3S	"
ἐσθίητε	VSPA--2P	"
ἔσθιον	VIIA--3P	see ἤσθιον
ἐσθίοντα	VPPAAM-S	ἐσθίω
ἐσθίοντας	VPPAAM-P	"
ἐσθίοντες	VPPANM-P	"
ἐσθίοντι	VPPADM-S	"
ἐσθιόντων	VPPAGM-P	"
ἐσθίουσι(ν)	VIPA--3P	"

ἐσθίω fut. mid. φάγομαι; 2aor. ἔφαγον; literally *eat* (MT 14.20); ἄρτον ἐσθίειν *have a meal, eat bread* or *food* (MT 15.2); idiomatically τὸν ἑαυτοῦ ἄρτον ἐσθίειν; (1) literally *eat one's own bread*, i.e. *earn a living* (2TH 3.12); (2) figuratively; (a) *consume, destroy* as if by rust or fire (HE 10.27); (b) metaphorically, as taking spiritual nourishment *eat, partake of* (JN 6.53)

ἐσθίων	VPPANM-S	ἐσθίω
ἐσθίωσι(ν)	VSPA--3P	"
ἔσθοντες	VPPANM-P	see ἐσθίοντες
ἔσθων	VPPANM-S	see ἐσθίων
ἐσίγησαν	VIAA--3P	σιγάω
ἐσίγησε(ν)	VIAA--3S	"
ἐσιώπα	VIIA--3S	σιωπάω
ἐσιώπων	VIIA--3P	"
ἐσκανδαλίζοντο	VIIP--3P	σκανδαλίζω
ἐσκανδαλίσθησαν	VIAP--3P	"
ἔσκαψε(ν)	VIAA--3S	σκάπτω
ἐσκήνωσε(ν)	VIAA--3S	σκηνόω
ἐσκίρτησε(ν)	VIAA--3S	σκιρτάω
ἐσκληρύνοντο	VIIP--3P	σκληρύνω
ἐσκόρπισε(ν)	VIAA--3S	σκορπίζω
ἐσκορπισμένα	VPRPAN-P	"
ἐσκοτίσθη	VIAP--3S	σκοτίζω
ἐσκοτισμένη	VPRPNF-S	"
ἐσκοτισμένοι	VPRPNM-P	"
ἐσκοτώθη	VIAP--3S	σκοτόω
ἐσκοτωμένη	VPRPNF-S	"
ἐσκοτωμένοι	VPRPNM-P	"
ἐσκυλμένοι	VPRPNM-P	σκύλλω
Ἐσλεί		Ἐσλί
Ἐσλί		"

Ἐσλί, ὁ (also **Ἐσλεί, Ἐσλί**) indeclinable; *Esli*, masculine proper noun

ἐσμέν	VIPA--1P	εἰμί
ἐσμυρνισμένον	VPRPAM-S	σμυρνίζω
ἔσομαι	VIFD--1S	εἰμί
ἐσόμεθα	VIFD--1P	"
ἐσόμενον	VPFDAN-S	"

ἔσονται	VIFD--3P	"

ἔσοπτρον, ου, τό as a piece of flat metal, polished to reflect an image *mirror*

ἐσόπτρου	N-GN-S	ἔσοπτρον
ἐσόπτρῳ	N-DN-S	"
ἐσπάραξε(ν)	VIAA--3S	σπαράσσω
ἐσπαργανωμένον	VPRPAN-S	σπαργανόω
ἐσπαργάνωσε(ν)	VIAA--3S	"
ἐσπαρμένον	VPRPAM-S	σπείρω
	VPRPAN-S	"
ἐσπαταλήσατε	VIAA--2P	σπαταλάω
ἔσπειρα	VIAA--1S	σπείρω
ἐσπείραμεν	VIAA--1P	"
ἔσπειρας	VIAA--2S	"
ἔσπειρε(ν)	VIAA--3S	"

ἑσπέρα, ας, ἡ as a time period between late afternoon and darkness *evening*

ἑσπέρα	N-NF-S	ἑσπέρα
ἑσπέραν	N-AF-S	"
ἑσπέρας	N-GF-S	"
ἔσπερες	VIIA--2S	σπείρω
ἑσπερινῇ	A--DF-S	ἑσπερινός

ἑσπερινός, ή, όν *in the evening*; ἡ ἑσπερινὴ φυλακή *the first watch of the night* (from 6:00 P.M. to 9:00 P.M.) (LU 12.38)

ἔσπευδε(ν)	VIIA--3S	σπεύδω
ἐσπιλωμένον	VPRPAM-S	σπιλόω
ἐσπλαγχνίσθη	VIAO--3S	σπλαγχνίζομαι
ἐσπούδασα	VIAA--1S	σπουδάζω
ἐσπουδάσαμεν	VIAA--1P	"
Ἐσρώμ		Ἐσρώμ

Ἐσρώμ, ὁ (also **Ἐσρώμ, Ἐσρών**) indeclinable; *Hezron*, masculine proper noun

Ἐσρών		Ἐσρώμ
ἐστάθη	VIAP--3S	ἵστημι
ἐστάθην	VIAP--1S	"
ἐστάθησαν	VIAP--3P	"
ἔσται	VIFD--3S	εἰμί
	VIFD--3S^VMPA--3S	
ἑστάναι	VNRA	ἵστημι
ἐσταυρώθη	VIAP--3S	σταυρόω
ἐσταυρωμένον	VPRPAM-S	"
ἐσταυρωμένος	VPRPNM-S	"
ἐσταύρωσαν	VIAA--3P	"
ἐσταυρώσατε	VIAA--2P	"
ἐσταύρωται	VIRP--3S	"
ἐστέ	VIPA--2P	εἰμί
ἔστειλε(ν)	VIAA--3S	στέλλω
ἐστέναξε(ν)	VIAA--3S	στενάζω
ἐστερεοῦντο	VIIP--3P	στερεόω
ἐστερεώθησαν	VIAP--3P	"
ἐστερέωσε(ν)	VIAA--3S	"
ἐστεφανωμένον	VPRPAM-S	στεφανόω
ἐστεφάνωσας	VIAA--2S	"
ἔστη	VIAA--3S	ἵστημι
ἕστηκα	VIRA--1S	"
ἑστήκαμεν	VIRA--1P	"
ἕστηκας	VIRA--2S	"
ἑστήκασι(ν)	VIRA--3P	"
ἑστήκατε	VIRA--2P	"
ἕστηκε(ν)	VIIA--3S	στήκω

ἕστηκε(ν)	VIRA--3S	ἵστημι
ἑστήκεσαν	VILA--3P	"
ἑστήκετε	VIRA--2P	"
ἑστηκός	VPRANN-S	"
ἑστηκότα	VPRAAM-S	"
ἑστηκότες	VPRANM-P	"
ἑστηκότων	VPRAGM-P	"
ἑστηκώς	VPRANM-S	"
ἑστηριγμένους	VPRPAM-P	στηρίζω
ἑστήρικται	VIRP--3S	"
ἑστήριξε(ν)	VIAA--3S	"
ἑστήρισε(ν)	VIAA--3S	"
ἔστησαν	VIAA--3P	ἵστημι
ἔστησε(ν)	VIAA--3S	"
ἐστί(ν)	VIPA--3S	εἰμί
ἐστός	VPRAAN-S	ἵστημι
	VPRANN-S	"
ἐστράφη	VIAP--3S	στρέφω
ἐστράφησαν	VIAP--3P	"
ἔστρεψε(ν)	VIAA--3S	"
ἐστρηνίασε(ν)	VIAA--3S	στρηνιάω
ἐστρωμένον	VPRPAN-S	στρωννύω
ἐστρώννυον	VIIA--3P	"
ἔστρωσαν	VIAA--3P	"
ἔστω	VMPA--3S	εἰμί
ἑστώς	VMPA--3S	see ἔστω
ἑστώς	VPRANM-S	ἵστημι
ἑστῶσα	VPRANF-S	"
ἑστῶσαι	VPRANF-P	"
ἔστωσαν	VMPA--3P	εἰμί
ἑστῶτα	VPRAAM-S	ἵστημι
	VPRAAN-P	"
ἑστῶτας	VPRAAM-P	"
ἑστῶτες	VPRANM-P	"
ἑστῶτος	VPRAGM-S	"
ἑστώτων	VPRAGM-P	"
ἐσυκοφάντησα	VIAA--1S	συκοφαντέω
ἐσύλησα	VIAA--1S	συλάω
ἔσυραν	VIAA--3P	σύρω
ἔσυρον	VIIA--3P	"
ἐσφάγης	VIAP--2S	σφάζω
ἐσφαγμένην	VPRPAF-S	"
ἐσφαγμένον	VPRPNN-S	"
ἐσφαγμένου	VPRPGN-S	"
ἐσφαγμένων	VPRPGM-P	"
ἔσφαξε(ν)	VIAA--3S	"
ἐσφράγισε(ν)	VIAA--3S	σφραγίζω
ἐσφραγίσθητε	VIAP--2P	"
ἐσφραγισμέναι	VPRPNF-P	"
ἐσφραγισμένοι	VPRPNM-P	"
ἐσφραγισμένων	VPRPGM-P	"
ἔσχατα	A--AN-P	ἔσχατος
	A--NN-P	"
ἐσχάταις	A--DF-P	"
ἐσχάτας	A--AF-P	"
ἐσχάτη	A--NF-S	"
ἐσχάτῃ	A--DF-S	"
ἔσχατοι	A--NM-P	"
ἔσχατον	AB	"
	A--AM-S	"
	A--AN-S	"

ἔσχατος, η, ον *last, final*, opposite πρῶτος (*first*) especially of meanings 2–4; (1) of place *farthest* (LU 14.9); substantivally τὸ ἔσχατον *the end, the farthest point* (AC 1.8); (2) of time *latest, last* (JN 6.39) τὰ ἔσχατα *the last state, the end* (MT 12.45); neuter ἔσχατον as an adverb *finally, last of all* (MK 12.6); (3) of rank *lowest, least important* (MT 19.30); (4) of a series *last, final* (RV 1.17)

ἔσχατος	A--NM-S	ἔσχατος
ἐσχάτου	A--GM-S	"
	A--GN-S	"
ἐσχάτους	A--AM-P	"
ἐσχάτῳ	A--DM-S	"
ἐσχάτων	A--GF-P	"
	A--GM-P	"

ἐσχάτως adverb; *finally*; idiomatically ἔχειν ἐ. literally *be in the last extremity*, i.e. *be very sick, be at the point of death* (MK 5.23)

ἐσχάτως	AB	ἐσχάτως
ἔσχε(ν)	VIAA--3S	ἔχω
ἔσχες	VIAA--2S	"
ἔσχηκα	VIRA--1S	"
ἐσχήκαμεν	VIRA--1P	"
ἔσχηκε(ν)	VIRA--3S	"
ἐσχηκότα	VPRAAM-S	"
ἐσχίσθη	VIAP--3S	σχίζω
ἐσχίσθησαν	VIAP--3P	"
ἐσχισμένον	VPRPNN-S	"
ἔσχομεν	VIAA--1P	ἔχω
ἔσχον	VIAA--1S	"
	VIAA--3P	"

ἔσω adverb of place; (1) *inside, within* (AC 5.23); (2) as an improper preposition with the genitive *within, inside, into* (MK 15.16); (3) of the moral and spiritual side of man ὁ ἔ. ἄνθρωπος *the inner being, the inner nature* (RO 7.22); (4) substantivally οἱ ἔ. of the Christian community *those within, insiders* (1C 5.12)

ἔσω	AB	ἔσω
	PG	"
ἐσώζοντο	VIIP--3P	σώζω
ἐσώζοντο	VIIP--3P	"

ἔσωθεν adverb of place, opposite ἔξωθεν (*from the outside*); (1) *from (the) inside* or *within* (LU 11.7); (2) *within, on the inside* (MT 7.15); τὸ ἔ. ὑμῶν *your inner nature, the inside of you* (LU 11.39)

ἔσωθεν	AB	ἔσωθεν
ἐσώθη	VIAP--3S	σώζω
ἐσώθημεν	VIAP--1P	"
ἔσωσας	VIAA--2S	"
ἔσωσε(ν)	VIAA--3S	"
ἐσωτέραν	A-MAF-S	ἐσώτερος
ἐσώτερον	PG	"

ἐσώτερος, τέρα, ον an adjectival comparative of the adverb ἔσω (*within*); (1) as indicating relative position within an area *inner, interior* (AC 16.24); (2) neuter accusative as an improper preposition with the genitive, indicating relative position between two areas, one more inward *beyond, farther in* (HE 6.19)

ἑταῖρε	N-VM-S	ἑταῖρος
ἑταίροις	N-DM-P	"

ἑταῖρος, ου, ὁ   (1) as one who is associated with another *comrade, friend, companion* (MT 11.16); (2) as a form of address, denoting a mutually binding relationship that should be recognized by the one being addressed *(my) friend, comrade* (MT 20.13)

ἔταξαν	VIAA--3P	τάσσω
ἐτάξατο	VIAM--3S	"
ἐταπείνωσε(ν)	VIAA--3S	ταπεινόω
ἐτάραξαν	VIAA--3P	ταράσσω
ἐτάραξε(ν)	VIAA--3S	"
ἐτάρασσε(ν)	VIIA--3S	"
ἐταράσσετο	VIIM--3S	"
	VIIP--3S	"
ἐταράχθη	VIAP--3S	
ἐταράχθησαν	VIAP--3P	
ἐτάφη	VIAP--3S	θάπτω
ἐτέθη	VIAP--3S	τίθημι
ἐτέθην	VIAP--1S	"
ἐτέθησαν	VIAP--3P	"
ἐτεθνήκει	VILA--3S	θνήσκω
ἔτει	N-DN-S	ἔτος
ἔτεκε(ν)	VIAA--3S	τίκτω
ἐτεκνοτρόφησε(ν)	VIAA--3S	τεκνοτροφέω
ἐτελειώθη	VIAP--3S	τελειόω
ἐτελείωσα	VIAA--1S	"
ἐτελείωσε(ν)	VIAA--3S	"
ἐτέλεσαν	VIAA--3P	τελέω
ἐτέλεσε(ν)	VIAA--3S	"
ἐτελέσθη	VIAP--3S	"
ἐτελέσθησαν	VIAP--3P	"
ἐτελεύτησε(ν)	VIAA--3S	τελευτάω
ἕτερα	A--AN-P	ἕτερος
ἑτέρα	A--NF-S	"
ἑτέρᾳ	A--DF-S	"
ἕτεραι	A--NF-P	"
ἑτέραις	A--DF-P	"
ἑτέραν	A--AF-S	"
ἑτέρας	A--GF-S	"
ἑτερογλώσσοις	A--DM-P	ἑτερόγλωσσος

ἑτερόγλωσσος, ον *speaking a foreign language, in a strange or unfamiliar language*; substantivally *a person speaking a foreign language* (1C 14.21)

ἑτεροδιδασκαλεῖ	VIPA--3S	ἑτεροδιδασκαλέω
ἑτεροδιδασκαλεῖν	VNPA	"

ἑτεροδιδασκαλέω *teach a different* (i.e. heretical) *doctrine, teach something other than the truth, teach error as if it were the truth*

ἑτεροζυγέω strictly *be yoked with an animal of a different kind*; hence *be mismatched, be wrongly associated together* (2C 6.14)

ἑτεροζυγοῦντες	VPPANM-P	ἑτεροζυγέω
ἕτεροι	A--NM-P	ἕτερος
ἑτέροις	A--DM-P	"
	A--DN-P	"
ἕτερον	A--AM-S	"
	A--AN-S	"
	A--NN-S	"

ἕτερος, τέρα, ον with a basic meaning *other, different*; (1) qualitatively *another of a different kind, different, not identical* with what was previously referred to (RO 7.23; GA 1.6); (2) numerically, denoting a new member dis-

tinct in kind from those that preceded *another, someone else, something else* (1C 12.8–10); in lists *some . . . some* (LU 8.6–8); (the first) *. . . the second . . . the third* (LU 14.19, 20); (3) substantivally ὁ ἕ. *one's neighbor, the other fellow* (RO 2.1); τῇ ἑτέρᾳ *on the next day* (AC 20.15); ἐν ἑτέρῳ *in another place, elsewhere* (HE 5.6); (4) as qualifying γλῶσσαι (*tongues*) *foreign or different languages* (AC 2.4)

ἕτερος	A--NM-S	ἕτερος
ἑτέρου	A--GM-S	"
ἑτέρους	A--AM-P	"
ἑτέρῳ	A--DM-S	"
	A--DN-S	"
ἑτέρων	A--GM-P	"
	A--GN-P	"

ἑτέρως adverb; *differently, otherwise* (PH 3.15)

ἑτέρως	AB	ἑτέρως
ἔτεσι(ν)	N-DN-P	ἔτος
ἐτέχθη	VIAP--3S	τίκτω
ἔτη	N-AN-P	ἔτος
	N-NN-P	"
ἐτηρεῖτο	VIIP--3S	τηρέω
ἐτήρησα	VIAA--1S	"
ἐτήρησαν	VIAA--3P	"
ἐτήρησας	VIAA--2S	"
ἐτήρουν	VIIA--1S	"
	VIIA--3P	"

ἔτι adverb; *yet, still*; (1) of time; (a) positively *still* (GA 1.10); (b) with a negative *(not) yet, (no) longer, (no) further* (LU 16.2); (2) in a nontemporal sense, as adding something *besides, in addition, furthermore* (HE 11.36); (3) to mark what is contrary to expectation *nevertheless, yet* (RO 9.19)

ἔτι	AB	ἔτι
ἐτίθει	VIIA--3S	τίθημι
ἐτίθεσαν	VIIA--3P	"
ἐτίθουν	VIIA--3P	"
ἔτιλλον	VIIA--3P	τίλλω
ἐτίμησαν	VIAA--3P	τιμάω
ἐτιμήσαντο	VIAM--3P	"
ἕτοιμα	A--AN-P	ἕτοιμος
	A--NN-P	"
ἑτοίμαζε	VMPA--2S	ἑτοιμάζω

ἑτοιμάζω 1aor. ἡτοίμασα; pf. ἡτοίμακα; pf. pass. ἡτοίμασμαι; 1aor. pass. ἡτοιμάσθην; *prepare, make ready*; (1) with a thing as the object *put* or *keep in readiness, prepare* (MT 26.19); (2) with a person as the object *make ready, prepare* (LU 1.17); (3) of what God provides for believers *prepare, have ready* (1C 2.9)

Ἑτοιμᾶς, ᾶ, ὁ (also Ἕτοιμος) *Hetoimas*, masculine proper noun

Ἑτοιμᾶς	N-NM-S	Ἑτοιμᾶς
ἑτοιμάσαι	VNAA	ἑτοιμάζω
ἑτοιμάσαντες	VPAANM-P	"
ἑτοιμάσας	VPAANM-S	"
ἑτοιμάσατε	VMAA--2P	"
ἑτοιμάσθη	VSAP--3S	"

ἑτοιμασία, ας, ἡ as a quality *readiness, preparedness, preparation* (EP 6.15)

ἑτοιμασία	N-DF-S	ἑτοιμασία
ἑτοιμάσομεν	VIFA--1P	ἑτοιμάζω

ἑτοίμασον	VMAA--2S	"
ἑτοιμάσω	VSAA--1S	"
ἑτοιμάσωμεν	VSAA--1P	"
ἑτοίμην	A--AF-S	ἕτοιμος
ἕτοιμοι	A--NF-P	"
	A--NM-P	"
ἕτοιμον	A--AN-S	"
Ἕτοιμος	N-NM-S	Ἕτοιμας

ἕτοιμος, η, ον *ready, prepared*; (1) of persons *ready, prepared* (LU 12.40); substantivally *a person who is ready* (MT 25.10); (2) of things *ready, put in readiness* (MK 14.15); substantivally τὰ ἕτοιμα *what has been prepared* (2C 10.16); (3) of time *ready, at hand, here* (JN 7.6)

ἕτοιμος	A--NM-S	ἕτοιμος
ἑτοίμους	A--AM-P	"
ἑτοίμῳ	A--DM-S	"
	A--DN-S	"

ἑτοίμως adverb; *readily*; ἑ. ἔχειν with an infinitive *be ready* or *willing to* (AC 21.13)

ἑτοίμως	AB	ἑτοίμως
ἐτόλμα	VIIA--3S	τολμάω
ἐτόλμησε(ν)	VIAA--3S	"
ἐτόλμων	VIIA--3P	"

ἔτος, ους, τό (1) *year* (AC 7.30); (2) in indications of age ἔτη ἔχειν, εἶναι ἐτῶν, or γίνεσθαι ἐτῶν with number *be x years old* (LU 2.42); (3) to denote duration in answer to the question "how long?" *for x years* (MT 9.20); in combination with prepositions, the kind of time notation is determined by the preposition: δι᾽ ἐτῶν πλειόνων *after several years* (AC 24.17); πρὸ ἐτῶν δεκατεσσάρων *fourteen years ago* (2C 12.2)

ἔτος	N-AN-S	ἔτος
ἐτράπει	VIAA--3S	τρέπω
ἐτρέχετε	VIIA--2P	τρέχω
ἔτρεχον	VIIA--3P	"
ἐτροποφόρησαν	VIAA--3P	τροποφορέω
ἐτροποφόρησε(ν)	VIAA--3S	"
ἐτροφοφόρησε(ν)	VIAA--3S	τροφοφορέω
ἐτρύγησε(ν)	VIAA--3S	τρυγάω
ἐτρυφήσατε	VIAA--2P	τρυφάω
ἐτύθη	VIAP--3S	θύω
ἐτυμπανίσθησαν	VIAP--3P	τυμπανίζω
ἔτυπτε(ν)	VIIA--3S	τύπτω
ἔτυπτον	VIIA--3P	"
ἐτύφλωσε(ν)	VIAA--3S	τυφλόω
ἐτῶν	N-GN-P	ἔτος

εὖ adverb; *fine, well, good*; (1) absolutely *well done! excellent!* (MT 25.21); (2) εὖ πράσσειν *do well, act correctly* (AC 15.29); (3) εὖ ποιεῖν *benefit, help, do good* (MK 14.7)

εὖ	AB	εὖ
Εὕαν	N-NF-S	Εὕα
Εὕαν	N-NF-S	"

Εὕα, ας, ἡ (also Εὔα, Εὖα) *Eve*, feminine proper noun

Εὕα	N-NF-S	Εὕα
εὐαγγελίζεσθαι	VNPM	εὐαγγελίζω
εὐαγγελίζεται	VIPM--3S	"
	VIPP--3S	"
εὐαγγελίζηται	VSPM--3S	"
εὐαγγελίζομαι	VIPM--1S	"
εὐαγγελιζόμεθα	VIPM--1P	"

εὐαγγελιζόμενοι	VPPMNM-P	"
εὐαγγελιζόμενος	VPPMNM-S	"
εὐαγγελιζομένου	VPPMGM-S	"
εὐαγγελιζομένῳ	VPPMDM-S	"
εὐαγγελιζομένων	VPPMGM-P	"
εὐαγγελίζονται	VIPP--3P	"

εὐαγγελίζω impf. mid. εὐηγγελιζόμην; 1aor. εὐηγγέλισα, mid. εὐηγγελισάμην; pf. pass. εὐηγγέλισμαι; 1aor. pass. εὐηγγελίσθην; active in Revelation, predominantly middle/passive in the rest of the NT; (1) generally *bring* or *announce good news* (LU 1.19); (2) predominantly in the NT, as making known God's message of salvation with authority and power *tell the good news, make known the gospel, evangelize* (AC 5.42); passive *have the gospel preached* to someone (MT 11.5)

εὐαγγελίζωμαι	VSPM--1S	εὐαγγελίζω

εὐαγγέλιον, ου, τό *good news*; in the NT only of God's message of salvation *gospel, good news*; (1) as denoting the act of proclamation *preaching of the gospel* (1C 4.15); (2) as denoting the work of evangelization *cause, service,* or *spread of the gospel* (PH 4.3); (3) as denoting the content of the message as an offer of salvation *gospel, good news, God's message* (1C 9.14a)

εὐαγγέλιον	N-AN-S	εὐαγγέλιον
	N-NN-S	"
εὐαγγελίου	N-GN-S	"
εὐαγγελίσαι	VNAA	εὐαγγελίζω
εὐαγγελισάμεθα	VIAM--1P	"
εὐαγγελισάμενοι	VPAMNM-P	"
εὐαγγελισαμένου	VPAMGM-S	"
εὐαγγελισαμένων	VPAMGM-P	"
εὐαγγελίσασθαι	VNAM	"
εὐαγγελίσηται	VSAM--3S	"
εὐαγγελισθέν	VPAPAN-S	"
	VPAPNN-S	"
εὐαγγελισθέντες	VPAPNM-P	"
εὐαγγελιστάς	N-AM-P	εὐαγγελιστής

εὐαγγελιστής, οῦ, ὁ *one who brings* or *announces good news*; in the NT *evangelist, preacher,* or *teacher of the gospel* (AC 21.8)

εὐαγγελιστής	N-NM-S	εὐαγγελιστής
εὐαγγελιστοῦ	N-GM-S	"
εὐαγγελίσωμαι	VSAM--1S	εὐαγγελίζω
εὐαγγελίῳ	N-DN-S	εὐαγγέλιον
Εὕαν	N-AF-S	Εὕα
Εὕαν	N-AF-S	"
Εὕαν	N-AF-S	"
εὐαρεστεῖται	VIPP--3S	εὐαρεστέω

εὐαρεστέω 1aor. εὐηρέστησα; pf. εὐηρέστηκα; (1) active *please (well), be pleasing, cause to be pleased* (HE 11.5, 6); (2) passive *take pleasure* or *delight in, be well-pleased with* (HE 13.16)

εὐαρεστηκέναι	VNRA	εὐαρεστέω
εὐαρεστῆσαι	VNAA	"
εὐάρεστοι	A--NM-P	εὐάρεστος
εὐάρεστον	A--AF-S	"
	A--AN-S	"
	A--NN-S	"

εὐάρεστος, ον *well-pleasing, acceptable*; (1) predominately of God's attitude toward human conduct (RO 14.18); absolutely τὸ εὐάρεστον *what is acceptable* (RO 12.2); (2)

of the conduct of slaves εὖ. εἶναι *give satisfaction, serve well* (TI 2.9)

εὐάρεστος	A--NM-S	εὐάρεστος
εὐαρέστους	A--AM-P	"

εὐαρέστως adverb; *acceptably, in an pleasing manner* (HE 12.28)

εὐαρέστως	AB	εὐαρέστως

Εὔβουλος, ου, ὁ *Eubulus*, masculine proper noun (2T 4.21)

Εὔβουλος	N-NM-S	Εὔβουλος

εὖγε as an exclamation expressing commendation *well done! excellent! bravo!* (LU 19.17)

εὖγε	QS	εὖγε
εὐγενεῖς	A--NM-P	εὐγενής
εὐγενέστεροι	A-MNM-P	"

εὐγενής, ές, gen. **οῦς** (1) as having a high status, especially socially *well-born, noble, important* (LU 19.12); substantivally *nobleman, important person* (1C 1.26); (2) as a commendable attitude *open-minded, without prejudice*; comparative εὐγενέστερος, τέρα, ον *more open-minded, less prejudiced* (AC 17.11)

εὐγενής	A--NM-S	εὐγενής

εὐγλωττία, ας, ἡ *fluency* or *glibness of speech, smooth talk* (RO 16.18)

εὐγλωττίας	N-GF-S	εὐγλωττία

εὐδία, ας, ἡ *fair* or *fine weather, cloudless day* (MT 16.2)

εὐδία	N-NF-S	εὐδία
εὐδοκεῖ	VIPA--3S	εὐδοκέω

εὐδοκέω impf. ηὐδόκουν and εὐδόκουν (1TH 2.8); 1aor. εὐδόκησα and ηὐδόκησα; (1) with ἐν and the dative of person *be well-pleased with, take pleasure* or *delight in, be glad in*, especially of God's approval (MT 3.17); (2) with an infinitive following *consider good, seem good to, consent to* (LU 12.32); (3) with a thing as the object *like, prefer, approve of* (2TH 2.12)

εὐδόκησα	VIAA--1S	εὐδοκέω
εὐδοκήσαμεν	VIAA--1P	"
εὐδόκησαν	VIAA--3P	"
εὐδοκήσαντες	VPAANM-P	"
εὐδόκησας	VIAA--2S	"
εὐδόκησε(ν)	VIAA--3S	"

εὐδοκία, ας, ἡ generally *what pleases*; (1) of people; (a) as having good intent *goodwill* (PH 1.15); (b) as a feeling of strong emotion in favor of something *desire, wish, good pleasure* (RO 10.1); (2) of God *good pleasure, favor, approval* (EP 1.5); (3) in LU 2.14 the possible readings allow differing meanings: (a) ἐν ἀνθρώποις εὐδοκίας *among people on whom his favor rests, among people with whom he is well-pleased*; (b) ἀνθρώποις εὐδοκίας *to* or *for people of goodwill*; (c) ἐν ἀνθρώποις εὐ. *goodwill among people*

εὐδοκία	N-NF-S	εὐδοκία
εὐδοκίαν	N-AF-S	"
εὐδοκίας	N-GF-S	"
εὐδοκοῦμεν	VIIA--1P	εὐδοκέω
	VIPA--1P	"
εὐδοκοῦντος	VPPANM-S	"
εὐδοκῶ	VIPA--1S	"

εὐεργεσία, ας, ἡ (1) *good service, well-doing* (1T 6.2); (2) as an individual act of kindness *benefit, good deed* (AC 4.9)

εὐεργεσία	N-DF-S	εὐεργεσία
εὐεργεσίας	N-GF-S	"
εὐεργέται	N-NM-P	εὐεργέτης

εὐεργετέω of beneficial activity *do good to, show kindness to, benefit* (AC 10.38)

εὐεργέτης, ου, ὁ *benefactor, helper*, often used as a title of honor for outstanding public leaders (LU 22.25)

εὐεργετῶν	VPPANM-S	εὐεργετέω
εὐηγγελίζετο	VIIM--3S	εὐαγγελίζω
εὐηγγελίζοντο	VIIM--3P	"
εὐηγγελισάμεθα	VIAM--1P	"
εὐηγγελισάμην	VIAM--1S	"
εὐηγγελίσαντο	VIAM--3P	"
εὐηγγελίσατο	VIAM--3S	"
εὐηγγέλισε(ν)	VIAA--3S	"
εὐηγγελίσθη	VIAP--3S	"
εὐηγγελισμένοι	VPRPNM-P	"
εὐηρεστηκέαι	VNRA	εὐαρεστέω
εὐθεῖα	A--NF-S	εὐθύς
εὐθεῖαν	A--AF-S	"
εὐθείας	A--AF-P	"
εὔθετον	A--AF-S	εὔθετος
	A--NN-S	"

εὔθετος, ον strictly *well-placed, arranged well*; hence (1) of persons *fit, useful, suitable* (LU 9.62); (2) of things *of value, useful* (LU 14.35)

εὔθετος	A--NM-S	εὔθετος

εὐθέως an adverb from εὐθύς (*straight*); *at once, immediately, right away*

εὐθέως	AB	εὐθέως

εὐθυδρομέω 1aor. εὐθυδρόμησα; *follow a straight course* to a destination; of a ship *steer* or *sail a straight course*

εὐθυδρομήσαμεν	VIAA--1P	εὐθυδρομέω
εὐθυδρομήσαντες	VPAANM-P	"
εὐθυμεῖ	VIPA--3S	εὐθυμέω
εὐθυμεῖν	VNPA	"
εὐθυμεῖτε	VMPA--2P	"

εὐθυμέω intransitively *be cheerful, take courage, cheer up*

εὔθυμοι	A--NM-P	εὔθυμος

εὔθυμος, ον *cheerful, encouraged, in good spirits*; comparative neuter as an adverb εὐθυμότερον *more confidently* (AC 24.10)

εὐθυμότερον	ABM	εὔθυμος

εὐθύμως adverb; *cheerfully, gladly, with encouragement* (AC 24.10)

εὐθύμως	AB	εὐθύμως
εὐθύνατε	VMAA--2P	εὐθύνω
εὐθύνοντος	VPPAGM-S	"

εὐθύνω 1aor. εὔθυνα; *cause to be straight*; (1) of a ship *steer, keep on a straight course*; ὁ εὐθύνων *the pilot* (JA 3.4); (2) of a road *make straight, straighten*; metaphorically, of John the Baptist's ministry as a forerunner of Jesus (JN 1.23)

εὐθύς, εῖα, ύ, gen. **έως** *straight*; (1) literally, of a roadway *straight* (AC 9.11); metaphorically, of moral and spiritual preparation for Jesus' appearing as Messiah εὐθείας τρίβους ποιεῖν literally *make straight paths*, i.e. *change behavior* (MT 3.3); substantivally (LU 3.5); figuratively, of moral integrity *upright, right, correct* (AC 8.21); (2) idiomatically εὐθεῖα ὁδός literally *straight* *road*, i.e. *correct behavior, right way* (2P 2.15); (3) neuter singular εὐθύ (and masculine singular εὐθύς) as an adverb *immediately, right away, at once* (MT 3.16); inferentially, of the immediately following event in a sequence *next* (MK 1.21); *right after that, then* (MK 1.30)

εὐθύ(ς)	AB	εὐθύς

εὐθύτης, ητος, ἡ literally *straightness*; figuratively, as a quality of life *honesty, integrity, justice* (HE 1.8)

εὐθύτητος	N-GF-S	εὐθύτης

εὐκαιρέω impf. εὐκαίρουν (MK 6.31) and ηὐκαίρουν (AC 17.21); 1aor. ηὐκαίρησα; (1) *have convenient time* or *leisure, find opportunity* (MK 6.31); (2) *enjoy doing, spend time enjoying* (AC 17.21)

εὐκαιρήσῃ	VSAA--3S	εὐκαιρέω

εὐκαιρία, ας, ἡ *favorable opportunity, convenient moment, the right time*

εὐκαιρίαν	N-AF-S	εὐκαιρία
εὔκαιρον	A--AF-S	εὔκαιρος

εὔκαιρος, ον *favorable, timely, at the right time*

εὐκαίρου	A--GF-S	εὔκαιρος
εὐκαίρουν	VIIA--3P	εὐκαιρέω

εὐκαίρως adverb; *conveniently* (MK 14.11); idiomatically εὐ. ἀκαίρως literally *in season or out of season*, i.e. *whether convenient or not* (2T 4.2)

εὐκαίρως	AB	εὐκαίρως

εὔκοπος, ον *easy*; only comparative in the NT εὐκοπώτερος, τέρα, ον; always impersonally, with ἐστί(ν) *it is easier*

εὐκοπώτερον	A-MNN-S	εὔκοπος

εὐλάβεια, ας, ἡ *godly fear* or *reverence, reverent regard, awe*

εὐλαβείας	N-GF-S	εὐλάβεια
εὐλαβεῖς	A--NM-P	εὐλαβής

εὐλαβέομαι 1aor. ptc. εὐλαβηθείς; only passive in the NT *give careful heed, be cautious* or *beware; be moved with reverent regard* (HE 11.7)

εὐλαβηθείς	VPAONM-S	εὐλαβέομαι

εὐλαβής, ές, gen. οῦς strictly *taking hold of well*; hence *cautious, devout, pious*, as a characteristic of one who carefully observes the law

εὐλαβής	A--NM-P	εὐλαβής
εὐλόγει	VIIA--3S	εὐλογέω
εὐλογεῖν	VNPA	"
εὐλογεῖται	VIPP--3S	"
εὐλογεῖτε	VMPA--2P	"

εὐλογέω impf. εὐλόγουν; fut. εὐλογήσω; 1aor. εὐλόγησα; pf. εὐλόγηκα; pf. pass. ptc. εὐλογημένος; 1fut. pass. εὐλογηθήσομαι; (1) of man's duty to speak well of God in the form of praise or thanksgiving *praise, extol* (LU 1.64); *give thanks* (1C 14.16); (2) as calling down God's gracious power on persons *bless, invoke a blessing on* (LU 24.50); on things *bless, consecrate, pronounce blessing on* (MT 26.26); (3) of God's action in bestowing blessing *confer favor* or *blessing on, graciously benefit, act kindly toward* (HE 6.14); passive *be blessed, be favored* (LU 1.42)

εὐλογηθήσονται	VIFP--3P	εὐλογέω
εὐλόγηκε(ν)	VIRA--3S	"
εὐλογημένη	VPRPNF-S	"
εὐλογημένοι	VPRPVM-P	"
εὐλογημένος	VPRPNM-S	"

εὐλογῇς	VSPA--2S	"
εὐλογήσας	VPAANM-S	"
εὐλόγησε(ν)	VIAA--3S	"
εὐλογήσῃς	VSAA--2S	"
εὐλογήσω	VIFA--1S	"

εὐλογητός, ή, όν *worthy of praise* or *blessing*; in the NT only of God and Christ *blessed, to be praised* (LU 1.68); substantivally ὁ εὐ. as a name for God *the Blessed One, the one who should be praised* (MK 14.61)

εὐλογητός	A--NM-S	εὐλογητός
εὐλογητοῦ	A--GM-S	"

εὐλογία, ας, ἡ (1) strictly *good* or *fine speech*; hence *praise, eulogy* (RV 5.12); (2) in a bad sense *flattery, plausible arguments* (RO 16.18); (3) of persons invoking God's favor on other persons *blessing, benediction* (JA 3.10); (4) of favor or benefit bestowed by God *blessing, bounty* (HE 12.17); (5) of benefit bestowed by people *gift, bounty* (2C 9.5); ἐπ᾽ εὐλογίαις *bountifully, liberally* (2C 9.6); (6) of things on which God's blessing has been pronounced *consecrated* (1C 10.16)

εὐλογία	N-NF-S	εὐλογία
εὐλογίᾳ	N-DF-S	"
εὐλογίαις	N-DF-P	"
εὐλογίαν	N-AF-S	"
εὐλογίας	N-GF-S	"
εὐλογοῦμεν	VIPA--1P	εὐλογέω
εὐλογοῦντα	VPPAAM-S	"
εὐλογοῦνται	VIPP--3P	"
εὐλογοῦντες	VPPANM-P	"
εὐλογῶν	VPPANM-S	"

εὐμετάδοτος, ον denoting a readiness to share *generous, liberal, bountiful* (1T 6.18)

εὐμεταδότους	A--AM-P	εὐμετάδοτος
Εὐνείκη	N-DF-S	Εὐνίκη

Εὐνίκη, ης, ἡ (also Εὐνείκη) *Eunice*, feminine proper noun (2T 1.5)

Εὐνίκη	N-DF-S	Εὐνίκη

εὐνοέω *be well-disposed toward, be friendly with*; ἴσθι εὐνοῶν ταχύ *go and settle matters quickly, come quickly to an agreement* (MT 5.25)

εὔνοια, ας, ἡ *goodwill, wholehearted zeal, good attitude* (EP 6.7)

εὔνοιαν	N-AF-S	εὔνοια
εὐνοίας	N-GF-S	"

εὐνουχίζω 1aor. εὐνούχισα; 1aor. pass. εὐνουχίσθην; literally, of depriving a male of the ability to reproduce *emasculate, castrate, make a eunuch of* (MT 19.12a); figuratively *impose sexual abstinence on oneself, be celibate* (MT 19.12b)

εὐνούχισαν	VIAA--3P	εὐνουχίζω
εὐνουχίσθησαν	VIAP--3P	"
εὐνοῦχοι	N-NM-P	εὐνοῦχος
εὐνοῦχον	N-AM-S	"

εὐνοῦχος, ου, ὁ from εὐνή (*bed*) and ἔχω (*hold*); (1) strictly *one in charge of the bed chamber*; hence *eunuch, castrated male* (MT 19.12b); often a trusted official in Middle Eastern courts (cf. AC 8.27–39); (2) of a male born without ability to reproduce (MT 19.12a); (3) figuratively, of one who imposes sexual abstinence on himself, *celibate* (MT 19.12c)

εὐνοῦχος	N-NM-S	εὐνοῦχος

εὐνοῶν	VPPANM-S	εὐνοέω
εὐξαίμην	VOAD--1S	εὔχομαι
εὐξάμην	VIAD--1S	"

Εὐοδία, ας, ἡ *Euodia, feminine proper noun* (PH 4.2)

Εὐοδίαν	N-AF-S	Εὐοδία
εὐοδοῦσθαι	VNPP	εὐοδόω
εὐοδοῦται	VIPP--3S	"

εὐοδόω 1fut. pass. εὐοδωθήσομαι; literally *lead along on a good path, guide well*; figuratively and only passive in the NT *prosper, succeed* (RO 1.10); θησαυρίζων ὅ τι ἐὰν εὐοδῶται *saving up whatever is possible, as much as one can* (1C 16.2)

εὐοδωθῇ	VSAP--3S	εὐοδόω
εὐοδωθήσομαι	VIFP--1S	"
εὐοδῶται	VSPP--3S	"
εὐπάρεδρον	AP-AN-S	εὐπάρεδρος

εὐπάρεδρος, ον strictly *sitting beside*; hence *devoted, constantly attending to*; neuter as a substantive τὸ εὐπάρεδρον *devotion* (1C 7.35)

εὐπειθής, ές, gen. **οῦς** strictly *easily persuaded*; hence *compliant, congenial, open to reason* (JA 3.17)

εὐπειθής	A--NF-S	εὐπειθής
εὐπερίσπαστον	A--AF-S	εὐπερίσπαστος

εὐπερίσπαστος, ον strictly *easy to pull away*; hence *easily distracting one's thinking* (HE 12.1)

εὐπερίστατον	A--AF-S	εὐπερίστατος

εὐπερίστατος, ον strictly *cleverly placing itself around, to exert tight control*; hence *easily entangling, controlling tightly* (HE 12.1)

εὐποιΐα, ας, ἡ *doing good, helpful kindness* (HE 13.16)

εὐποιΐας	N-GF-S	εὐποιΐα
εὐπορεῖτο	VIIM--3S	εὐπορέω

εὐπορέω impf. mid. εὐπορούμην; only middle in the NT *have plenty, be prosperous* (AC 11.29)

εὐπορία, ας, ἡ *prosperity, wealth, good income, easy living* (AC 19.25)

εὐπορία	N-NF-S	εὐπορία
εὐποροῦντο	VIIM--3P	εὐπορέω

εὐπρέπεια, ας, ἡ *fine appearance, beauty* (JA 1.11)

εὐπρέπεια	N-NF-S	εὐπρέπεια

εὐπρόσδεκτος, ον (1) *very acceptable, welcome* (RO 15.16); (2) of an opportunity *suitable, favorable* (2C 6.2)

εὐπρόσδεκτος	A--NF-S	εὐπρόσδεκτος
	A--NM-S	"
εὐπροσδέκτους	A--AF-P	"
εὐπρόσεδρον	AP-AN-S	εὐπρόσεδρος

εὐπρόσεδρος, ον strictly *sitting beside*; hence *devoted, constantly attending to*; neuter as a substantive εὐπρόσεδρον *devotion* (1C 7.35)

εὐπροσωπέω 1aor. εὐπροσώπησα; *make a good showing or impression, stand well (before others), appear plausible* (GA 6.12)

εὐπροσωπῆσαι	VNAA	εὐπροσωπέω
εὐρακήλων	N-NM-S	εὐρακύλων
εὐρακλύδων	N-NM-S	εὐροκλύδων
εὐρακοίδων	N-NM-S	"
εὐρακύκλων	N-NM-S	εὐρακύλων

εὐρακύλων, ωνος, ὁ (also εὐρακήλων, εὐρακύκλων, εὐτρακήλων) *Euraquilo, northeast wind*; as a nautical technical term *northeaster* a strong stormy wind blowing from the northeast (AC 27.14); some printed Greek texts capitalize this word

εὐρακύλων	N-NM-S	εὐρακύλων
εὔραμεν	VIAA--1P	εὑρίσκω
εὑράμενος	VPMMNM-S	"
εὑρεθείς	VPAPNM-S	"
εὑρέθη	VIAP--3S	"
εὑρεθῇ	VSAP--3S	"
εὑρέθημεν	VIAP--1P	"
εὑρέθην	VIAP--1S	"
εὑρεθῆναι	VNAP	"
εὑρέθησαν	VIAP--3P	"
εὑρεθήσεται	VIFP--3S	"
εὑρεθησόμεθα	VIFP--1P	"
εὑρεθῆτε	VSAP--2P	"
εὑρεθῶ	VSAP--1S	"
εὑρεθῶσι(ν)	VSAP--3P	"
εὑρεῖν	VNAA	"
εὗρε(ν)	VIAA--3S	"
εὗρες	VIAA--2S	"
εὕρῃ	VSAA--3S	"
εὕρηκα	VIRA--1S	"
εὑρήκαμεν	VIRA--1P	"
εὑρηκέναι	VNRA	"
εὕρῃς	VSAA--2S	"
εὑρήσει	VIFA--3S	"
εὑρήσεις	VIFA--2S	"
εὑρήσετε	VIFA--2P	"
εὑρήσῃς	VSAA--2S	"
εὑρήσομεν	VIFA--1P	"
εὑρήσουσι(ν)	VIFA--3P	"
εὑρήσων	VPFANM-S	"
εὑρήσωσι(ν)	VSAA--3P	"
εὕρητε	VSAA--2P	"
εὑρίσκει	VIPA--3S	"
εὑρίσκετο	VIIP--3S	"
εὑρισκόμεθα	VIPP--1P	"
εὑρίσκομεν	VIPA--1P	"
εὕρισκον	VIIA--3P	"
εὕρισκον	VPPANN-S	"
εὑρίσκοντες	VPPANM-P	"
εὑρίσκουσι(ν)	VIPA--3P	"

εὑρίσκω impf. εὕρισκον; fut. εὑρήσω; 2aor. εὗρον; pf. εὕρηκα; 1aor. pass. εὑρέθην; 1fut. pass. εὑρεθήσομαι; *find*; (1) to find after searching *discover, come on* (MT 7.7); (2) to find accidentally or without seeking *come across, come on* (MT 12.44); passive *be found, find oneself, be* (AC 8.40); (3) to experience for oneself *obtain, get, procure* (HE 9.12); (4) figuratively, of spiritual or intellectual discovery gained through observation, reflection, perception, investigation *find, discover, recognize* (RO 7.21); (5) passive *be found to be, appear, prove to be* (MT 1.18)

εὑρίσκω	VIPA--1S	εὑρίσκω
εὕροιεν	VOAA--3P	"
εὐροκλύδον	N-NM-S	εὐροκλύδων
εὐροκλύδω	N-NM-S	"

εὐροκλύδων, ωνος, ὁ (also εὐρακλύδων, εὐρακοίδων, εὐροκλοίδον, εὐροκλύδον, εὐροκλύδω, εὐρυκλύδων, εὐρωκλύδων) *Euroclydon, southeast wind*, explained as the stormy wind that stirs up broad waves (AC 27.14); some printed Greek texts capitalize this word

εὐροκλύδων	N-NM-S	εὐροκλύδων
εὐροκοίδον	N-NM-S	"
εὔρομεν	VIAA--1P	εὑρίσκω
εὑρόμενος	VPAMNM-S	see εὑράμενος
εὗρον	VIAA--1S	εὑρίσκω
	VIAA--3P	"
εὑρόντες	VPAANM-P	"
εὑροῦσα	VPAANF-S	"
εὑροῦσαι	VPAANF-P	"
εὐρυκλύδων	N-NM-S	εὐροκλύδων

εὐρύχωρος, ον spacious, roomy; of a road broad, wide (MT 7.13)

εὐρύχωρος	A--NF-S	εὐρύχωρος
εὕρω	VSAA--1S	εὑρίσκω
εὑρωκλύδων	N-NM-S	εὐροκλύδων
εὕρωμεν	VSAA--1P	εὑρίσκω
εὑρών	VPAANM-S	"
εὕρωσι(ν)	VSAA--3P	"

εὐσέβεια, ας, ἡ (1) generally, as a particular manner of life characterized by reverence toward God and respect for the beliefs and practices related to him religion, piety (1T 3.16); (2) as behavior directed dutifully toward God piety, devotion, godliness (1T 6.11); plural godly acts, godly living (2P 3.11)

εὐσέβεια	N-NF-S	εὐσέβεια
εὐσεβείᾳ	N-DF-S	"
εὐσεβείαις	N-DF-P	"
εὐσέβειαν	N-AF-S	"
εὐσεβείας	N-GF-S	"
εὐσεβεῖν	VNPA	εὐσεβέω
εὐσεβεῖς	A--AM-P	εὐσεβής
εὐσεβεῖτε	VIPA--2P	εὐσεβέω

εὐσεβέω (1) as conducting oneself with reverent regard for God worship (AC 17.23); (2) as putting religion into practice at home fulfill one's duties toward, be devoted to (one's own household members) (1T 5.4)

εὐσεβῆ	A--AM-S	εὐσεβής

εὐσεβής, ές of a manner of life lived reverently and respectfully toward God devout, godly, pious, opposite ἄδικος (ungodly, unjust); substantivally a person who respects God (2P 2.9)

εὐσεβής	A--NM-S	εὐσεβής

Εὐσέβιος, ου, ὁ Eusebius, masculine proper noun; referring to the church father of that name, often called Eusebius Pamphili, i.e. (the friend of) Pamphilius (MK 16 shorter ending)

Εὐσέβιος	N-NM-S	Εὐσέβιος

εὐσεβῶς adverb; in a godly manner; of life lived in a reverent relation to God piously, devotedly

εὐσεβῶς	AB	εὐσεβῶς
εὔσημον	A--AM-S	εὔσημος

εὔσημος, ον strictly, of something that gives an easily recognizable sign; hence clear, distinct; of language intelligible (1C 14.9)

εὔσπλαγχνοι	A--NM-P	εὔσπλαγχνος

εὔσπλαγχνος, ον tenderhearted, compassionate

εὔσχημον	A--AN-S	εὐσχήμων
εὐσχήμονα	A--NN-P	"
εὐσχήμονας	A--AF-P	"
εὐσχημονεῖ	VIPA--3S	εὐσχημονέω

εὐσχημονέω behave with dignity, act graciously; used in a bad sense with a negative in 1C 13.5, probably act superior or hypocritically, be snobbish, be outwardly good

εὐσχημόνων	A--GF-P	εὐσχήμων

εὐσχημόνως adverb; of honest and orderly behavior decently, properly, with propriety

εὐσχημόνως	AB	εὐσχημόνως

εὐσχημοσύνη, ης, ἡ as assuring proper external appearance presentability, modesty; εὐσχημοσύνην ἔχειν treat with modesty (1C 12.23)

εὐσχημοσύνην	N-AF-S	εὐσχημοσύνη

εὐσχήμων, ον, gen. **ονος** (1) of good or pleasing external appearance graceful, beautiful, presentable (1C 12.24); (2) of persons of high standing in the community prominent, reputable, honored (MK 15.43); (3) substantivally τὸ εὔσχημον good order, proper behavior (1C 7.35)

εὐσχήμων	A--NM-S	εὐσχήμων

εὐτόνως adverb; strictly at full stretch; hence vehemently, forcibly, vigorously

εὐτόνως	AB	εὐτόνως
εὐτρακήλων	N-NM-S	εὐρακύλων

εὐτραπελία, ας, ἡ from εὖ (easily) and τρέπω (turn); (1) in a good sense pleasantry, wittiness, urbanity; (2) in a bad sense coarse joking, clowning around, vulgar talk (EP 5.4)

εὐτραπελία	N-NF-S	εὐτραπελία

Εὔτυχος, ου, ὁ Eutychus, masculine proper noun (AC 20.9)

Εὔτυχος	N-NM-S	Εὔτυχος
εὔφημα	A--NN-P	εὔφημος

εὐφημία, ας, ἡ commendation, praise, good report (2C 6.8)

εὐφημίας	N-GF-S	εὐφημία

εὔφημος, ον strictly auspicious, of good omen; hence of good report, praiseworthy, commendable (PH 4.8)

εὐφορέω 1aor. εὐφόρησα; strictly bear well, bring forth well; hence, of farm land yield abundantly, produce well, bear good crops (LU 12.16)

εὐφόρησε(ν)	VIAA--3S	εὐφορέω
εὐφραίνεσθαι	VNPP	εὐφραίνω
εὐφραίνεσθε	VMPP--2P	"
εὐφραινόμενος	VPPPNM-S	"
εὐφραίνονται	VIPP--3P	"
εὐφραίνοντο	VIIP--3P	"
εὐφραίνου	VMPP--2S	"

εὐφραίνω impf. pass. εὐφραινόμην; 1aor. pass. ηὐφράνθην; (1) active make glad, cheer up someone (2C 2.2); (2) passive, of social and festive enjoyment be merry, enjoy oneself (LU 16.19); of religious and spiritual jubilation rejoice, celebrate, be jubilant (AC 2.26)

εὐφραίνων	VPPANM-S	εὐφραίνω
εὐφράνθη	VIAP--3S	"
εὐφρανθῆναι	VNAP	"
εὐφρανθήσονται	VIFP--3P	"
εὐφράνθητε	VMAP--2P	"
εὐφράνθητι	VMAP--2S	"
εὐφρανθῶ	VSAP--1S	"
εὐφρανθῶμεν	VSAP--1P	"
Εὐφράτη	N-DM-S	Εὐφράτης

Εὐφράτην | N-AM-S | "
Εὐφράτης, ου, ὁ | *Euphrates River*, a river in Mesopotamia
εὐφροσύνη, ης, ἡ | as a state of happiness *gladness, rejoicing, cheerfulness*

εὐφροσύνης	N-GF-S	εὐφροσύνη
εὐχαριστεῖ	VIPA--3S	εὐχαριστέω
εὐχαριστεῖν	VNPA	"
εὐχαριστεῖς	VIPA--2S	"
εὐχαριστεῖτε	VMPA--2P	"

εὐχαριστέω 1aor. εὐχαρίστησα and ηὐχαρίστησα (RO 1.21); (1) predominately as expressing gratitude to God *thank, give thanks to* (JN 11.41); (2) of a thanksgiving prayer, especially at meals *give* or *return thanks, bless* (MK 8.6); (3) as expressing gratitude generally *thank* (RO 16.4)

εὐχαριστηθῇ	VSAP--3S	εὐχαριστέω
εὐχαρίστησαν	VIAA--3P	"
εὐχαριστήσαντος	VPAAGM-S	"
εὐχαριστήσας	VPAANM-S	"
εὐχαρίστησε(ν)	VIAA--3S	"

εὐχαριστία, ας, ἡ (1) as an attitude *gratitude, thankfulness* (AC 24.3); (2) as an act of giving thanks *thanksgiving* (1C 14.16); (3) *Lord's Supper* (1C 10.16)

εὐχαριστία	N-NF-S	εὐχαριστία
εὐχαριστίᾳ	N-DF-S	"
εὐχαριστίαν	N-AF-S	"
εὐχαριστίας	N-AF-P	"
	N-GF-S	"
εὐχαριστιῶν	N-GF-P	"
εὐχάριστοι	A--NM-P	εὐχάριστος

εὐχάριστος, ον *thankful, grateful* (CO 3.15)

εὐχαριστοῦμεν	VIPA--1P	εὐχαριστέω
εὐχαριστοῦντες	VPPANM-P	"
εὐχαριστῶ	VIPA--1S	"
εὐχαριστῶν	VPPANM-S	"
εὔχεσθε	VMPD--2P	εὔχομαι
	VMPO--2P	"

εὐχή, ῆς, ἡ (1) *prayer* (JA 5.15); (2) as a solemn promise to God *vow, oath* (AC 18.18)

εὐχή	N-NF-S	εὐχή
εὐχήν	N-AF-S	"

εὔχομαι impf. ηὐχόμην; 1aor. εὐξάμην; (1) of petitionary prayer or appeal to God *pray, offer prayer, ask* (2C 13.7); (2) of a strong desire for something *want, wish for* (RO 9.3)

εὔχομαι	VIPD--1S	εὔχομαι
	VIPO--1S	"
εὐχόμεθα	VIPD--1P	"
	VIPO--1P	"
εὔχοντο	VIID--3P	see ηὔχοντο
	VIIO--3P	see ηὔχοντο
εὔχρηστον	A--AM-S	εὔχρηστος
	A--NN-S	"

εὔχρηστος, ον *very profitable, useful, serviceable*

εὔχρηστος	A--NM-S	εὔχρηστος

εὐψυχέω *be glad, cheered (up), become encouraged* (PH 2.19)

εὐψυχῶ	VSPA--1S	εὐψυχέω

εὐωδία, ας, ἡ *fragrance, sweet odor, aroma*; metaphorically, of sacrifices pleasing to God; (1) as those who serve God sacrificially (2C 2.15); (2) as a gift given sacrificially (PH 4.18); (3) as Christ's sacrifice of himself (EP 5.2)

εὐωδία	N-NF-S	εὐωδία
εὐωδίας	N-GF-S	"
εὐώνυμον	AP-AF-S	εὐώνυμος
	A--AM-S	"

εὐώνυμος, ον strictly *of good name, honorable, of good omen*; usually substantivally in both feminine singular and neuter plural, used by the Greeks as a euphemism for *left, the left hand, the left side*, as a replacement for ἀριστερός (*left*) in opposition to the right, since omens on the left were regarded as unfortunate (MT 20.21)

εὐωνύμων	AP-GN-P	εὐώνυμος

εὐωχία, ας, ἡ *banquet, feasting* (JU 12)

εὐωχίαις	N-DF-P	εὐωχία
ἐφ'	PA	ἐπί
	PD	"
	PG	"
ἔφαγε(ν)	VIAA--3S	ἐσθίω
ἐφάγετε	VIAA--2P	"
ἐφάγομεν	VIAA--1P	"
ἔφαγον	VIAA--1S	"
	VIAA--3P	"

ἐφάλλομαι 2aor. ἐφαλόμην; *leap* or *jump on* someone, *assault* (AC 19.16)

ἐφαλλόμενος	VPPDNM-S	ἐφάλλομαι
	VPPONM-S	"
ἐφαλόμενος	VPADNM-S	"
ἐφανερώθη	VIAP--3S	φανερόω
ἐφανερώθησαν	VIAP--3P	"
ἐφανέρωσα	VIAA--1S	"
ἐφανέρωσε(ν)	VIAA--3S	"
ἐφάνη	VIAP--3S	φαίνω
ἐφάνησαν	VIAP--3P	"

ἐφάπαξ adverb; (1) as a numerical time concept *at the same time, at once, all together* (probably 1C 15.6); (2) as a single occurrence *once, one time only* (possibly 1C 15.6); (3) as a religious technical term for the uniqueness and singularity of the Christ's death and the resultant redemption *once (and) for all* (HE 10.10)

ἐφάπαξ	AB	ἐφάπαξ
ἔφασκε(ν)	VIIA--3S	φάσκω
ἐφείσατο	VIAD--3S	φείδομαι
ἔφερε(ν)	VIIA--3S	φέρω
ἐφερόμεθα	VIIP--1P	"
ἔφερον	VIIA--3S	"
ἐφέροντο	VIIP--3P	"
Ἐφεσίνης	A--GF-S	Ἐφέσιος
Ἐφέσιοι	AP-VM-P	"
Ἐφέσιον	A--AM-S	"

Ἐφέσιος, ία, ον (also Ἐφεσῖνος) *Ephesian*; substantivally οἱ Ἐφέσιοι *the Ephesians*, people belonging to or living in Ephesus

Ἐφεσίου	AP-GM-S	Ἐφέσιος
Ἐφεσίων	AP-GM-P	"
Ἔφεσον	N-AF-S	Ἔφεσος

Ἔφεσος, ου, ἡ *Ephesus*, a leading seaport in western Asia Minor where the Cayster River empties into the Aegean Sea

Ἐφέσου	N-GF-S	Ἔφεσος
ἐφέστηκε(ν)	VIRA--3S	ἐφίστημι
ἐφεστώς	VPRANM-S	"

ἐφεστῶτα	VPRAAM-S	"
Ἐφέσῳ	N-DF-S	Ἔφεσος
ἐφευρετάς	N-AM-P	ἐφευρετής

ἐφευρετής, οῦ, ὁ as one who thinks up ways of doing things *inventor, contriver, deviser* (RO 1.30)

ἔφη	VIAA--3S	φημί
	VIIA--3S	"

ἐφημερία, ας, ἡ strictly *daily order* or *course* of duty; hence *daily service* of the temple; used of a group of priests performing daily duties in the temple for a week in rotation *division, class, priestly order* (LU 1.5, 8)

ἐφημερίας	N-GF-S	ἐφημερία

ἐφήμερος, ον *for the day, lasting for the day*; of necessary food *daily* (JA 2.15)

ἐφημέρου	A--GF-S	ἐφήμερος
ἐφημίσθη	VIAP--3S	φημίζω
ἔφθακε(ν)	VIRA--3S	φθάνω
ἐφθάσαμεν	VIAA--1P	"
ἐφθάσατε	VIAA--2P	"
ἔφθασε(ν)	VIAA--3S	"
ἐφθείραμεν	VIAA--1P	φθείρω
ἔφθειρε(ν)	VIIA--3S	"
ἐφικέσθαι	VNAD	ἐφικνέομαι

ἐφικνέομαι 2aor. ἐφικόμην; *come to, reach, arrive*

ἐφικνούμενοι	VPPDNM-P	ἐφικνέομαι
	VPPONM-P	"
ἐφίλει	VIIA--3S	φιλέω
ἐφιμώθη	VIAP--3S	φιμόω
ἐφίμωσε(ν)	VIAA--3S	"
ἔφιπποι	AP-NM-P	ἔφιππος

ἔφιππος, ον *on horseback*; substantivally, plural *men on horses*; as part of an army *cavalry* (RV 19.14)

ἐφίσταται	VIPM--3S	ἐφίστημι

ἐφίστημι 2aor. ἐπέστην; pf. ptc. ἐφεστώς; only with an intransitive sense in the NT; (1) present and aorist; (a) of persons *stand near, approach, appear (suddenly)* (LU 2.9); *stand ready, be always alert to* (2T 4.2); (b) of events *come on (suddenly), happen without previous warning* (1TH 5.3); (2) perfect; (a) of persons *stand by, be present* (AC 22.20); (b) of events *be at hand, be imminent* (2T 4.6); διὰ τὸν ὑετὸν τὸν ἐφεστῶτα *because the rain had set in, it had begun to rain* (AC 28.2)

ἐφνίδιος	A--NF-S	αἰφνίδιος
ἐφοβεῖτο	VIIP--3S	φοβέω
ἐφοβήθη	VIAP--3S	"
ἐφοβήθην	VIAP--1S	"
ἐφοβήθησαν	VIAP--3P	"
ἐφοβούμην	VIIP--1S	"
ἐφοβοῦντο	VIIP--3P	"
ἐφόνευσαν	VIAA--3P	φονεύω
ἐφονεύσατε	VIAA--2P	"
ἐφορέσαμεν	VIAA--1P	φορέω

Ἐφραίμ, ὁ (also Ἐφραίμ) indeclinable; *Ephraim*, masculine proper noun; name of a town (JN 11.54)

Ἐφραίμ		Ἐφραίμ
ἔφραξαν	VIAA--3P	φράσσω
ἐφρονεῖτε	VIIA--2P	φρονέω
ἐφρόνουν	VIIA--1S	"
ἐφρούρει	VIIA--3S	φρουρέω
ἐφρουρούμεθα	VIIP--1P	"
ἐφρύαξαν	VIAA--3P	φρυάσσω

ἐφυγάδευσε(ν)	VIAA--3S	φυγαδεύω
ἔφυγε(ν)	VIAA--3S	φεύγω
ἔφυγον	VIAA--3P	"
ἐφύλαξα	VIAA--1S	φυλάσσω
ἐφυλαξάμην	VIAM--1S	"
ἐφυλάξατε	VIAA--2P	"
ἐφύλαξε(ν)	VIAA--3S	"
ἐφύλασσον	VIIA--3P	"
ἐφυσιώθησαν	VIAP--3P	φυσιόω
ἐφύτευον	VIIA--3P	φυτεύω
ἐφύτευσα	VIAA--1S	"
ἐφύτευσε(ν)	VIAA--3S	"

ἐφφαθά indeclinable; an Aramaic word translated διανοίχθητι *be opened* (MK 7.34)

ἐφώνει	VIIA--3S	φωνέω
ἐφώνησαν	VIAA--3P	"
ἐφώνησε(ν)	VIAA--3S	"
ἐφώτισε(ν)	VIAA--3S	φωτίζω
ἐφωτίσθη	VIAP--3S	"
ἔχ	VSPA--3S	see ἔχῃ
ἔχαιρε(ν)	VIIA--3S	χαίρω
ἔχαιρον	VIIA--3P	"
ἐχαλάσθην	VIAP--1S	χαλάω
ἐχάρη	VIAO--3S	χαίρω
ἐχάρημεν	VIAO--1P	"
ἐχάρην	VIAO--1S	"
ἐχάρησαν	VIAO--3P	"
ἐχάρητε	VIAO--2P	"
ἐχαρίσατο	VIAD--3S	χαρίζομαι
ἐχαρίσθη	VIAP--3S	"
ἐχαρίτωσε(ν)	VIAA--3S	χαριτόω
ἔχε	VMPA--2S	ἔχω
ἔχει	VIPA--3S	"
ἔχειν	VNPA	"
ἔχεις	VIPA--2S	"
ἔχετε	VIPA--2P	"
	VMPA--2P	"
ἐχέτω	VMPA--3S	"
ἔχῃ	VSPA--3S	"
ἔχητε	VSPA--2P	"

ἐχθές adverb of time; (1) of the immediate past *yesterday* (JN 4.52); (2) generally *in the past* in contrast to the present (σήμερον) (HE 13.8)

ἐχθές	AB	ἐχθές

ἔχθρα, ας, ἡ *enmity, hostility, hatred*, both as an inner disposition and objective opposition (RO 8.7); plural, of hostile feelings and acts *animosities, hostilities, discord, feuds* (GA 5.20)

ἔχθρα	N-NF-S	ἔχθρα
ἔχθρᾳ	N-DF-S	"
ἔχθραι	N-NF-P	"
ἔχθραν	N-AF-S	"
ἐχθρέ	AP-VM-S	ἐχθρός
ἐχθροί	AP-NM-P	"
	A--NM-P	"
ἐχθρόν	AP-AM-S	"

ἐχθρός, ά, όν used of personal enemies, national foes, enemies of God; (1) active *hostile, hating* (MT 13.28); substantivally *enemy, adversary* (LU 19.27); (2) passive *hated, regarded as an enemy* (RO 11.28)

ἐχθρός	AP-NM-S	ἐχθρός
	A--NM-S	"

ἐχθροῦ	AP-GM-S	"
ἐχθρούς	AP-AM-P	"
ἐχθρῶν	AP-GM-P	"

ἔχιδνα, ης, ἡ literally *viper, poisonous serpent, snake* (AC 28.3); figuratively, of persons *evil and despised person* (MT 3.7)

ἔχιδνα	N-NF-S	ἔχιδνα
ἐχιδνῶν	N-GF-P	"
ἐχλεύαζον	VIIA--3P	χλευάζω
ἔχοι	VOPA--3S	ἔχω
ἔχοιεν	VOPA--3P	"
ἔχομεν	VIPA--1P	"
ἐχόμενα	VPPMAN-P	"
ἐχομένας	VPPMAF-P	"
ἐχομένη	VPPMDF-S	"
ἐχομένῳ	VPPMDN-S	"
ἔχον	VPPAAN-S	"
	VPPANN-S	"
ἔχοντα	VPPAAM-S	"
	VPPANN-P	"
ἔχοντας	VPPAAM-P	"
ἔχοντες	VPPANM-P	"
ἔχοντι	VPPADM-S	"
ἔχοντος	VPPAGM-S	"
	VPPAGN-S	"
ἐχόντων	VPPAGM-P	"
ἐχορτάσθησαν	VIAP--3P	χορτάζω
ἐχορτάσθητε	VIAP--2P	"
ἔχουσα	VPPANF-S	ἔχω
ἔχουσαι	VPPANF-P	"
ἐχούσαις	VPPADF-P	"
ἔχουσαν	VPPAAF-S	"
ἐχούσῃ	VPPADF-S	"
ἐχούσης	VPPAGF-S	"
ἔχουσι(ν)	VIPA--3P	"
ἐχρημάτισαν	VIAA--3P	χρηματίζω
ἐχρηματίσθη	VIAP--3S	"
ἐχρησάμεθα	VIAD--1P	χράομαι
ἐχρησάμην	VIAD--1S	"
ἔχρισας	VIAA--2S	χρίω
ἔχρισε(ν)	VIAA--3S	"
ἐχρῶντο	VIID--3P	χράομαι
	VIIO--3P	"

ἔχω impf. εἶχον; fut. ἕξω; 2aor. ἔσχον; pf. ἔσχηκα; with a basic meaning *have, hold,* with a wide range of meanings derived from the contexts and accompanying terms; the following are represented; **I.** active, transitively; (1) as using the hand to grasp something *have, hold* (RV 1.16); (2) of clothing, weapons, etc. *have on, wear* (JN 18.10); (3) literally and figuratively, as holding something safely *keep, preserve* (1T 3.9); (4) of emotional states taking hold of someone *seize, grip* (MK 16.8); (5) legally, of property *have (at one's disposal), possess, own, enjoy* (MK 10.22); (6) of a binding or close relationship with a person *have* (a husband), *be married* (JN 4.17); *have* (a friend) (LU 11.5); *have* (a master) (CO 4.1); (7) of conditions of body and soul; *have* (a disease) (AC 28.9); *be possessed by* (a demon), *have* (an evil spirit) (MK 5.15); (8) idiomatically, with indications of time ἔτη ἔχειν literally *have years,* i.e. *be x years old* (JN 8.57); ἡμέρας ἔχειν ἐν literally *have days in,* i.e. *be in a certain* situation *for x days* (JN 11.17); (9) as bearing or possessing abstract qualities, spiritual gifts, and powers *have, possess, enjoy* (JN 3.16); with ἐν *have something within* oneself (2C 1.9); (10) as holding an opinion *have, consider, regard as* (MT 14.5); (11) with the object expressed or implied and followed by an infinitive *have the possibility of, can, be able to* (MT 18.25; AC 4.14); with a sense of compulsion *must, have to* (LU 12.50); **II.** active, intransitively, with an adverb or adverbial expressions determining the sense *be, be situated, get along* in such a way; καλῶς ἔχειν *be well, be healthy* (MK 16.18), κακῶς ἔχειν *be sick* (MT 4.24), ἑτοίμως ἔχειν with an infinitive following *be ready to, be prepared to* (2C 12.14), ἐν γαστρὶ ἔχειν *be pregnant* (MK 13.17), etc.; **III.** middle (only as a participle in the NT); (1) of inherent association *belong to* (HE 6.9); (2) of close association of place *neighboring, nearby* (MK 1.38); (3) of close association of time τῇ ἐχομένῃ (ἡμέρᾳ) *on the next day, on the following day* (LU 13.33; AC 20.15)

ἔχω	VIPA--1S	ἔχω
	VSPA--1S	"
ἔχωμεν	VSPA--1P	"
ἔχων	VPPANM-S	"
ἐχωρίσθη	VIAP--3S	χωρίζω
ἔχωσι(ν)	VSPA--3P	ἔχω
ἐψευδομαρτύρουν	VIIA--3P	ψευδομαρτυρέω
ἐψεύσω	VIAD--2S	ψεύδομαι
ἐψηλάφησαν	VIAA--3P	ψηλαφάω
ἐῶν	VPPANM-S	ἐάω
ἑώρακα	VIRA--1S	ὁράω
ἑωράκαμεν	VIRA--1P	"
ἑώρακαν	VIRA--3P	"
ἑώρακας	VIRA--2S	"
ἑωράκασι(ν)	VIRA--3P	"
ἑωράκατε	VIRA--2P	"
ἑωράκει	VILA--3S	"
ἑώρακε(ν)	VIRA--3S	"
ἑωρακέναι	VNRA	"
ἑώρακες	VIRA--2S	see ἑώρακας
ἑωρακότες	VPRANM-P	ὁράω
ἑωρακώς	VPRANM-S	"
ἑώρων	VIIA--3P	"

ἕως (1) as a temporal conjunction; (a) to link the event marking the end of a time period to another element in the sentence *till, until* (MT 2.9); (b) to link to an event the circumstances on which the beginning of that event depends *until* (MT 2.13); (c) to denote the contemporaneous aspect of a time period *while, as long as* (MK 6.45; JN 9.4); (2) as an improper preposition with the genitive; (a) to denote time *until* (MK 15.33); (b) with historical names *up to the time of* (AC 13.20); (c) to denote place *as far as, to* (MT 24.27); (d) to denote order in a series *to* (MT 20.8); (e) to denote the upper limit of degree or measure *(up) to* (this point), *as much as, to the extent of* (MK 6.23)

ἕως	CS	ἕως
	PG	"

ἑωσφόρος, ον *bringing the morning;* substantivally ὁ ἑ. *the morning star* (2P 1.19)

ἑωσφόρος	AP-NM-S	ἑωσφόρος

ζ Z

ζʹ indeclinable; the sixth letter of the Greek alphabet; as a cardinal number *seven* (AC 12.10); as an ordinal number *seventh*

ζαβαφθανεί   σαβαχθάνι
ζαβαφθάνι   "
ζαβαχθάνι   "

Ζαβουλών, ὁ indeclinable; *Zebulun*, masculine proper noun; name of a tribe of Israel (RV 7.8); name used for its tribal territory (MT 4.13)

Ζακχαῖε   N-VM-S   Ζακχαῖος
Ζακχαῖος, ου, ὁ *Zacchaeus*, masculine proper noun
Ζακχαῖος   N-NM-S   Ζακχαῖος
Ζάρα, ὁ (also **Ζαρά, Ζάρε**) indeclinable; *Zerah*, masculine proper noun (MT 1.3)

Ζαρά   Ζάρα
Ζάρε   "
Ζαρούχ   Σερούχ
ζαφθανεί   σαβαχθάνι
ζαφθάνι   "
Ζαχαρία   N-VM-S   Ζαχαρίας
Ζαχαρίαν   N-AM-S   "
Ζαχαρίας, ου, ὁ *Zechariah*, masculine proper noun
Ζαχαρίας   N-NM-S   Ζαχαρίας
Ζαχαρίου   N-GM-S   "

ζάω contracted form ζῶ; impf. ἔζων; fut. ζήσω, mid. ζήσομαι; 1aor. ἔζησα; *live*; (1) of natural physical life; (a) *live, be living, be alive* (1C 15.45), opposite ἀποθνήσκω (*die*); (b) of return from death *become alive again* (MT 9.18); (c) of recovery from sickness *get well, recover, be well* (JN 4.50); (d) with mention of the sphere or basis of life *live in* (AC 17.28); *live by* (MT 4.4); (2) of supernatural, spiritual life, including resurrected life for the body and eternal life for the soul (JN 11.25, 26); (3) of the conduct of life *live (as)* (GA 2.14); *continue (to sin)* (RO 6.2); *live (for)* (2C 5.15); (4) participle ζῶν *living*, of things deriving from God as the source of life (1P 1.3)

Ζεβεδαῖον   N-AM-S   Ζεβεδαῖος
Ζεβεδαῖος, ου, ὁ *Zebedee*, masculine proper noun
Ζεβεδαίου   N-GM-S   Ζεβεδαῖος
ζέοντες   VPPANM-P   ζέω
ζεστός, ή, όν strictly *boiled, boiling*; hence *hot*; figuratively *fervent, zealous* (RV 3.15, 16), opposite ψυχρός (*indifferent*)

ζεστός   A--NM-S   ζεστός
ζεύγη   N-AN-P   ζεῦγος
ζεῦγος, ους, τό *yoke*; by metonymy, of two animals united by a yoke, as a *yoke* of oxen *pair, team* (LU 14.19); of two turtledoves *pair, couple* (LU 2.24)

ζεῦγος   N-AN-S   ζεῦγος
ζευκτηρία, ας, ἡ as equipment for tying two objects together *fastening, band*; on a ship, *rope* for tying the rudder, *rudder-band* (AC 27.40)

ζευκτηρίας   N-AF-P   ζευκτηρία
Ζεύς, Διός, ὁ, accusative **Δία** and **Δίαν** *Zeus*, masculine proper noun; name of the Greek supreme god, Jupiter to the Romans (AC 14.12, 13)

ζέω literally *well up, bubble, boil*; figuratively, of spiritual fervor *be very eager, show enthusiasm* (AC 18.25)

ζέων   VPPANM-S   ζέω
ζῇ   VIPA--3S   ζάω
ζήλευε   VMPA--2S   ζηλεύω
ζηλεύω *be zealous* or *earnest, greatly desire* (RV 3.19)
ζηλοῖ   VIPA--3S   ζηλόω
ζηλοῖς   N-DM-S   ζῆλος
ζῆλον   N-AM-S   "
ζῆλος, ου, ὁ and **ζῆλος, ους, τό** strictly *ferment of spirit*; (1) in a good sense, as a human emotion expressing active enthusiasm, ardent affection, keen interest *zeal, ardor, jealousy* (2C 7.7); (2) of the intensity of divine action *extremity* πυρὸς ζ. *fiery indignation, fierceness of fire* (HE 10.27); (3) in a bad sense *jealousy, envy* (GA 5.20)

ζῆλος   N-AN-S   ζῆλος
       N-NM-S   "
       N-NN-S   "
ζήλου   N-GM-S   "
ζήλους   N-AM-P   "
ζηλοῦσθαι   VNPM   ζηλόω
       VNPP   "
ζηλοῦσθε   VMPM--2P   "
       VMPP--2P   "
ζηλοῦσι(ν)   VIPA--3P   "
ζηλοῦτε   VIPA--2P   "
       VMPA--2P   "
       VSPA--2P   "
ζηλόω 1aor. ἐζήλωσα; (1) as commendably striving for something *desire, show zeal (for), set one's heart on* (1C 12.31); (2) of a strong personal concern for someone *be zealous* or *jealous* (over) (2C 11.2); (3) of an attitude of misplaced zeal *be zealous for, eagerly seek, try to win over* (GA 4.17); (4) in a bad sense of hostile emotion based on resentment *(be moved with) envy, be filled with jealousy, be jealous of* (AC 17.5)

ζηλῶ   VIPA--1S   ζηλόω
ζήλῳ   N-DM-S   ζῆλος
ζηλώσαντες   VPAANM-P   ζηλόω
ζήλωσον   VMAA--2S   "
ζηλωταί   N-NM-P   ζηλωτής
ζηλωτήν   N-AM-S   "
ζηλωτής, οῦ, ὁ (1) as one stirred to action by a strong emotion *zealot, enthusiast, one who is zealous* or *eager* (TI 2.14); (2) as a Jew with great personal concern for the Mosaic law *devoted adherent, zealot* (AC 22.3); (3) as a member of a fanatically patriotic group in Palestine

wanting to be independent of Rome *zealot, nationalist* (LU 6.15)

ζηλωτής	N-NM-S	ζηλωτής

ζημία, ας, ἡ as coming into a worsened situation from previous advantage *loss, damage, disadvantage*

ζημίαν	N-AF-S	ζημία
ζημίας	N-GF-S	"

ζημιόω 1aor. pass. ἐζημιώθην; 1fut. pass. ζημιωθήσομαι; only passive in the NT, as being set at a disadvantage *suffer loss* or *damage, suffer injury, forfeit* (1C 3.15)

ζημιωθείς	VPAPNM-S	ζημιόω
ζημιωθῇ	VSAP--3S	"
ζημιωθῆναι	VNAP	"
ζημιωθήσεται	VIFP--3S	"
ζημιωθῆτε	VSAP--2P	"
ζῆν	VNPA	ζάω
Ζηνᾶν	N-AM-S	Ζηνᾶς

Ζηνᾶς, ὁ, accusative ᾶν *Zenas*, masculine proper noun (TI 3.13)

Ζήνων, ωνος, ὁ *Zeno*, masculine proper noun

Ζήνωνα	N-AM-S	Ζήνων
ζῇς	VIPA--2S	ζάω
ζήσασα	VPAANF-S	"
ζήσει	VIFA--3S	"
ζήσεσθε	VIFM--2P	"
ζήσεται	VIFM--3S	"
ζήσετε	VIFA--2P	"
ζήσῃ	VIFM--2S	"
	VSAA--3S	"
ζησόμεθα	VIFM--1P	"
ζήσομεν	VIFA--1P	"
ζήσονται	VIFM--3P	"
ζήσουσι(ν)	VIFA--3P	"
ζήσω	VSAA--1S	"
ζήσωμεν	VSAA--1P	"
ζῆτε	VIPA--2P	"
ζήτει	VMPA--2S	ζητέω
ζητεῖ	VIPA--3S	"
ζητεῖν	VNPA	"
ζητεῖς	VIPA--2S	"
ζητεῖται	VIPP--3S	"
ζητεῖτε	VIPA--2P	"
	VMPA--2P	"
ζητείτω	VMPA--3S	"

ζητέω impf. ἐζήτουν; fut. ζητήσω; 1aor. ἐζήτησα; 1fut. pass. ζητηθήσομαι; (1) as a searching for what is lost *seek, try to find, look for* (LU 19.10); (2) of man's quest for God and what can be obtained only from him *seek, search for, try to obtain* (AC 17.27); (3) of what God requires or expects from man *seek, demand* (LU 12.48); (4) as making inquiry or investigation *examine, question, deliberate* (JN 16.19); (5) of man's effort to obtain something *pursue, endeavor to obtain, strive for* (MT 6.33); (6) of man's desire toward something *seek for, wish for, want* (1C 10.24)

ζητηθήσεται	VIFP--3S	ζητέω

ζήτημα, ατος, τό *issue, (controversial) question, dispute*

ζήτημα	N-NN-S	ζήτημα
ζητήματα	N-AN-P	"
	N-NN-P	"
ζητήματος	N-GN-S	"

ζητημάτων	N-GN-P	"
ζητῆσαι	VNAA	ζητέω
ζητησάτω	VMAA--3S	"
ζητήσει	VIFA--3S	"
ζητήσεις	N-AF-P	ζήτησις
ζητήσετε	VIFA--2P	ζητέω
ζητήσεως	N-GF-S	ζήτησις
ζητήσῃ	VSAA--3S	ζητέω
ζήτησιν	N-AF-S	ζήτησις

ζήτησις, εως, ἡ strictly *seeking*; (1) as a philosophical inquiry *discussion, debate, dispute* (JN 3.25); (2) as profitless disputing *disputation, controversy, questioning* (2T 2.23); (3) as a legal technical term *investigation, inquiry* (AC 25.20)

ζήτησις	N-NF-S	ζήτησις
ζήτησον	VMAA--2S	ζητέω
ζητήσουσι(ν)	VIFA--3P	"
ζητοῦμεν	VIPA--1P	"
ζητοῦν	VPPANN-S	"
ζητοῦντες	VPPANM-P	"
ζητοῦντι	VPPADM-S	"
ζητούντων	VPPAGM-P	"
ζητοῦσι(ν)	VIPA--3P	"
	VPPADM-P	"
ζητῶ	VIPA--1S	"
ζητῶν	VPPANM-S	"
ζιζάνια	N-AN-P	ζιζάνιον
	N-NN-P	"

ζιζάνιον, ου, τό a weed resembling wheat but producing poisonous seeds *zizanium, darnel, tare*

ζιζανίων	N-GN-P	ζιζάνιον
Ζμύρναν	N-AF-S	Σμύρνα
Ζμύρνη	N-DF-S	"
Ζοροβάβελ		Ζοροβαβέλ

Ζοροβαβέλ, ὁ (also **Ζοροβάβελ**) indeclinable; *Zerubbabel*, masculine proper noun

ζόφον	N-AM-S	ζόφος

ζόφος, ου, ὁ *gloom, darkness* (HE 12.18); as a designation for the underworld *thick darkness, gloomy hell* (2P 2.17)

ζόφος	N-NM-S	ζόφος
ζόφου	N-GM-S	"
ζόφῳ	N-DM-S	"
ζυγόν	N-AM-S	ζυγός

ζυγός, οῦ, ὁ strictly *crossbeam* or *crossbar*; (1) *yoke*; figuratively in the NT, of any binding burden *strict requirements, heavy obligations* (GA 5.1); (2) *lever of a balance*; by synecdoche *pair of scales, balance* (RV 6.5)

ζυγός	N-NM-S	ζυγός
ζυγῷ	N-DM-S	"

ζύμη, ης, ἡ (1) literally, as a small amount of dough kept over to start a new batch of bread dough *yeast, leaven* (MT 13.33); used proverbially to demonstrate great effect from little causes (GA 5.9); (2) metaphorically; (a) as corruption of thinking and conduct, identified as hypocrisy (LU 12.1); (b) identified as teachings based on unspiritual value systems (MT 16.12); (c) as sin within a believing community, identified as wicked ways (1C 5.8)

ζύμη	N-NF-S	ζύμη
ζύμη	N-DF-S	"
ζύμην	N-AF-S	"

ζύμης   N-GF-S   "

ζυμοῖ   VIPA--3S   ζυμόω

ζυμόω 1aor. pass. ἐζυμώθην; *(cause to) ferment, use yeast* or *leaven* to cause bread dough to rise

ζῶ   VIPA--1S   ζάω

ζῷα   N-NN-P   ζῷον

ζῷα   N-NN-P   "

ζωγρέω pf. pass. ptc. ἐζωγρημένος; literally *capture alive*; of fish and animals *catch*; metaphorically, of winning people for God's kingdom *attract* (LU 5.10); figuratively and passive, of being taken and held by the devil as his prisoner of war *be taken, be brought under control* (2T 2.26)

ζωγρῶν   VPPANM-S   ζωγρέω

ζωή, ῆς, ἡ *life*; (1) physical *life* (RO 8.38), opposite θάνατος (*death*); (2) supernatural *life*, opposite τὸ θνητόν (*what is subject to dying*) and φθορά (*destruction, death*), received by believers as a gift from God (JN 3.36; 1J 5.11), experienced both now (RO 6.4) and eternally (MK 10.30); (3) viewed as an attribute of God (1J 5.20) and Christ (JN 5.26b)

ζωή   N-NF-S   ζωή

ζωῇ   N-DF-S   "

ζωήν   N-AF-S   "

ζωῆς   N-GF-S   "

ζῶμεν   VIPA--1P   ζάω

    VSPA--1P   "

ζῶν   VPPAAN-S   "

    VPPANM-S   "

ζώνας   N-AF-P   ζώνη

ζώνη, ης, ἡ *belt, girdle*; as an article of clothing for men, bound around the waist; (1) for fastening up or shortening a garment for labor or service (RV 1.13); (2) for protection in battle (cf. EP 6.14); (3) for forming a pocket for carrying money (MK 6.8)

ζώνη   N-NF-S   ζώνη

ζώνην   N-AF-S   "

ζωννύω or **ζώννυμι** impf. ἐζώννυον; fut. ζώσω; 1aor. mid. imperative second-person singular ζῶσαι; (1) active *gird on, put on*, as a belt or piece of armor (JN 21.18); (2) middle, of fastening up a loose garment for working or walking *gird oneself* (AC 12.8)

ζῶντα   VPPAAM-S   ζάω

    VPPAAN-P   "

ζῶντας   VPPAAM-P   "

ζῶντες   VPPANM-P   "

ζῶντι   VPPADM-S   "

ζῶντος   VPPAGM-S   "

    VPPAGN-S   "

ζώντων   VPPAGM-P   "

ζῳογονεῖσθαι   VNPP   ζῳογονέω

ζῳογονέω fut. ζῳογονήσω; 1aor. inf. ζῳογονῆσαι; (1) *give life to, make alive* (1T 6.13); (2) *preserve life, keep alive* (LU 17.33)

ζῳογονῆσαι   VNAA   ζῳογονέω

ζῳογονήσει   VIFA--3S   "

ζῳογονοῦντος   VPPAGM-S   "

ζῷον, ου, τό (also **ζῶον**) (1) generally of any nonhuman living creature *living creature, living being* (RV 4.6); (2) *animal, beast* (JU 10)

ζῷον   N-NN-S   ζῷον

ζωοποιεῖ   VIPA--3S   ζωοποιέω

ζωοποιεῖται   VIPP--3S   "

ζωοποιέω fut. ζωοποιήσω; 1aor. ἐζωοποίησα; 1aor. pass. ἐζωοποιήθην; literally, of God's action *make alive, give life to* (JN 5.21); figuratively and passive, of the sprouting of seed *come to life, be given new life* (1C 15.36)

ζωοποιηθείς   VPAPNM-S   ζωοποιέω

ζωοποιηθήσονται   VIFP--3P   "

ζωοποιῆσαι   VNAA   "

ζωοποιήσει   VIFA--3S   "

ζωοποιοῦν   VPPAAN-S   "

    VPPANN-S   "

ζωοποιοῦντος   VPPAGM-S   "

ζῴου   N-GN-S   ζῷον

ζῶσα   VPPANF-S   ζάω

ζῶσαι   VMAM--2S   ζωννύω

ζῶσαν   VPPAAF-S   ζάω

ζώσας   VPPAAF-P   "

ζώσει   VIFA--3S   ζωννύω

ζῶσι(ν)   VIPA--3P   ζάω

    VSPA--3P   "

ζώσουσι(ν)   VIFA--3P   "

ζῴων   N-GN-P   ζῷον

ζῴων   N-GN-P   "

η Η

ἤ conjunction; (1) as a disjunctive; (a) conjoining opposites *or* (RV 3.15); ἤ . . . ἤ *either . . . or* (MK 13.35); (b) in negative statements *nor, or* (RV 13.17); (c) joining rhetorical or parallel questions to preceding statements or questions *or* (MT 7.9, 10); (d) joining alternatives πότερον . . . ἤ *whether . . . or* (JN 7.17); (2) as a comparative particle; (a) between the two members of the comparison, following a comparative *than* (MT 10.15); (b) with the comparative implied or expressed by μᾶλλον *more . . . than, rather . . . than* (MT 18.13; JN 3.19); (c) after the positive degree καλόν ἐστιν . . . ἤ *it is better . . . than* (MT 18.8, 9); (d) used with other particles: πρὶν ἤ with an infinitive *before* (MT 1.18); subjunctive *before* (LU 2.26); optative *before* (AC 25.16); ἀλλ᾽ ἤ *but rather* (LU 12.51)

ἤ	CC	ἤ
	CC+	"
	CH	"
	CS	"

ἦ adverb; *truly*; variation for εἰ (*if*) in the Hebraistic oath formula ἦ μήν in HE 6.14, expressing a strong affirmation *surely, certainly*

ἦ	AB	ἦ
ᾖ	VSPA--3S	εἰμί
ἡ	DNFS	ὁ
	DNFS+	"
	DNFS^APDNF-S	"
	DVFS	"
	DVFS+	"
ἥ	APRNF-S	ὅς
ᾗ	APRDF-S	"
ἠβουλήθην	VIAO--1S	βούλομαι
ἤγαγε(ν)	VIAA--3S	ἄγω
ἠγάγετε	VIAA--2P	"
ἤγαγον	VIAA--3P	"
ἠγαλλιάσατο	VIAM--3S	ἀγαλλιάω
ἠγαλλίασε(ν)	VIAA--3S	"
ἠγαλλιᾶτο	VIIM--3S	"
ἠγανάκτησαν	VIAA--3P	ἀγανακτέω
ἠγανάκτησε(ν)	VIAA--3S	"
ἠγάπα	VIIA--3S	ἀγαπάω
ἠγαπᾶτε	VIIA--2P	"
ἠγαπήκαμεν	VIRA--1P	"
ἠγαπηκόσι	VPRADM-P	"
ἠγαπημένην	VPRPAF-S	"
ἠγαπημένοι	VPRPNM-P	"
	VPRPVM-P	"
ἠγαπημένοις	VPRPDM-P	"
ἠγαπημένῳ	VPRPDM-S	"
ἠγάπησα	VIAA--1S	"
ἠγαπήσαμεν	VIAA--1P	"
ἠγάπησαν	VIAA--3P	"

ἠγάπησας	VIAA--2S	"
ἠγαπήσατε	VIAA--2P	"
ἠγάπησε(ν)	VIAA--3S	"
ἠγάπομεν	VIIA--1P	"
ἠγγάρευσαν	VIAA--3P	ἀγγαρεύω
ἤγγειλαν	VIAA--3P	ἀγγέλλω
ἤγγιζε(ν)	VIIA--3S	ἐγγίζω
ἤγγικαν	VIRA--3P	"
ἤγγικε(ν)	VIRA--3S	"
ἤγγισαν	VIAA--3P	"
ἤγγισε(ν)	VIAA--3S	"
ἤγειραν	VIAA--3P	ἐγείρω
ἤγειρε(ν)	VIAA--3S	"
ἡγεῖσθαι	VNPD	ἡγέομαι
	VNPO	"
ἡγεῖσθε	VMPD--2P	"
	VMPO--2P	"
ἡγείσθωσαν	VMPD--3P	"
	VMPO--3P	"
ἡγεμόνα	N-AM-S	ἡγεμών
ἡγεμόνας	N-AM-P	"
ἡγεμονεύοντος	VPPAGM-S	ἡγεμονεύω

ἡγεμονεύω *be leader, command, rule*; in the NT of a Roman provincial officer *be governor* (LU 2.2); of Pilate *be procurator, be governor* (LU 3.1)

ἡγεμόνι	N-DM-S	ἡγεμών

ἡγεμονία, ας, ἡ as leadership in high office *reign, government, rule* (LU 3.1)

ἡγεμονίας	N-GF-S	ἡγεμονία
ἡγεμόνος	N-GM-S	ἡγεμών
ἡγεμόνων	N-GM-P	"
ἡγεμόσι(ν)	N-DM-P	"

ἡγεμών, όνος, ὁ as one holding high office *prince, leader* (MT 2.6); as a Roman imperial provincial officer *governor* (MT 10.18)

ἡγεμών	N-NM-S	ἡγεμών
ἦγε(ν)	VIIA--3S	ἄγω

ἡγέομαι 1aor. ἡγησάμην; pf. ἥγημαι; (1) in the NT, as a present participle related to ἡγεμών (*leading, governing*) (AC 15.22); participle as a substantive ὁ ἡγούμενος *the leader* (AC 14.12); plural οἱ ἡγούμενοι *the (community) leaders* (HE 13.7); (2) as making a decision after weighing the facts or circumstances *consider, think, have an opinion* (JA 1.2); *regard, esteem* with a double accusative (PH 2.3)

ἠγέρθη	VIAP--3S	ἐγείρω
ἠγέρθησαν	VIAP--3P	"
ἤγεσθε	VIIP--2P	ἄγω
ἤγετο	VIIP--3S	"
ἥγημαι	VIRD--1S	ἡγέομαι
	VIRO--1S	"
ἡγησάμενος	VPADNM-S	"

ἡγησάμην	VIAD--1S	"
ἡγήσασθε	VMAD--2P	"
ἡγήσατο	VIAD--3S	"
ἡγίασε(ν)	VIAA--3S	ἁγιάζω
ἡγιάσθη	VIAP--3S	"
ἡγιάσθητε	VIAP--2P	"
ἡγιασμένη	VPRPNF-S	"
ἡγιασμένοι	VPRPNM-P	"
ἡγιασμένοις	VPRPDM-P	"
ἡγιασμένον	VPRPNN-S	"
ἡγίασται	VIRP--3S	"
ἡγνικότες	VPRANM-P	ἁγνίζω
ἡγνισμένον	VPRPAM-S	"
ἠγνοεῖται	VIPP--3S	see ἀγνοεῖται
ἠγνοήσαμεν	VIAA--1P	ἀγνοέω
ἠγνόουν	VIIA--3P	"
ἤγοντο	VIIP--3P	ἄγω
ἠγόραζον	VIIA--3P	ἀγοράζω
ἠγόρασα	VIAA--1S	"
ἠγόρασαν	VIAA--3P	"
ἠγόρασας	VIAA--2S	"
ἠγόρασε(ν)	VIAA--3S	"
ἠγοράσθησαν	VIAP--3P	"
ἠγοράσθητε	VIAP--2P	"
ἠγορασμένοι	VPRPNM-P	"
ἡγοῦμαι	VIPD--1S	ἡγέομαι
	VIPO--1S	"
ἡγούμενοι	VPPDNM-P	"
	VPPONM-P	"
ἡγουμένοις	VPPDDM-P	"
	VPPODM-P	"
ἡγούμενον	VPPDAM-S	"
	VPPOAM-S	"
ἡγούμενος	VPPDNM-S	"
	VPPONM-S	"
ἡγουμένους	VPPDAM-P	"
	VPPOAM-P	"
ἡγουμένων	VPPDGM-P	"
	VPPOGM-P	"
ἡγοῦνται	VIPD--3P	"
	VIPO--3P	"
ἠγωνίζοντο	VIID--3P	ἀγωνίζομαι
	VIIO--3P	"
ἠγώνισμαι	VIRD--1S	"
	VIRO--1S	"
ᾔδει	VILA--3S	οἶδα
ᾔδειν	VILA--1S	"
ᾔδεις	VILA--2S	"
ᾔδεισαν	VILA--3P	"
ᾔδειτε	VILA--2P	"

ἡδέως adverb; *gladly, with pleasure* (MK 6.20); superlative ἥδιστα *very gladly* (2C 12.15)

ἡδέως	AB	ἡδέως

ἤδη adverb; (1) of time *by this time, now* (MT 3.10); ἤ. ποτέ *now at length, at last* (RO 1.10); (2) logically *already* (MT 5.28; JN 3.18)

ἤδη	AB	ἤδη
ᾔδητε	VILA--2P	οἶδα
ἠδίκηκα	VIRA--1S	ἀδικέω
ἠδίκησα	VIAA--1S	"
ἠδικήσαμεν	VIAA--1P	"

ἠδικήσατε	VIAA--2P	"
ἠδίκησε(ν)	VIAA--3S	"
ἡδίονα	A-MAF-S	ἡδύς
ἥδιστα	ABS	ἡδέως
ἡδοναῖς	N-DF-P	ἡδονή

ἡδονή, ῆς, ἡ *pleasure, enjoyment*; in the NT in a bad sense, as indulgence and lack of control of natural appetites *(sensual) pleasure, passion, lust* (2P 2.13)

ἡδονήν	N-AF-S	ἡδονή
ἡδονῶν	N-GF-P	"
ἡδύναντο	VIID--3P	δύναμαι
	VIIO--3P	"
ἠδυνάσθη	VIID--2P	"
	VIIO--2P	"
ἠδύνατο	VIID--3S	"
	VIIO--3S	"
ἠδυνήθη	VIAO--3S	"
ἠδυνήθημεν	VIAO--1P	"
ἠδυνήθην	VIAO--1S	"
ἠδυνήθησαν	VIAO--3P	"
ἠδυνήθητε	VIAO--2P	"

ἡδύοσμον, ου, τό as a garden plant used for seasoning *mint*

ἡδύοσμον	N-AN-S	ἡδύοσμον

ἡδύς, εῖα, ὑ literally *sweet* to taste, smell, or hearing; figuratively *pleasing, pleasant*; comparative ἡδίων *more pleasing* (HE 11.4)

ἤθελαν	VIIA--3P	θέλω
ἤθελε(ν)	VIIA--3S	"
ἤθελες	VIIA--2S	"
ἠθέλησα	VIAA--1S	"
ἠθελήσαμεν	VIAA--1P	"
ἠθέλησαν	VIAA--3P	"
ἠθέλησας	VIAA--2S	"
ἠθελήσατε	VIAA--2P	"
ἠθέλησε(ν)	VIAA--3S	"
ἤθελον	VIIA--1S	"
	VIIA--3P	"
ἠθέτησαν	VIAA--3P	ἀθετέω
ἤθη	N-AN-P	ἦθος

ἦθος, ους, τό as a fixed pattern of behavior *habit, custom, usage*; plural *morals, habits, character* (1C 15.33)

ἠθροισμένους	VPRPAM-P	ἀθροίζω
ἠκαιρεῖσθε	VIID--2P	ἀκαιρέομαι
	VIIO--2P	"
ἥκασι(ν)	VIRA--3P	ἥκω
ἥκει	VIPA--3S	"
ἤκμασαν	VIAA--3P	ἀκμάζω
ἤκμασε(ν)	VIAA--3P	"
ἠκολούθει	VIIA--3S	ἀκολουθέω
ἠκολουθήκαμεν	VIRA--1P	"
ἠκολουθήσαμεν	VIAA--1P	"
ἠκολούθησαν	VIAA--3P	"
ἠκολούθησε(ν)	VIAA--3S	"
ἠκολούθουν	VIIA--3P	"
ἦκον	VIIA--3P	ἥκω
ἤκουε(ν)	VIIA--3S	ἀκούω
ἤκουον	VIIA--3P	"
ἤκουσα	VIAA--1S	"
ἠκούσαμεν	VIAA--1P	"
ἤκουσαν	VIAA--3P	"

189

ἤκουσας	VIAA--2S	"
ἠκούσατε	VIAA--2P	"
ἤκουσε(ν)	VIAA--3S	"
ἠκούσθη	VIAP--3S	"
ἤκουσι(ν)	VIPA--3P	ἤκω
ἠκρίβωσε(ν)	VIAA--3S	ἀκριβόω
ἠκυρώσατε	VIAA--2P	ἀκυρόω

ἤκω present stem with third-person plural perfect ending ἤκασι; impf. ἤκον; fut. ἤξω; 1aor. ἤξα; (1) of persons; (a) as the result of moving toward and reaching a point *be, come, arrive* (LU 15.27); (b) as being in a place *be here, be there* (HE 10.7); (2) impersonally, of events *happen, take place, come* (JN 2.4); used especially to express the certainty of future events happening (2P 3.10)

ἤκω	VIPA--1S	ἤκω
ἤλατο	VIAD--3S	ἅλλομαι
ἠλαττόνησε(ν)	VIAA--3S	ἐλαττονέω
ἠλαττωμένον	VPRPAM-S	ἐλαττόω
ἠλάττωσας	VIAA--2S	"
ἠλαύνετο	VIIP--3S	ἐλαύνω
ἠλέγχοντο	VIIP--3P	ἐλέγχω
ἠλεήθημεν	VIAP--1P	ἐλεέω
ἠλεήθην	VIAP--1S	"
ἠλεήθητε	VIAP--2P	"
ἠλεημένοι	VPRPNM-P	"
ἠλεημένος	VPRPNM-S	"
ἠλέησα	VIAA--1S	"
ἠλέησε(ν)	VIAA--3S	"
Ἠλεί		Ἠλί
ἠλεί		ἠλί
ἠλεί		"
Ἠλεία	N-DM-S	Ἠλίας
Ἠλεία	N-GM-S	see Ἠλείου
Ἠλεία	N-DM-S	Ἠλίας
Ἠλείαν	N-AM-S	"
Ἠλείαν	N-AM-S	"
Ἠλείας	N-NM-S	"
Ἠλείας	N-NM-S	"
Ἠλείου	N-GM-S	"
ἤλειφε(ν)	VIIA--3S	ἀλείφω
ἤλειφον	VIIA--3P	"
ἤλειψας	VIAA--2S	"
ἤλειψε(ν)	VIAA--3S	"
ἠλευθέρωσε(ν)	VIAA--3S	ἐλευθερόω
ἤλθαμεν	VIAA--1P	ἔρχομαι
ἤλθαν	VIAA--3P	"
ἤλθατε	VIAA--2P	"
ἤλθε(ν)	VIAA--3S	"
ἤλθες	VIAA--2S	"
ἤλθετε	VIAA--2P	"
ἤλθομεν	VIAA--1P	"
ἤλθον	VIAA--1S	"
	VIAA--3P	"
ἤλθοσαν	VIAA--3P	"

Ἠλί, ὁ (also **Ἠλεί, Ἠλί**) indeclinable; *Heli*, masculine proper noun (LU 3.23)

Ἠλί		Ἠλί

ἠλί (also **ἀηλί, ἠλεί, ἠλεί, ἠλί**) transliterated from the Hebrew word meaning *my God*; see also ἐλωΐ

ἠλί		ἠλί

Ἠλία	N-DM-S	Ἠλίας
Ἠλία	N-DM-S	"
Ἠλίαν	N-AM-S	"
Ἠλίαν	N-AM-S	"

Ἠλίας, ου, ὁ (also **Ἠλείας, Ἠλείας, Ἠλίας**) *Elijah*, masculine proper noun

Ἠλίας	N-NM-S	Ἠλίας
Ἠλίας	N-NM-S	"
ἠλίκην	A-TAF-S	ἠλίκος

ἠλικία, ας, ἡ (1) as the time of a person's life on earth *age, years, span of life* (probably MT 6.27 and LU 12.25; perhaps LU 2.52); (2) as a particular period of life *of mature age, adulthood, maturity*; ἡλικίαν ἔχειν *be of age, be mature* (JN 9.21, 23); figuratively (EP 4.13); (3) as dimension of the physical body *stature, size* (LU 19.3; perhaps MT 6.27; LU 2.52; 12.25)

ἠλικία	N-DF-S	ἠλικία
ἠλικίαν	N-AF-S	"
ἠλικίας	N-GF-S	"
ἠλίκοις	A-TDN-P	ἠλίκος
ἠλίκον	A-TAM-S	"
	A-TNN-S	"

ἠλίκος, η, ον as an interrogative occurring in indirect questions; (1) as a measure of size *how great, how large, how extensive* (JA 3.5); (2) as a measure of intensity *how severe, how much* (CO 2.1)

ἤλιον	N-AM-S	ἤλιος

ἤλιος, ου, ὁ *sun* (MT 5.45); by metonymy, for what comes from the sun *heat* (RV 7.16); *light* (AC 13.11)

ἤλιος	N-NM-S	ἤλιος
Ἠλίου	N-GM-S	Ἠλίας
Ἠλίου	N-GM-S	"
ἠλίου	N-GM-S	ἤλιος
ἠλίῳ	N-DM-S	"
ἠλκωμένος	VPRPNM-S	ἑλκόω
ἤλλαξαν	VIAA--3P	ἀλλάσσω
ἠλλάξαντο	VIAM--3P	"
ἤλλετο	VIID--3S	ἅλλομαι
	VIIO--3S	"
ἠλλοιώθη	VIAP--3S	ἀλλοιόω

ἤλος, ου, ὁ *nail*; as used in crucifying *iron spike*

ἤλπιζε(ν)	VIIA--3S	ἐλπίζω
ἠλπίζομεν	VIIA--1P	"
ἠλπίκαμεν	VIRA--1P	"
ἠλπίκατε	VIRA--2P	"
ἤλπικε(ν)	VIRA--3S	"
ἠλπικέναι	VNRA	"
ἠλπικότες	VPRANM-P	"
ἠλπίσαμεν	VIAA--1P	"
ἤλων	N-GM-P	ἤλος
ἥμαρτε(ν)	VIAA--3S	ἁμαρτάνω
ἥμαρτες	VIAA--2S	"
ἡμαρτήκαμεν	VIRA--1P	"
ἡμαρτήσαμεν	VIAA--1P	"
ἡμάρτομεν	VIIA--1P	"
ἥμαρτον	VIAA--1S	"
	VIAA--3P	"
ἡμᾶς	NPA-1P	ἐγώ
ἤμεθα	VIIM--1P	εἰμί
ἡμεῖς	NPN-1P	ἐγώ
ἠμέλησα	VIAA--1S	ἀμελέω

ἤμελλε(ν)	VIIA--3S	μέλλω
ἤμελλες	VIIA--2S	"
ἤμελλον	VIIA--1S	"
ἦμεν	VIIA--1P	εἰμί

ἡμέρα, ας, ἡ *day*; (1) as a natural time interval between sunrise and sunset *day, daytime, sunlight* (2P 2.13), opposite νύξ (*night*); (2) as a twenty-four-hour measure of time from sunrise to sunrise or from sunset to sunset *day* (MT 6.34); (3) idiomatically ἡμέρᾳ καὶ ἡμέρᾳ literally *day and day*, i.e. *day by day, every day* (2C 4.16); ἡμέραν ἐξ ἡμέρας literally *day out of day*, i.e. *from day to day, continually, for a long time* (2P 2.8); καθ᾽ ἑκάστην ἡμέραν *every day, daily* (HE 3.13); (4) as a longer period *time* (HE 8.9); plural *time(s), lifetime* (HE 5.7); (5) figuratively, as a period of time appointed for a special purpose, as for salvation (2C 6.2) or judgment (AC 17.31)

ἡμέρα	N-NF-S	ἡμέρα
ἡμέρᾳ	N-DF-S	"
ἡμέραι	N-NF-P	"
ἡμέραις	N-DF-P	"
ἡμέραν	N-AF-S	"
ἡμέρας	N-AF-P	"
	N-GF-S	"
ἡμερῶν	N-GF-P	"
ἡμετέρα	A--NF1S	ἡμέτερος
ἡμετέραις	A--DF1P	"
ἡμετέραν	A--AF1S	"
ἡμετέρας	A--GF1S	"
ἡμέτεροι	A--NM1P	"
ἡμετέροις	A--DM1P	"
ἡμέτερον	A--AM1S	"

ἡμέτερος, τέρα, ον *our*, a possessive adjective of the first-person plural, used emphatically (2T 4.15); substantivally οἱ ἡμέτεροι *our people*, i.e. *believers* (TI 3.14)

ἡμετέρῳ	A--DN1S	ἡμέτερος
ἡμετέρων	A--GF1P	"
ἤμην	VIIM--1S	εἰμί
ἡμιθανῆ	A--AM-S	ἡμιθανής

ἡμιθανής, ές *half-dead, about to die* (LU 10.30)

ἡμῖν	NPD-1P	ἐγώ
ἡμίσεα	A--AN-P	see ἡμίσια
ἡμίσεια	A--AN-P	see ἡμίσια
ἡμίση	A--AN-P	ἥμισυς
ἡμίσια	A--AN-P	"
ἡμίσους	A--GN-S	"
ἥμισυ	A--AN-S	"

ἥμισυς, εια, υ, gen. **ἡμίσους** *half* (RV 11.9); substantivally τὸ ἥμισυ *one-half* (RV 12.14)

ἡμιώριον	N-AN-S	ἡμίωρον

ἡμίωρον, ου, τό (also **ἡμιώριον**) *half an hour, half-hour* (RV 8.1)

ἡμίωρον	N-AN-S	ἡμίωρον
ἡμύνατο	VIAD--3S	ἀμύνομαι
ἡμφιεσμένον	VPRPAM-S	ἀμφιέννυμι
ἡμῶν	NPG-1P	ἐγώ
ἦν	VIIA--1S	εἰμί
	VIIA--3S	"
ἥν	APRAF-S	ὅς
	A-RAF-S	"
ἠνάγκαζον	VIIA--1S	ἀναγκάζω

ἠναγκάσατε	VIAA--2P	"
ἠνάγκασε(ν)	VIAA--3S	"
ἠναγκάσθη	VIAP--3S	"
ἠναγκάσθην	VIAP--1S	"
ἤνεγκα	VIAA--1S	φέρω
ἤνεγκαν	VIAA--3P	"
ἤνεγκε(ν)	VIAA--3S	"
ἠνείχεσθε	VIIM--2P	see ἀνείχεσθε
ἠνέστη	VIAA--3S	see ἀνέστη
ἠνεσχόμην	VIAM--1S	ἀνέχω
ἠνέχθη	VIAP--3S	φέρω
ἠνεῳγμένη	VPRPNF-S	ἀνοίγω
ἠνεῳγμένην	VPRPAF-S	"
ἠνεῳγμένον	VPRPAM-S	"
	VPRPAN-S	"
ἠνεῳγμένων	VPRPGM-P	"
ἠνέῳξε(ν)	VIAA--3S	"
ἠνεῴχθη	VIAP--3S	"
ἠνεῴχθησαν	VIAP--3P	"

ἡνίκα a conjunctive particle conjoining time *when, at the time when*; with the present subjunctive and ἄν *whenever* (2C 3.15); with the aorist subjunctive and ἐάν *every time that, when* (2C 3.16)

ἡνίκα	CS	ἡνίκα
ἠνοίγη	VIAP--3S	ἀνοίγω
ἠνοίγησαν	VIAP--3P	"
ἠνοιγμένων	VPRPGM-P	"
ἤνοιξαν	VIAA--3P	"
ἤνοιξε(ν)	VIAA--3S	"
ἠνοίχθη	VIAP--3S	"
ἠνοίχθησαν	VIAP--3P	"
ἠντληκότες	VPRANM-P	ἀντλέω
ἥξει	VIFA--3S	ἥκω
ἥξῃ	VSAA--3S	"
ἠξίου	VIIA--3S	ἀξιόω
ἠξίουν	VIIA--3P	"
ἠξίωσα	VIAA--1S	"
ἠξίωται	VIRP--3S	"
ἥξουσι(ν)	VIFA--3P	ἥκω
ἥξω	VIFA--1S	"
	VSAA--1S	"
ἥξωσι(ν)	VSAA--3P	"
ἠπατήθη	VIAP--3S	ἀπατάω
ἠπείθησαν	VIAA--3P	ἀπειθέω
ἠπειθήσατε	VIAA--2P	"
ἠπείθουν	VIIA--3P	"
ἠπείλει	VIIA--3S	ἀπειλέω

ἤπερ comparative conjunction; *than, than indeed*, intensive form of ἤ (*than*) (JN 12.43)

ἤπερ	CS	ἤπερ
ἤπιοι	A--NM-P	ἤπιος
ἤπιον	A--AM-S	"

ἤπιος, ία, ον *gentle, kind* (2T 2.24)

ἠπίστησαν	VIAA--3P	ἀπιστέω
ἠπίστουν	VIIA--3P	"
ἠπόρει	VIIA--3S	ἀπορέω
ἠπορεῖτο	VIIM--3S	"
ἥπτοντο	VIIM--3P	ἅπτω

Ἤρ, ὁ indeclinable; *Er*, masculine proper noun (LU 3.28)

ἦραν	VIAA--3P	αἴρω
ἤρατε	VIAA--2P	"

ἠργάζετο	VIID--3S	ἐργάζομαι
	VIIO--3S	"
ἠργάζοντο	VIID--3P	"
	VIIO--3P	"
ἠργασάμεθα	VIAD--1P	"
ἠργάσατο	VIAD--3S	"
ἠρέθισε(ν)	VIAA--3S	ἐρεθίζω
ἤρεμον	A--AM-S	ἤρεμος
ἤρεμος, ον	as a manner of life *quiet, tranquil, peaceful*	
ἦρε(ν)	VIAA--3S	αἴρω
ἤρεσε(ν)	VIAA--3S	ἀρέσκω
ἤρεσκον	VIIA--1S	"
ἠρέτισα	VIAA--1S	αἱρετίζω
ἠρημώθη	VIAP--3S	ἐρημόω
ἠρημωμένην	VPRPAF-S	"
ἤρθη	VIAP--3S	αἴρω
ἠριθμημέναι	VPRPNF-P	ἀριθμέω
ἠρίθμηνται	VIRP--3P	"
ἠρίστησαν	VIAA--3P	ἀριστάω
ἦρκε(ν)	VIRA--3S	αἴρω
ἠρμένον	VPRPAM-S	"
ἡρμοσάμην	VIAM--1S	ἁρμόζω
ἠρνεῖτο	VIID--3S	ἀρνέομαι
	VIIO--3S	"
ἠρνημένοι	VPRDNM-P	"
	VPRONM-P	"
ἠρνήσαντο	VIAD--3P	"
ἠρνήσασθε	VIAD--2P	"
ἠρνήσατο	VIAD--3S	"
ἠρνήσω	VIAD--2S	"
ἤρνηται	VIRD--3S	"
	VIRO--3S	"
ἤρξαντο	VIAM--3P	ἄρχω
ἤρξατο	VIAM--3S	"
Ἡροδίωνα	N-AM-S	Ἡρῳδίων
ἡρπάγη	VIAP--3S	ἁρπάζω
ἥρπασε(ν)	VIAA--3S	"
ἡρπάσθη	VIAP--3S	"
ἠρτυμένος	VPRPNM-S	ἀρτύω
ἤρχετο	VIID--3S	ἔρχομαι
	VIIO--3S	"
ἤρχοντο	VIID--3P	"
	VIIO--3P	"
ἤρχου	VIID--2S	"
	VIIO--2S	"
Ἡρώδη	N-DM-S	Ἡρῴδης
Ἡρῴδη	N-DM-S	"
Ἡρώδην	N-AM-S	"
Ἡρῴδην	N-AM-S	"
Ἡρῴδης	N-NM-S	"

Ἡρῴδης, ου, ὁ (also **Ἡρώδης**) *Herod*, masculine proper noun

Ἡρῴδης	N-NM-S	Ἡρῴδης
Ἡρωδιάδα	N-AF-S	Ἡρῳδιάς
Ἡρῳδιάδα	N-AF-S	"
Ἡρωδιάδος	N-GF-S	"
Ἡρῳδιάδος	N-GF-S	"

Ἡρῳδιανοί, ῶν, οἱ (also **Ἡρωδιανοί**) *Herodians, followers of Herod*, supporters of Herod the Great and his dynasty

Ἡρῳδιανῶν	N-GM-P	Ἡρῳδιανοί
Ἡρωδιανῶν	N-GM-P	"
Ἡρῳδιάς	N-NF-S	Ἡρῳδιάς

Ἡρῳδιάς, άδος, ἡ (also **Ἡρωδιάς**) *Herodias*, feminine proper noun

Ἡρῳδιάς	N-NF-S	Ἡρῳδιάς

Ἡρῳδίων, ωνος, ὁ (also **Ἡροδίων, Ἡρωδίων**) *Herodion*, masculine proper noun (RO 16.11)

Ἡρῳδίωνα	N-AM-S	Ἡρῳδίων
Ἡρωδίωνα	N-AM-S	"
Ἡρῴδου	N-GM-S	Ἡρῴδης
Ἡρώδου	N-GM-S	"
ἠρώτα	VIIA--3S	ἐρωτάω
ἠρώτησαν	VIAA--3P	"
ἠρώτησε(ν)	VIAA--3S	"
ἠρώτουν	VIIA--3P	"
ἠρώτων	VIIA--3P	"
ἦς	VIIA--2S	εἰμί
ἦς	VSPA--2S	"
ἧς	APRGF-S	ὅς
	A-RGF-S	"
Ἠσαΐᾳ	N-DM-S	Ἠσαΐας
Ἠσαΐᾳ	N-DM-S	"
Ἠσαΐᾳ	N-DM-S	"
Ἠσαΐαν	N-AM-S	"
Ἠσαΐαν	N-AM-S	"
Ἠσαΐαν	N-AM-S	"
Ἠσαΐας	N-NM-S	"

Ἠσαΐας, ου, ὁ (also **Ἡσαΐας, Ἠσαΐας, Ἰησάϊος**) *Isaiah*, masculine proper noun

Ἠσαΐας	N-NM-S	Ἠσαΐας
Ἠσαΐας	N-NM-S	"
Ἠσαΐου	N-GM-S	"
Ἠσαΐου	N-GM-S	"
Ἠσαΐου	N-GM-S	"
ἦσαν	VIIA--3P	εἰμί

Ἠσαῦ, ὁ indeclinable; *Esau*, masculine proper noun

ἠσέβησαν	VIAA--3P	ἀσεβέω
ἦσθα	VIIM--2S	εἰμί
ἠσθένει	VIIA--3S	ἀσθενέω
ἠσθενήκαμεν	VIRA--1P	"
ἠσθένησα	VIAA--1S	"
ἠσθενήσαμεν	VIAA--1P	"
ἠσθένησε(ν)	VIAA--3S	"
ἤσθιον	VIIA--3P	ἐσθίω
ἠσπάζοντο	VIID--3P	ἀσπάζομαι
	VIIO--3P	"
ἠσπάσατο	VIAD--3S	"

ἡσσάομαι or **ἡττάομαι** pf. pass. ἥττημαι; 1aor. ἡσσήθην; only passive in the NT; related to ἥσσων and ἥττων (*lesser, inferior, worse*); (1) strictly *be put to the worse*, hence *be defeated, conquered* (2P 2.19, 20); (2) *be treated as inferior to, be treated worse than* (2C 12.13)

ἧσσον	ABM	ἥσσων
	A-MAN-S	"
ἡσσώθητε	VIAO--2P	ἡσσάομαι

ἥσσων and **ἥττων, ον,** gen. **ονος** comparative without a positive degree; (1) *lesser, inferior* (MT 20.28); (2) substantivally τὸ ἧσσον *the worse* (1C 11.17), opposite τὸ κρεῖττον (*the more profitable thing*); (3) neuter ἧσσον as an adverb; (a) *less, to a lesser degree* (2C 12.15); (b) as less than satisfactory in quality *worse* (1C 11.17)

ἠστόχησαν	VIAA--3P	ἀστοχέω
ἡσυχάζειν	VNPA	ἡσυχάζω

ἡσυχάζω 1aor. ἡσύχασα; (1) as being inwardly calm *live quietly, keep calm* (1TH 4.11); (2) as keeping prescribed Sabbath rules *rest* (LU 23.56); (3) as being outwardly silent *be quiet, remain silent, keep still* (LU 14.4)

ἡσυχάσαμεν	VIAA--1P	ἡσυχάζω
ἡσύχασαν	VIAA--3P	"

ἡσυχία, ας, ἡ (1) as characterized by inward calm *tranquillity, quietness* (2TH 3.12); (2) of giving calm attention *silence, quietness* (AC 22.2)

ἡσυχία	N-DF-S	ἡσυχία
ἡσυχίαν	N-AF-S	"
ἡσυχίας	N-GF-S	"
ἡσύχιον	A--AM-S	ἡσύχιος

ἡσύχιος, ον as possessing inward calm *quiet, tranquil, peaceful, at rest*

ἡσυχίου	A--GN-S	ἡσύχιος
ἠσφαλίσαντο	VIAM--3P	ἀσφαλίζω
ἠσφαλίσατο	VIAM--3S	"
ἠτακτήσαμεν	VIAA--1P	ἀτακτέω
ἦτε	VIIA--2P	εἰμί
	VSPA--2P	"
ἠτένιζον	VIIA--3P	ἀτενίζω
ᾐτήκαμεν	VIRA--1P	αἰτέω
ᾐτήσαμεν	VIAA--1P	"
ᾔτησαν	VIAA--3P	"
ᾐτήσαντα	VIAM--3P	see ᾐτήσαντο
ᾐτήσαντο	VIAM--3P	αἰτέω
ᾔτησας	VIAA--2S	"
ᾐτήσασθε	VIAM--2P	"
ᾐτήσατε	VIAA--2P	"
ᾐτήσατο	VIAM--3S	"
ᾐτιασάμεθα	VIAD--1P	αἰτιάομαι
ἠτίμασαν	VIAA--3P	ἀτιμάζω
ἠτιμάσατε	VIAA--2P	"
ἠτιμασμένον	VPRPAM-S	"
ἠτίμησαν	VIAA--3P	ἀτιμάω
ἠτιμωμένον	VPRPAM-S	ἀτιμόω
ἥτις	APRNF-S	ὅστις

ἤτοι conjunction; an intensified form of the disjunctive ἤ (*or*); ἤτοι . . . ἤ *whether . . . or, either . . . or* (RO 6.16)

ἤτοι	CC	ἤτοι
ἡτοίμαθαι	VNRP	see ἡτοίμασθαι
ἡτοίμακα	VIRA--1S	ἑτοιμάζω
ἡτοίμασα	VIAA--1S	"
ἡτοίμασαν	VIAA--3P	"
ἡτοίμασας	VIAA--2S	"
ἡτοίμασε(ν)	VIAA--3S	"
ἡτοίμασθαι	VNRP	"
ἡτοίμασθε	VIAM--2P	"
ἡτοιμασμένην	VPRPAF-S	"
ἡτοιμασμένοι	VPRPNM-P	"
ἡτοιμασμένοις	VPRPDM-P	"
ἡτοιμασμένον	VPRPAM-S	"
	VPRPAN-S	"
	VPRPNN-S	"
ἡτοιμασμένῳ	VPRPDM-S	"
ἡτοίμασται	VIRP--3S	"

ᾐτοῦντο	VIIM--3P	αἰτέω
ἡττήθητε	VIAO--2P	see ἡσσώθητε

ἥττημα, ατος, τό as the result of being overthrown *defeat, failure, fall* (RO 11.12)

ἥττημα	N-NN-S	ἥττημα
ἥττηται	VIRP--3S	ἡσσάομαι
ἧττον	ABM	ἥσσων
ἥττονα	A-MAM-S	"
ἥττων	A-MNM-S	"
ἡττῶνται	VIPP--3P	ἡσσάομαι
ἤτω	VMPA--3S	εἰμί
ηὐδόκησα	VIAA--1S	εὐδοκέω
ηὐδοκήσαμεν	VIAA--1P	"
ηὐδόκησαν	VIAA--3P	"
ηὐδόκησας	VIAA--2S	"
ηὐδόκησε(ν)	VIAA--3S	"
ηὐκαίρουν	VIIA--3P	εὐκαιρέω
ηὐλήσαμεν	VIAA--1P	αὐλέω
ηὐλίζετο	VIID--3S	αὐλίζομαι
	VIIO--3S	"
ηὐλίσθη	VIAO--3S	"
ηὐλόγει	VIIA--3S	εὐλογέω
ηὐλόγηκε(ν)	VIRA--3S	"
ηὐλόγησε(ν)	VIAA--3S	"
ηὔξανε(ν)	VIIA--3S	αὐξάνω
ηὐξήθητε	VIAP--2P	"
ηὔξησε(ν)	VIAA--3S	"
ηὐπορεῖτο	VIIM--3S	εὐπορέω
ηὑρίσκετο	VIIP--3S	εὑρίσκω
ηὕρισκον	VIIA--3P	"
ηὐφόρησε(ν)	VIAA--3S	εὐφορέω
ηὐφράνθη	VIAP--3S	εὐφραίνω
ηὐχαρίστησαν	VIAA--3P	εὐχαριστέω
ηὐχόμην	VIID--1S	εὔχομαι
	VIIO--1S	"
ηὔχοντο	VIID--3P	"
	VIIO--3P	"
ἤφιε(ν)	VIIA--3S	ἀφίημι
ἦχε(ν)	VIIA--3S	see εἶχε(ν)

ἠχέω intransitively, as sounding or ringing out; (1) of brass gonglike instruments *boom out, resound*; metaphorically in 1C 13.1 of helping no one by what one says χαλκὸς ἠχῶν *resounding cymbal, clanging brass*; (2) of the sea *roar* (LU 21.25)

ἤχθη	VIAP--3S	ἄγω
ἤχθημεν	VIAP--1P	"
ᾐχμαλώτευσε(ν)	VIAA--3S	αἰχμαλωτεύω

ἦχος, ου, ὁ (I) *sound*; of a trumpet *blast* (HE 12.19)

ἦχος, ους, τό (II) (1) *sound, noise* (AC 2.2); (2) *rumor, report, news* (LU 4.37); (3) of the sea *roaring* (LU 21.25)

ἦχος	N-NN-S	ἦχος (II)
ἤχους	N-GN-S	"
ἠχούσης	VPPAGF-S	ἠχέω
ἠχρεώθησαν	VIAP--3P	ἀχρειόω
ἤχῳ	N-DM-S	ἦχος (I)
ἠχῶν	VPPANM-S	ἠχέω
ἥψαντο	VIAM--3P	ἅπτω
ἥψατο	VIAM--3S	"

θ Θ

θά see μαράνα θά
θᾶ see μαράνα θᾶ
θάβιτα ταλιθά
θαβιτά "
Θαδαῖον N-AM-S Θαδδαῖος
Θαδδαῖον N-AM-S "
Θαδδαῖος, ου, ὁ (also **Δαδδαῖος, Θαδαῖος, Ταδδαῖος**) *Thaddeus*, masculine proper noun (MK 3.18)
Θαδδαῖος N-NM-S Θαδδαῖος
θάλασσα, ης, ἡ (1) generally, as a large body of water *sea* (MK 9.42), in contrast to γῆ (*land*); (2) of specific seas: (a) Mediterranean Sea (AC 10.32); (b) Red Sea (AC 7.36); (3) *lake, inland sea*; the sea in Galilee: *the Sea* (MT 8.24), *Sea of Galilee* (MT 4.18), *Sea of Tiberias* (JN 21.1), *Galilean Sea of Tiberias* (JN 6.1); cf. Gennesaret Lake (λίμνη) (LU 5.1)
θάλασσα N-NF-S θάλασσα
θάλασσαν N-AF-S "
θαλάσσῃ N-DF-S "
θαλάσσης N-GF-S "
θάλπει VIPA--3S θάλπω
θάλπῃ VSPA--3S "
θάλπω strictly *impart warmth*; hence *cherish, comfort, tenderly care for* (1TH 2.7)
Θάμαρ Θαμάρ
Θαμάρ, ἡ (also **Θάμαρ**) indeclinable; *Tamar*, feminine proper noun (MT 1.3)
θαμβέω impf. pass. ἐθαμβούμην; 1aor. pass. ἐθαμβήθην; only passive in the NT *be amazed, be startled, be astonished*
θαμβηθέντες VPAPNM-P θαμβέω
θάμβος, ους, τό and **θάμβος, ου, ὁ** as an emotion in which awe and fear are mingled *astonishment, amazement*
θάμβος N-NM-S θάμβος
N-NN-S "
θάμβους N-GN-S "
θαμβῶν VPPANM-S θαμβέω
θανάσιμον AP-AN-S θανάσιμος
θανάσιμος, ον *deadly, poisonous*; substantivally τὸ θανάσιμον as something that causes death *deadly thing* (MK 16.18)
θάνατε N-VM-S θάνατος
θανατηφόρος, ον *deadly, death-bringing* (JA 3.8)
θανατηφόρου A--GM-S θανατηφόρος
θανάτοις N-DM-P θάνατος
θάνατον N-AM-S "
θάνατος, ου, ὁ *death*; with every form of it in the NT treated not as a natural process but always as a destroying power related to sin and its consequences; (1) physically, as the separation of soul from body *(physical) death* (JN 11.13); (2) as a legal technical term, of capital punishment *(physical) death* (MT 26.66); (3)

spiritually, as the separation of soul from God *(spiritual) death* (JN 5.24; JA 1.15), opposite ζωή (*life*); (4) spiritually, as the separation of soul from spirit or from the possibility of knowing God, as the result of judgment *(eternal) death* (RO 1.32); called *second death* in RV 2.11; 20.6; (5) by metonymy *deadly disease, pestilence* (RV 6.8)
θάνατος N-NM-S θάνατος
θανάτου N-GM-S "
θανατούμεθα VIPP--1P θανατόω
θανατούμενοι VPPPNM-P "
θανατοῦτε VIPA--2P "
θανατόω fut. θανατώσω; 1aor. ἐθανάτωσα; 1aor. pass. ἐθανατώθην; *deprive of life, put to death*; (1) literally, of physical death *condemn to death, deliver up to death, hand over to be killed* (MK 14.55); (2) figuratively; (a) *put a stop to, exterminate, cause tc cease* (RO 8.13); (b) passive, as ending one's relation to something *become dead to, stop completely* (RO 7.4)
θανάτῳ N-DM-S θάνατος
θανατωθείς VPAPNM-S θανατόω
θανάτων N-GM-P θάνατος
θανατῶσαι VNAA θανατόω
θανατώσουσι(ν) VIFA--3P "
θανατώσωσι(ν) VSAA--3P "
θάπτω 1aor. ἔθαψα; 2aor. pass. ἐτάφην; of a dead person *bury, put into a grave, entomb*
Θάρα, ὁ (also **Θαρά, Θάρρα**) indeclinable; *Terah*, masculine proper noun (LU 3.34)
Θαρά Θάρα
Θάρρα
θαρρέω 1aor. ἐθάρρησα; (1) of an attitude *be confident (in), be cheerful (about), rely (on)* (2C 7.16); (2) of a manner of approach *be bold* or *courageous* (HE 13.6); see θαρσέω for the imperative
θαρρῆσαι VNAA θαρρέω
θαρροῦμεν VIPA--1P "
θαρροῦντας VPPAAM-P "
θαρροῦντες VPPANM-P "
θαρρῶ VIPA--1S "
θάρσει VMPA--2S θαρσέω
θαρσεῖτε VMPA--2P "
θαρσέω only imperativally in the NT *be of good cheer! don't be afraid! take courage!*
Θαρσόν N-AF-S see Ταρσόν
θάρσος, ους, τό *courage, confidence*; idiomatically λαμβάνειν θ. literally *take courage*, i.e. *become confident* (AC 28.15)
θάρσος N-AN-S θάρσος
θαῦμα, ατος, τό (1) as an object of wonder *marvel, wonderful thing* (2C 11.14); (2) as an attitude that has been inspired *astonishment, amazement, surprise* (RV 17.6)

θαῦμα	N-AN-S	θαῦμα
	N-NN-S	"
θαυμάζειν	VNPA	θαυμάζω
θαυμάζετε	VIPA--2P	"
	VMPA--2P	"
θαυμάζητε	VSPA--2P	"
θαυμάζοντες	VPPANM-P	"
θαυμαζόντων	VPPAGM-P	"

θαυμάζω impf. ἐθαύμαζον; fut. θαυμάσομαι; 1aor. ἐθαύμασα; 1aor. pass. ἐθαυμάσθην; 1fut. pass. θαυμασθήσομαι; (1) intransitively; (a) as expressing human response when confronted by divine revelation in some form *wonder, be astonished, marvel* (MT 9.33); (b) with ὅτι following *be astonished* or *surprised that* (GA 1.6); (2) transitively; (a) *admire, wonder at* something (AC 7.31); (b) *be amazed* or *marvel at* someone (LU 7.9); (c) passive *be filled with wonder, be amazed* (RV 17.8); (d) as a Hebraism in JU 16 θαυμάζειν πρόσωπον literally *admire the face*, i.e. *flatter, praise insincerely*

θαυμάζω	VIPA--1S	θαυμάζω
θαυμάζων	VPPANM-S	"
θαυμάσαι	VNAA	"
θαυμάσαντες	VPAANM-P	"
θαυμάσατε	VMAA--2P	"
θαυμάση	VSAA--3S	"
θαυμάσης	VSAA--2S	"
θαυμάσητε	VSAA--2P	"
θαυμασθῆναι	VNAP	"
θαυμασθήσονται	VIFP--3P	"
θαυμάσια	A--AN-P	θαυμάσιος

θαυμάσιος, ία, ον *wonderful, marvelous, excellent*; substantivally τὰ θαυμάσια *remarkable things, wonderful deeds* (MT 21.15)

θαυμάσονται	VIFM--3P	θαυμάζω
θαυμαστά	A--NN-P	θαυμαστός
θαυμαστή	A--NF-S	"
θαυμαστόν	A--AN-S	"
	A--NN-S	"

θαυμαστός, ή, όν (1) of things relating to God and beyond human comprehension *wonderful, marvelous, remarkable*; (2) substantivally τὸ θαυμαστόν of what is unexpected and worthy of notice *the amazing thing* (JN 9.30)

θάψαι	VNAA	θάπτω
θαψάντων	VPAAGM-P	"

θεά, ᾶς, ἡ feminine of θεός (*god*) *goddess, female deity* (AC 19.27)

θεαθῆναι	VNAP	θεάομαι
θεάν	N-AF-S	θεά

θεάομαι 1aor. mid. ἐθεασάμην; pf. τεθέαμαι; 1aor. pass. (with passive meaning) ἐθεάθην; *see, look at, behold*; a verb of seeing, generally with special meanings: (1) with attentive regard *behold, look at, look over, see* (MT 22.11; 1J 1.1); (2) with a supernatural impression *watch, behold, gaze on* (JN 1.14, 32); (3) as remarking something significant *notice, take note of, see* (LU 5.27); (4) in the sense of visit *(come to) see* (RO 15.24)

θεᾶς	N-GF-S	θεά
θεασάμενοι	VPADNM-P	θεάομαι
θεασαμένοις	VPADDM-P	"
θεασάμενος	VPADNM-S	"
θεάσασθαι	VNAD	"
θεάσασθε	VMAD--2P	"
θεατριζόμενοι	VPPPNM-P	θεατρίζω

θεατρίζω publicly *put to shame make a spectacle of*; passive, of reproaches and afflictions *be publicly exposed to, be held up to* (HE 10.33)

θέατρον, ου, τό (1) *theater, amphitheater*, as a place for public spectacles and assemblies (AC 19.29); (2) by metonymy, of what is enacted in the theater *spectacle, show*; metaphorically in 1C 4.9

θέατρον	N-AN-S	θέατρον
	N-NN-S	"
θεέ	N-VM-S	θεός
θείας	A--GF-S	θεῖος
θεῖναι	VNAA	τίθημι

θεῖον, ου, τό *sulfur, brimstone*; anciently regarded as divine incense to purify and prevent contagion; in the NT always associated with supernaturally kindled fire and thus possibly the neuter of θεῖος (*divine*) (LU 17.29)

θεῖον	AP-AN-S	θεῖος
	N-AN-S	θεῖον
	N-NN-S	"

θεῖος, θεία, θεῖον as related to God by nature *divine* (2P 1.3); substantivally τὸ θεῖον *the divine nature, the divine being* (AC 17.29), opposite ἐπίγειος (*human*)

θειότης, ητος, ἡ of the state of being God *divinity, divine nature, deity* (RO 1.20)

θειότης	N-NF-S	θειότης
θείου	N-GN-S	θεῖον
θείς	VPAANM-S	τίθημι
θείῳ	N-DN-S	θεῖον
θειώδεις	A--AM-P	θειώδης

θειώδης, ες *sulfurous, of brimstone*; as a color *yellow as sulfur* (RV 9.17)

Θέκλα, ης, ἡ *Thecla*, feminine proper noun (2T 3.11)

Θέκλαν	N-AF-S	Θέκλα
θέλει	VIPA--3S	θέλω
θέλειν	VNPA	"
θέλεις	VIPA--2S	"
θέλετε	VIPA--2P	"
θέλῃ	VSPA--3S	"

θέλημα, ατος, τό generally, as the result of what one has decided *will*; (1) objectively *will, design, purpose, what is willed*; (a) used predominately of what God has willed: creation (RV 4.11), redemption (EP 1.5), callings (CO 1.9), etc.; (b) of what a person intends to bring about by his own action *purpose* (LU 22.42); (c) of one's sensual or sexual impulse *desire* (JN 1.13; EP 2.3); (d) of what a person intends to bring about through the action of another *purpose* (LU 12.47); (2) subjectively *act of willing* or *wishing*; (a) predominately of the exercise of God's *will* (GA 1.4); (b) of the exercise of the human will *desire, wish* (2P 1.21)

θέλημα	N-AN-S	θέλημα
	N-NN-S	"
θελήματα	N-AN-P	"
θελήματι	N-DN-S	"
θελήματος	N-GN-S	"
θέλῃς	VSPA--2S	θέλω
θελήσαντας	VPAAAM-P	"
θελήσει	VIFA--3S	"
θελήση	VSAA--3S	"

θέλησιν	N-AF-S	θέλησις

θέλησις, εως, ἡ as an action *willing, will, desiring*; used of God's will (HE 2.4)

θελήσω	VSAA--1S	θέλω
θελήσωσι(ν)	VSAA--3P	"
θέλητε	VSPA--2P	"
θέλοι	VOPA--3S	"
θέλομεν	VIPA--1P	"
θέλοντα	VPPAAM-S	"
θέλοντας	VPPAAM-P	"
θέλοντες	VPPANM-P	"
	VPPAVM-P	"
θέλοντι	VPPADM-S	"
θέλοντος	VPPAGM-S	"
θελόντων	VPPAGM-P	"
θέλουσα	VPPANF-S	"
θέλουσι(ν)	VIPA--3P	"

θέλω impf. ἤθελον; fut. θελήσω; 1aor. ἠθέλησα; as exercising the will; (1) from a motive of desire *wish, want, desire* (JN 15.7); (2) from a readiness or inclination, followed by an infinitive *consent to, be ready to, be pleased to, wish to* (MT 1.19); (3) from resolve, decision, or design *will, intend, purpose, aim*, with a following infinitive either expressed or implied from the context (RV 11.5); often used of God (1T 2.4), of Christ (MK 3.13), and of the authoritative dealings of the apostles (1TH 4.13)

θέλω	VIPA--1S	θέλω
	VSPA--1S	"
θέλων	VPPANM-S	"
θέλωσι(ν)	VSPA--3P	"

θέμα, ατος, τό *deposit*, especially *prize* consisting of money (1T 6.19)

θέμα	N-AN-S	θέμα
θεμέλια	N-AN-P	θεμέλιον
θεμέλιοι	N-NM-P	θεμέλιος

θεμέλιον, ου, τό as the base on which a building stands *foundation* (AC 16.26)

θεμέλιον	N-AM-S	θεμέλιος
	N-AN-S	θεμέλιον

θεμέλιος, ου, ὁ literally, of buildings *foundation, foundation stone* (RV 21.14); figuratively, as elementary beginnings of a community *foundation* (RO 15.20); as elementary or basic teachings *basis* (HE 6.1); as *what is necessary* for belief or practice (1C 3.11)

θεμέλιος	N-NM-S	θεμέλιος
θεμελίου	N-GN-S	θεμέλιον
θεμελίους	N-AM-P	θεμέλιος

θεμελιόω fut. θεμελιώσω; 1aor. ἐθεμελίωσα; pf. pass. τεθεμελίωμαι; pluperfect pass. τεθεμελιώμην; literally *provide with a foundation, found, lay the foundation of* (MT 7.25); figuratively, as providing a firm basis for belief or practice *establish, strengthen, settle, cause to be firm and unwavering* (1P 5.10)

θεμελίῳ	N-DM-S	θεμέλιος
θεμελιῶσαι	VNAA	θεμελιόω
θεμελιώσει	VIFA--3S	"
θέμενος	VPAMNM-S	τίθημι
θέντες	VPAANM-P	"
θέντος	VPAAGM-S	"
θεοδίδακτοι	A--NM-P	θεοδίδακτος

θεοδίδακτος, ον		*taught by God, divinely instructed* (1TH 4.9)
θεοί	N-NM-P	θεός
θεοῖς	N-DM-P	"

θεομαχέω *fight against God, oppose God's will* (AC 23.9)

θεομάχοι	A--NM-P	θεομάχος

θεομάχος, ον denoting conflict with God *being God's enemy, fighting against God* (AC 5.39)

θεομαχῶμεν	VSPA--1P	θεομαχέω
θεόν	N-AF-S	θεός
	N-AM-S	"

θεόπνευστος, ον of the Scriptures as communication that has been ordained by God's authority and produced by the enabling of his Spirit; strictly *God-breathed*; hence *divinely inspired, inspired by God* (2T 3.16)

θεόπνευστος	A--NF-S	θεόπνευστος

θεός, οῦ, ὁ and ἡ (1) as the supreme divine being, the true, living, and personal *God* (MT 1.23; possibly JN 1.1b); (2) as an idol *god* (AC 14.11); feminine *goddess* (AC 19.37); (3) of the devil as the ruling spirit of this age *god* (2C 4.4a); (4) as an adjective *divine* (probably JN 1.1b); (5) figuratively; (a) of persons worthy of reverence and respect as magistrates and judges *gods* (JN 10.34); (b) of the belly when the appetite is in control *god* (PH 3.19)

θεός	N-NM-S	θεός
	N-VM-S	"

θεοσέβεια, ας, ἡ as beliefs and practices relating to worship of a deity *religion, reverence for God, godliness* (1T 2.10)

θεοσέβειαν	N-AF-S	θεοσέβεια

θεοσεβής, ές of one who worships God *God-fearing, devout* (JN 9.31), opposite εἰδωλολάτρης (*idol worshiper*)

θεοσεβής	A--NM-S	θεοσεβής
θεοστυγεῖς	A--AM-P	θεοστυγής

θεοστυγής, ές originally in the passive sense *hated by God, God-forsaken*; in the NT in the active sense *God-hating, hateful toward God*; substantively *a person who hates God* (RO 1.30)

θεότης, ητος, ἡ as an abstract noun for θεός (*god*); *divinity, deity, Godhead, divine nature* (CO 2.9)

θεότητος	N-GF-S	θεότης
θεοῦ	N-GM-S	θεός
θεούς	N-AM-P	"
Θεόφιλε	N-VM-S	Θεόφιλος

Θεόφιλος, ου, ὁ *Theophilus*, masculine proper noun

θεραπεία, ας, ἡ *service, care*; (1) as medical care *healing, treatment* (LU 9.11); figuratively, as prosperity for the nations *healing, cure* (RV 22.2); (2) plural, by metonymy, of those who render service, as synonymous with οἰκετεία *household, household attendants, servants* (LU 12.42)

θεραπείαν	N-AF-S	θεραπεία
θεραπείας	N-GF-S	"
θεραπεύει	VIPA--3S	θεραπεύω
θεραπεύειν	VNPA	"
θεραπεύεσθαι	VNPP	"
θεραπεύεσθε	VMPP--2P	"
θεραπεύεται	VIPP--3S	"
θεραπεύετε	VMPA--2P	"
θεραπευθῆναι	VNAP	"

θεραπεύοντες	VPPANM-P	"
θεραπεῦσαι	VNAA	"
θεραπεύσει	VIFA--3S	"
θεράπευσον	VMAA--2S	"
θεραπεύσω	VIFA--1S	"

θεραπεύω impf. ἐθεράπευον, pass. ἐθεραπευόμην; fut. θεραπεύσω; 1aor. ἐθεράπευσα; pf. pass. τεθεράπευμαι; 1aor. pass. ἐθεραπεύθην; (1) of divine worship and service (synonymous with λειτουργέω) *serve, be of service* (AC 17.25); (2) of medical treatment *heal, cure, restore* (MT 4.23)

θεραπεύων	VPPANM-S	θεραπεύω

θεράπων, οντος, ὁ as a trusted servant, one who serves freely *helper, attendant, minister*; used in the NT only of Moses (HE 3.5)

θεράπων	N-NM-S	θεράπων
θερίζειν	VNPA	θερίζω
θερίζεις	VIPA--2S	"
θερίζουσι(ν)	VIPA--3P	"

θερίζω fut. θερίσω; 1aor. ἐθέρισα; 1aor. pass. ἐθερίσθην; opposite σπείρω (*sow, scatter*); (1) literally *reap, harvest, gather in* (MT 6.26); (2) figuratively; (a) proverbially, of receiving consequences of one's act *reap* (reward or punishment), *get what one deserves, get what God decides one deserves* (GA 6.7); (b) of the last judgment as an end-time event *reap, get what God decides one deserves* (RV 14.15)

θερίζω	VIPA--1S	θερίζω
θερίζων	VPPANM-S	"
θερίσαι	VNAA	"
θερισάντων	VPAAGM-P	"
θερίσει	VIFA--3S	"
θερισμόν	N-AM-S	θερισμός

θερισμός, οῦ, ὁ from θέρος (*summer*); *harvest (time)*; (1) literally, as the process of harvesting, *reaping, harvest* (JN 4.35); (2) metaphorically; (a) as what results from the spread of the gospel *harvest, outcome* (LU 10.2); (b) as the time of judgment at the end of this age (MT 13.30, 39)

θερισμός	N-NM-S	θερισμός
θερισμοῦ	N-GM-S	"
θερίσομεν	VIFA--1P	θερίζω
θέρισον	VMAA--2S	"
θερισταί	N-NM-P	θεριστής
θερισταῖς	N-DM-P	"

θεριστής, οῦ, ὁ as one who gathers in a crop *harvester, reaper*; metaphorically, of the angels who are active at the time of judgment (MT 13.30, 39)

θερμαίνεσθε	VMPM--2P	θερμαίνω
θερμαινόμενον	VPPMAM-S	"
θερμαινόμενος	VPPMNM-S	"

θερμαίνω impf. mid. ἐθερμαινόμην; only middle in the NT; (1) *warm oneself* (at a fire) (MK 14.54); (2) of clothing *dress warmly, keep warm* (JA 2.16)

θέρμη, ης, ἡ *heat, warmth* (AC 28.3)

θέρμης	N-GF-S	θέρμη

θέρος, ους, τό as the warm season of the year *summer*; in tropical countries, the primary season for growth

θέρος	N-NN-S	θέρος
θέσθε	VMAM--2P	τίθημι

Θεσσαλία, ας, ἡ *Thessaly*, a region in northeastern Greece (AC 17.15)

Θεσσαλίαν	N-AF-S	Θεσσαλία

Θεσσαλονικεύς, έως, ὁ *Thessalonian, inhabitant of Thessalonica*

Θεσσαλονικέων	N-GM-P	Θεσσαλονικεύς
Θεσσαλονικέως	N-GM-S	"

Θεσσαλονίκη, ης, ἡ *Thessalonica*, a port city in Macedonia on the Aegean Sea

Θεσσαλονίκη	N-DF-S	Θεσσαλονίκη
Θεσσαλονίκην	N-AF-S	"
Θεσσαλονίκης	N-GF-S	"
θέτε	VMAA--2P	τίθημι

Θευδᾶς, ᾶ, ὁ *Theudas*, masculine proper noun (AC 5.36)

Θευδᾶς	N-NM-S	Θευδᾶς
θεῷ	N-DM-S	θεός
θεωρεῖ	VIPA--3S	θεωρέω
θεωρεῖν	VNPA	"
θεωρεῖς	VIPA--2S	"
θεωρεῖτε	VIPA--2P	"
	VMPA--2P	"

θεωρέω impf. ἐθεώρουν; 1aor. ἐθεώρησα; a verb of seeing; (1) through sense perception *watch, look on* (as a spectator) (MT 27.55); (2) through mental perception *understand, perceive, notice* (AC 17.22); (3) through spiritual perception *perceive, behold, see* (JN 14.17); figuratively *experience, know, undergo* (JN 8.51)

θεωρῇ	VSPA--3S	θεωρέω
θεωρῆσαι	VNAA	"
θεωρήσαντες	VPAANM-P	"
θεωρησάντων	VPAAGM-P	"
θεωρήσει	VIFA--3S	"
θεωρήσῃ	VSAA--3S	"
θεωρήσητε	VSAA--2P	"
θεωρήσουσι(ν)	VIFA--3P	"
θεωρήσωσι(ν)	VSAA--3P	"
θεωρῆτε	VSPA--2P	"

θεωρία, ας, ἡ objectively in the NT, of what one looks at *spectacle, sight* (LU 23.48)

θεωρίαν	N-AF-S	θεωρία
θεωροῦντας	VPPAAM-P	θεωρέω
θεωροῦντες	VPPANM-P	"
θεωροῦντι	VPPADM-S	"
θεωροῦντος	VPPAGM-S	"
θεωρούντων	VPPAGM-P	"
θεωροῦσαι	VPPANF-P	"
θεωροῦσι(ν)	VIPA--3P	"
θεωρῶ	VIPA--1S	"
θεωρῶν	VPPANM-S	"
θεωρῶσι(ν)	VSPA--3P	"
θῇ	VSAA--3S	τίθημι

θήκη, ης, ἡ *receptacle* for putting something in for safekeeping; for a sword *sheath, scabbard, leather case* (JN 18.11)

θήκην	N-AF-S	θήκη
θηλαζομέναις	VPPPDF-P	θηλάζω
θηλαζόντων	VPPAGM-P	"
θηλαζούσαις	VPPADF-P	"

θηλάζω 1aor. ἐθήλασα; from θηλή (*nipple*); (1) as feeding a baby at the breast *nurse, suckle* (MT 24.19); (2) of the child *suck, nurse* (LU 11.27)

θήλειαι	AP-NF-P	θῆλυς
θηλείας	AP-GF-S	"
θῆλυ	AP-AN-S	"
	AP-NN-S	"
	A--AN-S	"
	A--NN-S	"

θῆλυς, εια, υ *female, of the female sex*, opposite ἄρσην (*male*); substantively τὸ θῆλυ *female child, the female sex* (MT 19.4); αἱ θήλειαι *the females, the women* (RO 1.26)

θήρα, ας, ἡ from θήρ (*wild beast*); *trap, net*; metaphorically *means of (sudden) ruin, way of being brought under control* (RO 11.9)

θήραν	N-AF-S	θήρα
θηρεῦσαι	VNAA	θηρεύω

θηρεύω 1aor. ἐθήρευσα; *hunt, catch*; metaphorically, of using treachery to gain advantage over someone who makes a mistake *catch off guard* someone making a mistake (LU 11.54)

θηρία	N-AN-P	θηρίον
	N-NN-P	"

θηριομαχέω 1aor. ἐθηριομάχησα; as a form of punishment *fight with wild beasts*; probably metaphorically in 1C 15.32 in the sense of being exposed to furious mobs *have a great conflict*

θηρίον, ου, τό diminutive of θήρ but equivalent in meaning; (1) literally *wild animal, beast* (MK 1.13); figuratively *wicked person* (TI 1.12); (2) as supernatural animal-like beings, especially demonic and satanic powers (RV 11.7)

θηρίον	N-AN-S	θηρίον
	N-NN-S	"
θηρίου	N-GN-S	"
θηρίῳ	N-DN-S	"
θηρίων	N-GN-P	"
θησαυρίζειν	VNPA	θησαυρίζω
θησαυρίζεις	VIPA--2S	"
θησαυρίζετε	VMPA--2P	"

θησαυρίζω 1aor. ἐθησαύρισα; pf. pass. τεθησαύρισμαι; (1) literally *lay up, store up* as treasure (MT 6.19); of offerings of money *lay by, put* or *set aside* (1C 16.2); (2) figuratively; (a) of spiritually valuable things accomplished *store up, cause to be recorded* (MT 6.20); (b) of divine wrath *make more intense, cause to be more extensive* (RO 2.5); (c) of God's plan for the future of the heaven and earth *reserve, keep, save up* (2P 3.7)

θησαυρίζων	VPPANM-S	θησαυρίζω
θησαυροί	N-NM-P	θησαυρός
θησαυρόν	N-AM-S	"

θησαυρός, οῦ, ὁ (1) as a place for storing valuables; (a) literally *treasury, treasure box* or *chest* (MT 2.11); *storeroom, storehouse*; (b) figuratively, of the heart as a storage place for spiritual possessions (LU 6.45); (2) as the valuables stored up; (a) literally *treasure, store* (MT 13.44); (b) figuratively *spiritually valuable things stored up* in heaven (MT 19.21); of the gospel *knowledge, divine illumination* (2C 4.7) and what it affords (CO 2.3)

θησαυρός	N-NM-S	θησαυρός
θησαυροῦ	N-GM-S	"
θησαυρούς	N-AM-P	"
θησαυρῷ	N-DM-S	"
θησαυρῶν	N-GM-P	"

θήσει	VIFA--3S	τίθημι
θήσεις	VIFA--2S	"
θήσω	VIFA--1S	"
	VSAA--1S	"

θιγγάνω 2aor. ἔθιγον; (1) as coming in contact with a thing *touch* (CO 2.21); (2) as expressing hostility toward a person *get to, harm, kill* (HE 11.28)

θίγῃ	VSAA--3S	θιγγάνω
θίγῃς	VSAA--2S	"
θλίβεσθαι	VNPP	θλίβω
θλιβόμεθα	VIPP--1P	"
θλιβόμενοι	VPPPNM-P	"
θλιβομένοις	VPPPDM-P	"
θλίβουσι(ν)	VPPADM-P	"

θλίβω pf. pass. τέθλιμμαι; strictly *press, rub together*; hence *compress, make narrow*; (1) metaphorically and passive τεθλιμμένη ἡ ὁδὸς ἡ ἀπάγουσα εἰς τὴν ζωήν literally *restricted is the road that leads to life*, i.e. in order to receive eternal life, one must live as God requires (MT 7.14); (2) *press* or *crowd against, throng* (MK 3.9); (3) figuratively *afflict, oppress, cause trouble to* (2TH 1.6); passive *experience hardship, be afflicted* (2C 1.6)

θλίβωσι(ν)	VSPA--3P	θλίβω
θλίψει	N-DF-S	θλῖψις
θλίψεις	N-NF-P	"
θλίψεσι(ν)	N-DF-P	"
θλίψεων	N-GF-P	"
θλίψεως	N-GF-S	"
θλῖψιν	N-AF-S	"

θλῖψις, εως, ἡ literally *pressure, pressing together*; figuratively in the NT, of suffering brought on by outward circumstances *affliction, oppression, trouble* (RO 5.3); especially to be regarded as participation in the sufferings of Christ (CO 1.24); of sufferings of the end-time *tribulation, trouble, distress* (MK 13.19); called ἡ μεγάλη θ. *the great tribulation, the time of great trouble* (MT 24.21; RV 7.14)

θλῖψις	N-NF-S	θλῖψις

θνήσκω pf. τέθνηκα; only perfect in the NT *have died, be dead*; literally, of physical death (MT 2.20); figuratively, of a spiritual state of separation from God (1T 5.6)

θνητά	A--AN-P	θνητός
θνητῇ	A--DF-S	"
θνητόν	A--AN-S	"
	A--NN-S	"

θνητός, ή, όν *mortal, subject to death*, opposite ἀθάνατος (*deathless, immortal*); substantively τὸ θνητόν *what is subject to dying* (1C 15.53; 2C 5.4), opposite ἀθανασία (*immortality, endless existence*) and ζωή (*life*)

θνητῷ	A--DN-S	θνητός
θορυβάζῃ	VIPP--2S	θορυβάζω

θορυβάζω *cause trouble*; only passive in the NT, of emotional disturbance *be troubled, be upset* (LU 10.41)

θορυβεῖσθαι	VNPP	θορυβέω
θορυβεῖσθε	VIPP--2P	"
	VMPP--2P	"

θορυβέω impf. ἐθορύβουν; (1) active *throw into disorder, disturb*; θορυβεῖν τὴν πόλιν *start a riot in the city, set the city in an uproar* (AC 17.5); (2) passive *be troubled, be completely upset* (AC 20.10); of a crowd *make a commotion, be all disturbed* (MT 9.23)

θόρυβον   N-AM-S   θόρυβος

θόρυβος, ου, ὁ (1) as an excited throng milling about *uproar, tumult, noise* (AC 21.34); (2) as mob action *outcry, clamor, uproar* (AC 24.18); (3) as a wailing and mourning scene *commotion, confusion, groaning* (MK 5.38)

θόρυβος   N-NM-S   θόρυβος
θορύβου   N-GM-S   "
θορυβούμενον   VPPPAM-S   θορυβέω
θορυβοῦντες   VPPANM-P   "

θραυματίζω *break* (LU 4.18)

θραύσασα   VPAANF-S   θραύω

θραύω pf. pass. ptc. τεθραυσμένος; literally *break in pieces*, as pottery; figuratively and passive, of persons broken in spirit by oppression *be downtrodden, be overwhelmed with trouble* (LU 4.18)

θρέμμα, ατος, τό from τρέφω (*nourish, feed*); plural, of animals kept by people for their use *flocks, cattle, livestock*

θρέμματα   N-NN-P   θρέμμα

θρηνέω impf. ἐθρήνουν; fut. θρηνήσω; 1aor. ἐθρήνησα; from θρέομαι (*shriek out*); (1) intransitively *mourn, lament, sing funeral songs* (MT 11.17); (2) transitively *mourn for, lament* someone (LU 23.27)

θρηνήσετε   VIFA--2P   θρηνέω

θρῆνος, ου, ὁ as a song expressing grief and mourning for someone who has died *(funeral) dirge, lamentation, wailing* (MT 2.18)

θρῆνος   N-NM-S   θρῆνος

θρησκεία, ας, ἡ (also **θρησκία**) *religion, religious service* or *worship* (CO 2.18); especially as expressed in a system of external observances (AC 26.5)

θρησκεία   N-NF-S   θρησκεία
θρησκείᾳ   N-DF-S   "
θρησκείας   N-GF-S   "
θρησκία   N-NF-S   "
θρησκίᾳ   N-DF-S   "
θρησκίας   N-GF-S   "

θρησκός, όν of one preoccupied with religious observances *religious, God-fearing, pious* (JA 1.26)

θρησκός   A--NM-S   θρησκός
θριαμβεύοντι   VPPADM-S   θριαμβεύω
θριαμβεύσας   VPAANM-S   "

θριαμβεύω 1aor. ἐθριάμβευσα; strictly *celebrate a triumph, lead in a triumphal procession*; hence (1) of God's overcoming power *triumph over* (CO 2.15); (2) of God's enabling believers to overcome *cause to be victorious, make to triumph* (possibly 2C 2.14); (3) *lead in triumph* (perhaps 2C 2.14)

θρίξ, τριχός, ἡ used of human or animal *hair*

θρίξ   N-NF-S   θρίξ
θριξί(ν)   N-DF-P   "
θροεῖσθαι   VNPP   θροέω
θροεῖσθε   VMPP--2P   "

θροέω 1aor. pass. ἐθροήθην; only passive in the NT, as being suddenly troubled inwardly *be disturbed, be alarmed, be startled*

θροηθέντες   VPAPNM-P   θροέω
θρόμβοι   N-NM-P   θρόμβος

θρόμβος, ου, ὁ as flowing blood *drop* (LU 22.44); as thickened or congealed blood *clot*

θρόνοι   N-NM-P   θρόνος

θρόνον   N-AM-S   "

θρόνος, ου, ὁ (1) *throne* a raised seat with a footstool, used by rulers (LU 1.52); (2) heaven as God's throne (MT 5.34); (3) by metonymy, for what the throne stands for *dominion, rule, kingly power, sovereignty* (LU 1.32); (4) plural, of powerful spirit-beings who rule *potentates, rulers* (CO 1.16)

θρόνος   N-NM-S   θρόνος
θρόνου   N-GM-S   "
θρόνους   N-AM-P   "
θρόνῳ   N-DM-S   "
θρόνων   N-GM-P   "
θρυπτόμενον   VPPPNN-S   θρύπτω

θρύπτω *break in pieces, crush*; passive *be broken, be crushed*; of the bodily sufferings of Christ (1C 11.24)

Θυάτειρα, ων, τά (also Θυάτειρα [ας, ἡ], Θυάτηρα, Θυάτιρα) *Thyatira*, a city in Lydia in Asia Minor (AC 16.14; RV 2.18)

Θυάτειρα   N-AN-P   Θυάτειρα
Θυάτειραν   N-AF-S   "
Θυατείρη   N-DF-S   "
Θυατείροις   N-DN-P   "
Θυατείρων   N-GN-P   "
Θυατήροις   N-DN-P   "
Θυατίροις   N-DN-P   "
Θυατίρων   N-GN-P   "
θύγατερ   N-VF-S   θυγάτηρ
θυγατέρα   N-AF-S   "
θυγατέραν   N-AF-S   see θυγατέρα
θυγατέρας   N-AF-P   θυγάτηρ
θυγατέρες   N-NF-P   "
     N-VF-P   "
θυγατέρων   N-GF-P   "

θυγάτηρ, τρός, ἡ *daughter*; (1) literally, as parents' female offspring (MT 9.18); (2) figuratively; (a) plural, as female descendants of one ancestor, the female members of a tribe or clan (LU 1.5); (b) as a friendly address to a girl or woman (MT 9.22); (c) plural, as female inhabitants of a city (LU 23.28); (d) as female followers of God (2C 6.18); (e) as a poetic designation for Jerusalem and its inhabitants θ. Σιών *daughter (of) Zion* (MT 21.5; JN 12.15)

θυγάτηρ   N-NF-S   θυγάτηρ
     N-VF-S   "
θυγατρί   N-DF-S   "

θυγάτριον, ου, τό diminutive of θυγάτηρ; *little daughter*; possibly denotes endearment *dear daughter*

θυγάτριον   N-NN-S   θυγάτριον
θυγατρός   N-GF-S   θυγάτηρ
θύει   VIPA--3S   θύω
θύειν   VNPA   "

θύελλα, ης, ἡ as a storm characterized by strong and sudden winds *tempest, squall, whirlwind* (HE 12.18)

θυέλλη   N-DF-S   θύελλα
θύεσθαι   VNPP   θύω
θύϊνον   A--AN-S   θύϊνος

θύϊνος, η, ον as a kind of wood *from the citron tree, thyine, citron (wood)* (RV 18.12)

θυμίαμα, ατος, τό (1) singular and plural *incense* (RV 5.8); (2) by metonymy *incense offering, burning of in-*

cense (LU 1.10); (3) τὸ θυσιαστήριον τοῦ θυμιάματος *the altar of incense, the incense altar* (LU 1.11)

θυμιάματα	N-AN-P	θυμίαμα
	N-NN-P	"
θυμιάματος	N-GN-S	"
θυμιαμάτων	N-GN-P	"
θυμιᾶσαι	VNAA	θυμιάω

θυμιατήριον, ου, τό strictly *container for burning incense, censer;* by metonymy, the place for offering incense, situated immediately before and "belonging to" (ἔχουσα) the innermost shrine of the temple *incense altar* (HE 9.4)

| θυμιατήριον | N-AN-S | θυμιατήριον |

θυμιάω 1aor. ἐθυμίασα; *burn incense, make the incense offering* (LU 1.9)

| θυμοί | N-NM-P | θυμός |

θυμομαχέω *be enraged* or *very angry at* someone (probably AC 12.20); *quarrel angrily* (possibly AC 12.20)

| θυμομαχῶν | VPPANM-S | θυμομαχέω |
| θυμόν | N-AM-S | θυμός |

θυμός, οῦ, ὁ from θύω (*move violently, rush along*); (1) as a strong passion of soul or mind *wrath, rage;* used for divine (RV 15.1), satanic (RV 12.12), and human *wrath* (LU 4.28); (2) in contrast with ὀργή as settled indignation, θ. is used of *anger* that boils up and subsides again, *swelling up of anger, hot temper, angry outburst* (2C 12.20); (3) the difficult phrase in RV 14.8 ἐκ τοῦ οἴνου τοῦ θυμοῦ τῆς πορνείας αὐτῆς πεπότικεν τὰ ἔθνη *she has made all nations drink of the wine of the wrath of her fornication* probably refers to the godlessness with which Babylon ensnared the nations and brought them under God's wrath, rather than to "the wine of her passionate immorality"

| θυμός | N-NM-S | θυμός |
| θυμοῦ | N-GM-S | " |

θυμόω 1aor. pass. ἐθυμώθην; *provoke to anger, make angry;* only passive in the NT *become angry, be enraged* (MT 2.16)

| θύουσι(ν) | VIPA--3P | θύω |

θύρα, ας, ἡ (1) *door;* literally, as an opening for entrance and exit; (a) of a house *door* (MK 1.33); (b) of a courtyard *outer door, gate* (AC 12.13); (c) of the temple *gate* (AC 3.2); (d) of a tomb *door, entrance* (MK 15.46); (e) of heaven *door* (RV 4.1); (2) figuratively; (a) ἐπὶ θύραις as a spatial image to denote temporal imminency *soon* (MK 13.29); (b) as what is possible or feasible opportunity (RV 3.8); (c) as an extended metaphor of Jesus as the one who provides salvation, spiritual safety, and nourishment (JN 10.7, 9)

θύρα	N-NF-S	θύρα
θύρᾳ	N-DF-S	"
θύραι	N-NF-P	"
θύραις	N-DF-P	"
θύραν	N-AF-S	"
θύρας	N-AF-P	"
	N-GF-S	"
θυρεόν	N-AM-S	θυρεός

θυρεός, οῦ, ὁ originally a large, oblong stone used to close an entrance *doorway;* later, *shield,* large, oblong, and four-cornered in shape (EP 6.16)

| θυρίδι | N-DF-S | θυρίς |
| θυρίδος | N-GF-S | " |

θυρίς, ίδος, ἡ diminutive of θύρα; *window, small opening in a wall*

| θυρῶν | N-GF-P | θύρα |

θυρωρός, οῦ, ὁ and ἡ as one who controls who is allowed to enter a place *doorkeeper, porter*

θυρωρός	N-NF-S	θυρωρός
	N-NM-S	"
θυρωρῷ	N-DF-S	"
	N-DM-S	"
θύσατε	VMAA--2P	θύω
θύσῃ	VSAA--3S	"

θυσία, ας, ἡ *sacrifice, offering;* (1) predominately in the NT, as what is sacrificed *sacrificial offering* (LU 2.24); (2) figuratively; (a) of the death of Christ as an offering of himself to God (EP 5.2); (b) of the life of believers as a self-offering to God (RO 12.1); (c) as providing acceptable service and faith as an offering to God (HE 13.15)

θυσία	N-NF-S	θυσία
θυσίᾳ	N-DF-S	"
θυσίαι	N-NF-P	"
θυσίαις	N-DF-P	"
θυσίαν	N-AF-S	"
θυσίας	N-AF-P	"
	N-GF-S	"
θυσιαστήρια	N-AN-P	θυσιαστήριον

θυσιαστήριον, ου, τό *altar;* (1) literally; (a) the altar of burnt offering in the court of the tabernacle or temple (HE 7.13); (b) the altar of incense before the innermost shrine (LU 1.11); (c) of altars in heaven (RV 8.3); (2) figuratively in HE 13.10 probably for the cross where Jesus "suffered outside the gate" (as noted in HE 13.12)

θυσιαστήριον	N-AN-S	θυσιαστήριον
	N-NN-S	"
θυσιαστηρίου	N-GN-S	"
θυσιαστηρίῳ	N-DN-S	"
θυσιῶν	N-GF-P	θυσία
θῦσον	VMAA--2S	θύω

θύω impf. ἔθυον; 1aor. ἔθυσα; pf. pass. τέθυμαι; 1aor. pass. ἐτύθην; (1) *sacrifice, offer, slaughter in sacrifice* (AC 14.13); (2) *slay, kill* (for food) (LU 15.23)

θῶ	VSAA--1S	τίθημι
Θωμᾶ	N-VM-S	Θωμᾶς
Θωμᾷ	N-DM-S	"
Θωμᾶν	N-AM-S	"

Θωμᾶς, ᾶ, ὁ *Thomas,* masculine proper noun corresponding to the Aramaic word for *twin* (JN 11.16)

Θωμᾶς	N-NM-S	Θωμᾶς
θῶμεν	VSAA--1P	τίθημι
θώρακα	N-AM-S	θώραξ
θώρακας	N-AM-P	"

θώραξ, ακος, ὁ (1) as a protective piece of armor *breastplate* (RV 9.9b; possibly 9.9a); figuratively, of righteousness (EP 6.14) or faith (1TH 5.8) as affording spiritual protection; (2) as the part of the body covered by the breastplate *chest, breast* (possibly RV 9.9a)

Ἰάειρος   N-NM-S   Ἰάϊρος

ἰαθείς   VPAPNM-S   ἰάομαι

ἰαθέντος   VPAPGM-S   "

ἰάθη   VIAP--3S   "

ἰαθῇ   VSAP--3S   "

ἰάθημεν   VIAP--1P   "

ἰαθῆναι   VNAP   "

ἰαθήσεται   VIFP--3S   "

ἰάθητε   VIAP--2P   "

ἰαθῆτε   VSAP--2P   "

ἰαθήτω   VMAP--3S   "

Ἰάϊρος, ου, ὁ (also **Ἰάειρος**) *Jairus*, masculine proper noun

Ἰάϊρος   N-NM-S   Ἰάϊρος

Ἰακώβ, ὁ indeclinable; *Jacob*, masculine proper noun

Ἰάκωβον   N-AM-S   Ἰάκωβος

Ἰάκωβος, ου, ὁ *James*, masculine proper noun; Greek form of the Hebrew name *Jacob*

Ἰάκωβος   N-NM-S   Ἰάκωβος

Ἰακώβου   N-GM-S   "

Ἰακώβῳ   N-DM-S   "

ἴαμα, ατος, τό *healing, cure*; χαρίσματα ἰαμάτων literally *gifts of healings*, i.e. power to heal, ability to cause people to be well again (1C 12.9)

ἰαμάτων   N-GN-P   ἴαμα

Ἰαμβρῆς, ὁ (also **Μαμβρῆς**) indeclinable; *Jambres*, masculine proper noun (2T 3.8)

Ἰαννά   Ἰανναί

Ἰανναί, ὁ (also **Ἰαννά**) indeclinable; *Jannai*, masculine proper noun (LU 3.24)

Ἰάννης, ὁ (also **Ἰαννῆς**) indeclinable; *Jannes*, masculine proper noun (2T 3.8)

Ἰαννῆς   Ἰάννης

ἰάομαι impf. ἰώμην; 1aor. mid. ἰασάμην; passive forms with passive meaning: pf. pass. ἴαμαι; 1aor. pass. ἰάθην; 1fut. pass. ἰαθήσομαι; *heal, cure*; literally, of deliverance from physical diseases and afflictions *heal* someone (LU 22.51); passive *be healed* or *cured* (MK 5.29); figuratively, of deliverance from sin and its evil consequences *restore, make whole, renew* (MT 13.15); passive *be restored, recover, be healed* (1P 2.24)

Ἰάρεδ   Ἰάρετ

Ἰαρέδ   "

Ἰάρεθ   "

Ἰάρετ, ὁ (also **Ἰάρεδ, Ἰαρέδ, Ἰάρεθ**) indeclinable; *Jared*, masculine proper noun

ἰάσασθαι   VNAD   ἰάομαι

ἰάσατο   VIAD--3S   "

ἰάσεις   N-AF-P   ἴασις

ἰάσεως   N-GF-S   "

ἰάσηται   VSAD--3S   ἰάομαι

ἰᾶσθαι   VNPD   "

     VNPO   "

ἴασιν   N-AF-S   ἴασις

ἴασις, εως, ἡ as an action *healing, cure*

ἰάσομαι   VIFD--1S   ἰάομαι

Ἰάσονα   N-AM-S   Ἰάσων

Ἰάσονι   N-DM-S   "

Ἰάσονος   N-GM-S   "

ἰάσπιδι   N-DF-S   ἴασπις

ἴασπις, ιδος, ἡ *jasper*, a precious stone of very fine-grained silica deposited from circulating water, found in various colors and ordinarily opaque

ἴασπις   N-NF-S   ἴασπις

ἰάσωμαι   VSAD--1S   ἰάομαι

Ἰάσων, ονος, ὁ *Jason*, masculine proper noun

Ἰάσων   N-NM-S   Ἰάσων

ἴαται   VIRP--3S   ἰάομαι

ἰᾶται   VIPD--3S   "

     VIPO--3S   "

ἰᾶτο   VIID--3S   "

     VIIO--3S   "

ἰατρέ   N-VM-S   ἰατρός

ἰατροῖς   N-DM-P   "

ἰατρός, οῦ, ὁ *physician, healer*

ἰατρός   N-NM-S   ἰατρός

ἰατροῦ   N-GM-S   "

ἰατρούς   N-AM-P   "

ἰατρῶν   N-GM-P   "

ιβ' indeclinable; from the Greek letters for ten (ι') and two (β'); as a cardinal number *twelve* (AC 1.26)

ἴδαν   VIAA--3P   see εἶδαν

ἴδε (also **εἶδε**) strictly, the second-person singular imperative of εἶδον (*see, perceive, look at*); used as a demonstrative particle to prompt attention, with a basic meaning *pay attention*, and followed by the nominative case or a statement to identify who or what is to be given attention; (1) to focus attention; (a) on a significant participant in a narrative, like *behold!*; *here is (are), this in none other than* (MK 3.34; JN 1.29); (b) on a significant place (MK 16.6); (2) to introduce something for special attention; (a) because it is contrary to the hearer's expectation *there now! take note! look!* (JN 3.26); (b) because it requires the hearer's response *listen! see there! pay attention now!* (MK 15.4)

ἴδε   QS   ἴδε

     VMAA--2S   εἶδον

ἰδέα   N-NF-S   εἰδέα

ἰδεῖν   VNAA   εἶδον

ἴδε(ν)   VIAA--3S   see εἶδε(ν)

ἴδετε   VMAA--2P   εἶδον

     VMAA--2P^QS   "

ἴδῃ   VSAA--3S   "

ἴδῃς   VSAA--2S   "

ἴδητε   VSAA--2P   "

ἴδια	AP-AN-P	ἴδιος
	A--AN-P	"
	A--NN-P	"
ἰδίᾳ	AB	"
	A--DF-S	"
ἰδίαις	A--DF-P	"
ἰδίαν	A--AF-S	"
ἰδίας	A--AF-P	"
	A--GF-S	"
ἴδιοι	AP-NM-P	"
ἰδίοις	A--DM-P	"
	A--DN-P	"
ἴδιον	AP-AN-S	"
	A--AM-S	"
	A--AN-S	"

ἴδιος, ία, ον *one's own*; (1) belonging to a particular thing or person *private, one's own*, in contrast to public property (κοινός *common*) or what belongs to another (ἀλλότριος *belonging to another*) (AC 4.32); (2) as a simple possessive like ἑαυτοῦ, ἑαυτῶν (*oneself*) (EP 5.22); (3) substantivally οἱ ἴδιοι *one's own people, family, household, countrymen* (JN 1.11b; 1T 5.8); τὰ ἴδια *one's own home, property, possessions* (JN 1.11a; 19.27); *one's own affairs* (1TH 4.11); (4) of what is appropriate to an individual by nature (LU 6.44) or by capability (MT 25.15); (5) adverbially ἰδίᾳ and κατ᾽ ἰδίαν *privately, individually, by oneself* (1C 12.11)

ἴδιος	A--NM-S	ἴδιος
ἰδίου	A--GM-S	"
	A--GN-S	"
ἰδίους	AP-AM-P	"
	A--AM-P	"
ἰδίῳ	A--DM-S	"
	A--DN-S	"
ἰδίων	AP-GM-P	"
	AP-GN-P	"
	A--GF-P	"
	A--GM-P	"
ἰδιῶται	N-NM-P	ἰδιώτης

ἰδιώτης, ου, ὁ strictly, one in private life *layman* or *nonspecialist*, with the specific sense taken from contrast in the context; (1) *uneducated, unlearned* (AC 4.13); (2) *nonmember* of a community, *uninstructed person, inquirer* (1C 14.16, 23, 24); (3) *unskilled, untrained* (2C 11.6)

ἰδιώτης	N-NM-S	ἰδιώτης
ἰδιώτου	N-GM-S	
ἴδον	VIAA--1S	εἶδον
ἰδόντες	VPAANM-P	"

ἰδού strictly, the second-person singular aorist middle imperative of εἶδον (*see, perceive, look at*) is ἰδοῦ; but with an acute accent (ἰδού) when used as a demonstrative particle to prompt attention, followed by the nominative case to designate what is being pointed out; *pay attention, (you) see, look*; (1) to arouse attention *listen!* (LU 22.10); (2) to introduce something new and extraordinary *indeed! (you) see!* (MT 1.20); (3) to emphasize the size, degree, amount, or importance of something in the context *indeed* (LU 13.16); (4) to call for close consideration *listen! remember! consider!* (MT 10.16); (5) to make prominent a noun that is without a finite verb, like *behold!*; *here* or *there is, here* or *there comes* (MT 12.10; 25.6)

ἰδού	QS	ἰδού

Ἰδουμαία, ας, ἡ *Idumea*, Greek form of *Edom* in the Old Testament, a mountainous district south of Judea (MK 3.8)

Ἰδουμαίας	N-GF-S	Ἰδουμαία
ἰδοῦσα	VPAANF-S	εἶδον

ἱδρώς, ῶτος, ὁ *sweat, perspiration* (LU 22.44)

ἱδρώς	N-NM-S	ἱδρώς
ἴδω	VSAA--1S	εἶδον
ἴδωμεν	VSAA--1P	"
ἰδών	VPAANM-S	"
ἰδώς	VPRANM-S	see εἰδώς
ἴδωσι(ν)	VSAA--3P	εἶδον

Ἰεζάβελ, ἡ (also **Ἰεζαβέλ, Ἰεζαβήλ, Ἰεσαβήλ**) indeclinable; *Jezebel*, feminine proper noun (RV 2.20)

Ἰεζαβέλ		Ἰεζάβελ
Ἰεζαβήλ		"
Ἱερᾷ	A--DF-S	Ἱεράπολις
ἱερά	A--AN-P	ἱερός
Ἱεραπόλει	N-DF-S	Ἱεράπολις

Ἱεράπολις, ἡ (also **Ἱερὰ Πόλις**) *Hierapolis*, a city of Phrygia in Asia Minor, on the Lycus River opposite Laodicea (CO 4.13)

ἱερατεία, ας, ἡ *priesthood, priestly office, priestly ministry*

ἱερατείαν	N-AF-S	ἱερατεία
ἱερατείας	N-GF-S	
ἱερατεύειν	VNPA	ἱερατεύω

ἱεράτευμα, ατος, τό *priesthood, order* or *body of priests*

ἱεράτευμα	N-AN-S	ἱεράτευμα
	N-NN-S	"

ἱερατεύω *officiate as priest, serve in the priestly office* (LU 1.8)

ἱερέα	N-AM-S	ἱερεύς
ἱερεῖ	N-DM-S	"
ἱερεῖς	N-AM-P	"
	N-NM-P	"
Ἱερειχώ		Ἱεριχώ
Ἱερειχώ		"
Ἱερεμίαν	N-AM-S	Ἱερεμίας
Ἱερεμίαν	N-AM-S	"

Ἱερεμίας, ου, ὁ (also **Ἱερεμίας**) *Jeremiah*, masculine proper noun

Ἱερεμίου	N-GM-S	Ἱερεμίας
Ἱερεμίου	N-GM-S	"

ἱερεύς, έως, ὁ (1) literally; (a) one who officiates at or performs sacred rites *priest* (MT 8.4); (b) under the old covenant a common *priest* (AC 6.7), in contrast to ἀρχιερεύς (*high priest*); (2) figuratively; (a) of Christ as a valid priest in the non-levitical order of Melchizedek (HE 5.6); (b) of believers serving God under the new covenant (RV 1.6)

ἱερεύς	N-NM-S	ἱερεύς
ἱερεῦσι(ν)	N-DM-P	"
ἱερέων	N-GM-P	"
ἱερέως	N-GM-S	"

Ἱεριχώ, ἡ (also **Ἱερειχώ, Ἱεριχώ, Ἱεριχώ**) indeclinable; *Jericho*, a city in Judea near the Jordan River

Ἱεριχώ		Ἱεριχώ
ἱερόθυτον	A--NN-S	ἱερόθυτος

ἱερόθυτος, ον   of meat from sacrificed animals *offered in sacrifice, sacrificed to idols* (1C 10.28)

ἱερόν	AP-AN-S	ἱερός
	A--AN-S	"
ἱεροπρεπεῖ	A--DN-S	ἱεροπρεπής
ἱεροπρεπεῖς	A--AF-P	"

ἱεροπρεπής, ές   strictly *befitting* or *suitable to what is sacred*; hence, of persons who honor God in their conduct *fitting for religious persons, reverent in behavior* (TI 2.3)

ἱερός, ά, όν   (1) with a basic meaning *what belongs to divinity, sacred, holy* (2T 3.15), opposite βέβηλος (*profane*); (2) substantivally; (a) τὸ ἱερόν as a sacred enclosed area under the protection of a god *temple* (AC 19.27); (b) predominately of the temple of God at Jerusalem, including the whole sacred area with its buildings, courts, walls, and gates (MT 21.12); (c) τὰ ἱερά as everything that belongs to the temple and its service *the holy* or *sacred things* (1C 9.13)

Ἱεροσόλυμα	N-AN-P	Ἱεροσόλυμα
	N-NF-S	"
	N-NN-P	"

Ἱεροσόλυμα, ων, τά and ἡ (also Ἱεροσόλυμα) and Ἱερουσαλήμ, ἡ (also Ἱερουσαλήμ) indeclinable   *Jerusalem*; (1) literally; (a) as the name of the city (MK 3.8); (b) in reference to its inhabitants (MT 2.3); (2) figuratively, as the spiritual home of God and his people; ἡ ἄνω Ἱ. *the Jerusalem above* (GA 4.26); Ἱ. ἐπουράνιος *heavenly Jerusalem* (HE 12.22); ἡ καινὴ Ἱ. *the new Jerusalem* (RV 3.12)

Ἱεροσόλυμα	N-AN-P	Ἱεροσόλυμα
	N-NF-S	"
	N-NN-P	"
Ἱεροσολυμεῖται	N-NM-P	Ἱεροσολυμίτης
Ἱεροσολυμεῖται	N-NM-P	"
Ἱεροσολυμειτῶν	N-GM-P	"
Ἱεροσολυμειτῶν	N-GM-P	"
Ἱεροσολυμῖται	N-NM-P	"

Ἱεροσολυμίτης, ου, ὁ (also Ἱεροσολυμείτης, Ἱεροσολυμείτης, Ἱεροσολυμίτης)   *citizen* or *inhabitant of Jerusalem, Jerusalemite*

Ἱεροσολυμιτῶν	N-GM-P	Ἱεροσολυμίτης
Ἱεροσολύμοις	N-DN-P	Ἱεροσόλυμα
Ἱεροσολύμοις	N-DN-P	"
Ἱεροσολύμων	N-GN-P	"
Ἱεροσολύμων	N-GN-P	"
ἱεροσυλεῖς	VIPA--2S	ἱεροσυλέω

ἱεροσυλέω   as removing sacred property from a sacred site *rob temples, commit sacrilege* (RO 2.22)

ἱερόσυλος, ον   *guilty of sacrilege*; substantivally *temple robber*; more generally, one who acts disrespectfully or violently against a holy place *sacrilegious person, desecrator* (AC 19.37)

| ἱεροσύλους | AP-AM-P | ἱερόσυλος |
| ἱεροῦ | AP-GN-S | ἱερός |

ἱερουργέω   *minister in sacred service, serve as priest*; ἱερουγεῖν τὸ εὐαγγέλιον *serve as priest of the gospel, minister the gospel* (RO 15.16)

ἱερουργοῦντα	VPPAAM-S	ἱερουργέω
Ἱερουσαλήμ		Ἱεροσόλυμα
Ἱερουσαλήμ		"

| ἱερῷ | AP-DN-S | ἱερός |

ἱερωσύνη, ης, ἡ   *priesthood, priestly office*

ἱερωσύνην	N-AF-S	ἱερωσύνη
ἱερωσύνης	N-GF-S	"
Ἰεσαβήλ		Ἰεζάβελ

Ἰεσσαί, ὁ (also Ἰεσσαί)   indeclinable; *Jesse*, masculine proper noun

| Ἰεσσαί | | Ἰεσσαί |

Ἰεφθάε, ὁ   indeclinable; *Jephthah*, masculine proper noun (HE 11.32)

| Ἰεχονίαν | N-AM-S | Ἰεχονίας |

Ἰεχονίας, ου, ὁ   *Jechoniah*, masculine proper noun

Ἰεχονίας	N-NM-S	Ἰεχονίας
Ἠσαίου	N-GM-S	Ἠσαίας
Ἰησοῦ	N-DM-S	Ἰησοῦς
	N-GM-S	"
	N-VM-S	"
Ἰησοῦν	N-AM-S	"

Ἰησοῦς, οῦ, ὁ   (1) *Joshua*, masculine proper noun meaning *Lord (Yahweh) saves*, designating Moses' successor (AC 7.45; HE 4.8); (2) *Joshua* or *Jesus*, a common name among Jews (CO 4.11; LU 3.29); (3) predominately *Jesus*, as the name borne by the Messiah, Jesus Christ, and used in relation to his humanity (PH 2.5), his Davidic ancestry (MT 1.1), and his life in fulfillment of the divine promise of a coming Savior (MT 1.21)

Ἰησοῦς	N-NM-S	Ἰησοῦς
ἱκανά	A--AN-P	ἱκανός
ἱκαναί	A--NF-P	"
ἱκαναῖς	A--DF-P	"
ἱκανάς	A--AF-P	"
ἱκανοί	A--NM-P	"
ἱκανοῖς	A--DM-P	"
ἱκανόν	AP-AN-S	"
	A--AM-S	"
	A--AN-S	"
	A--NN-S	"

ἱκανός, ή, όν   from a root ἱκ- and related to ἱκνέομαι (*reach, attain*); used of implied measurement that reaches to a certain stage *sufficient, enough, adequate*; (1) of number and quantity *large (enough), considerable, much* (MK 10.46); substantivally τὸ ἱκανόν *the amount of money needed for release* from custody, *bond, bail* (AC 17.9); idiomatically ἱκανὸν ποιεῖν literally *do what is enough*, i.e. *please, satisfy* (MK 15.15); (2) of time *considerable, long* (LU 8.27); plural, of days or years *many, considerable number of* (AC 9.23); (3) of persons *fit, worthy* (MT 8.8); *qualified, adequate, competent* (2C 2.16)

| ἱκανός | A--NM-S | ἱκανός |

ἱκανότης, ητος, ἡ   as a state of being qualified for something *adequacy, capacity, fitness* (2C 3.5)

ἱκανότης	N-NF-S	ἱκανότης
ἱκανοῦ	A--GM-S	ἱκανός
ἱκανούς	A--AM-P	"

ἱκανόω   1aor. ἱκάνωσα; *make sufficient, qualify, make adequate* or *competent for* something

ἱκανῷ	A--DM-S	ἱκανός
ἱκανῶν	A--GM-P	"
	A--GN-P	

ἱκανώσαντι	VPAADM-S	ἱκανόω
ἱκάνωσε(ν)	VIAA--3S	"

ἱκετηρία, ας, ἡ strictly *olive branch* entwined with white wool and fillets and *carried by a suppliant*; by metonymy *supplication* made to God, *prayer* (HE 5.7)

ἱκετηρίας	N-AF-P	ἱκετηρία
ἱκμάδα	N-AF-S	ἰκμάς

ἰκμάς, άδος, ἡ *moisture*, as needed in the soil for plant growth (LU 8.6)

Ἰκόνιον, ου, τό *Iconium*, a city in Lycaonia in southern Galatia

Ἰκόνιον	N-AN-S	Ἰκόνιον
Ἰκονίου	N-GN-S	"
Ἰκονίῳ	N-DN-S	"
ἱλαρόν	A--AM-S	ἱλαρός

ἱλαρός, ά, όν *happy, cheerful, joyful*, as a quality of genuine benevolence (2C 9.7)

ἱλαρότης, ητος, ἡ *cheerfulness, gladness*, as a mark of genuine benevolence (RO 12.8)

ἱλαρότητι	N-DF-S	ἱλαρότης
ἱλάσθητι	VMAP--2S	ἱλάσκομαι
ἱλάσκεσθαι	VNPD	"

ἱλάσκομαι 1aor. pass. imperative ἱλάσθητι; (1) *show kindness and compassion* toward one who does not deserve it, *have mercy on, pardon, forgive* (LU 18.13); (2) *bring about reconciliation, make acceptable to, provide for forgiveness*, with focus on the means of reconciliation

ἱλασμόν	N-AM-S	ἱλασμός

ἱλασμός, οῦ, ὁ with focus on atoning sacrifice for sin *means of forgiveness, way of reconciling* (1J 2.2; 4.10)

ἱλασμός	N-NM-S	ἱλασμός
ἱλαστήριον	AP-AN-S	ἱλαστήριος

ἱλαστήριος, ον with focus on the means by which sins are forgiven *having atoning power, bringing about reconciliation*; substantively τὸ ἱλαστήριον *means of forgiveness* (RO 3.25); by metonymy, with a focus on the place where sins are forgiven by means of the blood from an atoning sacrifice placed there *place of forgiveness, place where God forgives sins*, often translated *mercy seat* (HE 9.5)

ἵλεως, gen. ων (1) as an attribute of God *merciful, gracious, favorable* (HE 8.12); (2) in a Hebraistic formula ἵ. σοι *may God spare you this! God forbid! may that never happen to you!* (MT 16.22)

ἵλεως	A--NM-S	ἵλεως

Ἰλλυρικόν, οῦ, τό *Illyricum*, a district across the Adriatic Sea from Italy (RO 15.19)

Ἰλλυρικοῦ	N-GN-S	Ἰλλυρικόν
ἱμάντα	N-AM-S	ἱμάς

ἱμάς, άντος, ὁ *strap* or *thong* of leather; used for shoelaces (MK 1.7); for binding or beating criminals; τοῖς ἱμᾶσιν in AC 22.25 may be the instrumental dative *with the thongs* or the dative of purpose *for the thongs, lash, whip*

ἱμᾶσι(ν)	N-DM-P	ἱμάς
ἱμάτια	N-AN-P	ἱμάτιον
	N-NN-P	"

ἱματίζω pf. pass. ptc. ἱματισμένος; *clothe, dress*; passive *be clothed*

ἱματίοις	N-DN-P	ἱμάτιον

ἱμάτιον, ου, τό (1) generally *garment* (MT 9.16); plural *clothing* (LU 7.25); (2) as the outer garment distinct from the tunic or knee-length garment (χίτων) worn next to the skin, *cloak, robe, coat* (MT 5.40)

ἱμάτιον	N-AN-S	ἱμάτιον
	N-NN-S	"
ἱματίου	N-GN-S	"
ἱματισμένον	VPRPAM-S	ἱματίζω
ἱματισμόν	N-AM-S	ἱματισμός

ἱματισμός, οῦ, ὁ *clothing, apparel, garments*

ἱματισμός	N-NM-S	ἱματισμός
ἱματισμοῦ	N-GM-S	"
ἱματισμῷ	N-DM-S	"
ἱματίῳ	N-DN-S	ἱμάτιον
ἱματίων	N-GN-P	"

ἱμείρομαι *long for someone, dearly love* (1TH 2.8)

ἱμειρόμενοι	VPPDNM-P	ἱμείρομαι
	VPPONM-P	"

ἵνα conjunction; (1) used to introduce clauses that show a purpose or goal *that, in order that, so that*; (a) predominately with the present or aorist subjunctive (JN 10.10; RO 1.11); (b) occasionally with the future indicative ἵ. ἐρεῖ σοι (LU 14.10); ἵ. δώσουσι (LU 20.10); (c) rarely with the optative; (2) used to introduce the content of a discourse, especially when a purpose or command is implied; (a) as introducing the subjunctive clause of impersonal verbs *that* (MT 5.29; 1C 4.3); (b) as introducing the objective clause after verbs of saying, desiring, requesting, praying, etc. *that* (MT 14.36; MK 14.35); (3) elliptically, with the preceding verb to be supplied from the context; (a) used to introduce a purpose *so that, in order that* (JN 9.3); (b) used to introduce the content of a command (MK 5.23 ἵ. ἐπιθῇς . . . *(please) come and put your hands on (her)!*); (4) used to introduce a result clause, especially when a purpose was implied in the background *so that, with the result that* (JN 9.2; RO 11.11); (5) used to introduce an identifying or explanatory clause after a demonstrative, such as οὗτος, αὕτη, τοῦτο (*this*) *namely, that is* (JN 15.13; 18.37)

ἵνα	ABR	ἵνα
	CC	"
	CH	"
	CS	"

ἱνατί an interrogative adverb often written separately ἵνα τί; strictly *so that what might happen?* hence *why? for what reason?* (MT 9.4)

ἱνατί	ABT	ἱνατί

Ἰνδία, ας, ἡ *India*, a country of southern Asia (AC 2.9)

Ἰνδίαν	N-AF-S	Ἰνδία

Ἰόππη, ης, ἡ *Joppa*, a port city on the Mediterranean coast of Palestine, modern Jaffa

Ἰόππη	N-DF-S	Ἰόππη
Ἰόππην	N-AF-S	"
Ἰόππης	N-GF-S	"
Ἰορδάνῃ	N-DM-S	Ἰορδάνης
Ἰορδάνην	N-AM-S	"

Ἰορδάνης, ου, ὁ *Jordan River*, flowing from Mount Hermon south through the Sea of Galilee to the Dead Sea

Ἰορδάνου	N-GM-S	Ἰορδάνης

ἰός, οῦ, ὁ   (1) *venom, poison*, as of snakes; metaphorically, of deceitful words (JA 3.8); (2) *rust, tarnish*, as of metals (JA 5.3)

ἰός	N-NM-S	ἰός
ἰοῦ	N-GM-S	"
Ἰούδα	N-GM-S	Ἰούδας
	N-VM-S	"
Ἰούδᾳ	N-DM-S	"

Ἰουδαία, ας, ἡ   (1) as the southern district of Palestine *Judea* (MT 2.1); by metonymy, as its inhabitants (MT 3.5); (2) in a broader sense, the whole of Palestine as occupied by the Jewish nation *Jewish country* (AC 26.20), *Jewish territory* (MT 19.1)

Ἰουδαία	A--NF-S	Ἰουδαῖος
	N-NF-S	Ἰουδαία
Ἰουδαίᾳ	A--DF-S	Ἰουδαῖος
	N-DF-S	Ἰουδαία
Ἰουδαίαν	A--AF-S	Ἰουδαῖος
	N-AF-S	Ἰουδαία
Ἰουδαίας	A--GF-S	Ἰουδαῖος
	N-GF-S	Ἰουδαία
Ἰουδαΐζειν	VNPA	Ἰουδαΐζω

Ἰουδαΐζω   *live like a Jew, live according to Jewish customs* (GA 2.14)

| Ἰουδαϊκοῖς | A--DM-P | Ἰουδαϊκός |

Ἰουδαϊκός, ή, όν   as related to Jews *Jewish* (TI 1.14)

Ἰουδαϊκῶς   adverb; *in a Jewish manner, according to Jewish custom* (GA 2.14)

Ἰουδαϊκῶς	AB	Ἰουδαϊκῶς
Ἰουδαῖοι	AP-NM-P	Ἰουδαῖος
	AP-VM-P	"
	A--NM-P	"
	A--VM-P	"
Ἰουδαίοις	AP-DM-P	"
Ἰουδαῖον	AP-AM-S	"
	A--AM-S	"

Ἰουδαῖος, αία, ον   (1) as an adjective *Jewish* (AC 10.28); (2) predominately substantively; (a) *Jew* in respect to race or religion as opposed to non-Jews (Ἕλλην *Greek*; τὰ ἔθνη *nations, Gentiles*) (CO 3.11); (b) ἡ Ἰουδαία *the Jew* (AC 24.24); (c) οἱ Ἰουδαῖοι *the Jews*, the people of Palestine, especially as known by foreigners (MT 2.2); (d) in John's Gospel occasionally in a narrower sense of those hostile to Jesus, especially the national leaders (JN 2.18)

Ἰουδαῖος	AP-NM-S	Ἰουδαῖος
	A--NM-S	"
Ἰουδαίου	AP-GM-S	"
	A--GM-S	"
Ἰουδαίους	AP-AM-P	"

Ἰουδαϊσμός, οῦ, ὁ   the Jewish way of life as represented in their beliefs and practices *Judaism, Jewish religion*

Ἰουδαϊσμῷ	N-DM-S	Ἰουδαϊσμός
Ἰουδαίῳ	AP-DM-S	Ἰουδαῖος
	A--DM-S	"
Ἰουδαίων	AP-GM-P	"
	A--GM-P	"
Ἰούδαν	N-AM-S	Ἰούδας

Ἰούδας, α, ὁ   (1) *Judah*, masculine proper noun; as the name of the son of Jacob (MT 1.2), a tribe of Israel (HE 7.14), and the region occupied by the tribe of Judah (MT 2.6a); (2) *Judas*, masculine proper noun; as the name of an apostle (LU 6.16), a householder in Damascus (AC 9.11), and an ancestor of Jesus (LU 3.30); (3) *Jude*, the brother of Jesus (MT 13.55) and regarded by some as the writer of Jude (JU 1)

| Ἰούδας | N-NM-S | Ἰούδας |

Ἰουλία, ας, ἡ (also Ἀουλία, Ἰουνία) *Julia*, feminine proper noun (RO 16.15; possibly 16.7; see Ἰουνιᾶς)

| Ἰουλίαν | N-AF-S | Ἰουλία |

Ἰουλιανός, οῦ, ὁ   *Julian*, masculine proper noun (AC 27.3)

| Ἰουλιανός | N-NM-S | Ἰουλιανός |

Ἰούλιος, ου, ὁ   *Julius*, masculine proper noun (AC 27.1)

Ἰούλιος	N-NM-S	Ἰούλιος
Ἰουλίῳ	N-DM-S	"
Ἰουνίαν	N-AF-S	Ἰουλία
	N-AM-S	Ἰουνιᾶς
Ἰουνιᾶν	N-AM-S	"

Ἰουνιᾶς, ᾶ, ὁ (also Ἰουνίας) *Junias*, masculine proper noun (probably RO 16.7; see Ἰουλία)

Ἰοῦστος, ου, ὁ   *Justus*, masculine proper noun

Ἰοῦστος	N-NM-S	Ἰοῦστος
Ἰούστου	N-GM-S	"
ἱππεῖς	N-AM-P	ἱππεύς

ἱππεύς, έως, ὁ   as a soldier who fights on horseback *horseman, cavalryman*

ἱππικός, ή, όν   *pertaining to a horseman, equestrian*; substantivally τὸ ἱππικόν *the cavalry* (RV 9.16)

| ἱππικοῦ | AP-GN-S | ἱππικός |
| ἵπποις | N-DM-P | ἵππος |

ἵππος, ου, ὁ   *horse* (JA 3.3); used chiefly in battles for mounted warriors or for war chariots; symbolically in Revelation with varying roles depicted by horses of various colors (RV 6.2–8)

ἵππος	N-NM-S	ἵππος
ἵππου	N-GM-S	"
ἵππους	N-AM-P	"
ἵππων	N-GM-P	"

ἶρις, ιδος, ἡ   basically *circle of light*; (1) *rainbow* (RV 10.1); (2) *halo, radiance, circle of radiance* (RV 4.3, but *rainbow* is also possible here)

ἶρις	N-NF-S	ἶρις
ἴσα	AB	ἴσος
	A--AN-P	"
	A--NN-P	"
ἴσα	A--AN-P	"

Ἰσαάκ, ὁ   indeclinable; *Isaac*, masculine proper noun

| ἰσάγγελοι | A--NM-P | ἰσάγγελος |

ἰσάγγελος, ον   *like* or *equal to an angel* (LU 20.36)

ἴσαι	A--NF-P	ἴσος
ἴσασι(ν)	VIRA--3P	οἶδα
Ἰσαχάρ		Ἰσσαχάρ
ἴση	A--NF-S	ἴσος
ἴσην	A--AF-S	"
ἴσθι	VMPA--2S	εἰμί
Ἰσκαιώθ		Ἰσκαριώθ
Ἰσκαριώτην	N-AM-S	"

Ἰσκαριώθ, ὁ (also Ἰσκαιώθ, Σκαριώτα, Σκαριώθ) indeclinable and Ἰσκαριώτης, ου, ὁ (also Ἰσκαριότης, Ἰσκαριώτις, Σκαριότης, Σκαριώτης) *Iscariot* or *Scariot*, masculine proper noun; surname of the Judas who became Jesus' betrayer; usually understood as his place of origin *from Kerioth*, a town in southern Judea (MT 10.4; MK 3.19; JN 6.71)

Ἰσκαριώτη	N-NM-S	Ἰσκαριώθ
Ἰσκαριώτη	N-DM-S	"
Ἰσκαριώτην	N-AM-S	"
Ἰσκαριώτης	N-NM-S	"
Ἰσκαριώτιν	N-AM-S	"
Ἰσκαριώτου	N-GM-S	"
Ἰσκαρώτης	N-NM-S	see Ἰσκαριώτης
ἴσμεν	VIRA--1P	οἶδα
ἴσον	A--AM-S	ἴσος

ἴσος, η, ον (also **ἴσος**) *equal, like*; (1) of number, dimension, quantity *equal, same* (RV 21.16); (2) of agreement in content *consistent, identical* (MK 14.56); (3) of equality of essence *equal* (JN 5.18); (4) neuter as an adverb ἴσον and ἴσα *equal, alike* (PH 2.6); (5) substantively τὰ ἴσα *equal amount* (LU 6.34)

ἰσότης, ητος, ἡ (1) of value *equality* (2C 8.14); ἐξ ἰσότητος *as a matter of equality, as a question of fairness* (2C 8.13); (2) as due rights and obligations *fairness, what is equitable* (CO 4.1)

ἰσότης	N-NF-S	ἰσότης
ἰσότητα	N-AF-S	"
ἰσότητος	N-GF-S	"
ἰσότιμον	A--AF-S	ἰσότιμος

ἰσότιμος, ον *equally valuable* or *precious, of the same kind, equal to* (2P 1.1)

ἴσους	A--AM-P	ἴσος
ἰσόψυχον	A--AM-S	ἰσόψυχος

ἰσόψυχος, ον *of the same mind, like-minded, with a similar attitude* (PH 2.20)

Ἰσραήλ, ὁ indeclinable; *Israel*, masculine proper noun; (1) the surname given to the patriarch Jacob (RO 9.6a; PH 3.5); (2) the natural descendants of the patriarch *(people of) Israel* (AC 4.10), *(house of) Israel* (MT 10.6); (3) as the people with whom God made a covenant *(nation of) Israel* (MT 27.42), *(twelve tribes of) Israel* (RV 21.12); (4) the northern kingdom of *Israel* as opposed to the southern kingdom of Judah (HE 8.8); (5) geographically, Palestine as *(land of) Israel* (MT 2.20); (6) figuratively, of Christians as the new covenant people of God *Israel* (GA 6.16)

Ἰσραηλεῖται	N-NM-P	Ἰσραηλίτης
	N-VM-P	"
Ἰσραηλείτης	N-NM-S	"
Ἰσραηλῖται	N-NM-P	"
	N-VM-P	"

Ἰσραηλίτης, ου, ὁ (also **Ἰσραηλείτης**) *Israelite, descendant of Israel*

Ἰσραηλίτης	N-NM-S	Ἰσραηλίτης

Ἰσσαχάρ, ὁ (also **Ἰσαχάρ**) indeclinable; *Issachar*, masculine proper noun; name of one of the tribes of Israel (RV 7.7)

ἰστάνομεν	VIPA--1P	ἵστημι
ἰστάνω	VIPA--1S	"
ἴστε	VIRA--2P	οἶδα
	VMRA--2P	"

ἵστημι and **ἰστάνω** (and **ἰστάω**) fut. στήσω, mid. στήσομαι; 1aor. ἔστησα; 2aor. ἔστην; pf. ἕστηκα and ἔστακα; pluperfect εἱστήκειν; 1aor. pass. ἐστάθην; 1fut. pass.

στаθήσομαι; the meaning often derived from the context, tense, and surrounding relations; **I.** transitively (present active, imperfect active, future active, first aorist active) basically, as causing to stand still; (1) of persons *place, put forward, appoint, cause to come* (MT 4.5; AC 1.23); (2) of things, generally *set up, arrange*; (a) as arranging payment by putting things on the scales and bringing them to rest *weigh out, pay* (MT 26.15); (b) of time *set, appoint* (AC 17.31); (3) of abstract things, as law, covenants, plan for righteousness, etc. *bring into force, establish, make valid, confirm* (RO 3.31; HE 10.9); **II.** intransitively (second aorist active, perfect active, pluperfect active, future middle/passive, first aorist passive); (1) aorist and future; (a) *stand still, stop* (AC 8.38); (b) *stand* or *appear* before someone (MK 13.9); (c) *stand up to, offer resistance to* (EP 6.11); (d) *stand firm, hold one's ground* (RV 6.17); (e) *stand up* (firmly on one's feet) (RV 11.11); (2) perfect and pluperfect; (a) *stand* (from some other possible position) (JN 7.37; LU 23.10); (b) with an accompanying adverb or prepositional phrase to indicate place *be, exist, stand* (MK 11.5); (c) figuratively, of remaining firm on a commitment or stand one has taken (1C 10.12)

ἵστησι(ν)	VIPA--3S	ἵστημι
ἱστία	N-AN-P	ἱστίον

ἱστίον, ου, τό of a ship *sail* (AC 27.15, 17)

ἱστόν	N-AM-S	ἱστός

ἱστορέω 1aor. ἱστόρησα; *learn by inquiry; visit in order to get to know* someone, *visit with* (GA 1.18)

ἱστορῆσαι	VNAA	ἱστορέω

ἱστός, οῦ, ὁ as the upright pole on a ship to support the sails *mast* (AC 27.38)

ἴστω	VMPA--3S	see ἔστω
ἱστῶμεν	VIPA--1P	ἵστημι
ἰσχύει	VIPA--3S	ἰσχύω
ἰσχύειν	VNPA	"
ἴσχυε(ν)	VIIA--3S	"
ἰσχύϊ	N-DF-S	ἰσχύς
ἰσχύν	N-AF-S	"
ἴσχυον	VIIA--3P	ἰσχύω
ἰσχύοντες	VPPANM-P	"
ἰσχύοντος	VPPAGM-S	"
ἰσχύος	N-GF-S	ἰσχύς
ἰσχυρά	A--AN-P	ἰσχυρός
	A--NF-S	"
	A--VF-S	"
ἰσχυρᾷ	A--DF-S	"
ἰσχυραί	A--NF-P	"
ἰσχυράν	A--AF-S	"
ἰσχυρᾶς	A--GF-S	"
ἰσχυροί	A--NM-P	"
ἰσχυρόν	A--AM-S	"

ἰσχυρός, ά, όν *strong, powerful, mighty*; (1) of physical strength *strong, robust* (MT 12.29), opposite ἀσθενής (*weak, sick*); (2) of political or military status *great, mighty* (RV 6.15); (3) of spirit-beings *powerful, mighty* (RV 18.8); substantively ὁ ἰ. *the strong one*, probably a reference to Satan (MT 12.29); (4) of things, with the meaning fitting the context: *violent* (wind) (MT 14.30); *loud* (thunder) (RV 19.6); *weighty, serious* (letters) (2C

10.10); *severe* (famine) (LU 15.14); *strong* (encouragement) (HE 6.18); substantively τὸ ἰσχυρόν *strong thing* (1C 1.27), opposite τὸ ἀσθενές (*weak thing*); (5) comparative ἰσχυρότερος, τέρα, ον *stronger, mightier, more powerful* (MK 1.7)

ἰσχυρός	A--NM-S	ἰσχυρός
ἰσχυρότεροι	A-MNM-P	"
ἰσχυρότερον	A-MNN-S	"
ἰσχυρότερος	A-MNM-S	"
ἰσχυροῦ	A--GM-S	"
ἰσχυρῶν	A--GF-P	"
	A--GM-P	"

ἰσχύς, ύος, ἡ *strength, power, might*; used of the ability of human beings (MK 12.30), of angelic power (2P 2.11), and as an attribute of God (RV 5.12)

ἰσχύς	N-NF-S	ἰσχύς
ἰσχύσαμεν	VIAA--1P	ἰσχύω
ἴσχυσαν	VIAA--3P	"
ἴσχυσας	VIAA--2S	"
ἰσχύσατε	VIAA--2P	"
ἴσχυσε(ν)	VIAA--3S	"
ἰσχύσῃ	VSAA--3S	"
ἰσχύσουσι(ν)	VIFA--3P	"

ἰσχύω fut. ἰσχύσω; 1aor. ἴσχυσα; (1) of physical power *be strong, be powerful, be able* (MK 5.4); as being in possession of one's powers *be in good health, be healthy* (MK 2.17); (2) of intellectual power *be competent, have power, be able* (PH 4.13); (3) of spiritual or supernatural power *avail, prevail, be mighty* (AC 19.20; JA 5.16); (4) as a legal technical term, of law and institutions *have meaning, be valid, be in force* (HE 9.17)

ἰσχύω	VIPA--1S	ἰσχύω

ἴσως adverb; *probably, perhaps*, as qualifying something agreeable to what might be expected (LU 20.13)

ἴσως	AB	ἴσως

Ἰταλία, ας, ἡ *Italy*, name of a country extending into the Mediterranean Sea from the north, with Rome as its capital

Ἰταλίαν	N-AF-S	Ἰταλία
Ἰταλίας	N-GF-S	"
Ἰταλικῆς	A--GF-S	Ἰταλικός

Ἰταλικός, ή, όν *Italian, belonging to Italy* (AC 10.1)

Ἰτουραίας	A--GF-S	Ἰτουραῖος

Ἰτουραῖος, αία, ον *belonging to Iturea*, a region along the Lebanon and Anti-Lebanon mountain ranges west of Damascus; Ἰτουραία χώρα *territory of Iturea* (LU 3.1)

ἰχθύας	N-AM-P	ἰχθύς
ἰχθύδια	N-AN-P	ἰχθύδιον

ἰχθύδιον, ου, τό diminutive of ἰχθύς; *small fish*

ἰχθύες	N-NM-P	ἰχθύς
ἰχθύν	N-AM-S	"
ἰχθύος	N-GM-S	"

ἰχθύς, ύος, ὁ *fish*, generally referring to creatures with fins and scales, inhabiting the water of rivers, lakes, or seas (MT 17.27; perhaps 7.10); of such creatures prepared as food *fish* (MT 14.17); *piece of fish* (possibly MT 7.10)

ἰχθύων	N-GM-P	ἰχθύς
ἴχνεσι(ν)	N-DN-P	ἴχνος

ἴχνος, ους, τό literally *footprint, footstep*; plural, of a continuous line of such impressions *trail, track*; figura-

tively in the NT, to designate the record left by someone's conduct or manner of life as an example for others (1P 2.21)

Ἰωαθάμ		Ἰωαθάμ

Ἰωαθάμ, ὁ (also Ἰωάθαμ) indeclinable; *Jotham*, masculine proper noun

Ἰωακείμ		Ἰωακείμ

Ἰωακίμ, ὁ (also Ἰωακείμ) indeclinable; *Jehoiakim*, masculine proper noun (MT 1.11)

Ἰωάνα	N-NF-S	Ἰωάννα
Ἰωανᾶ	N-GM-S	Ἰωνᾶ

Ἰωανάν, ὁ (also Ἰωανᾶς [ᾶ], Ἰωαννάν) usually indeclinable; *Joanan*, masculine proper noun (LU 3.27)

Ἰωάνει	N-DM-S	see Ἰωάνῃ
Ἰωάνῃ	N-DM-S	Ἰωάννης
Ἰωάνην	N-AM-S	"
Ἰωάνης	N-NM-S	"

Ἰωάννα, ας, ἡ (also Ἰωάνα) *Joanna*, feminine proper noun (LU 8.3)

Ἰωάννα	N-NF-S	Ἰωάννα
Ἰωαννά		see Ἰωανάν
Ἰωαννᾶ	N-GM-S	Ἰωανάν
	N-GM-S	Ἰωνᾶς
Ἰωαννάν		Ἰωανάν
Ἰωάννει	N-DM-S	see Ἰωάννῃ
Ἰωάννῃ	N-DM-S	Ἰωάννης
Ἰωάννην	N-AM-S	"

Ἰωάννης, ου, ὁ (also Ἰωάνης) *John*, masculine proper noun; several prominent NT persons bear this name: (1) *John* the Baptist (MT 3.1); (2) *John* the son of Zebedee, one of the twelve apostles (MT 4.21; probably RV 1.1); (3) *John* Mark, cousin of Barnabas and writer of the Second Gospel (AC 12.25); (4) *John* father of Peter (JN 1.42); (5) *John*, a member of the high council (AC 4.6)

Ἰωάννης	N-NM-S	Ἰωάννης
Ἰωάννου	N-GM-S	"
Ἰωάνου	N-GM-S	"

Ἰωάς, ὁ indeclinable; *Joash*, masculine proper noun (MT 1.8)

Ἰώβ, ὁ indeclinable; *Job*, masculine proper noun (JA 5.11)

Ἰωβήδ, ὁ (also Ἰωβήλ, Ὠβήδ, Ὠβήδ, Ὠβήλ) indeclinable; *Obed*, masculine proper noun

Ἰωβήλ		Ἰωβήδ

Ἰωδά, ὁ indeclinable; *Joda*, masculine proper noun (LU 3.26)

Ἰωήλ, ὁ indeclinable; *Joel*, masculine proper noun (AC 2.16)

ἰώμενος	VPPDNM-S	ἰάομαι
	VPPONM-S	"
Ἰωνᾶ	N-GM-S	Ἰωνᾶς

Ἰωνάθας, ου, ὁ *Jonathas*, masculine proper noun (AC 4.6)

Ἰωνάθας	N-NM-S	Ἰωνάθας

Ἰωνάμ, ὁ (also Ἰωνάν) indeclinable; *Jonam*, masculine proper noun (LU 3.30)

Ἰωνάν		Ἰωνάμ
		see Ἰωανάν

Ἰωνᾶς, ᾶ, ὁ (also Ἰωανᾶς, Ἰωαννᾶς) (1) *Jonah*, masculine proper noun; name of the Old Testament prophet (MT

207

12.39); (2) *Jonah* father of Simon Peter and Andrew (MT 16.17)

| Ἰωνᾶς | N-NM-S | Ἰωνᾶς |
| ἰῶντο | VIIP--3P | ἰάομαι |

Ἰωράμ, ὁ   indeclinable; *Joram*, masculine proper noun

| Ἰωρείμ | | Ἰωρίμ |

Ἰωρίμ, ὁ (also Ἰωρείμ)   indeclinable; *Jorim*, masculine proper noun (LU 3.29)

Ἰωσαφάτ, ὁ   indeclinable; *Jehoshaphat*, masculine proper noun

Ἰωσείαν	N-AM-S	Ἰωσίας
Ἰωσείας	N-NM-S	"
Ἰωσή	N-GM-S	see Ἰωσῆ
Ἰωσῆ	N-GM-S	Ἰωσῆς
		see Ἰωσήφ

Ἰωσῆς, ῆτος (or ῆ), ὁ   *Joses*, masculine proper noun (MK 15.40); equivalent in MK 6.3 to Ἰωσήφ the brother of Jesus in MT 13.55

| Ἰωσῆς | N-NM-S | Ἰωσῆς |
| Ἰωσῆτος | N-GM-S | " |

Ἰωσήφ, ὁ   indeclinable; *Joseph*, masculine proper noun; several prominent biblical persons bear this name: (1) the patriarch, son of Jacob (JN 4.5); (2) husband of Mary mother of Jesus (MT 1.16); (3) a brother of Jesus (MT 13.55); (4) *Joseph* of Arimathea, Sanhedrin member who provided a tomb for Jesus (LU 23.50); (5) *Joseph* surnamed Barnabas, Paul's missionary companion (AC 4.36); (6) two of this name in the genealogy of Jesus (LU 3.24, 30); (7) *Joseph* surnamed Barsabbas (AC 1.23); (8) son of Mary (MT 27.56)

Ἰωσήχ, ὁ   indeclinable; *Josech*, masculine proper noun (LU 3.26)

| Ἰωσίαν | N-AM-S | Ἰωσίας |

Ἰωσίας, ου, ὁ (also Ἰωσείας)   *Josiah*, masculine proper noun (MT 1.10)

| Ἰωσίας | N-NM-S | Ἰωσίας |

ἰῶτα, τό   indeclinable; *iota*, the Greek equivalent for the smallest Aramaic letter *yod*; hence *minutest part, tiny bit* (MT 5.18)

κάβος, ου, ὁ *cab*, a measure equivalent to approximately 2 quarts or 2 liters (LU 16.6)

κάβους   N-AM-P   κάβος

κἀγώ, dative κἀμοί, accusative κἀμέ contracted from καί (*and, also*) and ἐγώ (*I*); (1) as a coordinate *and I* (LU 2.48); (2) as a contrastive *but I* (JA 2.18a); (3) as an additive *I also, I too* (1C 7.40); (4) consecutively *I, for my part; I, in turn* (RV 3.10); (5) to introduce as illustration a supposed case from one's life *I for instance, I in particular* (RO 3.7)

κἀγώ   AB&NPN-1S   κἀγώ
     CC&NPN-1S   "
     CH&NPN-1S   "
     CS&NPN-1S   "

κάδος, ου, ὁ *jar, barrel, cask*, a container for liquids (LU 16.6)

κάδους   N-AM-P   κάδος
καθ᾽   PA   κατά
     PG   "

καθά subordinating conjunction; a poetic form of κατά; *just as* (MT 27.10)

καθά   CS   καθά
καθαίρει   VIPA--3S   καθαίρω
καθαιρεῖσθαι   VNPP   καθαιρέω
καθαίρεσιν   N-AF-S   καθαίρεσις

καθαίρεσις, εως, ἡ as an action; literally *taking down, destruction, demolition* (2C 10.4); figuratively *weakening, causing to be less able* (2C 13.10), opposite οἰκοδομή (*edifying, building up*)

καθαιρέω 2fut. καθελῶ; 2aor. καθεῖλον; (1) literally; (a) *take* or *bring down from above, lower* someone (MK 15.46); (b) of buildings *pull* or *tear down, demolish* (LU 12.18); (2) figuratively; (a) of opponents *destroy, overthrow, conquer* (AC 13.19); (b) of a person in an important position *take away power, put down, overthrow* (LU 1.52); (c) of causing a state to cease *do away with, eliminate, bring to nothing* (AC 19.27)

καθαιροῦντες   VPPANM-P   καθαιρέω

καθαίρω *make clean* by taking away an undesirable part; of a vine *prune, cut back, take away* some of the branches (JN 15.2)

καθάπερ subordinating conjunction; (1) to introduce supporting quotations *just as, exactly as* (RO 4.6); (2) to introduce a comparison *just as* (RO 12.4)

καθάπερ   CS   καθάπερ

καθάπτω 1aor. καθῆψα; *take hold of, seize on*; of a snake *fasten on* (AC 28.3)

καθαρά   A--NF-S   καθαρός
     A--NN-P   "
καθαρᾷ   A--DF-S   "
καθαρᾶς   A--GF-S   "
καθαριεῖ   VIFA--3S   καθαρίζω

καθαρίζει   VIPA--3S   "
καθαρίζεσθαι   VNPP   "
καθαρίζεται   VIPP--3S   "
καθαρίζετε   VIPA--2P   "
     VMPA--2P   "
καθαρίζον   VPPANM-S   "
καθαρίζονται   VIPP--3P   "

καθαρίζω fut. καθαριῶ; 1aor. ἐκαθάρισα; pf. pass. κεκαθάρισμαι; 1aor. pass. ἐκαθαρίσθην; (1) literally, as thoroughly cleansing for sacred use *wash, make clean, cleanse* (LU 11.39); (2) figuratively; (a) of ritual cleansing, making levitically clean, as foods *cleanse, purify, declare clean* (AC 10.15); (b) of healing of diseases that render ceremonially unclean, as leprosy *cleanse, make ritually clean* (MK 1.40); (c) of religious and moral purity, as from sin and a guilty conscience *cleanse, make pure, make acceptable to God* (1J 1.7)

καθαρίζων   VPPANM-S   καθαρίζω
καθαρίσαι   VNAA   "
καθαρίσας   VPAANM-S   "
καθαρίσατε   VMAA--2P   "
καθαρισάτω   VMAA--3S   "
καθαρίσει   VIFA--3S   "
καθαρίση   VSAA--3S   "
καθαρίσθητε   VMAP--2P   "
καθαρίσθητι   VMAP--2S   "
καθαρισμόν   N-AM-S   καθαρισμός

καθαρισμός, οῦ, ὁ *purification, cleansing* literally, in the ritual sense (JN 3.25); figuratively, as moral and spiritual cleansing (HE 1.3)

καθαρισμοῦ   N-GM-S   καθαρισμός
καθάρισον   VMAA--2S   καθαρίζω
καθαρίσωμεν   VSAA--1P   "
καθαροί   A--NM-P   καθαρός
καθαροῖς   A--DM-P   "
καθαρόν   A--AM-S   "
     A--AN-S   "
     A--NN-S   "

καθαρός, ά, όν *clean, pure*; (1) literally; (a) as free from dirt *clean* (HE 10.22; perhaps MT 27.59), opposite ῥυπαρός (*dirty, foul*); used in metaphors relating to a way of life *clean, free from wrong* (MT 23.26; JN 13.10); (b) as without mixture; free from adulteration *pure* (RV 21.18; probably MT 27.59); (2) figuratively; (a) in a ritual sense of food declared acceptable *clean, undefiled* (RO 14.20), opposite κοινός (*common*); (b) morally and spiritually, as free from wrongdoing *pure, good in God's eyes, without sin* (JN 13.10); substantivally οἱ καθαροί (MT 5.8)

καθαρός   A--NM-S   καθαρός

καθαρότης, ητος, ἡ ceremonial *purity, cleanness, ritual acceptability* (HE 9.13)

καθαρότητα	N-AF-S	καθαρότης
καθαρούς	A--AM-P	καθαρός
καθαρῷ	A--DM-S	"
	A--DN-S	"

καθέδρα, ας, ἡ literally *seat, chair* (MT 21.12); idiomatically ἐπὶ τῆς Μωϋσέως καθέδρας καθιστάναι literally *sit on Moses' seat*, i.e. *have authority to interpret Mosaic law* (MT 23.2)

καθέδρας	N-AF-P	καθέδρα
	N-GF-S	"
καθέζησθε	VSPD--2P	καθέζομαι

καθέζομαι impf. ἐκαθεζόμην; fut. καθεσθήσομαι; (1) as occupying a position of respect or authority, such as teacher, councilor *sit* (MT 26.55); (2) as taking the position of a learner *sit* (LU 2.46); (3) reflexively *sit down, seat oneself* (JN 4.6)

καθεζόμενοι	VPPDNM-P	καθέζομαι
	VPPONM-P	"
καθεζόμενον	VPPDAM-S	"
	VPPOAM-S	"
καθεζόμενος	VPPDNM-S	"
	VPPONM-S	"
καθεζομένους	VPPDAM-P	"
	VPPOAM-P	"
καθεῖλε(ν)	VIAA--3S	καθαιρέω

καθεῖς from καθ᾿ εἷς (*according to one*); *one by one, one after another* (1C 14.31)

καθεῖς	AB	καθεῖς
καθελεῖν	VNAA	"
καθελόντες	VPAANM-P	"
καθελῶ	VIFA--1S	"
καθελών	VPAANM-S	"

καθεξῆς adverb; (1) denoting sequence in time, space, or logic *in order, one after the other, point by point* (LU 1.3); (2) substantivally, with the article οἱ κ. *the successors, those since* (AC 3.24); (3) idiomatically ἐν τῷ κ. literally *in the next*, i.e. *afterward, later* (LU 8.1)

καθεξῆς	AB	καθεξῆς
καθεσθήσεσθε	VIFO--2P	καθέζομαι
καθεσθίουσι(ν)	VIPA--3P	κατεσθίω
καθεύδει	VIPA--3S	καθεύδω
καθεύδειν	VNPA	"
καθεύδεις	VIPA--2S	"
καθεύδετε	VIPA--2P	"
	VMPA--2P	"
καθεύδῃ	VSPA--3S	"
καθεύδοντας	VPPAAM-P	"
καθεύδοντες	VPPANM-P	"
καθεύδουσι(ν)	VIPA--3P	"

καθεύδω impf. ἐκάθευδον; (1) literally *sleep, be fast asleep* (MT 13.25); (2) figuratively; (a) as a euphemism for death *sleep, die* (1TH 5.10); (b) as an attitude of spiritual laziness or indifference *sleep, pay no attention* (EP 5.14)

καθεύδωμεν	VSPA--1P	καθεύδω
καθεύδων	VPPANM-S	"
	VPPAVM-S	"
κάθη	VIPD--2S	κάθημαι
	VIPO--2S	"
καθηγηταί	N-NM-P	καθηγητής

καθηγητής, οῦ, ὁ strictly *guide, leader*; in the NT *teacher, instructor*

καθηγητής	N-NM-S	καθηγητής
καθηγορῆσαι	VNAA	see κατηγορῆσαι
καθῆκαν	VIAA--3P	καθίημι
καθῆκε(ν)	VIIA--3S	καθήκω
καθῆκον	VPPANN-S	"
καθήκοντα	VPPAAN-P	"

καθήκω strictly *extend to, reach to*; hence *be fit* or *suitable*; impersonally καθήκει *it is fitting* or *proper* (AC 22.22); in a moral sense τὰ μὴ καθήκοντα *improper things, what ought not to be done* (RO 1.28)

κάθημαι imperative κάθου; impf. ἐκαθήμην; fut. καθήσομαι; (1) literally; (a) *sit (down), be sitting* (MT 27.61); (b) as sitting in a certain place as a mark of high distinction *sit, be seated* (MT 26.64); (c) imperatively *sit down* (MT 22.44); (2) figuratively, as remaining in a certain place or condition *stay, reside, dwell* (MT 4.16; LU 21.35)

κάθημαι	VIPD--1S	κάθημαι
	VIPO--1S	"
καθήμεναι	VPPDNF-P	"
	VPPONF-P	"
καθημένην	VPPDAF-S	"
	VPPOAF-S	"
καθημένης	VPPDGF-S	"
	VPPOGF-S	"
καθήμενοι	VPPDNM-P	"
	VPPONM-P	"
καθημένοις	VPPDDM-P	"
	VPPDDN-P	"
	VPPODM-P	"
	VPPODN-P	"
καθήμενον	VPPDAM-S	"
	VPPDAN-S	"
	VPPOAM-S	"
	VPPOAN-S	"
καθήμενος	VPPDNM-S	"
	VPPONM-S	"
καθημένου	VPPDGM-S	"
	VPPOGM-S	"
καθημένους	VPPDAM-P	"
	VPPOAM-P	"
καθημένῳ	VPPDDM-S	"
	VPPODM-S	"
καθημένων	VPPDGM-P	"
	VPPOGM-P	"
καθημερινῇ	A--DF-S	καθημερινός

καθημερινός, ή, όν from καθ᾿ ἡμέραν (*according to day*); *daily, day by day* (AC 6.1)

κάθηνται	VIPD--2S	κάθημαι
	VIPO--2S	"
καθήσεσθε	VIFD--2P	"
καθῆσθαι	VNPD	"
	VNPO	"
κάθησθε	VSPD--2P	"
	VSPO--2P	"
κάθηται	VIPD--3S	"
	VIPO--3S	"
καθήψατο	VIAM--3S	καθάπτω
καθῆψε(ν)	VIAA--3S	"

καθιεμένην	VPPPAF-S	καθίημι
καθιέμενον	VPPPAN-S	"
καθίζει	VIPA--3S	καθίζω
καθίζετε	VIPA--2P	"

καθίζω fut. καθίσω and καθιῶ; 1aor. ἐκάθισα; pf. κεκάθικα; (1) transitively *cause to sit down, seat, set*, often in a place of power or authority (AC 2.30); figuratively *appoint, install, put in charge of* (1C 6.4); (2) intransitively; (a) *sit (down)* (MT 5.1); (b) as remaining in a certain place *stay, tarry, settle* (AC 18.11); (c) middle reflexively *sit down* (MT 19.28)

καθίημι 1aor. καθῆκα; *let down, lower* from a higher to a lower place

καθίσαι	VNAA	καθίζω
καθίσαντες	VPAANM-P	"
καθίσαντος	VPAAGM-S	"
καθίσας	VPAANM-S	"
καθίσατε	VMAA--2P	"
καθίσει	VIFA--3S	"
καθίσεσθε	VIFM--2P	"
καθίσῃ	VSAA--3S	"
καθίσησθε	VSAM--2P	"
κάθισον	VMAA--2S	"
καθιστάνοντες	VPPANM-P	καθίστημι
καθίσταται	VIPP--3S	"

καθίστημι and **καθιστάνω** fut. καταστήσω; 1aor. κατέστησα; 1aor. pass. κατεστάθην; 1fut. pass. καταστα-θήσομαι; (1) *conduct, bring, lead to* (AC 17.15); (2) set in an elevated position *appoint, put in charge* (LU 12.42); (3) with a double accusative *make* someone something, *cause to be in a certain position* or *state* (2P 1.8); passive *be made, become* (JA 4.4)

καθίστησι(ν)	VIPA--3S	καθίστημι
καθιστῶντες	VPPANM-P	"
καθίσωμεν	VSAA--1P	καθίζω
καθίσωσι(ν)	VSAA--3P	"
καθιῶ	VIFA-1S	"

καθό adverb; (1) of kind or manner *as* (RO 8.26); (2) of degree *to the degree that, insofar as* (1P 4.13)

καθό	CS	καθό

καθόλου adverb; *entirely, completely*; negatively μὴ κ. *not at all* (AC 4.18)

καθόλου	AB	καθόλου

καθοπλίζω pf. pass. ptc. καθωπλισμένος; *completely arm with weapons, fully equip*; passive *be fully armed* (LU 11.21)

καθορᾶται	VIPP--3S	καθοράω

καθοράω *clearly see, perceive, learn about*, implying sense perception combined with an intellectual apprehension

καθότι conjunction; (1) with ἄν (particle indicating contingency) to express manner *as, according to what, in proportion to* (AC 2.45); (2) as a causal *because, in view of the fact that* (LU 1.7)

καθότι	CS	καθότι
κάθου	VMPD--2S	κάθημαι
	VMPO--2S	"
καθωπλισμένος	VPRMNM-S	καθοπλίζω

καθώς a conjunction from κατά (*down*) and ὥς (*as*); (1) a comparative often with οὕτω(ς) (*so, in this way*) following *according as, just as* (LU 11.30); (2) as express-

ing manner *as, in proportion as, to the degree that* (AC 11.29); (3) as a causal *because, since, in as much as* (JN 17.2; RO 1.28); (4) temporally *as, when* (AC 7.17); (5) to introduce indirect discourse in the sense of πῶς *how* (AC 15.14)

καθώς	CS	καθώς

καθώσπερ a conjunction denoting an emphatic comparison *just as, exactly as* (HE 5.4)

καθώσπερ	CS	καθώσπερ

καί a coordinating conjunction with the sense varying according to its circumstances; **I.** as a connective; (1) connecting single words *and* (MT 2.11d); (2) as a continuative, connecting clauses and sentences *and* (MT 21.23c); (3) as coordinating time with an event *when* (MK 15.25); (4) to introduce a result from preceding circumstances *and then, and so* (MT 4.19); (5) to introduce an abrupt question expressing a contrasting feeling *then, in that case* (2C 2.2); (6) as emphasizing an unexpected fact *and yet, nevertheless, and in spite of that* (MT 3.14); (7) to explain what preceded *and so, that is, namely* (MT 8.33b; JN 1.16); (8) κ. . . . κ. *both . . . and, not only . . . but also* (AC 26.29); **II.** adverb; (1) as an adjunctive *also, too* (MT 5.39); (2) as an ascensive, introducing something unusual *even* (MT 5.46); (3) to reinforce a contrast or comparison *also* (2C 8.11b; HE 8.6)

καί	AB	καί
	CC	"
	CC+	"
	CH	"
	CS	"
Καιάφα	N-GM-S	Καϊάφας
Καϊάφα	N-GM-S	"
Καιάφαν	N-AM-S	"
Καϊάφαν	N-AM-S	"
Καϊάφας	N-NM-S	"

Καϊάφας, α, ὁ (also **Καιάφας, Καΐφας**) *Caiaphas*, masculine proper noun

Καϊάφας	N-NM-S	Καϊάφας

καίγε from καί (*and*) and γέ (*even*); *at least, were it only* (LU 19.42); *and even, yes too* (AC 2.18)

καίγε	AB	καίγε
	CC	"
καίεται	VIPP--3S	καίω
Κάιν		Κάϊν

Κάϊν, ὁ (also **Κάιν**) indeclinable; *Cain*, masculine proper noun

καινά	A--AN-P	καινός
	A--NN-P	"
καινοῖς	A--DF-P	"
Καινάμ		Καϊνάμ

Καϊνάμ, ὁ (also **Καινάμ, Καινάν, Καϊνάν**) indeclinable; *Cainan*, masculine proper noun

Καινάν		Καϊνάμ
Καϊνάν		"
καινή	A--NF-S	καινός
καινήν	A--AF-S	"
καινῆς	A--GF-S	"
καινόν	A--AM-S	"
	A--AN-S	"
	A--NN-S	"

καινοποιέω   *make new, renew* (RV 21.5)

| καινοποιῶ | VIPA--1S | καινοποιέω |

καινός, ή, όν   *new*, opposite παλαιός (*old*); (1) of what was not there before *new, recently made, not yet used, fresh* (MT 9.17); neuter as a substantive τὸ καινόν *new piece, new part* (MK 2.21); (2) of what was not known before *strange, unheard of, unusual* (MK 1.27); (3) of what was not possessed before *newly gained, newly acquired* (MT 13.52); (4) by way of contrast with the old or obsolete *better, superior, different* (HE 8.8); substantivally *new (and better) one* (HE 8.13); (5) comparative καινότερος, τέρα, ον *quite new*; colloquially *latest* (AC 17.21)

| καινότερον | A-MAN-S | καινός |

καινότης, ητος, ἡ   as depicting something not only recent and different but extraordinary *newness*

καινότητι	N-DF-S	καινότης
καινοῦ	A--GN-S	καινός
καινούς	A--AM-P	"

καινοφωνία, ας, ἡ   as a negative term for new expressions *new-fashioned talk, latest slang, newfangled* or *novel words* (1T 6.20; 2T 2.16)

| καινοφωνίας | N-AF-P | καινοφωνία |

καινόω   fut. καινώσω; *make new, innovate, introduce something new* (1C 9.15)

καινῶ	A--DN-S	καινός
καινώσει	VIFA--3S	καινόω
καιόμεναι	VPPPNF-P	καίω
καιομένη	VPPPNF-S	"
καιομένη	VPPPDF-S	"
καιομένην	VPPPAF-S	"
καιομένης	VPPPGF-S	"
καιόμενοι	VPPPNM-P	"
καιόμενον	VPPPNN-S	"
καιόμενος	VPPPNM-S	"
καίουσι(ν)	VIPA--3P	"

καίπερ   from καί (*even*) and πέρ (enclitic particle with an intensive force); a conjunction used to conjoin concession *although, even though, but nevertheless*

καίπερ	CS	καίπερ
καιροί	N-NM-P	καιρός
καιροῖς	N-DM-P	"
καιρόν	N-AM-S	"

καιρός, οῦ, ὁ   *time*; (1) as a measure of time, either as a point of time, past, present, or future *time, moment* (MT 11.25), or as a fixed period of time marked by suitableness *season, (favorable) time, opportunity* (2C 6.2); (2) as a specific and decisive point, often divinely allotted *time, season* (MK 1.15); (3) as a future period of time marked by characteristic circumstances *(the) last times, (the) end-time, (the) messianic times* (MT 16.3; 1T 4.1)

καιρός	N-NM-S	καιρός
καιροῦ	N-GM-S	"
καιρούς	N-AM-P	"
καιρῷ	N-DM-S	"
καιρῶν	N-GM-P	"

Καῖσαρ, αρος, ἡ   *Caesar*; originally a surname of Julius Caesar, later taken as a title by the chief Roman ruler *emperor*

| Καίσαρα | N-AM-S | Καῖσαρ |

Καισάρεια, ας, ὁ (also **Καισαρία**)   *Caesarea*, name of a city; (1) on the Mediterranean coast of Palestine (AC 9.30); (2) *Caesarea Philippi*, at the foot of Mount Hermon (MT 16.13)

Καισαρεία	N-DF-S	Καισάρεια
Καισάρειαν	N-AF-S	"
Καισαρείας	N-GF-S	"
Καίσαρι	N-DM-S	Καῖσαρ
Καισαρία	N-DF-S	Καισάρεια
Καισαρίαν	N-AF-S	"
Καισαρίας	N-GF-S	"
Καίσαρος	N-GM-S	Καῖσαρ

καίτοι   from καί (*even*) and τοί (enclitic particle emphasizing reliability); concessive conjunction *and yet, although, even though*

| καίτοι | CH | καίτοι |
| | CS | " |

καίτοιγε   from καίτοι (*and yet*) and γέ (*even*); emphatic concessive conjunction *and yet, although indeed* (JN 4.2)

καίτοιγε	CS	καίτοιγε
Καϊάφα	N-GM-S	Καϊάφας
Καϊάφαν	N-AM-S	"
Καϊάφας	N-NM-S	"

καίω   pf. pass. κέκαυμαι; 1aor. pass. ἐκαύθην; 1fut. pass. καυθήσομαι; (1) active *light* something, *kindle, ignite* (MT 5.15); (2) passive *be lit, burn* (JN 15.6); figuratively, of fervent emotion *burn, have strong feelings* (LU 24.32); (3) of consuming by fire *burn (up)*; passive *be burned*; καυθήσομαι in 1C 13.3 is understood as either martyrdom or voluntary burning of oneself

κακά	A--AN-P	κακός
	A--NN-P	"
κακαί	A--NF-P	"

κἀκεῖ   an adverb contracted from καί (*and, also*) and ἐκεῖ (*there*); (1) as a connective conjunction *and there* (MT 5.23); (2) as an adjunctive *there also, there too* (AC 17.13)

| κἀκεῖ | AB&AB | κἀκεῖ |
| | CC&AB | " |

κἀκεῖθεν   an adverb contracted from καί (*and*) and ἐκεῖθεν (*from there*); (1) denoting extension of place *and from there, and from that place* (MK 9.30); (2) denoting extension of time *and then, and afterward* (AC 13.21)

κἀκεῖθεν	CC&AB	κἀκεῖθεν
	CH&AB	"
κἀκεῖνα	AB&APDAN-P	κἀκεῖνος
	CC&APDAN-P	"
	CC&APDNN-P	"
κἀκείνη	CC&APDNF-S	"
κἀκεῖνοι	AB&APDNM-P	"
	CC&APDNM-P	"
	CH&APDNM-P	"
κἀκείνοις	CC&APDDM-P	"
κἀκεῖνον	AB&APDAM-S	"
	CC&APDAM-S	"
	CH&APDAM-S	"

κἀκεῖνος, η, ο   a demonstrative pronoun contracted from καί (*and, also*) and ἐκεῖνος (*that*); (1) as a relatively distant demonstrative; (a) *and he, and that one* (LU 11.7); (b) adjunctively *he also, that one too* (AC 15.11); (2) as a relatively near demonstrative *and he, and this one* (MT 15.18); adjunctively *he also, that one too* (JN 14.12)

κἀκεῖνος	AB&APDNM-S	κἀκεῖνος
	CC&APDNM-S	"
	CH&APDNM-S	"
κἀκείνους	CC&APDAM-P	"

κἀκεῖσε an adverb contracted from καί (*and*) and ἐκεῖσε (*there*); *and there, and in that place* (AC 27.6)

κἀκεῖσε	CC&AB	κἀκεῖσε
κακήν	A--AF-S	κακός

κακία, ας, ἡ having the quality of κακός (*evil, bad*) *evil, badness*; (1) morally *depravity, vice, wickedness* (JA 1.21), opposite ἀρετή (*virtue*); (2) behaviorally *dislike, ill will, hatefulness* (TI 3.3), opposite κοινωνία (*fellowship*); (3) as adverse circumstances *evil, trouble, misfortune* (MT 6.34)

κακία	N-NF-S	κακία
κακίᾳ	N-DF-S	"
κακίαν	N-AF-S	"
κακίας	N-GF-S	"

κακοήθεια, ας, ἡ as a disposition for producing mischief *wickedness, malice, spitefulness* (RO 1.29)

κακοηθείας	N-GF-S	κακοήθεια
κακοί	A--NM-P	κακός
κακολάλους	AP-AM-P	see καταλάλους

κακολογέω 1aor. inf. κακολογῆσαι; as using unjustified and abusive language against someone or something *speak evil of, revile, denounce, insult* (MT 15.4; AC 19.9)

κακολογῆσαι	VNAA	κακολογέω
κακολογοῦντες	VPPANM-P	"
κακολογῶν	VPPANM-S	"
κακόν	A--AN-S	κακός
	A--NN-S	"
κακοπαθεῖ	VIPA--3S	κακοπαθέω

κακοπάθεια, ας, ἡ (1) passive, of evil circumstances coming on someone *suffering, affliction, misery* (perhaps JA 5.10); (2) active, of facing evil circumstances courageously *perseverance, endurance* (probably JA 5.10)

κακοπαθείας	N-GF-S	κακοπάθεια

κακοπαθέω 1aor. ἐκακοπάθησα; (1) passive *suffer trouble, misfortunes* or *afflictions* (2T 2.9); (2) active, as meeting hardships courageously *bear affliction, endure hardships* (2T 4.5)

κακοπάθησον	VMAA--2S	κακοπαθέω
κακοπαθῶ	VIPA--1S	"

κακοποιέω 1aor. ἐκακοποίησα; (1) *do wrong, be an evildoer* or *criminal* (1P 3.17; perhaps MK 3.4 and LU 6.9), opposite ἀγαθοποιέω (*do good*); (2) *cause harm to, hurt, injure* someone (probably MK 3.4 and LU 6.9)

κακοποιῆσαι	VNAA	κακοποιέω

κακοποιός, όν *doing evil, mischievous*; substantively *evildoer, criminal* (1P 2.12), opposite ἀγαθοποιός (*well-doer, one who does right*)

κακοποιός	AP-NM-S	κακοποιός
	A--NM-S	"
κακοποιοῦντας	VPPAAM-P	κακοποιέω
κακοποιοῦντες	VPPANM-P	"
κακοποιοῦσι(ν)	VIPA--3P	"
κακοποιῶν	AP-GM-P	κακοποιός
	VPPANM-S	κακοποιέω
κακοπονούμενοι	VPPPNM-P	see καταπονούμενοι

κακός, ή, όν basically, denoting a lack of something *bad, not as it ought to be*, opposite καλός (*sound, good*) and ἀγαθός (*good*); (1) morally, of persons characterized by godlessness *evil, bad* (MT 24.48); substantivally *evildoer* (RV 2.2); (2) as moral conduct, attitudes, plans of godless people *evil, base, wicked* (MK 7.21); (3) neuter as a substantive τὸ κακόν *evil* as being present in the world (RO 13.3); plural κακά *evil deeds* (RO 1.30); (4) of circumstances and conditions that come on a person *harmful, evil, injurious* (RV 16.2); substantively τὰ κακά *ruin, harm, misfortunes, evils* (LU 16.25); (5) as characterized by reprehensible lack of accuracy *wrong, incorrect* (JN 18.23)

κακός	A--NM-S	κακός
κακοῦ	A--GN-S	"
κακοῦργοι	AP-NM-P	κακοῦργος

κακοῦργος, ον *doing evil, villainous*; substantively *criminal, evildoer, villain* (LU 23.32)

κακοῦργος	AP-NM-S	κακοῦργος
κακούργους	AP-AM-P	"
κακούργων	AP-GM-P	"
κακούς	A--AM-P	κακός
κἀκούσασαι	CC&VPAANF-P	see καί and ἀκούω

κακουχέω *mistreat, torment, cause to suffer*; passive *be ill-treated, be tormented*

κακουχούμενοι	VPPPNM-P	κακουχέω
κακουχουμένων	VPPPGM-P	"

κακόω fut. κακώσω; 1aor. ἐκάκωσα; (1) physically *harm, mistreat, ill-treat* (AC 7.6); (2) morally *embitter, poison* someone's mind against, *turn* someone against (AC 14.2)

κακῷ	A--DN-S	κακός
κακῶν	A--GM-P	"
	A--GN-P	"

κακῶς adverb; *badly*; (1) physically *severely* (MT 21.41); idiomatically κ. ἔχειν literally *have badly*, i.e. *be ill, be sick* (MT 4.24); (2) morally, of a manner of speaking *wrongly, incorrectly, with wrong motives* (JN 18.23)

κακῶς	AB	κακῶς
κακῶσαι	VNAA	κακόω
κάκωσιν	N-AF-S	κάκωσις

κάκωσις, εως, ἡ as an action of abuse or ill usage *mistreatment, affliction, oppression* (AC 7.34)

κακώσουσι(ν)	VIFA--3P	κακόω
κακώσων	VPFANM-S	"
καλά	A--AN-P	καλός
	A--NN-P	"

καλάμη, ης, ἡ as building material for thatching roofs *straw, stalk(s)* (1C 3.12)

καλάμην	N-AF-S	καλάμη
κάλαμον	N-AM-S	κάλαμος

κάλαμος, ου, ὁ as the (dried) stalk of tall plants; (1) *reed* (LU 7.24); (2) *staff* (MT 27.29); (3) *measuring stick, rod* (RV 11.1); (4) as an writing instrument *reed pen* (3J 13)

κάλαμος	N-NM-S	κάλαμος
καλάμου	N-GM-S	"
καλάμῳ	N-DM-S	"
κάλει	VMPA--2S	καλέω
καλεῖ	VIPA--3S	"
καλεῖν	VNPA	"

καλεῖσθαι	VNPP	"
καλεῖται	VIPP--3S	"
καλεῖτε	VIPA--2P	"
	VMPA--2P	"
καλέσαι	VNAA	"
καλέσαντα	VPAAAM-S	"
καλέσαντες	VPAANM-P	"
καλέσαντι	VPAADM-S	"
καλέσαντος	VPAAGM-S	"
καλέσας	VPAANM-S	"
καλέσατε	VMAA--2P	"
καλέσεις	VIFA--2S	"
	VIFA--2S^VMAA--2S	"
καλέσητε	VSAA--2P	"
κάλεσον	VMAA--2S	"
καλέσουσι(ν)	VIFA--3P	"
καλέσω	VIFA--1S	"

καλέω impf. ἐκάλουν; fut. καλέσω; 1aor. ἐκάλεσα; pf. κέκληκα; pf. pass. κέκλημαι; 1aor. pass. ἐκλήθην; *call*, with nuances of meaning varying with the context; (1) *call*; (a) *name, provide with a name*, with a double accusative (LU 1.59); passive *have as a name, be called* (LU 1.61); (b) *address as, designate, call*, with a double accusative (LU 6.46); (c) of an invitation *call to, invite* (MT 22.3); (d) of a summons, often with a legal sense *call in, summon, call together* (MT 2.7; AC 4.18); (2) figuratively; (a) of God's invitation to salvation or summons to discipleship *call* (MT 4.21; 1P 2.9); (b) of an appointment to a task *call* (HE 5.4)

καλῇ	A--DF-S	καλός
καλήν	A--AF-S	"
καλῆς	A--GF-S	"
καλλιέλαιον	N-AF-S	καλλιέλαιος

καλλιέλαιος, ου, ἡ *cultivated olive tree, garden olive* (RO 11.24), opposite ἀγριέλαιος (*wild olive tree*)

κάλλιον	ABM	καλός
κάλλιστα	A-SAN-P	"

καλοδιδάσκαλος, ον *teaching what is good, teaching right behavior* (TI 2.3)

καλοδιδασκάλους	A--AF-P	καλοδιδάσκαλος
καλοί	A--NM-P	καλός

Καλοὶ Λιμένες, οἱ from καλός and λιμήν; *Fair Havens*, a bay on the southern coast of the island of Crete in the Mediterranean Sea (AC 27.8)

καλοῖς	A--DM-P	καλός
	A--DN-P	"

καλοκἀγαθία, ας, ἡ contracted from καλός καὶ ἀγαθός; *excellence of character, nobility and goodness* (JA 5.10)

καλοκἀγαθίας	N-GF-S	καλοκἀγαθία
καλόν	A--AM-S	καλός
	A--AN-S	"
	A--NN-S	"

καλοποιέω *do what is right, do well* (2TH 3.13)

καλοποιοῦντες	VPPANM-P	καλοποιέω

καλός, ή, όν *good, beautiful*, with a basic meaning *healthy, sound, fit*, opposite κακός (*bad, evil*) and αἰσχρός (*ugly, deformed*); (1) of outward appearance *handsome, beautiful, lovely* (LU 21.5); (2) as a quality of freedom from defects *good, useful, fine* (MT 13.8; possibly MK 9.50); neuter as a substantive τὸ καλόν *good thing* (possibly MK 9.50); (3) of a sound moral disposition *good, noble,*

praiseworthy, synonymous with ἀγαθός (RO 7.18); of things *excellent*; substantivally τὸ καλόν *what is good, what passes the test* (1TH 5.21); (4) socially, of a mode of life and behavior, especially as καλὰ ἔργα *good works* (1T 5.10); (5) impersonally καλόν (ἐστιν) *it is good, expedient* or *advantageous* (MT 17.4); *it is (morally) good* (MT 15.26); *it is better* (MT 26.24); (6) comparative καλλίων, κάλλιον *better, more beautiful*; neuter singular as an adverb *very well* (AC 25.10); (7) superlative κάλλιστος, ίστη, ον *very beautiful*; substantivally τὰ κάλλιστα *the really good ones* (MT 13.48)

καλός	A--NM-S	καλός
καλοῦ	A--GN-S	"
καλουμένη	VPPPNF-S	καλέω
καλουμένη	VPPPDF-S	"
καλουμένην	VPPPAF-S	"
καλουμένης	VPPPGF-S	"
καλούμενον	VPPPAM-S	"
	VPPPAN-S	"
καλούμενος	VPPPNM-S	"
καλουμένου	VPPPGM-S	"
	VPPPGN-S	"
καλοῦνται	VIPM--3P	"
	VIPP--3P	"
καλοῦντες	VPPANM-P	"
καλοῦντος	VPPAGM-S	"
Καλούς	A--AM-P	Καλοὶ Λιμένες
καλούς	A--AM-P	καλός
καλοῦσα	VPPANF-S	καλέω
καλοῦσι(ν)	VIPA--3S	"

κάλυμμα, ατος, τό literally, a piece of thin cloth worn over the head or face *head-covering, veil* (2C 3.13); figuratively, of mental or spiritual hindrance to understanding (2C 3.14)

κάλυμμα	N-AN-S	κάλυμμα
	N-NN-S	"
καλύπτει	VIPA--3S	καλύπτω
καλύπτεσθαι	VNPP	"

καλύπτω fut. καλύψω; 1aor. ἐκάλυψα; pf. pass. κεκάλυμμαι; literally, as removing from view *conceal, hide, cover* (MT 8.24); *bury, cover up* (LU 23.30); figuratively, as preventing spiritual comprehension *keep secret, hide*; passive *be hidden* (2C 4.3); as showing a kind attitude toward the failures of others *conceal, keep secret* (JA 5.20; 1P 4.8)

καλύψατε	VMAA--2P	καλύπτω
καλύψει	VIFA--3S	"
καλῶ	VIPA--1S	καλέω
καλῷ	A--DN-S	καλός
καλῶν	A--GN-P	"
	VPPANM-S	καλέω

καλῶς adverb; *beautifully, well*; (1) of things done in the right way *fitly, well, appropriately* (1C 14.17); (2) in a moral sense *commendably, honorably, well* (HE 13.18); (3) of behavior *rightly, correctly, well* (MK 12.28; 3J 6); (4) as an exclamation expressing a positive evaluation *well said! quite right! that is true!* (RO 11.20); (5) idiomatically κ. ἔχειν literally *have well*, i.e. *be in good health, be well* (MK 16.18); (6) as acting beneficially κ. ποιεῖν *do good* (MT 12.12); (7) as characterized by value of importance *in a good place* (possibly JA 2.3); (8) as making a polite request *please!* (possibly JA 2.3)

καλῶς	AB	καλῶς
κάμέ	AB&NPA-1S	κάγώ
	CC&NPA-1S	"
κάμηλον	N-AF-S	κάμηλος

κάμηλος, ου, ὁ and ἡ *camel* (MT 3.4); proverbially in MT 19.24; 23.24

κάμηλος	N-NM-S	κάμηλος
καμήλου	N-GF-S	"
κάμητε	VSAA--2P	κάμνω
κάμιλον	N-AM-S	κάμιλος

κάμιλος, ου, ὁ *rope, ship's cable* (MT 19.24; MK 10.25; LU 18.25)

| κάμινον | N-AF-S | κάμινος |

κάμινος, ου, ἡ literally *oven, furnace, kiln* (RV 1.15); figuratively, of hell κ. τοῦ πυρός *fiery furnace* (MT 13.42)

| καμίνου | N-GF-S | κάμινος |
| καμίνῳ | N-DF-S | " |

καμμύω 1aor. ἐκάμμυσα; *shut, close*; idiomatically καμμύειν τοὺς ὀφθαλμούς literally *shut the eyes*, i.e. *refuse to learn, fail to acknowledge* (MT 13.15)

| κάμνοντα | VPPAAM-S | κάμνω |

κάμνω 2aor. ἔκαμον; *be weary*; idiomatically κάμνειν τῇ φυχῃ literally *be weary in soul*, i.e. *be discouraged* (HE 12.3); *be sick* or *ill* (JA 5.15)

κάμοί	AB&NPD-1S	κάγώ
	CC&NPD-1S	"
	CH&NPD-1S	"

κάμπτω fut. κάμψω; 1aor. ἔκαμψα; a Hebrew idiom meaning *worship*; (1) transitively, with γόνυ as the object *bend, bow the knee* (RO 11.4); (2) intransitively, with γόνυ as the subject *bend, bow down* (RO 14.11)

κάμπτω	VIPA--1S	κάμπτω
κάμψει	VIFA--3S	"
κάμψῃ	VSAA--3S	"

κἄν contracted from καί (*and, also*) and ἐάν (*if*); (1) to coordinate conditions *and if, but if* (JN 8.55); *whether . . . whether* (LU 12.38); (2) adverbially, to add ascensive force *even if, even though* (JN 10.38); (3) as a particle of emphasis by adding redundancy to ἄν (particle indicating contingency) *at least, at all events* (MK 5.28; AC 5.15)

κἄν	AB&CS	κἄν
	AB&QV	"
	CC&CS	"

Κανά, ἡ (also Κανᾶ) usually indeclinable; *Cana*, a city of Galilee

Κανᾶ		Κανά
Κανᾷ	N-DF-S	"
Κανααν		Χανάαν
Καναναῖον	N-AM-S	Καναναῖος

Καναναῖος, ου, ὁ *Cananaean*, surname of Simon, one of the apostles, meaning in Aramaic *zealot, enthusiast*; cf. ζηλωτής (*zealot, nationalist*) in LU 6.15 and AC 1.13

| Καναναῖος | N-NM-S | Καναναῖος |
| Κανανίτην | N-AM-S | Κανανίτης |

Κανανίτης, ου, ὁ *Cananite, man from Cana* (MT 10.4; MK 3.18)

| Κανανίτης | N-NM-S | Κανανίτης |

Κανδάκη, ης, ἡ *Candace*, feminine proper noun; interpreted by some as a title for the queen of Ethiopia *the Candace* (AC 8.27)

Κανδάκης	N-GF-S	Κανδάκη
κανόνα	N-AM-S	κανών
κανόνι	N-DM-S	"

κανονίζω 1aor. ἐκανόνισα; from κανών (*measure, norm*); *canonize, declare valid, recognize as part of biblical canon with the authority of divinely revealed truth* (MK 16 shorter ending)

| κανόνος | N-GM-S | κανών |

κανών, όνος, ὁ from the Hebrew for *cane* or *reed*; (1) literally *measuring rod* or *rule*; figuratively, as a measure of assessment of a prescribed norm of action or duty *standard, rule, principle* (GA 6.16); (2) as a sphere of activity or influence *area, limits* (2C 10.13–16)

| Καπερναούμ | | Καφαρναούμ |
| καπηλεύοντες | VPPANM-P | καπηλεύω |

καπηλεύω literally, of a petty retail merchant who sells deceitfully *hawk, peddle, be a huckster*; figuratively in 2C 2.17 of (a) peddling the gospel message for personal gain or (b) adulterating the gospel (so-called from the tricks of hucksters)

| καπνόν | N-AM-S | καπνός |

καπνός, οῦ, ὁ as the visible vapors or fumes given off by something burning or smoldering *smoke*

| καπνός | N-NM-S | καπνός |
| καπνοῦ | N-GM-S | " |

Καππαδοκία, ας, ἡ *Cappadocia*, a province in the interior of Asia Minor

| Καππαδοκίαν | N-AF-S | Καππαδοκία |
| Καππαδοκίας | N-GF-S | " |

καραδοκία, ας, ἡ strictly *watching with head outstretched*; hence *eager expectation* (PH 1.20)

| καραδοκίαν | N-AF-S | καραδοκία |

καρδία, ας, ἡ *heart*; in the NT *inner self*; (1) viewed as the seat of physical vitality (AC 14.17); (2) viewed as the innermost self, the source and seat of functions of soul and spirit in the emotional life (AC 2.26), the volitional life (2C 9.7), the rational life (AC 7.23); (3) viewed as the human dwelling place of heavenly beings and powers (RO 5.5; 2C 1.22; EP 3.17); (4) figuratively, of the depths of the earth *interior, center* (MT 12.40)

καρδία	N-NF-S	καρδία
καρδίᾳ	N-DF-S	"
καρδίαι	N-NF-P	"
καρδίαις	N-DF-P	"
καρδίαν	N-AF-S	"
καρδίας	N-AF-P	"
	N-GF-S	"
καρδιογνῶστα	N-VM-S	καρδιογνώστης

καρδιογνώστης, ου, ὁ *one who knows what people are thinking about, one who knows the heart, searcher of hearts*

καρδιογνώστης	N-NM-S	καρδιογνώστης
καρδιῶν	N-GF-P	καρδία
καρπόν	N-AM-S	καρπός

Κάρπος, οῦ, ὁ *Carpus*, masculine proper noun (2T 4.13)

καρπός, οῦ, ὁ (1) literally *fruit*; (a) of the produce of trees and vines *fruit* (MK 11.14); (b) of the produce of a field *crop, harvest* (MK 4.29); (2) figuratively *outcome, product*; (a) idiomatically, as the result of procreation, of the role of the mother κ. τῆς κοιλίας literally *fruit of the womb*, i.e. *child, baby* (LU 1.42); of the role of the father κ. τῆς ὀσφύος literally *fruit of the genitals*, i.e. *offspring, descendant* (AC 2.30); (b) as the result of words or actions *outcome, consequence* (HE 12.11); (c) as the working out of a matter to a good outcome *advantage, gain, profit* (PH 4.17)

καρπός	N-NM-S	καρπός
καρποῦ	N-GM-S	"
καρπούς	N-AM-P	"
καρποφορεῖ	VIPA--3S	καρποφορέω

καρποφορέω 1aor. ἐκαρποφόρησα; (1) literally *bear fruit* or *crops* (MK 4.28); (2) figuratively; (a) of the outcome in behavior from righteousness or evil in the inner life *cause results* (CO 1.10); (b) middle, of the effect of the gospel *be effective, bring about good results* (CO 1.6)

καρποφορῆσαι	VNAA	καρποφορέω
καρποφορήσωμεν	VSAA--1P	"
καρποφόρον	A--AN-S	καρποφόρος

καρποφόρος, ον *fruit-bearing, fruitful* (AC 14.17); neuter as a substantive, of a fruit tree branch τὸ καρποφόρον *the fruit-bearing one* (JN 15.2)

καρποφορούμενον	VPPMNN-S	καρποφορέω
καρποφοροῦντες	VPPANM-P	"
καρποφόρους	A--AM-P	καρποφόρος
καρποφοροῦσι(ν)	VIPA--3P	καρποφορέω
Κάρπῳ	N-DM-S	Κάρπος
καρπῶν	N-GM-P	καρπός
Καρράν		Χαρράν

καρτερέω 1aor. ἐκαρτέρησα; from κράτος (*strong*); *endure patiently, persevere, persist* (HE 11.27)

Καρυώτος, ου, ὁ *Carioth* or *Kerioth*, a place in southern Judea (JN 6.71; 13.2)

Καρυώτου	N-GM-S	Καρυώτος

κάρφος, ους, τό any small dry piece of straw, wood, etc. *speck, splinter, chaff*

κάρφος	N-AN-S	κάρφος
κατ'	PA	κατά
	PG	"

κατά preposition; generally downward movement; **I.** with the genitive; (1) of place; (a) *down from* (MK 5.13); figuratively *down into*; ἡ κ. βάθους πτωχεία *extreme poverty* (2C 8.2); (b) *throughout* (LU 4.14); (2) figuratively, with verbs of oath-taking *by* (MT 26.63); (3) figuratively, in a hostile sense *against* (1P 2.11); **II.** with the accusative; (1) of place; (a) as showing extension in space *on, through, over, (down) along* (LU 8.4; 10.4); (b) as indicating direction *toward, to, down to* (LU 10.32); (c) as indicating isolation or separation καθ' ἑαυτόν *by oneself* (AC 28.16); κ. μόνος *alone, by oneself* (MK 4.10); *in* (a separated place) (RO 16.5); (d) as a distributive *from* (place) *to* (place) (AC 5.42); *in every single* (place) (AC 15.21; TI 1.5); (2) of time; (a) as indicating the time within the range of which something takes place *during* (HE 3.8); *at* (AC 12.1), *in* (HE 1.10); *in agreement with* (MT 2.16); (b) as indicating indefinite time *toward, about* (AC 16.25); (c) distributively *every* καθ' ἡμέραν *daily* (MT 26.55); κ. πᾶν σάββατον *weekly* (AC 13.27); κ. μῆνα *monthly* (RV 22.2); κατ' ἔτος *annually* (LU 2.41); (3) distributively, with numerals: καθ' ἓν ἕκαστον *one by one, in detail* (AC 21.19), κ. δύο ἢ τρεῖς *two* or *three at a time* (1C 14.27), εἷς κ. εἷς *one after the other* (MK 14.19), etc.; (4) to indicate goal or purpose *for the purpose of, to, for* (JN 2.6); (5) to indicate standard or norm *in agreement with, corresponding to, in conformity with* (MT 9.29; 16.27; LU 1.38); (6) to indicate reason *because of, in accordance with* (EP 3.3); *on the basis of, as a result of* (MT 19.3; EP 1.5); (7) to denote relationship to something; (a) *in respect to, in relation to* (RO 1.3, 4); (b) with the κ. phrase qualifying like an adjective (EP 6.5); showing possession like a pronoun (AC 17.28) or a noun (AC 26.3)

κατά	PA	κατά
	PG	
καταβά	VMAA--2S	καταβαίνω
καταβαίνει	VIPA--3S	"
καταβαίνειν	VNPA	"
καταβαινέτω	VMPA--3S	"
καταβαίνῃ	VSPA--3S	"
καταβαῖνον	VPPAAN-S	"
	VPPANN-S	"
καταβαίνοντα	VPPAAM-S	"
καταβαίνοντας	VPPAAM-P	"
καταβαίνοντες	VPPANM-P	"
καταβαίνοντος	VPPAGM-S	"
	VPPAGN-S	"
καταβαινόντων	VPPAGM-P	"
καταβαίνουσα	VPPANF-S	"
καταβαίνουσαν	VPPAAF-S	"
καταβαινούσης	VPPAGF-S	"

καταβαίνω impf. κατέβαινον; fut. mid. καταβήσομαι; 2aor. κατέβην; pf. καταβέβηκα; with a basic meaning *step down*; (1) literally; (a) of persons *come down, go down, climb down, descend* (MT 27.40); from a boat *get out, disembark* (MT 14.29); (b) of things *come down* (AC 10.11); of a storm *come down, descend on* (LU 8.23); of a fire *fall down, come down* (LU 9.54); of a road *lead down, go down* (AC 8.26); (2) figuratively, of a ruinous downfall *fall*; passive *be brought down* (MT 11.23)

καταβαίνων	VPPANM-S	καταβαίνω
καταβαλλόμενοι	VPPMNM-P	καταβάλλω
	VPPPNM-P	"

καταβάλλω only middle/passive in the NT; (1) active *throw down, cast down, strike down*; figuratively and passive *be cast down, be struck down* (2C 4.9); (2) middle *lay* (a foundation), *found*; figuratively, of a spiritual foundation *put down, lay* (HE 6.1)

καταβάν	VPAAAN-S	καταβαίνω
καταβάντες	VPAANM-P	"
καταβάντι	VPAADM-S	"
καταβάντος	VPAAGM-S	"

καταβαπτίζω 1aor. κατεβάπτισα; *dip down* or *into, wash* (MK 7.4)

καταβαπτίσωνται	VSAM-3P	καταβαπτίζω

καταβαρέω 1aor. κατεβάρησα; strictly *weigh down*; hence *overburden, be a burden to* someone (2C 12.16)

καταβαρούμενοι	VPPPNM-P	καταβαρέω
καταβαρυνόμενοι	VPPPNM-P	καταβαρύνω

καταβαρύνω   *weigh down, burden, overload*; passive and idiomatically ἦσαν αὐτῶν οἱ ὀφθαλμοὶ καταβαρυνόμενοι literally *their eyes were very heavy*, i.e. *they were very sleepy* (MK 14.40)

καταβάς	VPAANM-S	καταβαίνω
καταβάσει	N-DF-S	κατάβασις

κατάβασις, εως, ἡ   as a place for descending *descent, downward road, slope* (LU 19.37)

καταβάτω	VMAA--3S	καταβαίνω
καταβέβηκα	VIRA--1S	"
καταβεβηκέναι	VNRA	"
καταβεβηκότες	VPRANM-P	"
καταβῇ	VSAA--3S	"
κατάβηθι	VMAA--2S	"
καταβῆναι	VNAA	"
καταβήσεται	VIFD--3S	"
καταβήσῃ	VIFD--2S	"

καταβιβάζω   1aor. κατεβίβασα; 1aor. pass. κατεβιβάσθην; 1fut. pass. καταβιβασθήσομαι; literally *make someone come down, bring* or *drive down* (AC 19.33); figuratively and passive, of a ruinous downfall *be brought down* (MT 11.23; LU 10.15)

καταβιβασθεῖσα	VPAPNF-S	καταβιβάζω
καταβιβασθήσῃ	VIFP-2S	"

καταβοάω   *cry out* or *complain (against), shout down* (AC 18.13)

καταβολή, ῆς, ἡ   (1) strictly *casting down*; hence *foundation, beginning* (MT 25.34); (2) as a technical term for putting seed into the ground, it is also used of the role of the male in impregnating the female; δύναμιν εἰς καταβολήν in HE 11.11 is best understood by the context and continuation of the subject to refer to the sexual function of the male in the sense *receive strength to become a father*; the phrase καὶ αὐτὴ Σάρρα στεῖρα (*Sarah herself also (was) barren*) is then taken as parenthetical

καταβολήν	N-AF-S	καταβολή
καταβολῆς	N-GF-S	"
καταβοῶντες	VPPANM-P	καταβοάω
καταβραβευέτω	VMPA-3S	καταβραβεύω

καταβραβεύω   literally, of an umpire *decide against, rob of a prize*; figuratively, of depriving of a spiritual reward *disqualify, judge unworthy* (CO 2.18)

καταγαγεῖν	VNAA	κατάγω
καταγάγῃ	VSAA--3S	"
καταγάγῃς	VSAA--2S	"
καταγαγόντες	VPAANM-P	"
καταγαγών	VPAANM-S	"

καταγγελεύς, έως, ὁ   literally, one who makes a solemn announcement *herald, proclaimer*; figuratively, one on a divine mission *proclaimer, preacher* (AC 17.18)

καταγγελεύς	N-NM-S	καταγγελεύς
καταγγέλλειν	VNPA	καταγγέλλω
καταγγέλλεται	VIPP-3S	"
καταγγέλλετε	VIPA--2P	"
καταγγέλλομεν	VIPA--1P	"
καταγγέλλουσι(ν)	VIPA--3P	"
	VPPADM-P	"

καταγγέλλω   impf. κατήγγελλον; 1aor. κατήγγειλα; 2aor. pass. κατηγγέλην; used of solemn religious messages; (1) *proclaim (solemnly), announce* something (AC 4.2); (2) *proclaim, tell about* someone (PH 1.17)

καταγγέλλω	VIPA--1S	καταγγέλλω
καταγγέλλων	VPPANM-S	"
καταγγελομένη	VPPPNF-S	"
καταγεινώσκη	VSPA--3S	see καταγινώσκη

καταγελάω   impf. κατεγέλων; *laugh at, ridicule, scornfully mock*

καταγινώσκει	VIPA--3S	καταγινώσκω
καταγινώσκῃ	VSPA--3S	"

καταγινώσκω   pf. pass. ptc. κατεγνωσμένος; as denoting accurate detection of evil in oneself (1J 3.20) or someone else (GA 2.11) *condemn, declare to be wrong, judge to be guilty*

καταγινώσκω	VSPA--1S	καταγινώσκω

κατάγνυμι   fut. κατεάξω; 1aor. κατέαξα; 2aor. pass. κατεάγην; *break off* or *in two* (MT 12.20); of the legs *break* (JN 19.31)

καταγράφω   impf. κατέγραφον; of emphasized, firm writing or drawing *write, draw*

κατάγω   2aor. κατήγαγον; 1aor. pass. κατήχθην; *lead* or *bring* down; geographically, to a (destination of a) lower elevation (AC 9.30); passive, as a nautical technical term, of ships and seafarers *land (at), put in (at)* (AC 27.3)

καταγωνίζομαι   1aor. κατηγωνισάμην; *defeat, conquer, overcome* (HE 11.33)

καταδέω   1aor. κατέδησα; *bind down*; of a wound *bandage* (LU 10.34)

κατάδηλον	A--NN-S	κατάδηλος

κατάδηλος, ον   *very clear, quite evident, easy to understand* (HE 7.15)

καταδικάζετε	VMPA--2P	καταδικάζω

καταδικάζω   1aor. κατεδίκασα; 1aor. pass. κατεδικάσθην; as a legal technical term *condemn, give judgment against, declare guilty*

καταδικασθήσει	VIFP--2S	see καταδικασθήσῃ
καταδικασθήσῃ	VIFP--2S	καταδικάζω
καταδικασθῆτε	VSAP--2P	"

καταδίκη, ης, ἡ   as a judicial sentence *condemnation, judgment against* someone (AC 25.15)

καταδίκην	N-AF-S	καταδίκη

καταδιώκω   1aor. κατεδίωξα; *search for (eagerly), track down, hunt for* someone (MK 1.36)

καταδουλοῖ	VIPA--3S	καταδουλόω

καταδουλόω   *make a slave of* someone, *enslave*; figuratively, of imposing control over someone for one's own ends *make subservient* (2C 11.20)

καταδουλώσουσι(ν)	VIFA--3P	καταδουλόω
καταδουλώσωνται	VSAM--3P	"
καταδυναστευομένους	VPPPAM-P	καταδυναστεύω
καταδυναστεύουσι(ν)	VIPA--3P	"

καταδυναστεύω   (1) denoting domination of the poor by the rich *oppress, exploit* (JA 2.6); (2) passive, of being under the devil's tyrannical power *be oppressed* (AC 10.38)

κατάθεμα, ατος, τό   as something that has been delivered over to divine wrath *accursed thing, anything accursed*

κατάθεμα	N-NN-S	κατάθεμα

καταθεματίζειν VNPA καταθεματίζω
καταθεματίζω *curse, call down curses*
καταθέσθαι VNAM κατατίθημι
καταισχύνει VIPA--3S καταισχύνω
καταισχύνετε VIPA--2P "
καταισχύνη VSPA--3S "
καταισχυνθῇ VSAP--3S "
καταισχυνθήσεται VIFP--3S "
καταισχυνθήσῃ VIFP--2S "
καταισχυνθῶμεν VSAP--1P "
καταισχυνθῶσι(ν) VSAP--3P "
καταισχύνω impf. pass. κατῃσχυνόμην; 1aor. pass.
κατῃσχύνθην; 1fut. pass. καταισχυνθήσομαι; (1) to denote adverse influence *bring to shame, disgrace, dishonor* (1C 11.4); (2) to denote unkind behavior *humiliate, put to shame* (1C 11.22); passive, of being shown
up as unkind *be shamed by* (1P 3.16); (3) to denote failure of expectation *disappoint, disillusion* (RO 5.5); passive *be disappointed, be embarrassed* (RO 9.33)
κατακαήσεται VIFP--3S κατακαίω
κατακαήσονται VIFP--3P "
κατακαίεται VIPP--3S "
κατακαίονται VIPP--3P "
κατακαίω impf. κατέκαιον; fut. κατακαύσω; 1aor.
κατέκαυσα; 2aor. pass. κατεκάην; 1fut. pass. κατακαυ-
θήσομαι; 2fut. pass. κατακαήσομαι; *destroy by fire, burn
(up), consume by fire*
κατακαλύπτεσθαι VNPM κατακαλύπτω
κατακαλυπτέσθω VMPM--3S "
κατακαλύπτεται VIPM--3S "
κατακαλύπτω (1) active *cover, veil*; (2) middle in the NT,
of covering one's head with a veil *veil oneself, wear a
veil*
κατακαυθήσεται VIFP--3S κατακαίω
κατακαῦσαι VNAA "
κατακαύσει VIFA--3S "
κατακαύσουσι(ν) VIFA--3P "
κατακαυχάομαι (1) as expressing a feeling of one's comparative superiority *boast against, exult over* (RO
11.18a); absolutely *boast, brag, look down on* (RO
11.18b; JA 3.14); (2) as expressing what is better or
victorious *triumph over, win out over, be more powerful
than* (JA 2.13)
κατακαυχᾶσαι VIPD--2S κατακαυχάομαι
 VIPO--2S "
κατακαυχᾶσθε VIPD--2P "
 VIPO--2P "
 VMPD--2P "
 VMPO--2P "
κατακαυχάσθω VMPD--3S "
 VMPO--3S "
κατακαυχᾶται VIPD--3S "
 VIPO--3S "
κατακαυχῶ VMPD--2S "
 VMPO--2S "
κατάκειμαι impf. κατεκείμην; *lie down*; (1) of someone
sick *lie* (MK 1.30); (2) of someone reclining on a couch
for a meal *recline, dine, eat a meal* (MK 2.15)
κατακείμενοι VPPDNM-P κατάκειμαι
 VPPONM-P "

κατακείμενον VPPDAM-S "
 VPPDNN-S "
 VPPOAM-S "
 VPPONN-S "
κατακειμένου VPPDGM-S "
 VPPOGM-S "
κατακεῖσθαι VNPD "
 VNPO "
κατάκειται VIPD--3S "
 VIPO--3S "
κατακεκλεισμένοις VPRPDN-P κατακλείω
κατακέκριται VIRP--3S κατακρίνω
κατακλάω 1aor. κατέκλασα; *break off*; of bread *break in
pieces*
κατακλεισμένοις VPRPDN-P see κατακεκλεισμένοις
κατακλείω 1aor. κατέκλεισα; pf. pass. κατακέκλεισμαι; of
prisoners *shut up, lock up, put in prison* (LU 3.20)
κατακληροδοτέω 1aor. κατεκληροδότησα; *parcel out by lot*
(AC 13.19)
κατακληρονομέω 1aor. κατεκληρονόμησα; from κατά
κλῆρος νέμω (*distribute by lot*); *give (over) in possession, give as an inheritance; divide out* something *valuable* (AC 13.19)
κατακλιθῆναι VNAP κατακλίνω
κατακλιθῇς VSAP--2S "
κατακλίνατε VMAA--2P "
κατακλίνω 1aor. κατέκλινα; 1aor. pass. κατεκλίθην; active
make to sit down or *recline to eat* (LU 9.14); passive *recline at table, sit down to eat* (LU 7.36)
κατακλύζω 1aor. pass. κατεκλύσθην; *flood, overwhelm*
or *deluge with water* (2P 3.6)
κατακλυσθείς VPAPNM-S κατακλύζω
κατακλυσμόν N-AM-S κατακλυσμός
κατακλυσμός, οῦ, ὁ *flood, inundation, deluge*
κατακλυσμός N-NM-S κατακλυσμός
κατακλυσμοῦ N-GM-S "
κατακολουθέω 1aor. κατηκολούθησα; *follow* someone
closely or *earnestly, come along behind*
κατακολουθήσασα VPAANF-S κατακολουθέω
κατακολουθήσασαι VPAANF-P "
κατακολουθοῦσα VPPANF-S "
κατακόπτω *break* or *cut in pieces*; of inflicting hurt with
stones *cut, bruise* (MK 5.5)
κατακόπτων VPPANM-S κατακόπτω
κατακρημνίζω 1aor. κατεκρήμνισα; *throw down from a
cliff, cast down headlong* (LU 4.29)
κατακρημνίσαι VNAA κατακρημνίζω
κατακριθείς VPAPNM-S κατακρίνω
κατακριθήσεται VIFP--3S "
κατακριθῆτε VSAP--2P "
κατακριθῶμεν VSAP--1P "
κατάκριμα, ατος, τό as a legal technical term for the result of judging, including both the sentence and its execution *condemnation, sentence of doom, punishment*
κατάκριμα N-AN-S κατάκριμα
 N-NN-S "
κατακρινεῖ VIFA--3S κατακρίνω
κατακρίνεις VIPA--2S "
κατακρίνῃ VSPA--3S "
κατακρινοῦσι(ν) VIFA--3P "

κατακρίνω   fut. κατακρινῶ; 1aor. κατέκρινα; pf. pass. κατακέκριμαι; 1aor. pass. κατεκρίθην; 1fut. pass. κατακριθήσομαι; as a legal technical term for pronouncing a sentence *condemn, pronounce judgment on*

κατακρίνω	VIPA--1S	κατακρίνω
κατακρινῶν	VPFANM-S	"
	VPPANM-S	"
κατακρίσεως	N-GF-S	κατάκρισις
κατάκρισιν	N-AF-S	"

κατάκρισις, εως, ἡ   as an action *condemnation* (2C 3.9); πρὸς κατάκρισιν οὐ λέγω *I do not say (this) to condemn, blame someone* (2C 7.3)

κατακύπτω   1aor. κατέκυψα; *bend* or *stoop down, bend over* (JN 8.8)

κατακυριεύοντες	VPPANM-P	κατακυριεύω
κατακυριεύουσι(ν)	VIPA--3P	"
κατακυρίευσαν	VPAANN-S	"
κατακυριεύσας	VPAANM-S	"

κατακυριεύω   1aor. κατεκυρίευσα; (1) *gain power over, overpower, subdue* (AC 19.16); (2) of exercising dominion for one's own advantage *lord it over, rule over, domineer over* (MK 10.42)

κατακύψας	VPAANM-S	κατακύπτω
καταλαβέσθαι	VNAM	καταλαμβάνω
καταλάβῃ	VSAA--3S	"
καταλάβητε	VSAA--2P	"
καταλαβόμενοι	VPAMNM-P	"
καταλαβόμενος	VPAMNM-S	"
καταλάβω	VSAA--1S	"
καταλαλεῖ	VIPA--3S	καταλαλέω
καταλαλεῖσθε	VIPP--2P	"
καταλαλεῖτε	VMPA--2P	"

καταλαλέω   as expressing hostility in speaking *speak (evil) against, slander, revile*

καταλαλιά, ᾶς, ἡ   as hostile speech *evil report, slander, disparagement*

καταλαλιαί	N-NF-P	καταλαλιά
καταλαλιάν	N-AF-S	"
καταλαλιάς	N-AF-P	"

κατάλαλος, ον   of one who spreads evil reports *slanderous, evil speaking*; substantively *slanderer* (RO 1.30)

καταλάλους	AP-AM-P	κατάλαλος
καταλαλοῦσι(ν)	VIPA--3P	καταλαλέω
καταλαλῶν	VPPANM-S	"
καταλαλῶσι(ν)	VSAP--3P	"
καταλαμβάνομαι	VIPM--1S	καταλαμβάνω

καταλαμβάνω   2aor. κατέλαβον; pf. κατείληφα; pf. pass. κατείλημμαι; 1aor. pass. κατελήμφθην; (1) with κατά adding intensity *seize, grasp with force* (MK 9.18); *overpower, gain control over* (possibly JN 1.5); (2) with κατά adding suddenness *catch, overtake, come on* (1TH 5.4); (3) with κατά adding certainty to possession *attain, win, make one's own* (PH 3.12b); (4) middle, of intellectual appropriation *find out about, comprehend, understand* (AC 4.13; perhaps JN 1.5 as active with a middle sense)

καταλεγέσθω	VMPP--3S	καταλέγω

καταλέγω   denoting selection and acceptance as a member of a group; of soldiers *enlist, enroll*; of elderly widows who need and qualify for support *select, enroll, put on the list* (1T 5.9)

κατάλειμμα, ατος, τό   as what has been left behind *remains, residue*; of persons *survivors* (RO 9.27)

κατάλειμμα	N-NN-S	κατάλειμμα
καταλείπει	VIPA--3S	καταλείπω
καταλείπεται	VIPP--3S	"
καταλειπομένης	VPPPGF-S	"
καταλείποντες	VPPANM-P	"

καταλείπω   impf. κατέλειπον; fut. καταλείψω; 1aor. κατέλειψα; 2aor. κατέλιπον; pf. pass. καταλέλειμμαι; 1aor. pass. κατελείφθην; *leave behind*; (1) of persons; (a) *leave (behind)* (MT 19.5); passive *be left behind* (AC 25.14); (b) *remain behind* for a purpose (1TH 3.1); (c) *be left (alone)* (LU 10.40); (2) of places *leave, abandon* (MT 4.13); figuratively *depart from, forsake* (2P 2.15); (3) of things; (a) *neglect, set to one side* (AC 6.2); (b) *abandon, leave behind* (MK 14.52); (c) *leave over, allow to remain*; figuratively *cause to continue to exist* (HE 4.1)

καταλειφθῆναι	VNAP	καταλείπω
καταλείψαντας	VPAAAM-P	"
καταλείψει	VIFA--3S	"
καταλελειμμένος	VPRPNM-S	"

καταλιθάζω   fut. καταλιθάσω; *stone to death, kill by hurling stones* (LU 20.6)

καταλιθάσει	VIFA--3S	καταλιθάζω
καταλίπῃ	VSAA--3S	καταλείπω
καταλιπόντες	VPAANM-P	"
καταλιπών	VPAANM-S	"
καταλλαγέντες	VPAPNM-P	καταλλάσσω
καταλλαγέντος	VPAPGM-S	"

καταλλαγή, ῆς, ἡ   literally *exchange, profit from exchange*; figuratively in the NT, as the reestablishing of personal relations *reconciliation, change from enmity to friendship* (2C 5.18, 19)

καταλλαγή	N-NF-S	καταλλαγή
καταλλαγήν	N-AF-S	"
καταλλαγῆς	N-GF-S	"
καταλλάγητε	VMAP--2P	καταλλάσσω
καταλλαγήτω	VMAP--3S	"
καταλλάξαντος	VPAAGM-S	"

καταλλάσσω   1aor. κατήλλαξα; 2aor. pass. κατηλλάγην; as restoring relationship between individuals or between God and man *reconcile, change from enmity to friendship* (2C 5.18); passive *be* or *become reconciled* (RO 5.10)

καταλλάσσων	VPPANM-S	καταλλάσσω
κατάλοιποι	A--NM-P	κατάλοιπος

κατάλοιπος, ον   *left, remaining*; substantively οἱ κατάλοιποι τῶν ἀνθρώπων *the rest of mankind* (AC 15.17)

κατάλυε	VMPA--2S	καταλύω
καταλυθῇ	VSAP--3S	"
καταλυθήσεται	VIFP--3S	"

κατάλυμα, ατος, τό   generally, a large place provided for rest or eating *inn, lodging place* (LU 2.7); more specifically *guest room, dining room* (MK 14.14)

κατάλυμα	N-NN-S	κατάλυμα
καταλύματι	N-DN-S	"
καταλύοντα	VPPAAM-S	καταλύω
καταλῦσαι	VNAA	"

καταλύσει   VIFA--3S   "
καταλύσω   VIFA--1S   "
καταλύσωσι(ν)   VSAA--3P   "

καταλύω fut. καταλύσω; 1aor. κατέλυσα; 1aor. pass. κατελύθην; 1fut. pass. καταλυθήσομαι; from the basic sense *put down, loosen*, various meanings are derived; (1) transitively; (a) literally, of buildings with their stones *destroy, demolish, dismantle* (MT 27.40), opposite οἰκοδομέω (*build*); (b) metaphorically, of the death of the body as a house or temple *tear down, destroy* (2C 5.1); (c) figuratively, of completely ruining someone's efforts *destroy* (RO 14.20); (d) figuratively, as invalidating an institution, such as law or sacrifice *do away with, annul, abolish* (MT 5.17); (2) intransitively, strictly *unharness* beasts of burden; hence *put up for the night, find lodging, rest* (LU 9.12)

καταλύων   VPPAVM-S   καταλύω
καταμάθετε   VMAA--2P   καταμανθάνω

καταμανθάνω 2aor. κατέμαθον; denoting intellectual awareness gained by thorough examination *consider, note well, learn (thoroughly) from* (MT 6.28)

καταμαρτυρέω as making a statement in witness against someone, with the genitive *bear witness against, testify against*

καταμαρτυροῦσι(ν)   VIPA--3P   καταμαρτυρέω
καταμένοντες   VPPANM-P   καταμένω

καταμένω fut. καταμενῶ; of temporary lodging *stay, lodge* (AC 1.13); *remain, continue with* (1C 16.6)

καταμενῶ   VIFA--1S   καταμένω

καταμόνας an adverb from κατά (*down*) and μόνος (*alone*); *alone, apart, in private* (MK 4.10)

καταμόνας   AB   καταμόνας

κατανάθεμα, ατος, τό as something that has been delivered over to divine wrath *accursed thing, anything cursed*

κατανάθεμα   N-NN-S   κατανάθεμα
καταναθεματίζειν   VNPA   καταναθεματίζω

καταναθεματίζω *curse* (MT 26.74)

καταναλίσκον   VPPANN-S   καταναλίσκω

καταναλίσκω *consume, destroy completely* (HE 12.29)

καταναρκάω fut. καταναρκήσω; 1aor. κατενάρκησα; strictly *be idle* to the disadvantage of someone, *be a dead weight on*; hence *be a financial burden to someone, weigh down*

καταναρκήσω   VIFA--1S   καταναρκάω

κατανεύω 1aor. κατένευσα; as giving a message by a hand gesture or nod of the head *beckon, signal* (LU 5.7)

κατανοεῖς   VIPA--2S   κατανοέω

κατανοέω impf. κατενόουν; 1aor. κατενόησα; (1) of intensive sensory perception *notice, perceive* (AC 27.39); (2) of attentive scrutiny of an object *study, examine* (JA 1.23); (3) of careful attention to a fact or process *consider, reflect on, discern* (LU 12.24); (4) of careful attention to a person or thing *consider, think about carefully, understand* (HE 3.1)

κατανοῆσαι   VNAA   κατανοέω
κατανοήσας   VPAANM-S   "
κατανοήσατε   VMAA--2P   "
κατανοοῦντι   VPPADM-S   "
κατανοῶμεν   VSPA--1P   "

κατανοῶν   VPPANM-S   "

καταντάω 1aor. κατήντησα; pf. κατήντηκα; *reach, come (to), arrive (at)*; (1) literally, as finishing a journey, with εἰς *come to, reach, arrive at* (AC 16.1); (2) figuratively; (a) as reaching a goal *attain to, arrive at* (PH 3.11); (b) of what comes to a person or community *come to, reach* (1C 14.36); *happen to, befall* (1C 10.11)

καταντῆσαι   VNAA   καταντάω
καταντήσαντες   VPAANM-P   "
καταντήσας   VPAANM-S   "
καταντήσειν   VNFA
καταντήσω   VSAA--1S   "
καταντήσωμεν   VSAA--1P   "
κατανύξεως   N-GF-S   κατάνυξις

κατάνυξις, εως, ἡ denoting a senseless mental condition as if in deep sleep *stupefaction, stupor, inability to think* (RO 11.8)

κατανύσσομαι 2aor. pass. κατενύγην; literally *be pierced through, be stabbed, be pricked deeply*; idiomatically, of the sharp pain felt in the heart from conviction or remorse κατανύσσεσθαι τὴν καρδίαν literally *be pierced through the heart*, i.e. *be greatly distressed, be very troubled* (AC 2.37)

καταξιόω 1aor. pass. κατηξιώθην; only passive in the NT *be considered* or *regarded as worthy, be thought of as deserving*

καταξιωθέντες   VPAPNM-P   καταξιόω
καταξιωθῆναι   VNAP   "
καταξιωθήσεται   VIFP--3S   "
καταξιωθῆτε   VSAP--2P   "
καταπατεῖν   VNPA   καταπατέω
καταπατεῖσθαι   VNPP

καταπατέω fut. καταπατήσω; 1aor. κατεπάτησα; 1aor. pass. κατεπατήθην; literally *tread down, trample underfoot* (MT 5.13); figuratively *treat contemptuously, despise, show disdain for* (HE 10.29)

καταπατήσας   VPAANM-S   καταπατέω
καταπατήσουσι(ν)   VIFA--3P   "
καταπατήσωσι(ν)   VSAA--3P   "
καταπαύσεως   N-GF-S   κατάπαυσις
κατάπαυσιν   N-AF-S

κατάπαυσις, εως, ἡ literally *ceasing from* one's work or activity *rest*; τόπος τῆς καταπαύσεως *place where one lives peacefully* (AC 7.49); metaphorically in HE 3.11 of the spiritual fulfillment God provides for his people

καταπαύω 1aor. κατέπαυσα; (1) transitively; (a) *cause to cease, restrain* (AC 14.18); (b) *bring to (a place of) rest; give rest to*; metaphorically, of spiritual rest provided for God's people (HE 4.8); (2) intransitively *rest, cease from (work)* (HE 4.4)

καταπεῖν   VNAA   see καταπιεῖν
καταπεσόντων   VPAAGM-P   καταπίπτω

καταπέτασμα, ατος, τό strictly *what is spread out downward*; hence *veil, curtain, cloth drape* (MT 27.51); metaphorically in HE 10.20 as symbolizing the flesh of Christ, assumed in his birth as a human being and "torn" in his atoning death to give access into God's holy presence

καταπέτασμα   N-AN-S   καταπέτασμα
    N-NN-S   "
καταπετάσματος   N-GN-S   "

καταπίει   VNAA   see καταπιεῖν

καταπιεῖν   VNAA   καταπίνω

καταπίῃ   VSAA--3S   "

καταπίμπρημι 1aor. κατέπρησα; *burn to ashes, burn down* (2P 2.6)

καταπῖν   VNAA   see καταπιεῖν

καταπίνοντες   VPPAVM-P   καταπίνω

καταπίνω 2aor. κατέπιον; 1aor. pass. κατεπόθην; (1) literally *drink* or *gulp down, swallow*; (a) of the ground absorbing liquids *take in* (RV 12.16); (b) of animals *devour*; used as part of a metaphor to denote the devil's activity against someone *completely overpower, bring under control* (1P 5.8); (2) figuratively *overcome, destroy*; (a) of waves of water overflowing someone *drown* (HE 11.29); (b) of heavy and continual sorrow happening to someone *overwhelm, prevail over, overcome* (2C 2.7); (c) of one force putting an end to another force *absorb completely, cause the end of* (2C 5.4)

καταπίπτειν   VNPA   καταπίπτω

καταπίπτω 2aor. κατέπεσον; *fall down, fall prostrate* (AC 26.14)

καταπλέω 1aor. κατέπλευσα; *sail toward* followed by εἰς and a destination (LU 8.26)

καταποθῇ   VSAP--3S   καταπίνω

καταπονέω *wear out* by toil or suffering, *oppress, torment*; only passive in the NT *be distressed* or *worn out* (2P 2.7); *be mistreated* (AC 7.24)

καταπονούμενοι   VPPPNM-P   καταπονέω

καταπονούμενον   VPPPAM-S   "

καταπονουμένῳ   VPPPDM-S   "

καταποντίζεσθαι   VNPP   καταποντίζω

καταποντίζω 1aor. pass. κατεποντίσθην; *throw into the sea, drown*; only passive in the NT *sink, be drowned* (MT 14.30)

καταποντισθῇ   VSAP--3S   καταποντίζω

κατάρα, ας, ἡ (1) as a legal action, of a supernatural power *curse* (GA 3.10); (2) as human utterance wishing evil on someone *imprecation, curse* (JA 3.10); (3) as the object of a curse *something accursed* (GA 3.13)

κατάρα   N-NF-S   κατάρα

κατάραν   N-AF-S   "

καταράομαι 1aor. κατηρασάμην; pf. pass. κατήραμαι; (1) middle, as stating that a supernatural power will cause harm to someone or something *curse* (LU 6.28); (2) passive *be doomed, be accursed* (MT 25.41)

κατάρας   N-GF-S   κατάρα

καταρᾶσθε   VMPD--2P   καταράομαι

        VMPO--2P   "

καταργεῖ   VIPA--3S   καταργέω

καταργεῖται   VIPP--3S   "

καταργέω fut. καταργήσω; 1aor. κατήργησα; pf. κατήργηκα; pf. pass. κατήργημαι; 1aor. pass. κατηργήθην; 1fut. pass. καταργηθήσομαι; from the basic sense *cause to be idle* or *useless*, the term always denotes a nonphysical destruction by means of a superior force coming in to replace the force previously in effect, as, e.g. light destroys darkness; (1) in relation to soil *use up, make barren* (LU 13.7); (2) as release by removal from a former sphere of control *free from*; passive *be discharged from, be freed from* (RO 7.2); (3) as destruction by replacement *abolish, destroy, cause to cease, put an end to* (1C 2.6; 13.11)

καταργηθῇ   VSAP--3S   καταργέω

καταργηθήσεται   VIFP--3S   "

καταργηθήσονται   VIFP--3P   "

καταργῆσαι   VNAA   "

καταργήσαντος   VPAAGM-S   "

καταργήσας   VPAANM-S   "

καταργήσει   VIFA--3S   "

καταργήσῃ   VSAA--3S   "

καταργοῦμεν   VIPA--1P   "

καταργουμένην   VPPPAF-S   "

καταργούμενον   VPPPNN-S   "

καταργουμένου   VPPPGN-S   "

καταργουμένων   VPPPGM-P   "

καταριθμέω pf. pass. κατηρίθμημαι; (1) *count*; (2) *count, number, reckon among*; only passive in the NT *belong to* (AC 1.17)

καταρτιεῖ   VIFA--3S   see καταρτίσει

καταρτίζεσθε   VMPP--2P   καταρτίζω

καταρτίζετε   VMPA--2P   "

καταρτίζοντας   VPPAAM-P   "

καταρτίζω fut. καταρτίσω; 1aor. κατήρτισα, mid. κατηρτισάμην; pf. pass. κατήρτισμαι; with a basic meaning *thoroughly prepare* something to meet demands; (1) *put in order, restore* to a former condition, *mend, repair* (MT 4.21; GA 6.1); (2) *prepare, make ready, complete* (HE 13.21); (3) *create, arrange, prepare* (HE 11.3); (4) as thoroughly equipping and adjusting Christian character *perfect, fully qualify, make fully adequate* (1C 1.10)

καταρτίσαι   VNAA   καταρτίζω

        VOAA--3S   "

καταρτίσει   VIFA--3S   "

κατάρτισιν   N-AF-S   κατάρτισις

κατάρτισις, εως, ἡ denoting ability gained through training, disciplining, and instructing *adequacy, full qualification, maturity* (2C 13.9)

καταρτισμόν   N-AM-S   καταρτισμός

καταρτισμός, οῦ, ὁ as a process of adjustment that results in a complete preparedness *equipping, perfecting, making adequate* (EP 4.12)

καταρώμεθα   VIPD--1P   καταράομαι

        VIPO--1P   "

καταρώμενον   VPPDAM-S   "

        VPPOAM-S   "

καταρωμένους   VPPDAM-P   "

        VPPOAM-P   "

κατασείσας   VPAANM-S   κατασείω

κατασείω 1aor. κατέσεισα; in the NT, as signaling with the hand *wave, motion (with), make a sign*

κατασκάπτω 1aor. κατέσκαψα; *demolish, tear down, raze to the ground*

κατασκευάζεται   VIPP--3S   κατασκευάζω

κατασκευαζομένης   VPPPGF-S   "

κατασκευάζω fut. κατασκευάσω; 1aor. κατεσκεύασα; pf. pass. ptc. κατεσκευασμένος; 1aor. pass. κατεσκευάσθην; (1) *prepare, make ready, put in readiness* (MK 1.2); of persons with mental and spiritual readiness *prepare*; passive *be prepared* (LU 1.17); (2) *build, construct, erect* (HE 11.7); (3) *furnish, equip* (HE 9.2)

κατασκευάσας   VPAANM-S   κατασκευάζω

κατασκευάσει   VIFA--3S   "
κατασκηνοῦν   VNPA   κατασκηνόω
κατασκηνοῦντες   VPPAVM-P   "

κατασκηνόω   fut. κατασκηνώσω; 1aor. κατεσκήνωσα; strictly *pitch one's tent* or *camp*; hence *rest, tarry, live* (AC 2.26); of birds *make a nest, settle* (MT 13.32)

κατασκηνώσει   VIFA--3S   κατασκηνόω
κατασκηνώσεις   N-AF-P   κατασκήνωσις

κατασκήνωσις, εως, ἡ   (1) as an action *taking up lodging, encamping*; (2) as a place to live in *lodging*; of birds *nest, nesting place* (MT 8.20)

κατασκιάζοντα   VPPANN-P   κατασκιάζω

κατασκιάζω   *overshadow, hover over* (HE 9.5)

κατασκοπέω   1aor. κατεσκόπησα; strictly *view closely*; hence *spy out, learn about by secret observation* (GA 2.4)

κατασκοπῆσαι   VNAA   κατασκοπέω

κατάσκοπος, ου, ὁ   as one who obtains information secretly *spy, scout* (HE 11.31)

κατασκόπους   N-AM-P   κατάσκοπος

κατασοφίζομαι   1aor. κατεσοφισάμην; *outwit, cunningly take advantage of, victimize by subtlety*, often with false arguments (AC 7.19)

κατασοφισάμενος   VPADNM-S   κατασοφίζομαι
κατασταθήσονται   VIFP--3P   καθίστημι
καταστείλας   VPAANM-S   καταστέλλω

καταστέλλω   1aor. κατέστειλα; pf. pass. ptc. κατεσταλμένος; transitively, as restoring order *restrain, bring under control, quiet down* (AC 19.35); participle κατεσταλμένος *calm, quiet*; δέον ἐστὶν ὑμᾶς κατεσταλμένους ὑπάρχειν *you must be calm* (AC 19.36)

κατάστημα, ατος, τό   strictly *state* or *condition*; hence *manner of life, behavior, demeanor* (TI 2.3)

καταστήματι   N-DN-S   κατάστημα
καταστήσει   VIFA--3S   καθίστημι
καταστήσῃς   VSAA--2S   "
καταστήσομεν   VIFA--1P   "
καταστήσω   VIFA--1S   "
καταστήσωμεν   VSAA--1P   "

καταστολή, ῆς, ἡ   strictly *arranging in order*; may denote an adjustment in behavior or dress; ἐν καταστολῇ κοσμίῳ in 1T 2.9 may be either *with proper behavior* or *in proper clothing*; the first seems preferable in view of the parallelism in 2.8 and the specific term for clothing in 2.9

καταστολῇ   N-DF-S   καταστολή

καταστρέφω   1aor. κατέστρεψα; pf. pass. ptc. κατεστραμμένος; (1) of a table *upset, overturn* (MT 21.12); (2) of a dwelling place *destroy*; perfect passive participle as a substantive τὰ κατεστραμμένα *the things destroyed, ruins*; figuratively, of a royal dynasty no longer in power *fallen* (AC 15.16)

καταστρηνιάσωσι(ν)   VSAA--3P   καταστρηνιάω

καταστρηνιάω   1aor. κατεστρηνίασα; as indulging sensual appetites to the point of giving up spiritual commitment *have strong (sexual) desires, burn with sensual desire* (1T 5.11)

καταστροφή, ῆς, ἡ   of a city *overthrow, ruin, destruction* (2P 2.6); figuratively, of the corrupting of persons *ruin, perversion, leading astray* (2T 2.14), opposite οἰκοδομή (*edifying, building up*)

καταστροφῇ   N-DF-S   καταστροφή

καταστρώννυμι   1aor. pass. κατεστρώθην; *cover by spreading over with* something; *scatter on the ground*; figuratively and passive in the NT, of dead bodies left to lie about over an area *be killed, die and be left unburied* (1C 10.5)

κατασύρῃ   VSPA--3S   κατασύρω

κατασύρω   as using force on someone *drag (away), drag* or *lead before* someone (LU 12.58)

κατασφάζω or **κατασφάττω**   1aor. κατέσφαξα; *kill, slay, strike down* (LU 19.27)

κατασφάξατε   VMAA--2P   κατασφάζω

κατασφραγίζω   pf. pass. ptc. κατεσφραγισμένος; as affixing documentary seals *seal (up)* (RV 5.1)

κατασχέσει   N-DF-S   κατάσχεσις
κατάσχεσιν   N-AF-S   "

κατάσχεσις, εως, ἡ   (1) *taking* or *holding fast in possession, possession* (AC 7.5); (2) *holding back, restraining, delaying* (AC 20.16)

κατάσχεσις   N-NF-S   κατάσχεσις
κατάσχωμεν   VSAA--1P   κατέχω

κατατίθημι   1aor. κατέθηκα; 2aor. mid. κατεθέμην; (1) *lay down, deposit*; of a burial *place* (in a tomb) (MK 15.46); (2) middle *deposit* or *lay up for oneself*; χάριτα καταθέσθαι in AC 24.27 and 25.9 probably means *gain goodwill* or *favor*, possibly *grant a favor*

κατατομή, ῆς, ἡ   strictly *cutting into*, as hacking or chopping up (sacrificial) meat; ironically in PH 3.2 as a contemptuous word for circumcision in outward state only *mutilation*; then by metonymy for those who practice such circumcision (PH 3.2)

κατατομήν   N-AF-S   κατατομή
κατατοξευθήσεται   VIFP--3S   κατατοξεύω

κατατοξεύω   1fut. pass. κατατοξευθήσομαι; *shoot down with an arrow* (HE 12.20)

κατατρέχω   2aor. κατέδραμον; *run down to*; of soldiers *charge down on* (AC 21.32)

καταυγάζω   1aor. inf. καταυγάσαι; literally *shine on, illuminate*; figuratively *enlighten, cause to understand* (2C 4.4)

καταυγάσαι   VNAA   καταυγάζω
κατάφαγε   VMAA--2S   κατεσθίω
καταφάγεται   VIFD--3S   "
καταφάγῃ   VSAA--3S   "
καταφάγοντι   VPAADM-S   "
καταφαγών   VPAANM-S   "
καταφερόμενος   VPPPNM-S   καταφέρω
καταφέροντες   VPPANM-P   "

καταφέρω   1aor. κατήνεγκα; 1aor. pass. κατηνέχθην; (1) strictly *bring* or *bear against*; hence, of legal charges *bring against, accuse of* (AC 25.7); of a judicial vote *cast against* (AC 26.10); (2) idiomatically, of being overpowered by sleep καταφέρεσθαι ὕπνῳ βαθεῖ literally *be carried away by deep sleep*, i.e. *become very sleepy* (AC 20.9); κατενεχθεὶς ἀπὸ τοῦ ὕπνου literally *having been carried away by sleep*, i.e. *being sound asleep* (AC 20.9)

καταφεύγω   2aor. κατέφυγον; literally *flee for refuge, take refuge* (AC 14.6); figuratively *have recourse to, turn to for (spiritual) safety* (HE 6.18)

καταφθαρήσονται   VIFP--3P   καταφθείρω

καταφθείρω   pf. pass. ptc. κατεφθαρμένος; literally *destroy* (2P 2.12); figuratively, of the mind *corrupt, deprave, ruin* (2T 3.8)

καταφιλέω   impf. κατεφίλουν; 1aor. κατεφίλησα; of a fervent or affectionate greeting *kiss tenderly*

καταφιλοῦσα	VPPANF-S	καταφιλέω
καταφρονεῖς	VIPA--2S	καταφρονέω
καταφρονεῖτε	VIPA--2P	"
καταφρονείτω	VMPA--3S	"
καταφρονείτωσαν	VMPA--3P	"

καταφρονέω   fut. καταφρονήσω; 1aor. κατεφρόνησα; (1) as treating with scornful contempt *look down on, despise, disparage* (1T 4.12); (2) as treating with neglect *disregard, slight, despise* (HE 12.2)

καταφρονήσας	VPAANM-S	καταφρονέω
καταφρονήσει	VIFA--3S	"
καταφρονήσητε	VSAA--2P	"
καταφρονηταί	N-VM-P	καταφρονητής

καταφρονητής, οῦ, ὁ   *scoffer, despiser, scorner* (AC 13.41)

καταφρονοῦντας	VPPAAM-P	καταφρονέω
καταφυγόντες	VPAANM-P	καταφεύγω

καταφωνέω   impf. κατεφώνουν; *cry out (loudly) against* someone, *shout against* (AC 22.24)

καταχέω   1aor. third-person singular κατέχεεν; of a liquid *pour out* or *down over*

καταχθέντες	VPAPNM-P	κατάγω

καταχθόνιος, ον   *under the earth, subterranean*; substantivally οἱ καταχθόνιοι *beings in the world below*, probably the realm of the dead (PH 2.10)

καταχθονίων	A--GM-P	καταχθόνιος
	A--GN-P	"

καταχράομαι   1aor. κατεχρησάμην; *make full use of, use to the uttermost* (1C 9.18); of an unrestrained use *be overdependent on, be preoccupied* with something (1C 7.31)

καταχρήσασθαι	VNAD	καταχράομαι
καταχρώμενοι	VPPDNM-P	"
	VPPONM-P	"

καταψηφίζομαι   1aor. pass. κατεψηφίσθην; *be enrolled, be voted in, be officially given a place* (AC 1.26)

καταψύξῃ	VSAA--3S	καταψύχω

καταψύχω   1aor. κατέψυξα; *cool (off), refresh, make cool* (LU 16.24)

κατεαγῶσι(ν)	VSAP--3P	κατάγνυμι
κατέαξαν	VIAA--3P	"
κατεάξει	VIFA--3S	"
κατέβαινε(ν)	VIIA--3S	καταβαίνω
κατεβάρησα	VIAA--1S	καταβαρέω
κατέβη	VIAA--3S	καταβαίνω
κατέβημεν	VIAA--1P	"
κατέβην	VIAA--1S	"
κατέβησαν	VIAA--3P	"
κατεβίβασαν	VIAA--3P	καταβιβάζω
κατεβλήθη	VIAP--3S	καταβάλλω
κατεγέλων	VIIA--3P	καταγελάω
κατέγνωσαν	VIAA--3P	καταγινώσκω
κατεγνωσμένος	VPRPNM-S	"
κατέγραφε(ν)	VIIA--3S	καταγράφω
κατέδησε(ν)	VIAA--3S	καταδέω
κατεδικάσατε	VIAA--2P	καταδικάζω
κατεδίωξαν	VIAA--3P	καταδιώκω

κατεδίωξε(ν)	VIAA--3S	"
κατέδραμε(ν)	VIAA--3S	κατατρέχω
κατέθηκε(ν)	VIAA--3S	κατατίθημι
κατείδωλον	A--AF-S	κατείδωλος

κατείδωλος, ον   *given to idolatry, full of idols, totally idolatrous* (AC 17.16)

κατειλημμένην	VPRPAF-S	καταλαμβάνω
κατείληπται	VIRP--3S	"
κατειληφέναι	VNRA	"
κατειλήφθη	VIAP--3S	"
κατειργάσατο	VIAD--3S	κατεργάζομαι
κατειργάσθαι	VNRD	"
	VNRO	"
κατειργάσθη	VIAP--3S	"
κατείχετο	VIIP--3S	κατέχω
κατειχόμεθα	VIIP--1P	"
κατεῖχον	VIIA--3P	"
κατεκάη	VIAP--3S	κατακαίω
κατέκαιον	VIIA--3P	"
κατέκειτο	VIID--3S	κατάκειμαι
	VIIO--3S	"
κατέκλασε(ν)	VIAA--3S	κατακλάω
κατέκλεισα	VIAA--1S	κατακλείω
κατέκλεισε(ν)	VIAA--3S	"
κατεκληροδότησε(ν)	VIAA--3S	κατακληροδοτέω
κατεκληρονόμησε(ν)	VIAA--3S	κατακληρονομέω
κατεκλίθη	VIAP--3S	κατακλίνω
κατέκλιναν	VIAA--3P	"
κατεκρίθη	VIAP--3S	κατακρίνω
κατεκρίθησαν	VIAP--3P	"
κατέκριναν	VIAA--3P	"
κατέκρινε(ν)	VIAA--3S	"
κατεκυρίευσαν	VIAA--3P	κατακυριεύω
κατεκυρίευσε(ν)	VIAA--3S	"
κατέλαβε(ν)	VIAA--3S	καταλαμβάνω
κατελάβη	VIAA--3S	see κατέλαβε(ν)
κατελαβόμην	VIAM--1S	καταλαμβάνω
κατέλειπε(ν)	VIIA--3S	καταλείπω
κατέλειπον	VIIA--3P	"
κατελείφθη	VIAP--3S	"
κατέλειψα	VIAA--1S	"
κατέλειψαν	VIAA--3P	"
κατελήμφθην	VIAP--1S	καταλαμβάνω
κατελήφθη	VIAP--3S	"
κατελήφθην	VIAP--1S	"
κατελθεῖν	VNAA	κατέρχομαι
κατελθόντα	VPAAM-S	"
κατελθόντες	VPAANM-P	"
κατελθόντων	VPAAGM-P	"
κατελθών	VPAANM-S	"
κατέλιπε(ν)	VIAA--3S	καταλείπω
κατέλιπον	VIAA--1S	"
	VIAA--3P	"
κατέλυσα	VIAA--1S	καταλύω

κατέναντι   adverb; (1) of place *opposite* (LU 19.30); (2) as an improper preposition with the genitive; (a) of place *opposite, over against* (MT 21.2); (b) *before, in the presence of* (MT 27.24); (c) figuratively *in the sight of, in the judgment of, in the view of* (RO 4.17)

κατέναντι	AB	κατέναντι
	PG	"

κατενάρκησα	VIAA--1S	καταναρκάω
κατένευσαν	VIAA--3P	κατανεύω
κατενεχθείς	VPAPNM-S	καταφέρω
κατενόησα	VIAA--1S	κατανοέω
κατενόησε(ν)	VIAA--3S	"
κατενόουν	VIIA--1S	"
	VIIA--3P	"
κατενύγησαν	VIAO--3P	κατανύσσομαι

κατενώπιον an adverb used as an improper preposition with the genitive; (1) of place *in the presence of, before* (JU 24); (2) figuratively *in the sight of, in the judgment of, in the view of* (EP 1.4)

κατενώπιον	PG	κατενώπιον
κατεξουσιάζουσι(ν)	VIPA--3P	κατεξουσιάζω

κατεξουσιάζω of the possession and exercise of authority *rule, reign, have dominion over* (MT 20.25); possibly in a negative sense *lord it over, tyrannize*

κατεπατήθη	VIAP--3S	καταπατέω
κατέπαυσαν	VIAA--3P	καταπαύω
κατέπαυσε(ν)	VIAA--3S	"
κατέπεσε(ν)	VIAA--3S	καταπίπτω
κατεπέστησαν	VIAA--3P	κατεφίστημι
κατέπιε(ν)	VIAA--3S	καταπίνω
κατέπλευσαν	VIAA--3P	καταπλέω
κατεπόθη	VIAP--3S	καταπίνω
κατεπόθησαν	VIAP--3P	
κατεποντίσθησαν	VIAP--3P	καταποντίζω
κατέπρησε(ν)	VIAA--3S	καταπίμπρημι
κατεργάζεσθαι	VNPD	κατεργάζομαι
	VNPO	"
κατεργάζεσθε	VMPD--2P	"
	VMPO--2P	"
κατεργάζεται	VIPD--3S	"
	VIPO--3S	"

κατεργάζομαι 1aor. mid. κατειργασάμην; pf. κατείργασμαι; 1aor. pass. κατειργάσθην; (1) as thoroughly working at something whether in a good sense (2C 12.12) or bad sense (RO 1.27) *do, accomplish, commit* (possibly EP 6.13); (2) as achieving an effect whether in a good sense (JA 1.3) or bad sense (RO 7.8) *produce, make, bring about*; (3) as working toward an effect *prepare, carefully fashion, make completely ready* (2C 5.5); (4) *prevail, overcome* (possibly EP 6.13)

κατεργάζομαι	VIPD--1S	κατεργάζομαι
	VIPO--1S	"
κατεργαζομένη	VPPDNF-S	"
	VPPONF-S	"
κατεργαζόμενοι	VPPDNM-P	"
	VPPONM-P	"
κατεργαζόμενος	VPPDNM-S	"
	VPPONM-S	"
κατεργαζομένου	VPPDGM-S	"
	VPPOGM-S	"
κατεργασάμενοι	VPADNM-P	"
κατεργασάμενον	VPADAM-S	"
κατεργασάμενος	VPADNM-S	"

κατέρχομαι 2aor. act. κατῆλθον; *come* or *go down*; (1) literally; (a) geographically, from a higher to a lower place *come* or *go down, descend* (LU 4.31); (b) of ships coming into harbor *arrive, put in at, land at* (AC 21.3);

(2) figuratively, of gifts sent from God *come (down)* (JA 3.15)

κατερχομένη	VPPDNF-S	κατέρχομαι
	VPPONF-S	"
κατερχόμενον	VPPDNN-S	"
	VPPONN-S	"
κατέσεισε(ν)	VIAA--3S	κατασείω
κατεσθίει	VIPA--3S	κατεσθίω
κατεσθίετε	VIPA--2P	"
κατεσθίοντες	VPPANM-P	"
κατεσθίουσι(ν)	VIPA--3P	"

κατεσθίω fut. mid. καταφάγομαι; 2aor. κατέφαγον; (1) literally *eat up, consume, devour* (MT 13.4); (2) figuratively *destroy*; (a) of fire *consume, burn up* (RV 11.5); (b) of illegal exploitation *rob, take complete advantage of* (MK 12.40); (c) of strife within a group *cause great division, destroy* (GA 5.15)

κατέσθοντες	VPPANM-P	see κατεσθίοντες
κατεσκαμμένα	VPRPAN-P	κατασκάπτω
κατέσκαψαν	VIAA--3P	"
κατεσκεύασε(ν)	VIAA--3S	κατασκευάζω
κατεσκευάσθη	VIAP--3S	"
κατεσκευασμένον	VPRPAM-S	"
κατεσκευασμένων	VPRPGN-P	"
κατεσκήνωσε(ν)	VIAA--3S	κατασκηνόω
κατεστάθησαν	VIAP--3P	καθίστημι
κατεσταλμένους	VPRPAM-P	καταστέλλω
κατέστησας	VIAA--2S	καθίστημι
κατέστησε(ν)	VIAA--3S	"
κατεστραμμένα	VPRPAN-P	καταστρέφω
κατεστρεμμένα	VPRPAN-P	see κατεστραμμένα
κατέστρεψε(ν)	VIAA--3S	καταστρέφω
κατεστρώθησαν	VIAP--3P	καταστρώννυμι
κατεσφραγισμένον	VPRPAN-S	κατασφραγίζω
κατευθῦναι	VOAA--3S	κατευθύνω
κατευθῦναι	VNAA	"
κατευθύνεται	VIPP--3S	"

κατευθύνω 1aor. κατεύθυνα; *cause to go straight, direct* or *guide in the right way*

κατευλόγει	VIIA--3S	κατευλογέω
κατευλογεῖ	VIIA--3S	"

κατευλογέω impf. κατευλόγουν; *bless, invoke a blessing on, ask God to be favorable toward* someone (MK 10.16)

κατέφαγε(ν)	VIAA--3S	κατεσθίω
κατέφαγον	VIAA--1S	"
κατεφθαρμένοι	VPRPNM-P	καταφθείρω
κατεφίλει	VIIA--3S	καταφιλέω
κατεφίλησε(ν)	VIAA--3S	"
κατεφίλουν	VIIA--3P	καταφιλέω

κατεφίστημι 2aor. κατεπέστην; *rise up against, assault, attack* (AC 18.12)

κατέφυγον	VIAA--3P	καταφεύγω
κατεφώνουν	VIIA--3P	καταφωνέω
κατέχεε(ν)	VIAA--3S	καταχέω
κατέχειν	VNPA	κατέχω
κατέχετε	VIPA--2P	"
	VMPA--2P	"
κατέχομεν	VIPA--1P	"
κατεχόμενοι	VPPPNM-P	"
κατεχόμενος	VPPPNM-S	"
κατέχον	VPPAAN-S	"

224

κατέχοντες	VPPANM-P	"
κατεχόντων	VPPAGM-P	"
κατέχουσι(ν)	VIPA--3P	"

κατέχω impf. κατεῖχον; 2aor. κατέσχον; (1) transitively, active; (a) *hold fast, keep in possession, possess* (2C 6.10); figuratively *hold in memory, keep in mind, continue believing* (1C 15.2); (b) *hold back, detain, prevent* (LU 4.42); figuratively *restrain, check* (2TH 2.6); (c) *hold down, suppress*; figuratively *suppress* (RO 1.18); (d) *take (over), occupy* (LU 14.9); (2) transitively, passive; (a) of law *be bound by* (RO 7.6); (b) of disease *be afflicted with* (JN 5.4); (3) intransitively, as a nautical technical term *hold one's course toward, head for, steer for* (AC 27.40)

κατέχωμεν	VSPA--1P	κατέχω
κατέχων	VPPANM-S	"
κατεψηφίσθη	VIAP--3S	καταψηφίζομαι
κατήγαγον	VIAA--1S	κατάγω
	VIAA--3P	"
κατηγγείλαμεν	VIAA--1P	καταγγέλλω
κατήγγειλαν	VIAA--3P	"
κατηγγέλη	VIAP--3S	"
κατήγγελλον	VIIA--3P	"
κατηγορεῖν	VNPA	κατηγορέω
κατηγορεῖσθαι	VNPP	"
κατηγορεῖται	VIPP--3S	"
κατηγορεῖτε	VIPA--2P	"
κατηγορείτωσαν	VMPA--3P	"

κατηγορέω impf. κατηγόρουν; fut. κατηγορήσω; 1aor. κατηγόρησα; (1) predominately as a legal technical term *accuse, bring charges against* (MT 12.10); (2) in a nonjudicial sense *accuse, reproach* (RO 2.15)

κατηγορῆσαι	VNAA	κατηγορέω
κατηγορήσω	VIFA--1S	"
κατηγορήσωσι(ν)	VSAA--3P	"

κατηγορία, ας, ἡ as a legal technical term *accusation, charge*

κατηγορίᾳ	N-DF-S	κατηγορία
κατηγορίαν	N-AF-S	"
κατήγοροι	N-NM-P	κατήγορος
κατηγόροις	N-DM-P	"

κατήγορος, ου, ὁ as a legal technical term *accuser*

κατήγορος	N-NM-S	κατήγορος
κατηγοροῦμεν	VIPA--1P	κατηγορέω
κατηγορούμενος	VPPPNM-S	"
κατηγόρουν	VIIA--3P	"
κατηγοροῦντες	VPPANM-P	"
κατηγορούντων	VPPAGM-P	"
κατηγόρους	N-AM-P	κατήγορος
κατηγοροῦσι(ν)	VIPA--3P	κατηγορέω
κατηγορῶν	VPPANM-S	"
κατηγωνίσαντο	VIAD--3P	καταγωνίζομαι

κατήγωρ, ορος, ὁ *accuser*, used as a designation for the devil (RV 12.10)

κατήγωρ	N-NM-S	κατήγωρ
κατήλθαμεν	VIAA--1P	κατέρχομαι
κατῆλθε(ν)	VIAA--3S	"
κατήλθομεν	VIAA--1P	"
κατῆλθον	VIAA--3P	"
κατηλλάγημεν	VIAP--1P	καταλλάσσω
κατήνεγκα	VIAA--1S	καταφέρω

κατηνέγκατε	VIAA--2P	"
κατήντηκε(ν)	VIRA--3S	καταντάω
κατηντήσαμεν	VIAA--1P	"
κατήντησαν	VIAA--3P	"
κατήντησε(ν)	VIAA--3S	"
κατηξιώθησαν	VIAP--3P	καταξιόω
κατηραμένοι	VPRPVM-P	καταράομαι
κατηράσω	VIAD--2S	"
κατηργάσατο	VIAD--3S	κατεργάζομαι
κατηργήθημεν	VIAP--1P	καταργέω
κατηργήθητε	VIAP--2P	"
κατήργηκα	VIRA--1S	"
κατήργηται	VIRP--3S	"
κατηριθμημένος	VPRPNM-S	καταριθμέω
κατηρτίσθαι	VNRP	καταρτίζω
κατηρτισμένα	VPRMAN-P	"
	VPRPAN-P	"
κατηρτισμένοι	VPRPNM-P	"
κατηρτισμένος	VPRPNM-S	"
κατηρτίσω	VIAM--2S	"
κατησχύνθην	VIAP--1S	καταισχύνω
κατησχύνοντο	VIIP--3P	"
κατηυλόγει	VIIA--3S	κατευλογέω

κατήφεια, ας, ἡ from κατὰ τὰ φαῆ (*with downcast eyes*); as a mental state *dejection, gloom, depression* (JA 4.9)

κατήφειαν	N-AF-S	κατήφεια

κατηχέω 1aor. κατήχησα; pf. pass. κατήχημαι; 1aor. pass. κατηχήθην; strictly *sound down against, make the ears ring*; hence *make oneself understood*; (1) of information being communicated *report, inform* (AC 21.21); (2) of beginning religious instruction *teach, instruct (carefully)* (AC 18.25)

κατηχήθης	VIAP--2S	κατηχέω
κατηχήθησαν	VIAP--3P	"
κατηχημένος	VPRPNM-S	"
κατήχηνται	VIRP--3P	"
κατήχησαν	VIAA--3P	"
κατηχήσω	VSAA--1S	"
κατήχθημεν	VIAP--1P	κατάγω
κατηχούμενος	VPPPNM-S	κατηχέω
κατηχοῦντι	VPPADM-S	"

κατιόω pf. pass. κατίωμαι; of the oxidation of metals *rust, corrode*; only passive in the NT *become tarnished* or *corroded* (JA 5.3)

κατίσχυον	VIIA--3P	κατισχύω
κατισχύσητε	VSAA--2P	"
κατισχύσουσι(ν)	VIFA--3P	"

κατισχύω impf. κατίσχυον; fut. κατισχύσω; 1aor. κατίσχυσα; (1) intransitively *be strong, able* or *powerful, be at full strength* (LU 21.36); absolutely *prevail, win out* (LU 23.23); (2) followed by the genitive *defeat, prevail against, overcome* (MT 16.18)

κατίωται	VIRP--3S	κατιόω
κατοικεῖ	VIPA--3S	κατοικέω
κατοικεῖν	VNPA	"
κατοικεῖς	VIPA--2S	"
κατοικεῖτε	VIPA--2P	"

κατοικέω 1aor. κατῴκησα; (1) intransitively; (a) literally, of a geographical place *live* or *dwell in, settle down in* (MT 2.23); (b) figuratively, of the possession of human beings by God, supernatural beings, religious virtues,

225

etc. *indwell, live* or *dwell in* (EP 3.17; 2P 3.13); (2) transitively *inhabit* (LU 13.4); substantivally οἱ κατοικοῦντες *the inhabitants* of a place (RV 17.2)

κατοικῆσαι	VNAA	κατοικέω
κατοικήσαντι	VPAADM-S	"
κατοικήσας	VPAANM-S	"
κατοίκησιν	N-AF-S	κατοίκησις

κατοίκησις, εως, ἡ   a settling down in a place *dwelling place, habitation* (MK 5.3)

κατοικητήριον, ου, τό   *dwelling place, abode, habitat*

κατοικητήριον	N-AN-S	κατοικητήριον
	N-NN-S	"

κατοικία, ας, ἡ   *habitat, dwelling place* (AC 17.26)

κατοικίας	N-GF-S	κατοικία

κατοικίζω   1aor. κατῴκισα; *cause to dwell, assign a dwelling place, send to live in* (JA 4.5)

κατοικίσαι	VNAA	κατοικίζω
κατοικοῦντας	VPPAAM-P	κατοικέω
κατοικοῦντες	VPPANM-P	"
	VPPAVM-P	"
κατοικοῦντι	VPPADM-S	"
κατοικούντων	VPPAGM-P	"
κατοίκουσαν	VIIA--3P	"
κατοικοῦσι(ν)	VPPADM-P	"
κατοικῶν	VPPANM-S	"
κατοπτριζόμεθα	VIPM--1P	κατοπτρίζω
κατοπτριζόμενοι	VPPMNM-P	"

κατοπτρίζω   *produce a clear reflection, show as in a mirror*; middle in the NT *look at* something *as in a mirror, see by reflection*; figuratively *reflect as in a mirror* (possibly 2C 3.18); the meaning *contemplate as in a mirror* is also possible in this passage

κατόρθωμα, ατος, τό   *right action*; plural *success, prosperity* (AC 24.2)

κατορθωμάτων	N-GN-P	κατόρθωμα

κάτω   adverb of place; (1) *downward, down* (MT 4.6); (2) *below* (MK 14.66), opposite ἄνω (*above*); (3) substantivally τὰ κ. *this world, here below* (JN 8.23), opposite τὰ ἄνω (*what is above, heaven*)

κάτω	AB	κάτω
κατῴκεισε(ν)	VIAA--3S	see κατῴκισε(ν)
κατῴκησαν	VIAA--3P	κατοικέω
κατῴκησε(ν)	VIAA--3S	"
κατῴκισε(ν)	VIAA--3S	κατοικίζω
κατώτερα	A-MAN-P	κατώτερος

κατώτερος, τέρα, ον   comparative of the adverb κάτω (*down, below*); used as an adjective *lower* (EP 4.9)

κατωτέρω   comparative adverb of κατώτερος (*lower*); used with numbers indicating age *under, less than* (MT 2.16)

κατωτέρω	ABM	κατωτέρω

Καῦδα, ἡ or **τό** (also **Γαύδην, Κλάδιν, Κλαῦδα, Κλαῦδαν, Κλαύδη, Κλαύδην, Κλαύδιον**)   indeclinable; *Cauda,* an island in the Mediterranean Sea off the southern coast of Crete; also called *Clauda* (AC 27.16)

καυθήσομαι	VIFP--1S	καίω
καυθήσωμαι	VIFP--1S	see καυθήσομαι

καῦμα, ατος, τό   *heat, burning* or *scorching heat*

καῦμα	N-AN-S	καῦμα
	N-NN-S	"

καυματίζω   1aor. ἐκαυμάτισα; 1aor. pass. ἐκαυματίσθην; (1) *harm by heat, burn up, scorch* (RV 16.8); (2) passive, of plants withering in the sun's extreme heat *be withered* or *scorched* (MT 13.6)

καυματίσαι	VNAA	καυματίζω

καυματόω   1aor. ἐκαυμάτωσα; 1aor. pass. ἐκαυματώθην; passive *be scorched by heat* (MT 13.6)

καῦσιν	N-AF-S	καῦσις

καῦσις, εως, ἡ   as an action *burning, consuming, being on fire* (HE 6.8)

καυσούμενα	VPPPNN-P	καυσόω

καυσόω   only passive in the NT *be intensely hot, be consumed by heat, be burned up*

καυστηριάζω   pf. pass. ptc. κεκαυστηριασμένος (and κεκαυτηριασμένος); active *brand with a red-hot iron*; of a slave *mark with a brand*; figuratively, of destroying the function of conscience *cause to be insensitive, make unfeeling, harden*; passive and idiomatically καυστηριάζεσθαι τὴν συνείδησιν literally *be seared in respect to the conscience,* i.e. *refuse to listen to one's conscience* (1T 4.2)

καυστηριασμένων	VPRPGM-P	see κεκαυστηριασμένων

καύσων, ωνος, ὁ   *heat*; of intense heat as from the sun or a scorching east wind *burning heat, scorching heat*

καύσων	N-NM-S	καύσων
καύσωνα	N-AM-S	"
καύσωνι	N-DM-S	"
καυτηριασμένων	VPRPGM-P	see κεκαυστηριασμένων

καυχάομαι   fut. καυχήσομαι; 1aor. ἐκαυχησάμην; pf. κεκαύχημαι; *boast*; (1) intransitively; (a) in a bad sense of self-glorying *boast, pride oneself on* (RO 2.23); (b) in a good sense of an attitude of confidence in God *rejoice in, glory in, boast in* (RO 5.11); (2) transitively, of achievements through divine help *boast about, glory in* (2C 11.30)

καυχᾶσαι	VIPD--2S	καυχάομαι
	VIPO--2S	"
καυχᾶσθαι	VNPD	"
	VNPO	"
καυχᾶσθε	VIPD--2P	"
	VIPO--2P	"
	VMPD--2P	"
	VMPO--2P	"
καυχάσθω	VMPD--3S	"
	VMPO--3S	"

καύχημα, ατος, τό   (1) what one is proud of *pride, boast, something to boast about* (RO 4.2); (2) what is said in boasting *boast, praise* (2C 9.3); *justification for boasting, right to boast* (1C 9.16)

καύχημα	N-AN-S	καύχημα
	N-NN-S	"
καυχήματος	N-GN-S	"
καυχήσασθαι	VNAD	καυχάομαι
καυχήσεως	N-GF-S	καύχησις
καυχήσηται	VSAD--3S	καυχάομαι
καύχησιν	N-AF-S	καύχησις

καύχησις, εως, ἡ   (1) as an action *boasting, glorying, pride*; in a good sense (RO 15.17); in a bad sense (RO 3.27); (2) as an object, of boasting, equivalent to καύχημα *boast* (2C 1.12); (3) as an attitude *pride*; in a good sense (2C 7.4)

καύχησις	N-NF-S	καύχησις
καυχήσομαι	VIFD--1S	καυχάομαι

καυχησόμεθα	VIFD--1P	"
καυχήσωμαι	VSAD--1S	"
καυχήσωνται	VSAD--3P	"
καυχῶμαι	VIPD--1S	"
	VIPO--1S	"
καυχώμεθα	VIPD--1P	"
	VIPO--1P	"
καυχῶμεν	VIPA--1P	see καυχώμεθα
καυχώμενοι	VPPDNM-P	καυχάομαι
	VPPONM-P	"
καυχώμενος	VPPDNM-S	"
	VPPONM-S	"
καυχωμένους	VPPDAM-P	"
	VPPOAM-P	"
καυχῶνται	VIPD--3P	"
	VIPO--3P	"

Καφαρναούμ, ἡ (also **Καπερναούμ**) indeclinable; *Capernaum*, a city on the northwestern shore of the Sea of Galilee

Κεγχρεαί, ῶν, αἱ (also **Κενχρεαί**) *Cenchrea*, the eastern seaport of Corinth, on the Saronic Gulf

Κεγχρεαῖς	N-DF-P	Κεγχρεαί
Κέδρος		Κεδρών

κέδρος, ου, ἡ *cedar tree* (JN 18.1)

Κέδρου		see Κεδρών
Κέδρου	N-GF-S	κέδρος
Κέδρων		Κεδρών

Κεδρών, ὁ (also **Κέδρος, Κέδρων**) indeclinable; *Kidron*, the name of a seasonal mountain stream and the valley through which it flows, between Jerusalem and the Mount of Olives on the east (JN 18.1)

Κεδρών		see Κεδρών

κεῖμαι impf. third-person singular ἔκειτο; *lie, recline*; (1) literally, spatially and predominately as the result of being placed or set; (a) *lie in or on* something (LU 2.12); (b) of things being situated somewhere *stand, set* (MT 5.14); (c) of storage of goods *be laid up, be in store* (LU 12.19); (2) figuratively; (a) of persons *be appointed, be set, destined* (LU 2.34); (b) as a legal technical term *be laid down, exist, be valid* (1T 1.9); (c) as being in a certain state or condition *be, find oneself (in), lie (in the power of)* (1J 5.19)

κεῖμαι	VIPD--1S	κεῖμαι
	VIPO--1S	"
κείμεθα	VIPD--1P	"
	VIPO--1P	"
κείμενα	VPPDAN-P	"
	VPPOAN-P	"
κείμεναι	VPPDNF-P	"
	VPPONF-P	"
κειμένη	VPPDNF-S	"
	VPPONF-S	"
κειμένην	VPPDAF-S	"
	VPPOAF-S	"
κείμενον	VPPDAM-S	"
	VPPDAN-S	"
	VPPOAM-S	"
	VPPOAN-S	"
κείμενος	VPPDNM-S	"
	VPPONM-S	"

κειμήλιον, ου, τό *anything stored up, treasure* (1T 6.19)

κειμήλιον	N-AN-S	κειμήλιον
κειράμενος	VPAMNM-S	κείρω
κείραντος	VPAAGM-S	"
κείρασθαι	VNAM	"
κειράσθω	VMAM--3S	"

κειρία, ας, ἡ as a wide strip of cloth for wrapping *bandage, swathe*; plural, as used in burial preparation *grave-clothes* (JN 11.44)

κειρίαις	N-DF-P	κειρία
κείροντος	VPPAGM-S	κείρω

κείρω 1aor. ἔκειρα, mid. ἐκειράμην; of a sheep *shear* (AC 8.32); of hair *cut off, shave off*; middle *cut one's hair, have one's hair cut off* (1C 11.6)

Κείς		Κίς
κεῖται	VIPD--3S	κεῖμαι
	VIPO--3S	"
κεκαθαρισμένους	VPRPAM-P	καθαρίζω
κεκαθαρμένους	VPRPAM-P	καθαίρω
κεκάθικε(ν)	VIRA--3S	καθίζω
κεκαλυμμένη	VPRPNF-S	καλύπτω
κεκαλυμμένον	VPRPNN-S	"
κεκαυμένῳ	VPRPDN-S	καίω
κεκαυστηριασμένων	VPRPGM-P	καυστηριάζω
κεκαυτηριασμένων	VPRPGM-P	see κεκαυστηριασμένων
κεκαύχημαι	VIRD--1S	καυχάομαι
	VIRO--1S	"
κεκένωται	VIRP--3S	κενόω
κεκερασμένου	VPRPGM-S	κεράννυμι
κεκλεισμένον	VPRPAN-S	κλείω
κεκλεισμένων	VPRPGF-P	"
κέκλεισται	VIRP--3S	"
κέκληκε(ν)	VIRA--3S	καλέω
κεκληκότι	VPRADM-S	"
κεκληκώς	VPRANM-S	"
κεκλημένοι	VPRPNM-P	"
κεκλημένοις	VPRPDM-P	"
κεκλημένος	VPRPNM-S	"
κεκλημένους	VPRPAM-P	"
κεκλημένων	VPRPGM-P	"
κεκληρονόμηκε(ν)	VIRA--3S	κληρονομέω
κέκληται	VIRP--3S	καλέω
κέκλικε(ν)	VIRA--3S	κλίνω
κέκμηκας	VIRA--2S	κάμνω
κεκοιμηθῇ	VSAO--3S	see κοιμηθῇ
κεκοιμημένων	VPRDGM-P	κοιμάομαι
	VPROGM-P	"
κεκοίμηται	VIRD--3S	"
	VIRO--3S	"
κεκοίνωκε(ν)	VIRA--3S	κοινόω
κεκοινωμένους	VPRPAM-P	"
κεκοινώνηκε(ν)	VIRA--3S	κοινωνέω
κεκονιαμένε	VPRPVM-S	κονιάω
κεκονιαμένοις	VPRPDM-P	"
κεκοπίακα	VIRA--1S	κοπιάω
κεκοπίακας	VIRA--2S	"
κεκοπιάκασι(ν)	VIRA--3P	"
κεκοπιάκατε	VIRA--2P	"
κεκοπίακες	VIRA--2S	"
κεκοπιακώς	VPRANM-S	"
κεκορεσμένοι	VPRPNM-P	κορέννυμι
κεκοσμημένην	VPRPAF-S	κοσμέω

κεκοσμημένοι	VPRPNM-P	"
κεκοσμημένον	VPRPAM-S	"
κεκόσμηται	VIRP--3S	"
κέκραγε(ν)	VIRA--3S	κράζω
κεκράξονται	VIFM--3P	"
κεκρατηκέναι	VNRA	κρατέω
κεκράτηνται	VIRP--3P	"
κέκρικα	VIRA--1S	κρίνω
κεκρίκατε	VIRA--2P	"
κεκρίκει	VILA--3S	"
κέκρικε(ν)	VIRA--3S	"
κεκριμένα	VPRPAN-P	"
κέκριται	VIRP--3S	"
κεκρυμμένα	VPRPAN-P	κρύπτω
κεκρυμμένον	VPRPNN-S	"
κεκρυμμένος	VPRPNM-S	"
κεκρυμμένου	VPRPGN-S	"
κεκρυμμένῳ	VPRPDM-S	"
κέκρυπται	VIRP--3S	"
κεκυρωμένην	VPRPAF-S	κυρόω
κελεύεις	VIPA--2S	κελεύω
κελευόντων	VPPAGM-P	"
κελεύσαντες	VPAANM-P	"
κελεύσαντος	VPAAGM-S	"
κελεύσας	VPAANM-S	"
κελεύσατε	VMAA--2P	"

κέλευσμα, ατος, τό *shout of command, signal call, summons* (1TH 4.16)

κελεύσματι	N-DN-S	κέλευσμα
κέλευσον	VMAA--2S	κελεύω

κελεύω impf. ἐκέλευον; 1aor. ἐκέλευσα; *command, order, direct*; usually followed by an infinitive to indicate what is expected as a response

κενά	A--AN-P	κενός
κενέ	A--VM-S	"
κενή	A--NF-S	"
κενῆς	A--GF-S	"

κενοδοξία, ας, ἡ *empty conceit, vain pride, (groundless) boasting* (PH 2.3)

κενοδοξίαν	N-AF-S	κενοδοξία
κενόδοξοι	A--NM-P	κενόδοξος

κενόδοξος, ον *as being proud without any good reason for it conceited, boastful* (GA 5.26)

κενοῖς	A--DM-P	κενός
κενόν	A--AM-S	"
	A--AN-S	"
	A--NN-S	"

κενός, ή, όν *empty, without content*; (1) literally, of containers *empty*; of persons *empty-handed* (MK 12.3); (2) figuratively; (a) of things that lack effectiveness *empty, futile, without result* (1TH 2.1); substantively εἰς κενόν literally *for an empty thing*, i.e. *in vain, to no purpose* (PH 2.16); κενά *worthless things* (AC 4.25); (b) of persons *vain, foolish* (JA 2.20)

κενός	A--NM-S	κενός
κενούς	A--AM-P	"

κενοφωνία, ας, ἡ *empty talk, chatter, foolish discussion*

κενοφωνίας	N-AF-P	κενοφωνία

κενόω fut. κενώσω; 1aor. ἐκένωσα; pf. pass. κεκένωμαι; 1aor. pass. ἐκενώθην; *make empty*; (1) literally *remove the content of* something; (2) figuratively; (a) as taking away the effectiveness of something *deprive of power* (1C 1.17); (b) as taking away the significance of something *destroy, make invalid, empty* (1C 9.15); (c) as taking away the prerogatives of status or position *empty, divest*; ἑαυτὸν ἐκένωσεν literally *he emptied himself*, i.e. *he took an unimportant position* (PH 2.7)

κέντρα	N-AN-P	κέντρον

κέντρον, ου, τό a sharp, pointed instrument used for piercing to hurt or kill; (1) literally, of insects with a poisonous tip *stinger* (RV 9.10); figuratively, of death *power to hurt* (1C 15.55); (2) literally, of prodding instruments *goad, spur*; proverbially, of a driving or impelling force that is hurtful to resist *strong conviction, emotional pain* (AC 26.14)

κέντρον	N-NN-S	κέντρον

κεντυρίων, ωνος, ὁ a Roman officer in charge of one hundred soldiers *centurion, commander, captain*

κεντυρίων	N-NM-S	κεντυρίων
κεντυρίωνα	N-AM-S	"
κεντυρίωνος	N-GM-S	"
Κενχρεαῖς	N-DF-P	Κεγχρεαί
κενωθῇ	VSAP--3S	κενόω

κενῶς adverb; of something done in an futile manner *idly, in vain, for no purpose* (JA 4.5)

κενῶς	AB	κενῶς
κενώσει	VIFA--3S	κενόω
κενώσῃ	VSAA--3S	"

κεραία, ας, ἡ literally *hornlike projection, little horn*; hence, the small diacritical marks in written letters for identifying accents, breathing, etc. *serif, point, tittle, dot*; used in MT 5.18 and LU 16.17 to represent a part considered small and insignificant

κεραία	N-NF-S	κεραία
κεραίαν	N-AF-S	"

κεραμεύς, έως, ὁ one who makes earthenware pots *potter*

κεραμεύς	N-NM-S	κεραμεύς
κεραμέως	N-GM-S	"
κεραμικά	A--NN-P	κεραμικός

κεραμικός, ή, όν of what is made of clay by a potter *earthen, ceramic* (RV 2.27)

κεράμιον, ου, τό *earthenware container*; with the meaning varying with the context *pitcher, jar, jug*

κεράμιον	N-AN-S	κεράμιον

κέραμος, ου, ὁ *clay*; by metonymy *clay roofing, tile* (LU 5.19)

κεράμους	N-AM-P	κέραμος
κεράμων	N-GM-P	

κεράννυμι 1aor. ἐκέρασα; pf. pass. ptc. κεκερασμένος; literally, of a wine or other alcoholic drink *mix*; figuratively, of God's wrath *cause to be at full strength, prepare* (RV 18.6); *pour out, cause to be fully experienced* (RV 14.10)

κέρας, ατος, τό (1) literally, of an animal *horn* used in the description of symbolic beasts, representing rulers (RV 12.3); (2) figuratively; (a) as symbolic of ruling power and might (LU 1.69); (b) of hornlike projections on an altar *horn, corner* (RV 9.13)

κέρας	N-AN-S	κέρας
κεράσατε	VMAA--2P	κεράννυμι

κέρατα	N-AN-P	κέρας
	N-NN-P	"

κεράτιον, ου, τό diminutive of κέρας; *little horn*; plural, the horn-shaped fruits of the carob tree *carob pods* (LU 15.16)

κερατίων	N-GN-P	κεράτιον
κέρατος	N-GN-S	κέρας
κεράτων	N-GN-P	"

κερδαίνω fut. κερδήσω and κερδανῶ; 1aor. ἐκέρδησα and ἐκέρδανα; 1fut. pass. κερδηθήσομαι; (1) *procure advantage* or *profit, get gain, make a profit* (JA 4.13); (2) figuratively *gain, win over* someone (MT 18.15; 1C 9.19); (3) of gain through avoiding a loss *spare, save oneself* something (AC 27.21)

κερδάνω	VSAA--1S	κερδαίνω
κερδανῶ	VIFA--1S	"
κέρδη	N-NN-P	κέρδος
κερδηθήσονται	VIFP--3P	κερδαίνω
κερδηθήσωνται	VIFP--3P	see κερδηθήσονται
κερδῆσαι	VNAA	κερδαίνω
κερδήσας	VPAANM-S	"
κερδήσῃ	VSAA--3S	"
κερδήσομεν	VIFA--1P	"
κερδήσω	VSAA--1S	"
κερδήσωμεν	VSAA--1P	"

κέρδος, ους, τό *gain, advantage, profit*

κέρδος	N-NN-S	κέρδος
κέρδους	N-GN-S	"

κέρμα, ατος, τό strictly *something cut small*; hence *piece of money, small change, coin* (JN 2.15)

κέρμα	N-AN-S	κέρμα
κέρματα	N-AN-P	"
κερματιστάς	N-AM-P	κερματιστής

κερματιστής, οῦ, ὁ one who exchanges one type of currency for another *money changer* (JN 2.14)

κεφαλαί	N-NF-P	κεφαλή

κεφάλαιον, ου, τό (1) in the progression of an argument *main* or *principal point* (HE 8.1); (2) of money *sum, price* (AC 22.28)

κεφάλαιον	N-NN-S	κεφάλαιον
κεφαλαίου	N-GN-S	"
κεφαλάς	N-AF-P	κεφαλή

κεφαλή, ῆς, ἡ *head*; (1) literally, of a human or animal *head* (MT 6.17); (2) figuratively; (a) metaphorically, of Christ as the head of which the church is the body (EP 1.22); (b) of persons, designating first or superior rank *head* (1C 11.3); (c) of things *uppermost part, extremity, end point*; of buildings *keystone, capstone* (MT 21.42); (d) *leading city, capital* (AC 16.12)

κεφαλή	N-NF-S	κεφαλή
κεφαλῇ	N-DF-S	"
κεφαλήν	N-AF-S	"
κεφαλῆς	N-GF-S	"
κεφαλίδι	N-DF-S	κεφαλίς

κεφαλιόω (or **κεφαλαιόω**) 1aor. ἐκεφαλίωσα (or ἐκεφαλαίωσα); *strike repeatedly on the head, wound in the head*

κεφαλίς, ίδος, ἡ diminutive of κεφαλή; *little head*; strictly, the top or round heads of wooden rolls used to roll up scrolls; by metonymy *roll* of a book consisting of several such rolls or sections, *scroll* (HE 10.7)

κεφαλῶν	N-GF-P	κεφαλή
κεχάρισμαι	VIRD--1S	χαρίζομαι
	VIRO--1S	"
κεχάρισται	VIRD--3S	"
	VIRO--3S	"
κεχαριτωμένη	VPRPVF-S	χαριτόω
κέχρημαι	VIRD--1S	χράομαι
	VIRO--1S	"
κεχρηματισμένον	VPRPNN-S	χρηματίζω
κεχρηματισμένος	VPRPNM-S	"
κεχρημάτισται	VIRP--3S	"
κεχρυσωμένη	VPRPNF-S	χρυσόω
	VPRPVF-S	"
κεχωρισμένος	VPRPNM-S	χωρίζω
κηδεῦσαι	VNAA	κηδεύω

κηδεύω 1aor. ἐκήδευσα; *bury, take care of* a corpse (MK 6.29)

κημόω fut. κημώσω; as putting something over the mouth of an ox treading grain *muzzle, keep from eating* (1C 9.9)

κημώσεις	VIFA--2S	κημόω
	VIFA--2S^VMAA--2S	"
κῆνσον	N-AM-S	κῆνσος

κῆνσος, ου, ὁ literally *census, enumeration* of people and property for taxing purposes; in the NT, taxes charged on the basis of such assessment *(poll) tax, tribute*

κήνσου	N-GM-S	κῆνσος
κῆπον	N-AM-S	κῆπος

κῆπος, ου, ὁ *garden*, as a place planted with trees and herbs

κῆπος	N-NM-S	κῆπος

κηπουρός, οῦ, ὁ *gardener, keeper of a garden* (JN 20.15)

κηπουρός	N-NM-S	κηπουρός
κήπῳ	N-DM-S	κῆπος

κηρίον, ου, τό *honeycomb, wax comb filled with honey* (LU 24.42)

κηρίον	N-AN-S	κηρίον
κηρίου	N-GN-S	"

κήρυγμα, ατος, τό as the content of a sacred message *what is preached, preaching, proclamation* (1C 2.4)

κήρυγμα	N-AN-S	κήρυγμα
	N-NN-S	"
κηρύγματι	N-DN-S	"
κηρύγματος	N-GN-S	"
κήρυκα	N-AM-S	κῆρυξ

κῆρυξ, υκος, ὁ *herald*, one who proclaims public announcements, *summons* to assemblies, *carries messages*, etc.; in the NT one who acts as God's official human messenger *preacher, proclaimer* (1T 2.7)

κῆρυξ	N-NM-S	κῆρυξ
κηρύξαι	VNAA	κηρύσσω
κηρύξας	VPAANM-S	"
κηρύξατε	VMAA--2P	"
κήρυξον	VMAA--2S	"
κηρύξουσι(ν)	VIFA--3P	"
κηρύξω	VSAA--1S	"
κηρύξωσι(ν)	VSAA--3P	"
κηρύσσει	VIPA--3S	"
κηρύσσειν	VNPA	"
κηρύσσεται	VIPP--3S	"
κηρύσσετε	VMPA--2P	"

κηρύσσομεν | VIPA--1P | "
κηρύσσοντα | VPPAAM-S | "
κηρύσσοντας | VPPAAM-P | "
κηρύσσοντος | VPPAGM-S | "
κηρύσσουσι(ν) | VIPA--3P | "

κηρύσσω impf. ἐκήρυσσον; fut. κηρύξω; 1aor. ἐκήρυξα; 1aor. pass. ἐκηρύχθην; 1fut. pass. κηρυχθήσομαι; (1) denoting the official activity of a herald *announce, publicly proclaim* (RV 5.2); (2) *make known extensively, tell everywhere* (MK 5.20); (3) in a religious sense, denoting proclamation of a sacred message *proclaim, preach, publish* (MT 4.23); (4) as proclaiming the necessity of a course of action *preach* (MK 1.4)

κηρύσσω | VIPA--1S | κηρύσσω
κηρύσσων | VPPANM-S | "
 | VPPAVM-S | "
κηρυχθείς | VPAPNM-S | "
κηρυχθέντος | VPAPGN-S | "
κηρυχθῇ | VSAP--3S | "
κηρυχθῆναι | VNAP | "
κηρυχθήσεται | VIFP--3S | "

κῆτος, ους, τό *sea monster, large fish* (MT 12.40)

κήτους | N-GN-S | κῆτος
Κηφᾷ | N-GM-S | Κηφᾶς
Κηφᾷ | N-DM-S | "
Κηφᾶν | N-AM-S | "

Κηφᾶς, ᾶ, ὁ *Cephas*, masculine proper noun, the Aramaic equivalent of the Greek name Πέτρος (*Peter*), surname of the apostle Simon Peter

Κηφᾶς | N-NM-S | Κηφᾶς
κιβώρια | N-AN-P | κιβώριον

κιβώριον, ου, τό (1) *ciborium*, the seed pod of the Egyptian *bean*; (2) *container* shaped like a bean pod (AC 19.24)

κιβωτόν | N-AF-S | κιβωτός

κιβωτός, οῦ, ἡ *box, chest*; in the NT; (1) the sacred box in the innermost shrine of the tabernacle or temple *ark, chest* (HE 9.4); (2) the boxlike boat built by Noah *ark, ship* (MT 24.38)

κιβωτός | N-NF-S | κιβωτός
κιβωτοῦ | N-GF-S | "

κιθάρα, ας, ἡ as a stringed musical instrument *lyre, harp*

κιθάρα | N-NF-S | κιθάρα
κιθάραις | N-DF-P | "
κιθάραν | N-AF-S | "
κιθάρας | N-AF-P | "
κιθαριζόμενον | VPPPNN-S | κιθαρίζω
κιθαριζόντων | VPPAGM-P | "

κιθαρίζω *play the lyre or harp*

κιθαρῳδός, οῦ, ὁ one who plays an accompaniment to his own singing *harpist, lyre player*

κιθαρῳδῶν | N-GM-P | κιθαρῳδός

Κιλικία, ας, ἡ *Cilicia*, a province in southeastern Asia Minor

Κιλικίαν | N-AF-S | Κιλικία
Κιλικίας | N-GF-S | "

Κίλιξ, ικος, ὁ *Cilician, inhabitant of Cilicia* (AC 23.34)

Κίλιξ | N-NM-S | Κίλιξ
κινάμωμον | N-AN-S | κιννάμωμον
κινδυνεύει | VIPA--3S | κινδυνεύω
κινδυνεύομεν | VIPA--1P | "

κινδυνεύω impf. ἐκινδύνευον; *be in danger* or *peril, run a risk* (LU 8.23); with an infinitive following *run the risk of* something (AC 19.27)

κινδύνοις | N-DM-P | κίνδυνος

κίνδυνος, ου, ὁ as a condition of threatening circumstances *danger, risk, peril*

κίνδυνος | N-NM-S | κίνδυνος
κινδύνου | N-GM-S | "

κινέω fut. κινήσω; 1aor. ἐκίνησα; 1aor. pass. ἐκινήθην; (1) as putting something in motion; (a) literally *move*; of moving the head as a sign of contempt *shake, wag* the head (MT 27.39); (b) figuratively, of a mental or spiritual impression that stimulates to action *move, arouse, stir up* (AC 21.30); politically *instigate, stir up, cause* (AC 24.5); (2) as moving something away *remove* (MT 23.4); (3) passive *move about, come and go, carry on* (AC 17.28)

κινῆσαι | VNAA | κινέω
κίνησιν | N-AF-S | κίνησις

κίνησις, εως, ἡ as an action *moving, agitation, motion* (JN 5.3)

κινήσω | VIFA--1S | κινέω

κιννάμωμον, ου, τό (also **κινάμωμον**) *cinnamon*, a yellowish brown spice made from the bark of a kind of laurel shrub (RV 18.13)

κιννάμωμον | N-AN-S | κιννάμωμον
κινναμώμου | N-GN-S | "
κινούμεθα | VIPP--1P | κινέω
κινοῦντα | VPPAAM-S | "
κινοῦντες | VPPANM-P | "

Κίς, ὁ (also **Κείς**) indeclinable; *Kish*, masculine proper noun (AC 13.21)

κίχρημι 1aor. ἔχρησα; *lend, allow the use of* something, expecting its return or its equivalent (LU 11.5)

Κλάδιν | | Καῦδα
κλάδοι | N-NM-P | κλάδος
κλάδοις | N-DM-P | "

κλάδος, ου, ὁ *branch* of a tree or woody shrub (MT 13.32); as a tender branch broken off for grafting *shoot*, used metaphorically in RO 11.16–21 of God's acceptance of Gentiles along with Jews

κλάδος | N-NM-S | κλάδος
κλάδους | N-AM-P | "
κλάδων | N-GM-P | "
κλαῖε | VMPA--2S | κλαίω
κλαίειν | VNPA | "
κλαίεις | VIPA--2S | "
κλαίετε | VIPA--2P | "
 | VMPA--2P | "
κλαίοντας | VPPAAM-P | "
κλαίοντες | VPPANM-P | "
 | VPPAVM-P | "
κλαιόντων | VPPAGM-P | "
κλαίουσα | VPPANF-S | "
κλαίουσαι | VPPANF-P | "
κλαίουσαν | VPPAAF-S | "
κλαίουσι(ν) | VIPA--3P | "
 | VPPADM-P | "

κλαίω impf. ἔκλαιον; fut. κλαύσω, mid. κλαύσομαι; 1aor. ἔκλαυσα; (1) intransitively, as expressing strong inner emotion *weep, cry, shed* tears (LU 6.21); (2) transitively *wail* or *lament over, weep for* someone (MT 2.18)

κλαίων	VPPANM-S	κλαίω
κλάσαι	VNAA	κλάω
κλάσας	VPAANM-S	"
κλάσει	N-DF-S	κλάσις

κλάσις, εως, ἡ as an action *breaking*; in the NT of bread only (LU 24.35)

κλάσμα, ατος, τό bread that has been broken into pieces *fragment, bite* or *piece of bread, crumb*

κλάσματα	N-AN-P	κλάσμα
κλασμάτων	N-GN-P	κλάσμα
Κλαῦδα		Καῦδα
Κλαῦδαν		"
Κλαύδη		"
Κλαύδην		"

Κλαυδία, ας, ἡ *Claudia*, feminine proper noun (2T 4.21)

Κλαυδία	N-NF-S	Κλαυδία
Κλαύδιον		Καῦδα
	N-AM-S	Κλαύδιος

Κλαύδιος, ου, ὁ *Claudius*, masculine proper noun

Κλαύδιος	N-NM-S	Κλαύδιος
Κλαυδίου	N-GM-S	"

κλαυθμός, οῦ, ὁ as an expression of strong inner emotion *weeping, crying, lamentation*

κλαυθμός	N-NM-S	κλαυθμός
κλαύσατε	VMAA--2P	κλαίω
κλαύσετε	VIFA--2P	"
κλαύση	VSAA--3S	"
κλαύσονται	VIFM--3P	"
κλαύσουσι(ν)	VIFA--3P	"

κλάω 1aor. ἔκλασα; *break, break off, break in pieces*; in the NT used only of the breaking of bread (MT 15.36); by metonymy *share a meal*, since by Jewish custom a host or head of household thus began the main part of the meal (AC 2.46)

κλεῖδα	N-AF-S	κλείς
κλεῖδας	N-AF-P	"
κλείει	VIPA--3S	κλείω
κλείετε	VIPA--2P	"
κλεῖν	N-AF-S	κλείς

κλείς, κλειδός, ἡ as anything used for locking *key*; figuratively in the NT; (1) as a symbol of authority (RV 1.18); (2) as a symbol of entrance into knowledge *means of acquiring* (LU 11.52)

κλείς	N-NF-S	κλείς
κλεῖς	N-AF-P	"
κλεῖσαι	VNAA	κλείω
κλείσας	VPAANM-S	"
κλείσει	VIFA--3S	"
κλείση	VSAA--3S	"
κλεισθῶσι(ν)	VSAP--3P	"

κλείω fut. κλείσω; 1aor. ἔκλεισα; pf. pass. κέκλεισμαι; 1aor. pass. ἐκλείσθην; literally *shut, lock, bar* (MT 25.10); figuratively *shut (out), close* (RV 3.7)

κλείων	VPPANM-S	κλείω

κλέμμα, ατος, τό as an act of wrongdoing *theft, stealing* (RV 9.21)

κλέμματα	N-NN-P	κλέμμα
κλεμμάτων	N-GN-P	"
Κλεόπας	N-NM-S	Κλεοπᾶς

Κλεοπᾶς, ᾶ, ὁ (also **Κλεόπας**) *Cleopas*, masculine proper noun (LU 24.18)

Κλεοπᾶς	N-NM-S	Κλεοπᾶς

κλέος, ους, τό as a good reputation *credit, honor, praise* (1P 2.20)

κλέος	N-NN-S	κλέος
κλέπται	N-NM-P	κλέπτης
κλέπτας	N-AM-P	"
κλέπτειν	VNPA	κλέπτω
κλέπτεις	VIPA--2S	"
κλεπτέτω	VMPA--3S	"

κλέπτης, ου, ὁ (1) literally *thief* (MT 6.19); (2) metaphorically; (a) of self-seeking religious leaders (JN 10.8); (b) figuratively, of what is sudden and unexpected in an event (2P 3.10)

κλέπτης	N-NM-S	κλέπτης
κλέπτουσι(ν)	VIPA--3P	κλέπτω

κλέπτω fut. κλέψω; 1aor. ἔκλεψα; *steal, take away* something *secretly*, without the owner's permission

κλέπτων	VPPANM-S	κλέπτω
κλέψεις	VIFA--2S^VMAA--2S	"
κλέψῃ	VSAA--3S	"
κλέψης	VSAA--2S	"
κλέψουσι(ν)	VIFA--3P	"
κλέψωσι(ν)	VSAA--3P	"
κληθείς	VPAPNM-S	καλέω
κληθέν	VPAPNN-S	"
κληθέντος	VPAPGM-S	"
κληθῆναι	VNAP	"
κληθῇς	VSAP--2S	"
κληθήσεται	VIFP--3S	"
κληθήσῃ	VIFP--2S	"
κληθήσονται	VIFP--3P	"
κληθῆτε	VSAP--2P	"
κληθῶμεν	VSAP--1P	"

κλῆμα, ατος, τό *branch, shoot*, especially of grapevines (JN 15.2)

κλῆμα	N-AN-S	κλῆμα
	N-NN-S	"
κλήματα	N-NN-P	"
Κλήμεντος	N-GM-S	Κλήμης

Κλήμης, εντος, ὁ *Clement*, masculine proper noun (PH 4.3)

κλῆρον	N-AM-S	κλῆρος
κληρονομεῖ	VIPA--3S	κληρονομέω
κληρονομεῖν	VNPA	"

κληρονομέω fut. κληρονομήσω; 1aor. ἐκληρονόμησα; pf. κεκληρονόμηκα; literally, as receiving a possession or gift from someone who has died *inherit, be an heir* (GA 4.30); figuratively, as receiving God's salvation, gifts, and benefits *obtain, gain possession of, receive* (LU 10.25; HE 12.17)

κληρονομῆσαι	VNAA	κληρονομέω
κληρονομήσατε	VMAA--2P	"
κληρονομήσει	VIFA--3S	"
κληρονομήση	VSAA--3S	"
κληρονομήσητε	VSAA--2P	"
κληρονομήσουσι(ν)	VIFA--3P	"
κληρονομήσω	VIFA--1S	"
	VSAA--1S	"
κληρονομήσωσι(ν)	VSAA--3S	"

κληρονομία, ας, ἡ   (1) literally, what is received as a gift from someone who has died *portion, inheritance, patrimony* (LU 12.13); figuratively, in a religious sense, as God's promised salvation, gifts, and benefits *inheritance, (eternal) possession* (AC 20.32); (2) the land of Canaan as the object of God's promise *possession, inheritance* (AC 7.5); (3) abstract for concrete, of God's people *heirs* (RO 11.1)

κληρονομία	N-NF-S	κληρονομία
κληρονομίαν	N-AF-S	"
κληρονομίας	N-GF-S	"
κληρονόμοι	N-NM-P	κληρονόμος
κληρονόμοις	N-DM-P	"
κληρονόμον	N-AM-S	"

κληρονόμος, ου, ὁ   *heir*; literally, one receiving an allotted portion *heir* (MT 21.38); figuratively, in a religious sense, one receiving what God has promised *heir, receiver* (RO 8.17)

κληρονόμος	N-NM-S	κληρονόμος
κληρονομούντων	VPPAGM-P	κληρονομέω
κληρονόμους	N-AM-P	κληρονόμος

κλῆρος, ου, ὁ   (1) strictly, a small object (pebble, twig, potsherd, etc.) thrown to determine a choice or assign a portion *lot* (MK 15.24); (2) as what is assigned or allotted *portion, share, possession* (AC 8.21); (3) plural, as parts of a congregation that have been entrusted to the oversight of individual leaders *responsibility, those entrusted to* someone's *care* (1P 5.3)

κλῆρος	N-NM-S	κλῆρος
κλήρου	N-GM-S	"
κλήρους	N-AM-P	"

κληρόω   1aor. pass. ἐκληρώθην; literally *choose by lot*; passive *obtain an inheritance, be appointed as heir*; used metaphorically in EP 1.11 to denote God's appointment of both Jews and Gentiles to partake of a spiritual inheritance through their relationship to Christ

κλήρων	N-GM-P	κλῆρος
κλήσει	N-DF-S	κλῆσις
κλήσεως	N-GF-S	"
κλῆσιν	N-AF-S	"

κλῆσις, εως, ἡ   as an action *calling, call, invitation*; (1) predominately in a religious sense in the NT, of the divine invitations (PH 3.14); (2) as one's temporal status and position in life *social role, vocation, situation, station* (1C 7.20)

κλῆσις	N-NF-S	κλῆσις
κλητοί	A--NM-P	κλητός
κλητοῖς	A--DM-P	"

κλητός, ή, όν   a verbal adjective from the aorist passive participle of καλέω (*call*); *called, invited*; (1) in the NT generally of one who has accepted a calling or an invitation to become a guest or member of a select group (1C 1.1); (2) substantivally, as a designation for Christians οἱ κλητοί *the called, those who are called* (RO 1.6); (3) as distinguished from οἱ ἐκλεκτοί (*elect, chosen*), which indicates that more than a superficial response to God's invitation is necessary (MT 22.14; RV 17.14)

| κλητός | A--NM-S | κλητός |
| κλίβανον | N-AM-S | κλίβανος |

κλίβανος, ου, ὁ   Attic κρίβανος; *oven, furnace*; especially a dome-shaped clay structure for baking bread (MT 6.30)

κλίμα, ατος, τό   strictly *slope*; from the idea of a supposed sloping of the earth from equator to poles; hence *region, tract of land*

| κλίμασι | N-DN-P | κλίμα |
| κλίματα | N-AN-P | " |

κλινάριον, ου, τό   diminutive of κλίνη; *couch, small bed, cot* (AC 5.15)

κλιναρίων	N-GN-P	κλινάριον
κλίνας	VPAANM-S	κλίνω
κλίνειν	VNPA	"

κλίνη, ης, ἡ   *bed, couch* for dining or resting (LU 17.34); as used for carrying a sick person *pallet, stretcher, mat* (MT 9.2)

κλίνη	VSAA--3S	κλίνω
	VSPA--3S	"
κλίνην	N-AF-S	κλίνη
κλίνης	N-GF-S	"

κλινίδιον, ου, τό   diminutive of κλίνη; *small bed, couch*; for carrying a sick person *mat, pallet, cot*

κλινίδιον	N-AN-S	κλινίδιον
κλινιδίῳ	N-DN-S	"
κλινουσῶν	VPPAGF-P	κλίνω

κλίνω   1aor. ἔκλινα; pf. κέκλικα; (1) transitively; (a) literally, of a movement of the body *bend, bow, incline* (JN 19.30); (b) idiomatically τὴν κεφαλὴν κλίνειν literally *lay down the head* (for sleep), i.e. *lie down to rest* (MT 8.20); κλίνειν τὸ πρόσωπον εἰς τὴν γῆν literally *lay the face to the ground*, i.e. *prostrate oneself before* someone (LU 24.5); (c) figuratively, of putting an army to headlong flight *defeat, put to rout* (HE 11.34); (2) intransitively, of the day *be about to end, be late* (LU 9.12)

| κλινῶν | N-GF-P | κλίνη |

κλισία, ας, ἡ   strictly *place for reclining to eat*; by metonymy *group* or *company sitting together* to eat (LU 9.14)

| κλισίας | N-AF-P | κλισία |
| κλοπαί | N-NF-P | κλοπή |

κλοπή, ῆς, ἡ   *theft, stealing*

κλύδων, ωνος, ὁ   from κλύζω (*dash* and *surge*, like waves); *violent wave, surge, billow*; κ. τοῦ ὕδατος *stormy sea, raging water* (LU 8.24); as a succession of waves *surf* (JA 1.6)

| κλύδωνι | N-DM-S | κλύδων |

κλυδωνίζομαι   *be tossed by waves*; figuratively, of unstable opinion *fluctuate, frequently change the way one thinks* or *believes* (EP 4.14)

κλυδωνιζόμενοι	VPPDNM-P	κλυδωνίζομαι
	VPPONM-P	"
κλῶμεν	VIPA--1P	κλάω
κλώμενον	VPPPNN-S	"
κλῶντες	VPPANM-P	"
Κλωπᾶ	N-GM-S	Κλωπᾶς

Κλωπᾶς, ᾶ, ὁ   *Clopas*, masculine proper noun (JN 19.25)

| κνηθόμενοι | VPPPNM-P | κνήθω |

κνήθω   *scratch, tickle, titillate*; only passive in the NT *itch*; idiomatically κνήθεσθαι τὴν ἀκοήν literally *itch with respect to hearing*, i.e. *crave to hear what one wants to hear* (2T 4.3)

Κνίδον	N-AF-S	Κνίδος

Κνίδος, ου, ἡ *Cnidus*, a peninsula with a city of the same name on the coast of Caria in southwestern Asia Minor (AC 27.7)

κοδράντην	N-AM-S	κοδράντης

κοδράντης, ου, ὁ *quadrans*, a Roman copper coin worth one-quarter of an assarion, equal to two λεπτά (*small coin, lepton*); *farthing, penny, cent* (MK 12.42)

κοδράντης	N-NM-S	κοδράντης

κοιλία, ας, ἡ from κοῖλος (*hollow*); (1) literally, the hollow part of the body; (a) where food is digested *stomach, belly* (MK 7.19); (b) where reproduction takes place *womb, uterus* (LU 1.15); (2) figuratively; (a) the inner self *innermost being, heart* (JN 7.38); (b) *desires, appetites* (RO 16.18)

κοιλία	N-NF-S	κοιλία
κοιλίᾳ	N-DF-S	"
κοιλίαι	N-NF-P	"
κοιλίαν	N-AF-S	"
κοιλίας	N-GF-S	"

κοιμάομαι pf. κεκοίμημαι; 1aor. ἐκοιμήθην; 1fut. κοιμηθήσομαι; only passive in the NT; literally *sleep, fall asleep* (AC 12.6); figuratively and euphemistically, for dying *fall asleep, die* (JN 11.11)

κοιμᾶται	VIPO--3S	κοιμάομαι
κοιμηθέντας	VPAOAM-P	"
κοιμηθέντες	VPAONM-P	"
κοιμηθῇ	VSAO--3S	"
κοιμηθησόμεθα	VIFO--1P	"
κοιμήσεως	N-GF-S	κοίμησις

κοίμησις, εως, ἡ as an action *sleeping, taking rest in sleep* (JN 11.13)

κοιμώμενος	VPPDNM-S	κοιμάομαι
	VPPONM-S	"
κοιμωμένους	VPPDAM-P	"
	VPPOAM-P	"
κοιμωμένων	VPPDGM-P	"
	VPPOGM-P	"
κοιμῶνται	VIPD--3P	"
	VIPO--3P	"
κοινά	A--AN-P	κοινός
	A--NN-P	"
κοιναῖς	A--DF-S	"
κοινήν	A--AF-S	"
κοινῆς	A--GF-S	"
κοινοῖ	VIPA--3S	κοινόω
κοινόν	A--AM-S	κοινός
	A--AN-S	"
	A--NN-S	"

κοινός, ή, όν *common*; (1) as belonging equally to several *mutual, communal, in common* (AC 2.44); (2) *not consecrated, common, ordinary* (RV 21.27), opposite ἅγιος (*holy, dedicated*); (3) *defiled, (ceremonially) unacceptable* (AC 10.14), opposite καθαρός (*clean, pure*); substantivally κοινόν *what is defiled* (AC 11.8)

κοίνου	VMPA--2S	κοινόω
κοινοῦν	VPPANN-S	"
κοινοῦντα	VPPANN-P	"

κοινόω 1aor. ἐκοίνωσα; pf. κεκοίνωκα; pf. pass. κεκοίνωμαι; (1) as violating ritual holiness *make common* or *unclean, defile, desecrate* (AC 21.28); (2) as making a

person ceremonially unclean *defile, make ritually unacceptable* (HE 9.13); (3) as making a person morally unclean *defile, pollute* (MK 7.15b); (4) of ceremonial disqualification *declare unclean, consider common, regard as ritually unacceptable* (AC 10.15)

κοινώνει	VMPA--2S	κοινωνέω
κοινωνεῖ	VIPA--3S	"
κοινωνεῖτε	VIPA--2P	"
κοινωνείτω	VMPA--3S	"

κοινωνέω 1aor. ἐκοινώνησα; pf. κεκοινώνηκα; (1) denoting common participation *share, have in common, take part with* someone (HE 2.14); (2) as giving so that others can share *contribute, share, give a part* (GA 6.6); (3) as equivalent to κοινόω *make unclean, defile, pollute*, either ritually or morally (MT 15.11)

κοινωνία, ας, ἡ (1) as a relationship characterized by sharing in common *fellowship, participation* (1J 1.3), opposite κακία (*dislike, hatefulness*); (2) as giving so that others can share *generosity, fellow feeling* (2C 9.13; PH 2.1); more concretely *willing contribution, gift* (RO 15.26)

κοινωνία	N-NF-S	κοινωνία
κοινωνίᾳ	N-DF-S	"
κοινωνίαν	N-AF-S	"
κοινωνίας	N-GF-S	"

κοινωνικός, ή, όν characterized by a readiness to share with others *liberal, generous, sociable* (1T 6.18)

κοινωνικούς	A--AM-P	κοινωνικός
κοινωνοί	N-NM-P	κοινωνός
κοινωνόν	N-AM-S	"

κοινωνός, οῦ, ὁ as one who fellowships and shares something in common with another *partner* (LU 5.10); *partaker* (1C 10.18); *fellow participant, companion* (HE 10.33)

κοινωνός	N-NM-S	κοινωνός
κοινωνοῦντες	VPPANM-P	κοινωνέω
κοινωνούς	N-AM-P	κοινωνός

κοινῶς (1) *commonly, publicly*; (2) *jointly, in common*, of the name Boanerges, which Jesus gave to James and John the sons of Zebedee (MK 3.17)

κοινῶς	AB	κοινῶς
κοινῶσαι	VNAA	κοινόω
κοίταις	N-DF-P	κοίτη

κοίτη, ης, ἡ (1) generally *bed* (LU 11.7); specifically *marriage bed* (HE 13.4); (2) euphemistically *sexual intercourse*; plural *sexual excesses, promiscuity, illicit affairs* (RO 13.13); (3) idiomatically κοίτην ἔχειν literally *have bed*, i.e. *conceive, become pregnant* (RO 9.10)

κοίτη	N-NF-S	κοίτη
κοίτην	N-AF-S	"

κοιτών, ῶνος, ὁ *bedroom, sleeping room*; by metonymy, as a title for an officer in charge of a ruler's sleeping quarters ὁ ἐπὶ τοῦ κοιτῶνος *chamberlain, personal attendant* (AC 12.20)

κοιτῶνος	N-GM-S	κοιτών
κοκκίνην	A--AF-S	κόκκινος
κόκκινον	AP-AN-S	"
	A--AN-S	"

κόκκινος, η, ον *scarlet, crimson, red*; neuter as a substantive τὸ κόκκινον *scarlet cloth*, dyed with κόκκος, a scarlet "berry," actually the female of a scale insect that clings to oak leaves, dried and crushed to prepare a red dye (RV 17.4)

κοκκίνου	AP-GN-S	κόκκινος
	A--GN-S	"
κοκκίνῳ	AP-DN-S	"
κόκκον	N-AM-S	κόκκος

κόκκος, ου, ὁ   (1) of grain or plants *seed, kernel*; (2) *scarlet "berry"*; see κόκκινος

κόκκος	N-NM-S	κόκκος
κόκκῳ	N-DM-S	"
κολαζόμενοι	VPPPNM-P	κολάζω
κολαζομένους	VPPPAM-P	"

κολάζω   1aor. mid. ἐκολασάμην; strictly *cut off, lop, trim*; hence *prune, trim*; figuratively in the NT, middle *punish, chastise, keep in line* (AC 4.21); passive *be punished* (2P 2.9)

κολακεία, ας, ἡ   *flattery, exaggerated praise*

κολακείας	N-GF-S	κολακεία
κολάσεως	N-GF-S	κόλασις
κόλασιν	N-AF-S	"

κόλασις, εως, ἡ   as an action *retribution, punishment* (MT 25.46); ὁ φόβος κόλασιν ἔχει *fear has to do with* or *involves punishment* (1J 4.18)

Κολασσαῖς	N-DF-P	Κολοσσαί
κολάσωνται	VSAM--3P	κολάζω
κολαφίζειν	VNPA	κολαφίζω
κολαφίζῃ	VSPA--3S	"
κολαφιζόμεθα	VIPP--1P	"
κολαφιζόμενοι	VPPPNM-P	"

κολαφίζω   1aor. ἐκολάφισα; literally, as beating or striking with the fist *box on the ear, cuff, buffet* (MT 26.67); generally *treat roughly, ill-treat* (1C 4.11); figuratively, denoting painful attacks from illness or adverse circumstances *buffet, afflict, cause difficulty* (2C 12.7)

| κολλᾶσθαι | VNPP | κολλάω |

κολλάω   1aor. pass. ἐκολλήθην; 1fut. pass. κολληθήσομαι; literally *join closely, glue together, unite*; figuratively and passive in the NT; (1) of things *cling to, adhere to, cleave to* (LU 10.11); (2) *come in close contact with, touch, reach to*; idiomatically κολλᾶσθαι ἄχρι τοῦ οὐρανοῦ literally *reach to heaven*, i.e. *increase greatly* (RV 18.5); (3) of persons, associate with closely, join oneself to (as a disciple) (AC 9.26); of a sexual partner *join oneself to, cleave to, unite with* (1C 6.16)

κολληθέντα	VPAPAM-S	κολλάω
κολληθέντες	VPAPNM-P	"
κολληθήσεται	VIFP--3S	"
κολλήθητι	VMAP--2S	"

κολλούριον, ου, τό (also **κολλύριον**)   diminutive of κολλύρα (*round cake*); a small cake prepared as an eye remedy *eyesalve* (RV 3.18)

| κολλούριον | N-AN-S | κολλούριον |

κολλυβιστής, οῦ, ὁ   from κόλλυβος (*small coin*); *money changer*

κολλυβιστῶν	N-GM-P	κολλυβιστής
κολλύριον	N-AN-S	κολλούριον
κολλώμενοι	VPPPNM-P	κολλάω
κολλώμενος	VPPPNM-S	"

κολοβόω   1aor. ἐκολόβωσα; 1aor. pass. ἐκολοβώθην; 1fut. pass. κολοβωθήσομαι; literally *maim, mutilate*; figura-

tively, as reducing in number or extent *decrease, shorten, cut short* (MT 24.22)

| κολοβωθήσονται | VIFP--3P | κολοβόω |

Κολοσσαί, ῶν, αἱ (also **Κολασσαί**)   *Colossae*, a city in Phrygia in Asia Minor (CO 1.2)

Κολοσσαῖς	N-DF-P	Κολοσσαί
κόλποις	N-DM-P	κόλπος
κόλπον	N-AM-S	"

κόλπος, ου, ὁ   (1) as the front of the body between the arms *chest, breast, bosom* (JN 13.23); idiomatically, as a place of honor and close fellowship at a meal ἀνακεῖσθαι ἐν τῷ κόλπῳ literally *recline on the bosom*, i.e. *dine in the place of honor* (JN 13.23); κ. Ἀβραάμ literally *Abraham's bosom*, i.e. as a place of honor among the righteous dead, *by Abraham's side, in Paradise* (LU 16.22); εἶναι εἰς τὸν κόλπον τοῦ πατρός literally *be in the bosom of the Father*, i.e. *be in close association with, be close beside the Father* (JN 1.18); (2) as the front fold of a garment formed into a large pocket *lap, fold* (LU 6.38); (3) as an inward extension of a sea *bay, inlet* (AC 27.39)

| κόλπῳ | N-DM-S | κόλπος |
| κολυμβᾶν | VNPA | κολυμβάω |

κολυμβάω   *swim*, as movement through water by the use of arms and legs (AC 27.43)

κολυμβήθρα, ας, ἡ   as a place constructed for holding water for swimming or bathing *pool* (JN 5.2)

| κολυμβήθρα | N-NF-S | κολυμβήθρα |
| κολυμβήθραν | N-AF-S | " |

κολωνία, ας, ἡ   *colony*, as a group of people settled in a distant land but remaining under the authority of their native land or still regarded as citizens of their native city (AC 16.12)

| κολωνία | N-NF-S | κολωνία |
| κομᾷ | VSPA--3S | κομάω |

κομάω   *wear long hair, let one's hair grow long*

κόμη, ης, ἡ   *hair*, especially *head of long hair* (1C 11.15)

κόμη	N-NF-S	κόμη
κομεῖσθε	VIFM--2P	κομίζω
κομεῖται	VIFM--3S	"
κομιζόμενοι	VPPMNM-P	"

κομίζω   fut. mid. κομίσομαι and κομιοῦμαι; 1aor. ἐκόμισα, mid. ἐκομισάμην; (1) active *bring, fetch* (LU 7.37); (2) middle, with a sense of receiving back as recompense or reward *get for oneself, obtain, receive (back)* (1P 1.9; 2P 2.13)

κομιούμενοι	VPFMNM-P	κομίζω
κομισάμενοι	VPAMNM-P	"
κομίσασα	VPAANF-S	"
κομίσεται	VIFM--3S	"
κομίσησθε	VSAM-2P	"
κομίσηται	VSAM-3S	"

κομψότερον   comparative adverb of κομψός (*well*); used idiomatically κ. ἔχειν literally *have better*, i.e. *get better, begin to improve* (JN 4.52)

| κομψότερον | ABM | κομψότερον |

κονιάω   pf. pass. ptc. κεκονιαμένος; as smearing something over with lime *whitewash, plaster over* (MT 23.27); idiomatically, of a person τοῖχος κεκονιαμένος literally *whitewashed wall*, i.e. *impostor, hypocrite* (AC 23.3)

| κονιορτόν | N-AM-S | κονιορτός |

κονιορτός, οῦ, ὁ   *dust stirred up, cloud of dust*; generally *dust*

κοπάζω   1aor. ἐκόπασα; of movement, such as wind *abate, die down, cease*

κοπετόν   N-AM-S   κοπετός

κοπετός, οῦ, ὁ   strictly *beating of the breast* as a sign of grief; hence *mourning, lamentation, wailing* (AC 8.2)

κοπή, ῆς, ἡ   strictly *cutting down*; hence *slaughter, smiting, (utter) defeat* (HE 7.1)

κοπῆς   N-GF-S   κοπή
κοπιᾷ   VIPA--3S   κοπιάω
κοπιάσαντες   VPAANM-P   "
κοπιάτω   VMPA--3S   "

κοπιάω   1aor. ἐκοπίασα; pf. κεκοπίακα; (1) physically *become weary* or *tired* (JN 4.6); (2) of strong exertions *work hard, strive, struggle* (1T 4.10); (3) emotionally *become discouraged, give up* (RV 2.3)

κοπιοῦσι(ν)   VIPA--3P   see κοπιῶσι(ν)
κοπιῶ   VIPA--1S   κοπιάω
κοπιῶμεν   VIPA--1P   "
κοπιῶντα   VPPAAM-S   "
κοπιῶντας   VPPAAM-P   "
κοπιῶντες   VPPANM-P   "
   VPPAVM-P   "
κοπιῶντι   VPPADM-S   "
κοπιώσας   VPPAAF-P   "
κοπιῶσι(ν)   VIPA--3P   "
κόποις   N-DM-P   κόπος
κόπον   N-AM-S   "

κόπος, ου, ὁ   strictly *beating*; (1) as exhausting physical or mental exertion *toil, labor, work* (JN 4.38); (2) as exhausting and wearisome difficulties encountered *trouble, burden, hardship* (MT 26.10)

κόπος   N-NM-S   κόπος
κόπου   N-GM-S   "
κόπους   N-AM-P   "
κόπρια   N-AN-P   κόπριον

κοπρία, ας, ἡ   as intended for fertilizer *manure pile, dung heap* (LU 14.35)

κοπρίαν   N-AF-S   κοπρία

κόπριον, ου, τό   as fertilizer *dung, manure* (LU 13.8)

κοπρίων   N-GN-P   κόπριον

κόπτω   impf. ἔκοπτον, mid. ἐκοπτόμην; fut. mid. κόψομαι; 1aor. ἔκοψα, mid. ἐκοψάμην; (1) active *cut (off)* (MT 21.8); (2) middle *beat one's breast* as a strong expression of grief or remorse; hence *mourn, lament* (RV 1.7)

κόπτω   VSPA--1S   κόπτω
κόπῳ   N-DM-S   κόπος
κόπων   N-GM-P   "
κόρακας   N-AM-P   κόραξ

κόραξ, ακος, ὁ   a large black bird *raven, crow* (LU 12.24)

κοράσιον, ου, τό   diminutive of κόρη; *little girl, maiden*

κοράσιον   N-NN-S   κοράσιον
   N-VN-S   "
κορασίῳ   N-DN-S   "

κορβᾶν, ὁ   indeclinable; from the Hebrew *corban* (*gift*), a word designating the whole burnt offering among the levitical sacrifices; equivalent to δῶρον in the NT, as a *gift, offering* used for fulfilling religious vows (MK 7.11)

κορβανᾶν   N-AM-S   κορβανᾶς

κορβανᾶς, ᾶ, ὁ   *sacred treasury, temple treasury* (MT 27.6)

κορβανᾶν   N-AM-S   see κορβανᾶν

Κόρε, ὁ (also Κορέ)   indeclinable; *Korah*, masculine proper noun (JU 11)

Κορέ   Κόρε

κορέννυμι   pf. pass. κεκόρεσμαι; 1aor. pass. ἐκορέσθην; *satiate, fill*; passive *get enough of, be satisfied with, have all one wants of* something (AC 27.38)

κορεσθέντες   VPAPNM-P   κορέννυμι
Κορίνθιοι   N-NM-P   Κορίνθιος
   N-VM-P   "

Κορίνθιος, ου, ὁ   *Corinthian, inhabitant of Corinth*

Κορινθίους   N-AM-P   Κορίνθιος
Κορινθίων   N-GM-P   "
Κόρινθον   N-AF-S   Κόρινθος

Κόρινθος, ου, ἡ   *Corinth*, a port city in Greece

Κορίνθου   N-GF-S   Κόρινθος
Κορίνθῳ   N-DF-S   "
Κορνήλιε   N-VM-S   Κορνήλιος

Κορνήλιος, ου, ὁ   *Cornelius*, masculine proper noun

Κορνήλιος   N-NM-S   Κορνήλιος
Κορνηλίου   N-GM-S   "
Κορνηλίῳ   N-DM-S   "

κόρος, ου, ὁ   *cor* or *kor*, the largest Hebrew dry measure, holding 11 bushels or about 390 liters (LU 16.7)

κόρους   N-AM-P   κόρος
κοσμεῖν   VNPA   κοσμέω
κοσμεῖτε   VIPA--2P   "

κοσμέω   impf. ἐκόσμουν; 1aor. ἐκόσμησα; pf. pass. κεκόσμημαι; from the basic sense of κόσμος (*order, adornment*); (1) *put in order, arrange*; of lamp wicks *trim* (MT 25.7); (2) *adorn, decorate* (MT 23.29); figuratively, of spiritual or moral attractiveness *adorn, make beautiful and attractive* (1P 3.5); of a way of life that recommends doctrinal teachings *do credit to, honor* (TI 2.10)

κοσμικάς   A--AF-P   κοσμικός
κοσμικόν   A--AN-S   "

κοσμικός, ή, όν   (1) *belonging to this world, earthly* (HE 9.1); (2) morally, of the systems or standards of the world that are hostile to God *worldly* (TI 2.12)

κόσμιον   A--AM-S   κόσμιος

κόσμιος, ον   strictly *well-arranged*; (1) of persons *disciplined, honorable, respectable* (1T 3.2); (2) of dress characterized by respectability *modest, sensible* (1T 2.9)

κοσμίῳ   A--DF-S   κόσμιος

κοσμίως   *modestly, respectably* (1T 2.9)

κοσμίως   AB   κοσμίως
κοσμοκράτορας   N-AM-P   κοσμοκράτωρ

κοσμοκράτωρ, ορος, ὁ   *one holding power over the world*; plural in the NT, for devilish forces, spirit-beings who control parts of the world system *world rulers* (EP 6.12)

κόσμον   N-AM-S   κόσμος

κόσμος, ου, ὁ   basically *something well-arranged*; (1) *adornment, adorning* (1P 3.3); (2) as the sum total of all created beings in heaven and earth *world, universe* (AC 17.24); (3) as all human beings *mankind, humanity, all people* (MK 16.15); (4) as this planet inhabited by mankind *world, earth* (MT 16.26; JN 11.9); (5) morally, mankind as alienated from God, unredeemed and hostile to him *world* (1J 5.19); (6) *sum total* of particulars in any one field of experience, *world, totality* (JA 3.6)

κόσμος	N-NM-S	κόσμος
κόσμου	N-GM-S	"
κόσμῳ	N-DM-S	"
κοσμῶσι(ν)	VSPA--3P	κοσμέω

Κούαρτος, ου, ὁ *Quartus*, masculine proper noun (RO 16.23)

Κούαρτος	N-NM-S	Κούαρτος
κούμ		κούμ

κούμ (also **κούμ, κούμι**) an imperative for the Aramaic *stand up, arise* (MK 5.41)

κούμι		κούμ

κουστωδία, ας, ἡ a detachment of soldiers *guard, watch* (MT 28.11); idiomatically ἔχειν κουστωδίαν literally *have guard*, i.e. *take a guard* (MT 27.65)

κουστωδίαν	N-AF-S	κουστωδία
κουστωδίας	N-GF-S	"

κουφίζω impf. ἐκούφιζον; *make light* or *less heavy*; of a ship *lighten* by throwing out cargo (AC 27.38)

κόφινοι	N-NM-P	κόφινος
κόφινον	N-AM-S	"

κόφινος, ου, ὁ *(hand)basket*, particularly a wicker basket typically used by Jews for carrying along levitically clean food

κοφίνους	N-AM-P	κόφινος
κοφίνων	N-GM-P	"
κόψαντες	VPAANM-P	κόπτω
κόψονται	VIFM--3P	"
κράβατον	N-AM-S	κράβαττος
κραβάττοις	N-DM-P	"
κράβαττον	N-AM-S	"

κράβαττος, ου, ὁ (also **κράβατος, κράββατος, κράββαττος, κρέβαττος**) *mat, pallet, cot* for one person, (poor person's) *bed*

κραβάττου	N-GM-S	κράβαττος
κραβάττων	N-GM-P	"
κραββάτοις	N-DM-P	"
κράββατον	N-AM-S	"
κραββάτου	N-GM-S	"
κράββαττον	N-AM-S	"
κραββάτῳ	N-DM-S	"
κραββάτων	N-GM-P	"
κράζει	VIPA--3S	κράζω
κράζειν	VNPA	"
κράζομεν	VIPA--1P	"
κράζον	VPPAAN-S	"
κράζοντα	VPPAAN-P	"
	VPPANN-P	"
κράζοντας	VPPAAM-P	"
κράζοντες	VPPANM-P	"
κραζόντων	VPPAGM-P	"
κράζουσι(ν)	VIPA--3P	"

κράζω impf. ἔκραζον; fut. κράξω, mid. κράξομαι and κεκράξομαι (LU 19.40); 1aor. ἔκραξα and ἐκέκραξα; pf. κέκραγα; (1) as speaking or demanding with a loud voice *cry (out), call (out), exclaim* (MT 9.27); (2) of the loud inarticulate cries of demons and demonized people *shriek, cry out, scream* (MK 5.5); (3) of urgent appeals for help *call, cry out* (MT 15.23); (4) figuratively, of urgent prophetic utterances *cry* (JN 1.15); (5) figuratively, of things personified as if uttering a loud protest *cry out* (LU 19.40)

κράζων	VPPANM-S	κράζω

κραιπάλη, ης, ἡ (1) as excessive wine drinking *carousing, dissipation, debauchery* (possibly LU 21.34); (2) as the dizziness and staggering that results from such behavior *intoxication, hangover* (probably LU 21.34)

κραιπάλη	N-DF-S	κραιπάλη

κρανίον, ου, τό *skull*, as the bony framework of the head

κρανίον	N-AN-S	κρανίον
κρανίου	N-GN-S	"
κράξαν	VPAANN-S	κράζω
κράξαντα	VPAAAM-S	"
κράξαντες	VPAANM-P	"
κράξας	VPAANM-S	"
κράξονται	VIFM--3P	"
κράξουσι(ν)	VIFA--3P	"
κράσπεδα	N-AN-P	κράσπεδον

κράσπεδον, ου, τό (1) as the outer limit of something; of a garment *hem, border, edge*; (2) in Jewish usage the *tassel* or *fringe* on the four corners of the outer garment, worn as a reminder to observe the commandments (cf. Numbers 15.38–41; Deuteronomy 22.12)

κρασπέδου	N-GN-S	κράσπεδον
κραταιάν	A-AF-S	κραταιός

κραταιός, ά, όν *strong, mighty, powerful* (1P 5.6)

κραταιοῦσθε	VMPP--2P	κραταιόω

κραταιόω impf. pass. ἐκραταιούμην; 1aor. pass. ἐκραταιώθην; (1) active *make strong, strengthen*; (2) passive in the NT *become strong, grow strong, be strengthened*

κραταιωθῆναι	VNAP	κραταιόω
κράτει	N-DN-S	κράτος
	VMPA--2S	κρατέω
κρατεῖν	VNPA	"
κρατεῖς	VIPA--2S	"
κρατεῖσθαι	VNPP	"
κρατεῖτε	VIPA--2P	"
	VMPA--2P	"

κρατέω impf. ἐκράτουν; fut. κρατήσω; 1aor. ἐκράτησα; pf. κεκράτηκα; pf. pass. κεκράτημαι; from a basic meaning *be strong* or *possess power*; (1) *take hold of* (forcibly), *seize, grasp* (MT 9.25); (2) *take into custody, seize, arrest* (MT 14.3); (3) *take control of, hold (fast)* (AC 2.24); (4) *hold back, restrain from, hinder, prevent* (LU 24.16); (5) of following a doctrine, creedal confession, or course of life *hold fast to, keep hold of, continue firmly in* (HE 4.14); of causing a state to continue *retain, keep* (JN 20.23)

κρατῆσαι	VNAA	κρατέω
κρατήσαντες	VPAANM-P	"
κρατήσας	VPAANM-S	"
κρατήσατε	VMAA--2P	"
κρατήσει	VIFA--3S	"
κρατήσωσι(ν)	VSAA--3P	"
κρατῆτε	VSPA--2P	"
κράτιστε	A-SVM-S	κράτιστος

κράτιστος, ίστη, ον superlative of κρατύς (*strong*); in the NT an honorary form of address to high officials *most excellent, most noble*

κρατίστῳ	A-SDM-S	κράτιστος

κράτος, ους, τό denoting the possession of force or strength that affords supremacy or control; (1) of God *sovereignty, power, might, dominion* (1T 6.16); (2) of the devil *power, control* (HE 2.14); (3) concretely *mighty deed, miracle* (LU 1.51)

κράτος	N-AN-S	κράτος
	N-NN-S	"
κρατοῦντας	VPPAAM-P	κρατέω
κρατοῦντες	VPPANM-P	"
κρατοῦντος	VPPAGM-S	"
κράτους	N-GN-S	κράτος
κρατοῦσι(ν)	VIPA--3P	κρατέω
κρατῶμεν	VSPA--1P	"
κρατῶν	VPPANM-S	"
κραυγάζοντα	VPPANN-P	κραυγάζω
κραυγαζόντων	VPPAGM-P	

κραυγάζω impf. ἐκραύγαζον; fut. κραυγάσω; 1aor. ἐκραύγασα; as speaking or demanding with a loud voice *cry out, shout*

κραυγάσει	VIFA--3S	κραυγάζω

κραυγή, ῆς, ἡ (1) as several voices speaking loudly at the same time *outcry, clamor, shouting* (MT 25.6); (2) as the loud sound of one voice *(loud) cry, shout* (LU 1.42); (3) as the loud sound accompanying weeping *crying, wailing* (RV 21.4)

κραυγή	N-NF-S	κραυγή
κραυγῇ	N-DF-S	"
κραυγῆς	N-GF-S	"
κρέα	N-AN-P	κρέας

κρέας, έως and **ατος, τό** of animals used for food *meat, flesh*

κρεβάττῳ	N-DM-S	κράβαττος
κρεῖσσον	ABM	κρείττων
	A-MAN-S	"
	A-MNN-S	"
κρείσσονα	A-MAN-P	"
κρεῖττον	ABM	"
	A-MAN-S	"
	A-MNN-S	"
κρείττονα	A-MAF-S	"
	A-MAN-P	"
κρείττονος	A-MGF-S	"
	A-MGM-S	"
	A-MGN-S	"
κρείττοσι(ν)	A-MDF-P	"
κρείττω	A-MAN-P	"

κρείττων, ον, gen. **ονος** and **κρείσσων** comparative of κρατύς (*strong*) used as a comparative of ἀγαθός (*good*); (1) of persons *superior, better, higher in rank* (HE 1.4); substantivally *more important person* (HE 7.7); (2) of what is *more advantageous, better, more useful* (1C 7.9); neuter as a substantive τὸ κρεῖττον *the advantage, the more profitable thing* (1C 11.17; perhaps HE 12.24), opposite τὸ ἧσσον (*the worse*); τὰ κρείσσονα *more useful things* (HE 6.9); (3) neuter as an adverb *(in a) better (way)* (probably HE 12.24)

κρείττων	A-MNM-S	κρείττων
κρεμάμενον	VPPMAN-S	κρεμάννυμι
κρεμάμενος	VPPMNM-S	"

κρεμάννυμι mid. κρέμαμαι; 1aor. ἐκρέμασα; 1aor. pass. ἐκρεμάσθην; (1) transitively; (a) literally *hang* something or someone *on* something (AC 5.30); (b) passive *be hung on* (MT 18.6); absolutely, of crucifixion *be hanged* (LU 23.39); (2) intransitively, middle *hang on,*

be suspended from (AC 28.4); figuratively, of laws and principles *depend on* (MT 22.40)

κρέμανται	VIPM--3P	κρεμάννυμι
κρεμάσαντες	VPAANM-P	"
κρεμασθέντων	VPAPGM-P	"
κρεμασθῇ	VSAP--3S	"
κρέμαται	VIPP--3S	"

κρημνός, οῦ, ὁ *steep slope* or *bank, cliff, precipice*

κρημνοῦ	N-GM-S	κρημνός

Κρής, ητός, ὁ *Cretan, inhabitant of Crete*, an island in the Mediterranean Sea

Κρήσκης, εντος, ὁ *Crescens*, masculine proper noun (2T 4.10)

Κρήσκης	N-NM-S	Κρήσκης
Κρῆτες	N-NM-P	Κρής

Κρήτη, ης, ἡ *Crete*, a large island in the Mediterranean Sea

Κρήτη	N-DF-S	Κρήτη
Κρήτην	N-AF-S	"
Κρήτης	N-GF-S	"

κριθή, ῆς, ἡ *barley (grain)* (RV 6.6)

κριθῆναι	VNAP	κρίνω
κριθῆς	N-GF-S	κριθή
κριθήσεσθε	VIFP--2P	κρίνω
κριθήσεται	VIFP--3S	"
κριθήσονται	VIFP--3P	"
κριθῆτε	VSAP--2P	"

κρίθινος, η, ον *made of barley flour*

κριθίνους	A--AM-P	κρίθινος
κριθίνων	A--GM-P	"
κριθῶν	N-GF-P	κριθή
κριθῶσι(ν)	VSAP--3P	κρίνω

κρίμα, ατος, τό (1) as an administrative decree, the result of κρίνω (*evaluate, judge*) *judgment, verdict, sentence* (LU 24.20); often in an unfavorable sense *condemnation, punishment* (2P 2.3); (2) as the function of a judge *authority to judge, judgment, judging* (RV 20.4); (3) as a legal action or process *lawsuit* (1C 6.7)

κρίμα	N-AN-S	κρίμα
	N-NN-S	"
κρίματα	N-AN-P	"
	N-NN-P	"
κρίματι	N-DN-S	"
κρίματος	N-GN-S	"
κρίνα	N-AN-P	κρίνον
κρῖναι	VNAA	κρίνω
κρίναντας	VPAAAM-P	"
κρίναντες	VPAANM-P	"
κρίναντος	VPAAGM-S	"
κρίνας	VPAANM-S	"
κρίνατε	VMAA--2P	"
κρινάτω	VMAA--3S	"
κρίνει	VIPA--3S	"
κρινεῖ	VIFA--3S	"
κρίνειν	VNPA	"
κρίνεις	VIPA--2S	"
κρίνεσθαι	VNPP	"
κρίνεται	VIPP--3S	"
κρίνετε	VIPA--2P	"
	VMPA--2P	"
κρινέτω	VMPA--3S	"

237

κρίνῃ	VSAA--3S	"
	VSPA--3S	"
κρίνομαι	VIPP--1S	"
κρινόμενοι	VPPPNM-P	"
κρινόμενος	VPPPNM-S	"

κρίνον, ου, τό *lily*; perhaps used as a general term for beautiful field flowers, such as the anemone

κρίνοντα	VPPAAM-S	κρίνω
κρίνοντες	VPPANM-P	"
κρίνοντι	VPPADM-S	"
κρινοῦμεν	VIFA--1P	"
κρινοῦσι(ν)	VIFA--3P	"

κρίνω impf. pass. ἐκρινόμην; fut. κρινῶ; 1aor. ἔκρινα; pf. κέκρικα; pf. pass. κέκραμαι; 1aor. pass. ἐκρίθην; 1fut. pass. κριθήσομαι; from a basic meaning *divide out* or *separate off*; (1) as making a personal evaluation *think of as better, prefer* (RO 14.5); (2) as forming a personal opinion *evaluate, think, judge* (AC 13.46); (3) as reaching a personal or group decision *resolve, determine, decide* (AC 16.4); (4) as passing a personal judgment on someone's actions *judge, criticize* (MT 7.1); often in a negative sense *condemn, find fault with* (JA 4.11); (5) as a legal technical term; (a) in a human court *judge, condemn, hand over for punishment* (JN 7.51); passive *be on trial, be judged* (AC 25.10); middle/passive *go to law, sue* (1C 6.6); (b) of God's judging *judge, administer justice*; with an obviously negative verdict *condemn, punish* (2TH 2.12); (6) Hebraistically, in a broader sense *rule, govern* (LU 22.30)

κρίνω	VIPA--1S	κρίνω
	VSAA--1S	"
	VSPA--1S	"
κρινῶ	VIFA--1S	"
κρίνωμεν	VSPA--1P	"
κρίνων	VPPANM-S	"
	VPPAVM-S	"
κρίσει	N-DF-S	κρίσις
κρίσεις	N-NF-P	"
κρίσεως	N-GF-S	"
κρίσιν	N-AF-S	"

κρίσις, εως, ἡ (1) as the action of a judge *decision, judgment* (JN 5.30); especially as the activity of God in a final time for judging ἡμέρα κρίσεως *day of judgment* (MT 10.15); in an unfavorable sense *condemnation, punishment* (RV 18.10); (2) as a personal evaluation of someone else's actions *judgment* (JN 7.24); (3) as the standard by which judgments and evaluations are to be made *right, justice* (MT 12.18); (4) as the basis on which a judgment is made *reason for a judgment* (JN 3.19)

κρίσις	N-NF-S	κρίσις
Κρίσπον	N-AM-S	Κρίσπος

Κρίσπος, ου, ὁ *Crispus*, masculine proper noun

Κρίσπος	N-NM-S	Κρίσπος
κριταί	N-NM-P	κριτής
κριτάς	N-AM-P	"
κριτῇ	N-DM-S	"
κριτήν	N-AM-S	"
κριτήρια	N-AN-P	κριτήριον

κριτήριον, ου, τό (1) as a place where justice is carried out *tribunal, law court* (JA 2.6); (2) of a legal process *case for judgment, lawsuit* (1C 6.2, 4)

κριτήριον	N-AN-S	κριτήριον
κριτηρίων	N-GN-P	"

κριτής, οῦ, ὁ (1) as one who makes decisions based on examination and evaluation *judge*, used of both divine and human judges (MT 5.25; AC 10.42); (2) in a specific historical sense, the leaders of Israel before the time of kings *judge* (AC 13.20)

κριτής	N-NM-S	κριτής

κριτικός, ή, όν *able to discern, skilled in judging* (HE 4.12)

κριτικός	A--NM-S	κριτικός
κρούειν	VNPA	κρούω
κρούετε	VMPA--2P	"
κρούοντι	VPPADM-S	"
κρούσαντος	VPAAGM-S	"

κρούω 1aor. ἔκρουσα; as seeking entrance *knock* (at a door or gate) (AC 12.13); figuratively, as seeking spiritual access *ask to be accepted* (RV 3.20)

κρούω	VIPA--1S	κρούω
κρούων	VPPANM-S	"
κρυβῆναι	VNAP	κρύπτω
κρυπτά	A--AN-P	κρυπτός
	A--NN-P	"

κρύπτη, ης, ἡ as a dark or hidden place *cellar, crypt, vault* (LU 11.33)

κρύπτην	N-AF-S	κρύπτη
κρυπτόν	A--NN-S	κρυπτός

κρυπτός, ή, όν (1) *hidden, secret, concealed* (MT 10.26); (2) neuter as a substantive (τὸ) κρυπτόν; (a) *hidden thing, secret* (LU 8.17); usually in a bad sense (2C 4.2); (b) *hidden place*; ἐν κρυπτῷ *in (a) secret (place)* (MT 6.4); (c) adverbially ἐν κρυπτῷ *in a secret way, privately* (JN 7.10)

κρυπτός	A--NM-S	κρυπτός

κρύπτω or **κρύβω** 1aor. ἔκρυψα; pf. pass. κέκρυμμαι; 2aor. pass. ἐκρύβην; with stress on the subjective element; literally, as preventing something from being seen *hide, conceal, cover* (MT 25.18); passive *hide* or *conceal oneself, be hidden* (JN 8.59); figuratively, as preventing something from being known *keep secret, conceal, hide* (LU 19.42); as preventing someone from being harmed by anything *keep safe, protect* (CO 3.3)

κρυπτῷ	A--DN-S	κρυπτός
κρυσταλλίζοντι	VPPADM-S	κρυσταλλίζω

κρυσταλλίζω *be clear as crystal, shine like crystal, shine brightly* (RV 21.11)

κρύσταλλον	N-AM-S	κρύσταλλος

κρύσταλλος, ου, ὁ from κρύος (*ice*); as clear rock *crystal*

κρυστάλλῳ	N-DM-S	κρύσταλλος

κρυφαῖος, αία, ον *hidden, secret*; substantivally ἐν τῷ κρυφαίῳ *in secret, in the hidden place* (MT 6.18)

κρυφαίῳ	A--DN-S	κρυφαῖος
κρυφῇ	AB	κρυφῇ

κρυφῇ (also **κρυφῆ**) adverb; *secretly, in secret*

κρυφῇ	AB	κρυφῇ
κρυφία	A--DF-S	κρύφιος

κρύφιος, ία, ιον *hidden, secret*; substantivally ἐν κρυφία *in secret, secretly* (MT 6.18)

κρύψατε	VMAA--2P	κρύπτω
κρύψετε	VMPA--2P	"

κτάομαι fut. κτήσομαι; 1aor. ἐκτησάμην; (1) as procuring something for oneself *get, obtain, acquire* (AC 1.18); (2) idiomatically; (a) σκεῦος κτᾶσθαι literally *possess a container*, i.e. *control one's sexual life*, derivative, derivation, derived from regarding σκεῦος (*container*) either as *one's body* or *one's wife* (1TH 4.4); (b) κτᾶσθαι τὴν ψυχήν literally *acquire one's soul*, i.e. *save oneself, protect one's life* (LU 21.19)

κτᾶσθαι	VNPD	κτάομαι
	VNPO	"

κτῆμα, ατος, τό as the result of gaining possession *possession, property* (MT 19.22); in later usage as landed property *field, estate, piece of ground* (AC 5.1)

κτῆμα	N-AN-S	κτῆμα
κτήματα	N-AN-P	"
κτήνη	N-AN-P	κτῆνος

κτῆνος, ους, τό strictly *possession*; generally plural, as property in animals kept by people for their use *cattle* (RV 18.13); as a tamed donkey *beast (of burden), (pack) animal* (LU 10.34); as animals for riding *mount*, possibly *horse* (AC 23.24)

κτῆνος	N-AN-S	κτῆνος
κτηνῶν	N-GN-P	"
κτήσασθε	VMAD--2P	κτάομαι
κτήσεσθε	VMPD--2P	"
κτήσησθε	VSAD--2P	"
κτήτορες	N-NM-P	κτήτωρ

κτήτωρ, ορος, ὁ *owner, possessor*, especially of houses and lands (AC 4.34)

κτίζω 1aor. ἔκτισα; pf. pass. ἔκτισμαι; 1aor. pass. ἐκτίσθην; (1) *create, call into being*; in the NT only of God's creative activity (1T 4.3); (2) of God's transforming activity in one's inner life *create, renew, change completely* (EP 2.10)

κτίσαντα	VPAAAM-S	κτίζω
κτίσαντι	VPAADM-S	"
κτίσαντος	VPAAGM-S	"
κτίσας	VPAANM-S	"
κτίσει	N-DF-S	κτίσις
κτίσεως	N-GF-S	"
κτίσῃ	VSAA--3S	κτίζω
κτισθέντα	VPAPAM-S	"
κτισθέντες	VPAPNM-P	"
κτίσιν	N-AF-S	κτίσις

κτίσις, εως, ἡ (1) in the NT generally as God's creative action *creation* (RO 1.20); (2) as what is created, animate and inanimate *creature, universe* (RO 8.39); as the sum total of everything created *creation, world* (MK 10.6); (3) as institutions created or established by God in which authority is entrusted to human beings *ordinance, ordering, authority* (1P 2.13)

κτίσις	N-NF-S	κτίσις

κτίσμα, ατος, τό in the NT the result of God's creative activity *creature*

κτίσμα	N-AN-S	κτίσμα
	N-NN-S	"
κτισμάτων	N-GN-P	"
κτίστῃ	N-DM-S	κτίστης

κτίστης, ου, ὁ *creator*; used only of God in the NT (1P 4.19)

κτῶμαι	VIPD--1S	κτάομαι
	VIPO--1S	"

κυβεία, ας, ἡ literally *playing at dice*; figuratively *craftiness, trickery, cheating* (EP 4.14)

κυβεία	N-DF-S	κυβεία
κυβερνήσεις	N-AF-P	κυβέρνησις

κυβέρνησις, εως, ἡ literally, the skill with which a pilot guides a ship; figuratively, of leadership skill *administrative ability, gift of leadership, managerial skill* (1C 12.28)

κυβερνήτῃ	N-DM-S	κυβερνήτης

κυβερνήτης, ου, ὁ of a ship *helmsman, pilot, captain*

κυβερνήτης	N-NM-S	κυβερνήτης

κυκλεύω 1aor. ἐκύκλευσα; *encircle* (JN 10.24); of an encampment *surround, encompass* (RV 20.9)

κυκλόθεν adverb of place; (1) as an adverb *on the outside* (RV 4.8); (2) as an improper preposition with the genitive *around, on all sides of, round about* (RV 4.3, 4)

κυκλόθεν	AB	κυκλόθεν
	PG	"
κυκλουμένην	VPPPAF-S	κυκλόω

κυκλόω 1aor. ἐκύκλωσα; 1aor. pass. ἐκυκλώθην; (1) *surround, encircle, encompass*, generally with hostile intent (JN 10.24); (2) of city walls *go around, circle round* (HE 11.30)

κύκλῳ adverb of place; literally *in a circle*; (1) as an adverb *all around* (RO 15.19); (2) as an adjective with the article *around, nearby* (MK 6.36); (3) as an improper preposition with the genitive *around* (RV 4.6)

κύκλῳ	AB	κύκλῳ
	PG	"
κυκλωθέντα	VPAPNN-P	κυκλόω
κυκλωσάντων	VPAAGM-P	"

κύλισμα, ατος, τό *roll* or *rolling*; *place for rolling* or *wallowing*, as mud for a pig (2P 2.22)

κύλισμα	N-AN-S	κύλισμα
κυλισμόν	N-AM-S	κυλισμός

κυλισμός, οῦ, ὁ strictly *rolling*; of swine in mud *wallowing, rolling about* (2P 2.22)

κυλίω impf. mid./pass. ἐκυλιόμην; 1aor. ἐκύλισα; (1) active *roll* something (LU 23.53); (2) middle or passive *roll oneself, wallow* (MK 9.20)

κυλλόν	A--AM-S	κυλλός

κυλλός, ή, όν *crooked, bent*; of bodily limbs *crippled, deformed* (MT 18.8); substantivally *cripple* (MT 15.30)

κυλλούς	A--AM-P	κυλλός

κῦμα, ατος, τό of the surging surface of the sea *wave, billow*

κύματα	N-NN-P	κῦμα
κυμάτων	N-GN-P	"

κύμβαλον, ου, τό *cymbal*, a shallow metal basin or disc producing a clanging sound when two are struck together (1C 13.1)

κύμβαλον	N-NN-S	κύμβαλον

κύμινον, ου, τό *cumin*, a Middle Eastern plant with tiny seeds, used as pungent seasoning (MT 23.23)

κύμινον	N-AN-S	κύμινον
κυνάρια	N-NN-P	κυνάριον
κυναρίοις	N-DN-P	"

κυνάριον, ου, τό diminutive of κύων; *little dog, house* or *lap dog*

κύνας	N-AM-P	κύων
κύνες	N-NM-P	"
Κύπριοι	N-NM-P	Κύπριος

Κύπριος, ου, ὁ *Cypriot, inhabitant of Cyprus*, a large island in the Mediterranean Sea

Κύπριος	N-NM-S	Κύπριος
Κυπρίῳ	N-DM-S	"
Κύπρον	N-AF-S	Κύπρος

Κύπρος, ου, ἡ *Cyprus*, a large island in the eastern part of the Mediterranean Sea

Κύπρου	N-GF-S	Κύπρος

κύπτω 1aor. ἔκυψα; *bend forward, stoop down*

Κυρείνου	N-GM-S	Κυρήνιος
Κυρηναῖοι	N-NM-P	Κυρηναῖος
Κυρηναῖον	N-AM-S	"

Κυρηναῖος, ου, ὁ *Cyrenian, inhabitant of Cyrene*, capital city of Cyrenaica, a Greek colony in northern Africa

Κυρηναῖος	N-NM-S	Κυρηναῖος
Κυρηναίου	N-GM-S	"
Κυρηναίων	N-GM-P	"

Κυρήνη, ης, ἡ *Cyrene*, capital city of the northern African district of Cyrenaica (AC 2.10)

Κυρήνην	N-AF-S	Κυρήνη

Κυρήνιος, ου, ὁ (also **Κυρεῖνος, Κυρίνιος, Κύρινος**) *Quirinius*, masculine proper noun (LU 2.2)

Κυρηνίου	N-GM-S	Κυρήνιος

κυρία, ας, ἡ feminine of κύριος (*strong, authoritative*); (1) as a title of respect for a woman, the *lady* of the house, *mistress* (possibly 2J 1, 5); (2) figuratively, for a church or congregation (probably 2J 1, 5; note the second-person plural in verses 6 and 12)

κυρία	N-VF-S	κυρία
κυρίᾳ	N-DF-S	"
κυριακῇ	A--DF-S	κυριακός
κυριακόν	A--AN-S	"

κυριακός, ή, όν generally *belonging to a lord* or *master*; as a religious technical term *belonging to the lord, the lord's, of the lord* (1C 11.20; RV 1.10)

κύριε	N-VM-S	κύριος
κυριεύει	VIPA--3S	κυριεύω
κυριεύομεν	VIPA--1P	"
κυριευόντων	VPPAGM-P	"
κυριεύουσι(ν)	VIPA--3P	"
κυριεύσας	VPAANM-S	"
κυριεύσει	VIFA--3S	"
κυριεύσῃ	VSAA--3S	"

κυριεύω fut. ἐκυριεύσω; 1aor. ἐκυρίευσα; (1) of persons being or becoming κύριος (*strong, authoritative*); *be lord* or *master over, rule, exercise dominion* (LU 22.25); (2) personification of various things that control human life, as law, sin, death *have dominion over, lord it over, exert mastery over* (RO 6.9)

Κυρινίου	N-GM-S	Κυρήνιος
Κυρίνου	N-GM-S	"
κύριοι	N-NM-P	κύριος
	N-VM-P	"
κυρίοις	N-DM-P	"
κύριον	N-AM-S	"

κύριος, ου, ὁ strictly, a substantive of the adjective κύριος (*strong, authoritative*); hence, one having legal power *lord, master*; (1) in a nonreligious sense; (a) one controlling his own property *owner, lord, master* (MK 12.9); (b) one having authority over persons *lord, master* (LU 12.43); (2) as a form of address showing respect *sir, lord* (JN 4.11); (3) in religious usage, as a designation and personal title for God (MT 1.20) and Jesus Christ (JN 20.18) *(the) Lord*; translation of the Hebrew *adonai*, which in the public reading of Scripture replaced the tetragrammaton *yhwh*

κύριος	N-NM-S	κύριος
	N-VM-S	"

κυριότης, ητος, ἡ (1) of power and position as lord *lordship, dominion* (JU 8); (2) plural, of supernatural beings possessing dominion, especially angelic powers *authorities, rulers, lordships* (CO 1.16)

κυριότητα	N-AF-S	κυριότης
κυριότητας	N-AF-P	"
κυριότητες	N-NF-P	"
κυριότητος	N-GF-S	"
κυρίου	N-GM-S	κύριος
κυρίῳ	N-DM-S	"
κυρίων	N-GM-P	"

κυρόω 1aor. ἐκύρωσα; pf. pass. κεκύρωμαι; (1) of legal action *confirm, validate, ratify* (GA 3.15); (2) of group decision in developing policy *publicly affirm, decide in favor of* (2C 2.8)

κυρῶσαι	VNAA	κυρόω
κυσί(ν)	N-DM-P	κύων
κύψας	VPAANM-S	κύπτω

κύων, κυνός, ὁ literally *dog* (LU 16.21); figuratively, as a term of reproach for persons regarded as unholy and impure (RV 22.15)

κύων	N-NM-S	κύων
Κῶ	N-AF-S	Κώς
κῶλα	N-NN-P	κῶλον

κῶλον, ου, τό literally *limb* or *member* of the body; plural in the NT *dead bodies* exposed and decaying, *corpses* (HE 3.17)

κωλύει	VIPA--3S	κωλύω
κωλύειν	VNPA	"
κωλύεσθαι	VNPP	"
κωλύετε	VMPA--2P	"
κωλύετω	VMPA--3S	"
κωλυθέντες	VPAPNM-P	"
κωλύοντα	VPPAAM-S	"
κωλυόντων	VPPAGM-P	"
κωλῦσαι	VNAA	"
κωλύσῃς	VSAA--2S	"
κωλύσητε	VSAA--2P	"

κωλύω impf. ἐκώλυον; 1aor. ἐκώλυσα; 1aor. pass. ἐκωλύθην; (1) of persons *hinder, prevent, forbid* (LU 18.16); (2) of things *restrain, forbid, prevent* (1T 4.3); (3) as keeping back something from someone *refuse, deny, withhold* (AC 10.47)

κώμας	N-AF-P	κώμη

κώμη, ης, ἡ *village, small town, country town* (MT 9.35); by metonymy *inhabitants of a village* (AC 8.25)

κώμη	N-DF-S	κώμη
κώμην	N-AF-S	"
κώμης	N-GF-S	"

κῶμοι	N-NM-P	κῶμος
κώμοις	N-DM-P	"
κωμοπόλεις	N-AF-P	κωμόπολις

κωμόπολις, εως, ἡ strictly *village-city*; hence *large open* or *unwalled village, town*; perhaps *market town* as opposed to a small village where field workers lived (MK 1.38)

κῶμος, ου, ὁ originally *festive procession* in honor of the wine god, *merrymaking*; in the NT always in a bad sense *carousing, revelry, excessive feasting*

Κῶν	N-AF-S	Κώς
κώνωπα	N-AM-S	κώνωψ

κώνωψ, ωπος, ὁ as a very small flying insect *gnat, wine gnat, midge* (MT 23.24)

Κώς, Κῶ, ἡ, accusative **Κῶ** (also **Κῶς**) *Cos*, a small island in the Aegean Sea (AC 21.1)

Κωσάμ, ὁ indeclinable; *Cosam*, masculine proper noun (LU 3.28)

κωφοί	A--NM-P	κωφός
κωφόν	A--AM-S	"
	A--NN-S	"
	A--VN-S	"

κωφός, ή, όν strictly *blunt, dull*, as a weapon; (1) as incapable of speaking *mute* (MT 9.32); substantivally (MT 15.31); (2) as incapable of hearing *deaf* (MK 9.25); substantivally (MT 11.5)

κωφός	A--NM-S	κωφός
κωφούς	A--AM-P	"

λ Λ

λ' indeclinable; as a cardinal number *thirty* (LU 3.23)

λάβε	VMAA--2S	λαμβάνω
λαβεῖν	VNAA	"
λάβετε	VMAA--2P	"
λαβέτω	VMAA--3S	"
λάβῃ	VSAA--3S	"
λάβῃς	VSAA--2S	"
λάβητε	VSAA--2P	"
λάβοι	VOAA--3S	"
λαβόντα	VPAAAM-S	"
λαβόντας	VPAAAM-P	"
λαβόντες	VPAANM-P	"
λαβόντων	VPAAGM-P	"
λαβοῦσα	VPAANF-S	"
λαβοῦσαι	VPAANF-P	"
λάβω	VSAA--1S	"
λάβωμεν	VSAA--1P	"
λαβών	VPAANM-S	"
λάβωσι(ν)	VSAA--3P	"

λαγχάνω 2aor. ἔλαχον; of what comes to someone always apart from his own efforts; (1) *cast lots* (JN 19.24); (2) *attain by lot, be appointed by lot, be chosen by lot* (LU 1.9); (3) of what comes by divine will *attain, receive, obtain* (2P 1.1)

Λάζαρε	N-VM-S	Λάζαρος
Λάζαρον	N-AM-S	"

Λάζαρος, ου, ὁ *Lazarus*, masculine proper noun

Λάζαρος	N-NM-S	Λάζαρος
λαθεῖν	VNAA	λανθάνω

λάθρα adverb; *secretly, in a secretive way* (MT 1.19)

λάθρα	AB	λάθρα
λαίλαπος	N-GF-S	λαῖλαψ

λαῖλαψ, απος, ἡ *furious gust of wind, hurricane, whirlwind*

λαῖλαψ	N-NF-S	λαῖλαψ
Λάσσα	N-NF-S	Λασαία

λακάω 1aor. ἐλάκησα; *burst apart, burst open* (AC 1.18)

λακτίζειν	VNPA	λακτίζω

λακτίζω literally, of animals *strike with the foot, kick*; figuratively, in a proverbial sense of a stubborn person *resist (unreasonably)* (AC 26.14)

λάλει	VMPA--2S	λαλέω
λαλεῖ	VIPA--3S	"
λαλεῖν	VNPA	"
λαλεῖς	VIPA--2S	"
λαλεῖσθαι	VNPP	"
λαλεῖται	VIPP--3S	"
λαλεῖτε	VIPA--2P	"
	VMPA--2P	
λαλείτω	VMPA--3S	"
λαλείτωσαν	VMPA--3P	"

λαλέω impf. ἐλάλουν; fut. λαλήσω; 1aor. ἐλάλησα; pf. λελάληκα; pf. pass. λελάλημαι; 1aor. pass. ἐλαλήθην; 1fut. pass. λαληθήσομαι; (1) of inanimate things *give forth sounds, sound out, speak* as with a message (RV 10.4); (2) of persons *speak, tell*, with focus on speaking rather than on logical reasoning as with λέγω (*say, speak*); (a) in contrast to keeping silent *speak, talk* (MK 1.34); (b) express oneself *speak (out)* (MT 10.20); (c) transitively *speak, assert, proclaim* something (MT 13.33); (d) the accompanying participle λέγων (*saying, speaking*) may be used to introduce the content of the speaking (MT 13.3)

λαλῇ	VSPA--3S	λαλέω
λαληθείς	VPAPNM-S	"
λαληθείσης	VPAPGF-S	"
λαληθέντος	VPAPGN-S	"
λαληθέντων	VPAPGN-P	"
λαληθῆναι	VNAP	"
λαληθήσεται	VIFP--3S	"
λαληθησομένων	VPFPGN-P	"
λαλήομεν	VIPA--1P	see λαλοῦμεν
λαλῆσαι	VNAA	λαλέω
λαλήσαντες	VPAANM-P	"
λαλήσαντος	VPAAGM-S	"
λαλήσας	VPAANM-S	"
λαλήσει	VIFA--3S	"
λαλήσετε	VIFA--2P	"
λαλήσῃ	VSAA--3S	"
λαλήσητε	VSAA--2P	"
λαλήσομεν	VIFA--1P	"
λαλήσουσι(ν)	VIFA--3P	"
λαλήσω	VIFA--1S	"
	VSAA--1S	"
λαλήσωμεν	VSAA--1P	"
λαλήσωσι(ν)	VSAA--3P	"

λαλιά, ᾶς, ἡ in the NT always in a good sense; (1) *what is said, speech, speaking*; διὰ τὴν σὴν λαλιάν *because of what you said* (JN 4.42); (2) as a manner of expressing oneself *way of speaking* (JN 8.43); as a peculiarity of dialect *accent* (MT 26.73)

λαλιά	N-NF-S	λαλιά
λαλιάν	N-AF-S	"
λαλοῦμεν	VIPA--1P	λαλέω
λαλουμένη	VPPPNF-S	"
λαλουμένοις	VPPPDN-P	"
λαλούμενον	VPPPAM-S	"
	VPPPNN-S	"
λαλοῦν	VPPANN-S	"
λαλοῦντα	VPPAAM-S	"
λαλοῦντας	VPPAAM-P	"
λαλοῦντες	VPPANM-P	"
λαλοῦντι	VPPADM-S	"
	VPPADN-S	"
λαλοῦντος	VPPAGM-S	"

λαλούντων	VPPAGM-P	"
λαλοῦσα	VPPANF-S	"
λαλοῦσαι	VPPANF-P	"
λαλοῦσαν	VPPAAF-S	"
λαλούσης	VPPAGF-S	"
λαλοῦσι(ν)	VIPA--3P	"
λαλῶ	VIPA--1S	"
	VSPA--1S	"
λαλῶν	VPPANM-S	"
λαλῶσι(ν)	VSPA--3P	"
λαμά		λεμά
λαμᾶ		"
λαμβάνει	VIPA--3S	λαμβάνω
λαμβάνειν	VNPA	"
λαμβάνεις	VIPA--2S	"
λαμβάνετε	VIPA--2P	"
	VMPA--2P	"
λαμβάνῃ	VSPA--3S	"
λαμβάνομεν	VIPA--1P	"
λαμβανόμενον	VPPPNN-S	"
λαμβανόμενος	VPPPNM-S	"
λαμβάνοντες	VPPANM-P	"
λαμβάνουσι(ν)	VIPA--3P	"

λαμβάνω impf. ἐλάμβανον; fut. mid. λήμψομαι (and λήψομαι); 2aor. ἔλαβον; pf. εἴληφα; (1) active, as bringing under one's control *take*; (a) with the hand *take hold of, grasp* (AC 27.35); (b) *take away, remove* (RV 3.11); (c) *take* for oneself, *take into possession* (LU 19.12); (d) as being seized by illness, demon attack, strong emotion *come on, seize* (LU 5.26); (e) as taking a due portion of something, as taxes, tithes, or collections *receive, accept, collect* (MT 17.24); (f) as taking to oneself someone's words, teaching, or testimony *receive, accept, come to believe* (MT 13.20); (g) figuratively *take advantage of, exploit* (2C 11.20); (2) passive, as being a recipient of something *receive*; (a) materially *receive, get, acquire* (2C 11.8); (b) spiritually, as being a recipient of God's grace, forgiveness, life, etc. *receive, obtain* (RO 1.5); (c) *be selected, be chosen* from one or more alternatives (HE 5.1)

λαμβάνω	VIPA--1S	λαμβάνω
λαμβάνων	VPPANM-S	"

Λάμεχ, ὁ indeclinable; *Lamech*, masculine proper noun (LU 3.36)

λαμμᾶ		λεμά
λαμπάδας	N-AF-P	λαμπάς
λαμπάδες	N-NF-P	"
λαμπάδων	N-GF-P	"

λαμπάς, άδος, ἡ (1) as a resinous burning brand of pine-covered or pitch-covered dry twigs *torch* (JN 18.3); (2) as an oil-fed light *lamp* (MT 25.1)

λαμπάς	N-NF-S	λαμπάς
λάμπει	VIPA--3S	λάμπω
λαμπρά	A--NN-P	λαμπρός
λαμπρᾷ	A--DF-S	"
λαμπράν	A--AF-S	"
λαμπρόν	A--AM-S	"
	A--AN-S	"

λαμπρός, ά, όν *shining, bright, radiant*; (1) of heavenly bodies *shining, bright* (RV 22.16); (2) of pure water *clear, sparkling* (RV 22.1); (3) of clothes *elegant, re-*

splendent, shining (LU 23.11); (4) neuter as a substantive τὰ λαμπρά as elegant things for luxurious living *dainties, splendor, lavish things* (RV 18.14)

λαμπρός	A--NM-S	λαμπρός

λαμπρότης, ητος, ἡ *brilliance, brightness* (AC 26.13)

λαμπρότητα	N-AF-S	λαμπρότης
λαμπρούς	A--AM-P	λαμπρός

λαμπρῶς adverb; of a luxurious way of life *splendidly, lavishly* (LU 16.19)

λαμπρῶς	AB	λαμπρῶς

λάμπω fut. λάμψω; 1aor. ἔλαμψα; intransitively in the NT; (1) literally *give light, shine, be bright*, with the sense varying according to the source of light: of a lamp *shine, give light*; of lightning *flash*; of light *gleam, shine*; (2) metaphorically, of spiritual light from God, Christ, and Spirit-filled human beings *shine forth, illuminate*; i.e. *show things as they really are* (MT 5.16; 2C 4.6)

λάμψαι	VNAA	λάμπω
λαμψάτω	VMAA--3S	"
λάμψει	VIFA--3S^VMAA--3S	"
λάμψουσι(ν)	VIFA--3P	"
λανθάνει	VIPA--3S	λανθάνω
λανθάνειν	VNPA	"
λανθανέτω	VMPA--3S	"
λανθάνουσι(ν)	VIPA--3P	"

λανθάνω 2aor. ἔλαθον; (1) as causing oneself to remain unknown or unrecognized *escape notice, be hidden* (LU 8.47); (2) as not having knowledge of something, followed by a participle *be unaware of, be ignorant of* (HE 13.2); (3) as failing to remain aware of the significance of something, followed by a ὅτι clause *ignore, forget* (2P 3.5, 8)

λαξευτός, ή, όν *cut in stone, hewn out of rock* or *stone* (LU 23.53)

λαξευτῷ	A--DN-S	λαξευτός

Λαοδίκεια, ας, ἡ (also **Λαοδικία**) *Laodicea*, a city in Phrygia in Asia Minor

Λαοδικεία	N-DF-S	Λαοδίκεια
Λαοδίκειαν	N-AF-S	"
Λαοδικείας	N-GF-S	"

Λαοδικεύς, έως, ὁ *Laodicean, inhabitant of Laodicea* in Phrygia (CO 4.16)

Λαοδικέων	N-GM-P	Λαοδικεύς
Λαοδικία	N-DF-S	Λαοδίκεια
Λαοδίκιαν	N-AF-S	"
Λαοδικίας	N-GF-S	"
λαοί	N-NM-P	λαός
λαοῖς	N-DM-P	"
λαόν	N-AM-S	"

λαός, οῦ, ὁ *people*; (1) relating to the general public, especially in Luke and Acts *crowd, populace, people* (LU 3.15); (2) nationally, as *people* making up a nation (RV 5.9); (3) as a religious technical term, of Israel as God's chosen *people* (AC 4.10), opposite τὰ ἔθνη (*Gentiles*); (4) in a religious sense, of the Christian community as the people of God (AC 15.14)

λαός	N-NM-S	λαός
	N-VM-S	"
λαοῦ	N-GM-S	"

λάρυγξ, γγος, ὁ   *throat, gullet,* by metonymy, for what is spoken by someone (RO 3.13)

λάρυγξ	N-NM-S	λάρυγξ

Λασαία, ας, ἡ (also Ἄλασσα, Λαίσσα, Λασέα, Λασία)   *Lasea,* a city on the southern coast of the island of Crete (AC 27.8)

Λασαία	N-NF-S	Λασαία
Λασέα	N-NF-S	"
Λασία	N-NF-S	"

λατομέω   1aor. ἐλατόμησα; pf. pass. λελατόμημαι; as carving or cutting from rock *hew out of, cut from*

λατρεία, ας, ἡ   in the NT, religious service based in worship *service (of God), divine service, worship*

λατρεία	N-NF-S	λατρεία
λατρείαν	N-AF-S	"
λατρείας	N-AF-P	"
	N-GF-S	"
λατρεύειν	VNPA	λατρεύω
λατρεύομεν	VIPA--1S	"
λατρεῦον	VPPANN-S	"
λατρεύοντα	VPPAAM-S	"
λατρεύοντας	VPPAAM-P	"
λατρεύοντες	VPPANM-P	"
λατρεύουσα	VPPANF-S	"
λατρεύουσι(ν)	VIPA--3P	"
λατρεύσεις	VIFA--2S^VMPA--2S	"
λατρεύσουσι(ν)	VIFA--3P	"
λατρεύσωμεν	VSAA--1P	"

λατρεύω   fut. λατρεύσω; 1aor. ἐλάτρευσα; in the NT, as carrying out religious duties in a spirit of worship *serve, minister, officiate* (HE 8.5); *worship, venerate* (MT 4.10)

λατρεύω	VIPA--1S	λατρεύω
λατρεύωμεν	VSPA--1P	"
λάχανα	N-AN-P	λάχανον

λάχανον, ου, τό   *garden herb, vegetable, edible plant*

λάχανον	N-AN-S	λάχανον
λαχάνων	N-GN-P	"
λαχοῦσι(ν)	VPAADM-P	λαγχάνω
λάχωμεν	VSAA--1P	"
λαῷ	N-DM-S	λαός
λαῶν	N-GM-P	"
Λεββαῖον	N-AM-S	Λεββαῖος

Λεββαῖος, ου, ὁ (also Λεββεδαῖος)   *Lebbaeus,* masculine proper noun (MT 10.3)

Λεββαῖος	N-NM-S	Λεββαῖος
Λεββεδαῖος	N-NM-S	"
λέγε	VMPA--2S	λέγω
λέγει	VIPA--3S	"
λέγειν	VNPA	"
λέγεις	VIPA--2S	"
λέγεσθαι	VNPP	"
λέγεται	VIPP--3S	"
λέγετε	VIPA--2P	"
	VMPA--2P	"
λεγέτω	VMPA--3S	"
λεγεών	N-NF-S	λεγιών
	N-NM-S	"
λεγεῶνα	N-AM-S	"
λεγεῶνας	N-AF-P	"
λεγεώνων	N-GF-P	"
λέγῃ	VSPA--3S	λέγω

λέγητε	VSPA--2P	"

λεγιών, ῶνος, ἡ (also λεγεών)   *legion, army;* literally, a Roman military unit of about 6,000 foot soldiers and 120 on horse, plus auxiliaries; figuratively in the NT, as powerful supernatural forces, whether angels (MT 26.53) or demons; the masculine ὁ λ. is understood (1) as the name of a group of many demons *Legion* (MK 5.9) or (2) as the descriptive designation for such a group *legion* (MK 5.15)

λεγιών	N-NF-S	λεγιών
	N-NM-S	"
λεγιῶνα	N-AM-S	"
λεγιῶνας	N-AF-P	"
λέγομεν	VIPA--1P	λέγω
λεγόμενα	VPPPAN-P	"
λεγομένη	VPPPNF-S	"
λεγομένην	VPPPAF-S	"
λεγομένης	VPPPGF-S	"
λεγόμενοι	VPPPNM-P	"
λεγομένοις	VPPPDN-P	"
λεγόμενον	VPPPAM-S	"
	VPPPAN-S	"
	VPPPNN-S	"
λεγόμενος	VPPPNM-S	"
λεγομένου	VPPPGM-S	"
λεγομένων	VPPPGM-P	"
λέγον	VPPANN-S	"
λέγοντα	VPPAAM-S	"
	VPPAAN-P	"
	VPPANN-P	"
λέγοντας	VPPAAM-P	"
λέγοντες	VPPANM-P	"
	VPPAVM-P	"
λέγοντι	VPPADM-S	"
λέγοντος	VPPAGM-S	"
	VPPAGN-S	"
λεγόντων	VPPAGM-P	"
λέγουσα	VPPANF-S	"
λέγουσαι	VPPANF-P	"
λέγουσαν	VPPAAF-S	"
λεγούσης	VPPAGF-S	"
λέγουσι(ν)	VIPA--3P	"

λέγω   impf. ἔλεγον; tenses beyond the present and imperfect supplied by εἶπον (q.v.); strictly *gather and lay in order;* hence, used of logical expression; (1) *say, speak, tell, narrate* (MT 3.9); (2) *tell of, report, recount* (MK 1.30); (3) with the sense derived from the context; (a) in direct discourse *ask, say* (MT 9.14); *answer, say* (MT 8.26); *order, command, recommend* (1J 5.16); *assure, assert,* especially in formulas such as ἀμὴν, ἀμὴν λ. ὑμῖν *truly, truly I say to you* (JN 1.51); *maintain, declare* (GA 4.1); (b) in designations *call, name* (MK 12.37); passive *be called, be named* (MT 1.16); (c) in explanatory foreign words *mean, interpret, translate* (JN 1.38)

λέγω	VIPA--1S	λέγω
	VSPA--1S	"
λέγωμεν	VSPA--1S	"
λέγων	VPPANM-S	"
	VPPAVM-S	"
λεγώνων	N-GF-P	λεγιών

λέγωσι(ν)	VSPA--3P	λέγω
λείας	A--AF-P	λεῖος
λειμά		λεμά

λεῖμμα, ατος, τό as what remains *small part, remnant*; in the NT especially of a community, a core of believers preserved by God *minority, small number, survivors* (RO 11.5)

λεῖμμα	N-NN-S	λεῖμμα

λεῖος, α, ον of a surface *smooth, level* (LU 3.5), opposite τραχύς (*rough, uneven*)

λείπει	VIPA--3S	λείπω
λείπεται	VIPM--3S	"
λείπῃ	VSPA--3S	"
λειπόμενοι	VPPMNM-P	"
	VPPPNM-P	"
λείποντα	VPPAAN-P	"

λείπω 2aor. ἔλιπον; (1) transitively *leave (behind)*; middle/passive *be left (behind), be inferior, fall short* (JA 1.4); with the genitive *be without, lack, be in need of* (JA 1.5); (2) intransitively, active with the dative *lack, fall short of* (LU 18.22)

λειτουργεῖν	VNPA	λειτουργέω

λειτουργέω 1aor. ἐλειτούργησα; strictly *perform a public service*; in the NT of religious and ritual service; (1) of a priest *officiate, minister, perform religious duties* (HE 10.11); (2) of a Christian's service to God through prayer, teaching, good works, etc. *serve, minister, worship* (AC 13.2)

λειτουργῆσαι	VNAA	λειτουργέω

λειτουργία, ας, ἡ strictly *public service* performed by an individual; in the NT of religious service; (1) as the ritual activity of priests *(priestly) service* (LU 1.23); (2) as the activity of Christians *service, ministry* (PH 2.30)

λειτουργία	N-DF-S	λειτουργία
λειτουργίας	N-GF-S	"
λειτουργικά	A--NN-P	λειτουργικός

λειτουργικός, ή, όν related to the performance of religious service *ministering, attending, serving* (HE 1.14)

λειτουργοί	N-NM-P	λειτουργός
λειτουργόν	N-AM-S	"

λειτουργός, οῦ, ὁ strictly, of one performing public service; in the NT of one who carries out God's will by serving others *servant, minister*

λειτουργός	N-NM-S	λειτουργός
λειτουργούντων	VPPAGM-P	λειτουργέω
λειτουργούς	N-AM-P	λειτουργός
λειτουργῶν	VPPANM-S	λειτουργέω

λείχω impf. ἔλειχον; of dogs *lick* (LU 16.21)

Λέκτρα, ας, ἡ *Lectra*, feminine proper noun

Λέκτραν	N-AF-S	Λέκτρα
λελάληκα	VIRA--1S	λαλέω
λελάληκε(ν)	VIRA--3S	"
λελαλημένοις	VPRPDN-P	"
λελάληται	VIRP--3S	"
λελατομημένον	VPRPNN-S	λατομέω
λελατομημένῳ	VPRPDN-S	"
λελουμένοι	VPRPNM-P	λούω
λελουμένος	VPRMNM-S	"
	VPRPNM-S	"
λελουσμένοι	VPRMNM-P	"
	VPRPNM-P	"

λελυμένα	VPRPNN-P	λύω
λελυμένον	VPRPNN-S	"
λελύπηκε(ν)	VIRA--3S	λυπέω
λέλυσαι	VIRP--2S	λύω

λεμά (also **λαμά, λαμᾶ, λαμμᾶ, λειμά, λημά, λιμά, λιμᾶ**) interrogative adverb; transliterated from the Aramaic; *why?* (MT 27.46)

λέντιον, ου, τό *linen cloth*; as used by servants *towel, apron*

λέντιον	N-AN-S	λέντιον
λεντίῳ	N-DN-S	"
λέοντι	N-DM-S	λέων
λέοντος	N-GM-S	"
λεόντων	N-GM-P	"
λεπίδες	N-NF-P	λεπίς

λεπίς, ίδος, ἡ literally, of a fish *scale*; of a seed *hull*; used metaphorically in AC 9.18 as a medical technical term for a thick layer of skin *flake, small incrustation*

λέπρα, ας, ἡ as a disease *leprosy*; probably used in reference to any of a group of infectious and inflammatory skin diseases, such as Hansen's disease (modern leprosy), ringworm, yaws, scabies, lupus, etc.

λέπρα	N-NF-S	λέπρα
λέπρας	N-GF-S	"
λεπροί	AP-NM-P	λεπρός
	A--NM-P	"

λεπρός, ά, όν originally *scaly, scabby*; of one afflicted with leprosy *leprous* (LU 17.12); substantivally ὁ λ. the *leper* (MT 8.2)

λεπρός	AP-NM-S	λεπρός
	A--NM-S	"
λεπροῦ	AP-GM-S	"
λεπρούς	AP-AM-P	"
λεπτά	AP-AN-P	λεπτός
λεπτόν	AP-AN-S	"

λεπτός, ή, όν *thin, small, tiny*; neuter as a substantive τὸ λεπτόν *small coin, lepton, mite*, a small copper coin worth a fraction of a cent

Λευεί		Λευί
	N-GM-S	"
Λευείν	N-AM-S	"
Λευείς	N-NM-S	"
Λευείτας	N-AM-P	Λευίτης
Λευείτης	N-NM-S	"
Λευείτης	N-NM-S	"
Λευειτικῆς	A--GF-S	Λευιτικός
Λευή		Λευί
Λευήν	N-AM-S	"
Λευής	N-NM-S	"

Λευί, ὁ (also **Λευεί, Λευή**) indeclinable, but generally Hellenized ὁ Λευίς, ί (also Λευείς, Λευής, Λευίς) *Levi*, masculine proper noun (LU 3.24, 29); father of one of the twelve tribes of Israel (HE 7.9); one of the twelve disciples (LU 5.27, 29)

Λευί		Λευί
	N-GM-S	"
Λευί	N-GM-S	"
Λευίν	N-AM-S	"
Λευίν	N-AM-S	"
Λευίς	N-NM-S	"
Λευίς	N-NM-S	"

Λευίτας	N-AM-P	Λευίτης
Λευίτας	N-AM-P	"

Λευίτης, ου, ὁ (also **Λευείτης, Λευΐτης**) *Levite*, descendant of Levi, a member of the tribe that performed tasks related to temple ritual and service

Λευίτης	N-NM-S	Λευίτης
Λευΐτης	N-NM-S	"
Λευιτικῆς	A--GF-S	Λευιτικός
Λευϊτικῆς	A--GF-S	"

Λευιτικός, ή, όν (also **Λευειτικός, Λευϊτικός**) *levitical*, pertaining to the Old Testament priesthood out of the tribe of Levi (HE 7.11)

λευκά	A--AN-P	λευκός
	A--NN-P	"
λευκαί	A--NF-P	"

λευκαίνω 1aor. ἐλεύκανα; *make white*; literally, of clothes *make white, whiten* through special treatment (MK 9.3); metaphorically, of spiritual robes representing righteousness *make pure* (RV 7.14)

λευκαῖς	A--DF-S	λευκός
λευκᾶναι	VNAA	λευκαίνω
λευκάς	A--AF-P	λευκός
λευκή	A--NF-S	"
λευκῇ	A--DF-S	"
λευκήν	A--AF-S	"
λευκοβύσσινον	AP-AN-S	λευκοβύσσινος

λευκοβύσσινος, η, ον *made of white linen*; neuter as a substantive τὸ λευκοβύσσινον *white linen garment* (RV 19.14)

λευκοῖς	A--DM-P	λευκός
	A--DN-P	"
λευκόν	A--AM-S	"
	A--AN-S	"
	A--NN-S	"

λευκός, ή, όν (1) of what is characterized by bright light, so bright it appears white *brilliant, shining, radiant*; used to describe clothes (MT 17.2), hair (RV 1.14), clouds (RV 14.14), etc., that are radiant with heavenly glory; (2) used for many shades of light or pale color, suitable to the context; of hair *gray, silvery* (MT 5.36); (3) of an overripe grain field *bleached, white, light yellow* (JN 4.35); (4) neuter as a substantive τὰ λευκά *white clothes, shining garments* (JN 20.12)

λευκός	A--NM-S	λευκός
Λευυί		see Λευί
λεχθέντων	VPAPGN-P	λέγω

λέων, οντος, ὁ literally, a violent beast of prey *lion* (HE 11.33); figuratively, of the Messiah as a strong overcomer (RV 5.5); probably figuratively in 2T 4.17 as a symbol of extreme danger from hostile and satanic forces; cf. Psalm 22.21

λέων	N-NM-S	λέων

λη´ indeclinable; from the Greek letters for thirty (λ´) and eight (η´); as a cardinal number *thirty-eight* (JN 5.5)

λήθη, ης, ἡ *forgetfulness*; idiomatically λήθην λαμβάνειν τινός literally *receive forgetfulness of something*, i.e. *forget something* (2P 1.9)

λήθην	N-AF-S	λήθη
λημά		λεμά
λήμψεσθε	VIFD--2P	λαμβάνω

λήμψεται	VIFD--3S	"
λήμψεως	N-GF-S	λῆμψις

λῆμψις, εως, ἡ (also **λῆψις**) as an action *receiving, credit*, related to the acceptance of monetary gifts (PH 4.15)

λημψόμεθα	VIFD--1P	λαμβάνω
λήμψονται	VIFD--3P	"
ληνόν	N-AF-S	ληνός

ληνός, οῦ, ἡ literally *tub* or *trough-shaped receptacle, vat, winepress* (MT 21.33); figuratively, as a judgment metaphor in which the treading out of grapes depicts God's judgment on his enemies (RV 19.15)

ληνός	N-NF-S	ληνός
ληνοῦ	N-GF-S	"

λῆρος, ου, ὁ *idle talk, nonsense, frivolous tale* (LU 24.11)

λῆρος	N-NM-S	λῆρος
λησταί	N-NM-P	λῃστής
λησταῖς	N-DM-P	"
λῃστάς	N-AM-P	"
λῃστήν	N-AM-S	"

λῃστής, οῦ, ὁ (1) *robber, bandit, highwayman*, one who seizes by violence, in contrast to a thief (κλέπτης), who uses stealth (LU 10.30); (2) politically *insurrectionist, revolutionary, rebel* who favors the use of force (JN 18.40); (3) figuratively, of unscrupulous, greedy, or overambitious leaders (JN 10.8)

λῃστής	N-NM-S	λῃστής
λῃστῶν	N-GM-P	"
λῃταιβόμενοι	VPPPNM-P	see πορευόμεναι
λήψεσθε	VIFD--2P	λαμβάνω
λήψεται	VIFD--3S	"
λήψεως	N-GF-S	λῆμψις
ληψόμεθα	VIFD--1P	λαμβάνω
λήψονται	VIFD--3P	"

λίαν adverb; *exceedingly, very, extremely*, adding a force of *too much* or *very much* to terms it qualifies

λίαν	AB	λίαν
λίβα	N-AM-S	λίψ
λίβανον	N-AM-S	λίβανος

λίβανος, ου, ὁ *frankincense*, a white resinous gum from a Middle East tree; in the NT the incense made from this resin

λιβανωτόν	N-AM-S	λιβανωτός

λιβανωτός, οῦ, ὁ *frankincense*; in the NT a container in which incense is burned *censer, incense burner*

Λιβερτῖνος, ου, ὁ *freedman*, a designation for a Jew who had gained freedom from slavery, or the descendant of such a Jew (AC 6.9)

Λιβερτίνων	N-GM-P	Λιβερτῖνος

Λιβύη, ης, ἡ (also **Λιβύα**) *Libya*, a district in northern Africa west of Egypt (AC 2.10)

Λιβύης	N-GF-S	Λιβύη

Λιβυστῖνος, ου, ὁ *Libyan, inhabitant of Libya* in northern Africa (AC 6.9)

Λιβυστίνων	N-GM-S	Λιβυστῖνος
λιθάζειν	VNPA	λιθάζω
λιθάζετε	VIPA--2P	"
λιθάζομεν	VIPA--1P	"

λιθάζω 1aor. ἐλίθασα; 1aor. pass. ἐλιθάσθην; *stone* someone, *kill by pelting with stones*, as a means of capital punishment

λιθάσαι	VNAA	λιθάζω

λιθάσαντες	VPAANM-P	"
λιθασθῶσι(ν)	VSAP--3P	"
λιθάσωσι(ν)	VSAA--3P	"
λίθινα	A--AN-P	λίθινος
λίθιναι	A--NF-P	"
λιθίναις	A--DF-P	"

λίθινος, η, ον *(made of) stone*

λιθοβολεῖσθαι	VNPP	λιθοβολέω

λιθοβολέω impf. ἐλιθοβόλουν; 1aor. ἐλιθοβόλησα; 1fut. pass. λιθοβοληθήσομαι; (1) *throw stones at* (MT 21.35); (2) *stone (to death)* (AC 7.58)

λιθοβοληθήσεται	VIFP--3S^VMAP--3S	λιθοβολέω
λιθοβοληθῆσαι	VNAA	"
λιθοβολήσαντες	VPAANM-P	"
λιθοβολοῦσα	VPPAVF-S	"
λίθοι	N-NM-P	λίθος
λίθοις	N-DM-P	"
λίθον	N-AM-S	"

λίθος, ου, ὁ (1) literally; (a) *stone, piece of rock* as used for various purposes: building material (MT 24.2), sealing graves (MT 27.60), millstones for processing food (RV 18.21), flat stones for engraved writing (2C 3.7), etc.; (b) of precious stones *jewels* (RV 4.3); (c) of idols *stone image* (AC 17.29); (2) metaphorically, of Christ as the keystone in God's spiritual temple (MT 21.42); of Christians as living stones in God's spiritual temple (1P 2.5)

λίθος	N-NM-S	λίθος
λιθόστρωτον	AP-AN-S	λιθόστρωτος

λιθόστρωτος, ον *paved with (blocks of) stone*; neuter as a substantive τὸ λιθόστρωτον *stone pavement, mosaic* (JN 19.13)

λίθου	N-GM-S	λίθος
λίθους	N-AM-P	"
λίθῳ	N-DM-S	"
λίθων	N-GM-P	"

λικμάω fut. λικμήσω; literally *winnow*, to separate grain from chaff; metaphorically in the NT, of destructive judgment *crush, grind into dust*, i.e. *punish very severely* (LU 20.18)

λικμήσει	VIFA--3S	λικμάω
λιμά		λεμά
λιμᾶ		"
λιμένα	N-AM-S	λιμήν
Λιμένας	N-AM-P	Καλοὶ Λιμένες
λιμένος	N-GM-S	λιμήν

λιμήν, ένος, ὁ *harbor, haven, port* along a sea

λίμνη, ης, ἡ as an area of standing water *lake, pool* (LU 5.1); figuratively, as the place of final punishment ἡ λ. τοῦ πυρός literally *the lake of fire*, i.e. *hell* (RV 20.14)

λίμνη	N-NF-S	λίμνη
λίμνῃ	N-DF-S	"
λίμνην	N-AF-S	"
λίμνης	N-GF-S	"
λιμοί	N-NF-P	λιμός
	N-NM-P	"
λιμόν	N-AF-S	"

λιμός, οῦ, ὁ and ἡ (1) as deprivation of food *hunger* (RO 8.35); (2) as scarcity of food or failure of grain harvests *famine* (MT 24.7)

λιμός	N-NF-S	λιμός
	N-NM-S	"
λιμῷ	N-DF-S	"
	N-DM-S	"
λίνα	N-AN-P	λίνον

λίνον, ου, τό *flax*; by metonymy; (1) *cloth or garments made from flax linen* (RV 15.6); (2) *lamp wick* (MT 12.20)

λίνον	N-AN-S	λίνον

Λίνος, ου, ὁ (also **Λῖνος**) *Linus*, masculine proper noun (2T 4.21)

Λίνος	N-NM-S	Λίνος
Λῖνος	N-NM-S	"
λινοῦν	AP-AN-S	λινοῦς

λινοῦς, ῆ, οῦν *(made of) linen*; substantivally ὁ λ. and τὸ λινοῦν *linen garment* (RV 15.6)

λινοῦς	AP-AM-P	λινοῦς
λιπαρά	A--NN-P	λιπαρός

λιπαρός, ά, όν literally *fat, oily*; figuratively in the NT, of a sleek, easy way of life *luxurious, costly*; neuter as a substantive τὰ λιπαρά *luxury, dainties, elegant things* (RV 18.14)

λίπῃ	VSAA--3S	λείπω

λίτρα, ας, ἡ *Roman pound*, a weight of 12 ounces in a Roman measure, about 325 grams

λίτραν	N-AF-S	λίτρα
λίτρας	N-AF-P	"

λίψ, λιβός, ὁ strictly *southwest wind*; by metonymy, of a part of the heavens *southwest*; of a harbor's situation κατὰ λίβα *toward the southwest, (open) to the southwest* (AC 27.12)

λογεία, ας, ἡ (also **λογία**) as an activity *collection*, a receiving of money voluntarily contributed

λογεῖαι	N-NF-P	λογεία
λογείας	N-GF-S	"
λόγια	N-AN-P	λόγιον
λογίαι	N-NF-P	λογεία
λογίας	N-AF-P	"
λογίζεσθαι	VNPP	λογίζομαι
λογίζεσθε	VIPD--2P	"
	VIPO--2P	"
	VMPD--2P	"
	VMPO--2P	"
λογιζέσθω	VMPD--3S	"
	VMPO--3S	"
λογίζεται	VIPD--3S	"
	VIPO--3S	"
	VIPP--3S	"
λογίζῃ	VIPD--2S	"
	VIPO--2S	"

λογίζομαι impf. ἐλογιζόμην; 1aor. mid. ἐλογισάμην; 1aor. pass. ἐλογίσθην; 1fut. λογισθήσομαι; from a basic meaning *think according to logical rules*; (1) as an objective reckoning; (a) as keeping a mental record *take into account, keep in mind, count (up)* (1C 13.5); (b) *charge or credit to* someone's account, *reckon to* (RO 4.11); (2) as the result of an objective evaluation *consider, look on as, regard as* (AC 19.27); (3) as a subjective act of thought *have in mind, ponder, think (about)* (1C 13.11); (4) as the result of a subjective evaluation *have an opin-*

ion, think, believe; followed by ὅτι (that) (RO 8.18); followed by the accusative and an infinitive (RO 3.28)

λογίζομαι	VIPD--1S	λογίζομαι
	VIPO--1S	"
λογιζόμεθα	VIPD--1P	"
	VIPO--1P	"
λογιζόμενος	VPPDNM-S	"
	VPPONM-S	"
λογιζομένους	VPPDAM-P	"
	VPPOAM-P	"
λογιζομένῳ	VPPDDM-S	"
	VPPODM-S	"
λογιζώμεθα	VSPD--1P	"
	VSPO--1P	"
λογικήν	A--AF-S	λογικός
λογικόν	A--AN-S	"

λογικός, ή, όν (1) rational, reasonable, belonging to the real nature of something (RO 12.1); (2) as belonging to the sphere of the mind and spirit spiritual (1P 2.2)

λόγιον, ου, τό plural in the NT oracles, sayings, message, originating from God and received as direct revelation; used of laws (AC 7.38), promises (RO 3.2), inspired utterances (1P 4.11), salvation history (HE 5.12)

λόγιος, ία, ον (1) eloquent, skilled in speech (perhaps AC 18.24); (2) learned, educated, skilled in knowledge (probably AC 18.24)

λόγιος	A--NM-S	λόγιος
λογισάμενος	VPADNM-S	λογίζομαι
λογίσασθαι	VNAD	"
λογίσηται	VSAD--3S	"
λογισθείη	VOAP--3S	"
λογισθῆναι	VNAP	"
λογισθήσεται	VIFP--3S	"

λογισμός, οῦ, ὁ plural in the NT, as the activity of one's reasoning powers thoughts, calculations, reflections (RO 2.15); in a negative sense misleading arguments (2C 10.4)

λογισμούς	N-AM-P	λογισμός
λογισμῶν	N-GM-P	"
λογίων	N-GN-P	λόγιον
λόγοι	N-NM-P	λόγος
λόγοις	N-DM-P	"
λογομάχει	VMPA--2S	λογομαχέω
λογομαχεῖν	VNPA	"

λογομαχέω argue, quarrel about words, wrangle over the meaning of terms (2T 2.14)

λογομαχία, ας, ἡ a dispute revolving around the meaning or use of words word battle, quarrel about words; by implication trivial dispute, petty controversy (1T 6.4)

λογομαχίας	N-AF-S	λογομαχία
λόγον	N-AM-S	λόγος

λόγος, ου, ὁ related to λέγω (arrange in order); (1) as a general term for speaking, but always with rational content word, speech (MT 22.46); often opposite ἔργον (deed) (1J 3.18); (2) with the specific translation depending on a wide variety of contexts; (a) question (MT 21.24); (b) prophecy (JN 2.22); (c) command (2P 3.5); (d) report (AC 11.22); (e) message, teaching (LU 4.32); (f) declaration, statement, assertion (MT 12.32), opposite μῦθος (legend); (g) plural, of words forming a unity of expression discourse, speech, teaching, conversation

(MT 7.24); (h) of what is being discussed subject, thing, matter (MK 9.10); (3) of divine revelation; (a) word, message (of God) (JN 10.35); (b) commandment(s) (MT 15.6); (c) of God's full self-revelation through Jesus Christ the Word (JN 1.1); (d) of the content of the gospel word, message (LU 5.1); (4) in a somewhat legal or technical sense; (a) accusation, matter, charge; (b) account, reckoning (RO 14.12); (c) reason, motive (AC 10.29)

λόγος	N-NM-S	λόγος
λόγου	N-GM-S	"
λόγους	N-AM-P	"

λόγχη, ης, ἡ strictly spear point, the iron head of a spear or javelin; by synecdoche spear, lance, javelin (JN 19.34)

λόγχη	N-DF-S	λόγχη
λόγχην	N-AF-S	"
λόγῳ	N-DM-S	λόγος
λόγων	N-GM-P	"
λοιδορεῖς	VIPA--2S	λοιδορέω

λοιδορέω 1aor. ἐλοιδόρησα; as hurling verbal abuse revile, shout insults, reproach

λοιδορία, ας, ἡ as verbal abuse intended to injure someone's reputation reviling, slander, insult

λοιδορίαν	N-AF-S	λοιδορία
λοιδορίας	N-GF-S	"
λοίδοροι	N-NM-P	λοίδορος

λοίδορος, ου, ὁ as one who intentionally abuses another with speech reviler, slanderer, abusive person

λοίδορος	N-NM-S	λοίδορος
λοιδορούμενοι	VPPPNM-P	λοιδορέω
λοιδορούμενος	VPPPNM-S	"
λοιμοί	N-NM-P	λοιμός (II)
λοιμόν	A--AM-S	λοιμός (I)

λοιμός, ή, όν (I) of a person dangerous to public welfare harmful, troublesome; possibly substantivally troublemaker, pest (AC 24.5)

λοιμός, οῦ, ὁ (II) pestilence, plague, (disease) epidemic (MT 24.7; LU 21.11)

λοιπά	A--AN-P	λοιπός
λοιπαί	A--NF-P	"
λοιπάς	A--AF-P	"
λοιποί	A--NM-P	"
λοιποῖς	A--DM-P	"
	A--DN-P	"
λοιπόν	AB	"
	A--AN-S	"

λοιπός, ή, όν (1) as an adjective remaining, left, other (RV 8.13); (2) as a substantive οἱ λοιποί the rest, the others, the remaining ones (LU 24.9); neuter as a substantive τὰ λοιπά the rest (of the things), other things (MK 4.19); (3) as an adverb; (a) to indicate time τὸ λοιπόν or τοῦ λοιποῦ from now on, henceforth, in the future (HE 10.13); (b) to mark a further fact furthermore, in addition, beyond that (1C 1.16); (c) to indicate a conclusion finally, for the rest (2C 13.11)

λοιποῦ	A--GN-S	λοιπός
λοιπούς	A--AM-P	"
λοιπῶν	A--GF-P	"
	A--GM-P	"
	A--GN-P	"

Λουκᾶς, ᾶ, ὁ Luke, masculine proper noun

Λουκᾶς N-NM-S Λουκᾶς

Λούκιος, ου, ὁ *Lucius*, masculine proper noun

Λούκιος N-NM-S Λούκιος
λουσαμένη VPAMNF-S λούω
λούσαντες VPAANM-P "
λούσαντι VPAADM-S "

λουτρόν, οῦ, τό *bath*; figuratively in the NT, as a baptismal term *(ceremonial) washing*

λουτροῦ N-GN-S λουτρόν
λουτρῷ N-DN-S "

λούω 1aor. ἔλουσα; pf. pass. λέλουμαι and λέλουσμαι; (1) active and literally, of cleansing someone *wash, bathe* (AC 16.33); (2) middle and literally *wash, bathe oneself*; metaphorically, of spiritual cleansing in JN 13.10; (3) figuratively, as a baptismal term *wash* (HE 10.22; RV 1.5)

Λύδδα, ας (also ης), **ἡ** *Lydda*, a city of Palestine southeast of Joppa on the road to Jerusalem

Λύδδα N-AF-S Λύδδα
Λύδδαν N-AF-S "
Λύδδας N-GF-S "
Λύδδης N-GF-S "

Λυδία, ας, ἡ *Lydia*, feminine proper noun

Λυδία N-NF-S Λυδία
Λυδίαν N-AF-S "
λύει VIPA--3S λύω
λύετε VIPA--2P "
λυθείσης VPAPGF-S "
λυθῇ VSAP--3S "
λυθῆναι VNAP "
λυθήσεται VIFP--3S "
λυθήσονται VIFP--3P "

Λυκαονία, ας, ἡ *Lycaonia*, a province in the interior of Asia Minor (AC 14.6)

Λυκαονίας N-GF-S Λυκαονία

Λυκαονιστί adverb; of the language spoken in Lycaonia *in Lycaonian (language)* (AC 14.11)

Λυκαονιστί AB Λυκαονιστί

Λυκία, ας, ἡ *Lycia*, a mountainous province of Asia Minor along the Mediterranean seacoast (AC 27.5)

Λυκίας N-GF-S Λυκία
λύκοι N-NM-P λύκος
λύκον N-AM-S "

λύκος, ου, ὁ as a fierce beast of prey *wolf* (MT 10.16); metaphorically, as a person with dangerous pretenses, such as a false prophet, false teacher, or false leader *vicious person, fierce person* (AC 20.29)

λύκος N-NM-S λύκος
λύκων N-GM-P "

λυμαίνω impf. mid. ἐλυμαινόμην; only middle in the NT, of irrational and relentless persecution *devastate, destroy, do great harm, severely injure* (AC 8.3)

λυόμενα VPPPNN-P λύω
λυομένων VPPPGN-P "
λύοντες VPPANM-P "
λυόντων VPPAGM-P "
λύουσι(ν) VIPA--3P "
λύπας N-AF-P λύπη
λυπεῖσθαι VNPP λυπέω
λυπεῖται VIPP--3S "
λυπεῖτε VMPA--2P "

λυπέω 1aor. ἐλύπησα; pf. λελύπηκα; 1aor. pass. ἐλυπήθην; 1fut. pass. λυπηθήσομαι; (1) active *(cause) pain, grieve, make sad* (EP 4.30); (2) passive *be sad, be sorrowful, be distressed* (MT 26.22); aorist *become distressed* or *sorry* (2C 7.9)

λύπη, ης, ἡ (1) physically *pain, suffering, distress* (JN 16.21); (2) mentally or spiritually *sorrow, grief, sadness, anxiety* (JN 16.6); (3) adverbially ἐκ λύπης *with a grieved spirit, reluctantly, grudgingly* (2C 9.7)

λύπη N-NF-S λύπη
λύπη N-DF-S "
λυπηθείς VPAPNM-S λυπέω
λυπηθέντας VPAPAM-P "
λυπηθέντες VPAPNM-P "
λυπηθῆναι VNAP "
λυπηθήσεσθε VIFP--2P "
λυπηθῆτε VSAP--2P "
λύπην N-AF-S λύπη
λύπης N-GF-S "
λυπῆσθε VSPP--2P λυπέω
λυπούμενοι VPPPNM-P "
λυπούμενος VPPPNM-S "
λυπῶ VIPA--1S "
λῦσαι VNAA λύω

Λυσανίας, ου, ὁ *Lysanias*, masculine proper noun (LU 3.1)

Λυσανίου N-GM-S Λυσανίας
λύσαντες VPAANM-P λύω
λύσαντι VPAADM-S "
λύσας VPAANM-S "
λύσατε VMAA--2P "
λύσῃ VSAA--3S "
λύσῃς VSAA--2S "
λύσητε VSAA--2P "

Λυσίας, ου, ὁ *Lysias*, masculine proper noun

Λυσίας N-NM-S Λυσίας
λύσιν N-AF-S λύσις

λύσις, εως, ἡ as an action *loosing, release, separation*; as release from the marriage bond *divorce* (1C 7.27)

λυσιτελεῖ VIPA--3S λυσιτελέω

λυσιτελέω *be advantageous, be better*; impersonally, with the dative λυσιτελεῖ *it is better, it is to* someone's *advantage* (LU 17.2)

λῦσον VMAA--2S λύω

Λύστρα, ας, ἡ and **ων, τά** *Lystra*, city in the province of Lycaonia

Λύστραν N-AF-S Λύστρα
Λύστροις N-DN-P "
λύσω VSAA--1S λύω

λύτρον, ου, τό as a price paid for release from slavery or captivity *ransom*; figuratively, of the cost to Christ in providing deliverance from sin *price of release, ransom, means of setting free*

λύτρον N-AN-S λύτρον
λυτροῦσθαι VNPM λυτρόω

λυτρόω 1aor. mid. ἐλυτρωσάμην; 1aor. pass. ἐλυτρώθην; only middle or passive in the NT; (1) middle *redeem, set free, deliver* (LU 24.21); (2) passive *be redeemed, be set free* (1P 1.18)

λυτρώσηται VSAM--3S λυτρόω
λύτρωσιν N-AF-S λύτρωσις

λύτρωσις, εως, ἡ   strictly *loosing*; (1) active *providing a ransom, releasing* from slavery or captivity; (2) figuratively and passive in the NT *deliverance, freedom, liberation*

λυτρώσωμαι	VSAM--1S	λυτρόω
λυτρωτήν	N-AM-S	λυτρωτής

λυτρωτής, οῦ, ὁ   one who sets free slaves or captives *liberator, deliverer* (AC 7.35)

λυχνία, ας, ἡ   as a place for setting a lamp, other than a candlestick *lampstand* (MT 5.15); metaphorically; (1) of a church as a place where people can learn things about God as they really are (RV 1.20); (2) of a witness who tells things as they really are (RV 11.4)

λυχνία	N-NF-S	λυχνία
λυχνίαι	N-NF-P	"
λυχνίαν	N-AF-S	"
λυχνίας	N-AF-P	"
	N-GF-S	"
λυχνιῶν	N-GF-P	"
λύχνοι	N-NM-P	λύχνος
λύχνον	N-AM-S	"

λύχνος, ου, ὁ   (1) literally *lamp* other than a candle, *light* (MT 5.15); figuratively, of the eye as the organ that admits light and enables understanding (MT 6.22); (2) metaphorically, of people or things that enable spiritual understanding: of prophecies (2P 1.19); of John the Baptist (JN 5.35); of Christ (RV 21.23); of the lives of believers (LU 12.35)

λύχνος	N-NM-S	λύχνος
λύχνου	N-GM-S	"
λύχνῳ	N-DM-S	"

λύω   impf. ἔλυον; 1aor. ἔλυσα; pf. pass. λέλυμαι; 1aor. pass. ἐλύθην; 1fut. pass. λυθήσομαι; from a basic meaning *loose*, translated with a variety of meanings from the specific contexts; (1) literally, as freeing someone or something tied or bound *loose, untie, set free, release* (MK 1.7; AC 22.30), opposite δέω (*bind*); figuratively, as freeing from a legal obligation *free, release* (1C 7.27); freeing from spiritual bondage *set free* (RV 1.5); (2) literally, as breaking something up into its component parts *destroy, tear down, break up* (2P 3.10); as breaking up a crowd *dismiss, disperse* (AC 13.43); figuratively, as bringing something to an end *do away with, undo* (1J 3.8); (3) of law, commandments, scriptures *set aside, annul, invalidate* (JN 7.23)

Λωΐδι	N-DF-S	Λωΐς
Λωΐδι	N-DF-S	"

Λωΐς, ΐδος, ἡ (also **Λωΐς**)   *Lois*, feminine proper noun (2T 1.5)

Λώτ, ὁ   indeclinable; *Lot*, masculine proper noun (LU 17.28) μʹ indeclinable; as a cardinal number *forty* (AC 10.41)

Μάαθ, ὁ (also **Μαάθ**) indeclinable; *Maath*, masculine proper noun (LU 3.26)

Μααθ		Μάαθ
Μαγαδά		Μαγαδάν

Μαγαδάν, ἡ (also **Μαγαδά, Μαγεδά, Μαγεδάν**) indeclinable; *Magadan*, a site on the western shore of the Sea of Galilee (MT 15.39)

Μαγδαλά, ἡ (also **Μαγδαλάν, Μαγεδάλ, Μαγεδαλά, Μελεγαδά**) indeclinable; *Magdala*, a town on the western shore of the Sea of Galilee, north of Tiberias (MT 15.39)

Μαγδαλάν		Μαγδαλά

Μαγδαληνή, ῆς, ἡ *Magdalene, woman from Magdala*, a site on the western shore of the Sea of Galilee

Μαγδαληνή	N-NF-S	Μαγδαληνή
Μαγδαληνῇ	N-DF-S	"
Μαγεδά		Μαγαδάν
Μαγεδάλ		Μαγδαλά
Μαγεδαλά		"
Μαγεδάν		Μαγαδάν
Μαγεδδών		Μαγεδών

Μαγεδών, τό (also **Μαγεδδών**) indeclinable; *Magedon*, part of a Hebrew place-name transliterated Ἁρ M. *Armageddon, Mount Magedon*, generally identified as the fortress of Megiddo, overlooking a pass through the Carmel Range into Galilee (RV 16.16); see also Ἁρμαγεδών

μαγεία, ας, ἡ *magic*; plural *magic arts, sorceries* (AC 8.11)

μαγείαις	N-DF-P	μαγεία

μαγεύω *practice magic or sorcery, be a magician, use witchcraft* (AC 8.9)

μαγεύων	VPPANM-S	μαγεύω
μάγοι	N-NM-P	μάγος
μάγον	N-AM-S	"

μάγος, ου, ὁ from Persian *magus* (*great*); (1) *magus*, plural *magi*, the high priestly caste of Persia; *wise man* of the Magian religion (MT 2.1); (2) *magician, sorcerer*, one using witchcraft or magic arts (AC 13.6)

μάγος	N-NM-S	μάγος
μάγους	N-AM-P	"

Μαγώγ, ὁ indeclinable; *Magog*, a people hostile to God in the last days (RV 20.8)

μάγων	N-GM-P	μάγος

Μαδιάμ, ὁ indeclinable; *Midian*, a district of Arabia, home of the Midianite people (AC 7.29)

μαζοῖς	N-DM-P	μαζός

μαζός, οῦ, ὁ *breast*; of a man (RV 1.13) or a woman

Μαθθάτ		Μαθθάτ
Μαθεάθ		"
μαθεῖν	VNAA	μανθάνω
μάθετε	VMAA--2P	"
μαθηταί	N-NM-P	μαθητής
μαθηταῖς	N-DM-P	"
μαθητάς	N-AM-P	"
μάθητε	VSAA--2P	μανθάνω
μαθητευθείς	VPAPNM-S	μαθητεύω
μαθητεύσαντες	VPAANM-P	"
μαθητεύσατε	VMAA--2P	"

μαθητεύω 1aor. ἐμαθήτευσα; 1aor. pass. ἐμαθητεύθην; (1) intransitively, active *be* or *become a disciple* of someone (MT 27.57); passive *become a disciple, be a follower* (MT 27.57); *be instructed, be trained* (MT 13.52); (2) transitively *make a disciple* of someone, *instruct, cause someone to become a follower* (MT 28.19)

μαθητῇ	N-DM-S	μαθητής
μαθητήν	N-AM-S	"

μαθητής, οῦ, ὁ (1) as one who directs his mind to something *learner, disciple, pupil* (LU 6.40); (2) in a more technical sense *disciple, apprentice*; specifically in the NT as one who attached himself to a spiritual leader, such as Jesus (MT 12.1), John the Baptist (JN 3.25); (3) in a broader sense *disciple, follower*, one who adhered intellectually and spiritually to religious leaders, such as Jesus (AC 11.26), the Pharisees (MT 22.16), John the Baptist (AC 19.1), Moses (JN 9.28b)

μαθητής	N-NM-S	μαθητής
μαθητοῦ	N-GM-S	"

μαθήτρια, ας, ἡ feminine of μαθητής (*disciple*); *female disciple, Christian woman* (AC 9.36)

μαθήτρια	N-NF-S	μαθήτρια
μαθητῶν	N-GM-P	μαθητής
Μαθθααάθ		Μαθθάτ
Μαθθάθ		"
Μαθθαθίου	N-GM-S	Ματταθίας
Μαθθαῖον	N-AM-S	Μαθθαῖος

Μαθθαῖος, ου, ὁ (also **Ματθαῖος**) *Matthew*, masculine proper noun (MT 10.3)

Μαθθαῖος	N-NM-S	Μαθθαῖος
Μαθθάν		Ματθάν

Μαθθάτ, ὁ (also **Μαθάτ, Μαθεάθ, Μαθθααάθ, Μαθθάθ, Ματθάτ, Ματτάθ, Μάττθ**) indeclinable; *Matthat*, masculine proper noun

Μαθθίαν	N-AM-S	Μαθθίας

Μαθθίας, ου, ὁ (also **Ματθίας**) *Matthias*, masculine proper noun

Μαθουσάλα		Μαθουσάλα

Μαθουσαλά, ὁ (also **Μαθουσάλα**) indeclinable; *Methuselah*, masculine proper noun (LU 3.37)

μαθών	VPAANM-S	μανθάνω
Μαϊνάν		Μεννά
μαίνεσθε	VIPD--2P	μαίνομαι
	VIPO--2P	"
μαίνεται	VIPD--3S	"
	VIPO--3S	"

μαίνη   VIPD--2S   "
       VIPO--2S   "

μαίνομαι   *be mad, be out of one's mind, be insane,* opposite σωφρονέω (*be of sound mind*)

μαίνομαι   VIPD--1S   μαίνομαι
       VIPO--1S   "
μακαρία   A--NF-S   μακάριος
μακάριαι   A--NF-P   "
μακαρίαν   A--AF-S   "
μακαρίζομεν   VIPA--1P   μακαρίζω

μακαρίζω   fut. μακαριῶ; as an evaluation of someone as happy because of favorable circumstances *regard as happy, think of as blessed, consider fortunate* (LU 1.48)

μακάριοι   A--NM-P   μακάριος
μακάριον   A--AM-S   "
       A--NN-S   "

μακάριος, ία, ον   (1) of persons characterized by transcendent happiness or religious joy *blessed, happy* (MT 5.3); without religious connotation *fortunate, lucky* (LU 23.29); (2) of parts of the body viewed as happy because of favorable circumstances (MT 13.16; LU 11.27); (3) of things closely related to God, as hope (TI 2.13); (4) comparative μακαριώτερος, τέρα, ον *more blessed, happier, better off* (1C 7.40)

μακάριος   A--NM-S   μακάριος
μακαρίου   A--GM-S   "
μακαριοῦσι(ν)   VIFA--3P   μακαρίζω
μακαρισμόν   N-AM-S   μακαρισμός

μακαρισμός, οῦ, ὁ   as a frame of mind produced by favorable circumstances *blessedness, happiness* (GA 4.15)

μακαρισμός   N-NM-S   μακαρισμός
μακαριωτέρα   A-MNF-S   μακάριος
μακαριωτερία   A-MNF-S   see μακαριωτέρα
Μακεδόνα   N-AM-S   Μακεδών
Μακεδόνας   N-AM-P   "
Μακεδόνες   N-NM-P   "

Μακεδονία, ας, ἡ   *Macedonia,* a Roman province north of Thessaly and west of Thrace in Greece

Μακεδονία   N-NF-S   Μακεδονία
Μακεδονίᾳ   N-DF-S   "
Μακεδονίαν   N-AF-S   "
Μακεδονίας   N-GF-S   "
Μακεδόνος   N-GM-S   Μακεδών
Μακεδόσι(ν)   N-DM-P   "

Μακεδών, όνος, ὁ   *Macedonian, native of Macedonia*

Μακεδών   N-NM-S   Μακεδών

μάκελλον, ου, τό   *food market,* a rectangular enclosed court with pillared walkways and booths on all sides; by synecdoche, one part of such a market *meat market* (1C 10.25)

μακέλλῳ   N-DN-S   μάκελλον
μακρά   AB   μακρός

μακράν   (1) as an adverb (originally an accusative of extent, with ὁδόν [*road*] implied); literally, of extent of space *far away, at a distance, far off* (MT 8.30); figuratively, of separation from God (EP 2.13, 17); (2) as an improper preposition with the genitive *far away from* (LU 7.6)

μακράν   AB   μακράν
       A--AF-S   μακρός

μακρόθεν   an adverb expressing location *from afar, from a distance, at a distance* (LU 18.13); ἀπὸ μ. *far away, from* or *at* a distance (MK 11.13)

μακρόθεν   AB   μακρόθεν
μακροθυμεῖ   VIPA--3S   μακροθυμέω
μακροθυμεῖτε   VMPA--2P   "

μακροθυμέω   1aor. ἐμακροθύμησα; (1) with an element of expectancy *wait (for), have patience (for)* (JA 5.7); (2) with an element of constraint *be patient* or *forbearing* (1C 13.4); (3) with an element of postponement *delay, be slow* (LU 18.7)

μακροθυμήσας   VPAANM-S   μακροθυμέω
μακροθυμήσατε   VMAA--2P   "
μακροθύμησον   VMAA--2S   "

μακροθυμία, ας, ἡ   as a state of emotional quietness in the face of unfavorable circumstances *patience, long-suffering*; (1) as patience under trial *endurance, steadfastness* (HE 6.12); (2) as constraint exercised toward others *forbearance, patience* (2C 6.6); (3) as God's constraint of his wrath *long-suffering, forbearance* (RO 2.4)

μακροθυμία   N-NF-S   μακροθυμία
μακροθυμίᾳ   N-DF-S   "
μακροθυμίαν   N-AF-S   "
μακροθυμίας   N-GF-S   "
μακροθυμῶν   VPPANM-S   μακροθυμέω

μακροθύμως   adverb; *patiently, with patience* (AC 26.3)

μακροθύμως   AB   μακροθύμως

μακρός, ά, όν   (1) of extension in time *long, long lasting*; neuter as an adverb μακρά *long* (MK 12.40); (2) of extension in space *far off* or *away, distant* (LU 15.13)

μακροχρόνιος, ον   of time *long lasting*; of a life span *long-lived* (EP 6.3)

μακροχρόνιος   A--NM-S   μακροχρόνιος
μαλακά   A--AN-P   μαλακός

μαλακία, ας, ἡ   strictly *softness*; in the NT a form of physical ailment resulting from disease *sickness, weakness, infirmity*

μαλακίαν   N-AF-S   μαλακία
μαλακοί   AP-NM-P   μαλακός
μαλακοῖς   A--DN-P   "

μαλακός, ή, όν   *soft*; (1) of clothes *soft (to the touch), delicate* (LU 7.25); neuter plural τὰ μαλακα as a substantive, *luxurious clothes* (MT 11.8); (2) figuratively, in a bad sense of men *effeminate, unmanly*; substantivally ὁ μ. especially of a man or boy who submits his body to homosexual lewdness *catamite, homosexual pervert* (1C 6.9)

Μαλαλεήλ   Μαλελεήλ

Μαλελεήλ, ὁ (also **Μαλαλεήλ, Μελελεήλ**) indeclinable; *Maleleel,* masculine proper noun (LU 3.37)

μαλιᾶς   N-GF-S   see τρυμαλιᾶς

μάλιστα   adverb (superlative of the adverb μάλα [*very much, exceedingly*]); as the highest point in the extent of something *most of all, especially, above all* (AC 20.38)

μάλιστα   ABS   μάλιστα

μᾶλλον   adverb (comparative of the adverb μάλα [*very much, exceedingly*]); as a higher point in the extent of something *more, rather*; (1) of degree *(even) more, to a greater degree* (PH 3.4); (2) of quality *for a better reason, (much) rather* (HE 12.9); (3) of increased certainty *more surely, more certainly* (MT 6.30); (4) of a preferred choice *rather, instead of* (MK 15.11); (5) μ. ἤ *rather than*, excluding consideration of what is introduced by ἤ (JN 3.19)

μᾶλλον	ABM	μᾶλλον

Μάλχος, ου, ὁ *Malchus*, masculine proper noun (JN 18.10)

Μάλχος	N-NM-S	Μάλχος
Μαμβρῆς		Ἰαμβρῆς

μάμμη, ης, ἡ originally *mother*; later, and in the NT, *grandmother* (2T 1.5)

μάμμη	N-DF-S	μάμμη
μαμμωνᾶ	N-GM-S	μαμωνᾶς
μαμμωνᾷ	N-DM-S	"
μαμωνᾶ	N-GM-S	"
μαμωνᾷ	N-DM-S	"

μαμωνᾶς, ᾶ, ὁ (also **μαμμωνᾶς**) transliterated from the Aramaic; usually in a derogatory sense *property, wealth, earthly goods* (LU 16.9); personification *Mammon*, the Syrian god of riches, *money* (MT 6.24)

Μαναήν, ὁ indeclinable; *Manaen*, masculine proper noun (AC 13.1)

Μανασσῆ, ὁ indeclinable and **Μανασσῆς**, gen. and accusative ἤ *Manasseh*, masculine proper noun; (1) a tribe of Israel descended from the son of Jacob by that name (RV 7.6); (2) a king of Israel son of Hezekiah (MT 1.10); Μανασσῆν in MT 1.10 is an irregular spelling of Μανασσῆ

Μανασσῆν	N-AM-S	Μανασσῆ
Μανασσῆς	N-NM-S	"
μανθάνειν	VNPA	μανθάνω
μανθανέτω	VMPA--3S	"
μανθανέτωσαν	VMPA--3P	"
μανθάνοντα	VPPAAN-P	"
μανθάνουσι(ν)	VIPA--3P	"

μανθάνω 2aor. ἔμαθον; from a basic meaning *learn*, i.e. of directing one's mind to something and producing an external effect; (1) as learning through instruction *be taught, learn* from someone (JN 7.15); (2) as learning through inquiry *ascertain, discover, find out* (AC 23.27); (3) as learning through practice or experience *come to know, come to realize* (PH 4.11; HE 5.8); (4) as achieving comprehension *understand, learn* (RV 14.3)

μανθάνωσι(ν)	VSPA--3P	μανθάνω

μανία, ας, ἡ as overcharged mental excitement *madness, frenzy, insanity* (AC 26.24)

μανίαν	N-AF-S	μανία

μάννα, τό indeclinable; *manna*, the food with which God miraculously fed the Israelites in the desert after the exodus from Egypt (JN 6.31); figuratively, of spiritual food (RV 2.17)

μαντεύομαι used of demonic divination in the NT *tell fortunes, predict future events* (AC 16.16)

μαντευομένη	VPPDNF-S	μαντεύομαι
	VPPONF-S	"

μαραίνω 1fut. pass. μαρανθήσομαι; only passive in the NT; literally, of plants losing beauty and vitality *fade away, dry up, wither*; figuratively, of persons *waste away, end up with nothing, lose out* (JA 1.11)

μαράν		μαράνα θά
μαράνα		"

μαράνα θά (also **μαράνα θά, μαρὰν ἀθά** or **μαρὰν ἀθᾶ**) an Aramaic formula used in early Christian liturgy; either (1) at the Lord's Supper *our Lord is present* or (2) as a petition for the Lord to return *O Lord, come!* the latter seems preferable in the context of 1C 16.22 (cf. RV 22.20)

μαραναθά		see μαράνα θά
μαράνθη	VIAP--3S	μαραίνω
μαρανθήσεται	VIFP--3S	"
μαργαρῖται	N-NM-P	μαργαρίτης
μαργαρίταις	N-DM-P	"
μαργαρίτας	N-AM-P	"
	N-GM-P	"
μαργαρίτῃ	N-DM-S	"
μαργαρίτην	N-AM-S	"

μαργαρίτης, ου, ὁ literally *pearl*, as a very valuable gem (1T 2.9); metaphorically, as something of supreme worth (proverbially in MT 7.6)

μαργαρίτης	N-NM-S	μαργαρίτης
μαργαρίτου	N-GM-S	"
μαργαρίτων	N-GM-P	"

Μάρθα, ας, ἡ *Martha*, feminine proper noun

Μάρθα	N-NF-S	Μάρθα
	N-VF-S	"
Μάρθαν	N-AF-S	"
Μάρθας	N-GF-S	"

Μαρία, ας, ἡ and **Μαριάμ** indeclinable feminine proper noun; (1) *Mary* (MT 1.16); (2) *Miriam*, the sister of Moses in the Old Testament; Μαριάμ is used as a byform for Μαρία in the NT (MT 13.55)

Μαρία	N-NF-S	Μαρία
Μαρίᾳ	N-DF-S	"
Μαριάμ		"
Μαρίαν	N-AF-S	"
Μαρίας	N-GF-S	"
Μάρκον	N-AM-S	Μάρκος
Μᾶρκον	N-AM-S	"
Μᾶρκος	N-NM-S	"

Μᾶρκος, ου, ὁ (also **Μάρκος**) *Mark*, masculine proper noun

Μᾶρκος	N-NM-S	Μᾶρκος
Μάρκου	N-GM-S	"

μάρμαρος, ου, ὁ as any valuable stone or rock with sparkling crystals in it *marble* (RV 18.12)

μαρμάρου	N-GM-S	μάρμαρος
μάρτυρα	N-AM-S	μάρτυς
μάρτυρας	N-AM-P	"
μαρτυρεῖ	VIPA--3S	μαρτυρέω
μαρτυρεῖν	VNPA	"
μαρτυρεῖς	VIPA--2S	"
μαρτυρεῖται	VIPP--3S	"
μαρτυρεῖτε	VIPA--2P	"
μάρτυρες	N-NM-P	μάρτυς

μαρτυρέω impf. ἐμαρτύρουν; fut. μαρτυρήσω; 1aor. ἐμαρτύρησα; pf. μεμαρτύρηκα; pf. pass. μεμαρτύρημαι; 1aor. pass. ἐμαρτυρήθην; used of the activity of a μάρτυς (*witness*); (1) of a human declaration of ascertainable facts based on firsthand knowledge or experience *bear witness to, declare, confirm* (RO 10.2); (2) absolutely, of a good report; (a) active *give a good report, speak well (of), approve (of)* (LU 4.22); (b) passive *receive a* good report, be well-spoken of, be approved, have a good reputation (AC 6.3); (3) of an emphatic declaration by an existing authority, such as God, the Spirit, Scripture *testify, declare, witness (solemnly)* (HE 7.17); (4) of religious witness to truth and the factual content of the gospel as revealed truth from God *be a witness, tell about, testify* (AC 23.11)

μαρτυρηθέντες	VPAPNM-P	μαρτυρέω
μαρτυρῆσαι	VNAA	"
μαρτυρήσαντος	VPAAGM-S	"
μαρτυρήσας	VPAANM-S	"
μαρτυρήσει	VIFA--3S	"
μαρτυρήση	VSAA--3S	"
μαρτύρησον	VMAA--2S	"
μαρτυρήσω	VSAA--1S	"

μαρτυρία, ας, ἡ as concrete and objective information given in proof of something *testimony*; (1) active *giving of a witness, testimony, declaration* (JN 1.7); (2) passive, as the witness given *testimony, evidence, record* (JN 1.19); (3) as facts presented in court *evidence, testimony* (MK 14.55); (4) as a good report received *reputation* (1T 3.7); (5) as divine and human witness, with Christ as the content *testimony, witness* (JN 3.33); as a formula for the gospel message μ. Ἰησοῦ *witness of (or about) Jesus* (RV 19.10)

μαρτυρία	N-NF-S	μαρτυρία
μαρτυρίαι	N-NF-P	"
μαρτυρίαν	N-AF-S	"
μαρτυρίας	N-GF-S	"

μαρτύριον, ου, τό an objective act, circumstance, or statement that serves as a means of proof *evidence, testimony, witness* (AC 4.33); ἡ σκηνὴ τοῦ μαρτυρίου *tent of testimony* (AC 7.44); εἰς μ. *for a testimony, to provide evidence, certify* (MT 8.4)

μαρτύριον	N-AN-S	μαρτύριον
	N-NN-S	"
μαρτυρίου	N-GN-S	"

μαρτύρομαι (1) as making an emphatic affirmation *seriously declare, testify, assert* (AC 20.26); (2) as making an emphatic demand *implore, insist, urge* (1TH 2.12)

μαρτύρομαι	VIPD--1S	μαρτύρομαι
	VIPO--1S	"
μαρτυρόμενοι	VPPDNM-P	"
	VPPONM-P	"
μαρτυρόμενος	VPPDNM-S	"
	VPPONM-S	"
μάρτυρος	N-GM-S	μάρτυς
μαρτυροῦμεν	VIPA--1P	μαρτυρέω
μαρτυρουμένη	VPPPNF-S	"
μαρτυρούμενοι	VPPMNM-P	"
μαρτυρούμενος	VPPPNM-S	"
μαρτυρουμένους	VPPPAM-P	"
μαρτυροῦν	VPPAGM-P	see μαρτυρούντων
	VPPANN-S	μαρτυρέω
μαρτυροῦντες	VPPANM-P	"
μαρτυροῦντι	VPPADM-S	"
μαρτυροῦντος	VPPAGM-S	"
μαρτυρούντων	VPPAGM-P	"
μαρτυροῦσαι	VPPANF-P	"
μαρτυρούσης	VPPAGF-S	"
μαρτυροῦσι(ν)	VIPA--3P	"

μαρτυρῶ	VIPA--1S	"
	VSPA--1S	"
μαρτύρων	N-GM-P	μάρτυς
μαρτυρῶν	VPPANM-S	μαρτυρέω

μάρτυς, μάρτυρος, ὁ *witness*; (1) as a witness to ascertainable facts; (a) legally (MT 26.65); (b) generally, as one who testifies to something (RO 1.9); (2) as one who declares facts directly known to himself; (a) from firsthand knowledge (AC 1.22) or (b) from firsthand experience (HE 12.1); (3) as one who tells what he believes, even though it results in his being killed for it *witness, martyr* (AC 1.8; RV 17.6)

μάρτυς	N-NM-S	μάρτυς
μάρτυσι(ν)	N-DM-P	"

μασάομαι impf. ἐμασώμην; of a reaction to extreme pain *bite (the lips), gnaw (the tongue)* (RV 16.10)

μάστιγας	N-AF-P	μάστιξ
μαστιγοῖ	VIPA--3S	μαστιγόω
μάστιγος	N-GF-S	μάστιξ

μαστιγόω fut. μαστιγώσω; 1aor. ἐμαστίγωσα; literally, as beating with a lash or whip *flog, scourge, whip* (MT 10.17); figuratively, of God's corrective punishment *chastise, punish severely* (HE 12.6)

μαστίγων	N-GF-P	μάστιξ
μαστιγῶσαι	VNAA	μαστιγόω
μαστιγώσαντες	VPAANM-P	"
μαστιγώσετε	VIFA--2P	"
μαστιγώσουσι(ν)	VIFA--3P	"
μαστίζειν	VNPA	μαστίζω

μαστίζω *scourge, beat* or *strike with a whip* (AC 22.25)

μάστιξ, ιγος, ἡ (1) *whip, lash, scourge*; plural *flogging, whipping* (AC 22.24); (2) as a distressing bodily disease *plague, affliction, ailment* (MK 3.10)

μάστιξι(ν)	N-DF-P	μάστιξ
μαστοί	N-NM-P	μαστός
μαστοῖς	N-DM-P	"

μαστός, οῦ, ὁ used of a male (RV 1.13) or female (LU 11.27) *breast*

Ματθίου	N-GM-S	Ματταθίας
ματαία	A--NF-S	μάταιος
ματαίας	A--GF-S	"
μάταιοι	A--NF-P	"
	A--NM-P	"

ματαιολογία, ας, ἡ *meaningless talk, empty prattle, idle discussion* (1T 1.6)

ματαιολογίαν	N-AF-S	ματαιολογία
ματαιολόγοι	AP-NM-P	ματαιολόγος

ματαιολόγος, ον *idly talking*; substantivally *idle talker, foolish prattler* (TI 1.10)

μάταιος, αία, ον of what is deceptive or ineffectual, not what it appears to be, translated according to the context; (1) of thoughts and speculations *empty, foolish, idle* (1C 3.20); (2) of unprofitable religion *futile, foolish, useless, worthless* (JA 1.26); neuter plural τὰ μάταια as a substantive *worthless things, idols* (AC 14.15)

μάταιος	A--NF-S	μάταιος

ματαιότης, ητος, ἡ strictly *nonsense, nothingness, emptiness* (2P 2.18); as a characteristic state of something *futility, frustration, purposelessness* (RO 8.20)

ματαιότητι	N-DF-S	ματαιότης
ματαιότητος	N-GF-S	"

ματαιόω   1aor. pass. ἐματαιώθην; only passive in the NT, as being given over to deceptive and meaningless thinking *become worthless* or *foolish, be unable to think clearly* or *correctly* (RO 1.21)

ματαίων	A--GN-P	μάταιος

μάτην   adverb; *senselessly, pointlessly, without result*

μάτην	AB	μάτην
Ματθαθαίου	N-GM-S	Ματταθίας
Ματθαῖον	N-AM-S	Μαθθαῖος
Ματθαῖος	N-NM-S	"

Ματθάν, ὁ (also **Μαθθάν**)   indeclinable; *Matthan*, masculine proper noun (MT 1.15)

Ματθάτ		Μαθθάτ
Ματθίαν	N-AM-S	Μαθθίας
Ματτάθ		Μαθθάτ

Ματταθά, ὁ (also **Μετταθά**)   indeclinable; *Mattatha*, masculine proper noun (LU 3.31)

Ματταθίας, ου, ὁ (also **Μαθθαθίας, Ματαθίας, Ματθαθίας**)   *Mattathias*, masculine proper noun (LU 3.25, 26)

Ματταθίου	N-GM-S	Ματταθίας
Μάττθ		Μαθθάτ
μάχαι	N-NF-P	μάχη

μάχαιρα, ης, ἡ   originally a large knife for killing and cutting up; in the NT *sword, saber*; literally, as a curved weapon for close combat *(small) sword, dagger* (JN 18.11); figuratively, as a symbol of violent death (RO 8.35), of hostility (MT 10.34), of the power of life and death (RO 13.4); metaphorically, for the penetrating power of words spoken by God (EP 6.17)

μάχαιρα	N-NF-S	μάχαιρα
μαχαίρᾳ	N-DF-S	"
μάχαιραι	N-NF-P	"
μάχαιραν	N-AF-S	"
μαχαίρας	N-GF-S	"
μαχαίρῃ	N-DF-S	"
μαχαίρης	N-GF-S	"
μαχαιρῶν	N-GF-P	"
μάχας	N-AF-P	μάχη
μάχεσθαι	VNPD	μάχομαι
	VNPO	"
μάχεσθε	VIPD--2P	"
	VIPO--2P	"

μάχη, ης, ἡ   literally, physical combat or a contest fought with weapons *battle, conflict, fight*; in the NT figuratively and plural, as battles fought with words only *disputes, quarrels, strifes* (2T 2.23)

μάχην	N-AF-S	μάχη

μάχομαι   impf. ἐμαχόμην; (1) of physical combat *fight* (AC 7.26); (2) figuratively, of word battles *quarrel, dispute, contend* (JN 6.52)

μαχομένοις	VPPDDM-P	μάχομαι
	VPPODM-P	
μέ	NPA-1S	ἐγώ
μέγα	A--AM-S	see μέγαν
	A--AN-S	μέγας
	A--NN-S	"
μεγάλα	A--AN-P	"
	A--NN-P	"
μεγάλαι	A--NF-P	"
μεγάλαις	A--DF-P	"
μεγάλας	A--AF-P	"
μεγαλαυχεῖ	VIPA--3S	μεγαλαυχέω

μεγαλαυχέω   *boast highly, speak haughtily* (JA 3.5)

μεγαλεῖα	AP-AN-P	μεγαλεῖος

μεγαλεῖος, εία, ον   *great, powerful, splendid*; neuter as a substantive τὰ μεγαλεῖα *the mighty acts, powerful works* (AC 2.11)

μεγαλειότης, ητος, ἡ   (1) as a demonstration of great power *mighty power, majesty, greatness* (2P 1.16); (2) as a state of greatness *importance, prominence* (AC 19.27)

μεγαλειότητα	N-AF-S	μεγαλειότης
μεγαλειότητι	N-DF-S	"
μεγαλειότητος	N-GF-S	"
μεγάλη	A--NF-S	μέγας
	A--VF-S	"
μεγάλῃ	A--DF-S	"
μεγάλην	A--AF-S	"
μεγάλης	A--GF-S	"
μεγάλοι	A--NM-P	"
	A--VM-P	"
μεγάλοις	A--DM-P	"

μεγαλοπρεπής, ές   as suitable to greatness *majestic, excellent, sublime* (2P 1.17)

μεγαλοπρεποῦς	A--GF-S	μεγαλοπρεπής
μεγάλου	A--GM-S	μέγας
μεγάλους	A--AM-P	"
μεγαλύνει	VIPA--3S	μεγαλύνω
μεγαλυνθῆναι	VNAP	"
μεγαλυνθήσεται	VIFP--3S	"
μεγαλυνόντων	VPPAGM-P	"
μεγαλύνουσι(ν)	VIPA--3P	"

μεγαλύνω   impf. ἐμεγάλυνον, mid. ἐμεγαλυνόμην; 1aor. pass. ἐμεγαλύνθην; 1fut. pass. μεγαλυνθήσομαι; *make great, magnify*; literally, of garment fringes *enlarge, make long* (MT 23.5); passive *be enlarged, increase* (2C 10.15); figuratively, as recognizing the greatness of someone's name or reputation *extol, praise, magnify* (AC 10.46); as recognizing the importance of someone *pay great respect to, highly honor* (AC 5.13)

μεγάλῳ	A--DM-S	μέγας
	A--DN-S	"
μεγάλων	A--GM-P	"

μεγάλως   adverb; *greatly*; when used to intensify a verb *very (much), greatly* (PH 4.10)

μεγάλως	AB	μεγάλως

μεγαλωσύνη, ης, ἡ   literally *prominence, greatness, importance*; used only of God *majesty* (JU 25); used as a name for God *the Majesty* (HE 1.3)

μεγαλωσύνη	N-NF-S	μεγαλωσύνη
μεγαλωσύνης	N-GF-S	"
μέγαν	A--AM-S	μέγας

μέγας, μεγάλη, μέγα   with a basic meaning *great*, translated to fit the context; (1) of extent of space *large, spacious, wide, long* (MK 4.32; 14.15); (2) of number and quantity *large, great, abundant* (HE 10.35); (3) of intensity and degree, opposite ὀλίγος (*little*); (a) in relation to natural phenomena *intense* (heat) (RV 16.9), *violent* (storm) (MK 4.37), *very bright* (light) (MT 4.16), etc.; (b) in relation to human and divine experience *loud* (voice) (MK 15.37), *loud* (lamentation) (AC 8.2), *in-*

tense (fever) (LU 4.38), etc.; (c) in relation to extraordinary and surprising events *mighty* (deeds) (RV 15.3); *severe* (trouble) (MT 24.21); neuter as a substantive μεγάλα *extraordinary things* (LU 1.49); (d) in relation to emotions *great* (joy) (MT 2.10), *deep* (sorrow) (RO 9.2), *fierce* (anger) (RV 12.12), *overwhelming* (astonishment) (MK 5.42), etc.; (4) of persons possessing power, rank, dignity *mighty, great, eminent* (TI 2.13); substantivally οἱ μεγάλοι *important people* (RV 11.18); (5) of things marked by importance *great, extraordinary, outstanding* (JN 19.31); especially of the time of judgment (AC 2.20; JU 6); (6) comparative μείζων, μεῖζον and μειζότερος, τέρα, ον *greater* (3J 4); *most important, very important* (1C 12.31); substantivally ὁ μείζων *the older one* (RO 9.12); (τὰ) μείζω *more outstanding things* (JN 1.50); (7) superlative μέγιστος, ίστη, ον *greatest, very great* (2P 1.4)

μέγας	A--NM-S	μέγας

μέγεθος, ους, τό of size, quantity, or degree *greatness* (EP 1.19)

μέγεθος	N-NN-S	μέγεθος
μέγιστα	A-SAN-P	μέγας

μεγιστάν, ᾶνος, ὁ *very important person*; only plural in the NT *great persons, very important people, nobles* (MK 6.21); *lords, chiefs* (RV 6.15)

μεγιστᾶνες	N-NM-P	μεγιστάν
μεγιστᾶσι(ν)	N-DM-P	"
μέγως	AB	see μεγάλως
μεθ᾽	PA	μετά
	PG	"
μέθαι	N-NF-P	μέθη
μέθαις	N-DF-P	"
μεθερμηνεύεται	VIPP--3S	μεθερμηνεύω
μεθερμηνευόμενον	VPPPNN-S	"
μεθερμηνευόμενος	VPPPNM-S	"

μεθερμηνεύω *translate, give the meaning* in a different language; passive *be translated* or *interpreted*

μέθη, ης, ἡ *drunkenness, intoxication*

μέθη	N-DF-S	μέθη
μεθιστάναι	VNPA	μεθίστημι
μεθιστάνειν	VNPA	"

μεθίστημι and **μεθιστάνω** 1aor. μετέστησα; 1aor. pass. μετεστάθην; literally *remove from one place to another, transfer* (1C 13.2); as causing a change in someone's official position *remove, dismiss, discharge* (AC 13.22); passive *be dismissed, lose one's job* (LU 16.4); figuratively, as causing someone to change sides mentally or spiritually *bring to a different view*; in a bad sense *turn away, mislead* (AC 19.26)

μεθοδεία, ας, ἡ (also **μεθοδία**) *method, procedure*; in the NT in a bad sense, as scheming to deceive *craftiness, cunning, deception* (EP 4.14); plural *stratagems, cunning attacks, tricks* (EP 6.11)

μεθοδείαν	N-AF-S	μεθοδεία
μεθοδείας	N-AF-P	"
μεθοδίας	N-AF-P	"
μεθόρια	N-AN-P	μεθόριον

μεθόριον, ου, τό *boundary, border, frontier*; plural, of the outer areas of any land or city *region, vicinity* (MK 7.24)

μεθύει	VIPA--3S	μεθύω

μεθύοντες	VPPANM-P	"
μεθυόντων	VPPAGM-P	"
μεθύουσαν	VPPAAF-S	"
μεθύουσι(ν)	VIPA--3P	"
μεθυσθῶσι(ν)	VSAP--3P	μεθύσκω
μεθύσκεσθαι	VNPP	"
μεθύσκεσθε	VMPP--2P	"
μεθυσκόμενοι	VPPPNM-P	"

μεθύσκω 1aor. pass. ἐμεθύσθην; *cause to become intoxicated*; only passive in the NT *be drunk, get drunk, become intoxicated* (LU 12.45); *drink freely* (JN 2.10); figuratively, of unrestrained and orgiastic cult activity *give oneself over* to something (RV 17.2)

μέθυσοι	N-NM-P	μέθυσος

μέθυσος, ου, ὁ *drunkard* (used of both men and women)

μέθυσος	N-NM-S	μέθυσος

μεθύω literally *drink a lot, get drunk* (1TH 5.7), opposite νήφω (*be sober*); metaphorically μεθύειν ἐκ τοῦ αἵματος of preoccupation with killing many people, literally *get drunk from blood*, i.e. *kill many* (RV 17.6)

μεῖζον	ABM	μέγας
	A-MAN-S	"
	A-MNN-S	"
μείζονα	A-MAF-S	"
	A-MAM-S	"
	A-MAN-P	"
μείζονας	A-MAF-P	"
μείζονες	A-MNM-P	"
μείζονος	A-MGF-S	"
	A-MGM-S	"
μειζοτέραν	A-MAF-S	"
μειζότερον	A-MAN-S	"
μείζω	A-MAF-S	"
	A-MAN-P	"
μείζων	A-MNF-S	"
	A-MNM-S	"
μεῖναι	VNAA	μένω
μείναντες	VPAANM-P	"
μείνατε	VMAA--2P	"
μείνῃ	VSAA--3S	"
μείνητε	VSAA--2P	"
μεῖνον	VMAA--2S	"
μείνοντες	VPAANM-P	"
μείνωσι(ν)	VSAA--3P	"
μέλαιναν	A--AF-S	μέλας
μέλανι	AP-DN-S	"
μέλανος	AP-GN-S	"

μέλας, μέλαινα, μέλαν, gen. ανος, αίνης, ανος *black, dark* (MT 5.36); neuter as a substantive τὸ μέλαν *ink* (2C 3.3)

μέλας	A--NM-S	μέλας

Μελεά, ὁ indeclinable (also possibly **Μελεᾶς, ᾶ, ὁ**) *Melea,* masculine proper noun (LU 3.31)

Μελεᾶ	N-GM-S	Μελεά
Μελεγαδά		Μαγδαλά

μέλει the third-person singular of μέλω; impf. ἔμελε; (*to care for, take an interest in*); (1) used impersonally with the dative of person *it is a care* or *concern* to someone (MT 22.16); (2) absolutely μή σοι μελέτω *never mind, don't worry about it* (1C 7.21)

μέλει	VIPA--3S	μέλει

Μελελεήλ		Μαλελεήλ
μέλεσι(ν)	N-DN-P	μέλος
μελέτα	VMPA--2S	μελετάω
μελετᾶτε	VMPA--2P	"

μελετάω 1aor. ἐμελέτησα; *give careful thought to, meditate on, think about* (1T 4.15); in a negative sense *plot, conspire, premeditate* (AC 4.25)

μελέτω	VMPA--3S	μέλει
μέλη	N-AN-P	μέλος
	N-NN-P	"
Μελητήνη	N-NF-S	Μελίτη

μέλι, ιτος, τό *honey* from bees

μέλι	N-AN-S	μέλι
	N-NN-S	

μελίσσειον, ου, τό (also **μελίσσιον**) *beehive* (LU 24.42)

μελίσσιος, ιον *of bees, made by bees*; μελίσσιον κηρίον *honeycomb* (LU 24.42)

μελισσίου	A--GN-S	μελίσσιος
	N-GN-S	μελίσσειον

Μελίτη, ης, ἡ (also **Μελητήνη, Μελιτήνη, Μελιτίνη, Μιλήτη, Μυτιλήνη**) *Malta,* an island south of Sicily in the Mediterranean Sea (AC 28.1)

Μελίτη	N-NF-S	Μελίτη
Μελιτήνη	N-NF-S	"
Μελιτίνη	N-NF-S	"
μέλλει	VIPA--3S	μέλλω
μέλλειν	VNPA	"
μέλλεις	VIPA--2S	"
μέλλετε	VIPA--2P	"
μέλλη	VSPA--3S	"
μελλήσετε	VIFA--2P	"
μελλήσω	VIFA--1S	"
μέλλομεν	VIPA--1P	"
μέλλον	VPPAAN-S	"
μέλλοντα	VPPAAM-S	"
	VPPAAN-P	"
	VPPANN-P	"
μέλλοντας	VPPAAM-P	"
μέλλοντες	VPPANM-P	"
μέλλοντι	VPPADM-S	"
	VPPADN-S	"
μέλλοντος	VPPAGM-S	"
	VPPAGN-S	"
μελλόντων	VPPAGM-P	"
	VPPAGN-P	"
μέλλουσαν	VPPAAF-S	"
μελλούσης	VPPAGF-S	"
μέλλουσι(ν)	VIPA--3P	"

μέλλω impf. ἔμελλον and ἤμελλον; fut. μελλήσω; (1) predominately with an infinitive following; (a) with the future infinitive μέλλειν ἔσεσθαι *will certainly take place, will come to pass* (AC 11.28); (b) with the aorist infinitive *be on the point of, be about to* (RV 3.2); *be destined to, be inevitable* (GA 3.23); (c) with the present infinitive *be about to, be going to, begin to* (MK 13.4); as a future or as a periphrasis for settled futurity *will, be going to* (HE 10.27); denoting intended action *have in mind to, intend to, want to* (MT 2.13); denoting an action resulting from a divine decree *be destined to, must, certainly will* (AC 26.22); (2) the present participle used absolutely to denote what is coming *future, to come,* coming (HE 2.5); neuter participle as a substantive, for an unlimited extent of time to come *the future* (1T 6.19); (3) as extending time because of indecision τί μέλλεις; *Why do you delay? What are you waiting for?* (AC 22.16)

μέλλω	VIPA--1S	μέλλω
μέλλων	VPPANM-S	"

μέλος, ους, τό literally, as any part of the human body *member, limb, part* (RO 12.4a); figuratively, of one who belongs to the Christian community as the body of Christ *member* (1C 6.15)

μέλος	N-NN-S	μέλος
μέλους	N-GN-S	"
Μελχεί		Μελχί

Μελχί, ὁ (also **Μελχεί**) indeclinable; *Melchi,* masculine proper noun

Μελχισέδεκ, ὁ (also **Μελχισεδέκ**) indeclinable; *Melchizedek,* masculine proper noun; meaning in Hebrew *king of righteousness*

Μελχισεδέκ		Μελχισεδέκ
μελῶν	N-GN-P	μέλος
μεμαθηκώς	VPRANM-S	μανθάνω
μεμαρτύρηκα	VIRA--1S	μαρτυρέω
μεμαρτύρηκας	VIRA--2S	"
μεμαρτύρηκε(ν)	VIRA--3S	"
μεμαρτύρηται	VIRP--3S	"

μεμβράνα, ης, ἡ as animal skins prepared for making scrolls and books *parchment*; by metonymy *books* made of parchment (2T 4.13)

μεμβράνας	N-AF-P	μεμβράνα
μεμενήκεισαν	VILA--3P	μένω
μεμέρικε(ν)	VIRA--3S	μερίζω
μεμέρισται	VIRP--3S	"
μεμεστωμένοι	VPRPNM-P	μεστόω
μεμιαμμένοις	VPRPDM-P	μιαίνω
μεμίανται	VIRP--3S	"
μεμιασμένοις	VPRPDM-P	"
μεμιγμένα	VPRPNN-P	μίγνυμι
μεμιγμένην	VPRPAF-S	"
μεμιγμένον	VPRPAM-S	"
μεμισήκασι(ν)	VIRA--3P	μισέω
μεμίσηκε(ν)	VIRA--3S	"
μεμισημένον	VPRPGN-S	"
μεμνημένος	VPRPNM-S	μιμνήσκω
μέμνησθε	VIRP--2P	"
μεμνησμένην	VPRPAF-S	μνάομαι
μεμνηστευμένη	VPRPDF-S	μνηστεύω
μεμνηστευμένην	VPRPAF-S	"
μεμονωμένη	VPRPNF-S	μονόω
μεμύημαι	VIRP--1S	μυέω
μέμφεται	VIPD--3S	μέμφομαι
	VIPO--3S	"

μέμφομαι *find fault with, blame, accuse*

μεμφόμενος	VPPDNM-S	μέμφομαι
	VPPONM-S	"
μεμψίμοιροι	A--NM-P	μεμψίμοιρος

μεμψίμοιρος, ον of one dissatisfied with his lot in life *faultfinding, complaining, constantly blaming*; substantivally *faultfinder, complainer* (JU 16)

μέμψιν	N-AF-S	μέμψις

μέμψις, εως, ἡ *reason for complaint* (CO 3.13)

μέν intensive particle (a weakened form of μήν [I]) *surely, indeed*; (1) used predominately with δέ (*but*) (MT 3.11) or ἀλλά (*but*) (RO 14.20) or πλήν (*but*) (LU 22.22), as a correlative to mark the affirmative in a concession or contrast *on the one hand . . . on the other hand, to be sure . . . but*; μ. may be left untranslated, but δέ in this combination always has adversative force (1C 1.12); (2) frequently μ. is found alone, with the contrast to be supplied from the context *indeed . . . (but), truly . . . (but)* (RO 7.12); (3) used to start a list in order to distinguish one thought from another in a series: πρῶτον μ. . . . ἔπειτα δέ *in the first place . . . then* (HE 7.2); ὃ μ. . . . ὃ δέ *the one . . . the other* (MT 13.8); τινὲς μ. . . . τινὲς δέ *some indeed . . . but others* (PH 1.15); (4) used to denote the concession, with δέ supplied from the context to mark the contraexpectation; λόγον μ. ἔχοντα σοφίας *even though they have a reputation for wisdom* (CO 2.23; see also 2C 12.12 and 1C 6.7); (5) found in combination with other particles: μ. οὖν denoting continuation *so, then* (AC 1.6); εἰ μ. οὖν *now if* (HE 7.11)

μέν	CC	μέν
	CS	"
	QS	"
Μεναν		Μεννά
μένε	VMPA--2S	μένω
μένει	VIPA--3S	"
μενεῖ	VIFA--3S	"
μένειν	VNPA	"
μένεις	VIPA--2S	"
μενεῖτε	VIFA--2P	"
μένετε	VIPA--2P	"
	VMPA--2P	"
μενέτω	VMPA--3S	"
μένῃ	VSPA--3S	"
μένητε	VSPA--2P	"

Μεννά, ὁ (also **Μαϊνάν, Μεναν, Μεννάν**) indeclinable; *Menna*, masculine proper noun (LU 3.31)

Μεννάν		Μεννά
μένομεν	VIPA--1P	μένω
μένον	VPPAAN-S	"
	VPPANN-S	"
μένοντα	VPPAAM-S	"
μένοντος	VPPAGM-S	"

μενοῦν particle; used especially in answers to emphasize or correct something *on the contrary, rather* (LU 11.28)

μενοῦν	QS	μενοῦν

μενοῦνγε particle; a reinforced form of μενοῦν (*on the contrary, rather*), used especially in answers to emphasize or correct *on the contrary, rather* (RO 9.20); *(yes) indeed* (RO 10.18); *even more* (PH 3.8)

μενοῦνγε	QS	μενοῦνγε
μένουσαν	VPPAAF-S	μένω
μένουσι(ν)	VIPA--3P	"

μέντοι particle; (1) used as an emphatic *indeed, truly* (JU 8); (2) used as a concessive *though, to be sure, indeed* (JN 4.27); (3) used as an adversative *nevertheless, yet, however* (JN 20.5); with δέ as a correlative to mark the adversative *on the one hand . . . but yet on the other hand* (JA 2.8–9)

μέντοι	CH	μέντοι

μένω impf. ἔμενον; fut. μενῶ; 1aor. ἔμεινα; pluperfect μεμενήκειν; *remain, abide*; (1) intransitively; (a) of someone or something remaining where it is *remain in a place, stay, tarry* (MT 10.11), opposite ἐξέρχομαι (*go away, depart*); (b) in a more permanent sense *dwell, live, lodge* (JN 1.38); (c) figuratively, as remaining unchanged in a sphere or realm *continue, abide, remain* (2T 2.13); (d) figuratively, as remaining in a fixed state or position *keep on, remain, abide* (1C 7.11; HE 7.3); (e) of persons continuing on through time *last, remain, continue to live* (JN 12.34), opposite ἀποθνῄσκω (*die, perish*); (f) of things continuing on through time *last, be permanent, endure* (HE 13.14); (2) transitively; (a) as expecting someone or something *wait for, await* (AC 20.5); (b) of things, such as danger, that threaten *await, face* (AC 20.23)

μένω	VIPA--1S	μένω
μενῶ	VIFA--1S	"
μένων	VPPANM-S	"
μέρει	N-DN-S	μέρος
μέρη	N-AN-P	"
μερίδα	N-AF-S	μερίς
μερίδος	N-GF-S	"

μερίζω 1aor. ἐμέρισα; pf. μεμέρικα; pf. pass. μεμέρισμαι; 1aor. pass. ἐμερίσθην; *divide, separate*; (1) as separating into component parts *divide* (MT 12.25); (2) as apportioning out something to someone *distribute, divide out, assign* (RO 12.3), opposite συνάγω (*gather*); middle *share* with someone (LU 12.13)

μέριμνα, ης, ἡ *care, concern* (2C 11.28); often in a negative sense *anxiety, worry, distraction* (LU 8.14)

μέριμνα	N-NF-S	μέριμνα
μεριμνᾷ	VIPA--3S	μεριμνάω
μέριμναι	N-NF-P	μέριμνα
μερίμναις	N-DF-P	"
μέριμναν	N-AF-S	"
μεριμνᾷς	VIPA--2S	μεριμνάω
μεριμνᾶτε	VIPA--2P	"
	VMPA--2P	"

μεριμνάω fut. μεριμνήσω; 1aor. ἐμερίμνησα; (1) in a good sense *care for, be concerned about* (1C 7.32); (2) in a bad sense *be anxious, be overly concerned about, be worried about* (PH 4.6)

μεριμνήσει	VIFA--3S	μεριμνάω
μεριμνήσητε	VSAA--2P	"
μεριμνῶν	N-GF-P	μέριμνα
	VPPANM-S	μεριμνάω
μεριμνῶσι(ν)	VSPA--3P	"

μερίς, ίδος, ἡ (1) *part* of a whole that has been chosen or divided up *share, portion* (LU 10.42); as a division of a country *district, region* (AC 16.12); (2) as an assigned portion *share, destiny, part* (CO 1.12)

μερίς	N-NF-S	μερίς
μερίσασθαι	VNAM	μερίζω
μερισθεῖσα	VPAPNF-S	"
μερισθῇ	VSAP--3S	"
μερισμοῖς	N-DM-P	μερισμός

μερισμός, οῦ, ὁ (1) as a process *dividing up, division, separation* (HE 4.12); (2) as a result *distribution, apportionment, distributed gifts* (HE 2.4)

μερισμοῦ	N-GM-S	μερισμός

μεριστήν N-AM-S μεριστής
μεριστής, οῦ, ὁ one who decides a dispute over inheritance *divider, arbitrator* (LU 12.14)

μέρος, ους, τό with a basic meaning *part, share*, translated according to the context; (1) as distinct from the whole *part, piece* (LU 24.42); (a) as a part of a country *district, region* (MT 2.22); (b) as a component of something *side* (of a boat or ship) (JN 21.6); (c) as a political or religious group *party* (AC 23.9); (d) as a line of business *trade* (AC 19.27); (e) adverbially, with prepositions: ἀνὰ μ. *in succession, one after the other* (1C 14.27); ἀπὸ μέρους *in part, partly* (RO 11.25); with respect to time *for a while* (RO 15.24); ἐκ μέρους *individually, in part* (1C 12.27); ἐν μέρει *in the matter of, with regard to* (CO 2.16); κατὰ μ. *in detail, part by part, point by point* (HE 9.5); (2) as a portion of the possible whole *share, place* (RV 20.6)

μέρος N-AN-S μέρος
  N-NN-S "
μέρους N-GN-S "
μέρων N-GN-P "
μεσαζούσης VPPAGF-S μεσάζω
μεσάζω of a time span *be in* or *at the middle (of)* (JN 7.14)

μεσημβρία, ας, ἡ (1) of time *midday, noon* (AC 22.6); (2) by metonymy, of place *south*; κατὰ μεσημβρίαν *toward the south*, from the position of the sun at midday (AC 8.26)

μεσημβρίαν N-AF-S μεσημβρία
μεσημβρίας N-GF-S "
μέσης A--GF-S μέσος
μεσιτεύω 1aor. ἐμεσίτευσα; *bring about a sure agreement, mediate, act as surety* of a contracted obligation, *guarantee* (HE 6.17)

μεσίτῃ N-DM-S μεσίτης
μεσίτης, ου, ὁ basically, a neutral and trusted person in the middle (μέσος); (1) one who works to remove disagreement *mediator, go-between, reconciler* (1T 2.5); (2) one who provides a guarantee of fulfillment of contracted obligation *mediator* (HE 9.15)

μεσίτης N-NM-S μεσίτης
μεσίτου N-GM-S "
μέσον AB μέσος
  A--AN-S "
  PG "
μεσονύκτιον, ου, τό *midnight, middle of the night*
μεσονύκτιον N-AN-S μεσονύκτιον
μεσονυκτίου N-GN-S "
Μεσοποταμία, ας, ἡ *Mesopotamia*, the region between the Tigris and Euphrates rivers
Μεσοποταμία N-DF-S Μεσοποταμία
Μεσοποταμίαν N-AF-S "
μέσος, η, ον with a basic meaning *middle, in the middle*, translated according to the context; (1) as an adjective *in the midst* or *middle of, between, among* (LU 22.55b); (2) substantivally τὸ μέσον *the middle, the midst*; with prepositions: ἀνὰ μέσον *among, at the center* (RV 7.17); of persons *between, among* (1C 6.5); διὰ μέσου *through the midst* (LU 4.30); εἰς τὸ μέσον *in* or *into the midst, in the middle* or *center, among* (LU 4.35); ἐν (τῷ) μέσῳ *in the middle, among, before* (AC 4.7); ἐκ (τοῦ) μέσου *from*

among, out of the way* (2TH 2.7); κατὰ μέσον τῆς νυκτός *about midnight* (AC 27.27); (3) neuter as an adverb *in the center* or as an improper preposition with the genitive *in the midst of* (PH 2.15)

μέσος A--NM-S μέσος
μεσότοιχον, ου, τό *partition, dividing wall*; figuratively *obstacle, barrier* that separates people from each other (EP 2.14)

μεσότοιχον N-AN-S μεσότοιχον
μέσου A--GN-S μέσος
μεσουράνημα, ατος, τό the highest point of the sun's circuit in the sky *zenith, midair, directly overhead*
μεσουρανήματι N-DN-S μεσουράνημα
μεσούσης VPPAGF-S μεσόω
μεσόω of a time period *be in the middle, be half over* (JN 7.14)

Μεσσίαν N-AM-S Μεσσίας
Μεσσίας, ου, ὁ *Messiah*; transliterated from the Hebrew; *Anointed One*; translated into Greek as Χριστός
Μεσσίας N-NM-S Μεσσίας
μεστή A--NF-S μεστός
μεστοί A--NM-P "
μεστόν A--AM-S "
  A--AN-S "
  A--NN-S "
μεστός, ή, όν of quantity beyond what could or should be expected *very full*; literally, with the genitive *full of, filled with* something (JN 21.11); figuratively, of a person, with the genitive *constantly preoccupied with, full of* something (MT 23.28; 2P 2.14)

μεστούς A--AM-P μεστός
μεστόω pf. pass. μεμέστωμαι; with the genitive *fill with*; passive *be full of, be glutted, be filled with* something (AC 2.13)

μέσῳ A--DN-S μέσος
μετ᾽ PA μετά
  PG "
μετά preposition with a basic meaning *in the midst of*; **I.** with the genitive *with*; (1) of a place *with, among* (MK 1.13); (2) of accompaniment *together with, in company with, accompanied by* (MT 16.27); (3) of close association εἶναι μ. τινος *be with someone, be on the side of* (MT 12.30); (4) of aid or help εἶναι μ. τινος *be with, stand by, help* (MT 28.20); (5) of hostility or conflict *with, against* (1C 6.6); (6) as closely connecting two concepts where emphasis is on the first *(along) with* (EP 6.23); (7) as denoting attendant circumstances *with* (LU 14.9); (8) as indicating means *by means of, through* (AC 2.28); **II.** with the accusative *after, behind*; (1) of place *behind, beyond* (HE 9.3); (2) of time *after* (MT 17.1; 24.29; AC 20.29); followed by an articular infinitive *after* (MT 26.32)

μετά PA μετά
  PG "
μετάβα VMAA--2S μεταβαίνω
μεταβαίνετε VMPA--2P "
μεταβαίνω fut. mid. μεταβήσομαι; 2aor. μετέβην; pf. μεταβέβηκα; (1) literally; (a) of persons *go from* one place to another, *pass from, depart* (JN 13.1); (b) of things *change, remove from* (MT 17.20); (2) figuratively, of going from one state to another *change* (JN 5.24)

μεταβαλλόμενοι	VPPMNM-P	μεταβάλλω

μεταβάλλω 2aor. mid. μετεβαλόμην; only middle in the NT *change one's mind, think differently than before* (AC 28.6)

μεταβαλόμενοι	VPAMNM-P	μεταβάλλω
μεταβάς	VPAANM-S	μεταβαίνω
μεταβεβήκαμεν	VIRA--1P	"
μεταβέβηκε(ν)	VIRA--3S	"
μεταβῇ	VSAA--3S	"
μετάβηθι	VMAA--2S	"
μεταβῆναι	VNAA	"
μεταβήσεται	VIFD--3S	"
μετάγεται	VIPP--3S	μετάγω
μετάγομεν	VIPA--1P	"

μετάγω 1aor. pass. μετήχθην; *guide in another direction*; of horses *turn (about), direct* (JA 3.3); passive, of ships *steer, pilot* (JA 3.4); of a body transferred to another burial place *be brought (back)* (AC 7.16)

μεταδιδόναι	VNPA	μεταδίδωμι
μεταδιδούς	VPPANM-S	"

μεταδίδωμι 2aor. subjunctive μεταδῶ, inf. μεταδοῦναι; as transferring something to another *impart, share, give*

μεταδότω	VMAA--3S	μεταδίδωμι
μεταδοῦναι	VNAA	"
μεταδῶ	VSAA--1S	"
μεταθέσεως	N-GF-S	μετάθεσις
μετάθεσιν	N-AF-S	"

μετάθεσις, θέσεως, ἡ literally, the act of transferring from one place to another *removal, taking up* or *away* (HE 11.5); figuratively *changeover* from one state or institution to another, *transformation, change* (HE 7.12)

μετάθεσις	N-NF-S	μετάθεσις

μεταίρω 1aor. μετῆρα; intransitively in the NT *go away, depart*

μετακάλεσαι	VMAM--2S	μετακαλέω
μετακαλέσομαι	VIFM--1S	"

μετακαλέω fut. mid. μετακαλέσομαι; 1aor. mid. μετεκαλεσάμην; only middle in the NT *have brought to oneself, summon, call to oneself*

μετακινέω *shift, remove*; figuratively and passive, as being led to give up one's confidence in something *be moved away from, be shifted away, be pushed from* (CO 1.23)

μετακινούμενοι	VPPPNM-P	μετακινέω
μετάλαβαν	VIAA--3P	see μετέλαβον
μεταλαβεῖν	VNAA	μεταλαμβάνω
μεταλαβών	VPAANM-S	"
μεταλαμβάνει	VIPA--3S	"
μεταλαμβάνειν	VNPA	"

μεταλαμβάνω impf. μετελάμβανον; 2aor. μετέλαβον; (1) followed by the genitive *receive (a portion of), partake of, take one's share of* (2T 2.6); of nourishment *take, share in* (AC 2.46); (2) followed by the accusative *take later*; idiomatically καιρὸν μεταλαμβάνειν literally *take opportunity later*, i.e. *find time* (AC 24.25)

μετάλημψιν	N-AF-S	μετάλημψις

μετάλημψις, εως, ἡ (also **μετάληψις**) as an action *receiving, sharing, partaking* (1T 4.3)

μετάληψιν	N-AF-S	μετάλημψις

μεταλλάσσω 1aor. μετήλλαξα; *exchange, alter, change*

μεταμεληθείς	VPAONM-S	μεταμέλομαι

μεταμεληθήσεται	VIFO--3S	"

μεταμέλομαι impf. μετεμελόμην; 1aor. μετεμελήθην; only passive in the NT; (1) *feel remorse, become concerned about afterward, regret* (MT 27.3); (2) *change one's mind, think differently afterward* (HE 7.21)

μεταμέλομαι	VIPD--1S	μεταμέλομαι
	VIPO--1S	"
μεταμορφούμεθα	VIPP--1P	μεταμορφόω
μεταμορφούμενοι	VPPPNM-P	"
μεταμορφοῦσθαι	VNPP	"
μεταμορφοῦσθε	VMPP--2P	"

μεταμορφόω 1aor. pass. μετεμορφώθην; only passive in the NT; (1) of an outwardly perceptible change of form *be transfigured, be changed in appearance* (MT 17.2); (2) of an inward change of nature *be changed, be transformed* (RO 12.2)

μεταμορφωθείς	VPAPNM-S	μεταμορφόω
μετανοεῖν	VNPA	μετανοέω
μετανοεῖτε	VMPA--2P	"

μετανοέω fut. μετανοήσω; 1aor. μετενόησα; strictly *perceive afterward*, with the implication of being too late to avoid consequences; (1) predominately of a religious and ethical change in the way one thinks about acts *repent, change one's mind, be converted* (MT 3.2); (2) as feeling remorse *regret, feel sorry* (LU 17.3, 4)

μετανοῆσαι	VNAA	μετανοέω
μετανοησάντων	VPAAGM-P	"
μετανοήσατε	VMAA--2P	"
μετανοήση	VSAA--3S	"
μετανοήσης	VSAA--2S	"
μετανοήσητε	VSAA--2P	"
μετανόησον	VMAA--2S	"
μετανοήσουσι(ν)	VIFA--3P	"
μετανοήσωσι(ν)	VSAA--3P	"
μετανοῆτε	VSPA--2P	"

μετάνοια, ας, ἡ strictly *later knowledge, subsequent correction*; (1) religiously and morally, as a change of mind leading to change of behavior *repentance, conversion, turning about* (MT 3.8; 2C 7.10); (2) as a change of opinion in respect to one's acts *regret, remorse* (a popular Greek usage not found in the NT)

μετάνοιαν	N-AF-S	μετάνοια
μετανοίας	N-GF-S	"
μετανοοῦντι	VPPADM-S	μετανοέω
μετανοῶ	VIPA--1S	"
μετανοῶσι(ν)	VSPA--3P	"

μεταξύ adverb; *between*; (1) of time, ἐν τῷ μ. *meanwhile, in the meantime* (JN 4.31); εἰς τὸ μ. σάββατον *on the next Sabbath* (AC 13.42); (2) of space, as an improper preposition with the genitive *between, in the middle of* (MT 23.35); (3) of mutual relation *between, among* (MT 18.15)

μεταξύ	AB	μεταξύ
	PG	
μεταπεμπόμενος	VPPMNM-S	μεταπέμπω

μεταπέμπω mid. μεταπέμπομαι; 1aor. mid. μετεπεμψάμην; 1aor. pass. μετεπέμφθην; (1) middle *send for, summon (to oneself)* (AC 10.5); (2) passive *be sent for* (AC 10.29)

μεταπεμφθείς	VPAPNM-S	μεταπέμπω
μετάπεμψαι	VMAM--2S	"
μεταπεμψάμενος	VPAMNM-S	"

μεταπέμψασθαι   VNAM   "

μεταπέμψηται   VSAM--3S   "

μετασταθῶ   VSAP--1S   μεθίστημι

μεταστειλάμενος   VPADNM-S   μεταστέλλομαι

μεταστέλλομαι   1aor. μετεστειλάμην; only middle in the NT *send for, summon (to oneself)* (AC 20.1)

μεταστήσας   VPAANM-S   μεθίστημι

μεταστραφήσεται   VIFP--3S   μεταστρέφω

μεταστραφήτω   VMAP--3S   "

μεταστρέφω   1aor. μετέστρεψα; 2aor. pass. μετεστράφην; 2fut. pass. μεταστραφήσομαι; (1) as turning something to its opposite state *change, alter, cause to be different* (GA 1.7); (2) passive, as experiencing a change of state *be changed, be turned* into something else (AC 2.20)

μεταστρέψαι   VNAA   μεταστρέφω

μετασχηματίζεται   VIPM--3S   μετασχηματίζω

μετασχηματιζόμενοι   VPPMNM-P   "

μετασχηματίζονται   VIPM--3P   "

μετασχηματίζω   fut. μετασχηματίσω; 1aor. μετεσχημάτισα; (1) physically, as changing the outward form of something *transform, transfigure, change* (PH 3.21); (2) middle, as altering the outward scheme of things so as to deceive *transform oneself, disguise oneself* (2C 11.14); (3) as illustrating something with the help of a figure of speech *adapt, apply, transfer* (1C 4.6)

μετασχηματίσει   VIFA--3S   μετασχηματίζω

μετατιθεμένης   VPPPGF-S   μετατίθημι

μετατιθέντες   VPPANM-P   "

μετατίθεσθε   VIPM--2P   "
   VIPP--2P   "

μετατίθημι   1aor. μετέθηκα; 1aor. pass. μετετέθην; (1) literally, as causing a change from one place to another *transfer, bring to, transplant* (HE 11.5b); passive *be taken, be transferred* (HE 11.5a); of a body transferred to another burial place *be brought back* (AC 7.16); (2) figuratively; (a) *change, alter* (HE 7.12); in a bad sense *pervert* (JU 4); (b) middle, as changing one's loyalty as a follower *turn from, desert, become apostate* (GA 1.6)

μετατραπήτω   VMAP--3S   μετατρέπω

μετατρέπω   2aor. pass. μετετράπην; as causing a change from one state to another *turn around*; passive *be turned* (JA 4.9)

μεταφυτεύθητι   VMAP--2S   μεταφυτεύω

μεταφυτεύω   1aor. pass. imperative μεταφυτεύθητι; *transplant*; passive *be transplanted* (LU 17.6)

μετέβαινε(ν)   VIIA--3S   μεταβαίνω

μετέβη   VIAA--3S   "

μετέθηκε(ν)   VIAA--3S   μετατίθημι

μετεκαλέσατο   VIAM--3S   μετακαλέω

μετέλαβον   VIAA--3P   μεταλαμβάνω

μετελάμβανον   VIIA--3P   "

μετεμελήθητε   VIAO--2P   μεταμέλομαι

μετεμελόμην   VIID--1S   "
   VIIO--1S   "

μετεμορφώθη   VIAP--3S   μεταμορφόω

μετενόησαν   VIAA--3P   μετανοέω

μετενόησε(ν)   VIAA--3S   "

μετέπειτα   adverb; *afterward, at a later time* (HE 12.17)

μετέπειτα   AB   μετέπειτα

μετεπέμψασθε   VIAM--2P   μεταπέμπω

μετεπέμψατο   VIAM--3S   "

μετέστησε(ν)   VIAA--3S   μεθίστημι

μετέσχε(ν)   VIAA--3S   μετέχω

μετέσχηκε(ν)   VIRA--3S   "

μετεσχημάτισα   VIAA--1S   μετασχηματίζω

μετετέθη   VIAP--3S   μετατίθημι

μετετέθησαν   VIAP--3P   "

μετέχειν   VNPA   μετέχω

μετέχομεν   VIPA--1P   "

μετέχουσι(ν)   VIPA--3P   "

μετέχω   2aor. μετέσχον; followed by the genitive *(have a) share in, participate in, partake of,* with the sharing always resulting from choosing to participate

μετέχω   VIPA--1S   μετέχω

μετέχων   VPPANM-S   "

μετεωρίζεσθε   VMPD--2P   μετεωρίζομαι
   VMPO--2P   "

μετεωρίζομαι   *lift up*; figuratively and passive in the NT *be unsettled, be in suspense, be anxious* about something (LU 12.29)

μετήλλαξαν   VIAA--3P   μεταλλάσσω

μετῆρε(ν)   VIAA--3S   μεταίρω

μετήχθησαν   VIAP--3P   μετάγω

μετοικεσία, ας, ἡ   as a (forced) removal to another place of habitation *deportation, exile, captivity*

μετοικεσίαν   N-AF-S   μετοικεσία

μετοικεσίας   N-GF-S   "

μετοικίζω   Attic fut. μετοικιῶ; 1aor. μετῴκισα; transitively *remove* someone *to another place, resettle* (AC 7.4); of forcible removal *deport, send into exile, banish* (AC 7.43)

μετοικιῶ   VIFA--1S   μετοικίζω

μετοχή, ῆς, ἡ   *sharing, participation*; as a participation in common *fellowship, partnership* (2C 6.14)

μετοχή   N-NF-S   μετοχή

μέτοχοι   AP-NM-P   μέτοχος
   AP-VM-P   "

μετόχοις   AP-DM-P   "

μέτοχος, ον   followed by the genitive *sharing* or *participating in* (HE 3.1); substantivally *partner, partaker, companion* (LU 5.7)

μετόχους   AP-AM-P   μέτοχος

μετρεῖτε   VIPA--2P   μετρέω

μετρέω   1aor. ἐμέτρησα; 1fut. pass. μετρηθήσομαι; *measure*; (1) literally; (a) *take the dimensions of, measure* (RV 11.1); (b) figuratively *evaluate, measure* (2C 10.12); (2) *apportion out, measure out, give out* (MT 7.2)

μετρηθήσεται   VIFP--3S   μετρέω

μετρήση   VSAA--3S   "

μετρήσης   VSAA--2S   "

μέτρησον   VMAA--2S   "

μετρήσουσι(ν)   VIFA--3P   "

μετρητάς   N-AM-P   μετρητής

μετρητής, οῦ, ὁ   strictly, a utensil for measuring liquids *measure*; in the NT a *measure* holding 39.4 liters or about 10.4 gallons (JN 2.6)

μετριοπαθεῖν   VNPA   μετριοπαθέω

μετριοπαθέω   *exercise moderation* toward someone in emotions and passions, *deal gently* (HE 5.2)

μετρίως   adverb; *moderately, in due measure*; οὐ μ. *not a little, greatly, much* (AC 20.12)

μετρίως   AB   μετρίως

μέτρον, ου, τό *measure*; (1) as an instrument for measuring *measure, standard* (MT 7.2); (2) as the result of measuring *measure*; figuratively *limit, extent* (RO 12.3); οὐκ ἐκ μέτρου *without measure, unlimited* (JN 3.34)

μέτρον	N-AN-S	μέτρον
μέτρου	N-GN-S	"
μετροῦντες	VPPANM-P	μετρέω
μέτρῳ	N-DN-S	μέτρον
Ματταθά		Ματταθά
μετῴκισε(ν)	VIAA--3S	μετοικίζω
μέτωπα	N-AN-P	μέτωπον

μέτωπον, ου, τό as the part of the face above the eyes *forehead*

μέτωπον	N-AN-S	μέτωπον
μετώπου	N-GN-S	"
μετώπων	N-GN-P	"

μέχρι, before vowels generally μέχρις *until*; (1) as an improper preposition with the genitive; (a) of space *as far as, to* (RO 15.19); (b) of time *until* (AC 20.7); (c) of degree or measure *to the point of, to* (2T 2.9); (2) as a conjunction with the subjunctive *until* (EP 4.13)

μέχρι	CS	μέχρι
	PG	"
μέχρις	PG	"

μή, negative particle *not*, used for assumed, hesitant, or indefinite denial; where οὐ (*not*) denies the fact, μή denies the idea; generally used with all moods except the factual indicative, including its use with the infinitive and participle; (1) used to negate an assumption (JN 3.18 ὅτι μὴ πεπίστευκεν *because he has not believed*); (2) used to introduce questions expecting a negative answer (1C 12.29, 30); (3) used with the aorist subjunctive and present imperative to express prohibitions; (a) with the aorist subjunctive it has an ingressive denotation signifying *don't begin to do* something (HE 3.8); (b) with the present imperative it signals to bring to an end an already existing condition; *stop doing* something, *don't do it any longer* (MT 14.27); if the action has not yet begun, it signifies *don't get into the habit of doing* something (CO 3.9); (4) with clauses used to express (a) a negative condition ἐὰν μή and εἰ μή *except, unless* (MT 5.20; 11.27); (b) a negative purpose ἵνα μή and μή πως (μήπως) *in order that not, so that not* (MT 24.20; 1C 8.9); (c) a negative result ὥστε μή with an infinitive *so that not*; (5) used in combination with οὐ to express a strong negative *never, in no way, under no circumstances, certainly not* (MT 5.18); (6) used as a conjunction after verbs of fearing *lest, for fear that* (AC 23.10) and warning *lest, that not* (HE 12.15); (7) μήγε in the formula εἰ δὲ μή γε *otherwise, but if not* (MT 6.1; 9.17)

μή	CC	μή
	CS	"
	QN	"
	QT	"

μήγε a strengthened form of μή, from μή (*not*) and γέ (*indeed, even*); in the formula εἰ δὲ μ. *otherwise* (MT 6.1)

μήγε	QN	μήγε
μηδ᾽	AB	μηδέ
	CC	"

μηδαμῶς an adverb denoting a negative reaction *by no means! in no way! never!*

μηδαμῶς	AB	μηδαμῶς

μηδέ negative disjunctive particle; from μή (*not*) and δέ (*and, but*); distinguished from μήτε (*and not*) in that μηδέ shows two things are progressively exclusive (not this . . . and not that), while μήτε shows parallel negations (neither this . . . nor that); (1) used to continue a preceding negative *and not, but not, nor* (MT 10.9); (2) used in the consequence clause of a conditional sentence *(then) neither, not (either)* (2TH 3.10); (3) as a negative ascensive *not even* (MK 2.2)

μηδέ	AB	μηδέ
	CC	"

μηδείς, μηδεμία, μηδέν (also μηθέν) negative of the numeral one, used where the negative particle μή (q.v.) would be appropriate in the construction; (1) as an adjective with a noun *not one, no* (1C 1.7); (2) as a substantive; (a) of a person *nobody, none, not one* (LU 5.14); with a double negative *nobody at all* (MK 11.14); (b) of a thing *not one thing, nothing* (MK 6.8); (c) adverbially ἐν μηδενί *in no way, in no respect* (2C 7.9)

μηδείς	APCNM-S	μηδείς
μηδεμίαν	A-CAF-S	"
μηδέν	APCAN-S	"
	APCNN-S	"
	A-CAN-S	"
μηδένα	APCAM-S	"
	A-CAM-S	"
μηδενί	APCDM-S	"
	APCDN-S	"
	A-CDN-S	"
μηδενός	APCGN-S	"
	A-CGN-S	"

μηδέποτε adverb; *never, not at any time* (2T 3.7)

μηδέποτε	AB	μηδέποτε

μηδέπω adverb; *not yet, still not* (HE 11.7)

μηδέπω	AB	μηδέπω
Μῆδοι	N-NM-P	Μῆδος

Μῆδος, ου, ὁ *Mede, inhabitant of Media* (AC 2.9)

μηθέν	APCAN-S	μηδείς
μηθενός	APCGN-S	"

μηκέτι adverb of time *no longer, no more*, in the same situations where μή (q.v.) is appropriate (JN 5.14); with a double negative *not ever again, no more after this*

μηκέτι	AB	μηκέτι

μῆκος, ους, τό as a measurement of space *length*

μῆκος	N-NN-S	μῆκος
μηκύνηται	VSPM--3S	μηκύνω

μηκύνω *make long, lengthen*; only passive in the NT, of sprouting grain *grow (long), come up* (MK 4.27)

μηλωταῖς	N-DF-P	μηλωτή

μηλωτή, ῆς, ἡ the raw, undressed skin of a sheep; used as clothing *sheepskin* (HE 11.37)

μήν (I) particle; Hebraistically, used with εἰ to make an oath formula more emphatic *surely, indeed* (HE 6.14)

μήν, μηνός, ὁ (II) using the moon's cycle as a measure of time *month* (LU 1.24); in reference to religious festivals held at the time of the new moon *new moon* (GA 4.10)

μήν	N-NM-S	μήν (II)
	QS	μήν (I)
μῆνα	N-AM-S	μήν (II)
μῆνας	N-AM-P	"
μηνί	N-DM-S	"
μηνυθείσης	VPAPGF-S	μηνύω
μηνύσαντα	VPAAAM-S	"
μηνύση	VSAA--3S	"

μηνύω 1aor. ἐμήνυσα; 1aor. pass. ἐμηνύθην; (1) as disclosing something previously unrealized *make known, point out, reveal* (LU 20.37); (2) *report* information (to authorities), *disclose, inform* (AC 23.30)

μήποτε from μή (*not*) and ποτέ (*at some time*); used as a negative particle in similar types of constructions as μή (q.v.); (1) with the indicative to reinforce negative time *never, at no time* (HE 9.17); (2) predominately as a conjunction as an emphatic form of μή; (a) after verbs of fearing and warning *lest (at any time), for fear that* (LU 21.34); (b) expressing anxiety about the future in negative purpose clauses *in order that not (at all), lest* (MT 4.6); (3) as an interrogative particle expressing a measure of doubt or uncertainty *whether perhaps* (LU 3.15); (4) as introducing a guess in a weakened negative *perhaps, probably* (MT 25.9)

μήποτε	AB	μήποτε
	CC	"
	CS	"
	QT	"

μήπου conjunction; *lest, that, that . . . somewhere* (AC 27.29)

μήπου	CS	μήπου

μήπω adverb; *not yet, still not*

μήπω	AB	μήπω

μήπως conjunction; *lest in anyway* (1C 9.27)

μήπως	CS	μήπως
μηρόν	N-AM-S	μηρός

μηρός, οῦ, ὁ the upper part of the leg *thigh* (RV 19.6)

μήτε a coordinating conjunction used to join negative ideas; (1) adding to a μή clause *not . . . (and) not, neither . . . nor* (MT 5.34); (2) as a disjunctive μ. . . . μ. *neither . . . nor* (AC 23.12)

μήτε	CC	μήτε
	CC+	"
μητέρα	N-AF-S	μήτηρ
μητέρας	N-AF-P	"

μήτηρ, τρός, ἡ (1) literally *mother* (MT 1.18); figuratively, of one respected as a mother (RO 16.13); (2) as a city in relation to its citizens; metaphorically, as the messianic community in relation to its members (GA 4.26); symbolically, of a city as a source of evil (RV 17.5)

μήτηρ	N-NF-S	μήτηρ

μήτι interrogative particle; (1) used when expecting an emphatic negative answer, often left untranslated or translated in such a way as to indicate a negative answer is expected *surely not, probably not*, e.g. μ. ἐγώ εἰμι, κύριε; *surely, Lord, it isn't I, is it?* (MT 26.22); (2) used to express doubt about an answer *perhaps* (MT 12.23)

μήτι	QT	μήτι

μήτιγε from μήτι (*surely not*) and γε (*indeed, even*); used to reinforce μήτι as an interrogative particle when a negative answer indicating contrast or comparison is expected *let alone, not to speak of, how much more* (1C 6.3)

μήτιγε	AB	μήτιγε

μήτρα, ας, ἡ in a female the organ in which offspring are formed before birth *womb*

μητραλοίαις	N-DM-P	see μητραλῴαις
μητραλῴαις	N-DM-P	μητρολῴας
μήτραν	N-AF-S	μήτρα
μήτρας	N-GF-S	"
μητρί	N-DF-S	μήτηρ
μητρολῴαις	N-DM-P	μητρολῴας

μητρολῴας, ου, ὁ (also **μητραλῴας**) *one who murders his mother, matricide* (1T 1.9)

μητρός	N-GF-S	μήτηρ
μία	APCNF-S	εἷς
	A-CNF-S	"
μιᾷ	APCDF-S	"
	A-CDF-S	"
μιαίνουσι(ν)	VIPA--3P	μιαίνω

μιαίνω 1aor. ἐμίανα; pf. pass. μεμίαμμαι; 1aor. pass. ἐμιάνθην; figuratively in the NT *defile, stain*; (1) of cultic and ceremonial impurity *defile, make unclean, cause to be unacceptable* (JN 18.28); (2) of religious and moral impurity *defile, deprave, corrupt* (HE 12.15)

μίαν	APCAF-S	εἷς
	A-CAF-S	"
μιάναντες	VPAANM-P	μιαίνω
μιανθῶσι(ν)	VSAP--3P	"
μιᾶς	APCGF-S	εἷς
	A-CGF-S	"

μίασμα, ατος, τό as a result *defilement, pollution*; figuratively in the NT *(moral) corruption* through evil and ungodly living, *(moral) impurity, corrupting influence* (2P 2.20)

μιάσματα	N-AN-P	μίασμα
μιασμόν	N-AM-S	μιασμός

μιασμός, οῦ, ὁ *pollution, corruption*; figuratively in the NT, as an action or state of moral uncleanness through crime and ungodly living ἐν ἐπιθυμίᾳ μιασμοῦ *through indulging unclean desires* (2P 2.10)

μιασμοῦ	N-GM-S	μιασμός

μίγμα, ατος, τό (also **σμῆγμα, σμίγμα**) a blend produced by mixing *mixture, compound, ointment* (JN 19.39)

μίγμα	N-AN-S	μίγμα

μίγνυμι or **μιγνύω** (or **μείγνυμι** or **μειγνύω**) 1aor. ἔμιξα; pf. pass. μέμιγμαι; (1) *mingle together* two or more substances (LU 13.1); (2) *mix, blend* into one substance (MT 27.34)

μικρά	A--NF-S	μικρός
μικράν	A--AF-S	"
μικροί	A--VM-P	"
μικροῖς	A--DM-P	"
μικρόν	A--AM-S	"
	A--AN-S	"
	A--NN-S	"
	A--VN-S	"

μικρός, ά, όν with a basic meaning *small, little*, translated according to the context; (1) of persons; (a) of physical size *small, little* (LU 19.3); (b) of age *young, little*; the substantive οἱ μικροὶ οὗτοι may belong here

(MT 18.10 etc.), but it possibly belongs to the following; (c) as measuring esteem or importance *insignificant, lowly, unimportant* (MT 10.42); comparative μικρότερος, τέρα, ον *least, most insignificant* (MT 11.11); (2) of things; (a) of quantity or mass *small, little, insignificant* (1C 5.6); neuter as a substantive μικρόν *little (bit)* (2C 11.16); (b) of time *short* (JN 7.33); neuter as a substantive *short time, little while* (JN 13.33); idiomatically μικρὸν ὅσον ὅσον literally *little, how much, how much,* i.e. *very soon, in a very little while* (HE 10.37); (c) of space, neuter as a substantive *little way, short distance* (MT 26.39)

μικρός	A--NM-S	μικρός
μικρότερον	A-MNN-S	"
μικρότερος	A-MNM-S	"
μικροῦ	A--GM-S	"
	A--GN-S	"
μικρούς	A--AM-P	"
μικρῷ	A--DM-S	"
μικρῶν	A--GM-P	"
	A--GN-P	"
Μιλήτη	N-NF-S	Μελίτη
Μίλητον	N-AF-S	Μίλητος

Μίλητος, ου, ἡ *Miletus*, a seaport city on the western coast of Asia Minor south of Ephesus

Μιλήτου	N-GF-S	Μίλητος
Μιλήτῳ	N-DF-S	"

μίλιον, ου, τό Roman *mile*, literally a thousand paces; as a fixed measure, a distance of 8 stades, about 4,850 feet, 1,480 meters, or 1.5 kilometers (MT 5.41)

μίλιον	N-AN-S	μίλιον
μιμεῖσθαι	VNPD	μιμέομαι
	VNPO	"
μιμεῖσθε	VMPD--2P	"
	VMPO--2P	"

μιμέομαι as following someone's actions or way of life *imitate, do* as someone else does, *follow* as an example

μιμηταί	N-NM-P	μιμητής

μιμητής, οῦ, ὁ one who follows another's example *imitator, follower*

μιμνήσκεσθε	VMPP--2P	μιμνήσκω
μιμνήσκω	VIPP--2S	"

μιμνήσκω pf. pass. μέμνημαι; 1aor. pass. ἐμνήσθην; 1fut. pass. μνησθήσομαι; (1) reflexively; (a) of recollection *remember, call to mind, think about again* (HE 10.17); (b) of solicitous concern *be mindful of, think of, care for* (LU 23.42); (2) passive *be mentioned, be noticed* (AC 10.31); the perfect passive has a derived meaning *have been reminded* equivalent to *remember* (2T 1.4)

μιμοῦ	VMPD--2S	μιμέομαι
	VMPO--2S	"
μισεῖ	VIPA--3S	μισέω
μισεῖν	VNPA	"
μισεῖς	VIPA--2S	"

μισέω impf. ἐμίσουν; fut. μισήσω; 1aor. ἐμίσησα; pf. μεμίσηκα; pf. pass. μεμίσημαι; *hate*; (1) of hostility of people for each other *hate, detest* (LU 6.27); (2) Hebraistically, requiring single-minded loyalty in discipleship *prefer less, love less* (LU 14.26); (3) of hostility toward God and the community of God *hate, detest* (LU 1.71); (4) *hate, reject, not choose* (RO 9.13), oppo-

site ἐκλέγω (*choose, select*) as divine election; (5) as strongly disapproving and rejecting evil *hate, abhor* (RV 2.6)

μισῇ	VSPA--3S	μισέω
μισήσει	VIFA--3S	"
μισήσεις	VIFA--2S	"
	VIFA--2S^VMPA--2S	"
μισήσουσι(ν)	VIFA--3P	"
μισήσωσι(ν)	VSAA--3P	"

μισθαποδοσία, ας, ἡ literally *payment of wages*; figuratively *recompense, reward*

μισθαποδοσίαν	N-AF-S	μισθαποδοσία

μισθαποδότης, ου, ὁ literally *one who pays wages*; figuratively, of God *rewarder, recompenser* (HE 11.6)

μισθαποδότης	N-NM-S	μισθαποδότης
μίσθιοι	AP-NM-P	μίσθιος

μίσθιος, ον *hired*; substantivally *hired worker, hired servant, day-laborer*

μισθίων	AP-GM-P	μίσθιος
μισθόν	N-AM-S	μισθός

μισθός, οῦ, ὁ *pay, wages*; literally, payment due for labor *wages, reward, compensation* (JA 5.4); figuratively, recompense for the moral quality of good or bad actions *reward, payment* (MT 6.2; AC 1.18); figuratively and in a positive sense, divine *recompense, reward* for obedience to God's will (MT 5.12); a negative divine payback for disobedience to God's will *punishment, reward* (RV 22.12)

μισθός	N-NM-S	μισθός
μισθοῦ	N-GM-S	"

μισθόω 1aor. mid. ἐμισθωσάμην; only middle in the NT *hire, engage* someone to work for oneself for pay (MT 20.1)

μίσθωμα, ατος, τό active *contract price, rent*; passive, of what has been rented *hired house, rented lodgings* (AC 28.30)

μισθώματι	N-DN-S	μίσθωμα
μισθώσασθαι	VNAM	μισθόω

μισθωτός, ή, όν *hired*; substantivally *hired worker, hireling, day-laborer*

μισθωτός	AP-NM-S	μισθωτός
μισθωτῶν	AP-GM-P	"
μισούμενοι	VPPPNM-P	μισέω
μισοῦντας	VPPAAM-P	"
μισοῦντες	VPPANM-P	"
μισούντων	VPPAGM-P	"
μισοῦσι(ν)	VPPADM-P	"
μισῶ	VIPA--1S	"
μισῶν	VPPANM-S	"

Μιτυλήνη, ης, ἡ *Mitylene*, chief city of the island of Lesbos in the Aegean Sea (AC 20.14)

Μιτυλήνην	N-AF-S	Μιτυλήνη

Μιχαήλ, ὁ indeclinable; *Michael*, name of the chief of the angels

μνᾶ, μνᾶς, ἡ *mina*; in the Old Testament a unit of weight equal to 100 shekels; in the NT a Greek unit of money equal to 100 drachmas or one-sixtieth of a talent

μνᾶ	N-NF-S	μνᾶ
μνᾶν	N-AF-S	"

μνάομαι pf. ptc. μεμνησμένος *woo* or *court for one's bride*; passive, of the woman *be engaged, be pledged to be married* (LU 1.27)

μνᾶς   N-AF-P   μνᾶ

Μνάσων, ωνος, ὁ   *Mnason*, masculine proper noun (AC 21.16)

Μνάσωνι   N-DM-S   Μνάσων

μνεία, ας, ἡ   (1) as a recalling to mind *memory, recollection, remembrance* ἔχειν μνείαν literally *have remembrance*, i.e. *think of* someone (1TH 3.6); (2) predominately of praying specifically for someone μνείαν ποιεῖσθαι *mention, make mention of* (RO 1.9)

μνείᾳ   N-DF-S   μνεία
μνείαις   N-DF-P   "
μνείαν   N-AF-S   "

μνῆμα, ατος, τό   literally *memorial, monument for the dead*; more generally *grave, tomb, sepulcher*

μνῆμα   N-AN-S   μνῆμα
    N-NN-S   "
μνήμασι(ν)   N-DN-P   "
μνήματα   N-AN-P   "
μνήματι   N-DN-S   "
μνημεῖα   N-AN-P   μνημεῖον
    N-NN-P   "
μνημείοις   N-DN-P   "

μνημεῖον, ου, τό   literally *memorial, monument* to commemorate the dead (MT 23.29); more generally *tomb, grave, sepulcher* (MT 8.28)

μνημεῖον   N-AN-S   μνημεῖον
    N-NN-S   "
μνημείου   N-GN-S   "
μνημείῳ   N-DN-S   "
μνημείων   N-GN-P   "

μνήμη, ης, ἡ   *remembrance, recollection, memory*; μνήμην ποιεῖσθαι literally *make remembrance*, i.e. *recall to mind, remember* (2P 1.15)

μνήμην   N-AF-S   μνήμη
μνημόνευε   VMPA--2S   μνημονεύω
μνημονεύει   VIPA--3S   "
μνημονεύειν   VNPA   "
μνημονεύετε   VIPA--2P   "
    VMPA--2P   "
μνημονεύητε   VSPA--2P   "
μνημονεύοντες   VPPANM-P   "
μνημονεύουσι(ν)   VIPA--3P   "
μνημονεύσητε   VSAA--2P   "

μνημονεύω   impf. ἐμνημόνευον; 1aor. ἐμνημόνευσα; (1) of recollection *recall, remember* (MT 16.9); (2) of solicitous concern *be mindful of, think of, remember* (GA 2.10); (3) of self-reflection *remember, keep in mind* (EP 2.11); (4) *speak (of), (make) mention (of)* (HE 11.22)

μνημονεύωμεν   VSPA--1P   μνημονεύω

μνημόσυνον, ου, τό   (1) of what is done that causes someone not to be forgotten *memorial, means of reminding* (MT 26.13); (2) of prayers recorded or kept in mind by God *memorial offering, means of reminding* (AC 10.4)

μνημόσυνον   N-AN-S   μνημόσυνον
μνησθῆναι   VNAP   μιμνήσκω
μνησθῇς   VSAP--2S   "
μνησθήσομαι   VIFP--1S   "
μνήσθητε   VMAP--2P   "

μνήσθητι   VMAP--2S   "
μνησθῶ   VSAP--1S   "
μνηστευθεῖσα   VPAPNF-S   μνηστεύω
μνηστευθείσης   VPAPGF-S   "

μνηστεύω   pf. pass. ptc. ἐμνηστευμένη and μεμνηστευμένη; 1aor. pass. ἐμνηστεύθην; active *woo and win* for marriage, *ask in marriage; pledge to marry*; only passive in the NT *be promised in marriage, become engaged*

μογγιλάλος, ον   *speaking in a hoarse* or *hollow voice*; substantivally *one with a speech impediment* (MK 7.35)

μογγιλάλου   A--GM-S   μογγιλάλος
μογιλάλον   A--AM-S   μογιλάλος

μογιλάλος, ον   of one who has a speech impediment *speaking with difficulty, tongue-tied, hardly able to talk*; substantivally *stammerer* (MK 7.32)

μόγις   adverb; *with difficulty, scarcely, hardly* (LU 9.39)

μόγις   AB   μόγις
μόδιον   N-AM-S   μόδιος

μόδιος, ίου, ὁ   *modius, one-peck measure*, a Roman grain measure holding 16 sextarii, equivalent to 2 English gallons or about 1 peck

μοί   NPD-1S   ἐγώ
μοιχαλίας   N-GF-S   μοιχεία
μοιχαλίδα   AP-AF-S   μοιχαλίς
μοιχαλίδες   AP-VF-P   "
μοιχαλίδι   A--DF-S   "
μοιχαλίδος   AP-GF-S   "

μοιχαλίς, ί, gen. ίδος   *adulterous, lustful*; figuratively, of religious unfaithfulness *unfaithful, treacherous, disloyal* (MT 12.39); substantivally *adulteress* (RO 7.3); ὀφθαλμοὶ μεστοὶ μοιχαλίδος literally *eyes full of adultery*, i.e. *ever on the lookout for an adulterous woman* (2P 2.14)

μοιχαλίς   AP-NF-S   μοιχαλίς
    A--NF-S   "
μοιχᾶσθαι   VNPP   μοιχάω
μοιχᾶται   VIPM--3S   "
    VIPP--3S   "

μοιχάω   (1) middle, of the man *commit adultery, be an adulterer* (MT 5.32; 19.9; MK 10.11); (2) passive, of the woman *commit adultery, be an adulteress* (MK 10.12)

μοιχεία, ας, ἡ (also **μοιχαλία**)   as an act of sexual intercourse with someone not one's own spouse *adultery* (JN 8.3)

μοιχεία   N-NF-S   μοιχεία
μοιχείᾳ   N-DF-S   "
μοιχεῖαι   N-NF-P   "
μοιχείας   N-GF-S   "
μοιχεύει   VIPA--3S   μοιχεύω
μοιχεύειν   VNPA   "
μοιχεύεις   VIPA--2S   "
μοιχευθῆναι   VNAP   "
μοιχευομένη   VPPPNF-S   "
μοιχευομένην   VPPPAF-S   "
μοιχεύοντας   VPPAAM-P   "
μοιχεύσεις   VIFA--2S^VMAA--2S   "
μοιχεύσῃς   VSAA--2S   "

μοιχεύω   fut. μοιχεύσω; 1aor. ἐμοίχευσα; 1aor. pass. ἐμοιχεύθην; (1) literally, of sexual intercourse with someone who is married to another *commit adultery* (MT 5.27); (a) active, as referring to the man alone with the feminine accusative as the object *commit adultery with*

(MT 5.28; LU 16.18); (b) passive, as referring to the woman *commit adultery* (MT 5.32; 19.9); (2) metaphorically, of spiritual unfaithfulness to God (RV 2.22)

| μοιχοί | N-NM-P | μοιχός |

μοιχός, οῦ, ὁ literally *adulterer, (unlawful) lover* (1C 6.9); metaphorically *one unfaithful to God* (JA 4.4)

| μοιχούς | N-AM-P | μοιχός |

μόλις adverb; (1) *with difficulty, hardly* (possibly AC 14.18); (2) *scarcely, just barely* (possibly AC 14.18 and RO 5.7); (3) *only rarely* (possibly RO 5.7)

| μόλις | AB | μόλις |

Μόλοχ, ὁ (also **Μολόχ**) indeclinable; *Moloch*, Canaanite-Phoenician sun god (AC 7.43)

Μόλοχ		Μόλοχ
μολύνεται	VIPP--3S	μολύνω
μολύνοντες	VPPANM-P	"

μολύνω 1aor. ἐμόλυνα; 1aor. pass. ἐμολύνθην; literally, as causing something to be dirty *soil, smear, stain*; metaphorically, as keeping the life spotless οὐκ ἐμόλυναν τὰ ἱμάτια αὐτῶν literally *they did not soil their garments*, i.e. *they have lived in the right way* (RV 3.4); figuratively, of religious and moral unfaithfulness *defile, make impure* (1C 8.7)

μολυσμός, οῦ, ὁ as a state *defilement*; figuratively, of moral and spiritual pollution *filthiness, uncleanness* (2C 7.1)

| μολυσμοῦ | N-GM-S | μολυσμός |

μομφή, ῆς, ἡ as a cause for grievance *complaint, reproach, blame* (CO 3.13)

μομφήν	N-AF-S	μομφή
μόνα	A--AN-P	μόνος
μοναί	N-NF-P	μονή
μόνας	A--AF-P	μόνος

μονή, ῆς, ἡ (1) *staying, tarrying* μονὴν ποιεῖσθαι literally *make a staying*, i.e. *live* or *stay with someone* (JN 14.23); (2) *dwelling place, abode, home* (JN 14.2)

μόνην	A--AF-S	μόνος
μόνην	N-AF-S	μονή
μονογενῆ	A--AM-S	μονογενής

μονογενής, ές of what is the only one of its kind of class *unique*; (1) an only child born to human parents *one and only* (LU 7.12; 8.42); substantivally *only child* (LU 9.38); (2) as a child born in a unique way; (a) used of God's Son Jesus *only, only begotten*; substantivally (JN 1.14); (b) used of Abraham's son Isaac *only*; substantivally ὁ μ. *his only true son* (HE 11.17)

μονογενής	A--NF-S	μονογενής
	A--NM-S	"
μονογενοῦς	A--GM-S	"
μόνοι	A--NM-P	μόνος
μόνοις	A--DM-P	"
μόνον	AB	"
	A--AM-S	"
	A--AN-S	"
	A--NN-S	"

μόνος, η, ον (1) as without accompaniment *alone* (MT 14.23); idiomatically κατὰ μόνας literally *throughout only places*, i.e. *alone* (MK 4.10); (2) as singly existing *only, lone* (JN 17.3); ὁ μ. *he alone* (1T 6.16); (3) as isolated from others; (a) of persons *alone, by oneself, solitary* (JN 16.32); (b) of things *by itself, single* (JN 12.24);

(4) neuter μόνον as an adverb; (a) used to limit or separate an action or state to the one designated in the verb *merely, only, alone* (MT 5.47); (b) used with negatives *not only . . . (but also)* (MT 21.21)

μόνος	A--NM-S	μόνος
μόνου	A--GM-S	"
μόνους	A--AM-P	"
μονόφθαλμον	A--AM-S	μονόφθαλμος

μονόφθαλμος, ον *deprived of sight in one eye, blind in one eye, one-eyed*

μονόω pf. pass. μεμόνωμαι; *make solitary, cause to be alone*; only passive in the NT *be without relatives, be left alone, be forsaken* (1T 5.5)

μόνῳ	A--DM-S	μόνος
	A--DN-S	"
μόνων	A--GF-P	"
	A--GM-P	"

μορφή, ῆς, ἡ (1) *form, external appearance*; generally, as can be discerned through the natural senses (MK 16.12); (2) of the nature of something, used of Christ's contrasting modes of being in his preexistent and human states *form, nature* (PH 2.6, 7)

| μορφῇ | N-DF-S | μορφή |
| μορφήν | N-AF-S | " |

μορφόω 1aor. pass. ἐμορφώθην; as giving shape to something *form, fashion*; figuratively and passive in the NT, as being caused to have a certain nature or character *be formed, become like* (GA 4.19)

| μορφωθῇ | VSAP--3S | μορφόω |
| μόρφωσιν | N-AF-S | μόρφωσις |

μόρφωσις, εως, ἡ (1) as an action *forming, shaping*; in the NT, as the result of shaping *outward form, (mere) appearance* (2T 3.5); (2) as what contains the essential features of something *embodiment, full content, complete expression* (RO 2.20)

| μόσχον | N-AM-S | μόσχος |

μοσχοποιέω 1aor. ἐμοσχοποίησα; *make calf (idol), form an image of a calf* (AC 7.41)

μόσχος, ου, ὁ as the young of cattle *calf* (LU 15.23); generally understood to refer to either sex, a bullock or a heifer

μόσχῳ	N-DM-S	μόσχος
μόσχων	N-GM-P	"
μού	NPG-1S	ἐγώ

μουσικός, ή, όν pertaining to music, *skilled in music*; substantivally *musician*; probably *singer, minstrel*, when mentioned as distinct from instrumentalists (RV 18.22)

| μουσικῶν | AP-GM-P | μουσικός |
| μόχθον | N-AM-S | μόχθος |

μόχθος, ου, ὁ as hard and difficult labor involving suffering *hardship, struggle, strenuous toil*; always combined with κόπος (*work*), as labor bringing to weariness and exhaustion

| μόχθῳ | N-DM-S | μόχθος |

μυελός, οῦ, ὁ literally, the soft filling of bone cavities *marrow*; figuratively, as denoting the inmost part of the being (HE 4.12)

| μυελῶν | N-GM-P | μυελός |

μυέω pf. pass. μεμύημαι; a religious technical term for initiation into sacred mystery religions *initiate, instruct*; figuratively in the NT; passive followed by an infinitive *learn the secret, be instructed* how to do something (PH 4.12)

μύθοις	N-DM-P	μῦθος

μῦθος, ου, ὁ   in the NT always in a negative sense *myth*; (1) *legend, fable* (2P 1.16), opposite λόγος (*declaration, assertion*); (2) *fiction, myth* (2T 4.4), opposite ἀλήθεια (*truth*)

μύθους	N-AM-P	μῦθος

μυκάομαι   of the loud resounding cry of fierce animals; of a lion *roar* (RV 10.3); of a bull *bellow*

μυκᾶται	VIPD--3S	μυκάομαι
	VIPO--3S	"
μυκτηρίζεται	VIPP--3S	μυκτηρίζω

μυκτηρίζω   from μυκτήρ (*nose*); strictly *turn up one's nose at*; hence *treat with contempt, mock, sneer at* (GA 6.7)

μυλικός, ή, όν   of a stone for grinding grain *belonging to a (hand) mill*; λίθος μ. *millstone* (LU 17.2)

μυλικός	A--NM-S	μυλικός
μύλινον	AP-AM-S	μύλινος

μύλινος, η, ον   *belonging to a mill*; substantively *millstone* (RV 18.21)

μύλον	N-AM-S	μύλος

μύλος, ου, ὁ   (1) *millstone* (MT 18.6); (2) often used for μύλη *mill* (MT 24.41)

μύλος	N-NM-S	μύλος
μύλου	N-GM-S	"
μύλῳ	N-DM-S	"

μυλών, ῶνος, ὁ (also μύλων)   as a place for grinding grain *millhouse* (MT 24.41)

μύλωνι	N-DM-S	μυλών
μυλῶνι	N-DM-S	"

μυλωνικός, ή, όν   *belonging to the millhouse* (MK 9.42)

μυλωνικός	A--NM-S	μυλωνικός

Μύρα, ων, τά (also Μύρρα)   *Myra*, a city on the southern coast of Lycia in Asia Minor (AC 27.5)

Μύρα	N-AN-P	Μύρα
μύρα	N-AN-P	μύρον
μυριάδας	N-AF-P	μυριάς
μυριάδες	N-NF-P	"
μυριάδων	N-GF-P	"

μυριάς, άδος, ἡ   (1) literally, as a number *myriad, ten thousand* (AC 19.19); (2) plural, in a more general sense of very large numbers *myriads, countless thousands* (RV 5.11)

μυριάσι(ν)	N-DF-P	μυριάς

μυρίζω   1aor. ἐμύρισα; *anoint*; of corpses *anoint* with perfumed ointments and spices as burial preparation (MK 14.8)

μύριοι, αι, α   as a cardinal number *ten thousand* (MT 18.24)

μυρίος, α, ον   as a large and indefinite number *countless, innumerable*

μυρίους	A--AM-P	μυρίος
μυρίσαι	VNAA	μυρίζω
μυρίων	A-CGM-P	μύριοι
	A-CGN-P	"

μύρον, ου, τό   *ointment, perfume*, sweet-smelling substance made not from animal fats but from plants

μύρον	N-AN-S	μύρον
	N-NN-S	"
μύρου	N-GN-S	"

Μύρρα	N-AN-P	Μύρα
μύρῳ	N-DN-S	μύρον

Μυσία, ας, ἡ   *Mysia*, a province in northwestern Asia Minor

Μυσίαν	N-AF-S	Μυσία
μυστήρια	N-AN-P	μυστήριον

μυστήριον, ου, τό   *mystery, secret*; (1) as a religious technical term in the cults of the Greco-Roman world, a religious *secret* confided only to the initiated, *secret rite*, not used in the NT; (2) in the NT; (a) as what can be known only through revelation mediated from God *what was not known before* (MT 13.11); (b) as a supreme redemptive revelation of God through the gospel of Christ *mystery* (RO 16.25; EP 3.9); (c) as the hidden meaning of a symbol with metaphorical significance *mystery* (EP 5.32)

μυστήριον	N-AN-S	μυστήριον
	N-NN-S	"
μυστηρίου	N-GN-S	"
μυστηρίῳ	N-DN-S	"
μυστηρίων	N-GN-P	"
Μυτιλήνη	N-NF-S	Μελίτη

μυωπάζω   *be nearsighted, see poorly*; figuratively in 2P 1.9 of spiritual shortsightedness *fail to understand*

μυωπάζων	VPPANM-S	μυωπάζω
μώλωπι	N-DM-S	μώλωψ

μώλωψ, ωπος, ὁ   the marks left by a blow *welt, bruise, wound* (that trickles with blood) (1P 2.24)

μωμάομαι   1aor. mid. ἐμωμησάμην; 1aor. pass. ἐμωμήθην; middle *find fault with, blame, censure* (2C 8.20); passive *be blamed, be criticized, be discredited* (2C 6.3)

μωμηθῇ	VSAP--3S	μωμάομαι
μωμήσηται	VSAD--3S	"
μῶμοι	N-NM-P	μῶμος

μῶμος, ου, ὁ   (1) *blame, disgrace, reproach*; (2) as what causes disgrace, either physically or morally *blemish, defect, flaw*; figuratively, of false teachers who mar the fellowship of believers (2P 2.13)

μῶν	NPG-1P	see ἡμῶν
μωρά	A--AN-P	μωρός
μωρᾷ	A--DF-S	"
μωραί	A--NF-P	"

μωραίνω   1aor. ἐμώρανα; 1aor. pass. ἐμωράνθην; (1) *make foolish, show to be foolish* (1C 1.20); passive *become foolish* (RO 1.22); (2) of the seasoning effect of salt *lose its strength, become tasteless*; metaphorically *become ineffective* (MT 5.13)

μωρανθῇ	VSAP--3S	μωραίνω
μωράς	A--AF-P	μωρός
μωρέ	A--VM-S	"

μωρία, ας, ἡ   what is considered foolish, intellectually weak, or irrational *foolishness, nonsense*

μωρία	N-NF-S	μωρία
μωρίαν	N-AF-S	"
μωρίας	N-GF-S	"
μωροί	A--NM-P	μωρός
	A--VM-P	"

μωρολογία, ας, ἡ   *foolish* or *idle talk, useless* or *silly speech* (EP 5.4)

μωρολογία	N-NF-S	μωρολογία
μωρόν	A--NN-S	μωρός

μωρός, ά, όν *foolish, stupid* always a term of reproach; (1) of persons considered to be intellectually weak, irrational, or lacking in foresight (MT 7.26), opposite σοφός (*wise*) and φρόνιμος (*intelligent*); substantively *foolish person* (MT 25.3); of one without respect for God (MT 23.17); the meaning of the substantive μωρέ in MT 5.22 is uncertain; as an insult it could mean *you fool! blockhead!*; (2) of things *foolish, useless* (2T 2.23); neuter as a substantive τὰ μωρά *what is thought of as foolish* (1C 1.27)

μωρός	A--NM-S	μωρός
μωρῷ	A--DM-S	"
Μωσέα	N-AM-S	Μωϋσῆς
Μωσεῖ	N-DM-S	"
Μωσέως	N-GM-S	"
Μωσῇ	N-DM-S	"

Μωσῆν	N-AM-S	"
Μωσῆς	N-NM-S	"
Μωυσέα	N-AM-S	"
Μωϋσέα	N-AM-S	"
Μωυσεῖ	N-DM-S	"
Μωϋσεῖ	N-DM-S	"
Μωυσέως	N-GM-S	"
Μωϋσέως	N-GM-S	"
Μωυσῇ	N-DM-S	"
Μωϋσῇ	N-DM-S	"
Μωυσῆν	N-AM-S	"
Μωϋσῆν	N-AM-S	"
Μωυσῆς	N-NM-S	"

Μωϋσῆς, έως, ὁ (also Μωσεύς, Μωσῆς, Μωυσεύς, Μωυσῆς) *Moses*, masculine proper noun

| Μωϋσῆς | N-NM-S | Μωϋσῆς |

Ναασσών, ὁ   indeclinable; *Nahshon*, masculine proper noun

Ναγγαί, ὁ   indeclinable; *Naggai*, masculine proper noun (LU 3.25)

Ναζαρά, ἡ (also **Ναζαράθ, Ναζαράτ, Ναζαρέδ, Ναζαρέθ, Ναζαρέτ**)   indeclinable; *Nazareth*, a town in Galilee

Ναζαράθ		Ναζαρά
Ναζαράτ		"
Ναζαρέδ		"
Ναζαρέθ		"
Ναζαρέτ		"
Ναζαρηνέ	A--VM-S	Ναζαρηνός
Ναζαρηνόν	A--AM-S	"

Ναζαρηνός, ή, όν (also **Ναζορηνός, Ναζωρηνός, Ναζωρινός**)   *of Nazareth, from Nazareth*; used substantivally and only of Jesus in the NT, in relation to his hometown (MK 1.24); substantivally, used as a designation of Jesus *the Nazarene* (MK 14.67)

Ναζαρηνός	A--NM-S	Ναζαρηνός
Ναζαρηνοῦ	AP-GM-S	"
	A--GM-S	"
Ναζοραῖος	N-NM-S	Ναζωραῖος
Ναζορηνός	A--NM-S	Ναζαρηνός
Ναζωραῖον	N-AM-S	Ναζωραῖος

Ναζωραῖος, ου, ὁ (also **Ναζοραῖος, Ναραῖος**)   *inhabitant of Nazareth, Nazarene*; used as a designation of Jesus (MT 2.23); plural, used of Christians in AC 24.5 in a derogatory sense *Nazarenes*

Ναζωραῖος	N-NM-S	Ναζωραῖος
Ναζωραίου	N-GM-S	"
Ναζωραίων	N-GM-P	"
Ναζαρηνός	A--NM-S	Ναζαρηνός
Ναζωρινός	A--NM-S	"

Ναθάμ, ὁ (also **Ναθάν**)   indeclinable; *Nathan*, masculine proper noun (LU 3.31)

Ναθάν		Ναθάμ

Ναθαναήλ, ὁ   indeclinable; *Nathanael*, masculine proper noun

ναί   particle expressing affirmation; (1) as denoting assent or agreement *yes* (MT 9.28); (2) as affirming the statements of others *certainly, that's so, quite so* (MT 15.27); (3) as emphasizing one's own previous answer to a rhetorical question *yes, indeed* (MT 11.9); (4) as an emphatic repetition of one's own statement *yes indeed, I tell you, even so* (MT 11.26); (5) v. v. used in strong affirmation instead of an oath formula *certainly yes, yes and amen* (MT 5.37; JA 5.12)

ναί	QS	ναί
Ναΐμ		Ναΐν

Ναιμάν, ὁ (also **Νεεμάν**)   indeclinable; *Naaman*, masculine proper noun (LU 4.27)

Ναΐν		Ναΐν

Ναΐν, ἡ (also **Ναΐμ, Ναίν**)   indeclinable; *Nain*, a town in Galilee (LU 7.11)

ναοί	N-NM-P	ναός
ναοῖς	N-DM-P	"
ναόν	N-AM-S	"

ναός, οῦ, ὁ   a building regarded as a dwelling place for a divine being; (1) in a narrower sense, the inner sanctuary within a sacred precinct (τὸ ἱερόν) where the divine being resides *shrine, (inner) temple* (MT 27.51); (2) in a broader yet specific sense, the sanctuary in Jerusalem consisting of the (outer) Holy Place and the (inner) Holy of Holies *temple* (MT 26.61); (3) the inner room of a pagan temple *shrine* (AC 17.24); (4) a small model of a temple or shrine *replica* (AC 19.24); (5) metaphorically, of Jesus and the individual Spirit-filled believer as a dwelling place for God on earth *shrine, temple* (JN 2.19; 1C 6.19); (6) metaphorically, of the church as the dwelling place of God on earth (EP 2.21); (7) the heavenly sanctuary *temple* (RV 14.15)

ναός	N-NM-S	ναός
ναοῦ	N-GM-S	"

Ναούμ, ὁ   indeclinable; *Nahum*, masculine proper noun (LU 3.25)

ναούς	N-AM-P	ναός
Ναραῖος	N-NM-S	Ναζωραῖος

νάρδος, ου, ἡ   (1) as a fragrant plant native to India *(spike)nard*; (2) as aromatic oil extracted from its roots *spikenard, oil, ointment, perfume of nard* (MK 14.3)

νάρδου	N-GF-S	νάρδος

Νάρκισσος, ου, ὁ   *Narcissus*, masculine proper noun (RO 16.11)

Ναρκίσσου	N-GM-S	Νάρκισσος

ναυαγέω   literally *suffer shipwreck, be shipwrecked* (2C 11.25); figuratively, as failing to continue to live with a clear conscience *be spiritually ruined, give up believing, no longer believe* (1T 1.19)

ναύκληρος, ου, ὁ   *shipmaster, owner of a ship* (AC 27.11)

ναυκλήρῳ	N-DM-S	ναύκληρος
ναῦν	N-AF-S	ναῦς

ναῦς, ἡ, accusative **ναῦν**   *ship*, a large boat used for traveling on oceans and large seas (AC 27.41)

ναῦται	N-NM-P	ναύτης

ναύτης, ου, ὁ   *sailor, seaman*, one who works on a ship

ναυτῶν	N-GM-P	ναύτης

Ναχώρ, ὁ   indeclinable; *Nahor*, masculine proper noun (LU 3.34)

ναῷ	N-DM-S	ναός
Νέαν	A--AF-S	Νέα Πόλις
νεανίαν	N-AM-S	νεανίας

νεανίας, ου, ὁ   *young man, youth*; (1) used of a man in the prime of life, between twenty-four and forty years old

(AC 7.58); (2) used of an *older boy, young (unmarried) man* (AC 23.17)

νεανίας	N-NM-S	νεανίας
νεανίου	N-GM-S	"
νεανίσκε	N-VM-S	νεανίσκος
νεανίσκοι	N-NM-P	"
	N-VM-P	
νεανίσκον	N-AM-S	"

νεανίσκος, ου, ὁ *young man, youth*; (1) used of a man in the prime of life, between twenty-four and forty years old (MT 19.20); (2) used of an *older boy, young (unmarried) man* (AC 23.18); (3) *servant* is the possible meaning in several passages (MK 14.51b; AC 5.10)

νεανίσκος	N-NM-S	νεανίσκος
Νεάπολιν	N-AF-S	Νέα Πόλις

Νέα Πόλις, ἡ (also **Νεάπολις**) from νέος (*new*) and πόλις (*city*); *Neapolis*, meaning *New City*, a port city along the Aegean Sea in Macedonia, serving as the harbor of Philippi (AC 16.11)

νέας	A--AF-P	νέος
	A--GF-S	"
Νεεμάν		Ναιμάν
νεῖκος	N-AN-S	νῖκος
	N-NN-S	"
νεκρά	A--NF-S	νεκρός
νεκράν	A--AF-S	"
νεκροί	A--NM-P	"
νεκροῖς	A--DM-P	"
νεκρόν	A--AM-S	"
	A--NN-S	"

νεκρός, ά, όν *dead*; (1) of persons; (a) literally; (i) of human beings and animals no longer physically alive *dead, lifeless, deceased* (AC 28.6; JA 2.26a); (ii) substantivally ὁ ν. *dead person* (LU 7.15); οἱ νεκροί *the dead, dead people* (MK 12.26); (b) figuratively; (i) of persons unable to respond to God because of moral badness or spiritual alienation *dead, powerless* (EP 2.1, 5); (ii) of persons regarded as dead because of separation *dead* (LU 15.24, 32); (iii) of persons no longer under the control of something *dead to* (RO 6.11); (2) of things; literally *lifeless* (e.g. idols); figuratively, of what is of no benefit morally or spiritually *utterly useless, completely ineffective* (HE 6.1; JA 2.26b)

νεκρός	A--NM-S	νεκρός
νεκροῦ	A--GM-S	"
νεκρούς	A--AM-P	"

νεκρόω 1aor. ἐνέκρωσα; pf. pass. νενέκρωμαι; literally *put to death, kill*; passive, as a medical condition, of a part of the body no longer useful because of illness or age *(as good as) dead, impotent* (RO 4.19); figuratively, as stopping the use of bodily members and functions for immoral purposes *deaden, do away with, cease completely* (CO 3.5)

νεκρῶν	A--GM-P	νεκρός
	A--GN-P	"
νεκρώσατε	VMAA--2P	νεκρόω
νεκρώσει	N-DF-S	νέκρωσις
νέκρωσιν	N-AF-S	"

νέκρωσις, εως, ἡ (1) as an action *putting to death, dying,* of the constant danger of being killed (2C 4.10); (2) as

a result *deadness, impotence*; of a part of the body, e.g. *barrenness* of the womb (RO 4.19)

νενεκρωμένον	VPRPAN-S	νεκρόω
νενεκρωμένου	VPRPGM-S	"
νενίκηκα	VIRA--1S	νικάω
νενικήκατε	VIRA--2P	"
νενομοθέτηται	VIRP--3S	νομοθετέω
νενομοθέτητο	VILP--3S	"

νεομηνία, ας, ἡ (also **νουμηνία**) as a time notation *new moon, first of the month*; often observed with religious festivities and ceremonies *new moon festival* (CO 2.16)

νεομηνίας	N-GF-S	νεομηνία
νέον	A--AM-S	νέος
	A--NN-S	"

νέος, α, ον (1) of time, as existing only recently *new, fresh*, synonymous with καινός (MT 9.17); (2) of what is superior in nature to the former *new*; figuratively, of persons *renewed in nature*; substantivally *new, renewed person* (CO 3.10); (3) of age *young*; substantivally αἱ νέαι *the young(er) women* (TI 2.4); mostly comparative νεώτερος, τέρα, ον *younger* (LU 15.12); substantivally οἱ νεώτεροι with little comparative force *young men, youths* (TI 2.6); αἱ νεώτεραι *young(er) women* (1T 5.14); (4) Νέα Πόλις *Neapolis*, meaning *New City*, the harbor of Philippi in Macedonia (AC 16.11)

νέος	A--NM-S	νέος
νεοσσούς	N-AM-P	νοσσός

νεότης, τητος, ἡ as an early period of life *youth*

νεότητος	N-GF-S	νεότης
νεόφυτον	A--AM-S	νεόφυτος

νεόφυτος, ον literally *newly planted*; figuratively, of one newly become a part of the Christian church *newly converted, only beginning* as a Christian; possibly substantivally *recent convert, new believer* (1T 3.6)

νεύει	VIPA--3S	νεύω

Νεύης, ὁ indeclinable; *Neues*, masculine proper noun (LU 16.19)

νεύσαντος	VPAAGM-S	νεύω

νεύω 1aor. ἔνευσα; as signaling to someone by a nod or gesture *(give a) nod, motion to, beckon*

νεφέλαι	N-NF-P	νεφέλη
νεφέλαις	N-DF-P	"

νεφέλη, ης, ἡ *cloud*

νεφέλη	N-NF-S	νεφέλη
νεφέλῃ	N-DF-S	"
νεφέλην	N-AF-S	"
νεφέλης	N-GF-S	"
νεφελῶν	N-GF-P	"
Νεφθαλείμ		Νεφθαλίμ

Νεφθαλίμ, ὁ (also **Νεφθαλείμ**) indeclinable; *Naphtali*, masculine proper noun; name of a tribe of Israel

νέφος, ους, τό *cloud, mass of clouds*; figuratively, of a dense throng of people *large crowd* (HE 12.1)

νέφος	N-AN-S	νέφος

νεφρός, οῦ, ὁ mostly plural *kidneys, veins*; figuratively, of the inner being, the source of thoughts, purposes, feelings *soul, mind* (RV 2.23)

νεφρούς	N-AM-P	νεφρός
νεωκόρον	N-AM-S	νεωκόρος

νεωκόρος, ου, ὁ literally *temple keeper, guardian of a temple*; in the NT of a city with a temple devoted to a deity (AC 19.35)

νεωτέρας	A-MAF-P	νέος
νεωτερικάς	A--AF-P	νεωτερικός

νεωτερικός, ή, όν of what is natural to a youth *youthful, adolescent, juvenile* (2T 2.22)

νεώτεροι	A-MNM-P	νέος
	A-MVM-P	"
νεώτερος	A-MNM-S	"
νεωτέρους	A-MAM-P	"

νή a particle (possible variation of ναί [*yes*]) used for strongly affirming oaths *by, on the basis of*, with the accusative of whom or what one uses for affirmation (1C 15.31)

νή	QS	νή
νήθει	VIPA--3S	νήθω
νήθουσι(ν)	VIPA--3P	"

νήθω as the process of making thread for cloth from plant or animal material *spin*

νηπιάζετε	VMPA--2P	νηπιάζω

νηπιάζω *be as a child, be childlike* (1C 14.20)

νήπιοι	AP-NM-P	νήπιος
	A--NM-P	"
νηπίοις	AP-DM-P	"
νήπιον	A--AM-S	"

νήπιος, ία, ον usually substantivally; (1) as a very young child *infant* (1C 13.11); plural *babes, infants* (MT 21.16); (2) figuratively, of adults; positively, of those unspoiled by worldly learning *childlike, innocent, simple people* (MT 11.25); negatively, of immature adults *childish, inexperienced people* (EP 4.14)

νήπιος	AP-NM-S	νήπιος
	A--NM-S	"
νηπίου	AP-GM-S	"
νηπίων	AP-GM-P	"
Νηρέα	N-AM-S	Νηρεύς
Νηρεί		Νηρί

Νηρεύς, έως, ὁ (also **Βηρεύς**) *Nereus*, masculine proper noun (RO 16.15)

Νηρί, ὁ (also **Νηρεί**) indeclinable; *Neri*, masculine proper noun (LU 3.27)

νησίον, ου, τό diminutive of νῆσος; *(small) island* (AC 27.16)

νησίον	N-AN-S	νησίον
νῆσον	N-AF-S	νῆσος

νῆσος, ου, ἡ *island*, an area of land entirely surrounded by water

νῆσος	N-NF-S	νῆσος
νήσου	N-GF-S	"

νηστεία, ας, ἡ (1) as deprivation of food *hunger* (2C 11.27); (2) as refusing to eat for religious purposes *fasting, fast* (MT 17.21); as a specific Jewish festival *Fast, Day of Atonement* (AC 27.9)

νηστεία	N-DF-S	νηστεία
νηστείαις	N-DF-P	"
νηστείαν	N-AF-S	"
νήστεις	A--AM-P	νῆστις
νηστειῶν	N-GF-P	νηστεία
νηστεύειν	VNPA	νηστεύω
νηστεύητε	VSPA--2P	"

νηστεύομεν	VIPA--1P	"
νηστεύοντες	VPPANM-P	"
νηστευόντων	VPPAGM-P	"
νηστεύουσι(ν)	VIPA--3P	"
νηστεῦσαι	VNAA	"
νηστεύσαντες	VPAANM-P	"
νηστεύσας	VPAANM-S	"
νηστεύσουσι(ν)	VIFA--3P	"

νηστεύω fut. νηστεύσω; 1aor. ἐνήστευσα; as going without food for religious purposes *fast*

νηστεύω	VIPA--1S	νηστεύω
νηστεύων	VPPANM-S	"

νῆστις, ὁ and **ἡ**, Ionic or Epic gen. ιος or εως, Attic gen. ιδος *hunger*; as an adjective *not eating, hungry* (MT 15.32)

νήσῳ	N-DF-S	νῆσος
νηφάλαιον	A--AM-S	νηφάλιος
νηφαλαίους	A--AF-P	"
	A--AM-P	"
νηφάλεον	A--AM-S	"
νηφαλέους	A--AF-P	"
	A--AM-P	"
νηφάλιον	A--AM-S	"

νηφάλιος, ία, ον (also **νηφάλαιος, αία, ον**; **νηφαλέος, α, ον**) strictly *holding no wine, without wine*; of persons *sober, temperate, abstinent*

νηφαλίους	A--AF-P	νηφάλιος
	A--AM-P	"
Νήφαν	N-AF-S	Νύμφα
νῆφε	VMPA--2S	νήφω
νήφοντες	VPPANM-P	"
νήφουσι(ν)	VIPA--3P	"

νήφω 1aor. ἔνηψα; literally *be sober*, opposite μεθύω (*be intoxicated*); figuratively in the NT, of being free from every form of mental and spiritual excess and confusion *be self-controlled, be clear-headed, be self-possessed*

νήφωμεν	VSPA--1P	νήφω
νήψατε	VMAA--2P	"

Νίγερ, ὁ indeclinable; *Niger*, masculine proper noun (AC 13.1)

νίθουσι(ν)	VIPA--3P	see νήθουσι(ν)
νίκα	VMPA--2S	νικάω
νικᾷ	VIPA--3S	"
Νικάνορα	N-AM-S	Νικάνωρ

Νικάνωρ, ορος, ὁ *Nicanor*, masculine proper noun (AC 6.5)

νικάω fut. νικήσω; 1aor. ἐνίκησα; pf. νενίκηκα; (1) intransitively *be victorious, win, prevail* (RV 2.7); of a legal action *win (out), prevail, win the case* (RO 3.4); (2) transitively *overcome, defeat, conquer* (LU 11.22)

νίκη, ης, ἡ *victory, success*; abstract for concrete *means for gaining victory, victorious principle*, such as faith (1J 5.4)

νίκη	N-NF-S	νίκη
νικῆσαι	VNAA	νικάω
νικήσασα	VPAANF-S	"
νικήσει	VIFA--3S	"
νικήσεις	VIFA--2S	"
νικήσῃ	VSAA--3S	"
νικήσῃς	VSAA--2S	"

Νικόδημος, ου, ὁ *Nicodemus*, masculine proper noun

Νικόδημος   N-NM-S   Νικόδημος

Νικολαΐτης, ου, ὁ   *Nicolaitan*, a follower of Nicolaus, founder of a sect

Νικολαϊτῶν   N-GM-P   Νικολαΐτης
Νικόλαον   N-AM-S   Νικόλαος

Νικόλαος, ου, ὁ   *Nicolaus*, masculine proper noun (AC 6.5)

Νικόπολιν   N-AF-S   Νικόπολις

Νικόπολις, εως, ἡ   *Nicopolis*, a city, usually taken to be in Epirus in western Greece, along the Adriatic Sea (TI 3.12)

νῖκος, ους, τό (also **νεῖκος**)   *victory*

νῖκος   N-AN-S   νῖκος
        N-NN-S   "
νικῶ   VMPP--2S   νικάω
νικῶν   VPPANM-S   "
νικῶντας   VPPAAM-P   "
νικῶντι   VPPADM-S   "
Νινευεῖται   N-NM-P   Νινευίτης
Νινευείταις   N-DM-P   "

Νινευή, ἡ (also **Νινευί**) indeclinable; *Nineveh*, capital of the later Assyrian Empire (LU 11.32)

Νινευί   Νινευή
Νινευῖται   N-NM-P   Νινευίτης
Νινευίταις   N-DM-P   "
Νινευίταις   N-DM-P   "

Νινευίτης, ου, ὁ (also **Νινευείτης, Νινευίτης**)   *Ninevite, inhabitant of Nineveh*, ancient capital of the Assyrian Empire, located along the Tigris River

νίπτειν   VNPA   νίπτω
νίπτεις   VIPA--2S   "

νιπτήρ, ῆρος, ὁ   *basin*, a container for washing hands and feet; cf. ποδονιπτήρ *foot basin* (JN 13.5)

νιπτῆρα   N-AM-S   νιπτήρ
νίπτονται   VIPM--3P   νίπτω

νίπτω   1aor. ἔνιψα, mid. ἐνιψάμην; (1) active *wash* someone or something (JN 13.5); used as a symbolic act *make morally clean* (JN 13.8); (2) middle, of washing parts of one's body, such as face, hands, or feet *wash (oneself)* (JN 9.7); used of ritual washings among followers of Judaism (MK 7.3); (3) idiomatically πόδας νίπτειν literally *wash the feet*, i.e. *show hospitality* (probably 1T 5.10); *humbly serve* (possibly 1T 5.10)

νίψαι   VMAM--2S   νίπτω
νιψάμενος   VPAMNM-S   "
νίψασθαι   VNAM   "
νίψῃς   VSAA--2S   "
νίψω   VSAA--1S   "
νίψωνται   VSAM--3P   "
νόει   VMPA--2S   νοέω
νοεῖτε   VIPA--2P   "
νοείτω   VMPA--3S   "

νοέω   1aor. ἐνόησα; with a basic meaning *direct one's mind* (νοῦς) to a subject; (1) of rational reflection or thought *perceive, understand, comprehend* (MT 15.17); (2) as perceiving through receiving sensory data *notice, think carefully about, recognize, consider* (MT 24.15); (3) as mental conception *imagine, conceive* (EP 3.20)

νόημα, ατος, τό   with a basic meaning *what results from directing one's mind* (νοῦς) to a subject; (1) as the content of thinking *thought, (what is in the) mind* (PH 4.7); (2) as the capacity for thinking *understanding, mind, reasoning power* (2C 3.14; 4.4); (3) as purposes conceived by thinking *design, scheme*; in a bad sense *stratagem, plot* (2C 2.11)

νόημα   N-AN-S   νόημα
νοήματα   N-AN-P   "
        N-NN-P   "
νοῆσαι   VNAA   νοέω
νοήσωσι(ν)   VSAA--3P   "
νόθοι   A--NM-P   νόθος

νόθος, η, ον   *born out of wedlock, illegitimate, bastard*; substantively and symbolically, to designate those who reject God's fatherly discipline (HE 12.8)

νοΐ   N-DM-S   νοῦς

νομή, ῆς, ἡ   (1) *pasture*, as a place where a flock may spread out to eat (JN 10.9); (2) figuratively *extension*; as a medical technical term for an ulcerous growth that spreads and eats the flesh ἔχειν νομήν *eat its way, spread, increase* (2T 2.17)

νομήν   N-AF-S   νομή
νομίζει   VIPA--3S   νομίζω
νομίζειν   VNPA   "
νομίζεις   VIPA--2S   "
νομίζοντες   VPPANM-P   "
νομιζόντων   VPPAGM-P   "

νομίζω   impf. ἐνόμιζον, pass. ἐνομιζόμην; 1aor. ἐνόμισα; related to νόμος (*custom*); (1) *use in common*; passive *be the custom* (AC 16.13); (2) as regarding something as already settled or established *suppose, think, presume* (MT 5.17)

νομίζω   VIPA--1S   νομίζω
νομίζων   VPPANM-S   "
νομικάς   A--AF-P   νομικός
νομικοί   AP-NM-P   "
νομικοῖς   AP-DM-P   "
νομικόν   AP-AM-S   "

νομικός, ή, όν   (1) *about law, pertaining to law* (TI 3.9); (2) *learned in law*; substantively ὁ ν. *lawyer, legal expert* (probably TI 3.13); predominately in the NT *interpreter of Jewish religious laws* (MT 22.35; perhaps TI 3.13)

νομικός   AP-NM-S   νομικός
νομικούς   AP-AM-P   "
νομικῶν   AP-GM-P   "

νομίμως   adverb; (1) *lawfully, in agreement with law, correctly* (1T 1.8); (2) of athletic contests *in agreement with rules, fairly* (2T 2.5)

νομίμως   AB   νομίμως
νομίσαντες   VPAANM-P   νομίζω
νομίσητε   VSAA--2P   "

νόμισμα, ατος, τό   *coin, money*, coinage that is sanctioned for common use by law or custom (MT 22.19)

νόμισμα   N-AN-S   νόμισμα
νομοδιδάσκαλοι   N-NM-P   νομοδιδάσκαλος

νομοδιδάσκαλος, ου, ὁ   in reference to Jewish teachers, *teacher of the law, interpreter of (the Mosaic system of) law*

νομοδιδάσκαλος   N-NM-S   νομοδιδάσκαλος
νομοδιδασκάλους   N-AM-P

νομοθεσία, ας, ἡ   literally *law-giving*; in the NT, as the result of law-giving *legislation, (possession of) law* (RO 9.4)

νομοθεσία	N-NF-S	νομοθεσία

νομοθετέω   pf. pass. νενομοθέτημαι; (1) of functioning as a law-giver *legislate, make laws*; passive *receive, be given law* (HE 7.11); (2) as ordering a matter by law *enact*; passive *be enacted, be established* (HE 8.6)

νομοθέτης, ου, ὁ   *law-giver*, one who decides on a system of laws (JA 4.12)

νομοθέτης	N-NM-S	νομοθέτης
νόμον	N-AM-S	νόμος

νόμος, ου, ὁ   with a basic meaning *law*, i.e. what is assigned or proper; (1) generally, any *law* in the judicial sphere (RO 7.1); (2) as rule governing one's conduct *principle, law* (RO 7.23); (3) more specifically in the NT of the Mosaic system of legislation as revealing the divine will (the Torah) *law (of Moses)* (LU 2.22); in an expanded sense, Jewish religious laws developed from the Mosaic law *(Jewish) law* (JN 18.31; AC 23.29); (4) as the collection of writings considered sacred by the Jews; (a) in a narrower sense, the Pentateuch, the first five books of the Bible, as comprising *the law* (MT 12.5; GA 3.10b); (b) in a wider sense, the Old Testament Scriptures as a whole (MT 5.18; RO 3.19); (5) figuratively, as the Christian gospel, the new covenant, as furnishing a new principle to govern spiritual life *law* (RO 8.2a; HE 10.16)

νόμος	N-NM-S	νόμος
νόμου	N-GM-S	"
νόμους	N-AM-P	"
νόμῳ	N-DM-S	"
νοός	N-GM-S	νοῦς
νοοῦμεν	VIPA--1P	νοέω
νοούμενα	VPPPNN-P	"
νοοῦντες	VPPANM-P	"

νοσέω   *be sick*; figuratively in the NT, of unwholesome ambition *have a morbid craving for, overly desire* something (1T 6.4)

νόσημα, ατος, τό   *disease, sickness* (JN 5.4)

νοσήματι	N-DN-S	νόσημα
νόσοις	N-DF-P	νόσος
νόσον	N-AF-S	"

νόσος, ου, ἡ   *sickness, disease*

νόσους	N-AF-P	νόσος
νοσσία	N-AN-P	νοσσίον

νοσσιά, ᾶς, ἡ   young birds hatched in a nest *brood, nest of birds* (LU 13.34)

νοσσιάν	N-AF-S	νοσσιά

νοσσίον, ου, τό   *nestling, chick*, the offspring of birds or fowls; plural *(the) young, chicks* (MT 23.37)

νοσσός, οῦ, ὁ (also νεοσσός)   *young of a bird*; δύο νοσσοὶ περιστερῶν *two young pigeons* or *doves* (LU 2.24)

νοσσούς	N-AM-P	νοσσός
νοσφιζομένους	VPPMAM-P	νοσφίζω

νοσφίζω   1aor. mid. ἐνοσφισάμην; only middle in the NT *put aside (secretly) for oneself, keep back funds for oneself* (AC 5.2); *misappropriate, steal, embezzle* (TI 2.10)

νοσφίσασθαι	VNAM	νοσφίζω
νόσων	N-GF-P	νόσος
νοσῶν	VPPANM-S	νοσέω

νότον	N-AM-S	νότος

νότος, ου, ὁ   (1) as a direction *south* (LU 13.29); (2) as a direction of the wind *south wind* (LU 12.55); (3) as a relative location of a country *south* (MT 12.42)

νότου	N-GM-S	νότος

νουθεσία, ας, ἡ   *teaching, admonition, warning*, ethical and corrective instruction in regard to belief or behavior

νουθεσίᾳ	N-DF-S	νουθεσία
νουθεσίαν	N-AF-S	"
νουθέτει	VMPA--2S	νουθετέω
νουθετεῖν	VNPA	"
νουθετεῖτε	VMPA--2P	"

νουθετέω   *admonish, warn, instruct*, as giving instructions in regard to belief or behavior

νουθετοῦντας	VPPAAM-P	νουθετέω
νουθετοῦντες	VPPANM-P	"
νουθετῶ	VIPA--1S	"
νουθετῶν	VPPANM-S	"
νουμηνίας	N-GF-S	νεομηνία
νοῦν	N-AM-S	νοῦς

νουνεχῶς   adverb; *sensibly, wisely, thoughtfully* (MK 12.34)

νουνεχῶς	AB	νουνεχῶς

νοῦς, νοός, ὁ, dative νοΐ, accusative νοῦν   with a basic meaning *direct one's inner sense to* an object; (1) as the faculty of intelligence *understanding, mind, intellect* (1C 14.15); (2) as the faculty of moral perception *(practical) reason, insight, awareness* (RO 7.25); (3) as the total inner orientation or moral attitude *way of thinking, mind (set), disposition* (RO 1.28); (4) as the result of mental activity *thought, judgment, resolve, opinion* (RO 14.5)

νοῦς	N-NM-S	νοῦς
νύκτα	N-AF-S	νύξ
νύκτας	N-AF-P	"
νυκτί	N-DF-S	"
νυκτός	N-GF-S	"

Νύμφα, ας, ἡ (also Νήφα)   *Nympha*, feminine proper noun (CO 4.15)

Νύμφαν	N-AF-S	Νύμφα
Νυμφᾶν	N-AM-S	Νυμφᾶς
Νύμφας	N-GF-S	Νύμφα

Νυμφᾶς, ᾶ, ὁ   *Nymphas*, masculine proper noun (CO 4.15)

νύμφη, ης, ἡ   (1) literally; (a) as a young woman engaged or newly married *bride, young wife* (JN 3.29); (b) in Jewish usage *daughter-in-law* (LU 12.53), in contrast to πενθερά *(mother-in-law)*; (2) metaphorically, of the church as the bride of Christ (RV 21.9; 22.17)

νύμφη	N-NF-S	νύμφη
νύμφην	N-AF-S	"
νύμφης	N-GF-S	"
νυμφίον	N-AM-S	νυμφίος

νυμφίος, ου, ὁ   *bridegroom, young husband* (JN 3.29)

νυμφίος	N-NM-S	νυμφίος
νυμφίου	N-GM-S	"
νυμφίῳ	N-DM-S	"
νυμφίων	N-GM-P	"

νυμφών, ῶνος, ὁ   (1) as the place where the wedding ceremonies are held *wedding hall* (MT 22.10); (2) as the place where the marriage is consummated *bridal chamber*; (3) idiomatically οἱ υἱοὶ τοῦ νυμφῶνος literally *sons of the wedding hall*, i.e. *the bridegroom's attendants* (MT 9.15)

νυμφῶνος   N-GM-S   νυμφῶν

νῦν   adverb of time *now*; (1) as an adverb; (a) designating a point of time not past or future *now, at the present time* (LU 6.21), opposite πρότερος (*earlier*); following the imperative, to urge immediate compliance *now, right now* (MT 27.42); (b) of time immediately before or after the present *just now, presently* (JN 11.8; PH 1.20); (c) with other particles to indicate more precise timing: ἀλλὰ ν. *but now* (LU 22.36), ν. δέ *but now* (JN 16.5), καὶ ν. *even now* (JN 11.22), ν. οὖν *so now* (AC 16.36), etc.; (2) as a noun used with the article τό: τὰ ν. *the present (time)* (AC 4.29); with prepositions: ἀπὸ τοῦ ν. *from now on, in the future* (LU 1.48); ἄχρι τοῦ ν. *until now* (RO 8.22); ἕως τοῦ ν. *until now, up to now* (MT 24.21); (3) as an adjective used with the article and joined to a noun *the present* (1T 6.17); (4) nontemporally; (a) as a connecting particle ἄγε ν. *come now* (JA 4.13; 5.1); καὶ ν. *and now* (AC 20.22); ν. οὖν *now therefore* (AC 10.33); (b) as a particle of logical antithesis used to shift from an unreal to a real state of affairs ν. δέ *but now, as it is; but, as a matter of fact* (LU 19.42)

νῦν   AB   νῦν

νυνί   adverb of time; an emphatic form of νῦν but not differing from it in meaning; (1) as a point of time not past or future *now, at the present time* (AC 24.13), opposite πρότερος (*earlier*); (2) as an adjective used with the article and joined to a noun *the present* (AC 22.1); (3) nontemporally, as a particle of logical antithesis used to shift from an unreal to a real state of affairs *but now; but, as a matter of fact* (1C 5.11); (4) ν. δέ used to introduce a summary of a situation *but now, and so* (RO 7.17; 1C 13.13)

νυνί   AB   νυνί

νύξ, νυκτός, ἡ   *night*; (1) literally; (a) as a period of time *night* (MT 4.2), opposite ἡμέρα (*day*); (b) genitive νυκτός answering the question "during what time?" *during the night, at night* (JN 3.2); with prepositions: διὰ νυκτός *at night, during the night* (AC 5.19); μέσης νυκτός *at midnight* (MT 25.6); (c) dative νυκτί answering the questions "when? at what point of time?" *at night*; ταύτῃ τῇ νυκτί *this very night, tonight* (MK 14.30); τῇ ἐπιούσῃ νυκτί *the following night* (AC 23.11); (d) accusative νύκτα answering the question "(for) how long?" *for a night, throughout the night* (MT 12.40); νύκτα καὶ ἡμέραν *(through) night and day* (MK 4.27); (2) figuratively; (a) as a symbol of death (JN 9.4); (b) as a sphere of moral darkness (1TH 5.5); (c) as a symbol of the present age (RO 13.12)

νύξ   N-NF-S   νύξ

νύξας   VPAANM-S   νύσσω

νύσσω   1aor. ἔνυξα; *prick, stab, pierce* (JN 19.34)

νυστάζει   VIPA--3S   νυστάζω

νυστάζω   1aor. ἐνύσταξα; literally *become drowsy, doze, get sleepy* (MT 25.5); figuratively *be idle* (as if asleep), *be inactive* (2P 2.3)

νυστάξει   VIFA--3S   νυστάζω

νυχθήμερον, ου, τό   *a night and a day, twenty-four hours* (2C 11.25)

νυχθήμερον   N-AN-S   νυχθήμερον

Νῶε, ὁ   indeclinable; *Noah*, masculine proper noun

νωθροί   A--NM-P   νωθρός

νωθρός, ά, όν   *sluggish, lazy*; in the NT used of being slow to understand or respond spiritually

νῶτον   N-AM-S   νῶτος

νῶτος, ου, ὁ   as a part of the body *back*; idiomatically συγκάμπτειν τὸν νῶτον literally *bend the back*, i.e. *burden with difficulties* (RO 11.10)

ξ Ξ

ξαίνουσι(ν) VIPA--3P ξαίνω
ξαίνω as processing wool for spinning and weaving *comb, card* (MT 6.28)
ξέναις A--DF-P ξένος
ξενία, ας, ἡ (1) as the entertaining of a guest *hospitality*; (2) in the NT, as the place where a guest is lodged *guest room, lodging*
ξενίαν N-AF-S ξενία
ξενίζεσθε VMPP--2P ξενίζω
ξενίζεται VIPP--3S "
ξενίζομαι VIPP--1S "
ξενίζοντα VPPAAN-P "
ξενίζονται VIPP--3P "
ξενίζω 1aor. ἐξένισα; 1aor. pass. ἐξενίσθην; (1) transitively; (a) active, of hospitality *receive as a guest, entertain, lodge* (AC 28.7); (b) passive *dwell as a guest, be entertained, stay* or *lodge with* (AC 10.6); (2) intransitively, of something new or strange; (a) active *surprise, astonish* (AC 17.20); (b) passive *be struck with, be amazed, wonder, think strange* (1P 4.12)
ξενίσαντες VPAANM-P ξενίζω
ξενισθῶμεν VSAP--1P "
ξενοδοχέω 1aor. ἐξενοδόχησα; of one who practices hospitality *entertain strangers, show hospitality to a guest* (1T 5.10)
ξένοι AP-NM-P ξένος
  A--NM-P "
ξένοις AP-DM-P "
ξένον A--AM-S "
ξένος, η, ον (1) *strange, foreign* (AC 17.18); substantivally: (a) *stranger, foreigner, alien* (MT 25.35), opposite πολίτης (*citizen*); (b) as one who extends hospitality *host* (RO 16.23); (2) of something strange in kind *surprising, unheard of* (1P 4.12); (3) figuratively, of being treated as an alien *excluded, estranged from* (EP 2.12)
ξένος AP-NM-S ξένος
  A--NM-S "
ξένου A--GN-S "
ξένους AP-AM-P "
ξένουσι(ν) VIPA--3P see ξαίνουσι(ν)
ξένων A--GN-P ξένος
ξέστης, ου, ὁ as a Roman liquid measure *sextarius*, a half-liter or a one-pint container *pitcher, jug* (MK 7.4)
ξεστῶν N-GM-P ξέστης
ξηρά A--NF-S ξηρός
ξηραίνεται VIPP--3S ξηραίνω
ξηραίνω 1aor. ἐξήρανα; pf. pass. ἐξήραμμαι; 1aor. pass. ἐξηράνθην; (1) literally *dry out, parch, cause to wither*

(JA 1.11); passive *become dry, dry up* (RV 16.12); of the flow of blood *stop* (MK 5.29); of plants *wither, dry up* (MT 13.6); of grain that has finished growing *ripe*; metaphorically, of conditions for judgment *ready* (RV 14.15); (2) figuratively and passive, of a damaged human body; of the whole body *stiffen (up), become rigid* (MK 9.18); of a limb *shrivel, wither, become useless* (MK 3.1)
ξηράν AP-AF-S ξηρός
  A--AF-S "
ξηρᾶς A--GF-S "
ξηρός, ά, όν *dry, dried (up)*; (1) literally, of land *dry* (HE 11.29); substantivally ἡ ξηρά *dry land* (MT 23.15); of plants *dry, parched*; used proverbially by Jesus in reference to a coming judgment on Jerusalem (LU 23.31); (2) of a damaged member of the body *paralyzed, withered, useless* (MT 12.10)
ξηρῷ A--DN-S ξηρός
ξηρῶν A--GM-P "
ξύλα N-AN-P ξύλον
ξύλινα A--AN-P ξύλινος
  A--NN-P "
ξύλινος, η, ον *wooden, made of wood*
ξύλον, ου, τό *wood, tree*; (1) of dead wood; as a building material (RV 18.12); used metaphorically in 1C 3.12 as inferior building material, representing less valuable teaching and lack of exemplary living; (2) of objects made of wood; (a) as an instrument of restraint *stocks* (AC 16.24); (b) as a weapon *cudgel, club, stick* (MT 26.47); (c) as an instrument for execution by crucifixion *cross, stake, tree* (AC 5.30); (3) of living wood *tree* (RV 2.7)
ξύλον N-AN-S ξύλον
  N-NN-S "
ξύλου N-GN-S "
ξύλῳ N-DN-S "
ξύλων N-GN-P "
ξύρασθαι VNAM see ξυράω
ξυρᾶσθαι VNPM ξυράω
  VNPP "
ξυράω present mid./pass. inf. ξυρᾶσθαι; fut. mid. ξυρήσομαι; 1aor. mid. inf. ξύρασθαι (as from ξύρω *shave*); pf. pass. ἐξύρημαι (as from ξυράω); middle *shave one's head, have oneself shaved* (AC 21.24; probably 1C 11.6 ξύρασθαι); passive *be shaved* (1C 11.5; possibly 11.6 ξυρᾶσθαι)
ξυρήσονται VIFM--3P ξυράω
ξυρήσωνται VSAM--3P "

275

o O

ὁ, ἡ, τό   a prepositive article; plural οἱ, αἱ, τά; in general the article imparts a component of individuality in any form of expression; its main usages are the following; **I.** as the definite article with nouns *the*; (1) to individualize nouns and provide focus (e.g. ὁ λόγος JN 1.1); (2) to refer to a common noun previously mentioned (e.g. τοὺς μάγους MT 2.7); (3) to individualize a common noun being given special attention (e.g. ὁ ἄνθρωπος JN 19.5); (4) generically, to single out an individual as representative of a class (e.g. ὁ ἐργάτης LU 10.7); (5) generally with proper nouns when the person is well known (e.g. ὁ Ἰωάννης MT 3.4; ὁ Ἰησοῦς MT 3.13); the article in such usage is untranslated; (6) with name of countries, rivers, seas, with the article left untranslated (e.g. τῆς Γαλιλαίας, τὸν Ἰορδάνην MT 3.13); (7) with nouns accompanied by a genitive to show possession, since the possession indicates a definite noun (e.g. τὸ ὄνομα αὐτοῦ MT 1.25); (8) preceding nouns modified by a demonstrative pronoun and positioned after the pronoun (e.g. οὗτος ὁ ἄνθρωπος LU 14.30); (9) with an abstract noun to give it a restricted and definite sense (e.g. ἡ ἀλήθεια JN 8.32); (10) placed before a nominative to mark it as a vocative (e.g. ὁ πατήρ MT 11.26); (11) to add emphasis by repeating the article with some word or phrase modifying a noun (e.g. ὁ λόγος ὁ τοῦ σταυροῦ 1C 1.18); (12) with the subject in a copulative sentence to distinguish it from the predicate (e.g. θεὸς ἦν ὁ λόγος *the Word was God* JN 1.1); **II.** the definite article with adjectives; (1) added to an adjective to mark it as a substantive (e.g. τοῦ πονηροῦ EP 6.16); (2) with numerals to refer to a part of an already known number (e.g. οἱ ἐννέα LU 17.17); **III.** as the definite article with a participle; (1) to mark the participle as a substantive (e.g. ὁ πειράζων MT 4.3); (2) to form the participle into a relative clause–like construction (e.g. ὁ πιστεύων JN 3.18); **IV.** the neuter article with an infinitive in forming an articular infinitive construction; (1) to stand for a noun (e.g. τὸ ἀναστῆναι *the rising* MK 9.10); (2) with prepositions to express logical relations, such as means, purpose, reason, circumstance, etc., with the meaning dependent on the case of the article and the prepositional construction governing the infinitive (e.g. μετὰ τὸ ἐγερθῆναί με *after I have risen* MT 26.32); **V.** as a pronoun; (1) as a demonstrative pronoun (its original use) *this one, that one, these, those* (e.g. οἱ ἀπὸ τῆς Ἰταλίας *those from Italy* HE 13.24); (2) as indicating alternatives (e.g. οἱ μὲν . . . οἱ δέ *some . . . others* AC 17.32); (3) as indicating a change of subject in the progress of a narrative (e.g. οἱ δέ *so they* MT 2.9); (4) as a possessive pronoun especially with parts of the body (e.g. τὰς χεῖρας *his hands* MK 6.5); **VI.** the sentential use: the neuter article placed before whole sentences or clauses to make a topic of the sentence or clause (e.g. τὸ οὐ φονεύσεις *the [one], you shall not kill* MT 19.18)

ὁ	DNMS	ὁ
	DNMS+	"
	DNMS^APDNM-S	"
	DVMS	"
	DVMS+	"
ὅ	APRAN-S	ὅς
	APRNN-S	"
	A-RAN-S	"

Ὀβήδ | | Ἰωβήδ

ὀγδόη | A-ODF-S | ὄγδοος

ὀγδοήκοντα   indeclinable; as a cardinal number *eighty*

ὀγδοηκοντατέσσαρες, gen. **τεσσάρων**   as a cardinal number *eighty-four* (LU 2.37)

ὀγδοηκοντατεσσάρων | A-CGN-P | ὀγδοηκοντατέσσαρες

ὄγδοον | A-OAM-S | ὄγδοος

ὄγδοος, η, ον   as an ordinal number *eighth*; substantivally *eighth one* (RV 21.20)

ὄγδοος | A-ONM-S | ὄγδοος

ὄγκον | N-AM-S | ὄγκος

ὄγκος, ου, ὁ   *weight, encumbrance, impediment*; figuratively *hindrance* (HE 12.1)

ὅδε, ἥδε, τόδε   demonstrative pronoun *this (one) here*; (1) to point to and focus on something that is going to be said, especially in the formula τάδε λέγει *this is what x says* (RV 2.1); (2) to point to someone previously mentioned *that (person), he, she, it* (LU 10.39); (3) to refer to someone or something in a suppositional case for the sake of illustration *such and such (a person or place), this or that (person or place)* (JA 4.13)

ὅδε | APDNM-S | ὅδε

ὁδεύω   *go, journey, travel* (LU 10.33)

ὁδεύων | VPPANM-S | ὁδεύω

ὁδηγεῖ | VIPA--3S | ὁδηγέω

ὁδηγεῖν | VNPA | "

ὁδηγέω   fut. ὁδηγήσω; literally *lead* someone *on the way, escort, guide* (MT 15.14); figuratively *instruct, teach, guide* in learning (AC 8.31)

ὁδηγῇ | VSPA--3S | ὁδηγέω

ὁδηγήσει | VIFA--3S | "

ὁδηγήση | VSAA--3S | "

ὁδηγοί | N-NM-P | ὁδηγός

| | N-VM-S | "

ὁδηγόν | N-AM-S | "

ὁδηγός, οῦ, ὁ   literally, one who leads on a path *guide, escort, leader* (AC 1.16); figuratively, one acting as instructor of the ignorant or inexperienced *guide, leader* (MT 23.16)

ὁδηγοῦ | N-GM-S | ὁδηγός

ὁδηγῶν | N-GM-P | "

276

ὁδοί	N-NF-P	ὁδός

ὁδοιπορέω   *journey, travel, be on the way* (AC 10.9)
ὁδοιπορία, ας, ἡ   *journey, travel, journeying*

ὁδοιπορίαις	N-DF-P	ὁδοιπορία
ὁδοιπορίας	N-GF-S	"
ὁδοιποροῦντες	VPPANM-P	ὁδοιπορέω
ὁδοιπορούντων	VPPAGM-P	"
ὁδοῖς	N-DF-P	ὁδός
ὁδόν	N-AF-S	"
ὀδόντα	N-AM-S	ὀδούς
ὀδόντας	N-AM-P	"
ὀδόντες	N-NM-P	"
ὀδόντος	N-GM-S	"
ὀδόντων	N-GM-P	"
ὁδοποιεῖν	VNPA	ὁδοποιέω

ὁδοποιέω   *make a way* or *path* (MK 2.23)

ὁδός, οῦ, ἡ   (1) literally; (a) as any place along which one travels, translated according to the context: *way* (MT 2.12), *road* (LU 10.31), *path* (MK 4.4), *street* (MT 22.10), *highway* (MT 4.15); (b) as an act of traveling *journey, way, course* (MT 10.10); (c) in adverbial expressions: ἐν τῇ ὁδῷ *en route, on the way* (MT 5.25); κατὰ τὴν ὁδόν *on* or *along the way* (LU 10.4); σαββάτου ὁ. literally *Sabbath day's journey*, i.e. about 800 meters or 2,000 paces (AC 1.12); ἡμέρας ὁ. *day's journey* (LU 2.44); (2) figuratively; (a) as a manner of living and acting *way of life, type of conduct* (JU 11); (b) as a system of doctrine, specifically Christianity *the Way* (AC 24.14); (c) as a means of entering into something *way* (MT 3.3; 7.13; HE 10.20)

ὁδός	N-NF-S	ὁδός
ὁδοῦ	N-GF-S	"

ὀδούς, ὀδόντος, ὁ   *tooth*

ὀδούς	N-AF-P	ὀδούς
ὀδύναις	N-DF-P	ὀδύνη
ὀδυνᾶσαι	VIPP--2S	ὀδυνάω

ὀδυνάω   pass. second-person singular ὀδυνᾶσαι; active *cause pain*; only passive in the NT; (1) of violent physical torment *feel pain, suffer torment, be in agony* (LU 16.24); (2) of spiritual or mental distress *be grieved, be pained, be anxious, be very worried* (LU 2.48)

ὀδύνει	VIPA--3S	see ὠδίνει

ὀδύνη, ης, ἡ   (1) physically *(severe and sudden) pain*; (2) as deep mental distress *grief, agitation, sorrow* (RO 9.2); (3) as remorse from a guilty conscience *pang, grief* (1T 6.10)

ὀδύνη	N-NF-S	ὀδύνη
ὀδυνῶμαι	VIPP--1S	ὀδυνάω
ὀδυνώμενοι	VPPPNM-P	"
ὀδύνων	N-GF-P	see ὠδίνων
ὀδυρμόν	N-AM-S	ὀδυρμός

ὀδυρμός, οῦ, ὁ   *wailing, lamentation*, a loud and grievous expression of mourning or remorse

ὀδυρμός	N-NM-S	ὀδυρμός
ὁδῷ	N-DF-S	ὁδός
ὁδῶν	N-GF-P	"
ὄζει	VIPA--3S	ὄζω
Ὀζείαν	N-AM-S	Ὀζίας
Ὀζείας	N-NM-S	"
Ὀζίαν	N-AM-S	"

Ὀζίας, ου, ὁ (also Ὀζείας)   *Uzziah*, masculine proper noun

Ὀζίας	N-NM-S	Ὀζίας

ὄζω   *give off an odor, smell*; of an unpleasant odor *stink, give off a stench* (JN 11.39)

ὅθεν   adverb; (1) of place *from where, from what place* (MT 25.24); (2) of source *from which (fact), out of which (circumstance), in consequence of which* (1J 2.18); (3) of cause *for which reason, because of which* (MT 14.7)

ὅθεν	ABR	ὅθεν
	CH	"
	CS	"

ὀθόνη, ης, ἡ   strictly *fine linen*; by metonymy *linen cloth, sheet*

ὀθόνην	N-AF-S	ὀθόνη
ὀθόνια	N-AN-P	ὀθόνιον
ὀθονίοις	N-DN-P	"

ὀθόνιον, ου, τό   diminutive of ὀθόνη; *piece of linen, bandage*; as used in burial preparations *swath, bandage, linen cloth, strip of linen*

ὀθονίων	N-GN-P	ὀθόνιον
οἱ	DNMP	ὁ
	DNMP+	"
	DNMP^APDNM-P	"
	DVMP	"
	DVMP+	"
οἵ	APRNM-P	ὅς
οἷα	APRNF-S	οἷος
	A-RNF-S	"
οἷα	APRAN-P	"
	APRNN-P	"

οἶδα   the perfect of the obsolete εἴδω (*see*) used as the present; second-person singular οἶδας, second-person plural οἴδατε, third-person plural οἴδασι (ἴσασι in AC 26.4), subjunctive εἰδῶ, inf. εἰδέναι, ptc. εἰδώς and εἰδυῖα; fut. εἰδήσω; pluperfect ᾔδειν; strictly *have seen*; hence *know*; (1) as having come to a perception or realization of something *know, understand, comprehend* (MK 4.13); (2) as having come to knowledge through experience *know (about), recognize, understand* (EP 1.18); (3) as having knowledge and ability to do something with an infinitive following *know how to, can, be able to* (MT 7.11); (4) of intimate or close relationship with someone *know, have knowledge of* (MT 26.72); (5) as a formula for introducing a well-known and accepted fact (e.g. οἴδαμεν ὅτι *we know that* . . . MT 22.16); for introducing a rhetorical question (e.g. οὐκ οἴδατε ὅτι *don't you know that*. . . ? 1C 3.16); (6) as giving deserved recognition to someone *respect, appreciate, have regard for* (1TH 5.12)

οἶδα	VIRA--1S	οἶδα
οἴδαμεν	VIRA--1P	"
οἶδας	VIRA--2S	"
οἴδασι(ν)	VIRA--3P	"
οἴδατε	VIRA--2P	"
οἶδε(ν)	VIRA--3S	"
οἰέσθω	VMPD--3S	οἴομαι
	VMPO--3S	"
οἰκεῖ	VIPA--3S	οἰκέω
οἰκεῖν	VNPA	"
οἰκεῖοι	AP-NM-P	οἰκεῖος

οἰκεῖος, ον (also οἰκίος)   literally *belonging to* or *standing in relation to a household*; substantively in the NT οἱ οἰκεῖοι *members of a family, relatives, household* (1T 5.8), opposite πάροικος (*stranger*); figuratively, of the members of God's spiritual family *(God's) household* (EP 2.19); οἰ. τῆς πίστεως *believers* (GA 6.10)

οἰκείους	AP-AM-P	οἰκεῖος
οἰκείων	AP-GM-P	"
οἰκέται	N-VM-P	οἰκέτης

οἰκετεία, ας, ἡ   of servants connected to a household *household servants* (MT 24.45)

οἰκετείας	N-GF-S	οἰκετεία
οἰκέτην	N-AM-S	οἰκέτης

οἰκέτης, ου, ὁ   literally *member of the household*; more specifically *house slave, domestic, servant*

οἰκέτης	N-NM-S	οἰκέτης
οἰκετῶν	N-GM-P	"

οἰκέω   (1) intransitively *dwell, live*; (a) literally, of marriage *live with, live together as husband and wife* (1C 7.12, 13); (b) figuratively, of spiritual indwelling *reside in* (1C 3.16); (2) transitively *inhabit, dwell in* something (1T 6.16)

οἴκημα, ατος, τό   *dwelling place*; (1) generally *room, quarters, apartment*; (2) euphemistically *prison* (AC 12.7)

οἰκήματι	N-DN-S	οἴκημα

οἰκητήριον, ου, τό   literally *dwelling place, habitation, abode* (JU 6); figuratively, of the body as the dwelling place of the soul *habitation, dwelling, home* (2C 5.2)

οἰκητήριον	N-AN-S	οἰκητήριον

οἰκία, ας, ἡ   (1) literally, as a building *house* (MT 2.11); by metonymy; (a) *family, household* (MT 10.12); (b) *property, possession, goods* (MK 12.40); (2) figuratively, of the body as the habitation of the soul *house* (2C 5.1)

οἰκία	N-NF-S	οἰκία
οἰκίᾳ	N-DF-S	
οἰκιακοί	N-NM-P	οἰκιακός
οἰκιακοῖς	N-DM-P	"

οἰκιακός, οῦ, ὁ   of children and servants under control of a head of household *member of a household, family*; *(extended) family, relatives* (MT 10.36)

οἰκιακούς	N-AM-P	οἰκιακός
οἰκίαν	N-AF-S	οἰκία
οἰκίας	N-AF-P	"
	N-GF-S	"
οἰκίοι	AP-NM-P	οἰκεῖος
οἰκιῶν	N-GF-P	οἰκία
οἰκοδεσποτεῖν	VNPA	οἰκοδεσποτέω

οἰκοδεσποτέω   *be master* or *mistress of a household, keep house, manage one's household* (1T 5.14)

οἰκοδεσπότῃ	N-DM-S	οἰκοδεσπότης
οἰκοδεσπότην	N-AM-S	"

οἰκοδεσπότης, ου, ὁ   literally *master of the house, head of the family, householder* (MT 24.43); figuratively, of God or Christ in NT figures and parables, as in charge of God's spiritual family (MT 10.25)

οἰκοδεσπότης	N-NM-S	οἰκοδεσπότης
οἰκοδεσπότου	N-GM-S	"
οἰκοδομαί	N-NF-P	οἰκοδομή
οἰκοδομάς	N-AF-P	"
οἰκοδομεῖ	VIPA--3S	οἰκοδομέω
οἰκοδομεῖν	VNPA	

οἰκοδομεῖσθαι	VNRP	see οἰκοδομῆσθαι
οἰκοδομεῖσθε	VIPP--2P	οἰκοδομέω
	VMPP--2P	"
οἰκοδομεῖται	VIPP--3S	
οἰκοδομεῖτε	VIPA--2P	
	VMPA--2P	"

οἰκοδομέω   impf. ᾠκοδόμουν; fut. οἰκοδομήσω; 1aor. ᾠκοδόμησα; 1aor. pass. ᾠκοδομήθην or οἰκοδομήθην (JN 2.20); 1fut. pass. οἰκοδομηθήσομαι; (1) literally; (a) as constructing houses, temples, tombs, etc. *build, erect* (LU 6.48); (b) absolutely *erect buildings* (LU 17.28); substantively οἱ οἰκοδομοῦντες *the builders* (MT 21.42); (c) *build again, restore* (MT 26.61), opposite καταλύω (*destroy, tear down*); (2) figuratively; (a) of the establishment and increase of a Christian community known as the house of God *build, establish* (1P 2.5); (b) of the process of spiritual growth and development of the spiritual community and each member within it *edify, make more able, strengthen* (1C 14.4); (c) in a negative sense, as setting up (again) a wall of separation between Jews and Gentiles *build (again), restore* (GA 2.18); (d) as imparting strength and courage to someone to do what is right (1TH 5.11) or wrong (1C 8.10) *strengthen, embolden*

οἰκοδομή, ῆς, ἡ   (1) as an action; (a) literally *building, construction*; (b) figuratively, of spiritual encouragement *making more able, edifying, building up* (1C 14.12; 2C 13.10), opposite καθαίρεσις (*weakening*) and καταστροφή (*leading astray*); (2) as a result; (a) literally *building, structure* (MT 24.1); (b) figuratively, especially of the church as the place for God's indwelling *building* (1C 3.9); (c) of the resurrected body in the future *something made* (by God), *building* (from God) (2C 5.1)

οἰκοδομή	N-NF-S	οἰκοδομή
οἰκοδομήθη	VIAP--3S	οἰκοδομέω
οἰκοδομηθήσεται	VIFP--3S	"
οἰκοδομήν	N-AF-S	οἰκοδομή
οἰκοδομῆς	N-GF-S	"
οἰκοδομῆσαι	VNAA	οἰκοδομέω
οἰκοδομήσαντι	VPAADM-S	"
οἰκοδόμησε(ν)	VIAA--3S	"
οἰκοδομήσετε	VIFA--2P	"
οἰκοδομῆσθαι	VNRP	"
οἰκοδομήσω	VIFA--1S	"

οἰκοδομία, ας, ἡ   *building*, both as process and result; figuratively *edification* (1T 1.4)

οἰκοδομίαν	N-AF-S	οἰκοδομία

οἰκοδόμος, ου, ὁ   *builder (of a house), architect* (AC 4.11)

οἰκοδομούμεναι	VPPPNF-P	οἰκοδομέω
οἰκοδομουμένη	VPPPNF-S	"
οἰκοδομοῦντες	VPPANM-P	"
οἰκοδομοῦντι	VPPADM-S	"
οἰκοδομούντων	VPPAGM-P	"
οἰκοδομῶ	VIPA--1S	"
	VSPA--1S	"
οἰκοδόμων	N-GM-P	οἰκοδόμος
οἰκοδομῶν	VPPAVM-S	οἰκοδομέω
οἴκοις	N-DM-P	οἶκος
οἶκον	N-AM-S	
οἰκονομεῖν	VNPA	οἰκονομέω

οἰκονομέω *hold the office of steward* (οἰκονόμος), *be (house) manager, be in charge of a household* (LU 16.2)

οἰκονομία, ας, ἡ (1) literally, relating to the task of an οἰκονόμος (*steward*) in household administration *stewardship, management* (LU 16.2); (2) figuratively; (a) of the apostolic office in God's redemptive work *task, responsibility, trusteeship* (CO 1.25); (b) of God's arrangements for mankind's redemption *plan, arrangement, purpose* (EP 3.9); 1T 1.4 may mean *(divine) training*, but *(divine) plan* is also possible

οἰκονομία	N-NF-S	οἰκονομία
οἰκονομίαν	N-AF-S	"
οἰκονομίας	N-GF-S	"
οἰκονόμοι	N-NM-P	οἰκονόμος
οἰκονόμοις	N-DM-P	"
οἰκονόμον	N-AM-S	"

οἰκονόμος, ου, ὁ (1) literally; (a) one put in charge of a household or estate *steward, manager* (LU 12.42); (b) a community official in charge of public funds and properties *treasurer, overseer* (RO 16.23); (2) figuratively, one entrusted by God with spiritual authority and administration *steward, administrator* (1C 4.1)

οἰκονόμος	N-NM-S	οἰκονόμος
οἰκονόμους	N-AM-P	"

οἰκος, ου, ὁ *house*; (1) as a place for habitation; literally *house, home, dwelling* (MT 9.6); of specific houses: as a king's house *palace* (MT 11.8), as God's house for prayer, worship, etc. *temple* (LU 11.51); in a wider sense of a city as the home of a community of people (MT 23.38); figuratively, of a community of believers as a spiritual house for God's indwelling (1P 2.5); (2) as those living within a house; literally *household, family* (LU 10.5); figuratively, as the members of God's family *household* (HE 3.6); (3) by extension, of the descendants from a common ancestor *house, nation, descendants* (MT 10.6)

οἰκος	N-NM-S	οἰκος
	N-VM-S	"
οἰκου	N-GM-S	"

οἰκουμένη, ης, ἡ (1) the inhabited part of the earth *world, inhabited earth* (MT 24.14); (2) as the inhabitants of the world *humanity, mankind, people* (RV 12.9); (3) in a more restricted sense, as the Roman Empire and its inhabitants (LU 2.1)

οἰκουμένη	N-NF-S	οἰκουμένη
οἰκουμένη	N-DF-S	"
οἰκουμένην	N-AF-S	"
οἰκουμένης	N-GF-S	"
οἰκοῦν	VPPAAN-S	οἰκέω

οἰκουργός, όν of one preoccupied with domestic affairs *working at home, domestic*; possibly substantivally *homemaker* (TI 2.5)

οἰκουργούς	A--AF-P	οἰκουργός

οἰκουρός, όν *watching* or *keeping the house, staying at home, domestic*; possibly substantivally *homemaker* (TI 2.5)

οἰκουρούς	A--AF-P	οἰκουρός
οἰκους	N-AM-P	οἰκος
οἰκοῦσα	VPPANF-S	οἰκέω
οἰκτειρήσω	VIFA--1S	οἰκτίρω
οἰκτείρω	VSPA--1S	"

οἰκτιρήσω	VIFA--1S	"
οἰκτιρμοί	N-NM-P	οἰκτιρμός
οἰκτίρμονες	A--NM-P	οἰκτίρμων

οἰκτιρμός, οῦ, ὁ as a motivating emotion *sympathy, mercy, pity*

οἰκτιρμοῦ	N-GM-S	οἰκτιρμός

οἰκτίρμων, ον *compassionate, merciful*

οἰκτίρμων	A--NM-S	οἰκτίρμων
οἰκτιρμῶν	N-GM-P	οἰκτιρμός

οἰκτίρω (and **οἰκτείρω**) fut. οἰκτιρήσω; as being moved or motivated by sympathy *have compassion on, pity*

οἰκτίρω	VSPA--1S	οἰκτίρω
οἰκω	N-DM-S	οἰκος
οἰκων	N-GM-P	"
οἰκῶν	VPPANM-S	οἰκέω
οἰμαι	VIPD--1S	οἰομαι
	VIPO--1S	"
οἰνον	N-AM-S	οἰνος

οἰνοπότης, ου, ὁ one who habitually drinks too much wine or alcoholic beverage *wine drinker, drunkard*

οἰνοπότης	N-NM-S	οἰνοπότης

οἰνος, ου, ὁ *wine*; (1) literally, of the juice of grapes, usually fermented (LU 1.15); (2) figuratively, in apocalyptic symbolism; (a) as indicating the wrath of God outpoured in judgment (RV 14.10); (b) as an enticement to immorality, like a love potion (RV 17.2)

οἰνος	N-NM-S	οἰνος
οἰνου	N-GM-S	"

οἰνοφλυγία, ας, ἡ strictly *bubbling over with wine*; hence *drunkenness, debauchery, drunken orgy* (1P 4.3)

οἰνοφλυγίαις	N-DF-P	οἰνοφλυγία
οἰνω	N-DM-S	οἰνος
οἰοι	APRNM-P	οἰος

οἰομαι contracted form οἰμαι; as making a mental evaluation but without certainty *think, suppose, presume*

οἰομαι	VIPD--1S	οἰομαι
	VIPO--1S	"
οἰόμενοι	VPPDNM-P	"
	VPPONM-P	"
οἰον	APRAM-S	"
	APRNN-S	"

οἰος, οἰα, ον a relative adjective predominately used as a relative pronoun; referring to quality in interrogative references *what sort of, of what kind* (1TH 1.5); showing similarity in quality *of such sort, such as* (MT 24.21)

οἰος	APRNM-S	οἰος
οἰου	A-RGN-S	"
οἰους	APRAM-P	"
	A-RAM-P	"
οἰς	APRDM-P	ὅς
	APRDN-P	"
οἰσει	VIFA--3S	φέρω
οἰσμαι	VIFD--1S	"
οἰσουσι(ν)	VIFA--3P	"
οἰτινες	APRNM-P	ὅστις
οἰω	A-RDN-S	οἰος

ὀκνέω 1aor. ὠκνησα; with an infinitive following *delay to, hesitate to, be slow to* (AC 9.38)

ὀκνηρέ	A--VM-S	ὀκνηρός
ὀκνηροί	A--NM-P	"
ὀκνηρόν	A--NN-S	"

ὀκνηρός, ά, όν (1) of being afraid to act *hesitating, shrinking, lazy* (MT 25.26); (2) of things arousing reluctance *bothersome, troublesome* (PH 3.1)

ὀκνῆσαι	VNAA	ὀκνέω
ὀκνήσῃς	VSAA--2S	"
ὄκνον	N-AM-S	ὄκνος

ὄκνος, ου, ὁ *cowardice, unreadiness, hesitation* (HE 12.1)

ὀκταήμερος, ον substantivally *on the eighth day*, related to the circumcision of a male child when it was a week old (PH 3.5)

ὀκταήμερος	A--NM-S	ὀκταήμερος

ὀκτώ indeclinable; as a cardinal number *eight*

ὅλαι	A--NF-P	ὅλος
ὀλέθριον	A--AF-S	ὀλέθριος

ὀλέθριος, ον *destructive, deadly* (2TH 1.9)

ὄλεθρον	N-AM-S	ὄλεθρος

ὄλεθρος, ου, ὁ in the NT always with a religious component *complete destruction, ruin, perdition*

ὄλεθρος	N-NM-S	ὄλεθρος
ὀλέθρου	N-GM-S	"
ὅλη	A--NF-S	ὅλος
ὅλῃ	A--DF-S	"
ὅλην	A--AF-S	"
ὅλης	A--GF-S	"
ὀλίγα	A--AN-P	ὀλίγος
ὀλίγαι	A--NF-P	"
ὀλίγαις	A--DF-P	"
ὀλίγας	A--AF-P	"
ὀλίγην	A--AF-S	"
ὀλίγης	A--GF-S	"
ὀλίγοι	A--AF-P	"
	A--NM-P	"
ὀλίγοις	A--DM-P	"
ὀλίγον	AB	"
	A--AM-S	"
	A--AN-S	"
	A--NN-S	"
ὀλιγόπιστε	A--VM-S	ὀλιγόπιστος

ὀλιγοπιστία, ας, ἡ *inadequacy* or *imperfection of faith* (MT 17.20)

ὀλιγοπιστίαν	N-AF-S	ὀλιγοπιστία
ὀλιγόπιστοι	A--VM-P	ὀλιγόπιστος

ὀλιγόπιστος, ον of one who does not believe or trust strongly *of little faith, not strong in trusting*; substantivally *a person not trusting firmly* (MT 8.26)

ὀλίγος, η, ον (1) of the number or size of a group *few, small* (MT 15.34), opposite πολλοί (*many*); substantivally ὀλίγοι *few people* (MT 7.14); ὀλίγα *few things* (RV 2.14); (2) of quantity *little, small* (LU 7.47a), opposite πολύ (*much*); substantivally τὸ ὀλίγον *small amount* (2C 8.15); (3) of degree *little, mild, slight* (AC 12.18), opposite μέγας (*great*); (4) of time duration *short* (RV 12.12); (5) neuter as an adverb ὀλίγον; (a) of distance *little (way), short distance* (MK 1.19); (b) of time *a little while, for a short time* (MK 6.31); (c) of degree *a little (bit), to a small extent* (LU 7.47b); (d) with prepositions: ἐν ὀλίγῳ of quantity *in brief, briefly, soon, quickly* (AC 26.28); πρὸς ὀλίγον of time *for a short time* (JA 4.14); of degree *for a little (bit)* (1T 4.8)

ὀλίγος	A--NM-S	ὀλίγος
ὀλίγου	A--GM-S	"

ὀλιγόψυχος, ον of one who feels his resources are too small for a given situation *fainthearted, despondent, discouraged*; substantivally *fainthearted person* (1TH 5.14)

ὀλιγοψύχους	A--AM-P	ὀλιγόψυχος
ὀλίγῳ	A--DM-S	ὀλίγος
	A--DN-S	"
ὀλίγων	A--GM-P	"
	A--GN-P	"
ὀλιγώρει	VMPA--2S	ὀλιγωρέω

ὀλιγωρέω as regarding something as having little value *think lightly of, make light of, disparage* (HE 12.5)

ὀλίγως adverb; *scarcely, just barely, only by a little* (2P 2.8)

ὀλίγως	AB	ὀλίγως

ὀλοθρευτής, οῦ, ὁ *destroyer*; in the NT an angel sent as the agent of divine punishment (1C 10.10)

ὀλοθρευτοῦ	N-GM-S	ὀλοθρευτής

ὀλοθρεύω as carrying out severe punishment *destroy, cause to perish* (HE 11.28)

ὀλοθρεύων	VPPANM-S	ὀλοθρεύω

ὁλοκαύτωμα, ατος, τό *whole burnt offering, sacrifice that is entirely burned*

ὁλοκαύτωμα	N-AN-S	ὁλοκαύτωμα
ὁλοκαυτώματα	N-AN-P	"
ὁλοκαυτωμάτων	N-GN-P	"

ὁλοκληρία, ας, ἡ *completeness*; as physical wholeness *perfect health, soundness in all parts of the body* (AC 3.16)

ὁλοκληρίαν	N-AF-S	ὁλοκληρία
ὁλόκληροι	A--NM-P	ὁλόκληρος
ὁλόκληρον	A--NN-S	"

ὁλόκληρος, ον of something complete in all its parts, with focus on quantity rather than quality *complete, whole, intact*; of a person *in every part of, in all aspects of, throughout the whole of* (1TH 5.23)

ὀλολύζοντες	VPPANM-P	ὀλολύζω

ὀλολύζω as making a loud and inarticulate *cry*, either in jubilation or terror; in the NT, as a reaction to desperate circumstances *howl, wail, lament*

ὅλον	A--AM-S	ὅλος
	A--AN-S	"
	A--NN-S	"

ὅλος, η, ον *whole, intact, entire, all (the)*; (1) used with a noun to indicate its totality (MK 1.33); occasionally with a noun supplied from the context (MT 13.33); (2) used with a pronoun σὺ ὅ. *you altogether, wholly* (JN 9.34); τοῦτο ὅλον *all this* (MT 1.22); (3) used substantivally with a preposition δι᾽ ὅλου literally *through the whole*, i.e. *throughout, all through* (JN 19.23)

ὅλος	A--NM-S	ὅλος
ὁλοτελεῖς	A--AM-P	ὁλοτελής

ὁλοτελής, ές a strengthened form of ὅλος (*whole, entire*), of something complete in all respects *through and through, wholly, altogether* (1TH 5.23)

ὅλου	A--GM-S	ὅλος
	A--GN-S	"
ὅλους	A--AM-P	"
Ὀλυμπᾶν	N-AM-S	Ὀλυμπᾶς

Ὀλυμπᾶς, ᾶ, ὁ *Olympas*, masculine proper noun (RO 16.15)

Ὀλυμπίδα   N-AM-S   see Ὀλυμπᾶν
ὄλυνθος, ου, ὁ   late or summer fig, unripe (late) fig (RV 6.13)
ὀλύνθους   N-AM-P   ὄλυνθος
ὄλῳ   A--DM-S   ὅλος
    A--DN-S   "
ὅλως   adverb; altogether, generally speaking; of a report actually, as a fact (1C 5.1); with a negative not at all (MT 5.34)
ὅλως   AB   ὅλως
ὄμβρος, ου, ὁ   heavy rain, thunderstorm, rainstorm (LU 12.54)
ὄμβρος   N-NM-S   ὄμβρος
ὀμείρομαι   as experiencing a strong feeling intensified by an inner attachment long for, have strong affection for, love very much (1TH 2.8)
ὀμειρόμενοι   VPPDNM-P   ὀμείρομαι
    VPPONM-P   "
ὁμιλεῖν   VNPA   ὁμιλέω
ὁμιλέω   impf. ὡμίλουν; 1aor. ὡμίλησα; converse or talk with, speak with
ὁμιλήσας   VPAANM-S   ὁμιλέω
ὁμιλία, ας, ἡ   of people intermingling in mutual relation association, companionship, company (1C 15.33)
ὁμιλίαι   N-NF-P   ὁμιλία
ὅμιλος, ου, ὁ   as people intermingling crowd, throng, multitude (RV 18.17)
ὅμιλος   N-NM-S   ὅμιλος
ὁμίχλαι   N-NF-P   ὁμίχλη
ὁμίχλη, ης, ἡ   cloudlike moisture close to the ground mist, fog (2P 2.17)
ὁμίχλη   N-NF-S   ὁμίχλη
ὄμμα, ατος, τό   as an organ of the body eye
ὄμματα   N-AN-P   ὄμμα
ὀμμάτων   N-GN-P   "
ὀμνύει   VIPA--3S   ὀμνύω
ὀμνύειν   VNPA   "
ὀμνύετε   VMPA--2P   "
ὀμνύναι   VNPA   "
ὀμνύουσι(ν)   VIPA--3P   "
ὀμνύω and ὄμνυμι   inf. ὀμνύναι (MK 14.71); 1aor. ὤμοσα; from a basic meaning grasp a sacred object; thus, swear, affirm, confirm by oath, with the accusative of person or object by which the oath is taken
ὁμοθυμαδόν   adverb; of action agreed on unanimously with one mind, with one purpose, by common consent
ὁμοθυμαδόν   AB   ὁμοθυμαδόν
ὅμοια   A--AN-P   ὅμοιος
    A--NN-P   "
ὁμοία   A--NF-S   "
ὁμοιάζει   VIPA-3S   ὁμοιάζω
ὁμοιάζετε   VIPA--2P   "
ὁμοιάζω   be like, resemble (MT 26.73; MK 14.70)
ὅμοιαι   A--NF-P   ὅμοιος
ὁμοίας   A-AF-P   "
ὅμοιοι   A--NM-P   "
ὁμοίοις   A--DM-P   "
ὅμοιον   A--AM-S   "
    A--AN-S   "
    A--NN-S   "
ὁμοιοπαθεῖς   A--NM-P   ὁμοιοπαθής

ὁμοιοπαθής, ές   (1) of the same (human) nature, similar in experience, as opposed to having superhuman nature (AC 14.15); (2) with the same feelings, experiencing similar sufferings, as opposed to having supernatural power and exemption from suffering (JA 5.17)
ὁμοιοπαθής   A--NM-S   ὁμοιοπαθής
ὅμοιος, οία, ον   as introducing similarity, usually with the dative following; (1) of the same nature or kind as, like to, resembling (AC 17.29); neuter as a substantive τὰ ὅμοια τούτοις things like these (GA 5.21); (2) of equal value, just as great (MT 22.39); (3) of equal power, as powerful as (RV 13.4)
ὅμοιος   A--NM-S   ὅμοιος
ὁμοιότης, ητος, ἡ   similarity, likeness; καθ᾽ ὁμοιότητα in the same way (HE 4.15)
ὁμοιότητα   N-AF-S   ὁμοιότης
ὁμοιόω   fut. ὁμοιώσω; 1aor. pass. ὡμοιώθην; (1) make like; passive become like, be like someone or something (AC 14.11; HE 2.17); (2) as portraying one thing or situation for purposes of comparison to another compare, liken (MT 11.16); passive be compared or likened to (MT 13.24)
ὁμοίῳ   A--DN-S   ὅμοιος
ὁμοιωθέντες   VPAPNM-P   ὁμοιόω
ὁμοιωθῆναι   VNAP   "
ὁμοιωθήσεται   VIFP--3S   "
ὁμοιωθῆτε   VSAP--2P   "
ὁμοίωμα, ατος, τό   as a result of making one thing like another; (1) abstractly what is made similar, likeness (RO 6.5); (2) concretely similarity, likeness, copy (RO 1.23); (3) as outward resemblance form, appearance (RV 9.7)
ὁμοίωμα   N-AN-S   ὁμοίωμα
    N-NN-S   "
ὁμοιώματα   N-NN-P   "
ὁμοιώματι   N-DN-S   "
ὁμοίως   adverb; likewise, similarly, in the same way
ὁμοίως   AB   ὁμοίως
ὁμοίωσιν   N-AF-S   ὁμοίωσις
ὁμοίωσις, εως, ἡ   as an action making similar or like; in the NT, as a state of similarity likeness, resemblance (JA 3.9)
ὁμοιώσω   VIFA--1S   ὁμοιόω
ὁμοιώσωμεν   VSAA--1P   "
ὁμολογεῖ   VIPA--3S   ὁμολογέω
ὁμολογεῖται   VIPP--3S   "
ὁμολογέω   impf. ὡμολόγουν; fut. ὁμολογήσω; 1aor. ὡμολόγησα; from a basic meaning say the same thing; (1) as binding a speaker to his word (solemnly) promise, assure (MT 14.7); (2) as confessing that something is true admit, agree (HE 11.13), opposite ἀρνέομαι (deny); of an acknowledgment of sins confess (1J 1.9); (3) in judicial matters make a binding statement, confess, bear witness (AC 24.14); as making a public acknowledgment of allegiance confess, declare, acknowledge (JN 9.22); (4) in a religious and moral sense, as making a public statement of what one believes profess, confess, acknowledge (RO 10.9, 10); (5) as acknowledging what is due to God praise (HE 13.15)
ὁμολογῇ   VSPA--3S   ὁμολογέω
ὁμολογήσαντες   VPAANM-P   "

ὁμολογήσει	VIFA--3S	"
ὁμολογήσῃ	VSAA--3S	"
ὁμολογήσῃς	VSAA--2S	"
ὁμολογήσω	VIFA--1S	"

ὁμολογία, ας, ἡ from a basic meaning *speaking in agreement with* a proposition or person; *confession*; (1) objectively, a statement of allegiance expressing binding assent and public commitment *profession, acknowledgment, confession* (HE 4.14); (2) subjectively, an inner commitment of loyalty to such a statement of allegiance that leads to a public expression *confessing, bearing witness* (2C 9.13)

ὁμολογίαν	N-AF-S	ὁμολογία
ὁμολογίας	N-GF-S	"
ὁμολογοῦμεν	VIPA--1P	ὁμολογέω

ὁμολογουμένως adverb; *with common consent, in the judgment of all, without controversy* (1T 3.16)

ὁμολογουμένως	AB	ὁμολογουμένως
ὁμολογοῦντες	VPPANM-P	ὁμολογέω
ὁμολογούντων	VPPAGM-P	"
ὁμολογοῦσι(ν)	VIPA--3P	"
ὁμολογῶ	VIPA--1S	"
ὁμολογῶμεν	VSPA--1P	"
ὁμολογῶν	VPPANM-S	"
ὁμόσαι	VNAA	ὀμνύω
ὁμόσας	VPAANM-S	"

ὁμόσε adverb; *to or in one and the same place, together* (AC 20.18)

ὁμόσε	AB	ὁμόσε
ὁμόσῃ	VSAA--3S	ὀμνύω
ὁμόσῃς	VSAA--2S	"
ὁμότεχνον	A--AM-S	ὁμότεχνος

ὁμότεχνος, ον *practicing the same trade* or *craft, of the same occupation* (AC 18.3)

ὁμοῦ adverb; *together*; (1) geographically *in the same place, together* (AC 2.1); (2) temporally *at the same time, together* (JN 4.36)

ὁμοῦ	AB	ὁμοῦ
ὁμόφρονες	A--NM-P	ὁμόφρων

ὁμόφρων, ον *of one mind, like-minded, united with others in the way one thinks* (1P 3.8)

ὅμως adverb; (1) as an adversative *nevertheless, yet, all the same* (JN 12.42); (2) in Pauline writings as a comparative *likewise, in the same way, also* (1C 14.7; GA 3.15)

ὅμως	AB	ὅμως
ὄν	VPPANN-S	εἰμί
ὅν	APRAM-S	ὅς
ὀναίμην	VOAM--1S	ὀνίνημι

ὄναρ, τό indeclinable; as a form of divine communication *dream*; κατ᾽ ὄ. *in a dream*; in the NT only in Matthew and replaced by ὅραμα (*vision*) after Pentecost

ὀνάριον, ου, τό diminutive of ὄνος; *(little) donkey, foal, donkey's colt* (JN 12.14)

ὀνάριον	N-AN-S	ὀνάριον
ὀνειδίζειν	VNPA	ὀνειδίζω
ὀνειδίζεσθε	VIPP--2P	"
ὀνειδιζόμεθα	VIPP--1P	"
ὀνειδιζόμενοι	VPPPNM-P	"
ὀνειδίζοντος	VPPAGM-S	"
ὀνειδιζόντων	VPPAGM-P	"

ὀνειδίζω impf. ὠνείδιζον; 1aor. ὠνείδισα; (1) as unjustifiably bringing reproach on someone *revile, disparage, insult* (MT 5.11); passive *suffer reproach* (1T 4.10); (2) as justifiably laying a charge on someone *scold, reproach, reprimand* (MT 11.20)

ὀνειδισμοί	N-NM-P	ὀνειδισμός
ὀνειδισμοῖς	N-DM-P	"
ὀνειδισμόν	N-AM-S	"

ὀνειδισμός, οῦ, ὁ (1) as unjustifiable verbal abuse inflicted by others *insult, reproach, reviling* (RO 15.3); (2) as justifiable reproach brought on oneself *disgrace* (1T 3.7)

ὀνειδίσωσι(ν)	VSAA--3P	ὀνειδίζω

ὄνειδος, ους, τό *disgrace, reproach* (LU 1.25)

ὄνειδος	N-AN-S	ὄνειδος
Ὀνήσιμον	N-AM-S	Ὀνήσιμος

Ὀνήσιμος, ου, ὁ *Onesimus*, masculine proper noun; the meaning of the name, *useful*, is significant to Paul's use of it in PM 10–11

Ὀνησίμῳ	N-DM-S	Ὀνήσιμος

Ὀνησίφορος, ου, ὁ *Onesiphorus*, masculine proper noun

Ὀνησιφόρου	N-GM-S	Ὀνησίφορος

ὀνικός, ή, όν *pertaining to a donkey*; in the NT in the combination μύλος ὀ., of an upper millstone so large it can be turned only by donkey power; hence *large (upper) millstone*

ὀνικός	A--NM-S	ὀνικός

ὀνίνημι 2aor. mid. optative ὀναίμην; *enjoy favor, receive profit* or *pleasure*; as a formula *may I be favored by someone, may I have (some) benefit from someone* (PM 20)

ὄνομα, ατος, τό with a basic meaning *name*, i.e. the result of distinguishing a person or thing by giving a designation; (1) used of a proper noun by which one is called (MT 1.21); (2) in the sense of repute or fame ἔχειν ὄ. *have a name* or *reputation* (RV 3.1); (3) plural, as designating indefiniteness *persons* or *people* who make up a group (AC 1.15); (4) as indicating rank or authority attributed to a representative *(in the) name (of)*; especially of authorization to represent God or Christ in praying, speaking, working miracles, etc. (LU 10.17; JN 14.14; JA 5.10); (5) as a designation for God or Jesus Christ as he is revealed through all his attributes, majesty, and perfections *(the) Name* (MT 6.9; HE 1.4; 3J 7); (6) predominately in reference to God or Christ in prepositional phrases; (a) διὰ τοῦ ὀνόματος *through the name, by the power of the name* (AC 10.43); (b) εἰς τὸ ὄ. *in regard to, in reference to, for the sake of the name* (MT 18.20); with πιστεύω to express saving faith *on, in the name* (JN 1.12); (c) ἐν (τῷ) ὀνόματι used to claim authority for something *in the name of, at the mention of the name of* (AC 4.7); in invocation of God's presence *(calling) on the name of* (1C 5.4); in approaching, worshiping, thanking God because of Christ's atoning work *in the name of* (EP 5.20); (d) with ἕνεκα and ἕνεκεν *for the sake of, because of the name* (MT 19.29); (e) ἐπὶ τῷ ὀνόματι used to claim association or representation *in the name of, with (the use of) the name of* (MT 24.5); (f) πρὸς τὸ ὄ. *against* or *contrary to the name of* (AC 26.9); (g) ὑπὲρ τοῦ ὀνόματος *in honor of* or *in behalf of the name* (AC 5.41)

ὄνομα	N-AN-S	ὄνομα
	N-NN-S	"
ὀνομάζειν	VNPA	ὀνομάζω
ὀνομαζέσθω	VMPP--3S	"
ὀνομάζεται	VIPP--3S	"
ὀνομαζόμενος	VPPPNM-S	"
ὀνομαζομένου	VPPPGN-S	"

ὀνομάζω 1aor. ὠνόμασα; 1aor. pass. ὠνομάσθην; *name, designate*; (1) as furnishing with a name *give a name, call, entitle, designate as* (MK 3.14); (2) as making use of a name because of the significance attached to it *mention, pronounce a name* (AC 19.13); passive *be named, be recognized, be known* (RO 15.20)

ὀνομάζων	VPPANM-S	ὀνομάζω
ὀνόματα	N-AN-P	ὄνομα
	N-NN-P	"
ὀνόματι	N-DN-S	"
ὀνόματος	N-GN-S	"
ὀνομάτων	N-GN-P	"
ὄνον	N-AF-S	ὄνος
	N-AM-S	"

ὄνος, ου, ὁ and ἡ *donkey*, male or female, a domesticated animal for burden-bearing or riding

ὄνος	N-NF-S	ὄνος
ὄνου	N-GF-S	"
ὄνπερ	APRAM-S	ὅσπερ
ὄντα	VPPAAM-S	εἰμί
	VPPAAN-P	"
	VPPANN-P	"
ὄντας	VPPAAM-P	"
ὄντες	VPPANM-P	"
ὄντι	VPPADM-S	"
ὄντος	VPPAGM-S	"
	VPPAGN-S	"
ὄντων	VPPAGM-P	"
	VPPAGN-P	"

ὄντως an adverb from the present participle of εἰμί (*be*); (1) of what is conformable to fact *truly, really, in reality* (MK 11.32); (2) with a noun, to attribute genuineness *real, true, indeed* (1T 5.3)

ὄντως	AB	ὄντως
ὀξεῖα	A--NF-S	ὀξύς
ὀξεῖαν	A--AF-S	"
ὀξεῖς	A--NM-P	"

ὄξος, ους, τό related to ὀξύς (*sharp*); *sour wine, wine vinegar*, a popular and inexpensive thirst-quenching drink

ὄξος	N-AN-S	ὄξος
ὄξους	N-GN-S	"
ὀξύ	A--AN-S	ὀξύς

ὀξύς, εῖα, ύ (1) of things *sharp* (RV 1.16); (2) of time *swift, hasty, quick* (RO 3.15)

ὀπαῖς	N-DF-P	ὀπή
ὅπερ	APRNN-S	ὅσπερ

ὀπή, ῆς, ἡ *opening, hole*; (1) as a place in the ground from which a spring of water flows *opening* (JA 3.11); (2) as a cleavage along rocky cliffs *cleft, crack, fissure* (HE 11.38)

ὀπῆς	N-GF-S	ὀπή

ὄπισθεν adverb; (1) of place *from behind* (MT 9.20); *behind, on the back* (RV 5.1), opposite ἔμπροσθεν (*in front, ahead*); (2) as an improper preposition with the genitive *behind, after* (MT 15.23)

ὄπισθεν	AB	ὄπισθεν
	PG	"

ὀπίσω adverb; (1) of place, with a verb of motion *behind, back* (MT 24.18); neuter as a substantive τὰ ὀ. *what is behind* (PH 3.13); idiomatically ἀπέρχεσθαι εἰς τὰ ὀ. literally *go back to what lies behind*, i.e. *no longer follow* (JN 6.66); (2) as an improper preposition with the genitive; (a) of place *behind* (MT 16.23); (b) of following in close relation *after* (MT 4.19); idiomatically ἀπέρχεσθαι ὀ. σαρκὸς ἑτέρας literally *go after strange flesh*, i.e. *practice homosexuality* (JU 7); (c) of time *after* (MT 3.11)

ὀπίσω	AB	ὀπίσω
	PG	"
ὅπλα	N-AN-P	ὅπλον
	N-NN-P	"

ὁπλίζω 1aor. mid. ὡπλισάμην; from a basic meaning *prepare, equip, arm*; only middle in the NT *arm* or *equip oneself with* something; figuratively *prepare, get ready* (1P 4.1)

ὁπλίσασθε	VMAM--2P	ὁπλίζω

ὅπλον, ου, τό (1) literally, any *tool* or *instrument* (probably figuratively in RO 6.13); (2) *weapon*; plural *arms, weapons* (JN 18.3); figuratively, as what is needed for successful Christian living, viewed as a spiritual warfare against evil *means to win out* (2C 10.4); possibly used in both negative and positive aspects of means for evil or good in RO 6.13

ὅπλων	N-GN-P	ὅπλον
ὁποίαν	A-TAF-S	ὁποῖος
ὁποῖοι	A-RNM-P	"
	A-TNM-P	"
ὁποῖον	A-RNN-S	"
	A-TNN-S	"

ὁποῖος, οία, ον correlative adjective of quality; (1) used as an indefinite relative pronoun *of whatever kind* (probably GA 2.6; possibly AC 26.29); (2) used as an indefinite interrogative pronoun *of what sort, what kind of, as* (JA 1.24; possibly AC 26.29 and GA 2.6)

ὁποῖος	A-RNM-S	ὁποῖος
	A-TNM-S	"

ὁπότε a subordinating conjunction indicating time, with reference to past events *when* (LU 6.3)

ὁπότε	CS	ὁπότε

ὅπου adverb of place; used as a subordinating conjunction for relative clauses; (1) literally, denoting place *where, to* or *in what* place (MT 6.21); as a conjunction for indefinite relative clauses ὅ. ἐάν or ὅ. ἄν *wherever, to* or *in whatever place* (MK 6.56); (2) figuratively, as a correlative introducing the more immediate circumstances or presuppositions, as e.g. in the proverb "where there's a will, there's a way," *where* (HE 9.16); as imparting a causal sense *whereas, insofar as, since* (1C 3.3)

ὅπου	ABR	ὅπου
	CS	"

ὀπτάνομαι a late present from ὤφθην, the first aorist passive of ὁράω (*see*); *be seen, appear* (AC 1.3)

ὀπτανόμενος	VPPDNM-S	ὀπτάνομαι
	VPPONM-S	"

ὀπτασία, ας, ἡ literally, as what appears to the mind by supernatural means *being seen*; in the NT of what God permits a human being to see of himself or angels *vision, appearance*

ὀπτασίᾳ	N-DF-S	ὀπτασία
ὀπτασίαν	N-AF-S	"
ὀπτασίας	N-AF-P	"

ὀπτός, ή, όν of food that has been prepared by fire or hot coals *roasted, baked, broiled*; of fish *broiled* (LU 24.42)

ὀπτοῦ	A--GM-S	ὀπτός

ὀπώρα, ας, ἡ as the season of ripening fruit, beginning with the rising of the star Sirius (Dog Star) in July; by metonymy, the *ripe fruit* itself; metaphorically *fruit*, i.e. *good things* (RV 18.14)

ὀπώρα	N-NF-S	ὀπώρα

ὅπως (1) as a relative adverb introducing indefiniteness means *how, in what way, by what means* (MT 22.15; LU 24.20); (2) as a conjunction; (a) with the subjunctive to indicate purpose, equivalent to ἵνα *so that* (MT 2.8); (b) with the subjunctive to connect object clauses after verbs of beseeching and asking *that* (MT 9.38)

ὅπως	ABR	ὅπως
	CC	"
	CH	"
	CS	"
ὅρα	VMPA--2S	ὁράω
ὁρᾷ	VIPA--3S	"

ὅραμα, ατος, τό (1) literally *what is seen, appearance, spectacle*; (2) in the NT a supernatural *vision*, given as a means of divine communication, to be distinguished from a dream (ὄναρ)

ὅραμα	N-AN-S	ὅραμα
	N-NN-S	"
ὁράματι	N-DN-S	"
ὁράματος	N-GN-S	"
ὁράσει	N-DF-S	ὅρασις
ὁράσεις	N-AF-P	"

ὅρασις, εως, ἡ (1) as an action *seeing, sight*; (2) in the NT of what is seen; (a) *appearance, sight*; ὁράσει *in appearance* (RV 4.3); (b) as a supernatural appearance *vision* (AC 2.17)

ὅρασις	N-NF-S	ὅρασις
ὁρατά	A--NN-P	ὁρατός
ὁρᾶτε	VIPA--2P	ὁράω
	VMPA--2P	"

ὁρατός, ή, όν a verbal adjective from ὁράω (*see*); *visible, what can be seen*; neuter as a substantive τὰ ὁρατά *visible things* (CO 1.16)

ὁράω impf. ἑώρων; fut. mid. ὄψομαι; 2aor. εἶδον; pf. ἑώρακα; 1aor. pass. ὤφθην; 1fut. pass. ὀφθήσομαι; see also εἶδον; (1) transitively; (a) of sense perception *see, perceive, catch sight of* (MT 24.30); *go to see, visit* (HE 13.23); (b) as seeing what is being communicated supernaturally *see* (LU 1.22); passive *become visible, appear* (AC 16.9); (c) in an experiential way as coming to knowledge *see, experience, know, witness* (JN 1.50); (d) of mental and spiritual perception *perceive, take note, recognize, find out* (AC 8.23); (2) intransitively; (a) *look*

at someone (JN 19.37); (b) predominately used in warnings and instructions *see to (it)* (MT 27.4); *take care (lest)* (MT 18.10); *look out for, watch out, be on guard (against)* (MT 16.6); elliptically ὅρα μή *don't do that!* (RV 19.10)

ὀργή, ῆς, ἡ as a vigorous upsurge of one's nature against someone or something *anger, wrath, indignation*; (1) as a human emotion *anger, wrath* (JA 1.20); (2) as the divine reaction against evil, bringing judgment and punishment both historically and in the future *wrath, indignation* (MT 3.7; RO 9.22); as a future culmination of judgment in an outpouring of the stored-up anger of God (ἡ) ἡμέρα (τῆς) ὀργῆς *(the) day of wrath* (RO 2.5; RV 6.17)

ὀργή	N-NF-S	ὀργή
ὀργῇ	N-DF-S	"
ὀργήν	N-AF-S	"
ὀργῆς	N-GF-S	"
ὀργίζεσθε	VMPD--2P	ὀργίζω
	VMPO--2P	"
ὀργιζόμενος	VPPDNM-S	"
	VPPONM-S	"

ὀργίζω 1aor. pass. ὠργίσθην; only passive in the NT, only of human and satanic anger *be* or *become angry, be* or *become furious, be* or *become enraged*

ὀργίλον	A--AM-S	ὀργίλος

ὀργίλος, η, ον *prone to anger, quick-tempered, wrathful* (TI 1.7)

ὀργισθείς	VPAONM-S	ὀργίζω

ὀργυιά, ᾶς, ἡ strictly, the distance measured by a man's arms outstretched *six feet, 1.85 meters*; as a nautical technical term *fathom*, a measure for gauging water depth

ὀργυιάς	N-AF-P	ὀργυιά
ὀρέγεται	VIPM--3S	ὀρέγω
ὀρεγόμενοι	VPPMNM-P	"
ὀρέγονται	VIPM--3P	"

ὀρέγω *stretch out*; only middle in the NT; literally *reach out for* something, *stretch oneself toward*; figuratively in the NT *strive for, aspire to, long for* (1T 3.1)

ὄρει	N-DN-S	ὄρος
ὀρεινῇ	AP-DF-S	ὀρεινός
ὀρεινήν	AP-AF-S	"

ὀρεινός, ή, όν *mountainous, hilly*; substantivally ἡ ὀρεινή *hill country, mountainous region*

ὀρέξει	N-DF-S	ὄρεξις

ὄρεξις, εως, ἡ literally *reaching out, striving* for something; figuratively, in an unfavorable sense *craving, lust, strong sexual desire* (RO 1.27)

ὄρεσι(ν)	N-DN-P	ὄρος
ὀρέων	N-GN-P	"
ὄρη	N-AN-P	"
	N-NN-P	"
ὀρθάς	A--AF-P	ὀρθός

ὀρθοποδέω literally *walk straight* or *upright*; figuratively, of man's conduct toward God or other persons *be straightforward, live uprightly, behave as one should* (GA 2.14)

ὀρθοποδοῦσι(ν)	VIPA--3P	ὀρθοποδέω

ὀρθός, ή, όν (1) of direction; literally *straight, in a straight line*; figuratively, of persevering on a correct course of life toward a goal *straight, right* (HE 12.13); (2) literally, of a standing position *upright, erect* (AC 14.10)

ὀρθός   A--NM-S   ὀρθός

ὀρθοτομέω   literally, as cutting a straight road through difficult terrain *make a straight path*; figuratively in the NT, with reference to correctly following and teaching God's message *hold to a straight course, teach accurately* (2T 2.15)

ὀρθοτομοῦντα   VPPAAM-S   ὀρθοτομέω
ὄρθριαι   A--NF-P   ὀρθρινός

ὀρθρίζω   impf. ὤρθριζον; *arise very early in the morning, be up with the dawn* (LU 21.38)

ὀρθριναί   A--NF-P   ὀρθρινός

ὀρθρινός, ή, όν (also **ὄρθριος**) *early in the morning, at daybreak* (LU 24.22)

ὄρθρον   N-AM-S   ὄρθρος

ὄρθρος, ου, ὁ   *dawn, early morning, daybreak*; ὄρθρου βαθέως literally *of depth of early morning*, i.e. *at the first streak of dawn, very early* (LU 24.1); ὄρθρου *early in the morning, at dawn* (JN 8.2); ὑπὸ τὸν ὄρθρον *about daybreak* (AC 5.21)

ὄρθρου   N-GM-S   ὄρθρος

ὀρθῶς   *correctly, rightly, in the right way*

ὀρθῶς   AB   ὀρθῶς
ὅρια   N-AN-P   ὅριον
ὁρίζει   VIPA--3S   ὁρίζω

ὁρίζω   1aor. ὥρισα; pf. pass. ὥρισμαι; 1aor. pass. ὡρίσθην; (1) as setting a boundary; (a) of time *fix, appoint* (HE 4.7); (b) of space *fix, determine* (AC 17.26); (2) of persons *appoint, designate* (AC 17.31); (3) as making a definite plan *appoint, decide, determine* (LU 22.22)

ὁρίοις   N-DN-P   ὅριον

ὅριον, ου, τό   *boundary*; plural in the NT, as a geographical area within boundaries *region, district, territory*

ὁρίσας   VPAANM-S   ὁρίζω
ὁρισθέντος   VPAPGM-S   "
ὁρίων   N-GN-P   ὅριον
ὁρκίζομεν   VIPA--1P   ὁρκίζω

ὁρκίζω   *cause to swear (an oath), put* someone *under oath, adjure*; the sense is not to be weakened to begging or imploring

ὁρκίζω   VIPA--1S   ὁρκίζω
ὅρκον   N-AM-S   ὅρκος

ὅρκος, ου, ὁ   as a formal and binding statement *oath*; by metonymy, what has been solemnly sworn *vow, oath*

ὅρκος   N-NM-S   ὅρκος
ὅρκου   N-GM-S   "
ὅρκους   N-AM-P   "
ὅρκῳ   N-DM-S   "

ὁρκωμοσία, ας, ἡ   *taking of an oath, swearing, confirmation by oath, oath*

ὁρκωμοσίας   N-GF-S   ὁρκωμοσία

ὁρμάω   1aor. ὥρμησα; of swift and violent forward motion uncontrolled by reason *rush* (AC 7.57); of a herd of animals in panic *rush headlong, stampede* (MT 8.32)

ὁρμή, ῆς, ἡ   (1) as swift and capricious mob action *rush, violent attempt, assault* (AC 14.5); (2) as a mental action *caprice, impulse* (JA 3.4)

ὁρμή   N-NF-S   ὁρμή

ὅρμημα, ατος, τό   as the result of a sudden and violent assault *violence, onrush, onset* (RV 18.21)

ὁρμήματι   N-DN-S   ὅρμημα
ὄρνεα   N-NN-P   ὄρνεον
ὀρνέοις   N-DN-P   "

ὄρνεον, ου, τό   *bird*

ὀρνέου   N-GN-S   ὄρνεον
ὄρνιξ   N-NF-S   ὄρνις

ὄρνις, ιθος, ὁ and ἡ (also **ὄρνιξ, ιχος**)   *bird, fowl*; in the NT a domesticated fowl *hen* (MT 23.37; LU 13.34)

ὄρνις   N-NF-S   ὄρνις

ὁροθεσία, ας, ἡ   strictly, as an action *placing boundaries*; by extension *fixed boundary, definite limit*; plural *boundaries* (AC 17.26)

ὁροθεσίαν   N-AF-S   ὁροθεσία
ὁροθεσίας   N-AF-P   "

ὄρος, ους, τό   (1) *mountain, hill* (MT 5.1); (2) *high country, mountain range* (MK 5.11); (3) plural τὰ ὄρη *mountains, hills, hilly* or *mountainous country* (MK 13.14)

ὄρος   N-AN-S   ὄρος
    N-NN-S   "

ὅρος, ου, ὁ   *boundary, limit*; (1) of space *boundary*; (2) of time *limit*; ὁ ὅ. τῶν ἐτῶν *the fixed number of years* (MK 16.14)

ὅρος   N-NM-S   ὅρος
ὄρους   N-GN-S   ὄρος

ὀρύσσω   1aor. ὤρυξα; as making a hole in the ground *dig, excavate*

ὀρφανός, ή, όν   literally, as being deprived of one's parents *orphaned*; substantivally in the NT *orphan* (JA 1.27); figuratively *abandoned, helpless, unprotected* (JN 14.18)

ὀρφανούς   AP-AM-P   ὀρφανός
ὀρφανῶν   AP-GM-P   "

ὀρχέομαι   1aor. ὠρχησάμην; *dance*

ὀρχησαμένης   VPADGF-S   ὀρχέομαι
ὁρῶ   VIPA--1S   ὁράω
ὁρῶμεν   VIPA--1P   "
ὁρῶν   VPPANM-S   "
ὁρῶντες   VPPANM-P   "
ὁρῶσαι   VPPANF-P   "

ὅς, ἥ, ὅ   (1) predominately as a relative pronoun agreeing with its antecedent in gender and number, its case determined by its use in its own clause, but occasionally attracted to the case of its antecedent, *who, which, that, what*, (MT 1.16); (2) as a demonstrative pronoun with the antecedent unexpressed ὅς *the one who* (MT 10.38); ὅ *that which, what* (MT 10.27); ὃς μὲν . . . ὃς δέ *the one . . . the other, one . . . another* (MT 22.5); in a series ὃ μὲν . . . ὃ δὲ . . . ὃ δέ *some . . . some (other) . . . some (other)* (MT 13.8); (3) used with prepositions to form conjunctions for subordinate clauses; (a) with ἀντί: ἀνθ᾽ ὧν *because* (LU 1.20), *therefore, for this reason* (LU 12.3); (b) with εἰς: εἰς ὅ *to this end, in view of this* (2TH 1.11); (c) with ἐν: ἐν ᾧ, ἐν οἷς *under which circumstance(s), in which (preceding) situation* (LU 12.1); (d) with ἐπί: ἐφ᾽ ᾧ *for the reason that, because* (RO 5.12); (e) οὗ χάριν *for the sake of which, that is why, therefore* (LU 7.47); (f) in time notations: ἀφ᾽ ἧς *from the time when, since* (LU 7.45), ἄχρι(ς) οὗ *until (the time when)* (AC 7.18), etc.; (4) οὗ (q.v.) as an adverb of place *where*

ὅς   APRNM-S   ὅς
    A-RNM-S   "

ὅσα	APRAN-P	ὅσος	
	APRNN-P	"	
ὅσαι	APRNF-P	"	

ὁσάκις relative adverb; *as often as*; with ἐάν *whenever*

ὁσάκις	CS	ὁσάκις	
ὅσας	APRAF-P	ὅσος	
ὅσια	AP-AN-P	ὅσιος	
ὅσιον	A--AM-S	"	

ὅσιος, ία, ον generally, of what is sanctioned by the supreme law of God; (1) of persons who live right before God *holy, devout, dedicated* (TI 1.8); by synecdoche, of hands lifted in prayer *holy, pure* (1T 2.8); (2) of the inherent nature of God and Christ *holy* (HE 7.26); substantivally ὁ ὅ. *the Holy One* (AC 2.27); (3) of things *holy, divine*; neuter as a substantive τὰ ὅσια *holy decrees, divine promises* (AC 13.34)

ὅσιος	A--NM-S	ὅσιος	
	A--VM-S	"	

ὁσιότης, τητος, ἡ as a disposition that acts out of regard for the moral law of God *dedication, holiness*

ὁσιότητι	N-DF-S	ὁσιότης	
ὁσίους	A--AF-P	ὅσιος	

ὁσίως an adverb marked by a conscientious regard for divine law *in a way pleasing to God, in a holy manner* (1TH 2.10)

ὁσίως	AB	ὁσίως	

ὀσμή, ῆς, ἡ *odor, fragrance, smell*; in the NT of pleasant odor; (1) literally *aroma, fragrance* (JN 12.3); (2) figuratively; (a) from the Middle Eastern concept that an odor from something is communicating its power *sweet smell, fragrance* (2C 2.14–16); (b) as a term for acceptable sacrifice *aroma, fragrance* (EP 5.2)

ὀσμή	N-NF-S	ὀσμή	
ὀσμήν	N-AF-S	"	
ὀσμῆς	N-GF-S	"	
ὅσοι	APRNM-P	ὅσος	
ὅσον	APRAM-S	"	
	APRAN-S	"	
	APRNN-S	"	

ὅσος, η, ον a correlative adjective with πόσος (*how great?*) and τοσοῦτος (*so great, so much*); used substantivally with measurements of space, time, number, size, degree in the sense *in such an amount as*; (1) of space *as far as, how far, as great as* (RV 21.16); (2) of time *as long as, while* (RO 7.1); idiomatically μικρὸν ὅσον ὅσον literally *little, how much, how much*, i.e. *very soon, in just a little while* (HE 10.37); (3) of number and quantity *as much (or many) as, how much (or many)* (JN 1.12; 6.11); πάντες ὅσοι *all who* (LU 4.40); πάντα ὅσα *everything that* (MT 13.46); absolutely ὅσοι *all those who* (MT 14.36); ὅσα *everything that, all that, whatever* (MT 17.12); (4) of measure and degree *as much as* (MK 7.36); καθ᾽ ὅσον *to the degree that, by so much as* (HE 3.3)

ὅσους	APRAM-P	ὅσος	

ὅσπερ, ἥπερ, ὅπερ intensive relative pronoun *the very one or thing* (MK 15.6)

ὀστέα	N-AN-P	ὀστέον	

ὀστέον, ου and **ὀστοῦν, οῦ, τό** *bone*

ὀστέων	N-GN-P	ὀστέον	

ὅστις, ἥτις, ὅ τι a relative pronoun usually occurring in the nominative case; (1) as an indefinite relative referring to anyone or anything in general *whoever, whatever, everyone who, anything that* (MT 5.39); (2) qualitatively, to indicate that a definite person or thing belongs to a certain class *which very one, (such a) one who* (MT 2.6; 21.41); (3) in a causal sense, to emphasize a characteristic quality that confirms the statement in the main clause by giving the grounds for it *who indeed, which to be sure, the kind who* (MT 7.15; RO 6.2); (4) as taking the place of the simple relative pronoun ὅς, ἥ, ὅ, especially when giving an associated comment to clarify or explain something about the antecedent (MT 27.62; LU 2.4); (5) with prepositions in fixed expressions: ἕως ὅτου *until* (LU 13.8); *while* (MT 5.25); (6) neuter ὅ τι and ὅτι as a relative; (a) used definitely *what, that which* (JN 8.25; AC 9.6); (b) used interrogatively as an adverb to introduce a direct question *why, for what reason* (MK 9.28); (c) used as an adverb to identify or explain whom a preceding demonstrative refers to *that is, namely (that)* (JN 3.19; 1J 5.11)

ὅστις	APRNM-S	ὅστις	
ὀστοῦν	N-NN-S	ὀστέον	
ὀστράκινα	A--NN-P	ὀστράκινος	
ὀστρακίνοις	A--DN-P	"	

ὀστράκινος, η, ον *made of clay, earthen(ware)*; used metaphorically to emphasize that something is fragile or lowly

ὄσφρησις, εως, ἡ *sense of smell, smelling* (1C 12.17)

ὄσφρησις	N-NF-S	ὄσφρησις	
ὀσφύας	N-AF-P	ὀσφῦς	
ὀσφύες	N-NF-P	"	
ὀσφύι	N-DF-S	"	
ὀσφύν	N-AF-S	"	
ὀσφύος	N-GF-S	"	

ὀσφῦς, ύος, ἡ (1) as the part of the body over which a belt of skin or cloth is worn *waist, loins* (MK 1.6); idiomatically περιζώννυναι τὴν ὀσφύν literally *tighten the belt around the waist*, i.e. *get ready, prepare oneself*; metaphorically, of readiness for spiritual activity (LU 12.35; EP 6.14); (2) Hebraistically *genitals, reproductive organs*; idiomatically ἐξέρχεσθαι ἐκ τῆς ὀσφύος literally *come out from the genitals*, i.e. *be a descendant* (HE 7.5)

ὀσφῦς	N-NF-S	ὀσφῦς	
ὅσῳ	APRDN-S	ὅσος	
ὅσων	APRGN-P	"	

ὅταν a temporal conjunction used to show indefinite time for repeated or contingent action *whenever, at the time that, when*; (1) with the present subjunctive to indicate action contemporaneous with the main clause *whenever, as long as, every time that* (MT 6.2); (2) with the aorist subjunctive to indicate action preceding the main clause *when* (MT 5.11); (3) with the indicative to indicate definite repeated action *whenever, at the time when* (RV 8.1)

ὅταν	ABR	ὅταν	
	CS	"	

ὅτε temporal adverb; (1) used as a conjunction *when, while, as long as* (MT 7.28); (2) used as a substitute for a relative pronoun after a noun denoting time *when, in which (time)* (MK 14.12)

ὅτε	ABR	ὅτε
	CS	"

ὅτερος A--NM-S see ἕτερος

ὅτι conjunction; (1) *that*; (a) used declaratively after speech verbs to turn a direct assertion into an indirect assertion (AC 20.26); (b) used after verbs of perception to introduce what is perceived (JN 4.19); (c) used after verbs of thinking, judging, believing to introduce the content of the thought processes (JN 11.13); (d) used after verbs denoting emotion such as fear, joy, amazement to introduce the cause of the emotion (LU 11.38); (2) *(that)*; to introduce direct discourse, untranslated but represented in written English conversation by quotation marks (MT 9.18); (3) *because, since, for (this reason)*, used to introduce a cause or reason based on an evident fact (JN 20.29)

ὅτι	ABR	ὅτι
	ABT	"
	APRAN-S	ὅστις
	CC	ὅτι
	CH	"
	CS	"

ὅτου	APRGM-S	ὅστις

οὐ οὐκ before a vowel, οὐχ before a rough-breathing vowel; an adverb negating an alleged fact, used predominately in the NT with the indicative mood *no, not* (MT 4.4); (1) with an accent οὔ as the negative answer *no* (JN 1.21); (2) in litotes, using a negative to emphasize a positive *not . . . (but)* (JN 1.13); (3) contrary to the general rule, occasionally with a participle; (a) to negate a single concept (HE 11.1); (b) to denote strong emphasis or contrast (HE 11.35); (c) in quotations from the Septuagint (GA 4.27); (4) used to negate the declarative future, forming a prohibition (MT 19.18); (5) used in direct questions to indicate that an affirmative answer is expected (MT 6.26); (6) in combination with other negatives, such as οὐ μή (MT 5.18), οὐκ οὐδέν (JN 6.63), to produce a strong negative or prohibition *never, not at all, by no means, certainly not*

οὐ	QN	οὐ
	QT	"
οὐ	QS	"

οὗ relative adverb (genitive of the relative pronoun ὅς) *where*; (1) with verbs of rest indicating locality *where, place in which* (MT 2.9); figuratively, to denote a situation in which something exists *where* (RO 4.15); (2) with verbs of motion *where, to which, whither* (LU 10.1)

οὗ	ABR	οὗ
	APRGM-S	ὅς
	APRGN-S	"
	CS	οὗ

οὐά particle of interjection expressing derisive amazement or scornful ridicule *aha! bah!* especially evoked by the overthrow of a boastful adversary (MK 15.29)

οὐά	QS	οὐά

οὐαί particle of interjection; (1) expressing extreme displeasure and calling for retributive pain on someone or something *woe! alas!* (MT 11.21); doubled or tripled for emphasis (RV 8.13; 18.10); (2) substantivally ἡ οὐ. indeclinable; *woe, disaster, calamity* (RV 9.12)

οὐαί	QS	οὐαί
οὐδ'	AB	οὐδέ
	CC	"
	CC+	"
	QT	"

οὐδαμῶς an adverb marking strongly emphatic negation *by no means, in no way, certainly not* (MT 2.6)

οὐδαμῶς	AB	οὐδαμῶς

οὐδέ negative conjunction; (1) used as a correlative to join negative sentences or clauses *and not, nor* (MT 6.20); (2) used to reinforce a negative alternative *also not, not either, neither* (MT 6.15); (3) used as an ascensive adverb *not even* (MT 6.29)

οὐδέ	AB	οὐδέ
	CC	"
	CC+	"
	QT	"

οὐδείς (also οὐθείς), οὐδεμία, οὐδέν (also οὐθέν) used for negating a referent; (1) as an adjective, used to negate a noun *no, not even one* (LU 4.24); (2) as a substantive; (a) οὐδείς and οὐδεμία *no one, nobody, none* (MT 6.24); οὐδέν *nothing* (MT 5.13); (b) to refer to invalid concepts *worthless, of no account, meaningless* (MT 23.16); (c) οὐδέν as an accusative of respect *in no way, in nothing at all* (GA 4.1)

οὐδείς	APCNM-S	οὐδείς
	A-CNM-S	"
οὐδεμία	A-CNF-S	"
οὐδεμίαν	APCAF-S	"
	A-CAF-S	"
οὐδέν	APCAN-S	"
	APCNN-S	"
	A-CAN-S	"
	A-CNN-S	"
οὐδένα	APCAM-S	"
οὐδενί	APCDM-S	"
	APCDN-S	"
	A-CDM-S	"
οὐδενός	APCGM-S	"
	APCGN-S	"
	A-CGM-S	"

οὐδέποτε an adverb negating a point of time *never, not at any time*

οὐδέποτε	AB	οὐδέποτε

οὐδέπω an adverb negating an extension of time *not yet, never yet* (JN 20.9); οὐ. οὐδείς *no one ever* (JN 19.41)

οὐδέπω	AB	οὐδέπω
οὐθείς	APCNM-S	οὐδείς
οὐθέν	APCAN-S	"
	A-CAN-S	"
οὐθενός	APCGM-S	"
	APCGN-S	"
οὐκ	QN	οὐ
	QT	"

οὐκέτι adverb; (1) literally, negating an extension of time beyond a certain point *no longer, no further, no more* (MK 12.34); (2) logically, to mark logical progression *then not, accordingly not* (RO 11.6a)

οὐκέτι	AB	οὐκέτι

οὔκουν   from the negative adverb οὐ (*not*) and the conjunction οὖν (*therefore*), *certainly not* (JN 18.37)

οὔκουν	AB	οὔκουν

οὔκοῦν   from the negative adverb οὐ (*not*) and the conjunction οὖν (*therefore*); (1) inferentially *not there, so not*; (2) interrogatively, when the question has inferential force for an emphatic affirmative response *so then? not therefore?* (JN 18.37)

οὔκοῦν	QN&CH	οὔκοῦν
	QT&CH	"

Οὐλαμμαούς   Ἐμμαούς

οὖν   conjunction; (1) inferentially, to introduce a logical result or inference from what precedes *therefore, so, consequently*; in this use it accompanies a finite verb in the main clause; (a) in declarative sentences (MT 7.24); (b) in commands (MT 5.48); (c) in real questions (MT 13.28); (d) in rhetorical questions (MT 12.12); (2) in historical narrative; (a) to resume the main narrative after background information has been given through an interruption *so, to go on, as I was saying* (predominately in John's Gospel, e.g. JN 4.6; 11.3); (b) to make a transition to a new thought or new phase of a narrative or discourse *now, then* (JN 3.25; AC 1.18; HE 7.11); (c) to indicate a response *in reply, in response, in turn* (JN 4.9; 6.53); (3) as an emphatic or intensive particle *surely, by all means, indeed, really, above all* (LU 14.34; JN 20.30; RV 3.3b); (4) as an adversative rendering a statement slightly adversative *however, but* (AC 26.22; 1C 11.20; JN 8.38); for a thorough treatment of οὖν see Dana and Mantey, *Manual Grammar of the Greek New Testament*, pages 252–58

οὖν	CC	οὖν
	CH	"
	QS	"

οὔπω   an adverb negating an extension of time beyond a certain point *not yet, still not* (MT 24.6); οὐδεὶς οὔ. *no one ever* (MK 11.2)

οὔπω	AB	οὔπω
	QT	"

οὐρά, ᾶς, ἡ   *tail*

οὐρά	N-NF-S	οὐρά
οὐραί	N-NF-P	"
οὐραῖς	N-DF-P	"
οὐρανέ	N-VM-S	οὐρανός
οὐρανίοις	A--DN-P	οὐράνιος

οὐράνιος, ον   of what dwells in heaven, comes from it, or appears in it *heavenly*; neuter as a substantive οὐράνια *heavenly things*

οὐράνιος	A--NM-S	οὐράνιος
οὐρανίου	A--GF-S	"
οὐρανίῳ	A--DF-S	"

οὐρανόθεν   adverb of place *from heaven, from the sky*

οὐρανόθεν	AB	οὐρανόθεν
οὐρανοί	N-NM-P	οὐρανός
	N-VM-P	"
οὐρανοῖς	N-DM-P	"
οὐρανόν	N-AM-S	"

οὐρανός, οῦ, ὁ   *heaven*, as a part of the universe (MT 5.18), opposite γῆ (*earth*); (1) as the atmosphere directly above the earth *sky, air, firmament* (MT 6.26; LU 17.24); (2) as the starry heaven *firmament, sky* (MT 24.29a); (3) as the dwelling place of God (MT 5.16), the angels (MT 22.30), and the righteous dead (2C 5.1, 2) *heaven*; (4) by metonymy, as synonymous with God or the inhabitants of heaven (LU 15.18; RV 12.12 [possibly personification]); (5) plural οἱ οὐρανοί *heaven, the heavens*, a Jewish concept, originally found in the Septuagint, that heaven is comprised of several spheres, with God dwelling in the highest heaven (2C 12.2; EP 1.10)

οὐρανός	N-NM-S	οὐρανός
οὐρανοῦ	N-GM-S	"
οὐρανούς	N-AM-P	"
οὐρανῷ	N-DM-S	"
οὐρανῶν	N-GM-P	"
οὐράς	N-AF-P	οὐρά
Οὐρβανόν	N-AM-S	Οὐρβανός

Οὐρβανός, οῦ, ὁ   *Urbanus*, masculine proper noun (RO 16.9)

Οὐρίας, ου, ὁ   *Uriah*, masculine proper noun (MT 1.6)

Οὐρίου	N-GM-S	Οὐρίας

οὖς, ὠτός, τό   literally, as the bodily organ of hearing *ear* (MK 7.33); idiomatically εἰς τὸ οὖς and πρὸς τὸ οὖς literally *into the ear*, i.e. *privately, in secret* (MT 10.27; LU 12.3); τιθέναι εἰς τὰ ὦτα literally *put into the ears*, i.e. *listen carefully, keep in mind* (LU 9.44); συνέχειν τὰ ὦτα literally *hold the ears closed*, i.e. *refuse to listen* or *pay attention* (AC 7.57); ἀπερίτμητος τοῖς ὠσίν literally *uncircumcised in ears*, i.e. *stubborn, unwilling to understand* (AC 7.51); τοῖς ὠσὶν βαρέως ἀκούειν literally *hear heavily with the ears*, i.e. *be slow to understand, be mentally dull* (MT 13.15); figuratively, in an extended sense of the activity of the ears *hearing* (LU 9.44)

οὖς	N-AN-S	οὖς
	N-NN-S	"
οὕς	APRAM-P	ὅς
οὖσα	VPPANF-S	εἰμί
οὖσαι	VPPANF-P	"
οὖσαν	VPPAAF-S	"
οὔσας	VPPAAF-P	"
οὔσῃ	VPPADF-S	"
οὔσης	VPPAGF-S	"

οὐσία, ας, ἡ   from εἰμί (*be*); what exists as one's own *property, goods, wealth*

οὐσίαν	N-AF-S	οὐσία
οὐσίας	N-GF-S	"
οὖσι(ν)	VPPADM-P	εἰμί
οὐσῶν	VPPAGF-P	"

οὔτε   adverb; (1) as a negative correlative equivalent to οὐδέ: *neither, and not*; predominately οὔ. . . . οὔ. *neither . . . nor* (MT 6.20); (2) used singly as an ascensive *not even* (JN 4.11)

οὔτε	CC	οὔτε
	CC+	"
οὗτοι	APDNM-P	οὗτος
	A-DNM-P	"

οὗτος, αὕτη, τοῦτο   the near demonstrative pronoun used to call attention to a designated person or object, often with special emphasis *this* (MT 3.17); (1) used as an adjective *this* (LU 2.25); (2) used as a substantive *this man, this woman, this thing, this one* (MT 12.23); (3) both adjectival and substantival forms may be used as a contemptuous sneer: οὑ. *this fellow* (MT 26.71); οὑ. ὁ τελώνης *this tax collector* (LU 18.11); (4) used resumptively to give special emphasis to a person or thing previously mentioned *the very one* (AC 7.36); plural *these very ones* (RO 9.8); (5) special uses of neuter τοῦτο *this*; (a) to refer to what preceded (LU 5.6); (b) plural ταῦτα may summarize what preceded (LU 8.8); (c) with prepositions the sense is derived from the preposition and the case of τοῦτο (e.g. διὰ τοῦτο *for this reason*); (d) cataphorically, to refer to what follows, introducing a statement, purpose, result, condition *this (is what I mean), this (namely)* (RO 6.6); (e) to indicate a correspondence τοῦτο μὲν . . . τοῦτο δέ *not only . . . but also, sometimes . . . sometimes* (HE 10.33)

οὗτος	APDNM-S	οὗτος
	A-DNM-S	"

οὕτω(ς) an adverb from the near demonstrative οὗτος *(this)*; *in this manner, in this way, thus, so*; (1) with reference to what preceded; (a) in combination with a correlative to produce a comparison *(just) as . . . so* (LU 11.30); (b) used absolutely to intensify what preceded *thus, so, in this way* (MT 11.26); (2) to refer to and introducing what follows *as follows, in this way* (MT 6.9); (3) before an adjective or adverb to denote degree of intensity *so* (RV 16.18)

οὕτω(ς)	AB	οὕτω(ς)
οὐχ	QN	οὐ
	QT	"

οὐχί strengthened form of the negative adverb οὐ *(not)*; (1) as a simple negative *not* (JN 13.11); (2) as an emphatic answer *no, by no means, not so* (LU 1.60); (3) predominately as an interrogative in questions expecting an affirmative answer *isn't it (so)?, is it not so?* (MT 5.46)

οὐχί	QN	οὐχί
	QS	"
	QT	"
ὀφειλάς	N-AF-P	ὀφειλή
ὀφείλει	VIPA--3S	ὀφείλω
ὀφείλεις	VIPA--2S	
ὀφειλέται	N-NM-P	ὀφειλέτης
ὀφειλέταις	N-DM-P	
ὀφείλετε	VIPA--2P	ὀφείλω
	VMPA--2P	"

ὀφειλέτης, ου, ὁ (1) literally *debtor*, one owing money or goods (MT 18.24); (2) figuratively; (a) of various obligations and duties *one who is obliged to, one who must* (RO 1.14); (b) of one who has committed a misdeed and owes it to the law to make it right *guilty person, offender, sinner* (MT 6.12)

ὀφειλέτης	N-NM-S	ὀφειλέτης

ὀφειλή, ῆς, ἡ *debt*; literally, a debt of goods or money (MT 18.32); figuratively *obligation, duty*; plural, of taxes *dues* (RO 13.7); as a euphemism for sexual intercourse that becomes a duty after a marriage vow *what should be done, conjugal duty* (1C 7.3)

ὀφείλημα, ατος, τό *debt*; (1) literally, what is owed *debt, sum owed*; in a broader sense of what is due *obligation* (RO 4.4); (2) morally, of guilt incurred *sin, offense* (MT 6.12; cf. τὰς ἁμαρτίας [*sins*] in LU 11.4)

ὀφείλημα	N-AN-S	ὀφείλημα
ὀφειλήματα	N-AN-P	"
ὀφειλήν	N-AF-S	ὀφειλή
ὀφείλητε	VSPA--2P	ὀφείλω
ὀφείλομεν	VIPA--1P	"
ὀφειλομένην	VPPPAF-S	"
ὀφειλόμενον	VPPPAN-S	"
ὀφείλοντες	VPPANM-P	"
ὀφείλοντι	VPPADM-S	"
ὀφείλουσι(ν)	VIPA--3P	"

ὀφείλω impf. ὤφειλον; *owe, be indebted (to)*; (1) literally, of financial indebtedness *owe something to someone* (PM 18); (2) figuratively; (a) of a sense of indebtedness to someone for something *ought, be under obligation* (RO 13.8); (b) predominately in the NT to express obligation, necessity, duty *be obligated*; with an infinitive following *must, ought to* (JN 13.14)

ὄφεις	N-AM-P	ὄφις
	N-NM-P	"
	N-VM-P	"

ὄφελον a fixed form, possibly the second aorist participle of ὀφείλω *(owe)*; used as a verbal particle to express an interjection concerning an unattainable wish *would that! if only!* (1C 4.8)

ὄφελον	QV	ὄφελον

ὄφελος, ους, τό *advantage, profit, benefit*

ὄφελος	N-NN-S	ὄφελος
ὄφεσι(ν)	N-DM-P	ὄφις
ὄφεων	N-GM-P	"
ὄφεως	N-GM-S	"
ὀφθαλμοδουλεία	N-DF-S	ὀφθαλμοδουλία
ὀφθαλμοδουλείαις	N-DF-P	"
ὀφθαλμοδουλείαν	N-AF-S	"

ὀφθαλμοδουλία, ας, ἡ (also ὀφθαλμοδουλεία) as service rendered without dedication or a sense of inner obligation but mainly to attract attention *eyeservice*

ὀφθαλμοδουλία	N-DF-S	ὀφθαλμοδουλία
ὀφθαλμοδουλίαις	N-DF-P	"
ὀφθαλμοδουλίαν	N-AF-S	"
ὀφθαλμοί	N-NM-P	ὀφθαλμός
ὀφθαλμοῖς	N-DM-P	"
ὀφθαλμόν	N-AM-S	"

ὀφθαλμός, οῦ, ὁ (1) literally, the bodily organ for seeing *eye* (MT 6.22); idiomatically ἐν ῥιπῇ ὀφθαλμοῦ literally *in a blink of an eye*, i.e. *suddenly* (1C 15.52); ἀνοίγειν τοὺς ὀφθαλμούς literally *open the eyes*, i.e. *cause to see, restore sight* (MT 9.30); ἐπαίρειν τοὺς ὀφθαλμούς literally *lift up the eyes*, i.e. *look, notice* (MT 17.8); ἦσαν αὐτῶν οἱ ὀφθαλμοὶ βεβαρημένοι literally *their eyes were weighed down*, i.e. *they were very sleepy* (MT 26.43); κατ' ὀφθαλμούς literally *according to eyes*, i.e. *in front of, in the presence of*; metaphorically *according to* someone's *understanding* (GA 3.1); (2) figuratively; (a) in an extended sense of the activity of the eyes *sight* (AC 1.9); (b) as the capacity to perceive and comprehend *understanding* (LU 19.42); idiomatically τυφλοῦν τοὺς ὀφθαλμούς literally *blind the eyes*, i.e. *cause to not understand* (JN 12.40); ὀ. πονηρός literally *evil eye*, i.e. *envy, greed*, perhaps *stinginess* (MT 20.15; MK 7.22)

ὀφθαλμός	N-NM-S	ὀφθαλμός
ὀφθαλμοῦ	N-GM-S	"
ὀφθαλμούς	N-AM-P	"

ὀφθαλμῷ	N-DM-S	"
ὀφθαλμῶν	N-GM-P	"
ὀφθείς	VPAPNM-S	ὁράω
ὀφθέντες	VPAPNM-P	"
ὀφθέντος	VPAPGM-S	"
ὀφθήσεται	VIFP--3S	"
ὀφθήσομαι	VIFP--1S	"
ὄφιν	N-AM-S	ὄφις

ὄφις, εως, ὁ *snake, serpent*; (1) literally (MT 10.16); used symbolically in JN 3.14 of a serpent figure made of brass and lifted up, referred to by Jesus from Numbers 21.6–9 as a symbol of the help God offers to people though Jesus' crucifixion; (2) metaphorically; (a) as a symbolic figure for the devil (2C 11.3); (b) as a depraved and hypocritical person *evil person* (MT 23.33)

ὄφις	N-NM-S	ὄφις
ὀφρύος	N-GF-S	ὀφρῦς

ὀφρῦς, ύος, ἡ literally *eyebrow*; figuratively, of any overhanging prominence on a hill, as a cliff *brow* (LU 4.29)

ὀχετόν	N-AM-S	ὀχετός

ὀχετός, οῦ, ὁ as any channel for water *canal, watercourse*; then *drain, sewer* for carrying off waste products (MK 7.19)

ὀχλέω *trouble, disturb*; passive, with unclean spirits as agents *be tormented* (AC 5.16)

ὄχλοι	N-NM-P	ὄχλος
ὄχλοις	N-DM-P	"
ὄχλον	N-AM-S	"

ὀχλοποιέω 1aor. ptc. ὀχλοποιήσας; *form a mob, create a tumult, start a riot* (AC 17.5)

ὀχλοποιήσαντες	VPAANM-P	ὀχλοποιέω

ὄχλος, ου, ὁ (1) *throng* of people milling around or closely pressed together, *crowd, multitude* (MT 5.1); (2) *(common) people*, in contrast to the authorities *populace, masses* (AC 24.12); used contemptuously of the lower classes *rabble* (JN 7.49); (3) *(specific) company* containing many people, *large number* (LU 6.17; AC 1.15); (4) plural *(hosts of) peoples*, along with other designations of the divisions of mankind, as λαοί (*peoples*), ἔθνη (*nations*), γλῶσσαι (*languages*) (RV 17.15)

ὄχλος	N-NM-S	ὄχλος
ὄχλου	N-GM-S	"
ὀχλούμενοι	VPPPNM-P	ὀχλέω
ὀχλουμένους	VPPPAM-P	"
ὄχλους	N-AM-P	ὄχλος
ὄχλῳ	N-DM-S	"
ὄχλων	N-GM-P	"
Ὀχοζίαν	N-AM-S	Ὀχοζίας

Ὀχοζίας, ου, ὁ *Ahaziah*, masculine proper noun (MT 1.8)

Ὀχοζίας	N-NM-S	Ὀχοζίας
ὀχυροί	A--NM-P	ὀχυρός

ὀχυρός, ά, όν *strong, firm*; substantively *bold persons* (LU 11.15)

ὀχύρωμα, ατος, τό literally, as a military technical term *fortified place, stronghold, bastion*; figuratively in the NT as a strong system of philosophy and reasoned arguments *false argument*, opposed to the true knowledge of God (2C 10.4)

ὀχυρωμάτων	N-GN-P	ὀχύρωμα
ὀψάρια	N-AN-P	ὀψάριον

ὀψάριον, ου, τό diminutive of ὄψον (*cooked food*); cooked food that is eaten with bread, *tidbit* of meat; especially *fish; fish sauce*

ὀψάριον	N-AN-S	ὀψάριον
ὀψαρίων	N-GN-P	"

ὀψέ adverb; *late, at a late hour*; (1) as a time beginning with the first watch of the night (from 6:00 P.M. to 9:00 P.M.) *evening* (MK 11.19); (2) as an improper preposition with the genitive *after*; ὀ. σαββάτων *at the close of, after the Sabbath* (MT 28.1)

ὀψέ	AB	ὀψέ
	PG	"
ὄψει	VIFA--2S	ὁράω
ὄψεσθε	VIFD--2P	"
	VIFD--2P^VMAA--2P	
ὄψεται	VIFD--3S	"
ὄψῃ	VIFD--2S	"
	VIFD--2S^VMAA--2S	"
ὄψησθε	VIFD--2P	see ὄψεσθε
	VSAD--2P	ὁράω
ὀψία	A--NF-S	ὄψιος
ὀψίας	AP-GF-S	"
	A--GF-S	"
ὄψιμον	AP-AM-S	ὄψιμος

ὄψιμος, ον *late in the season*; as a substantive ὁ ὄ. *the spring rain* needed to swell out the grain before harvest, *late rain*, opposite πρόϊμος (*early rain*); in the Middle East, the November-to-April rainy season is threefold, marked by early rain (at planting time), (heavy) winter rain, and late rain

ὄψιν	N-AF-S	ὄψις
ὀψινῆς	A--GF-S	ὄψιος

ὄψιος, ία, ον (also ὀψινός, ή, όν) (1) adjectivally, as a time of day, either before or just after sundown *late* (MK 11.11); (2) substantively ἡ ὀψία (ὥρα) *evening*; predominately in the phrase ὀψίας γενομένης *when evening came, when it was late* (MT 8.16)

ὄψις, εως, ἡ (1) as an action *seeing, sight*; (2) objectively in the NT; (a) *outward* or *external appearance* (JN 7.24); (b) *face, countenance* (JN 11.44)

ὄψις	N-NF-S	ὄψις
ὄψομαι	VIFD--1S	ὁράω
ὀψόμεθα	VIFD--1P	"
ὄψονται	VIFD--3P	"
ὀψώνια	N-NN-P	ὀψώνιον
ὀψωνίοις	N-DN-P	"

ὀψώνιον, ου, τό literally, as a military technical term for what is appointed to soldiers to buy food *ration (money), allowance, pay*; more generally *(subsistence) pay, wages, expense money* (LU 3.14; 1C 9.7); metaphorically, as pay for serving as a Christian soldier *money to live on* (2C 11.8); figuratively, of the compensation for serving sin *reward, end result* (RO 6.23)

ὀψώνιον	N-AN-S	ὀψώνιον

π Π

παγίδα	N-AF-S	παγίς
παγιδεύσωσι(ν)	VSAA--3P	παγιδεύω

παγιδεύω 1aor. ἐπαγίδευσα; as a hunting term *lay a snare, set a trap, entice into a trap*; figuratively in the NT *catch off guard, catch in a mistake, entrap* someone deliberately by provoking him to speak without forethought (MT 22.15)

παγίδος	N-GF-S	παγίς

παγίς, ίδος, ἡ (1) literally, anything that catches and holds fast *snare, trap, noose, net* (LU 21.35); (2) metaphorically; (a) used in RO 11.9 of a false sense of security that leads to a sudden and unexpected judgment *pitfall, concealed danger, source of error*; (b) as a stratagem of the devil for gaining control *deceitful trick, entanglement* (1T 3.7); (3) figuratively, as any allurement to wrongdoing *enticement, temptation, attraction* (1T 6.9)

παγίς	N-NF-S	παγίς
Πάγον	N-AM-S	Ἄρειος Πάγος
πάγον	N-AM-S	πάγος

πάγος, ου, ὁ *rocky hill*

Πάγου	N-GM-S	Ἄρειος Πάγος
πάγου	N-GM-S	πάγος
πάθει	N-DN-S	πάθος
παθεῖν	VNAA	πάσχω
πάθη	N-AN-P	πάθος
πάθη	VSAA--3S	πάσχω

πάθημα, ατος, τό (1) as what happens to a person and must be endured *suffering, misfortune* (HE 2.9); usually plural *sufferings* (HE 10.32); (2) as strong inward emotions, only plural *passions, impulses*; in the NT of uncontrolled sexual desires (RO 7.5)

πάθημα	N-AN-S	πάθημα
παθήμασι(ν)	N-DN-P	"
παθήματα	N-AN-P	"
	N-NN-P	"
παθημάτων	N-GN-P	"

παθητός, ή, όν a verbal adjective from πάσχω (*experience, suffer*); *subject to suffering*; in the case of Christ *destined to suffer* (AC 26.23)

παθητός	A--NM-S	παθητός
παθόντας	VPAAAM-P	πάσχω
παθόντος	VPAAGM-S	"

πάθος, ους, τό (1) as an experience *suffering, misfortune*; (2) as a strong emotion of desire or craving *passion*; in the NT only in a bad sense *uncontrolled sexual passion, lustful desire, evil craving* (CO 3.5)

πάθος	N-AN-S	πάθος
παθοῦσα	VPAANF-S	πάσχω
παθών	VPAANM-S	"
παῖδα	N-AM-S	παῖς
παιδαγωγόν	N-AM-S	παιδαγωγός

παιδαγωγός, οῦ, ὁ (1) literally *boy leader*, a trusted attendant who supervised the conduct and morals of a boy before he came of age *guardian, trainer, instructor*; (2) figuratively in the NT; (a) as a spiritual *instructor* (1C 4.15); (b) metaphorically, as the historical function of the Mosaic law under the old covenant *supervisor, guide, one in control* (GA 3.24, 25)

παιδαγωγός	N-NM-S	παιδαγωγός
παιδαγωγούς	N-AM-P	"
παιδαρίοις	N-DN-P	παιδάριον

παιδάριον, ου, τό diminutive of παῖς; *little boy* or *girl, lad* or *lass, child* (JN 6.9)

παιδάριον	N-NN-S	παιδάριον
παῖδας	N-AM-P	παῖς

παιδεία, ας, ἡ (1) active, of rearing and guiding a child toward maturity *training, instruction, discipline* (HE 12.11); as including Christian discipline and instruction (EP 6.4); as God's fatherly discipline of all believers *discipline, punishment, correction* (HE 12.5); (2) passive, of the result of such discipline *training, improved behavior* (HE 12.7)

παιδεία	N-NF-S	παιδεία
παιδείᾳ	N-DF-S	"
παιδείαν	N-AF-S	"
παιδείας	N-GF-S	"
παιδεύει	VIPA-3S	παιδεύω
παιδευθῶσι(ν)	VSAP--3P	"
παιδευόμεθα	VIPP--1P	"
παιδευόμενοι	VPPPNM-P	"
παιδευόμενος	VPPPNM-S	"
παιδεύοντα	VPPAAM-S	"
παιδεύουσα	VPPANF-S	"
παιδεύσας	VPAANM-S	"
παιδευτάς	N-AM-P	παιδευτής
παιδευτήν	N-AM-S	"

παιδευτής, οῦ, ὁ one who disciplines and corrects by punishment *instructor, trainer, corrector*

παιδεύω impf. ἐπαίδευον; 1aor. ἐπαίδευσα; pf. pass. πεπαίδευμαι; 1aor. pass. ἐπαιδεύθην; (1) as bringing up a child and guiding him toward maturity *instruct, train, educate* (AC 7.22); (2) as morally disciplining an adult *correct, give guidance to, discipline* (1T 1.20); (3) of flogging, as a form of legal punishment of a transgressor *punish, scourge, whip* (LU 23.16)

παιδεύω	VIPA--1S	παιδεύω
παιδία	N-AN-P	παιδίον
	N-NN-P	"
	N-VN-P	"

παιδιόθεν (also **παιδόθεν**) adverb; *from childhood* (MK 9.21)

παιδιόθεν	AB	παιδιόθεν
παιδίοις	N-DN-P	παιδίον

παιδίον, ου, τό diminutive of παῖς; (1) literally, of age; (a) as a newborn child *infant, babe* (HE 11.23); (b) as a small child *(young) child* (MT 2.8); (2) figuratively; (a) of undeveloped understanding *childish person* (1C 14.20); (b) spiritually, as God's children (HE 2.13); (c) plural, as an expression of fatherly affection (my) *little children*, (my) *dear children* (1J 2.14)

παιδίον	N-AN-S	παιδίον
	N-NN-S	"
	N-VN-S	"
παιδίου	N-GN-S	"
παιδίσκας	N-AF-P	παιδίσκη

παιδίσκη, ης, ἡ feminine diminutive of παῖς; in the NT a female servant *maid, servant girl, slave girl*

παιδίσκη	N-NF-S	παιδίσκη
παιδίσκην	N-AF-S	"
παιδίσκης	N-GF-S	"
παιδισκῶν	N-GF-P	"
παιδίων	N-GN-P	παιδίον
παιδόθεν	AB	παιδιόθεν
παιδός	N-GF-S	παῖς
	N-GM-S	"
παίδων	N-GM-P	"
παίζειν	VNPA	παίζω

παίζω as giving way to hilarity *play, amuse oneself*; as idolatrous worship *dance, carry on in boisterous revelry* (1C 10.7)

παῖς, παιδός, ὁ and ἡ *child*; (1) in reference to age *child*, either *boy* (MT 2.16) or *girl* (LU 8.51); (2) in reference to descent *son, daughter, child* (JN 4.51); (3) in reference to social position *servant, slave "boy"* (LU 7.7; cf. δοῦλος [*slave, servant*] in 7.2); as a servant in a ruler's household *attendant, courtier* (MT 14.2); (4) figuratively, in reference to relation to God *servant* (AC 4.25)

παῖς	N-NM-S	παῖς
	N-VF-S	"
παίσας	VPAANM-S	παίω
παίσῃ	VSAA--3S	"
παισί(ν)	N-DM-P	παῖς

παίω 1aor. ἔπαισα; *strike, hit, smite* (MT 26.68); of a scorpion's strike *sting* (RV 9.5)

πάλαι an adverb denoting time in the past in antithesis to the present; (1) as indicating the past in relation to the present *formerly* (2P 1.9); (2) as indicating past time generally *long ago, in time past* (MT 11.21; HE 1.1; possibly JU 4); (3) as covering a period of time, looking back from the present to a point of time; (a) *for a long time, all along, all this time* (2C 12.19; possibly JU 4); (b) denoting a short time *some time since, already* (MK 15.44)

πάλαι	AB	πάλαι
παλαιά	A--AN-P	παλαιός
	A--NF-S	"
παλαιᾷ	A--DF-S	"
παλαιάν	A--AF-S	"
παλαιᾶς	A--GF-S	"
παλαιόν	A--AM-S	"
	A--AN-S	"

παλαιός, ά, όν *old*; (1) literally; (a) opposite καινός (*new*); substantively (LU 5.39); (b) of what has existed for a long time, often with the idea of its being antiquated,

worn out, obsolete (MT 9.16); substantivally *old part* (MK 2.21); (c) of what has existed for a relatively long time *old*; neuter as a substantive παλαιά *old things, earlier teachings* (MT 13.52); (2) figuratively, of previous unregenerate behavior *former* (RO 6.6; 1C 5.7)

παλαιός	A--NM-S	παλαιός

παλαιότης, ητος, ἡ as a characteristic state *oldness, obsoleteness, old way* (RO 7.6)

παλαιότητι	N-DF-S	παλαιότης
παλαιοῦ	A--GN-S	παλαιός
παλαιούμενα	VPPPAN-P	παλαιόω
παλαιούμενον	VPPPNN-S	"
παλαιούς	A--AM-P	παλαιός

παλαιόω pf. πεπαλαίωκα; 1fut. pass. παλαιωθήσομαι; (1) active *make old, declare* or *treat as obsolete* (HE 8.13a); (2) passive *become old* (and therefore outmoded) (HE 8.13b); *wear out* (LU 12.33)

παλαιῷ	A--DN-S	παλαιός
παλαιωθήσονται	VIFP--3P	παλαιόω

πάλη, ης, ἡ literally *wrestling*, figuratively, of the believer's struggle against evil forces *conflict, struggle, fight* (EP 6.12)

πάλη	N-NF-S	πάλη

παλιγγενεσία, ας, ἡ from πάλιν (*again*) and γένεσις (*birth*); *regeneration*; (1) of the future as the restoration and renewal of the world *new age* (MT 19.28); (2) as spiritual and moral renewal of an individual *new birth, regeneration* (TI 3.5)

παλιγγενεσίᾳ	N-DF-S	παλιγγενεσία
παλιγγενεσίας	N-GF-S	"

πάλιν adverb; (1) with verbs of going, sending, turning, etc., denoting backward direction *back* (JN 11.7); (2) denoting a return to a previous state or activity *again* (JN 4.13); (3) denoting repetition *again, once more, anew* (MT 26.43, 44); (4) denoting continuation *furthermore, again*, often used in series of quotations or sayings introduced by a formula (MT 13.45; HE 1.5); (5) denoting a turn of thought *on the other hand, in turn, again* (1J 2.8)

πάλιν	AB	πάλιν

παμπληθεί (also πανπληθεί) adverb; of a large group acting in complete agreement *all together, one and all, all at once* (LU 23.18)

παμπληθεί	AB	παμπληθεί
παμπόλλου	A--GM-S	πάμπολυς

πάμπολυς, παμπόλλη, πάμπολυ of the size of a crowd *vast, very great* (MK 8.1)

Πάμφιλος, ου, ὁ *Pamphilius*, masculine proper noun, an elder in Caesarea (MK 16 shorter ending)

Παμφίλου	N-GM-S	Πάμφιλος
Παμφίρα	N-DF-S	see Σαπφίρη

Παμφυλία, ας, ἡ *Pamphylia*, a province along the Mediterranean coast in southern Asia Minor

Παμφυλίαν	N-AF-S	Παμφυλία
Παμφυλίας	N-GF-S	"
πᾶν	AP-AN-S	πᾶς
	AP-NN-S	"
	A--AN-S	"
	A--NN-S	"
πανδοχεῖ	N-DM-S	πανδοχεύς

πανδοχεῖον, ου, τό   as a lodging place for travelers *inn, caravansary, khan* (LU 10.34)

πανδοχεῖον   N-AN-S   πανδοχεῖον

πανδοχεύς, έως, ὁ   strictly *one who welcomes all*; hence, one who manages a lodging place for travelers *innkeeper, host* (LU 10.35)

πανηγύρει   N-DF-S   πανήγυρις

πανήγυρις, εως, ἡ   literally, as a festal gathering of a whole group *celebration, happy festive occasion*; καὶ μυριάσιν ἀγγέλων πανηγύρει *and to innumerable angels in joyful assembly* (HE 12.22)

πανοικεί (also πανοικί)   adverb; *with one's whole household* (AC 16.34)

πανοικεί   AB   πανοικεί
πανοικί   AB   "

πανοπλία, ας, ἡ   literally, the full preparation of a foot soldier for offense and defense *full armor, weapons and armor, complete suit of armor* (LU 11.22); metaphorically, of the spiritual characteristics of a believer for Christian warfare against evil

πανοπλίαν   N-AF-S   πανοπλία

πανουργία, ας, ἡ   strictly *capability for every work*; in the NT in a negative sense *cunning, craftiness, trickery*

πανουργία   N-DF-S   πανουργία
πανουργίαν   N-AF-S   "

πανοῦργος, ον   strictly *ready to do anything*; in the NT in a negative sense *clever, crafty, unscrupulous* (2C 12.16)

πανοῦργος   A--NM-S   πανοῦργος
πανπληθεί   AB   παμπληθεί
πάντα   AP-AM-S   πᾶς
    AP-AN-P   "
    AP-NN-P   "
    A--AM-S   "
    A--AN-P   "
    A--NN-P   "
    A--VN-P   "
πάντας   AP-AM-P   "
    A--AM-P   "

πανταχῇ   adverb; *everywhere, in every place, all over* (AC 21.28)

πανταχῇ   AB   πανταχῇ

πανταχόθεν   adverb; *from all parts, from every quarter* (MK 1.45)

πανταχόθεν   AB   πανταχόθεν

πανταχοῦ   adverb; *everywhere, in all directions, throughout*

πανταχοῦ   AB   πανταχοῦ
παντελές   A--AN-S   παντελής

παντελής, ές   of what is fully effective *(all) complete, perfect*; used adverbially with idioms; (1) εἰς τὸ παντελές literally *to the complete*, i.e. *completely, utterly, wholly* (probably HE 7.25) or *forever, for all time* (possibly HE 7.25); (2) ἀνακύψαι εἰς τὸ παντελές literally *straighten to the complete*, i.e. *stand fully erect, straighten oneself completely* (LU 13.11)

πάντες   AP-NM-P   πᾶς
    AP-VM-P   "
    A--NM-P   "
    A--VM-P   "

πάντη   adverb; *in every way, altogether* (AC 24.3)

πάντη   AB   πάντη

παντί   AP-DM-S   πᾶς
    AP-DN-S   "
    A--DM-S   "
    A--DN-S   "

πάντοθεν   adverb; *from all directions, from all sides* (LU 19.43); *on all sides, entirely* (HE 9.4)

πάντοθεν   AB   πάντοθεν
παντοκράτορος   N-GM-S   παντοκράτωρ

παντοκράτωρ, ορος, ὁ   a designation for God as the one holding all power and ruling all things *the Almighty, the All-Powerful, the Omnipotent (One)*

παντοκράτωρ   N-NM-S   παντοκράτωρ
    N-VM-S   "
παντός   AP-GM-S   πᾶς
    AP-GN-S   "
    A--GM-S   "
    A--GN-S   "

πάντοτε   adverb of time *at all times, always, ever(more)*

πάντοτε   AB   πάντοτε
πάντων   AP-GM-P   πᾶς
    AP-GN-P   "
    A--GM-P   "
    A--GN-P   "

πάντως   (1) to indicate extent *by all means, in every way* (1C 9.22); with a negative *not at all, in no way* (1C 16.12); (2) to indicate degree of certainty *certainly, surely, doubtless* (LU 4.23); with a negative *assuredly not, certainly not, by no means* (1C 5.10)

πάντως   AB   πάντως
παρ'   PA   παρά
    PD   "
    PG   "

παρά   preposition with a root meaning *beside*; **I.** with the genitive; (1) spatially, coming from the closeness of a person *from (beside)* (JN 6.46), *from (the presence of)* (JN 15.26); (2) to denote the author or originator of an action *from* (JN 1.6); (3) to denote the starting point from which an action takes place; after verbs of asking (JN 4.9), receiving (MK 12.2), hearing (JN 1.40), learning (2T 3.14); (4) in prepositional phrases; (a) used adjectively *from, by* (e.g. ἡ παρ' ἐμοῦ διαθήκη *my covenant* RO 11.27); (b) used substantivally to denote a close relationship (MK 3.21) or possession (MK 5.26); **II.** with the dative; (1) spatially, to denote nearness *near, by, beside*; (a) with things (JN 19.25); (b) with persons *beside, with, by* (LU 9.47); with plural objects *among* (MT 28.15); (2) legally, with reference to appearing before someone's judgment seat *before* (2P 2.11); (3) combining a legal and evaluative with a spatial sense *in the sight of, before, in the judgment of, with* (RO 2.13); **III.** with the accusative; (1) spatially; (a) to denote motion, as answering the question "to what place?" *to (the side of), toward* (MT 15.29); (b) to denote nearness, as answering the question "where?" *along(side) of, by, beside, at* (MT 13.1); (2) comparatively; (a) to denote superiority, whether real or imagined *more than, rather than, to the exclusion of* (RO 1.25; HE 1.9); (b) to denote preference, either positive or negative, *compared with, more than, beyond, in preference to* (LU 13.4); (3) differentially, from a basic sense *beyond*, to denote distance from and, hence, difference *with a difference of,* all but, less (2C 11.24); (4) adversatively *against, contrary to, without regard for, beyond* (RO 4.18; HE 11.11)

παρά	PA	παρά
	PD	"
	PG	"
παραβαίνετε	VIPA--2P	παραβαίνω
παραβαίνουσι(ν)	VIPA--3P	"

παραβαίνω 2aor. παρέβην; in the NT always in relation to wrongdoing; (1) intransitively *give up, turn aside* (AC 1.25); (2) transitively; (a) *overstep, offend (against)* (MT 15.2); (b) of going beyond what God's law allows *transgress, break, disregard* (MT 15.3); (c) absolutely ὁ παραβαίνων *the transgressor* (2J 9)

παραβαίνων	VPPANM-S	παραβαίνω

παραβάλλω 2aor. παρέβαλον; (1) intransitively, as a nautical technical term, of a ship approaching land *cross over to, come near, sail to* (AC 20.15); (2) transitively *set side by side*; figuratively *compare* (MK 4.30)

παραβάλομεν	VIFA--1P	παραβάλλω
παραβάλωμεν	VSAA--1P	"
παραβάσει	N-DF-S	παράβασις
παραβάσεων	N-GF-P	"
παραβάσεως	N-GF-S	"

παράβασις, εως, ἡ as wrongdoing in relation to law *overstepping, transgression, disobedience*

παράβασις	N-NF-S	παράβασις
παραβάται	N-NM-P	παραβάτης
παραβάτην	N-AM-S	"

παραβάτης, ου, ὁ as one who disobeys a specific divine commandment *transgressor, sinner*

παραβάτης	N-NM-S	παραβάτης

παραβιάζομαι 1aor. παρεβιασάμην; literally *use force*; figuratively *urge strongly, constrain, successfully persuade*

παραβολαῖς	N-DF-P	παραβολή
παραβολάς	N-AF-P	"

παραβολεύομαι 1aor. παρεβολευσάμην; strictly *hand over*; idiomatically παραβολεύεσθαι τὴν ψυχήν literally *hand over the life*, i.e. *expose oneself to danger, boldly risk one's life* (PH 2.30)

παραβολευσάμενος	VPADNM-S	παραβολεύομαι

παραβολή, ῆς, ἡ as a rhetorical figure of speech, setting one thing beside another to form a comparison or illustration; (1) in the Gospels *parable, illustration* (MT 13.3); (2) in Hebrews a prophetic *symbol, type, figure* (HE 9.9)

παραβολή	N-NF-S	παραβολή
παραβολῇ	N-DF-S	"
παραβολήν	N-AF-S	"
παραβολῆς	N-GF-S	"

παραβουλεύομαι 1aor. παρεβουλευσάμην; *show disregard, be careless* in relation to something; παραβουλεύεσθαι τῇ ψυχῇ *have no concern for one's life* (PH 2.30)

παραβουλευσάμενος	VPADNM-S	παραβουλεύομαι
παραγγείλαντες	VPAANM-P	παραγγέλλω
παραγγείλας	VPAANM-P	"
παραγγείλῃς	VSAA--2S	"
παραγγελεῖ	VIFA--3S	"

παραγγελία, ας, ἡ strictly, of passing on an announcement *proclaiming*; in the NT; (1) as a directive from an authoritative source *order, command, charge* (AC 16.24); (2) as doctrinal teaching about right living *instruction* (1TH 4.2)

παραγγελία	N-DF-S	παραγγελία
παραγγελίαν	N-AF-S	"
παραγγελίας	N-AF-P	"
	N-GF-S	"
παράγγελλε	VMPA--2S	παραγγέλλω
παραγγέλλει	VIPA--3S	"
παραγγέλλειν	VNPA	"
παραγγέλλομεν	VIPA--1P	"

παραγγέλλω impf. παρήγγελλον; fut. παραγγελῶ; 1aor. παρήγγειλα; strictly *pass on an announcement*; in the NT; (1) as issuing a directive from an authoritative source *command, give (strict) orders, direct, instruct* (MT 10.5); (2) followed by μή (*not*) and an infinitive *forbid* (LU 5.14); (3) absolutely *give instructions* (1C 11.17)

παραγγέλλω	VIPA--1S	παραγγέλλω
παραγγέλλων	VPPANM-S	"
παραγεγονέναι	VNRA	παραγίνομαι
παράγει	VIPA--3S	παράγω
παραγενόμενοι	VPADNM-P	παραγίνομαι
παραγενόμενον	VPADAM-S	"
παραγενόμενος	VPADNM-S	"
παραγενομένου	VPADGM-S	"
παραγενομένους	VPADAM-P	"
παραγενομένων	VPADGM-P	"
παραγένωμαι	VSAD--1S	"
παραγένωνται	VSAD--3P	"
παράγεται	VIPP--3S	παράγω
παραγίνεται	VIPD--3S	παραγίνομαι
	VIPO--3S	"

παραγίνομαι impf. παρεγινόμην; 2aor. παρεγενόμην; second perfect act. inf. παραγεγονέναι; (1) as reaching a place *arrive, come* (MT 2.1); (2) as showing up publicly at a place *appear, be present* (MT 3.1); (3) negatively, as arriving for a hostile purpose *come against* (LU 22.52); (4) positively, as arriving for a helpful purpose *stand by, come to the aid of* (2T 4.16)

παράγοντα	VPPAAM-S	παράγω
παράγοντι	VPPADM-S	"

παράγω impf. παρῆγον; (1) predominately intransitively in the NT *move along, go along* (MT 9.9); *pass by* (MT 20.30); (2) transitively, passive *be brought past, pass away, disappear* (1J 2.8, 17)

παράγων	VPPANM-S	παράγω
παραδεδομένοι	VPRPNM-P	παραδίδωμι
παραδέδοται	VIRP--3S	"
παραδεδώκεισαν	VILA--3P	"
παραδεδωκόσι(ν)	VPRADM-P	"
παραδειγματίζοντας	VPPAAM-P	παραδειγματίζω

παραδειγματίζω as intended to add to the punishment *publicly disgrace, make an example of, hold up to contempt* (HE 6.6)

παραδειγματίσαι	VNAA	παραδειγματίζω
παράδεισον	N-AM-S	παράδεισος

παράδεισος, ου, ὁ from Old Persian word for garden; *park, paradise*; (1) in the Old Testament the Garden of Eden and the Garden of God; (2) in the NT; (a) as a place of blessedness for the souls of the righteous dead

Paradise (LU 23.43); (b) as the heavenly place where God dwells (2C 12.4)

παραδείσου	N-GM-S	παράδεισος
παραδείσῳ	N-DM-S	"
παραδέξασθαι	VNAD	παραδέχομαι
παραδέξονται	VIFD--3P	"
παραδέχεσθαι	VNPD	"
	VNPO	"
παραδέχεται	VIPD--3S	"
	VIPO--3S	"

παραδέχομαι fut. παραδέξομαι; 1aor. pass. παρεδέχθην; (1) with a thing as the object *accept, acknowledge (as correct)* (AC 16.21); (2) with a person as the object *receive, welcome, accept* (AC 15.4)

παραδέχονται	VIPD--3P	παραδέχομαι
	VIPO--3P	"
παραδέχου	VMPD--2S	"
	VMPO--2S	"
παραδιατριβαί	N-NF-P	παραδιατριβή

παραδιατριβή, ῆς, ἡ   *useless occupation* (1T 6.5)

παραδιδοῖ	VSPA--3S	παραδίδωμι
παραδιδόμεθα	VIPP--1P	"
παραδιδόναι	VNPA	"
παραδιδόντα	VPPAAM-S	"
παραδιδόντες	VPPANM-P	"
παραδιδόντος	VPPAGM-S	"
παραδιδοσθαι	VNPP	"
παραδίδοται	VIPP--3S	"
παραδιδούς	VPPANM-S	"
παραδιδῷ	VSPA--3S	"

παραδίδωμι   impf. παρεδίδουν and παρεδίδοσαν (third-person plural); fut. παραδώσω; 1aor. παρέδωκα; 2aor. third-person plural παρέδοσαν; pf. παραδέδωκα; pluperfect παραδεδώκειν; 1aor. pass. παρεδόθην; 1fut. pass. παραδοθήσομαι; from a basic meaning *give over from one's hand to* someone or something; (1) of authoritative commitment of something to someone *entrust, commit, give* or *hand over, deliver* (MT 11.27; 25.20); (2) of a self-sacrificial love *give up, yield up, risk* (one's life) (AC 15.26); (3) as a legal technical term for passing someone along in the judicial process *hand over, turn over, deliver up* (MK 15.1); of an unjustified act of handing someone over to judicial authorities *betray* (MT 10.4); of God's judicial act of handing someone over to suffer the consequences of his wrongdoing *deliver up, hand over, give up (to)* (RO 1.24); of the church's authoritative disciplining *deliver over, hand over to the control of* (1C 5.5); (4) as a religious technical term for passing along traditions, decisions, teachings *hand down, transmit, pass on* (AC 16.4); (5) *permit, allow*; of a crop whose ripeness "hands it over" to harvesting (MK 4.29)

παραδίδως	VIPA--2S	παραδίδωμι
παραδιδῶσι(ν)	VSPA--3P	"
παραδοθείς	VPAPNM-S	"
παραδοθείση	VPAPDF-S	"
παραδοθείσης	VPAPGF-S	"
παραδοθῆναι	VNAP	"
παραδοθήσεσθε	VIFP--2P	"
παραδοθήσεται	VIFP--3S	"
παραδοθῶ	VSAP--1S	"

παραδοῖ	VSAA--3S	"
παραδόντος	VPAAGM-S	"
παράδοξα	A--AN-P	παράδοξος

παράδοξος, ον   of an unusual event that occurs contrary to belief or expectation *incredible, wonderful, remarkable*; neuter plural παράδοξα as a substantive *wonderful things* (LU 5.26)

παραδόσει	N-DF-S	παράδοσις
παραδόσεις	N-AF-P	"
παραδόσεων	N-GF-P	"
παράδοσιν	N-AF-S	"

παράδοσις, εως, ἡ   as an action *handing down* or *over*; in the NT in a passive sense, as teachings about ways of doing things that are handed down from generation to generation *tradition* (MT 15.2); as Christian doctrine handed down *teaching, instruction, tradition* (2TH 2.15)

παραδοῦναι	VNAA	παραδίδωμι
παραδούς	VPAANM-S	"
παραδῶ	VSAA--1S	"
παραδῷ	VSAA--3S	"
παραδώσει	VIFA--3S	"
παραδώσι(ν)	VSAA--3P	"
παραδώσουσι(ν)	VIFA--3P	"
παραδώσω	VIFA--1S	"
παραδώσων	VPFANM-S	"
παραδώσωσι(ν)	VSAA--3P	"
παραζηλοῦμεν	VIPA--1P	παραζηλόω

παραζηλόω   fut. παραζηλώσω; 1aor. παρεζήλωσα; of emotional excitement; (1) in a good sense, as inciting someone to act in a similar way *arouse to jealousy, provoke to imitation* (RO 11.11); (2) as inciting a protective reaction *provoke to jealousy, incite to indignation* (1C 10.22)

παραζηλῶσαι	VNAA	παραζηλόω
παραζηλώσω	VIFA--1S	"
	VSAA--1S	"
παραθαλασσίαν	A--AF-S	παραθαλάσσιος
παραθαλάσσιον	A--AF-S	"

παραθαλάσσιος, ία, ον   of what is situated beside a sea *by the sea, along the lake* (MT 4.13)

παραθεῖναι	VNAA	παρατίθημι
παραθέτε	VMAA--2P	"

παραθεωρέω   impf. παρεθεώρουν; *disregard, overlook, neglect*, as the result of making an unfavorable comparison (AC 6.1)

παραθήκη, ης, ἡ   as something that has been entrusted to another for faithful keeping *goods placed in trust, deposit*; in the NT of the spiritual heritage of gospel teaching entrusted to faithful Christians *what is entrusted* (1T 6.20); this passive meaning is to be preferred in 2T 1.12

παραθήκην	N-AF-S	παραθήκη
παραθῆναι	VNAA	see παραθεῖναι
παραθήσομαι	VIFM--1S	παρατίθημι
παραθήσω	VIFA--1S	"
παράθου	VMAM--2S	"
παραθῶσι(ν)	VSAA--3P	"

παραινέω   impf. παρῄνουν; *strongly advise, recommend, urge*

παραινῶ	VIPA--1S	παραινέω

παραινῶν	VPPANM-S	"
παραιτεῖσθαι	VNPD	παραιτέομαι
	VNPO	"

παραιτέομαι impf. παρητούμην; 1aor. παρητησάμην; pf. pass. παρήτημαι; (1) as a verb of asking *beg for, ask for, request for oneself* (MK 15.6); (2) with a negative denotation in the sense of declining; (a) as wanting to be excused from a positive response *beg off* (LU 14.18); (b) followed by an infinitive with the negative μή (*not*) *beg, ask that something not take place* (HE 12.19); (c) with the accusative of person *reject, not accept* someone, *disdain, spurn, refuse to listen* to someone (HE 12.25); *shun, avoid association with, have nothing to do with* someone (TI 3.10); (d) with the accusative of the thing *refuse to pay attention to, avoid* (1T 4.7)

παραιτησάμενοι	VPADNM-P	παραιτέομαι
παραιτήσησθε	VSAD--2P	"
παραιτοῦ	VMPD--2S	"
	VMPO--2S	"
παραιτοῦμαι	VIPD--1S	"
	VIPO--1S	"

παρακαθέζομαι 1aor. παρεκαθέσθην; *sit beside, sit down near*; aorist passive with a reflexive meaning *have taken one's place beside* (LU 10.39)

παρακαθεσθεῖσα	VPAONF-S	παρακαθέζομαι

παρακαθίζω 1aor. παρεκάθισα; *sit down beside* (LU 10.39)

παρακαθίσασα	VPAANF-S	παρακαθίζω
παρακάλει	VMPA--2S	παρακαλέω
παρακαλεῖ	VIPA--3S	"
παρακαλεῖν	VNPA	"
παρακαλεῖσθε	VMPP--2P	"
παρακαλεῖται	VIPP--3S	"
παρακαλεῖτε	VMPA--2P	"
παρακαλέσαι	VNAA	"
	VOAA--3S	"
παρακαλέσαντες	VPAANM-P	"
παρακαλέσας	VPAANM-S	"
παρακαλέσατε	VMAA--2P	"
παρακαλέσῃ	VSPA--3S	"
παρακάλεσον	VMAA--2S	"

παρακαλέω impf. παρεκάλουν; 1aor. παρεκάλεσα; pf. pass. παρακέκλημαι; 1aor. pass. παρεκλήθην; 1fut. pass. παρακληθήσομαι; from a basic meaning *call* someone to oneself; (1) *call to (one's side)*; (a) *summon, call for* (AC 28.20); (b) *invite* (AC 28.14); (c) *call on (for help), summon to one's aid* (MT 26.53); (2) as speaking with persistence *earnestly ask for, implore, beg* (AC 16.9); (3) as speaking authoritatively *exhort, urge, encourage* (AC 27.33); (4) as speaking to relieve sorrow or distress *comfort, cheer (up), encourage* (2C 1.4)

παρακαλούμεθα	VIPP--1P	παρακαλέω
παρακαλοῦμεν	VIPA--1P	"
παρακαλοῦντες	VPPANM-P	"
παρακαλοῦντος	VPPAGM-S	"
παρακαλοῦσι(ν)	VIPA--3P	"

παρακαλύπτω pf. pass. παρακεκάλυμμαι; *hide, conceal*; passive *be hidden, be a secret* (LU 9.45)

παρακαλῶ	VIPA--1S	παρακαλέω
παρακαλῶν	VPPANM-S	"
παρακαλῶνται	VSPP--3P	"
παρακαούσας	VPAANM-S	see παρακούσας

παρακαταθήκη, ης, ἡ		*deposit, thing committed to one's charge, trust*
παρακαταθήκην	N-AF-S	παρακαταθήκη

παράκειμαι *lie near, be adjacent*; figuratively in the NT *have (power) at one's disposal, be present, be at hand*

παράκειται	VIPD--3S	παράκειμαι
	VIPO--3S	"
παρακεκαλυμμένον	VPRPNN-S	παρακαλύπτω
παρακεκλήμεθα	VIRP--1P	παρακαλέω
παρακελεύσας	VPAANM-S	παρακελεύω

παρακελεύω 1aor. παρεκέλευσα; *urge, encourage* someone (AC 20.1)

παρακεχειμακότι	VPRADN-S	παραχειμάζω
παρακληθέντες	VPAPNM-P	παρακαλέω
παρακληθῆναι	VNAP	"
παρακληθήσονται	VIFP--3P	"
παρακληθῶσι(ν)	VSAP--3P	"
παρακλήσει	N-DF-S	παράκλησις
παρακλήσεως	N-GF-S	"
παράκλησιν	N-AF-S	"

παράκλησις, εως, ἡ from a basic meaning *calling* someone to oneself; (1) as a strong and persistent request *appeal, entreaty* (2C 8.4); (2) as an authoritative presentation of privileges and requirements *exhortation, encouragement* (1C 14.3); (3) as an offer of consoling help *consolation, comfort* (2C 1.4)

παράκλησις	N-NF-S	παράκλησις
παράκλητον	N-AM-S	παράκλητος

παράκλητος, ου, ὁ a verbal adjective with a basic meaning *one called alongside to help*; (1) as a legal technical term, as one who appears in another's behalf *advocate, defender, intercessor* (1J 2.1); (2) as one who gives protection, help, and security *helper, comforter, counselor* (JN 14.16)

παράκλητος	N-NM-S	παράκλητος

παρακοή, ῆς, ἡ as an unwillingness to listen *disobedience* (2C 10.6), opposite ὑπακοή (*obedience*)

παρακοή	N-NF-S	παρακοή
παρακοήν	N-AF-S	"
παρακοῆς	N-GF-S	"

παρακολουθέω fut. παρακολουθήσω; 1aor. παρηκολούθησα; pf. παρηκολούθηκα; literally *follow closely*; figuratively in the NT; (1) *go along with, happen along with, accompany* (MK 16.17); (2) as following a course of action with the mind *investigate, pursue* (LU 1.3); (3) as following a teaching with concentrated attention *faithfully follow, make one's own* (1T 4.6)

παρακολουθῆσαι	VNAA	παρακολουθέω
παρακολουθήσει	VIFA--3S	"
παρακούσας	VPAANM-S	παρακούω
παρακούσῃ	VSAA--3S	"
παρακούσομαι	VIFM--1S	"
παρακούσομεν	VIFA--1P	"

παρακούω 1aor. παρήκουσα; (1) as hearing what is not intended for one's ears *overhear* (possibly MK 5.36); (2) as being unwilling to hear *disregard, disobey, refuse to listen to* (MT 18.17); (3) *pay no attention, ignore* something (possibly MK 5.36)

παρακύπτω 1aor. παρέκυψα; from a basic meaning *stoop to see*, with the meaning modified by the situation of the observer; literally *stoop down (to look in)* (LU

24.12); figuratively *look intently into* (JA 1.25); *look into (a matter), investigate* (1P 1.12)

παρακύψαι	VNAA	παρακύπτω
παρακύψας	VPAANM-S	"
παράλαβε	VMAA--2S	παραλαμβάνω
παραλαβεῖν	VNAA	"
παραλαβόντα	VPAAAM-S	"
παραλαβόντες	VPAANM-P	"
παραλαβών	VPAANM-S	"
παραλαμβάνει	VIPA--3S	"
παραλαμβάνεται	VIPP--3S	"
παραλαμβάνοντες	VPPANM-P	"
παραλαμβάνουσι(ν)	VIPA--3P	"

παραλαμβάνω fut. mid. παραλήμψομαι (and παραλήψομαι); 2aor. παρέλαβον; 1fut. pass. παραλημθήσομαι; from a basic meaning *take to* oneself; (1) with a person as the object; (a) denoting accompaniment *take, take along* or *with, bring along* (MT 2.13); *lead aside, take aside* (MT 20.17); (b) denoting close fellowship and agreement *accept, receive to* oneself (JN 14.3); (2) with a thing as the object; (a) of an office *take over, receive* (CO 4.17); (b) of an inheritance *receive* (HE 12.28); of a spiritual legacy of doctrines and traditions *receive, learn by tradition, be taught* (MK 7.4; 1C 11.23)

παραλέγομαι impf. παρελεγόμην; as a nautical technical term *sail by* or *past, coast along*

παραλεγόμενοι	VPPDNM-P	παραλέγομαι
	VPPONM-P	"
παραλελυμένα	VPRPAN-P	παραλύω
παραλελυμένοι	VPRPNM-P	"
παραλελυμένος	VPRPNM-S	"
παραλελυμένῳ	VPRPDM-S	"
παραλημφθήσεται	VIFP--3S	παραλαμβάνω
παραλήμψομαι	VIFD--1S	"
παραληφθήσεται	VIFP--3S	see παραλημφθήσεται
παραλήψομαι	VIFD--1S	παραλαμβάνω

παράλιος, ον *located by the sea, maritime*; substantively *seacoast, coastal region* (LU 6.17)

παραλίου	AP-GF-S	παράλιος

παραλλαγή, ῆς, ἡ of the nature or character of something *variation, change* (JA 1.17)

παραλλαγή	N-NF-S	παραλλαγή
παραλογίζηται	VSPD--3S	παραλογίζομαι
	VSPO--3S	"

παραλογίζομαι strictly *reckon falsely*; (1) of persons *deceive, delude by false reasoning* (CO 2.4; JA 1.22); (2) of things *defraud, distort*

παραλογιζόμενοι	VPPDNM-P	παραλογίζομαι
	VPPONM-P	"
παραλυτικόν	AP-AM-S	παραλυτικός

παραλυτικός, ή, όν *paralytic, unable to walk, disabled*; substantively in the NT *paralyzed person, paralytic*

παραλυτικός	AP-NM-S	παραλυτικός
	A--NM-S	"
παραλυτικούς	AP-AM-P	"
παραλυτικῷ	AP-DM-S	"
παραλυτικῶν	AP-GM-P	"

παραλύω pf. pass. παραλέλυμαι; *weaken, disable*; only passive in the NT; perfect participle *paralyzed, enfeebled* (LU 5.18); as a substantive ὁ παραλελυμένος *the paralytic* (LU 5.24); idiomatically τὰ παραλελυμένα γό-

νατα ἀνορθοῦν literally *strengthen paralyzed knees*, i.e. *become encouraged again, renew courage, make a new effort* (HE 12.12)

παραμείνας	VPAANM-S	παραμένω
παραμένειν	VNPA	"

παραμένω fut. παραμενῶ; 1aor. παρέμεινα; *remain, stay (beside)*; (1) with the dative of person, often with the denotation of serving *stay, remain with* (PH 1.25); (2) *continue* in a state, *stay on* (HE 7.23); *continue* in a course of action, *keep on* (JA 1.25); (3) of temporarily lodging *remain, continue with* (1C 16.6)

παραμενῶ	VIFA--1S	παραμένω
παραμυθεῖσθε	VMPD--2P	παραμυθέομαι
	VMPO--2P	"

παραμυθέομαι 1aor. παρεμυθησάμην; from a basic meaning *come close to* someone's side *and speak in a friendly manner*; (1) as rousing up someone's will about what ought to be done *encourage, strengthen* (1TH 2.12); (2) as rousing up hope for a good outcome of what has happened *comfort, console* (JN 11.19)

παραμυθήσονται	VSAD--3P	παραμυθέομαι

παραμυθία, ας, ἡ as speaking to rouse up hope about what has happened *comfort, encouragement*; in distinction from παράκλησις (*exhortation, encouragement*), which aims to arouse the will to action (1C 14.3)

παραμυθίαν	N-AF-S	παραμυθία

παραμύθιον, ου, τό as persuasive power that points to a basis for hope and provides incentive *encouragement, comfort* (PH 2.1)

παραμύθιον	N-NN-S	παραμύθιον
παραμυθούμενοι	VPPDNM-P	παραμυθέομαι
	VPPONM-P	"

παράνοια, ας, ἡ *madness, folly, foolishness* (2P 2.16)

παράνοιαν	N-AF-S	παράνοια

παρανομέω as violating a specific law or established ordinance *act contrary to, disobey the law* (AC 23.3)

παρανομία, ας, ἡ as an act of lawbreaking that stems from habitual disregard for the law *wrongdoing, evildoing, (deliberate) transgression* (2P 2.16)

παρανομία	N-DF-S	παρανομία
παρανομίαν	N-AF-S	"
παρανομίας	N-GF-S	"
παρανομῶν	VPPANM-S	παρανομέω
παραπεσόντας	VPAAAM-P	παραπίπτω

παραπικραίνω 1aor. παρεπίκρανα; (1) in an absolute and intransitive sense *rebel, be disobedient* or *recalcitrant* (probably HE 3.16); (2) transitively *provoke, make angry* (possibly HE 3.16)

παραπικρασμός, οῦ, ὁ (1) *rebellion, revolt, hardheartedness* (probably HE 3.8, 15); (2) *embitterment, exasperation* (possibly HE 3.8, 15)

παραπικρασμῷ	N-DM-S	παραπικρασμός

παραπίπτω 2aor. παρέπεσον; literally *fall beside* or *aside, go astray, become lost*; figuratively in the NT of abandoning a former relationship *turn away, commit apostasy* (HE 6.6)

παραπλεῦσαι	VNAA	παραπλέω

παραπλέω 1aor. παρέπλευσα; *sail by* or *past* (AC 20.16)

παραπλήσιον	AB	παραπλήσιος

παραπλήσιος, ία, ον strictly *near, alongside*; hence *similar, almost the same as*; neuter as an adverb *nearly, almost* (PH 2.27)

παραπλησίως adverb; *similarly, in just the same way, likewise* (HE 2.14)

παραπλησίως	AB	παραπλησίως
παραπορεύεσθαι	VNPD	παραπορεύομαι
	VNPO	"

παραπορεύομαι impf. παρεπορευόμην; (1) *go* or *pass by* (MT 27.39); (2) *go through* (MK 2.23)

παραπορευόμενοι	VPPDNM-P	παραπορεύομαι
	VPPONM-P	"
παραπορευόμενον	VPPDAM-S	"
	VPPOAM-S	"

παράπτωμα, ατος, τό as a deviation from living according to what has been revealed as the right way to live *false step, sin, transgression*; used of serious offenses against both God (EP 1.7) and man (MT 6.15)

παράπτωμα	N-AN-S	παράπτωμα
	N-NN-S	"
παραπτώμασι(ν)	N-DN-P	"
παραπτώματα	N-AN-P	"
παραπτώματι	N-DN-S	"
παραπτώματος	N-GN-S	"
παραπτωμάτων	N-GN-P	"

παραρρέω 2aor. pass. subjunctive παραρυῶ; literally *slip from, off, away*; metaphorically in the NT of being like a ship drifting without anchorage *drift away from, gradually neglect* (HE 2.1)

παραρρυῶμεν	VSAA--1P	παραρρέω
παραρυῶμεν	VSAP--1P	"

παράσημος, ον strictly, of a distinguishing mark; hence, of a ship on which a figurehead is mounted *distinguished* or *marked (by), carrying an emblem* (probably AC 28.11); neuter as a substantive *emblem, figurehead, carved figure* (possibly AC 28.11)

παρασήμῳ	AP-DN-S	παράσημος
	A--DN-S	"
παρασκευαζόντων	VPPAGM-P	παρασκευάζω

παρασκευάζω fut. mid. παρασκευάσομαι; pf. mid./pass. παρεσκεύασμαι; (1) active *prepare* (a meal) (AC 10.10); (2) middle *get ready, prepare oneself* (1C 14.8); perfect *be ready, be prepared* (2C 9.2, 3)

παρασκευάσεται	VIFM--3S	παρασκευάζω

παρασκευή, ῆς, ἡ literally *preparation*; in Jewish, NT, and early Christian usage, only of a definite day, the sixth day of the week, the term for the Friday preceding the Sabbath, when all preparation for the Sabbath had to be completed and after which no work was permitted (MK 15.42; LU 23.54; JN 19.31, 42)

παρασκευή	N-NF-S	παρασκευή
παρασκευήν	N-AF-S	"
παρασκευῆς	N-GF-S	"

παραστάτις, ιδος, ἡ feminine of παραστάτης (*helper, defender*); one who stands by to help in the battle *helper, ally* (figuratively in RO 16.2)

παραστάτις	N-NF-S	παραστάτις
παραστῆναι	VNAA	παρίστημι
παραστῆσαι	VNAA	"
παραστήσατε	VMAA--2P	"
παραστήσει	VIFA--3S	"

παραστήσῃ	VSAA--3S	"
παραστησόμεθα	VIFM--1P	"
παραστήσωμεν	VSAA--1P	"
παραστῆτε	VSAA--2P	"
παρασχών	VPAANM-S	παρέχω
παρατεθῆναι	VNAP	παρατίθημι

παρατείνω 1aor. παρέτεινα; of an event *extend, prolong* (AC 20.7)

παρατηρεῖσθε	VIPM--2P	παρατηρέω

παρατηρέω impf. παρετήρουν, mid. παρετηρούμην; 1aor. παρετήρησα; with a general sense of directly perceiving something through close observation; active and middle have the same meaning; (1) *keep under observation, watch closely*; with a malicious intent *lie in wait for, lurk for, narrowly watch* with hidden intent (MK 3.2); (2) as being on guard *keep watch over, keep* (AC 9.24); (3) of scrupulous attitude in religious matters *observe, keep, carefully obey rules about* (GA 4.10)

παρατηρήσαντες	VPAANM-P	παρατηρέω
παρατηρήσεως	N-GF-S	παρατήρησις

παρατήρησις, εως, ἡ of the use of observable data to interpret events *observing, looking closely, watching* (LU 17.20)

παρατηρούμενοι	VPPMNM-P	παρατηρέω
παρατηροῦντες	VPPANM-P	"
παρατίθεμαι	VIPM--1S	παρατίθημι
παρατιθέμενα	VPPPAN-P	"
παρατιθέμενον	VPPPAN-S	"
παρατιθέμενος	VPPMNM-S	"
παρατιθέναι	VNPA	"
παρατιθέσθωσαν	VMPM--3P	"

παρατίθημι fut. παραθήσω; 1aor. παρέθηκα; 2aor. inf. παραθεῖναι, mid. παρεθέμην, imperative παράθου; 1aor. pass. παρετέθην; from a basic meaning *place beside, place before*; (1) active and literally, of food *place* or *set before* someone (MK 6.41); figuratively, of teaching *expound, point out, tell* (MT 13.24); (2) middle; (a) as a commercial technical term for giving something to someone in trust for safekeeping *commit, deposit, entrust*; figuratively in the NT (LU 23.46; 1T 1.18); (b) *present evidence, show to be true* (AC 17.3)

παρατίθημι	VIPA--1S	παρατίθημι
παρατιθῶσι(ν)	VSPA--3P	"
παρατυγχάνοντας	VPPAAM-P	παρατυγχάνω

παρατυγχάνω *happen to be near, chance to meet*; participle as a substantive οἱ παρατυγχάνοντες *people who happen to be there* or *come by* (AC 17.17)

παρατυχόντας	VPAAAM-P	παρατυγχάνω

παραυτίκα adverb; *for the moment, momentary, for a little while* (2C 4.17)

παραυτίκα	AB	παραυτίκα
παραφέρεσθε	VMPP--2P	παραφέρω
παραφερόμεναι	VPPPNF-P	"
παραφερόμενοι	VPPPNM-P	"

παραφέρω 2aor. παρήνεγκον; *carry away*; (1) literally and passive, of clouds *be carried away, be blown along* (JU 12); (2) figuratively; (a) as misleading someone from the true or right way *lead astray* (HE 13.9); (b) of an experience of suffering *take away, remove* (MK 14.36)

παραφιέναι	VNPA	παραφίημι

παραφίημι inf. παραφιέναι; *let go, leave undone* (LU 11.42) παραφρονέω *be completely irrational, be insane, be out of one's mind* (2C 11.23)

παραφρονία, ας, ἡ as mental derangement *madness, insanity, insane action* (2P 2.16)

παραφρονίαν	N-AF-S	παραφρονία
παραφρονῶν	VPPANM-S	παραφρονέω

παραφροσύνη, ης, ἡ *madness, insanity* (2P 2.16)

παραφροσύνην	N-AF-S	παραφροσύνη

παραχειμάζω fut. παραχειμάσω; 1aor. παρεχείμασα; pf. παρακεχείμακα; *spend the winter, stay in a place during the stormy season*

παραχειμάσαι	VNAA	παραχειμάζω

παραχειμασία, ας, ἡ *spending the stormy season* in a place, *wintering* (AC 27.12)

παραχειμασίαν	N-AF-S	παραχειμασία
παραχειμάσω	VIFA--1S	παραχειμάζω

παραχράομαι *misuse, act wrongly about* something (1C 7.31)

παραχρῆμα adverb; *immediately, at once, without delay*

παραχρῆμα	AB	παραχρῆμα
παραχρώμενοι	VPPDNM-P	παραχράομαι
	VPPONM-P	"
παρδάλει	N-DF-S	πάρδαλις

πάρδαλις, εως, ἡ *leopard, panther*, a large catlike animal (RV 13.2)

παρεβάλομεν	VIAA--1P	παραβάλλω
παρέβη	VIAA--3S	παραβαίνω
παρεβιάσαντο	VIAD--3P	παραβιάζομαι
παρεβιάσατο	VIAD--3S	"
παρεγένετο	VIAD--3S	παραγίνομαι
παρεγενόμην	VIAD--1S	"
παρεγένοντο	VIAD--3P	"
παρεγίνοντο	VIID--3P	"
	VIIO--3P	"
παρεδέχθησαν	VIAP--3P	παραδέχομαι
παρεδίδετο	VIIP--3S	παραδίδωμι
παρεδίδοσαν	VIIA--3P	"
παρεδίδοτο	VIIP--3S	"
παρεδίδου	VIIA--3S	"
παρεδίδουν	VIIA--3P	"
παρεδόθη	VIAP--3S	"
παρεδόθην	VIAP--1S	"
παρεδόθησαν	VIAP--3P	"
παρεδόθητε	VIAP--2P	"
παρέδοσαν	VIAA--3P	"
παρεδρεύοντες	VPPANM-P	παρεδρεύω

παρεδρεύω strictly *sit beside*; hence *concern oneself with, wait on*; of priestly work *serve* (1C 9.13)

παρέδωκα	VIAA--1S	παραδίδωμι
παρεδώκαμεν	VIAA--1P	"
παρέδωκαν	VIAA--3P	"
παρέδωκας	VIAA--2S	"
παρεδώκατε	VIAA--2P	"
παρέδωκε(ν)	VIAA--3S	"
παρέθεντο	VIAM--3P	παρατίθημι
παρεθεωροῦντο	VIIP--3P	παραθεωρέω
παρέθηκαν	VIAA--3P	παρατίθημι
παρέθηκε(ν)	VIAA--3S	"
πάρει	VIPA--2S	πάρειμι
παρειμένας	VPRPAF-P	παρίημι

πάρειμι ptc. παρών; impf. third-person plural παρῆσαν; fut. mid. third-person singular παρέσται; from παρά (*beside*) and εἰμί (*be*); (1) as being present; (a) of persons *be present, be here* (JN 11.28), opposite ἄπειμι (*be absent or away*); (b) of impersonal things; of time *(have) come* (JN 7.6); of what is at one's disposal *have, possess* (2P 1.9); neuter participle as a substantive τὰ πάροντα *what one has, one's possessions* (HE 13.5); (2) of persons, as appearing *arrive, show up, come* (LU 13.1); with the perfect sense *have come, be here* (AC 10.21)

παρεῖναι	VNAA	παρίημι
	VNPA	πάρειμι

παρεισάγω fut. παρεισάξω; *bring in from the outside*; with a negative sense, of heretical teachings *bring in (secretly), introduce on the sly* (2P 2.1)

παρείσακτος, ον a verbal adjective from παρά (*beside*) and εἰσάγω (*bring, lead*); with a negative sense *secretly brought in, sneaked* or *smuggled in, joined under false pretenses* (GA 2.4)

παρεισάκτους	A--AM-P	παρείσακτος
παρεισάξουσι(ν)	VIFA--3P	παρεισάγω

παρεισδύω or παρεισδύνω 1aor. παρεισέδυσα; 2aor. pass. παρεισεδύησα (JU 4); *slip in (stealthily), join a group unnoticed, worm one's way in*; second aorist passive with the intransitive meaning *sneak in*

παρεισεδύησαν	VIAA--3S	παρεισδύω
παρεισέδυσαν	VIAA--3P	"
παρεισενέγκαντες	VPAANM-P	παρεισφέρω

παρεισέρχομαι 2aor. παρεισῆλθον; (1) of the (Mosaic) law brought in to play a subordinate role *enter in alongside, come in (additionally)* (RO 5.20); (2) of people who join a group out of unworthy motives *slip in, sneak in* (GA 2.4)

παρεισῆλθε(ν)	VIAA--3S	παρεισέρχομαι
παρεισῆλθον	VIAA--3P	"
πάρεισι(ν)	VIPA--3P	πάρειμι
παρειστήκεισαν	VILA--3P	παρίστημι

παρεισφέρω 2aor. παρεισήνεγκα; as adding in a second effort *apply, bring into play*; idiomatically σπουδὴν πᾶσαν παρεισφέρειν literally *bring every effort to*, i.e. *do one's very best, try very hard* (2P 1.5)

παρεῖχαν	VIIA--3P	see παρεῖχον
παρεῖχε(ν)	VIIA--3S	παρέχω
παρείχετο	VIIM--3S	"
παρεῖχον	VIIA--3P	"
παρεκάλει	VIIA--3S	παρακαλέω
παρεκάλεσα	VIAA--1S	"
παρεκάλεσαν	VIAA--3P	"
παρεκάλεσας	VIAA--2S	"
παρεκάλεσε(ν)	VIAA--3S	"
παρεκαλοῦμεν	VIIA--1P	"
παρεκάλουν	VIIA--3P	"
παρεκλήθη	VIAP--3S	"
παρεκλήθημεν	VIAP--1P	"
παρεκλήθησαν	VIAP--3P	"

παρεκτός adverb; (1) of experiences coming from outside oneself *from the outside, external, in addition* (2C 11.28); (2) as an improper preposition with the genitive *apart from, except for* (MT 5.32)

παρεκτός	AB	παρεκτός
	PG	"

παρέκυψε(ν)	VIAA--3S	παρακύπτω
παρέλαβε(ν)	VIAA--3S	παραλαμβάνω
παρέλαβες	VIAA--2S	"
παρελάβετε	VIAA--2P	"
παρέλαβον	VIAA--1S	"
	VIAA--3S	"
παρελάβοσαν	VIAA--3P	"
παρελέγοντο	VIID--3P	παραλέγομαι
	VIIO--3P	"
παρελεύσεται	VIFD--3S	παρέρχομαι
παρελεύσονται	VIFD--3P	"
παρεληλυθέναι	VNRA	"
παρεληλυθώς	VPRANM-S	"
παρελθάτω	VMAA--3S	"
παρελθεῖν	VNAA	"
παρελθέτω	VMAA--3S	"
παρέλθη	VSAA--3S	"
παρελθόντες	VPAANM-P	"
παρελθών	VPAANM-S	"
παρέλθωσι(ν)	VSAA--3P	"

παρεμβάλλω fut. παρεμβαλῶ; as a military technical term expressing preparations to besiege a city *throw up a rampart of earthworks, surround with barricades* (LU 19.43)

παρεμβαλοῦσι(ν)	VIFA--3P	παρεμβάλλω
παρεμβολάς	N-AF-P	παρεμβολή

παρεμβολή, ῆς, ἡ as a military technical term; (1) for an army in the field *encampment, camp*; of the Israelite camp during the exodus period (HE 13.11); figuratively, for the Jewish religious community as developed in Judaism (HE 13.13); (2) for an army in battle array *battle line, army* (HE 11.34); (3) for a permanent army base *barracks, fortress, soldiers' quarters* (AC 21.34)

παρεμβολήν	N-AF-S	παρεμβολή
παρεμβολῆς	N-GF-S	"
παρενέγκαι	VNAA	παραφέρω
παρένεγκε	VMAA--2S	"
παρενεγκεῖν	VNAA	"
παρενοχλεῖν	VNPA	παρενοχλέω

παρενοχλέω *(cause) trouble, make it more difficult for, annoy* (AC 15.19)

παρέξει	VIFA--3S	παρέχω
παρέξη	VIFM--2S	"
	VSAM--2S	"
παρεπίδημοι	AP-NM-P	παρεπίδημος
παρεπιδήμοις	AP-DM-P	"

παρεπίδημος, ον of one who stays for awhile as an alien in a place *sojourning, staying*; substantivally *temporary resident, sojourner, stranger*; figuratively, of Christians as not counting this earth as their home (1P 1.1)

παρεπιδήμους	AP-AM-P	παρεπίδημος
παρεπίκραναν	VIAA--3P	παραπικραίνω
παρεπορεύοντο	VIID--3P	παραπορεύομαι
	VIIO--3P	"
παρέρχεσθε	VIPD--2P	παρέρχομαι
	VIPO--2P	"
παρέρχεται	VIPD--3S	"
	VIPO--3S	"

παρέρχομαι fut. παρελεύσομαι; 2aor. act. παρῆλθον; pf. act. παρελήλυθα; from a basic meaning *go* or *pass by*; (1) locally, of persons *go* or *pass by* (LU 18.37); *come near, arrive* (LU 12.37); (2) of time *pass* (1P 4.3); (3) figuratively; (a) of what is coming to an end *pass away, perish, disappear* (MK 13.31); (b) of what is losing force *pass away, become invalid, be left unfulfilled* (MT 24.35b); (c) of disregarding and acting contrary to law or custom *neglect, transgress, overlook* (LU 11.42)

πάρεσιν	N-AF-S	πάρεσις

πάρεσις, εως, ἡ *passing over, letting go, overlooking* (for the time being); of sins *letting go unpunished*; used of God's way of dealing with sins committed during Old Testament times and only symbolically atoned for by sacrifices until Christ should come and offer up himself as the adequate sacrifice; distinguished from ἄφεσις (*release, pardon*), which is a doing away with sins through an adequate atonement (RO 3.25; cf. HE 10.18)

παρεσκεύασαν	VIAA--3P	παρασκευάζω
παρεσκευασμένοι	VPRMNM-P	"
παρεσκεύασται	VIRM--3S	"
πάρεσμεν	VIPA--1P	πάρειμι
παρέσται	VIFD--3S	"
πάρεστε	VIPA--2P	"
παρέστη	VIAA--3S	παρίστημι
παρέστηκε(ν)	VIRA--3S	"
παρεστηκόσι(ν)	VPRADM-P	"
παρεστηκότων	VPRAGM-P	"
παρεστηκώς	VPRANM-S	"
παρέστησαν	VIAA--3P	"
παρεστήσατε	VIAA--2P	"
παρέστησε(ν)	VIAA--3S	"
πάρεστι(ν)	VIPA--3S	πάρειμι
παρεστώς	VPRANM-S	παρίστημι
παρεστῶσι(ν)	VPRADM-P	"
παρεστῶτα	VPRAAM-S	"
παρεστῶτες	VPRANM-P	"
παρεστώτων	VPRAGM-P	"
παρεσχεῖν	VNAA	παρέχω
παρέσχον	VIAA--3P	"
παρέτεινε(ν)	VIIA--3S	παρατείνω
παρετήρουν	VIIA--3P	παρατηρέω
παρετηροῦντο	VIIM--3P	"
πάρεχε	VMPA--2S	παρέχω
παρέχειν	VNPA	"
παρέχεσθε	VMPM--2P	"
παρέχετε	VIPA--2P	"
παρεχέτω	VMPA--3S	"
παρεχόμενος	VPPMNM-S	"
παρέχοντι	VPPADM-S	"
παρέχουσι(ν)	VIPA--3P	"

παρέχω impf. παρεῖχον, third-person plural παρεῖχαν, mid. παρειχόμην; fut. παρέξω, mid. second-person singular παρέξη; 2aor. παρέσχον; from a basic meaning *hold beside*; (1) active; (a) *hold out to, offer, present* (LU 6.29); (b) *supply, grant, show* something to someone (AC 28.2); (c) *cause, occasion, bring about* something for someone (MT 26.10); (d) *continue to be, keep on being*; (2) middle; (a) *show oneself to be* something (TI 2.7); (b) *grant* from one's own resources or power, *provide for* (LU 7.4; AC 19.24)

παρέχων	VPPANM-S	παρέχω
παρηγγείλαμεν	VIAA--1P	παραγγέλλω
παρήγγειλαν	VIAA--3P	"

παρηγγείλαντο	VIAM--3P	"
παρήγγειλε(ν)	VIAA--3S	"
παρήγγελλε(ν)	VIIA--3S	"
παρηγγέλλομεν	VIIA--1P	"
παρηγγελμένα	VPRPAN-P	"
παρῆγε(ν)	VIIA--3S	παράγω

παρηγορία, ας, ἡ *comfort, consolation, help* (CO 4.11)

παρηγορία	N-NF-S	παρηγορία
παρηκολούθηκας	VIRA--2S	παρακολουθέω
παρηκολουθηκότι	VPRADM-S	"
παρηκολούθησας	VIAA--2S	"
παρῆλθε(ν)	VIAA--3S	παρέρχομαι
παρῆλθον	VIAA--1S	"
παρῆν	VIIA--3S	πάρειμι
παρῄνει	VIIA--3S	παραινέω
παρῆσαν	VIIA--3P	πάρειμι
παρῃτημένον	VPRPAM-S	παραιτέομαι
παρῃτήσαντο	VIAD--3P	"
παρῃτοῦντο	VIID--3P	"
	VIIO--3P	"
παρθενείας	N-GF-S	see παρθενίας

παρθενία, ας, ἡ *virginity,* as having had no sexual intercourse (LU 2.36)

παρθενίας	N-GF-S	παρθενία
παρθένοι	N-NF-P	παρθένος
	N-NM-P	"
παρθένοις	N-DF-P	"
παρθένον	N-AF-S	"

παρθένος, ου, ἡ and ὁ (1) as an unmarried young woman *virgin, maiden, girl* (MT 25.1; perhaps 1C 7.36–38); figuratively, of the church as the bride pledged to Christ (2C 11.2); (2) in relation to the father in a household *virgin daughter* (probably 1C 7.36–38); (3) an adult male who has not had sexual intercourse with a woman *virgin*; perhaps metaphorically in RV 14.4 for members of a redeemed community maintaining moral purity *chaste men, pure persons*

παρθένος	N-NF-S	παρθένος
παρθένου	N-GF-S	"
παρθένων	N-GF-P	"
Πάρθοι	N-NM-P	Πάρθος

Πάρθος, ου, ὁ *Parthian, inhabitant of Parthia* in central Asia; Parthians were successors to Persians (AC 2.19)

παριδών	VPAANM-S	παροράω

παρίημι 2aor. inf. παρεῖναι; pf. pass. ptc. παρειμένος; from a basic meaning *send by, cause to go past*; (1) *neglect, leave undone, let go* (LU 11.42); (2) perfect passive participle, of a loosened grip of the hands *tired, drooping, slackened*; used metaphorically in HE 12.12 *discouraged, ready to give up*

παριστάνετε	VIPA--2P	παρίστημι
	VMPA--2P	"

παρίστημι and παριστάνω fut. παραστήσω, mid. παραστήσομαι; 1aor. παρέστησα; 2aor. παρέστην; pf. παρέστηκα, ptc. παρεστηκώς or παρεστώς; pluperfect παρειστήκειν; (1) transitively (present active, future active, first aorist active); (a) *place* someone or something *at* someone's *disposal, present* (RO 6.13); *furnish, provide* (AC 23.24); (b) *make ready, cause to be, present* (CO 1.22); (c) as a religious technical term in relation to sacrifice *offer, bring, present* (RO 12.1); (d) as a legal technical term

bring before (a judicial officer), *hand over* (AC 23.33); (e) legally *prove, show to be true* (AC 24.13); (2) intransitively (future middle, second aorist active, perfect active, pluperfect active); (a) *come before, approach, stand before* (AC 9.39); *be nearby* (MK 14.70); as a legal technical term *stand before* (AC 27.24); (b) *place oneself at* someone's *disposal* to assist, *come to the aid of, help* (RO 16.2); (c) perfect and pluperfect of persons *stand by, be present* (AC 1.10); of a point of time *be here, (have) come* (MK 4.29)

παρίστησι(ν)	VIPA--3S	παρίστημι
Παρμενᾶν	N-AM-S	Παρμενᾶς

Παρμενᾶς, ᾶ, ὁ *Parmenas,* masculine proper noun (AC 6.5)

πάροδος, ου, ἡ as a travel term *passing by*; ἐν παρόδῳ *in passing, while going through* a place (1C 16.7)

παρόδῳ	N-DF-S	πάροδος
παροικεῖς	VIPA--2S	παροικέω

παροικέω 1aor. παρῴκησα; as living in a place without holding citizenship *be an alien, live as a stranger, dwell temporarily*

παροικία, ας, ἡ literally, as a period spent in a foreign land *stay, time of temporary residence* (AC 13.17); metaphorically, of the Christian life viewed as a pilgrimage *life on earth* (1P 1.17)

παροικίᾳ	N-DF-S	παροικία
παροικίας	N-GF-S	"
πάροικοι	AP-NM-P	πάροικος
	A--NM-P	
πάροικον	A--NN-S	"

πάροικος, ον literally, of a noncitizen or resident alien *strange* (AC 7.6); predominately substantivally in the NT *stranger, alien, foreigner* (AC 7.29); metaphorically, of a Christian whose real home is in heaven *stranger, one who lives for awhile on earth* (1P 2.11); of a Gentile not yet belonging to God's covenant people *foreigner, nonmember of a family* (EP 2.19), opposite οἰκεῖος (*member of a family*)

πάροικος	AP-NM-S	πάροικος
παροίκους	AP-AM-P	"

παροιμία, ας, ἡ (1) *proverb, proverbial saying* (2P 2.22); (2) in John's Gospel a manner of speaking that conceals symbolic meaning and needs interpretation *veiled language, enigma, figure of speech* (JN 16.29); as a longer figurative discourse *allegory* (JN 10.6)

παροιμίαις	N-DF-P	παροιμία
παροιμίαν	N-AF-S	"
παροιμίας	N-GF-S	"
πάροινον	AP-AM-S	πάροινος
	A--AM-S	"

πάροινος, ον *addicted to wine, drunken,* of one who tends to be quarrelsome as he habitually drinks too much; substantivally *drunkard*

παροίχομαι pf. παρῴχημαι; of time *pass by, be gone* (AC 14.16)

παρόμοια	A--AN-P	παρόμοιος
παρομοιάζετε	VIPA--2P	παρομοιάζω

παρομοιάζω *be like, resemble closely, be very similar to* (MT 23.27)

παρόμοιος, ον *very similar, almost alike, closely resembling* (MK 7.13)

παρόν	VPPAAN-S	πάρειμι
παρόντα	VPPANN-P	"
παρόντες	VPPANM-P	"
παρόντος	VPPAGN-S	"
παροξύνεται	VIPP--3S	παροξύνω

παροξύνω impf. pass. παρωξυνόμην; literally *sharpen*; figuratively *arouse, excite, stimulate*; in a negative sense *provoke, irritate, cause to be upset*; only passive in the NT (AC 17.16; 1C 13.5)

παροξυσμόν	N-AM-S	παροξυσμός

παροξυσμός, οῦ, ὁ (1) in a positive sense *incitement, encouragement, stimulation* (HE 10.24); (2) in a negative sense *sharp argument, provocation, sharp disagreement* (AC 15.39)

παροξυσμός	N-NM-S	παροξυσμός
παροξυσμοῦ	N-GM-S	"

παροράω 2aor. παρεῖδον; *overlook, take no notice of* (AC 17.30)

παροργίζετε	VMPA--2P	παροργίζω

παροργίζω fut. παροργιῶ; *provoke to anger, exasperate, make angry*

παροργισμός, οῦ, ὁ in the passive sense, as a state of provocation to anger *angry mood, exasperation, anger* (EP 4.26)

παροργισμῷ	N-DM-S	παροργισμός
παροργιῶ	VIFA--1S	παροργίζω

παροτρύνω 1aor. παρώτρυνα; *stir up, arouse, incite*, often in a negative sense (AC 13.50)

παρούσῃ	VPPADF-S	πάρειμι

παρουσία, ας, ἡ (1) *being present, presence* (2C 10.10), opposite ἀπουσία (*absence, being away*); (2) *coming, arrival*; (a) of human beings (2C 7.6); (b) as a religious technical term, a future event when Jesus the Messiah returns to earth *coming, advent* (MT 24.3); (c) in a negative sense, of the appearance of Antichrist *coming* (2TH 2.9)

παρουσία	N-NF-S	παρουσία
παρουσίᾳ	N-DF-S	"
παρουσίαν	N-AF-S	"
παρουσίας	N-GF-S	"
παροῦσι(ν)	VPPADN-P	πάρειμι
παροψίδος	N-GF-S	παροψίς

παροψίς, ίδος, ἡ strictly, of food *dainty side dish*; by metonymy *dish, plate* for serving food (MT 23.25)

παρρησία, ας, ἡ as an attitude of openness that stems from freedom and lack of fear; (1) in speech *boldness, plainness, outspokenness* (AC 2.29); (2) in public work *openness*; παρρησίᾳ *publicly* (JN 7.13); (3) in the presence of high-ranking persons *courage, confidence, boldness* (AC 4.13); (4) in relation to God *confidence, boldness, joyful sense of freedom* (HE 10.35)

παρρησία	N-NF-S	παρρησία
παρρησίᾳ	N-DF-S	"
παρρησιάζεσθαι	VNPD	παρρησιάζομαι
	VNPO	"

παρρησιάζομαι impf. ἐπαρρησιαζόμην; 1aor. ἐπαρρησιασάμην; as acting with an attitude of openness that comes from freedom and lack of fear; (1) of openness in speech *speak freely, openly, boldly* (AC 9.27); (2) followed by an infinitive *be bold to, have courage to, dare to* (1TH 2.2)

παρρησιαζόμενοι	VPPDNM-P	παρρησιάζομαι
	VPPONM-P	"
παρρησιαζόμενος	VPPDNM-S	"
	VPPONM-S	"
παρρησίαν	N-AF-S	παρρησία
παρρησίας	N-GF-S	"
παρρησιασάμενοι	VPADNM-P	παρρησιάζομαι
παρρησιάσωμαι	VSAD--1S	"
παρῴκησε(ν)	VIAA--3S	παροικέω
παρών	VPPANM-S	πάρειμι
παρωξύνετο	VIIP--3S	παροξύνω
παρώτρυναν	VIAA--3P	παροτρύνω
παρῳχημέναις	VPRDDF-P	παροίχομαι
	VPRODF-P	"

πᾶς, πᾶσα, πᾶν **I.** as an adjective; (1) without the article; (a) with elative significance, denoting highest degree *all, full, supreme, greatest* (e.g. μετὰ παρρησίας πάσης *with all boldness, most boldly* AC 4.29); (b) with distributive significance, denoting each individual in a class *each, every, all* (LU 4.37); (c) with summarizing significance, designating everything belonging to a class *all (manner of), every kind of, all sorts of* (e.g. πᾶσα νόσος *every kind of disease* MT 4.23); (d) indefinitely, denoting any individual within a class *every, just any, each and every* (e.g. μὴ παντὶ πνεύματι πιστεύετε *do not believe just any spirit* 1J 4.1); (e) geographically, implying inclusion of all parts of a place *all, whole* (e.g. πᾶσα Ἱεροσόλυμα *all Jerusalem* MT 2.3); (f) with a pronoun to reinforce the inclusiveness *all* (e.g. πάντες ἡμεῖς *we all* AC 2.32); (2) with the article in the predicate position; singular *all, (the) whole, entire* (MK 16.15); plural *all, one and all, the whole group* (MT 2.4); (3) with the article in the attributive position, emphasizing total content of something *whole, as a whole, generally* (e.g. τὸν πάντα χρόνον *the whole time* AC 20.18); (4) with the article and followed by a participial phrase or a substantival prepositional phrase, to reinforce the inclusiveness *all those (who), all the ones who* (MT 5.15; LU 1.66); **II.** substantivally, as a noun; (1) without the article; (a) singular *each one, everyone* (LU 16.16); (b) plural *all, everyone* (MT 10.22); in an absolute sense πάντα *all things, everything* (LU 10.22); (c) with a preposition in an adverbial sense εἰς πάντα *in every way, in all respects* (2C 2.9); ἐν πᾶσιν *in every way, in all respects* (1T 3.11); πρὸ πάντων *above all, especially* (JA 5.12); (2) with the article to imply inclusion of all members or parts of a category *all* (MK 14.64); absolutely τὰ πάντα *all things, the universe, everything* (RO 11.36)

πᾶς	AP-NM-S	πᾶς
	A--NM-S	"
	A--VM-S	"
πᾶσα	AP-NF-S	"
	A--NF-S	"
πᾶσαι	AP-NF-P	"
	A--NF-P	"
πάσαις	A--DF-P	"
πᾶσαν	A--AF-S	"
πάσας	A--AF-P	"
πάσῃ	A--GF-S	see πάσης
πάσῃ	A--DF-S	πᾶς
πάσης	A--GF-S	"

πᾶσι(ν)   AP-DM-P   "
     AP-DN-P   "
     A--DM-P   "
     A--DN-P   "

πάσχα, τό indeclinable; *Passover*; (1) as the Jewish festival that includes the Feast of Unleavened Bread (LU 2.41); (2) in a narrower sense of the actual Passover meal, as ordained in the Old Testament (MK 14.1); (3) by metonymy, the lamb slain for the Passover meal *Passover* or *Paschal lamb* (MK 14.12a); figuratively, of Christ Jesus in his sacrificial death (1C 5.7)

πάσχει   VIPA--3S   πάσχω
πάσχειν   VNPA   "
πάσχετε   VIPA--2P   "
πασχέτω   VMPA--3S   "
πάσχοιτε   VOPA--2P   "
πάσχομεν   VIPA--1P   "
πάσχοντες   VPPANM-P   "

πάσχω 2aor. ἔπαθον; pf. πέπονθα; (1) basically, of what happens to a person *experience, undergo* something; (2) in a good sense *experience* (possibly GA 3.4); (3) predominately in a bad sense *suffer, undergo, endure* (MT 16.21; probably GA 3.4); euphemistically *die, suffer death* (LU 22.15)

πάσχω   VIPA--1S   πάσχω
πάσχων   VPPANM-S   "
πασῶν   A--GF-P   πᾶς
πατάξαι   VNAA   πατάσσω
πατάξας   VPAANM-S   "
πατάξῃ   VSAA--3S   "
πατάξομεν   VIFA--1P   "
πατάξω   VIFA--1S   "

Πάταρα, ων, τά *Patara*, a city in Lycia on the southwestern coast of Asia Minor (AC 21.1)

Πάταρα   N-AN-P   Πάταρα
πατάσσῃ   VSAA--3S   πατάσσω

πατάσσω fut. πατάξω; 1aor. ἐπάταξα; *strike, hit*; (1) as inflicting a heavy or fatal blow *strike (down), smite* (MT 26.31); (2) as giving a light or gentle blow *touch, strike* (AC 12.7)

πατεῖ   VIPA--3S   πατέω
πατεῖν   VNPA   "
πάτερ   N-VM-S   πατήρ
πατέρα   N-AM-S   "
πατέρας   N-AM-P   "
πατέρες   N-NM-P   "
     N-VM-P   "
πατέρων   N-GM-P   "

πατέω fut. πατήσω; 1aor. pass. ἐπατήθην; *tread on, step on*; (1) transitively *tread, trample* something (RV 14.20); in a hostile sense *tread down, trample*; figuratively *subdue by force, plunder, treat contemptuously* (LU 21.24); (2) intransitively *walk, step on* (LU 10.19)

πατήρ, πατρός, ὁ *father*; (1) literally; (a) as an immediate male ancestor (MT 4.21); (b) as a more remote or racial ancestor *(fore)father, progenitor* (MT 3.9); (2) as a title for God; (a) as the creator and sovereign ruler of all (JA 1.17); (b) as the Father of Jesus Christ (LU 2.49); (c) as the Father of Christians (RO 1.7); (3) figuratively; (a) of spiritual fatherhood (1C 4.15); (b) as a title of honor or respect (AC 7.2); (c) as the first of a class of

persons *archetype, founder* (RO 4.11); (d) of the devil as the first of the class of persons who partake of his nature as murderers, liars, etc. *leader, archetype, model* (JN 8.44)

πατήρ   N-NM-S   πατήρ
     N-VM-S   "
πατήσουσι(ν)   VIFA--3P   πατέω

Πάτμος, ου, ἡ *Patmos*, a small bare and rocky island in the Aegean Sea (RV 1.9)

Πάτμῳ   N-DF-S   Πάτμος
πατουμένη   VPPPNF-S   πατέω
πατραλοίαις   N-DM-P   see πατρολῴαις
πατραλῴαις   N-DM-P   πατρολῴας
πατράσι(ν)   N-DM-P   πατήρ
πατρί   N-DM-S   "

πατριά, ᾶς, ἡ (1) as one's ancestry derived through the father *family, clan, tribe* (LU 2.4); (2) plural, in a broader sense of all *peoples* of earth, as deriving from God the Father of mankind *families, nations* (AC 3.25); (3) in a unique sense, as the idea of a group of people forming a family, patterned after God's fatherhood, *family* (EP 3.15)

πατριά   N-NF-S   πατριά
πατριαί   N-NF-P
πατριάρχαι   N-NM-P   πατριάρχης
πατριάρχας   N-AM-P   "

πατριάρχης, ου, ὁ strictly *chief father*; used of an important male ancestor *patriarch, father of a tribe* or *nation, progenitor, chief of a family*

πατριάρχης   N-NM-S   πατριάρχης
πατριάρχου   N-GM-S   "
πατριᾶς   N-GF-S   πατριά
πατρίδα   N-AF-S   πατρίς
πατρίδι   N-DF-S   "

πατρικός, ή, όν of what is handed down from one's ancestors *ancestral, paternal, hereditary* (GA 1.14)

πατρικῶν   A--GF-P   πατρικός

πατρίς, ίδος, ἡ (1) literally; (a) as one's native country *fatherland, homeland* (JN 4.44); (b) in a more restricted sense *hometown, native city* (MT 13.54); (2) figuratively, as the believer's heavenly home where God dwells *country* (HE 11.14)

Πατρόβαν   N-AM-S   Πατροβᾶς
Πατροβᾶν   N-AM-S   "

Πατροβᾶς, ᾶ, ὁ (also Πατρόβας) *Patrobas*, masculine proper noun (RO 16.14)

πατρολῴαις   N-DM-P   πατρολῴας

πατρολῴας, ου, ὁ (also πατραλῴας) *one who kills his father, patricide* (1T 1.9)

πατροπαράδοτος, ον *inherited from ancestors, handed down from one's father* or *forefather, traditional* (1P 1.18)

πατροπαραδότου   A--GF-S   πατροπαράδοτος
πατρός   N-GM-S   πατήρ
πατρῴοις   A--DN-P   πατρῷος

πατρῷος, ῴα, ον of what belongs to or is derived from one's father or ancestors *paternal, inherited, ancestral*

πατρῴου   A--GM-S   πατρῷος
πατρῴῳ   A--DM-S
παύεται   VIPM--3S   παύω
Παῦλε   N-VM-S   Παῦλος
Παῦλον   N-AM-S   "

Παῦλος, ου, ὁ (1) *Paul*, name of the apostle (AC 13.9); (2) *Paulus*, name of the Roman deputy in Cyprus (AC 13.7)

Παῦλος	N-NM-S	Παῦλος
Παύλου	N-GM-S	"
Παύλῳ	N-DM-S	"
παύομαι	VIPM--1S	παύω
παυόμεθα	VIPM--1P	"
παύσασθαι	VNAM	"
παυσάτω	VMAA--3S	"
παῦσε	VMAA--2S	"
παύσῃ	VIFM--2S	"
παύσονται	VIFM--3P	"

παύω impf. mid. ἐπαυόμην; fut. mid. παύσομαι; 1aor. ἔπαυσα, mid. ἐπαυσάμην; pf. mid. πέπαυμαι; (1) active *(cause to) stop, restrain, keep* something from something (1P 3.10); (2) middle *stop (oneself), cease, leave off* (LU 5.4)

Πάφος, ου, ἡ *Paphos*, a city on the western coast of the island of Cyprus in the Mediterranean Sea

Πάφου	N-GF-S	Πάφος

παχύνω 1aor. pass. ἐπαχύνθην; literally *make fat, thicken*; figuratively *make impervious, insensitive, dull*; only passive in the NT *become dull* or *insensitive, be unable to understand*

πέδαις	N-DF-P	πέδη
πέδας	N-AF-P	"

πέδη, ης, ἡ what is used to bind the feet *fetter, shackle, ankle chain*

πεδινός, ή, όν of the shape of the terrain *flat, level, even* (LU 6.17)

πεδινοῦ	A--GM-S	πεδινός
πεζεύειν	VNPA	πεζεύω

πεζεύω *travel by land, go on foot* (AC 20.13)

πεζῇ adverb; of the kind of travel *on foot, by land*, in contrast to ἐν πλοίῳ (*by boat*)

πεζῇ	AB	πεζῇ
πεζοί	A--NM-P	πεζός

πεζός, ή, όν *going by land* or *on foot* (MT 14.13)

πειθαρχεῖν	VNPA	πειθαρχέω

πειθαρχέω 1aor. ἐπειθάρχησα; *obey* one in authority; generally *obey* (AC 5.29), *follow advice, listen to* (AC 27.21)

πειθαρχήσαντας	VPAAAM-P	πειθαρχέω
πειθαρχοῦσι(ν)	VPPADM-P	"
πείθεις	VIPA--2S	πείθω
πείθεσθαι	VNPP	"
πείθεσθε	VMPP--2P	"
πείθῃ	VIPP--2S	"
πειθοῖ	N-DF-S	πειθώ
πειθοῖς	A--DM-P	πειθός
πείθομαι	VIPP--1S	πείθω
πειθόμεθα	VIPP--1P	"
πείθομεν	VIPA--1P	"
πειθομένοις	VPPPDM-P	"
πειθομένου	VPPMGM-S	"
	VPPPGM-S	"

πειθός, ή, όν *persuasive, able to convince* (possibly 1C 2.4; see πειθώ)

πείθω impf. ἔπειθον, mid./pass. ἐπειθόμην; fut. πείσω; 1aor. ἔπεισα; second perfect πέποιθα; pluperfect ἐπεποίθειν; pf. pass. πέπεισμαι; 1aor. pass. ἐπείσθην; 1fut. pass. πεισθήσομαι; (1) active (except for second per-

fect and pluperfect); (a) *convince, persuade* (AC 18.4); (b) in a bad sense *seduce (by persuasion), mislead, coax* (MT 27.20); (c) in a milder sense *win over, strive to please* (possibly with bribes or promises) (AC 12.20); (d) as allaying fears *assure, conciliate* (MT 28.14; 1J 3.19); (2) second perfect and pluperfect with the present meaning; (a) strictly *have become convinced*; hence *trust (firmly) in, rely on, be confident about* (MT 27.43); (b) as an evaluative orienter for indirect statements *be convinced* or *persuaded, be sure* or *confident* that (RO 2.19; 2C 2.3); (3) passive (except perfect); (a) *be convinced* or *persuaded, believe* (LU 16.31); (b) as an evaluative orienter *believe (that)* (HE 13.18); (c) *obey, follow*, with the dative of person or thing (HE 13.17); (d) perfect passive *be convinced* or *certain of* something (LU 20.6)

πείθω	VIPA--1S	πείθω

πειθώ, οῦς, ἡ a skillful ability to persuade people to one's way of thinking *persuasive art, persuasiveness, ability to convince* (possibly 1C 2.4; see πειθός)

πείθωμεν	VSPA--1P	πείθω
πείθων	VPPANM-S	"
Πειλᾶτον	N-AM-S	Πιλᾶτος
Πειλᾶτον	N-AM-S	"
Πειλᾶτος	N-NM-S	"
Πειλάτου	N-GM-S	"
Πειλάτῳ	N-DM-S	"
πεῖν	VNAA	πίνω
πεινᾷ	VIPA--3S	πεινάω
	VSPA--3S	"
πεινᾶν	VNPA	"
πεινάσετε	VIFA--2P	"
πεινάσῃ	VSAA--3S	"
πεινάσουσι(ν)	VIFA--3P	"

πεινάω fut. πεινάσω; 1aor. ἐπείνασα; literally *be hungry, hunger* (MT 4.2); figuratively *strongly desire* something, *long for, want very much* (MT 5.6)

πεινῶμεν	VIPA--1P	πεινάω
πεινῶντα	VPPAAM-S	"
πεινῶντας	VPPAAM-P	"
πεινῶντες	VPPANM-P	"
	VPPAVM-P	"

πεῖρα, ας, ἡ (1) active *attempt, trial, test*; idiomatically πεῖραν λαμβάνειν literally *take an attempt*, i.e. *make an attempt at, try* (HE 11.29); (2) passive and idiomatically πεῖράν τινος λαμβάνειν literally *receive trial of something*, i.e. *experience* (HE 11.36)

πειράζει	VIPA--3S	πειράζω
πειράζεται	VIPP--3S	"
πειράζετε	VIPA--2P	"
	VMPA--2P	"
πειράζῃ	VSPA--3S	"
πειράζομαι	VIPP--1S	"
πειραζόμενοι	VPPPNM-P	"
πειραζομένοις	VPPPDM-P	"
πειραζόμενος	VPPPNM-S	"
πειράζοντες	VPPANM-P	"

πειράζω impf. ἐπείραζον; fut. πειράσω; 1aor. ἐπείρασα, mid. ἐπειρασάμην; pf. pass. πεπείρασμαι; 1aor. pass. ἐπειράσθην; (1) *make an attempt, try*, followed by an infinitive to indicate what is being attempted (AC 9.26);

(2) *put to the test, examine, try* (RV 2.2); in a good sense of God's actions toward his people *prove, put to the test, try* (HE 11.17); in a bad sense of a person's hostile intent toward God or Christ *test, try, prove* (MT 16.1); also in a bad sense of enticement to sin *tempt* (GA 6.1); participle as a substantive ὁ πειράζων *the tempter*, a descriptive title for the devil (MT 4.3)

πειράζων	VPPANM-S	πειράζω
πεῖραν	N-AF-S	πεῖρα
πειράομαι	impf. ἐπειρώμην; *try, attempt, endeavor* (AC 26.21)	
πειράσαι	VNAA	πειράζω
πειράσεις	VIFA--2S	"
	VIFA--2S^VMAA--2S	"
πειρασθείς	VPAPNM-S	"
πειρασθῆναι	VNAP	"
πειρασθῇς	VSAP--2S	"
πειρασθῆτε	VSAP--2P	"
πειρασμοῖς	N-DM-P	πειρασμός
πειρασμόν	N-AM-S	"

πειρασμός, οῦ, ὁ (1) as God's examination of man *test, trial* (1P 4.12); (2) as enticement to sin, either from without or within *temptation, testing* (LU 4.13); (3) of man's (hostile) intent *putting (God) to the test* (HE 3.8)

πειρασμός	N-NM-S	πειρασμός
πειρασμοῦ	N-GM-S	"
πειρασμῷ	N-DM-S	"
πειρασμῶν	N-GM-P	"
πείσαντες	VPAANM-P	πείθω
πείσας	VPAANM-S	"
πεισθέντες	VPAPNM-P	"
πεισθῇς	VSAP--2S	"
πεισθήσονται	VIFP--3P	"

πεισμονή, ῆς, ἡ as referring to the means (probably) or the process (possibly) of convincing *(persistent) persuasion, solicitation, enticement* (GA 5.8)

πεισμονή	N-NF-S	πεισμονή
πείσομεν	VIFA--1P	πείθω
πείσωμεν	VSAA--1P	"
πελάγει	N-DN-S	πέλαγος

πέλαγος, ους, τό (1) the open sea where ships may sail *depths, open sea, high sea* (MT 18.6); (2) as a large expanse of water *sea* (AC 27.5)

πέλαγος	N-AN-S	πέλαγος

πελεκίζω pf. pass. πεπελέκισμαι; *behead* (with an axe, πελεκύς), *strike* or *cut off the head with an axe* (RV 20.4)

πέμπει	VIPA--3S	πέμπω
πέμπειν	VNPA	"
πεμπομένοις	VPPPDM-P	"
πέμποντα	VPPAAM-S	"
πέμπουσι(ν)	VIPA--3P	"
πεμπταῖοι	A--NM-P	πεμπταῖος

πεμπταῖος, αία, ον *on the fifth day*; ἤλθομεν πεμπταῖοι *we came in five days* (AC 20.6)

πέμπτην	A-OAF-S	πέμπτος

πέμπτος, η, ον as an ordinal number *fifth* (RV 6.9); substantivally *fifth one* (RV 21.20)

πέμπτος	A-ONM-S	πέμπτος

πέμπω fut. πέμψω; 1aor. ἔπεμψα; 1aor. pass. ἐπέμφθην; from a basic meaning *send*, of causing movement from one place to another; (1) of persons *send, dispatch* (MT

2.8); especially of those sent as God's representatives (LU 4.26); in a more abstract sense *instruct, appoint* (JN 1.33); in distinction from ἀποστέλλω (*send forth, send out*), where the primary focus is on the authoritative commission behind the sending, π. focuses rather on the sender who is being represented and on the act of sending (JN 5.37; cf. 3.17); (2) of things *send* something to someone (RV 11.10); idiomatically, of harvesting πέμπειν τὸ δρέπανον literally *thrust in the sickle*, i.e. *begin to harvest*; figuratively in RV 14.15, 18 of the time of judgment at the end of this age

πέμπω	VIPA--1S	πέμπω
πεμφθέντες	VPAPNM-P	"
πέμψαι	VNAA	"
πέμψαντα	VPAAAM-S	"
πέμψαντες	VPAANM-P	"
πέμψαντι	VPAADM-S	"
πέμψαντος	VPAAGM-S	"
πέμψας	VPAANM-S	"
πέμψασι(ν)	VPAADM-P	"
πέμψει	VIFA--3S	"
πέμψῃς	VSAA--2S	"
πέμψον	VMAA--2S	"
πέμψουσι(ν)	VIFA--3P	"
πέμψω	VIFA--1S	"
	VSAA--1S	"

πένης, ες, gen. **ητος** (1) adjectivally *poor, needy*; (2) substantivally in the NT ὁ π. *the poor person*; used of one who has few possessions and consequently must work hard to support himself; distinguished from πτωχός (*beggar*) and ἐνδεής (*impoverished person*) (2C 9.9)

πένησι(ν)	AP-DM-P	πένης
πενθεῖν	VNPA	πενθέω
πενθεῖτε	VMPA--2P	"

πενθερά, ᾶς, ἡ the mother of one's spouse *mother-in-law* (MK 1.30), in contrast to νύμφη (*daughter-in-law*)

πενθερά	N-NF-S	πενθερά
πενθεράν	N-AF-S	"
πενθερᾶς	N-GF-S	"

πενθερός, οῦ, ὁ *father-in-law*, the father of one's spouse (JN 18.13)

πενθερός	N-NM-S	πενθερός

πενθέω fut. πενθήσω; 1aor. ἐπένθησα; (1) intransitively *mourn, grieve, be sad* (MK 16.10); (2) transitively *grieve for, lament* or *mourn over* (2C 12.21)

πενθήσατε	VMAA--2P	πενθέω
πενθήσετε	VIFA--2P	"
πενθήσουσι(ν)	VIFA--3P	"
πενθήσω	VSAA--1S	"

πένθος, ους, τό as an outward expression of sorrow *grief, lamentation, mourning* (JA 4.9)

πένθος	N-AN-S	πένθος
	N-NN-S	"
πενθοῦντες	VPPANM-P	πενθέω
πενθοῦσι(ν)	VIPA--3P	"
	VPPADM-P	"
πενιχράν	A--AF-S	πενιχρός

πενιχρός, ά, όν of one without possessions or money *(very) poor, (quite) needy* (LU 21.2)

πένται		see πέντε

πεντάκις adverb; *five times* (2C 11.24)

πεντάκις	AB	πεντάκις

πεντακισχίλιοι, αι, α as a cardinal number *five thousand* (MT 14.21); substantivally *five thousand people* (MK 8.19)

πεντακισχίλιοι	A-CNM-P	πεντακισχίλιοι
πεντακισχιλίους	APCAM-P	"
πεντακισχιλίων	APCGM-P	"
πεντακόσια	A-CAN-P	πεντακόσιοι

πεντακόσιοι, αι, α as a cardinal number *five hundred*

πεντακοσίοις	A-CDM-P	πεντακόσιοι
πεντακοσίων	A-CGM-P	"

πέντε indeclinable; as a cardinal number *five*

πεντεκαιδέκατος, η, ον as an ordinal number *fifteenth* (LU 3.1)

πεντεκαιδεκάτῳ	A-ODN-S	πεντεκαιδέκατος

πεντήκοντα indeclinable; as a cardinal number *fifty*

πεντηκοστή, ῆς, ἡ a substantine from the feminine of πεντηκοστός (*fiftieth*); strictly *fiftieth (day)*; in the NT the Jewish harvest feast held on the fiftieth day after the Passover *Pentecost* (AC 2.1; 20.16; 1C 16.8)

πεντηκοστῆς	N-GF-S	πεντηκοστή
πεπαιδευμένος	VPRPNM-S	παιδεύω
πεπαλαίωκε(ν)	VIRA--3S	παλαιόω
πέπαυται	VIRM--3S	παύω
πεπειραμένον	VPRPAM-S	πειράομαι
πεπειρασμένον	VPRPAM-S	πειράζω
πέπεισμαι	VIRP--1S	πείθω
πεπείσμεθα	VIRP--1P	"
πεπεισμένος	VPRPNM-S	"
πεπελεκισμένων	VPRPGM-P	πελεκίζω
πεπήρωκε(ν)	VIRA--3S	πηρόω
πεπιεσμένον	VPRPAN-S	πιέζω
πεπίστευκα	VIRA--1S	πιστεύω
πεπιστεύκαμεν	VIRA--1P	"
πεπίστευκας	VIRA--2S	"
πεπιστεύκατε	VIRA--2P	"
πεπιστεύκεισαν	VILA--3P	"
πεπίστευκε(ν)	VIRA--3S	"
πεπιστευκόσι(ν)	VPRADM-P	"
πεπιστευκότας	VPRAAM-P	"
πεπιστευκότες	VPRANM-P	"
πεπιστευκότων	VPRAGM-P	"
	VPRAGN-P	"
πεπιστευκώς	VPRANM-S	"
πεπίστευμαι	VIRP--1S	"
πεπλανημένοις	VPRPDN-P	πλανάω
πεπλάνησθε	VIRP--2P	"
πεπλάτυνται	VIRP--3S	πλατύνω
πεπληροφορημένοι	VPRPNM-P	πληροφορέω
πεπληροφορημένων	VPRPGN-P	"
πεπληρώκατε	VIRA--2P	πληρόω
πεπλήρωκε(ν)	VIRA--3S	"
πεπληρωκέναι	VNRA	"
πεπλήρωμαι	VIRP--1S	"
πεπληρωμένα	VPRPAN-P	"
πεπληρωμένη	VPRPNF-S	"
πεπληρωμένην	VPRPAF-S	"
πεπληρωμένοι	VPRPNM-P	"
πεπληρωμένους	VPRPAM-P	"
πεπλήρωνται	VIRP--3P	"
πεπληρῶσθαι	VNRP	"

πεπλήρωται	VIRP--3S	"
πεπλούτηκα	VIRA--1S	πλουτέω
πεποίηκα	VIRA--1S	ποιέω
πεποιήκαμεν	VIRA--1P	"
πεποιήκατε	VIRA--2P	"
πεποιήκει	VILA--3S	"
πεποιήκεισαν	VILA--3P	"
πεποίηκε(ν)	VIRA--3S	"
πεποιηκέναι	VNRA	"
πεποιηκόσι(ν)	VPRADM-P	"
πεποιηκότες	VPRANM-P	"
πεποιηκότος	VPRAGM-S	"
πεποιηκότων	VPRAGM-P	"
πεποιηκώς	VPRANM-S	"
πεποιημένων	VPRPGN-P	"
πέποιθα	VIRA--1S	πείθω
πεποίθαμεν	VIRA--1P	"
πέποιθας	VIRA--2S	"
πέποιθε(ν)	VIRA--3S	"
πεποιθέναι	VNRA	"
πεποιθήσει	N-DF-S	πεποίθησις
πεποίθησιν	N-AF-S	"

πεποίθησις, εως, ἡ *confidence, trust*; (1) as reliance on others (2C 1.15); (2) as reliance on God (EP 3.12); (3) as reliance on oneself *self-confidence, assurance* (2C 10.2)

πεποιθότας	VPRAAM-P	πείθω
πεποιθότες	VPRANM-P	"
πεποιθώς	VPRANM-S	"
πεπολίτευμαι	VIRD--1S	πολιτεύομαι
	VIRO--1S	"
πεπόνθασι(ν)	VIRA--3P	πάσχω
πέπονθε(ν)	VIRA--3S	"
πεπορευμένους	VPRDAM-P	πορεύομαι
	VPROAM-P	"
πεπότικε(ν)	VIRA--3S	ποτίζω
πεπραγμένον	VPRPNN-S	πράσσω
πέπρακε(ν)	VIRA--3S	πιπράσκω
πεπραμένος	VPRPNM-S	"
πέπραχα	VIRA--1S	πράσσω
πεπραχέναι	VNRA	"
πεπρησμένος	VPRPNM-S	πίμπρημι
πέπτωκαν	VIRA--3P	πίπτω
πέπτωκας	VIRA--2S	"
πεπτώκασι(ν)	VIRA--3P	"
πέπτωκε(ν)	VIRA--3S	"
πεπτωκότα	VPRAAM-S	"
πεπτωκυῖαν	VPRAAF-S	"
πεπυρωμένα	VPRPAN-P	πυρόω
πεπυρωμένης	VPRPGF-S	"
πεπυρωμένοι	VPRPNM-P	"
πεπυρωμένον	VPRPAN-S	"
πεπυρωμένῳ	VPRPDM-S	"
	VPRPDN-S	"
πέπωκαν	VIRA--3P	πίνω
πεπώκασι(ν)	VIRA--3P	"
πέπωκε(ν)	VIRA--3S	"
πεπώρωκε(ν)	VIRA--3S	πωρόω
πεπωρωμένη	VPRPNF-S	"
πεπωρωμένην	VPRPAF-S	"
περ᾽	PA	περί

πέρ   *very*; an enclitic particle with intensive and extensive force, generally written as a suffix to another particle but may be written separately following

πέρ	QV	πέρ

Πέραια, ας, ἡ   from the adverb πέραν (*beyond, on the other side*); *Perea*, meaning *shore* or *land on the other side*, the territory east of the Jordan River (LU 6.17)

Περαίας	N-GF-S	Πέραια

περαιτέρω   an adverb of περαίτερος, τέρα, ον, the comparative of πέρα (*beyond, further*); *further, more, in addition* (AC 19.39)

περαιτέρω	ABM	περαιτέρω

πέραν   adverb of place *on the other side, beyond*; (1) as a substantive, with the article τὸ π. *the opposite shore, the farther side*; εἰς τὸ π. *to the other side* (MT 8.18); (2) as an improper preposition with the genitive; (a) to answer "to what place?" *to the other side, beyond* (JN 6.1); (b) to designate the territory east of the Jordan River, often called Perea (MT 4.25)

πέραν	AB	πέραν
	PG	"

πέρας, ατος, τό   (1) of place *limit, boundary, end* (MT 12.42); (2) of a settled issue *end, conclusion* (HE 6.16)

πέρας	N-NN-S	πέρας
πέρατα	N-AN-P	"
περάτων	N-GN-P	"
Πέργαμον	N-AF-S	Πέργαμος
	N-AN-S	"

Πέργαμος, ου, ἡ and **Πέργαμον, ου, τό**   *Pergamus* or *Pergamum*, a city in Mysia in northwestern Asia Minor

Περγάμῳ	N-DF-S	Πέργαμος
	N-DN-S	"

Πέργη, ης, ἡ   *Perga*, a city in Pamphylia near the southern coast of Asia Minor

Πέργη	N-DF-S	Πέργη
Πέργην	N-AF-S	"
Πέργης	N-GF-S	"

περί   preposition with a basic meaning *around, on all sides*; **I.** with the genitive to denote the purpose, object, or person to which an action relates; (1) to denote a mental activity or spoken expression relating to someone or something *about, concerning* (AC 8.34); (2) to designate the object of or reason for questioning, censuring, praising, punishing, etc. *regarding* (AC 15.2), *concerning* (MT 2.8), *because of* (LU 3.19), *for* (JN 10.33), *on account of* (LU 19.37); (3) at the beginning of a sentence, to indicate what is under discussion *with regard to, with reference to* (1C 7.1); (4) in intercessory prayer, to denote in whose interest the petition is being made *for, on behalf of* (LU 4.38); (5) in the phrase π. ἁμαρτίας, to denote benefaction *for, to take away, to atone for sin* (RO 8.3; HE 10.18); (6) in the phrase τὰ π. τινος, to refer to someone's circumstances, situation, condition *what concerns someone, the things concerning, the reports about* (LU 24.27; AC 23.15); **II.** with the accusative; (1) of place *around, about, near* (LU 13.8); (2) of an object encircled by something *around* (MT 3.4); (3) of persons around someone, translated according to the context: *those standing about* (MK 4.10), *companions of* (AC 13.13), etc.; (4) of time *about, near* a point of time (MT 20.3);

(5) of preoccupation with something *with, about* (LU 10.40); (6) to specify a topic *with respect to, with regard to* (2T 2.18)

περί	PA	περί
	PG	"
περιάγειν	VNPA	περιάγω
περιάγετε	VIPA--2P	"
περιάγοντας	VPPAAM-P	"

περιάγω   impf. περιῆγον; (1) transitively *lead about, take someone along* (1C 9.5); (2) intransitively *go around* or *about* (AC 13.11); with the accusative of place, specifically of geographical district *travel in* or *through* (MT 9.35)

περιάγων	VPPANM-S	περιάγω
περιαιρεῖται	VIPP--3S	περιαιρέω

περιαιρέω   impf. pass. περιῃρούμην; 2aor. inf. περιελεῖν, ptc. περιελών; (1) literally *take away, remove* (2C 3.16); figuratively, of hope *stop, give up* (AC 27.20); of sin *take away, remove, do away with* (HE 10.11); (2) as a nautical technical term, of an anchor *lift, raise* (AC 28.13); *cut off, cast off* (AC 27.40)

περιάπτω   1aor. ptc. περιάψας; *kindle, light* (a fire) (LU 22.55)

περιαστράπτω   1aor. περιήστραψα; as giving out light with lightninglike quality; (1) transitively *shine around* someone (AC 9.3); (2) intransitively, with περί (accusative) *shine around* someone (AC 22.6)

περιαστράψαι	VNAA	περιαστράπτω
περιαψάντων	VPAAGM-P	περιάπτω
περιβαλεῖται	VIFM--3S	περιβάλλω
περιβάλῃ	VSAM--2S	"
περιβάληται	VSAM--3S	"

περιβάλλω   fut. περιβαλῶ; 2aor. περιέβαλον, mid. περιεβαλόμην; pf. pass. περιβέβλημαι; (1) literally, as preparation for besieging a city *throw up a rampart around, build an embankment around* (LU 19.43); (2) predominately of clothing; active *clothe* someone, *put something on* someone (MT 25.36); middle *wear* (clothes), *put on* (MK 14.51), *clothe oneself* with something (RV 3.5), *dress oneself* (MT 6.29); perfect passive *have put on*; hence *wear, be clothed in, be dressed in* (MK 16.5)

περιβαλοῦ	VMAM--2S	περιβάλλω
περιβαλοῦσι(ν)	VIFA--3P	"
περιβαλώμεθα	VSAM--1P	"
περιβαλών	VPAANM-S	"
περιβεβλημένη	VPRMNF-S	"
	VPRMVF-S	"
περιβεβλημένοι	VPRMNM-P	"
περιβεβλημένον	VPRMAM-P	"
περιβεβλημένος	VPRMNM-S	"
περιβεβλημένους	VPRMAM-P	"

περιβλέπω   impf. mid. περιεβλεπόμην; 1aor. mid. περιεβλεψάμην; only middle in the NT *look around (at), glance around* (MK 3.5)

περιβλεψάμενοι	VPAMNM-P	περιβλέπω
περιβλεψάμενος	VPAMNM-S	"

περιβόλαιον, ου, τό   from a basic meaning *covering thrown around*; (1) as an article of outer clothing *mantle, cloak* (HE 1.12); (2) as the effect of long hair *covering* (1C 11.15)

περιβόλαιον	N-AN-S	περιβόλαιον
περιβολαίου	N-GN-S	"

περιδέω pluperfect pass. περιεδεδόμην; *bind about, wrap around* (JN 11.44)

περιδραμόντες	VPAANM-P	περιτρέχω
περιεβάλετε	VIAA--2P	περιβάλλω
περιεβάλετο	VIAM--3S	"
περιεβάλομεν	VIAA--1P	"
περιέβαλον	VIAA--3P	"
περιεβλέπετο	VIIM--3S	περιβλέπω
περιεδέδετο	VILP--3S	περιδέω
περιέδραμον	VIAA--3P	περιτρέχω
περιεζωσμέναι	VPRPNF-P	περιζώννυμι
περιεζωσμένη	VPRPNF-S	"
περιεζωσμένοι	VPRMNM-P	"
περιεζωσμένον	VPRMAM-S	"
περιέθηκαν	VIAA--3P	περιτίθημι
περιέθηκε(ν)	VIAA--3S	"
περιέκρυβε(ν)	VIIA--3S	περικρύβω
περιέλαμψε(ν)	VIAA--3S	περιλάμπω
περιελεῖν	VNAA	περιαιρέω
περιέλειχον	VIIA--3P	περιλείχω
περιελθόντες	VPAANM-P	περιέρχομαι
περιελθόντων	VPAAGM-P	"
περιελόντες	VPAANM-P	περιαιρέω
περιέμεινε(ν)	VIAA--3S	περιμένω
περιεπάτει	VIIA--3S	περιπατέω
περιεπάτεις	VIIA--2S	"
περιεπατήσαμεν	VIAA--1P	"
περιεπατήσατε	VIAA--2P	"
περιεπάτησε(ν)	VIAA--3S	"
περιεπάτουν	VIIA--3P	"
περιέπειραν	VIAA--3P	περιπείρω
περιεπεπατήκει	VILA--3S	περιπατέω
περιέπεσε(ν)	VIAA--3S	περιπίπτω
περιεποιήσατο	VIAM--3S	περιποιέω
περίεργα	AP-AN-P	περίεργος

περιεργάζομαι *be a busybody, bustle about uselessly, be preoccupied with trifling matters* (2TH 3.11)

περιεργαζομένους	VPPDAM-P	περιεργάζομαι
	VPPOAM-P	"
περίεργοι	A--NF-P	περίεργος

περίεργος, ον strictly *overcareful, overdoing*; (1) of persons *meddlesome*; substantivally *busybody* (1T 5.13); (2) of things *intriguing, curious*; neuter plural τὰ περίεργα as a substantive *magic arts, sorcery, witchcraft* (AC 19.19)

περιέρχομαι 2aor. act. περιῆλθον; *wander about, rove, go from place to place* (HE 11.37); as a manner of sailing *take a circuitous course, sail around* (AC 28.13)

περιερχόμεναι	VPPDNF-P	περιέρχομαι
	VPPONF-P	"
περιερχομένων	VPPDGM-P	"
	VPPOGM-P	"
περιεσπᾶτο	VIIP--3S	περισπάω
περιέστησαν	VIAA--3P	περιΐστημι
περιέστραψε(ν)	VIAA--3S	see περιήστραψε(ν)
περιεστῶτα	VPRAAM-S	περιΐστημι
περιέσχε(ν)	VIAA--3S	περιέχω
περιέσωσε(ν)	VIAA--3S	περισῴζω
περιέτεμε(ν)	VIAA--3S	περιτέμνω
περιετμήθητε	VIAP--2P	"

περιέφερον	VIIA--3P	περιφέρω
περιέχει	VIPA--3S	περιέχω
περιέχουσαν	VPPAAF-S	"

περιέχω 2aor. περιέσχον; (1) literally *encircle, surround*; figuratively, of unexpected circumstances and emotions *come on* someone, *seize*; θάμβος περιέσχεν αὐτόν *he was amazed* (LU 5.9); (2) of the content of a document *contain*; impersonally περιέχει ἐν γράφῃ *it says* or *is contained in Scripture* (1P 2.6)

περιζώννυμι or **περιζωννύω** 1fut. mid. περιζώσομαι; 1aor. mid. περιεζωσάμην; pf. pass. περιέζωσμαι; as preparation for work or activity *gird about*, from the custom of shortening a garment by tightening the cloth belt around the waist; (1) active *gird* someone with something; passive *be girded* or *fastened*, with the accusative of the thing (LU 12.35); (2) middle *gird oneself, bind about oneself* (LU 12.37); with the accusative of what one is girded with (RV 1.13; 15.6); with the accusative of body part being encircled (EP 6.14); figuratively, girding denotes readiness for activity, ungirding denotes rest; idiomatically περιζώννυναι τὴν ὀσφύν literally *tighten the belt around the waist*, i.e. *get ready, prepare oneself* (EP 6.14)

περίζωσαι	VMAM--2S	περιζώννυμι
περιζωσάμενοι	VPAMNM-P	"
περιζωσάμενος	VPAMNM-S	"
περιζώσεται	VIFM--3S	"
περιῆγε(ν)	VIIA--3S	περιάγω
περιῆλθε(ν)	VIAA--3S	περιέρχομαι
περιῆλθον	VIAA--3P	"
περιῃρεῖτο	VIIP--3S	περιαιρέω
περιήστραψε(ν)	VIAA--3S	περιαστράπτω
περιθείς	VPAANM-S	περιτίθημι
περιθέντες	VPAANM-P	"
περιθέσεως	N-GF-S	περίθεσις

περίθεσις, εως, ἡ as an action *putting around*; of ornaments *putting on, wearing* (1P 3.3)

περιΐστασο	VMPM--2S	περιΐστημι

περιΐστημι 2aor. περιέστην; pf. ptc. περιεστώς; (1) of people forming a group around a person *stand around* (JN 11.42); (2) middle, as going out around something so as to keep aloof from it *avoid, shun*; figuratively in 2T 2.16 and TI 3.9

περικάθαρμα, ατος, τό what is removed or thrown out as a result of sweeping all around; the metaphorical meaning of its only use (1C 4.13) is uncertain; (1) *dirt, garbage, rubbish*; (2) *scapegoat, propitiatory offering*, from the Greek custom of offering victims to remove public defilement; the first alternative, denoting ill treatment, is generally preferred

περικαθάρματα	N-NN-P	περικάθαρμα

περικαθίζω 1aor. περιεκάθισα; *sit around* (LU 22.55)

περικαθισάντων	VPAAGM-P	περικαθίζω
περικαλύπτειν	VNPA	περικαλύπτω

περικαλύπτω 1aor. περιεκάλυψα; pf. pass. περικεκάλυμμαι; *put a covering all around, cover (completely), conceal* (MK 14.65); passive *be covered on all sides* (HE 9.4)

περικαλύψαντες	VPAANM-P	περικαλύπτω

περίκειμαι (1) middle *be around, surround*; (2) passive *have around* oneself, *be surrounded by*; figuratively in

HE 12.1; (3) passive *have* something *placed around* oneself; of fetters *wear* (AC 28.20); of a millstone *be hung about* something (MK 9.42); figuratively, of a hindering weakness *be beset by, be subject to, experience in many ways* (HE 5.2)

περίκειμαι	VIPD--1S	περίκειμαι
	VIPO--1S	"
περικείμενον	VPPDAN-S	"
	VPPOAN-S	"
περίκειται	VIPD--3S	"
	VIPO--3S	"
	VIPP--3S	"
περικεκαλυμμένην	VPRPAF-S	περικαλύπτω

περικεφαλαία, ας, ἡ *head-covering*; as a military head-covering *helmet*; metaphorically, of the spiritual protection afforded by salvation (EP 6.17); putting on the helmet marked the beginning of battle

περικεφαλαίαν	N-AF-S	περικεφαλαία
περικρατεῖς	A--NM-P	περικρατής

περικρατής, ές *having full power over, being in control of* something (AC 27.16)

περικρύβω impf. περιέκρυβον; *hide, (entirely) conceal* (LU 1.24)

περικυκλόω fut. περικυκλώσω; *surround, encircle* (LU 19.43)

περικυκλώσουσι(ν)	VIFA--3P	περικυκλόω

περιλάμπω 1aor. περιέλαμψα; transitively in the NT, of a light *shine around* someone

περιλάμψαν	VPAAAN-S	περιλάμπω
περιλείπεται	VIPP--3S	περιλείπομαι

περιλείπομαι only passive in the NT *be left behind*; hence *remain, survive* (1TH 4.15)

περιλειπόμενοι	VPPPNM-P	περιλείπομαι

περιλείχω impf. περιέλειχον; *lick all around, lick clean* (LU 16.21)

περίλυπον	A--AM-S	περίλυπος

περίλυπος, ον *afflicted beyond measure, deeply grieved, very sad*

περίλυπος	A--NF-S	περίλυπος
	A--NM-S	"
περιμένειν	VNPA	περιμένω

περιμένω *wait for, expect, await* (AC 1.4)

πέριξ adverb; *round about, all around, neighboring* (AC 5.16)

πέριξ	AB	πέριξ

περιοικέω *live around* or *nearby, live in the vicinity, be a neighbor* (LU 1.65)

περίοικοι	AP-NM-P	περίοικος

περίοικος, ον *living around, neighboring*; substantivally in the NT οἱ περίοικοι *the neighbors* (LU 1.58)

περιοικοῦντας	VPPAAM-P	περιοικέω
περιούσιον	A--AM-S	περιούσιος

περιούσιος, ον strictly, of property owned as a rich and distinctive possession; metaphorically in the NT, of God's redeemed people as his costly possession and a distinctive treasure *special, choice, chosen* (TI 2.14)

περιοχή, ῆς, ἡ what is contained in a document; its use in AC 8.32 may mean either (1) *passage* or *portion* or (2) *content* or *wording*; the first is generally preferred

τεριοχή	N-NF-S	περιοχή
περιπάτει	VMPA--2S	περιπατέω

περιπατεῖ	VIPA--3S	"
περιπατεῖν	VNPA	"
περιπατεῖς	VIPA--2S	"
περιπατεῖτε	VIPA--2P	"
	VMPA--2P	"
περιπατείτω	VMPA--3S	"

περιπατέω impf. περιεπάτουν; fut. περιπατήσω; 1aor. περιεπάτησα; (1) literally; (a) with a connotation of spending some time in a place *walk around, go about* (MK 11.27); (b) with an indication of how one is dressed *go about* (MK 12.38); (c) generally *walk, go (along)* (MT 4.18); (2) figuratively, of how one conducts one's daily life *behave, live* (CO 1.10); with the dative to denote attendant circumstances, manner, and kind of life (GA 5.16); with a prepositional phrase *behave* in such a way (EP 2.10); with an adverb (EP 4.1)

περιπατῇ	VSPA--3S	περιπατέω
περιπατῆσαι	VNAA	"
περιπατήσαντες	VPAANM-P	"
περιπατήσει	VIFA--3S	"
περιπατήσῃ	VSAA--3S	"
περιπατήσουσι(ν)	VIFA--3P	"
περιπατήσωμεν	VSAA--1P	"
περιπατῆτε	VSPA--2P	"
περιπατοῦμεν	VIPA--1P	"
περιπατοῦντα	VPPAAM-S	"
	VPPAAN-P	"
περιπατοῦντας	VPPAAM-P	"
περιπατοῦντες	VPPANM-P	"
περιπατοῦντι	VPPADM-S	"
περιπατοῦντος	VPPAGM-S	"
περιπατοῦσι(ν)	VIPA--3P	"
	VPPADM-P	"
περιπατῶμεν	VSPA--1P	"
περιπατῶν	VPPANM-S	"

περιπείρω 1aor. περιέπειρα; *pierce through, impale, wound deeply*; figuratively in the NT *experience, undergo* something severe (1T 6.10)

περιπεπατήκει	VILA--3S	περιπατέω
περιπέσητε	VSAA--2P	περιπίπτω
περιπεσόντες	VPAANM-P	"

περιπίπτω 2aor. περιέπεσον; as coming onto a situation accidentally and becoming innocently involved; literally, of mishaps *encounter*; of robbers *fall into the hands of, be seized by* (LU 10.30); of a ship on a reef *strike* (AC 27.41); figuratively, of trials *be involved in, experience* (JA 1.2)

περιποιέω 1aor. mid. περιεποιησάμην; only middle in the NT; (1) *preserve (for oneself), save* (LU 17.33); (2) *gain* or *acquire (for oneself), obtain* (1T 3.13); *pay the price for, acquire with much effort* (AC 20.28)

περιποιήσασθαι	VNAM	περιποιέω
περιποιήσεως	N-GF-S	περιποίησις
περιποίησιν	N-AF-S	"

περιποίησις, εως, ἡ as an action; (1) *preserving for oneself, saving, keeping* (HE 10.39); (2) *acquiring for oneself, obtaining* (1TH 5.9); (3) *possessing for oneself, possession* (1P 2.9)

περιποιοῦνται	VIPM--3P	περιποιέω

περιραίνω pf. pass. περιρέραμμαι; *sprinkle around* or *on all sides* (RV 19.13)

περιραντίζω

περιραντίζω pf. pass. περιρεράντισμαι; *sprinkle around on, sprinkle* (RV 19.13)

| περιρεραμμένον | VPRPAN-S | περιραίνω |
| περιρεραντισμένον | VPRPAN-S | περιραντίζω |

περιρήγνυμι (or **περιρρήγνυμι**) 1aor. περιέρηξα (or περιέρρηξα); *break off, tear off (all around)*; of clothes *strip* or *tear off* (AC 16.22)

περιρήξαντες	VPAANM-P	περιρήγνυμι
περιρρήξαντες	VPAANM-P	"
περισευθήσεται	VIFP--3S	see περισσευθήσεται

περισπάω impf. pass. third-person singular περιεσπᾶτο; only passive in the NT; literally *be pulled* or *dragged from all around*; figuratively *be* or *become distracted, be anxious* (LU 10.40)

περισσεία, ας, ἡ superabundance in anything *surplus*; of things accompanying salvation *abundance, fullness, overflowing* (RO 5.17); of wickedness *prevalence, excessive amount* (JA 1.21)

περισσεία	N-NF-S	περισσεία
περισσείαν	N-AF-S	"
περισσεύει	VIPA--3S	περισσεύω
περισσεύειν	VNPA	
περισσεύετε	VIPA--2P	"
περισσεύῃ	VSPA--3S	"
περισσεύητε	VSPA--2P	"
περισσευθήσεται	VIFP-3S	"

περίσσευμα, ατος, τό (1) of things *surplus, excess, abundance* (MK 8.8); (2) what is expressed as an overflow from one's heart *abundance, fullness* (MT 12.34)

περίσσευμα	N-AN-S	περίσσευμα
	N-NN-S	"
περισσεύματα	N-AN-P	
περισσεύματος	N-GN-S	
περισσεύομεν	VIPA--1P	περισσεύω
περισσεῦον	VPPAAN-S	"
περισσεύονται	VIPM--3P	"
περισσεύοντες	VPPANM-P	"
περισσεύοντος	VPPAGN-S	"
περισσεύουσα	VPPANF-S	"
περισσεύουσι(ν)	VIPA--3P	"
περισσεῦσαι	VOAA--3S	"
περισσεῦσαι	VNAA	"
περισσεῦσαν	VPAANN-S	"
περισσεύσαντα	VPAAAN-P	"
περισσεύσῃ	VSAA--3S	"

περισσεύω impf. ἐπερίσσευον; fut. περισσεύσω; 1aor. ἐπερίσσευσα; 1fut. pass. περισσευθήσομαι; (1) intransitively; (a) of things *be present in abundance, exceed, surpass* (MT 5.20); (b) of what is in excess *be left over, be more than enough* (MT 14.20); with the dative to indicate in what respects the abundance is expressed *overflow with, be (extremely) rich in* (2C 3.9); (c) of persons *have an advantage, be better off* (1C 8.8); *have an abundance of, have more than enough* (LU 15.17); *be outstanding in, excel in* (CO 2.7); (2) transitively; (a) of things *provide for in abundance, cause to increase* (2C 4.15); (b) of God's working *cause to abound, grant richly, provide a great deal of* (2C 9.8)

περισσεύω	VIPA--1S	περισσεύω
περισσόν	AP-AN-S	περισσός
	AP-NN-S	"
	A--NN-S	"

περισσός, ή, όν (1) of what exceeds usual expectation *extraordinary, remarkable* (MT 5.47); neuter as a substantive τὸ περισσόν *the advantage* (RO 3.1); adverbially ἐκ περισσοῦ *exceedingly, greatly* (MK 6.51); (2) of what exceeds necessity *abundant*; περισσόν ἔχειν *have abundantly* (JN 10.10); (3) *superfluous, unnecessary* (2C 9.1); (4) as a colloquial substitute for comparative τὸ περισσόν *what is more than, what goes beyond* (MT 5.37); (5) comparative περισσότερος, τέρα, ον, used as a popular substitute for πλείων (*more*) and μᾶλλον (*more, rather*); (a) as adding a degree of intensity to a noun *greater, more severe, more excellent, more abundant*, etc. (MK 12.40; 1C 12.23); (b) περισσότερον with the genitive of comparison *much more than, even more than* (MK 12.33; LU 7.26); (c) neuter singular περισσότερον as an adverb *even more, exceedingly, more abundantly* (HE 6.17)

περισσοτέρα	A-MDF-S	περισσός
περισσοτέραν	A-MAF-S	"
περισσότερον	ABM	"
	APMAN-S	"
	A-MAM-S	"
	A-MAN-S	"
	A-MNN-S	"

περισσοτέρως adverb; (1) used as a comparative to denote that a state or action is beyond what is ordinary or expected *to a greater degree, so much (the) more, far more* (HE 2.1); (2) as an elative *especially, all the more, more earnestly* (1TH 2.17)

| περισσοτέρως | ABM | περισσοτέρως |
| περισσοῦ | AP-GN-S | περισσός |

περισσῶς adverb; (1) *in an unusual manner, beyond measure* (AC 26.11); (2) as an elative *even more, all the more* (MT 27.23)

| περισσῶς | AB | περισσῶς |

περιστερά, ᾶς, ἡ *dove, pigeon*

περιστεραί	N-NF-P	περιστερά
περιστεράν	N-AF-S	"
περιστεράς	N-AF-P	"
περιστερῶν	N-GF-P	"

περισῴζω 1aor. περιέσωσα; *save from death, rescue* (MK 6.51)

περιτεμεῖν	VNAA	περιτέμνω
περιτέμνειν	VNPA	"
περιτέμνεσθαι	VNPP	"
περιτεμνέσθω	VMPP--3S	"
περιτέμνετε	VIPA--2P	"
περιτέμνημένοι	VPRPNM-P	see περιτετμημένοι
περιτέμνησθε	VSPP--2P	περιτέμνω
περιτεμνόμενοι	VPPPNM-P	"
περιτεμνομένῳ	VPPPDM-S	"

περιτέμνω 2aor. περιέτεμον; pf. pass. περιτέτμημαι; 1aor. pass. περιετμήθην; from a basic meaning *cut (off) around*; literally, as a religious rite *circumcise* the foreskin of a male (JN 7.22); passive *be circumcised, receive circumcision* (AC 15.1); figuratively, of spiritual and moral consecration in covenant relationship, possibly through Christian baptism (CO 2.11)

περιτετμημένοι	VPRPNM-P	περιτέμνω
περιτετμημένος	VPRPNM-S	"
περιτιθέασι(ν)	VIPA--3P	περιτίθημι

περιτίθεμεν VIPA--1P "

περιτίθημι 1aor. περιέθηκα; 2aor. περιέθην; literally *put* or *place* something *around* or *on* (MT 21.33); of a crown or wreath *place on* (MK 15.17); of clothing *put on* someone (MT 27.28); figuratively *invest* an object with something, τιμὴν περιτιθέναι *assign honor, treat honorably* (1C 12.23)

περιτμηθῆναι VNAP περιτέμνω
περιτμηθῆτε VSAP--2P "

περιτομή, ῆς, ἡ *circumcision*; (1) literally, as a religious rite signifying covenant participation with God (JN 7.22); figuratively, as spiritual circumcision denoting separation from sin and consecration to God in covenant relationship (RO 2.29); (2) by metonymy, for those who are circumcised; literally *the circumcised*, i.e. *Jews* (RO 3.30), opposite ἀκροβυστία (literally *the uncircumcised*, i.e. *Gentiles*); figuratively, of Christians (PH 3.3)

περιτομή N-NF-S περιτομή
περιτομῇ N-DF-S "
περιτομήν N-AF-S "
περιτομῆς N-GF-S "
περιτρέπει VIPA--3S περιτρέπω

περιτρέπω *turn about* (from one state to its opposite); εἰς μανίαν περιτρέπειν *drive* someone *crazy, cause to be insane* (AC 26.24)

περιτρέχω 2aor. περιέδραμον; *run around, go about in* an area (MK 6.55)

περιφέρειν VNPA περιφέρω
περιφέρεσθε VMPP--2P "
περιφερόμεναι VPPPNF-P "
περιφερόμενοι VPPPNM-P "
περιφέροντες VPPANM-P "

περιφέρω literally *carry about from one place to another, carry here and there* (MK 6.55); figuratively, of an effect on one's life *experience in different ways* (2C 4.10); metaphorically, of the effect of diverse doctrines on the mental and spiritual life *cause to think one way and then another* (EP 4.14)

περιφρονείτω VMPA--3S περιφρονέω

περιφρονέω *despise, look down on, disregard* (TI 2.15)

περίχωρον AP-AF-S περίχωρος

περίχωρος, ον *neighboring, adjacent*; substantivally in the NT, as a geographical designation ἡ π. *neighborhood, the region around* (MT 14.35); by metonymy *the inhabitants of a region* (MT 3.5)

περίχωρος AP-NF-S περίχωρος
περιχώρου AP-GF-S "
περιχώρῳ AP-DF-S "

περίψημα, ατος, τό what is removed by wiping or scraping clean all around; as used in 1C 4.13 it may be either (1) *scum, offscouring, dregs* or (2) *sacrificed victim, (expiatory) ransom*, from the Greek custom of offering victims regarded as the scum of society to remove public defilement (see also περικάθαρμα [*rubbish; scapegoat*]); the first alternative is generally preferred

περίψημα N-NN-S περίψημα
περπερεύεται VIPD--3S περπερεύομαι
VIPO--3S "

περπερεύομαι as speaking arrogantly *boast, brag; behave as a braggart* or *windbag* (πέρπερος) (1C 13.4)

Περσίδα N-AF-S Περσίς

Περσίς, ίδος, ἡ *Persis*, feminine proper noun (RO 16.12)

πέρυσι adverb; *last year, a year ago*

πέρυσι AB πέρυσι
πέσατε VMAA--2P see πέσετε
πεσεῖν VNAA πίπτω
πεσεῖται VIFD--3S "
πέσετε VMAA--2P "
πέσῃ VSAA--3S "
πέσητε VSAA--2P "
πεσόν VPAANN-S "
πεσόντα VPAAAM-S "
πεσόντας VPAAAM-P "
πεσόντες VPAANM-P "
πεσοῦνται VIFD--3P "
πεσών VPAANM-S "
πέσωσι(ν) VSAA--3P "
πετεινά AP-AN-P πετεινός
AP-NN-P "

πετεινός, ή, όν *winged, flying*; neuter as a substantive in the NT τὸ πετεινόν *bird, fowl*

πετεινῶν AP-GN-P πετεινός
πέτηται VSPD--3S πέτομαι
VSPO--3S "

πέτομαι (and **πετάομαι**) *fly*

πετομένοις VPPPDDN-P πέτομαι
VPPPODN-P "
πετόμενον VPPDAM-S "
VPPOAM-S "
πετομένου VPPDGM-S "
VPPOGM-S "
πετομένῳ VPPPDDM-S "
VPPPODM-S "

πέτρα, ας, ἡ (1) literally, living *rock, bedrock* (MT 7.24), in contrast to πέτρος (isolated *stone*); *cliff rock*, in which tombs may be hewn out (MK 15.46) or caves and clefts may be found (RV 6.15); *rocky ground* or *soil* (LU 8.6); (2) metaphorically, of Christ; (a) as the antitype fulfilling the event foreshadowed by the rock in the wilderness, offering "living water" when struck (1C 10.4); (b) as the rock of offense to Israel when it rejected him as the spiritual cornerstone or capstone of the invisible temple of God (RO 9.33; 1P 2.8); (3) figuratively, as the spiritual foundation of the church (MT 16.18), interpreted variously to refer to the affirmation Peter made (MT 16.16), to the apostle Peter (ὁ Πέτρος) as the leader of the apostolate, or to Christ himself

πέτρα N-NF-S πέτρα
πέτρᾳ N-DF-S "
πέτραι N-NF-P "
πέτραις N-DF-P "
πέτραν N-AF-S "
πέτρας N-AF-P "
N-GF-S "
Πέτρε N-VM-S Πέτρος
Πέτρον N-AM-S "

Πέτρος, ου, ὁ *Peter*, masculine proper noun given as a descriptive title to Simon, one of the apostles (MK 3.16); the meaning of the name, *stone*, is probably the Greek equivalent of an Aramaic word transliterated as Κηφᾶς (JN 1.42)

Πέτρος N-NM-S Πέτρος

Πέτρου	N-GM-S	"
Πέτρῳ	N-DM-S	"
πετρῶδες	AP-AN-S	πετρώδης
πετρώδη	AP-AN-P	"

πετρώδης, ες   *rocky, stony*; neuter singular τὸ πετρῶδες and plural τὰ πετρώδη as substantives *rocky ground* or *soil*

πετωμένοις	VPPDDN-P	πέτομαι
	VPPODN-P	"
πετώμενον	VPPDAM-S	"
	VPPOAM-S	"
πετωμένου	VPPDGM-S	"
	VPPOGM-S	"
πετωμένῳ	VPPDDM-S	"
	VPPODM-S	"
πεφανερώμεθα	VIRP--1P	φανερόω
πεφανερῶσθαι	VNRP	"
πεφανέρωται	VIRP--3S	"
πεφιλήκατε	VIRA--2P	φιλέω
πεφίμωσο	VMRP--2S	φιμόω
πεφορτισμένοι	VPRPVM-P	φορτίζω
πεφυσιωμένοι	VPRPNM-P	φυσιόω
πεφυσιωμένων	VPRPGM-P	"
πεφυτευμένην	VPRPAF-S	φυτεύω
πεφωτισμένους	VPRPAM-P	φωτίζω
πηγαί	N-NF-P	πηγή

πήγανον, ου, τό   *rue*, an aromatic garden herb with thick, fleshy leaves, used for seasoning (LU 11.42)

πήγανον	N-AN-S	πήγανον
πηγάς	N-AF-P	πηγή

πηγή, ῆς, ἡ   (1) literally *spring, fountain, (living) well*, as a source of water; to be distinguished from φρέαρ (*cistern* or *reservoir* for storing surface water) (cf. JN 4.6 and 4.11); (2) metaphorically, the *fountain* of the water of life, identified in JN 4.14 as eternal life; (3) figuratively in MK 5.29 as a hemorrhaging, *issue* or *flow* of blood; (4) metaphorically and plural in 2P 2.17 presumptuous sinners who resemble dried up *springs*

πηγή	N-NF-S	πηγή
πηγῇ	N-DF-S	"
πηγῆς	N-GF-S	"

πήγνυμι   1aor. ἔπηξα; *make firm, fix*; of a building *erect, put together*; of a tent *pitch, set up* (HE 8.2)

πηδάλιον, ου, τό   as the steering gear of a ship *rudder, steering paddle*

πηδαλίου	N-GN-S	πηδάλιον
πηδαλίων	N-GN-P	"
πηλίκοις	A-TDN-P	πηλίκος

πηλίκος, η, ον   interrogative correlative pronoun; used in the NT in exclamations; literally, of size *how large, how great* (GA 6.11); figuratively, of dignity *how great, how distinguished* (HE 7.4)

πηλίκος	A-TNM-S	πηλίκος
πηλόν	N-AM-S	πηλός

πηλός, οῦ, ὁ   (1) as soil suitable for making pottery *clay, loam* (RO 9.21); (2) as a mixture of earth and water *mud, moist earth* (JN 9.6)

πηλοῦ	N-GM-S	πηλός

πήρα, ας, ἡ   *knapsack, pouch, bag*, a leather bag or sack with a strap, used by travelers for carrying food provisions

πήραν	N-AF-S	πήρα
πήρας	N-GF-S	"

πηρόω   1aor. ἐπήρωσα; pf. πεπήρωκα; *maim, disable*; idiomatically πηροῦν τὴν καρδίαν literally *maim the heart*, i.e. *cause not to learn, close the mind; make unable to learn* (JN 12.40)

πηρώσει	N-DF-S	πήρωσις

πήρωσις, εως, ἡ   *disabling*, especially in the form of *short-sightedness, blindness*; figuratively in MK 3.5 *lack of ability to understand*

πῆχυν	N-AM-S	πῆχυς

πῆχυς, εως, ὁ, gen. plural **πηχῶν**   strictly *forearm*; as a measure of length, as long as the forearm *cubit, ell*; equivalent to 17.5 inches, 1.5 feet, or 0.46 meter

πηχῶν	N-GM-P	πῆχυς

πιάζω   1aor. ἐπίασα; 1aor. pass. ἐπιάσθην; (1) in a neutral sense *take (hold of)* (AC 3.7); (2) with hostile intent *seize, arrest, lay hold of* (JN 7.30); (3) of animals or fish *catch* (JN 21.3)

πιάσαι	VNAA	πιάζω
πιάσας	VPAANM-S	"
πιάσωσι(ν)	VSAA--3P	"
πίε	VMAA--2S	πίνω

πιέζω   pf. pass. πεπίεσμαι; as packing down something in a measure *press (down)* (LU 6.38)

πιεῖν	VNAA	πίνω
πίεσαι	VIFD--2S	"
πίεσθε	VIFD--2P	"
πίεται	VIFD--3S	"
πίετε	VMAA--2P	"
πίῃ	VSAA--3S	"
πίητε	VSAA--2P	"

πιθανολογία, ας, ἡ   *persuasive speech, plausible arguments* that are not necessarily true (CO 2.4)

πιθανολογίᾳ	N-DF-S	πιθανολογία
πιθοῖς	A--DM-P	πιθός

πιθός, ή, όν   *persuasive* (1C 2.4)

πικραίνεσθε	VMPP--2P	πικραίνω

πικραίνω   fut. πικρανῶ; 1aor. pass. ἐπικράνθην; literally *make bitter*; of waters *cause to be undrinkable*; passive *become bitter* (RV 8.11); of the stomach *sour* (RV 10.9, 10); figuratively and passive *become angry, become resentful, become bitter* (CO 3.19)

πικρανεῖ	VIFA--3S	πικραίνω

πικρία, ας, ἡ   *bitterness*; literally, of plants that produce inedible or poisonous fruit ῥίζα πικρίας *root that bears bitter fruit*; used metaphorically of a person whose influence or actions become harmful to a community *one who causes trouble* (HE 12.15; cf. Deuteronomy 29.18–19); figuratively, as a hostile attitude *(angry) resentment, animosity* (EP 4.31)

πικρία	N-NF-S	πικρία
πικρίας	N-GF-S	"
πικρόν	A--AM-S	πικρός
	A--AN-S	"

πικρός, ά, όν   strictly *sharp, piercing*; literally, of what sharply penetrates the senses; of taste *bitter*, opposite γλυκύς (*sweet*); of water unfit for drinking *bitter, brackish*; neuter as a substantive τὸ πικρόν (ὕδωρ) *bitter water* (JA 3.11); figuratively, of a resentful attitude *bitter, harsh, cruel* (JA 3.14) πικρῶς   adverb; *bitterly*; used of violent and uncontrolled weeping that expresses despair (MT 26.75)

πικρῶς	AB	πικρῶς
Πιλᾶτον	N-AM-S	Πιλᾶτος
Πιλᾶτον	N-AM-S	"
Πιλάτος	N-NM-S	"

Πιλᾶτος, ου, ὁ (also **Πειλᾶτος, Πιλάτος**)   *Pilate*, masculine proper noun

Πιλᾶτος	N-NM-S	Πιλᾶτος
Πιλάτου	N-GM-S	"
Πιλάτῳ	N-DM-S	"

πίμπλημι   1aor. ἔπλησα; 1aor. pass. ἐπλήσθην; 1fut. pass. πλησθήσομαι; *fill, fulfill*; (1) literally; (a) spatially *fill with* (LU 5.7); (b) passive, of intellectual and spiritual processes *be filled with, experience completely* (LU 1.15); (2) figuratively and passive; (a) of prophecies *be fulfilled, happen* (LU 21.22); (b) of time periods *come to an end, be fulfilled* (LU 1.23)

πίμπρασθαι	VNPP	πίμπρημι

πίμπρημι   pass. πίμπραμαι; pf. pass. ptc. πεπρησμένος; only passive in the NT; used as a medical technical term to describe feverish disorders; (1) *burn with fever*; (2) *swell up* (from inflammation), *become swollen* is probably the meaning in AC 28.6, evidenced by its quick visibility to onlookers

πίνακι	N-DM-S	πίναξ

πινακίδιον, ου, τό   diminutive of πίναξ; *small wooden tablet, writing tablet* (LU 1.63)

πινακίδιον	N-AN-S	πινακίδιον
πίνακος	N-GM-S	πίναξ

πίναξ, ακος, ὁ   strictly *pine board, plank*; as a relatively flat container for serving food *wooden platter, plate, dish*

πίνει	VIPA--3S	πίνω
πίνειν	VNPA	"
πίνετε	VIPA--2P	"
πινέτω	VMPA--3S	"
πίνῃ	VSPA--3S	"
πίνητε	VSPA--2P	"
πίνοντες	VPPANM-P	"
πίνουσι(ν)	VIPA--3P	"

πίνω   impf. ἔπινον; fut. mid. πίομαι, second-person singular πίεσαι; 2aor. ἔπιον, inf. πιεῖν (contracted form πεῖν); pf. πέπωκα; *drink*; (1) literally, of consuming liquids *drink* (MT 6.25); (2) figuratively, of the ground taking in rain *absorb, soak up* (HE 6.7); (3) idiomatically πίνειν ποτήριον literally *drink a cup*, i.e. *suffer severely* (MT 20.22); (4) metaphorically, of spiritual experience πίνειν ἐκ τοῦ ὕδατος οὗ ἐγὼ δώσω *drink the water that I* (Jesus) *will give*, i.e. *receive eternal life* (JN 4.14); (5) symbolically, as benefiting from Jesus' atoning blood πίνειν αὐτοῦ τὸ αἷμα literally *drink his blood*, i.e. *receive help from his death* (JN 6.53)

πίνω	VIPA--1S	πίνω
	VSPA--1S	"
πίνων	VPPANM-S	"

πιότης, τητος, ἡ   *fatness*; of flourishing plants *rich quality*; metaphorically in RO 11.17 of Israel's covenant privileges *richness, great value*

πιότητος	N-GF-S	πιότης
πιοῦσα	VPAANF-S	πίνω
πιπρασκομένων	VPPPGN-P	πιπράσκω

πιπράσκω   impf. ἐπίπρασκον; pf. πέπρακα; pf. pass. πέπραμαι; 1aor. pass. ἐπράθην; (1) literally; (a) of things *sell* (MT 13.46); passive *be sold* (MT 26.9); (b) of persons *be sold* (as a slave) (MT 18.25); (2) figuratively, of becoming enslaved to sin, personified as a master who gains control (RO 7.14)

πίπτει	VIPA--3S	πίπτω
πίπτοντες	VPPANM-P	"
πιπτόντων	VPPAGN-P	"

πίπτω   impf. ἔπιπτον; fut. mid. πεσοῦμαι; 2aor. ἔπεσον and ἔπεσα; pf. πέπτωκα; *fall*; (1) literally; (a) as coming down forcefully from a higher to lower level *fall, drop* (AC 20.9); (b) of buildings and walls *collapse, fall into ruins* (HE 11.30); (c) of a person, as suddenly dropping from an upright position *fall down, tumble* (AC 9.4); (d) as intentionally falling, prostrating oneself as a sign of worship or devotion *fall down, throw oneself down* (MT 18.26); (e) as suddenly experiencing something bad *fall on, happen to* (AC 13.11); (2) figuratively; (a) of things; idiomatically, of throwing the lot to decide something πίπτει ὁ κλῆρος ἐπί τινα literally *the lot falls on someone*, i.e. *someone is chosen by lot* (AC 1.26); (b) of what fades or comes to an end *cease, fall, fail* (1C 13.8); (c) of persons, in a religious and moral sense, as going astray or becoming guilty of wrongdoing *fall away, be ruined, fall* (into sin) (1C 10.12); of what results from judgment *fall, be ruined* (RO 11.11), opposite στήκω (*stand*); (3) euphemistically, of a violent death *fall, die* (1C 10.8)

Πισιδία, ας, ἡ   *Pisidia*, a mountainous region in south central Asia Minor (AC 14.24)

Πισιδίαν	A--AF-S	Πισίδιος
	N-AF-S	Πισιδία
Πισιδίας	N-GF-S	"

Πισίδιος, ία, ον   *Pisidian*, belonging to the country of Pisidia in south central Asia Minor (AC 13.14)

πιστά	A--AN-P	πιστός
πιστάς	A--AF-P	"
πιστέ	A--VM-S	"
πίστει	N-DF-S	πίστις
πίστευε	VMPA--2S	πιστεύω
πιστεύει	VIPA--3S	"
πιστεύειν	VNPA	"
πιστεύεις	VIPA--2S	"
πιστεύεται	VIPP--3S	"
πιστεύετε	VIPA--2P	"
	VMPA--2P	"
πιστεύῃ	VSPA--3S	"
πιστεύητε	VSPA--2P	"
πιστευθῆναι	VNAP	"
πιστεύομεν	VIPA--1P	"
πιστεύοντα	VPPAAM-S	"
πιστεύοντας	VPPAAM-P	"
πιστεύοντες	VPPANM-P	"
πιστεύοντι	VPPADM-S	"
πιστευόντων	VPPAGM-P	"
πιστεύουσι(ν)	VIPA--3P	"
	VPPADM-P	"
πιστεῦσαι	VNAA	"
πιστεύσαντας	VPAAAM-P	"
πιστεύσαντες	VPAANM-P	"

πιστευσάντων	VPAAGM-P	"
πιστεύσας	VPAANM-S	"
πιστεύσασα	VPAANF-S	"
πιστεύσασι(ν)	VPAADM-P	"
πιστεύσατε	VMAA--2P	"
πιστεῦσε	VMAA--2S	"
πιστεύσει	VIFA--3S	"
πιστεύσετε	VIFA--2P	"
πιστεύσῃ	VSAA--3S	"
πιστεύσῃς	VSAA--2S	"
πιστεύσητε	VSAA--2P	"
πιστεύσομεν	VIFA--1P	"
πίστευσον	VMAA--2S	"
πιστεύσοντες	VPFANM-P	"
πιστευσόντων	VPFAGM-P	"
πιστεύσουσι(ν)	VIFA--3P	"
πιστεύσω	VIFA--1S	"
	VSAA--1S	"
πιστεύσωμεν	VSAA--1P	"
πιστεύσωσι(ν)	VSAA--3P	"

πιστεύω impf. ἐπίστευον; fut. πιστεύσω; 1aor. ἐπίστευσα; pf. πεπίστευκα; pluperfect πεπιστεύκειν; pf. pass. πεπίστευμαι; 1aor. pass. ἐπιστεύθην; (1) as primarily an intellectual evaluation *believe*; (a) with what one is convinced of added as an object *believe (in), be convinced of* (JN 11.26b); (b) as an evaluative orienter, using ὅτι or the accusative and an infinitive *believe that* (AC 9.26; 15.11); (c) as having confidence in what is spoken or written, using the dative *believe, give credence to, think to be true* (JN 2.22); (d) as having confidence in a person, using the dative *believe, give credence to* someone (MK 16.14); (2) as primarily a religious commitment, especially with God or Christ as the object of faith *believe (in), trust*; (a) with the object in the dative *have faith in, believe* (AC 16.34); (b) especially denoting the exercise of saving faith, with the object expressed by using εἰς or ἐπί and the accusative, *believe in* or *on* (JN 3.16; AC 9.42); (c) as denoting relying on God for help *have confidence, believe* (MT 21.22); (3) as committing something to someone *entrust, trust* (LU 16.11); passive, as having something committed to someone *be entrusted with* (RO 3.2)

πιστεύω	VIPA--1S	πιστεύω
πιστεύων	VPPANM-S	
πίστεως	N-GF-S	πίστις
πιστή	A--NF-S	πιστός
πιστή	A--DF-S	"
πιστήν	A--AF-S	"
πιστῆς	A--GF-S	"
πιστικῆς	A--GF-S	πιστικός

πιστικός, ή, όν *trustworthy, faithful*; as qualifying a substance *pure, genuine, unadulterated*

πίστιν	N-AF-S	πίστις

πίστις, εως, ἡ (1) active, as belief directed toward a person or thing *confidence, faith, trust, reliance on* (MT 9.2); (2) absolutely, without an object; (a) as the essential Christian religion *(the) faith* (CO 1.23); (b) as recognition and acceptance of Christian teaching *faith* (JA 2.17); (c) as a decision to be faithful and loyal to the Christian religion *promise, pledge, commitment* (1T 5.12); (d) as a *conviction* that brings certainty *faith,*

assurance (RO 14.22); (e) as a Christian virtue, especially along with hope and love characterizing believers (1TH 1.3); (3) passive; (a) of what brings trust and confidence from others *faithfulness, fidelity, reliability* (TI 2.10); (b) as what inspires confidence *pledge, (means of) proof, guarantee* (AC 17.31); (4) objectively, as the content of what is believed *doctrine, (the) faith* (RO 1.5; JU 3)

πίστις	N-NF-S	πίστις
πιστοί	A--NM-P	πιστός
πιστοῖς	A--DM-P	"
πιστόν	A--AM-S	"
	A--AN-S	"
	A--NN-S	"

πιστός, ή, όν (1) active; (a) of persons *trusting, believing, full of faith, confiding* (JN 20.27); (b) absolutely, as an adjective *believing* (in Christ) (AC 16.1); as a substantive *believer* (2C 6.15); οἱ πιστοί literally *the believers,* i.e. *Christians* (1T 4.3); πιστή *female believer, Christian woman* (1T 5.16); (2) passive; (a) of persons *trustworthy, faithful, dependable* (CO 4.7), opposite ἄδικος (*dishonest*); (b) of God *trustworthy, faithful* (HE 10.23); (c) of things, especially of what one says *sure, reliable, trustworthy* (1T 1.15)

πιστός	A--NM-S	πιστός
πιστοῦ	A--GM-S	"
πιστούς	A--AM-P	"

πιστόω 1aor. pass. ἐπιστώθην; only passive in the NT *be firmly persuaded* or *convinced of* something, *believe* (2T 3.14)

πιστῷ	A--DM-S	πιστός
πιστῶν	A--GM-P	"
πίω	VSAA--1S	πίνω
πίωμεν	VSAA--1P	"
πιών	VPAANM-S	"
πίωσι(ν)	VSAA--3P	"
πλάκες	N-NF-P	πλάξ
πλανᾷ	VIPA--3S	πλανάω
πλανᾶσθαι	VNPP	"
πλανᾶσθε	VIPP--2P	"
	VMPP--2P	"
πλανάτω	VMPA--3S	"

πλανάω fut. πλανήσω; 1aor. ἐπλάνησα; pf. pass. πεπλάνημαι; 1aor. pass. ἐπλανήθην; (1) active *lead astray, cause to wander*; figuratively *mislead, deceive, cause to be mistaken* (MT 24.5); (2) passive; (a) literally *go astray* (MT 18.12), *wander about* (HE 11.38); (b) figuratively, as blameworthy and mistaken evaluation *be deceived* or *led astray, be mistaken, be deluded* (1C 6.9; GA 6.7); as abandoning what is true and committing oneself to error *err* (in heart) (HE 3.10; JA 5.19)

πλάνη, ης, ἡ *going astray, wandering*; figuratively in the NT; (1) as a straying from the truth *error, delusion, deception* (MT 27.64; 1J 4.6), opposite ἀλήθεια (*truth*); (2) as completely wrong behavior *perversion* (RO 1.27)

πλάνη	N-NF-S	πλάνη
πλάνη	N-DF-S	"
πλανηθῇ	VSAP--3S	πλανάω
πλανηθῆναι	VNAP	"
πλανηθῆτε	VSAP--2P	"

πλάνης, ητος, ὁ   *wanderer*; as a star or planet that appears not to stay on course, equivalent to πλανήτης (JU 13)

πλάνης	N-GF-S	πλάνη
πλανῆσαι	VNAA	πλανάω
πλανήσῃ	VSAA--3S	"
πλανήσουσι(ν)	VIFA--3P	"
πλανῆται	A--NM-P	πλανήτης
πλάνητες	N-NM-P	πλάνης

πλανήτης, ου, ὁ   *wanderer*; used to qualify ἀστέρες in JU 13 *wandering stars*

πλάνοι	AP-NM-P	πλάνος
	A--NM-P	"
πλάνοις	A--DN-P	"

πλάνος, ον   *causing to be mistaken, leading astray, deceitful* (1T 4.1); substantivally ὁ π. *deceiver, impostor* (MT 27.63)

πλάνος	AP-NM-S	πλάνος
πλανῶμεν	VIPA--1P	πλανάω
πλανώμενα	VPPPNN-P	"
πλανώμενοι	VPPMNM-P	"
	VPPPNM-P	"
πλανωμένοις	VPPPDM-P	"
πλανώμενον	VPPPAN-S	"
πλανῶν	VPPANM-S	"
πλανῶνται	VIPP--3P	"
πλανῶντες	VPPANM-P	"
πλανῶντων	VPPAGM-P	"

πλάξ, πλακός, ἡ   a flat, broad surface, as a *plain, mesa, tableland*; in the NT *flat stone* to inscribe on, *tablet*; plural, of stones engraved with the law *tables, tablets* (HE 9.4)

πλαξί(ν)	N-DF-P	πλάξ
πλάσαντι	VPAADM-S	πλάσσω

πλάσμα, ατος, τό   *what has been formed* or *molded* by an artisan, *figure, container, thing formed* (RO 9.20)

πλάσμα	N-NN-S	πλάσμα

πλάσσω   1aor. ἔπλασα; 1aor. pass. ἐπλάσθην; as what an artisan does *form, fashion, shape* (RO 9.20); of God's creative work *form, make* (1T 2.13)

πλαστοῖς	A--DM-P	πλαστός

πλαστός, ή, όν   a verbal adjective from πλάσσω (*form, fashion, shape*); *formed, made*; figuratively, of the man-made arguments of false teachers *fabricated, counterfeit, made-up* (2P 2.3)

πλατεῖα	AP-NF-S	πλατύς
	A--NF-S	"
πλατείαις	AP-DF-P	"
πλατείας	AP-AF-S	"
	AP-GF-S	"
πλατειῶν	AP-GF-P	"

πλάτος, ους, τό   *breadth, width*

πλάτος	N-AN-S	πλάτος
	N-NN-S	"
πλατύνθητε	VMAP--2P	πλατύνω
πλατύνουσι(ν)	VIPA--3P	"

πλατύνω   pf. pass. third-person singular πεπλάτυνται; 1aor. pass. ἐπλατύνθην; literally *make broad, enlarge* (MT 23.5); idiomatically ἡ καρδία ἡμῶν πεπλάτυνται literally *our heart is broadened*, i.e. *we have great affection for you, we love you very much* (2C 6.11)

πλατύς, εῖα, ύ   *broad, wide* (MT 7.13); the feminine πλατεῖα, with ὁδός to be supplied, serves as a substantive *broad way, open street, wide road* (MT 6.5), in contrast to ῥύμη (*alley*)

πλέγμα, ατος, τό   anything entwined or interwoven; as hair elaborately dressed with interwoven ornaments *plaited* or *braided hair* (1T 2.9)

πλέγμασι(ν)	N-DN-P	πλέγμα
πλεῖν	VNPA	πλέω
πλεῖον	ABM	πολύς
	A-MAN-S	"
	A-MNN-S	"
πλείονα	A-MAF-S	"
	A-MAM-S	"
	A-MAN-P	"
πλείονας	A-MAF-P	"
	A-MAM-P	"
πλείονες	A-MNM-P	"
πλείονος	A-MGF-S	"
πλειόνων	A-MGM-P	"
	A-MGN-P	"
πλείοσι(ν)	A-MDM-P	"
πλείους	A-MAF-P	"
	A-MNF-P	"
	A-MNM-P	"
πλεῖσται	A-SNF-P	"
πλεῖστοι	A-SNM-P	"
πλεῖστον	A-SAN-S	"
πλεῖστος	A-SNM-S	"
πλείω	A-MAN-P	"

πλέκω   1aor. ἔπλεξα; *weave, intertwine, plait*, as when making a wreath

πλέξαντες	VPAANM-P	πλέκω
πλέον	ABM	πολύς
	A-MAN-S	"
	VPPAAN-S	πλέω
πλεονάζει	VIPA--3S	πλεονάζω
πλεονάζοντα	VPPAAM-S	"
	VPPANN-P	"

πλεονάζω   1aor. ἐπλεόνασα; *be more than enough*; (1) intransitively; (a) with an abstract subject *increase, greatly abound, become more and more* (RO 5.20); (b) with a person as the subject *have more than enough* (2C 8.15); (2) transitively *cause to increase, make to abound, make more intense* (1TH 3.12)

πλεονάσαι	VOAA--3S	πλεονάζω
πλεονάσασα	VPAANF-S	"
πλεονάσῃ	VSAA--3S	"
πλεονέκται	N-NM-P	πλεονέκτης
πλεονέκταις	N-DM-P	"
πλεονεκτεῖν	VNPA	πλεονεκτέω

πλεονεκτέω   1aor. ἐπλεονέκτησα; 1aor. pass. ἐπλεονεκτήθην; from πλέον ἔχειν; with a basic meaning *have more than* another; (1) of persons, in regard to material possessions *take advantage of, exploit, cheat* (2C 7.2; 1TH 4.6); (2) of Satan's activity *outwit, get the better of* (2C 2.11)

πλεονεκτηθῶμεν	VSAP--1P	πλεονεκτέω

πλεονέκτης, ου, ὁ   as one who wants more than his share, especially of material possessions *covetous, greedy* or *grasping person* (1C 5.10; EP 5.5) πλεονέκτης   N-NM-S   πλεονέκτης

πλεονεξία, ας, ἡ   as bad behavior, a disposition to have more than one's share *greed, covetousness, avarice* (LU 12.15); ὡς π. *as a matter of being compelled to, as what is grudgingly given* (2C 9.5)

πλεονεξία	N-NF-S	πλεονεξία
πλεονεξίᾳ	N-DF-S	"
πλεονεξίαι	N-NF-P	"
πλεονεξίαις	N-DF-P	"
πλεονεξίαν	N-AF-S	"
πλεονεξίας	N-GF-S	"
πλέοντας	VPPAAM-P	πλέω
πλέοντι	VPPADM-S	"
πλεόντων	VPPAGM-P	"

πλευρά, ᾶς, ἡ   as a part of the body *side, rib*

πλευράν   N-AF-S   πλευρά

πλέω   impf. ἔπλεον; *sail, go by sea*; ὁ ἐπὶ τόπον πλέων *one who sails from place to place, seafarer, voyager* (RV 18.17)

πλέων	VPPANM-S	πλέω
πληγαί	N-NF-P	πληγή
πληγαῖς	N-DF-P	"
πληγάς	N-AF-P	"

πληγή, ῆς, ἡ   (1) literally *blow* (LU 10.30); as laid on by a whiplike instrument *stroke, stripe*, plural *beating* (LU 12.48); (2) as the result of blows or stripes *wound, bruise* (AC 16.33); (3) as a blow or stroke of judgment sent by God *plague, calamity* (RV 9.18)

πληγή	N-NF-S	πληγή
πληγῇ	N-DF-S	"
πληγήν	N-AF-S	"
πληγῆς	N-GF-S	"
πληγῶν	N-GF-P	"
πλήθει	N-DN-S	πλῆθος
πλήθη	N-NN-P	"

πλῆθος, ους, τό   strictly *fullness, magnitude*; (1) with the stress on largeness of number; (a) of persons *crowd, throng, multitude* (LU 6.17); (b) of things *large number (of), great many (of), multitude (of)* (HE 11.12); (2) as denoting the whole of a great number; (a) in religious usage *community, church, group* (AC 19.9); (b) in civic usage *populace, people, population* (AC 2.6)

πλῆθος	N-AN-S	πλῆθος
	N-NN-S	"
πλήθους	N-GN-S	"
πληθῦναι	VOAA--3S	πληθύνω
πληθύνει	VIPA--3S	"
πληθυνεῖ	VIFA--3S	"
πληθύνῃ	VSAA--3S	"
πληθυνθείη	VOAP--3S	"
πληθυνθῆναι	VNAP	"
πληθυνόντων	VPPAGM-P	"

πληθύνω   impf. pass. ἐπληθυνόμην; fut. πληθυνῶ; 1aor. pass. ἐπληθύνθην; (1) transitively; (a) active *cause to increase, multiply, give in abundance* (HE 6.14); (b) passive *be multiplied, grow, increase* (AC 7.17); (2) intransitively *increase, grow* (AC 6.1)

πληθυνῶ	VIFA--1S	πληθύνω
πληθύνων	VPPANM-S	"
πλήκτην	N-AM-S	πλήκτης

πλήκτης, ου, ὁ   strictly *striker*; hence *pugnacious person, bully, quarrelsome person*

πλήμμυρα, ης, ἡ (also **πλήμυρα**)   *flood, high water* (LU 6.48)

πλημμύρας	N-GF-S	πλήμμυρα
πλημμύρης	N-GF-S	"
πλημύρας	N-GF-S	"
πλημύρης	N-GF-S	"

πλήν   from πλέον (*more*); (1) an adverb used as a conjunction; (a) as an adversative equivalent to ἀλλά *but* (LU 23.28); (b) predominately used to restrict a previous statement *nevertheless, however, in spite of that* (LU 22.42); (c) used to break off a discussion and point out parenthetically what was important in it *in any case, however, only one thing* (PH 3.16; RV 2.25); (d) used to add in an exception π. ὅτι *except that* (AC 20.23); (2) as an improper preposition with the genitive *except, besides* (MK 12.32)

πλήν	CC	πλήν
	CH	"
	PG	"
πλήρεις	A--AF-P	πλήρης
	A--AM-P	"
	A--NM-P	"
πλῆρες	A--AN-S	"
πλήρη	A--AM-S	"

πλήρης, ες   sometimes indeclinable; (1) of space fully occupied *full (of), filled (with)*, with the genitive of what the filling consists; (a) literally, of things *full of, filled with* (MK 8.19); (b) figuratively, of persons *full of, filled with, rich* or *abounding in, thoroughly endowed with* (LU 4.1; AC 9.36); (2) of a totality of something or someone with nothing lacking *complete, in full, wholly filled* (JN 1.14); of grain *fully ripe* (MK 4.28)

πλήρης	A--NF-S	πλήρης
	A--NM-S	see πλήρη
	A--NM-S	πλήρης
	A--VM-S	"
πληροῖς	VSPA--2S	πληρόω
πληρούμενον	VPPPNN-S	"
πληρουμένου	VPPMGM-S	"
πληροῦν	VNPA	"
πληροῦσθε	VMPP--2P	"
πληροῦται	VIPP--3S	"
πληροφορείσθω	VMPP--3S	πληροφορέω

πληροφορέω   1aor. ἐπληροφόρησα; pf. pass. πεπληροφόρημαι; 1aor. pass. ἐπληροφορήθην; (1) *bring to fullness* or *to a full measure*; figuratively in the NT; (a) with a thing as the object *fill (completely), fulfill, accomplish* (2T 4.5); passive, of what is carried through to completion *be accomplished, be achieved* (LU 1.1); (b) passive, with a person as the subject *be brought to full measure, be complete* (possibly CO 4.12); (2) passive, of persons *be fully convinced, be completely certain, be fully assured* (RO 4.21; 14.5; possibly CO 4.12)

πληροφορηθείς	VPAPNM-S	πληροφορέω
πληροφορηθῇ	VSAP--3S	"
πληροφορηθῆτε	VSAP--2P	"
πληροφορῆσαι	VOAA--3S	"
πληροφόρησον	VMAA--2S	"

πληροφορία, ας, ἡ   *full assurance, complete certainty, full confidence*

πληροφορία   N-DF-S   πληροφορία

πληροφορίαν	N-AF-S	"
πληροφορίας	N-GF-S	"

πληρόω impf. ἐπλήρουν, pass. ἐπληρούμην; fut. πληρώσω; 1aor. ἐπλήρωσα; pf. πεπλήρωκα; pf. pass. πεπλήρωμαι; 1aor. pass. ἐπληρώθην; 1fut. pass. πληρωθήσομαι; (1) literally, with an idea of totality *make full, fill (up) completely* (AC 2.2); passive *become full, be filled with* (MT 13.48); figuratively, as filling something or someone with intangible things or qualities *fill* (MT 23.32; AC 5.28); mostly passive *be full of, become filled with*; (a) with the genitive of the thing (AC 13.52); (b) with the dative of the thing (LU 2.40); (c) with the accusative of the thing (PH 1.11); (d) absolutely *be well-supplied* (PH 4.18); (2) of a set span of time *complete, reach an end, fill (up)*; only passive in the NT *be fulfilled* (MK 1.15); (3) of foreknown laws, promises, prophecies, predictions, purposes *fulfill*; (a) active *bring to fulfillment, give true meaning to* (AC 3.18); (b) predominately passive *be fulfilled* (MT 1.22); (4) as fulfilling commandments, duties, demands; in the NT only with reference to the will of God *carry out, perform, accomplish* (CO 4.17); (5) as bringing an activity to completion *finish, bring to an end, complete* (LU 7.1; AC 12.25)

πληρωθείσης	VPAPGF-S	πληρόω
πληρωθέντων	VPAPGN-P	"
πληρωθῇ	VSAP--3S	"
πληρωθῆναι	VNAP	"
πληρωθήσεται	VIFP--3S	"
πληρωθήσονται	VIFP--3P	"
πληρωθῆτε	VSAP--2P	"
πληρωθῶ	VSAP--1S	"
πληρωθῶσι(ν)	VSAP--3P	"

πλήρωμα, ατος, τό (1) *what fills up*; (a) *(full) content(s), enough to fill up, fullness* (MK 6.43); (b) of cloth used to fill a torn place *patch* (MK 2.21); (2) as entirety of measurement *sum total, full measure, complete amount* (EP 3.19; possibly RO 11.25); (3) as what is beyond measure *overflowing amount, wealth, abundance* (RO 15.29); (4) of what is brought to a desired end *fulfillment, completion* (probably RO 11.25); (5) as the act of filling *fulfilling, completing* (RO 13.10); (6) as a period of time, when all intended within it has been accomplished *end, completion* (GA 4.4; EP 1.10)

πλήρωμα	N-AN-S	πλήρωμα
	N-NN-S	"
πληρώματα	N-AN-P	"
πληρώματι	N-DN-S	"
πληρώματος	N-GN-S	"
πληρῶσαι	VOAA--3S	πληρόω
πληρῶσαι	VNAA	"
πληρώσαντες	VPAANM-P	"
πληρώσας	VPAANM-S	"
πληρώσατε	VMAA--2P	"
πληρώσει	VIFA--3S	"
πληρώσεις	VIFA--2S	"
πληρώσετε	VMPA--2P	"
πληρώσῃ	VSAA--3S	"
πληρώσονται	VIFM--3P	"
πληρώσουσι(ν)	VIFA--3P	"
πληρώσωσι(ν)	VSAA--3P	"
πλήσαντες	VPAANM-P	πίμπλημι

πλήσας	VPAANM-S	"
πλησθείς	VPAPNM-S	"
πλησθέντων	VPAPGN-P	"
πλησθῆναι	VNAP	"
πλησθῇς	VSAP--2S	"
πλησθήσεται	VIFP--3S	"
πλησθήσονται	VIFP--3P	"

πλησίον neuter of πλησίος, α, ον (*near, close*); (1) as an adverb; (a) *near, close by*; (b) substantivally ὁ π. *the neighbor, the one near by, fellow man* (MT 5.43); with the meaning supplied from the context; *fellow countryman* (AC 7.27); *fellow believer* (RO 15.2); (2) as an improper preposition with the genitive *near, close to* something (JN 4.5)

πλησίον	AB	πλησίον
	PG	"

πλησμονή, ῆς, ἡ (1) as a condition of fullness *satisfaction, gratification*; (2) in a negative sense, in combination with σάρξ (*flesh*) in its only occurrence in CO 2.23 *indulgence*; this admittedly obscure passage appears to be constructed as a concession-contraexpectation in somewhat the following sense: "Even though such rules and regulations (verses 20–22) have a reputation for wisdom because they advocate man-made religion, self-abasement, and severe asceticism, still they do not advocate anything worthwhile at all, since they only cause people to indulge their sensual desires."

πλησμονήν	N-AF-S	πλησμονή

πλήσσω 2aor. pass. ἐπλήγην; *strike, smite*; figuratively and passive, of violence that comes to a person or thing *be struck, be damaged* (RV 8.12)

πλοῖα	N-AN-P	πλοῖον
	N-NN-P	"
πλοιάρια	N-AN-P	πλοιάριον
	N-NN-P	"

πλοιάριον, ου, τό diminutive of πλοῖον; *small boat or ship, skiff*

πλοιάριον	N-NN-S	πλοιάριον
πλοιαρίῳ	N-DN-S	"
πλοιαρίων	N-GN-P	"

πλοῖον, ου, τό (1) as a seagoing craft *ship* (JA 3.4); (2) as a small fishing craft *boat* (MT 4.21); ἐν πλοίῳ *by boat* in contrast to πεζῇ (*on foot, by land*)

πλοῖον	N-AN-S	πλοῖον
	N-NN-S	"
πλοίου	N-GN-S	"
πλοίῳ	N-DN-S	"
πλοίων	N-GN-P	"

πλοκή, ῆς, ἡ strictly *web*; hence, as adornment of the hair by interwoven ornaments *braiding, braid* (1P 3.3)

πλοκῆς	N-GF-S	πλοκή

πλόος and **πλοῦς, ὁ,** gen. **πλόος** as the movement of a boat through water *voyage, sailing, navigation*

πλοός	N-GM-S	πλόος
πλοῦν	N-AM-S	"
πλούσιοι	A--NM-P	πλούσιος
	A--VM-P	"
πλουσίοις	A--DM-P	"
πλούσιον	A--AM-S	"

πλούσιος, ία, ον (1) literally, in a material sense; (a) adjectivally *rich, wealthy, well-to-do* (MT 27.57); (b) substantivally ὁ π. *rich* or *wealthy person* (LU 6.24); (2) figuratively, of many and valuable spiritual virtues and eternal possessions *rich, abounding* in (JA 2.5)

πλούσιος	A--NM-S	πλούσιος
πλουσίου	A--GM-S	"
πλουσίους	A--AM-P	"

πλουσίως *richly, abundantly, in an abundant way*

πλουσίως	AB	πλουσίως
πλουτεῖν	VNPA	πλουτέω

πλουτέω 1aor. ἐπλούτησα; pf. πεπλούτηκα; literally, of material possessions; present *be rich* (1T 6.9); aorist *become rich* (RV 18.15); perfect *have become rich* (RV 3.17); figuratively *be rich* in something, *have much of, abound* in (1T 6.18); *give generously* (RO 10.12)

πλουτήσαντες	VPAANM-P	πλουτέω
πλουτήσῃς	VSAA--2S	"
πλουτήσητε	VSAA--2P	"
πλουτιζόμενοι	VPPPNM-P	πλουτίζω
πλουτίζοντες	VPPANM-P	"

πλουτίζω 1aor. pass. ἐπλουτίσθην; literally *make someone rich, enrich*; figuratively, of spiritual enrichment *cause to have an abundance* (2C 6.10); passive *be made rich* in, *be caused to have an abundance* of (1C 1.5)

πλοῦτον	N-AM-S	πλοῦτος

πλοῦτος, ου, ὁ and **πλοῦτος, ου, τό** literally, as material prosperity *riches, wealth* (MT 13.22); figuratively, as spiritual abundance or prosperity, followed by the genitive *abundance of, great amount of, extreme value of* something (RO 9.23; EP 1.7)

πλοῦτος	N-AN-S	πλοῦτος
	N-NM-S	"
	N-NN-S	"
πλούτου	N-GM-S	
πλουτοῦντας	VPPAAM-P	πλουτέω
πλουτῶν	VPPANM-S	"
πλύνοντες	VPPANM-P	πλύνω

πλύνω impf. ἔπλυνον; 1aor. ἔπλυνα; *wash*; literally, of fishing nets *wash* (LU 5.2); metaphorically πλύνειν τὰς στολάς literally *wash one's garments*, i.e. *make one's life pure* as cleansing the spiritual life from sin (RV 7.14)

πνέῃ	VSPA--3S	πνέω
πνεῖ	VIPA--3S	"
πνέοντα	VPPAAM-S	"
πνέοντος	VPPAGM-S	"
πνεούσῃ	VPPADF-S	"

πνεῦμα, ατος, τό (1) as derived from πνέω (*blow*), of the movement of air; (a) *blowing, wind* (probably JN 3.8a and HE 1.7); (b) *breathing, breath* (2TH 2.8; possibly MT 27.50 in the sense "he breathed his last"); (2) as a condition and agent of life *breath (of life), life spirit, soul* (LU 8.55; possibly MT 27.50 in the sense "he dismissed his spirit"); (3) as the immaterial part of the human personality, *spirit* in contrast to the outward and visible aspects of σάρξ (*flesh*) and σῶμα (*body*) (1C 5.3; 2C 7.1); (4) as the seat of the inner spiritual life of man, the capacity to know God, *spirit* (AC 18.25; RO 8.16b); (5) as a disposition or way of thinking *spirit, attitude* (GA 6.1); (6) as an independent spiritual being, not perceivable by the physical senses; (a) of God himself *spirit* (JN 4.24a); (b) as the third person of the Trinity, possessed by and proceeding from God or Christ *(Holy) Spirit* (MT 3.11; AC 16.7; 1TH 4.8; possibly JN 3.8a); (c) as a demonic nonmaterial being, only evil in the NT *spirit* (MT 8.16; MK 1.23); (d) of an angel as a spirit-being (HE 1.14; perhaps 1.7); (e) as a bodiless human being *ghost, specter, spirit* (LU 24.37, 39)

πνεῦμα	N-AN-S	πνεῦμα
	N-NN-S	"
	N-VN-S	"
πνεύμασι(ν)	N-DN-P	"
πνεύματα	N-AN-P	"
	N-NN-P	"
πνεύματι	N-DN-S	"
πνευματικά	AP-AN-P	πνευματικός
	A--AN-P	"
πνευματικαῖς	A--DF-P	"
πνευματικάς	A--AF-P	"
πνευματικῇ	A--DF-S	"
πνευματικήν	A--AF-S	"
πνευματικῆς	A--GF-S	"
πνευματικοί	A--NM-P	"
πνευματικοῖς	AP-DM-P	"
	AP-DN-P	"
πνευματικόν	AP-NN-S	"
	A--AN-S	"
	A--NN-S	"

πνευματικός, ή, όν *spiritual, pertaining to the spirit*, opposite σαρκικός (*fleshly, carnal*) and σάρκινος (*worldly, earthly*); (1) as distinguishing the nonmaterial from the material part of man; (2) predominately as distinguishing what belongs to the supernatural world from what belongs to the natural world (1C 15.44, 46); substantivally ὁ π. *the spiritual person, the Spirit-filled person*, i.e. a person possessing and governed by the Spirit of God (1C 2.15); neuter plural τὰ πνευματικά *spiritual things* or *matters* (1C 9.11); *spiritual gifts* or *enablements* (1C 14.1); (3) as an adjective expressing the qualifying characteristic of impersonal things under the divine order *spiritual* (RO 7.14); (4) as an adjective denoting relationship to satanic forces; neuter plural τὰ πνευματικὰ τῆς πονηρίας as a substantive *spiritual forces of evil, supernatural evil powers* (EP 6.12)

πνευματικός	AP-NM-S	πνευματικός
	A--NM-S	"
πνευματικούς	A--AM-P	"
πνευματικῶν	AP-GM-P	"
	AP-GN-P	"
	A--GN-P	"

πνευματικῶς adverb; *spiritually, in a spiritual manner*; (1) with reference to the inner life of a human being, the faculty of spiritual awareness *spiritually, in a spiritual sense* (1C 2.13; possibly 2.14); (2) with reference to the divine Spirit as enabling discernment in spiritual matters *spiritually, with the aid of the Spirit, consistent with the Spirit* (probably 1C 2.14); (3) denoting a nonliteral sense *symbolically, allegorically, so to speak* (RV 11.8)

πνευματικῶς	AB	πνευματικῶς
πνεύματος	N-GN-S	πνεῦμα
πνευμάτων	N-GN-P	"
πνεύσῃ	VSAA--3S	πνέω

πνέω   1aor. ἔπνευσα; in the NT only of the wind *blow*; substantivally ἡ πνέουσα (with αὔρα [*breeze*] understood) *the breeze* (AC 27.40)

πνίγω   impf. ἔπνιγον; 1aor. ἔπνιξα; *choke, strangle, suffocate* someone (MT 18.28); passive *be choked, choke*; as suffocating by falling into water *be drowned* (MK 5.13); figuratively, of plants overcrowded by other plants *cause to die* (MT 13.7)

πνικτόν	A--AN-S	πνικτός

πνικτός, ή, όν   *choked*; of animals killed by strangling, so that the blood is not drained from them *strangled, choked (to death)*; neuter as a substantive τὸ πνικτόν *what has been strangled*, i.e. *strangled animals* (AC 15.20)

πνικτοῦ	A--GN-S	πνικτός
πνικτῶν	A--GN-P	"

πνοή, ῆς, ἡ   (1) *wind* (AC 2.2); (2) with ζωή *breath* (AC 17.25)

πνοή	N-DF-S	πνοή
πνοήν	N-AF-S	"
πνοῆς	N-GF-S	"
πόδα	N-AM-S	πούς
πόδας	N-AM-P	"
πόδες	N-NM-P	"
ποδήρη	AP-AM-S	ποδήρης

ποδήρης, ες   of a long flowing garment *reaching to the feet, down to the feet*; substantivally *long robe* (RV 1.13)

ποδονιπτήρ, ῆρος, ὁ   *basin for washing feet* (JN 13.5)

ποδονιπτῆρα	N-AM-S	ποδονιπτήρ
ποδός	N-GM-S	πούς
ποδῶν	N-GM-P	"

πόθεν   interrogative adverb; (1) of place *from where? from what place?* (JN 3.8); (2) of origin *from what source? born of what parentage?* (JN 7.27); (3) of reason *how is it that? in what way?* (MK 12.37); in a question expressing surprise *why?* (LU 1.43)

πόθεν	ABT	πόθεν
πόθον	N-AM-S	πόθος

πόθος, ου, ὁ   as a desire for what is absent *longing, wish, yearning after* (CO 4.13)

ποία	A-TNF-S	ποῖος
ποῖα	APTAN-P	"
ποία	A-TDF-S	"
ποίαν	A-TAF-S	"
ποίας	APTAF-P	"
	APTGF-S	"
	A-TGF-S	"
ποίει	VIPA--3S	see ποιεῖ
	VMPA--2S	ποιέω
ποιεῖ	VIPA--3S	"
ποιεῖν	VNPA	"
ποιεῖς	VIPA--2S	"
ποιεῖσθαι	VNPM	"
	VNPP	"
ποιεῖσθε	VMPM--2P	"
ποιεῖται	VIPM--3S	"
ποιεῖτε	VIPA--2P	"
	VMPA--2P	"
ποιείτω	VMPA--3S	"

ποιέω   impf. ἐποίουν, mid. ἐποιούμην; fut. ποιήσω; 1aor. ἐποίησα, mid. ἐποιησάμην; pf. πεποίηκα; pluperfect πε-

ποιήκειν; pf. mid./pass. πεποίημαι, pass. ptc. πεποιημένος; **I.** active, with a basic meaning *make, do,* and the translation varying widely to suit the context; (1) of human activity involving external things *make, construct, form* (MT 17.4); (2) of God's creative activity *create* (MT 19.4); (3) of undertaking actions, bringing about states or conditions *accomplish, do* (a work) (JN 8.41), *perform* (miracles) (MT 7.22), *bring about* or *make* (peace) (EP 2.15), *prepare* or *give* (a feast) (LU 14.12), *keep* (a festival) (MT 26.18), *appoint* (followers) (MK 3.14), *establish* (a covenant) (HE 8.9), *wage* (war) (RV 11.7), *do* (good or evil) (RO 13.3), *acquire* or *make* (a gain) (LU 19.18), etc.; (4) of the natural processes of growth *produce, yield, bear, send out, bring forth* (MT 3.10); (5) with the accusative and an infinitive to indicate the result of an action *cause* someone *to, make* or *force* someone *to, bring it about that* someone (MT 5.32; MK 1.17); (6) with a double accusative as the object and predicate *make* someone or something *(to be)* something (MT 4.19; 21.13); (7) used with a noun to form a periphrasis for a simple verb of doing (e.g. ποιεῖν τὴν ἐκδίκησιν literally *make the vengeance,* i.e. *avenge* LU 18.7; ἐνέδραν ποιεῖν literally *make an ambush,* i.e. *plot, lie in wait* AC 25.3); (8) with the manner of the action indicated by an adverb *do* (well) (MT 12.12), *act* (wisely) (LU 16.8), *proceed* (in the same way) (MT 20.5); **II.** middle, with basic meanings *make* or *do* something *for oneself* or *perform with one's own resources;* (1) periphrastically, for a simple verbal idea: μονὴν ποιεῖσθαι literally *do a tarrying,* i.e. *make one's home with* (JN 14.23); ἐκβολὴν ποιεῖσθαι literally *make a throwing out,* i.e. *jettison (cargo)* (AC 27.18); μνήμην ποιεῖσθαι literally *make a remembrance,* i.e. *remember, keep in mind* (2P 1.15); etc.; (2) with a double accusative as the object and predicate βεβαίαν τὴν κλῆσιν ποιεῖσθαι literally *make firm the call,* i.e. *make one's calling (to be) sure* (2P 1.10)

ποιῇ	VSPA--3S	ποιέω

ποίημα, ατος, τό   *what has been made, work*; in the NT only of the works of God as creator *creation, things made, workmanship* (RO 1.20); figuratively, of Christians as God's handiwork *workmanship, product, what he has made* (EP 2.10)

ποίημα	N-NN-S	ποίημα
ποιήμασι(ν)	N-DN-P	"
ποιῇς	VSPA--2S	ποιέω
ποιῆσαι	VNAA	"
ποιήσαιεν	VOAA--3P	"
ποιησάμενοι	VPAMNM-P	"
ποιησάμενος	VPAMNM-S	"
ποιησαμένου	VPAMGM-S	"
ποιήσαντα	VPAAAM-S	"
ποιήσαντες	VPAANM-P	"
ποιήσαντι	VPAADM-S	"
ποιήσας	VPAANM-S	"
ποιήσασαν	VPAAAF-S	"
ποιήσασθαι	VNAM	"
ποιήσατε	VMAA--2P	"
ποιησάτω	VMAA--3S	"
ποιήσει	N-DF-S	ποίησις
	VIFA--3S	ποιέω

ποιήσειαν	VOAA--3P	"
ποιήσεις	VIFA--2S	"
	VIFA--2S^VMAA--2S	"
ποιήσετε	VIFA--2P	"
ποιήσῃ	VSAA--3S	"
ποιήσῃς	VSAA--2S	"
ποιήσητε	VSAA--2P	"
ποιήσθε	VSPM--2P	"
ποίησιν	N-AF-S	ποίησις

ποίησις, εως, ἡ as an action *doing, working, what one is doing* (JA 1.25)

ποιήσομαι	VIFM--1S	ποιέω
ποιησόμεθα	VIFM--1P	"
ποιήσομεν	VIFA--1P	"
ποίησον	VMAA--2S	"
ποιήσουσι(ν)	VIFA--3P	"
ποιήσω	VIFA--1S	"
	VSAA--1S	"
ποιήσωμεν	VSAA--1P	"
ποιήσων	VPFANM-S	"
ποιήσωσι(ν)	VSAA--3P	"
ποιηταί	N-NM-P	ποιητής
ποιῆτε	VSPA--2P	ποιέω

ποιητής, οῦ, ὁ (1) as one who does something as his occupation *maker, doer*; more specifically an author *poet* (AC 17.28); (2) as one who keeps the law *doer, observer* (RO 2.13)

ποιητής	N-NM-S	ποιητής
ποιητῶν	N-GM-P	
ποικίλαις	A--DF-P	ποικίλος
ποικίλης	A--GF-S	"
ποικίλοις	A--DM-P	"
	A--DN-P	"

ποικίλος, η, ον strictly *many-colored*; as indicating diversity *of many kinds, diverse, various* (MT 4.24)

ποίμαινε	VMPA--2S	ποιμαίνω
ποιμαίνει	VIPA--3S	"
ποιμαίνειν	VNPA	
ποιμαίνοντα	VPPAAM-S	"
ποιμαίνοντες	VPPANM-P	"

ποιμαίνω fut. ποιμανῶ; 1aor. ἐποίμανα; literally, as one who takes care of a group of animals, especially shepherding a flock *tend, feed, pasture* (LU 17.7); metaphorically, of administrative and protective activity in relation to a community of believers; *guide, care for, look after* (AC 20.28); with emphasis on the governing aspects of administration *rule* (RV 2.27)

ποιμάνατε	VMAA--2P	ποιμαίνω
ποιμανεῖ	VIFA--3S	"
ποιμένα	N-AM-S	ποιμήν
ποιμένας	N-AM-P	"
ποιμένες	N-NM-P	"
ποιμένων	N-GM-P	"

ποιμήν, ένος, ὁ (1) literally, one who takes care of a group of animals *shepherd, sheep herder* (LU 2.8); (2) metaphorically, one who assumes leadership over a group of believers; (a) as picturing Christ as the head of the church (HE 13.20); (b) as human leaders over a community of believers *pastor, minister* (EP 4.11)

ποιμήν	N-NM-S	ποιμήν

ποίμνη, ης, ἡ (1) literally *flock*, especially a group of sheep (LU 2.8); (2) metaphorically; (a) as Jesus' band of disciples (MT 26.31); (b) as the church or community of believers *followers of Christ* (JN 10.16)

ποίμνη	N-NF-S	ποίμνη
ποίμνην	N-AF-S	"
ποίμνης	N-GF-S	"

ποίμνιον, ου, τό (1) literally *flock*, especially a group of sheep; (2) metaphorically in the NT; (a) as the community of Jesus' followers *disciples* (LU 12.32); (b) as the *church* (AC 20.28)

ποίμνιον	N-AN-S	ποίμνιον
	N-VN-S	"
ποιμνίου	N-GN-S	"
ποιμνίῳ	N-DN-S	"
ποῖον	A-TAM-S	ποῖος
	A-TAN-S	"
	A-TNN-S	

ποῖος, ποία, ον an interrogative adjective referring to one among several of anything, used in direct and indirect questions; (1) with qualitative force *of what kind?* used with a noun *of what kind, of what sort?* (JN 12.33; 1P 1.11); (2) with less qualitative force, as nearly equivalent to τίς, τί; (a) used with a noun *which, what* (MT 22.36); (b) with the noun omitted ποῖα (ταῦτα) *what sort of things?* (LU 24.19); with the genitive ποίας (ὁδοῦ) *by what way* or *means, how?* (LU 5.19)

ποῖος	A-TNM-S	ποῖος
ποίου	A-TGM-S	"
ποιοῦμαι	VIPM--1S	ποιέω
ποιοῦμεν	VIPA--1P	"
ποιούμενοι	VPPMNM-P	"
ποιούμενος	VPPMNM-S	"
ποιοῦν	VPPANN-S	
ποιοῦντα	VPPAAM-S	
	VPPANN-P	
ποιοῦνται	VIPM--3P	
ποιοῦντας	VPPAAM-P	
ποιοῦντες	VPPANM-P	
ποιοῦντι	VPPADM-S	
	VPPADN-S	
ποιοῦντος	VPPAGM-S	
ποιοῦσι(ν)	VIPA--3P	
	VPPADM-P	
ποιῶ	VIPA--1S	
	VSPA--1S	
ποίῳ	A-TDM-S	ποῖος
	A-TDN-S	
ποιῶμεν	VSPA--1P	ποιέω
ποιῶν	VPPANM-S	
	VPPAVM-S	
ποιῶσι(ν)	VSPA--3P	
πόλει	N-DF-S	πόλις
πόλεις	N-AF-P	
	N-NF-P	
πολεμεῖ	VIPA--3S	πολεμέω
πολεμεῖτε	VIPA--2P	

πολεμέω fut. πολεμήσω; 1aor. ἐπολέμησα; literally *make war, war* (against), *fight* (with) (RV 12.7); figuratively as expressing hostile attitudes within a community *fight, be against* (JA 4.2)

πολεμῆσαι	VNAA	πολεμέω
πολεμήσουσι(ν)	VIFA--3P	"
πολεμήσω	VIFA--1S	"
πόλεμοι	N-NM-P	πόλεμος
πόλεμον	N-AM-S	"

πόλεμος, ου, ὁ literally *armed conflict, war* (MT 24.6), opposite εἰρήνη (*peace*); as a single engagement *battle, fight* (1C 14.8); figuratively and negatively, as a word battle within a community *strife, quarrel, conflict* (JA 4.1)

πόλεμος	N-NM-S	πόλεμος
πολέμους	N-AM-P	"
πολέμῳ	N-DM-S	"
πολέμων	N-GM-P	"
πόλεσι(ν)	N-DF-P	πόλις
πόλεων	N-GF-P	"
πόλεως	N-GF-S	"
Πόλιν	N-AF-S	Νέα Πόλις
πόλιν	N-AF-S	πόλις

πόλις, εως, ἡ literally, as an enclosed and usually fortified town *city* (MT 5.14), in contrast to χώρα (*countryside*); by metonymy, as the inhabitants of a city (MK 1.33); figuratively, as the heavenly place called New Jerusalem *the* (holy) *city* (RV 21.2)

πόλις	N-NF-S	πόλις
	N-VF-S	"
πολῖται	N-NM-P	πολίτης
πολιτάρχαι	N-NM-P	πολιτάρχης
πολιτάρχας	N-AM-P	"

πολιτάρχης, ου, ὁ strictly *city ruler*; as a member of a governing council in Macedonian cities *politarch, chief magistrate* (AC 17.6, 8)

πολιτεία, ας, ἡ literally, as the civic rights belonging to members of a political entity *citizenship* (AC 22.28); figuratively, as the privileged religious position of Israel in God's plan *people, community* (EP 2.12)

πολιτείαν	N-AF-S	πολιτεία
πολιτείας	N-GF-S	"
πολιτεύεσθε	VMPD--2P	πολιτεύομαι
	VMPO--2P	"

πολίτευμα, ατος, τό literally, what has been made into a civic entity *commonwealth, state*; figuratively in the NT, of belonging to God's kingdom *place of citizenship, homeland* (PH 3.20)

πολίτευμα	N-NN-S	πολίτευμα

πολιτεύομαι pf. πεπολίτευμαι; only middle in the NT; literally *live as a citizen, have one's citizenship* or *home*; figuratively in the NT, of how one lives as belonging to God's kingdom *live, behave, conduct oneself*

πολίτην	N-AM-S	πολίτης

πολίτης, ου, ὁ (1) one who shares in the political organization and rights of a city or city-state *citizen* (AC 21.39), opposite δοῦλος (*slave, servant*) and ξένος (*foreigner, alien*); (2) as an associate in a particular civic group *fellow citizen, fellow countryman* (LU 19.14)

πολίτης	N-NM-S	πολίτης
πολιτῶν	N-GM-P	"
πολλά	AB	πολύς
	A--AN-P	"
	A--NN-P	"
πολλαί	A--NF-P	

πολλαῖς	A--DF-P	"

πολλάκις adverb; *often, frequently, many times*

πολλάκις	AB	πολλάκις
πολλαπλασίονα	A--AN-P	πολλαπλασίων

πολλαπλασίων, ον, gen. ονος of quantity *manifold*; neuter plural as a substantive *many times more, many times as much*

πολλάς	A--AF-P	πολύς
πολλή	A--NF-S	"
πολλῇ	A--DF-S	"
πολλήν	A--AF-S	"
πολλῆς	A--GF-S	"
πολλοί	A--NM-P	"
πολλοῖς	A--DM-P	"
	A--DN-P	"
πολλοῦ	A--GM-S	"
	A--GN-S	"
πολλούς	A--AM-P	"
πολλῷ	A--DM-S	"
	A--DN-S	"
πολλῶν	A--GF-P	"
	A--GM-P	"
	A--GN-P	"
πολύ	AB	"
	A--AN-S	"
	A--NN-S	"

πολυεύσπλαγχνος, ον as an attribute of God *rich in compassion, very compassionate* (JA 5.11)

πολυεύσπλαγχνος	A--NM-S	πολυεύσπλαγχνος

πολυλογία, ας, ἡ *using many words, long speaking, talkativeness*, always in a negative sense (MT 6.7)

πολυλογία	N-DF-S	πολυλογία

πολυμερῶς adverb; *in many parts* or *portions, bit by bit* (HE 1.1)

πολυμερῶς	AB	πολυμερῶς
πολύν	A--AM-S	πολύς

πολυπλήθεια, ας, ἡ *large crowd* (AC 14.7)

πολυπλήθεια	N-NF-S	πολυπλήθεια

πολυποίκιλος, ον a strengthened form of ποικίλος (*of many kinds, diverse, various*), of something that is manifested in a great variety of forms *many-sided, most varied, manifold* (EP 3.10)

πολυποίκιλος	A--NF-S	πολυποίκιλος

πολύς, πολλή, πολύ, gen. πολλοῦ, ῆς, οῦ **I.** positive degree *much, many*; (1) adjectivally; (a) of number *many, numerous* (MT 7.22), opposite ὀλίγος (*few*); (b) of extent or magnitude *great, large, much, many, plentiful* (MT 19.22; JN 3.23); (c) of quantity; with a singular noun *much, large, great* (MT 14.14), opposite ὀλίγος (*little*); of things that occur in a mass or in large quantities: *much* (fruit) (JN 12.24), *long* (speech) (AC 15.32); of time: *long* (time) (JN 5.6), *late* (hour) (MK 6.35); (d) to denote degree, with the translation suiting the context: *great* (love) (EP 2.4), *long* (abstinence) (AC 27.21), *great* (peace) (AC 24.2), *deep* or *profound* (mourning) (MT 2.18), *severe* (loss) (AC 27.10), *severe* or *heavy* (affliction) (1TH 2.2), etc.; (2) substantivally; (a) πολλοί *many (persons)* (MT 7.22); (b) with the article οἱ πολλοί; (i) with an exclusive (Greek) sense *most (but not all), the majority* (only MT 24.12 and 2C 2.17); (ii) with an inclusive (Semitic) sense elsewhere; *all (present), the* *whole community, the whole (crowd)* (HE 12.15); (c) πολλοί in reference to the saving work of Jesus in MK 10.45; 14.24; RO 5.16; and HE 9.28, the Semitic inclusive sense is to be understood, i.e. Jesus died for all (cf. JN 6.51; 1T 2.6; HE 2.9); (d) accusative neuter singular πολύ and plural πολλά as adverbs *greatly, earnestly, strictly, often, loudly,* translated to intensify the action in a verb (MK 1.45; RO 16.6); **II.** comparative πλείων, πλεῖον, genitive πλείονος *more*; (1) an adjective followed by the genitive when used as a comparative; (a) of quantity *more, large(r) number of, greater amount, many* (AC 21.10); (b) of quality *superior, greater, more excellent* (MT 5.20); (2) substantivally οἱ πλείους *the majority, the most* (AC 19.32); πλείονες *many more, even more* (AC 28.23); (3) neuter accusative as an adverb *more, in greater measure, to a greater degree* (LU 7.42); of place ἐπὶ πλεῖον *any further* (AC 4.17); of time ἐπὶ πλεῖον *at length, for a long time* (AC 20.9); *too long, any longer* (AC 24.4); **III.** superlative πλεῖστος, η, ον *most*; (1) adjectivally *(the) most (of), (the) majority (of)* (MT 11.20); in an elative sense *very great, very large* (MK 4.1); (2) neuter as a substantive τὸ πλεῖστον *at the most* (1C 14.27)

πολύς	A--NM-S	πολύς

πολύσπλαγχνος, ον *very compassionate, full of pity, very merciful* (JA 5.11)

πολύσπλαγχνος	A--NM-S	πολύσπλαγχνος
πολυτελεῖ	A--DM-S	πολυτελής
πολυτελές	A--NN-S	"

πολυτελής, ές *very costly, expensive* (MK 14.3); figuratively *of great value, very precious* (1P 3.4)

πολυτελοῦς	A--GF-S	πολυτελής
πολύτιμον	A--AM-S	πολύτιμος

πολύτιμος, ον literally *of great price, very valuable, costly* (MT 13.46); figuratively, comparative πολυτιμότερος, τέρα, ον *(much) more precious, far more valuable* (1P 1.7)

πολυτιμότερον	A-MNN-S	πολύτιμος
πολυτίμου	A--GF-S	"

πολυτρόπως adverb; *in various ways, in many kinds of ways* (HE 1.1)

πολυτρόπως	AB	πολυτρόπως

πόμα, ατος, τό literally *drink* (HE 9.10); metaphorically, of spiritual sustenance symbolized by water supplied miraculously in the exodus period, probably prefiguring the communion elements (1C 10.4)

πόμα	N-AN-S	πόμα
πόμασι(ν)	N-DN-P	"
πονηρά	AP-AN-P	πονηρός
	AP-NN-P	"
	A--AN-P	"
	A--NF-S	"
	A--NN-P	"
	A--VF-S	"
πονηρᾷ	A--DF-S	"
πονηραί	A--NF-P	"
πονηράν	A--AF-S	"
πονηρᾶς	A--GF-S	"
πονηρέ	A--VM-S	"

πονηρία, ας, ἡ only in a moral and ethical sense in the NT, of intentionally practiced ill will *evil, wickedness, mal-*ice (LU 11.39); plural, for various expressions of evil-mindedness *wicked ways, evil doings, malicious deeds* (AC 3.26)

πονηρία	N-NF-S	πονηρία
πονηρίᾳ	N-DF-S	"
πονηρίαι	N-NF-P	"
πονηρίαν	N-AF-S	"
πονηρίας	N-GF-S	"
πονηριῶν	N-GF-P	"
πονηροί	A--NM-P	πονηρός
πονηροῖς	A--DM-P	"
	A--DN-P	"
πονηρόν	AP-AM-S	"
	AP-NM-S	"
	A--AN-S	"
	A--NN-S	"

πονηρός, ά, όν comparative πονηρότερος, α, ον; (1) adjectivally; (a) as what is physically disadvantageous *bad, harmful, evil, painful* (EP 5.16; RV 16.2); (b) of persons and things, as of little worth to anyone *useless, unprofitable, unserviceable* (MT 7.18; 18.32; perhaps MT 6.23 and LU 11.34); (c) in a moral sense of persons and things characterized by ill will *evil, wicked, malicious* (MT 12.35; probably MT 6.23 and LU 11.34); (2) substantivally; (a) of persons *evildoer, wicked person, bad person* (MT 13.49); (b) as a term for the devil ὁ π. *the evil* or *wicked one* (MT 13.19); the phrase τοῦ πονηροῦ (MT 5.37; 6.13) may belong here or it may be neuter, as in the following; (c) neuter (τὸ) πονηρόν generally *evil* (MT 5.11)

πονηρός	AP-NM-S	πονηρός
	A--NM-S	"
πονηρότερα	A-MAN-P	"
πονηροῦ	AP-GM-S	"
	AP-GN-S	"
	A--GM-S	"
	A--GN-S	"
πονηρούς	AP-AM-P	"
	A--AM-P	"
πονηρῷ	AP-DM-S	"
	AP-DN-S	"
πονηρῶν	AP-GN-P	"
	A--GM-P	"
	A--GN-P	"
πόνον	N-AM-S	πόνος

πόνος, ου, ὁ (1) as hard, exhaustive work that produces stress or demonstrates concern *toil, labor, great exertion* (CO 4.13); (2) as distress caused by hard, difficult circumstances *pain, affliction, anguish* (RV 16.10)

πόνος	N-NM-S	πόνος
πόνου	N-GM-S	"
Ποντικόν	A--AM-S	Ποντικός

Ποντικός, ή, όν of a native of Pontus in Asia Minor *from Pontus, Pontian* (AC 18.2)

Πόντιος, ου, ὁ *Pontius,* masculine proper noun, Pilate's Roman first name or clan-name

Πόντιος	N-NM-S	Πόντιος
Ποντίου	N-GM-S	"
Ποντίῳ	N-DM-S	"
Πόντον	N-AM-S	Πόντος
πόντον	N-AM-S	πόντος

Πόντος, ου, ὁ   *Pontus*, originally the name of the Black Sea; in the NT of the region in northeastern Asia Minor next to the Black Sea, a Roman province

πόντος, ου, ὁ   *sea*, especially *open sea, high sea* (RV 18.17)

Πόντου	N-GM-S	Πόντος
πόνων	N-GM-P	πόνος

Πόπλιος, ου, ὁ (also Πούπλιος)   *Publius*, masculine proper noun

Ποπλίου	N-GM-S	Πόπλιος
Ποπλίῳ	N-DM-S	

πορεία, ας, ἡ   strictly *going*; literally *journey, trip* (LU 13.22); plural, of business comings and goings *undertakings, pursuits* (probably JA 1.11); figuratively *way of life*; plural *ways* (possibly JA 1.11)

πορείαις	N-DF-P	πορεία
πορείαν	N-AF-S	"
πορεύεσθαι	VNPD	πορεύομαι
	VNPO	"
πορεύεσθε	VMPD--2P	"
	VMPO--2P	"
πορεύεται	VIPD--3S	"
	VIPO--3S	"
πορευθείς	VPAONM-S	"
πορευθεῖσα	VPAONF-S	"
πορευθεῖσαι	VPAONF-P	"
πορευθέντα	VPAOAM-P	"
πορευθέντες	VPAONM-P	"
πορευθέντι	VPAODM-S	"
πορευθῇ	VSAO--3S	"
πορευθῆναι	VNAO	"
πορευθῆτε	VSAO--2P	"
πορεύθητι	VMAO--2S	"
πορευθῶ	VSAO--1S	"
πορευθῶσι(ν)	VSAO--3P	"

πορεύομαι   impf. ἐπορευόμην; fut. πορεύσομαι; pf. ptc. πεπορευμένος; 1aor. ἐπορεύθην; *go, journey, travel, proceed*; (1) literally; (a) of going from one place to another *go, travel* (LU 13.33); (b) with an indication of the point of origin *depart* (from) (MT 25.41; LU 13.31); (c) with an indication of destination *go* (to), *proceed* (toward) (AC 1.25; 18.6); (2) figuratively; (a) euphemistically and idiomatically πορεύεσθαι (εἰς θάνατον) literally *go (to one's death)*, i.e. *die, leave this life* (LU 22.22, 33); (b) of behavior, *conduct oneself, live, behave* (LU 1.6); (c) imperative πορεύου, πορεύθητι as a command involving a sense of mission *go* (MT 2.20; 8.9); Hebraistically, the participle followed by an imperative has a similar imperatival sense (MT 9.13); (d) with ὀπίσω in the sense of seeking a close relation with someone or something *go* or *follow after, act in the same way* (LU 21.8; 2P 2.10)

πορεύομαι	VIPD--1S	πορεύομαι
	VIPO--1S	"
πορευόμεναι	VPPDNF-P	"
	VPPONF-P	"
πορευομένη	VPPDNF-S	"
	VPPONF-S	"
πορευόμενοι	VPPDNM-P	"
	VPPONM-P	"
πορευομένοις	VPPDDM-P	"
	VPPODM-P	"
πορευόμενον	VPPDAM-S	"
	VPPDNN-S	"
	VPPOAM-S	"
	VPPONN-S	"
πορευόμενος	VPPDNM-S	"
	VPPONM-S	"
πορευομένου	VPPDGM-S	"
	VPPOGM-S	"
πορευομένους	VPPDAM-P	"
	VPPOAM-P	"
πορευομένῳ	VPPDDM-S	"
	VPPODM-S	"
πορευομένων	VPPDGM-P	"
	VPPOGM-P	"
πορεύου	VMPD--2S	"
	VMPO--2S	"
πορεύσεται	VIFD--3S	"
πορεύσῃ	VIFD--2S	"
πορεύσομαι	VIFD--1S	"
πορευσόμεθα	VIFD--1P	"
πορεύσονται	VIFD--3P	"
πορευσώμεθα	VSAD--1P	"
πορεύωμαι	VSPD--1S	"
	VSPO--1S	"

πορθέω   impf. ἐπόρθουν; 1aor. ἐπόρθησα; *destroy, devastate, attack* (GA 1.13); as directed against persons *destroy, kill* (AC 9.21)

πορθήσας	VPAANM-S	πορθέω
πορισμόν	N-AM-S	πορισμός

πορισμός, οῦ, ὁ   as a process *means of gain, way to make money* (1T 6.5); figuratively *advantage, profit* (1T 6.6)

πορισμός	N-NM-S	πορισμός
Πόρκιον	N-AM-S	Πόρκιος

Πόρκιος, ου, ὁ   *Porcius*, Roman clan-name of Festus the procurator (AC 24.27)

πόρναι	N-NF-P	πόρνη

πορνεία, ας, ἡ   (1) generally, of every kind of extramarital, unlawful, or unnatural sexual intercourse *fornication, sexual immorality, prostitution* (1C 5.1); (2) when distinguished from adultery (μοιχεία) in the same context *extramarital intercourse, sexual immorality, fornication* (MT 15.19); (3) as a synonym for μοιχεία *(marital) unfaithfulness, adultery* (MT 5.32); (4) metaphorically, as apostasy from God through idolatry *(spiritual) immorality, unfaithfulness* (RV 19.2)

πορνεία	N-NF-S	πορνεία
πορνείᾳ	N-DF-S	"
πορνεῖαι	N-NF-P	"
πορνείαν	N-AF-S	"
πορνείας	N-AF-P	"
	N-GF-S	"
πορνευομένους	VPPPAM-P	πορνεύω
πορνεῦσαι	VNAA	"
πορνεύσαντες	VPAANM-P	"
πορνεύσῃς	VSAA--2S	"

πορνεύω   1aor. ἐπόρνευσα; (1) generally *practice sexual immorality, commit fornication, live without sexual restraint* (1C 6.18); (2) metaphorically *practice idolatry* (RV 17.2)

πορνεύωμεν	VSPA--1P	πορνεύω
πορνεύων	VPPANM-S	"

πόρνη, ης, ἡ from πέρνημι (*sell*); literally, a woman who practices sexual immorality as a means of making a living *harlot, prostitute, whore* (1C 6.15); metaphorically, from the Old Testament, a government hostile to God *harlot* (RV 17.1)

πόρνη	N-NF-S	πόρνη
πόρνῃ	N-DF-S	"
πόρνην	N-AF-S	"
πόρνης	N-GF-S	"
πόρνοι	N-NM-P	πόρνος
πόρνοις	N-DM-P	"

πόρνος, ου, ὁ in the NT a man who has sexual intercourse with a prostitute *fornicator, sexually immoral person* (1C 5.9); distinguished from μοιχός (*adulterer*) in 1C 6.9 and ἀρσενοκοίτης (*sodomite* or *homosexual*) in 1T 1.10

πόρνος	N-NM-S	πόρνος
πόρνους	N-AM-P	"
πορνῶν	N-GF-P	πόρνη

πόρρω adverb; *far (away), great way off, at a distance* (LU 14.32); comparative πορρώτερον *farther* (LU 24.28); πορρωτέρω *farther* (LU 24.28)

πόρρω	AB	πόρρω

πόρρωθεν adverb; *from afar; afar off, at a distance* (LU 17.12); as a prior point of time *long before, far ahead of time* (HE 11.13)

πόρρωθεν	AB	πόρρωθεν
πορρώτερον	ABM	πόρρω
πορρωτέρω	ABM	"

πορφύρα, ας, ἡ strictly, a species of shellfish yielding costly purple dye; in the NT of expensive garments made from cloth dyed purple *purple garment* (LU 16.19); *(royal) purple robe* (MK 15.17); *purple cloth* (RV 18.12)

πορφύρα	N-DF-S	πορφύρα
πορφύραν	N-AF-S	"
πορφύρας	N-GF-S	"

πορφυρόπωλις, ιδος, ἡ *(female) dealer in purple goods, (woman) seller of purple cloth* (AC 16.14)

πορφυρόπωλις	N-NF-S	πορφυρόπωλις
πορφύρου	AP-GN-S	πορφυροῦς
πορφυροῦν	AP-AN-S	"
	A--AN-S	"

πορφυροῦς, ᾶ, οῦν *purple (in color), made of purple fabric* (JN 19.2, 5); neuter as a substantive τὸ πορφυροῦν *purple clothing* (RV 17.4)

πόσα	APTAN-P	πόσος
πόσαι	A-TNF-P	"

ποσάκις interrogative adverb; *how many times? how often?*

ποσάκις	ABT	ποσάκις
πόσας	A-TAF-P	πόσος
πόσει	N-DF-S	πόσις
πόσην	A-TAF-S	πόσος
ποσί(ν)	N-DM-P	πούς

πόσις, εως, ἡ (1) as an action *drinking* (RO 14.17); (2) as what one drinks *drink* (JN 6.55)

πόσις	N-NF-S	πόσις
πόσοι	A-TNM-P	πόσος
πόσον	APTAN-S	"
	A-TNN-S	"

πόσος, η, ον an interrogative correlative to ὅσος (*in such an amount as*), used in exclamations and direct or indirect questions; (1) to denote degree *how great? how much? to what extent?* (MT 6.23); π. χρόνος *how long?* (MK 9.21); with a comparative following *how much greater? how much more?* (HE 10.29); (2) to denote quantity, with or without a noun; in the plural *how many?* (MT 15.34); in the singular *how much?* (LU 16.5); (3) in an exclamation *how great* (MT 6.23); *how much* (2C 7.11)

πόσος	A-TNM-S	πόσος
πόσου	A-TGN-S	"
πόσους	A-TAM-P	"
πόσῳ	APTDN-S	"
πόσων	A-TGF-P	"
ποταμοί	N-NM-P	ποταμός
ποταμόν	N-AM-S	

ποταμός, οῦ, ὁ literally, of flowing water *river, stream* (MT 3.6); plural, of water rushing down ravines after heavy rains *floods, torrents* (MT 7.25); metaphorically, of the water of life as a flowing river, denoting fullness of life from God (JN 7.38)

ποταμός	N-NM-S	ποταμός
ποταμοῦ	N-GM-S	
ποταμούς	N-AM-P	
ποταμοφόρητον	A--AF-S	ποταμοφόρητος

ποταμοφόρητος, ον *carried away by a river, swept away by a flood, overwhelmed by a torrent* (RV 12.15)

ποταμῷ	N-DM-S	ποταμός
ποταμῶν	N-GM-P	"
ποταπαί	A-TNF-P	ποταπός
ποταπή	A-TNF-S	"
ποταπήν	A-TAF-S	"
ποταποί	A-TNM-P	"

ποταπός, ή, όν an interrogative adjective referring to quality *of what sort* or *kind?* (LU 7.39); substantivally ποταποί *what sort of people* (2P 3.11); in exclamations expressing admiration *how great, how wonderful* (1J 3.1)

ποταπός	A-TNM-S	ποταπός
ποταπούς	A-TAM-P	"

ποταπῶς an interrogative adverb of ποταπός (*of what sort* or *kind?*); *in what way? how?* (AC 20.18)

ποταπῶς	ABT	ποταπῶς

πότε an interrogative adverb of time used in direct and indirect questions *when? at what time?* (MT 24.3); ἕως π. *until when? how long?* (MT 17.17)

πότε	ABT	πότε

ποτέ an enclitic indefinite adverb of time *at some time* or *other*; (1) of past time *once, formerly* (GA 1.13); (2) of future time *when (once)* (LU 22.32); (3) of present time ἤδη π. *now at last* (PH 4.10); (4) after a negative *ever, at any time* (1TH 2.5); (5) in rhetorical questions expecting a negative answer *ever* (HE 1.5)

ποτέ	ABI	ποτέ

πότερον an interrogative adverb used with ἤ (*or*) in a disjunctive question *whether . . . or (whether)* (JN 7.17)

πότερον	ABT	πότερον

ποτήριον, ου, τό literally *cup, drinking container* (MK 7.4); by metonymy, for what the cup contains and is offered as a drink (1C 11.25a); metaphorically, of one's destiny, either good or bad (JN 18.11; RV 14.10); idiomatically πίνειν π. literally *drink a cup*, i.e. *suffer severely* (MK 10.38); παραφέρειν π. ἀπό τινος literally *take away a cup from someone*, i.e. *cause someone not to suffer severely* (MK 14.36)

ποτήριον	N-AN-S	ποτήριον
	N-NN-S	"
ποτηρίου	N-GN-S	"
ποτηρίῳ	N-DN-S	"
ποτηρίων	N-GN-P	"
πότιζε	VMPA--2S	ποτίζω
ποτίζει	VIPA--3S	"

ποτίζω impf. ἐπότιζον; 1aor. ἐπότισα; pf. πεπότικα; 1aor. pass. ἐποτίσθην; (1) of persons *give to drink, cause to drink* (MT 10.42); (2) of plants and animals *(give) water (to)* (LU 13.15; 1C 3.6); metaphorically, as giving faithful instruction in the maturing ministry of a church; literally *water*, i.e. *teach* (1C 3.6–8); (3) metaphorically *cause to experience* (1C 12.13; RV 14.8)

ποτίζων	VPPANM-S	ποτίζω

Ποτίολοι, ων, οἱ *Puteoli*, a city on the Bay of Naples south of Rome in Italy (AC 28.13)

Ποτιόλους	N-AM-P	Ποτίολοι
ποτίσῃ	VSAA--3S	ποτίζω
πότοις	N-DM-P	πότος

πότος, ου, ὁ *drinking*; especially *drinking bout, carousal, drinking party* (1P 4.3)

πού enclitic indefinite adverb; (1) of place *somewhere*; with quotations from Scripture *in a certain place, somewhere* (HE 2.6); (2) with numbers, indicating an approximation *nearly, about, somewhere around* (RO 4.19); (3) in combination μή που *lest somewhere* (AC 27.29)

πού	ABI	πού

ποῦ an interrogative adverb of place; (1) *where? in what place?* (MT 2.2); (2) in a rhetorical question expecting a negative answer *where is?* (LU 8.25); (3) used as a conjunction to introduce a direct question followed by the indicative *where?* (MK 14.12); to introduce an indirect question followed by the indicative *where* (MT 2.4); followed by the subjunctive *(any)where, (any)place* (MT 8.20); (4) for ποῖ *to what place? whither?* (JN 7.35; HE 11.8)

ποῦ	ABT	ποῦ

Πούδης, εντος, ὁ *Pudens*, masculine proper noun (2T 4.21)

Πούδης	N-NM-S	Πούδης
Ποπλίῳ	N-DM-S	Πόπλιος

πούς, ποδός, ὁ *foot*; (1) literally, as the part of the body used for standing or walking *foot* (MT 4.6); (2) idiomatically, from various oriental customs involving feet; (a) πόδας νίπτειν literally *wash feet*, i.e. *show hospitality, welcome guests* (possibly 1T 5.10), also, *serve humbly* (JN 13.14; possibly 1T 5.10); (b) καθῆσθαι παρὰ τοὺς πόδας τινός literally *sit at someone's feet*, i.e. *learn from, be taught by* (LU 8.35); (c) κατευθύνειν τοὺς πόδας literally *guide the feet straight*, i.e. *guide behavior, teach how to live* (LU 1.79); (d) ὑπὸ τοὺς πόδας τινός literally *under someone's feet*, i.e. *under someone's control* (1C 15.25); τιθέναι τινά ὑποπόδιον τῶν ποδῶν τινος literally *make someone a footstool for someone's feet*, i.e. *give*

someone complete control over someone (else), from the ancient custom of depicting a ruler's conquered enemies on the footstool before his throne (LU 20.43; HE 1.13); (e) τιθέναι τινά πρὸς τοὺς πόδας τινός literally *place something at the feet of someone*, i.e. *turn something over, put at someone's disposal* (AC 4.37); (3) as a measure of limited space βῆμα ποδός literally *step of a foot, stride*, i.e. *about a square meter* or *square yard* (AC 7.5)

πούς	N-NM-S	πούς

πρᾶγμα, ατος, τό (1) as the result of activity *what has been done, deed, act, event* (AC 5.4); (2) as obligatory activity to be done *task, business, undertaking* (RO 16.2); (3) generally, of anything relating to human action *(some)thing, matter, affair* (MT 18.19); (4) as a legal process *lawsuit, dispute* (1C 6.1); (5) as something disgraceful τὸ π. in 1TH 4.6 may refer euphemistically in this context to unlawful sexual intercourse, but the sense of a business transaction is also possible

πρᾶγμα	N-AN-S	πρᾶγμα
	N-NN-S	"

πραγματεία, ας, ἡ plural in the NT *undertakings, affairs, activities*; αἱ τοῦ βίου πραγματεῖαι *the affairs of everyday life* (2T 2.4)

πραγματείαις	N-DF-P	πραγματεία
πραγματεύεσθαι	VNPD	πραγματεύομαι
πραγματεύεσθε	VMPD--2P	"

πραγματεύομαι 1aor. ἐπραγματευσάμην; of business affairs *trade, do business, carry on (profitably)* (LU 19.13)

πραγματεύσασθαι	VNAD	πραγματεύομαι
πραγματεύσασθε	VMAD--2P	"
πράγματι	N-DN-S	πρᾶγμα
πράγματος	N-GN-S	"
πραγμάτων	N-GN-P	"
πραεῖς	A--NM-P	πραΰς
πραέως	A--GN-S	"
πραθέν	VPAPNN-S	πιπράσκω
πραθῆναι	VNAP	"

πραιτώριον, ου, τό *pretorium*; originally the headquarters in a Roman field camp; in the Gospels the governor's official residence *palace, fortress* (MT 27.27); in Acts the *fortress* complex attached to a palace (AC 23.25); in Paul's prison letters, the *quarters* or *living place* for the emperor's guard in Rome (PH 1.13)

πραιτώριον	N-AN-S	πραιτώριον
	N-NN-S	"
πραιτωρίῳ	N-DN-S	"
πράκτορι	N-DM-S	πράκτωρ

πράκτωρ, ορος, ὁ strictly, an agent for carrying out a task *official*; in the NT the *court officer* who carries out an imposed sentence in a debtor's prison, *bailiff, constable*

πράκτωρ	N-NM-S	πράκτωρ
πρᾶξαι	VNAA	πράσσω
πράξαντες	VPAANM-P	"
πραξάντων	VPAAGM-P	"
πράξας	VPAANM-S	"
πράξατε	VMAA--2P	"
πράξει	N-DF-S	πρᾶξις
πράξεις	N-AF-P	"
πράξεσι(ν)	N-DF-P	"
πράξετε	VIFA--2P	πράσσω

πράξεων	N-GF-P	πρᾶξις
πράξης	VSAA--2S	πράσσω
πράξητε	VSAA--2P	"
πρᾶξιν	N-AF-S	πρᾶξις

πρᾶξις, εως, ἡ (1) as what one does *work, activity, practice* (MT 16.27); as the activity of bodily members *function* (RO 12.4); with a derogatory sense, plural *(evil) practices, (bad) habits* (RO 8.13); as deceptive actions *(magical) practices* (AC 19.18); (2) as a completed action *deed, act* (title of Acts)

πραότητα	N-AF-S	πραΰτης
πραότητι	N-DF-S	"

πρασιά, ᾶς, ἡ literally *garden bed, garden plot*; figuratively πρασιαὶ πρασιαί *group by group, in colorful groups*, a vivid metaphor of a landscape dotted with groups of people in colorful clothes (MK 6.40)

πρασιαί	N-NF-P	πρασιά
πράσσει	VIPA--3S	πράσσω
πράσσειν	VNPA	"
πράσσεις	VIPA--2S	"
πράσσετε	VMPA--2P	"
πράσσῃς	VSPA--2S	"
πράσσοντας	VPPAAM-P	"
πράσσοντες	VPPANM-P	"
πράσσοντι	VPPADM-S	"
πράσσουσι(ν)	VIPA--3P	"
	VPPADM-P	"

πράσσω (and **πράττω**) fut. πράξω; 1aor. ἔπραξα; pf. πέπραχα; pf. pass. πέπραγμαι; 1aor. pass. ἐπράχθην; (1) transitively; (a) of pressing through on an action *carry out, do, accomplish* (AC 26.20); (b) predominately with a negative evaluation *commit, do* (AC 5.35); (c) as denoting intense preoccupation with something *busy oneself with, practice* (AC 19.19); in regard to law *practice, observe* (RO 2.25); in regard to taxes, interest, toll duties *collect, demand, exact* (LU 19.23); (2) intransitively, with a qualifying adverb or phrase; (a) to qualify how someone is acting *do* (AC 3.17; perhaps 15.29); (b) to denote one's condition *be, be situated, be faring* (EP 6.21; perhaps AC 15.29)

πράσσω	VIPA--1S	πράσσω
πράσσων	VPPANM-S	"
πράτητα	N-AF-S	see πραΰτητα
πράττειν	VNPA	πράσσω
πραττόμενα	VPPPAN-P	"
πράττουσι(ν)	VIPA--3P	"
πραϋπάθειαν	N-AF-S	πραϋπαθία

πραϋπαθία, ας, ἡ (also **πραϋπάθεια**) as a calm disposition *gentleness, composure* (1T 6.11)

πραϋπαθίαν	N-AF-S	πραϋπαθία

πραΰς, πραεῖα, πραΰ as a mild and friendly disposition *gentle, kind, considerate, meek* (in the older sense of strong but accommodating); substantively οἱ πραεῖς *gentle, unassuming people* (MT 5.5)

πραΰς	A--NM-S	πραΰς

πραΰτης, ητος, ἡ (also **πραότης**) as a quality of gentle friendliness *gentleness, meekness* (as strength that accommodates to another's weakness), *consideration*

πραΰτης	N-NF-S	πραΰτης
πραΰτητα	N-AF-S	"
πραΰτητι	N-DF-S	

πραΰτητος	N-GF-S	"
πρέπει	VIPA--3S	πρέπω
πρέπον	VPPANN-S	"

πρέπω impf. third-person singular ἔπρεπε; (1) impersonally πρέπει, with an implication of moral judgment *it is fitting, suitable, proper* (HE 2.10); (2) neuter participle with ἐστίν *it is fitting, right, proper* (1C 11.13)

πρεσβεία, ας, ἡ as a body of ambassadors or legates *embassy, delegation, representatives*

πρεσβείαν	N-AF-S	πρεσβεία
πρεσβεύομεν	VIPA--1P	πρεσβεύω

πρεσβευτής, οῦ, ὁ *ambassador* (PM 9)

πρεσβευτής	N-NM-S	πρεσβευτής

πρεσβεύω literally *be an ambassador* or *envoy*; figuratively in the NT, of apostolic ministry *be an ambassador, be a representative* sent by Christ

πρεσβεύω	VIPA--1S	πρεσβεύω
πρεσβύτας	N-AM-P	πρεσβύτης
πρεσβυτέρας	APMAF-P	πρεσβύτερος

πρεσβυτέριον, ου, τό as a group of elders functioning with administrative authority *body* or *council of elders* (1) in Jerusalem equivalent to the Sanhedrin, the Jewish high court (LU 22.66); (2) as a Christian church council *presbytery, group of elders* (1T 4.14)

πρεσβυτέριον	N-NN-S	πρεσβυτέριον
πρεσβυτερίου	N-GN-S	"
πρεσβυτέροι	APMNM-P	πρεσβύτερος
	AP-NM-P	"
	AP-VM-P	"
	A-MNM-P	"
πρεσβυτέροις	APMDM-P	"
	AP-DM-P	"

πρεσβύτερος, τέρα, ον comparative of πρέσβυς (*old*); *older* (1) as an adjective, as denoting greater age *older* (of two) (LU 15.25); with loss of the comparative sense *old*; as a substantive οἱ πρεσβύτεροι *the older generation, the old ones* (AC 2.17); (2) as a substantive; (a) as denoting previous generations οἱ πρεσβύτεροι *forefathers, ancestors, people who lived long ago* (HE 11.2) (b) as designating honorable officials in local councils, synagogues, etc. *elder* (LU 7.3); (c) as designating lay members of the Sanhedrin from important families as distinct from priests and scribes *elder* (MK 11.27); (d) as denoting leaders who preside over Christian assemblies *elder* (AC 14.23; 15.2); (e) in Revelation denoting (human) members of a heavenly council around God's throne *elder* (RV 4.4)

πρεσβύτερος	AP-NM-S	πρεσβύτερος
	A-MNM-S	"
πρεσβυτέρου	AP-GM-S	"
πρεσβυτέρους	AP-AM-P	"
πρεσβυτέρῳ	APMDM-S	"
πρεσβυτέρων	APMGM-P	"
	AP-GM-P	"

πρεσβύτης, ου, ὁ as a designation of age *old man, aged person*

πρεσβύτης	N-NM-S	πρεσβύτης
πρεσβύτιδας	N-AF-P	πρεσβῦτις

πρεσβῦτις, ιδος, ἡ *old(er) woman, elderly lady* (TI 2.3)

πρηνής, ές, gen. οὖς as a bodily position in falling *head-foremost, headfirst, prostrate*; π. γενόμενος *falling head-long* (AC 1.18)

| πρηνής | A--NM-S | πρηνής |

πρίζω or πρίω 1aor. pass. ἐπρίσθην; as a method of execution *saw (in two), cut in two with a saw* (HE 11.37)

πρίν (1) literally, an adverb of time *before, formerly, previously*; (2) used as a temporal conjunction in the NT π. or π. ἥ *before*; followed by the aorist subjunctive (LU 2.26) or the accusative and an aorist infinitive (JN 4.49); (3) as an improper preposition used to indicate time; (a) with the genitive *before* (MT 26.34); (b) with the accusative *before, previous to* (MK 15.42)

πρίν	AB	πρίν
	CS	"
	PA	"
	PG	"

Πρίσκα and Πρίσκιλλα, ης, ἡ *Prisca* and its diminutive *Priscilla*, feminine proper noun

Πρίσκα	N-NF-S	Πρίσκα
Πρίσκαν	N-AF-S	"
Πρίσκιλλα	N-NF-S	"
Πρίσκιλλαν	N-AF-S	"

πρό preposition with the genitive *before*; (1) spatially *before, in front of, at* (AC 12.6); figuratively *before, ahead of* someone (MT 11.10); (2) temporally *before* (MT 24.38; CO 1.17); (3) denoting primary importance π. πάντων *above all, especially* (JA 5.12)

πρό	PG	πρό
προαγαγεῖν	VNAA	προάγω
προαγαγών	VPAANM-S	"
προάγει	VIPA--3S	"
προάγειν	VNPA	"
προάγοντες	VPPANM-P	"
προάγουσαι	VPPANF-P	"
προαγούσας	VPPAAF-P	"
προαγούσης	VPPAGF-S	"
προάγουσι(ν)	VIPA--3P	"

προάγω impf. προῆγον; fut. προάξω; 2aor. προήγαγον; (1) transitively *lead* or *bring out* (AC 16.30); of a law court *bring before* (AC 25.26); (2) intransitively *go before, precede, lead the way*; (a) spatially *go in front of* (MT 2.9); (b) temporally *come first, happen before* (1T 1.18); figuratively, of sins preceding sinners to the judgment *go ahead of time* (1T 5.24); of failing to obey properly *go too far, go beyond* (2J 9)

προάγω	VIPA--1S	προάγω
προάγων	VPPANM-S	"
προαιρεῖται	VIPM--3S	προαιρέω

προαιρέω pf. mid. προῄρημαι; only middle in the NT *choose (for oneself), prefer, decide ahead of time* (2C 9.7)

προαιτιάομαι 1aor. προῃτιασάμην; from πρό (*before*) and αἰτία (*accusation*); *accuse beforehand, previously convict*; προῃτιασάμεθα *we have already charged that* (RO 3.9)

προακούω 1aor. προήκουσα; *hear beforehand*; aorist *have heard before* (CO 1.5)

προαμαρτάνω pf. προημάρτηκα; *sin previously*; perfect *have sinned in the past*

| προάξω | VIFA--1S | προάγω |

προαύλιον, ου, τό the front part of a Roman-type house *forecourt, entranceway, courtyard* (MK 14.68)

| προαύλιον | N-AN-S | προαύλιον |

προβαίνω 2aor. προέβην; pf. προβέβηκα; literally *go forward, advance, go on* (MT 4.21); idiomatically, of old age προβεβηκέναι ἐν ταῖς ἡμέραις literally *be advanced in days*, i.e. *be very old* (LU 1.7)

| προβαλλόντων | VPPAGM-P | προβάλλω |

προβάλλω 2aor. προέβαλον; *project, put before*; (1) of persons *put* or *urge forward* (AC 19.33); (2) of plants *put out, sprout* (leaves, blossoms, etc.) (LU 21.30)

προβάλλωσι(ν)	VSPA--3P	προβάλλω
προβαλόντων	VPAAGM-P	"
προβάλωσι(ν)	VSAA--3P	"
προβάς	VPAANM-S	προβαίνω
πρόβατα	N-AN-P	πρόβατον
	N-NN-P	"
προβάτια	N-AN-P	προβάτιον
	N-NN-P	"
προβατικῇ	AP-DF-S	προβατικός

προβατικός, ή, όν *pertaining to sheep*; substantivally ἡ προβατική (πύλη) *sheep gate*, a gate in the northern city wall of Jerusalem (JN 5.2)

προβάτιον, ου, τό diminutive of πρόβατον without diminutive sense; *sheep* (JN 21.16)

πρόβατον, ου, τό *sheep*; (1) literally, domestic sheep, as distinguished from wild sheep on mountain ranges (LU 15.4); (2) metaphorically, of followers of any master; of mankind in need of a Savior (1P 2.25); of the people of Israel as God's covenant people (MT 10.6); of the followers of Christ (JN 10.11); at the time of judgment, of those who have done God's will, as distinguished from those who have not, in contrast to ἔριφος (*goat*) (MT 25.33); (3) idiomatically ἔρχεσθαι ἐν ἐνδύμασιν προβάτων literally *come in sheep's clothing*, i.e. *act hypocritically, pretend to be good* (MT 7.15)

πρόβατον	N-AN-S	πρόβατον
	N-NN-S	"
προβάτου	N-GN-S	"
προβάτων	N-GN-P	"
προβεβηκότες	VPRANM-P	προβαίνω
προβεβηκυῖα	VPRANF-S	"

προβιβάζω (or προσβιβάζω) 1aor. προεβίβασα and προσεβίβασα; 1aor. pass. προεβιβάσθην; *cause to step forward, push forward* (AC 19.33); figuratively *prompt, urge on, incite* (MT 14.8)

| προβιβασθεῖσα | VPAPNF-S | προβιβάζω |

προβλέπω 1aor. mid. προεβλεψάμην; *foresee*; only middle in the NT *plan* or *provide beforehand* (HE 11.40)

προβλεψαμένου	VPAMGM-S	προβλέπω
προγεγονότων	VPRAGN-P	προγίνομαι
προγεγραμμένοι	VPRPNM-P	προγράφω

προγίνομαι pf. act. προγέγονα; *happen before, be done earlier*; of sins *be previously done* or *committed* (RO 3.25)

| προγινώσκοντες | VPPANM-P | προγινώσκω |

προγινώσκω 2aor. προέγνων; (1) *know something beforehand* or *in advance* (2P 3.17); (2) *know someone previously* (AC 26.5); (3) *select in advance, choose* or *appoint beforehand* (RO 8.29)

| προγνώσει | N-DF-S | πρόγνωσις |

πρόγνωσιν   N-AF-S   "

πρόγνωσις, εως, ἡ   *advance knowledge, foreknowledge, what is known ahead of time*

προγόνοις   AP-DM-P   πρόγονος

πρόγονος, ον   *born early* or *before*; substantivally, plural πρόγονοι *parents and grandparents* (1T 5.4); *forefathers, ancestors* (2T 1.3)

προγόνων   AP-GM-P   πρόγονος

προγράφω   1aor. προέγραψα; pf. pass. προγέγραμμαι; 2aor. pass. προεγράφην; (1) *write before* or *previously*; (a) in the same document *write above* (EP 3.3); (b) passive, of what was found in an older document ὅσα προεγράφη *what was previously written* (RO 15.4); *be written about* (JU 4); (2) metaphorically, in the sense of a figure drawn or portrayed before the eyes of people *proclaim publicly, describe clearly, vividly portray* (GA 3.1)

πρόδηλα   A--NN-P   πρόδηλος
πρόδηλοι   A--NF-P   "
πρόδηλον   A--NN-S   "

πρόδηλος, ον   as something easily understood by all *clear, evident, quite plain*; with ἐστίν implied *it is quite evident* (that) (HE 7.14)

προδίδωμι   1aor. προέδωκα; 2aor. subjunctive third-person singular προδοῖ; (1) *precede in giving to* someone, *give first, pay in advance* (RO 11.35); (2) *hand over, betray* (MK 14.10)

προδοῖ   VSAA--3S   προδίδωμι
προδόται   N-NM-P   προδότης

προδότης, ου, ὁ   *betrayer, traitor*

προδότης   N-NM-S   προδότης
προδραμών   VPAANM-S   προτρέχω

πρόδρομος, ον   of one who goes on ahead to prepare the way *going before*; substantivally *forerunner*; metaphorically, of Jesus in his high priestly work in entering God's presence after his resurrection, ahead of his followers and on their behalf (HE 6.20)

πρόδρομος   AP-NM-S   πρόδρομος
προεβίβασαν   VIAA--3P   προβιβάζω
προέγνω   VIAA--3S   προγινώσκω
προεγνωσμένου   VPRPGM-S   "
προεγράφη   VIAP--3S   προγράφω
προέγραψα   VIAA--1S   "
προέδραμε(ν)   VIAA--3S   προτρέχω
προέδωκε(ν)   VIAA--3S   προδίδωμι
προεθέμην   VIAM--1S   προτίθημι
προέθετο   VIAM--3S   "
προειδομένου   VPRMGM-S   πρόοιδα
προειδώς   VPRANM-S   "
προείπαμεν   VIAA--1P   προεῖπον
προεῖπε(ν)   VIAA--3S   "
προείπομεν   VIAA--1P   "

προεῖπον   the second aorist with no present in use (προλέγω [*announce beforehand, forewarn*] [q.v.] is used instead); pf. προείρηκα; (1) in reference to future events *foretell, tell beforehand, predict* (AC 1.16); (2) aorist or perfect in reference to what was said previously *have already said, have mentioned previously* (GA 5.21)

προεῖπον   VIAA--1S   προεῖπον
προείρηκα   VIRA--1S   "
προειρήκαμεν   VIRA--1P   "
προείρηκε(ν)   VIRA--3S   "

προειρηκέναι   VNRA   "
προειρημένων   VPRPGN-P   "
προείρηται   VIRP--3S   "
προέκοπτε(ν)   VIIA--3S   προκόπτω
προέκοπτον   VIIA--1S   "
προέκοψε(ν)   VIAA--3S   "
προέλαβε(ν)   VIAA--3S   προλαμβάνω
προελέγομεν   VIIA--1P   προλέγω
προελεύσεται   VIFD--3S   προέρχομαι
προελθόντες   VPAANM-P   "
προελθών   VPAANM-S   "
προέλθωσι(ν)   VSAA--3P   "

προελπίζω   pf. προήλπικα; *hope before* or *first, be the first to hope*; used in reference to early Jewish converts to Christianity (EP 1.12)

προενάρχομαι   1aor. προενηρξάμην; with reference to past time *begin before* or *ahead of time* (2C 8.6, 10)

προενήρξασθε   VIAD--2P   προενάρχομαι
προενήρξατο   VIAD--3S   "

προεπαγγέλλω   1aor. mid. προεπηγγειλάμην; (1) middle *promise previously* or *beforehand* (RO 1.2); (2) passive *be promised* or *announced previously* (2C 9.5)

προέπεμπον   VIIA--3P   προπέμπω
προεπηγγείλατο   VIAM--3S   προεπαγγέλλω
προεπηγγελμένην   VPRPAF-S   "

προέρχομαι   impf. προηρχόμην; fut. προελεύσομαι; 2aor. act. προῆλθον; (1) *advance, go forward* (MT 26.39); (2) of advance travel *go on ahead* (of someone), *go before, precede* (AC 20.5); figuratively, as a forerunner *go before* (LU 1.17); (3) as showing the way *go before, lead* (LU 22.47)

προεστῶτες   VPRANM-P   προΐστημι
προέτειναν   VIAA--3S   προτείνω
προέτεινε(ν)   VIAA--3S   "

προετοιμάζω   1aor. προητοίμασα; *prepare beforehand*; used only of God's work in the NT *make ready in advance*

προευαγγελίζομαι   1aor. προευηγγελισάμην; *bring good news in advance*, with a restricted meaning in the NT *tell* or *announce the gospel beforehand* (GA 3.8)

προευηγγελίσατο   VIAD--3S   προευαγγελίζομαι
προεφήτευον   VIIA--3P   προφητεύω
προεφητεύσαμεν   VIAA--1P   "
προεφήτευσαν   VIAA--3P   "
προεφήτευσε(ν)   VIAA--3S   "
προέφθασε(ν)   VIAA--3S   προφθάνω
προεχειρίσατο   VIAD--3S   προχειρίζομαι
προεχόμεθα   VIPM--1P   προέχω
    VIPP--1P

προέχω   (1) intransitively, active *be first, excel*; passive *be excelled*, i.e. *be in a worse position, be worse off*; (2) intransitively, middle *have advantage*; (3) transitively, middle *hold before oneself for protection*, i.e. *make excuses*; depending on the antecedent of "we" in RO 3.9, any of the three meanings is possible but the second is to be preferred

προεχώμεθα   VSPM--1P   προέχω
προεωρακότες   VPRANM-P   προοράω
προήγαγε(ν)   VIAA--3S   προάγω
προήγαγον   VIAA--1S   "
προῆγε(ν)   VIIA--3S   "

προηγέομαι (1) *lead the way, be the leader*; figuratively in the NT *outdo others* (possibly RO 12.10); (2) *prefer, consider better, esteem more highly* (possibly RO 12.10)

προηγούμενοι	VPPDNM-P	προηγέομαι
	VPPONM-P	"
προηγουμένων	VPPDGM-P	"
	VPPOGM-P	"
προηκούσατε	VIAA--2P	προακούω
προῆλθε(ν)	VIAA--3S	προέρχομαι
προήλθομεν	VIAA--1P	"
προῆλθον	VIAA--3P	"
προηλπικότας	VPRAAM-P	προελπίζω
προημαρτηκόσι(ν)	VPRADM-P	προαμαρτάνω
προημαρτηκότων	VPRAGM-P	"
προῄρηται	VIRM--3S	προαιρέω
προήρχετο	VIID--3S	προέρχομαι
	VIIO--3S	"
προητιασάμεθα	VIAD--1P	προαιτιάομαι
προητοίμασε(ν)	VIAA--3S	προετοιμάζω
προθέσει	N-DF-S	πρόθεσις
προθέσεως	N-GF-S	"
πρόθεσιν	N-AF-S	"

πρόθεσις, εως, ἡ (1) *placing before, setting forth, presentation*; idiomatically, in reference to the sacred bread set out weekly in the tabernacle or temple οἱ ἄρτοι τῆς προθέσεως literally *the bread of the placing before*, i.e. *consecrated bread, loaves placed before God* (MT 12.4); (2) *plan, purpose, design*; of people (AC 11.23); of God (RO 8.28)

πρόθεσις	N-NF-S	πρόθεσις

προθεσμία, ας, ἡ *time fixed beforehand, appointed day, set time* (GA 4.2)

προθεσμίας	N-GF-S	προθεσμία

προθυμία, ας, ἡ as a determined disposition of mind *readiness, zeal* (AC 17.11); *willingness, eagerness* (2C 8.11)

προθυμία	N-NF-S	προθυμία
προθυμίαν	N-AF-S	"
προθυμίας	N-GF-S	"
πρόθυμον	A--NN-S	πρόθυμος

πρόθυμος, ον *ready, willing, eager* (MT 26.41); neuter as a substantive in RO 1.15 τὸ κατ' ἐμὲ πρόθυμον *my eagerness*, i.e. *I am eager*

πρόθυμος	A--NM-S	πρόθυμος

προθύμως adverb; *eagerly, willingly, readily* (1P 5.2)

προθύμως	AB	προθύμως
προϊδοῦσα	VPAANF-S	προοράω
προϊδών	VPAANM-S	
πρόϊμον	AP-AM-S	πρόϊμος

πρόϊμος, ον (also **πρώϊμος**) *early*; substantivally in the NT *early rain* (JA 5.7), opposite ὄψιμος (*late rain*); in the Middle East, the early rains come in late autumn (around November) and enable the new planting of grain

προϊστάμενοι	VPPMNM-P	προΐστημι
προϊστάμενον	VPPMAM-S	"
προϊστάμενος	VPPMNM-S	"
προϊσταμένους	VPPMAM-P	"
προϊστανόμενος	VPPMNM-S	see προϊστάμενος
προϊστανομένους	VPPMAM-P	see προϊσταμένους
προΐστασθαι	VNPM	προΐστημι

προΐστημι 2aor. προέστην; pf. ptc. προεστώς; intransitively in the NT; (1) middle *put oneself (responsibly) at the head, lead, direct, rule* (1T 5.17); (2) active, of a protective leadership *care for, help, give aid* (1TH 5.12); (3) of responsible preoccupation with something *devote oneself to, engage in, strive for* (TI 3.8)

προκαλέω *call forth*; only middle in the NT *challenge (to combat), provoke, irritate* (GA 5.26)

προκαλούμενοι	VPPMNM-P	προκαλέω
προκαταγγείλαντας	VPAAAM-P	προκαταγγέλλω

προκαταγγέλλω 1aor. προκατήγγειλα; *announce beforehand*; of prophecy *foretell, predict*

προκαταρτίζω 1aor. subjunctive προκαταρτίσω; *make ready beforehand, arrange in advance* (2C 9.5)

προκαταρτίσωσι(ν)	VSAA--3P	προκαταρτίζω
προκατεχόμεθα	VIPM--1P	προκατέχω
	VIPP--1P	"
προκατέχομεν	VIPA--1P	"

προκατέχω *gain possession of previously, preoccupy*; figuratively and middle in the NT *have a prior advantage* (RO 3.9)

προκατήγγειλαν	VIAA--3P	προκαταγγέλλω
προκατήγγειλε(ν)	VIAA--3S	"
προκατηγγελμένην	VPRPAF-S	"

πρόκειμαι (1) *lie before, be on public display*; of dead bodies *be exposed to view*; of destroyed cities exhibited as an example *exist for all to see* (JU 7); (2) figuratively, of a prescribed goal or prospect *lie ahead, be set before* (HE 12.1); (3) of an attitude *be present, be there* (2C 8.12)

προκειμένης	VPPDGF-S	πρόκειμαι
	VPPOGF-S	"
προκείμενον	VPPDAM-S	"
	VPPOAM-S	"
πρόκεινται	VIPD--3P	"
	VIPO--3P	"
πρόκειται	VIPD--3S	"
	VIPO--3S	"
προκεκηρυγμένον	VPRPAM-S	προκηρύσσω
προκεκυρωμένην	VPRPAF-S	προκυρόω
προκεχειρισμένον	VPRPAM-S	προχειρίζομαι
προκεχειροτονημένοις	VPRPDM-P	προχειροτονέω
προκηρύξαντος	VPAAGM-S	προκηρύσσω

προκηρύσσω 1aor. προεκήρυξα; (1) *proclaim publicly, speak forth*; (2) in a temporal sense of the preaching of John the Baptist *tell ahead of time, announce beforehand* (AC 13.24)

προκοπή, ῆς, ἡ *advancement, progress* (PH 1.25)

προκοπή	N-NF-S	προκοπή
προκοπήν	N-AF-S	

προκόπτω impf. προέκοπτον; fut. προκόψω; 1aor. προέκοψα; intransitively in the NT; (1) of persons *go forward, make progress, advance* (LU 2.52); *cause to increase* (2T 2.16); (2) of time *be advanced, be nearly over* (RO 13.12)

προκόψουσι(ν)	VIFA--3P	προκόπτω

πρόκριμα, ατος, τό as the result of a prior unjustified decision *prejudgment, prejudice, partiality* (1T 5.21)

προκρίματος	N-GN-S	πρόκριμα

προκυρόω   pf. pass. προκεκύρωμαι; of a will or covenant *cause to be in force earlier, make valid in advance, previously ratify* (GA 3.17)

προλαβών	VPAANM-S	προλαμβάνω
προλαμβάνει	VIPA--3S	"

προλαμβάνω   2aor. προέλαβον; 1aor. pass. προελήμφθην; *take beforehand*; (1) with the προ- prefix relating to time *anticipate, do* something *beforehand* (MK 14.8); (2) *surprise, overtake, detect*; passive *be overtaken, be caught (unawares)* (GA 6.1)

προλέγω   impf. προελέγον; προεῖπον (q.v.) serves as the second aorist, with προείρηκα as the perfect; *announce beforehand, tell in advance, forewarn*; with ὅτι (*that*) following (2C 13.2)

προλέγω	VIPA--1S	προλέγω
προλημφθῇ	VSAP--3S	προλαμβάνω
προληφθῇ	VSAP--3S	"

προμαρτύρομαι (and **προμαρτυρέομαι**)   *testify beforehand, declare in advance, predict* (1P 1.11)

προμαρτυρόμενον	VPPDNN-S	προμαρτύρομαι
	VPPONN-S	"
προμαρτυρούμενον	VPPDNN-S	"
	VPPONN-S	"
προμελετᾶν	VNPA	προμελετάω
προμελετᾶν	VNPA	"

προμελετάω   of a speech *practice beforehand, premeditate*; of court defense *prepare (beforehand)* (LU 21.14)

προμελετῶντες	VPPANM-P	προμελετάω
προμεριμνᾶτε	VMPA--2P	προμεριμνάω

προμεριμνάω   *be anxious* or *concerned beforehand, worry ahead of time* (MK 13.11)

προνοεῖ	VIPA--3S	προνοέω
προνοεῖται	VIPM--3S	"

προνοέω   (1) generally *think of beforehand, perceive ahead of time, foresee*; (2) *provide for* someone, *take thought for* (1T 5.8); (3) active and middle with the same meaning *give attention to doing* something, *provide, be concerned to show* (RO 12.17; 2C 8.21)

πρόνοια, ας, ἡ   *forethought, foresight* (AC 24.2); πρόνοιαν ποιεῖσθαι *be concerned about, plan a way to provide for* (RO 13.14)

πρόνοιαν	N-AF-S	πρόνοια
προνοίας	N-GF-S	"
προνοοῦμεν	VIPA--1P	προνοέω
προνοούμενοι	VPPMNM-P	"

πρόοιδα   pf. ptc. προειδώς; *know beforehand* (AC 2.31; HE 11.40)

προοράω   impf. mid. προορώμην; 2aor. προεῖδον; pf. προεώρακα; (1) of time, looking back from the present *see earlier* or *previously* (AC 21.29); (2) of time, looking to the future *foresee, see in advance* (AC 2.31); (3) figuratively and middle, with a spatial sense envisioned *see before oneself, hold before one's eyes, think about as if present* (AC 2.25)

προορίζω   1aor. προώρισα; 1aor. pass. προωρίσθην; *decide on beforehand, determine in advance*

προορίσας	VPAANM-S	προορίζω
προορισθέντες	VPAPNM-P	"
προορισθέντος	VPAPGM-S	"
προορώμην	VIIM--1S	προοράω
προπαθόντες	VPAANM-P	προπάσχω

προπάσχω   2aor. προέπαθον; with time orientation *suffer before* or *previously*; aorist *already have suffered* (1TH 2.2)

προπάτορα	N-AM-S	προπάτωρ

προπάτωρ, ορος, ὁ   as a founder of a family or nation *forefather, ancestor, progenitor* (RO 4.1)

προπεμπόντων	VPPAGM-P	προπέμπω

προπέμπω   impf. προέπεμπον; 1aor. προέπεμψα; 1aor. pass. προεπέμφθην; (1) with an attitude of respect *accompany, escort* (AC 20.38); (2) as furnishing things necessary for someone's travel *help on one's journey, send on one's way* (1C 16.11)

προπεμφθέντες	VPAPNM-P	προπέμπω
προπεμφθῆναι	VNAP	"
προπέμψας	VPAANM-S	"
προπέμψατε	VMAA--2P	"
προπέμψεις	VIFA--2S	"
προπέμψητε	VSAA--2P	"
πρόπεμψον	VMAA--2S	"
προπετεῖς	A--NM-P	προπετής
προπετές	A--AN-S	"

προπετής, ές, gen. **οῦς**   literally *falling headlong, precipitous*; figuratively in the NT, of behavior *rash, reckless, thoughtless*

προπορεύομαι   fut. προπορεύσομαι; (1) *precede, go (on) before* someone (LU 1.76); (2) *lead, show the way* (AC 7.40)

προπορεύσεται	VIFD--3S	προπορεύομαι
προπορεύσῃ	VIFD--2S	"
προπορεύσονται	VIFD-3P	"

πρός   preposition; **I.** with the genitive to show advantage *necessary for, beneficial toward* (AC 27.34); **II.** with the dative to show a near position *at, by, close to, before* (MK 5.11; LU 19.37); **III.** predominately with the accusative; (1) literally, to show motion toward a person or thing *to, toward*; after verbs of going (MK 1.33), sending (AC 25.21), leading (LU 19.35); figuratively, after verbs of attracting or drawing (JN 12.32); (2) literally, to show movement toward an object and implied reaction from it *against* (MT 4.6; AC 26.14); (3) figuratively, to show close relationship to a person; (a) in a friendly, peaceful manner *with, before, toward* (RO 5.1; CO 4.5); (b) in an unfriendly, hostile manner *against, toward* (AC 24.19); (c) to show interrelationship *among, with* (MT 13.56); (4) to show time; (a) of approaching a point in time *to, toward* (LU 24.29); (b) of marking a given (and probably approximate) span of time *at, about* (HE 12.11); idiomatically π. καιρόν literally *about a season*, i.e. *for a while, for a time* (LU 8.13); π. καιρὸν ὥρας literally *about a season of an hour*, i.e. *for a little while, for a short time* (1TH 2.17); π. ὥραν literally *about an hour*, i.e. *for a short time, briefly* (JN 5.35); π. ὀλίγας ἡμέρας literally *about a few days*, i.e. *for a little while, for a short time* (HE 12.10); (5) to show purpose; (a) to introduce the purpose or goal of an action *for the purpose of, for the sake of, in order to* (JN 11.4; AC 3.10); (b) to introduce a near purpose in relation to an ultimate goal *for the purpose of, with a view to* (EP 4.12; 1P 4.12); (6) to show result, looking toward the end point of a set of circumstances *up to the point of, ending up in, so as to result in* (MT 5.28; JN

4.35); (7) to show a close connection of content; (a) when people are involved *with reference to, about* (MK 12.12); (b) when things are involved *with regard to, as concerns* (perhaps MT 27.14; HE 6.11); (c) when agreement or harmony is involved *in line with, corresponding to* (LU 12.47; GA 2.14); **IV.** absolutely, as an adverb *besides, over and above* (probably MT 27.14)

πρός	AB	πρός
	PA	"
	PD	"
	PG	"

προσάββατον, ου, τό literally *day before Sabbath*, i.e. *Friday, Sabbath eve* (MK 15.42)

προσάββατον	N-NN-S	προσάββατον
προσάγαγε	VMAA--2S	προσάγω
προσαγαγεῖν	VNAA	"
προσαγάγῃ	VSAA--3S	"
προσαγαγόντες	VPAANM-P	"
προσάγειν	VNPA	"
προσαγορευθείς	VPAPNM-S	προσαγορεύω

προσαγορεύω 1aor. pass. προσηγορεύθην; (1) *greet, address*; (2) in the NT *designate, call, give a name* or *title to* (HE 5.10)

προσάγω 2aor. προσήγαγον; 1aor. pass. προσήχθην; (1) transitively *bring (forward)* someone to another, *conduct into the presence of* (LU 9.41); figuratively, of Christ's reconciling work in bringing people to God (1P 3.18); (2) intransitively *come near, approach* (AC 27.27)

προσαγωγή, ῆς, ἡ as a means of admission into the presence of a person in high position *access, approach, privilege of entrance*

προσαγωγήν	N-AF-S	προσαγωγή

προσαιτέω *beg, earnestly ask for* (JN 9.8)

προσαίτης, ου, ὁ *beggar*

προσαίτης	N-NM-S	προσαίτης
προσαιτῶν	VPPANM-S	προσαιτέω

προσαναβαίνω 2aor. προσανέβην, imperative προσανάβηθι; as being put into a place of honor *move up, go up higher*, i.e. *to a more important place* (LU 14.10)

προσανάβηθι	VMAA--2S	προσαναβαίνω

προσαναλαμβάνω *take in* or *receive in addition, welcome* (AC 28.2)

προσαναλίσκω or **προσαναλόω** 1aor. ptc. προσαναλώσας; strictly *spend in addition*; hence, of money or property *use up, expend, spend a great amount* (LU 8.43)

προσαναλώσασα	VPAANF-S	προσαναλίσκω
προσαναπληροῦσα	VPPANF-S	προσαναπληρόω

προσαναπληρόω 1aor. προσανεπλήρωσα; strictly *fill up by addition*; hence *replenish*; of someone's needs *supply, fully provide for*

προσανατίθημι 2aor. mid. προσανεθέμην; only middle in the NT; (1) as presenting one's cause to another for approval or judgment *confer with, ask advice* (GA 1.16); (2) *contribute, add* something to someone (GA 2.6)

προσανεθέμην	VIAM--1S	προσανατίθημι
προσανέθεντο	VIAM--3P	"
προσανελάμβανον	VIIA-3P	προσαναλαμβάνω
προσανεπλήρωσαν	VIAA--3P	προσαναπληρόω
προσανέχειν	VNPA	προσανέχω

προσανέχω *appear ahead of, rise up in front of* someone, as a shoreline coming into view ahead (AC 27.27)

προσαπειλέω 1aor. mid. προσηπειλησάμην; only middle in the NT *threaten further, make more threats* (AC 4.21)

προσαπειλησάμενοι	VPAMNM-P	προσαπειλέω
προσαχεῖν	VNPA	προσαχέω

προσαχέω Doric form for προσηχέω (*resound, reecho*); of an echo created by the surf pounding against the shore, indicating land is near *resound* (AC 27.27)

προσβλέπω 1aor. προσέβλεψα; *look on, look at* (HE 11.40)

προσβλεψαμένου	VPAMGM-S	προσβλέπω

προσδαπανάω 1aor. προσεδαπάνησα; *spend besides* or *in addition* (LU 10.35)

προσδαπανήσῃς	VSAA--2S	προσδαπανάω
προσδεξάμενοι	VPADNM-P	προσδέχομαι
προσδέξησθε	VSAD--2P	"

προσδέομαι *have need of* something *else*; negatively, of absolute self-sufficiency *need (nothing)* (AC 17.25)

προσδεόμενος	VPPDNM-S	προσδέομαι
	VPPONM-S	"
προσδέχεσθε	VMPD--2P	προσδέχομαι
	VMPO--2P	"
προσδέχεται	VIPD--3S	"
	VIPO--3S	"

προσδέχομαι impf. προσεδεχόμην; 1aor. προσεδεξάμην; (1) with a person as the object *accept, receive, welcome* (LU 15.2); as indicating active agree with something *accept* (AC 24.15); (2) predominately as having a sense of expectancy *await*; (a) of those who wait for the kingdom of God *expect, look for* (MK 15.43); (b) of the object of Christian expectation, such as resurrection, the fulfillment of all that God has promised, future glory, mercy, completed redemption *wait for* (TI 2.13; JU 21)

προσδεχόμενοι	VPPDNM-P	προσδέχομαι
	VPPONM-P	"
προσδεχομένοις	VPPDDM-P	"
	VPPODM-P	"
προσδεχόμενος	VPPDNM-S	"
	VPPONM-S	"
προσδέχονται	VIPD--3P	"
	VIPO--3P	"

προσδίδωμι impf. προσεδίδουν; *give (over), hand (over) to* (LU 24.30)

προσδοκᾷ	VIPA--3S	προσδοκάω

προσδοκάω impf. προσεδόκων; *wait for, look for, expect, anticipate*, with an added element of tension arising from hope or fear

προσδοκία, ας, ἡ *expectation, anticipation*

προσδοκίας	N-GF-S	προσδοκία
προσδοκῶμεν	VIPA--1P	προσδοκάω
	VSPA--1P	
προσδοκῶν	VPPANM-S	"
προσδοκῶντας	VPPAAM-P	"
προσδοκῶντες	VPPANM-P	"
προσδοκῶντος	VPPAGM-S	"
προσδοκώντων	VPPAGM-P	"
προσδραμών	VPAANM-S	προστρέχω

προσεάω *allow to approach, permit to go farther* (AC 27.7)

προσεβίβασαν	VIAA--3P	προβιβάζω
προσεγγίζειν	VNPA	προσεγγίζω
προσεγγίζοντος	VPPAGM-S	"

προσεγγίζω 1aor. προσήγγισα; *approach, come near to* (MK 2.4)

προσεγγίσαι	VNAA	προσεγγίζω
προσεδέξασθε	VIAD--2P	προσδέχομαι
προσεδέχετο	VIID--3S	"
	VIIO--3S	"
προσεδίδου	VIIA--3S	προσδίδωμι
προσεδόκων	VIIA--3P	προσδοκάω
προσέδραμεν	VIAA--1P	προστρέχω
προσεδρεύοντες	VPPANM-P	προσεδρεύω

προσεδρεύω strictly *sit near*; of temple service *serve, wait on, attend constantly* (1C 9.13)

προσέθετο	VIAM--3S	προστίθημι
προσέθηκε(ν)	VIAA--3S	"
προσειργάσατο	VIAD--3S	προσεργάζομαι
προσεῖχον	VIIA--3P	προσέχω
προσεκαλεῖτο	VIIM--3S	προσκαλέω
προσεκαλέσατο	VIAM--3S	"
προσεκαρτέρουν	VIIA--3P	προσκαρτερέω
προσεκληρώθησαν	VIAP--3P	προσκληρόω
προσεκλίθη	VIAP--3S	προσκλίνω
προσεκολλήθη	VIAP--3S	προσκολλάω
προσέκοψαν	VIAA--3P	προσκόπτω
προσέκρουσαν	VIAA--3P	προσκρούω
προσεκύλισε(ν)	VIAA--3S	προσκυλίω
προσεκύνει	VIIA--3S	προσκυνέω
προσεκύνησα	VIAA--1S	"
προσεκύνησαν	VIAA--3P	"
προσεκύνησε(ν)	VIAA--3S	"
προσεκύνουν	VIIA--3P	"
προσελάβετο	VIAM--3S	προσλαμβάνω
προσέλαβον	VIAA--3P	"
προσελάβοντο	VIAM--3P	"
προσελάμβανον	VIIA--3P	"
προσέλεγε(ν)	VIIA--3S	προσλέγω
προσελεύσεται	VIFD--3S	προσέρχομαι
προσεληλύθατε	VIRA--2P	"
πρόσελθε	VMAA--2S	"
προσελθεῖν	VNAA	"
προσελθόντες	VPAANM-P	"
προσελθόντι	VPAADM-S	"
προσελθόντων	VPAAGM-P	"
προσελθοῦσα	VPAANF-S	"
προσελθοῦσαι	VPAANF-P	"
προσελθών	VPAANM-S	"
προσενέγκαι	VNAA	προσφέρω
προσενέγκας	VPAANM-S	"
προσένεγκε	VMAA--2S	"
προσενεγκεῖν	VNAA	"
προσένεγκη	VSAA--3S	"
προσένεγκον	VMAA--2S	"
προσενεχθείς	VPAPNM-S	"
προσενεχθῇ	VSAP--3S	"
προσενήνοχε(ν)	VIRA--3S	"
προσέπεσαν	VIAA--3P	προσπίπτω
προσέπεσε(ν)	VIAA--3S	"
προσέπεσον	VIAA--3P	"
προσέπιπτε(ν)	VIIA--3S	"
προσέπιπτον	VIIA--3P	"
προσεποιεῖτο	VIIM--3S	προσποιέω
προσεποιήσατο	VIAM--3S	"

προσεργάζομαι 1aor. προσηργασάμην; as trading *gain, earn in addition, make more* (LU 19.16)

προσέρηξε(ν)	VIAA--3S	προσρήσσω
προσέρρηξαν	VIAA--3P	"
προσέρρηξε(ν)	VIAA--3S	"
προσέρχεσθαι	VNPD	προσέρχομαι
	VNPO	"
προσερχέσθωσαν	VMPD--3P	"
	VMPO--3P	"
προσέρχεται	VIPD--3S	"
	VIPO--3S	"

προσέρχομαι impf. προσηρχόμην; fut. προσελεύσομαι; 2aor. act. προσῆλθον; pf. act. προσελήλυθα; (1) literally *come* or *go to, approach* (MT 4.3); *come to visit, associate with* (AC 10.28); (2) figuratively; (a) in a cultic sense, as approaching a deity *come before, come to* (HE 10.1); (b) in the sense of being occupied with a matter *turn to, devote oneself to*; mentally *accede to, agree with* (1T 6.3)

προσερχόμεθα	VIPD--1P	προσέρχομαι
	VIPO--1P	"
προσερχόμενοι	VPPDNM-P	"
	VPPONM-P	"
προσερχόμενον	VPPDAM-S	"
	VPPOAM-S	"
προσερχομένου	VPPDGM-S	"
	VPPOGM-S	"
προσερχομένους	VPPDAM-P	"
	VPPOAM-P	"
προσέρχονται	VIPD--3P	"
	VIPO--3P	"
προσερχώμεθα	VSPD--1P	"
	VSPO--1P	"
προσέσχε(ν)	VIAA--3S	προσέχω
προσέσχηκε(ν)	VIRA--3S	"
προσέταξε(ν)	VIAA--3S	προστάσσω
προσετέθη	VIAP--3S	προστίθημι
προσετέθησαν	VIAP--3P	"
προσετίθει	VIIA--3S	"
προσετίθεντο	VIIP--3P	"
πρόσευξαι	VMAD--2S	προσεύχομαι
προσευξάμενοι	VPADNM-P	"
προσευξάμενος	VPADNM-S	"
προσεύξασθαι	VNAD	"
προσευξάσθωσαν	VMAD--3P	"
προσεύξηται	VSAD--3S	"
προσεύξομαι	VIFD--1S	"
προσευξόμεθα	VIFD--1P	"
προσεύξωμαι	VSAD--1S	"
προσευξώμεθα	VSAD--1P	"
προσευχαί	N-NF-P	προσευχή
προσευχαῖς	N-DF-P	"
προσευχάς	N-AF-P	"
προσεύχεσθαι	VNPD	προσεύχομαι
	VNPO	"
προσεύχεσθε	VIPD--2P	"
	VIPO--2P	"
	VMPD--2P	"
	VMPO--2P	"
προσευχέσθω	VMPD--3S	"
	VMPO--3S	"
προσεύχεται	VIPD--3S	"
	VIPO--3S	"

προσευχή, ῆς, ἡ (1) as a religious technical term, a request for help, made by speaking to a deity, usually in the form of a petition, vow, or wish *prayer* (1P 3.7); (2) by metonymy, a place where people go in order to talk to a deity *place for prayer* (AC 16.13, 16)

προσευχή	N-NF-S	προσευχή
προσεύχη	VSPD--2S	προσεύχομαι
	VSPO--2S	"
προσευχῇ	N-DF-S	προσευχή
προσευχήν	N-AF-S	"
προσευχῆς	N-GF-S	"
προσεύχησθε	VSPD--2P	προσεύχομαι
	VSPO--2P	"

προσεύχομαι impf. προσηυχόμην; fut. προσεύξομαι; 1aor. προσηυξάμην; as a religious technical term for talking to a deity in order to ask for help, usually in the form of a request, vow, or wish *pray, speak to (God), ask* (MT 6.6)

προσεύχομαι	VIPD--1S	προσεύχομαι
	VIPO--1S	"
προσευχόμεθα	VIPD--1P	"
	VIPO--1P	"
προσευχομένη	VPPDNF-S	"
	VPPONF-S	"
προσευχόμενοι	VPPDNM-P	"
	VPPONM-P	"
προσευχόμενον	VPPDAM-S	"
	VPPDNN-S	"
	VPPOAM-S	"
	VPPONN-S	"
προσευχόμενος	VPPDNM-S	"
	VPPONM-S	"
προσευχομένου	VPPDGM-S	"
	VPPOGM-S	"
προσεύχονται	VIPD--3P	"
	VIPO--3P	"
προσεύχωμαι	VSPD--1S	"
	VSPO--1S	"
προσευχῶν	N-GF-P	προσευχή
προσέφερε(ν)	VIIA--3S	προσφέρω
προσέφερον	VIIA--3P	"
προσεφώνει	VIIA--3S	προσφωνέω
προσεφώνησε(ν)	VIAA--3S	"
πρόσεχε	VMPA--2S	προσέχω
προσέχειν	VNPA	"
προσέχεται	VIPM--3S	"
προσέχετε	VMPA--2P	"
προσέχοντας	VPPAAM-P	"
προσέχοντες	VPPANM-P	"

προσέχω impf. προσεῖχον; 2aor. προσέσχον; pf. προσέσχηκα; (1) active, as turning or holding one's mind to someone or something; (a) with the dative of person *give heed to, pay attention to* (AC 8.10); (b) with the dative of the thing *give* or *pay close attention to* (AC 8.6); (c) as a warning when followed by ἀπό (*from, of*), μή (*not*) plus an infinitive, or μήποτε (*lest*): *watch out for, beware (of), be on guard (against), take care (not to)* (MT 6.1; 7.15; LU 21.34); (d) as occupying one's mind with something *devote oneself to, attend to* (1T 4.13); of wine *be addicted to* (1T 3.8); (2) middle *cling to*; figuratively *continue to firmly believe* (1T 6.3)

προσεῶντος	VPPAGM-S	προσεάω
πρόσεως	N-GF-S	see προσθέσεως
προσῆλθαν	VIAA--3P	προσέρχομαι
προσῆλθε(ν)	VIAA--3S	"
προσῆλθον	VIAA--3P	"

προσηλόω 1aor. προσήλωσα; *nail to, fasten with nails*; used metaphorically in CO 2.14 of canceling a sinner's record of guilt through Christ's death on the cross

προσήλυτοι	N-NM-P	προσήλυτος
προσήλυτον	N-AM-S	"

προσήλυτος, ου, ὁ probably derived from the perfect of προσέρχομαι (*come to, approach*); in the sense of *one who has come over, arrived at*; in the NT a religious technical term for one who has come over into Judaism from another religion, becoming a full Jew by being circumcised and by accepting the obligation of observing Jewish laws *proselyte, convert*; to be distinguished from the non-Jewish God-fearers (σεβόμενοι) who attended the Jewish synagogue but did not receive circumcision (cf. AC 13.43 and 17.4)

προσηλύτων	N-GM-P	προσήλυτος
προσηλώσας	VPAANM-S	προσηλόω
προσήνεγκα	VIAA--1S	προσφέρω
προσήνεγκαν	VIAA--3P	"
προσηνέγκατε	VIAA--2P	"
προσήνεγκε(ν)	VIAA--3S	"
προσηνέχθη	VIAP--3S	"
προσηνέχθησαν	VIAP--3P	"
προσήργασα	VIAD--3S	see προσηργάσατο
προσηργάσατο	VIAD--3S	προσεργάζομαι
προσήρχετο	VIID--3S	προσέρχομαι
	VIIO--3S	"
προσήρχοντο	VIID--3P	"
	VIIO--3P	"
προσηυξάμεθα	VIAD--1P	προσεύχομαι
προσηύξαντο	VIAD--3P	"
προσηύξατο	VIAD--3S	"
προσηύχετο	VIID--3S	"
	VIIO--3S	"
προσηχεῖν	VNPA	προσηχέω

προσηχέω *resound* or *reecho* (AC 27.27)

προσήχθη	VIAP--3S	προσάγω
προσθεῖναι	VNAA	προστίθημι
προσθείς	VPAANM-S	"
πρόσθες	VMAA--2S	"
προσθέσεως	N-GF-S	πρόσθεσις

πρόσθεσις, εως, ἡ *adding to, application; provision, assignment*; οἱ ἄρτοι τῆς προσθέσεως *consecrated bread, loaves placed before God* (MK 2.26)

προσθῶ	VSAA--1S	προστίθημι
προσθῶμεν	VSAA--1P	"
πρόσκαιρα	A--NN-P	πρόσκαιρος
πρόσκαιροι	A--NM-P	"
πρόσκαιρον	A--AF-S	"
	A--NN-S	"

πρόσκαιρος, ον of what continues only for a limited time *temporary, transitory, for a time* (MT 13.21), opposite αἰώνιος (*eternal, everlasting*); neuter as a substantive, of things in the visible world τὸ πρόσκαιρον *the temporary nature* (2C 4.17)

πρόσκαιρος	A--NM-S	πρόσκαιρος

προσκαλεῖται	VIPM--3S	προσκαλέω
προσκαλεσάμενοι	VPAMNM-P	"
προσκαλεσάμενος	VPAMNM-S	"
προσκαλεσάσθω	VMAM--3S	"
προσκαλέσηται	VSAM--3S	"

προσκαλέω 1aor. mid. προσεκαλεσάμην; pf. mid. προσκέκλημαι; (1) literally; (a) *call to oneself, summon* (MT 10.1); (b) as a legal technical term *summon, call in* (AC 5.40); (2) figuratively, of a divine call; (a) to faith and salvation *call, invite* (AC 2.39); (b) to a special task *call, appoint* (AC 13.2)

προσκαρτερεῖτε	VMPA--2P	προσκαρτερέω

προσκαρτερέω fut. προσκαρτερήσω; with a basic meaning *persist at, stay by*; (1) with the dative of person *be loyal to, attach oneself to, associate closely with* (AC 8.13); *serve personally, wait on* (AC 10.7); of a boat *be continually ready for* someone, *stand ready* (MK 3.9); (2) with the dative of the thing; (a) *occupy oneself diligently with, pay persistent attention to, be devoted to* (AC 6.4); (b) *hold fast to, cling to, persevere in* (AC 1.14; 2.42); (3) followed by ἐν and a place *spend much time in, continually be in* (AC 2.46)

προσκαρτερῇ	VSPA--3S	προσκαρτερέω
προσκαρτερήσει	N-DF-S	προσκαρτέρησις

προσκαρτέρησις, εως, ἡ *perseverance, unremitting persistence* (EP 6.18)

προσκαρτερήσομεν	VIFA--1P	προσκαρτερέω
προσκαρτεροῦντες	VPPANM-P	"
προσκαρτερούντων	VPPAGM-P	"
προσκαρτερῶν	VPPANM-S	"
προσκέκλημαι	VIRM--1S	προσκαλέω
προσκέκληται	VIRM--3S	"

προσκεφάλαιον, ου, τό as a headrest *pillow*; in a boat *boat cushion* (MK 4.38)

προσκεφάλαιον	N-AN-S	προσκεφάλαιον

προσκληρόω 1aor. pass. προσεκληρώθην; *allot, assign by lot*; only passive in the NT, of conscious self-attachment *join, attach oneself to, throw in one's lot with* (AC 17.4)

πρόσκλησιν	N-AF-S	πρόσκλησις

πρόσκλησις, εως, ἡ *invitation*; as a legal technical term *summons* (1T 5.21)

προσκλίνω 1aor. pass. προσεκλίθην; *cause to lean on* or *against*; figuratively and only passive in the NT, with the dative of person *attach oneself to, be loyal to, join up with* (AC 5.36)

πρόσκλισιν	N-AF-S	πρόσκλισις

πρόσκλισις, εως, ἡ *inclination*; in the NT in a negative sense *bias, partiality, prejudice* (1T 5.21)

προσκολλάω 1fut. pass. προσκολληθήσομαι; figuratively and only passive in the NT, of the attachment of a husband to his wife *be joined to, cleave to, be united with* (MK 10.7)

προσκολληθήσεται	VIFP--3S	προσκολλάω

πρόσκομμα, ατος, τό (1) as an action *stumbling*; λίθος προσκόμματος *stone that causes people to stumble*; metaphorically, of the effect of Christ's claim on the nation of Israel once they rejected him in RO 9.32, 33 and 1P 2.8; (2) as a result of an action *obstacle, hindrance*; figuratively, as an occasion for making a misstep *opportunity to do wrong* (RO 14.13; 1C 8.9)

πρόσκομμα	N-AN-S	πρόσκομμα
	N-NN-S	"
προσκόμματος	N-GN-S	"

προσκοπή, ῆς, ἡ literally, as an occasion for making a misstep *cause of stumbling, hindrance, reason to fall*; figuratively *opportunity* or *reason to do wrong* (2C 6.3)

προσκοπήν	N-AF-S	προσκοπή
προσκόπτει	VIPA--3S	προσκόπτω
προσκόπτουσι(ν)	VIPA--3P	"

προσκόπτω 1aor. προσέκοψα; (1) literally; (a) transitively *strike* something *against* (MT 4.6); (b) intransitively, with the dative *beat on, dash against* (MT 7.27); metaphorically, of Israel's failure to recognize the importance of Christ's saving work in God's plan for them *stumble against*, i.e. *take offense at, be angry at, reject* (RO 9.32); (2) figuratively *make a misstep* (JN 11.9); *find occasion for doing wrong* (RO 14.21)

προσκόψῃς	VSAA--2S	προσκόπτω

προσκρούω 1aor. προσέκρουσα; *strike* or *beat against* (MT 7.25, 27)

προσκυλίσας	VPAANM-S	προσκυλίω

προσκυλίω 1aor. προσεκύλισα; as moving a large stone to cover an opening *roll to* or *against*

προσκυνεῖ	VIPA--3S	προσκυνέω
προσκυνεῖν	VNPA	"
προσκυνεῖτε	VIPA--2P	"

προσκυνέω impf. προσεκύνουν; fut. προσκυνήσω; 1aor. προσεκύνησα; (1) from a basic sense *bow down to kiss* someone's feet, garment hem, or the ground in front of him; (2) in the NT of worship or veneration of a divine or supposedly divine object, expressed concretely with falling face down in front of someone *worship, venerate, do obeisance to*; (a) toward God (MT 4.10); (b) toward Jesus (MT 2.2); (c) toward the devil and demons (MT 4.9; RV 9.20); (d) toward idols (AC 7.43); (e) toward human beings as given or claiming to have divine power or authority (RV 3.9; 13.4b)

προσκυνῆσαι	VNAA	προσκυνέω
προσκυνήσαντες	VPAANM-P	"
προσκυνήσατε	VMAA--2P	"
προσκυνησάτωσαν	VMAA--3P	"
προσκυνήσει	VIFA--3S	"
προσκυνήσεις	VIFA--2S	"
	VIFA--2S^VMPA--2S	"
προσκυνήσετε	VIFA--2P	"
προσκυνήσῃς	VSAA--2S	"
προσκύνησον	VMAA--2S	"
προσκυνήσουσι(ν)	VIFA--3P	"
προσκυνήσω	VSAA--1S	"
προσκυνήσων	VPFANM-S	"
προσκυνήσωσι(ν)	VSAA--3P	"
προσκυνηταί	N-NM-P	προσκυνητής

προσκυνητής, οῦ, ὁ *worshiper*, as one who displays devotion toward a deity (JN 4.23)

προσκυνοῦμεν	VIPA--1P	προσκυνέω
προσκυνοῦντας	VPPAAM-P	"
προσκυνοῦντες	VPPANM-P	"
προσκυνοῦσα	VPPANF-S	"
προσκυνοῦσι(ν)	VIPA--3P	"
προσλαβεῖν	VNAA	προσλαμβάνω
προσλαβόμενοι	VPAMNM-P	

προσλαβόμενος VPAMNM-S "
προσλαβοῦ VMAM--2S "
προσλαλέω 1aor. προελάλησα; *speak to, converse with, address*
προσλαλῆσαι VNAA προσλαλέω
προσλαλοῦντες VPPANM-P "
προσλαμβάνεσθε VMPM--2P προσλαμβάνω
προσλαμβανόμενοι VPPMNM-P "
προσλαμβάνω 2aor. προσέλαβον, mid. προσελαβόμην; (1) *take aside, take hold of and lead aside* (MT 16.22); (2) *take along with oneself* (AC 17.5); (3) *receive hospitably, accept, welcome* (PM 17); (4) *take, partake of* food (AC 27.33)
προσλέγω impf. προσέλεγον; *answer, reply* followed by ὅτι (*that*) of direct discourse (MK 16.14)
πρόσλημψις, εως, ἡ (also **πρόσληψις**) as an action *receiving, acceptance* (RO 11.15)
πρόσλημψις N-NF-S πρόσλημψις
πρόσληψις N-NF-S "
προσμεῖναι VNAA προσμένω
προσμείνας VPAANM-S "
προσμένει VIPA--3S "
προσμένειν VNPA "
προσμένουσι(ν) VIPA--3P "
προσμένω 1aor. προσέμεινα; (1) absolutely *remain, stay on* (AC 18.18; 1T 1.3); (2) with the dative *remain* or *stay with* someone (MK 8.2); figuratively, with the dative of person *remain loyal to* (AC 11.23); with the dative of the thing *continue in, persevere in, keep on doing* (1T 5.5)
προσορμίζω 1aor. pass. προσωρμίσθην; from πρό (*before*) and ὅρμος (*station for tying up ships*); active *bring a ship into harbor*; only passive in the NT *come into (an inner) harbor, come to anchor, moor* (MK 6.53)
προσοφείλεις VIPA--2S προσοφείλω
προσοφείλω *owe besides, owe in return* (PM 19)
προσοχθίζω 1aor. προσώχθισα; *be angry, be offended, be vexed*
πρόσπεινος, ον as a physical state *very hungry* (AC 10.10)
πρόσπεινος A--NM-S πρόσπεινος
προσπεσοῦσα VPAANF-S προσπίπτω
προσπήγνυμι 1aor. προσέπηξα; *fix* or *fasten to* something; absolutely, of the crucifixion *nail to the cross, crucify* (AC 2.23)
προσπήξαντες VPAANM-P προσπήγνυμι
προσπίπτω impf. προσέπιπτον; 2aor. προσέπεσον or προσέπεσα; (1) with the dative of person *prostrate oneself, fall down before* or *at the feet of* someone (MK 3.11); (2) with the dative of the thing *fall on, strike against*; of forceful winds *beat on, rush against* (MK 7.25)
προσποιέω 1aor. mid. προσεποιησάμην; only middle in the NT; (1) *make as though, act as if, pretend* (LU 24.28); (2) with μή *act as if* something *does not exist, take no notice* (JN 8.6)
προσποιούμενος VPPMNM-S προσποιέω
προσπορεύομαι *approach, come near to* (MK 10.35)
προσπορεύονται VIPD--3P προσπορεύομαι
VIPO--3P "
προσρήσσω or **προσρήγνυμι** 1aor. προσέρηξα (or προσέρρηξα); intransitively in the NT, with the dative of the thing *dash against, burst on* (LU 6.48; MT 7.25, 27)

προστάσσω 1aor. προσέταξα; pf. pass. προστέταγμαι; (1) of those who have a valid right to command *order, tell, instruct* (MT 1.24); (2) perfect passive, of historical epochs of mankind's history as arranged by God προστεταγμένοι καιροί *appointed* or *prescribed periods of times* (AC 17.26)
προστάτις, ιδος, ἡ as a woman who renders assistance from her resources *protector, helper, patron* (RO 16.2)
προστάτις N-NF-S προστάτις
προστεθῆναι VNAP προστίθημι
προστεθήσεται VIFP--3S "
προστεταγμένα VPRPAN-P προστάσσω
προστεταγμένους VPRPAM-P "
προστῆναι VNAA προΐστημι
προστίθεται VIPP--3S προστίθημι
προστίθημι impf. προσετίθουν; 1aor. προσέθηκα; 2aor. inf. προσθεῖναι, ptc. προσθείς, imperative second-person singular πρόσθες, mid. προσεθέμην; 1aor. pass. προσετέθην; 1fut. pass. προστεθήσομαι; (1) *put to, add to*; (a) as adding to what is already present (MT 6.27); (b) as uniting people into a society already existing (AC 2.41); (c) passive, as a Hebraism of one joining his forefathers through death *be buried with, be laid away with, be gathered to* (AC 13.36); (2) *provide, give, grant* (MT 6.33; LU 17.5); (3) as a Hebraism denoting continuation or repetition when followed by an infinitive, literally *add* to do something, i.e. do *again, do further* (LU 19.11); (4) as a Hebraism followed by an infinitive to mark an event that immediately follows *proceed to do* (AC 12.3)
προστρέχοντες VPPANM-P προστρέχω
προστρέχω 2aor. προσέδραμον; *run up to* someone
προσφάγιον, ου, τό as anything eaten with bread *relish*; *fish* in JN 21.5
προσφάγιον N-AN-S προσφάγιον
πρόσφατον A--AF-S πρόσφατος
πρόσφατος, ον strictly *freshly killed*; in the NT *fresh, newly made, new and different* (HE 10.20)
προσφάτως adverb of time *recently, shortly before* (AC 18.2)
προσφάτως AB προσφάτως
πρόσφερε VMPA--2S προσφέρω
προσφέρει VIPA--3S "
προσφέρειν VNPA "
προσφέρεται VIPP--3S "
προσφέρῃ VSPA--3S "
προσφέρῃς VSPA--2S "
προσφερόμεναι VPPPNF-P "
προσφέρονται VIPP--3P "
προσφέροντες VPPANM-P "
προσφερόντων VPPAGM-P "
προσφέρουσι(ν) VIPA--3P "
προσφέρω 1aor. προσήνεγκα; 2aor. προσήνεγκον; pf. προσενήνοχα; 1aor. pass. προσηνέχθην; (1) active *bring to*; passive *be brought to*; (a) with the accusative of person *bring* someone to someone (MT 4.24); as a legal technical term *hand over, bring before* a magistrate (LU 23.14); (b) with the accusative of the thing *bring, offer, hand* something to someone (MT 22.19); (2) of offerings, gifts, sacrifices, prayers to a deity *present, bring,*

offer (MT 2.11; AC 7.42; HE 5.7); (3) passive with the dative of person *deal with, treat, act toward* (HE 12.7)

προσφέρων	VPPANM-S	προσφέρω
προσφέρωσι(ν)	VSPA--3P	"
προσφιλῆ	A--NN-P	προσφιλής

προσφιλής, ές in a passive sense of what is pleasing *acceptable, lovely* (PH 4.8); of persons *friendly*

προσφορά, ᾶς, ἡ used of sacrifice and gifts to a deity; (1) as a religious activity *offering, presenting, sacrificing* (HE 10.10); (2) literally and figuratively, as referring to what is brought *gift, offering, sacrifice* (HE 10.5)

προσφορά	N-NF-S	προσφορά
προσφορᾷ	N-DF-S	"
προσφοράν	N-AF-S	"
προσφοράς	N-AF-P	"
προσφορᾶς	N-GF-S	"
προσφωνεῖ	VIPA--3S	προσφωνέω

προσφωνέω impf. προσεφώνουν; 1aor. προσεφώνησα; (1) with the dative of person *call out to, address, speak to* (LU 7.32); (2) *call to oneself, summon* (LU 6.13)

προσφωνοῦντα	VPPANN-P	προσφωνέω
προσφωνοῦσι(ν)	VPPADN-P	"
προσχαίροντες	VPPANM-P	προσχαίρω

προσχαίρω *be glad* (MK 9.15)

πρόσχυσιν	N-AF-S	πρόσχυσις

πρόσχυσις, εως, ἡ as an action *sprinkling* or *pouring on* or *against* something, *affusion* (HE 11.28)

προσψαύετε	VIPA--2P	προσψαύω

προσψαύω *touch (lightly)*; metaphorically *touch in a concerned way*, i.e. *help in some way* (LU 11.46)

πρόσωπα	N-AN-P	πρόσωπον
	N-NN-P	"
προσωπολημπτεῖτε	VIPA--2P	προσωπολημπτέω

προσωπολημπτέω (or **προσωπολημπτέω**) *show partiality* or *favoritism, treat one person better than another* (JA 2.9)

προσωπολήμπτης, ου, ὁ (also **προσωπολήπτης**) *one who shows partiality, prejudiced person, one who treats one person better than another* (AC 10.34)

προσωπολήμπτης	N-NM-S	προσωπολήμπτης

προσωπολημψία, ας, ἡ (also **προσωποληψία**) *partiality, favoritism, prejudice*

προσωπολημψία	N-NF-S	προσωπολημψία
προσωπολημψίαις	N-DF-P	"
προσωποληπτεῖτε	VIPA--2P	προσωπολημπτέω
προσωπολήπτης	N-NM-S	προσωπολήμπτης
προσωποληψία	N-NF-S	προσωπολημψία
προσωποληψίαις	N-DF-P	"

πρόσωπον, ου, τό (1) *face, countenance*; literally, as a part of the body *face* (MT 6.16); figuratively; (a) as denoting personal presence *in person* (1TH 2.17); idiomatically, with the sense varied by controlling prepositions: π. πρὸς π. *face to face* (1C 13.12); ἀπὸ προσώπου *directly from* (AC 3.20); εἰς π. *before, in front of* (2C 8.24); ἐν προσώπῳ *in the presence of* (2C 2.10); κατὰ π. *face to face, in person* (AC 3.13), *openly, personally, to one's face* (GA 2.11); μετὰ προσώπου *with the presence of, by being with* someone (AC 2.28); πρὸ προσώπου *in front of, ahead of* (MT 11.10); (b) as denoting the front side of something *face*; of the earth *surface* (LU 21.35); (c) as denoting the external form of something *appearance*

(2C 5.12; JA 1.11); (2) by synecdoche *person, individual* (2C 1.11)

πρόσωπον	N-AN-S	πρόσωπον
	N-NN-S	"
προσώπου	N-GN-S	"
προσώπῳ	N-DN-S	"
προσώπων	N-GN-P	"
προσωρμίσθησαν	VIAP--3P	προσορμίζω
προσώχθισα	VIAA--1S	προσοχθίζω
προσώχθισε(ν)	VIAA--3S	"

προτάσσω pf. pass. ptc. προτεταγμένος; *determine beforehand, prearrange* (AC 17.26)

προτείνω 1aor. προέτεινα; *extend before, stretch out*, of one's hands being bound for flogging (AC 22.25)

προτέρᾳ	A-MDF-S	πρότερος
προτέραν	A-MAF-S	"
πρότερον	ABM	"
	A-MAN-S	"

πρότερος, τέρα, ον comparative of πρό (*before*); used in reference to time; (1) adjectivally *earlier, former, prior* (EP 4.22), opposite νῦν and νυνί (*now, at the present time*); (2) substantivally, neuter accusative singular πρότερον as an adverb *before, formerly, in former times* (2C 1.15); *in the first place, to begin with* (HE 7.27); with the article τὸ πρότερον *before, once, the first time* (JN 6.62; GA 4.13)

προτεταγμένους	VPRPAM-P	προτάσσω

προτίθημι 2aor. mid. προεθέμην; only middle in the NT; (1) *put forward publicly, present, offer* (RO 3.25); (2) strictly *set before oneself*; hence *intend, purpose, plan* (RO 1.13)

προτρέπω 1aor. mid. προετρεψάμην; only middle in the NT, with an infinitive following *encourage, urge on, persuade* to do something (AC 18.27)

προτρέχω 2aor. προέδραμον; *run (on) ahead, run before*

προτρεψάμενοι	VPAMNM-P	προτρέπω

προϋπάρχω impf. προϋπῆρχον; as a previous state or way of acting *be formerly, exist before*

προϋπάρχων	VPPANM-S	προϋπάρχω
προϋπῆρχε(ν)	VIIA--3S	"
προϋπῆρχον	VIIA--3P	"
προφάσει	N-DF-S	πρόφασις
πρόφασιν	N-AF-S	"

πρόφασις, εως, ἡ generally, of what is made to appear to others to hide the true state of things, opposite ἀλήθεια (*truth*); (1) as what is said *pretext, excuse* (JN 15.22); (2) as what is done *pretense, cover-up* (AC 27.30)

προφέρει	VIPA--3S	προφέρω

προφέρω *bring forth* or *out, produce*

προφῆται	N-NM-P	προφήτης
	N-VM-P	"
προφήταις	N-DM-P	"
προφήτας	N-AM-P	"

προφητεία, ας, ἡ *prophecy*; (1) as the gift (χάρισμα) of inspired speaking granted to believers by the Spirit *prophecy, ability to prophesy* (RO 12.6); (2) as the utterance of a prophet *prophetic words, inspired saying, prophecy* (1C 14.6); (3) as a foretelling of future events *prediction, prophecy* (MT 13.14); (4) as the work of a prophet *prophetic activity, prophesying* (RV 11.6)

προφητεία	N-NF-S	προφητεία

προφητεία	N-DF-S	"
προφητεῖαι	N-NF-P	"
προφητείαν	N-AF-S	"
προφητείας	N-AF-P	"
	N-GF-S	"
προφητεύειν	VNPA	προφητεύω
προφητεύητε	VSPA--2P	"
προφητεύομεν	VIPA--1P	"
προφητεύουσα	VPPANF-S	"
προφητεύουσαι	VPPANF-P	"
προφητεῦσαι	VNAA	"
προφητεύσαντες	VPAANM-P	"
προφήτευσον	VMAA--2S	"
προφητεύσουσι(ν)	VIFA--3P	"

προφητεύω impf. ἐπροφήτευον; fut. προφητεύσω; 1aor. ἐπροφήτευσα and προεφήτευσα (JU 14); *prophesy*; (1) generally, of speaking with the help of divine inspiration *proclaim what God wants to make known, preach, expound* (AC 2.17; 1C 11.4); (2) as speaking out divinely imparted knowledge of future events *foretell, prophesy* (MK 7.6; JN 11.51; RV 10.11); (3) as bringing to light what was concealed and outside the possibility of naturally acquired knowledge *prophetically reveal, prophesy* (MT 26.68)

προφητεύων	VPPANM-S	προφητεύω
προφητεύωσι(ν)	VSPA--3P	"
προφήτῃ	N-DM-S	προφήτης
προφήτην	N-AM-S	"

προφήτης, ου, ὁ *prophet*; (1) generally one who speaks for God, proclaiming what God wants to make known; used of Old Testament prophetic personalities (MT 2.23), of John the Baptist (MT 14.5), of Jesus (MT 21.11), of believers endowed with the gift of προφητεία (*prophecy*) (AC 15.32; EP 4.11), and once of a pagan prophet (TI 1.12); (2) the προ- prefix may indicate either a sense of place (before, in front of, publicly) or time (previously, in advance), and the context must be used to determine the presence of either or both elements; (a) with the prefix primarily of place, the *prophet* is one who declares God's message publicly as a *forth teller*, as teacher, admonisher, preacher (1C 14.29); (b) with the prefix denoting time, the *prophet* is a *foreteller* with special knowledge of the future (MT 24.15); (c) the Christian prophet is one with a special gift and calling to proclaim the divine message, interpret the times, and urge people to believe in Christ for salvation (EP 3.5); (3) plural οἱ προφῆται collectively, as a group *the prophets* (MT 5.12); by metonymy, for their writings *the prophetic books, the prophets, what the prophets wrote* (AC 24.14); idiomatically, of all the sacred writings of the Old Testament ὁ νόμος καὶ οἱ προφῆται literally *the law and the prophets*, i.e. *the Scriptures* (MT 7.12)

προφήτης	N-NM-S	προφήτης
προφητικόν	A--AM-S	προφητικός

προφητικός, ή, όν in reference to Old Testament Scripture *prophetic, spoken by a prophet*

προφητικῶν	A--GF-P	προφητικός
προφῆτιν	N-AF-S	προφῆτις

προφῆτις, ιδος, ἡ *prophet(ess)*, feminine form of προφήτης (*prophet*), a woman gifted by the Spirit for prophesying (LU 2.36; cf. AC 2.18)

προφῆτις	N-NF-S	προφῆτις
προφήτου	N-GM-S	προφήτης
προφητῶν	N-GM-P	"

προφθάνω 1aor. προέφθασα; as being beforehand in doing something *anticipate, be first before, be ahead of*, followed by the accusative (MT 17.25)

προχειρίζομαι 1aor. προεχειρισάμην; pf. pass. προκεχείρισμαι; strictly *handpick beforehand*; hence *choose in advance, ordain, appoint* (AC 22.14); passive *be appointed* (AC 3.20)

προχειρίσασθαι	VNAD	προχειρίζομαι

προχειροτονέω pf. pass. προκεχειροτόνημαι; *choose in advance, appoint beforehand, select previously* (AC 10.41)

Πρόχορον	N-AM-S	Πρόχορος

Πρόχορος, ου, ὁ *Prochorus*, masculine proper noun (AC 6.5)

προώρισε(ν)	VIAA--3S	προορίζω
προωρώμην	VIIM--1S	προοράω

πρύμνα, ης, ἡ *stern*, the back part of a ship or boat

πρύμνα	N-NF-S	πρύμνα
πρύμνῃ	N-DF-S	"
πρύμνης	N-GF-S	"

πρωΐ adverb of time *early, in the (early) morning*; in Jewish time reckoning, the fourth watch of the night (from 3:00 A.M. to 6:00 A.M.)

πρωΐ	AB	πρωΐ

πρωΐα, ας, ἡ feminine of πρώϊος (*early*) with ὥρα (*hour*) supplied; *(early) morning, morning hour*

πρωΐας	N-GF-S	πρωΐα
πρώϊμον	AP-AM-S	πρόϊμος
πρωϊνόν	A--AM-S	πρωϊνός

πρωϊνός, ή, όν *early, belonging to the morning*; metaphorically in RV 2.28 and 22.16 ὁ ἀστὴρ ὁ π. *the morning star*

πρωϊνός	A--NM-S	πρωϊνός

πρῷρα, ης, ἡ (also **πρῶρα**) *bow, prow*, the forepart of a ship or boat

πρῷρα	N-NF-S	πρῷρα
πρώρας	N-GF-S	"
πρῴρας	N-GF-S	"
πρῴρης	N-GF-S	"
πρῶτα	A-OAN-P	πρῶτος
	A-ONN-P	"

πρωτεύω *be first, have first place, hold highest rank* or *dignity* (CO 1.18)

πρωτεύων	VPPANM-S	πρωτεύω
πρώτη	A-ONF-S	πρῶτος
πρώτῃ	A-ODF-S	"
πρώτην	A-OAF-S	"
πρώτης	A-OGF-S	"
πρῶτοι	A-ONM-P	"
πρώτοις	A-ODM-P	"
	A-ODN-P	"

πρωτοκαθεδρία, ας, ἡ as a seat of honor in a meeting place *most important place, place of honor, best seat*

πρωτοκαθεδρίαν	N-AF-S	πρωτοκαθεδρία
πρωτοκαθεδρίας	N-AF-P	"

πρωτοκλισία, ας, ἡ   seat of honor at a dinner or banquet, usually beside the host, most important place, place of honor, best seat

πρωτοκλισίαν	N-AF-S	πρωτοκλισία
πρωτοκλισίας	N-AF-P	"
πρωτομάρτυρος	N-GM-S	πρωτόμαρτυς

πρωτόμαρτυς, υρος, ὁ   first martyr, used of Stephen in AC 22.20

πρῶτον	ABO	πρῶτος
	A-OAM-S	"
	A-OAN-S	"
	A-ONN-S	"

πρῶτος, η, ον   I. adjectivally first of several; (1) of time; (a) in comparison of past and present earlier, first, former (RV 2.5); (b) in antithesis between the beginning and the end first, before anything else (RV 1.17), opposite ἔσχατος (last, final); (2) of rank and value first (of all), foremost, chief, most important of all; (a) of things (MT 22.38); (b) substantivally, of persons οἱ πρῶτοι the leading men, the most important persons (MK 6.21); (3) of number or sequence first (MT 21.28; HE 10.9); (4) spatially front; substantivally ἡ πρώτη the outer (tent) (HE 9.2, 6, 8); II. substantivally, neuter singular πρῶτον as an adverb; (1) of time at first, to begin with, (for) the first time (RO 1.16); before, earlier (JN 15.18); (2) of priority or value first of all (MT 5.24); of degree above all, especially, in the first place (MT 6.33)

πρῶτος	ABO	πρῶτος
	A-ONM-S	"
πρωτοστάτην	N-AM-S	πρωτοστάτης

πρωτοστάτης, ου, ὁ   as one stationed in the front ranks of an army leader; in a negative sense ringleader (AC 24.5)

πρωτότοκα	A--AN-P	πρωτότοκος
πρωτοτοκείας	N-AF-P	πρωτοτόκια

πρωτοτόκια, ων, τά (also πρωτοκεία, ας, ἡ)   birthright, rights of the firstborn, special status and inheritance rights belonging to the firstborn son (HE 12.16)

πρωτοτόκια	N-AN-P	πρωτοτόκια
πρωτότοκον	AP-AM-S	πρωτότοκος
	A--AM-S	"

πρωτότοκος, ον   firstborn, existing before; (1) literally, as the oldest son in a family (LU 2.7; HE 11.28); (2) figuratively and substantivally; (a) singular ὁ π. used of Jesus Christ, as the unique preexistent Son of the heavenly Father (HE 1.6); as the one existing before all creation (CO 1.15); as the first to be resurrected from the dead (CO 1.18); as the head of a spiritual family of "many siblings" (RO 8.29); (b) plural οἱ πρωτότοκοι, of redeemed mankind as God's honored family (HE 12.23)

πρωτότοκος	AP-NM-S	πρωτότοκος
	A--NM-S	"
πρωτοτόκων	AP-GM-P	"
πρώτου	A-OGM-S	πρῶτος
	A-OGN-S	"
πρώτους	A-OAM-P	"
πρώτῳ	A-ODM-S	"
	A-ODN-S	"
πρώτων	A-OGF-P	"
	A-OGM-P	"
	A-OGN-P	"

πρώτως   adverb of time first, for the first time (AC 11.26)

πρώτως	ABO	πρώτως
πταίει	VIPA--3S	πταίω
πταίομεν	VIPA--1P	"
πταίσει	VIFA--3S	"
πταίσῃ	VSAA--3S	"
πταίσητε	VSAA--2P	"

πταίω   1aor. ἔπταισα; from a basic meaning stumble against something; intransitively and figuratively in the NT, of failing to do God's will stumble, err, sin

πτέρνα, ης, ἡ   heel; idiomatically, of treating someone maliciously, as with a kick ἐπαίρειν τὴν πτέρναν ἐπί τινα literally raise one's heel against someone, i.e. oppose, turn against someone (JN 13.18)

πτέρναν	N-AF-S	πτέρνα
πτέρυγας	N-AF-P	πτέρυξ
πτέρυγες	N-NF-P	"

πτερύγιον, ου, τό   diminutive of πτέρυξ; little wing; figuratively, of the pointed extremity of anything tip, edge; of a building pinnacle, apex, summit

πτερύγιον	N-AN-S	πτερύγιον
πτερύγων	N-GF-P	πτέρυξ

πτέρυξ, υγος, ἡ   wing of any creature that flies

πτηνός, όν   feathered, winged; neuter plural τὰ πτηνά as a substantive, as any kind of bird the birds (1C 15.39)

πτηνῶν	AP-GN-P	πτηνός

πτοέω   1aor. pass. ἐπτοήθην; terrify, frighten; only passive in the NT be startled, be terrified, be alarmed (LU 21.9)

πτοηθέντες	VPAPNM-P	πτοέω
πτοηθῆτε	VSAP--2P	"
πτόησιν	N-AF-S	πτόησις

πτόησις, εως, ἡ   (1) in an active sense terrifying, intimidation; (2) in a passive sense something fearful, what is alarming; both meanings are possible in 1P 3.6; the active sense (as not fearing human intimidation) may be preferable

Πτολεμαΐδα	N-AF-S	Πτολεμαΐς

Πτολεμαΐς, ΐδος, ἡ   Ptolemais, a seaport along the Phoenician coast, called Acco in Old Testament times, now called Acre (AC 21.7)

πτύξας	VPAANM-S	πτύσσω

πτύον, ου, τό   winnowing shovel, fan, a forklike shovel for throwing threshed grain up into the wind to allow the chaff to be blown away

πτύον	N-NN-S	πτύον
πτυρόμενοι	VPPPNM-P	πτύρω

πτύρω   frighten, scare; only passive in the NT be intimidated, be afraid, be terrified (PH 1.28)

πτύσας	VPAANM-S	πτύω

πτύσμα, ατος, τό   saliva, spittle (JN 9.6)

πτύσματος	N-GN-S	πτύσμα

πτύσσω   1aor. ἔπτυξα; of a garment fold up; of a scroll roll up (LU 4.20)

πτύω   1aor. ἔπτυσα; spit

πτῶμα, ατος, τό   what has fallen; of people and other animated creatures corpse, dead body, carcass

πτῶμα	N-AN-S	πτῶμα
	N-NN-S	"
πτώματα	N-AN-P	"
	N-NN-P	"
πτώσεως	N-GF-S	πτῶσις
πτῶσιν	N-AF-S	"

πτῶσις, εως, ἡ   literally, as an action *falling, fall, crash*; of a house *collapse* (MT 7.27); figuratively, of a worsening condition *downfall, ruin, destruction* (LU 2.34)

πτῶσις	N-NF-S	πτῶσις
πτωχά	A--AN-P	πτωχός

πτωχεία, ας, ἡ   strictly *life of a beggar*; hence *(extreme) poverty, (complete) destitution*

πτωχεία	N-NF-S	πτωχεία
πτωχείᾳ	N-DF-S	"
πτωχείαν	N-AF-S	"

πτωχεύω   1aor. ἐπτώχευσα; intransitively and literally *lead the life of a beggar, be destitute, be (extremely) poor*; figuratively, of Christ's earthly humility and lowly life *be* or *become poor* (2C 8.9)

πτωχή	A--NF-S	πτωχός
πτωχοί	AP-NM-P	"
	AP-VM-P	"
	A--NM-P	"
πτωχοῖς	AP-DM-P	"
πτωχόν	AP-AM-S	"

πτωχός, ή, όν   literally, of one dependent on others for support *poor, destitute* (MK 12.42); predominately substantivally οἱ πτωχοί *the poor* (MT 19.21); figuratively, of those in special need of God's help *poor, lowly* (MT 5.3); figuratively, in a negative sense *of little value, worthless, powerless* (GA 4.9)

πτωχός	AP-NM-S	πτωχός
πτωχούς	AP-AM-P	"
πτωχῷ	AP-DM-S	"
πτωχῶν	AP-GM-P	"

πυγμή, ῆς, ἡ   *fist*; adverbially πυγμῇ, of Jewish ceremonial hand-washing *carefully, properly*, perhaps by rubbing with the fist or up to the elbow or with a fistful of water (MK 7.3)

πυγμῇ	N-DF-S	πυγμή
πυθέσθαι	VNAD	πυνθάνομαι

Πύθιος, ία, ον   *Pythian, Delphian*, of a person of Delphi, a city north of Corinth in Greece; substantivally (AC 20.4)

Πυθίου	AP-GM-S	Πύθιος
πυθόμενος	VPADNM-S	πυνθάνομαι

πύθων, ωνος, ὁ   (also Πύθων)   *Python*; in Greek mythology, a giant snake guarding the oracular sanctuary at Delphi until slain by the god Apollo; later, *soothsaying ventriloquist*; πνεῦμα πύθωνα literally *python spirit*, i.e. *fortune-telling spirit, spirit of divination* (AC 16.16)

Πύθωνα	N-AM-S	πύθων
πύθωνα	N-AM-S	"
Πύθωνος	N-GM-S	"
πύθωνος	N-GM-S	"
πυκμῇ	N-DF-S	see πυγμή
πυκνά	AB	πυκνός
πυκνάς	A--AF-P	"

πυκνός, ή, όν   *frequent, numerous* (1T 5.23); substantivally, neuter accusative plural πυκνά as an adverb *frequently, often* (LU 5.33); neuter of the comparative as an adverb πυκνότερον *more often* or *frequently*; in an elative sense *very often, as often as possible* (AC 24.26)

πυκνότερον	ABM	πυκνός

πυκτεύω   as the art of a boxer *fight (with fists), box*; metaphorically, of self-discipline *strictly control one's behavior* (1C 9.26)

πυκτεύω	VIPA--1S	πυκτεύω
πύλαι	N-NF-P	πύλη
πύλας	N-AF-P	"

πύλη, ης, ἡ   *gate*; (1) literally; (a) *city gate* (HE 13.12); (b) *temple gate* (AC 3.10); (c) *prison gate* (AC 12.10); (2) metaphorically, of access or entrance either to eternal life or eternal death (MT 7.13, 14); (3) as a Semitism πύλαι ᾅδου *gates of Hades*, a synecdoche possibly denoting the powers of evil, underworld forces that cannot win out against the church; the meaning *death* is also possible (MT 16.18; cf. RV 6.8)

πύλη	N-NF-S	πύλη
πύλῃ	N-DF-S	"
πύλην	N-AF-S	"
πύλης	N-GF-S	"

πυλών, ῶνος, ὁ   a large *gateway* serving as entrance to a walled city (RV 21.12), to a temple (AC 14.13), to a palace complex (MT 26.71), to a house (AC 10.17); translated according to the context: *portal, forecourt, porch, vestibule, gateway*

πυλῶνα	N-AM-S	πυλών
πυλῶνας	N-AM-P	"
πυλῶνες	N-NM-P	"
πυλῶνος	N-GM-S	"
πυλώνων	N-GM-P	"
πυλῶσι(ν)	N-DM-P	"
πυνθάνεσθαι	VNPD	πυνθάνομαι
	VNPO	"

πυνθάνομαι   impf. ἐπυνθανόμην; 2aor. ἐπυθόμην; (1) *inquire, ask, investigate* (MT 2.4); (2) with ὅτι following *learn (by inquiry), find out* (AC 23.34)

πυνθάνομαι	VIPD--1S	πυνθάνομαι
	VIPO--1S	"
πυνθανόμενοι	VPPDNM-P	"
	VPPONM-P	"

πῦρ, πυρός, τό   *fire*; (1) literally, as an earthly phenomenon (MT 17.15); (2) figuratively; (a) in the future, of divine judgment *place of punishment* (MT 3.10); (b) as a destructive force (JA 3.5); (c) of trials as a purifying force (1P 1.7); (d) as a sign of the divine presence (AC 7.30; RV 1.14)

πῦρ	N-AN-S	πῦρ
	N-NN-S	"

πυρά, ᾶς, ἡ   as a pile of burning fuel *fire*

πυράν	N-AF-S	πυρά
πύργον	N-AM-S	πύργος

πύργος, ου, ὁ   *tower*; as a raised structure built for a fortification (perhaps LU 13.4); for a dwelling or a farm building (perhaps LU 14.28); for watching over a field or vineyard *watchtower* (MK 12.1)

πύργος	N-NM-S	πύργος
πυρέσσουσα	VPPANF-S	πυρέσσω
πυρέσσουσαν	VPPAAF-S	"

πυρέσσω   *be sick with fever, be feverish*

πυρετοῖς	N-DM-P	πυρετός

πυρετός, οῦ, ὁ   *fever, high temperature, feverish heat*

πυρετός	N-NM-S	πυρετός
πυρετῷ	N-DM-S	"

πυρί N-DN-S πῦρ

πύρινος, η, ον literally *of fire, fiery, burning*; figuratively, as a color *fiery red, red as fire* (RV 9.17)

πυρίνους A--AM-P πύρινος

πυρός N-GN-S πῦρ

πυροῦμαι VIPP--1S πυρόω

πυρούμενοι VPPPNM-P "

πυροῦσθαι VNPP "

πυρόω pf. pass. πεπύρωμαι; 1aor. pass. ἐπυρώθην; only passive in the NT *make fiery hot*; (1) literally; (a) *be destroyed by fire, be burned up* (2P 3.12); (b) of tested and refined metals *become fiery hot* (RV 1.15; 3.18); metaphorically βέλη πεπυρωμένα *flaming arrows*, i.e. *temptations* sent by Satan (EP 6.16); (2) figuratively; (a) of sexual passion *burn with desire, be sexually aroused* (1C 7.9); (b) of active sympathy and indignation arising from great concern *burn*, i.e. *be very worried and distressed* (2C 11.29)

Πύρρα N-GM-S see Πύρρου

πυρράζει VIPA--3S πυρράζω

πυρράζω *be (fiery) red*, of the color of a morning or evening sky

Πύρρος, ου, ὁ *Pyrrhus*, masculine proper noun (AC 20.4)

πυρρός, ά, όν as a color *fiery red, red (as fire)*

πυρρός A--NM-S πυρρός

Πύρρου N-GM-S Πύρρος

πυρώσει N-DF-S πύρωσις

πυρώσεως N-GF-S "

πύρωσις, εως, ἡ literally, as an action *burning* (RV 18.9); figuratively, of suffering sent by God for the spiritual refinement of believers *fiery test, painful suffering* (1P 4.12)

πωλεῖ VIPA--3S πωλέω

πωλεῖται VIPP--3S "

πωλεῖτε VIPA--2P "

πωλέω impf. ἐπώλουν; 1aor. ἐπώλησα; as exchanging possessions for money *sell*; passive *be offered for sale, be sold*

πωλῆσαι VNAA πωλέω

πωλήσας VPAANM-S "

πωλήσατε VMAA--2P "

πωλησάτω VMAA--3S "

πωλήσει VIFA--3S "

πώλησον VMAA--2S "

πῶλον N-AM-S πῶλος

πῶλος, ου, ὁ as the young of the horse or donkey *colt, foal*; in the NT a donkey's colt *young donkey*

πωλούμενον VPPPAN-S πωλέω

πωλοῦνται VIPP--3P "

πωλοῦντας VPPAAM-P "

πωλοῦντες VPPANM-P "

πωλούντων VPPAGM-P "

πωλοῦσι(ν) VPPADM-P "

πώποτε adverb; of an indefinite point of time *ever (yet), at any time*

πώποτε ABI πώποτε

πωρόω 1aor. ἐπώρωσα; pf. πεπώρωκα (JN 12.40); pf. pass. πεπώρωμαι; 1aor. pass. ἐπωρώθην; (1) literally *harden, petrify*; as a medical technical term *cover with thick skin* or *callous*; of body organs *thicken*; (2) figuratively in the NT; (a) active, of judicial hardening as a consequence of refusing to listen to God *cause to have a closed mind* (JN 12.40); (b) passive, of the self-hardening of unbelievers *be unwilling to hear, become stubborn* (MK 8.17)

πωρώσει N-DF-S πώρωσις

πώρωσιν N-AF-S "

πώρωσις, εως, ἡ literally, as a medical technical term, of covering with a callous or a thick growth of skin *hardening*; of the eyes *dulling, blindness*; figuratively in the NT, of unwillingness to learn *insensibility, obstinacy, stubbornness*

πώρωσις N-NF-S πώρωσις

πώς enclitic indefinite adverb; *somehow, in some way, perhaps*; used in combination with εἰ (e.g. εἴπως or εἴ π.) or μή (e.g. μήπως) *if somehow, if perhaps, if possibly* (AC 27.12); *lest in some way, that in no way* (2C 11.3)

πώς ABI πώς

πῶς interrogative adverb; (1) in direct questions; (a) to determine how something happens *how? in what way? by what means?* (LU 1.34); (b) in questions indicating surprise *how is it (possible) that? I do not understand how* (JN 4.9); (c) in questions intending disapproval *how dare you? with what right? how can you?* (MT 7.4); (d) in rhetorical questions rejecting an assumption *how could one? it is impossible that* (MT 12.26); (e) in deliberative questions followed by the subjunctive *how will something take place? how is something to be done?* (MT 26.54; MK 4.30); (2) in indirect questions; (a) with the indicative following *how? in what way?* (MT 6.28); (b) with the deliberative subjunctive following *how? in what manner?* (MT 10.19); (3) as an exclamatory particle *how . . .! how greatly!* (MK 10.24; LU 12.50)

πῶς AB πῶς

ABT "

CC "

Ῥαάβ, ἡ   indeclinable; *Rahab*, feminine proper noun

ῥαββεί   ῥαββί

ῥαββί, ὁ (also ῥαββεί)   indeclinable; transliterated from the Hebrew; literally *my great one*; used in the NT as a respectful term of address for a scribe or one recognized as an outstanding teacher of the law, interpreted in JN 1.38 as διδάσκαλε (*teacher*), *Rabbi, my teacher* or *master*

ῥαββονί   ῥαββουνί

ῥαββουνεί   "

ῥαββουνί, ὁ (also ῥαββονί, ῥαββουνεί, ῥαββωνί, ῥαβουνί)   indeclinable; transliterated from the Hebrew; a heightened form of ῥαββί (*my teacher*), used as a title of great honor and reverence *Rabboni, my lord, my master*

ῥαββωνί   ῥαββουνί

ῥαβδίζειν   VNPA   ῥαβδίζω

ῥαβδίζω   1aor. pass. ἐραβδίσθην; *beat with a rod* or *stick*; in the NT only of the Roman punishment by scourging (AC 16.22)

ῥάβδον   N-AF-S   ῥάβδος

ῥάβδος, ου, ἡ   *rod, staff*; (1) as a measuring stick of undefined length (RV 11.1); (2) as an instrument for punishment *stick, rod* (1C 4.21); (3) metaphorically, of a shepherd's authority over his sheep *staff* (RV 2.27); (4) as what the traveler carries *staff, walking stick* (MK 6.8); (5) as the aged's support *cane, staff* (HE 11.21); (6) as a symbol of a ruler's authority *scepter*; by metonymy *governing, rule* (HE 1.8)

ῥάβδος   N-NF-S   ῥάβδος

ῥάβδου   N-GF-S   "

ῥάβδους   N-AF-P   "

ῥαβδοῦχοι   N-NM-P   ῥαβδοῦχος

ῥαβδοῦχος, ου, ὁ   from ῥάβδος (*rod, staff*) and ἔχω (*have, hold*); strictly *one who holds the rod* or *staff*; in Roman government, a police officer who carried the fasces or bundles of sticks tied to an axe as a symbol of authority *lictor*; equivalent to *constable, sergeant, police officer*

ῥαβδούχους   N-AM-P   ῥαβδοῦχος

ῥάβδῳ   N-DF-S   ῥάβδος

ῥαβιθά   ταλιθά

ῥαβουνί   ῥαββουνί

Ῥαγάβ   Ῥαγαύ

Ῥαγαύ, ὁ (also Ῥαγάβ, Ῥαγαῦ)   indeclinable; *Reu*, masculine proper noun (LU 3.35)

Ῥαγαῦ   Ῥαγαύ

ῥαδιούργημα, ατος, τό   *thoughtless, reckless action, prank*, regarded as a serious offense against law; ῥ. πονηρόν *vicious crime, wicked wrongdoing* (AC 18.14)

ῥαδιούργημα   N-NN-S   ῥαδιούργημα

ῥαδιουργία, ας, ἡ   from ῥάδιος (*light, loose*); as taking life too lightly by lack of self-discipline and neglect of re-

sponsibilities *unscrupulousness, wickedness, recklessness* (AC 13.10)

ῥαδιουργίας   N-GF-S   ῥαδιουργία

ῥαίνω   1aor. ἔρρανα; pf. pass. ptc. ῥεραμμένος; *spatter, sprinkle* with a liquid (RV 19.13)

Ῥαιφάν, ὁ (also Ῥεμφά, Ῥεμφάμ, Ῥεμφάν, Ῥεμφφάν, Ῥεφά, Ῥεφάν, Ῥομφά, Ῥομφάν)   indeclinable; *Rephan*, a pagan deity, thought to be the Egyptian name for the Roman god Saturn, worshiped by some Israelites (AC 7.43)

ῥακά (also ῥαχά)   indeclinable; *raka*; transliterated from the Aramaic; used as a term of verbal abuse *blockhead! numskull! fool!* (MT 5.22)

ῥάκος, ους, τό   *piece of (torn off) cloth, patch*

ῥάκους   N-GN-S   ῥάκος

Ῥαμά, ἡ   indeclinable; *Rama*, a city of Judea about 6 miles or 9 kilometers north of Jerusalem (MT 2.18)

ῥαντίζουσα   VPPANF-S   ῥαντίζω

ῥαντίζω   1aor. ἐράντισα (and ἐρράντισα); pf. pass. ῥεράντισμαι; (1) of a purification rite *sprinkle* someone or something with something (HE 9.13); (2) middle; (a) *cleanse, wash oneself* (MK 7.4); (b) figuratively, of inward cleansing *purify, purge oneself* (HE 10.22)

ῥαντισμόν   N-AM-S   ῥαντισμός

ῥαντισμός, οῦ, ὁ   as ritual purifying *sprinkling*; figuratively, of Jesus' atoning sacrifice αἷμα ῥαντισμοῦ *blood that is sprinkled* to take away sin (HE 12.24)

ῥαντισμοῦ   N-GM-S   ῥαντισμός

ῥαντίσωνται   VSAM--3P   ῥαντίζω

ῥαπίζει   VIPA--3S   ῥαπίζω

ῥαπίζω   1aor. ἐράπισα; (1) as striking a blow with the palm of the hand, *slap, hit* (MT 5.39; possibly 26.67); (2) as striking a blow with an instrument, such as a club, rod, or whip *beat, hit, whip* (possibly MT 26.67)

ῥαπίσει   VIFA--3S   ῥαπίζω

ῥάπισμα, ατος, τό   (1) as a blow with the open hand, especially on the face or ear *slap, cuff* (JN 18.22; possibly MK 14.65 and JN 19.3); (2) as a strike with a club or stick *blow, hit* (possibly MK 14.65 and JN 19.3)

ῥάπισμα   N-AN-S   ῥάπισμα

ῥαπίσμασι(ν)   N-DN-P   "

ῥαπίσματα   N-AN-P   "

ῥάσσει   VIPA--3S   ῥήγνυμι

ῥαφίδος   N-GF-S   ῥαφίς

ῥαφίς, ίδος, ἡ   from ῥάπτω (*sew*); *needle*

ῥαχά   ῥακά

Ῥαχάβ, ἡ   indeclinable; *Rahab*, feminine proper noun (MT 1.5)

Ῥαχήλ, ἡ   indeclinable; *Rachel*, feminine proper noun (MT 2.18)

Ῥεβέκκα, ας, ἡ   *Rebecca*, feminine proper noun (RO 9.10)

Ῥεβέκκα   N-NF-S   Ῥεβέκκα

ῥέδη, ης, ἡ *chariot, carriage, wagon*, a four-wheeled carriage for traveling (RV 18.13)

ῥεδῶν	N-GF-P	ῥέδη
Ῥεμφά		Ῥαιφάν
Ῥεμφάμ		"
Ῥεμφάν		"
Ῥεμφφάν		"
ῥεραμμένον	VPRPAN-S	ῥαίνω
ῥεραντισμένοι	VPRPNM-P	ῥαντίζω
ῥεραντισμένον	VPRPAN-S	"
ῥεριμμένοι	VPRPNM-P	ῥίπτω
ῥεύσουσι(ν)	VIFA--3P	ῥέω
Ῥεφά		Ῥαιφάν
Ῥεφάν		"

ῥέω fut. ῥεύσω; *flow*, as a river; used metaphorically in JN 7.38 of the effect of the Spirit's presence in a life

Ῥήγιον, ου, τό *Rhegium*, a city at the southwestern extremity of Italy (AC 28.13)

Ῥήγιον	N-AN-S	Ῥήγιον

ῥῆγμα, ατος, τό *what has been split open and broken collapse, ruin, destruction* (LU 6.49)

ῥῆγμα	N-NN-S	ῥῆγμα

ῥήγνυμι and ῥήσσω (also ῥάσσω) fut. ῥήξω; 1aor. ἔρηξα or ἔρρηξα, imperative ῥῆξον; (1) *tear (in pieces), rip, burst* (MK 2.22); passive *be torn, burst* (MT 9.17); of an attack by rabid animals *tear in pieces* (with their teeth) (MT 7.6); of a demonic attack on a demon-possessed person *throw into a fit, dash to the ground* (MK 9.18); (2) absolutely *burst* into a shout, *break forth* in a cry of joy and freedom (GA 4.27)

ῥήγνυνται	VIPP--3P	ῥήγνυμι
ῥηθείς	VPAPNM-S	εἶπον
ῥηθέν	VPAPAN-S	"
	VPAPNN-S	"
ῥηθέντα	VPAPAN-P	"

ῥῆμα, ατος, τό (1) as what has definitely been stated, with focus on content, *(single) word, saying, utterance* (MT 27.14); often translated according to the context: *prediction* or *prophecy* (MT 26.75), *command* or *direction* (LU 5.5), *threat* (AC 6.13); plural, as a unified communication *sermon, proclamation, speech* (LU 7.1); *message* (JN 3.34), *teachings, doctrine* (JN 5.47); (2) Hebraistically, as a happening *thing, matter, business, transaction* (MT 18.16; LU 1.37)

ῥῆμα	N-AN-S	ῥῆμα
	N-NN-S	"
ῥήμασι(ν)	N-DN-P	"
ῥήματα	N-AN-P	"
	N-NN-P	"
ῥήματι	N-DN-S	"
ῥήματος	N-GN-S	"
ῥημάτων	N-GN-P	"
ῥήξει	VIFA--3S	ῥήγνυμι
ῥῆξον	VMAA--2S	"
ῥήξωσι(ν)	VSAA--3P	"

Ῥησά, ὁ indeclinable; *Rhesa*, masculine proper noun (LU 3.27)

ῥήσσει	VIPA--3S	ῥήγνυμι
ῥήσσεσθαι	VNPP	"
ῥήτορος	N-GM-S	ῥήτωρ

ῥήτωρ, ορος, ὁ *orator, public speaker*; as a court speaker *attorney, lawyer* (AC 24.1)

ῥητῶς adverb; *expressly, explicitly, in these exact words* (1T 4.1)

ῥητῶς	AB	ῥητῶς

ῥίζα, ης, ἡ *root*; (1) literally, of plants (MT 13.6); figuratively *cause, reason* (1T 6.10); metaphorically *origin, source* (RO 11.16–18); (2) figuratively and Hebraistically, of a *descendant*, as a shoot or sprout *offspring, scion* (RO 15.12)

ῥίζα	N-NF-S	ῥίζα
ῥίζαν	N-AF-S	"
ῥίζης	N-GF-S	"

ῥιζόω pf. pass. ἐρρίζωμαι; literally *cause to take root*; passive *be rooted, take root*; figuratively and only passive in the NT, of spiritual stability *be firmly established, be strengthened* (CO 2.7)

ῥιζῶν	N-GF-P	ῥίζα

ῥιπή, ῆς, ἡ as a rapid throwing movement *jerk*; of the eye *wink, twinkling, blink*; idiomatically ἐν ῥιπῇ ὀφθαλμοῦ literally *in the blinking of an eye*, i.e. *suddenly* (1C 15.52)

ῥιπῇ	N-DF-S	ῥιπή
ῥιπιζομένῳ	VPPPDM-S	ῥιπίζω

ῥιπίζω from ῥιπίς (*fan* or *bellows* that creates a puff of air); of the gusts and swirling of wind *blow here and there*; as the effect on waves *toss*; only passive in the NT *be tossed about* (JA 1.6)

ῥιπτούντων	VPPAGM-P	ῥίπτω

ῥίπτω and ῥιπτέω 1aor. ἔρριψα; pf. pass. ἔρριμμαι; (1) *throw*, with the translation suited to the context: *hurl* or *cast* (MT 27.5), *throw* or *toss off* (clothing) (AC 22.23), *throw* or *toss out* (from a ship) (AC 27.19); (2) of persons *throw (into)* (LU 17.2); with no denotation of violence *put* or *lay down* (sick people) (MT 15.30); perfect passive participle *lying on the ground, lying helpless*; figuratively *be discouraged, be dejected* (MT 9.36)

ῥῖψαν	VPAANN-S	ῥίπτω
ῥίψαντες	VPAANM-P	"
ῥίψας	VPAANM-S	"

Ῥοβοάμ, ὁ indeclinable; *Rehoboam*, masculine proper noun (MT 1.7)

Ῥόδη, ης, ἡ *Rhoda*, feminine proper noun (AC 12.13)

Ῥόδη	N-NF-S	Ῥόδη
Ῥόδον	N-AF-S	Ῥόδος

Ῥόδος, ου, ὁ *Rhodes*, an island off the southwestern coast of Asia Minor (AC 21.1)

ῥοιζηδόν adverb; of a noise, indicating sudden and violent movement *with a roar, with a loud rush* (2P 3.10)

ῥοιζηδόν	AB	ῥοιζηδόν
Ῥομφά		Ῥαιφάν

ῥομφαία, ας, ἡ strictly, a long Thracian *javelin*; later a large and broad *sword*; (1) in the NT simply *two-edged sword* (RV 2.12); (2) by metonymy *war* (RV 6.8); figuratively; (a) as the word of severe judgment that Christ speaks (RV 2.16); (b) as a feeling of sharp pain or anguish that comes to the heart (LU 2.35)

ῥομφαία	N-NF-S	ῥομφαία
ῥομφαίᾳ	N-DF-S	"
ῥομφαίαν	N-AF-S	"
ῥομφαίας	N-GF-S	"

Ῥομφάν | | Ῥαιφάν

ῥοπή, ῆς, ἡ   a sudden downward movement *inclination downward*, as when one side of a balance scale goes down; as the sudden lowering of the eyelid *blink, twinkling* (1C 15.52)

ῥοπή	N-NF-S	ῥοπή
ῥοπῇ	N-DF-S	"
ῥοπῆς	N-GF-S	"

Ῥουβήν, ὁ   indeclinable; *Reuben*, masculine proper noun; name of a tribe of Israel (RV 7.5)

Ῥούθ, ἡ   indeclinable; *Ruth*, feminine proper noun (MT 1.5)

Ῥοῦφον	N-AM-S	Ῥοῦφος

Ῥοῦφος, ου, ὁ   *Rufus*, masculine proper noun (RO 16.13)

Ῥούφου	N-GM-S	Ῥοῦφος
ῥύεσθαι	VNPD	ῥύομαι
	VNPO	"
ῥύεται	VIPD--3S	"
	VIPO--3S	"
ῥυήσεται	VIFP--3S	"
ῥύμαις	N-DF-P	ῥύμη
ῥύμας	N-AF-P	

ῥύμη, ης, ἡ   as an urban passageway shut in by buildings on both sides *narrow street, lane, alley*, in contrast to πλατεῖα (*broad way, open street*)

ῥύμην	N-AF-S	ῥύμη

ῥύομαι   fut. ῥύσομαι; 1aor. mid. ἐρρυσάμην; 1aor. pass. ἐρρύσθην; of bringing someone out of severe and acute danger *save, deliver, rescue*; in the NT always with God as the deliverer and with a person as the object (MT 6.13)

ῥυόμενον	VPPDAM-S	ῥύομαι
	VPPOAM-S	"
ῥυόμενος	VPPDNM-S	"
	VPPONM-S	"

ῥυπαίνω   1aor. pass. ἐρρυπάνθην; literally *make dirty, soil*; figuratively, of moral uncleanness *defile, pollute*; only passive in the NT *be impure, be completely bad* (RV 22.11)

ῥυπανθήτω	VMAP--3S	ῥυπαίνω
ῥυπαρᾷ	A--DF-S	ῥυπαρός
ῥυπαρευθήτω	VMAP--3S	ῥυπαρεύω

ῥυπαρεύω   literally *make dirty*; figuratively, of moral uncleanness *make impure, entangle in (moral) evil* (RV 22.11)

ῥυπαρία, ας, ἡ   literally *filth, dirt*; figuratively, as bad behavior *moral uncleanness, impurity, filthiness* (JA 1.21)

ῥυπαρίαν	N-AF-S	ῥυπαρία

ῥυπαρός, ά, όν   literally *dirty, filthy, foul* (JA 2.2), opposite καθαρός (*clean, pure*); figuratively, of bad behavior

morally impure, degenerate, completely bad; substantivally, a *morally filthy person* (RV 22.11)

ῥυπαρός	A--NM-S	ῥυπαρός

ῥύπος, ου, ὁ   *dirt, filth* (1P 3.21)

ῥύπου	N-GM-S	ῥύπος

ῥυπόω   *be filthy*; figuratively *be polluted* morally (RV 22.11)

ῥυπῶν	VPPANM-S	ῥυπόω
ῥυπωσάτω	VMAA--3S	"
ῥῦσαι	VMAD--2S	ῥύομαι
ῥύσασθαι	VNAD	"
ῥυσάσθω	VMAD--3S	"
ῥύσει	N-DF-S	ῥύσις
ῥύσεται	VIFD--3S	ῥύομαι
ῥυσθέντας	VPAPAM-P	"
ῥυσθῶ	VSAP--1S	"
ῥυσθῶμεν	VSAP--1P	"
ῥυσθῶσι(ν)	VSAP--3P	"

ῥύσις, εως, ἡ   of the movement of a liquid *flowing, issue*; of blood *hemorrhage, flow*

ῥύσις	N-NF-S	ῥύσις
ῥυτίδα	N-AF-S	ῥυτίς

ῥυτίς, ίδος, ἡ   *wrinkle*; metaphorically, as what mars the fellowship, unity, or testimony of the church (EP 5.27)

Ῥωμαϊκοῖς	A--DN-P	see Ῥωμαϊκοῖς
Ῥωμαϊκοῖς	A--DN-P	Ῥωμαϊκός

Ῥωμαϊκός, ή, όν   of the language *Roman, Latin* (LU 23.38)

Ῥωμαῖοι	AP-NM-P	Ῥωμαῖος
Ῥωμαίοις	AP-DM-P	"
	A--DM-P	"
Ῥωμαῖον	AP-AM-S	"
	A--AM-S	"

Ῥωμαῖος, αία, ον   *Roman* (AC 22.25); substantivally *Roman, Roman citizen* (AC 22.26); plural οἱ Ῥωμαῖοι *the Romans, the Roman people, the citizens of the Roman Empire* (AC 2.10)

Ῥωμαῖος	AP-NM-S	Ῥωμαῖος
Ῥωμαίους	A--AM-P	"

Ῥωμαϊστί   adverb; *in Latin, in the Latin* or *Roman language* (JN 19.20)

Ῥωμαϊστί	AB	Ῥωμαϊστί
Ῥωμαίων	AP-GM-P	Ῥωμαῖος

Ῥώμη, ης, ἡ   *Rome*, the capital city of Italy; ancient seat of the Roman Empire (RO 1.7)

Ῥώμῃ	N-DF-S	Ῥώμη
Ῥώμην	N-AF-S	"
Ῥώμης	N-GF-S	"

ῥώννυμι   pf. pass. ἔρρωμαι; literally *strengthen, make firm*; passive *be strong, be well, enjoy good health*; perfect imperative singular ἔρρωσο and plural ἔρρωσθε as a conclusion to letters *farewell, good-bye* (AC 15.29; 23.30)

σ Σ

σά | A--AN2P | σός
 | A--NN2P | "
σαβακθανεί | | σαβαχθάνι
σαβακθάνι | | "
σαβακθανί | | "
σαβακτανεί | | "
σαβακτάνι | | "
σαβαχθανεί | | "

σαβαχθάνι (also ζαβαφθανεί, ζαβαφθάνι, ζαβαχθάνι, ζαφθανεί, ζαφθάνι, σαβακθανεί, σαβακθάνι, σαβακθανί, σαβακτανεί, σαβακτάνι, σαβαχθανεί, σαβαχθανί, σαφθάνι) transliterated from the Aramaic *sabachthani* (*forsake*); *you* (singular) *have forsaken me*; interrogative λεμα σ. is interpreted as *why have you forsaken me?* (MT 27.46; MK 15.34)

σαβαχθανί | | σαβαχθάνι

Σαβαώθ, ὁ indeclinable; transliterated from the Hebrew *sabaoth* (*armies, hosts*); used in a title for God *Lord of hosts, Lord of the armies, the Almighty One* (RO 9.29; JA 5.4)

σάββασι(ν) | N-DN-P | σάββατον
σάββατα | N-AN-P | "

σαββατισμός, οῦ, ὁ *period of rest, Sabbath rest*; figuratively in HE 4.9, as a state of spiritual rest entered into by a commitment made in faith

σαββατισμός | N-NM-S | σαββατισμός

σάββατον, ου, τό *Sabbath*; strictly *ceasing from labor, rest*; (1) both singular and plural used for the seventh day of the week (Saturday) (MT 12.1, 2); (2) as the sacred festival held each week on the seventh day, beginning with sundown Friday evening and ending at sundown Saturday evening (JN 19.31); (3) singular and plural as a designation for the span of seven days *week* (MT 28.1b; LU 18.12); (4) combined into phrases κατὰ πᾶν σ. (*on*) *every Sabbath* (AC 13.27); σαββάτου ὁδός literally *Sabbath day's journey*, i.e. 2,000 cubits or paces, about 800 meters or 875 yards, denoting the distance the traditional law allowed a Jew to travel on the Sabbath (AC 1.12); κατὰ μίαν σαββάτου *every Sunday, on the first day of every week* (1C 16.2); (ἡ) μία (τῶν) σαββάτων *the first day of the week* (JN 20.1); δὶς τοῦ σαββάτου *twice a week* (LU 18.12)

σάββατον | N-AN-S | σάββατον
 | N-NN-S | "
σαββάτου | N-GN-S | "
σαββάτῳ | N-DN-S | "
σαββάτων | N-GN-P | "

σαγήνη, ης, ἡ as a long fishing net lowered into the water and hanging vertically with floats along the top and weights along the bottom *dragnet, seine* (MT 13.47)

σαγήνη | N-DF-S | σαγήνη
Σαδδουκαῖοι | N-NM-P | Σαδδουκαῖος

Σαδδουκαῖος, ου, ὁ *Sadducee*; only plural in the NT *Sadducees*, members of a Jewish religious and political party in Jerusalem consisting largely of priests claiming descent from the Davidic high priest Zadok, along with their supporters

Σαδδουκαίους | N-AM-P | Σαδδουκαῖος
Σαδδουκαίων | N-GM-P | "

Σαδώκ, ὁ indeclinable; *Zadok*, masculine proper noun

σαίνεσθαι | | VNPP | σαίνω

σαίνω only passive in the NT; (1) originally of dogs *wag the tail, move the tail to and fro, fawn*; figuratively, of persons *fawn over, flatter*; passive *be deceived* or *deluded*; (2) figuratively and passive, as being carried away emotionally by circumstances *be shaken, be disturbed, be unsettled*; either meaning makes good sense in 1TH 3.3, but ancient versions and Greek expositors prefer the second

σάκκος, ου, ὁ *haircloth*, a dark coarse fabric made from hair; by metonymy *sackcloth*, a sacklike garment made from haircloth and worn by mourners, penitents, and prophets; goat-hair was predominately used to make this rough cloth

σάκκος | N-NM-S | σάκκος
σάκκους | N-AM-P | "
σάκκῳ | N-DM-S | "

Σαλά, ὁ (also **Σαλμάν**) indeclinable; *Shelah*, masculine proper noun

Σαλαθιήλ, ὁ indeclinable; *Shealtiel* or *Salathiel*, masculine proper noun (LU 3.27)

Σαλαμῖνι | N-DF-S | Σαλαμίς

Σαλαμίς, ῖνος, ἡ *Salamis*, a city on the eastern coast of the island of Cyprus in the Mediterranean Sea (AC 13.5)

Σαλείμ, τό (also **Σαλέμ, Σαλήμ, Σαλίμ, Σαλλείμ**) indeclinable; *Salim*, a place of uncertain location, probably along the western side of the Jordan River valley about 20 miles or 32 kilometers south of the Sea of Galilee, near the springs in that area (JN 3.23)

Σαλέμ | | | Σαλέμ
σαλευθῆναι | VNAP | σαλεύω
σαλευθήσονται | VIFP--3P | "
σαλευθῶ | VSAP--1S | "
σαλευόμενα | VPPPNN-P | "
σαλευόμενον | VPPPAM-S | "
σαλευομένων | VPPPGN-P | "
σαλεύοντες | VPPANM-P | "
σαλεῦσαι | VNAA | "

σαλεύω 1aor. ἐσάλευσα; pf. pass. σεσάλευμαι; 1aor. pass. ἐσαλεύθην; 1fut. pass. σαλευθήσομαι; transitively in the NT; (1) literally, as the unexpected and disastrous shaking of what would be thought to be stable, e.g. earth or sky *shake, cause to move to and fro, cause to waver* or *totter, make to rock* (AC 16.26); (2) figuratively; (a) of stirring up a crowd *incite, move, agitate* (AC 17.13); (b) mentally, of an individual *agitate*; passive *be distressed, be upset, be shaken* (2TH 2.2)

Σαλήμ, ἡ indeclinable; *Salem,* name of a city, probably the ancient name for Jerusalem (cf. Josephus, *Jewish Antiquities* 1.10.2 §180; Psalm 76.2); interpreted as meaning *peace* in HE 7.2

Σαλήμ		Σαλείμ
		Σαλήμ
Σαλίμ		Σαλείμ
Σαλλείμ		"
Σαλμάν		Σαλά

Σαλμών, ὁ indeclinable; *Salmon,* masculine proper noun

Σαλμώνη, ης, ἡ *Salmone,* a high ridge of land on the northeastern corner of the island of Crete in the Mediterranean Sea (AC 27.7)

Σαλμώνην	N-AF-S	Σαλμώνη

σάλος, ου, ὁ *rolling* or *tossing motion*; especially of the restless movement of the sea in its tidal rise and fall *billow, surf, surging waves* (LU 21.25)

σάλου	N-GM-S	σάλος
σάλπιγγα	N-AF-S	σάλπιγξ
σάλπιγγας	N-AF-P	"
σάλπιγγες	N-NF-P	"
σάλπιγγι	N-DF-S	"
σάλπιγγος	N-GF-S	"
σαλπίγγων	N-GF-P	"

σάλπιγξ, ιγγος, ἡ (1) as a long metal wind instrument with a mouthpiece made of horn *trumpet* (RV 1.10); (2) by metonymy, the sound or signal blown through it *trumpet call, blast, trumpet signal* (MT 24.31)

σάλπιγξ	N-NF-S	σάλπιγξ
σαλπίζειν	VNPA	σαλπίζω

σαλπίζω fut. σαλπίσω; 1aor. ἐσάλπισα; as producing a blast on a trumpet *sound* or *blow the trumpet*

σαλπίσει	VIFA--3S	σαλπίζω
σαλπίσῃς	VSAA--2S	"

σαλπιστής, οῦ, ὁ *one who blows a trumpet, trumpeter* (RV 18.22)

σαλπιστῶν	N-GM-P	σαλπιστής
σαλπίσωσι(ν)	VSAA--3P	σαλπίζω

Σαλώμη, ης, ἡ *Salome,* feminine proper noun

Σαλώμη	N-NF-S	Σαλώμη
Σαλωμών		Σολομών

Σαμάρεια, ας, ἡ (also **Σαμαρία**) *Samaria,* in NT times the territory or province in west central Palestine from the Plain of Jezreel south to Judea (JN 4.4)

Σαμάρεια	N-NF-S	Σαμάρεια
Σαμαρείᾳ	N-DF-S	"
Σαμάρειαν	N-AF-S	"
Σαμαρείας	N-GF-S	"
Σαμαρεῖται	N-NM-P	Σαμαρίτης
Σαμαρείταις	N-DM-P	"
Σαμαρείτης	N-NM-S	"
Σαμαρείτιδος	N-GF-S	Σαμαρῖτις
Σαμαρεῖτις	N-NF-S	"
Σαμαρειτῶν	N-GM-P	Σαμαρίτης
Σαμαρία	N-NF-S	Σαμάρεια
Σαμαρίᾳ	N-DF-S	"
Σαμαρίαν	N-AF-S	"
Σαμαρίας	N-GF-S	"
Σαμαρῖται	N-NM-P	Σαμαρίτης
Σαμαρίταις	N-DM-P	"

Σαμαρίτης, ου, ὁ (also **Σαμαρείτης**) *Samaritan man, inhabitant of Samaria* (LU 17.16)

Σαμαρίτης	N-NM-S	Σαμαρίτης
Σαμαρίτιδος	N-GF-S	Σαμαρῖτις

Σαμαρῖτις, ιδος, ἡ (also **Σαμαρεῖτις**) *Samaritan woman*; ἡ γυνὴ ἡ Σ. *the Samaritan woman* (JN 4.9)

Σαμαρῖτις	N-NF-S	Σαμαρῖτις
Σαμαριτῶν	N-GM-P	Σαμαρίτης

Σαμοθράκη, ης, ἡ *Samothrace,* an island in the northern Aegean Sea (AC 16.11)

Σαμοθράκην	N-AF-S	Σαμοθράκη
Σάμον	N-AF-S	Σάμος

Σάμος, ου, ἡ *Samos,* an island in the Aegean Sea off the western coast of Asia Minor near Ephesus (AC 20.15)

Σαμουήλ, ὁ indeclinable; *Samuel,* masculine proper noun (HE 11.32)

Σαμφουρείν or **Σαμφουρίν, ἡ** indeclinable; *Samphourin,* thought by some to be *Sepphoris* in Galilee (JN 11.54)

Σαμφουρίν		Σαμφουρείν

Σαμψών, ὁ indeclinable; *Samson,* masculine proper noun (HE 11.32)

σανδάλια	N-AN-P	σανδάλιον

σανδάλιον, ου, τό wooden or leather sole bound to the foot with thongs or straps *sandal*

σανίς, ίδος, ἡ *board, plank* (AC 27.44)

σανίσι(ν)	N-DF-P	σανίς

Σαούλ, ὁ indeclinable; *Saul,* masculine proper noun (AC 9.4); see also Σαῦλος

σαπρά	A--AN-P	σαπρός
σαπρόν	A--AM-S	"
	A--AN-S	"
	A--NN-S	"

σαπρός, ά, όν *decayed, rotting, rotten*; literally, of decaying fish or fruit no longer useful for food; more generally *useless, of no value, unfit* (MT 7.17); neuter as a substantive τὰ σαπρά *the unusable ones* (MT 13.48); figuratively, of unedifying speech *harmful, bad, unprofitable* (EP 4.29)

σαπρός	A--NM-S	σαπρός
σαπρούς	A--AM-P	"
Σαπφείρα	N-DF-S	Σάπφιρα
Σαπφείρῃ	N-DF-S	"
σάπφειρος	N-NF-S	σάπφιρος

Σάπφιρα, ης, ἡ (also **Σαπφείρα, Σαπφείρῃ**) *Sapphira,* feminine proper noun (AC 5.1)

Σαπφίρη	N-DF-S	Σάπφιρα

σάπφιρος, ου, ἡ (also **σάπφειρος**) *sapphire,* a precious stone, a blue-colored gem (RV 21.19)

σάπφιρος	N-NF-S	σάπφιρος

σαργάνη, ης, ἡ strictly *twisted* or *braided work*; as a network of cords woven together *(rope) basket, hamper* (2C 11.33)

σαργάνῃ	N-DF-S	σαργάνη

Σάρδεις, εων, αἱ *Sardis,* the ancient capital of Lydia in western Asia Minor

Σάρδεις	N-AF-P	Σάρδεις
Σάρδεσι(ν)	N-DF-P	"

σάρδινος, ου, ὁ *sardine,* a precious stone of blood red color (RV 4.3)

σαρδίνῳ	N-DM-S	σάρδινος

σάρδιον, ου, τό *sardius, sard, carnelian*, a precious stone, a gem of reddish or ruby color (RV 21.20)

σάρδιον	N-NN-S	σάρδιον

σάρδιος, ία, ον as the color of a precious stone or gem *deep orange-red, brownish-red*; ὁ σ. substantivally, as a variety of translucent quartz regarded as a precious stone *sardius, sard, carnelian*, regarded as equivalent to a ruby (RV 21.20)

σάρδιος	AP-NM-S	σάρδιος
σαρδίῳ	N-DN-S	σάρδιον

σαρδόνυξ, υχος, ὁ *sardonyx*, a precious agate stone marked by layers of colors of the red sardius and white onyx (RV 21.20)

σαρδόνυξ	N-NM-S	σαρδόνυξ

Σάρεπτα, ων, τά (also **Σάρεφθα**) *Zarephath* (Hebrew) or *Sarepta* (Greek), a city on the Phoenician coast between Tyre and Sidon (LU 4.26)

Σάρεπτα	N-AN-P	Σάρεπτα
Σάρεφθα	N-AN-P	"
σάρκα	N-AF-S	σάρξ
σάρκας	N-AF-P	"
σαρκί	N-DF-S	"
σαρκικά	A-AN-P	σαρκικός
	A-NN-P	"
σαρκικῇ	A--DF-S	"
σαρκικῆς	A--GF-S	"
σαρκικοί	A--NM-P	"
σαρκικοῖς	A--DN-P	"

σαρκικός, ή, όν *fleshly, in the manner of the flesh, carnal*, opposite πνευματικός (*spiritual, pertaining to the spirit*); (1) belonging to the earthly sphere of existence *material, physical* (2C 10.4); neuter as a substantive τὰ σαρκικά *material things* (RO 15.27); (2) of behavior, having the characteristics of σάρξ (*flesh*) in its sensual, sinful tendencies *worldly, carnal* (1C 3.3); (3) as human in quality *natural* (2C 1.12)

σαρκικός	A--NM-S	σαρκικός
σαρκικῶν	A--GF-P	"
σαρκίναις	A--DF-P	σάρκινος
σαρκίνη	A--DF-S	"
σαρκίνης	A--GF-S	"
σάρκινοι	A--NM-P	"
σαρκίνοις	A--DM-P	"

σάρκινος, η, ον (1) *consisting of flesh, composed* or *made of flesh, fleshly*, as the body that is capable of sensitive feeling (2C 3.3); (2) as relating to the earthly sphere of existence *worldly, earthly* (possibly 1C 3.1 and HE 7.16), opposite πνευματικός (*spiritual, pertaining to the spirit*); in distinction from σαρκικός (*fleshly, carnal*), σ. has to do with the body and living in the body; σαρκικός has to do with living for the body, i.e. to satisfy bodily desires; (3) as relating to human existence *natural* (possibly 1C 3.1 and HE 7.16); substantivally σάρκινοι *mere human beings*

σάρκινος	A--NM-S	σάρκινος
σαρκός	N-GF-S	σάρξ
σαρκῶν	N-GF-P	"

σάρξ, σαρκός, ἡ *flesh*; (1) literally, as the muscular part that covers the bones of a human or animal body *flesh* (1C 15.39); (2) by synecdoche, the physical body as a whole *body, flesh* (AC 2.31); (3) as a human being *person, man (of flesh and blood)* (JN 1.14); (4) euphemistically, as the seat of the sexual or procreative drive *flesh* (JN 1.13); (5) as relating to the earthly sphere of existence *human* or *mortal nature, earthly descent, blood relation* (RO 4.1); *ethnic group, race* (RO 11.14); (6) as distinguishing the corruptible from the incorruptible part of man *corporeality, earthly life, physical limitation* (1C 7.28; CO 1.22); (7) in a negative sense, the external side of life as an object of trust *flesh* (PH 3.3); κατὰ σάρκα *from a (purely) human point of view, by human standards, as far as outward circumstances are concerned* (JN 8.15; 2C 11.18); (8) in an ethical sense in Paul's epistles; (a) as a sinful and sensual power tending toward sin and opposing the Spirit's working *flesh* (RO 7.25; GA 5.17), opposite πνεῦμα (*spirit*); (b) as life apart from the Spirit of God and controlled by sin in its expressions *flesh* (RO 7.5; 8.9)

σάρξ	N-NF-S	σάρξ
σαροῖ	VIPA--3S	σαρόω
Σαρούκ		Σερούχ
Σαρούχ		"

σαρόω 1aor. ἐσάρωσα; pf. pass. σεσάρωμαι; 1aor. pass. ἐσαρώθην; *sweep, clean with a broom*

Σάρρα, ας, ἡ *Sarah*, feminine proper noun (RO 4.19)

Σάρρα	N-NF-S	Σάρρα
Σάρρᾳ	N-DF-S	"
Σάρρας	N-GF-S	"
Σαρρῶνα	N-AM-S	Σαρών
Σάρων	N-AM-S	see Σάρωνα

Σαρών, ῶνος, ὁ (also **Ἀσσάρων, Σαρρῶνα, Σάρων**) *Sharon*, a plain along the Mediterranean coast of Israel from Caesarea to Joppa (AC 9.35)

Σάρωνα	N-AM-S	Σαρών
Σαρῶνα	N-AM-S	"
Σαρωνᾶν	N-AM-S	see Σαρῶνα
σάτα	N-AN-P	σάτον
Σατᾶν		Σατανᾶς
σατᾶν		"
Σατανᾶ	N-GM-S	"
	N-VM-S	"
Σατανᾷ	N-DM-S	"
Σατανᾶν	N-AM-S	"

Σατανᾶς, ᾶ, ὁ (also **Σατᾶν** or **σατᾶν** indeclinable) *Satan*; literally *Adversary*, the constant enemy of God and man, a supernatural evil being (MT 16.23; 1TH 2.18); in a more positive sense, permitted to be God's agent to present moral choice to man (LU 22.31; cf. MT 4.1)

Σατανᾶς	N-NM-S	Σατανᾶς

σάτον, ου, τό *seah, measure*, a Hebrew measure for grain equivalent to a Roman *satum*, in size 1.5 modii, about 1.5 English pecks, 12 quarts, or 13.5 liters (MT 13.33)

Σαῦλον	N-AM-S	Σαῦλος

Σαῦλος, ου, ὁ *Saul*; masculine proper noun; Greek form of the Hebrew name *Saul*; see also Σαούλ

Σαῦλος	N-NM-S	Σαῦλος
Σαύλου	N-GM-S	"
Σαύλῳ	N-DM-S	"
σαυτόν	NPAM2S	see σεαυτόν
σαφθάνι		σαβαχθάνι

σβέννυμι   fut. σβέσω; 1aor. ἔσβεσα; literally *extinguish, quench, put out* something, as fire (MK 9.48) or lamps (MT 25.8); metaphorically, of an activity *cause to cease, thwart, block* (MT 12.20; EP 6.16); figuratively *stifle, suppress, restrain* (1TH 5.19)

σβέννυνται	VIPP--3P	σβέννυμι
σβέννυται	VIPP--3S	"
σβέννυτε	VMPA--2P	"
σβέσαι	VNAA	"
σβέσει	VIFA--3S	"
σέ	NPA-2S	σύ
σεαυτόν	NPAM2S	σεαυτοῦ

σεαυτοῦ, ῆς   reflexive pronoun of second-person singular, used only in oblique cases *yourself*

σεαυτοῦ	NPGM2S	σεαυτοῦ
σεαυτῷ	NPDM2S	"

σεβάζομαι   1aor. ἐσεβάσθην; *worship, show reverence to, venerate*; first aorist passive with active sense (RO 1.25)

σέβασμα, ατος, τό   (1) *object of worship* or *veneration* (2TH 2.4; possibly AC 17.23); (2) a place held in veneration or reverent awe *sanctuary, altar* (possibly AC 17.23)

σέβασμα	N-AN-S	σέβασμα
σεβάσματα	N-AN-P	"
Σεβαστῆς	A--GF-S	σεβαστός
Σεβαστόν	AP-AM-S	"

σεβαστός, ή, όν   transliterated from the Latin *augustus* (*sacred, revered, worthy of veneration*); substantivally ὁ Σ. as a title for the Roman supreme ruler *His Majesty the Emperor* (AC 25.21, 25); σπεῖρα Σεβαστή *Augustan band, imperial cohort* or *regiment* (AC 27.1)

Σεβαστοῦ	AP-GM-S	σεβαστός
σέβεσθαι	VNPM	σέβω
σέβεται	VIPM--3S	"
σεβομένας	VPPMAF-P	"
σεβομένη	VPPMNF-S	"
σεβομένοις	VPPMDM-P	"
σεβομένου	VPPMGM-S	"
σεβομένων	VPPMGM-P	"
σέβονται	VIPM--3P	"

σέβω   only middle in the NT and always of the worship of a deity *worship, venerate, adore* (MK 7.7); as a religious technical term applied to Gentiles who accepted Judaism's belief in one God and attended the synagogue but did not become Jewish proselytes by undergoing male circumcision; σεβόμενοι τὸν θεόν *God-fearers, worshipers of God* (AC 17.17)

Σειλεᾷ	N-DM-S	Σιλᾶς
σειομένη	VPPPNF-S	σείω

σειρά, ᾶς, ἡ   *chain, cord, rope* (2P 2.4)

σειραῖς	N-DF-P	σειρά
σειροῖς	N-DM-P	σιρός
σείσας	VPAANM-S	σείω
σεισμοί	N-NM-P	σεισμός
σεισμόν	N-AM-S	"

σεισμός, οῦ, ὁ   as a series of violent movements *shaking, agitation*; of the earth *earthquake* (MT 24.7); of the sea when high winds cause huge waves *tempest, (violent) storm* (MT 8.24)

σεισμός	N-NM-S	σεισμός
σεισμῷ	N-DM-S	"

σείσω	VIFA--1S	σείω

σείω   fut. σείσω; 1aor. pass. ἐσείσθην; literally, as causing violent movement or disturbance, especially of universal dimension *shake, agitate, cause to quake* (HE 12.26); passive, of the earth *be shaken, quake* (MT 27.51); figuratively, of mental or spiritual agitation *disturb, stir up* (MT 28.4); of a populace *incite, move, cause an uproar* (MT 21.10)

σείω	VIPA--1S	σείω
Σέκουνδος	N-NM-S	Σεκοῦνδος

Σεκοῦνδος, ου, ὁ (also Σέκουνδος)   *Secundus*, masculine proper noun (AC 20.4)

Σέκουνδος	N-NM-S	Σεκοῦνδος

Σελεύκεια, ας, ἡ (also Σελευκία)   *Seleucia*, seaport of Antioch in Syria, along the Mediterranean Sea (AC 13.4)

Σελεύκειαν	N-AF-S	Σελεύκεια
Σελευκίαν	N-AF-S	"

σελήνη, ης, ἡ   *moon*

σελήνη	N-NF-S	σελήνη
σελήνη	N-DF-S	"
σελήνης	N-GF-S	"
σεληνιάζεται	VIPD--3S	σεληνιάζομαι
	VIPO--3S	"

σεληνιάζομαι   as being mentally out of control of oneself *be moonstruck, be lunatic*; distinguished from δαιμονίζομαι (*be tormented by, be demonized*) in which one is controlled by a demon (MT 4.24)

σεληνιαζομένους	VPPDAM-P	σεληνιάζομαι
	VPPOAM-P	"
Σεμεεί		Σεμεΐν
Σεμεείν		"
Σεμεί		"
Σεμεΐ		"

Σεμεΐν, ὁ (also Σεμεεί, Σεμεείν, Σεμεί, Σεμεΐ)   indeclinable; *Semein*, masculine proper noun (LU 3.26)

σεμίδαλιν	N-AF-S	σεμίδαλις

σεμίδαλις, εως, ἡ   *fine flour*, made from the finest wheat (RV 18.13)

σεμνά	A--NN-P	σεμνός
σεμνάς	A--AF-P	"

σεμνός, ή, όν   (1) of persons, that which in a human being calls forth veneration and respect from others *honorable, of good character, worthy of respect* (1T 3.8); (2) of things *worthy, honorable, noble* (PH 4.8)

σεμνότης, τητος, ἡ   as serious and worthy conduct that earns reverence and respect *dignity, seriousness, propriety*

σεμνότητα	N-AF-S	σεμνότης
σεμνότητι	N-DF-S	"
σεμνότητος	N-GF-S	"
σεμνούς	A--AM-P	σεμνός

Σέργιος, ου, ὁ   *Sergius*, masculine proper noun (AC 13.7)

Σεργίῳ	N-DM-S	Σέργιος
Σερούκ		Σερούχ

Σερούχ, ὁ (also Ζαρούχ, Σαρούκ, Σαρούχ, Σερούκ)   indeclinable; *Serug*, masculine proper noun (LU 3.35)

σεσαλευμένον	VPRPAN-S	σαλεύω
σεσαρωμένον	VPRPAM-S	σαρόω
σέσηπε(ν)	VIRA--3S	σήπω
σεσιγημένου	VPRPGN-S	σιγάω
σεσοφισμένοις	VPRPDM-P	σοφίζω

σέσωκε(ν)	VIRA--3S	σῴζω
σεσωρευμένα	VPRPAN-P	σωρεύω
σεσωσμένοι	VPRPNM-P	σῴζω
σέσωσται	VIRP--3S	"
σέσωται	VIRP--3S	"
σῇ	A--DF2S	σός

Σήθ, ὁ indeclinable; *Seth*, masculine proper noun (LU 3.38)

Σήμ, ὁ indeclinable; *Shem*, masculine proper noun (LU 3.36)

σημαίνω impf. ἐσήμαινον; 1aor. ἐσήμανα; with a basic meaning *intentionally produce an impression* to signal or signify something; (1) as making something clear *signify, indicate, show* (AC 25.27); (2) prophetically *foretell, signify (beforehand)* (JN 12.33)

σημαίνων	VPPANM-S	σημαίνω
σημᾶναι	VNAA	"
σημεῖα	N-AN-P	σημεῖον
	N-NN-P	"
σημείοις	N-DN-P	"

σημεῖον, ου, τό (1) basically, as what serves as a pointer to aid perception or insight *sign, mark, distinguishing characteristic*; (2) as what distinguishes one person or thing from another *sign, token, mark* (LU 2.12; RO 4.11); (3) as a miraculous event contrary to the usual course of nature and intended as a pointer or means of confirmation, often used with τέρας *(wonder) sign* (MK 13.22); as a miraculous event resulting from personal action *sign, miracle* (JN 2.11; RV 13.13)

σημεῖον	N-AN-S	σημεῖον
	N-NN-S	"
σημειοῦσθε	VMPM--2P	σημειόω

σημειόω *denote, signal* something; middle in the NT *take special note of, mark (out), publicly identify* (2TH 3.14)

σημείων	N-GN-P	σημεῖον

σήμερον adverb of time; (1) generally designating the present *today, this day* (MT 11.23), in contrast to ἐχθές (*in the past*); (2) as an unspecified period of time between past and future periods *for the present, at this time* (LU 13.32, 33); (3) as the twenty-four-hour period beginning at sundown *today, this very day* (MK 14.30); (4) as designating the same period of time as the day of the discourse *today* (MT 21.28); (5) as a religious technical term identifying the limits of the time God has put at man's disposal for some purpose *today* (HE 3.13)

σήμερον	AB	σήμερον
σήν	A--AF2S	σός

σήπω second perfect σέσηπα; literally, of organic matter *cause to decay*; passive *decay, rot*; figuratively and second perfect active, of riches or treasures *become corrupted* or *spoiled* (JA 5.2)

σηρικός, ή, όν *silk, of silk, silken* (RV 18.12); cf. σιρικός

σηρικοῦ	AP-GN-S	σηρικός

σής, σητός, ὁ *moth*, a small butterflylike insect whose larva feeds on cloth

σής	N-NM-S	σής
σῆς	A--GF2S	σός
σητόβρωτα	A--NN-P	σητόβρωτος

σητόβρωτος, ον of clothing eaten into by moths *moth-eaten* (JA 5.2)

σθενόω fut. σθενώσω; *strengthen, make strong, cause to be more able* (1P 5.10)

σθενώσαι	VNAA	σθενόω
σθενώσει	VIFA--3S	"
σιαγόνα	N-AF-S	σιαγών

σιαγών, όνος, ἡ strictly *jaw, jawbone*; in the NT *cheek*

σιαίνεσθαι	VNPP	σιαίνομαι

σιαίνομαι *be disturbed, be annoyed* (1TH 3.3)

σιγᾶν	VNPA	σιγάω
σιγάτω	VMPA--3S	"
σιγάτωσαν	VMPA--3P	"

σιγάω 1aor. ἐσίγησα; pf. pass. σεσίγημαι; (1) intransitively *be silent, keep still*; (a) *say nothing, keep silent* (LU 20.26); (b) *become silent, stop speaking* (LU 18.39); (c) *keep quiet, say nothing* about something (LU 9.36); (2) transitively *conceal, keep as a secret* (RO 16.25)

σιγή, ῆς, ἡ *silence, quiet*, as the absence of all noise or speaking

σιγή	N-NF-S	σιγή
σιγῆς	N-GF-S	"
σιγῆσαι	VNAA	σιγάω
σιγήσῃ	VSAA--3S	"
σιγήσουσι(ν)	VIFA--3P	"
σιγῶσι(ν)	VSPA--3P	"
σιδηρᾷ	A--DF-S	σιδηροῦς
σιδηρᾶν	A--AF-S	"

σίδηρος, ου, ὁ as a metal *iron* (RV 18.12)

σιδήρου	N-GM-S	σίδηρος

σιδηροῦς, ᾶ, οῦν *(made of) iron* (AC 12.10); metaphorically ἐν ῥάβδῳ σιδηρᾷ literally *with an iron rod*, i.e. *with strict, merciless rule* (RV 2.27)

σιδηροῦς	A--AM-P	σιδηροῦς

Σιδών, ῶνος, ἡ *Sidon*, a Phoenician coastal city north of Tyre

Σιδῶνα	N-AF-S	Σιδών
Σιδῶνι	N-DF-S	"
Σιδωνίας	AP-GF-S	Σιδώνιος
Σιδωνίοις	AP-DM-P	"

Σιδώνιος, ία, ον *belonging to Sidon, Sidonian*; substantivally; (1) ἡ Σιδωνία (χώρα) *the country* or *district around Sidon, the territory of Sidon* (LU 4.26); (2) οἱ Σιδώνιοι *the Sidonians* (AC 12.20)

Σιδῶνος	N-GF-S	Σιδών

σικάριος, ου, ὁ one armed with a dagger *assassin, bandit, cutthroat*; especially used of fanatical armed guerrilla bands hostile to foreign overlordship *terrorist* (AC 21.38)

σικαρίων	N-GM-P	σικάριος

σίκερα, τό indeclinable; *strong drink*, a sweet intoxicating beverage usually made from something other than grapes (e.g. barley beer) (LU 1.15)

Σίλα	N-DM-S	Σιλᾶς
Σιλᾷ	N-DM-S	"
Σίλαν	N-AM-S	"
Σιλᾶν	N-AM-S	"
Σίλας	N-NM-S	"

Σιλᾶς, ᾶ, ὁ and **Σίλας** (also Σειλεᾶς, Σιλεᾶς) *Silas*, masculine proper noun (AC 15.22)

Σιλᾶς	N-NM-S	Σιλᾶς
Σιλεᾶ	N-DM-S	"

Σιλουανός, οῦ, ὁ *Silvanus*, masculine proper noun, generally regarded as referring to Silas (1TH 1.1)

Σιλουανός   N-NM-S   Σιλουανός
Σιλουανοῦ   N-GM-S   "

Σιλωάμ, ὁ indeclinable; *Siloam*, a pool that is part of a water system near Jerusalem (JN 9.7)

Σιμαίαν   N-AM-S   Σιμαίας

Σιμαίας, ου, ὁ *Simaias*, masculine proper noun (2T 4.19)

σιμικίνθια   N-AN-P   σιμικίνθιον

σιμικίνθιον, ου, τό *apron*, a linen covering used by workers and servants to cover the front of the body to protect clothing (AC 19.12)

Σίμων, ωνος, ὁ *Simon*, masculine proper noun

Σίμων   N-NM-S   Σίμων
        N-VM-S   "
Σίμωνα   N-AM-S   "
Σίμωνι   N-DM-S   "
Σίμωνος   N-GM-S   "
Σινά   Σινᾶ

Σινᾶ, τό (also **Σινά**) indeclinable; *Sinai*, the mountain or mountain range in the peninsula of the same name, between Egypt and modern Arabia; used in an extended metaphor in GA 4.25 τὸ δὲ Ἁγὰρ Σ. ὄρος ἐστὶν ἐν τῇ Ἀραβίᾳ *but the name Hagar stands for Mount Sinai in Arabia*

σινάπεως   N-GN-S   σίναπι

σίναπι, εως, τό *mustard plant*, an herb or shrub with extremely small pungent seeds (MT 13.31)

σινδόνα   N-AF-S   σινδών
σινδόνι   N-DF-S   "

σινδών, όνος, ἡ *linen cloth*; (1) as a loosely fitting sleeping garment *tunic, (night)shirt* (MK 14.51); (2) as a cloth used to wrap a corpse for burial *linen cloth, sheet* (MT 27.59)

σινιάζω 1aor. ἐσινίασα; *sift, shake in a sieve, winnow*, as separating chaff from grain; figuratively, of character refinement *test out, take away the bad from the good* (LU 22.31)

σινιάσαι   VNAA   σινιάζω

σιρικός, ή, όν strictly *pertaining to Seres*, a people of China; *made of silk, silken*; neuter as a substantive τὸ σιρικόν *silk, silk cloth* or *garments* (RV 18.12); cf. σηρικός

σιρικοῦ   AP-GN-S   σιρικός
σιροῖς   N-DM-P   σιρός

σιρός, οῦ, ὁ (also **σειρός**) *pit, (underground) cave, deep hole* (2P 2.4)

σῖτα   N-AN-P   σῖτος
σιτευτόν   A--AM-S   σιτευτός

σιτευτός, ή, όν *fattened, fatted*, of animals kept in a stall and fed grain to prepare them for slaughter as food (possibly LU 15.27); of the resulting condition *prized, valuable* (possibly LU 15.27)

σιτία   N-AN-P   σιτίον

σιτίον, ου, τό diminutive of σῖτος; plural in the NT, as food prepared from grain *food, victuals, provisions* (AC 7.12)

σιτιστά   AP-NN-P   σιτιστός

σιτιστός, ή, όν from σῖτος (*grain*); of young animals fed grain to prepare them for slaughter *fattened*; neuter plural τὰ σιτιστά as a substantive *fattened cattle, fatlings* (MT 22.4)

σιτομέτριον, ου, τό *ration, food allowance, share of food*, a measured portion of grain or food (LU 12.42)

σιτομέτριον   N-AN-S   σιτομέτριον
σῖτον   N-AM-S   σῖτος

σῖτος, ου, ὁ *wheat*; more generally *grain* (MT 3.12); irregular neuter plural τὰ σῖτα as a substantive (AC 7.12)

σῖτος   N-NM-S   σῖτος
σίτου   N-GM-S   "
Σιχάρ   Συχάρ

Σιών, ἡ indeclinable; *Zion*; (1) (Mount) *Zion*, a hill within Jerusalem (RV 14.1); (2) as a name for Jerusalem and its inhabitants (MT 21.5); (3) as the theocratic community that centers in Jerusalem, made up of the people of Israel (RO 9.33); (4) figuratively, as the Christian community that centers in the heavenly or New Jerusalem (HE 12.22)

σιώπα   VMPA--2S   σιωπάω

σιωπάω impf. ἐσιώπων; fut. σιωπήσω; 1aor. ἐσιώπησα; *be silent*; (1) *be silent, make no sound, keep quiet* (MK 3.4); (2) *become quiet*; (a) of persons *stop speaking, become silent* (MT 20.31); (b) figuratively, of wind and waves *quiet down, become calm* (MK 4.39); (3) *be silent, be unable to speak* (LU 1.20)

σιωπή, ῆς, ἡ *silence*; as an adverb σιωπῇ *quietly, privately* (JN 11.28)

σιωπῇ   N-DF-S   σιωπή
σιωπήσῃ   VSAA--3S   σιωπάω
σιωπήσῃς   VSAA--2S   "
σιωπήσουσι(ν)   VIFA--3P   "
σιωπήσωσι(ν)   VSAA--3P   "
σιωπῶν   VPPANM-S   "
σκάνδαλα   N-AN-P   σκάνδαλον
σκανδαλίζει   VIPA--3S   σκανδαλίζω
σκανδαλίζεται   VIPP--3S   "
σκανδαλίζῃ   VSPA--3S   "
σκανδαλίζονται   VIPP--3P   "

σκανδαλίζω impf. pass. ἐσκανδαλιζόμην; 1aor. ἐσκανδάλισα; 1aor. pass. ἐσκανδαλίσθην; 1fut. pass. σκανδαλισθήσομαι; *cause to stumble*; figuratively in the NT; (1) active, as occasioning transgression *cause to do wrong* or *sin* (MT 5.29); passive *be led into sin, be caused to do wrong* (2C 11.29); in an absolute sense *fall away, give up believing* (MT 13.21); (2) passive, as taking offense at Jesus or refusing to believe in him *be offended* (MT 11.6); (3) as furnishing an occasion for someone to be shocked or angered *give offense to, offend* (MT 17.27)

σκανδαλίζωμεν   VSPA--1P   σκανδαλίζω
σκανδαλίσῃ   VSAA--3S   "
σκανδαλισθῇ   VSAP--3S   "
σκανδαλισθήσεσθε   VIFP--2P   "
σκανδαλισθήσομαι   VIFP--1S   "
σκανδαλισθήσονται   VIFP--3P   "
σκανδαλισθῆτε   VSAP--2P   "
σκανδαλίσω   VSAA--1S   "
σκανδαλίσωμεν   VSAA--1P   "

σκάνδαλον, ου, τό (1) strictly, the movable bait stick or trigger in a trap *trap stick*; by synecdoche, the trap itself *snare*; (2) metaphorically *trap*, i.e. *what causes a person to sin, cause of ruin, occasion of falling* (RO 11.9); (3) figuratively; (a) as an *enticement* to sin or apostasy *temptation, offense* (MT 18.7); (b) as what gives offense or arouses opposition *stumbling block, offense* (1C 1.23)

σκάνδαλον	N-AN-S	σκάνδαλον
	N-NN-S	"
σκανδάλου	N-GN-S	"
σκανδάλων	N-GN-P	"
σκάπτειν	VNPA	σκάπτω

σκάπτω 1aor. ἔσκαψα; intransitively; (1) *dig, excavate (in) the ground* (LU 6.48); (2) *till, spade up the ground,* as in gardening (LU 13.8)

Σκαριότα		Ἰσκαριώθ
Σκαριώθ		"
Σκαριώτη	N-DM-S	"
Σκαριώτης	N-NM-S	"
Σκαριώτου	N-GM-S	"

σκάφη, ης, ἡ strictly *anything dug out* or *hollowed*; hence *small boat, skiff,* as a ship's boat (AC 27.16)

σκάφην	N-AF-S	σκάφη
σκάφης	N-GF-S	"
σκάψω	VSAA--1S	σκάπτω
σκέλη	N-AN-P	σκέλος

σκέλος, ους, τό *leg,* as the limb of the body from hip to toes (JN 19.31)

σκέπασμα, ατος, τό strictly *covering material,* either in the form of clothing or shelter; in the NT probably restricted to *clothing* (1T 6.8)

σκεπάσματα	N-AN-P	σκέπασμα
Σκευᾶ	N-GM-S	Σκευᾶς

Σκευᾶς, ᾶ, ὁ *Sceva,* masculine proper noun (AC 19.14)

σκεύει	N-DN-S	σκεῦος
σκεύεσι(ν)	N-DN-P	"
σκεύη	N-AN-P	"
	N-NN-P	"

σκευή, ῆς, ἡ *apparatus, equipment, (household) furnishings*; of a ship *gear, tackle, rigging* (AC 27.19)

σκευήν	N-AF-S	σκευή

σκεῦος, ους, τό a container of any material used for a specific purpose, with the meaning varying according to the context; (1) literally; (a) generally *object, thing, utensil* (MK 11.16); (b) as a container in a household *jar, dish, jug,* etc. (JN 19.29); (c) as used in religious service *utensil, equipment* (HE 9.21); (d) on a ship *gear,* probably *sea anchor* (AC 27.17), used in an effort to slow down a storm-driven ship; (2) figuratively, of persons in certain respects; (a) as chosen for specific divine service *person, instrument* (AC 9.15); (b) euphemistically and Hebraistically, of a wife as her husband's sexual *partner* (1P 3.7; probably 1TH 4.4); (c) of the body as the container of the soul *container* (2C 4.7; possibly 1TH 4.4); (d) as a recipient of God's wrath or mercy *object* (RO 9.22, 23)

σκεῦος	N-AN-S	σκεῦος
	N-NN-S	"
σκηναῖς	N-DF-P	σκηνή
σκηνάς	N-AF-P	"
σκήνει	N-DN-S	σκῆνος

σκηνή, ῆς, ἡ *tent, booth*; (1) generally, of transitory, movable lodging places for nomads, pilgrims, herdsmen, soldiers, constructed of various materials *tent, lodging, dwelling* (HE 11.9); (2) as the portable divine sanctuary *Tabernacle, Tent* (HE 8.5); (3) as referring to the temple in Jerusalem (HE 13.10); (4) as referring to the outer and inner rooms of the Tabernacle, comprising the Holy Place and the Holy of Holies (HE 9.2–8); (5) as a portable case for an idol *shrine* (AC 7.43); (6) figuratively, of the heavenly *dwelling place* of God, *sanctuary* (RV 13.6); (7) plural, as the eternal habitations of the righteous *dwellings, homes* (LU 16.9); (8) figuratively, as a ruling dynasty or lineage *ruling family, kingdom* (AC 15.16)

σκηνή	N-NF-S	σκηνή
σκηνῇ	N-DF-S	"
σκηνήν	N-AF-S	"
σκηνῆς	N-GF-S	"

σκηνοπηγία, ας, ἡ as a technical term in Jewish religion *pitching* or *erecting a tent* or *booth*; as the name of the annual religious festival *Feast of Tabernacles, Festival of Booths, Celebration of Tents* (often with ἑορτή [*feast*]) (JN 7.2)

σκηνοπηγία	N-NF-S	σκηνοπηγία
σκηνοποιοί	N-NM-P	σκηνοποιός

σκηνοποιός, οῦ, ὁ as a trade *tentmaker* (AC 18.3)

σκῆνος, ους, τό *tent, tabernacle*; normally used in a figurative sense of the *(human) body* in its temporary and corruptible state (2C 5.1); idiomatically εἶναι ἐν τῷ σκήνει literally *be in the tent,* i.e. *be physically alive* (2C 5.4)

σκηνοῦντας	VPPAAM-P	σκηνόω
σκηνοῦντες	VPPAVM-P	"
σκηνούντων	VPPAGM-P	"
σκήνους	N-GN-S	σκῆνος

σκηνόω fut. σκηνώσω; 1aor. ἐσκήνωσα; *live, dwell (temporarily)*; literally *live* or *camp in a tent*; figuratively in the NT *dwell, take up one's residence, come to reside (among)* (JN 1.14)

σκήνωμα, ατος, τό strictly, what has been set up as an abode *tent, tentlike dwelling*; figuratively in the NT; (1) as a temple for God's habitation on earth *dwelling place, habitation* (AC 7.46); (2) the physical *body*; idiomatically εἶναι ἐν τούτῳ τῷ σκηνώματι literally *be in this tent,* i.e. *remain alive* (2P 1.13); ἡ ἀπόθεσις τοῦ σκηνώματος literally *the putting off of the tent-dwelling,* i.e. *death* (2P 1.14)

σκήνωμα	N-AN-S	σκήνωμα
σκηνώματι	N-DN-S	"
σκηνώματος	N-GN-S	"
σκηνώσει	VIFA-3S	σκηνόω

σκιά, ᾶς, ἡ (1) literally *shadow, shade* (MK 4.32); (2) figuratively; (a) idiomatically, as the sphere of those alienated from God ἐν σκιᾷ θανάτου literally *in shadow of death,* i.e. *about to die* (MT 4.16); (b) as the antithesis of reality *shadow* (HE 8.5); (c) prophetically, of the relation of type to antitype *foreshadowing* (CO 2.17)

σκιά	N-NF-S	σκιά
σκιᾷ	N-DF-S	"
σκιάν	N-AF-S	"

σκιρτάω 1aor. ἐσκίρτησα; as an expression of joy *leap about, jump* (for joy), *show that one is very happy*

σκιρτήσατε	VMAA--2P	σκιρτάω

σκληροκαρδία, ας, ἡ   as a stubborn attitude toward changing one's behavior *hardness of heart, stubbornness, insensitivity*

σκληροκαρδίαν	N-AF-S	σκληροκαρδία
σκληρόν	A--NN-S	σκληρός

σκληρός, ά, όν   (1) of things, literally *hard, dry, rough*; figuratively in the NT; (a) of words *harsh, unpleasant, hard to take, intolerable* (JN 6.60); neuter as a substantive τὰ σκληρά *harsh talk* (JU 15); (b) of winds *fierce, powerful* (JA 3.4); (2) of persons *strict, unmerciful, demanding* (MT 25.24); (3) impersonally, neuter with an infinitive σκληρόν σοι *it is hard for you* (AC 26.14)

σκληρός	A--NM-S	σκληρός

σκληρότης, ητος, ἡ   literally *hardness*; figuratively, as a resistant attitude denoting unreceptivity *stubbornness, obstinacy* (RO 2.5)

σκληρότητα	N-AF-S	σκληρότης
σκληροτράχηλοι	A--VM-P	σκληροτράχηλος

σκληροτράχηλος, ον   figuratively, of resistance against changing one's behavior *stiff-necked, headstrong, stubborn*; substantivally *stubborn person* (AC 7.51)

σκληρύνει	VIPA--3S	σκληρύνω
σκληρύνητε	VSAA--2P	"
σκληρυνθῇ	VSAP--3S	"

σκληρύνω   impf. pass. ἐσκληρυνόμην; 1aor. ἐσκλήρυνα; 1aor. pass. ἐσκληρύνθην; (1) literally and passive, as a medical technical term *harden, become thick*; (2) figuratively in the NT; (a) active and metaphorically σκληρύνειν τὴν καρδίαν literally *cause one's heart to be hard*, i.e. *act stubbornly, refuse to change one's attitude* (HE 3.8); of God's judicial action *cause someone to be stubborn, make someone refuse to listen* (RO 9.18); (b) passive *be or become stubborn, refuse to yield* (HE 3.13)

σκληρῶν	A--GM-P	σκληρός
	A--GN-P	"
σκολιά	A--NN-P	σκολιός
σκολιᾶς	A--GF-S	"
σκολιοῖς	A--DM-P	"

σκολιός, ά, όν   (1) literally *crooked, bent*; (2) figuratively; (a) of social behavior *crooked, dishonest*; neuter plural τὰ σκολιά as a substantive *dishonest ways* (LU 3.5); (b) of personal behavior *unscrupulous, unfair, dishonest*; substantivally οἱ σκολιοί of those in charge of workers *harsh masters* (1P 2.18)

σκόλοψ, οπος, ὁ   literally, something pointed *stake*; as an injurious sharp object *splinter, thorn*; figuratively, as a sharply painful affliction or disability; idiomatically σ. τῇ σαρκί literally *thorn in the flesh*, i.e. *serious difficulty, painful trouble*, possibly a recurring physical illness, such as malaria (2C 12.7)

σκόλοψ	N-NM-S	σκόλοψ
σκόπει	VMPA--2S	σκοπέω
σκοπεῖν	VNPA	"
σκοπεῖτε	VMPA--2P	"
σκοπείτω	VMPA--3S	"

σκοπέω   (1) *keep a watchful eye on, notice carefully, watch out* (RO 16.17); (2) of self-examination based on inspection of a model or example before one *consider, be concerned about, keep thinking about* (GA 6.1)

σκοπόν	N-AM-S	σκοπός

σκοπός, οῦ, ὁ   *goal*; as a metaphor drawn from athletics for what one aims to achieve in the Christian life *mark, goal* (PH 3.14)

σκοποῦντες	VPPANM-P	σκοπέω
σκοπούντων	VPPAGM-P	"
σκοπῶν	VPPANM-S	"
σκορπίζει	VIPA--3S	σκορπίζω

σκορπίζω   1aor. ἐσκόρπισα; 1aor. pass. ἐσκορπίσθην; literally *scatter, disperse* (JN 10.12), opposite συνάγω (*gather*); as a metaphor drawn from seed sowing, for what one does to help those in need *distribute, disperse, give generously* (2C 9.9)

σκορπίοι	N-NM-P	σκορπίος
σκορπίοις	N-DM-P	"
σκορπίον	N-AM-S	"

σκορπίος, ου, ὁ   *scorpion*, a large crab-shaped insect of the same family as spiders, with a poisonous stinger in its tail

σκορπίου	N-GM-S	σκορπίος
σκορπίσει	VIFA--3S	σκορπίζω
σκορπισθῆτε	VSAP--2P	"
σκορπίων	N-GM-P	σκορπίος
σκότει	N-DN-S	σκότος
σκοτεινόν	A--AN-S	σκοτεινός
	A--NN-S	"

σκοτεινός, ή, όν   *in the dark*; figuratively, as characterized by lack of moral and spiritual perception *full of darkness*, i.e. *unable to know the difference between right and wrong*

σκοτία, ας, ἡ   as a quality *darkness, obscurity*; literally, as the absence of natural light *darkness* (JN 6.17); idiomatically ἐν τῇ σκοτίᾳ literally *in the dark*, i.e. *secretly* (MT 10.27); figuratively, of what is characterized by lack of religious and moral perception *darkness, evil* (MT 4.16); personified in Johannine usage of forces hostile to God *realm of evil, all that opposes God* (JN 1.5)

σκοτία	N-NF-S	σκοτία
σκοτίᾳ	N-DF-S	"
σκοτίας	N-GF-S	"

σκοτίζω   pf. pass. ἐσκότισμαι; 1aor. pass. ἐσκοτίσθην; 1fut. pass. σκοτισθήσομαι; only passive in the NT; literally *be or become dark, be unable to give light* (MT 24.29); figuratively, of the lack of religious and moral perception *be unable to understand* (RO 1.21)

σκοτισθέντος	VPAPGM-S	σκοτίζω
σκοτισθῇ	VSAP--3S	"
σκοτισθήσεται	VIFP--3S	"
σκοτισθήτωσαν	VMAP--3P	"

σκότος, ους, τό   *darkness*; (1) literally, as an enveloping sphere where light (φῶς) is absent *darkness, gloom, obscurity* (MT 27.45); in relation to the world, as the primitive chaos before light was created (2C 4.6); idiomatically τὸ σ. τὸ ἐξώτερον literally *the outer darkness*, i.e. *the place of punishment*, as the region of future exclusion from the kingdom of God (MT 8.12); (2) figuratively, as an absence of moral and spiritual renewal *ignorance, lack of understanding* (AC 26.18); metaphorically, as the domain under the authority of the devil and demons *realm of evil, evil world* (LU 22.53; EP 6.12)

σκότος	N-AN-S	σκότος
	N-NN-S	"
σκότους	N-GN-S	"

σκοτόω pf. pass. ἐσκότωμαι; 1aor. pass. ἐσκοτώθην; only passive in the NT; literally *be* or *become darkened* (RV 9.2); figuratively, of the lack of religious and moral perception *be darkened*, i.e. *unable to understand* (EP 4.18)

σκότῳ	N-DM-S	σκότος
σκύβαλα	N-AN-P	σκύβαλον

σκύβαλον, ου, τό anything that is to be treated as worthless and thrown out, translated according to the context *dung, rubbish, garbage, offscourings* (PH 3.8)

Σκύθης, ου, ὁ *Scythian, inhabitant of Scythia* (modern southern Russia) (CO 3.11)

Σκύθης	N-NM-S	Σκύθης
σκυθρωποί	A--NM-P	σκυθρωπός

σκυθρωπός, ή, όν as a characteristic of the appearance of the face *with a sad* or *gloomy countenance, sad-appearing, sullen*

σκῦλα	N-AN-P	σκῦλον
σκύλλε	VMPA--2S	σκύλλω
σκύλλεις	VIPA--2S	"
σκύλλου	VMPP--2S	"

σκύλλω pf. pass. ἔσκυλμαι; strictly *flay, skin*; figuratively in the NT; (1) *harass, weary* someone (MT 9.36); (2) *bother, annoy, trouble* someone (MK 5.35); passive *trouble oneself, bother* (LU 7.6)

σκῦλον, ου, τό plural in the NT, for what is stripped off a fallen enemy *spoils, booty* (LU 11.22)

σκωληκόβρωτος, ον *eaten by worms, worm-eaten* (AC 12.23)

σκωληκόβρωτος	A--NM-S	σκωληκόβρωτος

σκώληξ, ηκος, ὁ *worm, maggot* that eats dead flesh; metaphorically, of the unending torment that characterizes punishment in hell (MK 9.48)

σκώληξ	N-NM-S	σκώληξ

σμαράγδινος, η, ον *(made of) emerald* (RV 4.3); substantivally *emerald stone* (RV 4.3)

σμαραγδίνῳ	A--DM-S	σμαράγδινος
σμαραγδίνων	AP-GM-P	"

σμάραγδος, ου, ὁ *emerald*, a transparent bright green precious stone (RV 21.19)

σμάραγδος	N-NM-S	σμάραγδος
σμαράγδῳ	N-DM-S	"
σμῆγμα	N-AN-S	μίγμα
σμίγμα	N-AN-S	"

Σμύρνα, ης, ἡ (also **Ζμύρνα**) *Smyrna*, a city on the western coast of Asia Minor north of Ephesus

σμύρνα, ης, ἡ *myrrh*, a resinous gum oozing from a kind of balsam tree, used for incense and ointments

Σμυρναῖος, α, ον *Smyrnian, inhabiting Smyrna*; substantivally *citizen of Smyrna, Smyrnian* (RV 2.8)

Σμυρναίων	AP-GM-P	Σμυρναῖος
Σμύρναν	N-AF-S	Σμύρνα
σμύρναν	N-AF-S	σμύρνα
Σμύρνῃ	N-DF-S	Σμύρνα
σμύρνης	N-GF-S	σμύρνα

σμυρνίζω pf. pass. ἐσμύρνισμαι; *mix with myrrh*; of wine *flavor* or *spice with myrrh* to create a stupefying effect (MK 15.23)

Σόδομα, ων, τά *Sodom*, a city by the Dead Sea, destroyed by a judgmental rain of sulfur and fire (cf. Genesis 19.24); figuratively in RV 11.8, for Jerusalem as a center of wickedness

Σόδομα	N-NN-P	Σόδομα
Σοδόμοις	N-DN-P	"
Σοδόμων	N-GN-P	"
σοί	A--NM2P	σός
	NPD-2S	σύ

Σολομών, ῶνος, ὁ and **Σολομῶν, ῶντος, ὁ** (also **Σαλωμών** indeclinable) *Solomon*, masculine proper noun

Σολομών	N-NM-S	Σολομών
Σολομῶν	N-NM-S	"
Σολομῶνα	N-AM-S	"
Σολομῶνος	N-GM-S	"
Σολομῶντα	N-AM-S	"
Σολομῶντος	N-GM-S	"
σόν	A--AN2S	σός
	A--NN2S	"

σορός, οῦ, ἡ *coffin*; in the NT *bier, funeral couch*, an open frame used to carry a dead person to burial (LU 7.14)

σοροῦ	N-GF-S	σορός

σός, σή, σόν a possessive adjective of the second-person singular used for emphasis or contrast *your, yours*; (1) with a noun *your, yours* (MT 7.3); (2) substantivally; (a) masculine οἱ σοί *your own people* or *family* (MK 5.19); (b) neuter as a substantive τὸ σόν *what is yours, what belongs to you* (MT 20.14); plural τὰ σά *your things* or *goods* (LU 6.30)

σός	A--NM2S	σός
σοῦ	A--GM2S	"
	A--GN2S	"
	NPG-2S	σύ
σουδάρια	N-AN-P	σουδάριον

σουδάριον, ου, τό *face cloth, handkerchief, napkin* (LU 19.20); as used to bind shut the jaws or wrap the head of a corpse *cloth, kerchief* (JN 11.44)

σουδάριον	N-AN-S	σουδάριον
σουδαρίῳ	N-DN-S	"
σούς	A--AM2P	σός

Σουσάννα, ης, ἡ *Susanna*, feminine proper noun (LU 8.3)

Σουσάννα	N-NF-S	Σουσάννα

σοφία, ας, ἡ *wisdom*; (1) generally, the ability to use knowledge for correct behavior *insight, understanding* (CO 4.5) or in a clever way *skill, cleverness* (1C 1.17); (2) naturally, human wisdom *wisdom, cleverness*, often as opposed to divine wisdom; used of human philosophy (1C 1.21b), scientific learning (AC 7.22), natural moral intelligence (AC 6.3); (3) spiritually; (a) as the supreme intelligence of God and Christ (CO 2.3; possibly LU 11.49); (b) of Christ as the embodiment of God's wisdom (1C 1.24); (c) as enlightenment given through divine revelation (2P 3.15); (d) as God's plan of salvation as revealed in the gospel (1C 2.7); (4) as the title of a book containing wise sayings *Wisdom* (possibly LU 11.49)

σοφία	N-NF-S	σοφία
σοφίᾳ	N-DF-S	"
σοφίαν	N-AF-S	"
σοφίας	N-GF-S	"

σοφίζω 1aor. ἐσόφισα; pf. pass. σεσόφισμαι; (1) active *make someone wise, instruct, give wisdom* (2T 3.15); (2) middle *reason out skillfully, devise*; (3) passive, of false wisdom *be cleverly thought up, be cunningly devised* (2P 1.16)

σοφίσαι	VNAA	σοφίζω
σοφοί	AP-NM-P	σοφός
	A--NM-P	"
σοφοῖς	AP-DM-P	"

σοφός, ή, όν *wise*; (1) generally, of acquired intelligence characterized by the ability to use knowledge for correct behavior (1C 6.5) or human skill (1C 3.10) *wise, skillful, clever, learned*, opposite ἀνόητος (*without understanding, foolish*); substantively ὁ σ. *wise person, philosopher* (1C 1.20); (2) of conduct and action governed by divinely given insight and moral integrity *wise, understanding* (1C 3.18), opposite μωρός (*foolish, stupid*); (3) comparative σοφώτερος, τέρα, ον *wiser* (1C 1.25)

σοφός	AP-NM-S	σοφός
	A--NM-P	"
σοφούς	AP-AM-P	"
	A--AM-P	"
σοφῷ	A--DM-S	"
σοφῶν	AP-GM-P	"
σοφώτερον	A-MNN-S	"

Σπανία, ας, ἡ *Spain*, a country or region bordering the northwestern part of the Mediterranean Sea

Σπανίαν	N-AF-S	Σπανία
σπαράξαν	VPAANN-S	σπαράσσω
σπαράξας	VPAANM-S	"
σπαράσσει	VIPA--3S	"

σπαράσσω 1aor. ἐσπάραξα; *tear, pull (apart), pull to and fro*; figuratively, as designating the effect of demonization of a person *convulse, throw into a fit, distort by convulsions*

σπαργανόω 1aor. ἐσπαργάνωσα; pf. pass. ἐσπαργάνωμαι; as providing initial care for newborn children by wrapping them in long strips of cloth *swathe, wrap up in swaddling cloths* (σπάργανα) (LU 2.7)

σπαρείς	VPAPNM-S	σπείρω
σπαρέντες	VPAPNM-P	"
σπαρῇ	VSAP--3S	"
σπασάμενος	VPAMNM-S	σπάω

σπαταλάω 1aor. ἐσπατάλησα; of a self-indulgent way of life *live luxuriously, riotously*, for sensual gratification (1T 5.6)

σπαταλῶσα	VPPANF-S	σπαταλάω

σπάω 1aor. mid. ἐσπασάμην; *draw, pull*; middle in the NT, as taking a sword from its sheath *draw*

σπεῖρα, ης, ἡ *cohort, battalion*, a Roman military technical term for the tenth part of a legion, normally containing 600 troops (AC 10.1); as a detachment of soldiers *troop, band, company* (JN 18.3)

σπεῖρα	N-NF-S	σπεῖρα
σπεῖραι	VNAA	σπείρω
σπεῖραν	N-AF-S	σπεῖρα
σπείραντι	VPAADM-S	σπείρω
σπείραντος	VPAAGM-S	"
σπείρας	VPAANM-S	"
σπείρει	VIPA--3S	"

σπείρειν	VNPA	"
σπείρεις	VIPA--2S	"
σπείρεται	VIPP--3S	"
σπείρῃ	VSAA--3S	"
	VSPA--3S	"
σπείρης	N-GF-S	σπεῖρα
σπειρόμενοι	VPPPNM-P	σπείρω
σπειρόμενον	VPPPAN-S	"
σπείροντι	VPPADM-S	"
σπείροντος	VPPAGM-S	"
σπείρουσι(ν)	VIPA--3P	"

σπείρω 1aor. ἔσπειρα; pf. pass. ἔσπαρμαι; 2aor. pass. ἐσπάρην; (1) literally, of seed *sow, scatter* (MT 6.26), opposite θερίζω (*reap, gather*); participle as a substantive ὁ σπείρων *the sower* (MT 13.3); (2) metaphorically; (a) as telling the Word of God, spread the gospel as divine seed (MK 4.14); (b) of the natural human body as destined for resurrection (1C 15.42–44); (c) as acting in ways that will bring multiplied consequences of good or evil (GA 6.8)

σπείρων	VPPANM-S	σπείρω
σπεκουλάτορα	N-AM-S	σπεκουλάτωρ

σπεκουλάτωρ, ορος, ὁ literally *spy, scout*; when attached to a ruling official *member of a bodyguard, messenger, executioner* (MK 6.27)

σπεκουλάτωρα	N-AM-S	σπεκουλάτωρ
σπένδομαι	VIPP--1S	σπένδω

σπένδω *offer a libation, pour out a drink offering*; metaphorically and passive in the NT, of martyrdom *be poured out as a libation*, i.e. *be put to death, have one's life blood poured out*

σπέρμα, ατος, τό *seed*; (1) literally; (a) of plants (MT 13.24); (b) of human or animal semen *sperm, seed*; by metonymy, as human descendants *offspring, posterity, children* (MK 12.19); (2) figuratively; (a) as a surviving remnant from which to build a new posterity (RO 9.29); (b) as a principle of life implanted by the Spirit *imparted nature* (1J 3.9)

σπέρμα	N-AN-S	σπέρμα
	N-NN-S	"
σπέρμασι(ν)	N-DN-P	"
σπέρματι	N-DN-S	"
σπέρματος	N-GN-S	"
σπερμάτων	N-GN-P	"

σπερμολόγος, ον literally *picking up seeds*, of birds, such as rooks and crows; figuratively and substantively in the NT, of one who lounges in the marketplace and subsists on scraps, what falls off loads, etc. *rag-picker, parasite*; figuratively, of a false teacher who picks up and passes on scraps of truth or information *babbler, chatterer, empty talker* (AC 17.18)

σπερμολόγος	AP-NM-S	σπερμολόγος
σπεύδοντας	VPPAAM-P	σπεύδω

σπεύδω impf. ἔσπευδον; 1aor. ἔσπευσα; (1) intransitively, as doing something as quickly as possibly *hurry, make haste, hasten* (AC 22.18); participle as an adverb *hastily, quickly* (LU 2.16); (2) transitively *urge on, be eager for, cause to happen soon* (2P 3.12)

σπεύσαντες	VPAANM-P	σπεύδω
σπεύσας	VPAANM-S	"
σπεῦσον	VMAA--2S	"

σπήλαια   N-AN-P   σπήλαιον
σπηλαίοις   N-DN-P   "
σπήλαιον, ου, τό   (1) *cave* (JN 11.38); (2) *den* as used by robbers for hiding away from justice and for storing loot; metaphorically, of the misuse and abuse of temple privileges by a dishonest priesthood *hideout, refuge* (MT 21.13)
σπήλαιον   N-AN-S   σπήλαιον
    N-NN-S   "
σπηλαίῳ   N-DN-S   "
σπιλάδες   N-NF-P   σπιλάς
σπιλάς, άδος, ἡ   *rock over which the sea washes, reef, hidden rock*; metaphorically in JU 12 of ungodly people who wreck the lives of others before danger is suspected *hidden danger*
σπίλοι   N-NM-P   σπίλος
σπίλοι   N-NM-P   "
σπίλον   N-AM-S   "
σπίλος, ου, ὁ (also **σπῖλος**)   *spot, stain, blemish*; figuratively, as a moral imperfection *something wrong, fault, blemish* (EP 5.27); plural, of immoral people attached to a godly community *those who bring shame* or *cause disgrace* (2P 2.13)
σπιλοῦσα   VPPANF-S   σπιλόω
σπιλόω   pf. pass. ἐσπίλωμαι; *stain, defile, spot*; metaphorically in the NT, as bringing about moral impurity *cause disgrace, make shameful* (JU 23)
σπλάγχνα   N-AN-P   σπλάγχνον
    N-NN-P   "
σπλαγχνίζομαι   1aor. ἐσπλαγχνίσθην; *be moved with compassion for, feel sympathy with, take pity on* someone (MT 18.27)
σπλαγχνίζομαι   VIPD--1S   σπλαγχνίζομαι
    VIPO--1S   "
σπλαγχνισθείς   VPAONM-S   "
σπλάγχνοις   N-DN-P   σπλάγχνον
σπλάγχνον, ου, τό   of the body *inward part*, such as heart, bowels, liver; only plural in the NT; (1) literally *intestines, viscera, inward parts* of the body, located in the belly (AC 1.18); (2) figuratively; (a) the deep, inner seat of tender emotions in the whole personality, in differing cultures conceived of as *heart, stomach, bowels* (2C 7.15); (b) the heartfelt emotion itself, translated to fit the context *affection, love, deep feeling, compassion* (PH 1.8)
σπόγγον   N-AM-S   σπόγγος
σπόγγος, ου, ὁ   *sponge*, the lightweight skeleton of a porous sea animal, with remarkable power to absorb liquids
σποδός, οῦ, ἡ   what is left after something is burned *ash, ashes*
σποδός   N-NF-S   σποδός
σποδῷ   N-DF-S   "
σπορά, ᾶς, ἡ   (1) as an activity *sowing*; (2) as what is sown *seed*; metaphorically, of the power of God's Word to produce spiritual life (1P 1.23)
σπορᾶς   N-GF-S   σπορά
σπόριμος, ον   *sown*; neuter as a substantive τὰ σπόριμα *sown fields, fields of grain, standing crops*
σπορίμων   AP-GN-P   σπόριμος
σπόρον   N-AM-S   σπόρος

σπόρος, ου, ὁ   (1) literally *seed* (MK 4.26); (2) metaphorically; (a) as God's Word, able to produce spiritual life (LU 8.11); (b) as reciprocal benefits from generosity *crop*, i.e. *results of good deeds, much good brought about* (2C 9.10)
σπόρος   N-NM-S   σπόρος
σπουδάζοντες   VPPANM-P   σπουδάζω
σπουδάζω   fut. σπουδάσω; 1aor. ἐσπούδασα; intransitively; (1) with an infinitive following to show the area of urgency *make haste to, hurry to, do your best to* (2T 4.9); (2) with an infinitive following to show the area of concern *be eager to, make every effort to, try hard to* (HE 4.11)
σπουδάζω   VIPA--1S   σπουδάζω
σπουδαῖον   A--AM-S   σπουδαῖος
σπουδαῖος, αία, ον   *diligent, zealous, eager* (2C 8.22); comparative σπουδαιότερος, τέρα, ον *very earnest, more diligent* (2C 8.17); substantivally, neuter accusative singular as an adverb *very diligently* (2T 1.17)
σπουδαιότερον   ABM   σπουδαῖος
    A-MAM-S   "
σπουδαιότερος   A-MNM-S   "
σπουδαιοτέρως   ABM   σπουδαίως
σπουδαίως   an adverb used to add intensity and emphasis to verbs of asking *earnestly* (LU 7.4), seeking *diligently* (2T 1.17), sending *urgently* (TI 3.13); comparative σπουδαιοτέρως with the superlative meaning *as quickly as possible* (PH 2.28)
σπουδαίως   AB   σπουδαίως
σπουδάσατε   VMAA--2P   σπουδάζω
σπούδασον   VMAA--2S   "
σπουδάσω   VIFA--1S   "
σπουδάσωμεν   VSAA--1P   "
σπουδή, ῆς, ἡ   (1) *haste, speed*; μετὰ σπουδῆς *with haste, in a hurry* (LU 1.39); (2) as a quality of genuine commitment *zeal, diligence, eagerness* (RO 12.11); (3) as an expression of active concern *devotion, care, goodwill* (2C 7.11)
σπουδῇ   N-DF-S   σπουδή
σπουδήν   N-AF-S   "
σπουδῆς   N-GF-S   "
σπυρίδας   N-AF-P   σπυρίς
σπυρίδι   N-DF-S   "
σπυρίδων   N-GF-P   "
σπυρίς, ίδος, ἡ   *(large) basket, hamper*; used by Jews especially on longer journeys, for carrying along levitically clean provisions, such as food and hay for sleeping on (MT 15.37); equivalent to σαργάνη *hamper, basket made of braided ropes* (cf. AC 9.25 and 2C 11.33)
στάδια   N-AN-P   στάδιον
στάδιον, ου, τό   (1) as an oval area surrounded by tiers of seats for spectators, used for public contests *arena, stadium, racecourse* (1C 9.24); (2) as a measure of distance; cf. στάδιος (*stade*) in JN 6.19
στάδιος, ου, ὁ   as an established measure of distance, in length around 600 feet, 200 yards, 190 meters, or one-eighth Roman mile, almost a furlong *stade, stadium* (MT 14.24; JN 6.19)
σταδίου   N-GM-S   στάδιος
σταδίους   N-AM-P   "
σταδίῳ   N-DN-S   στάδιον

σταδίων	N-GM-P	στάδιος
σταθείς	VPAPNM-S	ἵστημι
σταθέντα	VPAPAM-S	"
σταθέντες	VPAPNM-P	"
σταθῇ	VSAP--3S	"
σταθῆναι	VNAP	"
σταθήσεσθε	VIFP--2P	"
σταθήσεται	VIFP--3S	"
	VIFP--3S^VMAP--3S	"
σταθῆτε	VSAP--2P	"

στάμνος, ου, ἡ *earthen jar, pot, urn* (HE 9.4)

στάμνος	N-NF-S	στάμνος
στάντες	VPAANM-P	ἵστημι
στάντος	VPAAGM-S	"
στάς	VPAANM-S	"
στᾶσα	VPAANF-S	"
στάσει	N-DF-S	στάσις
στάσεις	N-AF-P	"
στάσεως	N-GF-S	"

στασιαστής, οῦ, ὁ *rebel, revolutionary*, one who takes part in an insurrection (MK 15.7)

στασιαστῶν	N-GM-P	στασιαστής
στάσιν	N-AF-S	στάσις

στάσις, εως, ἡ from a basic meaning *standing*; (1) as the continuance of an old order *unchanged existence*; στάσιν ἔχειν literally *have standing*, i.e. *be in existence, be standing* (HE 9.8); (2) politically *taking a stand*, especially a rebellious *insurrection, uprising, revolt* (LU 23.19, 25; probably MK 15.7); (3) as civil strife that threatens political security *uproar* (AC 19.40; perhaps MK 15.7); (4) as sharp dissension or unrest within a community *strife, heated quarrel, conflict* (AC 15.2)

στάσις	N-NF-S	στάσις

στατήρ, ῆρος, ὁ *stater*, a silver *coin* worth four Attic drachmas, equivalent to one Jewish shekel (MT 17.27)

στατῆρα	N-AM-S	στατήρ
στατῆρας	N-AM-P	"
σταυρόν	N-AM-S	σταυρός

σταυρός, οῦ, ὁ (1) literally *cross*, an instrument of capital punishment, an upright pointed stake, often with a crossbeam above it, or intersected by a crossbeam (MT 27.32); (2) by metonymy, as the means of atonement *punishment of the cross, crucifixion* (PH 2.8); as a religious technical term representing the significance of the atoning death of Jesus in the Christian religion *cross* (1C 1.18); metaphorically, the dedication of life and the self-denial that a believer must be prepared to take on himself in following Christ (LU 14.27)

σταυρός	N-NM-S	σταυρός
σταύρου	VMPA--2S	σταυρόω
σταυροῦ	N-GM-S	σταυρός
σταυροῦνται	VIPP--3P	σταυρόω
σταυροῦσι(ν)	VIPA--3P	"

σταυρόω fut. σταυρώσω; 1aor. ἐσταύρωσα; pf. pass. ἐσταύρωμαι; 1aor. pass. ἐσταυρώθην; literally *nail* or *affix to a cross, crucify* (MT 20.19); metaphorically, of a believer's renouncing his old sinful way of living to be united to his Lord *crucify, put to death*, i.e. *be done with* (GA 5.24)

σταυρῷ	N-DM-S	σταυρός
σταυρωθέντες	VPAPNM-P	σταυρόω

σταυρωθῇ	VSAP--3S	"
σταυρωθῆναι	VNAP	"
σταυρωθήτω	VMAP--3S	"
σταυρῶσαι	VNAA	"
σταυρώσαντες	VPAANM-P	"
σταυρώσατε	VMAA--2P	"
σταυρώσετε	VIFA--2P	"
σταύρωσον	VMAA--2S	"
σταυρώσουσι(ν)	VIFA--3P	"
σταυρώσω	VSAA--1S	"
σταυρώσωσι(ν)	VSAA--3P	"
σταφυλαί	N-NF-P	σταφυλή
σταφυλάς	N-AF-P	"

σταφυλή, ῆς, ἡ *(cluster* or *bunch of) grapes*

σταφυλή	N-NF-S	σταφυλή
σταφυλήν	N-AF-S	"
σταφυλήνας	N-AF-P	see σταφυλάς
στάχυας	N-AM-P	στάχυς
στάχυϊ	N-DM-S	"
Στάχυν	N-AM-S	Στάχυς
στάχυν	N-AM-S	στάχυς

Στάχυς, υος, ὁ *Stachys*, masculine proper noun (RO 16.9)

στάχυς, υος, ὁ of growing grain *head, ear*

στέγει	VIPA--3S	στέγω

στέγη, ης, ἡ *(flat) roof, covering* for a room or house

στέγην	N-AF-S	στέγη
στέγομεν	VIPA--1P	στέγω
στέγοντες	VPPANM-P	"

στέγω related to στέγη *(roof)*; (1) strictly *put a roof on*; hence *cover, keep silent about, keep confidential* (1C 13.7); (2) *endure, bear* (1TH 3.1); (3) *refrain from, put up with* (1C 9.12)

στέγων	VPPANM-S	στέγω

στεῖρα, ας, ἡ from the adjective στεῖρος, α, ον (*barren, sterile*); *barren woman, woman incapable of bearing a child* (LU 1.7; HE 11.11)

στεῖρα	N-NF-S	στεῖρα
	N-VF-S	"
στείρα	N-DF-S	"
στεῖραι	N-NF-P	"
στέλλεσθαι	VNPM	στέλλω
στελλόμενοι	VPPMNM-P	"

στέλλω only middle in the NT; from the active sense *place in set order, arrange, make ready* arises the sense of disciplining oneself in relation to disorderly (ἀτάκτως) elements within a community; (1) of persons *hold oneself aloof, keep away* from someone (2TH 3.6); (2) of things *try to avoid, steer clear of, be on guard against* (2C 8.20)

στέμμα, ατος, τό *wreath* or *garland* (of flowers or wool interwoven with flowers and leaves) put on an animal just before it is killed as a sacrifice (AC 14.13)

στέμματα	N-AN-P	στέμμα
στεναγμοῖς	N-DM-P	στεναγμός

στεναγμός, οῦ, ὁ *sigh, groan, groaning*

στεναγμοῦ	N-GM-S	στεναγμός
στενάζετε	VMPA--2P	στενάζω
στενάζομεν	VIPA--1P	"
στενάζοντες	VPPANM-P	"

στενάζω 1aor. ἐστέναξα; *sigh, groan*, either inwardly or openly (MK 7.34); as discontent directed against another *complain strongly, mutter, grumble* (JA 5.9)

στενή	A--NF-S	στενός
στενῆς	A--GF-S	"

στενός, ή, όν of space *narrow*; metaphorically, of the strict requirements relating to the entrance and path to eternal life *narrow, strict, exacting* (MT 7.13)

στενοχωρεῖσθε	VIPP--2P	στενοχωρέω

στενοχωρέω literally *confine, squeeze into a narrow tight place, restrict*; figuratively and passive in the NT, as having a cramped or narrow feeling *be restricted, be severely limited* (2C 6.12); *be completely overwhelmed with difficulty* (2C 4.8)

στενοχωρία, ας, ἡ literally *narrowness, tight* or *narrow place*; figuratively, as the restrictiveness and pressures brought on by inner or outer problems *distress, difficulty, trouble*

στενοχωρία	N-NF-S	στενοχωρία
στενοχωρίαις	N-DF-P	"
στενοχωρούμενοι	VPPPNM-P	στενοχωρέω
στερεά	A--NF-S	στερεός
στερεᾶς	A--GF-S	"
στερεοί	A--NM-P	"

στερεός, ά, όν (1) *solid, firm, strong*; of a foundation *firm*; figuratively *basic* (2T 2.19); (2) of adult food *solid*, in contrast to γάλα (*milk*); figuratively, of advanced or deeper doctrine *mature* (HE 5.12, 14); (3) figuratively, of faith *steadfast, strong* (1P 5.9)

στερεός	A--NM-S	στερεός

στερεόω impf. pass. ἐστερεούμην; 1aor. ἐστερέωσα; 1aor. pass. ἐστερεώθην; *make strong, firm, hard*; literally, of physical strength *make strong, strengthen* (AC 3.16); passive *become firm* or *strong* (AC 3.7); figuratively, of firm beliefs and attitudes *be strengthened* (AC 16.5)

στερέωμα, ατος, τό strictly *solid body* or *part*, as what has been made solid or firm; hence, as a quality of faith that is strong and unchanging *stability, steadfastness, firmness* (CO 2.5)

στερέωμα	N-AN-S	στερέωμα
Στεφανᾶ	N-GM-S	Στεφανᾶς

Στεφανᾶς, ᾶ, ὁ *Stephanas*, masculine proper noun (1C 1.16)

Στεφανᾶς	N-NM-S	Στεφανᾶς
στέφανοι	N-NM-P	στέφανος
στέφανον	N-AM-S	Στέφανος
στέφανον	N-AM-S	στέφανος

Στέφανος, ου, ὁ *Stephen*, masculine proper noun (AC 6.5)

Στέφανος	N-NM-S	Στέφανος

στέφανος, ου, ὁ *crown, wreath*; (1) literally, as an adornment worn around the head, given as an award in athletic contests (1C 9.25a); metaphorically; (a) of success achieved in life viewed as a race *reward, sign of accomplishment* (understood in 1C 9.25b); (b) as a community of believers who exist as proof of a worker's success (1TH 2.19); (c) as a symbol of heavenly honor and authority (RV 4.4); (2) literally, as the symbol of authority worn by a ruler *crown*, scornfully accorded to Jesus as a crown made of thorns (MT 27.29)

στέφανος	N-NM-S	στέφανος
	N-VM-S	"

Στεφάνου	N-GM-S	Στέφανος
στεφάνους	N-AM-P	στέφανος
στεφανοῦται	VIPP--3S	στεφανόω

στεφανόω 1aor. ἐστεφάνωσα; pf. pass. ἐστεφάνωμαι; *place a wreath around, crown*; (1) literally, as rewarded to a victor in the games (2T 2.5); (2) figuratively, of the dignity and exaltation accorded to Jesus for victoriously achieving the atonement *honor, reward* (HE 2.7, 9)

Στεφάνῳ	N-DM-S	Στέφανος
στήθη	N-AN-P	στῆθος
στῆθι	VMAA--2S	ἵστημι

στῆθος, ους, τό as the front part of the upper body *breast, chest*; idiomatically, from the Mediterranean custom for guests to recline on couches around a table at a meal ἀναπίπτειν ἐπὶ τὸ σ. literally *lean back on the breast*, i.e. *dine in the place of honor* (JN 13.25)

στῆθος	N-AN-S	στῆθος
στήκει	VIPA--3S	στήκω
στήκετε	VIPA--2P	"
	VMPA--2P	"
στήκητε	VSPA--2P	"
στήκοντες	VPPANM-P	"

στήκω impf. ἔστηκον (RV 12.4); a new verb from ἔστηκα, the perfect of ἵστημι (*place, put*); (1) literally *stand* (MK 11.25); (2) figuratively; (a) as demonstrating stability *stand firm, be steadfast* (1C 16.13); (b) as gaining approval when examined *stand* (RO 14.4), opposite πίπτω (*fall*)

στῆναι	VNAA	ἵστημι

στηριγμός, οῦ, ὁ *steadfastness, perseverance, firm position*, as a state of inner stability (2P 3.17)

στηριγμοῦ	N-GM-S	στηριγμός

στηρίζω fut. στηρίξω and στηρίσω; 1aor. ἐστήριξα and ἐστήρισα; pf. pass. ἐστήριγμαι; 1aor. pass. ἐστηρίχθην; literally, as setting up something so that it remains immovable *fix (firmly), establish, support* (LU 16.26); Hebraistically *set* in a certain position or direction; αὐτὸς τὸ πρόσωπον ἐστήρισεν τοῦ πορεύεσθαι εἰς Ἰερουσαλήμ literally *he fixed his face to go to Jerusalem*, i.e. *he firmly decided to journey to Jerusalem* (LU 9.51); figuratively *strengthen, confirm, stabilize* someone (LU 22.32)

στηρίζων	VPPANM-S	στηρίζω
στηρίξαι	VNAA	"
	VOAA--3S	"
στηρίξατε	VMAA--2P	"
στηρίξει	VIFA--3S	"
στηριξον	VMAA--2S	"
στηρίσει	VIFA--3S	"
στήρισον	VMAA--2S	"
στηριχθῆναι	VNAP	"
στῆσαι	VNAA	ἵστημι
στήσαντες	VPAANM-P	"
στήσει	VIFA--3S	"
στήσεσθε	VIFM--2P	"
στήσῃ	VSAA--3S	"
στήσῃς	VSAA--2S	"
στήσητε	VSAA--2P	"
στήσονται	VIFM--3P	"
στῆτε	VMAA--2P	"
	VSAA--2P	"
στιβάδας	N-AF-P	στιβάς

στιβάς, άδος, ἡ (also στοιβάς) bed of straw, reeds, leaves, etc., litter; by metonymy, of such materials soft foliage, leafy twigs, field grasses (MK 11.8)

στίγμα, ατος, τό literally, what is pricked in or branded as a mark of ownership on the body of a soldier, servant, religious devotee, etc. mark, brand, tattoo; figuratively, probably the wounds and scars received in service and identifying a faithful servant of Jesus; idiomatically βαστάζειν στίγματα literally bear marks, i.e. endure suffering in the service of someone (GA 6.17)

στίγματα	N-AN-P	στίγμα

στιγμή, ῆς, ἡ strictly point; of time moment, instant (LU 4.5)

στιγμῇ	N-DF-S	στιγμή
στίλβοντα	VPPANN-P	στίλβω

στίλβω as an effect of radiating very bright light shine, glisten, be radiant (MK 9.3)

στοά, ᾶς, ἡ portico, porch, cloister, a covered colonnade attached to a building, for walking and standing about

στοᾷ	N-DF-S	στοά
στοαῖς	N-DF-P	"
στοάς	N-AF-P	"
Στογυλίῳ	N-DN-S	Τρωγύλλιον
στοιβάδας	N-AF-P	στιβάδας

Στοϊκός, ή, όν (also Στωϊκός) Stoic, pertaining to Stoic philosophy (AC 17.18)

Στοϊκῶν	A--GM-P	Στοϊκός
στοιχεῖα	N-AN-P	στοιχεῖον
	N-NN-P	"
στοιχεῖν	VNPA	στοιχέω

στοιχεῖον, ου, τό strictly small upright post; hence first beginning, element or principle; only plural in the NT; (1) generally, the rudimentary elements of anything, what belongs to a basic series in any field of knowledge; in grammar, the ABCs; in speech, basic sounds; in physics, the four basic elements (earth, air, fire, water); in geometry, the axioms; in philosophy, the givens; (2) as used in the NT; (a) as a religious technical term elementary doctrines, fundamental teachings, basic principles (HE 5.12; perhaps CO 2.8, 20 and GA 4.3, 9); (b) in a negative sense, humanistic teachings common to Jewish and pagan religions, involving binding traditions, taboos, prohibitions, ordinances, ceremonies, etc., teachings involving either supernatural elemental or animating spirits (probably CO 2.8, 20), or basic material elements (probably GA 4.3, 9) elements, elemental things; (c) in relation to the natural world (basic) elements, natural substances (2P 3.10, 12)

στοιχεῖς	VIPA--2S	στοιχέω
στοιχείων	N-GN-P	στοιχεῖον

στοιχέω fut. στοιχήσω; strictly be drawn up or advance in line, belong in the ranks; figuratively in the NT be in harmony or agreement with someone or something, hold to, live in conformity with (GA 5.25); idiomatically στοιχεῖν τοῖς ἴχνεσίν τινος literally walk in someone's steps, i.e. imitate (RO 4.12)

στοιχήσουσι(ν)	VIFA-3P	στοιχέω
στοιχήσωσι(ν)	VSAA-3P	"
στοιχοῦσι(ν)	VIPA-3P	"
	VPPADM-P	"
στοιχῶμεν	VSPA--1P	"

στολαί	N-NF-P	στολή
στολαῖς	N-DF-P	"
στολάς	N-AF-P	"

στολή, ῆς, ἡ equipping, fitting out; by metonymy dress, clothes; in the NT robe, especially long flowing garment or robe worn as an upper or outer garment

στολή	N-NF-S	στολή
στολήν	N-AF-S	"

στόμα, ατος, τό (1) as the bodily organ for eating and speaking mouth, jaws (MT 15.11); (2) by synecdoche, of someone speaking person, individual (MT 12.34); idiomatically σ. πρὸς σ. literally mouth to mouth, i.e. person to person (2J 12); (3) by metonymy, for what the mouth utters word, speech (MT 18.16); Hebraistically ἀνοίγειν τὸ σ. open the mouth, begin to speak (MT 13.35); idiomatically ἐν ἑνὶ στόματι literally with one mouth, i.e. with one voice, in unison (RO 15.6); (4) figuratively, of a sword edge (LU 21.24); of the earth large fissure (RV 12.16)

στόμα	N-AN-S	στόμα
	N-NN-S	"
στόματα	N-AN-P	"
στόματι	N-DN-S	"
στόματος	N-GN-S	"
στομάτων	N-GN-P	"
στόμαχον	N-AM-S	στόμαχος

στόμαχος, ου, ὁ as the bodily organ for digestion stomach (1T 5.23)

στρατεία, ας, ἡ literally, as the activity of an army campaign, expedition; metaphorically resistance against evil, spiritual warfare (2C 10.4), struggle, fight (1T 1.18)

στρατείαν	N-AF-S	στρατεία
στρατείας	N-GF-S	"
στρατεύεται	VIPM--3S	στρατεύω
στρατεύῃ	VSPM--2S	"

στράτευμα, ατος, τό army (MT 22.7); as a smaller detachment of soldiers corps, band of soldiers, armed force (AC 23.10); plural troops, guards, bodyguard (LU 23.11)

στράτευμα	N-AN-S	στράτευμα
στρατεύμασι(ν)	N-DN-P	"
στρατεύματα	N-AN-P	"
	N-NN-P	"
στρατεύματι	N-DN-S	"
στρατεύματος	N-GN-S	"
στρατευμάτων	N-GN-P	"
στρατευόμεθα	VIPM--1P	στρατεύω
στρατευόμενοι	VPPMNM-P	"
στρατευόμενος	VPPMNM-S	"
στρατευομένων	VPPMGF-P	"
στρατεύονται	VIPM--3P	"
στρατεύσῃ	VSAA--2S	"

στρατεύω 1aor. mid. ἐστρατευσάμην; only middle in the NT; (1) literally perform military service, serve as a soldier, go to fight (1C 9.7); (2) metaphorically, of intensified spiritual warfare brought about by the presence of evil; (a) positively, of a Christian worker resist evil, struggle against evil forces (2C 10.3; 1T 1.18); (b) negatively, as depicting the effect of worldly lusts and pleasures on a life cause conflict, oppose spiritual welfare (1P 2.11)

στρατηγοί	N-NM-P	στρατηγός

357

στρατηγοῖς N-DM-P "

στρατηγός, οῦ, ὁ *military leader*, with the title translated according to the context; (1) over the temple precincts *captain* (LU 22.4); (2) over a Roman colony *(chief) magistrate, (high) official, (military) governor* (AC 16.20)

στρατηγός N-NM-S στρατηγός
στρατηγούς N-AM-P "

στρατιά, ᾶς, ἡ *army, host*; in a nonmilitary sense of angels *multitude, throng* (LU 2.13); of heavenly bodies, as the stars, etc. that were worshiped as symbols of celestial powers *supernatural spirit-beings* (AC 7.42)

στρατιᾷ N-DF-S στρατιά
στρατιᾶς N-GF-S "
στρατιῶται N-NM-P στρατιώτης
στρατιώταις N-DM-P "
στρατιώτας N-AM-P "
στρατιώτῃ N-DM-S "
στρατιώτην N-AM-S "

στρατιώτης, ου, ὁ literally *soldier, legionary* (MT 8.9); figuratively, of one serving Christ in the warfare against evil (2T 2.3)

στρατιώτης N-NM-S στρατιώτης
στρατιωτῶν N-GM-P "

στρατολογέω 1aor. ἐστρατολόγησα; *enlist (soldiers)* for military service, *gather an army* (2T 2.4)

στρατολογήσαντι VPAADM-S στρατολογέω
στρατοπεδάρχῃ N-DM-S στρατοπεδάρχης

στρατοπεδάρχης, ου, ὁ *camp commander*; the *commander of the Pretorian guards* at Rome, troops attached to an emperor or high-ranking magistrate (AC 28.16)

στρατοπέδαρχος, ου, ὁ *military commander, commanding officer of a (Roman) camp* (AC 28.16)

στρατοπεδάρχῳ N-DM-S στρατοπέδαρχος

στρατόπεδον, ου, τό from στρατός (*army*) and πέδον (*ground, plain*); as a military technical term *campsite, encampment, camp*; by metonymy *army, legion* (LU 21.20)

στρατοπέδων N-GN-P στρατόπεδον
στραφείς VPAPNM-S στρέφω
στραφεῖσα VPAPNF-S "
στραφέντες VPAPNM-P "
στραφῆτε VSAP--2P "
στραφῶσι(ν) VSAP--3P "
στρεβλοῦσι(ν) VIPA--3P στρεβλόω

στρεβλόω strictly *twist* or *wrench* limbs on an instrument for torturing people called a rack; hence *torture, torment*; figuratively *distort, twist, misinterpret* words to a false meaning (2P 3.16)

στρεβλώσουσι(ν) VIFA--3P στρεβλόω
στρέφειν VNPA στρέφω
στρεφόμεθα VIPP--1P "

στρέφω 1aor. ἔστρεψα; 2aor. pass. ἐστράφην; (1) active transitively; (a) *turn something toward* someone (MT 5.39); (b) as making a change of substance *turn, change* something into something (RV 11.6); (c) *return* something to someone, *take back to* (MT 27.3); (2) passive with a reflexive meaning; (a) *turn around, turn toward* (MT 7.6; LU 7.9); (b) figuratively, of establishing a relation with someone *begin to relate to, turn to* (AC 13.46); *turn back to* (AC 7.39); (c) *turn* or *change inwardly, change one's ways, be converted* (MT 18.3)

στρέψον VMAA--2S στρέφω
στρηνιάσαντες VPAANM-P στρηνιάω

στρηνιάω 1aor. ἐστρηνίασα; *live sensually* or *luxuriously, indulge, revel* (RV 18.3)

στρῆνος, ους, τό *luxury, sensuality*, a way of life characterized by headstrong pride

στρήνους N-GN-S στρῆνος
Στρογγυλίῳ N-DN-S Τρωγύλλιον
στρουθία N-NN-P στρουθίον

στρουθίον, ου, τό diminutive of στρουθός (*sparrow*); *little bird*; more specifically *sparrow*

στρουθίων N-GN-P στρουθίον

στρωννύω or **στρώννυμι** impf. ἐστρώννυον; 1aor. ἔστρωσα; pf. pass. ἔστρωμαι; *spread out, disperse by scattering* (MT 21.8); as preparing a bed or couch either before or after use *make up, spread* (AC 9.34); passive, of a supper room *be spread with couches, be furnished* (MK 14.15)

στρῶσον VMAA--2S στρωννύω
στυγητοί A--NM-P στυγητός

στυγητός, ή, όν *hated, hateful, detestable* (TI 3.3)

στυγνάζω 1aor. ἐστύγνασα; (1) *be appalled* or *shocked* (perhaps MK 10.22); (2) *be* or *become gloomy* or *dark*; as a facial expression *be downcast* (perhaps MK 10.22); of a cloud-covered sky *be overcast* or *threatening* (MT 16.3)

στυγνάζων VPPANM-S στυγνάζω
στυγνάσας VPAANM-S "
στῦλοι N-NM-P στῦλος
στῦλον N-AM-S "

στῦλος, ου, ὁ literally *pillar, column* (RV 10.1); metaphorically, of an authoritative *leader* in the community, *very important person* (GA 2.9); of the church, as upholding true doctrine *pillar*, i.e. *support* (1T 3.15)

στῦλος N-NM-S στῦλος
Στωϊκῶν A--GM-P Στοϊκός

σύ second-person personal pronoun σοῦ (σου), σοί (σοι), σέ (σε); plural ὑμεῖς, ὑμῶν, ὑμῖν, ὑμᾶς; *you*; (1) in the nominative case; (a) denoting contrast to another (MT 3.14); (b) emphasizing the subject (MK 14.30); (c) emphasizing a vocative noun (MT 2.6); (2) in oblique cases: accented forms denote contrast or emphasis (LU 2.35); after prepositions, the accented form appears without special emphasis (e.g. ἐν σοί *in you* MT 6.23)

σύ NPN-2S σύ

συγγένεια, ας, ἡ *(blood) relationship, kinship*; concretely *kindred, relatives, family* (LU 1.61)

συγγενείᾳ N-DF-S συγγένεια
συγγένειαν N-AF-S "
συγγενείας N-GF-S "
συγγενεῖς AP-AM-P συγγενής
           AP-NM-P "
συγγενέσι(ν) AP-DM-P "
συγγενεῦσι(ν) AP-DM-P "
συγγενή AP-AM-S "
συγγενῆν AP-AM-S see συγγενή

συγγενής, ές (also **συγγενεύς**) (1) literally *of common origin, related (by blood), akin to*; substantively in the NT *relative* (JN 18.26); plural οἱ συγγενεῖς *relatives, kinsfolk* (LU 1.58); (2) in a broader sense of the same race or people *fellow countryman, fellow citizen* (RO 9.3;

probably 16.21); (3) passive, of close relationship in Christ *close companion, intimate friend, (spiritual) kinsman* (perhaps RO 16.21)

συγγενής	AP-NM-S	συγγενής

συγγενίς, ίδος, ἡ *kinswoman, (female) relative* (LU 1.36)

συγγενίς	N-NF-S	συγγενίς
συγγενῶν	AP-GM-P	συγγενίς

συγγνώμη, ης, ἡ (also **συνγνώμη**) strictly *agreement to meet* someone *halfway*; hence *concession, permission, allowance* (1C 7.6)

συγγνώμην	N-AF-S	συγγνώμη

συγκάθημαι (and **συνκάθημαι**) *sit down with* someone, *sit in company with*

συγκαθήμενοι	VPPDNM-P	συγκάθημαι
	VPPONM-P	"
συγκαθήμενος	VPPDNM-S	"
	VPPONM-S	"

συγκαθίζω (or **συνκαθίζω**) 1aor. συνεκάθισα; (1) transitively *cause to sit down with, seat together with* (EP 2.6); (2) intransitively *sit down together with* (LU 22.55)

συγκαθισάντων	VPAAGM-P	συγκαθίζω

συγκακοπαθέω (or **συνκακοπαθέω**) 1aor. συνεκακοπάθησα; *undergo affliction* or *hardship along with* someone, *suffer together with, join in suffering*

συγκακοπάθησον	VMAA--2S	συγκακοπαθέω
συγκακουχεῖσθαι	VNPD	συγκακουχέομαι
	VNPO	"

συγκακουχέομαι (and **συνκακουχέομαι**) *suffer* or *be mistreated along with* someone, *share ill treatment, endure trouble with* (HE 11.25)

συγκαλεῖ	VIPA--3S	συγκαλέω
συγκαλεῖται	VIPM--3S	"
συγκαλεσάμενοι	VPAMNM-P	"
συγκαλεσάμενος	VPAMNM-S	"
συγκαλέσασθαι	VNAM	"

συγκαλέω (and **συνκαλέω**) 2aor. συνεκάλεσα, mid. συνεκαλεσάμην; (1) active *call together* (MK 15.16); (2) middle *call to one's side, call to oneself, summon* (LU 9.1)

συγκαλοῦσι(ν)	VIPA--3P	συγκαλέω

συγκαλύπτω (and **συνκαλύπτω**) pf. pass. συγκεκάλυμμαι; *cover up (completely), conceal* (LU 12.2)

συγκάμπτω (or **συνκάμπτω**) 1aor. συνέκαμψα; *cause to bend down*; idiomatically τὸν νῶτόν τινος συγκάμπτειν literally *bend someone's back* in bondage, i.e. *overwhelm someone with trouble, cause great difficulty for someone* (RO 11.10)

σύγκαμψον	VMAA--2S	συγκάμπτω

συγκαταβαίνω (or **συνκαταβαίνω**) 2aor. συγκατέβην; geographically, as going from a higher to a lower place or altitude *go* or *come down with* someone (AC 25.5)

συγκαταβάντες	VPAANM-P	συγκαταβαίνω

συγκατάθεσις, εως, ἡ (also **συνκατάθεσις**) *mutual agreement, harmony*, arrived at by a group decision, as when there is a deposit of votes (2C 6.16)

συγκατάθεσις	N-NF-S	συγκατάθεσις
συγκατανεύσαντος	VPAAGM-S	συγκατανεύω

συγκατανεύω (or **συνκατανεύω**) 1aor. συγκατένευσα; *agree, consent* (AC 18.27)

συγκατατεθειμένος	VPRDNM-S	συγκατατίθεμαι
	VPRONM-S	"

συγκατατίθεμαι (and **συνκατατίθεμαι**) pf. συγκατατέθειμαι; strictly, from a custom of putting something into a pot as a vote *deposit one's vote in the same urn as* another; hence *consent to, agree with* (LU 23.51)

συγκατατιθέμενος	VPPDNM-S	συγκατατίθεμαι
	VPPONM-S	"
συγκατατιθεμένων	VPPDGM-P	"
	VPPOGM-P	"

συγκαταψηφίζομαι (or **συνκαταψηφίζομαι**) 1aor. pass. συγκατεψηφίσθην; *choose (by a vote) together with, (officially) give a place along with, count with* (AC 1.26)

συγκατεψηφίσθη	VIAP--3S	συγκαταψηφίζομαι

σύγκειμαι *recline together* (MT 9.10)

συγκεκαλυμμένον	VPRPNN-S	συγκαλύπτω
συγκεκεραμένους	VPRPAM-P	συγκεράννυμι
συγκεκεραμμένοι	VPRPNM-P	"
συγκεκερασμένος	VPRPNM-S	"
συγκεκερασμένους	VPRPAM-P	"
συγκεκλησμένοι	VPRPNM-P	συγκλείω
συγκεκραμένος	VPRPNM-S	συγκεράννυμι
συγκεκραμένους	VPRPAM-P	"

συγκεράννυμι (or **συνκεράννυμι**) 1aor. συνεκέρασα; pf. pass. συγκεκέρασμαι or συγκεκέραμαι (HE 4.2) or συγκεκέραμμαι (HE 4.2); (1) active *mix* or *mingle together, blend, unite*; figuratively, of unifying a group into one body *compose, put together, combine* (1C 12.24); (2) figuratively and passive *be united with*; a great variety of manuscript readings in HE 4.2 point toward two general possible meanings: λόγος . . . μὴ συγκεκερασμένος *the message was not mingled with faith in the hearers* and μὴ συγκεκερασμένους *those people were not united with those who heard in faith*; the former is more suitable to the context

συγκεχυμένη	VPRPNF-S	συγχέω
συγκέχυται	VIRP--3S	"

συγκινέω (or **συνκινέω**) 1aor. συνεκίνησα; *incite, put into a commotion, stir up* (people) (AC 6.12)

συγκλειόμενοι	VPPPNM-P	συγκλείω

συγκλείω (and **συνκλείω**) 1aor. συνέκλεισα; literally *encircle, enclose*, as fish in a net (LU 5.6); figuratively *restrict, cause to happen* within imposed restrictions, *confine*, used of the compelling force of God's will in working out the issues of his grace and mercy (RO 11.32)

συγκληρονόμα	A--AN-P	συγκληρονόμος
συγκληρονόμοι	AP-NM-P	"
συγκληρονόμοις	AP-DM-P	"

συγκληρονόμος, ον (also **συνκληρονόμος**) of receiving possessions along with another *inheriting together with*; metaphorically, of the Christian expectation in relation to Christ; substantivally *fellow heir with, joint heir, fellow receiver*, followed by the genitive of person one inherits with

συγκληρονόμος	AP-NM-S	συγκληρονόμος
συγκληρονόμους	AP-AM-P	"
συγκληρονόμῳ	AP-DM-S	"
συγκληρονόμων	AP-GM-P	"
συγκοινωνεῖτε	VMPA--2P	συγκοινωνέω

συγκοινωνέω (and **συνκοινωνέω**) 1aor. συνεκοινώνησα; *share together in, associate with, participate with in* something (EP 5.11); with a sympathetic attitude *share with* (PH 4.14)

συγκοινωνήσαντες   VPAANM-P   συγκοινωνέω

συγκοινωνήσητε   VSAA--2P   "

συγκοινωνός, οῦ, ὁ (also **συνκοινωνός**) as one who takes part in something along with another *fellow participant, partner*

συγκοινωνός   N-NM-S   συγκοινωνός

συγκοινωνούς   N-AM-P   "

συγκομίζω (or **συνκομίζω**) 1aor. συνεκόμισα; literally, of harvest sheaves *bring in, collect* to the threshing floor or barn; figuratively and euphemistically, of burial *help to prepare for burial, arrange to bury* (AC 8.2)

συγκρίναι   VNAA   συγκρίνω

συγκρίνοντες   VPPANM-P   "

συγκρίνω (and **συνκρίνω**) 1aor. συνέκρινα; (1) of things brought together for explanation *interpret, explain, combine* (1C 2.13); (2) of persons *set together for comparison, compare* (2C 10.12)

συγκύπτουσα   VPPANF-S   συγκύπτω

συγκύπτω (and **συνκύπτω**) of a disabled person *be bent over, be doubled up* (LU 13.11)

συγκυρία, ας, ἡ *coincidence, chance*; κατὰ συγκυρίαν *by coincidence, by chance, accidentally* (LU 10.31)

συγκυρίαν   N-AF-S   συγκυρία

συγχαίρει   VIPA--3S   συγχαίρω

συγχαίρετε   VMPA--2P   "

συγχαίρω (and **συνχαίρω**) impf. συνέχαιρον; 2aor. pass. συνεχάρην; of persons *rejoice with, share joy with* (LU 15.6; probably LU 1.58 and PH 2.17, 18); *congratulate* (perhaps LU 1.58 and PH 2.17, 18)

συγχαίρω   VIPA--1S   συγχαίρω

συγχάρητε   VMAO--2P   "

συγχέω and **συγχύννω** (and **συνχέω, συνχύννω, συνχύνω**) impf. συνέχεον (AC 21.27) and συνέχυννον; pf. pass. συγκέχυμαι; 1aor. pass. συνεχύθην; literally *pour together, mingle*; figuratively in the NT *confuse, stir up, cause dismay* (AC 21.27); passive *be amazed, be bewildered, be confused* (AC 2.6)

συγχράομαι *have dealings with, associate with* in a friendly way (JN 4.9)

συγχρῶνται   VIPD--3P   συγχράομαι

      VIPO--3P

συγχύνεται   VIPP--3S   συγχέω

συγχύννεται   VIPP--3S   "

συγχύσεως   N-GF-S   σύγχυσις

σύγχυσις, εως, ἡ of disorderly mob reaction *confusion, tumult, uproar* (AC 19.29)

συγχωρέω 1aor. mid. imperative συγχωρῆσαι; *grant to, permit* someone (AC 21.39)

συγχωρῆσαι   VNAA   συγχωρέω

συζάω (and **συνζάω**) fut. συζήσω; 1aor. ἐσύζησα; *live together with*; figuratively *have a permanent place in one's affections* (2C 7.3); of identification with the resurrected and exalted Christ *be alive together with, live with* (RO 6.8)

συζεύγνυμι 1aor. συνέζευξα; literally *yoke together, pair together*; figuratively *join together, unite*, especially in marriage

συζῆν   VNPA   συζάω

συζήσομεν   VIFA--1P   "

συζήσωμεν   VSAA--1P   "

συζητεῖν   VNPA   συζητέω

συζητεῖτε   VIPA--2P   "

συζητέω (and **συνζητέω**) impf. συνεζήτουν; (1) *inquire together, discuss, question* (MK 9.10); (2) in a negative sense *dispute, debate, argue with* (AC 6.9)

συζητήσεως   N-GF-S   συζήτησις

συζήτησιν   N-AF-S   "

συζήτησις, εως, ἡ as forceful expressions of differences of opinion *heated discussion, debate, dispute* (AC 28.29)

συζητητής, οῦ, ὁ (also **συνζητητής**) strictly *one who investigates with*; hence, as one skilled in arguing *disputer, disputant, debater* (1C 1.20)

συζητητής   N-NM-S   συζητητής

συζητοῦντας   VPPAAM-P   συζητέω

συζητοῦντες   VPPANM-P   "

συζητούντων   VPPAGM-P   "

σύζυγε   AP-VM-S   σύζυγος

σύζυγος, ον (also **σύνζυγος**) literally *yoked together*; figuratively and substantivally in PH 4.3 γνήσιε σύζυγε *genuine fellow worker, true comrade*; some see a proper noun *Syzygus* here, but the adjectival qualifier makes this unlikely

συζωοποιέω 1aor. συνεζωοποίησα; figuratively, as a religious technical term, of an effect of union with Christ *make alive together with, cause to live together with* (EP 2.5; CO 2.13)

σῦκα   N-AN-P   σῦκον

συκάμινος, ου, ἡ *sycamine, mulberry*, a black mulberry tree with a strong root system (LU 17.6)

συκαμίνῳ   N-DF-S   συκάμινος

συκῆ, ῆς, ἡ *fig tree*

συκῆ   N-NF-S   συκῆ

συκῇ   N-DF-S   "

συκῆν   N-AF-S   "

συκῆς   N-GF-S   "

συκομοραίαν   N-AF-S   see συκομωραίαν

συκομορέα, ας, ἡ (also **συκομωραία**) *sycamore fig, fig mulberry*, a tree with strong and spreading branches; probably so-called because the leaves resemble those of the mulberry and its fruit resembles figs (LU 19.4)

συκομορέαν   N-AF-S   συκομορέα

συκομωραίαν   N-AF-S   "

συκομωρέαν   N-AF-S   see συκομορέαν

σῦκον, ου, τό as the fruit of the fig tree *fig*, especially *late* or *ripe fig*

συκοφαντέω 1aor. ἐσυκοφάντησα; from an Athenian term for an informer against illegal exporters of figs; (1) *accuse falsely, bring false charges, blackmail*; more generally *harass, oppress* (LU 3.14); (2) as exacting money by using false information *extort, defraud, cheat* (LU 19.8)

συκοφαντήσητε   VSAA--2P   συκοφαντέω

συκωμοραίαν   N-AF-S   see συκομωραίαν

σύκων   N-GN-P   σῦκον

συλαγωγέω literally *carry off (as) booty* or *captive*; *rob*; figuratively, of victimizing or brainwashing someone with religious error or false teaching *take control of, lead astray, prey on* someone spiritually (CO 2.8)

συλαγωγῶν   VPPANM-S   συλαγωγέω

συλάω   1aor. ἐσύλησα; as taking money without earning it *rob, encroach on*; figuratively and exaggerated for effect, of Paul's feeling about accepting support from one church while ministering in another *rob* (2C 11.8)

συλλαβεῖν	VNAA	συλλαμβάνω
συλλαβέσθαι	VNAM	"
συλλαβόμενοι	VPAMNM-P	"
συλλαβόντες	VPAANM-P	"
συλλαβοῦσα	VPAANF-S	"
συλλαβοῦσι(ν)	VPAADM-P	"

συλλαλέω (and συνλαλέω)   impf. συνελάλουν; 1aor. συνελάλησα; *talk, converse, discuss with*

συλλαλήσαντες	VPAANM-P	συλλαλέω
συλλαλήσας	VPAANM-S	"
συλλαλοῦντες	VPPANM-P	"
συλλαμβάνου	VMPM--2S	συλλαμβάνω

συλλαμβάνω   fut. mid. συλλήμψομαι; 2aor. συνέλαβον, mid. συνελαβόμην; pf. συνείληφα; 1aor. pass. συνελήμφθην; (1) active (as well as future middle); (a) as taking prisoners into custody *seize, arrest* (MT 26.55); (b) as taking animals or fish *catch* (LU 5.9); (c) sexually, of conception *conceive, be* or *become pregnant* (LU 1.24); metaphorically, of the union of a desire (lust) with the will that results in a sinful act *conceive* (JA 1.15); (2) middle; (a) *seize, arrest* (AC 26.21); (b) *help, assist, come to the aid of* (LU 5.7)

συλλέγεται	VIPP--3S	συλλέγω
συλλέγετε	VMPA--2S	"
συλλέγοντες	VPPANM-P	"
συλλέγουσι(ν)	VIPA--3P	"

συλλέγω   fut. συλλέξω; 1aor. συνέλεξα; *gather (in), collect*; of fruit *pick* (MT 7.16); of weeds *pull out* or *up* (MT 13.28)

συλλέξατε	VMAA--2P	συλλέγω
συλλέξουσι(ν)	VIFA--3P	"
συλλέξωμεν	VSAA--1P	"
συλλημφθέντα	VPAPAM-S	συλλαμβάνω
συλλημφθῆναι	VNAP	"
συλλήμψῃ	VIFD--2S	"
συλληφθέντα	VPAPAM-S	"
συλληφθῆναι	VNAP	"
συλλήψῃ	VIFD--2S	"

συλλογίζομαι   1aor. συνελογισάμην; as thinking and talking over something with someone else *debate, reason, discuss* (LU 20.5)

συλλυπέω   *grieve* or *hurt with* or *at the same time*; passive *be (deeply) grieved with* someone, *be disturbed, feel distressed* (MK 3.5)

συλλυπούμενος	VPPPNM-S	συλλυπέω
συμβαίνειν	VNPA	συμβαίνω
συμβαίνοντος	VPPAGN-S	"

συμβαίνω   impf. συνέβαινον; 2aor. συνέβην; pf. συμβέβηκα; of circumstances coming together to form an event *come about, turn out, happen*

συμβαλεῖν	VNAA	συμβάλλω
συμβάλλειν	VNPA	"
συμβάλλουσα	VPPANF-S	"

συμβάλλω   impf. συνέβαλλον; 2aor. συνέβαλον; strictly *throw together*; (1) active; (a) transitively; (i) with λόγους (*words*) understood *confer, consult* (AC 4.15); (ii) con-

sider, ponder, think about seriously (LU 2.19); (iii) *quarrel, dispute* (AC 17.18); (b) intransitively *meet, fall in with* (AC 20.14); in a hostile sense *meet in battle, wage war with, fight* (LU 14.31); (2) middle *help, give assistance to, contribute to* (AC 18.27)

συμβάντων	VPAAGM-P	συμβαίνω
συμβασιλεύσομεν	VIFA--1P	συμβασιλεύω
συμβασιλεύσωμεν	VSAA--1P	"

συμβασιλεύω   fut. συμβασιλεύσω; 1aor. συνεβασίλευσα; as a religious technical term, of participating with Christ in his future kingdom *rule* or *reign together with* (2T 2.12); ironically in 1C 4.8 *become king, ascend the throne*

συμβέβηκε(ν)	VIRA--3S	συμβαίνω
συμβεβηκότι	VPRADN-S	"
συμβεβηκότων	VPRAGN-P	"
συμβιβαζόμενον	VPPPNN-S	συμβιβάζω
συμβιβάζοντες	VPPANM-P	"

συμβιβάζω   fut. συμβιβάσω; 1aor. συνεβίβασα; 1aor. pass. συνεβιβάσθην; strictly *cause to stand together*; hence (1) *unite, bring together*; (a) literally and passive, of the physical body *be held together, be united* (EP 4.16); (b) figuratively, of the church as the body of Christ *be united together, be joined* (CO 2.2, 19); (2) intellectually; (a) *prove conclusively, demonstrate* (AC 9.22); (b) *conclude, infer* (AC 16.10); (c) *instruct, inform, advise* (1C 2.16); as a Semitism in AC 19.33 ἐκ τοῦ ὄχλου συνεβίβασαν Ἀλέξανδρον *some of the crowd advised/informed Alexander* (what to say, i.e. that the trouble was about the Christian "way," not Judaism; cf. 19.23)

συμβιβάζων	VPPANM-S	συμβιβάζω
συμβιβάσει	VIFA--3S	"
συμβιβασθέντες	VPAPNM-P	"
συμβιβασθέντων	VPAPGM-P	"
συμβιβασθῶσι(ν)	VSAP--3P	"
συμβουλεύσας	VPAANM-S	συμβουλεύω

συμβουλεύω   1aor. συνεβούλευσα; (1) active *advise, counsel, give advice* (JN 18.14); (2) middle *consult, consider*; in a negative sense *plot, plan against* (MT 26.4)

συμβουλεύω	VIPA--1S	συμβουλεύω

συμβούλιον, ου, τό   what is related to consultation; (1) as its result *plan, purpose*; as a Latinism σ. λαμβάνειν *form a plan*; in a negative sense *plot* (MT 22.15); σ. διδόναι and σ. ποιεῖν *take counsel, hold a consultation* (MK 3.6); σ. ἑτοιμάζειν *reach a decision* (MK 15.1); (2) as an assembly of councilors *council* (AC 25.12)

συμβούλιον	N-AN-S	συμβούλιον
συμβουλίου	N-GN-S	"

σύμβουλος, ου, ὁ   *counselor, adviser* (RO 11.34)

σύμβουλος	N-NM-S	σύμβουλος

Συμεών, ὁ   indeclinable; *Simeon, Symeon*, masculine proper noun

συμμαθηταῖς	N-DM-P	συμμαθητής

συμμαθητής, οῦ, ὁ   *fellow disciple* (JN 11.16)

συμμαρτυρεῖ	VIPA--3S	συμμαρτυρέω

συμμαρτυρέω   as not making a totally authoritative assertion but as giving confirmation *testify* or *bear witness with, add testimony in support* (RO 8.16); more generally *confirm, agree with* (RO 2.15)

συμμαρτυροῦμαι	VIPM--1S	συμμαρτυρέω
συμμαρτυροῦντος	VPPAGM-S	"

361

συμμαρτυρούσης VPPAGF-S "
συμμερίζονται VIPM--3P συμμερίζω
συμμερίζω only middle in the NT *divide up with, share with, partake with* (1C 9.13)
συμμέτοχα A--AN-P συμμέτοχος
συμμέτοχοι AP-NM-P "
 A--NM-P "
συμμέτοχος, ον *partaking in jointly, casting one's lot with, sharing with*; substantivally ὁ σ. *partner, sharer* (EP 5.7)
συμμιμηταί N-NM-P συμμιμητής
συμμιμητής, οῦ, ὁ *fellow imitator*; συμμιμηταί μου γίνεσθε *join (with others) in following me as an example* (PH 3.17)
συμμορφιζόμενος VPPPNM-S συμμορφίζω
συμμορφίζω *conform to the same form*; passive in the NT, only of relationship to Christ *be made to conform to, become like*, denoting an inward similarity of attitudes and character (PH 3.10)
σύμμορφον A--AN-S σύμμορφος
σύμμορφος, ον of similarity of form or nature *having the same form as, conformed to, similar in form* or *nature* (RO 8.29)
συμμορφούμενος VPPPNM-S συμμορφόω
συμμόρφους A--AM-P σύμμορφος
συμμορφόω *give the same form*; passive *be conformed to, take on the same form* (PH 3.10)
συμπαθεῖς A--NM-P συμπαθής
συμπαθέω 1aor. συνεπάθησα; as showing a disposition to help because of fellow feeling *feel sympathy for, be compassionate toward*
συμπαθής, ές *sympathetic, compassionate, sharing the same feelings with* another (1P 3.8)
συμπαθῆσαι VNAA συμπαθέω
συμπαραγενόμενοι VPADNM-P συμπαραγίνομαι
συμπαραγίνομαι (or **συνπαραγίνομαι**) 2aor. συμπαρεγενόμην; (1) *come* or *arrive together, convene, gather together* (LU 23.48); (2) *come to the aid of* someone (2T 4.16)
συμπαρακαλέω (or **συνπαρακαλέω**) 1aor. pass. συμπαρεκλήθην; *encourage together*; only passive in the NT *share in mutual encouragement, be mutually encouraged, be comforted together* (RO 1.12)
συμπαρακληθῆναι VNAP συμπαρακαλέω
συμπαραλαβεῖν VNAA συμπαραλαμβάνω
συμπαραλαβόντες VPAANM-P "
συμπαραλαβών VPAANM-S "
συμπαραλαμβάνειν VNPA "
συμπαραλαμβάνω (and **συνπαραλαμβάνω**) 2aor. συμπαρέλαβον; *bring* someone *along, take as a companion* (GA 2.1)
συμπαραμένω fut. συμπαραμενῶ; *stay with* someone *to help, stay among* (PH 1.25)
συμπαραμενῶ VIFA--1S συμπαραμένω
συμπαρεγένετο VIAD--3S συμπαραγίνομαι
συμπάρειμι (and **συνπάρειμι**) *be present with* someone, *be with* (AC 25.24)
συμπαρόντες VPPAVM-P συμπάρειμι
συμπάσχει VIPA--3S συμπάσχω
συμπάσχομεν VIPA--1P "
συμπάσχω (and **συνπάσχω**) (1) *suffer with, share the same kind of sufferings* (RO 8.17); (2) of the physical body

in relation to its members *be involved in suffering, suffer along with* (1C 12.26)
συμπέμπω 1aor. συνέπεμψα; *send along with, send at the same time*
συμπεριεχόντων VPPAGM-P συμπεριέχω
συμπεριέχω *surround, stand around together* (LU 12.1)
συμπεριλαβών VPAANM-S συμπεριλαμβάνω
συμπεριλαμβάνω 2aor. συμπεριέλαβον; *embrace, throw one's arms around* someone (AC 20.10)
συμπίνω 2aor. συνέπιον; *drink with* someone (AC 10.41)
συμπίπτω 2aor. συνέπεσον; *fall in (ruins), collapse into a heap* (LU 6.49)
συμπληροῦσθαι VNPP συμπληρόω
συμπληρόω impf. pass. συνεπληρούμην; only passive in the NT *fill completely, fill up*; (1) literally, as a nautical technical term, of a ship in heavy waves *be filled with water, be swamped* (LU 8.23); (2) figuratively, of a span of time in God's planning *be fulfilled, come to an end* (LU 9.51)
συμπνίγει VIPA--3S συμπνίγω
συμπνίγειν VNPA "
συμπνίγονται VIPP--3P "
συμπνίγουσι(ν) VIPA--3P "
συμπνίγω (and **συνπνίγω**) impf. συνέπνιγον; 1aor. συνέπνιξα; *choke, throttle*; literally, of weeds too thickly surrounding plants *choke, cause to die*; metaphorically, of things causing a message to be ineffective in a life *crowd out*, i.e. *overwhelm, take over* (MK 4.19); exaggerated for effect, of a thronging crowd *suffocate, almost crush, crowd in around* (LU 8.42)
συμπολῖται N-NM-P συμπολίτης
συμπολίτης, ου, ὁ *fellow citizen*; figuratively and plural, as Gentiles who become Christians and are thus in the kingdom of God (EP 2.19)
συμπορεύομαι impf. συνεπορευόμην; (1) *go along with, accompany* (LU 7.11); (2) of a crowd *come together to* someone, *gather around* (MK 10.1)
συμπορεύονται VIPD--3P συμπορεύομαι
 VIPO--3P "
συμπόσια N-AN-P συμπόσιον
συμποσία, ας, ἡ *common meal, eating together* (MK 6.39)
συμποσίαν N-AF-S συμποσία
συμπόσιον, ου, τό strictly *drinking together, banquet*; by metonymy *festive company*; συμπόσια συμπόσια *in groups, in parties, in companies* (MK 6.39)
συμπρεσβύτερος, ου, ὁ *fellow elder, elder along with others*, as church leaders possessing authority and dignity in common (1P 5.1)
συμπρεσβύτερος N-NM-S συμπρεσβύτερος
συμφέρει VIPA--3S συμφέρω
συμφέρομεν VIPA--1P "
συμφέρον VPPAAN-S "
 VPPANN-S "
συμφερόντων VPPAGN-P "
συμφέρω 1aor. συνήνεγκα; (1) transitively *bring together, gather, collect* (AC 19.19); (2) intransitively; (a) *be of use, be profitable* or *advantageous* (1C 6.12); (b) impersonally, with the dative followed by a ἵνα clause or an infinitive *it is better, advantageous* (MT 5.29; 19.10); neuter participle as a substantive τὸ σύμφερον *profit,*

advantage (HE 12.10); πρὸς τὸ σύμφερον *for the common good* (1C 12.7)

σύμφημι (and **σύνφημι**) strictly *affirm with*; hence *agree, assent* (RO 7.16)

σύμφημι	VIPA--1S	σύμφημι
σύμφορον	AP-AN-S	σύμφορος

σύμφορος, ον *beneficial, advantageous, profitable*; neuter as a substantive τὸ σύμφορον *benefit, advantage, profit*, with the genitive of person (1C 7.35)

συμφυείσαι	VPAPNF-P	συμφύω

συμφυλέτης, ου, ὁ strictly *one of the same tribe*; hence *one's own countryman, one's own people, fellow citizen* (1TH 2.14)

συμφυλετῶν	N-GM-P	συμφυλέτης
σύμφυτοι	A--NM-P	σύμφυτος

σύμφυτος, ον literally *planted together, grown together*; figuratively *united with, closely identified with, one with* (RO 6.5)

συμφύω (or **συνφύω**) 2aor. pass. ptc. συμφυείς (or συνφυείς); of plants *make to grow together*; intransitively and passive in the NT *grow* or *spring up together with something* (LU 8.7)

συμφωνεῖ	VIPA--3S	συμφωνέω

συμφωνέω fut. συμφωνήσω; 1aor. συνεφώνησα; 1aor. pass. συνεφωνήθην; strictly *sound together*; (1) of things *fit together, correspond with, match* (AC 15.15); (2) of persons *be of one mind, make an agreement with, agree* (MT 18.19)

συμφωνήσας	VPAANM-S	συμφωνέω
συμφωνήσει	VIFA--3S	"

συμφώνησις, εως, ἡ *agreement, harmony, joint decision* (2C 6.15)

συμφώνησις	N-NF-S	συμφώνησις
συμφωνήσουσι(ν)	VIFA--3P	συμφωνέω
συμφωνήσωσι(ν)	VSAA--3P	"

συμφωνία, ας, ἡ strictly *sounding together*; hence, as a concert of instruments *music, band*; as from a single instrument, perhaps *double flute* or *bagpipe music*; LU 15.25 is variously interpreted

συμφωνίας	N-GF-S	συμφωνία

σύμφωνος, ον literally *agreeing in sound, harmonious*; figuratively *agreeing*; substantivally in the NT ἐκ συμφώνου *by agreement, by mutual consent* (1C 7.5)

συμφώνου	AP-GN-S	σύμφωνος
συμφωνοῦσι(ν)	VIPA--3P	συμφωνέω

συμψηφίζω 1aor. συνεψήφισα; *calculate, count up, add up* (AC 19.19)

σύμψυχοι	A--NM-P	σύμψυχος

σύμψυχος, ον (also **σύνψυχος**) of total agreement in attitude *united in spirit, in full agreement, harmonious* (PH 2.2)

σύν preposition with the dative *with*; (1) of persons, denoting a togetherness, often an inner agreement, fellowship, or harmony of experience (LU 8.51; AC 5.1; RO 16.14); as denoting close association σ. τινι εἶναι *be with someone, follow, attend* (MK 2.26; PH 1.23); (2) as combining things *accompanied by, together with* (MT 25.27); (3) as introducing a new factor to be reckoned in *besides, in addition to* (LU 24.21)

σύν	PD	σύν
συναγαγεῖν	VNAA	συνάγω

συναγάγετε	VMAA--2P	"
συναγάγῃ	VSAA--3S	"
συναγαγόντες	VPAANM-P	"
συναγαγούσῃ	VPAADF-S	"
συναγαγών	VPAANM-S	"
συνάγε	VMPA--2S	"
συνάγει	VIPA--3S	"
συνάγεσθε	VMPP--2P	"
συνάγεται	VIPP--3S	"
συνάγετε	VMPA--2P	"
συνάγονται	VIPP--3P	"
συνάγουσι(ν)	VIPA--3P	"

συνάγω fut. συνάξω; 2aor. συνήγαγον; pf. pass. συνῆγμαι; 1aor. pass. συνήχθην; 1fut. pass. συναχθήσομαι; (1) of things; (a) *gather in, gather up, collect* (MT 13.47), opposite σκορπίζω (*scatter*) and μερίζω (*distribute, divide out*); (b) *store, keep safe* (LU 12.17); (c) *turn into cash, convert into money* (LU 15.13); (2) of persons; (a) *bring or call together, assemble* (MT 22.10); (b) as showing hospitality *take in, invite in* (MT 25.35); (c) passive *assemble, come together, be gathered together* (MT 18.20)

συνάγω	VIPA--1S	συνάγω
συναγωγαῖς	N-DF-P	συναγωγή
συναγωγάς	N-AF-P	"

συναγωγή, ῆς, ἡ strictly *assembling* or *bringing together*; hence (1) as a (formal) assembly for worship *meeting* (AC 13.43); (2) specifically, as Jews meeting together *congregation, synagogue* (AC 9.2); (3) predominately, as the building where Jewish congregations met *synagogue, place of assembly* (MT 4.23)

συναγωγή	N-NF-S	συναγωγή
συναγωγῇ	N-DF-S	"
συναγωγήν	N-AF-S	"
συναγωγῆς	N-GF-S	"
συναγωγῶν	N-GF-P	"
συνάγων	VPPANM-S	συνάγω

συναγωνίζομαι 1aor. συνηγωνισάμην; as helping someone with great effort *join in a struggle, fight along with, help* (RO 15.30)

συναγωνίσασθαι	VNAD	συναγωνίζομαι

συναθλέω 1aor. συνήθλησα; as laborers working together in a common cause *toil by the side of, (earnestly) cooperate with, strive together with*

συναθλοῦντες	VPPANM-P	συναθλέω

συναθροίζω 1aor. συνήθροισα; pf. pass. συνήθροισμαι; *gather, assemble, call together* (AC 19.25); passive *be gathered, meet* (AC 12.12)

συναθροίσας	VPAANM-S	συναθροίζω
συναίρει	VIPA--3S	συναίρω
συναίρειν	VNPA	"

συναίρω 1aor. inf. συνᾶραι; *take up a thing with* someone; συναίρειν λόγον *settle (up) accounts* (MT 18.23)

συναιχμάλωτος, ου, ὁ from σύν, αἰχμή, and ἁλωτός literally *taken with the spear*, i.e. *fellow prisoner (of war), fellow captive*; in Pauline usage probably used figuratively to describe certain fellow workers who shared his hardships (RO 16.7; CO 4.10; PM 23); Paul always uses δέσμιος (*prisoner*) of himself as a prisoner (EP 3.1; PM 1)

συναιχμάλωτος	N-NM-S	συναιχμάλωτος
συναιχμαλώτους	N-AM-P	"

συνακολουθέω impf. συνηκολούθουν; 1aor. συνηκολούθησα; *accompany, follow along with* (MK 5.37)

συνακολουθῆσαι	VNAA	συνακολουθέω
συνακολουθήσασα	VPAANF-P	"
συνακολουθοῦσαι	VPPANF-P	"

συναλίζομαι (and συναυλίζομαι) only passive in the NT; AC 1.4 is interpreted variously; (1) *bring together, assemble*; passive *come together, meet with*; (2) *eat* (*salt*, ἅλς) *with*; (3) *stay with, be with* (reading συναυλιζόμενος); the first interpretation presents the least difficulties

συναλιζόμενος	VPPDNM-S	συναλίζομαι
	VPPONM-S	

συναλίσκομαι passive *be taken captive together* (AC 1.4)

συναλισκόμενος	VPPDNM-S	συναλίσκομαι
	VPPONM-S	

συναλλάσσω impf. συνήλλασσον; *reconcile*; conative imperfect in AC 7.26 *attempt to reconcile*

συναναβαίνουσι(ν)	VIPA--3P	συναναβαίνω

συναναβαίνω 2aor. συνανέβην; as traveling from a lower to a higher place in a company *come* or *go up with* or *together, ascend with*

συναναβᾶσαι	VPAANF-P	συναναβαίνω
συναναβᾶσι(ν)	VPAADM-P	"

συνανάκειμαι impf. συνανεκείμην; from the Mediterranean custom for guests to recline on couches around a table at a meal *recline at table with, eat with*

συνανακείμενοι	VPPDNM-P	συνανάκειμαι
	VPPONM-P	"
συνανακειμένοις	VPPDDM-P	
	VPPODM-P	
συνανακειμένους	VPPDAM-P	
	VPPOAM-P	
συνανακειμένων	VPPDGM-P	
	VPPOGM-P	

συναναμίγνυμι active *mix, mingle together*, as when mixing ingredients for medicine; figuratively and only middle or passive in the NT *mingle oneself with, intermingle, associate with* (1C 5.9)

συναναμίγνυσθαι	VNPM	συναναμίγνυμι
	VNPP	"
συναναμίγνυσθε	VMPM--2P	"
	VMPP--2P	

συναναπαύομαι 1aor. συνανεπαυσάμην; literally *lie down with, sleep with*; figuratively in the NT *find rest* or *refreshment with* or *in company of* someone (RO 15.32)

συναναπαύσομαι	VIFD--1S	συναναπαύομαι
συναναπαύσωμαι	VSAD--1S	"

συναναστρέφω 2aor. pass. συνανεστράφην; *associate with, go with* (AC 10.41)

συνανατρέφω 1aor. pass. συνανεχύθην; *pour on together with* (AC 11.26)

συναναχυθῆναι	VNAP	συναναχέω
συνανέκειντο	VIID--3P	συνανάκειμαι
	VIIO--3P	"
συνανεστράφημεν	VIAP--1P	συναναστρέφω

συναντάω fut. συναντήσω; 1aor. συνήντησα; literally, of persons *meet (with), encounter* (LU 9.37); figuratively, of events *happen to, befall* (AC 20.22)

συναντήσας	VPAANM-S	συναντάω

συναντήσει	VIFA--3S	"
συνάντησιν	N-AF-S	συνάντησις

συνάντησις, εως, ἡ *meeting (with)*; εἰς συνάντησίν τινι *to meet someone* (MT 8.34)

συναντήσοντα	VPFAAN-P	συναντάω
συναντιλάβηται	VSAD--3S	συναντιλαμβάνομαι
συναντιλαμβάνεται	VIPD--3S	"
	VIPO--3S	"

συναντιλαμβάνομαι 2aor. συναντελαβόμην; strictly *grasp hold of with* someone; hence *(helpfully) take up a matter with*; generally *help, come to the aid of* (RO 8.26)

συνάξαντες	VPAANM-P	συνάγω
συνάξει	VIFA--3S	"
συνάξω	VIFA--1S	"
συναπαγόμενοι	VPPPNM-P	συναπάγω

συναπάγω 1aor. pass. συναπήχθην; figuratively and only passive in the NT; (1) in a positive sense; (a) of things *accommodate oneself to, go along with* (perhaps RO 12.16); (b) of persons *associate with, condescend to* (probably RO 12.16); (2) in a negative sense *be carried off along with, be led astray* (GA 2.13)

συναπαχθέντες	VPAPNM-P	συναπάγω
συναπεθάνομεν	VIAA--1P	συναποθνήσκω
συναπέστειλα	VIAA--1S	συναποστέλλω
συναπήχθη	VIAP--3S	συναπάγω
συναποθανεῖν	VNAA	συναποθνήσκω

συναποθνήσκω 2aor. συναπέθανον; literally *die together with* someone (MK 14.31); metaphorically, of the believer's acceptance of Christ's death as his own (2T 2.11); as expressing a close bond of relationship (2C 7.3)

συναπόλλυμι 2aor. mid. συναπωλόμην; (1) active *destroy with*; (2) only middle in the NT *be destroyed, perish with* (HE 11.31)

συναποστέλλω 1aor. συναπέστειλα; as dispatching a messenger *send with* someone, *send at the same time* (2C 12.18)

συναπώλετο	VIAM--3S	συναπόλλυμι
συνᾶραι	VNAA	συναίρω

συναρμολογέω *fit together, join together*, used of the parts of the body or the stones of the building; figuratively and only passive in the NT, of the inner relation of Christ and the Christian community (EP 2.21; 4.16)

συναρμολογουμένη	VPPPNF-S	συναρμολογέω
συναρμολογούμενον	VPPPNN-S	"

συναρπάζω 1aor. συνήρπασα; pluperfect συνηρπάκειν; 1aor. pass. συνηρπάσθην; *seize (suddenly and violently)*, *drag away* someone (AC 6.12); of demon activity *seize* (LU 8.29); passive, of a ship in a storm *be caught, be forced off course* by the wind and swept on (AC 27.15)

συναρπάσαντες	VPAANM-P	συναρπάζω
συναρπασθέντος	VPAPGN-S	"
συναυλιζόμενος	VPPDNM-S	συναλίζομαι
	VPPONM-S	"
συναυξάνεσθαι	VNPP	συναυξάνω

συναυξάνω only passive in the NT *grow together, grow side by side* (MT 13.30)

συναχθέντες	VPAPNM-P	συνάγω
συναχθέντων	VPAPGM-P	"
συναχθῆναι	VNAP	"
συναχθήσεται	VIFP--3S	"

συναχθήσονται   VIFP--3P   "
συνάχθητε   VMAP--2P   "
συνβάλλουσα   VPPANF-S   συμβάλλω
συγγνώμην   N-AF-S   συγγνώμη
συνδεδεμένοι   VPRPNM-P   συνδέω
σύνδεσμον   N-AM-S   σύνδεσμος

σύνδεσμος, ου, ὁ (1) literally, as the middle item that joins two or more things together *link, joint, bond*; of the body *sinew, ligament, muscle* (CO 2.19); (2) figuratively; (a) in a positive sense of spiritual forces that unite people *bond, what ties together* (CO 3.14); (b) in a negative sense, of unspiritual forces that enslave people *bondage, fetter, what causes to be under control* (AC 8.23)

σύνδεσμος   N-NM-S   σύνδεσμος
συνδέσμῳ   N-DM-S   "
συνδέσμων   N-GM-P   "

συνδέω pf. pass. συνδέδεμαι; only passive in the NT; literally, of prisoners bound with the same chains *be bound together with*; more generally *be fellow prisoners, be in prison with* (HE 13.3)

συνδοξάζω 1aor. pass. συνεδοξάσθην; only passive in the NT *glorify together with*; of the participation of believers in Christ's rule *receive honor with, be put in an important position with* (RO 8.17)

συνδοξασθῶμεν   VSAP--1P   συνδοξάζω
σύνδουλοι   N-NM-P   σύνδουλος
σύνδουλον   N-AM-S   "

σύνδουλος, ου, ὁ literally *fellow slave, fellow servant* (MT 24.49); figuratively, of believers, ministers, angels, any who relate in service together under Christ as Lord (CO 1.7; RV 19.10)

σύνδουλος   N-NM-S   σύνδουλος
συνδούλου   N-GM-S   "
συνδούλους   N-AM-P   "
συνδούλων   N-GM-P   "

συνδρομή, ῆς, ἡ as the forming of a mob *running together*; ἐγένετο σ. τοῦ λαοῦ literally *running together of the people took place*, i.e. *the people rushed together* (AC 21.30)

συνδρομή   N-NF-S   συνδρομή
συνέβαινε(ν)   VIIA--3S   συμβαίνω
συνέβαινον   VIIA--3P   "
συνέβαλε(ν)   VIAA--3S   συμβάλλω
συνεβάλετο   VIAM--3S   "
συνέβαλλε(ν)   VIIA--3S   "
συνεβάλλετο   VIIM--3S   "
συνέβαλλον   VIIA--3P   "
συνέβαλον   VIAA--3P   "
συνέβη   VIAA--3S   συμβαίνω
συνεβίβασαν   VIAA--3P   συμβιβάζω
συνεβουλεύσαντο   VIAM--3P   συμβουλεύω

συνεγείρω 1aor. συνήγειρα; 1aor. pass. συνηγέρθην; literally *cause to rise up* or *wake up with another*; figuratively, of the believer's participation in the resurrection life and power of Jesus; (1) active *raise up together* (EP 2.6); (2) passive *be raised up with* (CO 2.12)

συνέδραμε(ν)   VIAA--3S   συντρέχω
συνέδραμον   VIAA--3P   "
συνέδρια   N-AN-P   συνέδριον

συνέδριον, ου, τό (1) generally, as a governing body *council, assembly*; (2) predominately as the Jewish supreme court in Jerusalem *Sanhedrin, High Council* (MT 26.59); plural, of local Jewish courts *town councils* (MT 10.17)

συνέδριον   N-AN-S   συνέδριον
   N-NN-S   "
συνεδρίου   N-GN-S   "
συνεδρίους   AP-AM-P   σύνεδρος
συνεδρίῳ   N-DN-S   συνέδριον

σύνεδρος, ον (also **συνέδριος**) *sitting together in council, assembled together in council*; substantively *councilor, council member* (AC 5.35)

συνέζευξε(ν)   VIAA--3S   συζεύγνυμι
συνεζήτει   VIIA--3S   συζητέω
συνεζωοποίησε(ν)   VIAA--3S   συζωοποιέω
συνέθεντο   VIAM--3P   συντίθημι
συνέθλιβον   VIIA--3P   συνθλίβω
συνειδήσει   N-DF-S   συνείδησις
συνειδήσεσι(ν)   N-DF-P
συνειδήσεως   N-GF-S
συνείδησιν   N-AF-S

συνείδησις, εως, ἡ (1) as a perceptive *awareness* within oneself, *consciousness* (HE 10.2; 1P 2.19); (2) as the faculty of moral consciousness or awareness by which moral judgments relating to right and wrong are made *conscience* (AC 23.1)

συνείδησις   N-NF-S   συνείδησις
συνειδύης   VPRAGF-S   see συνειδυίης
συνειδυίας   VPRAGF-S   σύνοιδα
συνειδυίης   VPRAGF-S   "
συνείληφε(ν)   VIRA--3S   συλλαμβάνω
συνειληφυῖα   VPRANF-S   "

σύνειμι (I) ptc. συνόντος; impf. third-person plural συνῆσαν; from σύν (*with*) and εἰμί (*be*); *be with, accompany* (LU 8.4; 9.18; AC 13.31; 22.11)

σύνειμι (II) ptc. συνιόντος; from σύν (*with*) and εἶμι (*go*); *go* or *come together, gather* (LU 8.4)

συνείπετο   VIID--3S   συνέπομαι
   VIIO--3S   "
συνείποντο   VIID--3P   "
   VIIO--3P   "

συνεισέρχομαι 2aor. act. συνεισῆλθον; *enter with, go with* someone *into* a place

συνεισῆλθε(ν)   VIAA--3S   συνεισέρχομαι
συνεισῆλθον   VIAA--3P   "
σύνεισι(ν)   VIPA--3P   σύνειμι (I)
συνείχετο   VIIP--3S   συνέχω
συνείχοντο   VIIP--3P   "
συνεκάθισε(ν)   VIAA--3S   συγκαθίζω
συνεκάλεσαν   VIAA--3P   συγκαλέω

συνέκδημος, ου, ὁ *traveling companion, fellow traveler*

συνέκδημος   N-NM-S   συνέκδημος
συνεκδήμους   N-AM-P   "
συνέκειντο   VIID--3P   σύγκειμαι
   VIIO--3P   "
συνεκέρασε(ν)   VIAA--3S   συγκεράννυμι
συνεκίνησαν   VIAA--3P   συγκινέω
συνέκλεισαν   VIAA--3P   συγκλείω
συνέκλεισε(ν)   VIAA--3S   "
συνεκλεκτή   AP-NF-S   συνεκλεκτός

365

συνεκλεκτός, ή, όν *chosen together with*; substantivally ἡ ἐν Βαβυλῶνι συνεκλεκτή *your sister in Babylon, chosen together with you* probably refers to a church rather than an individual woman (1P 5.13)

συνεκόμισαν	VIAA--3P	συγκομίζω

συνεκπορεύομαι impf. συνεξεπορευόμην; *go out of* a place *with* someone (AC 3.11)

συνέλαβε(ν)	VIAA--3S	συλλαμβάνω
συνέλαβον	VIAA--3P	"
συνελάλησε(ν)	VIAA--3S	συλλαλέω
συνελάλουν	VIIA--3P	"

συνελαύνω 1aor. συνήλασα; *drive* or *force* (AC 7.26)

συνέλεξαν	VIAA--3P	συλλέγω
συνεληλύθει	VILA--3S	συνέρχομαι
συνεληλύθεισαν	VILA--3P	"
συνεληλυθότας	VPRAAM-P	"
συνεληλυθότες	VPRANM-P	"
συνεληλυθυῖαι	VPRANF-P	"
συνελθεῖν	VNAA	"
συνέλθη	VSAA--3S	"
συνελθόντα	VPAAAM-S	"
συνελθόντας	VPAAAM-P	"
συνελθόντες	VPAANM-P	"
συνελθόντος	VPAAGM-S	"
συνελθόντων	VPAAGM-P	"
συνελθούσαις	VPAADF-P	"
συνελογίζοντο	VIID--3P	συλλογίζομαι
	VIIO--3P	"
συνελογίσαντο	VIAD--3P	"
συνενέγκαντες	VPAANM-P	συμφέρω
συνεξεπορεύετο	VIID--3S	συνεκπορεύομαι
	VIIO--3S	"
συνέξουσι(ν)	VIFA--3P	συνέχω
συνεπαθήσατε	VIAA--2P	συμπαθέω
συνεπέθεντο	VIAM--3P	συνεπιτίθημι
συνεπέμψαμεν	VIAA--1P	συμπέμπω
συνέπεσε(ν)	VIAA--3S	συμπίπτω
συνεπέστη	VIAA--3S	συνεφίστημι
συνεπέστησαν	VIAA--3P	"

συνεπιμαρτυρέω *testify at the same time, confirm, add one's witness to* (HE 2.4)

συνεπιμαρτυροῦντος	VPPAGM-S	συνεπιμαρτυρέω
συνεπίομεν	VIAA--1P	συμπίνω
συνεπισκόποις	N-DM-P	συνεπίσκοπος

συνεπίσκοπος, ου, ὁ *fellow bishop, fellow overseer* (PH 1.1)

συνεπιτίθημι 2aor. mid. συνεπεθέμην; only middle in the NT *join in attacking* or *accusing, support an accusation* (AC 24.9)

συνεπληροῦντο	VIIP--3P	συμπληρόω
συνέπνιγον	VIIA--3P	συμπνίγω
συνέπνιξαν	VIAA--3P	"

συνέπομαι impf. συνειπόμην; *accompany* someone, *follow* (AC 20.4)

συνεπορεύετο	VIID--3S	συμπορεύομαι
	VIIO--3S	"
συνεπορεύοντο	VIID--3P	"
	VIIO--3P	"
συνεργεῖ	VIPA--3S	συνεργέω

συνεργέω impf. συνήργουν; (1) of persons *work (together) with, help, cooperate (with)* (1C 16.16); (2) of things *join together, unite with* (JA 2.22); in RO 8.28 manuscripts vary between πάντα (*all*) and ὁ θεός (*God*) as the subject; a third possible subject is πνεῦμα (*Spirit*) in 8.27

συνεργοί	AP-NM-P	συνεργός
συνεργόν	AP-AM-S	"

συνεργός, όν *working together with, helping*; predominately substantivally in the NT *fellow worker, helper, fellow laborer*

συνεργός	AP-NM-S	συνεργός
συνεργοῦντες	VPPANM-P	συνεργέω
συνεργοῦντι	VPPADM-S	"
συνεργοῦντος	VPPAGM-S	"
συνεργούς	AP-AM-P	συνεργός
συνεργῷ	AP-DM-S	"
	A--DM-S	"
συνεργῶν	AP-GM-P	"
συνέρχεσθε	VIPD--2P	συνέρχομαι
	VIPO--2P	"
συνέρχεται	VIPD--3S	"
	VIPO--3S	"
συνέρχησθε	VSPD--2P	"
	VSPO--2P	"

συνέρχομαι impf. συνηρχόμην; 2aor. act. συνῆλθον; pf. act. συνελήλυθα; pluperfect act. συνεληλύθειν; (1) *come together*; (a) of persons *assemble, gather* (MK 3.20); (b) as a religious technical term, of Christians assembling in a congregation *hold meetings, meet* (1C 11.17); (c) euphemistically, as having sexual intercourse *come together, live together (as husband and wife)* (MT 1.18); (2) *go with, travel with* (AC 15.38)

συνερχόμενοι	VPPDNM-P	συνέρχομαι
	VPPONM-P	"
συνερχομένων	VPPDGM-P	"
	VPPOGM-P	"
συνέρχονται	VIPD--3P	"
	VIPO--3P	"
συνέσει	N-DF-S	σύνεσις
συνέσεως	N-GF-S	"
συνεσθίει	VIPA--3S	συνεσθίω
συνεσθίειν	VNPA	"

συνεσθίω impf. συνήσθιον; 2aor. συνέφαγον; of social association *eat together, associate with* on familiar terms

σύνεσιν	N-AF-S	σύνεσις

σύνεσις, εως, ἡ from συνίημι (*bring together*); strictly *sending together, union*, as of two rivers; hence (1) as a natural intellectual faculty *comprehension, understanding, intelligence* (1C 1.19); (2) as granted by God through spiritual revelation *insight, understanding* (EP 3.4)

συνεσπάραξε(ν)	VIAA--3S	συσπαράσσω
συνεσταλμένος	VPRPNM-S	συστέλλω
συνεσταυρώθη	VIAP--3S	συσταυρόω
συνεσταύρωμαι	VIRP--1S	"
συνεσταυρωμένοι	VPRPNM-P	"
συνέστειλαν	VIAA--3P	συστέλλω
συνέστηκε(ν)	VIRA--3S	συνίστημι
συνεστήσατε	VIAA--2P	"
συνεστραμμένων	VPRPGM-P	συστρέφω
συνεστράφημεν	VIAP--1P	"
συνεστῶσα	VPRANF-S	συνίστημι

συνεστῶσαι	VPRANF-P	"
συνεστώσης	VPRAGF-S	"
συνεστῶτα	VPRANN-P	"
συνεστῶτας	VPRAAM-P	"
συνέσχον	VIAA--3P	συνέχω
συνέταξε(ν)	VIAA--3S	συντάσσω
συνετάραξε(ν)	VIAA--3S	συνταράσσω
συνετάφημεν	VIAP--1P	συνθάπτω
σύνετε	VMAA--2P	συνίημι
συνετέθειντο	VILM--3P	συντίθημι
συνετέλεσε(ν)	VIAA--3S	συντελέω
συνετελέσθη	VIAP--3S	"
συνετελέσθησαν	VIAP--3P	"
συνετήρει	VIIA--3S	συντηρέω

συνετός, ή, όν *having understanding, intelligent, wise* (AC 13.7); plural συνετοί as a substantive *wise people, (naturally) intelligent people* (MT 11.25)

συνετῷ	A--DM-S	συνετός
συνετῶν	A--GM-P	"
συνευδοκεῖ	VIPA--3S	συνευδοκέω
συνευδοκεῖν	VNPA	"
συνευδοκεῖτε	VIPA--2P	"

συνευδοκέω strictly *approve along with another*; hence *approve of, consent to* (AC 8.1); with an infinitive following *be willing to, agree to* (1C 7.12, 13)

συνευδοκοῦντες	VPPANM-P	συνευδοκέω
συνευδοκοῦσι(ν)	VIPA--3P	"
συνευδοκῶν	VPPANM-S	"

συνεύχομαι *pray with* or *together, join in praying* (JU 12)

συνευχόμενοι	VPPDNM-P	συνεύχομαι

συνευωχέομαι only passive in the NT *feast together* (2P 2.13; JU 12)

συνευωχούμενοι	VPPDNM-P	συνευωχέομαι
	VPPONM-P	"
συνέφαγε(ν)	VIAA--3S	συνεσθίω
συνέφαγες	VIAA--2S	"
συνεφάγομεν	VIAA--1P	"

συνεφίστημι 2aor. συνεπέστην; intransitively in the middle and the second aorist active *rise up against, join in attacking, set on together* (AC 16.22)

συνεφωνήθη	VIAP--3S	συμφωνέω
συνεφώνησας	VIAA--2S	"
συνεφώνησε(ν)	VIAA--3S	"
συνέχαιρον	VIIA--3P	συγχαίρω
συνέχεαν	VIIA--3P	see συνέχεον
συνέχει	VIPA--3S	συνέχω
συνέχειν	VNPA	"
συνέχεον	VIIA--3P	συγχέω
συνέχομαι	VIPP--1S	συνέχω
συνεχομένη	VPPPNF-S	"
συνεχόμενον	VPPPAM-S	"
συνεχομένους	VPPPAM-P	"
συνέχοντες	VPPANM-P	"
συνέχουσι(ν)	VIPA--3P	"
συνεχύθη	VIAP--3S	συγχέω
συνεχυθῆναι	VNAP	"
συνεχύθησαν	VIAP--3P	"
συνέχυνε(ν)	VIIA--3S	"
συνέχυννε(ν)	VIIA--3S	"

συνέχω impf. mid./pass. συνειχόμην; fut. συνέξω; 2aor. συνέσχον; from a basic meaning *hold* something to-

gether; (1) *hold together, sustain*; (2) *enclose, lock up, close by holding (together)*; of the ears *stop*; idiomatically συνέχειν τὰ ὦτα literally *hold the ears shut*, i.e. *refuse to listen* (AC 7.57); of imprisonment *hold in custody, hold prisoner* (LU 22.63); (3) of crowds *surround, hem in, crowd around* (LU 8.45); (4) passive; (a) of being gripped by difficult circumstances, such as severe illness *be seized by, suffer from, be tormented by* (MT 4.24); (b) of severe emotional stress *be gripped by, be seized with* (LU 8.37); (c) of being totally claimed by a task *devote oneself completely to, be occupied with*; συνείχετο τῷ λόγῳ *he was wholly absorbed in preaching* (AC 18.5); (5) *constrain, impel, urge on* (2C 5.14); passive and idiomatically συνέχεσθαι ἐκ τῶν δύο literally *be pulled from two directions*, i.e. *have conflicting thoughts* (PH 1.23)

συνεψήφισαν	VIAA--3P	συμψηφίζω
συνεψηφίσθη	VIAP--3S	"
συνζῆν	VNPA	συζάω
συνζήσομαι	VIFA--1P	"
συνζήσομεν	VIFA--1P	"
συνζήσωμεν	VSAA--1P	"
συνζητεῖν	VNPA	συζητέω
συνζητεῖτε	VIPA--2P	"
συνζητήσεως	N-GF-S	συζήτησις
συνζήτησιν	N-AF-S	"
συνζητητής	N-NM-S	συζητητής
συνζητοῦντας	VPPAAM-P	συζητέω
συνζητοῦντες	VPPANM-P	"
συνζητοῦντων	VPPAGM-P	"
σύνζυγε	AP-VM-S	σύζυγος
συνήγαγε(ν)	VIAA--3S	συνάγω
συνηγάγετε	VIAA--2P	"
συνηγάγομεν	VIAA--1P	"
συνήγαγον	VIAA--3P	"
συνήγειρε(ν)	VIAA--3S	συνεγείρω
συνηγέρθητε	VIAP--2P	"
συνηγμένα	VPRPAN-P	συνάγω
συνηγμένη	VPRPNF-S	"
συνηγμένοι	VPRPNM-P	"
συνηγμένων	VPRPGM-P	"

συνήδομαι passive *delight in, happily approve, feel good about* (RO 7.22)

συνήδομαι	VIPD--1S	συνήδομαι
	VIPO--1S	"

συνήθεια, ας, ἡ as an established practice; (1) objectively *custom, usage, habit* (JN 18.39); (2) as a state, a being habituated by repeated actions into a pattern of behavior *becoming used to, being accustomed to* (1C 8.7)

συνήθεια	N-NF-S	συνήθεια
συνηθείᾳ	N-DF-S	"
συνήθειαν	N-AF-S	"
συνήθλησαν	VIAA--3P	συναθλέω
συνηθροισμένοι	VPRPNM-P	συναθροίζω
συνηθροισμένους	VPRPAM-P	"
συνῆκαν	VIAA--3P	συνίημι
συνήκατε	VIAA--2P	"
συνηκολούθει	VIIA--3S	συνακολουθέω
συνήλασε(ν)	VIAA--3S	συνελαύνω
συνῆλθαν	VIAA--3P	συνέρχομαι
συνῆλθε(ν)	VIAA--3S	"

συνῆλθον	VIAA--3P	"
συνηλικιώτας	N-AM-P	συνηλικιώτης

συνηλικιώτης, ου, ὁ   *one of the same age, contemporary* (GA 1.14)

συνήλλασσε(ν)	VIIA--3S	συναλλάσσω
συνήντησαν	VIAA--3P	συναντάω
συνήντησε(ν)	VIAA--3S	"
συνήργει	VIIA--3S	συνεργέω
συνηρπάκει	VILA--3S	συναρπάζω
συνήρπασαν	VIAA--3P	"
συνήρχετο	VIID--3S	συνέρχομαι
	VIIO--3S	"
συνήρχοντο	VIID--3P	"
	VIIO--3P	"
συνῆσαν	VIIA--3P	σύνειμι (I)
συνήσθιε(ν)	VIIA--3S	συνεσθίω
συνήσθιον	VIIA--3P	"
συνήσουσι(ν)	VIFA--3P	συνίημι
συνῆτε	VSAA--2P	"
συνήχθη	VIAP--3S	συνάγω
συνήχθησαν	VIAP--3P	"

συνθάπτω   2aor. pass. συνετάφην; *bury (together) with* or *at the same time*; figuratively, of identifying with Christ through baptism in accepting his death and burial as one's own (RO 6.4)

συνθλασθήσεται	VIFP--3S	συνθλάω

συνθλάω   1fut. pass. συνθλασθήσομαι; *crush (together), dash to pieces, shatter*

συνθλίβοντα	VPPAAM-S	συνθλίβω

συνθλίβω   impf. συνέθλιβον; *press together*; of a crowd *throng, press in on* someone, *crowd around*

συνθρύπτοντες	VPPANM-P	συνθρύπτω

συνθρύπτω   *crush, break in pieces*; figuratively and idiomatically συνθρύπτειν τὴν καρδίαν τινός literally *break the heart of someone*, i.e. *cause someone to feel very sad* (AC 21.13)

συνιᾶσι(ν)	VIPA--3P	συνίημι
συνιδόντες	VPAANM-P	συνοράω
συνιδών	VPAANM-S	"
συνιείς	VPPANM-S	συνίημι
συνιέναι	VNPA	"
συνιέντες	VPPANM-P	"
συνιέντος	VPPAGM-S	"
συνίετε	VIPA--2P	"
	VMPA--2P	"
συνιέτω	VMPA--3S	"

συνίημι and **συνίω**   inf. συνιέναι (AC 7.25a); fut. συνήσω; 1aor. συνῆκα; 2aor. subjunctive συνῶ; from a basic meaning *bring together*; with the attitude affecting ability to comprehend *understand (thoroughly), perceive clearly, gain insight into* (MK 6.52)

συνιόντος	VPPAGM-S	σύνειμι (II)
συνίουσι(ν)	VIPA--3P	συνίημι
συνίσασι(ν)	VIRA--3S	σύνοιδα
συνιστᾶν	VNPA	συνίστημι
συνιστάνειν	VNPA	"
συνιστάνομεν	VIPA--1P	"
συνιστάνοντες	VPPANM-P	"
συνιστανόντων	VPPAGM-P	"
συνίσταντες	VPPANM-P	"
συνιστάνω	VIPA--1S	"
συνιστάνων	VPPANM-S	"
συνίστασθαι	VNPP	"

συνίστημι and **συνιστάνω** (and **συνιστάω**)   1aor. συνέστησα; pf. συνέστηκα, ptc. συνεστῶς; from a basic meaning *put together*; (1) transitively; (a) active, as making known one's approval *commend, recommend* (RO 16.1); passive *be recommended* (2C 12.11); (b) as making known by action *demonstrate, show, bring out* (RO 3.5); (2) intransitively (present middle and perfect active); (a) *stand together, stand with* or *by* (LU 9.32); (b) *exist, have existence, continue* (CO 1.17; 2P 3.5)

συνίστημι	VIPA--1S	συνίστημι
συνίστησι(ν)	VIPA--3S	"
συνιστῶν	VPPANM-S	"
συνιστῶντες	VPPANM-P	"
συνίων	VPPANM-S	συνίημι
συνιών	VPPANM-S	"
συνιῶν	VPPANM-S	"
συνιῶσι(ν)	VSPA--3P	"
συνκαθήμενοι	VPPDNM-P	συγκάθημαι
	VPPONM-P	"
συνκαθήμενος	VPPDNM-S	"
	VPPONM-S	"
συνκαθίσαι	VNAA	"
συνκαθισάντων	VPAAGM-P	συγκαθίζω
συνκακοπάθησον	VMAA--2S	συγκακοπαθέω
συνκακουχεῖσθαι	VNPD	συγκακουχέομαι
	VNPO	"
συνκαλεῖ	VIPA--3S	συγκαλέω
συνκαλεῖται	VIPM--3S	"
συνκαλεσάμενος	VPAMNM-S	"
συνκαλέσασθαι	VNAM	"
συνκαλοῦσι(ν)	VIPA--3P	"
σύνκαμψον	VMAA--2S	συγκάμπτω
συνκαταβάντες	VPAANM-P	συγκαταβαίνω
συνκατάθεσις	N-NF-S	συγκατάθεσις
συνκατανεύσαντος	VPAAGM-S	συγκατανεύω
συνκατατεθειμένος	VPRDNM-S	συγκατατίθεμαι
	VPRONM-S	"
συνκατατιθέμενος	VPPDNM-S	"
	VPPONM-S	"
συνκατεψηφίσθη	VIAP--3S	συγκαταψηφίζομαι
συνκεκαλυμμένον	VPRPNN-S	συγκαλύπτω
συνκεκεραμμένοι	VPRPNM-P	συγκεράννυμι
συνκεκραμένους	VPRPAM-P	"
συνκεχυμένη	VPRPNF-S	συγχέω
συνκέχυται	VIRP--3S	"
συνκλειόμενοι	VPPPNM-P	συγκλείω
συνκληρονόμα	A--AN-P	συγκληρονόμος
συνκληρονόμοι	AP-NM-P	"
συνκληρονόμοις	AP-DM-P	"
συνκληρονόμων	AP-GM-P	"
συνκοινωνεῖτε	VMPA--2P	συγκοινωνέω
συνκοινωνήσαντες	VPAANM-P	"
συνκοινωνήσητε	VSAA--2P	"
συνκοινωνός	N-NM-S	συγκοινωνός
συνκοινωνούς	N-AM-P	"
συνκρῖναι	VNAA	συγκρίνω
συνκρίνοντες	VPPANM-P	"
συνκύπτουσα	VPPANF-S	συγκύπτω

συλλαλοῦντες VPPANM-P συλλαλέω
συμμαρτυρούσης VPPAGF-S συμμαρτυρέω
συνοδεύοντες VPPANM-P συνοδεύω
συνοδεύω *journey* or *travel with, accompany on a journey* (AC 9.7)
συνοδία, ας, ἡ literally *journeying together*; by metonymy *caravan, company of fellow travelers* (LU 2.44)
συνοδίᾳ N-DF-S συνοδία
σύνοιδα pf. ptc. feminine singular συνειδυῖα; perfect with the present meaning; (1) *know something with someone*; *share in the knowledge of* (AC 5.2); (2) reflectively σ. ἐμαυτῷ *I know (within myself), I am aware, I am conscious*; with οὐδέν *I am clear* (1C 4.4)
σύνοιδα VIRA--1S σύνοιδα
συνοικέω *live with*; specifically of husband and wife *live together* (1P 3.7)
συνοικοδομεῖσθε VIPP--2P συνοικοδομέω
συνοικοδομέω *build up (together)*; metaphorically and only passive in the NT, of the community of Christ being formed into a dwelling place for God *be built up together* (EP 2.22)
συνοικοῦντες VPPANM-P συνοικέω
σύνολον A--AN-S σύνολος
σύνολος, ον *all together*; neuter substantive as an adverb τὸ σύνολον *on the whole, in general* (AC 23.14)
συνομιλέω strictly *be in company with*; hence *talk* or *converse with* (AC 10.27)
συνομιλοῦντες VPPANM-P συνομιλέω
συνομιλῶν VPPANM-S "
συνομορέω of a place *border on, be next (door) to, adjoin* (AC 18.7)
συνομοροῦσα VPPANF-S συνομορέω
συνόντος VPPAGM-S σύνειμι (I)
συνόντων VPPAGM-P "
συνοράω 2aor. συνεῖδον; in the NT of mental perception *perceive, become aware of, learn about* (AC 14.6)
συνορία, ας, ἡ *neighboring country* (MT 4.24)
συνορίαν N-AF-S συνορία
συνοχή, ῆς, ἡ from a basic meaning *holding together, compression*; literally *prison*; figuratively in the NT, as being gripped by a severe emotional stress *anxious fear, dismay, distress*
συνοχή N-NF-S συνοχή
συνοχῆς N-GF-S "
συνπαραγενόμενοι VPADNM-P συμπαραγίνομαι
συνπαρακληθῆναι VNAP συμπαρακαλέω
συνπαραλαβόντες VPAANM-P συμπαραλαμβάνω
συνπαραλαμβάνειν VNPA "
συνπαρόντες VPPAVM-P συμπάρειμι
συνπάσχομεν VIPA--1P συμπάσχω
συνπεριλαβών VPAANM-S συμπεριλαμβάνω
συνπνίγονται VIPP--3P συμπνίγω
συνσχηματίζεσθαι VNPM συσχηματίζω
VNPP "
συνσχηματίζεσθε VMPM--2P "
VMPP--2P "
συνσχηματιζόμενοι VPPMNM-P "
VPPPNM-P "
συνταράσσω 1aor. συνετάραξα; *throw into complete confusion, profoundly disturb, greatly vex* (LU 9.42)

συντάσσω 1aor. συνέταξα; strictly *arrange* or *place in order together*; hence *order, command, instruct* (MT 21.6)
συνταφέντες VPAPNM-P συνθάπτω
συντέλεια, ας, ἡ as the point of time marking the close of an age *end, conclusion, completion* (MT 13.39)
συντέλεια N-NF-S συντέλεια
συντελείᾳ N-DF-S "
συντελείας N-GF-S "
συντελεῖσθαι VNPP συντελέω
συντελέσας VPAANM-S "
συντελεσθεισῶν VPAPGF-P "
συντελέσω VIFA--1S "
συντελέω fut. συντελέσω; 1aor. pass. συνετελέσθην; (1) of an activity *bring to an end, complete, finish* (LU 4.13); (2) of a predicted event *accomplish, carry out, fulfill* (MK 13.4); (3) of a time span *come to an end, be over* (AC 21.27); (4) of a new undertaking *cause to exist, bring about, establish* (HE 8.8)
συντελουμένης VPPPGF-S συντελέω
συντελῶν VPPANM-S "
συντέμνω literally *cut short, chop off, shorten*; figuratively, of an allotted time *cut short, abruptly end* (RO 9.28)
συντέμνων VPPANM-S συντέμνω
συντετμημένον VPRPAM-S "
συντετριμμένον VPRPAM-S συντρίβω
συντετριμμένους VPRPAM-P "
συντετριφέναι VNRA "
συντετρίφθαι VNRP "
συντεχνίται N-NM-P συντεχνίτης
συντεχνίτης, ου, ὁ *one who works at the same trade, fellow craftsman* (AC 19.25)
συντηρέω impf. συνετήρουν; (1) *(carefully) keep in mind, preserve in memory* (LU 2.19); (2) *guard, protect, keep safe and sound* (MK 6.20); passive *be preserved* (MT 9.17)
συντηροῦνται VIPP--3P συντηρέω
συντίθημι 2aor. mid. συνεθέμην; pluperfect mid. συνετεθείμην; only middle in the NT; (1) as coming to a mutual understanding *agree together, come to an agreement with* someone (LU 22.5); (2) as coming to a mutual decision within a group *decide, agree* (JN 9.22)
συντόμως adverb; (1) of time *in a short time, promptly* (MK 16 shorter ending); (2) of speaking *concisely, briefly* (AC 24.4)
συντόμως AB συντόμως
συντρεχόντων VPPAGM-P συντρέχω
συντρέχω 2aor. συνέδραμον; *run together*; literally, of people hurrying to the same place *run together* (MK 6.33); figuratively, of close association in a type of behavior *go (along) with, (eagerly) join in with* (1P 4.4)
συντρίβεται VIPP--3S συντρίβω
συντριβήσεται VIFP--3S "
συντρῖβον VPPANN-S "
συντρίβω fut. συντρίψω; 1aor. συνέτριψα; pf. pass. συντέτριμμαι, inf. συντετρῖφθαι; 2aor. pass. συνετρίβην; 2fut. pass. συντριβήσομαι; strictly *rub hard together*; hence *smash, crush*; (1) of things *break (in pieces), shatter* (MK 14.3); (2) of persons *mistreat, bruise, beat severely* (LU 9.39); of enemies *overcome completely, crush*

(RO 16.20); (3) figuratively, of mental and emotional states *deprive of strength, break down*; passive *be heartbroken, be in despair* (LU 4.18)

σύντριμμα, ατος, τό what is broken or shattered *destruction, ruin, calamity* (RO 3.16)

σύντριμμα	N-NN-S	σύντριμμα
συντρίψαι	VOAA--3S	συντρίβω
συντρίψασα	VPAANF-S	"
συντρίψει	VIFA--3S	"

σύντροφος, ον *nourished* or *brought up with* someone; substantivally ὁ σ. *childhood companion, foster brother, intimate friend,* of children raised in the same household but not blood relatives (AC 13.1)

σύντροφος	AP-NM-S	σύντροφος

συντυγχάνω 2aor. συνέτυχον; *get (near) to, meet, join* (LU 8.19)

συντυχεῖν	VNAA	συντυγχάνω

Συντύχη, ης, ἡ *Syntyche,* feminine proper noun (PH 4.2)

Συντύχην	N-AF-S	Συντύχη

συντυχία, ας, ἡ *occurrence, happening, incident;* κατὰ συντυχίαν *by chance, by coincidence* (LU 10.31)

συντυχίαν	N-AF-S	συντυχία
συντυχών	VPAANM-S	συντυγχάνω
συνυπεκρίθησαν	VIAO--3P	συνυποκρίνομαι

συνυποκρίνομαι 1aor. συνυπεκρίθην; *join in pretending* or *playing a part;* figuratively *speak* or *act falsely along with, join in hypocrisy* (GA 2.13)

συνυπουργέω *join in helping, cooperate with by means of* something, as prayer (2C 1.11)

συνυπουργούντων	VPPAGM-P	συνυπουργέω
σύνφημι	VIPA--1S	σύμφημι
συνφυεῖσαι	VPAPNF-P	συμφύω
συνχαίρει	VIPA--3S	συγχαίρω
συνχαίρετε	VMPA--2P	"
συνχαίρω	VIPA--1S	"
συνχάρητε	VMAP--2P	"
συνχρῶνται	VIPD--3P	συγχράομαι
	VIPO--3P	"
συνχύννεται	VIPP--3P	συγχέω
σύνψυχοι	A--NM-P	σύμψυχος
συνωδίνει	VIPA--3S	συνωδίνω

συνωδίνω literally, as suffering birth pangs in common with others *travail together;* metaphorically, of creation in all its parts awaiting its future regeneration *groan together (as in childbirth), be in travail, suffer agony together* (RO 8.22)

συνωμοσία, ας, ἡ *taking an oath together;* in a negative sense, of a plan against someone *conspiracy, plot* (AC 23.13)

συνωμοσίαν	N-AF-S	συνωμοσία
συνῶσι(ν)	VSAA--3P	συνίημι

Σύρα, ας, ἡ *Syrian woman* (MK 7.26)

Σύρα	N-NF-S	Σύρα

Συράκουσαι, Συρακουσῶν, αἱ *Syracuse,* a large city on the eastern coast of Sicily, an island off the southwestern tip of Italy (AC 28.12)

Συρακούσας	N-AF-P	Συράκουσαι
Σύραν	N-AF-S	Σύρα
Συραφοινίκισσα	N-NF-S	Συροφοινίκισσα
σύρει	VIPA--3S	σύρω

Συρία, ας, ἡ *Syria;* in the NT a large country and later a Roman province in western Asia

Συρίαν	N-AF-S	Συρία
Συρίας	N-GF-S	"
σύροντες	VPPANM-P	σύρω

Σύρος, ου, ὁ *Syrian, inhabitant of Syria* (LU 4.27)

Σύρος	N-NM-S	Σύρος

Συροφοινίκισσα, ης, ἡ (also Σύρα Φοινίκισσα, Συραφοινίκισσα, Σύρα Φοίνισσα, Συροφοίνισσα, Τυροφοινίκισσα) *Syrophoenician woman,* a woman from Phoenicia within the Roman province of Syria (MK 7.26)

Συροφοινίκισσα	N-NF-S	Συροφοινίκισσα
Συροφοίνισσα	N-NF-S	"

συρρέω fut. mid. συρρυήσομαι; *flow together* (2P 3.10)

συρρυήσεται	VIFD--3S	συρρέω
Σύρτιν	N-AF-S	Σύρτις
σύρτιν	N-AF-S	σύρτις

Σύρτις, εως, ἡ *Syrtis,* name of two shallow gulfs along the northern African coast, full of shifting sandbanks, called Greater and Lesser Syrtis; AC 27.17 refers to the former, near Cyrenaica

σύρτις, εως, ἡ *shoal, sandbank, place dangerous on account of shoals* (AC 27.17)

σύρω impf. ἔσυρον; as moving someone or something along by force *drag (away), pull (along), draw* (AC 14.19); of a fish net *drag in* (JN 21.8); of stars *sweep away* out of the sky (RV 12.4)

σύρων	VPPANM-S	σύρω

συσπαράσσω 1aor. συνεσπάραξα; *pull about, rend in pieces, tear;* as the effect of a demonic attack on the human body *convulse, throw into convulsions, cause a fit*

σύσσημον, ου, τό *signal, sign,* very carefully stipulated and arranged beforehand (MK 14.44)

σύσσημον	N-AN-S	σύσσημον
σύσσωμα	A--AN-P	σύσσωμος

σύσσωμος, ον *belonging to the same body;* figuratively in EP 3.6, of Gentile believers as fellow members in the church, the spiritual body of Christ

συστασιαστής, οῦ, ὁ *fellow insurrectionist, one who takes part in a sedition, fellow rioter* (MK 15.7)

συστασιαστῶν	N-GM-P	συστασιαστής

συστατικός, ή, όν of speaking good words on behalf of another *commendatory, introductory;* substantivally *recommendation;* συστατικὴ ἐπιστολή *letter of recommendation* (2C 3.1)

συστατικῶν	A--GF-P	συστατικός

συσταυρόω pf. pass. συνεσταύρωμαι; 1aor. pass. συνεσταυρώθην; only passive in the NT; literally *be crucified (together) with* (MT 27.44); figuratively, of spiritual identification with Christ in his death, as a believer counts Christ's death as his own (RO 6.6)

συσταυρωθέντες	VPAPNM-P	συσταυρόω
συσταυρωθέντος	VPAPGM-S	"
συστείλαντες	VPAANM-P	συστέλλω

συστέλλω 1aor. συνέστειλα; pf. pass. συνέσταλμαι; (1) *draw together, contract;* passive, of an extent of time *be limited, be short, be near the end* (1C 7.29); (2) οἱ νεώτεροι συνέστειλαν αὐτόν in AC 5.6 is variously understood: (a) *wrap up, enshroud;* (b) *snatch up;* (c) *re-*

move; the first is to be preferred in view of the subsequent participle ἐξενέγκαντες (*carried out*)

συστενάζει   VIPA--3S   συστενάζω

συστενάζω *sigh* or *groan together*, as when all share pain in common; metaphorically, of creation pictured as anxiously awaiting its time for regeneration *groan throughout (all its parts)* (RO 8.22)

συστοιχεῖ   VIPA--3S   συστοιχέω
συστοιχεῖν   VNPA   "

συστοιχέω strictly *be in a series with*; literally, of soldiers *be in the same row* or *rank, stand in the same line*; figuratively, in logical discussions of things that have distinctive features that fit in the same category *correspond to* (GA 4.25)

συστοιχοῦσα   VPPANF-S   συστοιχέω
συστρατιώτη   N-DM-S   συστρατιώτης
συστρατιώτην   N-AM-S   "

συστρατιώτης, ου, ὁ *fellow soldier*; figuratively *associate* or *fellow worker* in the cause of Christ

συστραφέντες   VPAPNM-S   συστρέφω
συστραφῶσι(ν)   VSAA--3P   "
συστρεφομένων   VPPPGM-P   "

συστρέφω 1aor. συνέστρεψα; pf. pass. ptc. συνεστραμμένος (AC 11.28); 2aor. pass. συνεστράφην; (1) *gather (up), bring together, collect* (AC 28.3); (2) passive, of people *be gathered, come together* (AC 10.41); (3) *be all together, go around together* (MT 17.22)

συστρέψαντος   VPAAGM-S   συστρέφω

συστροφή, ῆς, ἡ as a disorderly gathering for a negative purpose *commotion, riot, uproar* (AC 19.40); as involving an unlawful purpose *conspiracy, plot*; ποιεῖν συστροφήν *hold a secret meeting, form a conspiracy* (AC 23.12)

συστροφήν   N-AF-S   συστροφή
συστροφῆς   N-GF-S   "
συσχηματίζεσθαι   VNPM   συσχηματίζω
   VNPP   "
συσχηματίζεσθε   VMPM--2P   "
   VMPP--2P   "
συσχηματιζόμενοι   VPPMNM-P   "
   VPPPNM-P   "

συσχηματίζω (and **συνσχηματίζω**) as fashioning something by using a shaped container *form, mold*; figuratively in the NT; (1) middle *conform oneself to, change one's behavior to be like* (perhaps RO 12.2 and 1P 1.14); (2) passive *allow oneself to be changed to be like, be conformed to, be made like* (probably RO 12.2 and 1P 1.14)

Συχάρ, ἡ (also **Σιχάρ**) indeclinable; *Sychar*, a small city of Samaria, probably near Jacob's well at the base of Mount Ebal (JN 4.5)

Συχέμ, ὁ and **ἡ** indeclinable; (1) ἡ Σ. *Shechem*, a city of Samaria at the base of Mount Gerizim, modern Nablus (JN 4.5; AC 7.16); (2) ὁ Σ. *Shechem*, masculine proper noun (AC 7.16)

σφαγή, ῆς, ἡ literally *slaughter(ing)* by cutting or slashing the throat; πρόβατα σφαγῆς *sheep (destined) for slaughter* (RO 8.36); idiomatically ἐν ἡμέρᾳ σφαγῆς literally *in a day of slaughter* in JA 5.5 is variously understood: (1) *for a day marked for* or *characterized by slaughter*, in reference to a time of destructive judgment; (2) *in a day of slaughter*, in reference to rich people fattening

themselves, i.e. amassing more wealth at the expense of poor people in a troubled time; the first alternative is to be preferred in view of James's threatening tone against the rich in 5.1–3

σφαγήν   N-AF-S   σφαγή
σφαγῆς   N-GF-S   "
σφάγια   N-AN-P   σφάγιον

σφάγιον, ου, τό as a sacrificed animal *victim*; plural *(sacrificed) offerings* (AC 7.42)

σφάζω fut. σφάξω; 1aor. ἔσφαξα; pf. pass. ἔσφαγμαι; 2aor. pass. ἐσφάγην; (1) of animals, especially when killed as a sacrifice *slaughter, slay*; metaphorically, of Jesus' atoning death as the Lamb of God (RV 5.6, 9); (2) of persons *put to death by violence, kill, murder* (1J 3.12); ὡς ἐσφαγμένη εἰς θάνατον *as if mortally wounded* (RV 13.3)

σφαλήσεται   VIFP--3S   σφάλλω

σφάλλω 2fut. pass. σφαλήσομαι; *make to fall, cause to stumble*; passive *fall, stumble, be tripped up* (MT 15.14)

σφάξουσι(ν)   VIFA--3P   σφάζω
σφάξωσι(ν)   VSAA--3P   "

σφόδρα adverb; *exceedingly, extremely, greatly, very much*

σφόδρα   AB   σφόδρα

σφοδρῶς *exceedingly, greatly, violently*

σφοδρῶς   AB   σφοδρῶς
σφραγῖδα   N-AF-S   σφραγίς
σφραγῖδας   N-AF-P   "
σφραγίδων   N-GF-P   "

σφραγίζω 1aor. ἐσφράγισα, mid. ἐσφραγισάμην; pf. pass. ἐσφράγισμαι; 1aor. pass. ἐσφραγίσθην; *seal*; (1) literally *seal up, secure by putting a seal on* (MT 27.66); figuratively, as keeping something secret *seal (up), conceal* (RV 10.4); (2) as providing a sign of identification or ownership *(mark with a) seal* (RV 7.3); metaphorically, of endowment with the Spirit (EP 1.13); (3) figuratively, from the idea of an official seal on a document; (a) *confirm, attest, certify* (JN 3.33); (b) metaphorically, as a commercial technical term indicating a safely accomplished transaction σφραγίζειν τινί τὸν καρπὸν τοῦτον literally *seal to someone this fruit*, i.e. *safely turn over to someone this kind provision* (RO 15.28)

σφραγίς, ίδος, ἡ *seal*; (1) literally; (a) as the instrument for producing a seal or stamp *seal* (RV 7.2); (b) by metonymy, as the impression made *seal, mark* (RV 9.4); metaphorically *identifying authentication, way to recognize* (2T 2.19); (2) figuratively, in the sense of an official mark showing authenticity *certification, confirmation, proof* (RO 4.11; 1C 9.2)

σφραγίς   N-NF-S   σφραγίς
σφραγισάμενος   VPAMNM-S   σφραγίζω
σφραγίσαντες   VPAANM-P   "
σφραγίσης   VSAA--2S   "
σφραγῖσι(ν)   N-DF-P   σφραγίς
σφράγισον   VMAA--2S   σφραγίζω
σφραγίσωμεν   VSAA--1P   "
σφυδρά   N-NN-P   σφυδρόν

σφυδρόν, οῦ, τό as a part of the body *ankle* (AC 3.7)

σφυρά   N-NN-P   σφυρόν

σφυρόν, οῦ, τό (1) *ankle*; (2) *heel*; either meaning is possible in AC 3.7; the former is to be preferred

σχεδόν adverb; *nearly, almost*

σχεδόν	AB	σχεδόν

σχῆμα, ατος, τό as what may be known from without about a person or thing; (1) of persons *outward appearance, form, bearing* (PH 2.7); (2) of a way of life *(distinctive) form, nature, present scheme of things* (1C 7.31)

σχῆμα	N-NN-S	σχῆμα
σχήματι	N-DN-S	"
σχῆτε	VSAA--2P	ἔχω
σχίζει	VIPA--3S	σχίζω
σχιζομένους	VPPPAM-P	"

σχίζω fut. σχίσω; 1aor. ἔσχισα; 1aor. pass. ἐσχίσθην; literally *split, divide, tear (apart), rend* (MT 27.51); figuratively, of the effect of contrary views *cause division, divide*; passive *become divided* or *disunited* (AC 14.4)

σχίσας	VPAANM-S	σχίζω
σχίσει	VIFA--3S	"

σχίσμα, ατος, τό literally *split, rift, division*; in a garment *tear, rent* (MT 9.16); figuratively, of doctrinal differences and divided loyalties within a group *schism, division of opinion, discord* (JN 7.43; 1C 12.25)

σχίσμα	N-NN-S	σχίσμα
σχίσματα	N-AN-P	"
	N-NN-P	"
σχίσωμεν	VSAA--1P	σχίζω
σχοινία	N-AN-P	σχοινίον

σχοινίον, ου, τό strictly *cord made of* (the fibers from) *rushes*; generally *rope, cord*

σχοινίων	N-GN-P	σχοινίον
σχολάζητε	VSPA--2P	σχολάζω
σχολάζοντα	VPPAAM-S	"

σχολάζω 1aor. ἐσχόλασα; *be at leisure, have time*; (1) of persons, with the dative *give one's time to, devote oneself to* (1C 7.5); (2) of a building *be unoccupied, stand empty*; metaphorically, of a person after demons have been caused to leave (MT 12.44)

σχολάσητε	VSAA--2P	σχολάζω

σχολή, ῆς, ἡ strictly *freedom from occupation*; hence, a place where there is leisure for learning *school, lecture hall* (AC 19.9)

σχολῇ	N-DF-S	σχολή
σχῶ	VSAA--1S	ἔχω
σχῶμεν	VSAA--1P	"
σχῶσι(ν)	VSAA--3P	"
σῷ	A--DM2S	σός
	A--DN2S	"
σώζει	VIPA--3S	σώζω
σώζει	VIPA--3S	"
σώζειν	VNPA	"
σώζειν	VNPA	"
σώζεσθαι	VNPP	"
σώζεσθαι	VNPP	"
σώζεσθε	VIPP--2P	"
σώζεσθε	VIPP--2P	"
σώζεται	VIPP--3S	"
σώζεται	VIPP--3S	"
σώζετε	VMPA--2P	"
σώζετε	VMPA--2P	"
σωζόμενοι	VPPPNM-P	"
σωζόμενοι	VPPPNM-P	"
σωζομένοις	VPPPDM-P	"
σωζομένοις	VPPPDM-P	"
σωζομένους	VPPPAM-P	"
σωζομένους	VPPPAM-P	"
σωζομένων	VPPPGM-P	"
σώζοντος	VPPAGM-S	"
σώζοντος	VPPAGM-S	"

σώζω (and **σώζω**) impf. pass. ἐσωζόμην; fut. σώσω; 1aor. ἔσωσα; pf. σέσωκα; pf. pass. σέσωσμαι; 1aor. pass. ἐσώθην; 1fut. pass. σωθήσομαι; *save, preserve from harm, rescue*; (1) of natural dangers and afflictions; (a) in relation to acute physical danger *deliver, save, rescue* (AC 27.20); (b) in relation to a stressful and threatening situation *save, bring out safely* (JN 12.27); (c) in relation to sickness and disease *heal, cure, restore to health* (MT 9.21); (2) in a religious sense, in relation to spiritual dangers and threat of eternal death; (a) *save, rescue from sin, bring to salvation* (RO 5.9; EP 2.8); (b) of human beings mediating the divine salvation (RO 11.14; 1C 7.16); (c) of the instrumentality of spiritual things, as God's Word, baptism, faith, that lead to salvation *save, deliver* (JA 1.21; 2.14; 1P 3.21)

σωθῇ	VSAP--3S	σώζω
σωθῆναι	VNAP	"
σωθήσει	VIFA--3S	"
σωθήσεται	VIFP--3S	"
σωθήσῃ	VIFP--2S	"
σωθήσομαι	VIFP--1S	"
σωθησόμεθα	VIFP--1P	"
σώθητε	VMAP--2P	"
σωθῆτε	VSAP--2P	"
σωθῶ	VSAP--1S	"
σωθῶμεν	VSAA--1P	"
σωθῶσι(ν)	VSAP--3P	"

σῶμα, ατος, τό *body*; (1) literally; (a) as the *living body* of a human being or animal (MT 6.25; JA 3.3); (b) as the *dead body* of a human being or animal *corpse* (MK 15.43; HE 13.11); (c) plural, by metonymy, of persons valued impersonally as bodies for serving *slaves* (RV 18.13); (d) as the distinctive form of created things, as plants (1C 15.37, 38), and sun, moon, or stars (1C 15.40); (e) as the seat of mortal life and subject to immortal life through resurrection *body* (1C 15.44); (f) as the material part of man in distinction from soul and spirit *body* (1TH 5.23); (g) in relation to the sexual function, the reproductive powers (RO 4.19; 1C 6.13; 7.4); (2) figuratively; (a) as *substance* or *reality* in contrast to shadow (CO 2.17); (b) as a group of people united by a mystical union *body*, used of the church as the *body* of which Christ is the head (RO 12.5)

σῶμα	N-AN-S	σῶμα
	N-NN-S	"
σώμασι(ν)	N-DN-P	"
σώματα	N-AN-P	"
	N-NN-P	"
σώματι	N-DN-S	"
σωματική	A--NF-S	σωματικός

σωματικός, ή, όν (1) having the form and characteristics of a body *bodily, tangible* (LU 3.22); (2) pertaining to the body *physical* (1T 4.8)

σωματικῷ	A--DN-S	σωματικός

σωματικῶς   adverb; *bodily, corporeally*; in CO 2.9 τὸ πλήρωμα τῆς θεότητος σ. *the fullness of the Godhead bodily*
has two possible meanings: (1) *in bodily form, in the
form of a body*, i.e. a resurrected body; (2) *in reality*,
contrasted with shadow in 2.17; the former, as referring
to the true and permanent humanity of Jesus, is to be
preferred, especially in correlation with 1.19

σωματικῶς	AB	σωματικῶς
σώματος	N-GN-S	σῶμα
σωμάτων	N-GN-P	"

Σώπατρος, ου, ὁ   *Sopater*, masculine proper noun (AC
20.4)

Σώπατρος	N-NM-S	Σώπατρος
σωρεύσεις	VIFA--2S	σωρεύω

σωρεύω   fut. σωρεύσω; pf. pass. σεσώρευμαι; (1) *pile on,
heap up*; idiomatically, in correlation with Proverbs
25.21–22, of overcoming hostility against oneself by
showing kindness, σωρεύειν ἄνθρακας πυρὸς ἐπὶ τὴν
κεφαλήν literally *heap coals of fire on the head*, i.e. *cause
to feel ashamed, help to become different* (RO 12.20);
(2) figuratively and passive, of persons *be overwhelmed
by* something, *be burdened with, be much involved with*
(2T 3.6)

σῶσαι	VNAA	σῴζω
σώσαντος	VPAAGM-S	"
σώσας	VPAANM-S	"
σωσάτω	VMAA--3S	"
σώσει	VIFA--3S	"
σώσεις	VIFA--2S	"
σώσετε	VIFA--2P	"
Σωσθένην	N-AF-S	Σωσθένης

Σωσθένης, ους, ὁ   *Sosthenes*, masculine proper noun

Σωσθένης	N-NM-S	Σωσθένης
Σωσθένους	N-GM-S	"

Σωσίπατρος, ου, ὁ   *Sosipater*, masculine proper noun (RO
16.21)

Σωσίπατρος	N-NM-S	Σωσίπατρος
σῶσον	VMAA--2S	σῴζω
σώσω	VIFA--1S	"
	VSAA--1S	"
σώσων	VPFANM-S	"

σωτήρ, ῆρος, ὁ   as the agent of salvation or deliverance
savior, deliverer, rescuer; (1) used of God as the source
of salvation *Savior* (TI 1.3); (2) used of Jesus Christ as
the agent sent by God to bring deliverance to mankind
Savior (AC 13.23)

σωτήρ	N-NM-S	σωτήρ
σωτῆρα	N-AM-S	"
σωτῆρι	N-DM-S	"

σωτηρία, ας, ἡ   *salvation, deliverance*; (1) physically, as
rescue from danger *deliverance, preservation, safety*
(HE 11.7); (2) as a religious technical term *safety of

the soul in a spiritual sense *salvation* (2C 7.10); (3) of
the messianic deliverance at the end of the present age
salvation (RO 13.11)

σωτηρία	N-NF-S	σωτηρία
σωτηρίαν	N-AF-S	"
σωτηρίας	N-GF-S	"
σωτήριον	AP-AN-S	σωτήριος
	AP-NN-S	"

σωτήριος, ον   of what is related to the means of salvation *rescuing, bringing salvation, delivering* (TI 2.11);
neuter as a substantive τὸ σωτήριον *the (messianic)
salvation* (LU 3.6); by metonymy, the Messiah himself
as mediating *salvation* or *deliverance* (LU 2.30)

σωτήριος	A--NF-S	σωτήριος
σωτηρίου	AP-GN-S	"
σωτῆρος	N-GM-S	σωτήρ
σώφρονα	A--AM-S	σώφρων
σώφρονας	A--AF-P	"
	A--AM-P	"
σωφρονεῖν	VNPA	σωφρονέω

σωφρονέω   1aor. ἐσωφρόνησα; *be of sound mind*; (1) of
mental health *be sane, be in one's right mind, think
straight* (MK 5.15), opposite μαίνομαι (*be out of one's
mind, be insane*); (2) of intellectual soundness *be sensible, use good sense, be reasonable* (2C 5.13); (3) of a
measured and ordered way of life *be self-controlled, be
moderate, be sober* (RO 12.3)

σωφρονήσατε	VMAA--2P	σωφρονέω
σωφρονίζουσι(ν)	VIFA--3P	σωφρονίζω

σωφρονίζω   strictly *bring someone to be self-controlled,
be sensible*; hence *train, teach, advise* (TI 2.4)

σωφρονίζωσι(ν)	VSPA--3P	σωφρονίζω

σωφρονισμός, οῦ, ὁ   (1) as a process *teaching of moderation, making temperate, advice for making wise decisions* (possibly 2T 1.7); (2) as the resultant state *self-
control, discipline, sensible behavior* (probably 2T 1.7)

σωφρονισμοῦ	N-GM-S	σωφρονισμός
σωφρονοῦμεν	VIPA--1P	σωφρονέω
σωφρονοῦντα	VPPAAM-S	"

σωφρόνως   adverb; *sensibly, with self-control, temperately*
(TI 2.12)

σωφρόνως	AB	σωφρόνως

σωφροσύνη, ης, ἡ   (1) as a quality of life characterized
by the ability to restrain passions and impulses *self-
control, moderation, sensibleness* (1T 2.9); (2) as intellectual soundness *rationality, reasonableness, good sense*
(AC 26.25)

σωφροσύνης	N-GF-S	σωφροσύνη

σώφρων, ον, gen. **ονος**   strictly *having a sound* or *healthy
mind*; as having ability to curb desires and impulses
so as to produce a measured and orderly life *self-controlled, sensible*

τ T

τά DANP ὁ
    DANP+ "
    DNNP "
    DNNP+ "
    DVNP "
Ταβειθά Ταβιθά
ταβέρνη, ης, ἡ from Latin *tabernae*; *inn, shop, store*; plural, as a staging post on the Appian Way 33 Roman miles southeast of Rome, Τρεῖς Ταβέρναι *Three Shops* (AC 28.15)
Ταβερνῶν N-GF-P ταβέρνη
Ταβηθά see Ταβιθά
Ταβιθά, ἡ (also **Ταβειθά**) indeclinable; transliterated from the Aramaic; *Tabitha*, feminine proper noun, interpreted in AC 9.36 as meaning Δορκάς (*gazelle*), a small antelope or deer
ταβιθά ταλιθά
τάγμα, ατος, τό (1) as what is placed in order or ranked *right order, (appointed) position*; (2) as a group of persons made into a unit *class, division*; as the order in which a series of events takes place *order, turn, place (in line)* (1C 15.23)
τάγματι N-DN-S τάγμα
Ταδδαῖον N-AM-S Θαδδαῖος
τάδε APDAN-P ὅδε
ταῖς DDFP ὁ
    DDFP+ "
τακήσεται VIFP--3S τήκω
τακτῆ A--DF-S τακτός
τακτός, ή, όν of an arranged day or time *fixed, decided on, appointed* (AC 12.21)
ταλαιπωρέω 1aor. ἐταλαιπώρησα; intransitively in the NT, of emotion resulting from inner or outer torment *be wretched* or *sorrowful*; by metonymy, as expressing a miserable feeling *show grief* or *remorse, lament* (JA 4.9)
ταλαιπωρήσατε VMAA--2P ταλαιπωρέω
ταλαιπωρία, ας, ἡ as an emotional condition that arises from inner or outer torment *misery, wretchedness*; plural *hardships, miseries* (JA 5.1)
ταλαιπωρία N-NF-S ταλαιπωρία
ταλαιπωρίαις N-DF-P "
ταλαίπωρος, ον as feeling inwardly or outwardly tormented *miserable, wretched, distressed* (RO 7.24); substantivally ὁ τ. *the miserable one* (RV 3.17)
ταλαίπωρος A--NM-S ταλαίπωρος
τάλαντα N-AN-P τάλαντον
ταλαντιαία A--NF-S ταλαντιαῖος
ταλαντιαῖος, αία, ον *weighing a talent, of the weight of a talent*; the Hebrew talent was equivalent to 3,000 shekels or 40 kilograms or 90 sixteen-ounce pounds; the Babylonian talent varied from 28 to 36 kilograms,

or 60 to 80 sixteen-ounce pounds (RV 16.21; cf. RSV *heavy as a hundredweight*)
τάλαντον, ου, τό *talent*; (1) as a measure of weight varying in size from 28 to 36 kilograms, or 60 to 80 sixteen-ounce pounds, equivalent to 3,000 Hebrew shekels; (2) as a large unit of money varying in value with the metal involved, whether gold, silver, or copper, it is possible to translate variously as *millions, thousands,* or *hundreds* (of dollars, francs, pesos, etc.)
τάλαντον N-AN-S τάλαντον
ταλάντων N-GN-P "
ταλειθά ταλιθά
ταλιθά, ἡ (also **θάβιτα, θαβιτά, ῥαβιθά, ταβιθά, ταλειθά**) indeclinable; transliterated from the Aramaic; interpreted in MK 5.41 as τὸ κοράσιον *(little) girl, maiden*
ταμείοις N-DN-P ταμείον
ταμείον, ου, τό (also **ταμιείον**) (1) as a place for storage *storehouse* (LU 12.24); (2) more generally of the interior rooms of a house reserved for privacy *private room, inner chamber* (MT 6.6)
ταμείον N-AN-S ταμείον
    N-NN-S "
ταμιείοις N-DN-P "
ταμίοις N-DN-P see ταμείοις
τανῦν an adverb from τά (neuter plural article) and νῦν (*now*); *now*
τανῦν AB τανῦν
ταξάμενοι VPAMNM-P τάσσω
τάξει N-DF-S τάξις
τάξιν N-AF-S "
τάξις, εως, ἡ (1) as an arrangement for temple service *sequence, fixed succession, order* (LU 1.8); (2) as a distinctive class characterized by fixed appointment and position *kind, type, order* (HE 5.6); (3) as a characteristic of well-regulated conduct *good order, orderliness* (CO 2.5); κατὰ τάξιν *in an orderly manner* (1C 14.40)
ταπεινοῖς A--DM-P ταπεινός
    A--DN-P "
ταπεινός, ή, όν (1) literally, of situation *low*, opposite ὑψηλός (*high*); (2) figuratively in the NT; (a) of persons, of trivial power or significance *lowly, poor, undistinguished* (JA 1.9); substantivally ταπεινοί *unimportant people* (LU 1.52); (b) as an emotional state *downhearted, depressed* (2C 7.6); substantivally οἱ ταπεινοί *the downhearted people* (2C 7.6); (c) as an attitude; in a bad sense *servile, abject, subservient* (probably 2C 10.1); in a good sense *lowly, humble, gentle* (MT 11.29; perhaps 2C 10.1); substantivally ταπεινοί *humble people* (JA 4.6); (d) neuter plural τὰ ταπεινά as a substantive, of things *humble tasks* (probably RO 12.16), opposite τὰ ὑψηλά (*high things, lofty things*)
ταπεινός A--NM-S ταπεινός

374

ταπεινούς A--AM-P "
ταπεινοῦσθαι VNPP ταπεινόω
ταπεινόφρονες A--NM-P ταπεινόφρων

ταπεινοφροσύνη, ης, ἡ in the NT, as a quality of voluntary submission and unselfishness *humility, self-effacement* (AC 20.19), opposite ὑπερηφανία (*arrogance, pride*); in a negative sense, as a misdirected submission in cultic behavior *self-abasement, (false) humility, self-mortification* (CO 2.18, 23)

ταπεινοφροσύνη N-DF-S ταπεινοφροσύνη
ταπεινοφροσύνην N-AF-S "
ταπεινοφροσύνης N-GF-S "

ταπεινόφρων, ον, gen. **ονος** as having a modest opinion of oneself *humble, having a humble attitude* (1P 3.8)

ταπεινόω fut. ταπεινώσω; 1aor. ἐταπείνωσα; 1aor. pass. ἐταπεινώθην; 1fut. pass. ταπεινωθήσομαι; (1) literally *lower, make low*; of a mountain *level off* (LU 3.5); (2) figuratively; (a) in a negative sense, of assigning someone or oneself to a lower place in order to abase *humiliate, humble, degrade* (2C 11.7); (b) passive, in a positive sense, of voluntary submission *humble (oneself), become humble* (JA 4.10); as disciplining oneself to live without abundance *be in need, be poor* (PH 4.12)

ταπεινωθήσεται VIFP--3S ταπεινόω
ταπεινώθητε VMAP--2P "
ταπεινῶν VPPANM-S "
ταπεινώσει N-DF-S ταπείνωσις
 VIFA--3S ταπεινόω
ταπεινώσεως N-GF-S ταπείνωσις
ταπεινώσῃ VSAA--3S ταπεινόω
ταπείνωσιν N-AF-S ταπείνωσις

ταπείνωσις, εως, ἡ (1) as an experience of being abased *humiliation* (JA 1.10); (2) as a state *low status, humility, lowly condition* (LU 1.48)

ταρασσέσθω VMPP--3S ταράσσω
ταράσσοντες VPPANM-P

ταράσσω impf. ἐτάρασσον; 1aor. ἐτάραξα; pf. pass. τετάραγμαι; 1aor. pass. ἐταράχθην; (1) literally *shake* or *stir up* (JN 5.4, 7); (2) figuratively, of a crowd *cause an uproar* (AC 17.8); of acute mental or spiritual agitation *disturb, unsettle, throw into confusion* (AC 15.24); passive *be troubled, be upset, be agitated* (MT 2.3); with an added component of fear *be frightened, be terrified* (MT 14.26); with an added component of threat *be intimidated* (1P 3.14)

ταράσσων VPPANM-S ταράσσω
ταραχαί N-NF-P ταραχή

ταραχή, ῆς, ἡ literally, as a disturbance in the usual order of things; of water *stirring up* (JN 5.4); figuratively *tumult, (rebellious) commotion, riot* (MK 13.8)

ταραχήν N-AF-S ταραχή
ταραχθῇ VSAP--3S ταράσσω
ταραχθῆτε VSAP--2P "

τάραχος, ου, ὁ (1) as mental agitation *extreme anxiety, confusion* (AC 12.18); (2) as public excitement *commotion, serious disturbance, tumult* (AC 19.23)

τάραχος N-NM-S τάραχος
Ταρσέα N-AM-S Ταρσεύς

Ταρσεύς, έως, ὁ *person from Tarsus*, a native from Tarsus, capital city of Cilicia in southeastern Asia Minor

Ταρσεύς N-NM-S Ταρσεύς

Ταρσόν N-AF-S Ταρσός

Ταρσός, οῦ, ἡ *Tarsus*, the capital of Cilicia in southeastern Asia Minor

Ταρσῷ N-DF-S Ταρσός

ταρταρόω 1aor. ἐταρτάρωσα; strictly *hurl into Tartarus*, regarded by the Greeks as a place of torment and punishment below Hades; probably so regarded in Jewish apocalyptic literature also; *consign to Tartarus, throw into hell* (2P 2.4)

ταρταρώσας VPAANM-S ταρταρόω
τάς DAFP ὁ
 DAFP+ "
τασσόμενος VPPPNM-S τάσσω

τάσσω 1aor. ἔταξα, mid. ἐταξάμην; pf. τέταχα; pf. pass. τέταγμαι; (1) *assign to a place* or *task, appoint, decide* (AC 15.2); passive, in relation to properly constituted authority *be instituted, be appointed, be established* (RO 13.1); (2) passive, with an abstract noun ὅσοι ἦσαν τεταγμένοι εἰς ζωὴν αἰώνιον *as many as had become disposed toward eternal life* (possibly AC 13.48) or *all those who were appointed to eternal life* (probably AC 13.48); (3) as determining a fixed time or course of events, middle for active *arrange, order, appoint* (MT 28.16; AC 28.23); (4) as doing something regularly and devotedly *give oneself to* (1C 16.15)

ταῦροι N-NM-P ταῦρος

ταῦρος, ου, ὁ *bull, ox*

ταύρους N-AM-P ταῦρος
ταύρων N-GM-P "
ταῦτα APDAN-P οὗτος
 APDNN-P "
 A-DAN-P "
 A-DNN-P "

ταὐτά by crasis for τὰ αὐτά, *the same things*

ταὐτά DANP&AP-AN-P ταὐτά
ταύταις APDDF-P οὗτος
 A-DDF-P "
ταύτας APDAF-P "
 A-DAF-P "
ταύτῃ APDDF-S "
 A-DDF-S "
ταύτην APDAF-S "
 A-DAF-S "
ταύτης APDGF-S "
 A-DGF-S "

ταφή, ῆς, ἡ *burial*; by metonymy *burial place, grave, burying ground* (MT 27.7)

ταφήν N-AF-S ταφή
τάφοις N-DM-P τάφος
τάφον N-AM-S "

τάφος, ου, ὁ literally *grave, tomb, sepulcher* (MT 23.27); metaphorically, as the throat of an evil person who speaks destructively *means of speaking harmfully* (RO 3.13)

τάφος N-NM-S τάφος
τάφου N-GM-S "
τάφους N-AM-P "

τάχα adverb; *perhaps, possibly, probably*

τάχα AB τάχα
τάχει N-DN-S τάχος

ταχέως an adverb of ταχύς (*quick*); (1) as qualifying an action *quickly, at once, without delay* (LU 14.21); (2) as qualifying time *soon* (1C 4.19); (3) in an unfavorable sense *hastily, with too much haste* (GA 1.6)

ταχέως	AB	ταχέως
ταχινή	A--NF-S	ταχινός
ταχινήν	A--AF-S	"

ταχινός, ή, όν as indicating what is near at hand or impending *imminent, swift, coming soon*

τάχιον	ABM	ταχύς
τάχιστα	ABS	"

τάχος, ους, τό *speed, haste, swiftness*; adverbially ἐν τάχει *without delay, at once, speedily*

ταχύ	AB	ταχύς

ταχύς, εῖα, ύ (1) as an adjective *quick, prompt, ready* (JA 1.19), opposite βραδύς (*slow*); (2) predominately, neuter singular ταχύ as an adverb; (a) as qualifying action *quickly, swiftly, rapidly* (MT 28.7); (b) as qualifying time *without delay, right away, at once, soon (afterward)* (MT 5.25); (3) comparative τάχιον; (a) *more quickly, faster, sooner* (JN 20.4); (b) without a time comparison *quickly, without delay* (JN 13.27); (4) superlative τάχιστα *very quickly*; with ὡς *as soon as possible* (AC 17.15)

ταχύς	A--NM-S	ταχύς

τέ an enclitic particle used as a conjunction, closely coordinating concepts, clauses, and occasionally whole sentences; (1) used alone, indicating close or corresponding relationship; (a) between clauses *and, likewise, and so* (JN 4.42; AC 2.40); (b) between single concepts (HE 6.5); τὲ . . . τέ *not only . . . but also, both . . . and* (AC 2.46; RO 14.8); (2) τὲ . . . καί and τε καί *and, both . . . and* (AC 5.24; HE 5.1)

τέ	AB	τέ
	CC	"
	CC+	"
	CH	"
	CS	"
τεθέαμαι	VIRD--1S	θεάομαι
	VIRO--1S	"
τεθεάμεθα	VIRD--1P	"
	VIRO--1P	"
τεθέαται	VIRD--3S	"
	VIRO--3S	"
τέθεικα	VIRA--1S	τίθημι
τεθείκατε	VIRA--2P	"
τεθεικώς	VPRANM-S	"
τεθειμένος	VPRPNM-S	"
τέθειται	VIRP--3S	"
τεθεμελιωμένοι	VPRPNM-P	θεμελιόω
τεθεμελιωμένων	VPRPGM-P	"
τεθεμελίωτο	VILP--3S	"
τεθεραπευμέναι	VPRPNF-P	θεραπεύω
τεθεραπευμένον	VPRPAM-S	"
τεθεραπευμένῳ	VPRPDM-S	"
τεθεράπευσθε	VIRP--2P	"
	VMRP--2P	"
τεθῇ	VSAP--3S	τίθημι
τεθῆναι	VNAP	"
τεθησαυρισμένοι	VPRPNM-P	θησαυρίζω
τεθλιμμένη	VPRPNF-S	θλίβω
τεθνάναι	VNRA	θνήσκω

τεθνήκασι(ν)	VIRA--3P	"
τέθνηκε(ν)	VIRA--3S	"
τεθνηκέναι	VNRA	"
τεθνηκότα	VPRAAM-S	"
τεθνηκότος	VPRAGM-S	"
τεθνηκώς	VPRANM-S	"
τεθραμμένος	VPRPNM-S	τρέφω
τεθραυματισμένους	VPRPAM-P	θραυματίζω
τεθραυμένους	VPRPAM-P	θραύω
τεθραυσμένους	VPRPAM-P	"
τεθυμένα	VPRPNN-P	θύω
τεθῶσι(ν)	VSAP--3P	τίθημι
τείχη	N-NN-P	τεῖχος

τεῖχος, ους, τό *wall*, especially of a city or town, used as a strong fortification

τεῖχος	N-AN-S	τεῖχος
	N-NN-S	"
τείχους	N-GN-S	"
τεκεῖν	VNAA	τίκτω
τέκη	VSAA--3S	"
τεκμηρίοις	N-DN-P	τεκμήριον

τεκμήριον, ου, τό used of a sign or evidence that removes doubt *clear* or *convincing proof* (AC 1.3)

τέκνα	N-AN-P	τέκνον
	N-NN-P	"
	N-VN-P	"
τεκνία	N-VN-P	τεκνίον

τεκνίον, ου, τό diminutive of τέκνον; *little child*; figuratively, as a term of affectionate address *my dear children, my good friends* (JN 13.33)

τεκνογονεῖν	VNPA	τεκνογονέω

τεκνογονέω of motherhood *bear children, have children* (1T 5.14)

τεκνογονία, ας, ἡ *bearing children, childbearing, motherhood* (1T 2.15)

τεκνογονίας	N-GF-S	τεκνογονία
τέκνοις	N-DN-P	τέκνον

τέκνον, ου, τό (1) literally *child*; (a) from the standpoint of origin and without reference to sex distinction *child* (AC 7.5); (b) plural, generically *descendants, posterity, children* (MT 2.18); (c) where the sex is made clear by the context *son* (MT 21.28a); (2) figuratively; (a) often as a form of familiar or affectionate address *my son, my child* (MT 9.2); (b) spiritually, as a convert, follower, disciple *child, son* (1C 4.17); (c) plural, as the members of a church *children* (2J 1); (d) plural, as those who share the faith or nature of a spiritual "ancestor," as Abraham (MT 3.9) or Sarah (1P 3.6); (e) as believers, in relation to God as the heavenly Father (JN 1.12); (f) Hebraistically, the inhabitants of a city (MT 23.37); of a person, as characterized by some condition or quality *child of, one obedient to* (EP 5.8), *person of* (1P 1.14), *one subject to* (2P 2.14)

τέκνον	N-AN-S	τέκνον
	N-NN-S	"
	N-VN-S	"

τεκνοτροφέω 1aor. ἐτεκνοτρόφησα; *bring up children, rear a family* (1T 5.10)

τέκνου	N-GN-S	τέκνον

τεκνόω 1aor. ἐτέκνωσα; of a father's part *father*; of a mother's part *bear (a child)* (HE 11.11)

τέκνῳ	N-DN-S	τέκνον
τέκνων	N-GN-P	"
τεκνῶσαι	VNAA	τεκνόω
τέκτον	N-NM-S	see τέκτων
τέκτονος	N-GM-S	τέκτων

τέκτων, ονος, ὁ   *carpenter, builder, craftsman*

τέκτων	N-NM-S	τέκτων
τελεῖ	VIPA--3S	τελέω
τελεία	A--NF-S	τέλειος
τέλειοι	A--NM-P	"
τελείοις	A--DM-P	"
τέλειον	A--AM-S	"
	A--AN-S	"
	A--NN-S	"

τέλειος, εία, ον   *complete, perfect*; (1) with its chief component as totality, as opposed to partial or limited; (a) of things *in full measure, undivided, complete, entire* (RO 12.2); substantivally τὸ τέλειον *the finish, completeness* (1C 13.10); comparative τελειότερος, τέρα, ον *more complete* or *perfect* (HE 9.11); (b) of persons *complete, perfect* (MT 5.48; 19.21); (2) with its chief component being full development as opposed to immaturity; (a) of persons *full grown, mature* (1C 14.20); substantivally οἱ τέλειοι *adults, mature persons*; used of spiritually mature persons (1C 2.6); (b) of things *fully developed, complete* (JA 1.4; 1J 4.18); (3) with its chief component being full preparation or readiness *complete, perfect* (CO 1.28; JA 3.2); in all its meanings τ. carries the component of a purpose that has been achieved

τέλειος	A--NM-S	τέλειος
τελειοτέρας	A-MGF-S	"

τελειότης, ητος, ἡ   as a state of being *completion, perfection*; (1) with a component of totality *wholeness, perfect unity* (CO 3.14); (2) with a component of having achieved a purpose *maturity, perfection* (HE 6.1)

τελειότητα	N-AF-S	τελειότης
τελειότητος	N-GF-S	"
τελειοῦμαι	VIPM--1S	τελειόω
	VIPP--1S	"
τελείους	A--AM-P	τέλειος
τελειοῦται	VIPP--3S	τελειόω

τελειόω   1aor. ἐτελείωσα; pf. τετελείωκα; pf. pass. τετελείωμαι; 1aor. pass. ἐτελειώθην; (1) from the standpoint of complete preparation, bringing something to its goal *complete, fulfill, accomplish*; (a) of Jesus *perfect, make perfect, completely prepare* (HE 2.10); (b) of promises, prophecies, plans *fulfill, carry out, make happen* (JN 19.28); (c) of dying, as finishing one's earthly course of life successfully; passive *be perfected* (LU 13.32; HE 12.23); (2) from the standpoint of totality, of executing something fully *accomplish, complete, carry out* (JN 4.34; AC 20.24); (3) spiritually, as qualifying someone to stand before God and dwell in his presence, especially in Hebrews *perfect, make perfect* (HE 7.19; 10.14)

τελεῖται	VIPP--3S	τελέω
τελεῖτε	VIPA--2P	"
τελειωθείς	VPAPNM-S	τελειόω
τελειωθῇ	VSAP--3S	"
τελειωθῶμεν	VSAP--1P	"
τελειωθῶσι(ν)	VSAP--3P	"

τελείωμαι	VSPP--1S	"
τελείων	A--GM-P	τέλειος

τελείως   adverb; *fully, completely, altogether* (1P 1.13)

τελείως	AB	τελείως
τελειῶσαι	VNAA	τελειόω
τελειωσάντων	VPAAGM-P	"
τελειώσας	VPAANM-S	"

τελείωσις, εως, ἡ   as designating an action; (1) as actualization of a promise *fulfillment, accomplishment* (LU 1.45); (2) as a completion of spiritual preparation *perfection* (HE 7.11)

τελείωσις	N-NF-S	τελείωσις
τελειώσω	VSAA--1S	τελειόω
τελειωτήν	N-AM-S	τελειωτής

τελειωτής, οῦ, ὁ   *perfecter, finisher*; specifically in HE 12.2 as a designation for Jesus, the one who brings faith to its highest attainment, either in himself as an example or in others through his high priestly ministry

τελέσει	VIFA--3S	τελέω
τελέσητε	VSAA--2P	"
τελεσθῇ	VSAP--3S	"
τελεσθῆναι	VNAP	"
τελεσθήσεται	VIFP--3S	"
τελεσθήσονται	VIFP--3P	"
τελεσθῶσι(ν)	VSAP--3P	"

τελεσφορέω   *bring to maturity*; of fruit *bring to ripeness, produce ripe fruit*; used metaphorically of spiritual character in LU 8.14 *become all that one should be*

τελεσφοροῦσι(ν)	VIPA--3P	τελεσφορέω
τελέσωσι(ν)	VSAA--3P	τελέω
τελευτᾷ	VIPA--3S	τελευτάω
τελευτᾶν	VNPA	"
τελευτάτω	VMPA--3S	"

τελευτάω   1aor. ἐτελεύτησα; pf. τετελεύτηκα; intransitively in the NT *come to an end*; euphemistically *die*

τελευτή, ῆς, ἡ   *end*; euphemistically, of the end of life *death, decease* (MT 2.15)

τελευτῆς	N-GF-S	τελευτή
τελευτήσαντος	VPAAGM-S	τελευτάω
τελευτῶν	VPPANM-S	"

τελέω   fut. τελέσω; 1aor. ἐτέλεσα; pf. τετέλεκα; pf. pass. τετέλεσμαι; 1aor. pass. ἐτελέσθην; 1fut. pass. τελεσθήσομαι; (1) as completing something *bring to an end, conclude, complete* (MT 7.28); (2) as obeying a rule or ritual *carry out, fulfill, perform* (LU 2.39); (3) of obligatory taxes, tolls, dues *pay* (MT 17.24); (4) passive, of duration of time *be over, end, be finished* (RV 20.3)

τέλη	N-AN-P	τέλος
	N-NN-P	"

τέλος, ους, τό   (1) as an action *achievement, carrying out, fulfillment* (LU 22.37); (2) as a closing act *end, termination, cessation* (2C 3.13; 1P 4.7), opposite ἀρχή (*beginning*); (3) as a goal toward which movement is being directed *outcome, end (result), purpose* (1T 1.5); (4) as civic payment of what is owed *tribute, tax, customs (duties)* (RO 13.7); (5) in adverbial expressions; (a) accusative τὸ τ. *finally* (1P 3.8); (b) εἰς τ., with either a temporal or quantitative sense according to the context *to the end* (MK 13.13), *finally, at last* (possibly 1TH 2.16), *in full measure, fully, completely* (JN 13.1; possibly 1TH 2.16); (c) with ἕως, μέχρι, ἄχρι(ς) *to the end, to the last* or *fully, altogether*, depending on the context

τέλος	N-AN-S	τέλος
	N-NN-S	"
τέλους	N-GN-S	"
τελοῦσα	VPPANF-S	τελέω
τελῶναι	N-NM-P	τελώνης
τελώνην	N-AM-S	"

τελώνης, ου, ὁ *tax collector, revenue officer, toll collector*; in the NT unpopular Jewish subordinates who hired out to foreign officials holding tax-collecting contracts

| τελώνης | N-NM-S | τελώνης |

τελώνιον, ου, τό *toll house, revenue* or *tax office, toll collector's booth*

τελώνιον	N-AN-S	τελώνιον
τελωνῶν	N-GM-P	τελώνης
τέξεται	VIFD--3S	τίκτω
τέξῃ	VIFD--2S	"

τέρας, ατος, τό *wonder, marvel, portent*, something so unusual it arouses close observation; only plural in the NT and combined with σημεῖα (*signs*)

τέρασι(ν)	N-DN-P	τέρας
τέρατα	N-AN-P	
	N-NN-P	
τεράτων	N-GN-P	
Τερέντιος	N-NM-S	Τέρτιος

Τέρτιος, ου, ὁ (also **Τερέντιος**) *Tertius*, masculine proper noun (RO 16.22)

| Τέρτιος | N-NM-S | Τέρτιος |
| Τερτίου | N-GM-S | " |

Τέρτυλλος, ου, ὁ *Tertullus*, masculine proper noun (AC 24.2)

Τέρτυλλος	N-NM-S	Τέρτυλλος
Τερτύλλου	N-GM-S	"
τέσσαρα	A-CAN-P	τέσσαρες
	A-CNN-P	"
τεσσαράκοντα		τεσσεράκοντα
τεσσαρακονταετῆ	A--AM-S	τεσσερακονταετής
τέσσαρας	A-CAF-P	τέσσαρες
	A-CAM-P	"

τέσσαρες, gen. **τεσσάρων** as a cardinal number *four* (AC 21.9); substantively *four people* (MK 2.3)

τέσσαρες	A-CNF-P	τέσσαρες
	A-CNM-P	"
τεσσαρεσκαιδεκάτη	A-ONF-S	τεσσαρεσκαιδέκατος
τεσσαρεσκαιδεκάτην	A-OAF-S	"

τεσσαρεσκαιδέκατος, η, ον as an ordinal number *fourteenth*

τέσσαρσι(ν)	A-CDF-P	τέσσαρες
	A-CDM-P	"
	A-CDN-P	"
τεσσάρων	APCGM-P	"
	A-CGM-P	"
	A-CGN-P	"

τεσσεράκοντα (also **τεσσαράκοντα**) indeclinable; as a cardinal number *forty* (RV 21.17)

τεσσερακονταετη	A--AM-S	τεσσερακονταετής
τεσσερακονταετῆ	A--AM-S	"
τεσσερακονταετήν	A--AM-S	"

τεσσερακονταετής, ές (also **τεσσαρακονταετής**) *of forty years*; τ. χρόνος *period of forty years* (AC 7.23)

τεσσερακονταετής	A--NM-S	τεσσερακονταετής
τεταγμέναι	VPRPNF-P	τάσσω
τεταγμένοι	VPRPNM-P	"
τεταγμένους	VPRPAM-P	"
τέτακται	VIRP--3S	"
τεταραγμένοι	VPRPNM-P	ταράσσω
τετάρακται	VIRP--3S	"

τεταρταῖος, αία, ον *on the fourth day*; substantivally τ. ἐστιν *it is the fourth day* (since he died), i.e. *he has been dead four days* (JN 11.39)

τεταρταῖος	A--NM-S	τεταρταῖος
τετάρτη	A-ODF-S	τέταρτος
τετάρτην	A-OAF-S	"
τετάρτης	A-OGF-S	"
τέταρτον	A-OAN-S	"
	A-ONN-S	"

τέταρτος, η, ον as an ordinal number *fourth* (MT 14.25); masculine as a substantive *fourth one* (RV 16.8); neuter as a substantive τὸ τέταρτον as the fourth part of anything, *one-fourth, one part out of four* (RV 6.8)

τέταρτος	A-ONM-S	τέταρτος
τετάρτου	A-OGN-S	"
τετεχέναι	VNRA	τάσσω
τετελείωκε(ν)	VIRA--3S	τελειόω
τετελείωμαι	VIRP--1S	"
τετελειωμένη	VPRPNF-S	"
τετελειωμένοι	VPRPNM-P	"
τετελειωμένον	VPRPAM-S	"
τετελειωμένων	VPRPGM-P	"
τετελείωται	VIRP--3S	"
τετέλεκα	VIRA--1S	τελέω
τετέλεσται	VIRP--3S	"
τετελευτηκότος	VPRAGM-S	τελευτάω
τέτευχε(ν)	VIRA--3S	τυγχάνω
τετήρηκα	VIRA--1S	τηρέω
τετήρηκαν	VIRA--3P	"
τετήρηκας	VIRA--2S	"
τετηρήκασι(ν)	VIRA--3P	"
τετήρηκε(ν)	VIRA--3S	"
τετηρημένην	VPRPAF-S	"
τετηρημένοις	VPRPDM-P	"
τετηρημένους	VPRPAM-P	"
τετήρηται	VIRP--3S	"
τετιμημένου	VPRPGM-S	τιμάω

τετρααρχέω (and **τετραρχέω**) strictly *be ruler of a fourth part* of a kingdom, *be tetrarch*; in the NT *be provincial sovereign* under the Roman emperor, ruling over some portion of Herod the Great's former kingdom, *govern* a region (LU 3.1)

τετραάρχης, ου, ὁ (also **τετράρχης**) strictly *ruler over the fourth part* of a kingdom, *tetrarch*; in the NT a petty prince subordinate to the Roman emperor, *governor* of a region

τετραάρχης	N-NM-S	τετραάρχης
τετραάρχου	N-GM-S	"
τετρααρχοῦντος	VPPAGM-S	τετρααρχέω

τετράγωνος, ον of a place having four equal sides; *laid out in a quadrangle, (four)square, as a square* (RV 21.16)

| τετράγωνος | A--NF-S | τετράγωνος |
| τετραδίοις | N-DN-P | τετράδιον |

378

τετράδιον, ου, τό   strictly *set of four*; as a military technical term *detachment* or *squad of four soldiers, quaternion* (AC 12.4)

τετρακισχίλιοι, αι, α   as a cardinal number *four thousand* (MT 15.38); substantivally *four thousand people* (MK 8.9)

τετρακισχίλιοι	APCNM-P	τετρακισχίλιοι
	A-CNM-P	"
τετρακισχιλίους	APCAM-P	"
	A-CAM-P	"
τετρακισχιλίων	APCGM-P	"
τετρακόσια	A-CAN-P	τετρακόσιοι

τετρακόσιοι, αι, α   as a cardinal number *four hundred* (AC 7.6); substantivally *four hundred people* (AC 5.36)

τετρακοσίοις	A-CDN-P	τετρακόσιοι
τετρακοσίων	APCGM-P	"
τετράμηνον	AP-NN-S	τετράμηνος

τετράμηνος, ον   *lasting four months*; substantivally in the NT ἔτι τ. ἐστιν *four months more* (JN 4.35)

τετράμηνος	AP-NM-S	τετράμηνος
τετραπλοῦν	A--AN-S	τετραπλοῦς

τετραπλοῦς, ῆ, οῦν   *fourfold, quadruple*; neuter as a substantive τετραπλοῦν *four times as much* (LU 19.8)

τετράποδα	AP-AN-P	τετράπους
	AP-NN-P	"
τετραπόδων	AP-GN-P	"

τετράπους, ουν, gen. ποδος   *four-footed*; neuter plural τὰ τετράποδα as a substantive *four-footed animals* or *beasts, quadrupeds*

τετράρχης	N-NM-S	τετραάρχης
τετράρχου	N-GM-S	"
τετραρχοῦντος	VPPAGM-S	τετρααρχέω

τετράς, άδος, ἡ   as a cardinal number *four* (AC 10.11)

τέτρασι(ν)	N-DF-P	τετράς
τετραυματισμένους	VPRPAM-P	τραυματίζω
τετραχηλισμένα	VPRPNN-P	τραχηλίζω
τετύφλωκε(ν)	VIRA--3S	τυφλόω
τετυφωμένοι	VPRPNM-P	τυφόω
τετύφωται	VIRP--3S	"
τέτυχε(ν)	VIRA--3S	τυγχάνω
τετύχηκε(ν)	VIRA--3S	"

τεφρόω   1aor. ἐτέφρωσα; *reduce to ashes, burn to ashes, burn up completely* (2P 2.6)

τεφρώσας	VPAANM-S	τεφρόω
τεχθείς	VPAPNM-S	τίκτω

τέχνη, ης, ἡ   *trade, skill, craft*

τέχνη	N-DF-S	τέχνη
τέχνης	N-GF-S	"
τεχνῖται	N-NM-P	τεχνίτης
τεχνίταις	N-DM-P	"
τεχνίτας	N-AM-P	"

τεχνίτης, ου, ὁ   as a skilled workman *craftsman, artisan* (AC 19.24); as a designer of a city *architect*; metaphorically, of God as providing an eternal home for believers (HE 11.10)

τεχνίτης	N-NM-S	τεχνίτης
τῇ	DDFS	ὁ
	DDFS+	"
τῇδε	APDDF-S	ὅδε
τήκεται	VIPP--3S	τήκω

τήκω   transitively *melt (down), render liquid*; only passive in the NT *be melted, dissolve into liquid* (2P 3.12)

τηλαυγῶς (also **δηλαυγῶς**)   adverb; strictly *shining clearly*; hence *quite distinctly, very clearly* (MK 8.25)

τηλαυγῶς	AB	τηλαυγῶς
τηλικαῦτα	A-DNN-P	τηλικοῦτος
τηλικαύτης	A-DGF-S	"
τηλικοῦτον	A-DAN-S	"

τηλικοῦτος, αύτη, οῦτο   a demonstrative intensifier adjective correlated to ἡλίκος (*how great*); (1) of size *so great, so large* (JA 3.4); (2) of degree *so important, so great, so mighty* (2C 1.10; HE 2.3)

τηλικοῦτος	A-DNM-S	τηλικοῦτος
τηλικούτου	A-DGM-S	"
τηλικούτων	A-DGM-P	"
τήν	DAFS	ὁ
	DAFS+	"
τήνδε	A-DAF-S	ὅδε
τήρει	VMPA--2S	τηρέω
τηρεῖ	VIPA--3S	"
τηρεῖν	VNPA	"
τηρεῖσθαι	VNPP	"
τηρεῖτε	VMPA--2P	"

τηρέω   impf. ἐτήρουν; fut. τηρήσω; 1aor. ἐτήρησα; pf. τετήρηκα; pf. pass. τετήρημαι; 1aor. pass. ἐτηρήθην; from a basic meaning *keep in view, take note, watch over*; (1) literally; (a) *guard* (AC 12.6); (b) *keep, hold in reserve, preserve* for a purpose or until a suitable time (JN 2.10); passive, of custody of people or angelic beings *hold in custody* (AC 25.4; 2P 2.4); (c) *maintain, keep* (JU 6a), opposite ἀπόλλυμι (*forfeit, lose*); (d) *protect, keep intact, keep inviolate* (1C 7.37); (2) figuratively; (a) spiritually, of persons *guard, preserve, protect* (JN 17.11); (b) as maintaining the essence of the Christian life *keep* (2T 4.7); (c) with reference to doctrine, commandments, precepts *observe, obey* (MT 19.17)

τηρῇ	VSPA--3S	τηρέω
τηρηθείη	VOAP--3S	"
τηρηθῆναι	VNAP	"
τηρηθήσεται	VIFP--3S	"
τηρῆσαι	VNAA	"
τηρήσαντας	VPAAAM-P	"
τηρήσατε	VMAA--2P	"
τηρήσει	N-DF-S	τήρησις
	VIFA--3S	τηρέω
τηρήσετε	VIFA--2P	"
τηρήσῃ	VSAA--3S	"
τηρήσῃς	VSAA--2S	"
τηρήσητε	VSAA--2P	"
τήρησιν	N-AF-S	τήρησις

τήρησις, εως, ἡ   as an action *watching, keeping*; literally *custody, imprisonment*; by metonymy *prison, jail* (AC 4.3); figuratively, of commandments and precepts *keeping, observance, obeying* (1C 7.19)

τήρησις	N-NF-S	τήρησις
τήρησον	VMAA--2S	τηρέω
τηρήσουσι(ν)	VIFA--3P	"
τηρήσω	VIFA--1S	"
τηρήσωμεν	VSAA--1P	"
τηρῆτε	VSPA--2P	"

τηροῦμεν	VIPA--1P	"
τηρούμενοι	VPPPNM-P	"
τηρουμένους	VPPPAM-P	"
τηροῦνται	VIFP--3P	"
τηροῦντες	VPPANM-P	"
τηρούντων	VPPAGM-P	"
τηρῶ	VIPA--1S	"
τηρῶμεν	VSPA--1P	"
τηρῶν	VPPANM-S	"
τῆς	DGFS	ὁ
	DGFS+	"
τι	APIAN-S	τὶς
	APINN-S	"
	A-IAN-S	"
	A-INN-S	"
τί	ABT	τίς
	APTAN-S	"
	APTNN-S	"
	A-TAN-S	"
	A-TNN-S	"
Τιβεριάδος	N-GF-S	Τιβεριάς

Τιβεριάς, άδος, ἡ *Tiberias*; (1) a city on the western shore of the Sea of Galilee or the Lake of Gennesaret (JN 6.23); (2) as one name for the lake itself (JN 6.1)

Τιβέριος, ου, ὁ *Tiberius*; the third Roman emperor (LU 3.1)

Τιβερίου	N-GM-S	Τιβέριος
τιθέασι(ν)	VIPA--3P	τίθημι
τιθείς	VPPANM-S	"
τιθέναι	VNPA	"
τιθέντες	VPPANM-P	"
τίθεται	VIPP--3S	"
τιθέτω	VMPA--3S	"

τίθημι impf. ἐτίθουν; fut. θήσω, mid. θήσομαι; 1aor. ἔθηκα; 2aor. subjunctive θῶ, second-person plural imperative θέτε, inf. θεῖναι, ptc. θείς, mid. ἐθέμην; pf. τέθεικα; pf. pass. τέθειμαι; 1aor. pass. ἐτέθην; a bland verb with a basic meaning *put, place, lay* and the sense often derived from its object and the context; **I.** active/passive; (1) generally in a local sense; *lay* (a foundation) (LU 14.29), *lay out* to be seen by someone passing by (MK 6.56), *lay away, bury* (MK 6.29); *lay on* (the hands) (MK 8.25); *put, place* (a light) (MK 4.21); (2) figuratively, of endowment with the Spirit *put* (MT 12.18); *put down* (enemies) (MT 22.44); economically *invest, deposit* (money) (LU 19.21); *set aside, store up* (money) (1C 16.2); (3) idiomatically τιθέναι τὰ γόνατα literally *place the knees*, i.e. *bend the knees, kneel down* (MK 15.19); τιθέναι ἐν καρδίᾳ literally *place in the heart* or *mind*, i.e. *make up one's mind, decide, purpose* (LU 21.14); τιθέναι ἐν τῷ πνεύματι literally *place in the spirit*, i.e. *make up one's mind, resolve* (AC 19.21); τιθέναι τὴν ψυχήν literally *lay down one's life*, i.e. *die voluntarily* (JN 10.11); etc.; (4) with a double accusative *establish, appoint, make* someone something, *destine* someone to or for something (AC 13.47; RO 4.17); **II.** middle, with same meanings but with more self-involvement; (1) especially of God's designed self-activity *arrange, establish, fix, entrust* (AC 1.7; 2C 5.19; 1T 1.12); (2) *keep in mind, think of, resolve* (LU 1.66; AC 5.4)

τίθημι	VIPA--1S	τίθημι

τίθησι(ν)	VIPA--3S	"
τίκτει	VIPA--3S	τίκτω
τίκτη	VSPA--3S	"
τίκτουσα	VPPANF-S	"
	VPPAVF-S	"

τίκτω fut. mid. τέξομαι; 2aor. ἔτεκον; 1aor. pass. ἐτέχθην; literally *bear, give birth to, bring forth* (children) (MT 1.21); metaphorically, of the earth *produce, bring forth, yield* (HE 6.7); of the evil consequence of indulging one's lust *bring forth, cause, produce* (JA 1.15)

τίλλειν	VNPA	τίλλω
τίλλοντες	VPPANM-P	"

τίλλω impf. ἔτιλλον; *pluck, pick*; of heads of standing grain *pick* or *pluck off*

τίμα	VMPA--2S	τιμάω
τιμᾷ	VIPA--3S	"

Τίμαιος, ου, ὁ (also **Τιμαῖος**) *Timaeus*, masculine proper noun (MK 10.46)

Τιμαίου	N-GM-S	Τίμαιος
τιμαῖς	N-DF-P	τιμή
τιμάς	N-AF-P	"
τιμᾶτε	VMPA--2P	τιμάω

τιμάω fut. τιμήσω; 1aor. ἐτίμησα, mid. ἐτιμησάμην; pf. pass. τετίμημαι; (1) as ascribing worth to someone *honor, revere, respect* (MT 15.4); (2) as assigning value to something or to a person considered as property, such as a slave, *set a price on, assess the value of, estimate* (MT 27.9); (3) as providing for someone financially as a means of showing due respect *assist, support* (1T 5.3)

τιμή, ῆς, ἡ basically, the worth ascribed to a person or the value ascribed to a thing; (1) as the recognition of another's worth; (a) active *honor, reverence, respect* (RO 12.10); (b) passive *recognition, esteem, dignity bestowed* (JN 4.44); concretely, as a position of honor *office, place of honor* (HE 2.9; 5.4); (c) *honorarium, compensation, payment received for service* (1T 5.17); (2) as the value ascribed to a thing; (a) *price, value, price received* or *paid back* (AC 4.34); (b) figuratively *value, benefit, usefulness* (CO 2.23)

τιμή	N-NF-S	τιμή
τιμῇ	N-DF-S	"
τιμήν	N-AF-S	"
τιμῆς	N-GF-S	"
τιμήσατε	VMAA--2P	τιμάω
τιμήσει	VIFA--3S	"
τιμήση	VSAA--3S	"
τίμια	A--AN-P	τίμιος
τιμία	A--NF-S	"
τιμίαν	A--AF-S	"
τίμιον	A--AM-S	"

τίμιος, ία, ον (1) literally, of things *valuable, costly, precious* (RV 17.4); used metaphorically of the quality of one's service (1C 3.12); figuratively, as honor and value attributed to something *precious, of great worth, held in honor* (1P 1.19); (2) literally, of persons *honored, highly regarded, respected* (AC 5.34); (3) superlative τιμιώτατος, τάτη, ον *most valuable, very expensive* (RV 18.12)

τίμιος	A--NM-S	τίμιος

τιμιότης, ητος, ἡ *costliness*; concretely *valuable merchandise, abundance of costly things* (RV 18.19)

Greek	Parse	Lemma
τιμιότητος	N-GF-S	τιμιότης
τιμίου	A--GM-S	τίμιος
τιμίους	A--AM-P	"
τιμίῳ	A--DM-S	"
	A--DN-S	"
τιμιωτάτου	A-SGN-S	"
τιμιωτάτῳ	A-SDM-S	"
τιμιώτερον	A-MNN-S	"
Τιμόθεε	N-VM-S	Τιμόθεος
Τιμόθεον	N-AM-S	"

Τιμόθεος, ου, ὁ *Timothy*, masculine proper noun

Greek	Parse	Lemma
Τιμόθεος	N-NM-S	Τιμόθεος
Τιμοθέου	N-GM-S	"
Τιμοθέῳ	N-DM-S	"
τιμῶ	VIPA--1S	τιμάω

Τίμων, ωνος, ὁ *Timon*, masculine proper noun (AC 6.5)

Greek	Parse	Lemma
τιμῶν	VPPANM-S	τιμάω
Τίμωνα	N-AM-S	Τίμων

τιμωρέω 1aor. pass. ἐτιμωρήθην; *punish, have someone punished*; passive *receive punishment, be punished*

Greek	Parse	Lemma
τιμωρηθῶσι(ν)	VSAP--3P	τιμωρέω

τιμωρία, ας, ἡ *punishment* (HE 10.29)

Greek	Parse	Lemma
τιμωρίας	N-GF-S	τιμωρία
τιμωρῶν	VPPANM-S	τιμωρέω
τιμῶσι(ν)	VIPA--3P	τιμάω
	VSPA--3P	"
τίνα	APTAM-S	τίς
	APTNN-P	"
	A-TAF-S	"
	A-TAM-S	"
τινά	APIAM-S	τὶς
	APIAN-P	"
	A-IAF-S	"
	A-IAM-S	"
	A-IAN-P	"
	A-INN-P	"
τίνας	APTAM-P	τίς
	A-TAF-P	"
τινάς	APIAM-P	τὶς
	A-IAF-P	"
	A-IAM-P	"
τίνες	APTNM-P	τίς
τινές	APINF-P	τὶς
	APINM-P	"
	A-INF-P	"
	A-INM-P	"
τίνι	APTDM-S	τίς
	APTDN-S	"
	A-TDF-S	"
	A-TDM-S	"
τινί	APIDM-S	τὶς
	APIDN-S	"
	A-IDF-S	"
	A-IDM-S	"
	A-IDN-S	"
τίνος	APTGF-S	τίς
	APTGM-S	"
	APTGN-S	"
τινός	APIGM-S	τὶς
	APIGN-S	"
	A-IGF-S	"
	A-IGM-S	"

τίνω fut. τίσω; of a penalty *pay*; of punishment *undergo, incur, experience retribution* (2TH 1.9)

Greek	Parse	Lemma
τίνων	APTGM-P	τίς
	APTGN-P	"
τινῶν	APIGM-P	τὶς
	APIGN-P	"
	A-IGF-P	"
	A-IGM-P	"

τίς, τί, gen. **τίνος** an interrogative pronoun used in direct, indirect, and rhetorical questions; (1) as a substantive; (a) *who? which one? what?* (MT 3.7); (b) in the sense of ποῖος (*of what kind?*), *what sort of person? who?* (JN 1.22); (c) as equivalent to πότερος *which of two?* (MT 27.17); (d) neuter τί with prepositions: διὰ τί *why? for what reason?* (MT 9.11); εἰς τί *why? for what purpose?* (MT 26.8); ἐν τίνι *with what?* (MT 5.13), *through whom?* (LU 11.19); πρὸς τί *why? for what (immediate) purpose?* (JN 13.28); χάριν τίνος *thanks to what? for what reason? why?* (1J 3.12); (e) special uses of neuter τί: as a substitute for a relative pronoun *anything that, that which, what* (MK 14.36); as an adverb using the accusative of respect *for what reason? why?* (MT 16.8); in an exclamation *how!* (LU 12.49); (2) as an adjective *which, what* (MT 5.46)

Greek	Parse	Lemma
τίς	APTNF-S	τίς
	APTNM-S	"
	A-TNF-S	"
	A-TNM-S	"

τὶς, τὶ, gen. **τινός** enclitic indefinite pronoun; (1) as a substantive; (a) used indefinitely *someone, something; any(one), anything; somebody, anybody* (MT 5.23; 12.29); plural, of persons *some, a number of, several* (MT 9.3); *certain things* (AC 17.20); (b) used definitely *a certain person, one* (LU 8.49); plural *certain persons* (RO 3.8); of things *some* (AC 27.44); (c) as indicating a claim to prestige *a person of importance, somebody (great)* (AC 5.36); (2) as an adjective; (a) used with a substantive *some, any, a certain* (LU 1.5); plural *several, some, a number of* (LU 8.2); (b) with a proper noun *a certain* (LU 23.26); (c) as rendering an expression less definite *a kind of, a sort of* (JA 1.18); (d) as heightening quality or quantity in rhetorical emphasis *only* (HE 2.7, 9; 10.27), *considerable* (AC 18.23), *in some part, partly* (1C 11.18)

Greek	Parse	Lemma
τὶς	APINM-S	τὶς
	A-INF-S	"
	A-INM-S	"
τίσι(ν)	APTDM-P	τίς
τισί(ν)	APIDM-P	τὶς
	APIDN-P	"
	A-IDM-P	"
τίσουσι(ν)	VIFA--3P	τίνω

Τίτιος, ου, ὁ *Titius*, masculine proper noun (AC 18.7)

Greek	Parse	Lemma
Τιτίου	N-GM-S	Τίτιος
τίτλον	N-AM-S	τίτλος

τίτλος, ου, ὁ as a brief notice used for identification *inscription, writing*; as an affixed notice giving a reason for execution *title, inscription* (JN 19.19)

Greek	Parse	Lemma
Τίτον	N-AM-S	Τίτος

Τίτος, ου, ὁ *Titus*, masculine proper noun

Greek	Parse	Lemma
Τίτος	N-NM-S	Τίτος

Τίτου	N-GM-S	"
Τίτῳ	N-DM-S	"
τό	DANS	ὁ
	DANS+	"
	DNNS	"
	DNNS+	"
	DVNS	"
τοιᾶσδε	A-DGF-S	τοιόσδε
τοιαῦτα	APDAN-P	τοιοῦτος
	A-DAN-P	"
τοιαῦται	A-DNF-P	"
τοιαύταις	A-DDF-P	"
τοιαύτας	APDAF-P	"
τοιαύτη	APDNF-S	"
	A-DNF-S	"
τοιαύτην	A-DAF-S	"

τοιγαροῦν from τοί (emphatic particle), γάρ (*for, because*), and οὖν (*therefore, so*); a particle strongly introducing an inference from preceding facts *for that very reason therefore, therefore in the light of that*; the τοί particle itself strengthens a statement by assuring its reliability

τοιγαροῦν	CH	τοιγαροῦν

τοίνυν a strengthened inferential particle *therefore, in agreement with that, so indeed*

τοίνυν	CH	τοίνυν

τοιόσδε, άδε, όνδε as pointing to the distinctiveness of something *such as this, of such a kind* (2P 1.17)

τοιοῦτο	A-DAN-S	τοιοῦτος
τοιοῦτοι	APDNM-P	"
	A-DNM-P	"
τοιούτοις	APDDM-P	"
	APDDN-P	"
τοιοῦτον	APDAM-S	"
	A-DAM-S	"

τοιοῦτος, αύτη, οῦτον (1) a qualitative correlative with οἷος (*what sort of, of what kind*): *such as* (the one is) . . . *so* (is the other) (1C 15.48); (2) as an adjective with a noun *such, such as this, of such a kind, of this sort* (MT 9.8); (3) as a substantive; (a) of persons, referring to a definite individual with special characteristics or certain qualities *such a one, a person like that* (AC 22.22; 1C 5.5); (b) of things *things like that, such things* (RO 1.32)

τοιοῦτος	APDNM-S	τοιοῦτος
	A-DNM-S	"
τοιούτου	APDGM-S	"
τοιούτους	APDAM-P	"
	A-DAM-P	"
τοιούτῳ	APDDM-S	"
τοιούτων	APDGM-P	"
	APDGN-P	"
	A-DGN-P	"
τοῖς	DDMP	ὁ
	DDMP+	"
	DDNP	"
	DDNP+	"
τοῖχε	N-VM-S	τοῖχος

τοῖχος, ου, ὁ *wall* of a house or building, distinguished from τεῖχος (city *wall*); idiomatically, as an insult τοῖχε

κεκονιαμένε literally *you whitewashed wall*, i.e. *you hypocrite, impostor* (AC 23.3)

τοίχῳ	N-DM-S	τοῖχος

τόκος, ου, ὁ strictly, the result of bringing forth *offspring*; figuratively, as what is produced by lending money *interest, usury*

τόκῳ	N-DM-S	τόκος
τολμᾷ	VIPA--3S	τολμάω
	VSPA--3S	"
τολμᾶν	VNPA	"

τολμάω impf. ἐτόλμων; fut. τολμήσω; 1aor. ἐτόλμησα; as being bold enough to defy danger or opposition; (1) predominately with an infinitive following; (a) in a negative sense, with a component of fear or anxiety *dare to, be brave enough to, have courage to* (JN 21.12); (b) in a negative sense, with a component of boldness or insolence *dare to, presume to* (1C 6.1); (c) in a weakened sense, as possibly doing something beyond normal expectation *dare to, might be prepared to* (RO 5.7); (d) in a positive sense *dare, have courage to, be brave enough to* (PH 1.14); (2) absolutely *summon up courage, venture* (MK 15.43)

τολμηρός, ά, όν *bold, daring*; comparative neuter as an adverb τολμηρότερον *more boldly, rather freely, a little boldly* (RO 15.15); comparative adverb τολμηροτέρως *rather boldly* (RO 15.15)

τολμηρότερον	ABM	τολμηρός
	A-MAN-S	"
τολμηροτέρως	ABM	"
τολμῆσαι	VNAA	τολμάω
τολμήσας	VPAANM-S	"
τολμήσω	VIFA--1S	"
τολμηταί	N-NM-P	τολμητής

τολμητής, οῦ, ὁ *bold* or *daring person*; in the NT only in a bad sense *arrogant* or *presumptuous person* (2P 2.10)

τολμῶ	VIPA--1S	τολμάω
τολμῶμεν	VIPA--1P	"

τομός, ή, όν *cutting, sharp*; comparative τομώτερος, τέρα, ον *sharper*; metaphorically, for the power of God's Word *having capacity to penetrate deeply* (HE 4.12)

τομώτερος	A-MNM-S	τομός
τόν	DAMS	ὁ
	DAMS+	"

τόξον, ου, τό *bow*, an instrument for launching arrows (RV 6.2)

τόξον	N-AN-S	τόξον

τοπάζιον, ου, τό *topaz*, a greenish-yellow precious stone, perhaps the modern chrysolite (RV 21.20)

τοπάζιον	N-NN-S	τοπάζιον
τόποις	N-DM-P	τόπος
τόπον	N-AM-S	"

τόπος, ου, ὁ *place*; (1) to denote a specific and defined area *district, territory, land, region* (AC 12.17); (2) under Semitic influence, to denote the site of an event *place, location* (JN 10.40); (3) to denote an inhabited *place*, as a city, village, seaport, etc. (MT 14.35; AC 27.2); by metonymy *the people of a place* (MK 6.11); (4) to denote an inhabited *space*, as a room, building, temple, etc. *place* (MT 24.15; AC 4.31); (5) to refer to the *location* of a passage in a book (LU 4.17); (6) to denote a *po-*

sition, office, task (AC 1.25a); (7) figuratively, to refer to an *opportunity, occasion, chance* (AC 25.16)

τόπος	N-NM-S	τόπος
τόπου	N-GM-S	"
τόπους	N-AM-P	"
τόπῳ	N-DM-S	"
τόπων	N-GM-P	"
τοσαῦτα	APDAN-P	τοσοῦτος
	A-DAN-P	"
	A-DNN-P	"
τοσαύτην	A-DAF-S	"
τοσοῦτο	APDAN-S	"
τοσοῦτοι	APDNM-P	"
	A-DNM-P	"
τοσοῦτον	APDAN-S	"
	A-DAM-S	"
	A-DAN-S	"

τοσοῦτος, αὕτη, οῦτον and **οῦτο** an adjective correlated to ὅσος (*in such an amount as*), with the meaning derived from the context; (1) quantitatively *so great, so large, so much, so far* (AC 5.8; HE 12.1); plural *so many* (JN 6.9); (2) qualitatively *so strong, so great* (MT 8.10); (3) of time *so long* (JN 14.9); (4) a correlative with a comparative corresponding to ὅσος *so much* (greater, more, better) *than, to the degree that* (HE 1.4)

τοσοῦτος	A-DNM-S	τοσοῦτος
τοσούτου	APDGN-S	"
τοσούτους	APDAM-P	"
τοσούτῳ	APDDN-S	"
	A-DDM-S	"
τοσούτων	APDGM-P	"

τότε an adverb of subsequent time, correlated to ὅτε (*when, while, as long as*); (1) used correlatively with ὅτε *when . . . then* (MT 13.26); (2) as a time marker *at that time, then* (MT 2.17); (3) in narration to introduce what follows in time *then, thereupon* (MT 2.7)

τότε	AB	τότε
τοῦ	DGMS	ὁ
	DGMS+	"
	DGNS	"
	DGNS+	"
τοὐναντίον	AB	see τό and ἐναντίον
τοὔνομα	DANS&N-AN-S	see τό and ὄνομα
τούς	DAMP	ὁ
	DAMP+	"
	DAMP^APDAM-P	"
τοῦτ'	APDNN-S	see τοῦτο

τουτέστι(ν) by crasis for τοῦτ' ἔστιν; *that is, which signifies, which implies*

τουτέστι(ν)	QS	τουτέστι(ν)
τοῦτο	APDAN-S	οὗτος
	APDNN-S	"
	A-DAN-S	"
	A-DNN-S	"
τούτοις	APDDM-P	"
	APDDN-P	"
	A-DDM-P	"
	A-DDN-P	"
τοῦτον	APDAM-S	"
	A-DAM-S	"

τούτου	APDGM-S	"
	APDGN-S	"
	A-DGM-S	"
	A-DGN-S	"
τούτους	APDAM-P	"
	A-DAM-P	"
τούτῳ	APDDM-S	"
	APDDN-S	"
	A-DDM-S	"
	A-DDN-S	"
τούτων	APDGF-P	"
	APDGM-P	"
	APDGN-P	"
	A-DGF-P	"
	A-DGM-P	"
	A-DGN-P	"

τράγος, ου, ὁ *male goat*; in the NT as a sacrificial animal (HE 9.12)

τράγων	N-GM-P	τράγος

τράπεζα, ης, ἡ *table*; (1) as a piece of furniture on which something can be placed *table* (HE 9.2); (2) as a place for spreading out meals, either on the ground or on an article of furniture, *table, dining table* (MT 15.27); by metonymy, as what is put on the table *meal, food* (probably AC 6.2); (3) as a place to display wares or money changers' coins *table* (MT 21.12); by metonymy *bank* (LU 19.23; perhaps AC 6.2)

τράπεζα	N-NF-S	τράπεζα
τραπέζαις	N-DF-P	"
τράπεζαν	N-AF-S	"
τραπέζας	N-AF-P	"
τραπέζης	N-GF-S	"
τραπεζίταις	N-DM-P	τραπεζίτης

τραπεζίτης, ου, ὁ *money changer, banker, broker* (MT 25.27)

τραῦμα, ατος, τό as the result of an injury or severe beating *wound* (LU 10.34)

τραύματα	N-AN-P	τραῦμα

τραυματίζω 1aor. ἐτραυμάτισα; pf. pass. τετραυμάτισμαι; *wound, cause to be wounded, hurt*

τραυματίσαντες	VPAANM-P	τραυματίζω
τραχεῖαι	A--NF-P	τραχύς
τραχεῖς	A--AM-P	"

τραχηλίζω pf. pass. ptc. τετραχηλισμένος; strictly *take hold of by the neck*; only passive in the NT, as a metaphor drawn from ancient custom, either of making an enemy face his conquerors by a sword fixed under his chin, of fastening a lock grip on an opponent in wrestling, or of bending back the head of a sacrificial victim, ready for the knife *be exposed*, i.e. *be easily known* (HE 4.13)

τράχηλον	N-AM-S	τράχηλος

τράχηλος, ου, ὁ literally *neck, throat* (MT 18.6); idiomatically ἐπιπίπτειν ἐπὶ τὸν τράχηλον literally *fall on the neck*, i.e. *embrace, hug* (LU 15.20); metaphorically ὑποτιθέναι τὸν τράχηλον literally *lay one's neck under* the executioner's sword, i.e. *risk one's life* (RO 16.4); ἐπιθεῖναι ζυγὸν ἐπὶ τὸν τράχηλον literally *put a yoke on the neck*, i.e. *impose burdensome rules, load down with obligations* (AC 15.10) τραχύς, εῖα, ύ   rough; of a road uneven; opposite λεῖος (smooth); substantivally αἱ τραχεῖαι uneven places (LU 3.5); of a seashore rocky (AC 27.29)

Τραχωνίτιδος   A--GF-S   Τραχωνῖτις

Τραχωνῖτις, gen. ιδος   of Trachonitis, a district or region south of Damascus (LU 3.1)

τρεῖς, τρία, gen. τριῶν, dative τρισίν   as a cardinal number three (MT 12.40); substantivally τ. three people (1C 14.27); τρία three things (1C 13.13)

τρεῖς	APCAM-P	τρεῖς
	APCNM-P	"
	A-CAF-P	"
	A-CAM-P	"
	A-CNF-P	"
	A-CNM-P	"

Τρεῖς Ταβέρναι, αἱ   from τρεῖς (three) and ταβέρνη (inn); Three Taverns or Inns (AC 28.15)

τρέμουσα	VPPANF-S	τρέμω
τρέμουσι(ν)	VIPA--3P	"

τρέμω   (1) literally tremble, quiver (MK 5.33); (2) figuratively be afraid of, fear (possibly 2P 2.10); respect (possibly 2P 2.10)

τρέμων	VPPANM-S	τρέμω

τρέπω   2aor. ἔτραπον; change (AC 28.16)

τρέφει	VIPA--3S	τρέφω
τρέφεσθαι	VNPP	"
τρέφεται	VIPP--3S	"
τρέφηται	VSPP--3S	"
τρέφουσι(ν)	VIPA--3S	"

τρέφω   1aor. ἔθρεψα; pf. pass. τέθραμμαι; (1) feed, take care of, provide for (MT 6.26); (2) as raising children rear, educate, bring up; passive grow up (LU 4.16); (3) figuratively and in a bad sense of overindulgence in revelry that will result in judgment fatten, gorge, pamper (JA 5.5; cf. Jeremiah 12.3)

τρέφωσι(ν)	VSPA--3P	τρέφω
τρέχει	VIPA--3S	τρέχω
τρέχετε	VMPA--2P	"
τρέχῃ	VSPA--3S	"
τρέχοντες	VPPANM-P	"
τρέχοντος	VPPAGM-S	"
τρεχόντων	VPPAGM-P	"
τρέχουσι(ν)	VIPA--3P	"

τρέχω   impf. ἔτρεχον; 2aor. ἔδραμον; run; (1) literally, as moving forward rapidly run, rush forward (MK 5.6); (2) figuratively; (a) as a course of conduct, from a metaphor of footraces strive to advance, exert oneself, make good progress (GA 5.7); (b) of the spread of the gospel message progress freely, spread rapidly (2TH 3.1)

τρέχω	VIPA--1S	τρέχω
	VSPA--1S	"
τρέχωμεν	VSPA--1P	"

τρῆμα, ατος, τό   opening, hole; of a needle eye (LU 18.25)

τρήματος	N-GN-S	τρῆμα
τρία	APCNN-P	τρεῖς
	A-CAN-P	"

τριάκοντα   indeclinable; as a cardinal number thirty

τριακόσιοι, αι, α   as a cardinal number three hundred

τριακοσίοις	A-CDN-P	τριακόσιοι
τριακοσίων	A-CGN-P	"

τρίβολος, ου, ὁ   from an adjective meaning three-pronged; plural, of various prickly plants thistles, briars, burrs, thorns (MT 7.16)

τριβόλους	N-AM-P	τρίβολος
τριβόλων	N-GM-P	"

τρίβος, ου, ἡ   as a well-worn track (beaten) path, thoroughfare, (high)way (MK 1.3)

τρίβους	N-AF-P	τρίβος

τριετία, ας, ἡ   period of three years, for three years (AC 20.31)

τριετίαν	N-AF-S	τριετία
τρίζει	VIPA--3S	τρίζω

τρίζω   make harsh and creaking sounds; as made with the teeth grind, gnash (MK 9.18)

τρίμηνον	AP-AM-S	τρίμηνος

τρίμηνος, ον   of three months; the masculine accusative is used adverbially as a substantive τρίμηνον period of three months, for three months (HE 11.23)

τρίς   adverb; three times, thrice (MT 26.34); substantivally ἐπὶ τ. as many as three times, (yet) a third time (AC 10.16)

τρίς	AB	τρίς
τρισί(ν)	APCDM-P	τρεῖς
	A-CDF-P	"
	A-CDM-P	"

τρίστεγον, ου, τό   of a building third story, third floor (American usage), second story (British usage) (AC 20.9)

τριστέγου	N-GN-S	τρίστεγον
τρισχίλιαι	A-CNF-P	τρισχίλιοι

τρισχίλιοι, αι, α   as a cardinal number three thousand (AC 2.41)

τρισχίλιοι	A-CNM-P	τρισχίλιοι
τρίτη	A-ONF-S	τρίτος
τρίτη	A-ODF-S	"
τρίτην	A-OAF-S	"
τρίτης	A-OGF-S	"
τρίτον	ABO	"
	A-OAM-S	"
	A-OAN-S	"
	A-ONN-S	"

τρίτος, η, ον   as an ordinal number third; (1) as an adjective often with the noun supplied from the context (MT 22.26; 2C 12.2); (2) neuter as a substantive τὸ τρίτον the third part, one-third, followed by the genitive (RV 8.7–12); (3) neuter as an adverb (τὸ) τρίτον (for) the third time (LU 23.22); in enumerations in the third place (1C 12.28)

τρίτος	A-ONM-S	τρίτος
τρίτου	A-OGM-S	"
	A-OGN-S	"
τρίχα	N-AF-S	θρίξ
τρίχας	N-AF-P	"
τρίχες	N-NF-P	"

τρίχινος, η, ον   made of hair, hairy (RV 6.12)

τρίχινος	A--NM-S	τρίχινος
τριχῶν	N-GF-P	θρίξ
Τριῶν	A-CGF-P	Τρεῖς Ταβέρναι
τριῶν	APCGM-P	τρεῖς
	A-CGF-P	"
	A-CGM-P	"

τρόμος, ου, ὁ *trembling, shaking*, as an outward sign of fear or of being seized with great awe (1C 2.3)

τρόμος	N-NM-S	τρόμος
τρόμου	N-GM-S	"
τρόμῳ	N-DM-S	"

τροπή, ῆς, ἡ as a turning around *turn, return*; (1) of heavenly bodies in their courses *return*; (2) metaphorically, of the unchangeableness of God οὐ τροπῆς ἀποσκίασμα literally *not a shadow cast by turning*, i.e. *no change at all* (JA 1.17)

τροπή	N-NF-S	τροπή
τροπῆς	N-GF-S	"
τρόπον	N-AM-S	τρόπος

τρόπος, ου, ὁ strictly *turn, direction*; (1) *manner, way, fashion*; κατὰ μηδένα τρόπον *by no means, in no way* (2TH 2.3); ἐν παντὶ τρόπῳ *in every way, by all means* (2TH 3.16); καθ᾽ ὃν τρόπον *in the same way as* (AC 15.11); ὃν τρόπον *in the manner in which, just as* (MT 23.37); (2) as customary behavior *way of life, character* (HE 13.5)

τρόπος	N-NM-S	τρόπος

τροποφορέω 1aor. ἐτροποφόρησα; as being tolerant toward someone's disposition, manners, moods *bear, be very patient, put up with* (AC 13.18)

τρόπῳ	N-DM-S	τρόπος
τροφάς	N-AF-P	τροφή

τροφή, ῆς, ἡ literally *nourishment, food, provision* (MT 3.4); metaphorically, of spiritual or mental nourishment (HE 5.14)

τροφή	N-NF-S	τροφή
τροφήν	N-AF-S	"
τροφῆς	N-GF-S	"
Τρόφιμον	N-AM-S	Τρόφιμος

Τρόφιμος, ου, ὁ *Trophimus*, masculine proper noun

Τρόφιμος	N-NM-S	Τρόφιμος

τροφός, οῦ, ἡ as one who nourishes and rears up a child *nurse*, possibly *mother* (1TH 2.7)

τροφός	N-NF-S	τροφός

τροφοφορέω 1aor. ἐτροφοφόρησα; *bear up* or *carry in one's arms as a nurse*, i.e. *take care of*; metaphorically, of God's care of Israel in the exodus wanderings (AC 13.18)

τροχιά, ᾶς, ἡ literally *wheel track, course, path*; idiomatically, of the moral and ethical life τροχίας ὀρθὰς ποιεῖν τοῖς ποσίν literally *make straight wheel tracks for the feet*, i.e. *live in the right way, behave correctly* (HE 12.13)

τροχιάς	N-AF-P	τροχιά
τροχόν	N-AM-S	τροχός

τροχός, οῦ, ὁ literally *wheel*; figuratively, as an ordered pattern of events; ὁ τ. τῆς γενέσεως *the course of life, the whole round of existence* (probably JA 3.6); *the whole cycle of nature, how we live* (perhaps JA 3.6)

τρύβλιον, ου, τό *bowl, (deep) dish*

τρύβλιον	N-AN-S	τρύβλιον
τρυβλίῳ	N-DN-S	"

τρυγάω 1aor. ἐτρύγησα; literally *gather* or *harvest (fruit)*, especially *pick* (grapes) (LU 6.44); metaphorically, of God's judgments coming on the earth at the end of this age τρυγᾶν τὴν ἄμπελον τῆς γῆς literally *harvest the vine of the earth*, i.e. *cause people to receive the punishment they deserve* (RV 14.19)

τρύγησον	VMAA--2S	τρυγάω
τρυγόνων	N-GF-P	τρυγών

τρυγών, όνος, ἡ *turtledove, (wild) dove* (LU 2.24)

τρυγῶσι(ν)	VIPA--3P	τρυγάω

τρυμαλιά, ᾶς, ἡ *hole*; of a needle *eye* (MK 10.25)

τρυμαλιᾶς	N-GF-S	τρυμαλιά
τρυμαλίδος	N-GF-S	see τρυμαλιᾶς

τρύπημα, ατος, τό *that which is bored through, hole*; of a needle *eye* (MT 19.24)

τρυπήματος	N-GN-S	τρύπημα

Τρύφαινα, ης, ἡ *Tryphena*, feminine proper noun (RO 16.12)

Τρύφαιναν	N-AF-S	Τρύφαινα

τρυφάω 1aor. ἐτρύφησα; *revel, live in luxury, give oneself to self-indulgence* (JA 5.5)

τρυφή, ῆς, ἡ as a way of life *indulgence, reveling* (2P 2.13); *luxurious living, luxury* (LU 7.25)

τρυφῇ	N-DF-S	τρυφή
τρυφήν	N-AF-S	"
τρυφῆς	N-GF-S	"

Τρυφῶσα, ης, ἡ *Tryphosa*, feminine proper noun (RO 16.12)

Τρυφῶσαν	N-AF-S	Τρυφῶσα
Τρωάδα	N-AF-S	Τρωάς
Τρῳάδα	N-AF-S	"
Τρωάδι	N-DF-S	"
Τρῳάδι	N-DF-S	"
Τρωάδος	N-GF-S	"
Τρῳάδος	N-GF-S	"

Τρῳάς, άδος, ἡ *Troas*, a seaport colony in the northwestern corner of Asia Minor, near the site of ancient Troy (AC 20.6)

τρώγοντες	VPPANM-P	τρώγω
Τρωγυλία	N-DF-S	see Τρωγυλίῳ
Τρωγυλίῳ	N-DN-S	Τρωγύλλιον

Τρωγύλλιον, ου, τό (also Γύλλιον, Στογύλιον, Στρογγύλιον, Τρωγύλιον) *Trogyllium*, a seacoast town and promontory on the western coast of Asia Minor south of Ephesus (AC 20.15)

Τρωγυλλίῳ	N-DN-S	Τρωγύλλιον

τρώγω strictly *crunch*; literally, of animals *gnaw, nibble*; of human beings *eat, take food, partake of (a meal)* (MT 24.38); idiomatically τρώγειν τινός τὸν ἄρτον literally *eat someone's bread*, i.e. *be a close companion* (JN 13.18); figuratively and as a religious technical term, of deriving benefit from Christ's atoning death *benefit from, partake of* (JN 6.54–58)

τρώγων	VPPANM-S	τρώγω
τυγχάνοντα	VPPAAM-S	τυγχάνω
τυγχάνονταν	VPPAAM-S	"
τυγχάνοντες	VPPANM-P	"

τυγχάνω 2aor. ἔτυχον; pf. τέτευχα, τέτυχα, and τετύχηκα; strictly *hit* as a target, especially with an arrow; (1) with the genitive *experience* something, *meet up with, have happen to* (AC 24.2; 2T 2.10; HE 11.35); (2) as a litotes, what one doesn't experience or meet up with every day; (a) of miracles *extraordinary, uncommon* (AC 19.11); (b) of hospitality *unusual, unexpected* (AC 28.2); (3) intransitively *happen, turn out*; (a) *happen to be*; ἀφέντες ἡμιθανῆ τυγχάνοντα *leaving him for half-dead, as in fact he was* (LU 10.30); (b) idiomatically εἰ τύχοι literally *if it should happen*, i.e. *probably, perhaps* (1C 15.37); (c) neuter aorist participle τυχόν as an adverb *perhaps, if possible* (1C 16.6; AC 12.15)

τυμπανίζω 1aor. pass. ἐτυμπανίσθην; strictly *beat a drum, drum on*; hence *torture with the bastinado* or *tympanum*, a cudgel for beating the bottoms of the feet; more generally *beat* or *torture* with rods and clubs, often resulting in death (HE 11.35)

τυπικῶς adverb; *typically, as an example* or *warning, figuratively* (1C 10.11)

τυπικῶς	AB	τυπικῶς
τύποι	N-NM-P	τύπος
τύπον	N-AM-S	"

τύπος, ου, ὁ (1) literally *blow*; by metonymy, the impression made by the blow *mark, trace* (JN 20.25); as a figure formed by blows of the hammer or chisel *image, statue* (AC 7.43); as a small-scale form designed to be copied *pattern, model* (AC 7.44; HE 8.5); (2) figuratively; (a) of teaching or writing *form, content* (RO 6.17); (b) of behavior *example, pattern, model* (1T 4.12); (c) as a person or event serving as a prophetic symbol to prefigure a future person or event *type* (RO 5.14)

τύπος	N-NM-S	τύπος
τύπους	N-AM-P	"
τύπτειν	VNPA	τύπτω
τύπτεσθαι	VNPP	"
τυπτόμενος	VPPPNM-S	"
τύπτοντες	VPPANM-P	"
τύπτοντι	VPPADM-S	"

τύπτω impf. ἔτυπτον; (1) literally *strike, beat* (MT 24.49); (2) figuratively; (a) as judgment sent by God in the form of misfortunes or death *smite* (AC 23.3a); (b) in a psychological sense of causing someone to act against his conscience *wound, harm, injure* (1C 8.12)

Τυραννίου	N-GM-S	Τύραννος
τύραννοι	N-NM-P	τύραννος

Τύραννος, ου, ὁ (also **Τυράννιος**) *Tyrannus*, masculine proper noun (AC 19.9)

τύραννος, ου, ὁ *tyrant, absolute sovereign*, unlimited by law, usually applied to one who has made himself king by force (AC 5.39)

Τυράννου	N-GM-S	Τύραννος
τυρβάζῃ	VIPP--2S	τυρβάζω

τυρβάζω *trouble, stir up*; middle or passive *trouble oneself, be troubled about* something, *be in disorder* (LU 10.41)

Τυρίοις	N-DM-P	Τύριος

Τύριος, ου, ὁ *Tyrian, inhabitant of Tyre*, a seaport along the Mediterranean Sea in Phoenicia (AC 12.20)

Τύρον	N-AF-S	Τύρος

Τύρος, ου, ἡ *Tyre*, a seaport in Phoenicia along the Mediterranean Sea

Τύρου	N-GF-S	Τύρος
Τυροφοινίκισσα	N-NF-S	Συροφοινίκισσα
Τυρραννίου	N-GM-S	Τύραννος
Τύρῳ	N-DF-S	Τύρος
τυφλέ	A--VM-S	τυφλός
τυφλοί	A--NM-P	"
	A--VM-P	"
τυφλοῖς	A--DM-P	"

τυφλόν	A--AM-S	"

τυφλός, ή, όν (1) literally *blind, without sight* (JN 9.1); substantivally *blind person* (MT 9.27); (2) metaphorically, of mental and spiritual blindness, often the result of self-deception, *unable to understand* (MT 15.14); substantivally (MT 23.17)

τυφλός	A--NM-S	τυφλός
τυφλοῦ	A--GM-S	"
τυφλούς	A--AM-P	"

τυφλόω 1aor. ἐτύφλωσα; pf. τετύφλωκα; (1) literally *blind, make blind, deprive of the ability to see*; (2) metaphorically in the NT; (a) of God's judgment on those who refuse to receive the revelation of himself through Jesus *cause* someone *not to be able to understand, take away ability to comprehend* (JN 12.40; 2C 4.4); (b) spiritually and morally, of the consequence of hating one's fellow believer (1J 2.11)

τυφλῷ	A--DM-S	τυφλός
τυφλῶν	A--GM-P	"
τυφόμενον	VPPPAN-S	τύφω

τυφόω pf. pass. τετύφωμαι; 1aor. pass. ἐτυφώθην; (1) literally *wrap in smoke* or *mist, becloud*; (2) figuratively and only passive in the NT; (a) *be puffed up, be very proud* or *arrogant* (1T 3.6); (b) *be silly, be stupid, be absurd* from a sense of one's own importance (2T 3.4)

τύφω as burning slowly *give off smoke, raise a cloud of smoke*; only passive in the NT *smoke, smolder, flicker* (MT 12.20)

τυφωθείς	VPAPNM-S	τυφόω

τυφωνικός, ή, όν of a stormy impetuous wind *typhoonlike, like a whirlwind* or *hurricane* (AC 27.14)

τυφωνικός	A--NM-S	τυφωνικός
τύχα	N-AF-S	τύχη
τυχεῖν	VNAA	τυγχάνω

τύχη, ης, ἡ strictly *what one obtains*; hence *(good) fortune, luck, chance*, either good or bad; κατὰ τύχα *by chance* (LU 10.31)

Τύχικον	N-AM-S	Τυχικός
Τυχικόν	N-AM-S	"
Τύχικος	N-NM-S	"

Τυχικός, οῦ, ὁ (also **Τύχικος**) *Tychicus*, masculine proper noun

Τυχικός	N-NM-S	Τυχικός
τύχοι	VOAA--3S	τυγχάνω
τυχόν	VPAAAN-S	"
τυχοῦσαν	VPAAAF-S	"
τυχούσας	VPAAAF-P	"
τυχών	VPAANM-S	"
τύχωσι(ν)	VSAA--3P	"
τῷ	DDMS	ὁ
	DDMS+	"
	DDNS	"
	DDNS+	"
τῶν	DGFP	"
	DGFP+	"
	DGMP	"
	DGMP+	"
	DGNP	"
	DGNP+	"

ὑακίνθινος, ίνη, ον   *hyacinth-colored*, either dark sapphire blue or dark red, depending on which mineral or stone is used for comparison (RV 9.17)

ὑακινθίνους	A--AM-P	ὑακίνθινος

ὑάκινθος, ου, ὁ   *jacinth* or *hyacinth*, a precious stone either dark blue or dark red (RV 21.20)

ὑάκινθος	N-NM-S	ὑάκινθος
ὑαλίνη	A--NF-S	ὑάλινος
ὑαλίνην	A--AF-S	"

ὑάλινος, η, ον   *of glass, made of glass, transparent* (RV 4.6)

ὕαλος, ου, ἡ (also ὕελον)   *glass, crystal, transparent stone* (RV 21.18)

ὕαλος	N-NF-S	ὕαλος
ὑάλῳ	N-DF-S	"
ὕβρεσι(ν)	N-DF-P	ὕβρις
ὕβρεως	N-GF-S	"
ὑβρίζεις	VIPA--2S	ὑβρίζω
ὑβρίζοντες	VPPANM-S	"

ὑβρίζω   1aor. ὕβρισα; 1aor. pass. ὑβρίσθην; 1fut. pass. ὑβρισθήσομαι; transitively in the NT, with a basic meaning *act to invade* the sphere of another to his hurt, *violate* a divine or human right; (1) through insolent words *insult, scoff at, spitefully mock, revile* (note the lawyer's complaint to Jesus; LU 11.45); (2) through abusive actions *mistreat, punish in a humiliating way, outrage* (MT 22.6; 1TH 2.2)

ὕβριν	N-AF-S	ὕβρις

ὕβρις, εως, ἡ   only in a passive sense in the NT; (1) as the result of presumptuous invasion of one's rights by others through words or actions *insult, outrage, ignominious mistreatment* (2C 12.10); (2) as the result of natural forces, such as wind and weather *damage, injury, hardship* (AC 27.10)

ὑβρίσαι	VNAA	ὑβρίζω
ὕβρισαν	VIAA--3P	"
ὑβρισθέντες	VPAPNM-P	"
ὑβρισθήσεται	VIFP--3S	"
ὑβριστάς	N-AM-P	ὑβριστής
ὑβριστήν	N-AM-S	"

ὑβριστής, οῦ, ὁ   *insolent person, violent aggressor*, especially of one who takes a superior attitude and mistreats others out of his own revolt against God's revelation of truth

ὑγιαίνειν	VNPA	ὑγιαίνω
ὑγιαίνοντα	VPPAAM-S	"
ὑγιαίνοντας	VPPAAM-P	"
ὑγιαίνοντες	VPPANM-P	"
ὑγιαινόντων	VPPAGM-P	"
ὑγιαινούση	VPPADF-S	"
ὑγιαινούσης	VPPAGF-S	"
ὑγιαίνουσι(ν)	VPPADM-P	"

ὑγιαίνω   *be healthy* or *sound*; literally, of physical and mental soundness *be healthy, be well* (LU 7.10); figuratively, of doctrinal teaching *be correct, be accurate, be sound* (1T 1.10)

ὑγιαίνωσι(ν)	VSPA--3P	ὑγιαίνω
ὑγιεῖς	A--AM-P	ὑγιής
ὑγιῆ	A--AM-S	"

ὑγιής, ές   *healthy*, as being balanced and ordered throughout; literally, of physical and mental health *healthy, well, sound* (MT 12.13; MK 5.34); figuratively, of doctrinal teaching *correct, sound, accurate* (TI 2.8)

ὑγιής	A--NF-S	ὑγιής
	A--NM-S	
ὑγίους	A--AM-P	see ὑγιεῖς

ὑγρός, ά, όν   *moist, wet*; of wood before it is dried out *green* (LU 23.31)

ὑγρῷ	A--DN-S	ὑγρός
ὕδασι(ν)	N-DN-P	ὕδωρ
ὕδατα	N-AN-P	"
	N-NN-P	"
ὕδατι	N-DN-S	"
ὕδατος	N-GN-S	"
ὑδάτων	N-GN-P	"

ὑδρία, ας, ἡ   as a container for storing or transporting water *water jar, water pot*

ὑδρίαι	N-NF-P	ὑδρία
ὑδρίαν	N-AF-S	"
ὑδρίας	N-AF-P	"
ὑδροπότει	VMPA--2S	ὑδροποτέω

ὑδροποτέω   *drink (only) water; be a water drinker* (by abstaining from wine) (1T 5.23)

ὑδρωπικός, ή, όν   as a medical technical term *suffering from dropsy, dropsical*, due to an abnormal accumulation of fluids in bodily tissues and cavities, *swollen with water* (LU 14.2)

ὑδρωπικός	A--NM-S	ὑδρωπικός

ὕδωρ, ατος, τό   *water*; (1) literally, as a physical element used for drinking (MK 9.41) and cleansing (LU 7.44); found in springs (JA 3.12), wells (JN 4.7), rivers (RV 16.12), pools (JN 5.7), lakes (MT 14.28), seas (RV 14.2), floods (2P 3.6); (2) used symbolically in baptism (MT 3.11), ceremonial washings (JN 13.5; cf. MK 7.3–4); (3) used metaphorically; (a) to represent spiritual realities ὕ. ζῶν *living water*, i.e. *what gives eternal life* (JN 4.10; cf. 10.14); (b) plural, to represent the many peoples of the earth (RV 17.15)

ὕδωρ	N-AN-S	ὕδωρ
	N-NN-S	"
ὑέλῳ	N-DF-S	ὕαλος
ὑετόν	N-AM-S	ὑετός

ὑετός, οῦ, ὁ   *rain*; (1) as a substance *rain water* (HE 6.7); (2) as an event *rain, raining* (AC 14.17)

ὑετός	N-NM-S	ὑετός
ὑετούς	N-AM-P	"
υἱέ	N-VM-S	υἱός

υἱοθεσία, ας, ἡ *adoption*; used in the NT as a legal technical term but in a metaphorical sense; (1) of God's acceptance of the nation of Israel as his chosen people (RO 9.4); (2) of the sonship status bestowed on those who believe in Christ (GA 4.5); (3) of the status given in the resurrected state (RO 8.23)

υἱοθεσία	N-NF-S	υἱοθεσία
υἱοθεσίαν	N-AF-S	"
υἱοθεσίας	N-GF-S	"
υἱοί	N-NM-P	υἱός
	N-VM-P	"
υἱοῖς	N-DM-P	"
υἱόν	N-AM-S	"

υἱός, οῦ, ὁ *son*; (1) literally; (a) as an immediate male *offspring* (MT 1.21); (b) as a descendant (MT 27.9); (c) as one adopted as a son (AC 7.21); (d) as the immediate male *offspring* of an animal (MT 21.5); (2) figuratively; (a) as a pupil, disciple, follower, or spiritual son (MT 12.27; 1P 5.13); (b) in titles, denoting the relationship of Jesus to God ὁ υἱ. τοῦ θεοῦ (*Son of God*) (MT 16.16), to mankind ὁ υἱ. τοῦ ἀνθρώπου (*Son of Man*) (MT 9.6), to David's royal dynasty (MT 12.23); (c) as a person sharing a nature or quality characteristic of a group; (i) in a positive sense (AC 4.36); (ii) in a negative sense (EP 2.2); (d) spiritually, as a person who stands in a close relation to or belongs to God (RO 8.14), the devil (AC 13.10), this world (LU 20.34), God's kingdom (MT 8.12), etc.

υἱός	N-NM-S	υἱός
	N-VM-S	"
υἱοῦ	N-GM-S	"
υἱούς	N-AM-P	"
υἱῷ	N-DM-S	"
υἱῶν	N-GM-P	"

ὕλη, ης, ἡ *wood*; (1) as standing *forest, woodland* (probably JA 3.5); (2) as cut *wood, firewood, building material* (perhaps JA 3.5)

ὕλην	N-AF-S	ὕλη
ὑμᾶς	NPA-2P	σύ
ὑμεῖν	NPD-2P	see ὑμῖν
ὑμεῖς	NPN-2P	σύ

Ὑμέναιος, ου, ὁ *Hymenaeus*, masculine proper noun

Ὑμέναιος	N-NM-S	Ὑμέναιος
ὑμετέρα	A--NF2S	ὑμέτερος
ὑμετέρα	A--DF2S	"
ὑμετέραν	A--AF2S	"
ὑμετέρας	A--GF2S	"
ὑμέτερον	A--AM2S	"
	A--AN2S	"

ὑμέτερος, τέρα, ον a possessive adjectival form of the second-person plural pronoun *your, yours, belonging to you* (LU 6.20); substantively τὸ ὑμέτερον *your own property, what is yours* (LU 16.12), opposite τὸ ἀλλότριον (*belonging to another, not one's own*); in the subjective sense *proceeding from you* (JN 15.20); objectively *to you* (RO 11.31), *about you* (1C 15.31)

ὑμέτερος	A--NM2S	ὑμέτερος

ὑμετέρῳ	A--DM2S	"
	A--DN2S	"
ὑμῖν	NPD-2P	σύ

ὑμνέω impf. ὕμνουν; fut. ὑμνήσω; 1aor. ὕμνησα; (1) transitively *sing the praise of* someone (only of God in the NT), *sing praise to* (AC 16.25); (2) intransitively *sing (a hymn), recite (a psalm)* (MT 26.30)

ὑμνήσαντες	VPAANM-P	ὑμνέω
ὑμνήσω	VIFA--1S	"
ὕμνοις	N-DM-P	ὕμνος

ὕμνος, ου, ὁ *hymn, sacred song, song of praise to God*, especially used to express thanksgiving

ὕμνουν	VIIA--3P	ὑμνέω
ὑμῶν	NPG-2P	σύ
ὑοδήποτε	A-RDN-S&AB	see οἵῳ and δήποτε
ὑπ'	PA	ὑπό
	PG	"
ὕπαγε	VMPA--2S	ὑπάγω
ὑπάγει	VIPA--3S	"
ὑπάγειν	VNPA	"
ὑπάγεις	VIPA--2S	"
ὑπάγετε	VMPA--2P	"
ὑπάγῃ	VSPA--3S	"
ὑπάγῃς	VSPA--2S	"
ὑπάγητε	VSPA--2P	"
ὑπάγοντας	VPPAAM-P	"
ὑπάγοντες	VPPANM-P	"

ὑπάγω impf. ὑπῆγον; strictly *lead* or *bring under control*; intransitively in the NT; (1) as taking oneself away *go away, withdraw, leave* (JN 6.67); predominately in the Gospels as an intensive imperative ὕπαγε *be gone! be off! go away!* (MT 4.10) or with an indication of goal or direction *go* (MT 8.13; MK 2.11; 10.21); (2) as equivalent to πορεύομαι *go (off), proceed (to), journey* (JN 7.3); (3) euphemistically *depart* (from this life), *die, go* (to God) (MK 14.21; JN 7.33); (4) as experiencing a change of condition *undergo, go to* (RV 13.10; 17.8, 11)

ὑπάγω	VIPA--1S	ὑπάγω
ὑπάγωμεν	VSPA--1P	"
ὑπάγων	VPPANM-S	"

ὑπακοή, ῆς, ἡ (1) *obedience, submission, compliance* (RO 16.19), opposite παρακοή (*disobedience*); (2) *favorable hearing, compliance* with a request (PM 21)

ὑπακοή	N-NF-S	ὑπακοή
ὑπακοῇ	N-DF-S	"
ὑπακοήν	N-AF-S	"
ὑπακοῆς	N-GF-S	"
ὑπακούει	VIPA--3S	ὑπακούω
ὑπακούειν	VNPA	"
ὑπακούετε	VIPA--2P	"
	VMPA--2P	"
ὑπακούουσι(ν)	VIPA--3P	"
	VPPADM-P	"
ὑπακοῦσαι	VNAA	"
ὑπακούσασι(ν)	VPAADM-P	"

ὑπακούω impf. ὑπήκουον; 1aor. ὑπήκουσα; from a basic meaning *listen to*; (1) with the dative of person *obey, submit to, be subject to* (EP 6.1); (2) with the dative of the thing *yield to, obey, surrender to* (AC 6.7); (3) as the duty of a doorkeeper *hearken, answer* a knock, *open* (the door) (AC 12.13) ὕπανδρος, ον strictly *under authority of* or *(legally) bound to a man*; hence, of a woman *married* (RO 7.2)

ὕπανδρος	A--NF-S	ὕπανδρος

ὑπαντάω fut. ὑπαντήσω; 1aor. ὑπήντησα; *meet (someone)*, *come* or *go to meet*, *encounter* (MT 8.28); in a hostile sense *oppose, face* (LU 14.31)

ὑπαντῆσαι	VNAA	ὑπαντάω
ὑπαντήσει	VIFA--3S	"
ὑπάντησιν	N-AF-S	ὑπάντησις

ὑπάντησις, εως, ἡ as an action *going to meet* someone, *drawing near*; εἰς ὑπάντησίν τινι *to meet someone*

ὑπάρξεις	N-AF-P	ὕπαρξις
ὕπαρξιν	N-AF-S	"

ὕπαρξις, εως, ἡ *what exists, existence*; only plural in the NT, as equivalent to τὰ ὑπάρχοντα *what one has, property, belongings* (AC 2.45)

ὑπάρχει	VIPA--3S	ὑπάρχω
ὑπάρχειν	VNPA	"
ὑπάρχοντα	VPPAAM-S	"
	VPPAAN-P	"
	VPPANN-P	"
ὑπάρχοντας	VPPAAM-P	"
ὑπάρχοντες	VPPANM-P	"
ὑπάρχοντος	VPPAGM-S	"
	VPPAGN-S	"
ὑπαρχόντων	VPPAGM-P	"
	VPPAGN-P	"
ὑπάρχουσαι	VPPANF-P	"
ὑπαρχούσης	VPPAGF-S	"
ὑπάρχουσι(ν)	VIPA--3P	"
	VPPADN-P	"

ὑπάρχω impf. ὑπῆρχον; (1) *exist, be present, be at hand, be (found)* (AC 19.40; 1C 11.18); (2) as equivalent to εἰμι followed by a predicate noun *be* (LU 8.41) or to the participle ὤν followed by a predicate noun *who is, because he is* (AC 2.30; GA 1.14); (3) neuter plural τὰ ὑπάρχοντα as a substantive *what one has at one's disposal, property, possessions* (MT 19.21; LU 8.3)

ὑπάρχων	VPPANM-S	ὑπάρχω
ὑπάρχωσι(ν)	VSPA--3P	"
ὑπέβαλε(ν)	VIAA--3S	ὑποβάλλω
ὑπέβαλον	VIAA--3P	"
ὑπέδειξα	VIAA--1S	ὑποδείκνυμι
ὑπέδειξε(ν)	VIAA--3S	"
ὑπεδέξατο	VIAD--3S	ὑποδέχομαι
ὑπεδέχθησαν	VIAP--3P	"
ὑπέθηκαν	VIAA--3P	ὑποτίθημι
ὑπείκετε	VMPA--2P	ὑπείκω

ὑπείκω literally *yield, retire from, give way*; figuratively *submit* to someone's authority, *resist no longer, do* as someone says (HE 13.17)

ὑπέλαβε(ν)	VIAA--3S	ὑπολαμβάνω
ὑπελείφθην	VIAP--1S	ὑπολείπω
ὑπέμειναν	VIAA--3P	ὑπομένω
ὑπεμείνατε	VIAA--2P	"
ὑπέμεινε(ν)	VIAA--3S	"
ὑπέμενον	VIIA--3P	"
ὑπεμνήσθη	VIAP--3S	ὑπομιμνήσκω
ὑπεναντίον	A--NN-S	ὑπεναντίος

ὑπεναντίος, α, ον strictly *over against*; hence *contrary, hostile, opposed* (CO 2.14); substantively *opponent, adversary* (HE 10.27)

ὑπεναντίους	AP-AM-P	ὑπεναντίος
ὑπενεγκεῖν	VNAA	ὑποφέρω
ὑπενόουν	VIIA--1S	ὑπονοέω
	VIIA--3P	"
ὑπεπλεύσαμεν	VIAA--1P	ὑποπλέω

ὑπέρ preposition; literally *over, above*; used only in a nonliteral sense in the NT; (1) with the genitive; (a) with a component of protection and concern *on behalf of, for the sake of, for* (PH 4.10; CO 1.7); (b) after expressions relating to prayer *for, in behalf of* (MT 5.44); (c) after expressions relating to sacrifice *for, to atone for* someone (MK 14.24); *to atone, pay the price for* something (HE 10.12); (d) with a component of representation or substitution *in the place of, for, in the name of, instead of* (RO 9.3; 1C 15.29; PM 13); (e) to mark cause or reason *on account of, for the sake of, in view of* (AC 5.41; 2TH 1.5); (f) to mark general content *with reference to, about, concerning* (equivalent to περί) (JN 1.30; RO 9.27); (2) with the accusative; (a) with a component of excelling or surpassing *exceeding, above, more than* (2C 1.8b; EP 1.22); (b) preceded by a comparative *than* (LU 16.8; HE 4.12); (3) adverbially *to an even greater degree, more* (2C 11.23; cf. ἐγὼ μᾶλλον [*I (even) more*] in PH 3.4)

ὑπέρ	AB	ὑπέρ
	PA	"
	PG	"
ὑπεραίρομαι	VIPP--1S	ὑπεραίρω
ὑπεραιρόμενος	VPPMNM-S	"

ὑπεραίρω *lift up over*; only middle or passive in the NT; (1) middle *exalt oneself, proudly set oneself up* as something (2TH 2.4); (2) passive *be elated, be overly proud* (2C 12.7)

ὑπεραίρωμαι	VSPP--1S	ὑπεραίρω

ὑπέρακμος, ον strictly *beyond a high point* or *prime*; ἐὰν ᾖ ὑπέρακμος in 1C 7.36 is variously interpreted, depending on one's understanding of γαμίζω and whether ὑπέρ adds a temporal or intensifying role; (1) as referring to an unmarried woman, with the temporal sense *beyond the prime of life, past marriageable age*; (2) as referring to an unmarried man, with the intensifying sense *with (too) strong sexual desires*

ὑπέρακμος	A--NF-S	ὑπέρακμος
	A--NM-S	"

ὑπεράνω adverb; *above, far above*; used as an improper preposition with the genitive; (1) of location (HE 9.5); (2) of superior status (EP 1.21)

ὑπεράνω	PG	ὑπεράνω
ὑπερασπίζειν	VNPA	ὑπερασπίζω

ὑπερασπίζω strictly *hold a shield over*; hence *protect, preserve, keep* someone *safe* (JA 1.27)

ὑπεραυξάνει	VIPA--3S	ὑπεραυξάνω

ὑπεραυξάνω *grow wonderfully, increase very much* or *immeasurably*; figuratively, of the faith of believers (2TH 1.3)

ὑπερβαίνειν	VNPA	ὑπερβαίνω

ὑπερβαίνω (1) literally, of space *step over* (a boundary), *break over* (a barrier), *go beyond* (prescribed limits);

(2) figuratively; (a) of laws *break, transgress*; (b) absolutely *do wrong, sin*; (c) with a person as the object *cheat against, wrong* someone; in 1TH 4.6 two ideas are possible: (i) with the two verbs ὑ. and πλεονεκτέω (*have more than*) creating one reinforced idea and with πρᾶγμα (*deed, act, event*) meaning *business*, thus *ruthlessly defraud his brother in business*; (ii) with a demonstrative understood, with πρᾶγμα and pointing to the general context of sexual immorality and with ὑ. taken absolutely *do wrong and take advantage of his brother in this matter*

ὑπερβάλλον	VPPAAN-S	ὑπερβάλλω
	VPPANN-S	"
ὑπερβάλλοντα	VPPAAN-P	"

ὑπερβαλλόντως an adverb expressing degree *above measure, exceedingly*; in a comparative sense *more severely, to a much greater degree, many more times* (2C 11.23)

ὑπερβαλλόντως	AB	ὑπερβαλλόντως
ὑπερβάλλουσαν	VPPAAF-S	ὑπερβάλλω
ὑπερβαλλούσης	VPPAGF-S	"

ὑπερβάλλω strictly *throw over* or *beyond, excel in throwing*; in the NT, as expressing a degree beyond comparison *go beyond, surpass all measure, go beyond all comprehension*

ὑπερβολή, ῆς, ἡ strictly *throwing beyond*; (1) as an expression of extraordinary degree *excess, extraordinary amount* or *quality* of anything (2C 4.7); (2) adverbially καθ᾽ ὑπερβολήν with a basic meaning *to an extreme degree*, taking its specific sense from the context; *exceedingly, in the extreme, altogether* (RO 7.13); *far surpassing, very much better* (1C 12.31); καθ᾽ ὑπερβολὴν εἰς ὑπερβολήν *surpassing all measure, exceeding all else* (2C 4.17)

ὑπερβολή	N-NF-S	ὑπερβολή
ὑπερβολῇ	N-DF-S	"
ὑπερβολήν	N-AF-S	"

ὑπερέκεινα adverb of space *beyond, on the far side*; as an improper preposition with the genitive τὰ ὑ. ὑμῶν *the places beyond you* (2C 10.16)

ὑπερέκεινα	PG	ὑπερέκεινα

ὑπερεκπερισσοῦ adverb; *surpassingly, extremely*; of prayer *as earnestly as possible* (1TH 3.10); as the highest form of comparison imaginable *immeasurably more than* (EP 3.20)

ὑπερεκπερισσοῦ	AB	ὑπερεκπερισσοῦ

ὑπερεκπερισσῶς adverb; *beyond all measure, most highly* (1TH 5.13)

ὑπερεκπερισσῶς	AB	ὑπερεκπερισσῶς
ὑπερεκτείνομεν	VIPA--1P	ὑπερεκτείνω

ὑπερεκτείνω *overextend*; with ἑαυτόν *overextend oneself, go beyond (assigned) limits* (2C 10.14)

ὑπερεκχυννόμενον	VPPPAN-S	ὑπερεκχύννω

ὑπερεκχύννω (and **ὑπερεκχύνω**) *pour out over*; only passive in the NT *overflow* (LU 6.38)

ὑπερεκχυνόμενον	VPPPAN-S	ὑπερεκχύννω
ὑπερεντυγχάνει	VIPA--3S	ὑπερεντυγχάνω

ὑπερεντυγχάνω *plead, intercede for* another (RO 8.26)

ὑπερεπερίσσευσε(ν)	VIAA--3S	ὑπερπερισσεύω
ὑπερεπλεόνασε(ν)	VIAA--3S	ὑπερπλεονάζω
ὑπερέχον	VPPAAN-S	ὑπερέχω
ὑπερέχοντας	VPPAAM-P	"
ὑπερέχοντι	VPPADM-S	"
ὑπερέχουσα	VPPANF-S	"
ὑπερέχουσαι	VPPANF-P	"
ὑπερεχούσαις	VPPADF-P	"

ὑπερέχω strictly *hold above*; hence (1) of value *surpass, be better than, excel* (PH 4.7); (2) of power *be in authority (over), be in control* (1P 2.13)

ὑπερηφανία, ας, ἡ as a conscious effort to appear conspicuously above others *arrogance, pride, haughtiness* (MK 7.22), opposite ταπεινοφροσύνη (*humility*)

ὑπερηφανία	N-NF-S	ὑπερηφανία
ὑπερήφανοι	A--NM-P	ὑπερήφανος
ὑπερηφάνοις	A--DM-P	"

ὑπερήφανος, ον strictly *showing above*; hence, in a negative sense *arrogant, proud, haughty*, of an empty boaster who brags of his position and despises others (2T 3.2); substantivally ὑπερήφανοι *proud people* (JA 4.6)

ὑπερηφάνους	A--AM-P	ὑπερήφανος
ὑπεριδών	VPAANM-S	ὑπεροράω

ὑπερλίαν adverb; of an excessive degree of anything *exceedingly, extremely, superlatively*; used ironically in 2C 11.5 and 12.11 οἱ ὑ. ἀπόστολοι *the superapostles*

ὑπερλίαν	AB	ὑπερλίαν

ὑπερνικάω *be more than conqueror, be completely victorious, completely win out over* something (RO 8.37)

ὑπερνικῶμεν	VIPA--1P	ὑπερνικάω
ὑπέρογκα	A--AN-P	ὑπέρογκος

ὑπέρογκος, ον strictly *of excessive size, overgrown, (over)swollen*; hence, of speech *very boastful, bombastic, pompous*; substantivally ὑπέρογκα *boastful words* (JU 16)

ὑπεροράω 2aor. ὑπερεῖδον; *overlook, disregard* (AC 17.30)

ὑπεροχή, ῆς, ἡ (1) literally *elevation, prominence*; (2) figuratively in the NT; (a) *excellence, superiority* (1C 2.1); (b) *place of prominence*; οἱ ἐν ὑπεροχῇ ὄντες *those who are in authority* or *in an important position* (1T 2.2)

ὑπεροχῇ	N-DF-S	ὑπεροχή
ὑπεροχήν	N-AF-S	"
ὑπερπερισσεύομαι	VIPP--1S	ὑπερπερισσεύω

ὑπερπερισσεύω 1aor. ὑπερεπερίσσευσα; (1) intransitively; (a) of a great quantity *abound over and above, be more abundant, be present to a greater extent* (possibly RO 5.20); (b) of an extraordinary degree of anything *be present to a greater degree, be very much greater* or *stronger* (probably RO 5.20); (2) transitively *cause to overflow*; figuratively and passive *overflow, be full and running over* with something, *experience exceedingly* (2C 7.4)

ὑπερπερισσῶς adverb; *beyond (all) measure, exceedingly, to an extreme degree* (MK 7.37)

ὑπερπερισσῶς	AB	ὑπερπερισσῶς

ὑπερπλεονάζω 1aor. ὑπερεπλεόνασα; literally, as a measure of quantity of a container *fill to overflowing*; figuratively *be present in great abundance, abound exceedingly* (1T 1.14)

ὑπερυψόω 1aor. ὑπερύψωσα; of status *exalt highly* or *supremely, put* someone *in the most important position* of honor and power (PH 2.9)

ὑπερύψωσε(ν)	VIAA--3S	ὑπερυψόω
ὑπερφρονεῖν	VNPA	ὑπερφρονέω

ὑπερφρονέω _be haughty, be conceited, think too highly of oneself_ (RO 12.3)

ὑπερῷον, ου, τό as the upper part of a house _upper room, upstairs, upper story_

ὑπερῷον	N-AN-S	ὑπερῷον
ὑπερῴῳ	N-DN-S	"
ὑπεστειλάμην	VIAM--1S	ὑποστέλλω
ὑπέστελλε(ν)	VIIA--3S	"
ὑπέστρεφε(ν)	VIIA--3S	ὑποστρέφω
ὑπέστρεφον	VIIA--3P	"
ὑπέστρεψα	VIAA--1S	"
ὑπέστρεψαν	VIAA--3P	"
ὑπέστρεψε(ν)	VIAA--3S	"
ὑπεστρώννυον	VIIA--3P	ὑποστρωννύω
ὑπετάγη	VIAP--3S	ὑποτάσσω
ὑπετάγησαν	VIAP--3P	"
ὑπέταξας	VIAA--2S	"
ὑπέταξε(ν)	VIAA--3S	"
ὑπέχουσαι	VPPANF-P	ὑπέχω
ὑπέχουσι(ν)	VIPA--3P	"

ὑπέχω strictly _hold under_; hence _experience, undergo_; as a legal technical term δίκην ὑπέχειν _undergo punishment, suffer as one deserves_ (JU 7)

ὑπεχώρησε(ν)	VIAA--3S	ὑποχωρέω
ὑπῆγον	VIIA--3P	ὑπάγω
ὑπήκοοι	A--NM-P	ὑπήκοος

ὑπήκοος, ον _obedient, submissive_

ὑπήκοος	A--NM-S	ὑπήκοος
ὑπήκουε(ν)	VIIA--3S	ὑπακούω
ὑπήκουον	VIIA--3P	"
ὑπήκουσαν	VIAA--3P	"
ὑπηκούσατε	VIAA--2P	"
ὑπήκουσε(ν)	VIAA--3S	"
ὑπήνεγκα	VIAA--1S	ὑποφέρω
ὑπήντησαν	VIAA--3P	ὑπαντάω
ὑπήντησε(ν)	VIAA--3S	"
ὑπηρέται	N-NM-P	ὑπηρέτης
ὑπηρέταις	N-DM-P	"
ὑπηρέτας	N-AM-P	"
ὑπηρετεῖν	VNPA	ὑπηρετέω

ὑπηρετέω 1aor. ὑπηρέτησα; with the dative of person _serve, render assistance to, help, be helpful to_ someone

ὑπηρέτῃ	N-DM-S	ὑπηρέτης
ὑπηρέτην	N-AM-S	"

ὑπηρέτης, ου, ὁ from a basic meaning _one who acts under orders_ of another to carry out his will, _assistant, helper_ (AC 13.5); in a law court _officer, deputy_ (MT 5.25); in a synagogue _attendant, assistant_ (LU 4.20); in the Sanhedrin _officer, servant_ (MT 26.58; JN 18.12); in a king's household _attendant, servant_ (JN 18.36); as those who work with Christ to accomplish his purposes _trusted servant, minister, assistant_ (1C 4.1)

ὑπηρέτησαν	VIAA--3P	ὑπηρετέω
ὑπηρετήσας	VPAANM-S	"
ὑπηρετοῦντα	VPPAAM-S	"
ὑπηρετῶν	N-GM-P	ὑπηρέτης
ὑπῆρχε(ν)	VIIA--3S	ὑπάρχω
ὑπῆρχον	VIIA--3P	"

ὕπνος, ου, ὁ literally _sleep_ (MT 1.24); idiomatically βαρεῖσθαι ὕπνῳ literally _be burdened by sleep_, i.e. _be sound asleep_ (LU 9.32); καταφέρεσθαι ὕπνῳ literally _be carried away by sleep_, i.e. _become more and more sleepy_ (AC 20.9); metaphorically, in a negative sense, as spiritual apathy ἐξ ὕπνου ἐγερθῆναι literally _be roused out of sleep_, i.e. _wake up to reality, realize what is going on_ (RO 13.11)

ὕπνου	N-GM-S	ὕπνος
ὕπνῳ	N-DM-S	"

ὑπό preposition; (1) with the genitive; (a) with a person as the object and with a passive verb, denoting the immediate agent _by_ (MT 1.22); (b) with a thing and a passive verb, denoting cause or instrument _by, by means of_ (MT 8.24; LU 8.14); (c) with a person and a verb with a passive sense; πάσχειν ὑ. τινος _suffer at the hands of_ someone (MT 17.12); γίνεσθαι ὑ. τινος _be done by someone_ (LU 13.17); (d) with a person and a noun carrying a passive sense _by, at the hands of_ (2C 2.6); (e) with an active verb, implying an agent _with, by_ (RV 6.8); (2) with the accusative; (a) denoting place _under, below, underneath_ (MT 8.8; JN 1.48); (b) denoting submission or subjection to authority, rule, command, power _under_ (LU 7.8; GA 3.25); (c) denoting subjection or bondage to a moral force, such as sin (GA 3.22), law (GA 4.5), judgment (JA 5.12) _under the control of, subject to_; (d) denoting an approximate time, short of a specific point ὑ. τὸν ὄρθρον _about daybreak_ (AC 5.21)

ὑπό	PA	ὑπό
	PG	"

ὑποβάλλω 1aor. ὑπέβαλον; as hiring someone to do something illegal _secretly induce, (secretly) instigate, bribe_ (AC 6.11)

ὑπογραμμόν	N-AM-S	ὑπογραμμός

ὑπογραμμός, οῦ, ὁ (1) strictly _writing copy_ for beginners; hence _model, pattern_; (2) figuratively _example, guidelines_ (1P 2.21)

ὑποδέδεκται	VIRD--3S	ὑποδέχομαι
	VIRO--3S	"
ὑποδεδεμένους	VPRMAM-P	ὑποδέω

ὑπόδειγμα, ατος, τό (1) in a positive sense, as something to be imitated _example, model_ (JN 13.15); (2) in a negative sense, as something to be avoided _(warning) example_ (2P 2.6); (3) as a representative copy or likeness of what is original and genuine _imitation, image_ (HE 8.5)

ὑπόδειγμα	N-AN-S	ὑπόδειγμα
ὑποδείγματα	N-AN-P	"
ὑποδείγματι	N-DN-S	"

ὑποδείκνυμι or **ὑποδεικνύω** fut. ὑποδείξω; 1aor. ὑπέδειξα; (1) strictly _show secretly, give a glimpse of_; hence _intimate, suggest_; (2) figuratively, with the dative of person _show, make known, point out_ (LU 6.47; AC 9.16); in a negative sense _warn_ (MT 3.7)

ὑποδείξατε	VMAA--2P	ὑποδείκνυμι
ὑποδείξω	VIFA--1S	"
ὑποδεξαμένη	VPADNF-S	ὑποδέχομαι

ὑποδέχομαι 1aor. ὑπεδεξάμην; pf. ὑποδέδεγμαι; _welcome, receive, entertain as a guest_

ὑποδέω 1aor. mid. ὑπεδησάμην; pf. mid. ptc. ὑποδεδεμένος; only middle in the NT _tie_ or _bind beneath_; of shoes or sandals _put on_ (AC 12.8); perfect participle _have on as shoes, wear_ (MK 6.9)

ὑπόδημα, ατος, τό   as what is bound under the feet *sandal*, a leather sole bound to the foot by straps

ὑπόδημα	N-AN-S	ὑπόδημα
ὑποδήματα	N-AN-P	"
ὑποδήματος	N-GN-S	"
ὑποδημάτων	N-GN-P	"
ὑποδῆσαι	VMAM--2S	ὑποδέω
ὑποδησάμενοι	VPAMNM-P	"

ὑπόδικος, ον   as a legal technical term, of one who has lost all possibility of disproving a charge against him and thus has already lost his case *accountable, answerable, liable to punishment* (RO 3.19)

ὑπόδικος	A--NM-S	ὑπόδικος
ὑποδραμόντες	VPAANM-P	ὑποτρέχω

ὑποζύγιον, ου, τό   as a domesticated animal for pulling a plow or carrying a burden; in the NT *donkey, pack animal*

ὑποζύγιον	N-NN-S	ὑποζύγιον
ὑποζυγίου	N-GN-S	"

ὑποζώννυμι   ptc. ὑποζωννύς; as a nautical technical term, of a ship *undergird, brace, fasten ropes around* (AC 27.17)

ὑποζωννύντες	VPPANM-P	ὑποζώννυμι

ὑποκάτω   adverb; *underneath, below*; in the NT used only as an improper preposition with the genitive *under, below, beneath* (MK 7.28); *at the foot of, down before* (the altar) (RV 6.9); idiomatically ὑ. τῶν ποδῶν literally *under the feet*, i.e. *under the complete control of* (MT 22.44)

ὑποκάτω	PG	ὑποκάτω

ὑπόκειμαι   *lie below*; ὑποκεῖσθαι ἐν τῷ ὀφθαλμῷ *be found in the eye* (LU 6.42)

ὑπόκειται	VIPD--3S	ὑπόκειμαι

ὑποκρίνομαι   *pretend, act a part, make believe*; as assuming a counterfeit character *feign* (LU 20.20)

ὑποκρινομένους	VPPDAM-P	ὑποκρίνομαι
	VPPOAM-P	
ὑποκρίσει	N-DF-S	ὑπόκρισις
ὑποκρίσεις	N-AF-P	"
ὑποκρίσεως	N-GF-S	"
ὑπόκρισιν	N-AF-S	"

ὑπόκρισις, εως, ἡ   strictly *delivery* of a speech, along with interpretive gestures and imitation; in the NT only in a bad sense *pretense, hypocrisy, dissimulation*

ὑπόκρισις	N-NF-S	ὑπόκρισις
ὑποκριτά	N-VM-S	ὑποκριτής
ὑποκριταί	N-NM-P	"
	N-VM-P	

ὑποκριτής, οῦ, ὁ   strictly *actor, stage player*; figuratively in the NT, as a moral or religious counterfeit *hypocrite, pretender, dissembler*

ὑποκριτῶν	N-GM-P	ὑποκριτής
ὑπολαβών	VPAANM-S	ὑπολαμβάνω
ὑπολαμβάνειν	VNPA	"
ὑπολαμβάνετε	VIPA--2P	"

ὑπολαμβάνω   2aor. ὑπέλαβον; (1) *take up* someone *(from below)* (AC 1.9); (2) *receive as a guest, help, support* (3J 8); (3) to introduce a response to a question; (a) *take up* (a word) *and answer, reply, retort* (LU 10.30); (b) *take up* (an idea), *suppose, think, assume* (LU 7.43)

ὑπολαμβάνω	VIPA--1S	ὑπολαμβάνω

ὑπολαμβάνων	VPPANM-S	"
ὑπολαμπάδες	N-NF-P	ὑπολαμπάς

ὑπολαμπάς, άδος, ἡ   *window*, an opening in a building to allow light and air to enter (AC 20.8)

ὑπόλειμμα, ατος, τό   *remnant, small number, survivors* (RO 9.27)

ὑπόλειμμα	N-NN-S	ὑπόλειμμα

ὑπολείπω   1aor. pass. ὑπελείφθην; *leave remaining, leave behind*; passive *be left (surviving)* (RO 11.3)

ὑπολήνιον, ου, τό   as a container placed or a pit dug under an olivepress or winepress to receive the oil or juice *vat, trough* (MK 12.1)

ὑπολήνιον	N-AN-S	ὑπολήνιον

ὑπολιμπάνω   *leave behind* something for someone to use (1P 2.21)

ὑπολιμπάνων	VPPANM-S	ὑπολιμπάνω
ὑπομείναντας	VPAAAM-P	ὑπομένω
ὑπομείνας	VPAANM-S	"
ὑπομεμενηκότα	VPRAAM-S	"
ὑπομένει	VIPA--3S	"
ὑπομένειν	VNPA	"
ὑπομενεῖτε	VIFA--2P	"
ὑπομένετε	VIPA--2P	"
	VMPA--2P	"
ὑπομένομεν	VIPA--1P	"
ὑπομένοντας	VPPAAM-P	"
ὑπομένοντες	VPPANM-P	"

ὑπομένω   1aor. ὑπέμεινα; pf. ptc. ὑπομεμενηκώς; (1) with ἐν and the dative of place *remain behind, stay* (when others depart) (LU 2.43); (2) as refusing to flee *hold out, stand one's ground, endure* (MT 10.22); (3) with the accusative of the thing *be patient under, suffer, endure, put up with* (HE 12.2); (4) absolutely *endure, continue firm, persevere* (RO 12.12; JA 5.11)

ὑπομένω	VIPA--1S	ὑπομένω
ὑπομίμνησκε	VMPA--2S	ὑπομιμνήσκω
ὑπομιμνήσκειν	VNPA	"

ὑπομιμνήσκω   fut. ὑπομνήσω; 1aor. ὑπέμνησα; 1aor. pass. ὑπεμνήσθην; (1) with the accusative of person *remind* someone of something, *cause to think about again* (JN 14.26); (2) with the accusative of the thing *call to mind, suggest, remind of* (2T 2.14); (3) passive *remember, recall, think of* something (LU 22.61)

ὑπομιμνήσκω	VIPA--1S	ὑπομιμνήσκω
ὑπομνῆσαι	VNAA	"
ὑπομνήσει	N-DF-S	ὑπόμνησις
	VIFA--3S	ὑπομιμνήσκω
ὑπόμνησιν	N-AF-S	ὑπόμνησις

ὑπόμνησις, εως, ἡ   as recollection by a definite act of will; (1) active *reminding, putting in mind* (2P 1.13; 3.1); (2) passive *recollection, remembrance* (2T 1.5)

ὑπομνήσω	VIFA--1S	ὑπομιμνήσκω

ὑπομονή, ῆς, ἡ   (1) as a basic attitude or frame of mind *patience, steadfastness* (2C 12.12; probably 2TH 3.5); (2) as steadfast adherence to a course of action in spite of difficulties and testings *perseverance, endurance, fortitude* (RO 5.3, 4; probably HE 10.36; perhaps 2TH 3.5); (3) with a component of hope and confidence *expectation, patient waiting* (RV 1.9; perhaps HE 10.36)

ὑπομονή	N-NF-S	ὑπομονή
ὑπομονῇ	N-DF-S	"

ὑπομονήν N-AF-S "
ὑπομονῆς N-GF-S "
ὑπονοεῖτε VIPA--2P ὑπονοέω
ὑπονοέω impf. ὑπενόουν; strictly *secretly think*; hence, in a bad sense *suspect, hold a suspicion* (AC 25.18); generally *suppose, conjecture, assume* (AC 27.27); *regard as* (AC 13.25)
ὑπόνοια, ας, ἡ strictly *secret opinion*, often without sufficient evidence; hence, in a bad sense *suspicion, unfounded opinion, conjecture* (1T 6.4)
ὑπόνοιαι N-NF-P ὑπόνοια
ὑποπλέω 1aor. ὑπέπλευσα; as an effort to protect a ship from stormy winds *sail under the lee* or *sheltered side* of an island, usually the southern side in the Mediterranean Sea
ὑποπνεύσαντος VPAAGM-S ὑποπνέω
ὑποπνέω 1aor. ὑπέπνευσα; of the wind *blow gently* or *moderately* (AC 27.13)
ὑποπόδιον, ου, τό *footstool*, especially that placed before a throne; figuratively, of the earth as God's footstool (MT 5.35); idiomatically, in reference to a place for a conqueror's feet, from the ancient custom of depicting conquered enemies on a footstool ὑ. τῶν ποδῶν literally *footstool for the feet*, i.e. *under the complete control of* (MT 5.35)
ὑποπόδιον N-AN-S ὑποπόδιον
  N-NN-S "
ὑποστάσει N-DF-S ὑπόστασις
ὑποστάσεως N-GF-S "
ὑπόστασις, εως, ἡ as the objective aspect and underlying reality behind anything, with the specific meaning derived from the context; (1) as an undertaking *plan, project* (2C 9.4); (2) as God's substantial nature *real being, essence* (HE 1.3); (3) as the objective reality that gives a firm guarantee and basis for confidence or assurance *substance, ground of hope, foundation* (HE 3.14; 11.1)
ὑπόστασις N-NF-S ὑπόστασις
ὑποστείληται VSAM--3S ὑποστέλλω
ὑποστέλλω impf. ὑπέστελλον; 1aor. mid. ὑπεστειλάμην; (1) as consciously retreating from a position *withdraw, draw back* (GA 2.12); (2) in a negative sense *keep silent about, conceal* (AC 20.20); (3) middle, as expressing fear and lack of faith *draw back, shrink back* from a commitment (HE 10.38)
ὑποστολή, ῆς, ἡ strictly *lowering of sails*; hence *lack of steadfastness, shrinking back, giving up* (HE 10.39)
ὑποστολῆς N-GF-S ὑποστολή
ὑπόστρεφε VMPA--2S ὑποστρέφω
ὑποστρέφειν VNPA "
ὑποστρέφοντι VPPADM-S "
ὑποστρέφω impf. ὑπέστρεφον; fut. ὑποστρέψω; 1aor. ὑπέστρεψα; intransitively in the NT *turn back, return*; with εἰς and the accusative of place or state *be again in, return to* (LU 1.56); with ἀπό and the genitive *return from* (LU 4.1); with ἐκ and the genitive *turn away from* (2P 2.21)
ὑποστρέφων VPPANM-S ὑποστρέφω
ὑποστρέψαι VNAA "
ὑποστρέψαντες VPAANM-P "
ὑποστρέψαντι VPAADM-S "

ὑποστρέψας VPAANM-S "
ὑποστρέψασαι VPAANF-P "
ὑποστρέψω VIFA--1S "
ὑποστρέψωσι(ν) VSAA--3P "
ὑποστρωννύω impf. ὑπεστρώννυον; *scatter* something *under, spread out under* or *beneath* (LU 19.36)
ὑποταγέντων VPAPGM-P ὑποτάσσω
ὑποταγή, ῆς, ἡ only passive in the NT *submission, obedience, subjection*
ὑποταγῇ N-DF-S ὑποταγή
  VSAP--3S ὑποτάσσω
ὑποταγήσεται VIFP--3S "
ὑποταγησόμεθα VIFP--1P "
ὑποτάγητε VMAP--2P "
ὑποτάγωμεν VSAA--1P "
ὑποτάξαι VNAA "
ὑποτάξαντα VPAAAM-S "
ὑποτάξαντι VPAADM-S "
ὑποτάξαντος VPAAGM-S "
ὑποτάσσεσθαι VNPP "
ὑποτάσσεσθε VIPP--2P "
  VMPP--2P "
ὑποτασσέσθω VMPP--3S "
ὑποτασσέσθωσαν VMPP--3P "
ὑποτάσσεται VIPP--3S "
ὑποτάσσησθε VSPP--2P "
ὑποτασσόμεναι VPPPNF-P "
ὑποτασσομένας VPPPAF-P "
ὑποτασσόμενοι VPPPNM-P "
ὑποτασσόμενος VPPPNM-S "
ὑποτάσσω 1aor. ὑπέταξα; pf. pass. ὑποτέταγμαι; 2aor. pass. ὑπετάγην; 2fut. pass. ὑποταγήσομαι; (1) active *subject, bring under firm control, subordinate* (RO 8.20b); (2) passive with a middle sense; (a) with a component of compulsion *have to submit* (LU 10.17, 20); (b) with a component of voluntary submission *be submissive, obey, subject oneself* (LU 2.51; EP 5.21)
ὑποτεταγμένα VPRPAN-P ὑποτάσσω
ὑποτέτακται VIRP--3S "
ὑποτιθέμενος VPPMNM-S ὑποτίθημι
ὑποτίθημι 1aor. ὑπέθηκα; strictly *place under*; (1) active *lay down*; idiomatically τὸν τράχηλον ὑποτιθέναι literally *put down the neck*, i.e. *risk one's life* (RO 16.4); (2) middle *point out* something to someone, *advise, instruct* (1T 4.6)
ὑποτρέχω 2aor. ὑπέδραμον; *run in under*; as a nautical technical term, literally *sail under the lee*, i.e. *along the sheltered side* of a landmass (AC 27.16)
ὑποτύπωσιν N-AF-S ὑποτύπωσις
ὑποτύπωσις, εως, ἡ strictly *outline, sketch*; hence *pattern, model, example*
ὑποφέρει VIPA--3S ὑποφέρω
ὑποφέρω 1aor. ὑπήνεγκα; *bear up under* (a burden); of sufferings and testings *hold up under, endure (patiently)* (1C 10.13); *undergo, experience* (2T 3.11)
ὑποχωρέω 1aor. ὑπεχώρησα; as moving away a distance from a place *depart, withdraw, retreat, retire*
ὑποχωρήσαντες VPAANM-P ὑποχωρέω
ὑποχωρῶν VPPANM-S "
ὑπωπιάζῃ VSPA--3S ὑπωπιάζω

ὑπωπιάζω (1) literally *strike beneath the eye, give a black eye*; figuratively *annoy greatly, pester, wear out* (LU 18.5); (2) literally, in boxing *beat black and blue*; figuratively, of severe self-imposed discipline *treat severely, keep under*, i.e. *strictly control* one's body (1C 9.27)

ὑπωπιάζω	VIPA--1S	ὑπωπιάζω

ὗς, ὑός, ἡ as the female swine *sow, female pig* (2P 2.22)

ὗς	N-NF-S	ὗς

ὑσσός, οῦ, ὁ *javelin* (JN 19.29)

ὑσσῷ	N-DM-S	ὑσσός

ὕσσωπος, ου, ἡ and ὁ (also **ὕσσωπον, ου, τό**) *hyssop*, a plant used in purification rites; this aromatic Middle East plant can grow between the stones of a wall (cf. 1 Kings 4.33), and a liquid clings easily to its bushy leaves (JN 19.29)

ὑσσώπου	N-GF-S	ὕσσωπος
	N-GM-S	"
	N-GN-S	"
ὑσσώπῳ	N-DF-S	"
	N-DM-S	"
	N-DN-S	"
ὑστερεῖ	VIPA--3S	ὑστερέω
ὑστερεῖσθαι	VNPP	

ὑστερέω 1aor. ὑστέρησα; pf. ὑστέρηκα; 1aor. pass. ὑστερήθην; from a basic meaning *come too late* in time, *come after* in space; (1) active; (a) as coming too late through one's own fault *miss, fail to reach* (HE 4.1); *be excluded* (HE 12.15); (b) as having a need *be in need of, lack* (LU 22.35); (c) as falling short, behind someone else *be less than, be inferior to* (2C 11.5); (d) as falling short of expectations *lack, fail in, be wanting* (MK 10.21); (2) passive, with the genitive of the thing *come short of, come behind in* (RO 3.23); absolutely *go without, be in need* (LU 15.14; PH 4.12)

ὑστερηθείς	VPAPNM-S	ὑστερέω
ὑστερηκέναι	VNRA	"

ὑστέρημα, ατος, τό as what has become deficient; (1) in contrast to abundance *need, poverty, destitution* (LU 21.4); (2) as a defect that should be removed *shortcoming, lack* (1TH 3.10); (3) with a person as the object *absence, not being present* (1C 16.17)

ὑστέρημα	N-AN-S	ὑστέρημα
ὑστερήματα	N-AN-P	"
ὑστερήματος	N-GN-S	"
ὑστέρησα	VIAA--1S	ὑστερέω
ὑστερήσαντος	VPAAGM-S	"
ὑστερήσατε	VIAA--2P	"
ὑστερήσεως	N-GF-S	ὑστέρησις
ὑστέρησιν	N-AF-S	"

ὑστέρησις, εως, ἡ *need, want, poverty* (MK 12.44); καθ᾽ ὑστέρησιν *because of need, from want* (PH 4.11)

ὑστέροις	A-MDM-P	ὕστερος
ὕστερον	ABM	"

ὕστερος, τέρα, ον with a basic meaning *what is behind* or *after* in space or time; (1) as an adjective; (a) used as a comparative ὁ ὕ. *the last named, the latter, the second one* (MT 21.32); (b) used as a superlative as the final in a series of times *last*; possibly *later, future* times (1T 4.1); (2) neuter as an adverb; (a) in a comparative sense *in the second place, later, afterward* (MT 4.2); (b) in a

superlative sense *finally, lastly* (MT 21.37); ὕστερον πάντων *last of all* (MT 22.27)

ὕστερος	A-MNM-S	ὕστερος
ὑστερούμεθα	VIPP--1P	ὑστερέω
ὑστερούμενοι	VPPPNM-P	"
ὑστερουμένῳ	VPPPDN-S	"
ὑστεροῦνται	VIPP--3P	"
ὑστεροῦντι	VPPADN-S	"
ὑστερῶ	VIPA--1S	"
ὑστερῶν	VPPANM-S	"
ὑφ᾽	PA	ὑπό
	PG	"
ὑφαίνει	VIAA--3S	ὑφαίνω

ὑφαίνω *weave, make cloth* by interlacing threads (LU 12.27)

ὑφαντός, ή, όν of cloth *woven* (JN 19.23)

ὑφαντός	A--NM-S	ὑφαντός
ὕψει	N-DN-S	ὕψος
ὑψηλά	A--AN-P	ὑψηλός
ὑψηλοῖς	A--DM-P	"
	A--DN-P	"
ὑψηλόν	A--AN-S	"
	A--NN-S	"

ὑψηλός, ή, όν (1) literally, of place *high, lofty, tall* (MT 4.8), opposite ταπεινός (*low*); neuter plural ὑψηλά as a substantive, as referring to heaven *high places, on high, the world above* (HE 1.3); comparative ὑψηλότερος, τέρα, ον with the genitive of comparison *higher than, above* (HE 7.26); (2) figuratively; (a) neuter as a substantive τὸ ὑψηλόν *what is thought of as very valuable, what is considered greatest* (LU 16.15); τὰ ὑψηλά *high, lofty things*, opposite τὰ ταπεινά (*humble tasks*); (b) in a negative sense *arrogant, proud*; idiomatically ὑψηλά φρονεῖν literally *think high things*, i.e. *have proud thoughts, be haughty* (RO 12.16)

ὑψηλότερος	A-MNM-S	ὑψηλός
ὑψηλοῦ	A--GM-S	"
ὑψηλοφρόνει	VMPA--2S	ὑψηλοφρονέω
ὑψηλοφρονεῖν	VNPA	

ὑψηλοφρονέω *be proud, be arrogant, act haughtily*

ὑψίστοις	APSDN-P	ὕψιστος

ὕψιστος, η, ον superlative of the adverb ὕψι; *highest, most exalted*; (1) spatially *highest, loftiest*, neuter plural τὰ ὕψιστα as a substantive *the highest heights, heaven, the world above* (MT 21.9); (2) in relation to rank and power *most high*; substantively, as a name for God ὁ ὕ. *the Most High* (MK 5.7)

ὕψιστος	APSNM-S	ὕψιστος
ὑψίστου	APSGM-S	"
	A-SGM-S	"
ὑψίστῳ	APSDM-S	"

ὕψος, ους, τό literally, as a dimension of space *height* (EP 3.18); concretely *world above, heaven* (LU 1.78); εἰς ὕ. *on high, into heaven* (EP 4.8); figuratively *exaltation, important rank, high position* (JA 1.9)

ὕψος	N-AN-S	ὕψος
	N-NN-S	"
ὕψους	N-GN-S	"

ὑψόω fut. ὑψώσω; 1aor. ὕψωσα; 1aor. pass. ὑψώθην; 1fut. pass. ὑψωθήσομαι; literally *lift up, raise high* (JN 3.14a); euphemistically, of the method of Christ's death by crucifixion *lift up* (JN 3.14b); figuratively, of honor and position *uplift, exalt* (LU 1.52); in a negative sense ὑψοῦν ἑαυτόν *exalt oneself, think oneself better than others* (MT 23.12)

ὑψωθείς	VPAPNM-S	ὑψόω
ὑψωθεῖσα	VPAPNF-S	"
ὑψωθῆναι	VNAP	"
ὑψώθης	VIAP--2S	"
ὑψωθήσεται	VIFP--3S	"
ὑψωθήσῃ	VIFP--2S	"
ὑψωθῆτε	VSAP--2P	"
ὑψωθῶ	VSAP--1S	"

ὕψωμα, ατος, τό   literally *height, high place*; of space, the (created) sphere above the earth in which supernatural powers rule *(the) height, world on high* (RO 8.39); figuratively in a negative sense, of an exaggerated evaluation πᾶν ὕ. *all arrogance, every proud conceit* or *pretension* (like a fortress with high walls and great towers) (2C 10.5)

ὕψωμα	N-AN-S	ὕψωμα
	N-NN-S	"
ὑψῶν	VPPANM-S	ὑψόω
ὑψώσει	VIFA--3S	"
ὕψωσε(ν)	VIAA--3S	"
ὑψώσῃ	VSAA--3S	"
ὑψώσητε	VSAA--2P	"

φ Φ

φάγε	VMAA--2S	ἐσθίω
φαγεῖν	VNAA	"
φάγεσαι	VIFD--2S	"
φάγεται	VIFD--3S	"
φάγετε	VMAA--2P	"
φάγῃ	VSAA--3S	"
φάγῃς	VSAA--2S	"
φάγητε	VSAA--2P	"
φάγοι	VOAA--3S	"
φάγομαι	VIFD--1S	"
φάγονται	VIFD--3P	"
φαγόντες	VPAANM-P	"

φάγος, ου, ὁ as one who habitually eats too much *glutton*

φάγος	N-NM-S	φάγος
φάγω	VSAA--1S	ἐσθίω
φάγωμεν	VSAA--1P	"
φάγωσι(ν)	VSAA--3P	"
φαιλόνην	N-AM-S	φαιλόνης

φαιλόνης, ου, ὁ (also **φελόνης**) *cloak, traveling cloak*, a heavier outer garment for protection in wintry and stormy weather (2T 4.13)

φαίνει	VIPA--3S	φαίνω
φαίνεσθε	VIPM--2P	"
	VIPP--2P	"
	VMPM--2P	"
	VMPP--2P	"
φαίνεται	VIPM--3S	"
	VIPP--3S	"
φαίνῃ	VSPA--3S	"
φαινομένη	VPPMNF-S	"
	VPPPNF-S	"
φαινομένου	VPPMGM-S	"
	VPPPGM-S	"
φαινομένων	VPPMGN-P	"
	VPPPGN-P	"
φαίνονται	VIPP--3P	"
φαίνοντι	VPPADM-S	"

φαίνω fut. mid. φανοῦμαι; 1aor. ἔφανα; 2aor. pass. ἐφάνην; 2fut. pass. φανήσομαι; (1) active intransitively in the NT; (a) literally *shine, give light* (2P 1.19); (b) metaphorically, of a person who makes it possible to know something or someone (JN 5.35); of a source of spiritual truth and knowledge (JN 1.5; 1J 2.8); (2) passive; (a) literally, of light and its sources *shine, flash* (MT 24.27); (b) of someone or something one becomes aware of *appear, become visible, be revealed* (MT 1.20; 2.7); (c) of what becomes known, either in its true character (RO 7.13) or only in its superficial character (MT 23.28) *appear, seem to be, look as though*; (d) idiomatically ποῦ φανεῖται literally *where will it appear?* i.e. *what will happen to? what will become of?* (1P 4.18)

φαίνων	VPPANM-S	φαίνω

φαίνωσι(ν)	VSPA--3P	"
Φάλεγ		Φάλεκ

Φάλεκ, ὁ (also **Φάλεγ, Φαλέκ, Φάλεχ, Φαλέχ**) indeclinable; *Peleg*, masculine proper noun (LU 3.35)

Φαλέκ		Φάλεκ
Φάλεχ		"
Φαλέχ		"
φανεῖται	VIFM--3S	φαίνω
φανερά	A--NF-S	φανερός
	A--NN-P	"
φανεροί	A--NM-P	"
φανερόν	A--AM-S	"
	A--AN-S	"
	A--NN-S	"

φανερός, ά, όν (1) adjectivally; (a) of sensory perception *visible, clearly seen, apparent* (RO 1.19; 2.28); (b) of intellectual perception *recognized, (well-)known* (MT 12.16); *evident, clear, plain* (GA 5.19); (2) neuter as a substantive τὸ φανερόν *what is open and public*; εἰς φανερόν ἐλθεῖν *come to light, become widely known* (MK 4.22); (3) adverbially ἐν τῷ φανερῷ *outwardly, externally* (RO 2.28); (4) neuter comparative φανερώτερόν ἐστιν *it is very evident* (AC 4.16)

φανερός	A--NM-S	φανερός
φανερούμενοι	VPPPNM-P	φανερόω
φανερούμενον	VPPPNN-S	"
φανεροῦντι	VPPADM-S	"
φανερούς	A--AM-P	φανερός
φανεροῦται	VIPP--3S	φανερόω

φανερόω fut. φανερώσω; 1aor. ἐφανέρωσα; pf. πεφανέρωκα; pf. pass. πεφανέρωμαι; 1aor. pass. ἐφανερώθην; 1fut. pass. φανερωθήσομαι; (1) of a thing; (a) active, as a causative *make known, cause to be seen, show*, often as synonymous with ἀποκαλύπτω to indicate God's revelation of something (RO 1.19; 2C 2.14); (b) passive *become visible, be revealed, become known* (MK 4.22; JN 3.21); (2) of a person; (a) active *make oneself known, show* or *reveal oneself* (JN 7.4); (b) passive *become known, be shown, be in true character* (2C 5.11); *appear, become visible, be revealed* (JN 21.14; 1T 3.16)

φανερῷ	A--DN-S	φανερός
φανερωθείς	VPAPNM-S	φανερόω
φανερωθεῖσαν	VPAPAF-S	"
φανερωθέντες	VPAPNM-P	"
φανερωθέντος	VPAPGM-S	"
φανερωθῇ	VSAP--3S	"
φανερωθῆναι	VNAP	"
φανερωθήσεσθε	VIFP--2P	"
φανερωθήσεται	VIFP--3S	"
φανερωθῶσι(ν)	VSAP--3P	"
φανερῶν	VPPANM-S	"

φανερῶς   adverb; (1) in contrast to what is done in secret *openly, publicly* (MK 1.45); (2) in contrast to what is indistinct *plainly, clearly, distinctly* (AC 10.3)

φανερῶς	AB	φανερῶς
φανερώσαντες	VPAANM-P	φανερόω
φανερώσει	N-DF-S	φανέρωσις
	VIFA--3S	φανερόω

φανέρωσις, εως, ἡ   as an action *making public, clear announcement, disclosure* (2C 4.2); *evidencing, making known, revelation* (1C 12.7)

φανέρωσις	N-NF-S	φανέρωσις
φανέρωσον	VMAA--2S	φανερόω
φανερώσω	VSAA--1S	"
φανερώτερον	A-MNN-S	φανερός
φάνῃ	VSAA--3S	φαίνω
φανῇ	VSAP--3S	"
φανῇς	VSAP--2S	"
φανήσεται	VIFP--3S	"

φανός, οῦ, ὁ   originally *torch*; later, *lantern, lamp for use outdoors* (JN 18.3)

Φανουήλ, ὁ   indeclinable; *Phanuel*, masculine proper noun (LU 2.36)

φανταζόμενον	VPPPNN-S	φαντάζω

φαντάζω   *make visible, cause to appear* in an extraordinary way; only passive in the NT *become visible, appear*; τὸ φανταζόμενον *the sight, spectacle* (HE 12.21)

φαντασία, ας, ἡ   strictly *making visible*; in a negative sense, as an appearance made for effect, for showing off *cheap display, pomp, pageantry* (AC 25.23)

φαντασίας	N-GF-S	φαντασία

φάντασμα, ατος, τό   as an appearance phenomenon *apparition, ghost, phantom*

φάντασμα	N-NN-S	φάντασμα
φανῶμεν	VSAP--1P	φαίνω
φανῶν	N-GM-P	φανός
φανῶσι(ν)	VSAP--3P	φαίνω

φάραγξ, αγγος, ἡ   as a place narrowly enclosed by cliffs and precipices *valley, ravine* (LU 3.5)

φάραγξ	N-NF-S	φάραγξ
φάραξ	N-NF-S	see φάραγξ

Φαραώ, ὁ   indeclinable; *Pharaoh*, title of Egyptian kings (AC 7.13); also used as a masculine proper noun (AC 7.10)

Φάρες, ὁ   indeclinable; *Perez*, masculine proper noun

Φαρισαῖε	N-VM-S	Φαρισαῖος
Φαρισαῖοι	N-NM-P	"
	N-VM-P	"
Φαρισαίοις	N-DM-P	"
Φαρισαῖον	N-AM-S	"

Φαρισαῖος, ου, ὁ   transliterated from the Hebrew word meaning *one who is set apart, separatist*; *Pharisee*, a member or follower of the sect of the Pharisees, an organized society of Jews who claimed authority in interpreting the Scripture and setting rules for the observance of the law in daily life

Φαρισαῖος	N-NM-S	Φαρισαῖος
Φαρισαίου	N-GM-S	"
Φαρισαίους	N-AM-P	"
Φαρισαίων	N-GM-P	"

φαρμακεία, ας, ἡ   as the use of drugs of any kind for magical effect *sorcery, magic* (GA 5.20); plural *magic arts* (RV 9.21)

φαρμακεία	N-NF-S	φαρμακεία
φαρμακείᾳ	N-DF-S	"
φαρμακειῶν	N-GF-P	"

φαρμακεύς, έως, ὁ   *one who deals with drugs*; *enchanter, magician, sorcerer*

φαρμακεῦσι(ν)	N-DM-P	φαρμακεύς
φαρμακιῶν	N-GF-P	see φαρμακειῶν
φάρμακοι	N-NM-P	φάρμακος
φαρμακοί	N-NM-P	"
φαρμάκοις	N-DM-P	"
φαρμακοῖς	N-DM-P	"

φάρμακον, ου, τό   *magic potion, charm, drug*; plural *casting of magic spells, witchcraft, sorceries* (RV 9.21)

φάρμακος, ου, ὁ (also **φαρμακός**)   one who prepares and uses drugs for magical purposes or ritual witchcraft *sorcerer, poisoner, magician*

φαρμάκων	N-GN-P	φάρμακον
φασί(ν)	VIPA--3P	φημί

φάσις, εως, ἡ   *report, information, news*

φάσις	N-NF-S	φάσις
φάσκοντας	VPPAAM-P	φάσκω
φάσκοντες	VPPANM-P	"

φάσκω   impf. ἔφασκον; as speaking with certainty *assert, claim, declare*, followed by the accusative and an infinitive

φάτνη, ης, ἡ   (1) as a feeding place *stall, stable* (LU 13.15); (2) as a feed trough *manger, crib* (LU 2.7)

φάτνη	N-DF-S	φάτνη
φάτνης	N-GF-S	"
φαῦλα	A--AN-P	φαῦλος
φαῦλον	AB	"
	A--AN-S	"
	A--NN-S	"

φαῦλος, η, ον   of what is morally base or worthless *wicked, evil, bad* (JA 3.16); neuter as a substantive φαῦλον *something bad* (TI 2.8); φαῦλα *evil deeds* (JN 3.20); neuter as an adverb *in a worthless way, unhelpfully* (2C 5.10)

φέγγος, ους, τό   *light, radiance, glow*; in distinction from φῶς (beam of *light*), φ. is a softer, diffused light, such as given off by the moon

φέγγος	N-AN-S	φέγγος

φείδομαι   fut. φείσομαι; 1aor. ἐφεισάμην; (1) *spare* someone or something, *free* someone from something (RO 8.32; 1C 7.28); (2) *refrain from, avoid doing* something (2C 12.6)

φείδομαι	VIPD--1S	φείδομαι
	VIPO--1S	"
φειδόμενοι	VPPDNM-P	"
	VPPONM-P	"
φειδόμενος	VPPDNM-S	"
	VPPONM-S	"

φειδομένως   adverb; *in a limited way, sparingly*; figuratively, of miserly giving to help others (2C 9.6)

φειδομένως	AB	φειδομένως
φείσεται	VIFD--3S	φείδομαι
φείσηται	VSAD--3S	"
φείσομαι	VIFD--1S	"
φελόνην	N-AM-S	φαιλόνης

φέρε	VMPA--2S	φέρω
φέρει	VIPA--3S	"
φέρειν	VNPA	"
φέρεις	VIPA--2S	"
φέρεσθαι	VNPP	"
φέρεται	VIPP--3S	"
φέρετε	VIPA--2P	"
	VMPA--2P	"
φέρῃ	VSPA--3S	"
φέρητε	VSPA--2P	"
φερόμενα	VPPPNN-P	"
φερομένην	VPPPAF-S	"
φερομένης	VPPPGF-S	"
φερόμενοι	VPPPNM-P	"
φέρον	VPPAAN-S	"
φέροντες	VPPANM-P	"
φέρουσαι	VPPANF-P	"
φέρουσαν	VPPAAF-S	"
φέρουσι(ν)	VIPA--3P	"

φέρω impf. ἔφερον; fut. οἴσω; 1aor. ἤνεγκα; 2aor. inf. ἐνεγκεῖν; 1aor. pass. ἠνέχθην; from a basic meaning *bring, lead*; (1) literally *bring, bear, carry* (LU 23.26); figuratively; (a) of Christ's sustaining the universe *bear along, carry forward* (HE 1.3); (b) as experiencing difficulty from burdensome circumstances *bear patiently, endure, put up with* (HE 13.13); (2) *bring with one, bring along* (LU 24.1); (3) of plants *produce, bear* (fruit), *bring forth* (MK 4.8); (4) *move, drive, bear along*; (a) literally and passive *be moved, be driven* as by wind and weather (AC 27.15); (b) figuratively and passive *be moved, be borne along* as by God's Spirit (2P 1.21b); (5) (a) literally and passive with an intransitive sense, as what is borne along by natural forces, as the wind, *rush, sweep* (AC 2.2); (b) figuratively, as by spiritual forces *go forward, go on* (HE 6.1); (6) as bringing in evidence of validity, by a doctrine (2J 10), a pronouncement (2P 1.17), a legal charge (JN 18.29; AC 25.18), a valid attestation (HE 9.16) *present, express, convey*; (7) used absolutely of orienting movement in a certain direction, as by a road or gate *lead* (to) (AC 12.10)

φερώμεθα	VSPP--1P	φέρω
φέρων	VPPANM-S	"
φεῦγε	VMPA--2S	φεύγω
φεύγει	VIPA--3S	"
φεύγετε	VMPA--2P	"
φευγέτωσαν	VMPA--3P	"
φεύγοντας	VPPAAM-P	"

φεύγω fut. mid. φεύξομαι; 2aor. ἔφυγον; (1) absolutely *flee, take to flight* (MT 8.33); (2) with the accusative *escape* something (HE 11.34); (3) with the accusative in a moral sense *flee from, avoid, shun* (1C 6.18); (4) *vanish, quickly disappear* (RV 16.20)

φεύξεται	VIFD--3S	φεύγω
φεύξονται	VIFD--3P	"
Φήλικα	N-AM-S	Φῆλιξ
Φήλικι	N-DM-S	"
Φήλικος	N-GM-S	"

Φῆλιξ, ικος, ὁ *Felix*, masculine proper noun

Φῆλιξ	N-NM-S	Φῆλιξ
	N-VM-S	

φήμη, ης, ἡ *news, report, information*

φήμη	N-NF-S	φήμη

φημί third-person singular φησίν, third-person plural φασίν; impf./2aor. third-person singular ἔφη; (1) as introducing direct discourse *say, affirm* (MT 4.7); (2) as introducing quotations (JN 1.23; HE 8.5); (3) as introducing an interpretation of a statement *mean, imply* (1C 7.29; 10.19)

φημί	VIPA--1S	φημί

φημίζω 1aor. pass. ἐφημίσθην; *spread a report* or *rumor* (MT 28.15; AC 13.43)

φημισθῆναι	VNAP	φημίζω
φησί(ν)	VIPA--3S	φημί
Φῆστε	N-VM-S	Φῆστος
Φῆστον	N-AM-S	"

Φῆστος, ου, ὁ *Festus*, masculine proper noun

Φῆστος	N-NM-S	Φῆστος
Φήστου	N-GM-S	"
Φήστῳ	N-DM-S	"

φθάνω 1aor. ἔφθασα; pf. ἔφθακα; from a basic meaning *precede* someone, *be beforehand*; (1) *precede, go prior to, come* or *go before* (1TH 4.15); (2) followed by a preposition to indicate a goal or state *arrive at, reach, attain* (RO 9.31); *come on, happen to* someone (MT 12.28)

φθαρῇ	VSAP--3S	φθείρω
φθαρήσονται	VIFP--3P	"
φθαρτῆς	A--GF-S	φθαρτός
φθαρτοῖς	A--DN-P	"
φθαρτόν	A--AM-S	"
	A--AN-S	"
	A--NN-S	"

φθαρτός, ή, όν of what is subject to decay or destruction; (1) of persons *mortal* (RO 1.23); (2) of things *perishable, transitory, corruptible* (1P 1.18); neuter as a substantive τὸ φθαρτόν *perishable nature* (1C 15.53); φθαρτά *transitory things* (1P 1.18)

φθαρτοῦ	A--GM-S	φθαρτός
φθάσωμεν	VSAA--1P	φθάνω
φθέγγεσθαι	VNPD	φθέγγομαι
	VNPO	"

φθέγγομαι 1aor. ἐφθεγξάμην; strictly *produce a sound*; (1) *speak, utter, articulate* (2P 2.16); (2) *speak loud and clear*; ὑπέρογκα φθέγγεσθαι literally *speak puffed-up words*, i.e. *speak bombastically, make hollow boasts* (2P 2.18)

φθεγγόμενοι	VPPDNM-P	φθέγγομαι
	VPPONM-P	"
φθεγξάμενον	VPADNN-S	"
φθείρει	VIPA--3S	φθείρω
φθειρεῖ	VIFA--3S	see φθερεῖ
φθειρῇ	VIFA--3S	see φθερεῖ
φθειρόμενον	VPPPAM-S	φθείρω
φθείρονται	VIPP--3P	"
φθείρουσι(ν)	VIPA--3P	"

φθείρω fut. φθερῶ; 1aor. ἔφθειρα; 2aor. pass. ἐφθάρην; 2fut. pass. φθαρήσομαι; *ruin, destroy*; (1) in relation to outward circumstances *ruin, corrupt, cause harm to* (possibly 2C 7.2); (2) in morals and religion *seduce, corrupt, mislead* (RV 19.2; probably 2C 7.2); passive *be*

led astray (2C 11.3); *be corrupt, be depraved* (EP 4.22);
(3) of God's eternal punishment *destroy* (1C 3.17b)

φθερεῖ	VIFA--3S	φθείρω
φθηρεῖ	VIFA--3S	see φθερεῖ
φθινοπωρινά	A--NN-P	φθινοπωρινός

φθινοπωρινός, ή, όν   literally *belonging to late autumn,
autumnal*; of trees *autumn*, i.e. *fruitless, bare, worthless*; used metaphorically of false teachers *of no help
at all, useless* (JU 12)

φθόγγοις	N-DM-P	φθόγγος

φθόγγος, ου, ὁ   as distinctive sounds; of musical instruments *sound, tone* (1C 14.7); of persons *voice, message*
(RO 10.18)

φθόγγος	N-NM-S	φθόγγος
φθόγγου	N-GM-S	
φθονεῖτε	VIPA--2P	φθονέω

φθονέω   *envy, be jealous of* someone (GA 5.26)

φθόνοι	N-NM-P	φθόνος
φθόνον	N-AM-S	"

φθόνος, ου, ὁ   (1) in a negative sense *envy, jealousy* over the
good success of another (MT 27.18); (2) in a positive
sense of God's protective jealousy (perhaps JA 4.5 πρὸς
φθόνον *to the point of envy, even with envy*)

φθόνος	N-NM-S	φθόνος
φθόνου	N-GM-S	"
φθονοῦντες	VPPANM-P	φθονέω
φθόνους	N-AM-P	φθόνος
φθόνῳ	N-DM-S	"

φθορά, ᾶς, ἡ   *destruction, ruin, dissolution*; literally, as it
affects nature *corruptibility, subjection to decay* (RO
8.21); of the body at burial *dissolution, decomposition,
decay* (1C 15.42); of animals destined for food *slaughter, killing* (2P 2.12a); figuratively, in a moral sense *depravity, corruption* (2P 1.4); of the future as a final recompense *destruction, death, ruin* (GA 6.8; 2P 2.12b),
opposite ζωὴ αἰώνιος (*eternal life*)

φθορά	N-NF-S	φθορά
φθορᾷ	N-DF-S	"
φθοράν	N-AF-S	"
φθορᾶς	N-GF-S	"
φιάλας	N-AF-P	φιάλη

φιάλη, ης, ἡ   *bowl, shallow cup*, a container broad and
flat in shape (RV 5.8)

φιάλην	N-AF-S	φιάλη
φιλάγαθον	A--AM-S	φιλάγαθος

φιλάγαθος, ον   *liking what is good, loving goodness*, of
one who is tireless in activities prompted by love (TI
1.8)

Φιλαδέλφεια, ας, ἡ (also **Φιλαδελφία**)   *Philadelphia*, a city
in Lydia in west central Asia Minor

Φιλαδέλφεια	N-DF-S	Φιλαδέλφεια
Φιλαδέλφειαν	N-AF-S	"
Φιλαδελφίᾳ	N-DF-S	"

φιλαδελφία, ας, ἡ   *brotherly love, love for brother* or *sister*;
as a religious technical term in the NT, restricted to
love for fellow members of a religious group *affection
for a fellow believer*

φιλαδελφία	N-NF-S	φιλαδελφία
φιλαδελφίᾳ	N-DF-S	"
Φιλαδελφίαν	N-AF-S	Φιλαδέλφεια
φιλαδελφίαν	N-AF-S	φιλαδελφία

φιλαδελφίας	N-GF-S	"
φιλάδελφοι	A--NM-P	φιλάδελφος

φιλάδελφος, ον   *brother-loving, loving one's brother* or *sister*; as a religious technical term in the NT, restricted to
a loving disposition toward fellow believers (1P 3.8)

φίλανδρος, ον   as a loving disposition of a wife toward
her husband *loving one's husband, affectionate* (TI 2.4)

φιλάνδρους	A--AF-P	φίλανδρος

φιλανθρωπία, ας, ἡ   as a friendly disposition toward people
goodness, friendliness, love for mankind (TI 3.4); as a
humane action *hospitality, kindness* (AC 28.2)

φιλανθρωπία	N-NF-S	φιλανθρωπία
φιλανθρωπίαν	N-AF-S	"

φιλανθρώπως   adverb; of acting in a humane manner
kindly, in a friendly way (AC 27.3)

φιλανθρώπως	AB	φιλανθρώπως

φιλαργυρία, ας, ἡ   as a greedy disposition *love of money,
avarice, covetousness* (1T 6.10)

φιλαργυρία	N-NF-S	φιλαργυρία
φιλάργυροι	A--NM-P	φιλάργυρος

φιλάργυρος, ον   as having a greedy disposition *loving
money, covetous, wanting to be rich* (LU 16.14)

φίλας	AP-AF-P	φίλος
φίλαυτοι	A--NM-P	φίλαυτος

φίλαυτος, ον   *fond of oneself, self-loving, selfish* (2T 3.2)

φίλε	AP-VM-S	φίλος
φιλεῖ	VIPA--3S	φιλέω
φιλεῖς	VIPA--2S	"

φιλέω   impf. ἐφίλουν; 1aor. ἐφίλησα; pf. πεφίληκα; (1) *love*,
as devotion based in the emotions, often distinguished
from ἀγαπάω (*love*), which is devotion based in the
will *like, feel affection for*; with the accusative of person (MT 10.37; JN 11.3); with the accusative of the
thing (MT 23.6); (2) as an outward expression of affection *kiss* (MT 26.48); (3) followed by an infinitive
like to or *be accustomed to do* something (MT 6.5)

φιλήδονοι	A--NM-P	φιλήδονος

φιλήδονος, ον   used in a bad sense of what is against God
and spiritually destructive to oneself *intent on pleasure, abandoned to (sensual) pleasure, pleasure-loving*
(2T 3.4)

φίλημα, ατος, τό   *kiss*; used in the NT (1) as an expression
of greeting (LU 7.45; perhaps 22.48) or farewell; (2) as
a mark of special respect (probably LU 22.48); (3) as an
expression of intimate fellowship within a community
of believers, called φ. ἅγιον *holy kiss* (RO 16.16)

φίλημα	N-AN-S	φίλημα
φιλήματι	N-DN-S	"
Φιλήμονι	N-DM-S	Φιλήμων

Φιλήμων, ονος, ὁ   *Philemon*, masculine proper noun
(PM 1)

φιλῆσαι	VNAA	φιλέω
φιλήσω	VSAA--1S	"

Φίλητος, ου, ὁ (also **Φιλητός**)   *Philetus*, masculine proper
noun (2T 2.17)

Φίλητος	N-NM-S	Φίλητος
Φιλητός	N-NM-S	"

φιλία, ας, ἡ   *friendship, affection, love* (JA 4.4)

φιλία	N-NF-S	φιλία
Φίλιππε	N-VM-S	Φίλιππος
Φιλιππήσιοι	N-VM-P	Φιλιππήσιος

Φιλιππήσιος, ου, ὁ *Philippian, citizen of Philippi* (PH 4.15)

Φίλιπποι, ων, οἱ *Philippi*, a city in Macedonia, on the northern coast of the Aegean Sea, in southeastern Europe

Φιλίπποις	N-DM-P	Φίλιπποι
Φίλιππον	N-AM-S	Φίλιππος

Φίλιππος, ου, ὁ *Philip*, masculine proper noun

Φίλιππος	N-NM-S	Φίλιππος
Φιλίππου	N-GM-S	"
Φιλίππους	N-AM-P	Φίλιπποι
Φιλίππῳ	N-DM-S	Φίλιππος
Φιλίππων	N-GM-P	Φίλιπποι
φιλόθεοι	A--NM-P	φιλόθεος

φιλόθεος, ον *loving God, devout* (2T 3.4)

φίλοι	AP-NM-P	φίλος
	A--NM-P	"
φίλοις	AP-DM-P	"
Φιλόλογον	N-AM-S	Φιλόλογος

Φιλόλογος, ου, ὁ *Philologus*, masculine proper noun (RO 16.15)

φίλον	AP-AM-S	φίλος

φιλονεικία, ας, ἡ strictly *readiness to quarrel*; hence *dispute, controversy* (LU 22.24)

φιλονεικία	N-NF-S	φιλονεικία

φιλόνεικος, ον *contentious, quarrelsome, fond of dispute* (1C 11.16)

φιλόνεικος	A--NM-S	φιλόνεικος

φιλοξενία, ας, ἡ strictly *love for strangers* or *foreigners*; hence *hospitality, kindness to strangers* (RO 12.13)

φιλοξενίαν	N-AF-S	φιλοξενία
φιλοξενίας	N-GF-S	"
φιλόξενοι	A--NM-P	φιλόξενος
φιλόξενον	A--AM-S	"

φιλόξενος, ον strictly *stranger-loving*; hence *hospitable, kind to strangers* (1P 4.9)

φιλοπρωτεύω *strive to be first, like to be leader* (3J 9)

φιλοπρωτεύων	VPPANM-S	φιλοπρωτεύω

φίλος, η, ον (1) adjectivally; (a) with a passive sense *beloved, dear*; (b) with an active sense *loving, friendly, devoted* (AC 19.31); (2) substantivally; (a) *friend, congenial associate, close companion* (MT 11.19; LU 7.6); feminine φίλη *woman friend* (LU 15.9); (b) in special uses, as the "best man" in a wedding, responsible for arranging dowry and details for the wedding; used metaphorically of John the Baptist in relation to Jesus (JN 3.29); of Abraham, as standing in a close relation to God (JA 2.23)

φίλος	AP-NM-S	φίλος

φιλοσοφία, ας, ἡ *philosophy, love of wisdom, pursuit of wisdom*; in a negative sense in the NT, of a worldview opposed to that derived from divine revelation *human wisdom* or *understanding* (CO 2.8)

φιλοσοφίας	N-GF-S	φιλοσοφία

φιλόσοφος, ου, ὁ *philosopher, scholar*, one given to the pursuit of wisdom and learning, often from a particular worldview; a member of a philosophical school (AC 17.18)

φιλοσόφων	N-GM-P	φιλόσοφος
φιλόστοργοι	A--NM-P	φιλόστοργος

φιλόστοργος, ον *tenderly affectionate, very loving, (naturally) devoted*, particularly to members of one's family or in-group (RO 12.10)

φιλότεκνος, ον *loving one's children, be loving* as a mother (TI 2.4)

φιλοτέκνους	A--AF-P	φιλότεκνος
φιλοτιμεῖσθαι	VNPD	φιλοτιμέομαι
	VNPO	"

φιλοτιμέομαι followed by an infinitive *be ambitious to, endeavor earnestly to, aspire to* (1TH 4.11)

φιλοτιμοῦμαι	VIPD--1S	φιλοτιμέομαι
	VIPO--1S	"
φιλοτιμούμεθα	VIPD--1P	"
	VIPO--1P	"
φιλοτιμούμενον	VPPDAM-S	"
	VPPOAM-S	"
φιλοῦντας	VPPAAM-P	φιλέω
φιλούντων	VPPAGM-P	"
φίλους	AP-AM-P	φίλος
φιλοῦσι(ν)	VIPA--3P	φιλέω
φιλόφρονες	A--NM-P	φιλόφρων

φιλοφρόνως adverb; *affectionately, kindly, in a friendly manner*; as related to guests *hospitably, courteously* (AC 28.7)

φιλοφρόνως	AB	φιλοφρόνως

φιλόφρων, ον, gen. ονος *friendly, kind, kindly minded* (1P 3.8)

φιλῶ	VIPA--1S	φιλέω
	VSPA--1S	"
φίλων	AP-GM-P	φίλος
φιλῶν	VPPANM-S	φιλέω
φιμοῦν	VNPA	φιμόω

φιμόω fut. φιμώσω; 1aor. ἐφίμωσα; pf. pass. second-person singular imperative πεφίμωσο; 1aor. pass. ἐφιμώθην; *tie shut*, as done to an animal to prevent its snatching up grain while treading on a threshing floor *muzzle* (1C 9.9); figuratively *(put to) silence, deprive of an argument* (1P 2.15); passive *have nothing to say, be without an answer* (MT 22.12); as done to the sea waves *be quieted down, become calm* (MK 4.39)

φιμώθητι	VMAP--2S	φιμόω
φιμώσεις	VIFA--2S^VMAA--2S	"
Φλέγοντα	N-AM-S	Φλέγων

Φλέγων, οντος, ὁ *Phlegon*, masculine proper noun (RO 16.14)

φλόγα	N-AF-S	φλόξ
φλογί	N-DF-S	"
φλογιζομένη	VPPPNF-S	φλογίζω
φλογίζουσα	VPPANF-S	"

φλογίζω *set on fire, kindle*; figuratively *inflame, arouse, excite* (JA 3.6)

φλογός	N-GF-S	φλόξ

φλόξ, φλογός, ἡ *flame, blaze* (LU 16.24); ἐν πυρὶ φλογός *in flaming fire* (2TH 1.8)

φλόξ	N-NF-S	φλόξ

φλυαρέω from φλύω (*bubble up*); *talk nonsense, make empty charges against* someone, *prate against* (3J 10)

φλύαροι	A--NF-P	φλύαρος

φλύαρος, ον as indulging in empty and foolish talk *babbling, talking on and on, gossiping* (1T 5.13)

φλυαρῶν	VPPANM-S	φλυαρέω

φοβεῖσθαι	VNPP	φοβέω
φοβεῖσθε	VMPP--2P	"
φοβερά	A--NF-S	φοβερός
φοβερόν	A--NN-S	"

φοβερός, ά, όν   only in the active sense in the NT *inspiring fear, formidable, terrible, fearful* (HE 10.31)

φοβέω   impf. pass. ἐφοβούμην; 1aor. pass. ἐφοβήθην; 1fut. pass. φοβηθήσομαι; only passive in the NT; (1) *be afraid, become frightened*; (a) absolutely *be frightened, be alarmed, be afraid* (MT 10.31); φοβεῖσθαι ἀπό τινος *be afraid of someone* (MT 10.28a); with an infinitive following *be afraid to, shrink back from* doing something (MT 1.20); (b) transitively *fear* someone (JN 9.22); *fear* something (HE 11.23); (2) *reverence, have respect for, fear*; (a) toward God (LU 1.50); (b) toward a person (EP 5.33)

φοβῇ	VIPP--2S	φοβέω
φοβηθείς	VPAPNM-S	"
φοβηθεῖσα	VPAPNF-S	"
φοβηθέντες	VPAPNM-P	"
φοβηθῇ	VSAP--3S	"
φοβηθῆναι	VNAP	"
φοβηθῇς	VSAP--2S	"
φοβηθήσομαι	VIFP--1S	"
φοβήθητε	VMAP--2P	"
φοβηθῆτε	VSAP--2P	"
φόβηθρα	N-NN-P	φόβητρον
φοβηθῶμεν	VSAP--1P	φοβέω
φοβῆται	VSPP--3S	"
φόβητρα	N-NN-P	φόβητρον

φόβητρον, ου, τό (also **φόβηθρον**)   as something that inspires terror *terrible sight, fearful event, dreadful happening* (LU 21.11)

φόβοι	N-NM-P	φόβος
φόβον	N-AM-S	"

φόβος, ου, ὁ   (1) active *causing fear, source of fear, terror* (RO 13.3; probably 1P 3.14); (2) passive; (a) in a negative sense *fear, dread, alarm* (2C 7.5; possibly 1P 3.14); (b) in a positive sense *respect, reverence, awe, (wholesome) fear* (RO 3.18); *respect* for those in authority (EP 6.5)

φόβος	N-NM-S	φόβος
φόβου	N-GM-S	"
φοβοῦ	VMPP--2S	φοβέω
φοβοῦμαι	VIPP--1S	"
φοβούμεθα	VIPP--1P	"
φοβούμεναι	VPPPNF-P	"
φοβούμενοι	VPPPNM-P	"
	VPPPVM-P	"
φοβουμένοις	VPPPDM-P	"
φοβούμενος	VPPPNM-S	"
φοβουμένους	VPPPAM-P	"
φόβῳ	N-DM-S	φόβος

Φοίβη, ης, ἡ   *Phoebe*, feminine proper noun (RO 16.1)

Φοίβην	N-AF-S	Φοίβη
Φοίνικα	N-AM-S	Φοῖνιξ
φοίνικας	N-AM-P	φοῖνιξ
φοίνικες	N-NM-P	"

Φοινίκη, ης, ἡ   *Phoenicia*, a region of central Syria along the Mediterranean seacoast

Φοινίκην	N-AF-S	Φοινίκη

Φοινίκης	N-GF-S	"
Φοινίκισσα	N-NF-S	Συροφοινίκισσα
φοινίκων	N-GM-P	φοῖνιξ

Φοῖνιξ, ικος, ὁ   *Phoenix*, a harbor city on the southwestern coast of the island of Crete (AC 27.12)

φοῖνιξ and **φοίνιξ, ικος, ὁ**   *palm tree, date palm* (JN 12.13); by synecdoche *palm branches, palm leaves* (RV 7.9)

Φοίνισσα	N-NF-S	Συροφοινίκισσα
φονέα	N-AM-S	φονεύς
φονεῖς	N-AM-P	"
	N-NM-P	"
φονεύεις	VIPA--2S	φονεύω
φονεύετε	VIPA--2P	"

φονεύς, έως, ὁ   *murderer, slayer, killer* (MT 22.7)

φονεύς	N-NM-S	φονεύς
φονευσάντων	VPAAGM-P	φονεύω
φονεύσεις	VIFA--2S^VMAA--2S	"
φονεύσῃ	VSAA--3S	"
φονεύσῃς	VSAA--2S	"
φονεῦσι(ν)	N-DM-P	φονεύς

φονεύω   fut. φονεύσω; 1aor. ἐφόνευσα; 1fut. pass. φονευθήσομαι; *murder, kill, put to death* (MT 23.31); absolutely *commit murder, kill* (MT 5.21)

φόνοι	N-NM-P	φόνος
φόνον	N-AM-S	"

φόνος, ου, ὁ   *murder, slaughter, killing* (LU 23.19)

φόνος	N-NM-S	φόνος
φόνου	N-GM-S	"
φόνους	N-AM-P	"
φόνῳ	N-DM-S	"
φόνων	N-GM-P	"
φορεῖ	VIPA--3S	φορέω
φορέσομεν	VIFA--1P	"
φορέσωμεν	VSAA--1P	"

φορέω   fut. φορέσω; 1aor. ἐφόρεσα; a frequentative that replaces φέρω (*bring, lead*) when something is carried or borne regularly or for a considerable time; (1) literally, of clothing *wear* (MT 11.8); of a crown *wear* (JN 19.5); of a sword *bear, wear*; idiomatically φορεῖν τὴν μάχαιραν literally *bear the sword*, i.e. *have power to punish* (RO 13.4); (2) figuratively, of a name *bear*; of a likeness *bear, have* (1C 15.49)

φόρον, ου, τό   see Ἀππίου Φόρον; *forum*, the central market and administrative center of a Roman city (AC 28.15)

φόρον	N-AM-S	φόρος

φόρος, ου, ὁ   *tribute, tax*; in the NT, as paid to a foreign ruler, whether levied on houses, lands, or persons (LU 20.22)

Φόρου	N-GN-S	Ἀππίου Φόρον
φοροῦντα	VPPAAM-S	φορέω
φοροῦντες	VPPANM-P	"
φόρους	N-AM-P	φόρος
φορτία	N-AN-P	φορτίον
φορτίζετε	VIPA--2P	φορτίζω

φορτίζω   pf. pass. ptc. πεφορτισμένος; *cause* someone *to carry* something, *load, burden*; figuratively in the NT, of being weighed down with troubles and difficult circumstances (MT 11.28); metaphorically, of requiring burdensome legal observances *burden, cause to do many hard things* (LU 11.46)

φορτίοις | N-DN-P | φορτίον

φορτίον, ου, τό diminutive of φόρτος; as a burden borne for a worthy purpose; of a ship *cargo* (AC 27.10); figuratively, in a positive sense of the demands of practical discipleship *burden* (GA 6.5); in a negative sense of oppressive and legalistic requirements for keeping rules and ceremonies *burden* (LU 11.46)

φορτίον	N-AN-S	φορτίον
	N-NN-S	"
φορτίου	N-GN-S	"

φόρτος, ου, ὁ *burden*, especially *cargo* of a ship (AC 27.10)

φόρτου | N-GM-S | φόρτος

Φορτουνᾶτος, ου, ὁ (also **Φορτούνατος, Φορτουνάτος, Φουρτουνάτος**) *Fortunatus*, masculine proper noun (1C 16.17)

Φορτουνάτου	N-GM-S	Φορτουνᾶτος
φορῶν	VPPANM-S	φορέω
Φουρτουνάτου	N-GM-S	Φορτουνᾶτος

φραγέλλιον, ου, τό *whip, scourge, lash* (JN 2.15)

φραγέλλιον | N-AN-S | φραγέλλιον

φραγελλόω 1aor. ἐφραγέλλωσα; as inflicting punishment after the pronouncement of a death sentence and prior to execution *flog, scourge, beat with a whip*

φραγελλώσας	VPAANM-S	φραγελλόω
φραγῇ	VSAP--3S	φράσσω
φραγήσεται	VIFP--3S	"
φραγμόν	N-AM-S	φραγμός

φραγμός, οῦ, ὁ *fence, hedge* (MT 21.33); plural, by metonymy, hedgeside *paths* or *country lanes*, frequented by vagabonds and beggars (LU 14.23); figuratively, of a divisive element keeping two groups separated *wall, what separates* (EP 2.14)

φραγμοῦ	N-GM-S	φραγμός
φραγμούς	N-AM-P	"

φράζω 1aor. ἔφρασα; *tell distinctly*; in the NT *explain, interpret, give the meaning* (MT 13.36; 15.15)

φράσον | VMAA--2S | φράζω

φράσσω 1aor. ἔφραξα; 2aor. pass. ἐφράγην; 2fut. pass. φραγήσομαι; *shut, close, stop*; literally and idiomatically, in reference to lions φράσσειν στόμα literally *stop the mouth*, i.e. *keep from harming*; figuratively, in reference to speech *cause to cease, stop* (2C 11.10); idiomatically φράσσειν στόμα literally *stop the mouth*, i.e. *put to silence, remove any reason to speak* (RO 3.19)

φρέαρ, ατος, τό (1) as a place for storing runoff water *cistern, reservoir*, a sealed-in *well*, distinguished from πηγή (*spring, fountain*) (JN 4.11); (2) as the opening into a deep hole in the ground *shaft, pit* (RV 9.1, 2)

φρέαρ	N-AN-S	φρέαρ
	N-NN-S	"
φρέατος	N-GN-S	"
φρεναπατᾷ	VIPA--3S	φρεναπατάω
φρεναπάται	N-NM-P	φρεναπάτης

φρεναπατάω as causing someone to believe what is not true *deceive*; with ἑαυτόν *deceive oneself* (GA 6.3)

φρεναπάτης, ου, ὁ as one who causes people to no longer believe what is true *deceiver* (TI 1.10)

φρεσί(ν) | N-DF-P | φρήν

φρήν, φρενός, ἡ only plural in the NT αἱ φρένες; strictly *midriff, diaphragm, parts around the heart*, as the supposed seat of intellectual activity; by metonymy, the intellectual activity itself *understanding, way of thinking* (1C 14.20)

φρίσσουσι(ν) | VIPA--3P | φρίσσω

φρίσσω *shudder, shiver* from fear or dread, *be extremely afraid* (JA 2.19)

φρόνει	VMPA--2S	φρονέω
φρονεῖ	VIPA--3S	"
φρονεῖν	VNPA	"
φρονεῖς	VIPA--2S	"
φρονείσθω	VMPP--3S	"
φρονεῖτε	VIPA--2P	"
	VMPA--2P	"

φρονέω impf. ἐφρόνουν; fut. φρονήσω; (1) *think, have an opinion, have understanding* (AC 28.22; 1C 13.11); (2) followed by the accusative *ponder on, be intent on, keep thinking about* (PH 3.19); (3) as having an attitude or frame of mind *think in such a way, purpose, be inclined* (PH 2.5); (4) *have high regard for, honor, respect* (RO 14.6)

φρόνημα, ατος, τό as a result of thinking *mind-set, way of thinking, outlook, aim* (RO 8.6)

φρόνημα	N-NN-S	φρόνημα
φρονήσει	N-DF-S	φρόνησις
φρονήσετε	VIFA--2P	φρονέω

φρόνησις, εως, ἡ as relating to the action of thinking; (1) *way of thinking, wisdom, outlook* (LU 1.17); (2) *intelligence, understanding* (EP 1.8)

φρονῆτε	VSPA--2P	φρονέω
φρόνιμοι	A--NF-P	φρόνιμος
	A--NM-P	"
φρονίμοις	A--DF-P	"
	A--DM-P	"

φρόνιμος, ον as relating to the quality of one's thinking resulting from insight *wise, intelligent, sensible* (MT 7.24), opposite μωρός (*foolish, stupid*) and ἄφρων (*foolish, senseless*); substantivally φρόνιμοι *people with understanding* (MT 25.4); comparative φρονιμώτερος, τέρα, ον *more intelligent, shrewder* (LU 16.8)

φρόνιμος	A--NM-S	φρόνιμος
φρονίμῳ	A--DM-S	"

φρονίμως adverb; *shrewdly, wisely, with insight* (LU 16.8)

φρονίμως	AB	φρονίμως
φρονιμώτεροι	A-MNM-P	φρόνιμος
φρονοῦμεν	VIPA--1P	φρονέω
φρονοῦντες	VPPANM-P	"
φρονοῦσι(ν)	VIPA--3P	"

φροντίζω *think seriously about, be careful about, be concerned to*, followed by an infinitive (TI 3.8)

φροντίζωσι(ν)	VSPA--3P	φροντίζω
φρονῶμεν	VSPA--1P	φρονέω
φρονῶν	VPPANM-S	"

φρουρέω impf. ἐφρούρουν, pass. ἐφρουρούμην; fut. φρουρήσω; transitively in the NT; (1) *guard, keep watch over* something (2C 11.32); (2) *hold in custody, confine*; metaphorically and passive, of the effect of supervision by law *be kept under strict control, be restrained* (GA 3.23); (3) *garrison, guard*; figuratively *protect, keep*; in a transferred sense (PH 4.7); passive (1P 1.5)

φρουρήσει	VIFA--3S	φρουρέω
φρουρουμένους	VPPPAM-P	"

φρυάσσω 1aor. ἐφρύαξα; literally, of the actions of a high-spirited horse *snort and neigh, stomp*; figuratively *be arrogant, be insolent, rave angrily* (AC 4.25)

φρύγανον, ου, τό *dry stick*; plural φρύγανα *dry sticks for fuel, brushwood, firewood* (AC 28.3)

φρυγάνων	N-GN-P	φρύγανον

Φρυγία, ας, ἡ *Phrygia*, an inland district in central Asia Minor

Φρυγίαν	N-AF-S	Φρυγία

φυγαδεύω 1aor. ἐφυγάδευσα; intransitively *be a fugitive, live in exile* (AC 7.29)

φυγεῖν	VNAA	φεύγω
Φύγελλος	N-NM-S	Φύγελος

Φύγελος, ου, ὁ (also **Φύγελλος**) *Phygelus*, masculine proper noun (2T 1.15)

Φύγελος	N-NM-S	Φύγελος

φυγή, ῆς, ἡ *flight, escape* (MT 24.20)

φυγή	N-NF-S	φυγή
φύγητε	VSAA--2P	φεύγω
φυέν	VPAPNN-S	φύω
φυλαί	N-NF-P	φυλή
φυλαῖς	N-DF-P	"
φυλακαῖς	N-DF-P	φυλακή
φύλακας	N-AM-P	φύλαξ
φυλακάς	N-AF-P	φυλακή
φύλακες	N-NM-P	φύλαξ

φυλακή, ῆς, ἡ (1) as an action *guarding, watch*; idiomatically φυλάσσειν φυλακάς literally *guard a guarding*, i.e. *keep watch, do guard duty* (LU 2.8); (2) as a person keeping watch at a guard station or post *sentinel, guard* (AC 12.10); (3) by metonymy, as a place of guarding *prison, guardhouse* (MT 14.10); as a part of the underworld or a place of punishment *prison* (1P 3.19); as a place frequented or inhabited by demons *haunt, den, refuge* (RV 18.2); (4) as a division of nighttime, the length of duty for a sentinel *watch, night watch* (MT 14.25)

φυλακή	N-NF-S	φυλακή
φυλακῇ	N-DF-S	"
φυλακήν	N-AF-S	"
φυλακῆς	N-GF-S	"

φυλακίζω *imprison, throw into prison, put in jail* (AC 22.19)

φυλακίζων	VPPANM-S	φυλακίζω
φυλακτήρια	N-AN-P	φυλακτήριον

φυλακτήριον, ου, τό strictly *safeguard, preservative, means of protection*; as worn on a person *charm, amulet*; plural, as worn by Jews during prayer *phylacteries, containers*, small boxes encasing certain Scripture verses (MT 23.5)

φυλάκων	N-GM-P	φύλαξ

φύλαξ, ακος, ὁ *guard, sentinel, (prison) keeper* (AC 5.23)

φυλάξαι	VNAA	φυλάσσω
φυλάξατε	VMAA--2P	"
φυλάξει	VIFA--3S	"
φυλάξῃ	VSAA--3S	"
φυλάξῃς	VSAA--2S	"
φύλαξον	VMAA--2S	"
φυλάξωμεν	VSAA--1P	"
φυλάς	N-AF-P	φυλή
φυλάσσειν	VNPA	φυλάσσω

φυλάσσεσθαι	VNPM	"
	VNPP	"
φυλάσσεσθε	VMPM--2P	"
φυλάσσῃ	VSPA--3S	"
φυλάσσῃς	VSPA--2S	"
φυλασσόμενος	VPPPNM-S	"
φυλάσσοντες	VPPANM-P	"
φυλάσσοντι	VPPADM-S	"
φυλάσσου	VMPM--2S	"
φυλάσσουσι(ν)	VIPA--3P	"

φυλάσσω impf. ἐφύλασσον; fut. φυλάξω; 1aor. ἐφύλαξα, mid. ἐφυλαξάμην; (1) active, of the activity of a watchman; (a) *guard, protect, watch (over)*; idiomatically φυλάσσειν φυλακάς literally *guard a guarding*, i.e. *keep under watch, carefully guard, do guard duty* (LU 2.8); (b) *guard, keep (from escaping)* (AC 12.4); (c) *protect, preserve, guard (from theft)* (AC 22.20); (d) of law *keep, observe, follow* (AC 7.53); (2) middle; (a) *take care, be on guard against, look out for, avoid* (AC 21.25); (b) of law *observe, obey* (MK 10.20)

φυλάσσων	VPPANM-S	φυλάσσω

φυλή, ῆς, ἡ (1) as an ethnically related subdivision within a total community *tribe*, predominantly as one of the twelve tribes of Israel (LU 2.36); (2) in a broader sense, plural *peoples, nations* (MT 24.30)

φυλήν	N-AF-S	φυλή
φυλῆς	N-GF-S	"
φύλλα	N-AN-P	φύλλον
	N-NN-P	"

φύλλον, ου, τό *leaf* of a tree; plural *leaves*; in a collective sense *foliage* (MT 21.19)

φύλων	N-GF-P	φυλή
φύουσα	VPPANF-S	φύω

φύραμα, ατος, τό any substance that has been mixed and kneaded together; (1) of bread *dough, lump, batch* (1C 5.6); νέον φ. literally *fresh dough*, i.e. *without yeast*; used metaphorically of a morally clean community of believers (1C 5.7); (2) of potter's clay *lump* (RO 9.21)

φύραμα	N-AN-S	φύραμα
	N-NN-S	"
φυράματος	N-GN-S	"
φύσει	N-DF-S	φύσις
φύσεως	N-GF-S	"
φυσικά	A--NN-P	φυσικός
φυσικήν	A--AF-S	"

φυσικός, ή, όν (1) as belonging to the naturally regulated order of things *instinctive, natural, by nature* (RO 1.26, 27); (2) of animals *governed by natural instincts* (2P 2.12)

φυσικῶς *naturally, by (natural) instinct* (JU 10)

φυσικῶς	AB	φυσικῶς
φύσιν	N-AF-S	φύσις
φυσιοῖ	VIPA--3S	φυσιόω
φυσιούμενος	VPPPNM-S	"
φυσιοῦσθε	VIPP--2P	"
φυσιοῦται	VIPP--3S	"

φυσιόω pf. pass. ptc. πεφυσιωμένος; 1aor. pass. ἐφυσιώθην; literally *puff up, blow up*; figuratively in the NT *make proud* or *arrogant, cause to become haughty* (1C 8.1); passive *become conceited* or *proud* (1C 4.6)

403

φύσις, εως, ἡ *nature*; (1) as the naturally regulated order of things *nature* (RO 2.14); κατὰ φύσιν *according to nature, natural* (RO 11.21); παρὰ φύσιν *contrary to nature, unnatural* (RO 1.26); (2) as inherited or habituated characteristics natural to man *(human) nature* (JA 3.7b); (3) *natural endowment, native condition* inherited from one's ancestors (GA 2.15; EP 2.3); (4) as a *creature* produced naturally, *natural being, species, kind* (JA 3.7a); (5) as God's essential character *nature* (2P 1.4)

φύσις	N-NF-S	φύσις
φυσιώσεις	N-NF-P	φυσίωσις

φυσίωσις, εως, ἡ literally *puffing up, inflation*; figuratively *pride, conceit*; plural *acts of arrogance, conceited behavior* (2C 12.20)

φυτεία, ας, ἡ active *planting*; passive, as what is planted *plant*; metaphorically *correct teaching, true doctrine* (MT 15.13; cf. 15.9)

φυτεία	N-NF-S	φυτεία
φυτεύει	VIPA--3S	φυτεύω
φυτεύθητι	VMAP--2S	"

φυτεύω impf. ἐφύτευον; 1aor. ἐφύτευσα; pf. pass. πεφύτευμαι; 1aor. pass. ἐφυτεύθην; literally *plant* (MT 21.33); metaphorically, of introducing the gospel message into different communities *be the first to tell the message* (1C 3.6)

φυτεύων	VPPANM-S	φυτεύω

φύω 2aor. pass. ἐφύην, ptc. masculine φυείς, neuter φυέν; (1) active *grow (up)*; of plants *come up, sprout, germinate*; metaphorically, in a negative sense, of a person becoming a part of a group and by wrong conduct or doctrine leading others astray *appear, show up* (HE 12.15); (2) passive *be grown, grow* or *spring up* (LU 8.6)

φωλεός, οῦ, ὁ as a place used by an animal for shelter or habitation, with the translation varying according to a particular animal's habits *hole, den, burrow*

φωλεούς	N-AM-P	φωλεός
φωναί	N-NF-P	φωνή
φωναῖς	N-DF-P	"
φωνάς	N-AF-P	"
φώνει	VMPA--2S	φωνέω
φωνεῖ	VIPA--3S	"
φωνεῖτε	VIPA--2P	"

φωνέω impf. ἐφώνουν; fut. φωνήσω; 1aor. ἐφώνησα; 1aor. pass. ἐφωνήθην; (1) as producing a sound or noise in ordered sequence, so that it conveys significance, translated according to the context: of a cock *crow* (MT 26.34); of a person *call* or *cry out, speak loudly* (LU 8.8); of an angel *call, speak* (RV 14.18); of a demon in a person *scream, shriek, cry out* (MK 1.26); (2) *call, address* someone *as, name* (JN 13.13); (3) *summon to oneself, call into one's presence* (MT 20.32; AC 10.7); (4) *invite*, as to a feast (LU 14.12)

φωνή, ῆς, ἡ as the production of a sound, made to convey significance; (1) as produced through the throat of living creatures; (a) generally of man and supernatural beings *voice, speech, utterance* (MT 27.46; JN 5.37); idiomatically ἐπαίρειν φωνήν literally *raise the voice*, i.e. *speak loudly, cry out* (LU 11.27); (b) as what is being specifically expressed through speaking, as an *outcry* (AC 19.34), *(solemn) declaration* (2P 1.17), *cry* (MK 15.37), *message* (AC 13.27), *lamentation* (MT 2.18); (c)

of speech, as characteristic of human beings *language* (1C 14.10); (d) as the various cries and sounds made by animals and birds; (2) as produced by inanimate things *sound, tone, noise*, translated according to the source: as a *reverberation, rumbling* of thunder (RV 6.1), *sound, roar* of waters (RV 1.15b), *rush* of wings (RV 9.9a), *clatter* of chariot wheels (RV 9.9b), *grinding* of millstones (RV 18.22b), *melody* of musical instruments (1C 14.7), *signal* of a trumpet (1C 14.8), *rushing* of wind (JN 3.8)

φωνή	N-NF-S	φωνή
φωνῇ	N-DF-S	"
φωνηθῆναι	VNAP	φωνέω
φωνήν	N-AF-S	φωνή
φωνῆς	N-GF-S	"
φωνῆσαι	VNAA	φωνέω
φωνῆσαν	VPAANN-S	"
φωνήσαντες	VPAANM-P	"
φωνήσας	VPAANM-S	"
φωνήσατε	VMAA--2P	"
φωνήσει	VIFA--3S	"
φωνήση	VSAA--3S	"
φώνησον	VMAA--2S	"
φωνοῦντες	VPPANM-P	"
φωνοῦσι(ν)	VIPA--3P	"
φωνῶν	N-GF-P	φωνή

φῶς, φωτός, τό literally *light*; (1) by metonymy, of sources or bearers of illumination, as *(sun)light* (RV 22.5b); *(star)light*, as one of many heavenly lights (JA 1.17); *(fire)light* (MK 14.54); *(lamp)light* (LU 8.16); *(torch or lantern) light* (AC 16.29); (2) as a religious metaphor, used especially of God as the ultimate source of light and of the sphere where he exists (1T 6.16; 1J 1.5); (3) figuratively *openness*; idiomatically ἐν τῷ φωτί literally *in the light*, i.e. *openly, publicly* (MT 10.27); (4) figuratively; (a) as divine *illumination* or *understanding* given to the spirit and soul of human beings (MT 4.16); (b) as a person who bears or brings such illumination to others (RO 2.19); (c) as a person who guides the way he lives by such understanding (EP 5.8; 1TH 5.5)

φῶς	N-AN-S	φῶς
	N-NN-S	"

φωστήρ, ῆρος, ὁ (1) *light-giving body, luminary, star* (PH 2.15); (2) by metonymy, as a the state of brightness *radiance, shining, brilliance* (RV 21.11)

φωστήρ	N-NM-S	φωστήρ
φωστῆρες	N-NM-P	"

φωσφόρος, ον *bringing (morning) light*; substantivally in the NT *morning star, daystar*, referring to one of the brighter planets, usually Venus; figuratively, of Christ and his atoning work (2P 1.19)

φωσφόρος	AP-NM-S	φωσφόρος
φῶτα	N-AN-P	φῶς
φωτεινή	A--NF-S	φωτεινός
φωτεινόν	A--NN-S	"

φωτεινός, ή, όν (1) as describing what is composed of or full of light *illuminated, well-lit, clear* (MT 6.22); (2) as what is characterized by light *bright, shining, radiant* (MT 17.5)

φωτί	N-DN-S	φῶς
φωτιεῖ	VIFA--3S	φωτίζω
φωτίζει	VIPA--3S	"

φωτίζη   VSPA--3S   "

φωτίζω   fut. φωτίσω; 1aor. ἐφώτισα; pf. pass. ptc. πεφωτισμένος; 1aor. pass. ἐφωτίσθην; (1) intransitively; (a) *shine, give light*; (b) figuratively *give guidance* or *understanding* (RV 22.5); (2) transitively; (a) literally *give light to, light (up), illuminate* (LU 11.36); (b) figuratively *make clear, cause to fully know, cause to understand*; used of God's enlightenment through revelation (EP 1.18) or his making known what is hidden (1C 4.5; 2T 1.10)

φωτίσαι   VNAA   φωτίζω

φωτίσαντος   VPAAGM-S   "

φωτίσει   VIFA--3S   "

φωτισθέντας   VPAPAM-P   "

φωτισθέντες   VPAPNM-P   "

φωτισμόν   N-AM-S   φωτισμός

φωτισμός, οῦ, ὁ   *enlightenment, illumination, light*; figuratively in the NT, of God's message given through the gospel *what God has made known* (2C 4.4)

φωτός   N-GN-S   φῶς

φώτων   N-GN-P   "

χ X

χαῖρε   VMPA--2S   χαίρω
    VMPA--2S^QS   "
χαίρει   VIPA--3S   "
χαίρειν   VNPA   "
    VNPA^QS   "
χαίρετε   VMPA--2P   "
    VMPA--2P^QS   "
χαίρῃ   VSPA--3S   "
χαίρομεν   VIPA--1P   "
χαιρόμενος   VPPMNM-S   "
χαίροντες   VPPANM-P   "
χαιρόντων   VPPAGM-P   "
χαίρουσι(ν)   VIPA--3P   "

χαίρω impf. ἔχαιρον; 2aor. pass. ἐχάρην; 2fut. pass. χαρήσομαι; (1) *rejoice, be glad, be delighted* (JN 3.29); with the participle used adverbially with other verbs *gladly, with joy, joyfully* (LU 19.6); (2) used as a formula of greeting or address in the imperative implying a wish for well-being χαῖρε, χαίρετε *welcome, good morning, hail (to you), hello* (MT 26.49); at the beginning of a letter χαίρειν *greetings!* (AC 15.23; 23.26); at the end of a letter *farewell* (2C 13.11); (3) passive *be glad, be happy, rejoice* (LU 6.23; 2C 7.13)

χαίρω   VIPA--1S   χαίρω
χαίρωμεν   VSPA--1P   "
χαίρων   VPPANM-S   "

χάλαζα, ης, ἡ *hail, hailstones*, raindrops frozen into ice

χάλαζα   N-NF-S   χάλαζα
χαλάζης   N-GF-S   "
χαλάσαντες   VPAANM-P   χαλάω
χαλασάντων   VPAAGM-P   "
χαλάσατε   VMAA--2P   "
χαλάσω   VIFA--1S   "
χαλάσωμεν   VSAA--1P   "

χαλάω fut. χαλάσω; 1aor. ἐχάλασα; 1aor. pass. ἐχαλάσθην; *let down, lower* something (MK 2.4); *slacken, release gradually* (AC 27.17)

Χαλδαῖος, ου, ὁ *Chaldean*, a native of Chaldea, a country in central Asia near the Persian Gulf (AC 7.4)

Χαλδαίων   N-GM-P   Χαλδαῖος
χαλεποί   A--NM-P   χαλεπός

χαλεπός, ή, όν (1) *hard, difficult*; καιροὶ χαλεποί *troublesome, perilous times* (2T 3.1); (2) of persons *fierce, violent, dangerous* (MT 8.28)

χαλιναγωγέω 1aor. ἐχαλιναγώγησα; literally, of a horse *guide with a bit and bridle* (JA 3.2); figuratively *hold in check, restrain, control* (JA 1.26)

χαλιναγωγῆσαι   VNAA   χαλιναγωγέω
χαλιναγωγῶν   VPPANM-S   "

χαλινός, οῦ, ὁ *bit*, the mouthpiece of the bridle for a horse (JA 3.3); by synecdoche the *bridle* itself (RV 14.20)

χαλινούς   N-AM-P   χαλινός

χαλινῶν   N-GM-P   "
χαλκᾶ   A--AN-P   χαλκοῦς
χαλκείων   N-GN-P   see χαλκίων

χαλκεύς, έως, ὁ *worker in copper, coppersmith*; more generally *metalworker, worker in metals, (black)smith* (2T 4.14)

χαλκεύς   N-NM-S   χαλκεύς

χαλκηδών, όνος, ὁ *chalcedony*, a valuable stone that can be highly polished, like the modern agate, onyx, carnelian, chrysoprase (RV 21.19)

χαλκηδών   N-NM-S   χαλκηδών

χαλκίον, ου, τό *copper* or *brass container, kettle, bronze utensil* (MK 7.4)

χαλκίων   N-GN-P   χαλκίον

χαλκολίβανον, ου, τό and **χαλκολίβανος, ου, ὁ** a highly refined metal or alloy of uncertain identity, probably *burnished bronze, fine brass*; the old Latin translation has *aurichalcum*, an alloy of gold and copper

χαλκολιβάνῳ   N-DM-S   χαλκολίβανον
    N-DN-S   "
χαλκόν   N-AM-S   χαλκός

χαλκός, οῦ, ὁ (1) as the metal itself *copper, brass* (an alloy of copper and zinc), *bronze* (an alloy of copper and tin) (RV 18.12); (2) as anything made of this metal, such as *gong* (1C 13.1), *copper coins* (MT 10.9); more generally *money* (MK 12.41)

χαλκός   N-NM-S   χαλκός
χαλκοῦ   N-GM-S   "

χαλκοῦς, ῆ, οῦν *made of copper, brass*, or *bronze, brazen* (RV 9.20)

χαλῶσι   VIPA--3P   χαλάω

χαμαί *on the ground* (JN 9.6); *to the earth* (JN 18.6)

χαμαί   AB   χαμαί

Χανάαν, ἡ (also **Κανάαν, Χαναάν**) indeclinable; *Canaan*, the ancient name for Israel or Palestine, the land west of the Jordan River

Χανάαν   Χανάαν
Χαναναία   A--NF-S   Χαναναῖος

Χαναναῖος, αία, ον *Canaanite, belonging to the land* or *people of Canaan* (MT 15.22)

χαρά, ᾶς, ἡ (1) literally *joy*, as a feeling of inner happiness *rejoicing, gladness, delight* (MT 2.10); (2) by metonymy; (a) the person or thing that is the cause or object of joy or happiness (LU 2.10; PH 4.1); (b) a state or condition of happiness or blessedness (MT 25.21; HE 12.2)

χαρά   N-NF-S   χαρά
    N-VF-S   "
χαρᾷ   N-DF-S   "

χάραγμα, ατος, τό (1) *mark* or *stamp*, made by engraving, etching, imprinting, branding (RV 13.16); (2) by metonymy *likeness, handiwork, the thing formed* (AC 17.29)

χάραγμα	N-AN-S	χάραγμα
χαράγματα	N-AN-P	"
χαράγματι	N-DN-S	"
χαράγματος	N-GN-S	"
χάρακα	N-AM-S	χάραξ

χαρακτήρ, ῆρος, ὁ originally *engraver* or *engraving tool*; used figuratively in the NT of Christ in relation to God *exact representation, precise reproduction, impress* (HE 1.3)

χαρακτήρ	N-NM-S	χαρακτήρ
χαράν	N-AF-S	χαρά

χάραξ, ακος, ὁ *stake*; by synecdoche, as what is made by sharpened stakes *barricade, rampart, palisade*, a fortified fence constructed of wooden poles with earth, stones, pieces of wood packed between (LU 19.43)

χαράς	N-GF-S	χαρά
χαρῆναι	VNAO	χαίρω
χαρήσεται	VIFD--3S	"
χαρήσομαι	VIFD--1S	"
χαρήσονται	VIFD--3P	"
χάρητε	VMAO--2P	"
χαρῆτε	VSAO--2P	"
χαρίζεσθαι	VNPD	χαρίζομαι
	VNPO	"
χαρίζεσθε	VIPD--2P	"
	VIPO--2P	"

χαρίζομαι fut. χαρίσομαι; 1aor. mid. ἐχαρισάμην; pf. κεχάρισμαι; 1aor. pass. ἐχαρίσθην; 1fut. χαρισθήσομαι; from a basic meaning *give*, with the translation suited to the context; (1) *give freely* or *graciously, grant as a favor* (LU 7.21; AC 27.24; possibly GA 3.18); (2) (a) of a debt that is owed to someone *cancel, do away with* (LU 7.42); (b) figuratively, as a religious technical term, of a wrong that has been done to someone *give pardon, forgive* (CO 2.13); (3) as expressing pleasure toward someone *show oneself gracious* (possibly GA 3.18); (4) as a legal technical term, of putting someone under the control of another *hand over* (AC 25.16)

χαριζόμενοι	VPPDNM-P	χαρίζομαι
	VPPONM-P	

χάριν accusative of χάρις (*favor*); used as a postposition with the genitive, rarely as an improper preposition with the genitive; (1) to present a reason *on account of*; τούτου χ. *for this reason, on this account* (EP 3.1); οὗ χ. *for which reason, therefore* (LU 7.47); χ. τινός *for what reason? why?* (1J 3.12); (2) to present a goal or purpose *for the sake of, on behalf of*, i.e. *bring about* (GA 3.19); *to obtain* (JU 16); τούτου χ. *for this purpose* (TI 1.5)

χάριν	N-AF-S	χάρις
	PG	χάριν

χάρις, ιτος, ἡ *grace*; (1) as a quality that adds delight or pleasure *graciousness, attractiveness, charm* (LU 4.22); (2) as a favorable attitude; (a) active, of what is felt toward another *goodwill, favor* (AC 2.47); (b) as a religious technical term for God's attitude toward human beings *kindness, grace, favor, helpfulness* (JN 1.16, 17; EP 2.8); (3) concretely; (a) of exceptional effects produced by God's favor *ability, power, enabling* (RO 12.6; 1C 15.10); (b) of practical proofs of goodwill from one person to another *kind deed, benefit, favor* (AC 24.27; 2C

1.15); *collection* for the poor, *generous gift* (1C 16.3); (4) as an experience or state resulting from God's favor *state of grace, favored position* (RO 5.2); (5) as a verbal thank offering to God *gratitude, thanks* (1C 15.57; 2C 9.15); (6) as contained in formulas that express greetings or farewell in letters *goodwill, favor, blessing* (RO 1.7; 16.20)

χάρις	N-NF-S	χάρις
χαρισάμενος	VPADNM-S	χαρίζομαι
χαρίσασθαι	VNAD	"
χαρίσασθε	VMAD--2P	"
χαρίσεται	VIFD--3S	"
χαρισθέντα	VPAPAN-P	"
χαρισθῆναι	VNAP	"
χαρισθήσομαι	VIFP--1S	"

χάρισμα, ατος, τό a verbal noun from χαρίζομαι (*give*); denoting *what has been given, gift*; (1) as the result of a gracious act of God *gift of grace, favor bestowed, benefit*, with the meaning varying according to the context: *privileges granted* (RO 11.29), *rescue from danger* (2C 1.11), *gift of redemption* (RO 5.15–16); (2) as a concrete manifestation of grace in the form of extraordinary powers given to individuals, often in the plural *gifts, special abilities* (RO 12.6); the *ability* to be self-restrained in matters of sex (1C 7.7); the bestowal of *special ability* given through ordination *what God has given, endowment* (1T 4.14; 1P 4.10)

χάρισμα	N-AN-S	χάρισμα
	N-NN-S	"
χαρίσματα	N-AN-P	"
	N-NN-P	"
χαρίσματι	N-DN-P	"
χαρίσματος	N-GN-S	"
χαρισμάτων	N-GN-P	"
χάριτα	N-AF-S	χάρις
χάριτας	N-AF-P	"
χάριτι	N-DF-S	"
χάριτος	N-GF-S	"

χαριτόω 1aor. ἐχαρίτωσα; pf. pass. ptc. κεχαριτωμένος; *favor (highly), show kindness to, bless* someone (EP 1.6); in the NT used in reference to divine grace

Χαρράν, ἡ (also **Καρράν**) indeclinable; *Haran*, a city in northwestern Mesopotamia

χάρτης, ου, ὁ *piece of paper, sheet of papyrus* as used to write on (2J 12)

χάρτου	N-GM-S	χάρτης

χάσμα, ατος, τό strictly *yawning*; hence *chasm, gulf*, a gaping, unbridgeable space between two parts of a place (LU 16.26)

χάσμα	N-NN-S	χάσμα
χείλεσι(ν)	N-DN-P	χεῖλος
χειλέων	N-GN-P	"
χείλη	N-AN-P	"

χεῖλος, ους, τό, gen. plural **χειλέων** *lip*; plural, by metonymy, as what is spoken by the lips *speech* (HE 13.15); figuratively χ. τῆς θαλάσσης *seashore, edge* (HE 11.12)

χεῖλος	N-AN-S	χεῖλος
χειμαζομένων	VPPPGM-P	χειμάζω

χειμάζω *expose to bad weather, experience a tempest*; only passive in the NT, of a ship at sea *be storm-tossed, be driven about by a storm* (AC 27.18)

χείμαρρος or χειμάρρους, ου, ὁ as a stream that flows abundantly during the winter rainy season *(winter) torrent*; in other seasons *ravine, wadi* (JN 18.1)

χειμάρρου	N-GM-S	χείμαρρος

χειμών, ῶνος, ὁ (1) *rainy* or *stormy weather, bad weather* (MT 16.3); on the sea *tempest, storm* (AC 27.20); (2) by metonymy, as the season when bad weather comes *winter* (JN 10.22); χειμῶνος *in, during winter* (MT 24.20); πρὸ χειμῶνος *before winter* (2T 4.21)

χειμών	N-NM-S	χειμών
χειμῶνες	N-NM-P	"
χειμῶνος	N-GM-S	"

χείρ, χειρός, ἡ *hand*; (1) literally; (a) as a member of the body used for movement and action; generally *hand* (JN 11.44; probably MT 12.10); occasionally *arm* (LU 4.11; perhaps MT 12.10), *finger* (LU 15.22); or by synecdoche *person* (AC 17.25); (b) by metonymy, as the physical effect of using the hand *handwriting* (1C 16.21); (2) figuratively, as the expression of the activity of a supernatural or human being *control, power*; (a) of God's agency as creator (AC 7.50), ruler (AC 4.28), helper (LU 1.66), judge (AC 13.11); (b) of angelic agency (AC 7.35); (c) of human agency (AC 2.23)

χείρ	N-NF-S	χείρ
χεῖρα	N-AF-S	"

χειραγωγέω *lead by the hand* (AC 9.8)

χειραγωγός, οῦ, ὁ *one who leads another by the hand, guide* (AC 13.11)

χειραγωγούμενος	VPPPNM-S	χειραγωγέω
χειραγωγοῦντες	VPPANM-P	"
χειραγωγούς	N-AM-P	χειραγωγός
χείραν	N-AF-S	see χεῖρα
χεῖρας	N-AF-P	χείρ
χεῖρες	N-NF-P	"
χειρί	N-DF-S	

χειρόγραφον, ου, τό strictly *handwritten document*; in legal matters a *promissory note, record of indebtedness, bond*; figuratively in CO 2.14 not as the law itself, but as the *record of charges* (for breaking God's law), which stood against us and which God symbolically removed by "nailing it to the cross," *handwritten account, record of debts*

χειρόγραφον	N-AN-S	χειρόγραφον
χεῖρον	A-MAN-S	χείρων
	A-MNN-S	"
χείρονα	A-MNN-P	"
χείρονος	A-MGF-S	"
χειροποίητα	A--AN-P	χειροποίητος
χειροποιήτοις	A--DM-P	"
χειροποίητον	A--AM-S	"

χειροποίητος, ον *made* or *done by (human) hands, man-made*; substantivally οἱ χειροποίητοι *man-made dwelling places* (AC 7.48)

χειροποιήτου	A--GF-S	χειροποίητος
χειρός	N-GF-S	χείρ
χειροτονεῖν	VNPA	χειροτονέω

χειροτονέω 1aor. ἐχειροτόνησα; 1aor. pass. ἐχειροτονήθην; *choose, elect by raising a hand* to signify a vote; gener-

ally *appoint, install* (in an office) (AC 14.23); passive *be chosen, be appointed* (2C 8.19)

χειροτονηθείς	VPAPNM-S	χειροτονέω
χειροτονήσαντες	VPAANM-P	"

χείρων, ον, gen. ονος comparative of κακός (*bad*); *worse, more severe, very bad* (MT 9.16); idiomatically, of ill health εἰς τὸ χεῖρον ἐλθεῖν literally *come to the worse*, i.e. *become sicker, get worse* (MK 5.26)

χείρων	A-MNF-S	χείρων
	A-MNM-S	"
χειρῶν	N-GF-P	χείρ

Χερούβ, τό (also Χερουβείν, Χερουβίμ, Χερουβίν) indeclinable; *Cherub*, a winged supernatural living creature; plural Χερουβίν *Cherubim, cherubs* (HE 9.5)

Χερουβείν		Χερούβ
Χερουβίμ		"
Χερουβίν		"
χερσί(ν)	N-DF-P	χείρ
χήρα	AP-NF-S	χῆρος
	A--NF-S	"
χῆραι	AP-NF-P	"
χήραις	AP-DF-P	"
χήραν	AP-AF-S	"
	A--AF-S	"
χήρας	AP-AF-P	"
	A--GF-S	"
χήροις	AP-DM-P	"

χῆρος, α, ον (1) *bereaved, widowed* by the death of one's spouse (LU 2.37); (2) substantivally; (a) ἡ χήρα, ας *widow*, a woman whose husband has died (MK 12.43); metaphorically, of a city stripped of inhabitants and wealth (RV 18.7); (b) ὁ χ., ου *widower*, a man whose wife has died (1C 7.8)

χηρῶν	AP-GF-P	χῆρος

χθές *yesterday* (AC 7.28)

χθές	AB	χθές
χίλια	A-CAN-P	χίλιοι
	A-CNN-P	"
χιλιάδες	N-NF-P	χιλιάς
χιλιάδων	N-GF-P	"
χιλιάρχη	N-DM-S	χιλίαρχος
χιλιάρχης	N-NM-S	"
χιλίαρχοι	N-NM-P	"
χιλιάρχοις	N-DM-P	"
χιλίαρχον	N-AM-S	"

χιλίαρχος, ου, ὁ (also χιλιάρχης) *chiliarch, commander* of a thousand soldiers; in Roman military organization *tribune, commander* of a Roman cohort of about 600 soldiers; generally *high-ranking officer, chief captain*, equivalent to a major or colonel today

χιλίαρχος	N-NM-S	χιλίαρχος
χιλιάρχῳ	N-DM-S	"
χιλιάρχων	N-GM-P	"
χιλίας	A-CAF-P	χίλιοι

χιλιάς, άδος, ἡ as a number, often comprising a group, *one thousand* (LU 14.31); as referring to countless multitudes χιλιάδες χιλιάδων *thousands of thousands, myriads, millions* (RV 5.11)

χιλιάσι(ν)	N-DF-P	χιλιάς

χίλιοι, αι, α as a cardinal number *one thousand*

χιλίων	A-CGM-P	χίλιοι

Χίος, ου, ἡ   *Chios*, an island in the Aegean Sea off the western coast of Asia Minor (AC 20.15)

Χίου	N-GF-S	Χίος

χιτών, ῶνος, ὁ   *tunic*, an undergarment worn next to the skin by both men and women, a sleeveless *shirt* reaching below the knees; more generally *clothing, garment*; plural *clothes*

χιτών	N-NM-S	χιτών
χιτῶνα	N-AM-S	"
χιτῶνας	N-AM-P	"

χιών, όνος, ἡ   *snow*; used as a symbol of complete whiteness

χιών	N-NF-S	χιών
χλαμύδα	N-AF-S	χλαμύς

χλαμύς, ύδος, ἡ   *cloak*, a loose outer garment worn over the χιτών (*shirt*); as a military garment *short cloak, robe, mantle*, fastened by an ornamental pin on the right shoulder so as to hang over the left (MT 27.28)

χλευάζοντες	VPPANM-P	χλευάζω

χλευάζω   impf. ἐχλεύαζον; of derisive behavior *jeer, scoff, sneer* (AC 17.32)

χλιαρός, ά, όν   of temperature between cold and hot *lukewarm, tepid*; metaphorically, of a half-hearted condition of love and loyalty (RV 3.16)

χλιαρός	A--NM-S	χλιαρός

Χλόη, ης, ἡ   *Chloe*, feminine proper noun (1C 1.11)

Χλόης	N-GF-S	Χλόη
χλωρόν	AP-AN-S	χλωρός

χλωρός, ά, όν   literally, as the color of plants *green, pale green, yellowish green* (MK 6.39); neuter as a substantive τὸ χλωρόν *plant* (RV 9.4); figuratively, as the color of a sick person *pale*; symbolically ἵππος χ. *pale horse* ridden by Death (RV 6.8)

χλωρός	A--NM-S	χλωρός
χλωρῷ	A--DM-S	"

χξς′   indeclinable; from the alphabetic symbols for six hundred (ἑξακόσιοι), sixty (ἑξήκοντα), and six (ἕξ); as a cardinal number *six hundred sixty-six* (RV 13.18)

χοϊκοί	A--NM-P	χοϊκός

χοϊκός, ή, όν   of existence in this world *made of earth* or *dust, earthy, earthly* (1C 15.41); substantivally ὁ χ. *the person made of earth* (1C 15.48)

χοϊκός	A--NM-S	χοϊκός
χοϊκοῦ	A--GM-S	"
χοίνικες	N-NF-P	χοῖνιξ

χοῖνιξ, ικος, ἡ   *choenix*, a dry measure almost equal to *quart*, or slightly more than 1 liter, considered a daily grain ration sufficient for one person (RV 6.6)

χοῖνιξ	N-NF-S	χοῖνιξ
χοῖροι	N-NM-P	χοῖρος

χοῖρος, ου, ὁ   *young pig, porker*; more generally *swine* (MK 5.11)

χοίρους	N-AM-P	χοῖρος
χοίρων	N-GM-P	"
χολᾶτε	VIPA--2P	χολάω

χολάω   as having a strong feeling of displeasure *be very angry* (JN 7.23)

χολή, ῆς, ἡ   (1) as a bitter digestive fluid stored in the gall bladder in the body *gall, bile*; (2) as a bitter substance made from wormwood, a plant yielding a bitter-tasting dark-green oil that is alcoholic in its effect *gall*

(MT 27.34); (3) idiomatically, of a person εἰς χολὴν πικρίας εἶναι literally *be full of bitter poison*, i.e. *be very jealous, be bitterly envious* (AC 8.23)

χολῇ	N-DF-S	χολή
χολήν	N-AF-S	"
χολῆς	N-GF-S	"
Χοραζείν		Χοραζίν

Χοραζίν, ἡ (also Χοραζείν, Χωραζίν)   indeclinable; *Chorazin*, a city of Galilee in the foothills rising above the northeastern shore of the Sea of Galilee

χορηγεῖ	VIPA--3S	χορηγέω

χορηγέω   fut. χορηγήσω; strictly *lead a public chorus* for a drama or *pay the cost* for one; hence *furnish, supply, provide (abundantly)*

χορηγῆσαι	VOAA--3S	χορηγέω
χορηγήσει	VIFA--3S	"

χορηγία, ας, ἡ   strictly *paying the cost* of a public chorus for a drama; hence *abundance of means, wealth* (1P 4.11)

χορηγίαν	N-AF-S	χορηγία

χορός, οῦ, ὁ   *dancing*, as accompanied by music (LU 15.25)

χορτάζεσθαι	VNPP	χορτάζω
χορτάζεσθε	VMPM--2P	"

χορτάζω   1aor. ἐχόρτασα; 1aor. pass. ἐχορτάσθην; 1fut. pass. χορτασθήσομαι; literally *feed, satisfy, fill (up)* (MK 8.4); passive *eat one's fill, be satisfied* (MT 14.20); of an animal or bird that eats dead flesh *gorge itself* (RV 19.21); figuratively *be satisfied* (MT 5.6)

χορτάσαι	VNAA	χορτάζω
χορτασθῆναι	VNAP	"
χορτασθήσεσθε	VIFP--2P	"
χορτασθήσονται	VIFP--3P	"

χόρτασμα, ατος, τό   *sustenance, nourishment*, as *food* for people and *fodder* for flocks and herds (AC 7.11)

χορτάσματα	N-AN-P	χόρτασμα
χόρτον	N-AM-S	χόρτος

χόρτος, ου, ὁ   *feeding place* for grazing animals; by metonymy, what grows there *grass, hay, herbage* (MT 6.30); in reference to grain *growing plant* before it heads out *sprout, blade* (MT 13.26); as a building material *hay, (thatched) grass* (1C 3.12)

χόρτος	N-NM-S	χόρτος
χόρτου	N-GM-S	"
χόρτους	N-AM-P	"
χόρτῳ	N-DM-S	"
χορῶν	N-GM-P	χορός
Χουζᾶ	N-GM-S	Χουζᾶς

Χουζᾶς, ᾶ, ὁ   *Chuza*, masculine proper noun (LU 8.3)

χοῦν	N-AM-S	χοῦς

χοῦς, χοός, ὁ, accusative χοῦν   *loose earth, dust, soil* (MK 6.11)

χράομαι   impf. ἐχρώμην; 1aor. ἐχρησάμην; pf. κέχρημαι; (1) with the dative of the thing *use, make use of, employ* (AC 27.17); (2) with an adverb *act toward, deal with* in a certain way (2C 13.10); (3) with the dative of person *treat, behave toward* someone in a certain way (AC 27.3)

χρεία, ας, ἡ   (1) *need, lack, necessity*; χρείαν ἔχειν *have need of* someone or something (MT 3.14; MK 2.25); plural *needs, necessities* of life (AC 20.34); (2) abstractly *what is needed, what is useful* (EP 4.29); (3) *needful matter, business, duty* (AC 6.3)

χρεία	N-NF-S	χρεία
χρείαις	N-DF-P	"
χρείαν	N-AF-S	"
χρείας	N-AF-P	"
	N-GF-S	"
χρεοφειλέται	N-NM-P	χρεοφειλέτης

χρεοφειλέτης, ου, ὁ (also **χρεοφιλέτης, χρεωφειλέτης, χρεωφιλέτης**) *debtor, one who owes a debt* (LU 7.41)

χρεοφειλετῶν	N-GM-P	χρεοφειλέτης
χρεοφιλετῶν	N-GM-P	"
χρεωφειλέται	N-NM-P	"
χρεωφειλετῶν	N-GM-P	"
χρεωφιλετῶν	N-GM-P	"

χρή an impersonal verb followed by the accusative and an infinitive *it is necessary, it ought, it should* (JA 3.10)

χρή	VIPA--3S	χρή
χρῄζει	VIPA--3S	χρῄζω
χρῄζετε	VIPA--2P	"
χρῄζῃ	VSPA--3S	"
χρῄζομεν	VIPA--1P	"

χρῄζω *need, have need of, be without* (MT 6.32)

χρῆμα, ατος, τό *what has been acquired to meet one's needs*; (1) singular *sum of money* (AC 4.37); plural *money* (AC 8.18; 24.26); (2) more generally *property, wealth, riches* (MK 10.23)

χρῆμα	N-AN-S	χρῆμα
χρήμασι(ν)	N-DN-P	"
χρήματα	N-AN-P	"
	N-NN-P	"
χρηματίζοντα	VPPAAM-S	χρηματίζω

χρηματίζω fut. χρηματίσω; 1aor. ἐχρημάτισα; pf. pass. κεχρημάτισμαι; 1aor. pass. ἐχρηματίσθην; (1) of what God makes known; (a) active *impart a revelation, give a message* (HE 12.25); (b) passive *be warned, be instructed, be given a message* (MT 2.12); (2) active with a passive sense *bear a title* or *name, be called, be known as* (AC 11.26; RO 7.3)

χρηματίσαι	VNAA	χρηματίζω
χρηματίσει	VIFA--3S	"
χρηματισθείς	VPAPNM-S	"
χρηματισθέντες	VPAPNM-P	"

χρηματισμός, οῦ, ὁ as the content of what God makes known *answer, response from God, oracle* (RO 11.4)

χρηματισμός	N-NM-S	χρηματισμός
χρημάτων	N-GN-P	χρῆμα
χρῆσαι	VMAD--2S	χράομαι
χρησάμενος	VPADNM-S	"
χρήσηται	VSAD--3S	"
χρήσθ᾽	A--AN-P	see χρηστά
χρήσιμον	A--AN-S	χρήσιμος
	A--NN-S	"

χρήσιμος, η, ον *useful, profitable, beneficial* (2T 2.14); substantivally τὸ χρήσιμον *more profitable thing*

χρῆσιν	N-AF-S	χρῆσις

χρῆσις, εως, ἡ *use made of anything, usage*; more specifically of sexual intercourse *function, sexual use* (RO 1.26, 27)

χρῆσον	VMAA--2S	κίχρημι
χρηστά	A--AN-P	χρηστός

χρηστεύεται	VIPD--3S	χρηστεύομαι
	VIPO--3S	"

χρηστεύομαι *be kind, be gentle, behave kindly* (1C 13.4)

Χριστιανός	N-NM-S	see Χριστιανός
Χριστιανούς	N-AM-P	see Χριστιανούς
χρηστοί	A--NM-P	χρηστός

χρηστολογία, ας, ἡ *fine speaking, smooth* or *plausible speech, (deceptively) friendly words* (RO 16.18)

χρηστολογίας	N-GF-S	χρηστολογία
χρηστόν	A--NN-S	χρηστός

χρηστός, ή, όν with a basic meaning *being well adapted to fulfill a purpose*, i.e. *useful, suitable, excellent*; (1) of things *good, easy, pleasant*; of requirements *easy* (MT 11.30); comparative χρηστότερος, τέρα, ον *better, more pleasant* (LU 5.39); morally *upright, suitable, good* (1C 15.33); of value *superior, better* (LU 5.39); (2) of persons *kind, obliging, benevolent* (EP 4.32); of God *gracious, good* (1P 2.3); (3) neuter as a substantive τὸ χρηστόν *kindness* (RO 2.4)

χρηστός	A--NM-S	χρηστός
χρηστότερος	A-MNM-S	"

χρηστότης, ητος, ἡ (1) as a gracious attitude *goodness, kindness* (RO 2.4), opposite ἀποτομία (*severity*); (2) as moral integrity *uprightness, honesty* (2C 6.6); ποιεῖν χρηστότητα *do what is right* (RO 3.12)

χρηστότης	N-NF-S	χρηστότης
χρηστότητα	N-AF-S	"
χρηστότητι	N-DF-S	"
χρηστότητος	N-GF-S	"
χρήσωμαι	VSAD--1S	χράομαι
χρῆται	VSPD--3S	"
	VSPO--3S	"
χρίσας	VPAANM-S	χρίω

χρῖσμα, ατος, τό literally, as what has been spread on *ointment, unguent, anointing*, used in the Old Testament to symbolize appointment to and empowerment for a task; figuratively in the NT, as the gift and empowering of the Holy Spirit for a task *anointing, endowment, appointment* (1J 2.20)

χρῖσμα	N-AN-S	χρῖσμα
	N-NN-S	"
Χριστέ	N-VM-S	Χριστός
Χριστιανοί	N-NM-P	Χριστιανός
Χριστιανόν	N-AM-S	"

Χριστιανός, οῦ, ὁ *follower of Christ, Christian*

Χριστιανός	N-NM-S	Χριστιανός
Χριστιανούς	N-AM-P	"
Χριστόν	N-AM-S	Χριστός

Χριστός, οῦ, ὁ strictly *one who has been anointed*, symbolizing appointment to a task; as a title for Jesus, designating him as the *Messiah* sent from God (see JN 1.41), *Christ, (the) Anointed One* (MT 1.16); as a personal name for Jesus, *Christ* (RO 6.4)

Χριστός	N-NM-S	Χριστός
Χριστοῦ	N-GM-S	"
Χριστῷ	N-DM-S	"

χρίω 1aor. ἔχρισα; *anoint*; figuratively in the NT, of God's activity in appointing someone to an office, function, or privilege; *appoint, assign, give a task*; (1) of Jesus, the Christ (LU 4.18); (2) of Christian workers (2C 1.21)

χρονιεῖ	VIFA--3S	χρονίζω

χρονίζει   VIPA--3S   "
χρονίζειν   VNPA   "
χρονίζοντος   VPPAGM-S   "

χρονίζω fut. χρονίσω; (1) absolutely *be late, delay, fail to come for a long time* (MT 24.48); (2) with an infinitive following *delay, put off, take a long time* to do something (LU 12.45)

χρονίσει   VIFA--3S   χρονίζω
χρόνοις   N-DM-P   χρόνος
χρόνον   N-AM-S   "

χρόνος, ου, ὁ *time*; (1) predominately as a unit of time *period of time, span, set time* (AC 1.21); ἱκανὸς χ. *considerable time, long time* (LU 8.27); ὅσον χρόνον *as long as* (MK 2.19); plural χρόνοι *times*, as one long period made up of several shorter ones (RO 16.25); (2) as marking an event *point of time* (LU 1.57; AC 1.6); (3) accusative, as measuring time *for a time* (AC 13.18); (4) as time available for something *opportunity, occasion* (HE 11.32); (5) as time taken or allowed for something *respite, delay, opportunity* (RV 2.21; 10.6)

χρόνος   N-NM-S   χρόνος
χρονοτριβέω 1aor. inf. χρονοτριβῆσαι; *spend time, linger, lose time* (AC 20.16)

χρονοτριβῆσαι   VNAA   χρονοτριβέω
χρόνου   N-GM-S   χρόνος
χρόνους   N-AM-P   "
χρόνῳ   N-DM-S   "
χρόνων   N-GM-P   "
χρυσᾶ   A--AN-P   χρυσοῦς
    A--NN-P   "
χρυσαί   A--NF-P   "
χρυσᾶν   A--AF-S   "
χρυσᾶς   A--AF-P   "
χρυσέων   A--GF-P   "
χρυσῆ   A--NF-S   "
χρυσῆν   A--AF-S   "

χρυσίον, ου, τό (1) as a very valuable metal *gold* (1P 1.7); (2) by metonymy, of things made of gold; (a) *gold ornaments, jewelry* (1P 3.3); (b) *gold coins, gold, money* (AC 3.6)

χρυσίον   N-AN-S   χρυσίον
    N-NN-S   "
χρυσίου   N-GN-S   "
χρυσίῳ   N-DN-S   "
χρυσίων   N-GN-P   "

χρυσοδακτύλιος, ον *with gold ring(s) on one's finger(s), adorned with gold rings, wearing gold rings* (JA 2.2)

χρυσοδακτύλιος   A--NM-S   χρυσοδακτύλιος
χρυσοί   N-NM-P   χρυσός

χρυσόλιθος, ου, ὁ *chrysolite*, a gold-colored gem, known today as *topaz* (RV 21.20)

χρυσόλιθος   N-NM-S   χρυσόλιθος
χρυσόν   N-AM-S   χρυσός

χρυσόπρασος, ου, ὁ *chrysoprase*, a translucent gem, a variety of quartz of golden green color (RV 21.20)

χρυσόπρασος   N-NM-S   χρυσόπρασος

χρυσός, οῦ, ὁ (1) as a highly valued metal *gold* (RV 18.12); (2) by metonymy, as made into valuable products, such as *coins, money* (MT 10.9), *ornaments, jewelry* (1T 2.9), *idols* (AC 17.29), *crowns* (RV 9.7)

χρυσός   N-NM-S   χρυσός

χρυσοῦ   A--GN-S   χρυσοῦς
    N-GM-S   χρυσός
χρυσοῦν   A--AM-S   χρυσοῦς
    A--AN-S   "

χρυσοῦς, ῆ, οῦν *golden*; *made of* or *inlaid with gold* (2T 2.20); *overlaid with gold, gilt* (HE 9.4)

χρυσοῦς   A--AM-P   χρυσοῦς

χρυσόω pf. pass. ptc. κεχρυσωμένος; *make of gold*; only passive in the NT *be gilded* or *adorned with gold (ornaments)* (RV 17.4)

χρυσῷ   N-DM-S   χρυσός
χρυσῶν   A--GF-P   χρυσοῦς
χρῶ   VMPD--2S   χράομαι
    VMPO--2S   "
χρώμεθα   VIPD--1P   "
    VIPO--1P   "
χρώμενοι   VPPDNM-P   "
    VPPONM-P   "

χρώς, χρωτός, ὁ *skin, surface* or *covering of the body* (AC 19.12)

χρωτός   N-GM-S   χρώς
χωλοί   A--NM-P   χωλός
χωλόν   A--AM-S   "
    A--NN-S   "

χωλός, ή, όν literally *lame, crippled* (AC 3.2); substantivally χωλοί *lame people* (MT 11.5); *deprived of one foot, maimed* (MT 18.8); figuratively, of spiritual weakness; metaphorically, neuter as a substantive τὸ χωλόν *what is lame, weak limb*, used to denote believers wavering between two opinions within a Christian community (HE 12.13; cf. 1 Kings 18.21 Septuagint)

χωλός   A--NM-S   χωλός
χωλούς   A--AM-P   "
χωλῶν   A--GM-P   "

χώρα, ας, ἡ strictly *space* between two limits; (1) as a tract of land inhabited by a political entity or ethnic group *land, country* (MT 2.12); (2) as a part of a larger tract of land *territory, district, region* (MK 5.10); (3) *countryside, rural area* (JN 11.55), in contrast to πόλις (*city*); (4) *(dry) land* (AC 27.27), in contrast to θάλασσα (*sea*); (5) as a cultivated area *field, land, ground* (JN 4.35); (6) by metonymy, for the inhabitants of a region *land, people of a region* (MK 1.5)

χώρα   N-NF-S   χώρα
χώρᾳ   N-DF-S   "
Χωραζίν   Χοραζίν
χώραις   N-DF-P   χώρα
χώραν   N-AF-S   "
χώρας   N-AF-P   "
    N-GF-S   "
χωρεῖ   VIPA--3S   χωρέω
χωρεῖν   VNPA   "
χωρείτω   VMPA--3S   "

χωρέω fut. χωρήσω; 1aor. ἐχώρησα; from a basic meaning *make room for, give way to*; (1) as moving from one place to another; (a) as a motion forward *make progress, go forward*; figuratively *make headway* (probably JN 8.37); *come to, reach* (2P 3.9); (b) as a motion away from *withdraw, go out, move on* (MT 15.17; 20.28); (2) as having a large enough space for something *have room for, contain, hold* (MK 2.2); figuratively; (a) *find* *acceptance* (perhaps JN 8.37); (b) of persons *open one's heart to, be friendly toward* (2C 7.2); (c) intellectually *grasp, understand, accept* (MT 19.11)

χωρῆσαι	VNAA	χωρέω
χωρήσατε	VMAA--2P	"
χωρήσειν	VNFA	"
χωρία	N-NN-P	χωρίον
χωρίζεσθαι	VNPP	χωρίζω
χωριζέσθω	VMPP--3S	"
χωρίζεται	VIPP--3S	"
χωριζέτω	VMPA--3S	"

χωρίζω fut. χωρίσω; 1aor. ἐχώρισα; pf. pass. κεχώρισμαι; 1aor. pass. ἐχωρίσθην; (1) active *separate, divide, part* (MT 19.6); (2) passive; (a) *separate (oneself), be separated*, i.e. *be divorced* (1C 7.10); (b) *be separated from, depart from* a place (AC 1.4); (c) *be separate from, be different from* (HE 7.26); (d) *be at a distance from, be separate from* a person (PM 15)

χωρίον, ου, τό diminutive of χώρα or χῶρος; *place, spot* (MT 26.36); *piece of ground, field, place* (JN 4.5)

χωρίον	N-AN-S	χωρίον
χωρίου	N-GN-S	"

χωρίς adverb; (1) used as an adverb *separately, apart, by itself* (JN 20.7); (2) in the NT predominately as an improper preposition with the genitive *apart from, without*; (a) with the genitive of person *without, with no relationship to, separated from* (JN 15.5); *apart from* (someone's help), *independent of* (JN 1.3); without counting someone in *besides, except, in addition to* (MT 14.21); (b) with the genitive of the thing *outside of, apart from* (2C 12.3); *without making use of* (MT 13.34); *without any relation to* (HE 9.28)

χωρίς	AB	χωρίς
	PG	"
χωρίσαι	VNAA	χωρίζω
χωρίσει	VIFA--3S	"
χωρισθείς	VPAPNM-S	"
χωρισθῇ	VSAP--3S	"
χωρισθῆναι	VNAP	"

χωρισμός, οῦ, ὁ strictly *division, separation*; hence *quarreling, difference of opinion* (AC 4.32)

χωρισμός	N-NM-S	χωρισμός
χωρίων	N-GN-P	χωρίον
χῶρον	N-AM-S	χῶρος (II)

χῶρος, ου, ὁ (I) *place*; διὰ τῶν χώρων *throughout the region, in various places* (AC 11.2)

χῶρος, ου, ὁ (II) *northwest wind*; by metonymy, as the direction from which this wind blows *northwest* (AC 27.12)

χωροῦσαι	VPPANF-P	χωρέω
χωροῦσι(ν)	VIPA--3P	"
χώρων	N-GM-P	χῶρος (I)

ψαλλέτω   VMPA--3S   ψάλλω
ψάλλοντες   VPPANM-P   "
ψάλλω fut. ψαλῶ; strictly *strike the strings* of an instrument; hence *sing to the accompaniment of a harp*; in the NT *sing praises*

ψαλμοῖς   N-DM-P   ψαλμός
ψαλμόν   N-AM-S   "
ψαλμός, οῦ, ὁ *(Old Testament) psalm* (LU 20.42); as used among believers *song of praise, sacred song* (1C 14.26)

ψαλμῷ   N-DM-S   ψαλμός
ψαλμῶν   N-GM-P   "
ψαλῶ   VIFA--1S   ψάλλω
ψας   VPAANM-S   see ἐμβάψας
ψευδαδέλφοις   N-DM-P   ψευδάδελφος
ψευδάδελφος, ου, ὁ *false brother*, i.e. a Christian in name only (2C 11.26)

ψευδαδέλφους   N-AM-P   ψευδάδελφος
ψευδαπόστολοι   N-NM-P   ψευδαπόστολος
ψευδαπόστολος, ου, ὁ *false apostle*, i.e. one without a divine commission for the office (2C 11.13)

ψεύδει   N-DN-S   ψεῦδος
ψευδεῖς   AP-AM-P   ψευδής
    A--AM-P   "
ψεύδεσθε   VMPD--2P   ψεύδομαι
    VMPO--2P   "
ψευδέσι(ν)   AP-DM-P   ψευδής
ψευδής, ές *lying, false, deceitful* (AC 6.13), opposite ἀληθής *(truthful)*; substantivally *one who tells lies, liar* (RV 21.8)

ψευδοδιδάσκαλοι   N-NM-P   ψευδοδιδάσκαλος
ψευδοδιδάσκαλος, ου, ὁ *false teacher*, i.e. one who teaches what is not true (2P 2.1)
ψευδολόγος, ον *speaking falsely, lying*; substantivally in the NT *liar* (1T 4.2)

ψευδολόγων   AP-GM-P   ψευδολόγος
ψεύδομαι fut. ψεύσομαι; 1aor. ἐψευσάμην; (1) absolutely *lie, tell what is not true* (RV 3.9); (2) *deceive (by lying), mislead, lie to* (AC 5.3, 4)

ψεύδομαι   VIPD--1S   ψεύδομαι
    VIPO--1S   "
ψευδομάρτυρες   N-NM-P   ψευδόμαρτυς
ψευδομαρτυρέω impf. ἐψευδομαρτύρουν; fut. ψευδομαρτυρήσω; 1aor. ἐψευδομαρτύρησα; as lying to a judge after taking an oath to tell only what is true *bear false witness, give false testimony in court, commit perjury*

ψευδομαρτυρήσεις   VIFA--2S^VMAA--2S   ψευδομαρτυρέω
ψευδομαρτυρήσῃς   VSAA--2S   "
ψευδομαρτυρία, ας, ἡ of encouraging a false judgment *false witness* or *testimony, perjury*

ψευδομαρτυρίαι   N-NF-P   ψευδομαρτυρία
ψευδομαρτυρίαν   N-AF-S   "
ψευδομαρτύρων   N-GM-P   ψευδόμαρτυς

ψευδόμαρτυς, υρος, ὁ *one who gives false testimony, false witness*, as one who claims to be a witness and still says something untrue, thus promoting a false judgment, *perjurer*

ψευδόμεθα   VIPD--1P   ψεύδομαι
    VIPO--1P   "
ψευδόμενοι   VPPDNM-P   "
    VPPONM-P   "
ψεύδονται   VIPD--3P   "
    VIPO--3P   "
ψευδοπροφῆται   N-NM-P   ψευδοπροφήτης
ψευδοπροφήταις   N-DM-P   "
ψευδοπροφήτην   N-AM-S   "
ψευδοπροφήτης, ου, ὁ *false prophet*, one who falsely claims to be a prophet and thus prophesies falsely

ψευδοπροφήτης   N-NM-S   ψευδοπροφήτης
ψευδοπροφήτου   N-GM-S   "
ψευδοπροφητῶν   N-GM-P   "
ψεῦδος, ους, τό *lie, falsehood, deceit*, opposite ἀλήθεια *(truth)*; predominately in the NT as religious error; as what does not exist except as a false claim *the lie* (2TH 2.11); ποιεῖν ψ. *promote (religious) error, practice falsehood* (RV 21.27; 22.15)

ψεῦδος   N-AN-S   ψεῦδος
    N-NN-S   "
ψεύδους   N-GN-S   "
ψευδόχριστοι   N-NM-P   ψευδόχριστος
ψευδόχριστος, ου, ὁ *false Christ, false Messiah*, i.e. one who falsely claims to be the Messiah (MT 24.24)
ψευδώνυμος, ον *falsely named, falsely called* or *designated as something* (1T 6.20)

ψευδωνύμου   A--GF-S   ψευδώνυμος
ψεύσασθαι   VNAD   ψεύδομαι
ψεῦσμα, ατος, τό *falsehood, lie, what is not true* promoted as being truth (RO 3.7)

ψεύσματι   N-DN-S   ψεῦσμα
ψεῦσται   N-NM-P   ψεύστης
ψεύσταις   N-DM-P   "
ψεύστας   N-AM-P   "
ψεύστην   N-AM-S   "
ψεύστης, ου, ὁ *liar, one who speaks what is not true*; of persons (1T 1.10); of the devil (JN 8.44)

ψεύστης   N-NM-S   ψεύστης
ψηλαφαμένῳ   VPPPDN-S   see ψηλαφωμένῳ
ψηλαφάω 1aor. ἐψηλάφησα; (1) *feel about, grope one's way*, like a person who is blind or in the dark; figuratively, of those who seek to know God through natural and moral revelation apart from special revelation *try to find, want to know, feel one's way toward* (AC 17.27); (2) *feel, touch, handle* (LU 24.39); passive *be felt* or *touched* in a tangible way (HE 12.18)

ψηλαφήσαιε(ν)   VOAA--3P   ψηλαφάω

ψηλαφήσαισαν	VOAA--3P	see ψηλαφήσειαν
ψηλαφήσατε	VMAA--2P	ψηλαφάω
ψηλαφήσειαν	VOAA--3P	"
ψηλαφήσειε	VOAA--3S	"
ψηλαφομένῳ	VPPPDN-S	see ψηλαφωμένῳ
ψηλαφουμένῳ	VPPPDN-S	see ψηλαφωμένῳ
ψηλαφωμένῳ	VPPPDN-S	ψηλαφάω
ψηφίζει	VIPA--3S	ψηφίζω

ψηφίζω 1aor. ἐψήφισα; strictly *reckon* or *calculate with pebbles*; hence (1) *count up, reckon, add up* (LU 14.28; possibly RV 13.18); (2) *figure out, interpret*, come to *understand* the significance of a number (probably RV 13.18)

ψηφισάτω	VMAA--3S	ψηφίζω
ψῆφον	N-AF-S	ψῆφος

ψῆφος, ου, ἡ literally *small worn stone, pebble*, with the meaning derived from the uses to which such pebbles were put; (1) as a means of casting a judicial ballot *vote, voice* (AC 26.10); (2) *amulet, charm* as a protection against evil forces (perhaps RV 2.17); (3) *badge* or *token*, inscribed with a name that admits the bearer to special privileges in a guest-host relationship; used metaphorically of relation to Jesus (possibly RV 2.17)

ψιθυρισμοί	N-NM-P	ψιθυρισμός

ψιθυρισμός, οῦ, ὁ *whispering, hiss*; in a bad sense *gossip, tale-bearing, secret slandering* (2C 12.20)

ψιθυριστάς	N-AM-P	ψιθυριστής

ψιθυριστής, οῦ, ὁ *(habitual) gossiper, tale-bearer, secret slanderer* (RO 1.29)

ψιλαφωμένῳ	VPPPDN-S	see ψηλαφωμένῳ

ψίξ, ψιχός, ἡ *bit, morsel, crumb*, especially of bread (LU 16.21)

ψιχίον, ου, τό diminutive of ψίξ; *crumb, morsel, little bit* (of food) (MT 15.27)

ψιχίων	N-GN-P	ψιχίον
ψιχῶν	N-GF-P	ψίξ
ψυγήσεται	VIFP--3S	ψύχω
ψυχαί	N-NF-P	ψυχή
ψυχαῖς	N-DF-P	"
ψυχάς	N-AF-P	"
ψύχει	N-DN-S	ψῦχος

ψυχή, ῆς, ἡ *life, soul*; a many-sided word with the meaning derived from the context; (1) as the derivative existence of all living creatures, including human beings *life-principle, physical life, breath* (AC 20.10; RV 8.9); (2) as earthly existence in contrast to supernatural existence *life, natural life, one's life on earth* (MT 6.25; AC 20.24; RO 11.3); (3) as the nonmaterial inner life of human beings for which the body serves as a dwelling place *soul, inner self* (MT 11.29; 20.28); often with focus on various aspects of feeling, thinking, choosing in which the psychological being is involved; *mind, purpose* (PH 1.27); *heart* (MK 14.34); *desire* (LU 10.27); by metonymy, of a living being that possesses a soul *person, individual* (AC 2.43; 1C 15.45); plural *persons, people* (AC 2.41); in a first-person reference as equivalent to ἐγώ *I (myself)* (LU 1.47); *me (myself)* (LU 12.19); (4) idiomatically ἀπολλύναι τὴν ψυχήν literally *have*

one's life destroyed, i.e. *die* (MT 10.39); τὴν ψυχὴν τιθέναι literally *lay down one's life*, i.e. *die voluntarily* (JN 13.38); διδόναι ψυχήν literally *give one's life*, i.e. *die willingly* (MT 20.28); παραδιδόναι τὴν ψυχήν literally *hand over one's life*, i.e. *risk one's life, expose oneself to danger* (AC 15.26); παραβολεύεσθαι τῇ ψυχῇ literally *have no concern for one's life*, i.e. *risk one's life* (PH 2.30); ζητεῖν τὴν ψυχήν τινος literally *seek someone's life*, i.e. *want to kill* (MT 2.20); ψ. ζωῆς literally *living soul*, i.e. *(sea) creature* (RV 16.3); τὴν ψυχήν τινος αἴρειν literally *lift up someone's soul*, i.e. *keep someone in suspense* without being able to come to a conclusion (JN 10.24); κάμνειν τῇ ψυχῇ literally *become tired in soul*, i.e. *become discouraged* (HE 12.3)

ψυχή	N-NF-S	ψυχή
	N-VF-S	"
ψυχῇ	N-DF-S	"
ψυχήν	N-AF-S	"
ψυχῆς	N-GF-S	"
ψυχική	A--NF-S	ψυχικός
ψυχικοί	A--NM-P	"
ψυχικόν	A--NN-S	"

ψυχικός, ή, όν of life in the natural world and what pertains to it; (1) as governed by sensual appetites and lived apart from the Spirit of God *natural, unspiritual, worldly* (1C 2.14; JU 19); (2) as being a characteristic of the earthly body *physical, natural* (1C 15.44); neuter as a substantive τὸ ψυχικόν *what is physical* (1C 15.46)

ψυχικός	A--NM-S	ψυχικός
ψῦχος, ους, τό		of weather *cold, coolness, chill* (JN 18.18)
ψῦχος	N-AN-S	ψῦχος
	N-NN-S	"

ψυχρός, ά, όν literally *cold, chilly, cool*; neuter as a substantive τὸ ψυχρόν *cold water* (MT 10.42); figuratively, of one without enthusiasm; spiritually, of one alienated or nonspiritual *indifferent, heartless* (RV 3.15), opposite ζεστός (*fervent, zealous*)

ψυχρός	A--NM-S	ψυχρός
ψυχροῦ	A--GN-S	"
ψυχροῦν	A--AN-S	"

ψύχω 2fut. pass. ψυγήσομαι; *make cool* or *cold*; only passive in the NT *become* or *grow cold*; of fire *become extinguished, go out*; figuratively, of a loss of spiritual devotedness *become less, greatly diminish* (MT 24.12)

ψυχῶν	N-GF-P	ψυχή
ψώμιζε	VMPA--2S	ψωμίζω

ψωμίζω 1aor. ἐψώμισα; strictly *feed by morsels*; (1) of food *feed, supply* someone *with food* (RO 12.20); (2) of property *dole out, give away bit by bit* (1C 13.3)

ψωμίον, ου, τό diminutive of ψωμός (*morsel*); *mouthful, bit of bread*

ψωμίον	N-AN-S	ψωμίον
ψωμίσω	VSAA--1S	ψωμίζω
ψώχειν	VNPA	ψώχω
ψώχοντες	VPPANM-P	"

ψώχω *rub*; of grain *thresh out by rubbing* between the hands (LU 6.1)

Ω, ω indeclinable; *omega*, the last letter of the Greek alphabet; (1) figuratively *last* in a series, reflecting ultimate importance; related to *alpha* as ἀρχή (*beginning*) to τέλος (*end*); (2) Ω (or ᾿Ω) as a symbolic letter in combination with A (q.v.), the first letter of the Greek alphabet ΑΩ *beginning and end, first and last* (RV 1.11)

ὦ interjection *O! oh!* used in address or in an exclamation expressing admiration (MT 15.28; RO 11.33)

ὦ	QS	ὦ
	VSPA--1S	εἰμί
ᾧ	APRDM-S	ὅς
	APRDN-S	"
	A-RDM-S	"
	A-RDN-S	"
Ὠβήδ		Ἰωβήδ
Ὠβήλ		"
ᾠδαῖς	N-DF-P	ᾠδή

ὧδε an adverb of ὅδε (*here*); of place; (1) *to this place, hither, here* (MT 8.29); (2) *in this place, here* (MT 12.6); with the local sense weakened, denoting relevance *in this case, at this point, under these circumstances* (1C 4.2; RV 13.18)

ὧδε	AB	ὧδε

ᾠδή, ῆς, ἡ *song*; in the NT a religious song sung by a community gathered for worship (EP 5.19)

ᾠδήν	N-AF-S	ᾠδή

ὠδίν, ῖνος, ἡ (1) literally, as the pain that accompanies childbirth *birth pang, labor pain* (1TH 5.3); (2) metaphorically; (a) of intolerable anguish from calamities preceding the advent of the Messiah, usually plural *distress, great sufferings, agonies* (MT 24.8); (b) as the final agonies before death *pangs, pain, throes* (AC 2.24)

ὠδίν	N-NF-S	ὠδίν
ὠδῖνας	N-AF-P	"
ὠδίνει	VIPA-3S	ὠδίνω
ὠδίνουσα	VPPANF-S	"
	VPPAVF-S	"

ὠδίνω literally *suffer birth pains, be in travail* (to give birth) (RV 12.2); figuratively *suffer greatly* for a good purpose (GA 4.19); metaphorically and negatively, of the new covenant church οὐκ ὠδίνουσα *not having to suffer to give birth*, i.e. *not requiring obedience to old covenant rules and ceremonies* (GA 4.27)

ὠδίνω	VIPA-1S	ὠδίνω
ὠδίνων	N-GF-P	ὠδίν
ᾠκοδόμησε(ν)	VIAA-3S	οἰκοδομέω
ᾠκοδόμητο	VILP-3S	"
ᾠκοδόμουν	VIIA-3P	"
ὦμεν	VSPA--1P	εἰμί
ὡμίλει	VIIA-3S	ὁμιλέω
ὡμίλουν	VIIA-3P	"
ὡμοιώθη	VIAP-3S	ὁμοιόω

ὡμοιώθημεν	VIAP--1P	"
ὡμολόγησας	VIAA--2S	ὁμολογέω
ὡμολόγησε(ν)	VIAA-3S	"
ὡμολόγουν	VIIA-3P	"

ὦμος, ου, ὁ literally, as a part of the body *shoulder* (LU 15.5); metaphorically, of requiring legalistic and burdensome observances, like a load tied on the back or shoulders of a slave (MT 23.4)

ὤμοσα	VIAA--1S	ὀμνύω
ὤμοσε(ν)	VIAA-3S	"
ὤμους	N-AM-P	ὦμος
ὤν	VPPANM-S	εἰμί
	VPPAVM-S	"
ὧν	APRGF-P	ὅς
	APRGM-P	"
	APRGN-P	"
	A-RGN-P	"
ὠνειδιζόμεθα	VIIP--1P	ὀνειδίζω
ὠνείδιζον	VIIA-3P	"
ὠνείδισας	VIAA--2S	"
ὠνείδισε(ν)	VIAA-3S	"

ὠνέομαι 1aor. ὠνησάμην; *buy, purchase* something from someone, with the genitive of price (AC 7.16)

ὠνήσατο	VIAD-3S	ὠνέομαι
ὠνόμασε(ν)	VIAA-3S	ὀνομάζω
ὠνομάσθη	VIAP-3S	"

ᾠόν, ᾠοῦ, τό *egg*; in the NT *chicken egg* (LU 11.12)

ᾠόν	N-AN-S	ᾠόν

ὥρα, ας, ἡ (1) as a limited or measured segment of time *hour*, the twelfth part of a day (JN 11.9); (2) as the time set for something *hour, appointed time* (LU 14.17); (3) by metonymy, what takes place within an appointed time *events of an hour* or *time*, as for childbirth (her) *hour*, (her) *time* (JN 16.21); for Jesus' redemptive acts (my) *hour*, (my) *time* (JN 17.1); for future events (the coming) *time*, (the last) *hour* (1J 2.18; RV 3.10); (4) idiomatically, of a comparatively short period of time μία ὥρα literally *in a single hour*, i.e. *in an amazingly short time* (RV 18.10, 19); πρὸς ὥραν *for a while, for a season* (JN 5.35); *for a moment* (GA 2.5); ἡ ἄρτι ὥ. literally *the present hour*, i.e. *at this very time* (1C 4.11)

ὥρα	N-NF-S	ὥρα
ὥρᾳ	N-DF-S	"
ὥραι	N-NF-P	"
ὡραία	A--DF-S	ὡραῖος
ὡραίαν	A--AF-S	"
ὡραῖοι	A--NM-P	"

ὡραῖος, αία, ον strictly *timely, seasonable, ripe*; (1) of persons and things *beautiful, lovely* (MT 23.27); (2) of an appropriate time *timely, welcome* (RO 10.15)

ὡραῖος	A--NM-S	ὡραῖος
ὥραν	N-AF-S	ὥρα

ὥρας	N-AF-P	"
	N-GF-S	"
ὠργίσθη	VIAO--3S	ὀργίζω
ὠργίσθησαν	VIAO--3P	"
ὤρθριζε(ν)	VIIA--3S	ὀρθρίζω
ὥρισαν	VIAA--3P	ὁρίζω
ὥρισε(ν)	VIAA--3S	"
ὡρισμένη	VPRPDF-S	"
ὡρισμένον	VPRPAN-S	"
ὡρισμένος	VPRPNM-S	"
ὥρμησαν	VIAA--3P	ὁρμάω
ὥρμησε(ν)	VIAA--3S	"
ὤρυξε(ν)	VIAA--3S	ὀρύσσω

ὠρύομαι as the loud cry of animals, translated to fit the animal in the context, *roar, bellow, howl* (1P 5.8)

ὠρυόμενος	VPPDNM-S	ὠρύομαι
	VPPONM-S	"
ὠρχήσασθε	VIAD--2P	ὀρχέομαι
ὠρχήσατο	VIAD--3S	"
ὠρῶν	N-GF-P	ὥρα

ὡς conjunction; an adverbial form of the relative pronoun ὅς, ἥ, ὅ; (1) as a comparative conjunction introducing manner and used correlatively: οὕτω(ς) . . . ὡς *thus, so, in such a way . . . as* (EP 5.33); often with οὕτω(ς) omitted *as, in the same way as, like* (1C 13.11); (2) in indirect questions indicating manner *how* (LU 24.35); (3) used to introduce a comparison *as, like* (AC 8.32); often with one or both sides of the comparison abbreviated or understood *as, like* (MT 13.43); (4) Semitically, combined with a substantive to take the place of a substantive or adjective in expressing a comparison *as it were, something like, as* (RV 8.8); (5) used to introduce a characteristic quality that is real, claimed, or supposed *as* (1C 3.10); with the genitive *as of* (1P 1.19); (6) used with a participle when joining on a cause or reason *because* (AC 28.19; 2P 1.3); (7) as a time connector; (a) followed by the present, of times that are equal in extent *while, as long as* (LU 12.58; JN 12.35); (b) followed by the aorist, of time preceding an event *as, when, after* (JN 21.9); (c) followed by the subjunctive, of time that is uncertain or conditional, introduced by ὡς ἄν or ὡς ἐάν *when(ever), as soon as* (1C 11.34); (d) idiomatically, of a subsequent point of time ὡς τάχιστα literally *as very quickly*, i.e. *as soon as possible, in a hurry* (AC 17.15); (8) used to introduce a purpose *so as to, in order that* (AC 20.24); (9) used to introduce a consequence *and so, with the result that, consequently* (HE 3.11); (10) adverbially, with numerals *about, approximately* (JN 6.10); (11) used to introduce an example or illustration; (a) from Scripture *as* (MK 7.6); (b) from human opinion (LU 3.23; AC 17.28); (c) from customary behavior (MK 10.1)

ὡς	AB	ὡς
	ABR	"
	CC	"
	CH	"
	CS	"
ὡσάν	CS&QV	see ὡς and ἄν

ὡσαννά a particle transliterated from the Aramaic; strictly, a cry expressing an appeal for divine help *save!*

help, we pray! in a liturgical usage, a shout of praise and worship *hosanna, we praise you* (MT 21.9)

ὡσαννά	QS	ὡσαννά

ὡσαύτως adverb; *similarly, likewise, in just the same way*

ὡσαύτως	AB	ὡσαύτως

ὡσεί conjunction; literally *as if*; (1) as a conjunction introducing a comparative *as, as though, like, as it were* (MT 3.16); (2) adverbially, with numbers and measures *about, nearly* (MT 14.21)

ὡσεί	AB	ὡσεί
	CS	"
Ὡσηέ		Ὡσηέ

Ὡσηέ, ὁ (also **Ὠσηέ**) indeclinable; *Hosea*, masculine proper noun (RO 9.25)

ὦσι(ν)	VSPA--3P	εἰμί
ὠσί(ν)	N-DN-P	οὖς

ὥσπερ conjunction; *(just) as, like as*; (1) in the first part of a comparative with a finite verb and followed by οὕτω(ς) *(in this manner, thus, so)* with the second part *(just) as . . . so* (MT 12.40); (2) as an emphatic marker of similarity, connecting closely with what preceded *(just) as (indeed)* (MT 6.2; 1C 8.5); *like* (LU 18.11); *as if* (MT 18.17)

ὥσπερ	CS	ὥσπερ

ὡσπερεί a conjunction used to emphasize similarity between events or states *just as if, as it were, as though* (1C 15.8)

ὡσπερεί	CS	ὡσπερεί

ὥστε conjunction; (1) introducing inferential independent clauses, followed by the indicative or the imperative *therefore, for this reason, so then* (1C 5.8); (2) introducing dependent clauses, followed by the indicative or an infinitive; (a) to express actual result *so that, with the result that* (JN 3.16); (b) to express intended result *so as to, with a view to, for the purpose of* (MT 10.1); (c) to express negative result ὥ. μή followed by an infinitive *so that not* (MT 8.28)

ὥστε	CH	ὥστε
	CS	"
ὦτα	N-AN-P	οὖς
	N-NN-P	"

ὠτάριον, ου, τό diminutive of οὖς; as a part of the body *(outer) ear* (MK 14.47)

ὠτάριον	N-AN-S	ὠτάριον

ὠτίον, ου, τό diminutive of οὖς; *(outer) ear* (MT 26.51)

ὠτίον	N-AN-S	ὠτίον
ὠτίου	N-GN-S	"
ὤφειλε(ν)	VIIA--3S	ὀφείλω
ὠφείλετε	VIPA--2P	"
ὠφείλομεν	VIIA--1P	"
ὤφειλον	VIIA--1S	"
ὠφελεῖ	VIPA--3S	ὠφελέω

ὠφέλεια, ας, ἡ *usefulness, advantage, benefit* (RO 3.1)

ὠφέλεια	N-NF-S	ὠφέλεια
ὠφελείας	N-GF-S	"
ὠφελεῖται	VIPP--3S	ὠφελέω
ὠφελεῖτε	VIPA--2P	"

ὠφελέω fut. ὠφελήσω; 1aor. ὠφέλησα; 1aor. pass. ὠφελήθην; 1fut. pass. ὠφεληθήσομαι; *help, benefit, assist, be of use*; (1) with a person as the object *benefit someone* (1C 14.6); passive *receive help, be benefited* (MT 15.5);

(2) with a thing as the object *accomplish, do*; colloquially οὐδὲν ὠφελεῖ *he was getting nowhere* (MT 27.24); (3) with a thing as the subject *it is of value* (RO 2.25)

ὠφεληθεῖσα	VPAPNF-S	ὠφελέω
ὠφεληθῇς	VSAP--2S	"
ὠφελήθησαν	VIAP--3P	"
ὠφεληθήσεται	VIFP--3S	"
ὠφελήσει	VIFA--3S	"
ὠφέλησε(ν)	VIAA--3S	"

ὠφελήσω	VIFA--1S	"
ὠφέλιμα	A--NN-P	ὠφέλιμος
ὠφέλιμος, ον	*profitable, useful, beneficial* (TI 3.8)	
ὠφέλιμος	A--NF-S	ὠφέλιμος
ὠφελοῦμαι	VIPP--1S	ὠφελέω
ὤφθη	VIAP--3S	ὁράω
ὤφθην	VIAP--1S	"
ὤφθησαν	VIAP--3P	"

417

Appendix 1

Crossed-over Adjectives

Some New Testament adjectives have become nouns either totally or in some particular function.[1] Since first-century usage gives evidence of their adjectival status, we have retained their adjectival identification in the lexicon. Instances of "crossed-over" words in the following list are marked AP in *ANLEX*, while adjectives that are used substantively in the Greek New Testament appear as A- by virtue of their having been decontextualized in the pages of the lexicon. Three criteria were followed in making the "cross-over" decisions:

1. A term is generally regarded as a noun in isolation from its contextual meaning.
2. A term takes on distinctive meanings as a noun having its own components of meaning (e.g., σοφός, "philosopher"; ὕψιστος, "the Most High God").
3. A term is generally accepted as an adjective, but takes on substantive meaning within a given context. In such cases, the tag of the reflex shows A-, but in each case the substantival uses are shown in the lemma write-up. For a specific adjective in context, the user may refer to *AGNT*, where the tag will show if its contextual use is A- or AP. All crossed-over adjectives are also marked as substantives in the definitions of *ANLEX*. Conversely, not all items marked *substantive* or *substantivally* in the definitions are crossed-over adjectives.

---

1. Those that have become nouns in one or more particular functions include those of plurals (while the corresponding singular remains unaffected) and those of one or two genders (but not all).

Some words considered adjectives in our analysis (because they show both modifying and substantival functions) retain in *ANLEX* any *AGNT*-analyzed AP, even though they haven't crossed over. These include many that are intuitively traditional pronouns (μηδείς, οὐδείς, πᾶς, αὐτός [in its intensifying meaning]), demonstratives (ἕκαστος, ἕτερος, οὗτος, ἐκεῖνος, etc.), cardinal numbers (εἷς, δύο, τρεῖς, etc.), relative pronouns (ὅς, ὅστις, etc.), interrogatives (τίς, τί, etc.), and indefinites (τὶς, τὶ). On the other hand, ordinals are overwhelmingly A- and are given that analysis exclusively in *ANLEX*, with the exception of δεκάτη in its specialized meaning "tenth, tithe."

ἀγαθοεργός, οῦ, ὁ	well-doer
ἀγαθοποιός, οῦ, ὁ	one doing good works
ἀγενῆ, ῶν, τά	common people
ἅγια, ων, τά	sanctuary
ἅγιοι, ων, οἱ	saints, God's people
ἅγιον, ου, τό	sanctuary
ἀγοραῖοι, ων, αἱ	court days, court sessions
ἄδικος, ου, ὁ	unbeliever
ἀδύνατον, ου, τό	impossible thing
ἄζυμα, ων, τά	Jewish Feast of Unleavened Bread
Ἀθηναῖος, ου, ὁ	Athenian
Αἰγύπτιος, ου, ὁ	Egyptian
αἴτιον, ου, τό	crime
αἴτιος, ου, ὁ	cause, reason
ἀλλογενής, ους, ὁ	foreigner, stranger
ἀλλότριος, ου, ὁ	(1) foreigner; (2) enemy
ἀλλόφυλος, ου, ὁ	Gentile, non-Jew
ἁμαρτωλός, οῦ, ὁ	sinner
ἄνομος, ου, ὁ	(1) non-Jew; (2) lawless one (Antichrist)
ἄπιστος, ου, ὁ	pagan, heathen
ἀριστερά, ᾶς, ἡ	left hand
ἅρπαξ, αγος, ὁ	robber
ἄρσεν, ενος, τό	male child, (the) male sex
ἄρσην, ενος, ὁ	male, man
ἀσχήμονα, ων, τά	private body parts
ἄτομον, ου, τό	moment, instant
ἄτοπον, ου, τό	crime
βαθέα, έων, τά	deep secrets
βάρβαρος, ου, ὁ	non-Greek, barbarian
βασίλειον, ου, τό	palace
βασιλικός, οῦ, ὁ	royal official
Βεροιαῖος, ου, ὁ	Berean
βλάσφημος, ου, ὁ	blasphemer
βοηθός, οῦ, ὁ	helper
βύσσινον, ου, τό	fine linen, linen garment
Γαδαρηνός, οῦ, ὁ	Gadarene
Γαλιλαῖος, ου, ὁ	Galilean
γεννητός, οῦ, ὁ	one born, person, human being
Γερασηνός, οῦ, ὁ	Gerasene
γνωστός, οῦ, ὁ	acquaintance, friend
Δαμασκηνός, οῦ, ὁ	Damascene
δεκάτη, ης, ἡ	tenth part, tithe
δεξιά, ᾶς, ἡ	right hand
δεξιά, ῶν, τά	right hand
Δερβαῖος, ου, ὁ	Derbean
διάβολος, ου, ὁ	slanderer, devil
διοπετές, οῦς, τό	stone from heaven (goddess)
δίψυχος, ου, ὁ	doubter, hypocrite, fickle person
δυνατοί, ῶν, οἱ	important people, influential people
δυνατός, οῦ, ὁ	Mighty One
ἔγγυος, ου, ὁ	guarantor
ἐγκάθετος, ου, ὁ	spy
ἐθνικός, οῦ, ὁ	Gentile, pagan
εἰδωλόθυτον, ου, τό	idol food
εἰρηνοποιός, οῦ, ὁ	peacemaker
ἔκγονον, ου, τό	grandchild
ἔκδικος, ου, ὁ	avenger, punisher
ἐκλεκτός, οῦ, ὁ	(1) the elect; (2) the Chosen One
ἐλεύθερος, ου, ὁ	freeman
Ἑλληνική, ῆς, ἡ	Greek language
ἐνάλιον, ου, τό	sea creature
ἐντόπιοι, ων, οἱ	local residents
ἐπαρχεία, ας, ἡ	province
ἐπίορκος, ου, ὁ	perjurer
ἔρημος, ου, ἡ	desert, wilderness
εὐπάρεδρον, ου, τό	devotion
εὐπρόσεδρον, ου, τό	devotion
εὐώνυμα, ων, τά	left side (euphemism)
εὐώνυμος, ου, ἡ	left side (euphemism)
Ἐφέσιοι, ων, οἱ	Ephesians
ἔφιπποι, ων, οἱ	cavalry
ἐχθρός, οῦ, ὁ	enemy, adversary
ἑωσφόρος, ου, ὁ	morning star

θανάσιμον, ου, τό — deadly poison
θεῖον, ου, τό — divine being, deity
θήλειαι, ῶν, αἱ — women
θῆλυ, εος, τό — female child, (the) female sex

ἴδια, ων, τά — one's property
ἴδιοι, ιων, οἱ — one's family, one's people
ἱερόν, οῦ, τό — temple
ἱερόσυλος, ου, ὁ — temple robber, desecrator
ἱκανόν, ου, τό — security, peace bond
ἱλαστήριον, ου, τό — mercy seat, place of forgiveness

Ἰουδαῖοι, ων, οἱ — Jews
ἱππικόν, οῦ, τό — cavalry, horsemen
κακοποιός, ου, ὁ — evildoer, criminal
κακοῦργος, ου, ὁ — evildoer, criminal
κατάλαλος, ου, ὁ — slanderer
κόκκινον, ου, τό — scarlet cloth
λεπρός, οῦ, ὁ — leper
λεπτόν, οῦ, τό — mite, lepton, small coin
λευκοβύσσινον, ου, τό — white linen garment
λιθόστρωτον, ου, τό — stone pavement, mosaic
λινοῦν, οῦ, τό — linen garment
λινοῦς, οῦ, ὁ — linen garment
μαλακός, οῦ, ὁ — homosexual pervert
ματαιολόγος, ου, ὁ — idle talker
μεγαλεῖα, ων, τά — mighty deeds
μέλαν, ανος, τό — ink
μέτοχος, ου, ὁ — partner, companion
μίσθιος, ου, ὁ — hired worker, day-laborer
μισθωτός, οῦ, ὁ — hired worker, day-laborer
μοιχαλίς, ίδος, ἡ — adulteress
μουσικός, οῦ, ὁ — musician
μύλινος, ου, ὁ — millstone
Ναζαρηνός, οῦ, ὁ — Nazarene
νήπιος, ου, ὁ — infant, baby
νομικός, οῦ, ὁ — lawyer
ξένος, ου, ὁ — (1) stranger; (2) host
ξηρά, ᾶς, ἡ — dry land
οἰκεῖοι, ων, οἱ — household, relatives
ὀρεινή, ῆς, ἡ — hill country
ὀρφανός, οῦ, ὁ — orphan
ὅσια, ων, τά — divine promises
ὀψία, ας, ἡ — evening
ὄψιμος, ου, ὁ — spring rain, late rain
παράλιος, ου, ἡ — seacoast
παραλυτικός, οῦ, ὁ — paralytic
παράσημον, ου, τό — emblem, figurehead
παρεπίδημος, ου, ὁ — stranger
πάροικος, ου, ὁ — stranger, foreigner
πάροινος, ου, ὁ — drunkard
πένης, ητος, ὁ — poor person
περίεργα, ων, τά — sorcery, witchcraft
περίεργος, ου, ὁ — busybody
περίοικοι, ων, οἱ — neighbors

περισσόν, οῦ, τό — advantage
περίχωρος, ου, ἡ — neighborhood
πετεινόν, ου, τό — bird, fowl
πετρῶδες, ους, τό — rocky ground
πετρώδη, έων, τά — rocky ground
πλάνος, ου, ὁ — deceiver, impostor
πλατεῖα, ας, ἡ — wide street
πνευματικά, ῶν, τά — spiritual matters/gifts
πνευματικός, οῦ, ὁ — Spirit-filled person
ποδήρης, ους, ὁ — long robe
πονηρόν, οῦ, τό — evil thing/deed
πονηρός, οῦ, ὁ — (1) evil person; (2) devil
πορφυροῦν, οῦ, τό — purple clothing
πρεσβύτερος, ου, ὁ — elder, leader
προβατική, ῆς, ἡ — Sheep Gate
πρόγονοι, ων, οἱ — (1) parents and grandparents; (2) ancestors

πρόδρομος, ου, ὁ — forerunner
πρόϊμος, ου, ὁ — early rain
πρωτότοκοι, ων, οἱ — redeemed
πρωτότοκος, ου, ὁ — firstborn (messianic title)
πτηνά, ῶν, τά — birds
πτωχοί, ῶν, οἱ — poor
Πύθιος, ου, ὁ — Pythian, Delphian
Ῥωμαῖος, ου, ὁ — Roman, Roman citizen
σάρδιος, ου, ὁ — sardius, carnelian
Σεβαστός, οῦ, ὁ — his majesty the emperor
Σιδώνιος, ου, ὁ — Sidonian
σιρικόν, ου, τό — silk, silk cloth/garments
σιτιστά, ῶν, τά — fattened (grain-fed) cattle
σμαράγδινος, ου, ὁ — emerald
Σμυρναῖος, ου, ὁ — Smyrnian
σοφός, οῦ, ὁ — wise person, philosopher
σπερμολόγος, ου, ὁ — parasite, babbler
σπόριμα, ων, τά — grainfields
συγγενής, οῦς, ὁ — (1) relative; (2) fellow citizen
συγκληρονόμος, ου, ὁ — fellow receiver, fellow heir
σύζυγος, ου, ὁ — fellow worker
συμμέτοχος, ου, ὁ — partner, sharer
σύμφορον, ου, τό — benefit, advantage
σύμφωνον, ου, τό — agreement
σύνεδρος, ου, ὁ — councilor, council member
συνεκλεκτή, ῆς, ἡ — sister church
συνεργός, οῦ, ὁ — fellow worker
σύντροφος, ου, ὁ — foster brother, childhood companion
σωτήριον, ου, τό — salvation
τετράμηνος, ου, ὁ — four-month period, for four months
τετράποδα, ων, τά — quadrupeds
τρίμηνος, ου, ὁ — three-month period, for three months

ὑπεναντίος, ου, ὁ	adversary, opponent	χήρα, ας, ἡ	widow
ὕψιστα, ων, τά	heaven	χῆρος, ου, ὁ	widower
ὕψιστος, ου, ὁ	Most High (God)	χλωρόν, οῦ, τό	plant
φίλη, ης, ἡ	friend	ψευδής, οῦ, ὁ	liar
φίλος, ου, ὁ	friend	ψευδολόγος, ου, ὁ	liar
φωσφόρος, ου, ὁ	morning star		

Appendix 2

A Theory of Deponent Verbs

by Neva F. Miller

As a result of thinking creatively about Greek deponent verbs, I have tried to form a comprehensive and systematic view to explain the facts of the case. I put forward this theory in hopes that others will test it to confirm or falsify it.[1]

Deponent verbs are those for which no active forms are found. The term *deponent* basically means displaced or laid aside and is applied to verbs that are thought to have become defective. Deponency is found not only in Greek, but also, for example, in Latin. Much of what is said here could also apply to Latin verbs with equivalent meanings.

Deponency and Voice

As a grammatical term, the category of deponent verbs has to do with that form of a verb called voice. The voice of a verb is construed to show how the participants in the action expressed in a verb relate to that action. There are three voices in the Greek verb system: active, middle, and passive. In the active voice, the subject of a (transitive) verb performs the action expressed in it. The result of the action passes through to affect the expressed or implied object of the verb. For example, *The boy caught a big fish*.

---

1. The voice system used in *AGNT* and fully explained in its lengthy appendix was developed to classify verbs as to voice and "deponency" according to "majority perceptions." Until there is a paradigm shift with regard to voice, both *AGNT*'s system and this essay may stand as useful tools for enquiring users.

The middle voice shows that not only does the subject perform the action in the verb, but that the effect of the action comes back on him. He does the action with reference to himself. He is involved in the action in such a way that it reflects back on him. The action calls attention to him in some way. For example, *I washed myself*.

The passive voice differs from the active in that the subject is acted on, that is, receives the action expressed in the verb. For example, *The child was fed*. The passive voice differs from the middle in that the subject receives the result of the action from an agent other than himself. For example, *The child was washed by his mother*.

Grammarians recognize that as the Greek language moved through its various stages, the passive voice was a later development and gradually replaced the middle voice. That means that we sometimes find the reflexive quality of a verb constructed in a passive voice rather than in a middle voice. This essay reflects a synchronic view of the Greek language, that is, a view of its structure at a particular time, in this case the first century A.D., at the time the New Testament was written. Thus, in relation to deponency, we find the reflexive quality of a verb constructed sometimes in the middle voice, sometimes in the passive voice.

The Problem of Deponency

But a problem has developed in our efforts to understand the Greek verb system. Largely through failure to understand what is being communicated, verbs that show no active voice forms have been relegated to a category called deponent. These verbs occur only in the middle and/or passive voice. Two assumptions have often been drawn from this phenomenon: (1) in the earlier stages of the development of the language, every Greek verb had an active form; and (2) in later developments of the language some verbs lost their active forms and thus became "defective."

Why are verbs without active forms assumed to be defective? Likely, it is because we can easily see that the subject performs the action in the verb. For example, this category of verbs includes those meaning *help*, *fight*, *eat*, *think*, *learn*. At first glance, it appears as if these verbs are middle or passive in form but have an active meaning. Thus, grammars typically describe deponent verbs as those that are middle or passive in form but have an active meaning. It is thought that the original active form was somehow lost or laid aside.

Attempted Solutions

In line with this definition, some grammarians attempt to explain deponent verbs by saying that their voice forms do not conform to their meaning. That is, deponency occurs when the form of one voice (usually active) has been discarded in a particular tense, but the meaning that would have been intended by that form has been transferred to another voice. For example, the active form πίπτω ("I fall") has a future middle πεσοῦμαι, built on its second aorist stem ἔπεσον rather than on the present stem. This is called a deponent future in grammar texts. Beginning students are taught to translate such a future form as if it were active: "I will fall." The student can only conclude that since we do not understand and cannot explain the information that deponency intends to communicate, we should simply translate such verb forms as active, since they appear to communicate in a rather clumsy way concepts that appear clear enough in other languages as active verbs.

But that is not necessarily the case, as A. T. Robertson pointed out. Each occurrence of the middle should be examined for its own sake and allowed to express for itself the precise idea it communicates. As a class, so-called deponent verbs probably never had an active form at all and so never laid it aside.

Furthermore, if there is any language that is not clumsy or defective in its ability to communicate thoughts and ideas, it is the Greek language. In particular, its verbal system is rich in its growth and wealth of meaning, so that it became a finely tuned instrument for communicating various turns of thought. It has a wonderful ability to set forth ideas in a logical manner and to make vivid the action it is portraying. Philosophers searched deeply for origins and meanings relating to behavior and were able to use the Greek language to tell us clearly the conclusions they were coming to. Poets and others skilled in the art of speaking used it for the finest expressions of human thought. In this language, dramas were written and presented to teach people lasting social concepts. Alexander the Great, the youthful leader of the Macedonian Empire that spread over the Mediterranean world and as far east as India more than three hundred years before Jesus, had a high regard for the Greek language. Everywhere he spread his conquests, he founded Greek-style cities and required people to learn the Greek language and culture. As a result, the Greek language developed into the common language of the empire. In Alexandria, Egypt, Jewish scholars translated the Hebrew Scriptures into Greek (a version known as the Septuagint). The New Testament writers also wrote their accounts and letters in Greek. Thus the grand teachings of God's redemptive plan for mankind were originally expressed through Greek concepts, and the people could understand those teachings in the common language of their day.

And so it is unreasonable to suppose that such a fine and useful language should have developed in a clumsy way, with its ability to communicate precise meaning hindered by defective verbs. It is more reasonable to accept the challenge of explaining so-called deponent verbs on the basis of what the voice forms of those verbs communicate. In agreement with that, some grammarians contend that the term *deponent* is a misnomer and should not be used at all as a category of verbs. It has been suggested that it is more appropriate to call this category the dynamic middle, since the meaning in the verb involves significant movement that comes back in some way to cause the agent of the action also to become affected by that action. In other words, an emphasis is put on reflexive action, and the subject, when he is the agent of the action, becomes the center of gravity. The agent does something that benefits himself. The action is not transferred away from him, since the action in the verb does not pass through to affect an object that is only outside of him. He stays involved. For example, in the verb *fight*, the action in the verb is meaningless unless the subject stays involved in that action (recall the saying "It takes two to fight"). It is hard to imagine what the original active form, if such existed, would have had as its meaning for verbs like *answer, try, doubt, fear, touch*.

An Alternate Approach to Deponency

I propose, then, that we need to work toward a better understanding of those verbs for which no active form is found. We need to examine each such verb for its own sake and allow it to speak for itself. Since the middle voice signals that the agent is in some way staying involved in the action, it is appropriate to ask, How is the agent involved? Is he benefiting himself (e.g., *I eat*)? Is he interacting positively with someone else (*I welcome*)? Or is he interacting negatively with someone else (*I leap on*)? Could it be that he is communicating with someone else, so that if he did not stay involved as the speaker, the verb would become meaningless? And how could a person feel ashamed unless there were interaction with his own thoughts and feelings?

If we accept the theory that so-called deponent verbs express personal interest, self-involvement, or interaction of the subject with himself or with others in some way, we will be better able to accept that the non-active form of the verb is valid for communicating a meaning on its own, and we will be challenged to look for that meaning.

The following display is representative—not exhaustive—of New Testament deponent verbs and is intended to suggest an alternate way of thinking about them. The verbs are presented in such a way that the self-involvement of the subject in the action or state expressed in the verb is highlighted. In this way the middle forms of the verb can be understood as having valid meanings apart from active forms.

Class 1: Reciprocity

Some verbs involve situations where two parties are involved and where the removal of one party would render the verb meaningless and no action possible.

A. Positive Interaction

δέχομαι	welcome
δωρέομαι	bestow on
εἰσκαλέομαι	invite in
ἐναγκαλίζομαι	embrace
ἐπιμελέομαι	take care of
ἐπισκέπτομαι	visit, look after
ἰάομαι	heal, cure
ἱλάσκομαι	bring about reconciliation
συναντιλαμβάνομαι	help
χαρίζομαι	forgive

B. Negative Interaction

διαμάχομαι	contend with
δράσσομαι	catch, seize
ἐνάλλομαι	leap on
ἐπαγωνίζομαι	struggle against
ἐπιλαμβάνομαι	grasp, seize hold of
μάχομαι	fight
μέμφομαι	blame, find fault with

C. Positive and Negative Communication

αἰτιάομαι	accuse
ἀνατάσσομαι	narrate
ἀποκρίνομαι	answer
ἀποφθέγγομαι	declare
ἀρνέομαι	deny
ἀσπάζομαι	greet
διαβεβαιόομαι	speak confidently
διακατελέγχομαι	refute
διαμαρτύρομαι	warn
διηγέομαι	tell, relate
ἐξηγέομαι	interpret, describe
μαρτύρομαι	affirm, witness to
παραιτέομαι	request
ψεύδομαι	lie to

Class 2: Reflexivity

In reflexive verbs, the verbal concept inheres in the subject and is not deflected away from it. The action turns back or is reflected back on the subject.

ἀπολογέομαι	make a defense
ἐγκαυχάομαι	boast (pride oneself in)

ἐγκρατεύομαι	abstain (control oneself)
ἐπαναπαύομαι	rest (support oneself on)
μασάομαι	bite one's lips or tongue
μιμέομαι	imitate (pattern oneself after)
πειράομαι	try (exert oneself)

Some reflexive verbs express the notion of moving oneself in one direction or another:

ἀφικνέομαι	arrive
διαπορεύομαι	go through
διεξέρχομαι	come out
ἐξάλλομαι	leap up
ἐπανέρχομαι	return
ἐπεκτείνομαι	stretch toward
ἔρχομαι	come, go
ὀρχέομαι	dance
πορεύομαι	journey

Class 3: Self-Involvement

Some verbs intimately involve the self in the processes going on within the action. These have to do with thinking, feeling, deciding—processes that the subject alone can experience for himself. No one else can do the thinking, feeling, or deciding for him.

A. Intellectual Activities

αἰσθάνομαι	perceive
διαλογίζομαι	ponder
ἐνυπνιάζομαι	dream
ἐπιλανθάνομαι	forget
ἐπίσταμαι	understand
ἡγέομαι	consider
λογίζομαι	reckon
οἴομαι	suppose
πυνθάνομαι	learn

B. Emotional States

βδελύσσομαι	abhor, strongly hate
διαπονέομαι	be annoyed
ἐμβριμάομαι	be indignant
ἐμμαίνομαι	be enraged against
εὐλαβέομαι	feel reverence for
μετεωρίζομαι	be worried
ὀμείρομαι	long for

C. Volitional Activities

βούλομαι	will, wish
ἐναντιόομαι	oppose, set oneself against

Class 4: Self-Interest

Verbs occasionally show the subject acting in his own interest.

διαδέχομαι	succeed to
διαπραγματεύομαι	earn by trading
ἐμπορεύομαι	buy and sell
ἐργάζομαι	perform, accomplish
κτάομαι	get, acquire

Class 5: Receptivity

Sometimes the subject is the center of emphasis, the receiver of sensory perception.

γεύομαι	taste
ἐπακροάομαι	listen to
θεάομαι	see, behold (through visual impression)

Class 6: Passivity

If verbs show a passive subject, the verbal concept alludes to involuntary experiences. The subject is viewed as unable to avoid the experience depicted in the verb. Here may be found unavoidable passions (e.g., *fall in love*).

γίνομαι	(1) be born; (2) come into being
ἐπιγίνομαι	come on, approach (of the night)
κοιμάομαι	fall asleep, die
μαίνομαι	be mad (lunatic)
μαντεύομαι	divine, prophesy (by demon possession)

Class 7: State, Condition

Sometimes the subject is the center of gravity.

δύναμαι	be able, be powerful enough to
ἐπίκειμαι	lie on
καθέζομαι	sit down
κάθημαι	sit
κεῖμαι	lie (down)
παράκειμαι	be at hand, be ready

Conclusion

If the verbs in the above classes are understood as true middles—and if active forms could not have expressed such concepts—then it may be that categorizing such verbs as deponent is no longer relevant.

I do not claim that all the dust surrounding the issue of deponency is settled. The issue is a live one, and some questions remain unanswered. For example, what about semideponency? Was there an original active future form for verbs that now show a future middle built on a second aorist stem? And is there any difference in meaning to be found between middle and passive deponents, or is that a matter to be explained by a gradual displacement of middle forms with passive forms in the development of the language? Further, would diachronic study (i.e., comparison of the various stages of the language) be able to show if a displacement of active forms ever did occur? Much study remains to be done on the matter of deponency.

What I do assert in this essay is that it would be worthwhile for exegetes, students, and translators to look for the enriched meaning being communicated by this category of verbs by letting each middle or passive "deponent" verb speak with its own voice.

Glossary

absolute   a word or phrase whose meaning and/or use is considered apart from its usual context and grammatical construction. Example: transitive verb *eat*, as in *let's eat!*, used without its expected object (e.g. *eat a sandwich*).

abstract noun   a quality or quantity as a characteristic of an object or event; it is not the material object or event in itself. Examples: *light, love, goodness, darkness, beauty, length, breadth*. Cf. *concrete noun*.

accusative case   in many inflected languages, a grammatical set of forms usually functioning as the object of the action of a transitive verb or as the object of certain prepositions. English has retained only a few inflected accusative forms (e.g. *him, her, them, whom*). The subject of a Greek infinitive construction is also in the accusative case.

active voice   a form of the verb showing that the subject is the agent that performs the action expressed in the verb. Example: The boy *caught* a big fish.

adjective   a word that limits, describes, or qualifies a noun. Examples: *bright, yellow, small, strong*.

adjunctive   a connector that adds a grammatical unit equal in prominence. Example: The father *and* his son walked along together. See also *coordinating conjunction*.

adverb   a word or phrase that limits, describes, or qualifies the action or state of existence in a verb. It may also qualify an adjective or another adverb. Examples: *brightly, quietly, very soon, in a hurry*.

adversative   a connector introducing an opposite or contrasting proposition to something already stated, emphasizing differences rather than similarities. Examples: *but, nevertheless, however, instead, rather*.

agent   the person or thing that performs the action indicated in a verb. In active constructions, the agent is usually stated specifically. In passive constructions, the agent may be only implied or expressed in a subordinate role as the object of a preposition. Examples: *The boy* caught a big fish (active). That big fish was caught (by *the boy*) yesterday (passive).

allegory   an expanded metaphor in the form of a story, in which the participants and their actions vividly portray spiritual truth, human conduct or experiences, etc., presenting the point of comparison in a symbolic way. Example: the story of Abraham's two sons (GA 4).

anaphoric   a word or phrase referring back to something previously stated. Example: God loves us. *That* is what the prophet said to the people. Cf. *cataphoric*.

antecedent   a person, thing, or event that precedes or exists before someone or something else. In a later reference to the same person, thing, or event, the speaker or writer may use a pronoun. Example: *Abraham* was an important ancestor of the Jews. He was Isaac's father.

aorist tense   a set of verb forms that indicate that the action in the verb has been completed, without implying continuance or duration of time. When used in historical contexts, the aorist tense indicates an action completed in past time. Example: The people *built* a harbor where the river flows into the sea.

apodosis   the conclusion in a condition-consequence sentence, often expressing a result. Example: If you follow that path, *you will arrive at the lake*. Cf. *protasis*.

apposition   the placing of two expressions together, usually side by side, so that they both refer to the same person, thing, event, or idea, with the second adding information about the first. Example: The old man, *his grandfather*, taught the boy many things.

article   a grammatical class of words that indicate whether the accompanying noun refers to a definite or indefinite person, object, or idea. The English definite article is *the* and the indefinite article is *a* (or *an*). Examples: *The* house is built beside *a* river. *An* old tree stands beside it. See also *definite article*.

ascensive   a word or phrase that intensifies or makes more obvious the action or idea being expressed. Example: *Even* a strong man cannot lift that stone.

aspect   a form of the verb that makes specific the kind of action it expresses, whether the action is continuing, completed, uncompleted, repeated, etc. Example: Every day he *goes* (habitual action) to the river to fish. Cf. *tense*.

aspirate   in the Greek language, the *h*-sound (i.e. rough breathing) in front of a word-initial vowel or a word-initial *rho*.

assimilation   the process by which one speech sound is modified to make it easier to pronounce in combination with another sound preceding or following it. Example: ἐνβλέπω (*look at*) becomes ἐμβλέπω.

attributive   a word that limits or describes another word. Adjectives assign qualities to nouns, and adverbs assign qualities to verbs. Examples: *The* (article) *tall* (adjective) man talked *rapidly* (adverb).

auxiliary   a word closely joined to another word to specify certain important aspects of meaning. Auxiliary words (e.g. *shall, will, may, should, has, have, did*) are often joined to verbs to show the time or kind of action being expressed. Examples: My brother *has* learned to make fishing nets. He *will* teach you.

cardinal number   a number used in counting or showing how many. It may be used as an adjective. Example: Only *four* elders came to the meeting. More often it stands alone, with its noun implied from the context. Example: There were not many elders living in that village. Only *four* came to the meeting. Cf. *ordinal number*.

case   an inflectional form of a noun, pronoun, or adjective indicating its grammatical relation to other words. The five cases in the Greek language are nominative, genitive, dative, accusative, and vocative.

cataphoric   a word or phrase referring forward to an idea or event not yet expressed. Example: *This* is good for you, to eat some fresh fruit every day. Cf. *anaphoric*.

causative   a form of the verb that shows that someone or something caused the action in the verb to happen rather than doing it directly. Example: John *ran* the horse (i.e. John did not run, the horse ran; John *made* the horse *run*).

clause   a grammatical construction or unit of meaning that is part of a sentence, normally containing its own subject and verb. Examples: *When the man picked up a stick* (dependent clause), *the animal ran away* (independent clause).

collective   a number of persons or things thought of as a single unit, on the basis of traditional usage. Example: The *crowd* became angry.

collocate   putting a word together with its natural partner. In each culture, certain words naturally go together with certain other words. Examples: *bread and butter, black and white, rest and relaxation, heaven and earth, keep the law, drive a car, sing a song.*

colloquial   informal language expressions, sometimes called street language, spoken by the people of an area but not used in formal writing or speeches. Example: He *ain't* my brother.

comparative   the form of an adjective or adverb that shows that the object or event it describes has a certain quality in a degree greater than another object or event has. Examples: This man is *richer* than his brother. A grown person runs *faster* than a child. Cf. *positive degree* and *superlative*.

compensatory lengthening   a process whereby one or more consonants are dropped out and a preceding short vowel becomes a long vowel or diphthong. Example: λύονται (*they loose*) becomes λύουσι.

component   one of the parts or elements that together form the whole of an object. In relation to a word, the semantic components are the elements of meaning that give it a meaning of its own. Examples: *human, female,* and *mature* are semantic components of *woman.*

compound   a word or phrase made up of two or more parts that would otherwise be independent. Example: The *gatekeeper* (i.e. the keeper of the gate) asked the man whom he wanted to see.

conative   a form of the verb that expresses striving or attempted action, but does not indicate that the action was completed. Example: He *tried* to cut down a tree.

concession   a grammatical unit that allows or admits that something varies from the main thing being talked about. Such connectors (e.g. *although, even though*) are called concessives. Example: *Even though* the river flowed swiftly, the boy was able to swim across it.

concrete noun   an object or event existing in the material or actual world, without expressing any quality or characteristic of it. Examples: The *man* caught the *horse*, leaped on its *back*, and rode away. Cf. *abstract noun*.

condition   a grammatical unit that restricts the circumstances under which something may be true. Typical conditional connectors are *as if, whenever, if ever*. Example: *If you walk over there*, you will see my uncle's house.

conjunction   a word connecting words, sentences, and paragraphs and showing the relationship between them. Typical connectors are *and, but, if, because, so that*. Examples: He went to see his mother, *because* he heard that she was sick. *But* he hopes to return here soon.

connotation   positive or negative feelings aroused in a hearer or reader by the words a speaker or writer chooses to use. Such words have a secondary or implied meaning apart from their explicit and recognized meanings. This secondary meaning is aroused by sensitivity to cultural, religious, or national matters. Example: She dresses in such an *old-fashioned* way. Cf. *denotation*.

contraction   the making of a shorter word form by omitting or combining some consonants or vowels. Examples: If you *don't* (do not) go right now, *you'll* (you will) not see any of the parade, for it *isn't* (is not) very long. Cf. *crasis*.

coordinating conjunction   a connector that joins one grammatical unit to another without making either subordinate to the other. A coordinating conjunction (e.g. *and*) might indicate additional information, while a subordinating conjunction (e.g. *but*) might introduce contrasting information. Example: I have finished planting my garden, *and* now I will go work in my field.

copula or **copulative**   a coupling conjunction (e.g. *and, or, neither*) joining words or phrases into grammatically independent or coordinate constructions; also the verb *be* joining subject and predicate. Examples: He does not want to go; *neither* does his brother. He *is* tall.

correlative   the regular use of more than one connector to indicate mutual or complementary relation. Example: He is willing *either* to go back *or* to stay on here for awhile.

crasis   the combining of two words into one by merging them, often by omitting one or more letters. Example: κἀγώ from καί (*and*) and ἐγώ (*I*). Cf. *contraction*.

dative case   in many inflected languages, a grammatical set of forms usually functioning as the indirect or more remote object of the action in a verb. It may also convey other relevant information about the action in a verb: the instrument used to perform the action, the location where it takes place, or the means by which it is achieved. Examples: The boy carried some food *in a basket to his father in the forest* (three dative-case prepositional phrases, each independent of the others).

definite article   a grammatical modifier of a noun that marks it as an identifiable or particular person or thing. The English definite article is *the*. The Greek definite article reflects three genders: ὁ (masculine), ἡ (feminine), and τό (neuter). Examples: *The* place where *the* parents took *the* sick child is not far away.

demonstrative adjective   a grammatical modifier of a noun that points to a particular person or thing in order to separate it from the persons or things of the same kind with which it is associated. English demonstratives are *this* and *that, these* and *those*. The equivalent Greek demonstrative adjectives are οὗτος and ἐκεῖνος. Examples: *That* field is better for growing grain than *this* one.

denotation   the exact or primary meaning of a word apart from any secondary or implied meanings resulting from emotional response to it. Cf. *connotation*.

deponent   a grammatical term (meaning *displaced* or *laid aside*) designating a middle or passive verb form of which it is thought the corresponding active forms have been laid aside during the course of the development of the language. Cf. *middle deponent* and *passive deponent*.

determiner   see *definite article*.

dieresis   two small dots over the second of two adjacent vowels to show that the second vowel is to be pronounced separately. Example: Μωϋσῆς (*Moses*), pronounced Μω-υ-σῆς.

diminutive   the form of a word that shows a person to be dear or small in size, usually achieved by adding to or changing the word. Examples: κέρας (*horn*) and κεράτιον (*little horn*); Πρίσκα (*Prisca*, a woman's name) and Πρίσκιλλα (*Priscilla*, meaning *dear Prisca*).

direct object   the person or thing that receives the action in a verb. The action is directed toward that object. Example: The boy pulled *the fish* out of the river. Cf. *indirect object*.

discourse   a connected and continued communication of thought by means of spoken or written language. Example: Jesus' Sermon on the Mount (MT 5–7).

disjunctive   a word that joins together mutually exclusive ideas as alternatives. Examples of disjunctive conjunctives: *either, neither, nor, or, whether*; examples of disjunctive adverbs: *else, otherwise*.

distributive   a word referring not to a group as a whole but to the individual members of the group, separating them from one another. Example: Jesus sent his disciples *two by two* to preach the gospel.

double negative   the use of two or more negative words in the same sentence to produce a strong emphasis on the positive or negative meaning in the verb. English usually uses two negatives to produce a strong positive meaning. Example: I will *never* fail you *nor* will I ever abandon you (HE 13.5, five negatives in Greek). See also *negative particle*.

elative   a word or expression added to a proposition or grammatical unit to emphasize or indicate a greater degree of something. Example: This worker helped people *more* abundantly than the others did.

ellipsis   the use of normal shortcuts in a language, omitting one or more words to avoid repeating information when the sense is perfectly clear without them. An omitted word has been elided, and the sense has been expressed elliptically. Example: *No person ever spoke in such a way* (as this person speaks) (JN 7.46).

enclitic   a particle so closely connected to the preceding word that it loses its own accent and is pronounced with it as one word. Examples: γέ, ποτέ, πού, πώς, τὶς.

etymology   the meaning of a word as obtained from its derivation or the history of its use in a language.

euphemism   a figure of speech; a mild or indirect expression that means something different from what it seems to say. It is used to avoid mentioning what would seem blunt, disrespectful, or offensive (e.g. death or intimate sexual matters) within a cultural group. Example: I do not *know* a man (LU 1.34).

exclamation   a word or phrase that a speaker uses to show strong feelings. Examples: *help!* (expressing danger), *you're crazy!* (anger or frustration), *oh!* (surprise), *wait!* (sudden inspiration).

expletive   a word or phrase that replaces the subject or object in the normal word order, anticipating a word or phrase that will be spoken later to complete the meaning. Example: *It* is hard for you to kick against the goads (AC 26.14).

explicative   the introducing of a proposition with a word that indicates that it contains an explanation or description of what precedes. Examples: *that is*, *namely*, *so*.

feminine   one of several subclasses of nouns and pronouns according to gender. Cf. *masculine* and *neuter*.

figurative   words used in other than their literal or ordinary meanings for the purpose of communicating a secondary meaning via the comparison. Figurative meaning is often expressed by a metaphor. Examples: Above all, take up the *shield of faith*, with which you will be able to *quench* all the *fiery darts* of the wicked one (EP 6.16).

figure of speech   a way of saying something in order to catch attention or stir up feelings. The words used are not to be taken literally or in their ordinary sense. Figures of speech include euphemism, hyperbole, irony, litotes, metaphor, simile, and synecdoche (qq.v.).

finite verb   a form of the verb limited by indication of person, number, tense, mode, and aspect. In contrast, an infinitive does not specify agent or time involved in the action.

first person   a grammatical form of pronouns, adjectives, and verbs that indicates the person speaking or writing. Example: *I* told *my* brother about *my* problem.

frequentative   a form of the verb that expresses frequent repetition of the action in the underlying verb. Frequentative verbs related to the verb *talk* include *chatter*, *stutter*, *murmur*, *babble in an idle or senseless way*. Example: He *chattered* all the way to town.

future tense   a set of verb forms that indicate that at the time of the discourse the action in the verb had not yet happened; the action was still to come.

gender   a grammatical subclass that is partly arbitrary (οἶκος *house* = masculine; κρίμα *judgment* = neuter; κτίσις *creation* = feminine) and partly based on distinguishable characteristics, especially sex (ἀνήρ *man* = masculine; παιδίον *child* = neuter; γυνή *woman* = feminine). Gender determines the grammatical agreement between words and related inflectional forms.

genitive case   in many inflected languages, a grammatical set of forms that mainly indicate that a noun modifies another noun. The modifier often shows possession, but it may also indicate source, separation, measure, or characteristic. Example: The love *of God* is without limit.

Hebraism   see *Semitism*.

hyperbole   a figure of speech that makes use of exaggeration for emphasis or dramatic effect. A deliberate overstatement is made. Example: If your right eye offends you, *take it out and throw it away* (MT 5.29).

hyperordinate clause   equivalent to *superordinate clause* (q.v.).

hyperordinating conjunction   equivalent to *superordinating conjunction* (q.v.). An *AGNT* innovation, introduced to distinguish a superordinating conjunction (CH) from a subordinating conjunction (CS).

idiom or **idiomatic**   the combining of words into a unit of expression to convey a meaning different from the meaning conveyed by the individual words. Example: ἐπὶ τῆς Μωϋσέως καθέδρας καθιστάναι (literally *sit on Moses' seat*) means *have authority to interpret Mosaic law* (MT 23.2)

imperative mode   a form of the verb that indicates a command or strong request. Languages vary in the ways they give commands, making a difference between soft and hard commands, polite and abrupt commands, direct and indirect commands, etc. Example: *Resist* the devil, and he will flee from you (JA 4.7).

imperfect tense   a set of verb forms that indicate that at the time of the discourse the action in the verb was incomplete or continuing in the past. Example: We *were walking* along the seashore.

impersonal verb   a form of the verb or verbal expression that indicates an action but does not specify the agent. Some languages use the third-person singular verb form (*it is possible . . .*), the third-person plural (*they/people say . . .*), or the first-person plural (*we always say . . .*).

improper preposition   a preposition that cannot be pre-positioned as a prefix to a verb to form a compound verb. Adverbs that function as prepositions are also called improper prepositions. Examples: ἄχρι(ς), ἔμπροσθεν, ἐναντίον, ἔξωθεν, μέχρι(ς), πλήν, πρίν, ὑπεράνω, χάριν, χωρίς. Cf. *preposition*.

indeclinable   a noun that does not vary in form by inflectional endings, which ordinarily show case, number, and gender. Many Greek proper nouns are indeclinable, especially names borrowed from other languages.

indefinite pronoun   a pronoun that designates an unidentified person or thing somewhat out of focus. Examples: *anyone*, *someone*, *no one*.

indicative mode   a form of the verb that states an act

or condition as actual fact rather than as an unrealized condition, a possibility, or a wish. Example: He *sailed* his ship across the sea.

indirect object the person or thing that has a personal interest in the action of a verb, more remotely receiving a good or bad outcome from it than a *direct object* (q.v.) does. Examples: He sang a song of praise *to God*. He spoke kind words *to his father*.

infinitive mode a form of the verb that indicates an act or condition without specifying the agent or time. The infinitive form ordinarily functions as a noun phrase in the sentence, especially as the subject or object of the main verb. Example: I want *to thank* God for helping us.

intensive a word that increases the emphasis or force in any expression. Languages vary in the way they indicate emphasis: English uses words like *very* and *really*; Greek prefixes prepositions to verbs; and Hebrew uses a separate set of verb forms. Example: It rained *very* hard this afternoon.

interjection a word or phrase, usually invariable in form, that is thrown into a conversation to exclaim about something. It may be used to express emotion, indicate surprise, or call attention sharply to something. Examples: *oh! indeed! alas! hey!*

interrogative a pronoun or adjective that indicates that the speaker or writer is asking a question. Examples: *who? whose? whom? which? what?*

interrogative particle a small word whose grammatical form does not change in Greek and that a speaker uses in rhetorical questions to show whether he expects a *yes* or *no* answer or to show that what he asks is a probable or improbable possibility. Example: Come and see a man who told me everything I ever did. *Can* this *be* the Messiah? (JN 4.29).

intransitive a verb that does not need a direct object to complete its meaning. The action or state expressed in the verb is limited to the agent or subject. In contrast, the action in a transitive verb (q.v.) passes over to a direct object. Examples: He *ran*. She *slept*.

irony a figure of speech in which the speaker or writer openly pretends to agree with someone's point of view while in fact holding an opposite opinion. Sarcasm or humor is used to rebuke or ridicule. Example: They (the soldiers) began to salute him, "*Hail, King of the Jews!*" (MK 15.18).

iterative an aspect of a verb, usually in the present or imperfect tense, that expresses repeated or habitual action. Examples: And the Lord *kept adding* to the group the people who *were being saved* (AC 2.47).

Latinism a Latin idiom or manner of speech. Example: The Pharisees *took counsel* (i.e. plotted) how they might entangle him in his talk (MT 22.15).

lemma the headword in a dictionary or lexicon, along with information that identifies that word. Example: Ἀαρών, ὁ.

linguistics the study of the system and structure of language, including sounds (phonology), word formation (morphology), sentence structure (syntax), and meaning and meaning change (semantics).

literal the ordinary or natural meaning of an expression, its primary meaning, in contrast to its figurative or secondary meaning.

litotes a figure of speech making an emphatic statement by saying that the opposite idea is not true. An affirmative is thus expressed and reinforced by stating the negative of the contrary. Example: With God *nothing will be impossible* (LU 1.37).

masculine one of several subclasses of nouns and pronouns according to gender. Cf. *feminine* and *neuter*.

metaphor a figure of speech that illustrates a comparison (which is not stated explicitly). One object, event, or state is spoken of as if it were another. Each metaphor consists of a topic (the item being illustrated), an image (the representative figure), and a point of similarity (the particular aspect being compared). The hearer or reader is to understand the point of similarity by thinking about it. Example: *Feed my sheep* (JN 21.15) means *nurture my followers*. Cf. *simile*.

metathesis the exchange of position of two sounds in a word. Example: τίτκω (*give birth to*) became τίκτω.

metonym or **metonymy** a word referring to an associated idea. The name given to one idea stands for an idea associated with it (e.g. a scepter or ruler's stick may stand for the authority he possesses). Example: I have not come to bring peace, but a *sword* (MT 10.34).

middle deponent a verb for which in New Testament–era Greek no active-voice forms are supposed to have been in use; in the future and aorist tenses, only middle-voice forms have been observed. As with passive deponents, it may be that the middle-voice forms also share in the meaning of the action through personal interest, self-involvement, or interaction. Example: By *rejecting* (i.e. not listening to their) conscience, certain persons have made a shipwreck of their faith (1T 1.19). (See discussion in *AGNT* appendix.) Cf. *deponent* and *passive deponent*.

middle voice a form of the verb showing that the subject is the agent of the action in the verb and that the action reflects back on the agent in some way, often to show benefit. Examples: I *washed* (myself), and then I *ate* (fed myself).

mode, modal, mood a grammatical form that indicates the perspective of a speaker or writer toward what he says. The resultant verb form indicates whether the speaker or writer wants to express a statement of fact (indicative mode), a command (imperative mode), a condition (subjunctive mode), a wish or prayer (optative mode), etc. The Greek verb system has six modes: indicative, subjunctive, optative, imperative, infinitive, and participle.

modifier a word or phrase added to another in order to limit or qualify its meaning. Adjectives modify the meaning of nouns; adverbs modify the meaning of verbs. Examples: *The* (article) *big* (adjective) man walked *slowly* (adverb) toward *the* (article) center of *the* (article) circle.

morphology the study of word formation, inflectional forms, etc. in a language.

negative particle usually a small word that limits an expressed or implied verb to a negative meaning. In Greek, οὐ is used with the indicative mood, μή for all other moods. The negative meaning can show denial, disagreement, disapproval, prohibition, doubt, uncertainty. Example: Do *not* play with fire. See also *double negative*.

neuter one of several subclasses of nouns and pronouns according to gender. Cf. *feminine* and *masculine*.

nominative case in many inflected languages, a grammatical set of forms that name the subject or agent of the action in a verb and indicate which articles and adjectives modify it.

noun a word that names a person, thing, place, action, quality, or idea. It is used to specify the subject or object of a verb and the object of a preposition in a discourse. Examples: The big black *bird* flapped his *wings* in the *sky* overhead.

number a grammatical category, usually only singular or plural (i.e. some languages exhibit, e.g., dual forms), that points to quantity and is used to signal agreement among related words (e.g. article, adjective, noun).

numeral a word expressing quantity or number (whether cardinal or ordinal); also its conventional name or symbol.

object as a grammatical term, the noun or noun equivalent toward which the action in a verb is directed; also the word that a preposition governs. Examples: I see my *father* over there. I am going to tell *him* about my *lesson*. Cf. *direct object* and *indirect object*.

oblique case the inflectional form of a noun, pronoun, or adjective in any case other than the nominative and vocative (i.e. in the genitive, dative, or accusative case). Examples: I see *him* running along *my* garden path toward *me*.

optative mode a form of the verb that expresses a wish, prayer, or desire. Its most common New Testament use is in the prayer/command: μὴ γένοιτο (*may it not be!*), meaning *don't think such a thing!* (LU 20.16).

ordinal number a number put into a form that shows where it comes in a series. Examples: *first, second, tenth, hundredth, thousandth.* Cf. *cardinal number*.

orienter a verb, usually of saying, hearing, seeing,

thinking, etc., that serves to relate the following content to the rest of the discourse. Examples: He *saw* (that the situation was hopeless). He *told* her (that his disciples should meet him in Galilee).

participle mode a verbal adjective; a word formed from a verb and expressing action or existence like a verb and yet qualifying a noun like an adjective. Example: The *shining* sun rose high in the blue sky.

particle a small word whose grammatical form does not change (though its phonological shape may) and that expresses relation or connection between grammatical units. Common Greek particles are conjunctions, negatives, and prepositions.

passive deponent a verb for which in New Testament–era Greek no active-voice forms are supposed to have been in use; in the aorist tense, at least, only passive-voice forms have been observed. Passive deponents are otherwise the same in function and meaning as middle deponents, and often it is hard to distinguish between middle and passive deponency in some tenses. Cf. *deponent* and *middle deponent*.

passive voice a form of the verb showing that the grammatical subject is the person or thing to which the action in the verb is done. Often the agent of the action is not specified, so that for one reason or another, the agent may be kept out of focus. Example: Now Jesus, after he *was baptized*, immediately went up out of the water (MT 3.16).

perfect tense a set of verb forms that indicate that at the time of the discourse the action in the verb was already completed when another action takes place. In the Greek verb system, the perfect tense indicates that the effect of the action continues until the time of the discourse. Example: The messenger hurried into the meeting house and shouted, "The chief *has* already *arrived* and he is calling for you to come."

periphrasis the expressing of something in a roundabout way. Periphrasis may be achieved by combining the verb *be* with a participle to emphasize ongoing action or by choosing words to avoid using the divine name. Examples: I *am experiencing* (i.e. I experience) much hardship these days. In the future we will live in the *heavenly city* (i.e. the city that belongs to God).

person the grammatical form of pronouns, adjectives, and verbs that indicates the speaker or writer (first-person), the person spoken or written to (second-person), or the person or thing spoken or written about (third-person). Most nouns are third-person. Examples: *I* (first-person) will tell *you* (second-person) all about *it* (third-person).

personal pronoun a word that replaces a noun in the discourse and indicates the speaker or writer (first-person), the person spoken or written to (second-person), and the person or thing spoken or written about (third-person). Examples: *I* (first-person) will tell *you* (second-person) all about *it* (third-person).

phonology   the study of speech sounds and sound changes within a language.

phrase   a grammatical unit of two or more words that, though part of a sentence, does not express a complete thought by itself. Phrases are usually specified in agreement with their function, such as noun phrase, verb phrase, or prepositional phrase. Examples: *With thunder and lightning* (prepositional phrase), *the heavy rain* (noun phrase) *began beating down* (verb phrase).

pluperfect tense   a set of verb forms that indicate that at the time of the discourse the action in the verb had already been completed before another action took place. Sometimes referred to as the past perfect tense. Example: The chief *had* already *entered* the village before the messenger came to announce his arrival.

plural   a word form that indicates that more than one person or thing is involved. Examples: The *angels* were watching over him. God sent *them* to do that. Cf. *singular*.

positive degree   the simple or uncompared quality of an adjective or adverb. Example: *good* (positive), *better* (comparative), *best* (superlative). Cf. *comparative* and *superlative*.

possessive   a form of a noun, pronoun, or adjective that indicates ownership or possession. Examples: Jesus went back to *his Father's* house.

postpositive   a word, especially a particle, that cannot stand as the first word in its clause. It usually stands second. Examples: γάρ, γέ, δέ, δή, μέν, οὖν, τέ, τοίνυν. Cf. *prepositive*.

predicate   that part of a clause or sentence that complements the subject by expressing what is being said about it. A verb, whether explicit or implied, is part of the predicate. Example: The moon *was shining brightly*.

prefix   a letter or one or more syllables placed at the beginning of a word to change its meaning in some way. Example: κατά (*down* or *against*) plus κρίνω (*judge*) becomes κατακρίνω (*condemn*). Cf. *suffix*.

preposition   a word usually put before a noun or pronoun in order to relate it to another noun, pronoun, verb, or adjective. Prepositions are particles that do not usually change grammatical form (but do occasionally exhibit phonological change: e.g. ἐκ becomes ἐξ before vowels). Prepositions may be prefixed to verbs to form compound verbs (e.g. ἐπικαλέω). Examples: ἀνά, ἀντί, ἀπό, διά, εἰς, ἐκ, ἐν, ἐπί, κατά, μετά, παρά, περί, πρό, πρός, σύν, ὑπέρ, and ὑπό. Cf. *improper preposition*.

prepositive   a word, such as an article, that can be positioned only before the word it qualifies. Examples: *The* animal dashed into *the* forest. Cf. *postpositive*.

present tense   a set of verb forms that indicate that at the time of the discourse the action in the verb

was continuing or being repeated. Examples: I *am watching* what my brother *is doing*.

pronominal adjective   an adjective that stands for or replaces an expected noun. *AGNT/ANLEX* tags beginning with AP mark pronominal adjectives. Cf. *substantive*.

pronoun   a word used in place of a noun (third-person) or standing for the speaker/writer (first-person) or hearer/reader (second-person), often to avoid repeating the name of the person, thing, event, or idea. Examples: When *your* (second-person) father arrives, *I* (first-person) want to talk with *him* (third-person).

proper noun   a name given uniquely to a person (e.g. *Joseph*), place (*Jerusalem*), event (*the judgment*), group (*the Twelve*), organization (*the Sanhedrin*), position (*the King of Israel*), etc. English proper nouns are usually written with an initial capital letter.

protasis   the condition in a condition-consequence sentence; typically introduced by *if* or *whether*. Example: *If you follow that path*, you will arrive at the lake. Cf. *apodosis*.

purpose clause   words constructed together to indicate the purpose in some other action. A purpose clause was traditionally called final clause. Example: He wants to go home *so that he can see his mother*.

qualifier   a word that limits the meaning of another word. Articles, adjectives and adverbs are common qualifiers. Examples: *The* (article) *old* (adjective) man walked *slowly* (adverb).

reciprocal   words that express mutual relation (e.g. *each other*, *one another*). Example: The gospel teaches us to love *one another*.

referent   the person or thing referred to by a pronoun, phrase, or clause. Example: *Jesus* is coming again. He is the one who will rule over all the earth.

reflex   the particular inflected or conjugated form of a word used in a text. Example: υἱόν (JN 3.16) is the accusative, masculine, singular reflex of the lemma υἱός.

reflexive   pronouns or verbs in which the agent and goal are the same person. The action is passed back on the subject. Example: He washed *himself*.

relative clause   a clause in which a relative pronoun (e.g. *who, which, that*) joins a dependent clause containing a description or additional information to the person or thing to which it refers. Examples: The man *whom you met* is the headman, *who also happens to be my grandfather*.

relative pronoun   a pronoun referring to a noun in another clause; ordinarily used to mark the subordination of its own clause to that noun. The subordinated clause is called a *relative clause* (q.v.). Example: The boy, *who* ran faster than anyone else, won the race.

result or **resultative**   a proposition or grammatical unit connected together with words that show that the second one expresses the consequences or results of the first. A result clause was traditionally called a consecutive clause. Example: He worked hard *so that he finished his work quickly*.

rhetorical question   a question that is asked not for the purpose of getting information but to emphasize something else (e.g. a truth), to express surprise, to rebuke someone, to provoke thought, etc. Examples: *How can Satan cast out Satan?* (MK 3.23). *Why did you children go to the river when I told you not to go?*

second person   a grammatical form of pronouns, adjectives, and verbs that indicates the person spoken or written to. Examples: Are *you* taking *your* son to school?

semantics   the study of meaning of language forms, in contrast to grammar, which studies words according to their use in a discourse. Semantic categories include objects, events, abstracts.

Semitism   a Hebrew or Aramaic vocabulary or grammatical construction brought into the Greek text. Also called *Hebraism* or *Aramaism*.

sentential   a special use of the Greek neuter article τό when it stands before whole sentences or clauses to indicate that the sentence or clause functions as the topic in a larger sentence. Examples: The "you shall not commit adultery" is summed up in this saying, in *the* "you shall love your neighbor as yourself" (RO 13.9).

sentential particle   a word that in some way modifies its entire sentence, as opposed to modifying a single word or phrase. It frequently adds connotative sense to the sentence.

simile   a figure of speech that contains an explicitly stated comparison, introduced by *like* or *as*. As in a *metaphor* (q.v.), each simile consists of a topic (the item being illustrated), an image (the representative figure), and a point of similarity (the particular aspect being compared). Examples: All flesh is *like grass*, and all its glory is *like the flower of grass* (1P 1.24).

singular   a word form that indicates that only one person or thing is involved. Examples: The angels were watching over *him*. *God* sent them to do that. Cf. *plural*.

subjunctive mode   a form of the verb that indicates that an act or state is not actual fact, but is possible, desirable, probable, conditional, or wished for. Example: We would be happy if it *were* possible for us to go back to our own country.

subordinate clause   a grammatical construction related to and dependent on another construction or embedded within it. English subordinate clauses are introduced by conjunctions (e.g. *if, when, until, for, because, although*). Example: The chief will be happy *if his people live peacefully with each other*. Cf. *superordinate clause*.

subordinating conjunction   a word that casts the clause it heads into a subordinate relationship to some other (superordinated) clause in the sentence. Cf. *superordinating conjunction*.

substantive   a word or phrase that functions as a noun. Examples: The kind man invited both the *good* and the *bad* to his feast. Cf. *pronominal adjective*.

suffix   a letter or one or more syllables placed at the end of a word to change its meaning in some way. English nouns may be changed from singular to plural by adding *s*, and verbs may be changed into a participle or gerund by adding *ing*. Cf. *prefix*.

superlative   the form of an adjective or adverb that shows that the object or event it describes has a certain quality in a measure greater than any other object or event being compared in the context. It often has only elative force (e.g. *very*). Example: God lives in the *highest* heaven. Cf. *comparative* and *positive degree*.

superordinate clause   a grammatical construction related to and more prominent than another clause subordinated to it. Superordinate clauses may be introduced by the conjunctions ἄρα (*in that case*), διό (*therefore*), καί (*in addition*), μέντοι (*though, indeed*), οὐκοῦν (*isn't it so?*), or τοίνυν (*therefore, indeed*). Also called *hyperordinate clause*. Cf. *subordinate clause*.

superordinating conjunction   a word that casts the clause it heads into a superordinate relationship to some other (subordinated) clause in the sentence. Also called *hyperordinating conjunction*. Cf. *subordinating conjunction*.

synecdoche   a figure of speech in which a part of a thing refers to the whole thing or in which one attribute represents a person. Examples: *the Highest* (i.e. God), *daily bread* (i.e. our entire meal).

technical term   a word belonging to a particular field of knowledge or practice such as medicine, law, military matters, etc. Example: *jurisprudence* (law).

temporal clause   a clause that relates the time of another clause. Example: *When Jesus saw the people*, he felt compassion for them.

tense   a form of the verb that indicates time or kind of action in relation to a discourse or some event in a discourse. The New Testament–era Greek verb system has six tenses: present, imperfect, future, aorist, perfect, and pluperfect. Cf. *aspect*.

third person   a grammatical form of pronouns, adjectives, and verbs that indicates the person or thing being spoken or written about. Examples: *He* is waiting for *his* father to come home with *his* new bicycle.

transitive   a verb that needs a direct object to complete its meaning. The action in the verb passes over to affect its object. In contrast, the action in an intransitive verb (q.v.) is limited to the agent or subject. Example: The boat *struck* a rock in the shallow waters of the river.

transliterate   the process of changing a word from a source language into a receptor language not by translating the meaning but by representing or spelling the word in the characters of the receptor language. Such words are sometimes called loan-words. Examples: *Amen* (from Hebrew), *Hallelujah* (from Hebrew), *Christ* (from Greek).

verb   a grammatical class of words expressing action, emotion, or existence.

verbal   a word formed from a verb that takes on the function of nouns and adjectives. An infinitive functions as a noun; a participle functions as an adjective. Examples: *Writing* (participle) a letter is something I like to do. It makes me happy *to write* (infinitive) to my friends.

verbal particle   a Greek word that usually cannot be translated by a single word in English, but when used with a verb affects the meaning of the verb. The particles ἄν and ἐάν show that the action of the verb depends on some circumstance or condition. The particle ὄφελον introduces a wish that the speaker knows cannot come true. Example: *How I wish* you really had become kings! (1C 4.8).

verb stem   the basic core of a verb from which tense stems are formed by various changes to show the different aspects of a verb. Example: the stem of ἐλύθησαν (*they were released*; RV 9.15) is λυ.

vocative case   in many inflected languages, a grammatical set of forms that addresses someone directly. The person spoken to is named. Example: *My dear children*, listen well.

voice   a form of the verb that shows how a participant in the action relates to the action expressed in the verb. The three voices in the Greek verb system are active, middle, and passive.